THE ROUGH GUIDE TO

New England

D0094547

There are more than two hundred Rough Guide titles
covering destinations from Alaska to Zimbabwe
and subjects from Acoustic Guitar to Travel Health

Forthcoming travel guides include
Malta • Tenerife
Thailand Beaches and Islands • US Rockies

Forthcoming reference guides include
100 Essential Latin CDs • Personal Computers
Website Directory

Rough Guides Online
www.roughguides.com

ROUGH GUIDE CREDITS

Text editors: Mary Beth Maioli, Richard Koss
Series editor: Mark Ellingham
Editorial: Martin Dunford, Jonathan Buckley, Jo Mead, Kate Berens, Ann-Marie Shaw, Paul Gray, Helena Smith, Judith Bamber, Orla Duane, Olivia Eccleshall, Ruth Blackmore, Geoff Howard, Claire Saunders, Gavin Thomas, Alexander Mark Rogers, Polly Thomas, Joe Staines, Richard Lim, Duncan Clark, Peter Buckley, Sam Thorne, Lucy Ratcliffe, Clifton Wilkinson, David Glen, Alison Murchie, Matthew Teller (UK); Andrew Rosenberg, Stephen Timblin, Yuki Takagaki (US)
Production: Susanne Hillen, Andy Hilliard, Link Hall, Helen Prior, Julia Bovis, Michelle Draycott, Katie Pringle, Mike Hancock, Zoë Nobes, Rachel Holmes, Andy Turner

Cartography: Melissa Baker, Maxine Repath, Ed Wright, Katie Lloyd-Jones
Picture research: Louise Boulton, Sharon Martins
Online: Kelly Cross, Anja Mutić-Blessing, Jennifer Gold, Audra Epstein, Suzanne Welles (US)
Finance: John Fisher, Gary Singh, Edward Downey, Mark Hall, Tim Bill
Marketing & Publicity: Richard Trillo, Niki Smith, David Wearn, Chloë Roberts, Birgit Hartmann, Claire Southern (UK); Simon Carloss, David Wechsler, Kathleen Rushforth (US)
Administration: Tania Hummel, Demelza Dallow, Julie Sanderson

ACKNOWLEDGMENTS

Many thanks to Melissa Baker for maps, Jerry Williams and Rachel Holmes for typesetting, Anne Hegerty for proofreading, all the good production folk in London, Ruth Blackmore and Narrell Leffman for UK and Oz Basics help, Michael Millman for literary aid, Suzanne Welles for her film review, and Rob Shea for Gloucester listings.

Thanks to Aunt Sue and Jim in Vermont, Rozzy in Winchestah, and Mom and Dad for crash pads and loads of guidance; thanks to Susan at the Conway, NH hostel and to my ever-so-patient editor, Mary Beth; and, most of all, thanks to my wife, Yumiko.

Paul Tarrant would like to thank Pattie Woodbury, Barbara and George Wojtkiewicz, Ron Stalford, Becky Bovell, Joy Dawson, Pat Brown, Mike and Anthea Hagopian, Mary Peck, Allan and Joan Easterbrooks, Jean and Colin Hill and the friendly and helpful people of Maine, Connecticut and Rhode Island – my second home – for all their help and support along the way.

PUBLISHING INFORMATION

This second edition published July 2001 by Rough Guides Ltd, 62–70 Shorts Gardens, London WC2H 9AH.
Distributed by the Penguin Group:
Penguin Books Ltd, 27 Wrights Lane, London W8 5TZ
Penguin Putnam, Inc. 375 Hudson Street, NY 10014, USA
Penguin Books Australia Ltd, 487 Maroondah Highway, PO Box 257, Ringwood, Victoria 3134, Australia
Penguin Books Canada Ltd, 10 Alcorn Avenue, Toronto, Ontario, Canada M4V 1E4
Penguin Books (NZ) Ltd, 182–190 Wairau Road, Auckland 10, New Zealand
Typeset in Linotron Univers and Century Old Style to an original design by Andrew Oliver.
Printed in England by Clays Ltd, St Ives PLC.
Illustrations in Part One and Part Three by Edward Briant.

Illustrations on p.1 & p.533 by Henry Iles
© Rough Guides Ltd 2001
No part of this book may be reproduced in any form without permission from the publisher except for the quotation of brief passages in reviews.
592pp – Includes index
A catalogue record for this book is available from the British Library
ISBN 1-85828-707-3

The publishers and authors have done their best to ensure the accuracy and currency of all the information in *The Rough Guide to New England*, however, they can accept no responsibility for any loss, injury, or inconvenience sustained by any traveler as a result of information or advice contained in the guide.

THE ROUGH GUIDE TO

New England

written and researched by

David Tarr and
Paul Tarrant

ROUGH
GUIDES

TRAVEL GUIDES • PHRASEBOOKS • MUSIC AND REFERENCE GUIDES

 We set out to do something different when the first Rough Guide was published in 1982. Mark Ellingham, just out of university, was traveling in Greece. He brought along the popular guides of the day, but found they were all lacking in some way. They were either strong on ruins and museums but went on for pages without mentioning a beach or taverna. Or they were so conscious of the need to save money that they lost sight of Greece's cultural and historical significance. Also, none of the books told him anything about Greece's contemporary life – its politics, its culture, its people, and how they lived.

So with no job in prospect, Mark decided to write his own guidebook, one which aimed to provide practical information that was second to none, detailing the best beaches and the hottest clubs and restaurants, while also giving hard-hitting accounts of every sight, both famous and obscure, and providing up-to-the-minute information on contemporary culture. It was a guide that encouraged independent travelers to find the best of Greece, and was a great success, getting shortlisted for the Thomas Cook travel guide award, and encouraging Mark, along with three friends, to expand the series.

The Rough Guide list grew rapidly and the letters flooded in, indicating a much broader readership than had been anticipated, but one which uniformly appreciated the Rough Guide mix of practical detail and humor, irreverence and enthusiasm. Things haven't changed. The same four friends who began the series are still the caretakers of the Rough Guide mission today: to provide the most reliable, up-to-date and entertaining information to independent-minded travelers of all ages, on all budgets.

We now publish more than 150 titles and have offices in London and New York. The travel guides are written and researched by a dedicated team of more than 100 authors, based in Britain, Europe, the USA and Australia. We have also created a unique series of phrasebooks to accompany the travel series, along with an acclaimed series of music guides, and a best-selling pocket guide to the Internet and World Wide Web. We also publish comprehensive travel information on our Web site:

www.roughguides.com

HELP US UPDATE

We've gone to a lot of effort to ensure that the second edition of *The Rough Guide to New England* is accurate and up to date. However, things change – places get "discovered", opening hours are notoriously fickle, restaurants and rooms raise prices or lower standards. If you feel we've got it wrong or left something out, we'd like to know, and if you can remember the address, the price, the time, the phone number, so much the better.

We'll credit all contributions, and send a copy of the next edition (or any other Rough Guide if you prefer) for the best letters. Please mark letters: "Rough Guide New England Update" and send to:
Rough Guides, 62–70 Shorts Gardens, London WC2H 9AH, or Rough Guides, 4th Floor, 345 Hudson St, New York, NY 10014.
Or send email to: mail@roughguides.co.uk
Online updates about this book can be found on Rough Guides' Web site at www.roughguides.com

THE AUTHORS

Paul Tarrant worked on the first edition of *The Rough Guide to New England*, and is also co-author of *The Rough Guide to Scotland*. He has written travel features for publications as diverse as *Take a Break* and *The Church Times*. He lives in Dorset, England, with his golden retriever Tess.

A native of New England, David Tarr has recently returned to the region from eight years on the West Coast and in Asia. Novelist, poet and occasional vagabond, he resides in Cambridge, MA, with his wife, Yumiko, and a happy boy named Julian, who dropped into their lives during the research for this book.

READERS' LETTERS

John Connolly, Angela Kao, Alice Rosenfield, Darlene Salzer, Linda and Richard Schaye,

Peter Smith, Lisa Tigger, Joe and Helena Wygal, and Lisa and Mark Youngman

CONTENTS

• CHAPTER 3: CENTRAL AND WESTERN MASSACHUSETTS   210–244

• CHAPTER 4: RHODE ISLAND   245–280

• CHAPTER 5: CONNECTICUT   281–335

• CHAPTER 6: VERMONT   336–383

• CHAPTER 7: NEW HAMPSHIRE   384–455

• CHAPTER 8: MAINE

PART THREE CONTEXTS 533

LIST OF MAPS

MAP SYMBOLS

Railway; Interstate (55); U.S. Highway (2); State Highway (114); Canadian Autoroute (15); Tunnel; 4WD track; Pedestrianized road; Path; Ferry route; International boundary; State boundary; Chapter division boundary; River; General point of interest; Airport; Ⓣ station

Accommodation; Restaurant; Camp; Mountain peak; Waterfall; Spring/spa; Lighthouse; Museum; Monument; Stately home; Tourist office; Post office; Building; Church; Cemetery; Park; National park

BACKGROUND BOXES

INTRODUCTION

The six New England states of Massachusetts, Rhode Island, Connecticut, Vermont, New Hampshire, and Maine often regard themselves as the repository of all that is intrinsically American. In this version of history, the tangled streets of old Boston, the farms of Connecticut, and the villages of Vermont are the cradle of the nation. It's a picture which has some truth to it, however, and, although nostalgia plays a big part in the tourist trade here, and innumerable small towns have been dolled up to recapture a past that can occasionally be wishful thinking, the appeal of New England is undeniable. It is the most historic region of the United States; its towns and villages are often rustic and pretty, with white-spired churches sitting beside tidy greens and colonial churchyards; and its landscape can get surprisingly diverse – ranging from some of its stark coastlines to its green rolling hills and mountains further inland. Like most regions that have a well-developed tourist industry, though, the trick is to find the unspoiled corners, and to distinguish the bogus from the authentic.

Above all, New England packs an enormous amount of variety into what is by American standards a relatively small area. There are the region's literary connections – with well-visited shrines to Emily Dickinson, Mark Twain, and Edith Wharton, to name just a few New England writers. There is no shortage of inviting places to ski, hike, boat, or just watch the leaves change color and drop from the trees – which phenomenal numbers of people come to do each fall. And there are the historic sights, which manage to catalog all manner of New England architecture and design, not to mention Yankee pride and ingenuity. Boston especially is celebrated as the birthplace of American independence – so many of the seminal events of the Revolutionary War took place here, or just outside, in Lexington or Concord; and, although the genteel seaside towns of Massachusetts and Rhode Island can seem a far cry from the first European settlements in New England, plenty of traces of those early years remain. This is, after all, the stretch of the United States where the Pilgrim Fathers and other religious sects put down their stakes, their survival aided by groups of Native Americans who themselves were eventually displaced, though their legacy remains, too, in place names throughout the region. Later, as the European foothold on the continent became more secure, the coastline became increasingly prime real estate, lined with grand patrician homes, from the Vanderbilt mansions of Newport to the presidential compounds of the Bush and Kennedy families. Inland, the Ivy League colleges of Harvard, Yale, Brown, Dartmouth and others still embody New England's strong sense of its own superiority, and contribute to accusations of provincialism and snobbishness; in fact, the region's traditional role as home to the WASP elite is due more to the vagaries of history and ideology than to economic realities. Its thin soil and harsh climate made it difficult for the first pioneers to sustain an agricultural way of life, while the industrial prosperity of the nineteenth and early twentieth centuries is now but a distant memory. Indeed, New England has pockets, in Vermont and the other more northerly states, that are as poor as anywhere in the US; and the southern states have all the problems that are normally associated with long-established urban conglomerations.

Despite the apparent gulf between its interior and coast – and, too, its northern and southern halves – New England is compact and well defined, and quite easy to get around; only Maine, New England's biggest and most rural state by some way, takes any real time and effort to navigate. Most of its states offer the same mix (to differing

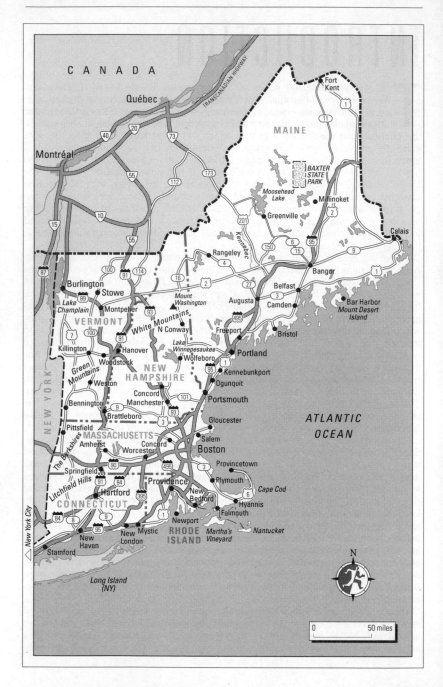

degrees) of picturesque small towns and villages and at times dramatic landscapes, though each has its own distinctive character. When you're working out where to go, plan to include coverage of at least parts of two to three states, in order to pick up on some of that difference. The southern states of Connecticut, Massachusetts and Rhode Island are more urban and historic and, where nature intervenes, it is usually along the region's spectacular coastline. Here, the tourist facilities are aimed as much at weekenders from the big cities as outsiders – Cape Cod, the Berkshires, Martha's Vineyard, all are convenient (and very popular) targets for moneyed locals. Further north, the lakes and mountains of Vermont, New Hampshire, and particularly Maine, offer wilderness to rival any in the nation.

Where to go and what to see

Boston is the undisputed capital of New England, perhaps America's most historic city, certainly one of its most elegant, full of enough colonial charm and contemporary culture to satisfy most appetites. Together with its energetic student neighbor, Cambridge, Boston has plenty to merit a visit of at least a few days, including a fine array of restaurants, bars and venues for both high- and lowbrow culture. The city also makes a good base for day-trips out to historic Lexington and Concord, the rocky North Shore, where the witch sights of Salem probably hold the most interest, and Cape Cod – an admittedly somewhat overrated, usually very crowded peninsula, but one which does at least have delightful, quirky Provincetown at its outermost tip.

West of Boston, there's the collegiate Pioneer Valley, which gives way to the Berkshires, a scenic if hopelessly twee retreat for Boston and New York's cultural elite – much like its Connecticut cousin, Litchfield Hills, just to its south. Southwest of Boston, along the coast, tiny Rhode Island's two main attractions are energetic Providence and wealthy Newport, beyond which you can take in the better parts of the Connecticut coast – the seaport of Mystic, and, further on, likeable New Haven, home to Yale University.

In the opposite direction from Boston, in the three states to the north, New England is more varied: the weekenders are thinner on the ground, there's a greater sense of space, and a simpler way of life rules. In Vermont, outside of the relaxed, pleasant towns of Brattleboro and Burlington, both worthy of exploration, you're best off just wandering the state's backroads in search of country inns, dairy farms, and some peace and quiet – unless of course you've come to make the pilgrimage to Ben & Jerry's in Waterbury, to see how an ice-cream empire began. Over in New Hampshire, the rugged glory of the White Mountains is the most dramatic lure, with the highest peaks in the area and countless outdoor opportunities; indeed, if you're an avid camper or hiker, you won't want to miss this area. Coastal Portsmouth is also as nice a town as you'll find most anywhere in the region. Finally, there's Maine, in the far northeast of the country, which has perhaps New England's most extreme blend of seaside towns (Portland, Bar Harbor) and untamed interior wilderness, in which you can spot moose outside of Rangeley, whitewater raft near Moosehead Lake, and do some remote hiking in Baxter State Park along the Appalachian Trail, which actually runs through all three of New England's northern states.

ROUGH GUIDE FAVORITES:
New England

We've listed by category some of our favorite cities, sights, and diversions in New England at the back of this book; see the index on pp.560–564 for more.

AVERAGE TEMPERATURES (°F) AND RAINFALL (INCHES) IN NEW ENGLAND											
	Jan	Feb	March	April	May	June	July	Aug	Sept	Oct	Nov	Dec
Bangor												
max	27	28	37	52	63	73	79	75	68	57	45	30
min	9	10	21	34	43	52	57	55	48	39	30	16
precipitation	3.0	2.9	3.2	3.3	3.5	3.3	3.3	3.3	3.4	3.4	4.6	3.9
Boston												
max	36	37	45	57	66	77	82	81	72	63	52	39
min	23	25	32	41	50	59	64	64	57	46	39	27
precipitation	3.6	3.6	3.7	3.6	3.3	3.1	2.8	3.2	3.1	3.3	4.2	4.0
Burlington												
max	25	27	37	54	66	75	81	79	70	57	45	30
min	9	9	21	34	45	54	59	57	48	39	30	16
rain	1.8	1.6	2.2	2.8	3.1	3.5	3.6	4.1	3.3	2.9	3.1	2.4
Hartford												
max	36	37	46	59	70	79	84	82	75	64	52	37
min	18	19	27	37	46	55	63	61	52	41	34	21
rain	3.3	3.0	3.4	3.9	4.0	3.8	3.6	3.5	3.5	3.5	3.7	3.6
Providence												
max	36	37	46	57	68	77	82	81	73	63	52	41
min	19	21	28	37	48	57	63	63	54	43	36	25
rain	3.9	3.6	4.0	4.1	3.8	3.3	3.2	3.6	3.5	3.7	4.5	4.4

When to go

New England can be a rather pricey place to visit, especially in late September and October, when visitors flock to see the magnificent fall foliage. The region is at its most beautiful during this time, which makes the crowds and prices understandable, if not more bearable. It can get quite cold, unsurprisingly, during winter months, but that's fine if you're thinking of skiing or other winter sports, or a cabin retreat of sorts. Bear in mind, though, that, whichever resort you choose, you likely won't be alone. Summers are warm and dry, but this is New England's prime season and it can get extremely crowded, especially in overpopulated getaway towns like those on Cape Cod, Martha's Vineyard, the Rhode Island coast and in southern Maine – though the upside of coming then is that at least you know everything will be open. On balance, late spring is probably the nicest time to come: the temperature is generally clement, if a little unpredictable, the crowds are more dispersed, and prices have yet to go up for the tourist season.

PART ONE

THE

BASICS

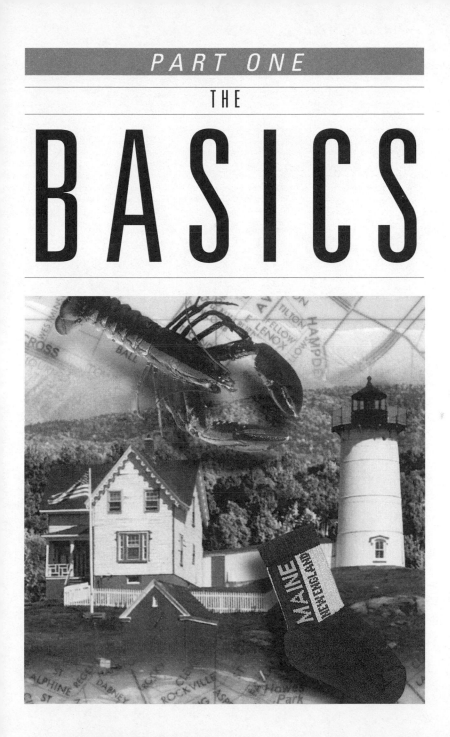

GETTING THERE FROM BRITAIN AND IRELAND

There are no direct flights to New England's small regional airports from the UK or Ireland; flights to Boston connect with services to Providence, Hartford, Burlington, Portland and Bangor. New York flights also connect to the smaller airports, which may be a cheaper option than flying via Boston, especially in the fall when some airlines keep their Boston prices high.

FARES AND AIRLINES

Although you can fly to the US from any of the regional airports, the only nonstop flights from Britain to Boston are from London, with one direct flight daily from Dublin and from Shannon. The nonstop **flight time** is around eight hours from London to Boston; following winds ensure that return flights are always up to an hour shorter than outward journeys. Because of the time difference (five hours), flights usually leave London mid-morning, while flights back from Boston tend to arrive early in the morning.

Britain remains one of the best places in Europe to obtain flight bargains, though **fares** vary widely according to season, availability, and the current level of inter-airline competition. The comments that follow can only act as a general guide, so be sure to shop around carefully for the best offers by checking the **travel ads** in the weekend papers, on the **holiday pages** of ITV's **Teletext** and, in London, scouring **Time Out** and London's **Evening Standard**. Giveaway magazines aimed at young travelers, like TNT, are also useful resources. In addition, **Web sites** such as

www.lastminute.com, *www.cheapflights.co.uk* and *www.deckchair.com* are good sources of discounted fares and last-minute deals.

Standby deals (open-dated tickets which you pay for and then decide later when you want to fly – if there's room on the plane) are few and far between, and don't give great savings: in general you're better off with an **Apex** ticket. The conditions on these are pretty standard whomever you fly with – seats must be purchased seven days or more in advance, and you must stay for at least one Saturday night; tickets are normally valid for up to six months. Some airlines also do less expensive **Super-Apex** tickets, which fall into two categories: the first are approximately £150 cheaper than an ordinary Apex but must be bought 21 days in advance and require a minimum stay of seven days and a maximum stay of one month, the second are around £100 less than an Apex, must be purchased fourteen days in advance and entail a minimum stay of a week and a maximum stay of two months – such tickets are usually non-refundable or changeable. **Open-jaw** tickets can be a good idea, allowing you to fly into New York, for example, and back from Boston for little or no extra charge; fares are calculated by halving the return fares to each destination and adding the two figures together. This makes a convenient option for those who want a fly-drive holiday (see p.4).

Generally, the most expensive time to fly is **high season**, roughly between June and August and around Christmas, though bear in mind that some airlines maintain higher prices throughout the fall season. May and September are slightly less pricey, and the rest of the year is considered **low season** and is cheaper still. Keep an eye out for slack season bargains and, additionally, make sure to check the exact dates of the seasons with your operator or airline; you might be able to make major savings by shifting your departure date by a week – or even a day. **Weekend rates** for all return flights tend to be around £20 more expensive than those in the week.

For an overview of the various offers, and unofficially discounted tickets, go straight to an **agent** specializing in low-cost flights (some are listed on p.4). Especially if you're under 26 or a student, they may be able to knock up to thirty percent off the regular Apex fares when there are no special airline deals. Agents will usually offer nonstop flights,

DIRECT FLIGHTS TO BOSTON FROM BRITAIN AND IRELAND

Aer Lingus ☎01/886 8888, *www.aerlingus.ie.* Daily flights from Dublin and Shannon. Low-season fares start from IR£269 plus IR£45.64 airport tax.

American Airlines ☎0345/789789, *www.aa.com.* Two flights daily from London Heathrow. Low-season fares start from £154 plus £49 tax.

British Airways ☎0845/773 3377, *www.british-airways.com.* Three flights daily from London Heathrow. Typical low-season fares are £211 plus £49 tax.

Virgin Atlantic ☎01293/747747, *www .flyvirgin.com/atlantic.* Daily flight from London Gatwick. A sample low-season fare comes out at £175 plus £55.20 tax.

FLIGHT AGENTS IN BRITAIN AND IRELAND

Bridge the World, 47 Chalk Farm Rd, London NW1 8AN (☎020/7916 0990, *www.bridgetheworld.com*). Good deals aimed at the backpacker market.

Flightbookers, 177–178 Tottenham Court Rd, London W1P 0LX (☎020/7757 2000); Gatwick Airport, south terminal, British Rail station (☎01293/568300; daily 8am–10pm); 34 Argyle Arcade, off Buchanan St, Glasgow G1 1RS (☎0141/204 1919), *www.ebookers.com.* Low fares on an extensive range of scheduled flights.

Joe Walsh Tours, 69 Upper O'Connell St, Dublin 2 (☎01/872 2555); 8–11 Lower Baggot St, Dublin 2 (☎01/676 3053); 117 St Patrick St, Cork (☎021/427 7959), *www.joewalshtours.ie.* Budget fares.

The London Flight Centre, 131 Earls Court Rd, London SW5 9RH (☎020/7244 6411); 47 Notting Hill Gate, London W11 3JS (☎020/7727 4290); Shop 33, The Broadway Centre, Hammersmith tube, London W6 9YE (☎020/8748 6777), *www.topdecktravel.co.uk.* Long-established agent dealing in discount flights.

North South Travel, Moulsham Mill Centre, Parkway, Chelmsford, Essex CM2 7PX (☎01245/608291, *www.northsouthtravel.co.uk*). Friendly, competitive travel agency, offering discounted fares worldwide – profits are used to support projects in the developing world, especially the promotion of sustainable tourism.

STA Travel 86 Old Brompton Rd, London SW7 3LH, 117 Euston Rd, London NW1 2SX; 38 Store St, London WC1E 7BZ (☎020/7361 6161); 11 Goodge St, London W1P; 25 Queen's Rd, Bristol BS8 1QE (☎0117/929 4399); 38 Sidney St,

or "direct" flights via another airport in the US, although you may be offered other, stranger, combinations (London to Boston via Reykjavik with Iceland Air, for less than £210 in low season) – all worth considering if the price is right.

The same agents also offer cut-price seats on **charter flights**. These are particularly good value if you're traveling from a British city other than London, although they tend to be limited to the summer season, be restricted to so-called "holiday destinations" and have fixed departure and return dates. Brochures are available in most high street travel agents, or contact the specialists direct. Finally, if you're planning to visit destinations outside New England, many airlines also offer air passes (see p.24), which allow foreign travelers to fly between a given number of US cities for one discounted price.

PACKAGES

Packages – fly-drive, flight/accommodation deals and guided tours (or a combination of all three) – can work out cheaper than arranging the same trip yourself, especially for a short-term stay. The obvious drawbacks are the loss of flexibility and the fact that most schemes use hotels in the mid-range bracket, but there is a wide variety of options available. High-street travel agents have plenty of brochures and information about the various combinations.

FLY-DRIVE

Fly-drive deals, which give cut-rate (sometimes free) car rental when you're buying a transatlantic ticket, always work out cheaper than renting on the spot and give especially great value if you intend to do a lot of driving. On the other hand, you'll probably have to pay more for the flight than if you booked it through a discount agent. Competition between airlines and tour operators means that it's well worth phoning to check on current special promotions.

Northwest Flydrive (see box on p.6) offers excellent deals for not much more than an ordinary Apex fare; for example, a return flight to Boston

Cambridge CB2 3HX (☎01223/366966); 75 Deansgate, Manchester M3 2BW (☎0161/834 0668); 36 George St, Oxford OX1 2OJ (☎01865/792800), *www.statravel.co.uk*. Also branches in Aberdeen, Birmingham, Canterbury, Cardiff, Coventry, Durham, Glasgow, Loughborough, Nottingham, Warwick and Sheffield. Specialists in low-cost flights for students and under-26s, though other customers welcome.

Trailfinders, 42–50 Earls Court Rd, London W8 6FT (☎020/7938 3366); 194 Kensington High St, London W8 7RG (☎020/7938 3939); 215 Kensington High St, London W6 6BD (☎020/7937 5400); 58 Deansgate, Manchester M3 2FF (☎0161/839 6969); 254–284 Sauchiehall St, Glasgow G2 3EH (☎0141/353 2224); 22–24 The Priory, Queensway, Birmingham B4 6BS (☎0121/236 1234); 48 Corn St, Bristol BS1 1HQ (☎0117/929 9000); 4–5 Dawson St, Dublin 2 (☎01/677 7888), *www.trailfinders.co.uk*. One of the best-informed and most efficient agents for independent travelers.

Travel Bag, 52 Regent St, London W1R 6DX; 373–375 The Strand, opposite the Savoy Hotel, London WC2R 0JF; 3–5 High St, Alton, Hants GU34 1BN; 28 Princess St, Knutsford, Cheshire WA16 6BU; 26–28 Drury Lane, Solihull, West Midlands B91 3BG (USA enquries and bookings ☎020/7287 5559, *www.travelbag.co.uk*).

Discount flights to USA and other long-haul destinations.

Travel Care, Florence Rd, Bray, Co Wicklow (☎01/286 4244, fax 01/282 8622, *www.travelcare.ie*). Discount flight specialists.

USIT CAMPUS, national call centre ☎0870/240 1010; 52 Grosvenor Gardens, London SW1W 0AG (☎020/7730 2101); 541 Bristol Rd, Selly Oak, Birmingham B29 6AU (☎0121/414 1848); 61 Ditchling Rd, Brighton BN1 4SD (☎01273/570226); 37–39 Queen's Rd, Clifton, Bristol BS8 1QE (☎0117/929 2494); 5 Emmanuel St, Cambridge CB1 1NE (☎01223/324283); 53 Forest Rd, Edinburgh EH1 2QP (☎0131/225 6111, tele-sales 668 3303); 122 George St, Glasgow G1 1RF (☎0141/553 1818); 166 Deansgate, Manchester M3 3FE (☎0161/273 1721); 105–106 St Aldates, Oxford OX1 1DO (☎01865/242067), *www.usitcampus.co.uk*. Student/youth travel specialists, with branches also in YHA shops and on university campuses all over Britain.

USIT Now, Fountain Centre, College St, Belfast BT1 6ET (☎028/9032 4073); 66 Oliver Plunkett St, Cork (☎021/427 0900); 4 Shipquay Place, Derry (☎028/7137 1888); 19 Aston Quay, Dublin 2 (☎01/602 1700); 16 Mary St, Galway (☎091/565177); Central Buildings, 51 O'Connell St, Limerick (☎061/415064); 36–37 Georges St, Waterford (☎051/872601). Student and youth specialists.

and a week's car rental costs around £450 per person in low season. Several of the other companies listed in the box offer similar, and sometimes cheaper, packages.

Watch out for hidden extras, such as local taxes, "drop-off" charges, which can be as much as a week's rental, and Collision Damage Waiver insurance. Remember, too, that while you can drive in the States with a British license, there can be problems renting vehicles if you're under 25. For complete car rental and driveaway details, see "Getting Around" (p.21).

FLIGHT AND ACCOMMODATION DEALS

There are plenty of combined **flight and accommodation deals** to New England, and although you can often do things cheaper independently, you won't be able to do the same things cheaper – in fact, the equivalent room booked separately will normally be a lot more expensive – and you can leave the organizational hassles to someone

else. Drawbacks include loss of flexibility and the fact that you'll probably have to stay in hotels in the mid-range to expensive bracket, even though less expensive accommodation is almost always available.

A handful of tour operators (see p.6) offer quite deluxe packages, of which Virgin Holidays are about the least expensive: three nights in Boston costs around £650 in high season. Discount agents can set up more basic packages for just over £500 per person. Pre-booked accommodation schemes, under which you buy vouchers for use in a specific group of hotels, are not normally good value.

TOURING AND ADVENTURE PACKAGES

A simple and exciting way to New England's remoter parts, without being hassled by too many practical considerations, is to take a specialist **touring and adventure package**, which typically includes transportation, accommodation, food, and a guide. Some of the more adventurous tours take small groups around on minibuses and use a combination of budget hotels and camping (equipment, except a sleeping bag, is provided).

Explore Worldwide is one UK-based company to

TOUR OPERATORS AND NEW ENGLAND SPECIALISTS

American Airlines Holidays, PO Box 5, 12 Coningsby Rd, Peterborough PE3 8XP (☎0870/605 0506). Flight-plus-accommodation and fly-drive deals.

American Adventures and Road Runner, 64 Mount Pleasant Ave, Tunbridge Wells, Kent TN1 1QY (☎01892/512700, *www.americanadventures.com*). Small-group camping adventure trips in the USA and Canada.

American Connections, 10 York Way, Lancaster Rd, High Wycombe, Bucks HP12 3PY (☎01494/473173, *www.connectionsworldwide.net*). Tailor-made packages plus escorted coach tours: the twelve-day "Charm of New England" package features Boston, Albany, the Berkshires and Rhode Island, amongst other attractions. The price ranges from £1045 to £1275 per person, depending on season.

Bon Voyage, 18 Bellevue Rd, Southampton, Hants SO15 2AY (☎023/8033 0332). Flight-plus-accommodation operator.

British Airways Holidays, Astral Towers, Bettsway, London Road, Crawley, West Sussex RH10 2XA (☎0870/242 4243, *www.baholidays.co.uk*). Boston city breaks and fly-drive deals. Seven-night self-drive tour of New England starts from around £460.

Contiki Travel, Wells House, 15 Elmfield Rd, Bromley, Kent BR1 1LS (☎020/8290 6777, *www.contiki.com*). All-inclusive coach tours of the States, taking in Boston. From £699 for nine days.

Cosmos, Wren Court, 17 London Rd, Bromley, Kent BR1 1DE (☎0870/264 6055, *www.cosmoscoach.co.uk*). Their eleven-day "New England Splendor and Cape Cod" tour of Massachusetts, Vermont, New Hampshire and Maine starts at around £1079.

The Destination Group, 14 Greville St, London EC1N 8SB (☎020/7400 7001, *www.destinationgroup.co.uk*). Tailor-made accommodation, fly-drive deals and tours in association with Amtrak.

Explore Worldwide, 1 Frederick St, Aldershot, Hants GU11 1LQ (☎01252/760000, *www.explore.co.uk*). Small-group adventure tours.

Individual Travellers, New England Country Homes, Manor Courtyard, Bignor, Pulborough,

RH20 1QD (☎0870/077 4774, fax 078 0190, *www.indiv-travellers.com*). Complete packages, including selected accommodation in traditional New England clapboard cottages, colonial houses, log houses, hunting lodges and beach houses.

Kuoni, 33 Maddox St, London W1S 1PX (☎020/7499 8636); 2a Barton Square, Manchester M2 7LW (☎0161/832 0667), *www.kuoni.co.uk*. Multi-center flight-plus-accommodation-plus-car deals.

North America Travel Service, 7 Albion St, Leeds LS1 5ER (☎0113/246 1466). Tailor-made holidays. An eight-day fly-drive holiday taking in Boston, Maine, White Mountains, Green Mountains and Cape Cod costs from £649 per person.

Northwest Flydrive, PO Box 45, Bexhill-on-Sea, East Sussex TN40 1PY (☎01424/224400, fax 223300, *www.flydriveusa.co.uk*). Flight-plus-accommodation and fly-drive specials. Boston weekend breaks start from £269.

Premier Holidays, Westbrook, Milton Road, Cambridge CB4 1YG (☎0870/789 3334, *www.directcollection.co.uk*). Flight-plus-accommodation deals.

Travel 4, Hamlyn House, Highgate Hill, London N19 5PR (☎0870/606 2444). City packages in the Boston area, and tailor-made trips elsewhere in New England.

Travelpack, Clarendon House, Clarendon Road, Eccles, Manchester M30 9TR (☎0870/574 7101, *www.travelpack.co.uk*). Boston city-breaks, escorted tours and tailor-made holidays.

United Vacations, PO Box 377, Bromley, Kent BA1 1LY (☎020/8466 7766, *www.unitedvacations.co.uk*). City breaks, tailor-mades and fly-drives.

Up & Away, 19 The Mall, Bromley, Kent BR1 1TT (☎020/8289 5050, *up.away@btinternet.com*). Tailor-made and fly-drive deals to Boston and other New England destinations.

Virgin Holidays, The Galleria, Station Road, Crawley, West Sussex RH10 1WW (☎01293/617181, *www.virginholidays.co.uk*). Fly-drive and accommodation packages, from Boston to the Berkshires.

offer such deals: their sixteen-day New England package includes canoeing in the Adirondacks, whitewater rafting and hiking the Haselton trail. It costs from around £1025 per person.

ENTRY REQUIREMENTS

Citizens of **Britain**, **Ireland**, and most European countries in possession of full passports do not require visas for trips to the United States of less than ninety days. Instead you are simply asked to fill in the **visa waiver form** handed out on incoming flights. Immigration control takes place at your initial point of arrival on US soil. For further details, contact your nearest **American embassy** or consulate: 24/31 Upper Grosvenor Square, London W1A 1AE (☎020/7499 9000; visa hotline ☎0891/200290); 3 Regent Terrace, Edinburgh EH7 5BW (☎0131/556 8315); Queens House, 14 Queen St, Belfast BT1 6EQ (☎028/9024 1279); or 42 Elgin Rd, Ballsbridge, Dublin 4 (☎01/668 8777).

GETTING THERE FROM AUSTRALIA AND NEW ZEALAND

There are no direct flights to Boston from Australia or New Zealand, and most people reach the eastern United States by way of the West Coast via gateway cities such as Los Angeles and San Francisco. You can do this by either buying an all-in ticket via LA or San Francisco, or simply flying to LA and using one of the domestic flight coupons you can buy with your international ticket. The latter can work out cheaper than opting for a straight-through fare, especially if you intend to take in other US cities besides Boston.

For example, a low-season return ticket to LA costs around A$1699/NZ$1899 and A$2099/NZ$2299 high season with Air New Zealand. By purchasing a domestic flight coupon for A$450/NZ$650 (for a minimum of three), it is one of the cheapest ways to get to Boston. In comparison a round-trip, 21-day advance ticket from Australia to Boston, Burlington, Hartford or Providence usually starts at around A$2300 during low season, and around A$2700 during high season; from New Zealand, look to pay NZ$2400–2800. There's always the option of getting off for a few days en route, often a welcome break on long-haul flights and also worth consideration if Boston is part of a wider US trip, and you have plenty of time, is to travel overland by either car, train or bus. There are fairly regular flights leaving from all the major US cities to Boston and, to a lesser extent, Burlington, Hartford, and Providence. Alternatively, if you don't mind going via Asia, Korean Airlines, Japan Airlines (JAL), Cathay Pacific and Singapore Airlines all offer good-value regular services as far as New York via their home cities.

FARES AND ROUTES

You can choose between booking direct through airlines, usually at published rates, or through **travel agents**, which often offer the best deals on fares and have the latest information on limited special offers. They can also point you to **fly-drive-accommodation packages**. Flight Centres and STA Travel generally offer the lowest fares. You might also want to have a look on the Internet: *www.travel.com.au* offers discounted fares as does *www.sydneytravel.com*. All the information below can only act as a general guide, so be sure to shop around a bit when choosing your ticket.

Remember that airfares are seasonal, and the differences can add up to as much as A$200/NZ$400. Generally speaking, the most expensive time to fly is **high season**, from mid-June to mid-July and mid-December to mid-January; **low season** is from February through March and

AIRLINES

Air New Zealand Australia ☎13/2476; New Zealand ☎09/357 3000, *www.airnz.com*.
Daily flights from Sydney and Auckland to Boston with a transfer in Los Angeles: code-shares with United Airlines.

America West Airlines Australia ☎02/9290 2232 & ☎1300/ 364 757, *www.americawest.com*.
Flight coupons for US domestic travel.

American Airlines Australia ☎1300/650 747; New Zealand ☎09/309 0735 or ☎0800/887 997, *www.aa.com*.
Daily flights from Sydney to Boston with a transfer in Los Angeles: code-shares with Qantas.

Cathay Pacific Australia ☎13/1747 or ☎02/9931 5500; New Zealand ☎09/379 086, *www.cathaypacific.com*.
Several flights a week from major Australasian cities to Los Angeles and New York with a transfer in Hong Kong.

Delta Airlines Australia ☎02/9251 3211 & ☎1800/500 992; New Zealand ☎09/379 3370 or ☎0800/440 876, *www.delta-air.com*.
Flight coupons for US domestic travel.

JAL Japan Airlines Australia ☎02/9272 1111; New Zealand ☎09/379 9906, *www.japanair.com*.
Several flights a week from Cairns, Brisbane, Sydney, Auckland and Christchurch to New York

and Boston with either a transfer or an overnight stopover in Tokyo.

Korean Air Australia ☎02/9262 6000; New Zealand ☎09/307 3687, *www.koreanair.com*.
Several flights a week from Sydney, Brisbane, and Auckland to Boston with an overnight stop in Seoul.

Northwest Airlines Australia ☎1300/303 747; New Zealand ☎09/302 1452, *www.nwa.com*.
Flight coupons for USA domestic travel.

Qantas Australia ☎13/1313; New Zealand ☎ 09/357 8900 or ☎0800/808 767, *www.qantas.com.au*.
Daily flights from major Australian cities and Auckland to Boston with a transfer in Los Angeles.

Singapore Airlines Australia ☎13/10 11 & ☎02/9350 0262; New Zealand ☎09/303 2129 or ☎0800/808 909, *www.singaporeair.com*.
Daily flights from Sydney, Perth, and Auckland to New York with a transfer in Singapore and Los Angeles.

United Airlines Australia ☎13/1777; New Zealand ☎09/379 3800, *www.ual.com*.
Daily flights from Sydney and Auckland to Boston with transfers in either San Francisco, Los Angeles or New York.

mid-October through November. The rest of the year is considered **shoulder season**. As for travel time from either Sydney or Auckland to Boston, including connections, count on basically a full 24-hour day. Fares from all eastern Australian capitals are generally the same (with Ansett and Qantas providing a free connecting service between these cities), whereas fares from Perth and Darwin are about A$200 more.

The **most direct flights** to Boston are with United Airlines in conjunction with Air New Zealand (from Sydney to Boston via Auckland and LA and Qantas/American Airlines via Los Angeles all starting at A$2399/NZ$2499 low season and A$2799/NZ$2899 during high season. The **lowest fares** are offered by Korean Airlines and Japan Airlines (JAL) and include a night's accommodation in their respective home cities of Seoul from A$1799/NZ$2250 to A$2499/NZ$2699 and Tokyo from A$1955/NZ$2399 to A$2599/NZ$2799. If you don't want to spend the night,

Cathay Pacific and Singapore Airlines can get you there from A$2099/NZ$2399 to A$2699/NZ$2899 with a transfer (but not an overnight stay) in their home cities of Hong Kong and Singapore.

ROUND THE WORLD

One possible option is to take in New England as part of a larger trip, in which case a **round-the-world** ticket may be right for you, often working out just a little more than an all-in ticket. Call your travel agent or airline for a rundown of the routes available; they'll likely be able to work to your itinerary. There are a number of airline combinations to choose from: for example, a straightforward ticket (no backtracking or side trips) from Sydney or Auckland to LA, New York/Boston, London, Paris, Bangkok, Singapore, and back home, starts at A$2099. More flexible mileage-based tickets such as the "Star Alliance 1" offered by Ansett Australia/Air New Zealand/United/Thai, starting at A$2499, and "One World Explorer" by

Qantas/British Airways/American Airlines/Cathay which starts at A$2599, allow side trips, backtracking and open-jaw travel within the USA.

FLY-DRIVE AND TOUR PACKAGES

There are virtually no fly-drive or flight/accommodation deals from Australia or New Zealand; however, if you're planning to travel in style, and especially if your visit is going to be short or geared around special interests, such as cycling or history, you may want to consider one of the **package tours** offered by the operators in the box below. Though these tours are inevitably more restrictive than independent travel, they may work out cheaper than making the same arrangements on

arrival and can help you make the most of time if you're on a tight schedule. Specialist agents and tour operators can usually arrange flights to fit in with your travel plans.

ENTRY REQUIREMENTS

Australian and New Zealand passport holders staying less than ninety days do not require a visa, providing they arrive on a commercial flight with an onward or return ticket. For longer stays, US multiple-entry visas cost A$80/NZ$110; a six-month visa costs around A$199/NZ$250. You'll need an application form, available from either the US visa information service (☎1902/941 641) or travel agencies, one signed passport photo and your passport. Post

---

DISCOUNT TRAVEL AGENTS

Anywhere Travel, 345 Anzac Parade, Kingsford, Sydney (☎02/9663 0411; *anywhere@ozemail.com.au*). Travel agent close to the airport offering discounted flights, as well as good deals on accommodation, tours and car rental.

Budget Travel, 16 Fort St, Auckland, plus branches around the city (☎09/366 0061 & 0800/808 040). Long-established travel agent dealing with budget airfares and accommodation packages.

Destinations Unlimited, 220 Queen St, Auckland (☎09/373 4033). Discount fares plus a good selection of tours and holiday packages.

Flight Centre Australia: 82 Elizabeth St, Sydney, plus branches nationwide (☎02/9235 3522, nearest branch ☎13/1600, *www.flightcentre.com.au*). New Zealand: 350 Queen St, Auckland (☎09/358 4310), plus branches nationwide. Competitive discounts on airfares, and a wide range of package holidays and adventure tours.

Northern Gateway, 22 Cavenagh St, Darwin (☎08/8941 1394, *oztravel@norgate.com.au*). Low-cost flights to the US from Darwin.

STA Travel, Australia: 855 George St, Sydney; 256 Flinders St, Melbourne; other offices in state capitals and major universities (nearest branch ☎13/1776, fastfare telesales ☎1300/360 960, *www.statravel.com.au*). New Zealand: 10 High St, Auckland (☎09/309 0458, fastfare telesales ☎09/366 6673), plus branches in Wellington, Christchurch, Dunedin, Palmerston

North, Hamilton and at major universities. Airfare discounts for students and those under 26, as well as visas, student cards and travel insurance.

Student Uni Travel, 92 Pitt St, Sydney (☎02/9232 8444, *sydney@backpackers.net*) plus branches in Brisbane, Cairns, Darwin, Melbourne and Perth. Student/youth flight discounts and travel information.

Thomas Cook, Australia: 175 Pitt St, Sydney (☎02/9231 2877, *www.thomascook.com.au*); 257 Collins St, Melbourne (☎03/9282 0222); plus branches in other state capitals (local branch ☎13/1771, Thomas Cook direct telesales ☎1800/801 002); New Zealand: 191 Queen St, Auckland (☎09/379 3920). Low-cost flights, also tours, accommodation, car rental and travellers cheques.

Trailfinders, 8 Spring St, Sydney (☎02/9247 7666; *www.trailfinders.com.au*); 91 Elizabeth St, Brisbane (☎07/3229 0887); Hides Corner, Shield St, Cairns (☎07/4041 1199). Independent travel specialist offering a wide selection of tours and discounted flights.

Travel.com.au, 76-80 Clarence St, Sydney (☎02/9249 5444 & 1800/000 447, *www.travel.com.au*). Online flight discounts.

USIT Beyond, cnr Shortland St and Jean Batten Place, Auckland (☎09/379 4224 or ☎0800/788 336, *www.usitbeyond.co.nz*) plus branches in Christchurch, Dunedin, Palmerston North, Hamilton and Wellington. Student/youth travel specialists.

SPECIALIST AGENTS AND TOUR OPERATORS

The Adventure Travel Company, 164 Parnell Rd, Parnell, Auckland (☎09/379 9755, *advakl@hot.co.nz*). NZ agent for Peregrine and Exodus.

America Town & Country Holidays, 127 Canterbury Rd, Blackburn South, Melbourne (☎03/9877 3322). Can arrange accommodation-car rental packages and Boston city mini-stays from A$400/NZ$650 for 3 nights (twin share) and cruises along the New England coast.

American Express Travel, 344 Queen St, Brisbane (☎07/3220 0878). All US travel arrangements.

Australian Pacific Tours, 475 Hampton Street, Hampton, Vic (☎03/9277 8444 or 1800/675 222, *apt.mail@apt.otc.au*); 2 Sutton Crescent, Hunters Corner, Auckland (☎09/279 6077). Offer 8-day luxury coach tours during September and October of the region's historical sights, architecture and scenery; from Boston via Cambridge, Lexington, Concord and Williamstown, then up through Vermont to St Johns, across to the coast of Main to Kennebunkport then back to Boston. Tours cost A$2580/NZ$3200.

Canada and America Travel Specialists, 343 Pacific Highway, Crows Nest, Sydney (☎02/9922 4600). Wholesalers of Greyhound Ameripasses plus flights and accommodation.

Connections, Level 2, 164 Wharf Street, Brisbane (☎1800/077 251, *mail@connections1835.com.au*). Pre-arranged and individually tailored group adventure tours for 18 to 35s.

Journeys Worldwide/ American Travel Centre, 333 Adelaide St, Brisbane (☎07/3221 4788 or ☎1300/734 788, *journey@atlasmail.com*). A selection of accommodation from A$250/NZ$310 per night for a double room, as well as coach tours and car rental.

Pacific and International Travel Company, Level 1, 91 York Street, Sydney (☎13/2747, *www.pitc.com.au*). Offer 13-day escorted deluxe coach tours that take in the sights and scenery from Boston, along the coast of Maine over to the White Mountains, down through Vermont to the Berkshires and Stockbridge, then on to Newport, Cape Cod and Martha's Vineyard. Tours from Sept to Oct and cost A$3120/NZ$3675.

Peregrine, 258 Lonsdale St, Melbourne (☎03/9662 2700 & 1300/655 433, *www.peregrine.net.au*), plus offices in Brisbane, Sydney, Adelaide and Perth. Adventure travel company and agents for Exodus' 8-day cycling tours from Cape Cod across Massachusetts to the Berkshire Hills. Prices start at A$2890/NZ$3850 (plus US$100 bike hire).

Sydney International Travel, 8/75 King St, Sydney (☎02/9299 8000, *www.sydneytravel.com.au*). A good selection of regional hotel accommodation, as well as Boston city stays, packaged and individually tailored tours and car rental.

Wiltrans/Maupintour, 10/189 Kent St, Sydney (☎02/9255 0899). Cruises along the New England coast as well as luxury five-star-all inclusive New England autumn coach tours from US$2285 (land only).

it or personally lodge it at an American embassy or consulate. Visa application forms OF156 are available online through the consulate's interactive websites (see addresses below).

In **Australia**, the US Embassy is at 21 Moonah Place, Canberra (☎02/6214 5600), and there's a consulate at Level 59, MLC Centre, Consular Section, 19 Martin Place, Sydney (☎02/9373 9200 or visa hotline ☎1902/941 641, *www.usembassy-australia.state.gov*). For postal applications in Australia, visa application payments can be made at any post office (US visa application payment form no. 828); you'll also need to include the receipt of payment and an

SAE. Processing takes about ten working days for postal applications; personal lodgements take two days – but check details with the consulate first.

In **New Zealand**, the US Consulate is on the 3rd Floor, Citibank Centre, 23 Customs Street, Auckland (☎09/303 2724, *www.consulateauckland.org.nz*). Application forms are available from the consulate or most travel agencies. For postal applications, you'll need to send application form, one passport photograph, fee as a bank cheque or money order and an SAE to the Non-Immigrant Visa Section, Locked Bag 92022, Auckland 1.

GETTING THERE FROM NORTH AMERICA

Getting to New England from anywhere else in North America is only problematic in the harsh winter months, when roads get icy and airports occasionally close due to inclement weather. All the main airlines operate daily scheduled flights to Boston's Logan Airport from across the country, and there are daily scheduled flights from Toronto and Vancouver as well. You should be aware that service to airports other than Boston's Logan Airport can be infrequent. Flying remains the best but most expensive way to travel, although if you're coming from the mid-Atlantic states, driving may make more sense. Train comes a slow but smooth second, and traveling by bus is the least expensive method, but it's also slow – and much less comfortable.

BY AIR

Boston's Logan International Airport is by far the biggest and most accessible in New England; direct flights are available from all the major hubs in North America – though you may find yourself connecting through Chicago, New York City, or another large East Coast city. Smaller airports in Manchester (NH), Portland (ME), Bangor (ME), Burlington (VT), and Windsor Locks (near Hartford, CT) are serviced less regularly by smaller aircraft; some have international terminals as well. It's also worth checking flights to New York City, as they are often cheap enough to make taking a bus, train, or rental car the rest of the way to New England worth it. Albany's (NY) international airport is also close by and a good bet for reasonable fares, especially if you're going on to Vermont, western Massachusetts, or Connecticut.

As airlines tend to match each other's prices, there's generally little difference in the quoted fares. Barring a fare war, round-trip prices to Boston start at around $120 from New York, $190 from Chicago, $180 from Atlanta, and about $240 from Houston. From San Francisco or Los Angeles, round-trip tickets run about $370. What makes more difference than your choice of carrier is the conditions governing the ticket – whether it's fully refundable, the time and day, and most importantly the time of year you travel. Least expensive of all is a non-summer-season midweek flight, booked and paid for at least three weeks in advance. Also keep in mind that one-way tickets are sometimes more expensive than

AIRPORTS IN NEW ENGLAND

Connecticut
Bradley International Airport, I-91, Exit 40, Windsor Locks, CT (☎203/627-3000).

Maine
Portland International Jetport, 1001 Westbrook St, Portland, ME (☎207/774-7301).

Massachusetts
Logan International Airport, East Boston, MA (☎1-800/235-6426).

New Hampshire
Manchester Airport, Brown Ave, Manchester, NH (☎603/624-6556). Pease International Tradeport, 601 Spaulding Turnpike, Portsmouth, NH (☎603/433-6088).

Rhode Island
TF Green State Airport, 2000 Post Rd, Warwick, RI (☎401/737-4000).

Vermont
Burlington International Airport, 1200 Airport Drive, South Burlington, VT (☎802/863-2874).

AIRLINES IN THE USA AND CANADA

Air Canada
☎1-888/247-2262; in Canada call directory inquiries for local toll-free number, *www.aircanada.ca*

Air Tran
☎1-800-AIRTRAN, *www.airtran.com*

Alaska Airlines
☎1-800/426-0333, *www.alaska-air.com*

America Trans Air
☎1-800/435-9282, *www.ata.com*

America West
☎1-800/2FLYAWA, *www.americawest.com*

American Airlines
☎1-800/433-7300, *www.americanair.com*

British Airways ☎1-800/247-9297; in Canada ☎1-800/668-1059, *www.british-airways.com*

Continental
☎1-800/525-0280, *www.flycontinental.com*

Delta Airlines
☎1-800/221-1212; in Canada, call directory inquiries for local toll-free number, *www.delta-air.com*

JetBlue Airlines
☎1-800/JETBLUE, *www.jetblue.com*

Northwest ☎1-800/225-2525, *www.nwa.com*

Southwest ☎1-800/435-9792, *www.iflyswa.com*

Trans World Airlines
☎1-800/221-2000, *www.twa.com*

United Airlines ☎1-800/241-6522, *www.ual.com*

US Airways
☎1-800/428-4322, *www.usairways.com*

Virgin Atlantic
☎1-800/862-8621, *www.fly.virgin.com/atlantic*

round-trip tickets. While it makes sense to call the airlines directly to get a sense of their official fares, it's also worth checking with a reputable travel agent to find out about any special deals or student/youth fares that may be available. You can also scout online at *www.travelocity.com, www.expedia.com, www.cheaptickets.com,* or *www.bestfares.com*.

In addition to the big-name airlines like United and American, a few lesser-known carriers run no-frills flights, which can prove to be very good value, especially if you have a flexible schedule and can stand a few delays. Southwest Airlines flies from a host of cities at rock-bottom prices, and although they don't fly to Boston Logan, they do service Providence (RI), Manchester (NH), and Hartford's Bradley International Airport.

From Canada

Travelers intending to fly from Canada are likely to find that, with less competition on these routes, fares are slightly higher than they are for flights wholly within the US. Canadian flies out of all major cities in Canada in conjunction with American Airlines to Boston and all other New England airports; Air Canada serves Boston and a host of other regional airports jointly with United Airlines. You may well find that it's worth the effort to get to a US city first, and fly on to New England from there. Flights to Boston from Toronto and Montréal tend to run from about CDN$300. From Vancouver to Boston, the lowest round-trip fare might be from around CDN$650.

BY TRAIN

If you have a bit more money and hanker after a few more creature comforts (all the trains have private cabins and dining cars that can be yours for a premium), or simply have the time and inclination to take in some of the rest of the US on your way to New England, then an **Amtrak train** may be just the ticket for you. The most spectacular train journey has to be the **Zephyr** in conjunction with the **Lakeshore Limited**, which runs all the way from San Francisco to Boston (73 hours, including a stopover in Chicago); bus to Emeryville (the nearest Zephyr station to San Francisco) departs San Francisco at 8am daily. Alternately, you can get an 8.45am train from Oakland's Jack London Square and connect with the Zephyr in Sacramento. After climbing alongside raging rivers through gorgeous mountain scenery east of Salt Lake City, the route drops down the eastern flank of the Rockies and races across the Midwest to Chicago where you

For all information on Amtrak fares and schedules, and to make reservations, use the toll-free number ☎1-800/USA-RAIL or visit *www.amtrak.com*. Do not call individual train stations.

change trains before hitting the rolling greenery of western Pennsylvania and upstate New York. Another major route, the **Crescent**, originates in New Orleans and crosses into Atlanta, before making its way north up the East Coast for Boston, traversing some nine states en route.

There are, of course, plenty of routes for shorter trips: Amtrak has ten trains daily from **New York** to Boston and nine daily from **Washington, DC** to Boston, including the new **Acela Express**, which cuts the ride time between New York and Boston to three and a half hours. The express departs New York's Penn Station at 8am and 6pm.

Fares are often more expensive than flying, though off-peak discounts and special deals can make the train an economical choice. One-way cross-country fares are around $170 or so, though if you're traveling round-trip you can take advantage of what they call "Explore America" fares, which are zone-based and allow three stopovers in between your origin and eventual return; you must complete your travels within 45 days. Travel within the Northeast Corridor (from New Orleans up to Vermont) costs $279 between August 15 and June 15 excluding Christmas, $299 from June to August and during the two weeks around Christmas; to add the Midwest zone (east of Denver) costs $359/$399; and for the entire USA the cost is $429/$499. If you want to travel in a bit more style, however, the cost rises quickly. Sleeping compartments, which include meals, small toilets and showers, start at around $285 per night for one or two people (this is in addition to the basic fare). Though you can usually reserve a sleeping compartment on the day of travel, to be safe call several days ahead to check for availability. Regular seats are rarely, if ever, sold out.

FROM CANADA

Amtrak offers services to and from several major Canadian cities, including Toronto, Montréal, and Vancouver. Via Rail Canada operates an extensive rail system within Canada, connecting these larger cities with smaller destinations all over the country. Contact their national information line (☎1-888/842-7733) for local train station contacts and details.

BY BUS

Bus travel is the most tedious and time-consuming way to get to New England, and, for all the trouble, won't really save you much money.

DISCOUNT AGENTS IN THE US AND CANADA

Council Travel
Head office, 205 E 42nd St, New York, NY 10017 (☎212/822-2700; nationwide information ☎1-800/226-8624) *www.counciltravel.com.*

STA Travel
10 Downing St, New York, NY 10014 (☎212/627-3111; nationwide information ☎1-800/777-0112), *www.sta-travel.com.*

Travel CUTS
Head office in Canada, 187 College St, Toronto, ON M5T 1P7 (☎416/979-2406), *www .voyagescampus.com.*

Greyhound (☎1-800/231-2222, *www.greyhound .com*) is the sole long-distance operator and has an extensive network of destinations in New England. Several smaller bus companies (see p.26) that operate within New England often have direct connections with Greyhound's longer routes. Some typical one-way fares (you don't really save getting round-trip tickets) are $40 from New York to Boston; $52 from Philadelphia ($49 with 7-day advance purchase), and $100 from Chicago ($69 with 7-day advance purchase, $79 with 14-day).

The real reason to go Greyhound is if you're planning to visit a number of other places en route; Greyhound's Ameripass is good for unlimited travel within a certain time, and costs $209 for seven days, $319 for fifteen days, $429 for thirty days, and $599 for sixty days. Foreign visitors can buy Ameripasses before leaving home (see p.24 for details). An alternative, in every sense, is the San Francisco-based Green Tortoise bus company, which services Boston in a leisurely coast-to-coast journey (see box).

FROM CANADA

From Canada you may be required to change buses en route. Greyhound Canada (☎1-800/661-8747, *www.greyhound.ca*) is the major carrier, with service from most larger cities. Their parent company, Greyhound, also issues tickets for Canada–USA trips (☎1-800/231-2222). In cases where Greyhound buses do not cover a particular area or destination, their customer service agents can usually issue a ticket through another bus company.

ENTRY REQUIREMENTS FOR CANADIAN VISITORS

Canadian citizens are in a particularly privileged position when it comes to crossing the border into the US. Though it is possible to enter the States without your passport, you should really have it with you on any trip that brings you as far as the New England coast. You only need a visa if you plan to stay for more than ninety days. Remember that without the proper paperwork, Canadians are legally barred from seeking gainful employment in the US.

US Embassy in Canada
100 Wellington St, Ottawa, ON K1P 5T1
(☎613/238-5335).

US Consulates in Canada (2 columns)

Suite 1050, 615 Macleod Trail, Calgary, AB T2G
4T8 (☎403/266-8962).

Suite 910, Cogswell Tower, Scotia Square,
Halifax, NS B3J 3K1 (☎902/429-2480).

Complex Desjardins, South Tower, Montréal, PQ
H5B 1G1 (☎514/398-9695).

2 Place Terrasse Dufferin, Québec City, PQ G1R
4T9 (☎418/692-2095).

360 University Ave, Toronto, ON M5G 1S4
(☎416/595-1700).

1095 W Pender St, Vancouver, BC V6E 2M6
(☎604/685-4311).

BY CAR

Driving your own car gives the greatest freedom and flexibility, but if you don't have one (or don't trust the one you do have), one option worth considering is a driveaway. Companies operate in most major cities, and are paid to find drivers to take a customer's car from one place to another – most commonly between California and New York. Deliveries terminating in Boston are also available. The company will normally pay for your insurance and your first tank of gas; after that, you'll be expected to drive along the most direct route and to average four hundred miles a day. Many drive-

GREEN TORTOISE

One alternative to Long-Distance Bus Hell is the slightly countercultural Green Tortoise, whose buses, complete with foam cushions, bunks, fridges and rock music, cross the country from California to New York and Boston during the summer. These transcontinental trips amount to mini-tours of the nation, taking 10–14 days at a current cost of $590–630 one-way (including most of the contributions to the food fund, which amounts to around $10 a day), and allowing plenty of stops for hiking, river-rafting and hot springs. Other Green Tortoise trips include excursions to the major national parks, south to Mexico and Central America and north to Alaska.

Main Office: 494 Broadway, San Francisco, CA 94133 (☎1-800/867-8647 or 415/956-7500, *www.greentortoise.com*).

away companies are keen to use foreign travelers (German tourists are ideal, it seems), but if you can convince them you are a safe bet they'll take something like a $250 deposit, which you get back after delivering the car in good condition. Get in touch in advance to spare yourself a week's wait for a car to turn up. Look under "Automobile transporters and driveaway companies" in the Yellow Pages and phone around for the latest offers, or try one of the ninety branches of Auto Driveaway, based at 310 S Michigan Ave in Chicago (☎312/341-1900).

Renting a car is the usual story of phoning the local branch of one of the majors (see box, p.21), of which Thrifty tends to be the cheapest. Most have offices at destination airports, and addresses and phone numbers are comprehensively documented in the Yellow Pages. Also worth considering are fly-drive deals, which give cut-rate (and sometimes free) car rental when buying an air ticket. They usually work out cheaper than renting on the spot and are especially good value if you intend to do a lot of driving. A car rented in Canada can normally be driven across the border into the US, but you will pay a much higher fee if you do not return it to its country of origin. Most of the larger companies have offices in Canada.

PACKAGE TOURS

Many tour operators run all-inclusive packages which combine plane tickets and hotel accommodation with (for example) sightseeing, wining and dining, or excursions to typical historic sights. Even if the "package" aspect doesn't thrill you to pieces, these deals can still be more convenient and sometimes even work out to be more economical than arranging the same thing yourself, providing that you don't mind losing a little flexibility. With such a vast range of packages available, it's impossible to give an overview – major travel agents will have brochures detailing what's available. So-called "leaf peeper" tours, where you're shuttled around from town to quaint town during the colorful fall foliage months, are particularly popular, as are all-inclusive ski packages.

HEALTH AND INSURANCE

Travel insurance policies vary: some are comprehensive while others cover only certain risks (accidents, illnesses, delayed or lost luggage, cancelled flights, etc). Whatever it is, though, it's worth having before you set off. In particular, ask whether the policy pays medical costs up front or reimburses you later, and whether it provides for medical evacuation to your home country.

For policies that include lost or stolen luggage, check exactly what is and isn't covered, and make sure the per-article limit will cover your most valuable possession.

Premiums vary as well; you might choose between a range of packages covering anywhere from a week to a year, and they range in cost accordingly. If you're planning to do any "dangerous sports" (skiing, mountaineering, etc.), be sure to ask whether these activities are covered: some companies levy a surcharge.

For **foreign visitors**, travel insurance is essential in view of the high costs of healthcare in the US. Bank and credit cards (particularly American Express) often have certain levels of medical or other insurance included, especially if you use them to pay for your trip. If you have a good all-risks home insurance policy it *may* cover your possessions against loss or theft even when overseas. Many private medical schemes such as BUPA or PPP also offer coverage plans for abroad, including baggage loss, cancellation or curtailment and cash replacement as well as sickness or accident.

North American travel policies apply only to items lost, stolen or damaged while in the custody of an identifiable, responsible third party – hotel porter, airline, luggage consignment, etc. Even in these cases you will have to contact the local police within a certain time limit to have a complete report made out so that your insurer can process the claim.

Insurance is available from most travel agents or direct from insurance companies for periods ranging from a few days to a year or even longer. Most policies are similar in premium and coverage but if you plan to indulge in high-risk activities such as mountaineering, bungee jumping or scuba diving without a certificate, check the policy carefully to make sure you'll be covered.

SAFETY

You're unlikely to incur any great risks traveling around New England, and while it pays to be cautious and safe, especially in big cities like Boston, or on lonely country roads, the area is pretty unforeboding. Emergency number for police is ☎911; numbers for lost or stolen credit cards, travelers' checks and the like can be found on p.19.

INFORMATION AND MAPS

Advance information for a trip to New England can be obtained by calling the appropriate state's information center (see box on p.18). If you're from the UK or Germany, a publicly funded firm called Discover New England, PO Box 3809, Stowe, VT 05672 (☎802/253-2500) can provide advance information; just write or call. They'll refer callers from other countries to the appropriate tourism board. In the UK, their offices are at 133a St Margaret's Rd, Twickenham, Middlesex TW1 1RG (☎0906/558 8555) and in Germany at Herzog HC GmbH, Borsigallee 17, D-60388, Frankfurt (☎069/420 8900).

Once you've arrived, you'll find most towns have visitor centers of some description – often called the **Convention and Visitors Bureau** (CVB) or **Chamber of Commerce**: many are listed in the Guide. These will give out detailed information on the local area and can often help with finding accommodation. Free **newspapers** in most places carry news of events and entertainment.

Most of the tourist offices we've mentioned here or in the *Guide* can supply you with good **maps**, either free or for a small charge, and, supplemented with our own, these should be enough

MAP AND TRAVEL BOOK SUPPLIERS

AUSTRALIA AND NEW ZEALAND

The Map Shop, 6 Peel St, Adelaide (☎08/8231 2033)

Mapland, 372 Little Bourke St, Melbourne (☎03/9670 4383).

Mapworld, 173 Gloucester Street, Christchurch (☎03/374 5399, fax 03/374 5633, www.mapworld.co.nz).

Perth Map Centre, 1/884 Hay St, Perth (☎08/9322 5733).

Specialty Maps, 46 Albert St, Auckland (☎09/307 2217).

Travel Bookshop, Shop 3, 175 Liverpool St, Sydney (☎02/9261 8200).

Walkers Bookshop, 96 Lake Street, Cairns (☎07/4051 2410).

Worldwide Maps and Guides, 187 George St, Brisbane (☎07/3221 4330).

CANADA

Open Air Books and Maps, 25 Toronto St, Toronto, ON M5C 2R1 (☎416/363-0719).

Ulysses Travel Bookshop, 4176 St-Denis St, Montréal PQ H2W 2M5 (☎514/843-9447).

World Wide Books and Maps, 736A Granville St, Vancouver, BC V6Z 1G3 (☎604/687-3320).

BRITAIN (excluding London)

Blackwell's, 50 Broad St, Oxford OX1 3BQ (☎01865/792792). General bookshop with good range of foreign maps. Mail order available. Also at 156–160 West St, Sheffield S1 3ST (☎0114/273 8906); 13–17 Royal Arcade, Cardiff CF1 2PR (☎029/2039 5036); Blackwell's University Bookshop, Alsop Building, Brownlow Hill, Liverpool L3 5TX (☎0151/709 8146); www.bookshop.blackwell.co.uk

Heffers Map and Travel, 20 Trinity St, Cambridge, CB2 1TJ (☎01223/586 586, www.heffers.co.uk). Mail order available.

James Thin Melven's Bookshop, 29 Union St, Inverness, IV1 1QA (☎01463/233500, www.jthin.co.uk). Established 1849; map department with all foreign maps; mail order specialist.

John Smith and Son, 50 Crouper St, Townhead, Glasgow G4 ODL (☎0141/552 4394, www.johnsmith.co.uk).

The Map Shop, 30A Belvoir St, Leicester LE1 6QH (☎0116/247 1400). Mail order available.

Newcastle Map Centre, 55 Grey St, Newcastle upon Tyne NE1 6EF (☎0191/261 5622, www.newtraveller.com).

Stanfords, 29 Corn St, Bristol BS1 1HT (☎0117/929 9966, www.stanfords.co.uk).

Waterstone's, 128 Princes St, Edinburgh DH2 4AD (☎0131/226 2666); 91 Deansgate, Manchester M3 2BW (☎0161/832 3000, www.waterstones.co.uk).

IRELAND

Easons Bookshop, 40 O'Connell St, Dublin 1 (☎01/873 3811).

Fred Hanna's Bookshop, 27–29 Nassau St, Dublin 2 (☎01/677 1255).

Hodges Figgis Bookshop, 56–58 Dawson St, Dublin 2 (☎01/677 4754).

Waterstone's, Queens Bldg, 8 Royal Ave, Belfast BT1 1DA (☎028/9024 7355); 7 Dawson St, Dublin 2 (☎01/679 1415); 69 St Patrick St, Cork (☎021/427 6522); www.waterstones.co.uk

LONDON

Daunt Books, 83 Marylebone High St, W1M 3DE (☎020/7224 2295, fax 020/7224 6893); 193 Haverstock Hill, NW3 4QL (☎020/7794 4006).

National Map Centre, 22–24 Caxton St, SW1H 0QU (☎020/7222 2466, www.mapsnmc.co.uk).

Stanfords, 12–14 Long Acre, WC2E 9LP (☎020/7836 1321, www.stanfords.co.uk). There's also a branch within the British Airways offices at 156 Regent St, W1B 5SN (☎020/7434 4744).

The Travel Bookshop, 13–15 Blenheim Crescent, W11 2EE (☎020/7229 5260, www.thetravelbookshop.co.uk).

USA

The Appalachian Mountain Club, 5 Joy St, Boston, MA 02108 (☎617/523-0636, www.outdoors.com).

The Complete Traveler, 3207 Fillmore St, San Francisco, CA 94123 (☎415/923-1511, www.completetraveler.com).

The Complete Traveler, 199 Madison Ave, New York, NY 10016 (☎212/685-9007).

Forsyth Travel Library, 226 Westchester Ave, White Plains, NY 10604 (☎1-800/367-7984, www.forsyth.com).

Gulliver's, 7 Commercial Alley, Portsmouth, NH 0380 (☎603/431-5556, www.gulliversbooks.com).

Phileas Fogg's Books & Maps, 87 Stanford Shopping Center, Palo Alto, CA 94304 (☎1-800/533-FOGG, www.foggs.com).

Rand McNally* 84 State St, Boston, MA 02109 (☎617/720-1125); 444 N Michigan Ave, Chicago, IL 60611 (☎312/321-1751); 150 E 52nd St, New York, NY 10022 (☎212/758-7488); 595 Market St, San Francisco, CA 94105 (☎415/777-3131); 10250 Santa Monica Blvd, Suite 681, Los Angeles, CA 90067 (☎310/556-2202).

The Savvy Traveller, 310 S Michigan Ave, Chicago, IL 60604 (☎312/913-9800, www.thesavvytraveller.com).

Sierra Club Bookstore, 85 Second St, San Francisco, CA 94105 (☎415/977-5600).

*Rand McNally now has 24 stores across the US; call ☎1-800/333-0136 (ext 2111) for the location of your nearest store, or for direct mail maps. On the web, you can find them at www.randmcnallystore.com.

NEW ENGLAND STATE INFORMATION CENTERS

Connecticut, 505 Hudson St, Hartford, CT 06106 (☎860/270-8080 or 1-800/282-6863, *www.ctbound.org*).

Maine, PO Box 3000, Hallowell, ME 04347-2300 (☎207/623-0363 or 1-888/624-6345, *www .visitmaine.com*).

Massachusetts, 100 Cambridge St, 13th floor, Boston, MA 02202 (☎617/727-3201 or 1-800/303-3972, *www.mass-vacation.com*).

New Hampshire, 172 Pembroke Rd, Concord, NH 03302 (☎603/271-2343 or 1-800/FUN-IN-NH, *www.visitnh.com*).

Rhode Island, One West Exchange St, Providence, RI 02903 (☎401/222-2601 or 1-800/556-2484, *www.visitrhodeisland.com*).

Vermont, 6 Baldwin St, Montpelier, VT 05633 (☎802/828-3236 or 1-800/VERMONT; *www .1-800-vermont.com*).

for general sightseeing and touring. Rand McNally produces a decent map of the East Coast ($15), and its **Road Atlas** ($10.95), covering the whole country plus Mexico and Canada, is a worthwhile investment if you're traveling further afield. For driving or cycling through rural areas, Maine-based DeLorme publishes their valuable Atlas & Gazetteer to each of the New England states (*www.delorme.com*; $16.95 each or $74.95 for all five New England states), with detailed city plans, marked campgrounds and reams of nation-al park and forest information. For something more detailed, say for hiking purposes, ranger stations in parks and wilderness areas all sell good-quality local hiking maps for $1–5, and camping stores generally have a good selection too. *The American Automobile Association* (☎1-800/922-8228, *www.aaa.com*) has offices in most large cities and provides excellent free maps and travel assistance to its members, and to British members of the AA and RAC. Most bookstores will have a range of local trail guides.

COSTS, MONEY, AND BANKS

To help with planning your vacation in New England, this book contains detailed price information for accommodation and eating. Unless otherwise stated, the hotel price codes (explained on p.28) are for the cheap-est double room throughout most of the year, exclusive of any local taxes, while meal prices include food only and not drinks or tip. For museums and similar attractions, the prices we quote are generally for adults; you can assume that children get in half-price. Naturally, costs will increase slightly over-all during the life of this edition, but the rel-ative comparisons should remain valid.

COSTS

Accommodation is likely to be your biggest single expense in New England. Few hotel or motel rooms cost under $40; you're likely to pay more than $80 for anything halfway decent in a city, and rates in rural areas are not much cheaper. In Boston, it may well be difficult to find anything at all for less than $75. Hostels offering dorm beds – usually for $15–20 – are available, but they are by no means everywhere, and they save little money for two or more people traveling together. Camping, of course, is cheap (anywhere from free to $25 per night), but rarely practical in the big cities.

As for **food**, $20 a day is enough to get an adequate life-support diet, while for a daily total of around $30 you can dine pretty well. Beyond this, everything hinges on how much sightseeing, taxi-cabbing, and drinking you do. Much of any of these – especially in the cities – and you're likely to be getting through upwards of $50 a day.

The rates for traveling around, especially on buses, and to a lesser extent on trains and planes, may look inexpensive on paper, but the distances involved mean that costs soon mount up. For a group of two or more, renting a car can be a very good investment (see "Getting Around" p.31), not least because it enables you to stay in the ubiquitous budget motels along the Interstate highways instead of relying on expensive downtown hotels.

Remember that a **sales tax** of 8.5 percent is added to virtually everything you buy in stores except for groceries, but isn't part of the marked price. In addition, many potential accommodations apply a hotel tax; this can add as much as fourteen percent to the total bill. New Hampshire, it should be noted, does not have a sales tax.

TRAVELERS' CHECKS AND BANKS

US dollar travelers' checks are the best way to carry money, for both American and foreign visitors; they offer the great security of knowing that lost or stolen checks will be replaced. You should have no problem using the better-known checks, such as American Express and Visa, in the same way as cash in shops, restaurants and gas stations (don't be put off by "no checks" signs, which only refer to personal checks). Be sure to have plenty of the $10 and $20 denominations for everyday transactions.

Banks are generally open from 9am until 5pm Monday to Thursday, and 9am to 6pm on Friday. Some have limited hours on Saturdays, and ATMs are usually accessible 24 hours a day. Most major banks change travelers' checks for their face value (not that there's much point in doing this – and some charge for the privilege, so ask before you do), and change foreign travelers' checks and currency. **Exchange bureaux**, always found at airports, tend to charge less commission: Thomas Cook and American Express are the biggest names. Rarely, if ever, do hotels change foreign currency. If your checks and/or credit cards are stolen or if you need to find the nearest bank that sells a particular brand of travelers' check, or to buy checks by

MONEY: A NOTE FOR FOREIGN TRAVELERS

Even when the exchange rate is at its least advantageous, most western European visitors find virtually everything – accommodation, food, gas, cameras, clothes, and more – to be better value in the US than it is at home. However, if you're used to traveling in the less expensive countries of Europe, let alone in the rest of the world, you shouldn't expect to scrape by on the same minuscule budget once you're in the US. Regular upheaval in the world money markets causes the relative value of the US dollar against the currencies of the rest of the world to vary considerably. Generally speaking, one pound sterling will buy between $1.40 and $1.80; one Canadian dollar is worth between $0.60 and $0.90; one Australian dollar is worth between $0.64 and $0.88; and one New Zealand dollar is worth between $0.50 and $0.72.

BILLS AND COINS

US currency comes in bills of $1, $5, $10, $20, $50, and $100, plus various larger (and rarer) denominations. All are the same size and color, making it necessary to check each bill carefully. The dollar is made up of 100 cents with coins of 1 cent (known as a penny), 5 cents (a nickel), 10 cents (a dime) and 25 cents (a quarter). New gold dollar coins were recently introduced in the US and are becoming more prevalent. Very occasionally you might find JFK half-dollars (50¢), Susan B. Anthony dollar coins, or a two-dollar bill. Change (quarters are the most useful) is needed for buses, vending machines, parking meters, and telephones, so always have some on hand.

phone, call the following numbers: American Express (☎1-800/673-3782), Citicorp (☎1-800/645-6556), MasterCard International/Thomas Cook (☎1-800/223-7373) and Visa (☎1-800/227-6811).

PLASTIC MONEY AND CASH MACHINES

If you don't already have a credit card, you should think seriously about getting one before you set off. For many services, it's simply taken for granted that you'll be paying with plastic. When renting a car (or even a bike) or checking into a hotel you may well be asked to show a credit card to establish your creditworthiness – even if you intend to settle the bill in cash. Visa, MasterCard (known elsewhere as Access), Diners Club, American Express and Discover are the most widely used.

With MasterCard or Visa it is also possible to withdraw cash at any bank displaying relevant stickers, or from appropriate **automatic teller machines** (ATMs). Diners Club cards can be used to cash personal checks at Citibank branches. American Express cards can only get cash, or buy travelers' checks, at American Express offices (check the **Yellow Pages**) or from the travelers' check dispensers at most major airports. Most Canadian credit cards issued by hometown banks are honored in the US. ATMs are everywhere in New England – in addition to banks, many supermarkets, convenience stores, and drug stores now have outlets where you can withdraw cash for a small transaction fee (usually around $2). ATM cards held by visitors from other parts of the country usually work in New England machines – check with your bank before you leave home. This method of obtaining cash is safer and more convenient and, if you're visiting from another country, it will usually be slightly cheaper than the commission fees charged by the exchange bureaus.

Most major credit cards issued by foreign banks are accepted in the US; so are cash-dispensing cards linked to international networks such as Cirrus, Plus, and Star – once again, check before you set off, as otherwise the machine may simply gobble up your plastic friend. Overseas visitors should also bear in mind that fluctuating exchange rates may result in spending more (or less) than expected when the item eventually shows up on a statement; the rate is dependent on the date of the transaction, not when the statement is issued.

> Each of the two main networks operates a toll-free line to let customers know the location of their nearest ATM; Plus System is ☎1-800/THE-PLUS and Cirrus is ☎1-800/4CIRRUS.

EMERGENCIES

Assuming you know someone who is prepared to send you money in a crisis, the quickest way is to have them take the cash to the nearest **Western Union** office (☎1-800/325-6000 in the US; ☎0800/833833 in the UK; ☎1800/395395 in the Republic of Ireland; ☎1800/649 565 in Australia; and ☎09/302 0143 in New Zealand; *www.westernunion.com*), and have it instantaneously wired to the office nearest you, subject to the deduction of five to ten percent commission: the bigger the transaction the lower the percentage. To send $500 for example, costs $43, while $1000 costs $75. For a little higher commission, you can send the money over the phone using a Visa or Mastercard. American Express Moneygram (☎1-800/543-4080) offers a similar service.

It's also possible to have money wired directly from a bank in your home country to a bank in the US, although this is somewhat less reliable because it involves two separate institutions. If you go this route, the person wiring the funds to you will need to know the telex number of the bank the funds are being wired to. It is never convenient or cheap, though, and should be considered a last resort.

If you have a few days' leeway, a postal money order, exchangeable at any post office through the mail, is a cheaper option. The equivalent for foreign travelers is the international money order, for which you need to allow up to seven days in the international air mail before arrival. An ordinary check sent from overseas takes two to three weeks to clear. Foreign travelers in difficulties have the final option of throwing themselves on the mercy of their nearest national consulate, which will – in worst cases only – repatriate you, but will never, under any circumstances, lend you money.

GETTING AROUND

Although rural areas can be nearly impossible to access if you don't have a car, getting from one large city to the next is seldom much of a problem on public transport in New England. Good bus links and reasonable, though limited, train service are nearly always available. Getting around after you arrive, however, is another story. If you plan to cover any range of different destinations, renting a car is highly recommended, but with adroit forward-planning, you can usually get to the main points of interest on local buses and charter services, details of which are in the relevant sections of the Guide.

BY CAR

Driving is by far the best way to get around New England. Things get confusing within the larger

---

CAR RENTAL COMPANIES

AUSTRALIA

Avis ☎13/6333, *www.avis.com*
Budget ☎1300/362 848, *www.budget.com*

Dollar ☎02/9223 1444 or 1800/358 008, *www.dollarcar.com.au*
Hertz , ☎1800/550 067, *www.hertz.com*

NEW ZEALAND

Avis ☎09/526 5231, ☎0800/655 111, *www.avis.com*
Budget ☎0800/ 652 227 or 09/375 2270, *www.budget.com*

Hertz ☎09/309 0989, 0800/655 955, *www.hertz.com*

NORTH AMERICA

Alamo ☎1-800/354-2322, *www.goalamo.com*
Avis ☎1-800/331-1212, *www.avis.com*
Budget ☎1-800/527-0700, *www.budgetrentacar.com*
Dollar ☎1-800/421-6868, *www.dollarcar.com*
Enterprise ☎1-800/325-8007, *www.enterprise.com*
Hertz ☎1-800/654-3131; in Canada ☎416/620-9620, *www.hertz.com*

National ☎1-800/CAR-RENT, *www.nationalcar.com*
Payless ☎1-800/729-5377, *www.paylesscar.com*
Rent-A-Wreck ☎1-800/535-1391, *www.rent-a-wreck.com*
Thrifty ☎1-800/367-2277, *www.thrifty.com*

UK AND IRELAND

Autos Abroad ☎0207/287 6000, *www.autosabroad.co.uk*
Avis ☎0870/606 0100; Eire ☎01/874 5844, *www.avis.com*
Budget ☎0800/181181; Eire ☎0800/973159, *www.budgetrentacar.com*
Europcar ☎0345/222525; Eire ☎01/874 5844, *www.europcar.com*

Hertz ☎0870/844 8844; Eire ☎01/676 7476, *www.hertz.com*
Holiday Autos ☎0870/400 0011; Eire ☎01/872 9366, *www.holidayautos.com*
National Car Rental ☎01895/233300, *www.nationalcar.com*
Thrifty ☎01494/442110, *www.thrifty.com*

DRIVING FOR FOREIGN VISITORS

UK nationals can drive in the US on a full UK **driving license** (International Driving Permits are not always regarded as sufficient). Fly-drive deals are good value if you want to rent a car, though you can save up to sixty percent simply by booking in advance with a major firm. If you choose not to pay until you arrive, be sure you take a written confirmation of the price with you. Remember that it's safer not to rent a car straight off a long transatlantic flight; and that standard rental cars have automatic transmissions.

It's also easier and cheaper to book **RVs** in advance from Britain. Most travel agents who specialize in the US can arrange RV rental, and usually do it cheaper if you book a flight through them as well. A price of £1000 for a five-berth van for two weeks is fairly typical. Once you have a vehicle, you'll find that **petrol** (US "gasoline") is fairly cheap; a self-served US gallon (3.8 liters) of unleaded – which most cars use – costs between $1.15 and $1.85, depending on the location of the gas station (and fluctuating markets). In New England, most petrol stations are **self-service**: when removing the nozzle from the pump, remember to lift or turn the lever to activate it. If you insist on having someone else pump your gas, you'll pay for it; full service pumps often charge upwards of $0.30 extra per gallon. American miles are the same as British miles but sometimes distances are given in hours – the length of time it should take to drive between any two places. There are obviously

other differences between driving in the US and in Britain, not least the fact that rules and regulations aren't always nationally fixed. Many foreign travelers have problems at first adjusting to driving on the right. This can be remarkably easy to forget – some people draw a cross or tie a ribbon on their right hand to remind them.

There are several types of road. The best for covering long distances quickly are the wide, straight and fast **Interstate highways**, usually at least six-lane motorways and always prefixed by "I" (eg I-5) – marked on maps by a red, white, and blue shield bearing the number. Even-numbered Interstates run east–west and those with odd numbers north–south. Driving on these roads is easier than it first appears, but you need to adapt quickly to the American habit of changing lanes: US drivers do this frequently, and overtake on both sides. In New England you are also permitted to stay in the fast lane (left lane) while being overtaken on the inside, although common courtesy dictates that slower drivers stay to the right.

Though most roads are free, some of the more traveled highways, known as **turnpikes**, charge anywhere from 50¢ to several dollars to cruise down their broad lanes. You'll be warned in advance that a toll booth is coming. If you're severely strapped for cash, you can usually get to the same destination on smaller – and considerably slower – roads, but the extra effort is usually not worth it.

A grade down, and broadly similar to British

cities such as Boston, where complicated freeway networks intertwine with narrow one-way city streets that were designed for horse-drawn carriages. Away from the cities, many places are almost impossible to reach without your own transportation; most national and state parks and forests are only served by infrequent public transportation as far as the main visitor center, if that. What's more, if you are planning on doing a fair amount of camping, renting a car can save you money by allowing access to less-expensive out-of-the-way campgrounds, not to mention easing the burden of carting your equipment around.

Drivers wishing to rent cars are supposed to have held their licenses for at least one year (though this is rarely checked); people **under 25 years old** may encounter problems, and will probably get lumbered with a higher than normal insurance premium. Car rental companies (see box on p.21) will also expect you to have a credit

card; if you don't they may let you leave a hefty deposit (at least $200), but don't count on it. The likeliest tactic for getting a good deal is to phone the major firms' toll-free numbers and ask for their best rate – most will try to beat the offers of their competitors, so it's worth haggling.

In general the **lowest rates** are available at the airport branches – $200 a week for a subcompact is a fairly standard budget rate. Always be sure to get free **unlimited mileage**, and be aware that leaving the car in a different state from the one in which you rented can incur a drop-off charge of up to $300 – however, many companies do not charge drop-off fees to certain cities so check before you book if you plan a one-way drive. Also, don't automatically go for the cheapest rate, as there's a big difference in the quality of cars from company to company; industry leaders like Hertz and Avis tend to have newer, lower-mileage cars, often with air-condi-

dual carriageways and main roads, are the **state highways** (eg Hwy-1) and the **US highways** (eg US-395). Some major roads in cities are technically state highways but are better known by their local name. Hwy-1 in Brunswick, Maine, for instance, is better known as Mill Street. In rural areas, you'll also find much smaller **county roads**, which are known as routes (eg Rte-11).

Although the law says that drivers must keep up with the flow of traffic, which is often hurtling along at 75mph, the **maximum speed limit** in New England is 65mph, with lower posted limits – usually around 25–35mph – in built-up areas. There are no spot fines but if given a ticket for speeding, your case will come to court and the size of the fine will be at the discretion of the judge; $100 is a rough minimum. If the police do flag you down, don't get out of the car, and don't reach into the glove compartment as the cops may think you have a gun. Simply sit still with your hands on the wheel, when questioned, be polite and don't attempt to make jokes.

As for other possible violations, US law requires that any alcohol be carried unopened in the boot (trunk) of the car, and it can't be stressed enough that driving while intoxicated (DWI) or driving under the influence (DUI) is a very serious offense. If a police officer smells alcohol on your breath or has reason to believe that you are under the influence, he/she is entitled to administer a breath, saliva or urine test. If you fail, you'll be locked up with other inebriates in the drunk tank of the nearest jail until you sober up. Your case will later be heard by a judge, who can fine you as much as $1000, or in extreme (or repeat) cases, imprison you for thirty days. Less serious offenses include making a U-turn on an Interstate or anywhere where a single unbroken line runs along the middle of the road; driving in car pool lanes with fewer than two people in the vehicle; parking on a highway; and front-seat passengers riding without fastened seatbelts. At junctions, one rule is crucially different from the UK: you can **turn right on a red light** if there is no traffic approaching from the left; otherwise red means stop. Stopping is also compulsory, in both directions, when you come upon a school bus disgorging passengers with its lights flashing. Blinking red lights should be treated as a stop sign, and blinking yellow lights indicate that you should cross the intersection with caution, but do not need to come to a complete stop.

Once at your destination, you'll find in cities at least that **parking meters** are commonplace. Charges for an hour range from 25¢ to $1. Car parks (US parking lots) charge up to $15 a day. If you park in the wrong place (such as within 10ft of a fire hydrant) your car is likely to be towed away or wheel-clamped; a ticket on the windshield tells you where to pay the $25 fine. Watch out for signs indicating the street cleaning schedule, as you mustn't park overnight before an early-morning clean. Validated parking, where your fee for parking in, say, a shopping mall's lot is waived if one of the stores has stamped your parking stub (just ask), is common, as is valet parking at even quite modest restaurants, for which a small tip is expected.

tioning and stereo cassette decks as standard equipment.

Alternatively, various **local companies** rent out new – and not so new (try Rent-a-Heap or Rent-a-Wreck) – vehicles. They are certainly cheaper than the big chains if you just want to spin around a city for a day, but you have to drop them back where you picked them up, and free mileage is seldom included. Addresses and phone numbers are listed in the **Yellow Pages**.

When you rent a car, read the small print carefully for details on **Collision Damage Waiver** (CDW), sometimes called Liability Damage Waiver (LDW), a form of insurance which often isn't included in the initial rental charge but is well worth considering. This specifically covers the car that you are driving yourself, as you are in any case insured for damage to other vehicles. At $9–13 a day, it can add substantially to the total cost, but without it you're liable for every scratch to the car – even those that aren't your fault. Some credit-card companies offer automatic CDW coverage to anyone using their card; read the fine print beforehand in any case.

You should also check your **third-party liability**. The standard policy often only covers you for the first $15,000 of the third party's claim against you, a paltry sum in litigation-conscious America. Companies strongly advise taking out third-party insurance, which costs a further $10–12 a day but indemnifies the driver for up to $2,000,000.

If you **break down** in a rented car, there'll be an emergency number pinned to the dashboard or tucked away in the glove compartment. You can summon the highway patrol on one of the new emergency phones stationed along freeways (usually at half-mile intervals) and many other remote highways (mostly every two miles) – although as the highway patrol and state police cruise by regularly, you can just sit tight and wait.

Raising your car hood is recognized as a call for assistance, although women traveling alone should be wary of doing this.

Another tip, for women especially, is to rent a **mobile telephone** from the car rental agency – you often only have to pay a nominal amount until you actually use it, and in larger cities they increasingly come built into the car. Having a phone can be reassuring at least, and a potential lifesaver should something go terribly wrong.

One variation on renting is a **driveaway**, whereby you drive a car from one place to another on behalf of the owner, paying only for the gas you use. The same rules as for renting apply, but look the car over before you take it, as you'll be charged with any repair costs, and a large fuel bill if the vehicle's a big drinker. The most common route in New England is between Boston and New York, although you may find something that takes you further up the coast. See p.14 for details.

RENTING AN RV

Besides cars, Recreational Vehicles or RVs (camper vans) can be rented for around $500 a week, although outlets are surprisingly rare, as people tend to own their RVs: near Boston, try Verc RVs, 63 Samoset St, Plymouth, MA 02360 (☎1-800/696-VERC or 508/747-1997). The Recreational Vehicle

---

ADVANCE PLANNING FOR OVERSEAS TRAVELERS

AMTRAK RAIL PASSES

Foreign travelers have a choice of four rail passes; including the Coastal Pass, which permits unlimited train travel on the East and West coasts, but not between the two.

	15-day (June–Sept 5)	15-day (Sept 6–May)	30-day (June–Sept 5)	30-day (Sept 6–May)
North East	£125	£113	£147	£138
East	£156	£128	£194	£159
Coastal	–	–	£172	£141
National	£266	£178	£334	£234

On production of a passport issued outside the US or Canada, the passes can be bought at Amtrak stations in the US. In the **UK**, you can buy them from most travel agents, including Trailfinders and USIT CAMPUS (see p.5 for addresses); in **Ireland**, contact USIT Now (☎01/602 1600); in **Australia**, Walshes World (☎02/9223 7111) or Thomas Cook (☎1300/361 941); and in **New Zealand**, Walshes World (☎09/379 3708).

GREYHOUND AMERIPASSES

Foreign visitors can buy a Greyhound **Ameripass**, offering unlimited travel within a set time limit, before leaving home: most travel agents can oblige. In the UK they cost £90 (4-day; Mon–Thurs only), £105 (7-day), £145 (10-day), £160 (15-day), £229 (30-day), £245 (45-day) or £307 (60-day). In Australia, contact by email at greyhound@crystalholidays.co.uk or Jetsave Travel (☎ 02/9434 2088), and in New Zealand, Greyhound World Travel (☎09/479 6555).

No daily extensions are available. The first time you use your pass, it will be dated by the ticket clerk (which becomes the commencement date of the ticket), and your destination is written on a page which the driver will tear out and keep as you board the bus. Repeat this procedure for every subsequent journey.

AIR PASSES

All the main American airlines offer air passes for visitors who plan to fly a lot within the US; these have to be bought in advance, and in the UK are usually sold with the proviso that you cross the Atlantic with the relevant airline. All the deals are broadly similar, involving the purchase of at least three coupons (for around £290 and around £75 for each additional coupon), each valid for a flight of any duration in the US.

The Visit USA scheme entitles foreign travelers to a thirty percent discount on any full-priced US domestic fare, provided you buy the ticket before you leave home.

Rental Association, 3930 University Drive, Fairfax, VA 22030 (☎1-800/336-0355 or 703/591-7130, *www.rvda.com*), publishes a newsletter and a directory of rental firms. Some of the larger companies offering RV rentals are Cruise America (☎1-800/327-7799, *www.cruiseamerica.com*) and Moturis (☎1-800/ 566-8874, *www.moturis.com*).

On top of the rental fees, take into account the cost of **gas** (some RVs do ten miles to the gallon or less) and any **drop-off charges**, in case you plan to do a one-way trip across the country. Also, it is rarely legal simply to pull up in an RV and spend the night at the roadside – you are expected to stay in designated parks that cost up to $30 per night.

BY PLANE

A plane is obviously the quickest way of getting around New England, and it can be less expensive than you may think. By keeping up with the ever-changing deals being offered by airlines – check with your local travel agent or read the ads in local newspapers – you may be able to take advantage of heavily discounted fares. Airlines with a strong route structure in the area include American Eagle (☎1-800/433-7300), Business Express (☎1-800/345-3400), Continental Express (☎1-800/525-0280), Delta Connection (☎1-800/345-3400), New England Air (☎1-800/464-2460), TWA Express (☎1-800/221-2000), United Express (☎1-800/241-6522), and US Air Express (☎1-800/428-4322).

Phone the airlines for **routes and schedules**, then buy your ticket from a travel agent using the computerized **Fare Assurance Program**, which processes all the available ticket options and searches for the lowest fare, taking into account the special needs of individual travelers. One agent using the service is Travel Avenue (☎1-800/333-3335). At off-peak times, flights between Boston and Portland (ME) cost around $140 round trip and may require a booking to be made 21 days in advance.

BY TRAIN

Amtrak's four main routes in New England provide decent, though limited, connections between the few major cities in western New England, as well as some of the minor ones. You're assured of a smooth journey with few if any delays and the carriages are clean, comfortable, tidy, and rarely crowded. Probably the prettiest route is the Vermonter, which winds from Washington, DC up

For all information on Amtrak fares and schedules in the US, use the toll-free number ☎1-800/USA-RAIL or visit the official Amtrak Web site: *www.amtrak.com*. Do not phone individual stations.

through upstate New York and Vermont all the way up to Montréal; it's particularly popular in the fall, though beautiful vistas whisk by your window at all times of the year. The other north-to-south Amtrak routes in and around New England, the Ethan Allen (Washington, DC to Rutland, VT), the Twilight Shoreliner (Boston, MA to Newport News, VA), and the Northeast Corridor (Washington, DC to Boston, MA), are almost as scenic, though they go no further east than Vermont. There's also a route that connects Boston with Toronto, Canada.

Americans can cut fares greatly by using one of three **Explore America** rail passes, each of which gives unlimited travel for 45 days (see p.13). The **coastal pass** available to foreign travelers (see box opposite) is not sold to US citizens.

BY BUS

If you're traveling on your own, and making a lot of stops, buses are by far the cheapest way to get around. There are several main bus companies which link the major cities and many smaller towns in New England (see box on p.26). Out in the country, buses are fairly scarce, sometimes appearing only once a day, and here you'll need to plot your route with care. But along the main highways, buses run around the clock to a fairly full timetable, stopping only for meal breaks (almost always fast-food dives) and driver changeovers.

The buses are slightly less uncomfortable than you might expect, too, and it's feasible to save on a night's accommodation by **traveling overnight** and sleeping on the bus – though you may not feel up to much the next day.

To avoid possible hassle, lone female travelers in particular should take care to sit as near to the driver as possible, and to arrive during **daylight hours**, as many bus stations are in fairly dodgy areas. It used to be that any sizeable community would have a bus station; in some places, now, the post office, a convenience store, or a gas station doubles as the bus stop and ticket office, and in many others the bus service has been canceled altogether. Reservations, either in person at the station or on the toll-free number, are not essential but recommended – if a bus is full you may be

Greyhound's nationwide toll-free information service can give you routes and times, plus phone numbers and addresses of local terminals. You can also make reservations: ☎1-800/231-2222 or *www.greyhound.com*.

forced to wait until the next one, sometimes overnight or longer.

Fares average about $0.10 a mile, which can add up quickly; indeed, for long-trip travel, the bus is not that much cheaper than flying. However, it's the best deal if you want to visit a lot of places, and Greyhound's **Ameripasses** for domestic travelers are good for unlimited travel nationwide for 7 days ($209), 15 days ($319), 30 days ($429), and 60 days ($599); the reduced rates for foreign travelers are on p.24.

The bus companies that specialize in New England each publish comprehensive timetables. Most tourist offices are well supplied with route information and schedules, particularly at Logan Airport.

CYCLING

In general, **cycling** is one of the best ways to get around New England. Some of the larger cities have cycle lanes and local buses equipped to carry bikes (strapped to the outside), and even the bustle of Boston can be easily escaped in half an hour by bicycle. Although the terrain is often slightly mountainous, there's nothing insurmount-

able to an experienced cyclist. One is rarely more than an hour's ride from a town or village, and the countryside in between is frequently idyllic, worth taking in at a leisurely pace on two wheels.

Bikes can be rented for less than $25 a day, $90–100 a week from most bike stores; the local visitor center will have details (we've listed rental options where applicable throughout the *Guide*). Be sure to carry warm clothing and rain gear on longer rides. Also remember that the further north you go, the lower the temperatures and the more frequent the rains become.

For **long-distance cycling** you'll need a good quality multispeed bike (but don't immediately splurge on a mountain bike, unless you are planning a lot of off-road use – good road conditions and trail restrictions in national parks make a touring bike an equally good or better choice), maps, spare tires, tools, panniers, and a helmet (not a legal necessity, but a very good idea). A route avoiding the Interstates (on which cycling is illegal) is essential, and it's also wise to cycle **north to south**, as the wind blows this way in the summer and can make all the difference between a pleasant trip and acute leg-ache. The main problem you'll encounter is **traffic**: wide, cumbersome recreational vehicles spew unpleasant exhaust in your face and, in northern Maine, and Vermont close to the Canadian border, enormous logging trucks have slipstreams that will pull you towards the middle of the road. Be particularly careful if you're planning to cycle along Hwy-1 on the Maine

NEW ENGLAND BUS COMPANIES

American Eagle (☎508/990-0000). Massachusetts only, Boston to New Bedford.

Bonanza, One Bonanza Way, Providence, RI (☎401/331-7500 or ☎1-800/556-3815, *www.bonanzabus.com*). Nonstop service between New York and Providence. Also covers Cape Cod, southern Massachusetts (including Boston), Connecticut, eastern New York, and Bennington, VT.

C&J Trailways, Sumner Drive, Dover, NH (☎1-800/258-7111 or 603/742-5111, *www.cjtrailways.com*). Service from Logan Airport and Boston's South Station to Dover, Durham, and Portsmouth, NH, and to Newburyport, MA.

Concord Trailways, Trailways Transportation Center, 30 Stickney Ave, Concord, NH

(☎1-800/639-3317, *www.concordtrailways.com*). Good coverage of New Hampshire and Maine, with connecting service to Logan Airport.

Peter Pan Trailways, PO Box 1776, Springfield, MA (☎1-800/343-9999, *www.peterpan-bus.com*). Relatively frequent and extensive service between Boston and New York, via Springfield and Hartford.

Plymouth and Brockton, Peter Pan Terminal, Boston (☎617/773-9401, *www.p-b.com*). Comprehensive service to Cape Cod.

Vermont Transit Lines, 345 Pine St, Burlington, VT (☎802/864-6811, *www.vermonttransit.com*). Service throughout most of New England, plus lines to New York, Toronto and Montréal. Direct connections with Greyhound.

coast, since besides heavy traffic, it has narrow shoulders; again, you're much better off on the quiet country roads that New England is known for.

When asking for directions, stick to other cyclists or bike shops; others will either look at you in disbelief, or give you directions along the most direct, and therefore the busiest and least scenic, route.

Good sources for **cycling information** in New England, including trail and bike store locations, are the New England Mountain Bike Association, PO Box 2221, Acton, MA 01720-6221 (☎1-800/576-3622, *www.nemba.org*), or the Web sites *www.neoactivities.com* and *www.velocipede.com*. If you're **camping** as well as cycling, contact the Adventure Cycling Association (formerly Bikecentennial), 150 E Pine St, Missoula, MT 59807 (☎406/721-1776); Backroads, 801 Cedar St, Berkeley, CA 94710-1800 (☎510/527-1555 or 1-800/462-2848); or consult the Web site *www.cybercycling.com* for information on special biker campgrounds as well as programs and scheduled group rides.

ACCOMMODATION

Accommodation standards in New England – as in the rest of the US – are high, and costs inevitably form a significant proportion of the expenses for any trip to the area. It is possible to haggle, however, especially in the chain motels, and if you're on your own, you can possibly pare costs by sleeping in dormitory-style hostels, where a bed will cost $12–18. However, groups of two or more will find it only a little more expensive to stay in the far more plentiful budget motels and hotels, where basic rooms away from the major cities typically cost around $40 per night. Many hotels will set up a third single bed for around $5–10 on top of the regular price, reducing costs for three people sharing. By contrast, the lone traveler will have a hard time of it: "singles" are usually double rooms at an only slightly reduced rate. Prices quoted by hotels and motels are almost always for the actual room rather than for each person using it.

Wherever you stay, unless you use a credit card, you'll be expected to **pay in advance**, at least for the first night and perhaps for further nights too, particularly if it's high season and the hotel's expecting to be busy. Payment can be in cash or in US dollar travelers' checks, though it's more common to give your credit-card number and sign for everything when you leave. **Reservations** are only held until 5pm or 6pm unless you've told them you'll be arriving late. Most of the larger chains have an advance booking form in their brochures and will make reservations at another of their premises for you.

Since cheap accommodation in the cities and on the popular sections of the coast is snapped up fast, **book ahead** whenever possible, using the suggestions in this book.

Hotels and motels are essentially the same thing, although motels tend to be located beside the main roads away from city centers – and thus are much more accessible to drivers. The budget ones are pretty basic affairs, but in general there's a uniform standard of comfort everywhere – double beds with bathroom, TV, and phone – and you don't get a much better deal by paying, say, $55 instead of $40. Over $55, the room and its fittings simply get bigger and more luxurious, and there'll probably be a swimming pool which guests can use for free. Paying over $100 brings you into the realms of the en-suite Jacuzzi and fireplace.

ACCOMMODATION PRICE CODES

Throughout this book, accommodation has been price-coded according to the cost of the least expensive double room throughout most of the year; we have given individual dollar prices for hostels and whole apartments. Expect prices in most places to jump into the next highest category on Friday and Saturday nights.

However, with the exception of the budget Interstate motels, there's rarely such a thing as a set rate for a room. A basic motel in a seaside or mountain resort may double its prices according to the season, while a big-city hotel which charges $200 per room during the week will often slash its tariff at the weekend when all the business types have gone home. As the high and low seasons for tourists vary widely across the region, astute planning can save a lot of money. Watch out also for local events, which can raise rates far above normal. Only where we explicitly say so do these room rates include local taxes.

① up to $30	④ $60–80	⑦ $130–175
② $30–45	⑤ $80–100	⑧ $175–250
③ $45–60	⑥ $100–130	⑨ $250+

A growing number of New England hotels provide a **complimentary breakfast**. Sometimes this will be no more than a cup of coffee and a sticky bun, but increasingly it is a sit-down affair likely to comprise fruit, cereals, muffins and toast, even made-to-order omelettes in the pricier spots. In most places you'll be able to find cheap one-off hotels and motels simply by keeping your eyes open – they're usually advertised by enormous roadside signs. Alternatively, there are a number of budget-priced chains whose rooms start at $45–60, such as Econolodge, Motel 6, and Travelodge. Mid-priced options include Best Western, Howard Johnson, and Ramada – though if you can afford to pay this much ($55–140) there's normally somewhere nicer and more personal to stay. When it's worth blowing a hunk of cash on somewhere really atmospheric we've said as much in the *Guide*. Bear in mind the most upscale establishments have all manner of services which may appear to be free but for which you'll be expected to tip in a style commensurate with the hotel's status – ie big.

DISCOUNTS AND RESERVATIONS

During off-peak periods many motels and hotels struggle to fill their rooms and it's worth haggling to get a few dollars off the asking price. Staying in the same place for more than one night may bring further reductions. Additionally, pick up the many discount coupons which fill tourist information offices. Read the small print, though: what appears to be an amazingly cheap room rate sometimes turns out to be a per-person charge for two people sharing, and limited to midweek.

BED AND BREAKFAST

Bed and breakfasts are everywhere in New England – nearly every town with any tourist traffic at all will have one – though some are nothing more than a converted room in the back of someone's home. Typically, the bed-and-breakfast inns, as they're usually known, are restored old buildings with fewer than ten rooms and plenty of antique furnishings. Television is refreshingly absent from most, as are in-room phones. Abundant flowers, stuffed cushions and a contrived homey atmosphere are commonplace. Then, of course, there's the breakfast, often an extravagant feast with French toast, eggs, fresh fruit, pastries, coffee and juice. It's often served around a common dining table (8–9am), which can be fun if you're a "morning person," but a nightmare if you'd rather down your poached pears in peace.

B&B prices vary greatly: anything from $60 to $300 depending on location, season, and facilities. Most fall between $80 and $130 per night for

HOTEL DISCOUNT VOUCHERS

For the benefit of overseas travelers, many of the higher-rung hotel chains offer pre-paid discount vouchers, which in theory save you money if you're prepared to pay in advance. To take advantage of such schemes, British travelers must purchase the vouchers in the UK, at a usual cost of £30–60 per night for a minimum of two people sharing. However, it's hard to think of a good reason to buy them; you may save a nominal amount on the fixed rates, but better-value accommodation is not exactly difficult to find in the US, and you may well regret the inflexibility imposed upon your travels. Most UK travel agents will have details of the various voucher schemes.

NEW ENGLAND B&B CONTACTS

American Country Collection
(☎1-800/810-4948 or 518/370-4948, *carolbnbres @msn.com*) Western Massachusetts and Vermont only.

B&B Cape Cod
PO Box 1312, Orleans, MA 02653-1312 (☎1-800/541-6226; international 1-800-1541-6226; from Republic of Ireland 1-800-220-164).

Boston Area B&B Reservations
(☎617/964-1606 or 1-800/832-2632, *www .bbreserve.com*). Includes areas of Maine, New Hampshire, and Vermont.

New England Inkeepers Association,
PO Box 1089, 29 Lafayette Rd, N Hampton, NH 03862 (☎603/964-6689).

Nutmeg B&B
(☎1-800/727-7592 or 860/236-6698). Connecticut only.

Yankee Magazine, PO Box 523, Dublin, NH 03444 (☎603/563-8111). Sells a New England B&B guide for $4.95.

a double, a little less for solo travelers. Bear in mind, too, that they are often booked well in advance, and even if they're not full, the cheaper rooms may already be taken. Also know that many charge hefty "service fees" or hotel taxes, which can add as much as 20 percent to the cost.

HOSTELS

At an average of $15 per night per person, hostels are clearly the cheapest accommodation option in New England other than camping. There are three main kinds of hostel-type accommodation in the US: YMCA/YWCA hostels (known as "Ys") offering accommodation for both sexes or, in a few cases, women-only accommodation; official HI-AYH hostels; and the growing AAIH (American Association of Independent Hostels) organization. There is a fairly good concentration of hostels in New England; HI-AYH are the most prevalent, though there are many unaffiliated hostels as well. For a complete listing of the hostels in the region, check out *www.hostels.com*.

Prices in YMCAs range from around $15 for a dormitory bed to $35 for a single or double room. Some Ys are basically health clubs and do not offer accommodation. As well, in recent years, many YMCAs have become exclusively long-term residential, and many more will follow, as urban gentrification pushes out residential hotels and

WORLDWIDE YOUTH HOSTEL INFORMATION

AUSTRALIA AND NEW ZEALAND

Youth Hostel Association (YHA), Australia, 422 Kent St, Sydney (☎02/9261 1111); 205 King St, Melbourne (☎03/9670 9611); 38 Stuart St, Adelaide (☎08/8231 5583); 154 Roma St, Brisbane (☎07/3236 1680); 236 William St, Perth (☎08/9227 5122); 69A Mitchell St, Darwin (☎08/8981 2560); 28 Criterion St, Hobart (☎03/6234 9617); *www.yha.com.au*.
New Zealand: PO Box 436, Christchurch (☎03/379 9970, *www.yha.co.nz*).

BRITAIN

Scottish Youth Hostel Association, 7 Glebe Crescent, Stirling, FK8 2JA (☎01786/451181, *www.syha.org.uk*).

Youth Hostel Association (YHA), Trevelyan House, 8 St Stephen's Hill, St Albans, Herts AL1 2DY (☎01727/855215, *www.yha/england /wales.org.uk*); London membership desk and booking office: 14 Southampton St, London WC2 7HY (☎020/7836 8541).

IRELAND

An Oige, 61 Mountjoy St, Dublin 7 (☎01/830 4555, *www.irelandyha.org*).

Youth Hostel Association of Northern Ireland, 22 Donegall Rd, Belfast BT12 5JN (☎028/9032 4733, *www.hini.org.uk*). Annual membership £10.

other low-income residence alternatives. Be sure to call in advance if you intend to stay at a YMCA. The Ys listed in the *Guide* do offer accommodation to travelers at the present time. Although they are often in older buildings in less than ideal neighborhoods, facilities can include a gymnasium, a swimming pool, and an inexpensive cafeteria.

You'll find HI-AYH hostels (the prefix is usually shortened to HI in listings) in major cities and popular hiking areas, including national and state parks, across New England. Most urban hostels have 24-hour access, while rural ones may have a curfew and limited daytime hours. HI also operates a couple of small "home hostels" in the region; though as with other hostels you need to reserve in advance or there may be no one there to receive you. Rates at HI hostels range from $12 to $24 for HI members; non-members generally pay an additional $3 per night. If you plan on staying in several hostels, it obviously makes sense to join — each place will have registration information.

It's advisable to book ahead through one of the specialist travel agents or international youth hostel offices: HI-AYH has a **free booking service** on ☎202/783-6161. Some HI hostels will allow you to use a sleeping bag, though officially they should (and many do) insist on a sheet sleeping bag, which can usually be rented at the hostel. The maximum stay at each hostel is technically three days, though this is again a rule that is often ignored if there's space. Few hostels provide meals but most have cooking facilities. Alcohol, smoking and, of course, drugs are banned.

The **independent hostels** in the AAIH group are usually a little less expensive than their HI counterparts, and have fewer rules. The quality is not as consistent; some can be quite poor, while others, which we've included in this book, are absolutely wonderful. There is often no curfew and, at some,

a party atmosphere is encouraged at barbecues and keg parties. Their independent status may be due to a failure to come up to the HI's (fairly rigid) criteria, but often it's simply because the owners prefer not to be tied down by HI regulations.

New England **hosteling information services** include Eastern New England Council, 1105 Commonwealth Ave, Boston, MA 02215 (☎617/779-0900, *www.tiac.net/users/hienec*), and Yankee Council, PO Box 87, Windsor, CT 06095 (☎860/683-2847, *www.pages.cthome.net/sevenoaks*). *The Hostel Handbook for the USA and Canada*, produced each May, lists over two hundred hostels and is available for $4 from Jim Williams, Sugar Hill House International Hostel, 722 Saint Nicholas Ave, New York, NY 10031 (☎212/926-7030). *Hosteling North America*, the HI guide to hostels in the USA and Canada, is available free of charge to any overnight guest at HI-AYH hostels or direct for $2 from the HI National Office, 733 15th St NW, Suite 840, Washington, DC 20005 (☎202/783-6161).

CAMPING

New England campgrounds range from the primitive (a flat piece of ground that may or may not have a water tap) to places more like open-air hotels, with shops, pools, game rooms, restaurants and washing facilities. Naturally enough, prices vary accordingly, from nothing for the most basic plots to $30 a night for something comparatively luxurious. There are plenty of campgrounds but often plenty of people intending to use them as well. Call ahead for reservations at the bigger parks, or anywhere at all during national holidays or the summer, when many grounds will be either full or very crowded. Many save a number of sites for same-day arrivals, but to claim one of these you

---

RESERVING A CAMPGROUND

Kampgrounds of America (KOA), PO Box 30558, Billings, MT 59114 (☎406/248-7444, *www.koakampgrounds.com*), privately oversees a multitude of campgrounds all over New England, although these are almost exclusively for RVs. More tent-friendly (and aesthetically pleasing) sites can be found in the state parks and public lands. These can be booked ahead (for a fee) through a centralized system in each state. To reserve a site at public campgrounds, contact the individual state's division of parks and recreation: CT (☎860/424-3200), MA (☎617/973-8700), ME (☎207/287-3821), NH (☎603/271-3556), RI (☎401/884-0088), and VT (☎802/879-6565). The Appalachian Mountain Club also has some very well-maintained camping areas and mountain huts; call their headquarters in Boston for reservation information (☎617/523-0636, *www.outdoors.org*). Additionally, the National Park Service runs a reservation system (☎1-800/365-2667, *www.nps.gov*), through which you can reserve several months in advance but not less than two days before you arrive.

should plan on arriving early in the day – before 9am to be safe. Vacancies often exist in the grounds outside the parks – where the facilities are usually marginally better – and some of the more basic campgrounds in isolated areas will often be empty whatever time of year you're there. If there's any charge at all you'll need to pay by leaving the money in the bin provided.

Much of the backcountry **forest land** in New England is owned by paper and logging companies, though many cooperate with campers (and hikers) who are hoping to make use of their pristine but soon to be destroyed lands. Contact the local chamber of commerce for information on land usage and **wilderness camping**. In other designated public lands you can camp rough pretty much anywhere you want provided you first obtain a wilderness permit (either free or about $2), and usually a campfire permit, from the nearest park rangers' office. You should also take the proper precautions: carry sufficient food and drink to cover emergencies, inform the park ranger of your travel plans, and watch out for bears, and the effect your presence can have on their environment; see "Backcountry Camping, Hiking and Wildlife" on p.40. For more information on these undeveloped regions – which are often protected within either "national parks" or "national forests" – contact the **US Forest Service**, Eastern Region, 310 W Wisconsin Ave, Room 500, Milwaukee, WI 53203 (☎414/297-3600, *www.fs.fed.us/r9*).

LONG-TERM ACCOMMODATION

Apartment-hunting is not the nightmare it is in, say, New York (with the possible exception of Boston). Accommodation is plentiful and not always expensive, though there is very little really cheap accommodation anywhere except in isolated country areas. Apartments will usually come unfurnished; expect to pay at least $900 a month for a studio or one-bedroom apartment and upwards of $1800 (or more) per month for two to three bedrooms in Boston. Elsewhere, prices can be half that. Most landlords will expect one month's rent as a deposit, plus one month in advance. There is no area-wide organization for long-term accommodation: near universities or college campuses, where apartment turnover is especially high, the best way to find somewhere is to ask around. Otherwise rooms for rent are often advertised in the windows of houses and local papers have "Apartments For Rent" sections. In Boston, the single best source is the Sunday edition of the *Boston Globe*. The *Yellow Pages* will also sometimes list "apartment-finder" firms under "Apartments", and you might try calling real estate offices for help as well (though rental agents may charge a hefty fee – usually one month's rent – in return).

FOOD AND DRINK

Food in New England is difficult to categorize, though in almost every city or town you'll find a mess of typically hearty all- **American family restaurants with lots of basic meat, seafood, and pasta dishes and little to say in the way of ambience.**

New England **seafood** is excellent and loved – lobster almost worshipped – and, especially along the coast, a multitude of "lobster pounds" and low-key seafood joints will try to tempt you with "wicked good" home-made clam-chowder ("chowdah"), oysters, clams, fish, and of course fresh lobsters. Any of these ocean creatures can be part of a traditional New England **clambake** (see box p.32), a delicious way of enjoying the fruits of the sea. Signature Boston baked beans, a once-popular salty stewed mix of pork, onions, and beans, are still found on more nostalgic New England menus. Good attempts at more refined American and international food are available in touristed areas and the larger urban centers, where New England's version of

A NEW ENGLAND CLAMBAKE

Clambake is not just the title of a particularly bad Elvis Presley movie, it's a local tradition older than New England itself. Long before the first white settlers arrived, Native Americans had perfected the ritual of cooking plentiful amounts of clams by what now seems a rather unconventional method. A deep pit is dug into a beach's sand, then lined with smooth rocks. Wood is added and ignited; its ashes are eventually swept away, with the rocks left hot enough to cook on. Before the cooking begins, seaweed is piled on these rocks; layers of sweet potatoes, onions, corn and clams – and/or sometimes lobsters – follow. Then comes another layer of seaweed, and finally a wet canvas covering everything to trap the steam. The result is an unforgettable, and messy, meal, usually eaten with bare hands. Clambakes are usually organized by churches and similar groups that hold fund-raisers; also, a few commercial organizations arrange clambakes in late summer and fall when the fresh corn is at its best. Your best bet if you want to participate in a clambake is to search out local papers for advertisements; towns along the southern coast of Rhode Island are the likeliest sites. In any case, don't think of just staging one on your own unless you want trouble from the authorities.

California cuisine – using fresh, locally grown ingredients – has caught on with the well-heeled crowds. Country inns and bed and breakfasts that serve dinner are good bets for high-quality food in a romantic setting; many have professional chefs on staff. And, of course, there's an abundance of pizza, hamburger, and fast-food places that have become the unfortunate (and not always accurate) symbol of American cuisine.

Even though New England is not particularly agriculturally rich, in season, larger grocery stores stock just about every type of **produce** imaginable – from mangos to avocados to chili peppers. The region also produces its own range of highly nutritious goodies: apples, strawberries, blueberries, peaches, plums, and cranberries are all grown locally. **Maple syrup** is a big product in the region, and every New England state produces at least some amount of the sweet gooey liquid. Vermont is known for its quality **dairy** products – cheese, milk, and yogurt – not to mention Ben and Jerry's Ice Cream.

BREAKFASTS

For the price, on average $5–8, breakfast is the best-value and most filling meal of the day. Go to a diner, or, slightly smarter, a café or coffee shop, all of which serve breakfast until at least 11am, with some diners serving them all day. There are often special deals at earlier times too, say 6–8am, when the price may be even lower.

The breakfasts themselves are pretty much what you'd find all over the country. Eggs are the staple ingredient, often accompanied by some form of meat: ham or bacon, streaky and fried to a crisp; or sausages, skinless and spicy, sometimes shaped as disc-like "sausage patties."

Many breakfasts come with toast: rye, white or whole-wheat bread generally, though tangy sourdough bread is also common. Alternatives are an English muffin (a toasted bread roll) or an American muffin, a fruitcake traditionally made with bran and sugar, often flavored with blueberries, poppyseed or chocolate chip. If you wish, you can add waffles, pancakes or French toast to the combination, consumed swamped in butter with lashings of sickly sweet syrup, flavored to mimic the more delicate and expensive maple syrup. Typically, fresh fruit such as apple, banana, grapefruit, orange, pineapple, or strawberry is available.

Wherever you eat, a dollar or so will entitle you to wash the meal down with as much **coffee** as you can stomach; **tea** is less common, but isn't hard to find.

LUNCH AND SNACKS

Most New England workers take their lunch break between 11.30am and 1.30pm, and during these hours you should look for the low-cost set menus on offer – generally excellent value. Chinese restaurants, for example, frequently have help-yourself rice, noodles, or dim sum feasts for $5–8, and many Japanese restaurants give you a chance to eat

FREE FOOD

Some bars are used as much by diners as drinkers, who take advantage of the free hors d'oeuvres often laid out between 5pm and 7pm Monday to Friday – an attempt to nab the commuting classes before they head off to the suburbs. For the price of a drink you can stuff yourself silly on chili, seafood, or pasta, though bear in mind that the food is more often than not downright unappetizing until you've had at least three drinks.

sushi much more cheaply ($8–12) than usual. Most diners are exceptionally well priced all the time: you can get a good-sized lunch for $5–10. Along the coast, look for seafood restaurants selling fish and chips: the fish is breaded and then fried, and the chips are real chipped potatoes rather than the American French fry matchsticks you normally find. A plateful is about $5. Look, too, for clam chowder, a thick, creamy shellfish soup served almost everywhere for $4–5, sometimes using a hollowed-out sourdough cottage loaf as a bowl.

As you'd expect, there's also **pizza**, available from chains like *Pizza Hut* or local restaurants. Most are dependable and have a similar range of offerings; count on paying around $10 for a basic two-person pizza.

For quick snacks, you'll find many **delis** do a range of sandwiches "to go," which can be meals in themselves: huge French rolls filled with a custom-built combination of meat, cheese, and vegetables. Mexican food is not as prevalent here as on the West Coast, but if you can find it, it will undoubtedly be cheap and goopy – tacos, burritos, quesadillas, and enchiladas are all standard. **Bagels** are available in larger towns: thick, chewy rolls with a hole in the middle, filled with anything you fancy, but generally cream cheese is the standard. **Street stands** sell hot dogs, burgers, or a slice of pizza for around $2 and most shopping malls have ethnic fast-food stalls that are usually edible and filling And of course the burger chains are as ubiquitous here as anywhere in the US: *Wendy's*, *Burger King* and *McDonald's* are the most familiar. Consider also a favorite healthy fast food: **frozen yogurt**, which is sold in most places by the tub for $2.

Besides sodas, available everywhere in any number of varieties, a wide stock of **juices** is also available at most casual restaurants; Snapple is a favorite, as are locally produced Nantucket Nectars. Each has at least a dozen different flavors, though when you read the fine print you'll be sorry to learn that both have no more than fifteen percent real fruit juice – and plenty of sweeteners. You're better off with a cold jug of **bottled water**, which is also available everywhere, despite the fact that New England tap water is clean and perfectly drinkable.

RESTAURANTS

Traditional American cooking – juicy burgers, steaks, fries, salads (invariably served before the main dish) and baked potatoes – is found all over New England. Seafood is particularly abundant along the coast, where it is served in both upscale

expensive gourmet restaurants and no-nonsense harborside shacks where you'll sit at an outdoor bench with other hungry tourists. Ethnic cuisines are plentiful too. Chinese food can be found in the most rural towns, and during lunchtime can often be very cheap. Japanese is more expensive and somewhat fashionable – though sushi is not worshipped here the way it is in, say, California. Italian food is very popular, but can be expensive once you leave the simple pizzas and pastas to explore the specialist Italian regional cooking that's fast catching on. French food, rarely found outside the larger cities, can be quite expensive. Thai, Korean, Vietnamese, Indian, and Indonesian foods are similarly city-based, though usually cheaper.

DRINKING

Typically American bars and cocktail lounges – long, dimly lit counters with a few customers perched on stools before a bartender cum guru, and tables and booths for those who don't want to join in the drunken bar-side debates – are prevalent across New England, although in college-dominated Boston the bars are particularly lively with plenty of young, white, extremely drunken revelers. Similarly, younger and more tourist-driven towns like Portland, ME, Portsmouth, NH, Burlington, VT, and Providence, RI, hold most of New England's worthwhile pubs and microbreweries.

To **buy and consume alcohol** in New England (or anywhere in the US) you need to be 21, and you could well be asked for ID even if you look much older. Alcohol can be bought and drunk any time between 6am and 2am, seven days a week; as well, bars, nightclubs and restaurants are nearly always fully licensed. In addition, it is sometimes permitted to take your own bottled wine into a restaurant, where the corkage fee will be $5–10. You can buy beer, wine or spirits more cheaply and easily in supermarkets, delis, and liquor stores. Beware that in some states it's illegal for stores to sell alcohol on Sundays, though you can still buy alcohol in bars and restaurants after noon. As well, many towns and cities have open-container laws, which make it a misdemeanor to carry an open container of alcohol in a public place, including parks and riversides. You'll probably get away with a warning to take it home, but you could get a fine.

American **beers** fall into two diametrically opposite categories: wonderful and tasteless. You'll probably be familiar with the latter, which are found everywhere: light, fizzy brands such as Budweiser, Miller, and Michelob, the only nationally sold variety likely to find fans among British beer drinkers. The alternative is a fabulous range of **"microbrewed"** beers, the product of a wave of backyard and in-house operations that swelled about ten years ago and has now matured to the point that many pump out over 150,000 barrels a year and are classed as "regional breweries." Head for one of the brewpubs (many are listed in the *Guide* along with breweries you can visit) and you'll find handcrafted beers such as crisp pilsners, wheat beers and stouts on tap, at prices only marginally above those of the national brews. Bottled microbrews like Boston's Harpoon are found on draft in most New England cities. Sam Adams, the self-proclaimed original microbrewery, is the largest of the regional beers and well known throughout the United States, while smaller Vermont-brewed Otter Creek is more difficult to find but worth the effort. Portsmouth Ale, found in many parts of northern New England, is also a satisfying choice.

Alternatively, you can always find a selection of **imported beers** from countries such as Japan, Mexico, and, of course, Europe. Expect to fork out $3 for a glass of draft beer, about the same for a bottle of imported beer. In all but the most pretentious bars, several people can save money by buying a (quart or half-gallon) "pitcher" of beer for $6–10. Six-packs from a supermarket should run $4–5 for domestic, $5–8 for imported brews.

If you're partial to **wines**, most people prefer the produce of California's innumerable, and invariably good, smaller wineries, which are available in most grocery stores, bars, and restaurants in New England. Wines are categorized by grape-type rather than place of origin: Cabernet Sauvignon is probably the most popular, a fruity and palatable red. Also widespread are the heavier reds – Burgundy, Merlot, and Pinot Noir. Among the whites, Chardonnay is very dry and flavorful, and generally preferred to Sauvignon Blanc or Fume Blanc, though these have their devotees. The most unusual is the strongly flavored Zinfandel, which comes in white (mocked by wine snobs, but popular nonetheless), red, or rosé. It's fairly inexpensive to buy the stuff: a decent glass of wine in a bar or restaurant costs about $4, a bottle $15–30. Buying from a supermarket is better still – a quality bottle can be purchased for as little as $7.

Cocktails are extremely popular, especially during happy hours (usually any time between 5pm and 7pm) when drinks are half-price and there's often a buffet thrown in (see "Free food" box, p.32). Varieties are innumerable, sometimes specific to a single bar or cocktail lounge, and they cost anything between $3 and $6.

An increasing alternative to drinking dens, **coffee shops** (look out for any joint with "Java" in the title) play a vibrant part in New England's social scene, and are havens of high-quality coffee far removed from the stuff served in diners and convenience stores. In larger towns and cities, cafes will boast of the quality of the roast, and offer specialties such as espresso with lemon peel as well as a full array of cappuccinos, lattes and the like, served straight, iced, organic, or flavored with syrups. Herbal teas and light snacks are often on the menu.

TELEPHONES, MAIL AND EMAIL

Communications in the US are typically speedy and efficient; New England is no exception to this high standard. Away from towns or cities, you may find it frustrating just getting to the nearest public phone – which may be many miles away – but in general keeping in touch is easy.

TELEPHONES

New England telephones are run by Verizon (☎1-800/474-9999) and Southern New England Telephone (☎1-800/348-6425), which were hived off from the previous Verizon monopoly – the successor to which is the nationwide AT&T network.

Public telephones invariably work, and in cities at any rate can be found everywhere – on street corners, in train and bus stations, hotels, bars, and restaurants. They take 5¢, 10¢, and 25¢

TELEPHONE AREA CODES IN NEW ENGLAND

Connecticut
Northeastern CT ☎860
Southwestern CT ☎203
Maine ☎207

Massachusetts
Boston ☎617
Suburban Boston ☎781
Cape Cod ☎508
Northern MA ☎978
Western MA ☎413

New Hampshire ☎603

Rhode Island ☎401

Vermont ☎802

USEFUL NUMBERS
Emergencies ☎911; ask for the appropriate emergency service: fire, police, or ambulance
Directory information (national) ☎411
Directory inquiries for toll-free numbers
☎1-800/555-1212

---

coins. The cost of a local call from a public phone (generally one within the same area code) varies from a minimum of 20¢, and is usually 35¢; when necessary, a voice comes on the line telling you to pay more.

Some numbers covered by the same area code are considered so far apart that calls between them count as **non-local** (zone calls) and cost much more. Pricier still are **long-distance calls** (ie to a different area code, and always preceded by a 1), for which you'll need plenty of change. Non-local calls and long-distance calls are much less expensive if made between 6pm and 8am – the cheapest rates are after 11pm – and calls from private phones are always much cheaper than those from public phones. Detailed rates are listed at the front of the telephone directory (the **White Pages**, a copious source of information on many matters).

Making telephone calls from **hotel rooms** is usually more expensive than from a pay phone, though some budget hotels offer free local calls from rooms – ask when you check in. An increasing number of phones accept **credit cards**, while anyone who has a US billing address can obtain an **AT&T calling card** (information on ☎1-800/451-4341). Foreign visitors will have to make do with **phone cards** – in denominations of $5, $10, and $20 – bought from general stores, some hostels and relatively few 7-Elevens. These provide you with a temporary account (just tap in the number printed on the card), and are a lot cheaper than feeding coins into a pay phone, especially if calling abroad.

Many government agencies, car rental firms, hotels and so on have **toll-free numbers**, which always have the prefix ☎1-800, ☎1-888, or, less frequently, ☎1-877. Within the US, you can dial any number starting with those digits free of charge, though some numbers only operate inside the state of their origin: it isn't apparent from the number until you try. Numbers with the

INTERNATIONAL TELEPHONE CALLS

International calls can be dialed direct from private or (more expensively) public phones. You can get assistance from the international operator (☎00), who may also interrupt every three minutes asking for more money, and call you back for any money still owed immediately after you hang up. The lowest rates for international calls to Europe are between 6pm and 7am, when a direct-dialed three-minute call will cost roughly $5.

In **Britain**, it's possible to obtain a free **BT Chargecard** (☎0800/800838), using which all calls from overseas can be charged to your quarterly domestic account. To use these cards in the US, or to make a **collect call** (to "reverse the charges") using a BT operator, contact the carrier: AT&T ☎1-800/225-5288; MCI ☎1-800/444-2162; or Sprint ☎1-800/888-8000. To avoid the international operator fee, BT credit-card calls can be made directly using an automated system: AT&T ☎1-800/445-5688; MCI ☎1-800/854-4826; or Sprint ☎1-800/825-4904.

British visitors who are going to be making a number of calls to the US, and who want to be able to call ☎1-800 numbers, otherwise inaccessible from outside the country, should take advantage of the **Swiftcall** telephone club, for which you need a touch-tone phone. Call your nearest office (daily 8am–midnight), and once you've paid by credit card for however many units you want, you are given a PIN. Any time you want to get an international line, simply dial ☎020/7488 0800, punch in your PIN, and then dial as you would were you in the US, putting a 1 before the area code, followed by the number. Calls to the USA – including ☎1-800 calls – cost about 14p per minute, a **saving** of over fifty percent.

Swiftcall numbers
UK ☎0800/769 5555
Ireland ☎0800/409278
USA ☎1-800/513-7325

Telephone cards such as Australia's Telstra Telecard and New Zealand Telecom Calling Card can be used to make calls abroad, which are charged back to a domestic account or credit card. Apply to Telstra ☎1800/038 000 or NZ Telecom ☎04/382 5818. The telephone code to dial TO the US from the outside world (excluding Canada) is 1.

To make international calls FROM the US, dial 011 followed by the country code:

Australia 61	Netherlands 31
Denmark 45	New Zealand 64
Germany 49	Sweden 46
Ireland 353	United Kingdom 44

prefix ☎1-900 are pay-per-call lines, generally quite expensive and almost always involving either sports information, psychics or phone sex. Some numbers, particularly those of consumer services, employ letters as part of their number. The letters are on the button, thus ☎1-800/GET-TAXI becomes ☎1-800/438-8294.

New England has numerous **area codes** – three-digit numbers which must precede the seven-figure number if you're calling from abroad or from a region with a different area code. With the exception of Massachusetts and Connecticut,

each state has its own specific area code. In this book, we've included the local area code with every phone number. With an ever-increasing number of phones and phone numbers, new area codes in New England are likely to become active. If you have trouble getting through, contact the operator or call Verizon (☎1-800/474-9999) for new area code information.

MAIL SERVICES

Post offices are usually open Monday to Friday from 9am until 5pm, and Saturday from 9am to 4pm, and there are blue mail boxes on many street corners. Ordinary mail within the US costs 34¢ for letters weighing up to an ounce. Stamps are also available (for a small extra fee) at some ATMs and grocery stores. Air mail from New England to Europe generally takes less than a week. Postcards, aerograms and letters weighing up to an ounce (a single sheet) cost 80¢.

The last line of the address is made up of the city name, an abbreviation denoting the state

---

New England State Abbreviations

Connecticut: CT
Maine: ME
Massachusetts: MA
New Hampshire: NH
Rhode Island: RI
Vermont: VT

(in Massachusetts "MA") and a five-digit number – the **zip code** – denoting the local post office. The additional four digits you will sometimes see appended to zip codes are not essential. Letters which don't carry the zip code are liable to get lost or at least delayed; if you don't know it, phone books carry a list for their service area, and post offices – even in Europe – have directories.

Letters can be sent **c/o General Delivery** (what's known elsewhere as poste restante) to the one relevant post office in each city, but must include the zip code and will only be held for thirty days before being returned to sender – so make sure there's a return address on the envelope. If you're receiving mail at someone else's address, it should include "c/o" and the regular occupant's name, or it is likely to be returned.

Rules on sending **parcels** are very rigid: packages must be sealed according to the instructions given at the start of the **Yellow Pages**. To send anything out of the country, you'll need a green customs declaration form, available from a post office. **Postal rates** for sending a parcel weighing up to 1lb regular airmail (delivery within 4–7 days) are $14 to Europe and $14.50 to Australia and New Zealand.

TELEGRAMS, FAXES AND EMAIL

To send a telegram (also known as a wire), don't go to a post office but to a Western Union office (listed in the Yellow Pages). Credit-card holders can dictate messages over the phone. International telegrams cost slightly less than the cheapest international phone call: one sent in the morning from New England should arrive at its destination the following day. For domestic telegrams ask for a mailgram, which will be delivered to any address in the country the next morning.

Public **fax machines**, which may require your credit card to be "swiped" through an attached device, are found at photocopy centers and, occasionally, bookstores.

Public access to **email** and the **Internet** is increasingly available in New England. So-called "Internet cafés," with terminals on each table, can be found in major cities – and even some smaller towns – charging up to $7 per hour for full access to the Internet. Additionally, many public libraries have computers available with Internet access – just ask at the circulation desk. If you don't already have one, you can set up **a free email account** at *www.rocketmail.com*, *www.hotmail.com*, *www.yahoo.com* or *www.juno.com* before you depart.

THE MEDIA

The two Boston daily newspapers, the **Boston Globe (www.boston.com) and the Boston Herald**, are both fairly well distributed throughout New England, although local papers are more commonly read. These small regional newspapers, such as the Hartford Courant (www.courant.com), the Bangor Daily News, and the Providence Journal (www.projo.com) tend to excel at reporting their own area but generally rely on agencies for foreign – and even some national – reports.

Major newspapers from other parts of the US such as the **New York Times**, and some overseas newspapers, tend to be found in vending machines, newsstands, and bookstores in major cities. While some weekly local papers are free, most cost anywhere from 50¢ to $1; massive Sunday papers cost more – the *New York Times* Sunday edition, for example, sells for a whopping $4.

Every community of any size has at least a few **free newspapers**, found in street distribution bins, in cafés, bars, or just lying around in piles. It's a good idea to pick up a full assortment: some simply cover local goings-on, while others provide specialist coverage of interests ranging from long-distance cycling to getting ahead in business – and the classified and personal ads can provide hours of entertainment. Many of them are also excellent sources for **listings information**; we've mentioned the most useful titles where relevant in the *Guide*.

TELEVISION

New England **TV** is pretty much the standard network barrage of sitcoms, newscasts and talk shows found all over the States, though PBS, the national public television station, broadcasts a steady stream of interesting documentaries, informative (if slightly dry) news programs, and educational children's television. **Cable television** is ubiquitous, and with up to seventy channels, there's bound to be programming of at least marginal interest. Most cable stations are in fact no better than the major networks (ABC, CBS, NBC, and FOX), though some of the more specialized channels are consistently interesting. The ARTS channel broadcasts enjoyable cultural features, imported TV plays and the like, while CNN (Cable News Network) and a whole host of imitators offer round-the-clock news. ESPN and its spin-off, ESPN2, cover sports 24 hours a day, and the latter is likely to broadcast more obscure competitions, including rugby and European football. HBO (Home Box Office) and Cinemax show recent big-bucks movies, and AMC (American Movie Channel) shows old black-and-white films. Finally, there are MTV, VH-1 and a number of other music stations.

To watch publicity-hyped **pay-per-view** events like world heavyweight boxing bouts you may have to pay as much as $40 to your motel; bars often put on live screenings for a cheaper admission fee. Many hotels and motels offer a choice of movies that have just finished their cinema run, also on a pay-per-view basis, for around $7 each.

RADIO

Radio stations are even more abundant than TV channels, and the majority, again, stick to a bland commercial format. Except for news and chat, stations on the AM band are best avoided in favor of FM, in particular the **nationally funded public** (NPR) and college stations, found between 88 and 92 FM. These provide diverse and listenable programming, be it bizarre underground rock, obscure theater, progressive jazz, or BBC newscasts, and they're also good sources for information on local nightlife.

The large cities boast good specialist music stations, but in between you'll probably have to resort to skipping up and down the frequencies, going from rerun Eagles tracks to fire-and-brimstone Bible thumpers and crazed phone-ins. Driving through rural areas can be especially frustrating, with sometimes only one or two (very dull) stations available in addition to NPR.

FESTIVALS AND PUBLIC HOLIDAYS

Someone, somewhere is always celebrating something in New England although, apart from national holidays, few festivities are shared throughout the entire region. Instead, there is a disparate multitude of local events:

art and craft shows, county fairs, ethnic celebrations, music festivals, rodeos, parades, and many others of every hue and shade.

NEW ENGLAND FESTIVALS AND EVENTS

New England has a number of major annual events and festivals. In addition, New England tourist offices can provide full lists, or you can just phone ahead to the visitor center in a particular region to ask what's coming up. The calendar opposite provides a good overview of unusual or unusually good area festivals.

PUBLIC HOLIDAYS

PUBLIC HOLIDAYS	
New Year's Day	January 1
Martin Luther King Jr's Birthday	January 15
Presidents' Day	Third Monday in February
Easter Monday	varies, usually early April
Memorial Day	Last Monday in May
Independence Day	July 4
Labor Day	First Monday in September
Columbus Day	Second Monday in October
Veterans' Day	November 11
Thanksgiving Day	Last Thursday in November
Christmas Day	December 25

The biggest and most all-American of the national holidays is Independence Day on the Fourth of July, when the entire country grinds to a standstill as people get drunk, salute the flag and take part in fireworks displays, marches, beauty pageants and more, all in commemoration of the signing of

NEW ENGLAND FESTIVALS AND EVENTS

JANUARY

Winter Carnival, Jackson, NH, first two weeks '
(☎603/383-9336, *www.jacksonnh.com*). Ice
sculptures, sleigh rides, and Nordic skiing.

Stowe Winter Carnival, Stowe, VT, last week
(☎1-800/247-8693, *www.stowecarnival.com*).
Similar to above, with more partying.

FEBRUARY

Railroad Show, West Springfield, MA, first
weekend (☎413/436-0242). An extravaganza of
trains, both model and real.

Beanpot Championship, Boston, MA, first two
Mondays (☎617/624-1000). Hockey tournament
pitting local colleges against one another.

Winter Festival, Newport, RI, second week
(☎1-800/976-5122, *www.newportevents.com*).
Discounts at area shops and restaurants with the
purchase of a festival button ($6), plus hayrides
and ice sculpting.

MARCH

Maine Boatbuilders Show, Portland, ME, mid-
March (☎207/774-1067). More than two hundred
boatbuilders come to show off their craft.

APRIL

Boston Marathon, Boston, MA, third Monday
(☎617/236-1652, *www.bostonmarathon.org*).
Perhaps the premier running event in the States.

Five Colleges Book Sale, Hanover, NH, late
April (☎603/643-3115). Tons of books, videos
and such.

MAY

Moose Mania, Greenville, ME, mid-May to mid-
June (☎207/695-2702). Moose-watching, boat
and bike races, and family activities.

Open Studios, VT (statewide), Memorial Day
weekend (☎802/223-3380). Artists open their
homes and studios to the public.

JUNE

Balloon and Craft Festival, Essex Junction, VT,
first weekend (☎802/425-4884). Rides, crafts,
and giant balloons.

Windjammer Days, Boothbay Harbor, ME, late
June (☎207/633-2353). Parade, fireworks, waterfront concerts, and antique boats.

One World, One Heart Festival, Warren, VT, late
June (☎802/651-9600). Concerts, food, and Ben
and Jerry's Ice Cream.

JULY

Schooner Days, Rockland, ME, second weekend (☎207/596-0376). Lobster bakes, schooner
rides, and a concurrent blues festival.

Yard Sale Day, Charlestown, NH, third Saturday
(☎603/826-5237). Coordinated sale in city drive-
ways.

Folk Festival, Lowell, MA, last weekend
(☎978/970-5000). Traditional music and dance on
six outdoor stages, plus food, parades, and
crafts.

AUGUST

Maine Lobster Festival, Rockland, ME, first
weekend (☎207/596-0376). Eight tons of boiled
lobster.

Native American Festival, Haddam, CT, third
week (☎1-800/486-3346). Dancing, music, crafts,
and food.

Crane Beach Sand Blast, Ipswich, MA,
late August (☎978/356-4351). Sandcastle building contest.

SEPTEMBER

World's Fair, Tunbridge, VT, second weekend
after Labor Day (☎802/889-5555). Agricultural
fair with butter-churning, cheesemaking,
sheepshearing, and the like.

Grand Old Brewers Festival, Portsmouth, NH,
last weekend (☎603/433 1100). Keg rolling, tug-
of-war, and, of course, lots of beer.

OCTOBER

Fryeburg Fair, Fryeburg, ME, first week
(☎207/935-3268). Crafts, axe-throwing, and harness racing.

Haunted Happenings, Salem, MA, late October
(☎978/744-0013). Learn to cast spells and visit
haunted houses in the days leading up to
Halloween.

NOVEMBER

Antiquarian Book Fair, Boston, MA, mid-
month (☎617/266-6540). Tons of old books.

Victorian Holiday, Portland, ME, weekend after
Thanksgiving (☎207/772-6828). Horse-drawn carriages and Victorian garb abound.

DECEMBER

Christmas Town Festival, Bethlehem, CT, first
weekend (☎203/266-5557). Caroling, crafts, and
the lighting of the town tree by Santa himself.

the Declaration of Independence in 1776. Halloween (October 31) lacks any such patriotic overtones, and is not a public holiday despite being one of the most popular yearly flings. Traditionally, costumed kids run around the streets banging on doors demanding "trick or treat," and receiving pieces of candy. These days that sort of activity is mostly confined to rural and suburban areas, while in bigger cities Halloween has grown into a massive drunken celebration of the macabre. More sedate is Thanksgiving Day, on the last Thursday in November, essentially a domestic affair, when relatives return to the

familial nest to stuff themselves with roast turkey, and (supposedly) fondly recall the first harvest of the Pilgrims in Massachusetts – though in fact Thanksgiving was already a national holiday before anyone thought to make that connection.

On the national public holidays listed in the box below, shops, banks and offices are liable to be **closed** all day. Many states also have their own additional holidays, and in some places Good Friday is a half-day holiday. The traditional summer season for tourism runs from Memorial Day to Labor Day; some tourist attractions are only open during that period.

BACKCOUNTRY CAMPING, HIKING AND WILDLIFE

New England has some fabulous backcountry and wilderness areas, coated by dense

forests, splashed with sparkling lakes, and capped by monumental mountains. Unfort-

BACKCOUNTRY DANGERS AND WILDLIFE

You're likely to meet many kinds of wildlife and come upon unexpected hazards on your travels through the wilderness, but only a few are likely to cause problems. With due care, many potential difficulties can be avoided.

Hiking in the foothills should not be problematic but you should check your clothes frequently for **ticks** – pesky blood-sucking burrowing insects which are known to carry **Lyme disease**, a health hazard especially in southern New England (it's named after a town in Connecticut). If you have been bitten, and especially if you get flu-like symptoms, get advice from a park ranger. Also annoying around water are **mosquitoes**; carry candles scented with citronella or insect repellent to keep them at bay. **Black flies** also come out in force around water in the warm summer months, and, with a tenacious appetite for human heads, ears, and faces, and a perpetual buzz, they can be tremendously annoying; again, carry insect repellent.

You're highly unlikely to encounter a **bear** in New England, though the American black bear is native to the region, and prevalent in the northern wilderness areas. To reduce the likelihood of encountering one, make noise (carrying bells in your pack isn't a bad idea) as you walk. If you do come across one, keep calm, and make sure it is aware of your presence by clapping, talking, singing, or making other sounds. If the bear does not leave immediately after seeing you, the pres-

ence of food may be encouraging him to stay; remove any sight or smell of food. Black bears will occasionally **charge** with no intention of attacking when attempting to steal food or if they feel threatened. If you are so unlucky, don't try to run, just slowly back away.

If a bear visits your camp, scare it off by **banging pots and pans** – if it doesn't go, you should. Leave backpacks open and lying on the ground so a bear can examine the contents without tearing them apart. It will be after your food, which should be stored in airtight containers when camping. Some campgrounds are equipped with bear-proof lockers, which you are obliged to use to store food when not preparing or eating it. Elsewhere, you should hang both food and garbage from a high branch (too weak to support the weight of a bear) some distance from your camp. **Never feed a bear**: it'll make the bear dependent on humans for food. Bears within state and national parks are protected, but if they spend too much time around people the park rangers are, depressingly, left with no option but to shoot them. Finally, never get between a mother and her cubs. Young animals are cute; irate mothers are not.

Moose, which live in the lush unpopulated regions near the Canadian border, seldom attack unless provoked: do not tease or try to approach them. The largest member of the deer family, they can be up to nine feet tall and weigh as much as

unately, while still immensely rewarding – and it's one of the compelling reasons for coming to New England – it isn't all as wild as it once was, thanks to the thousands who tramp through each year. If you're intending to do the same, you can help preserve the special qualities of the environment by observing a few simple rules. For practical information on traveling through the forest, see the box below.

The US's protected backcountry areas fall into a number of potentially confusing categories. Most numerous are **state parks**, owned and operated by the individual states. They include state beaches, state historic parks, and state recreational areas, often around sites of geological or historical importance and not necessarily in rural areas. **Daily fees** are usually $4–6, though a $40–75 annual pass gives free access to most sites for a year.

Acadia National Park in Maine, a large, federally controlled and preserved area of great natural beauty is the only national park in New England; entry is $5 for one person on foot, bicycle, or motorbike, or $10 for up to four in a car. Acadia is supplemented by the smaller national historic sites ($3–4), like St Gaudins in New Hampshire, with just one major feature, national forests, national monuments, and national seashores. If you plan to visit a few of these, invest in a **Golden Eagle Passport** ($65 cash from any national park entrance), which grants both driver and passengers (or if cycling or hiking, the holder's immediate family) access to all New England's national parks, monuments, seashores, and forests for a calendar year. Excellent free ranger programs – such as guided walks or slide shows – are held throughout the year. The federal government also operates national recreation areas. Campgrounds and equipment-rental outlets are always abundant.

1200 pounds. They are mostly active at night, but can also be seen at dusk and dawn, when they may gather to feed near lakes and streams. Though they may seem slow, tame, and passive at first, moose can be unpredictable, especially during the mating season in September and October. If you happen upon one in the forest, move slowly, avoid making any loud noises, and keep your distance. The best place to view a moose is from your automobile, though you should be careful when driving along northern country roads – collisions can be fatal for all parties involved.

Mountain lions (cougars, panthers or pumas) also live in the northern portion of the region. Sightings are rare in well-traveled areas, and there have been very few attacks on hikers, but to reduce the already slim chance of an unwanted encounter, avoid walking by yourself, especially after dark, when lions tend to hunt. Make noise as you walk, wield a stick and keep children close to you. If you encounter one, face the lion, try to appear larger by raising your arms or holding your coat above you and it will probably back away. If not, throw rocks and sticks in its vicinity.

Campsite critters – ground squirrels, chipmunks and raccoons – are usually just a nuisance though they tend to carry diseases and you should avoid contact. Only the **marmot** is a real pest, as it likes to chew through radiator hoses and car electrics to reach a warm engine on a cold night. Before setting off in the morning, check the motor for gnawed components, otherwise you might find yourself with a seized engine and a cooked or, at best, terrified marmot as a passenger. Boots and rucksacks also come in for marmot scrutiny.

Poison ivy is one thing that isn't going to come and get you, though you may come up against it, especially in the spring. Recognizable by its shiny configuration of variously notched leaves (which secrete an oily juice), greenish flowers, and whitish berries, this twiggy shrub or climbing vine is found in open woods or along stream banks throughout much of New England. It's highly allergenic, so avoid touching it. If you do, washing with strong soap, taking frequent dips in the sea, and applying cortisone cream usually help relieve the symptoms; in extreme cases, see a doctor.

In the mountains, your biggest dangers have nothing to do with the flora or fauna. **Late snows** are common, giving rise to the possibility of **avalanches** and **meltwaters**, which make otherwise simple stream crossings hazardous. Drowning in fast-flowing meltwater rivers is one of the biggest causes of death in New England wilderness areas. The riverbanks are often strewn with large, slippery boulders – keep well clear unless you are specifically there for river activities. Sudden changes in the weather are also common in more mountainous regions, when temperatures can fluctuate wildly and high winds and storms can appear out of nowhere; be sure to have enough warm clothing with you at all times, and check with park rangers before you set off for particularly long backcountry treks.

New England's two **national forests**, the Green Mountain National Forest in Vermont (see p.347) and the White Mountain National Forest in New Hampshire (see p.435), are huge, covering fifty percent of all public land in Vermont and an area larger than the state of Rhode Island in New Hampshire. They are federally administered (by the US Forest Service, *www.fs.fed.us*), but with much less protection than national parks. More roads run through national forests, and often there is some limited logging and other land-based industry operated on a sustainable basis.

All the above forms of protected land can contain **wilderness areas**, which aim to protect natural resources in their most native state. In practice this means there's no commercial activity at all; buildings, motorized vehicles and bicycles are not permitted, nor are firearms and pets. Overnight camping is allowed, but wilderness permits (free–$5) must be obtained in advance from the land management agency responsible. In New England, the White Mountains and the Green Mountains both have large wilderness areas, with only the regions near roads, visitor centers and buildings designated as less stringently regulated "front country."

CAMPING

When camping rough, check that fires are permitted before you start one; if they are, use a stove

ESSENTIAL EQUIPMENT

Many campgrounds are on rock with only a thin covering of soil, so driving pegs in can be a problem; freestanding dome-style tents are therefore preferable. Go for one with a large area of mosquito netting and a removable fly sheet: tents designed for harsh European winters can get horribly sweaty once the sun rises, unless, of course, you're camping in the winter.

Most developed campgrounds are equipped with fire rings with some form of grill for cooking, but many people prefer a Coleman stove, powered by white gas, a kind of super-clean gasoline. Both stoves and white gas are widely available in camping stores. Other camping stoves are less common. Equipment using butane and propane – Camping Gaz and, to a lesser extent, EPI gas, Scorpion, and Optimus – is on the rise, though outside of major camping areas you'll be pushed to find supplies, so stock up when you can.

In New England, the **Appalachian Mountain Club** (☎617/523-0636, *www.outdoors.org*) offers a range of backcountry hikes into otherwise barely accessible parts of the wilderness, with food and guide provided. The tours happen at all times of the year, cost anywhere from $50 to $800, last from a day to two weeks, and are heavily subscribed, making it essential to book well in advance. Club members pay around $20 less, though you'll also have to pay $40 to join. They also have some very well-maintained camping areas and mountain huts; call their headquarters in Boston for information on making reservations.

in preference to local materials – in some places firewood is scarce, although you may be allowed to use deadwood. No open fires are allowed in wilderness areas, where you should also try to camp on previously used sites. Where there are no toilets, bury human waste at least four inches into the ground and a hundred feet from the nearest water supply and camp. Burn rubbish, and what you can't burn, carry away. One potential problem is giardia, a water-borne protozoan causing an intestinal disease, symptoms of which are chronic diarrhea, abdominal cramps, fatigue and loss of weight, that requires treatment. To avoid catching it, never drink from rivers and streams, however clear and inviting they may look (you never know what unspeakable acts people – or animals – further upstream have performed in them). Water that isn't from taps should be boiled for at least five minutes, or cleansed with an iodine-based purifier (such as Potable Aqua) or a Giardia-rated filter, available from camping or sports stores.

Finally, don't use ordinary soaps or detergents in lakes and streams; you can buy special ecological soap for such a purpose.

HIKING

Wilderness areas start close to the main areas of national parks. There is normally no problem entering the wilderness for day walks, but overnight trips require wilderness permits (see above). In peak periods, a quota system operates for the most popular paths, so if there's a hike you specifically want to do, obtain your permit well ahead of time (at least two weeks, more for popular hikes). When completing the form for your permit, be sure to ask a park ranger for weather conditions and general information about the hike you're undertaking.

Hikes covered in the *Guide* are given with length and estimated walking time for a healthy but not especially fit adult. State parks have many graded trails designed for people who drive to the corner store, so anyone used to walking and with a moderate degree of fitness will find these ratings very conservative.

SPORTS AND OUTDOOR PURSUITS

Boston is the only city in New England with major professional sports teams; excepting football, they have one team in each of the primary sports – baseball, hockey, and basketball. The region's only professional football team is based slightly afield, in Foxboro, MA. Residents in smaller towns often choose instead to root for the teams at their local high school or university, though Boston's professional teams are followed closely in all New England newspapers. College basketball in the region is particularly competitive, and, more locally, minor league baseball teams draw enthusiastic crowds. Locals are also physically active; the most popular outdoor pursuits include fishing, hiking, river-rafting, canoeing, and kayaking.

FOOTBALL

Football in America attracts the most obsessive and devoted fans of any sport, perhaps because there are fewer games played – only sixteen in a season, which lasts throughout the fall. With many quick skirmishes and military-like movements up and down the field, the game is ideal for television, and nowhere is this more apparent than during the televised games which are a feature of many bars on Monday nights – though most games are played on Sundays.

The game lasts for four fifteen-minute quarters, with a fifteen-minute break at half time. But since time is only counted when play is in progress, matches can take up to **three hours** to complete, mainly due to interruptions for TV advertising. Commentators will discuss the game throughout to help your comprehension, though they use such a barrage of statistics to illustrate their remarks that you may feel hopelessly confused. Not that it matters – the spectacle of American football is fun to experience, even if you haven't a clue what's going on. Players tend to be huge, averaging about six foot five and weighing upwards of three hundred pounds; they look even bigger when they're suited up for battle in shoulder pads and helmets. The best players become nationally known celebrities, raking in millions of dollars in fees for product endorsements on top of astronomical salaries.

TEAMS AND TICKETS

All major teams play in the National Football League (NFL), the sport's governing body, which divides the teams into two conferences of equal stature, the National Football Conference (NFC) and the American Football Conference (AFC). In turn, each conference is split into three divisions, East, Central and West. For the end of season playoffs, the best team in each of the six divisions plus three wildcards from each conference fight it out for the title.

The NFL season begins in late summer and lasts through the end of January. New England's only team is the **New England Patriots**, who went to (and lost) the Super Bowl in 1996 but have since been rather mediocre. They are based outside of Boston in Foxboro, having withstood a plan to relocate to Hartford. There are no second division equivalents, though the region's college teams serve as a training ground for future NFL stars.

Tickets cost $20–80 for professional games, $5–15 for college games. To **book tickets** call either the NFL (☎212/450-2000, *www.nfl.com*) or the New England Patriots (☎508/543-8200, *www.patriots.com*).

BASEBALL

Baseball, much like cricket in its relaxed, summertime pace and seemingly Byzantine rules, is often called "America's pastime," though its image was tarnished by the bitter strike by players which shortened the 1994 season and saw the unthinkable canceling of the World Series.

Games are played – 162 each full season – all over the US almost every day from April to September, with the league championships and the World Series, the final best-of-seven playoff, lasting through October. Watching a game, even if you don't understand what's going on, can be at the least a pleasant day out, drinking beer and eating hot dogs in the bleachers and unshaded

AMERICAN SPORTS FOR FORIEGN VISITORS

THE RULES OF FOOTBALL

The **rules** of **American football** are fairly simple: the field is 100 yards long by 40 yards wide, plus two end zones at each end; there are two teams of eleven men. The game begins with a **kickoff**, after which the team in possession of the ball tries to move downfield to score a **touchdown**, while the opposing team tries to stop them. The attacking team has four chances to move the ball forward ten yards and gain a first down; otherwise they forfeit possession to the opposition. After the kickoff the **quarterback**, the leader of the attack, either hands the ball off to a **running back**, or throws the ball through the air downfield to a **receiver**. Play ends when the man with the ball is tackled to the ground (or runs out of bounds), or if the pass attempt falls incomplete.

A touchdown, worth six points, is made when a player crosses into the defending team's end zone carrying the ball; unlike in rugby, no actual touching down is necessary, it is enough just to carry the ball over the line. After a touchdown, the scoring team has one attempt at an **"extra point"** by either kicking a field goal (1 point) or crossing into the end zone (2 points) from three yards out. A regular field goal, worth three points, is scored when the **placekicker** – always the smallest man on the team and quite often the lone foreigner – kicks the ball, as in rugby, through the goalposts that stand in the end zone. If the attacking team has failed to move the ball within scoring range, and seems unlikely to gain the required ten yards for another first down, they can elect to **punt** the ball, kicking it to the other team. A change of possession can also occur if the opposition players manage to **intercept** an attempted pass or force a **fumble**, taking the ball away from a runner.

THE RULES OF BASEBALL

The setup for baseball looks like the English game of rounders, with four **bases** set at the corners of a 90-foot diamond. The base at the bottom corner is called **home plate**, and serves much the same purpose as do the stumps in cricket. Play begins when the **pitcher**, standing on a pitcher's mound in the middle of the diamond, throws the ball at upwards of a hundred miles an hour, making it curve and bend as it travels towards the **catcher**, who crouches behind home plate; seven other defensive players take up positions, one at each base and the others spread out around the field of play.

A **batter** from the opposing team stands beside home plate and tries to hit the ball. If the batter swings and misses, or if the pitched ball crosses the plate above the batter's knees and below his chest, it counts as a strike; if he doesn't swing and the ball passes outside this **strike** zone, it counts as a ball – equivalent to a "no ball" in cricket. If the batter gets three strikes against him he is **out**; four balls and he gets a free **walk**, and takes his place as a runner on first base. Foul balls, hit out of the field of play, count as a strike, but a player cannot strike out (get a third strike) on a foul ball.

If he succeeds in hitting the pitched ball into fair territory (the wedge between the first and third bases), the batter runs toward **first base**; if the opposing players catch the ball before it hits the ground, the batter is out. Otherwise they field the ball and attempt to relay it to first base before the batter gets there; if they fail he is **safe** – and stays there, being moved along by subsequent batters until he makes a complete circuit and scores a run. The most exciting moment in baseball is the **home run**, when a batter hits the ball over the outfield fences, a boundary some 400 feet away from home plate; he and any runners on base when he hits the ball each score a run. If there are runners on all three bases it's called a **grand slam**, and earns four runs.

The **nine players** per side bat in rotation; each side gets **three outs** per inning, and there are nine innings per game – the "top" of the innings is when the first team (usually the visiting team) is batting, or is about to bat; the "bottom" of the innings is during the second team's turn. Games normally last two to three hours, and are **never tied**; if the scores are level after nine innings, extra innings are played until one side pulls ahead and wins.

benches beyond the outfield; tickets are comparatively cheap ($18–20) and the crowds usually friendly and sociable.

TEAMS AND TICKETS

All Major League baseball teams play in either the **National League** or the **American League**, each of equal stature and split into three divisions, East, Central and West. For the end of season playoffs and the World Series, the best team in each of the six divisions plus a second-place wildcard from each league fight it out for the title.

New England's Major League club is the **Boston Red Sox**, though there's also a team across the border in Montréal, the **Expos**. In addition, there are also numerous minor league clubs, known as farm teams because they supply the top clubs with talent. Details are included in relevant chapters of the *Guide*.

Tickets for games cost $18–55 per seat, and are generally available on the day of the game.

BASKETBALL

Basketball is one of the few professional sports that is also actually played by many ordinary Americans, since all you need is a ball and a hoop. It's a particularly popular sport in low-income inner-city areas, where school playgrounds are packed with young hopefuls.

The professional game is played by athletes of phenomenal agility, seven-foot-tall giants who float through the air over a wall of equally tall defenders, seeming to change direction in mid-flight before slam-dunking the ball (smashing it through the hoop with such force that the backboard sometimes shatters) to score two points. Games last for an exhausting 48 minutes of playing time, around two hours total.

TEAMS AND TICKETS

New England's basketball club, the **Boston Celtics** (☎617/523-6050, *www.nba.com/celtics*), have been struggling ever since their domination ended in the late Eighties, when Larry Bird and company parted ways. The **University of Connecticut**, the **University of Massachusetts**, and **Providence University** all field perpetually competitive college basketball teams. Additionally, in recent years quite a lot of buzz has been generated around the University of Connecticut **women's basketball** team, the 2000 NCAA champions. **Tickets** cost $10–85 for professional

BASEBALL LEAGUE AND CLUB CONTACT INFORMATION
Major League ☎212/339-7800, *www.mlb.com*
National League ☎212/339-7700
American League ☎212/339-7600
Boston Red Sox ☎617/267-9440, *www.redsox.com*
Montréal Expos ☎514/253-3434, *www.montrealexpos.com*

games, $5–25 for college games. Call the National Basketball Association (☎212/407-8000) or National Collegiate Athletic Association (☎1-800/545-5201) for more ticket information.

ICE HOCKEY

Ice hockey enjoys considerable popularity in New England, not least because the cold winter weather is so conducive to the sport. Many children grow up playing the sport, and go on to compete at the area's highly competitive colleges and universities; a small percentage go on to play in the professional **National Hockey League** (NHL). A considerable rivalry has developed over the years between players from the United States and Canada, owing largely to Canada's fear of losing their longtime claim as the world's premier hockey nation. As heavy favorites in the 1998 Winter Olympics, however, the over-confident US and Canadian national teams were both humiliated by the Czech Republic, Russia, and Finland.

TEAMS AND TICKETS

New England has one NHL team, the **Boston Bruins** (☎617/624-1500, *www.bostonbruins.com*), and there's also a club in Montréal, the **Canadiens** (☎514/932-2582, *www.canadiens.com*); both manage to draw considerable crowds. Tickets start at about $20. Call the NHL (☎212/789-2000) for more information.

OUTDOOR PURSUITS

Hunting and fishing, if they can be considered sports, are probably the two most popular outdoor pursuits in New England, although the more physically challenging hiking, mountain biking, and kayaking all fall right behind. Duck, deer, and sometimes even the mighty moose are all popular targets, though hunting laws are strict and you'll need a **permit** (ask the local chamber of commerce how you can get one) before you start dropping victims in the forest. Streams, lakes, ponds, and rivers fill up with fishermen (and women) in season, though as with hunting, permits are required and laws are strict. Trout and salmon are found in most bodies of freshwater.

Hiking is huge, especially in the northern areas of New England, although you'll find good places to get out into nature just about anywhere outside of the main cities. Most state and federally operated parks maintain good networks of trails, not least the famous **Appalachian Trail**, which originates in Georgia and winds through the beautiful backcountry of New England before traversing New Hampshire's White Mountains and terminating in desolate northern Maine. We've given plenty more on hiking on p.42, and throughout the *Guide* as well.

Cycling is also extremely popular, particularly longer road rides on New England's many deserted, tree-shaded country roads or hectic trail rides in the mountains. Weekend enthusiasts put their knobby mountain bike tires to use on the countless trails that weave throughout New England's beautiful wilderness areas. Special mountain bike parks, most of them operating in summer only, exploit the groomed snow-free runs of Northern New Hampshire, Vermont, and Maine. In such places, and throughout New England, you can rent bikes for $20–30 a day; see "Getting Around," p.26, for more on general cycling.

Skiing is the biggest mass-market participant sport, with downhill resorts all over northeastern New England – where it snows heavily most winters. In fact, the mountains that cap the northern ends of Maine, New Hampshire, and Vermont offer the best skiing in the eastern US, particularly in **Killington, VT** (see p.354), and **Sugarloaf, ME** (see p.525). You can rent equipment for about $50 a weekend, plus another $40 to $60 a day for lift tickets. The Internet is a great source for additional information. For example, *www.skieast.com* has links to resort-cams, weather information, and most of the ski resorts. Another good bet is *www.newenglandskiresorts.com*, which locates all of the downhill ski resorts in the region on maps and provides extensive descriptions of each. A number of companies run all-inclusive ski trips (including transportation, lift-tickets, equipment, and accommodations) from the larger cities. In addition to convenience, these outfits usually offer good deals; consult the relevant section of the **Guide** or check the **Yellow Pages**.

A cheaper option is **cross-country skiing**, or ski-touring. A number of backcountry ski lodges offer a range of rustic accommodation, equipment rental, and lessons, from as little as $20 a day for skis, boots, and poles, up to about $200 for an all-inclusive weekend tour. For additional information, consult *www.nexcski.com*, an exhaustive reference pertaining to the sport in New England, with information on resorts, trail conditions, equipment, and ski shops.

TRAVELERS WITH DISABILITIES

Travelers with mobility problems or other physical disabilities are likely to find New England – as with the US in general – to be much more in tune with their needs than anywhere else in the world. All public buildings must be wheelchair-accessible and have suitable toilets; most city street corners have dropped curbs; subways have elevators, and most city buses are able to kneel to make access easier and are built with space and handgrips for wheelchair users. Most hotels, restaurants and theaters (certainly any built in the last ten years or so) have excellent wheelchair access.

GETTING AROUND

Most airlines, transatlantic and within the US, do whatever they can to ease your journey, and will usually let attendants of people with serious disabilities accompany them at no extra charge. The Americans with Disabilities Act (ADA) of 1990 obliged all air carriers to make the majority of their services accessible to travelers with disabilities within five to nine years.

Almost every Amtrak **train** includes one or more coaches with accommodation for disabled passengers. Guide dogs travel free, and Amtrak will provide wheelchair assistance at its train stations,

CONTACTS FOR DISABLED TRAVELERS

AUSTRALIA AND NEW ZEALAND

ACROD (Australian Council for Rehabilitation of the Disabled), PO Box 60, Curtin, ACT 2605 (☎ 02/6282 4333); 24 Cabarita Rd, Cabarita, NSW 2137 (☎02/9743 2699). *www.acrod.org* Lists of travel agencies and tour operators.

Disabled Persons Assembly, 4/173-175 Victoria St, Wellington (☎04/801 9100, *www.dpa.org.nz*). Resource centre with lists of travel agencies and tour operators for people with disabilities.

BRITAIN

Holiday Care Service, 2nd floor, Imperial Building, Victoria Rd, Horley, Surrey RH6 7PZ (☎01293/774535, fax 784647, minicom 776943, *www.holidaycare.org.uk*). Provides information on all aspects of travel.

Tripscope, The Courtyard, Evelyn Rd, London W4 5JL (☎020/8994 9294, fax 994 3618, *www.justmobility.co.uk/tripscope*). National telephone information service offering free advice on transport and travel.

IRELAND

Disability Action Group, 2 Annadale Ave, Belfast BT7 3JH (☎028/9029 7880, *www.disabilityaction.org*).

Irish Wheelchair Association, Blackheath Drive, Clontarf, Dublin 3 (☎01/833 8241, fax 833 3873, *iwa@iol.ie*).

USA

The Center for Independent Living, 2539 Telegraph Ave, Berkeley, CA 94704 (☎510/841-4776). Counseling services.

Mobility International USA, PO Box 10767, Eugene, OR 97440 (☎541/343-1284, *www.miusa.org*). Transportation queries.

Society for the Advancement of Travellers with Handicaps (SATH), 347 Fifth Ave, Suite 610, New York, NY 10016 (☎212/447-7284, *www.sath.org*). Travel industry group.

Twin Peaks Press, PO Box 129, Vancouver, WA 98666 (☎1-800/637-2256 or 360/694-2462). Publish *Travel for the Disabled, Wheelchair Vagabond* and *Directory of Travel Agencies for the Disabled*.

---

adapted seating on board and a fifteen percent discount on the regular fare, all provided 24 hours' notice is given. Passengers with hearing impairment can get information on ☎1-800/523-6590.

Traveling by Greyhound or regional **buses**, however, is not to be recommended. They are not equipped with lifts for wheelchairs, though staff will assist with boarding (inter-city carriers are required by law to do this), and the "Helping Hand" scheme offers two-for-the-price-of-one tickets to passengers unable to travel alone (carry a doctor's certificate).

The major **car rental firms** can, given sufficient notice, provide vehicles with hand controls (though these are usually only available on the more expensive models). The American Automobile Association produces the **Handicapped Driver's Mobility Guide** for drivers with disabilities (available free from AAA, Traffic Safety Dept, 150 Van Ness Ave, San Francisco, CA 94102, ☎415/565-2012). There are no longer differences in state parking regulations for disabled motorists: the Department of Transportation has decreed that all state licenses issued to disabled persons must

carry a three-inch square international access symbol, and each state must provide placards bearing this symbol to be hung from the rear-view mirror – the placards are blue for permanent disabilities, red for temporary (maximum of six months). More information can be obtained from your state motor vehicle office.

As in other parts of the world, the rise of the **self-service gas station** is unwelcome for many disabled drivers. The states of New England have addressed this by changing its laws so that most service stations are required to provide full service to disabled drivers at self-service prices.

INFORMATION

The State Tourism Offices (see p.18) all have **information** on "handicapped facilities" at places of accommodation and attractions. They should also be able to provide lists of "wheelchair-accessible" properties – hotels, motels, apartments, B&Bs, hostels, RV parks – in the cities and surrounding countryside; as always, call the property in question to confirm details.

ACCOMMODATION

The big motel and hotel chains are often the safest bet for **accessible accommodation**; there are plenty of excellent local alternatives, of course, but with a chain at least you'll know what to expect. At the higher end of the scale Embassy Suites (☎1-800/362-2779, voice; ☎1-800/458-4708, TDD) have been working to implement new standards of access which meet and exceed ADA requirements, involving both new construction and the retrofitting of their one hundred existing hotels, and providing special training to all employees. Although the President of Hyatt International Corporation (☎1-800/233-1234) summed up the hotel industry's initial reaction to the ADA as "the end of the world as we know it," Hyatt has also committed itself to extensive redesign to improve accessibility.

THE GREAT OUTDOORS

Citizens or permanent residents of the US who have been "medically determined to be blind or permanently disabled" can obtain the **Golden Access Passport**, a free lifetime entrance pass to those federally operated parks, monuments, historic sites, recreation areas, and wildlife refuges which charge entrance fees. The pass must be picked up in person from the areas described, and it also provides a fifty percent discount on fees charged for facilities such as camping, boat launching and parking. Each state also offers passes (free to the disabled) that give similar concessions to its state-run parks, beaches, and historic sites. Reduced rates are available for permanently disabled people who apply by mail

for a Disabled Discount Pass ($3.50 once-only payment) to the relevant state's Department of Parks and Recreation Disabled Discount Pass Program.

For visitors to **national parks** the somewhat outdated **Access America Guide: An Atlas of the National Parks** costs $44.95, from Northern Cartographic, Suite 131, 4050 Williston Rd, South Burlington, VT 05403 (☎802/860-2886). The guide contains all sorts of useful information for visitors with mobility impairments, or hearing, visual, or developmental disabilities.

Disabled Outdoors Magazine, Box 395, Grand Marnais, MN 55604 (☎218/387-9100), is a quarterly magazine covering outdoor activities for sportspersons with disabilities (US $10, Can $16 yearly). Also useful is **Easy Access to National Parks**, by Wendy Roth and Michael Tompane ($15), a detailed guide to all US national parks for people with disabilities, senior citizens, and families with young children, published by the Sierra Club, 85 Second St, San Francisco, CA 94105 (☎415/977-5500, voice; ☎415/977-5780, TDD). Acadia National Park, PO Box 177, Bar Harbor, ME 04609-0177 (☎207/288-3338), can also supply general information direct.

PACKAGES

Many US **tour companies** cater for disabled travelers or specialize in organizing disabled group tours. State tourist departments should be able to provide lists of such companies; failing that, ask the National Tour Association, 546 E Main St, PO Box 3071, Lexington, KY 40596 (☎1-800/755-8687 or 859/226-4444). They can put you in touch with operators whose tours match your needs.

WOMEN TRAVELERS

Practically speaking, though a woman traveling alone is certainly not the attention-grabbing spectacle in New England that she might be elsewhere in the world, you're likely to come across some sort of minor harassment. More serious than the odd offensive comment, rape statistics in the US are high, and it goes without saying that, even more than anyone else, women should never hitch alone – this is widely interpret-

ed as an invitation for trouble, and there's no shortage of weirdos to give it.

Similarly, if you have a car, be careful whom you pick up: just because you're in the driver's seat doesn't mean you're safe. If you can, avoid traveling **at night** by public transport – deserted bus stations, while not necessarily threatening, will do little to make you feel secure, and where possible you should team up with another woman. On buses, sit as near to the front – and the driver – as possible.

New England cities can feel very safe, but as with anywhere, particular care has to be taken at night, and a modicum of **common sense** can often avert disasters. Walking down unlit, empty streets is never a good idea, and you should take cabs wherever possible. The advice that women who look confident tend not to encounter trouble is, like all home truths, grounded in fact but not written in stone; those who stand around looking lost and a bit scared are prime targets, but nobody is immune. Provided you listen to advice, though, and stick to the better parts of a town, going into bars and clubs alone should pose no problems, especially in Boston, where there's generally a pretty healthy attitude towards women who choose to do so. If in doubt, gay and lesbian bars are usually a trouble-free alternative.

Small towns in rural areas are not blessed with the same liberal attitudes toward lone women travelers that you'll find in the cities. If your vehicle **breaks down** in a country area, walk to the nearest house or town for help; don't wait by the vehicle in the middle of nowhere hoping for somebody to stop – they will, but it may not be the help you're looking for. Should disaster strike, all major towns have some kind of rape counseling service available; if not, the local sheriff's office will make adequate arrangements for you to get help, counseling, and, if necessary, get you home.

The **National Organization for Women** is a women's issues group whose lobbying has done much to affect positive legislation. NOW branches, listed in local phone directories, can provide referrals for specific concerns such as rape crisis centers and counseling services, feminist bookstores and lesbian bars. Further back-up material can be found in *Women's Travel in Your Pocket* ($14; Ferrari Publications, PO Box 37887, Phoenix, AZ 85069, ☎602/863-2408), a guide for women travellers, last updated in 1999. Specific women's contacts are listed where applicable in the city sections of the *Guide*.

TRAVELING WITH CHILDREN

Traveling with kids in New England is relatively problem-free; children are readily accepted – indeed welcomed – in public places everywhere. Hotels and motels are used to them (although some bed and breakfasts have a minimum age requirement – ask when making reservations), most state and national parks organize children's activities, every town or city has clean and safe playgrounds, and there are plenty of commercial attractions that specialize in kids' entertainment – mini-golf, water slides, arcades and the like. Restaurants make considerable efforts to encourage parents to bring their offspring. All the national chains offer booster chairs and a special kids' menu, packed with huge, excellent-value (though not necessarily healthy) meals.

Local tourist offices (see p.18) can provide specific information on what their state has to offer children, and various **guidebooks** have been written for parents traveling with children, like the helpful **Trouble Free Travel with Children** ($6.95), available through Publishers Group West. John Muir Publications puts out a series of books for children, called *Kidding*

Around, which tell about the history and describe the various sights of major US cities.

GETTING AROUND

Most families choose to travel by car, and while this is the least problematic way to get around it's worth planning ahead to assure a pleasant trip. Don't set yourself unrealistic targets if you're hoping to enjoy a driving vacation with your kids – those long, boring journeys on the Interstate can be disastrous. If you're on a fly-drive vacation, note that when renting a car the company is legally obliged to provide free car seats for kids. RVs are also a good option for family travel, combining the convenience of built-in kitchens and bedrooms with freedom of the road (see "Getting Around," p.24).

Children under two years old **fly free** on domestic routes, and for ten percent of the adult fare on international flights – though that doesn't mean they get a seat, let alone frequent-flier miles. Kids between two and twelve are usually entitled to half-price tickets.

Traveling by **bus** is the most uncomfortable for kids. Under-twos travel (on your lap) for free; ages two to four are charged ten percent of the adult fare, as are any toddlers who take up a seat. Children under twelve years old are charged half the standard fare.

Taking the **train** is by far the best option for long journeys – not only does everyone get to enjoy the scenery, but you can get up and walk around,

relieving pent-up energy. Most cross-country trains have **sleeping compartments**, which may be quite expensive but are likely to be seen as a great adventure. On Amtrak, two children aged two to fifteen can travel at half-fare with each adult passenger.

SENIOR TRAVELERS

For many senior citizens, retirement brings the opportunity to explore the world in a style and at a pace that is the envy of younger travelers. As well as the obvious advantages of being free to travel for longer periods during the quieter – and less expensive – seasons, anyone over the age of 62 can enjoy a tremendous variety of discounts with suitable ID. Amtrak, Greyhound, local buses, and many US airlines offer (smallish) percentage reductions on fares to older passengers.

Any US citizen or permanent resident aged 62 or over is entitled to **free admission** for life to all national parks, monuments and historic sites using a **Golden Age Passport**, for which a once-only $10 fee is charged; it can be issued at any such site. This free entry also applies to any accompanying car passengers or, for those hiking or cycling, the passport-holder's immediate family. It also gives a

fifty percent reduction on fees for camping, parking, and boat launching.

The individual states offer Senior Citizen **discounts** on admission to state-run parks, beaches and historic sites; these give $1 off parking and $2 off family camping except where the fee is less than $3. Several states offer special senior citizen discount passes – contact the relevant state's tourist information center for details (see p.18).

Museums, art galleries and even hotels offer small discounts, and since the definition of "senior" can drop as low as 55, it is always worth asking. The **American Association of Retired Persons**, 601 E St NW, Washington, DC 20049 (☎202/434-2277 or 1-800/424-3410, *www.aarp.org*), membership of which is open to US residents aged fifty or over for an annual fee of $10, organizes group travel for senior citizens and can provide discounts on accommodation and vehicle rental.

GAY AND LESBIAN NEW ENGLAND

The gay scene in New England is rather subdued, and just about anywhere, even in Boston, homosexuals are still commonly oppressed. Sadly, especially in more rural areas, gay travelers would be well advised to watch their step to avoid hassles. Be careful, for example, with open displays of affection and the like. As difficult and as frustrating as this may be, it's usually the most effective way to keep narrow-minded bigots at bay.

This is not to say that the situation is entirely bleak; in **Maine**, for example, where you would expect there to be a backcountry-fueled opposi-

tion to anything different, locals are so obsessed with living life their own way that gays and lesbians are enjoying more public acceptance. **Vermont** is notoriously liberal, though slower to accept homosexuality than, say, the West Coast, while **New Hampshire** remains staunchly conservative. There are sizeable, predominantly gay areas in almost all the New England states – Massachusetts' **Provincetown**, Maine's **Ogunquit**, and the **South End** of Boston to name a few. However, tolerance is lacking just about everywhere else, the liberal attitudes of the major cities are not always reflected in the more isolated areas.

GAY AND LESBIAN PUBLICATIONS

Of **national publications** to look out for, most of which are available from any good bookstore, by far the best are the range produced by The Damron Company, PO Box 422458, San Francisco, CA 94142 (☎1-800/462-6654 or 415/255-0404). These include the *Address Book*, a pocket-sized yearbook full of listings of hotels, bars, clubs, and resources for gay men ($15.95); the *Women's Traveler*, which provides similar listings for lesbians ($12.95); the *Road Atlas*, which shows lodgings and entertainment in major cities ($15.95); and the *Damron Accommodations Guide* with color photos of gay-friendly places to stay in Canada and the US ($18.95). The *Gay Yellow Pages* (PO Box 533, Village Station, New York, NY 10014; $12) is also a valuable resource. Other works to look out for are the travel books published by Ferrari, PO Box 37887, Phoenix, AZ 85069 (☎602/863-2408), though neither of them is specific to New England; rather, the *Men's Travel In Your Pocket* ($16) and *Women's Travel In Your Pocket* ($14) guides cover general travel and entertainment information for gays and lesbians, respectively.

The Advocate (Liberation Publications, Suite 1000, 6922 Hollywood Blvd, Los Angeles, CA 90028; $3.95) is a bimonthly national gay news magazine, with features, general info, and classified ads (not to be confused with *Advocate Men*, which is a soft porn magazine). Another useful publication (albeit online) is *www.qtmagazine.com*, an exclusively gay and lesbian travel resource with monthly features, events guides, and helpful links.

Although gay life exploded into the public eye in the 1970s, the energies of gay men and women have been more recently directed to the protection of existing rights and to increasing support and help for victims of AIDS. Activist groups like ACT-UP (the AIDS Coalition To Unleash Power) and Queer Nation hold sit-ins as part of continuing efforts to maintain a high profile in the face of continued intolerance and isolation.

DIRECTORY

ADDRESSES Though initially confusing for overseas visitors, American addresses are masterpieces of logical thinking. Generally speaking, roads in built-up areas are laid out to a grid system, creating "blocks" of buildings: addresses of buildings refer to the block, which will be numbered in sequence, from a central point usually downtown; for example, 620 S Cedar will be six blocks south of downtown. In small towns, and parts of larger cities, "streets" and "avenues" often run north–south and east–west respectively; streets are usually named (sometimes alphabetically), avenues generally numbered.

CIGARETTES AND SMOKING Smoking is as much frowned upon in New England as the rest of the States (excepting the fanatic West Coast, °perhaps). Cigarettes are sold in almost any food shop, convenience store, drugstore, or bar. A packet of twenty costs upwards of $5.

DEPARTURE TAX All airport, customs and security taxes are included in the price of your ticket.

DRUGS Possession of under an ounce of the widely consumed marijuana is a misdemeanor in New England, and the worst you'll get is a $200 fine. Being caught with more than an ounce, however, means facing a criminal charge for dealing, and a possible prison sentence – stiffer if caught anywhere near a school. Other drugs are, of course, completely illegal and it's a much more serious offense if you're caught with any.

ELECTRICITY 110V AC. The insubstantial two-pronged plugs have now largely been replaced by a more sturdy three-pronged affair. Some travel plug adapters don't fit American sockets.

FLOORS In the US, what would be the ground floor in Britain is the first floor, the first floor the second floor and so on.

ID Should be carried at all times. Two pieces will diffuse any suspicion, one of which should have a photo: driving license, passport, and credit card(s) are your best bets.

MEASUREMENTS AND SIZES The US has yet to go metric, so measurements are in inches, feet, yards, and miles; weight in ounces, pounds, and tons. American pints and gallons are about four-fifths of Imperial ones. Clothing sizes are always two figures less than what they would be in Britain – a British women's size 12 is a US size 10 – while British shoe sizes are half a size below American ones for women, and one size below for men.

TAX Added on to your bill will invariably be some sort of surcharge, be it restaurant tax (5–8 percent), hotel tax (6–12 percent), or sales tax (5–8 percent). New Hampshire, however, has no sales tax; Vermont has none for hotels.

TIME New England runs on Eastern Standard Time (EST), five hours behind GMT in winter and three hours ahead of the West Coast. British Summer Time runs almost concurrent with US Daylight Saving Time – implemented from the last Sunday in April to the last Sunday in October – causing a four-hour time difference for two weeks of the year.

TIPPING You are, of course, expected to tip pretty much all service-related help, from waitstaff (15–20 percent) to bartenders (10–15 percent) to cab drivers (10–15 percent).

WHALE-WATCHING During November and December, huge playful whales migrate from the Arctic to their breeding grounds off the coast of Canada, making their return journey during February and March. Plenty of tours and events along the coast will be on offer during these months that will allow you to get a glimpse of the great creatures.

PART TWO

THE

GUIDE

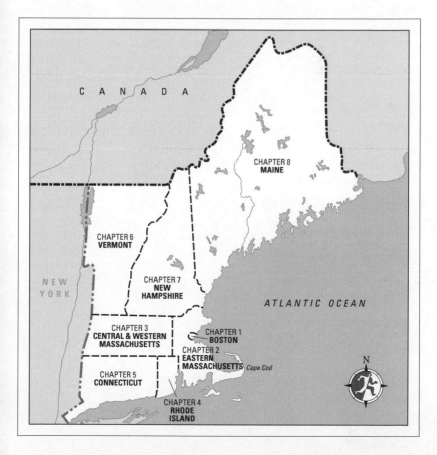

CHAPTER ONE

BOSTON

Boston might be as close to the Old World as the New World gets, an American city that proudly trades in on its colonial past, having served a crucial role in the country's development from a few wayward pilgrims right through the Revolutionary War. It occasionally takes this a bit too far — what's a faded relic anywhere else becomes a plaque-covered tourist sight here — but none of it detracts from the city's overriding historic charm, nor its present-day energy. Indeed, there are plenty of tall skyscrapers, thriving business concerns and cultural outposts that are part-and-parcel of modern urban America, not to mention excellent mergers of past and present, such as the redeveloped – and bustling – Quincy Market, a paradigm for successful urban renewal. True, nowhere else will you get a better feel for the events and personas behind the birth of a nation, all played out in Boston's wealth of emblematic and evocative colonial-era sights. But the city's cafés and shops, its attractive public spaces, and the diversity of its neighborhoods – student hives, ethnic enclaves, and stately districts of preserved town houses – are similarly alluring, and go some way to answering the twin accusations of elitism and provincialism to which Boston is perennially subjected.

As the undisputed commercial and cultural center of New England, Boston is the highlight of any trip to the region, truly unmissable because almost every road in the area leads to it (indeed Boston was, until the late 1700s, America's most populous and culturally important city). It's also the center of the American university system – more than sixty colleges call the area their home, including Harvard, in the neighboring city of Cambridge – and it enjoys a youthful buzz that again belies any reputation for stuffiness it might have. This academic connection has also played a key part in the city's left-leaning political tradition, the kind that spawned a line of ethnic mayors and, most famous, the Kennedy clan.

Today, Boston's relatively small size – both physically and in terms of population (eighteenth among US cities) – and its provincial feel actually serve the city to great advantage. Though it has expanded since it was first settled in 1630 through landfills and annexation, it has never lost its center, a tangle of streets clustered around Boston Common which can really only be explored on foot. Steeped in Puritan roots, the residents of these areas often display a slightly anachronistic Yankee pride, but it's one that has served to protect the city's identity, while groups of Irish and Italian descent have carved out authentically and often equally unchanged communities in areas like the North End, Charlestown and South Boston. Indeed, the districts around the Common exude almost a small-town atmosphere and, until recently at least, were relatively unmarred by chain stores and fast-food joints. Even as Boston has evolved from busy port to blighted city to the rejuvenated place it is today, it has remained, fundamentally, a city on a human scale.

Unless otherwise stated, all phone numbers in this chapter are prefixed by the code ☎617

Some history

Boston's first permanent settlement was started by **William Blackstone**, who split off from the Pilgrims' camp down in Plymouth for more isolated territory. He was soon joined by more Puritan settlers, to whom he sold most of the land he had staked out, then called the Shawmut Peninsula and soon renamed by the Puritans after their hometown in England: Boston.

Early Bostonians enjoyed almost total political autonomy, but with the restoration of the British monarchy in 1660, the crown began appointing governors to oversee the Massachusetts Bay Colony. The colonists clashed frequently with these appointees, their resentment growing with a series of acts over the next one hundred or so years that restricted various civil and commercial liberties. This culminated in such skirmishes as the Boston Massacre and the Boston Tea Party, events that went a long way towards propelling the **Revolutionary War**, which effectively started just outside Boston, in Lexington.

Post-Revolution, Boston emerged as a leading port city, eventually moving on to prominence in textiles and other industries. Its success in these fields brought wave after wave of nineteenth-century immigrants, notably Irish and Italian, ethnicities that still largely populate the city and that have made great inroads into local and regional politics. Despite a strong history of progressive thought in abolitionism, the city has been less successful in integrating African-Americans into the fold, and **racial tensions** flared up frequently in the twentieth century, most recently with the controversial advent of busing in the 1970s. This has been somewhat healed of late, as have any economic doldrums that plagued the city for the latter half of this century, and a new sense of confidence – so emblematic of Boston's storied past – has taken hold.

Recent US economic boom years have however substantially altered the city's physical and human landscape. In 1998, a group of crafty landlords succeeded in putting a motion to repeal the rent control laws in Boston, Cambridge and Somerville on a state-wide referendum, although the majority of the state was unaffected; it passed narrowly, and Boston rents have since skyrocketed. Ethnic and economic diversity have suffered accordingly, and all over Boston, Cambridge and Somerville, chainstores and apartment high rises are sprouting and local businesses are closing. It's hard to believe that the city will weather these changes.

Arrival, information, and getting around

Boston is the unchallenged travel hub of New England, and if it's not the only place in the region you'll visit, it almost certainly will be the first. Conveniently, all **points of arrival** are located inside the city boundaries, none more than a few miles away from downtown, and all are well connected to public transport.

By air

Logan International Airport (☎1-800/23-LOGAN) is usually quite busy with services both domestic and international. It sits on Boston's easternmost peninsula, which juts far out into Boston Harbor. The airport has five lettered terminals: you'll find **currency exchange** in terminals C and E (daily 2–6pm), plus information centers, car rental, and Automatic Teller Machines (ATMs) in all five. Each is connected by a series of courtesy buses, which also run to the Airport

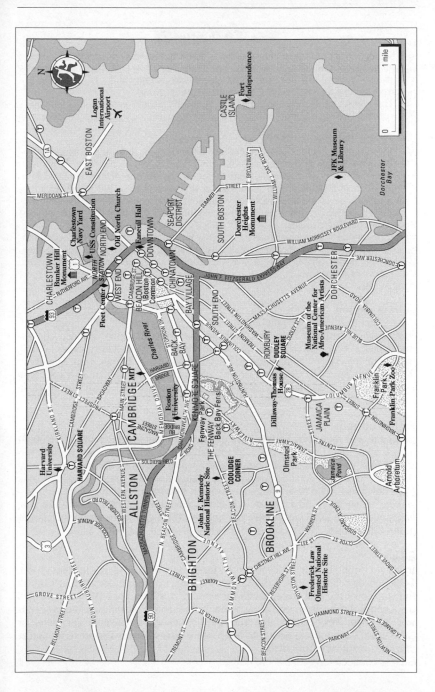

N

1 mile

0

Logan International Airport

EAST BOSTON

Fort Independence

CASTLE ISLAND

Dorchester Bay

JFK Museum & Library

MERIDIAN ST

SUMMER STREET

E. BROADWAY

WILLIAM J. DAY BLVD.

Charlestown Navy Yard

USS Constitution

Old North Church

Faneuil Hall

SEAPORT DISTRICT

SOUTH BOSTON

Dorchester Heights Monument

WILLIAM MORRISSEY BOULEVARD

CHARLESTOWN

Bunker Hill Monument

RUTHERFORD AVE

NORTH STATION

NORTH END

DOWNTOWN

WEST END

CHINATOWN

Fleet Center

CAMBRIDGE ST

Beacon Hill

Boston Common

BAY VILLAGE

SOUTH END

DORCHESTER

DORCHESTER AVE

JOHN F. FITZGERALD EXPRESSWAY

Charles River

STORROW DR.

BACK BAY

MASSACHUSETTS AVENUE

COLUMBIA ROAD

BLUE HILL AVENUE

COLUMBUS AVENUE

TREMONT STREET

WASHINGTON STREET

SOUTH STREET

Museum of the National Center for Afro-American Artists

ROXBURY

DUDLEY SQUARE

DUDLEY STREET

Harvard Bridge

MIT

CAMBRIDGE

MEMORIAL DRIVE

MAGAZINE STREET

Boston University

BU BRIDGE

COMMONWEALTH AVE.

KENMORE SQUARE

HUNTINGTON AVE.

Back Bay Fens

THE FENWAY

Fenway Park

Dillaway-Thomas House

COLUMBUS AVENUE

JAMAICA PLAIN

CENTRAL

JAMAICAWAY

Franklin Park

Franklin Park Zoo

WASHINGTON STREET

MAIN STREET

BROADWAY

PROSPECT STREET

KIRKLAND STREET

CAMBRIDGE STREET

Harvard University

HARVARD SQUARE

ALLSTON

SOLDIERS FIELD

WESTERN AVENUE

SOLDIERS FIELD RD.

N. BEACON STREET

CAMBRIDGE STREET

RIVERWAY

Olmsted Park

Jamaica Pond

Arnold Arboretum

GODDARD AVENUE

John F. Kennedy National Historic Site

COOLIDGE CORNER

BEACON STREET

BROOKLINE

Frederick Law Olmsted National Historic Site

CHESTNUT HILL AVE

WARREN ST.

LEE ST.

CLYDE ST.

GROVE STREET

RESERVOIR RD.

BOYLSTON STREET

HAMMOND STREET

PARKWAY

GROVE STREET

MOUNT AUBURN STREET

BELMONT STREET

COOLIDGE AVENUE

FOSTER ST.

TREMONT ST.

BRIGHTON

MARKET STREET

COMMONWEALTH AVENUE

BEACON STREET

NEWTON STREET

LA GRANGE ST.

MASSACHUSETTS AVENUE

THE BIG DIG

Whether you arrive in Boston by air, rail or highway, you're likely to notice a downtown in seeming disarray. This mess has been created by the **Big Dig**, a grand attempt – and one that has evolved into a political calamity and a logistical nightmare – to bury the city's central traffic artery underground.

The project, approved in 1987 and started in 1991, began as an attempt to alleviate central Boston's heinous traffic – roads are often gridlocked for ten hours a day – by relocating some seven and a half miles of highway underground, a move that would free up an estimated 27 acres of land for use as a downtown park.

The budget, originally estimated at $2.6 billion, is now expected to exceed $12 billion since an inquiry discovered that city planners had hidden over $2 billion of their project's cost overruns from the public. While the project is slated for completion in 2004, concerns about the cost overruns have led to talk of auctioning off the space to developers – a move that would change the central artery's proposed "green space" into a conglomeration of high-rise office buildings and parking garages.

If this modern civic blunder interests you, visit the **Big Dig Visitors' Center**, 70 East India Row, on the harbor (daily 10am–4.30pm; ☎951-6400). There, one can learn that during the dig "more earth will be moved than during the construction of the Great Pyramids."

subway station. From there, you can take the Blue Line to State or Government Center stations, in the heart of downtown; the ride is about fifteen minutes ($1). Just as quick, and a lot more fun, is the **water shuttle**, which connects the terminal buses with Rowes Wharf across the harbor (Mon–Thurs every 15min, 6am–8pm; Fri every 30min, 8am–11pm; Sat every 30min 10am–11pm; Sun every 30min 10am–8pm; $8). A **taxi** to downtown costs $15–20, plus an extra $4.30 in fees and tolls. For around the same price, you can ride in style with Boston Town Car (☎782-4000).

By bus or train

Boston is well served by both **bus** and **rail** travel. Peter Pan (☎1-800/343-9999) and Greyhound buses (☎1-800/231-2222), along with Amtrak trains (☎1-800/USA-RAIL), all arrive in (and depart from) Boston's **South Station**, at Summer Street and Atlantic Avenue, near the waterfront and just a short walk from downtown. The newly renovated station houses information booths, newsstands, restaurants, and a fantastic old clock, though no currency exchange. The easily accessible Red Line subway can quickly whisk you to the center of town or out to Cambridge.

By car

If you're coming **by car**, be aware of the three main highways that lead into town: **I-95** (locally referred to as Rte-128), which is part of the Interstate that runs all the way down the east coast, skirts the greater Boston area; **I-93**, locally called the Central Artery, is an expressway that runs through downtown and proceeds well up into New Hampshire; and **I-90** (the Massachusetts Turnpike, or "Masspike") is a toll highway that approaches Boston from due west, a popular entryway from New York State.

Information

Boston's main public tourist office is the **Boston Visitor Information Pavilion** on Boston Common, near the Park Street subway stop (Mon–Sat 8.30am–5pm, Sun 9am–5pm). You'll find loads of maps and brochures, plus information on historical sights, cultural events, accommodation, restaurants, and bus trips. Across the street from the Old State House, at 15 State St, is a **visitor's center** maintained by the Boston National Historical Park (daily 9am–5pm); it too has plenty of free brochures, plus a bookstore with lots of material on Boston, New England and Revolutionary history. In Back Bay, there is a visitor **kiosk** in the Prudential Center (Mon–Fri 8.30am–6pm, Sat 10am–6pm, Sun 11.30am–6pm). For advance information, the Greater Boston CVB maintains the free **Boston By Phone** service, which is especially helpful for accommodation bookings (Mon–Fri 9am–5pm; ☎1-800/888-5515).

The "Calendar" section in Thursday's *Boston Globe* (50¢), the city's premier newspaper, is a good source for up-to-date events listings. Still better is the some-

GUIDED TOURS OF BOSTON

Perhaps the best way to orient yourself in Boston, aside from walking, is by taking a **trolley tour**, on small open-air bus-like vehicles painted to look like streetcars. Most of the trolleys let you hop on and off at various locations and they make pickups at major hotels; full tours usually last about two hours, and there is little difference from tour to tour in what historical sights you'll actually see. For day-trips to Lexington, Concord, Plymouth, or Salem, Brush Hill Tours (☎720-6342) offer coach tours, a good option if you don't have a car.

NARRATED TROLLEY TOURS

Beantown Trolley (☎720-6342) is one of the oldest and most popular. $22.

Cityview Luxury Trolley Tours (☎363-7899) has more coach-like seats, more comfortable than most; $18. Admission to the Aquarium or a harbor cruise comes to $22.

Discover Boston Multilingual Trolley Tours (☎742-1440) narrates tours in English, but provides special audio devices that make it possible to hear descriptions in French, German, Italian, Japanese, Spanish, or Russian. $24.

Old Town Trolley Tours (☎269-7010) seem to be everywhere, and are distinguishable by their orange and green colors. $23.

OTHER CITY TOURS

Boston by Foot (☎367-2345) has guides leading informative ninety-minute tours of Beacon Hill, Copley Square, the waterfront, North End and the Underground (which takes in disused Ⓣ stations). $8.

Boston Duck Tours (☎723-DUCK) take advantage of the Boston Ducks, a fleet of restored and brightly painted World War II truck-boats that make the usual rounds and then dip into the Charles River. Be forewarned: you may be asked to quack. Tours depart from the Prudential Center, 101 Huntington Ave, every half hour starting at 9am until sunset. $21.

Boston National Historical Park Visitor's Center Freedom Trail Tours (☎242-5642) are led by park rangers and take in a few Freedom Trail sights. They run on the hour between 10am and 3pm.

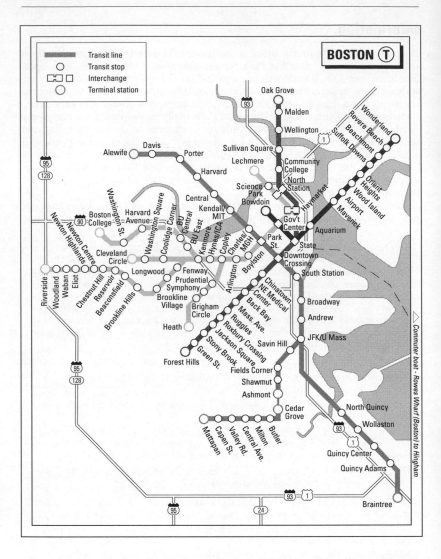

what alternative free weekly *Boston Phoenix*, published on Thursdays and available from street boxes, newsstands, coffee shops, and various other places. Other free publications include *The Improper Bostonian* and *Stuff @Night*, though both concentrate more on features than listings. The best source **of gay and lesbian information** is the weekly *Bay Windows*; pick up a copy for free at one of Boston's predominantly gay bookstores (see p.129).

The **Boston City Pass** (available all over; $30.25) is a ticket booklet that covers admission to the Isabella Stewart Gardner Museum, the John Hancock Tower, the Kennedy Museum, the Museum of Fine Arts, the New England Aquarium, and the Science Museum.

City transport

Much of the pleasure of visiting Boston comes from being in a city built long before cars were invented. Walking around the narrow, winding streets can be a joy; conversely, driving around them is a nightmare. If you have a car, park it for the duration of your trip and get around either by foot or by **public transport** – a system of subway lines and buses run by the Massachusetts Bay Transportation Authority (MBTA; ☎722-3200, *www.mbta.com*).

Subway (the "Ⓣ")

Four **subway** lines transect Boston and continue out into some of its more proximate neighbors. While not the most modern system (the Green Line was America's first underground train, built in the late nineteenth century), it's at least reasonably cheap and efficient.

Each line is keyed to a particular color and passes through downtown before continuing on to other districts. The **Red Line** is the most frequent, passing through South Boston and Dorchester to the south and Cambridge to the north; the **Green Line** hits Back Bay in addition to Kenmore Square, The Fenway, and Brookline; the infrequent **Orange Line** traverses the South End and continues down to Roxbury and Jamaica Plain; and the **Blue Line** heads out into East Boston, useful primarily for its stop at Logan Airport. All are fairly fast and safe; only some parts of the Orange Line after dark might be said to be unsafe. Free transit maps are available at any station. The fare is $1, payable with exact change or by tokens purchased at the station; trains generally run from 5.15am to 12.30am, though they start slightly later on Sundays. If you're planning to take public transport a lot, it's a good idea to buy a **visitor's passport**, for one ($6), three ($11) or seven days' ($22) unlimited subway and bus use. A cheaper option, depending on your timetable, may be the weekly combo commuter passes ($12.50), which are good from Sunday to Saturday, and are sold from the previous Thursday until the Wednesday of the week they're valid for. You can buy them at the Harvard, Kenmore, or Park St Ⓣ stations.

Buses

City **buses** run less frequently than the subway and are harder to navigate, but they hold three main advantages: they're slightly cheaper (75¢, exact change only), they provide service to many more points, and they allow you to see more of the city than you otherwise would in a train tunnel. It's a service used primarily by natives who have grown familiar with the byzantine system of routes. Be brave and arm yourself with the *Official Public Transport Map* and schedules available at all subway stations. Buses run from 5.30am to 1am.

Bikes

In and around Boston are some eighty miles of **bike trails**, making it an excellent city to explore on two wheels. You can rent bikes year-round at Back Bay Bikes & Boards, 333 Newbury St (☎247-2336) and from April through September at Community Bike Shop, 490 Tremont St (☎542-8623), among others. A copy of *Boston's Bike Map* ($4) will help you find all the trails and bike-friendly roads in the area.

Taxis

Given Boston's small scale and the efficiency of its public transport, **taxis** aren't as necessary or prevalent as in big cities like New York or London. You can generally hail one along the streets of downtown or Back Bay, though competition gets pretty stiff after 1am, when the subway has stopped running, and bars and clubs begin to close; in that case, go to a hotel, where cabs cluster, or where a bellhop can arrange one for you. In Cambridge, taxis mostly congregate around Harvard Square.

Boston Cab (☎262-2227) and Bay State Taxi Service (☎566-5000) have 24-hour service and accept all major credit cards; another option is Town Taxi (☎536-5000). In Cambridge, call the dispatcher at ☎495-8294 for Yellow Cabs or Ambassador Cabs or ☎547-3000 for Cambridge Cab.

Accommodation

For such a popular travel destination, Boston has a surprisingly limited range of well-priced **accommodation**. Though there are still bargains to be found, prices at many formerly moderate **hotels** have inched into the expense-account range. Your best bet is to come off-season, around November through April, when many hotels not only have more vacancies but offer special discounts too. At any other time of year, be sure to make reservations well in advance. September (start of the school year) and June (graduation) are particularly busy months, due to the large student population here. Even if Boston's hotels are not suited to every traveler's budget, they do cater to most tastes, and range from the usual assortment of **chains** to some excellent independently run hotels, the best of which, not to mention the highest concentration, are in Back Bay. Most of the business hotels are located in or around the Financial District.

Increasingly popular are **bed and breakfasts**, of which there are a surprising number tucked into renovated brownstones in Beacon Hill, Back Bay, and the South End. The industry is thriving, largely because it is so difficult to find accommodation here for under $100 a night – and many B&Bs offer just that. Some of the best are actually outside the city, in either Cambridge or Brookline. You can make reservations directly with the places we've listed; there are also numerous B&B **agencies** that can do the booking for you.

Short-term **furnished apartments**, spread throughout the city, are another option; most have two-week minimums. There are also a handful of decent **hostels** if you're looking for real budget accommodation, though definitely book

---

ACCOMMODATION PRICE CODES

All accommodation prices in this book have been coded using the symbols below; prices are for one night in the least expensive **double room** in each establishment. For a full explanation see p.28 in Basics. Individual rates rather than price codes are given for **hostels**.

① up to $30	④ $60–80	⑦ $130–175
② $30–45	⑤ $80–100	⑧ $175–250
③ $45–60	⑥ $100–130	⑨ $250+

ahead, especially in summer. Hotels and bed-and-breakfasts are listed below by neighborhood, with hostels listed separately.

Downtown

Boston Harbor Hotel, 70 Rowes Wharf (☎439-7000 or 1-800/752-7077, fax 345-6799). Aquarium Ⓣ. Opulent accommodation in an atmosphere of studied corporate elegance. There's a health club, pool, kowtowing concierge staff, and rooms with harbor and city views. Ⓨ.

Boston Marriot Long Wharf, 296 State St (☎227-0800, fax 227-2867). Aquarium Ⓣ. All the rooms here boast harbor views, but the awesome lobby is what really makes this Marriott stand out. The price isn't too bad either. Ⓖ–Ⓧ.

Harborside Inn, 185 State St (☎723-7500, fax 670-2010). State Ⓣ. Small hotel housed in a renovated mercantile warehouse across from Quincy Market, with reasonably priced rooms. Ⓖ.

Le Meridien, 250 Franklin St (☎451-1900 or 1-800/543-4300, fax 423-2844). State Ⓣ. Located in the heart of the Financial District, this stern granite building is, appropriately enough, the former Federal Reserve Bank of Boston. Modern rooms, but stiff atmosphere. Ⓧ.

Milner Hotel, 78 Charles St S (☎426-6220 or 1-800/453-1731). Boylston Ⓣ. Recently renovated, this uninspiring but affordable hotel is convenient to the Theater District, Bay Village, and the Public Garden. All room rates include a continental breakfast. Ⓓ–Ⓖ.

Omni Parker House, 60 School St (☎227-8600 or 1-800/843-6664, fax 742-5729). Park Ⓣ. No one can compete with the *Parker House* in the history department: it's the oldest continuously operating hotel in the US. Though the present building only dates from 1927, the lobby has been restored to its nineteenth-century splendor of dark oak and carved gilt moldings; the rooms are small and a bit dowdy. Ⓗ–Ⓨ.

Regal Bostonian Hotel, Faneuil Hall Marketplace (☎1-800/343-0922, fax 523-2454). State Ⓣ. Splendid quarters in the heart of downtown. Its rooms and lobby are festooned with portraits of famous Colonial figures. Ⓨ.

Tremont House, 275 Tremont St (☎426-1400 or 1-800/331-9998, fax 338-7881). Boylston Ⓣ. The opulent lobby of this 1925 hotel somewhat compensates for its rather small rooms, but if you want to be in the thick of the Theater District you can't do better. Ⓗ.

Beacon Hill and the West End

Beacon Hill Bed & Breakfast, 27 Brimmer St (☎523-7376). Charles Ⓣ. Only three rooms are available in this well-situated brick town house. There are sumptuous full breakfasts; two-night minimum, three on weekends. Completely non-smoking. Ⓨ.

Holiday Inn Select – Government Center, 5 Blossom St (☎742-7630 or 1-800/HOLIDAY, fax 742-4192). Bowdoin Ⓣ. Actually more convenient to Beacon Hill than Government Center, standard chain has modern accoutrements, plus a weight room and pool. Ⓧ.

The John Jeffries House, 14 Embankment Rd (☎367-1866, fax 742-0313). Charles Ⓣ. Midscale quarters at the foot of Beacon Hill. There's a cozy lounge for hotel guests, and all rooms include kitchenettes. Ⓖ–Ⓖ.

The Shawmut Inn, 280 Friend St (☎720-5544 or 1-800/350-7784). North Station Ⓣ. Located in the old West End near the FleetCenter, this hostelry has 66 rooms, all of which come equipped with kitchenettes. Ⓖ–Ⓧ.

Back Bay and the South End

463 Beacon Street Guest House, 463 Beacon St (☎536-1302). Hynes Ⓣ. The good-sized rooms in this renovated brownstone, in the heart of Back Bay, come equipped with kitchenettes and other hotel-style amenities. Ask for the top-floor room. Ⓖ–Ⓖ.

82 Chandler Street, 82 Chandler St (☎482-0408). Back Bay Ⓣ. One of Boston's best in-town B&Bs, a restored 1863 brownstone on an up-and-coming South End street. Good breakfasts served on the sun-splashed top floor – where you'll also find the best room in the house. Ⓧ.

Boston Park Plaza Hotel & Towers, 64 Arlington St (☎426-2000 or 1-800/225-2008, fax 426-5545). Arlington ⊤. The *Park Plaza* is practically its own neighborhood, housing the original *Legal Seafoods* restaurant alongside three other eateries, plus offices for American, United, and Delta airlines. Its old-school elegance and hospitality, however, make it stand out. ⑧.

The Chandler Inn, 26 Chandler St (☎482-3450 or 1-800/842-3450, fax 542-3428). Back Bay ⊤. Small, comfortable hotel that has retained its warm and homey feel despite recent renovations. Free continental breakfast. ⑤.

The Colonnade, 120 Huntington Ave (☎424-7000 or 1-800/962-3030, fax 424-1717). Prudential ⊤. With its beige poured concrete shell, the *Colonnade* is barely distinguishable from the buildings of the Church of Christ, Scientist, World Headquarters directly across the street. Still, there are spacious rooms and, in summer, a rooftop pool, the only one in Boston. ⑧.

Copley Square, 47 Huntington Ave (☎536-9000 or 1-800/225-7062, fax 267-3547). Copley ⊤. Situated on the eastern fringe of Copley Square. Low-key, with a European crowd. ⑨.

Eliot, 370 Commonwealth Ave (☎267-1607 or 1-800/442-5468, fax 536-9114). Hynes ⊤. West Back Bay's answer to the *Ritz*, this calm, plush nine-floor suite hotel has rooms with kitchenettes and luxurious Italian marble baths; they also serve a nice breakfast downstairs. ⑨.

Fairmont Copley Plaza, 138 St. James Ave (☎267-5300 or 1-800/795-3906, fax 375-9648). Copley ⊤. Built in 1912 and it shows, from the somewhat severe facade facing Copley Square to the old-fashioned rooms. It does boast Boston's most elegant and plush lobby, and even if you don't stay here, you should at least enjoy a martini in the fabulous *Oak Room* (p.121). ⑨.

Four Seasons, 200 Boylston St (☎338-4400 or 1-800/332-3442, fax 426-7199). Arlington ⊤. The tops in city accommodation, with 288 rooms that offer quiet, contemporary comfort. ⑨.

The Lenox, 710 Boylston St (☎536-5300 or 1-800/225-7676, fax 236-0351). Copley ⊤. Billed as Boston's version of the *Waldorf-Astoria* when its doors first opened in 1900, the *Lenox* is a far cry from that now, though it's still one of the most comfortably upscale and affordable hotels in the city. Many of the rooms have working fireplaces. ⑧–⑨.

Newbury Guest House, 261 Newbury St (☎437-7666, fax 262-4243). Copley ⊤. Big 32-room Victorian brownstone that still fills up whenever there's a large convention in town, so call in advance. Continental breakfast included. ⑥–⑦.

Nolan House Bed and Breakfast, 10 G St (☎269-1550 or 1-800/383-1550, *www .nolanhouse.com*). Broadway ⊤. Inviting B&B in an impressive 1860 Victorian home. The stylish rooms are spacious and clean with TV/VCR and air-conditioning plus they serve a full-sized, proper English breakfast. Free guest parking. ⑤–⑥.

Oasis Guest House, 22 Edgerly Rd (☎267-2262, fax 267-1920). Hynes/ICA ⊤. Sixteen comfortable, affordable rooms, some with shared baths, in a renovated brownstone near Symphony Hall. ④–⑤.

Ritz-Carlton, 15 Arlington St (☎536-5700 or 1-800/241-3333, fax 536-1335). Arlington ⊤. This is the *Ritz-Carlton* flagship, and even if the rooms can seem a bit cramped, the hotel retains a certain air of refinement, aided by a view overlooking the Public Garden. ⑨.

Kenmore Square, The Fenway, and Brookline

Beacon Inn, 1087 and 1750 Beacon St (☎566-0088). Dean ⊤. Lobby fireplaces and original woodwork enhance the relaxed atmosphere in these two nineteenth-century brownstones, under the same ownership. ④–⑤.

Brookline Manor Guest House, 32 Centre St (☎232-0003 or 1-800/535-5325, fax 734-5815). Coolidge Corner ⊤. This small guesthouse, on a pleasant stretch off Beacon Street, is just a short subway ride from Kenmore Square. ⑤–⑦.

Cambridge

A Cambridge House, 2218 Massachusetts Ave (☎491-6300 or 1-800/232-998, fax 868-2079, *www.acambridgehouse.com*). Porter ⊤. A classy B&B, with gorgeous rooms decked out with canopy beds, period pieces, and fireplaces, plus evening hors d'oeuvres in the parlor. Far out from points of interest, but worth the trek. ⑤–⑥.

B&B AGENCIES AND SHORT-TERM ACCOMMODATION

Beacon Inns & Guest Houses (☎262-1771 or 266-7142, fax 266-7276) books guest rooms with private baths and kitchenettes throughout Back Bay.

Bed & Breakfast Agency of Boston, 47 Commercial Wharf, Boston, MA 02110 (☎720-3540 or 1-800/248-9262, fax 523-5761), can book you a room in a brownstone, a waterfront loft or even on a yacht.

Bed & Breakfast Associates Bay Colony Ltd, PO Box 57166, Babson Park Branch, Boston, MA 02157 (☎449-5302 or 1-800/347-5088, fax 449-5958), lists some real finds in Back Bay and the South End.

Bed & Breakfast – Cambridge and Greater Boston (☎720-1492 or 1-800/888-0178, fax 227-0021, *www.bnbboston.com*) has listings for B&Bs, both hosted and unhosted, and furnished apartments throughout central Cambridge and Boston.

Boston Short Term Rental (☎262-3100) has furnished apartments throughout the city from $500 per week and up, with a two-week minimum stay.

A Friendly Inn, 1673 Cambridge St (☎547-7851). Harvard Ⓣ. This is a great deal, and just a few minutes' walk from Harvard Square. The rooms are nothing special, but they do have private bath and cable TV. ⑤–⑥.

Charles Hotel, 1 Bennett St (☎864-1200 or 1-800/882-1818). Harvard Ⓣ. The clean, bright rooms have a good array of amenities, including cable TV, three phones, minibar, Shaker furniture, and access to the adjacent WellBridge Health Spa. There's also an excellent jazz club, *Regattabar* (p.125), and restaurant, *Henrietta's Table* (p.119), on the premises. ⑧.

Harvard Square Hotel, 110 Mt Auburn St (☎864-5200 or 1-800/458-5886, fax 864-2409). Harvard Ⓣ. The rooms here are only adequate, but the price and Harvard Square location are right. ⑦–⑧.

Inn at Harvard, 1201 Massachusetts Ave (☎491-2222 or 1-800/458-5886, fax 492-4896). Harvard Ⓣ. This recently built hotel is carefully designed to give the impression of old-school grandeur, and it is so close to Harvard you can smell the ivy. Pleasant but rather small rooms. ⑨.

Mary Prentiss Inn, 6 Prentiss St (☎661-2929, fax 661-5989). Porter Ⓣ. Twenty clean, comfortable rooms in an impressively refurbished mid-nineteenth-century Greek Revival building. Homemade cookies at teatime. Rooms can be as high as $260. ⑥.

Prospect Place, 112 Prospect St (☎864-7500 or 1-800/769-5303). Harvard Ⓣ. Its Italianate edifice hides a restored parlor with nineteenth-century period antiques, including two grand pianos, plus newly redecorated rooms. ⑤–⑥.

Royal Sonesta, 5 Cambridge Parkway (☎491-3600 or 1-800/SONESTA, fax 661-5956). Kendall Ⓣ. Luxury quarters with views of the downtown Boston skyline. The fancy rooms have big, sparkling bathrooms; the vast lobby is festooned with strikingly bad art. ⑦–⑧.

Susse Chalet Cambridge, 211 Concord Turnpike (☎661-7800, fax 868-8153). Alewife Ⓣ. Modest, adequate rooms in a plain motor lodge located right off a highway (a mixed blessing) and next-door to a vintage bowling alley (a definite plus). Free continental breakfast. ⑤–⑥.

Hostels

Greater Boston YMCA, 316 Huntington Ave (☎536-7800, fax 267-4653). Symphony Ⓣ. Good budget rooms, and access to the Y's health facilities (pool, weight room, and so on). Singles are $41–56, but you can get a 4-person room for $96. Summers co-ed, rest of year men only.

HI - Back Bay Summer Hostel, 512 Beacon St (☎353-3294). Kenmore Ⓣ. This converted BU dorm has 63 beds, but is only open June 16 to Aug 15 (reservation requests to 1020 Commonwealth Ave, Boston, MA 02215; ☎739-3017). Members $24, nonmembers $27.

HI – Boston, 12 Hemenway St (☎536-1027, fax 424-6558). Hynes Ⓣ. Around the Back Bay–Fenway border, standard dorm accommodation with 3–6 beds per room. Members $24, nonmembers $27.

Irish Embassy Youth Hostel, 232 Friend St (☎973-4841, fax 720-3998). North Station Ⓣ. Boston's only independent youth hostel is above the West End's *Irish Embassy* pub, which holds gigs most nights that are free to lodgers. Dorm beds are $22.

Strathmore Manor, 1876 Beacon St (☎730-4118). Englewood Avenue Ⓣ. From the same people who own the *Irish Embassy*, this is another friendly, independent youth hostel. Dorm beds are $25.

YWCA, 7 Temple St (☎491-6050) Central Ⓣ. Spartan quarters for women only (men aren't allowed on the premises, even for a visit), but space is very limited, so call in advance. Members $40 per night, $150 per week, nonmembers $45/$175.

The City

Boston is small for an American city, and its tangle of old streets makes it far easier to get around on foot than by car, especially in the city center. Driving is particularly trying these days due to the ongoing **"Big Dig"** highway reconstruction project, wherein Interstate 93, which cuts through the heart of the city, is being put underground. Boston's **downtown** area is situated on a peninsula that juts into Boston Harbor; most of the other neighborhoods branch out south and west from here mainly along the thoroughfares of Washington, Tremont and Beacon streets.

Downtown really begins with Boston Common, a large public green that holds either on or near its grounds many of the city's major historical sights, including the State House, Old Granary Burying Ground and Old South Meeting House. Nothing, however, captures the spirit of the city better than downtown's Faneuil Hall, the so-called "Cradle of Liberty," and the always-animated Quincy Market, adjacent to the hall. On the other side of I-93 from the marketplace is the **North End**, which occupies the northeast corner of the peninsula; aside from being the city's Little Italy, it's home to Old North Church and the Paul Revere House. Just across Boston's Inner Harbor is **Charlestown**, the quiet home of the world's oldest commissioned warship, the *USS Constitution*.

North of the Common are the vintage gaslights and red-brick Federalist town houses that line the streets of **Beacon Hill**, the city's most exclusive residential neighborhood. Charles Street runs south along the base of the hill and separates Boston Common from the Public Garden, which marks the beginning of **Back Bay**. This similarly well-heeled neighborhood holds opulent row houses alongside modern landmarks like the John Hancock Tower, New England's tallest skyscraper; appended south of Back Bay is the gay enclave of the **South End**, known for its hip restaurants. The student domains of **Kenmore Square** and **Fenway** are west of Back Bay: the former has some of the area's best nightlife, while the latter is home to the Museum of Fine Arts, the Isabella Stewart Gardner Museum and Fenway Park. South of all these neighborhoods are Boston's vast **Southern Districts**, which don't hold too much of interest other than some links in Frederick Law Olmsted's series of parks known as the "Emerald Necklace," such as the dazzling Arnold Arboretum and Franklin Park, home to the city zoo. Across the Charles River from Boston lies **Cambridge**, a must for its excellent bookstore-and-café scene and, above all, the ivy-covered walls of Harvard University.

Downtown Boston

Boston's compact **downtown** encompasses both the colonial heart and contemporary core of the city, an assemblage of red-brick buildings and modern office towers that, if not rivaling the glamor of other American big-city centers, still holds a number of the best reasons for visiting. Quite lively by day, when commuters and tourists create a constant buzz, the streets thin out come nightfall, with a few exceptions: the touristy **Quincy Market** area, which has a decent, if somewhat downmarket, bar scene; **Chinatown**, with its ever-popular restaurants; and the **Theater District**, particularly animated on weekends.

King's Chapel, on Tremont, and the nearby **Old State House** mark the periphery of Boston's earliest town center, where the first church, market, newspaper and prison were all clustered. **Spring Lane**, a tiny pedestrian passage off Washington Street, recalls the location of one of the bigger springs that lured the earliest settlers over to the Shawmut Peninsula from Charlestown. The most evocative streets, however, are those whose character has been less diluted over the years – **School Street**, **State Street**, and the eighteenth-century enclave known as **Blackstone Block**, near Faneuil Hall.

You can get the flavor of Boston Harbor, once the world's third busiest, along the **waterfront**, now somewhat isolated on account of the elevated John F. Fitzgerald Expressway, a chunk of I-93 that's to be put underground. The **Freedom Trail**, a self-guided walking tour that connects an assortment of historic sights by a line of red bricks embedded in the pavement, begins in **Boston Common**, a king-sized version of the tidy green space at the core of innumerable New England villages. One of the many historic places it passes is the ever-popular meeting place **Faneuil Hall**, not far from the Common. South is the **Financial District**, its short streets still following the tangled patterns of colonial village lanes; west of it is the small but vibrant Chinatown and adjacent Theater District.

Boston Common and around

Boston's premier piazza is **Boston Common**, a fifty-acre chunk of green, neither meticulously manicured nor especially attractive, which effectively separates downtown from the posher Beacon Hill and Back Bay districts. It's the first thing you'll see emerging from the **Park Street Ⓣ station**, the central transfer point of America's first subway and, unfortunately, a magnet for panhandlers. Established in 1634 as "a trayning field" and "for the feeding of Cattell" – so a slate tablet opposite the station recalls – the Common is still primarily utilitarian, used by both pedestrian commuters on their way to downtown's office towers and tourists seeking the **Boston Visitor Information Pavilion** (see p.59), down Tremont Street from the Ⓣ and the official starting-point of the Freedom Trail. The shabbiness of the southern side of the Common is offset by the lovely **Beacon Street Promenade**, which runs the length of the northern side.

One of the few actual sights here is the **Central Burying Ground**, on the southeast corner of the Common, near the intersection of Boylston and Tremont streets. Artist **Gilbert Stuart**, best known for his portraits of George Washington – the most famous of which is replicated on the American one-dollar bill – died penniless and was interred in Tomb 61. Among the other notables buried here are members of the largest family to take part in the Boston Tea Party, various

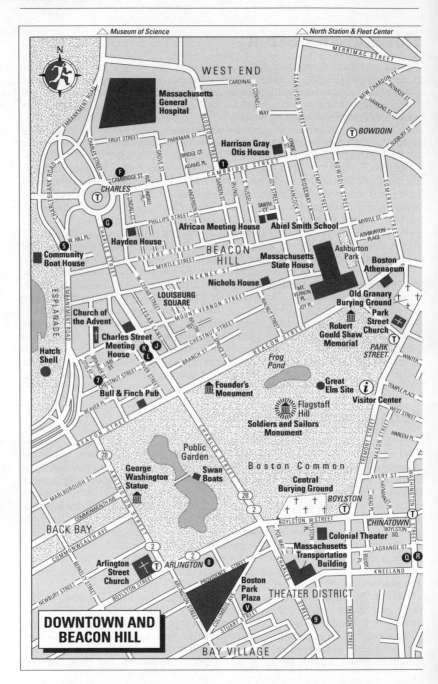

△ Museum of Science   △ North Station & Fleet Center

MERRIMAC STREET

WEST END

CARDINAL
O'CONNELL
WAY

**Massachusetts
General
Hospital**

FRUIT STREET   PARKMAN ST.

**Harrison Gray
Otis House**

CAMBRIDGE STREET

F CAMBRIDGE ST.

CHARLES
T

G

Hayden House

African Meeting House   **Abiel Smith School**

5

**Community
Boat House**

BEACON
HILL

Ashburton
Park

**Boston
Athenaeum**

**Massachusetts
State House**

Nichols House

PINCKNEY ST.

**LOUISBURG
SQUARE**

MOUNT VERNON STREET

**Old Granary
Burying Ground**

Park
Street
Church **T**

**Robert
Gould Shaw
Memorial**

*PARK
STREET*

**Church of
the Advent**

**Charles Street
Meeting
House**

K **J**

L

*Frog
Pond*

**Hatch
Shell**

ESPLANADE

7

Bull & Finch Pub

**Founder's
Monument**

**Great
Elm Site**

i

Visitor Center

**Flagstaff
Hill**

**Soldiers and Sailors
Monument**

Public
Garden

B o s t o n   C o m m o n

28

**George
Washington
Statue**

**Swan
Boats**

**Central
Burying Ground**

BOYLSTON
T

BACK BAY

MARLBOROUGH ST.

COMMONWEALTH AVE.

28

2

BOYLSTON STREET

CHINATOWN

Colonial Theater

**Massachusetts
Transportation
Building**

LAGRANGE ST.

Q **R**

KNEELAND

**Arlington
Street
Church**

ARLINGTON
T **8**

**Boston
Park
Plaza**

V

THEATER DISTRICT

9

**DOWNTOWN AND
BEACON HILL**

BAY VILLAGE

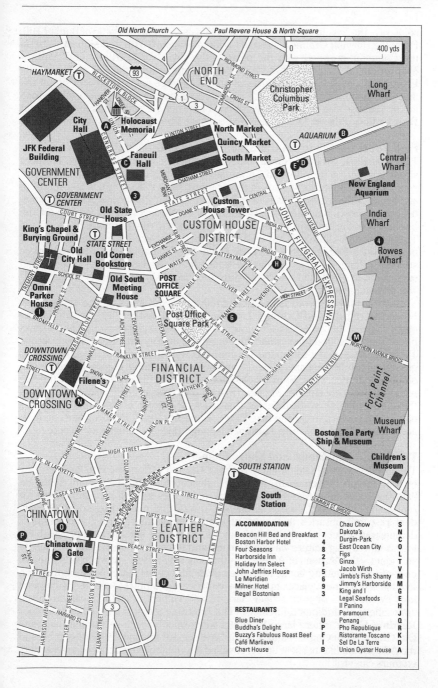

Old North Church △   △ Paul Revere House & North Square

0   400 yds

HAYMARKET

NORTH
END

Christopher
Columbus
Park

Long
Wharf

City
Hall

Holocaust
Memorial

North Market

Quincy Market

AQUARIUM

JFK Federal
Building

Faneuil
Hall

South Market

Central
Wharf

GOVERNMENT
CENTER

GOVERNMENT
CENTER

Old State
House

Custom
House Tower

New England
Aquarium

India
Wharf

King's Chapel &
Burying Ground

CUSTOM HOUSE
DISTRICT

Rowes
Wharf

Old
City Hall

STATE STREET

Old Corner
Bookstore

Omni
Parker
House

Old South
Meeting
House

POST
OFFICE
SQUARE

Post Office
Square Park

FINANCIAL
DISTRICT

DOWNTOWN
CROSSING

Filene's

DOWNTOWN
CROSSING

Fort Point Channel

Museum
Wharf

Boston Tea Party
Ship & Museum

Children's
Museum

SOUTH STATION

South
Station

CHINATOWN

LEATHER
DISTRICT

Chinatown
Gate

ACCOMMODATION		Chau Chow	S
Beacon Hill Bed and Breakfast	7	Dakota's	N
Boston Harbor Hotel	4	Durgin-Park	C
Four Seasons	8	East Ocean City	O
Harborside Inn	2	Figs	L
Holiday Inn Select	1	Ginza	T
John Jeffries House	5	Jacob Wirth	V
Le Meridien	6	Jimbo's Fish Shanty	M
Milner Hotel	9	Jimmy's Harborside	M
Regal Bostonian	3	King and I	G
		Legal Seafoods	E
		Il Panino	H
RESTAURANTS		Paramount	J
Blue Diner	U	Penang	Q
Buddha's Delight	P	Pho Republique	R
Buzzy's Fabulous Roast Beef	F	Ristorante Toscano	K
Café Marliave	I	Sel De La Terre	D
Chart House	B	Union Oyster House	A

soldiers of the Revolutionary Army, and Redcoats killed in the Battle of Bunker Hill. From the Burying Ground it's a short walk to **Flagstaff Hill**, the highest point on the Common, crowned with the pillar of the Civil War **Soldiers and Sailors Monument**. A former repository of colonial gunpowder, the hill overlooks the **Frog Pond**, once home to legions of unusually large amphibians and site of the first water pumped into the city. It's really just a kidney-shaped pool, used for wading in summer and ice skating in winter. From here, a path leads to the elegant **Brewer Fountain**, an 1868 bronze replica of one from the Paris Exposition of 1855.

Park Street Church to the Old Granary Burying Ground

The 1809 **Park Street Church**, on the northeast corner of Park and Tremont streets just across from Boston Common (July & Aug Tues-Sat 9am–3pm, rest of year by appointment for groups of ten or more; ☎523-3383; free), is an oversized, and rather uninteresting, mass of bricks and mortar, though its ornate 217-foot-tall white telescoping **steeple** is undeniably impressive. To get an idea of the immensity of the building, including the spire, walk to tiny Hamilton Place, across Tremont Street. Ultimately its reputation rests not on size but on events that took place inside: this is where William Lloyd Garrison delivered his first public address calling for the nationwide abolition of slavery (Massachusetts had scrapped it in 1783), and where the ditty *America* ("My country 'tis of thee . . .") was first sung, on July 4, 1831.

Adjacent to the church is one of the more peaceful stops on the always-busy Freedom Trail, the **Old Granary Burying Ground**, last resting place for numerous leaders of the American Revolution. Its odd name comes from a grain warehouse that once stood next door. The entrance, an Egyptian Revival arch, fronts Tremont Street, and it's from the Tremont sidewalk that some of the most famous gravesites can be best appreciated: the boulder and plaque commemorating revolutionary **James Otis**; **Samuel Adams**' tomb; and the group grave of the five people killed in the **Boston Massacre** of 1770. From any angle inside you can see the stocky **obelisk** at dead center that marks the grave of Benjamin Franklin's parents. Also further inside are **Peter Faneuil**, **Paul Revere**, and, at least according to the pillar, **John Hancock**, though this fact remains in dispute.

The Boston Athenaeum and King's Chapel

The loveliest view of Old Granary Burying Ground is from the fifth-floor balcony of the **Boston Athenaeum**, at 10 1/2 Beacon St (Mon 9am–8pm, Tues–Fri 9am–5pm; also Sept–May Sat 9am–4pm; tours Tues and Thurs 3pm; closed for renovations until 2002; free), established in 1807 and one of the oldest independent research libraries in the country. In naming their library, the founders demonstrated not only their high-minded classicism but marketing sensibility too, as its growing stature was a potent enough force to endow Boston with a lofty sobriquet – the "Athens of America" – that has stuck. Best known are its **special collections**, including books from the private library of George Washington. **Art**, too, has a prominent place: an impressive array of sculptures, coupled with paintings by the likes of John Singer Sargent and Gilbert Stuart, contribute to the atmosphere of studious refinement. The crowning glory is the sedate fifth-floor **Reading Room**, where large Palladian windows afford those stunning views of Old Granary Burying Ground and the skyscrapers beyond. Paying members of the Athenaeum like to roost up here, which is probably why only visitors on guided tours can visit it.

THE FREEDOM TRAIL

Boston's history is so visible that it often stands accused of living in the past; the presence of numerous tourist-friendly contrivances, none more conspicuous – or successful – than the **Freedom Trail**, surely adds to the notion. Like many American cities, Boston experienced an economic slump in the postwar years as people migrated to the suburbs. This urban flight engendered the kind of mentality that enabled civic officials to green-light a major highway that ripped through the most historic part of the city, the North End. So when in 1951, Boston residents William Schofield and Bob Winn came up with the idea of the Freedom Trail, it seemed like a sure way to lure visitors and their money back into town – and it has become Boston's chief attraction in the process.

The trail is delineated by a 2.5-mile red-brick stripe in the sidewalk, which links sixteen historical sights that reach from the downtown area up into Charlestown, and while it simplifies their identification, it belies the complexity of early Bostonian (and American) history. Though it's easy to assume each spot played an important part in the struggle to overthrow British rule, this is not entirely the case. While there's no denying the Revolutionary-era role of the **Old North Church** and **Faneuil Hall**, two of the most popular stops on the trail, historians would be hard pressed to pinpoint the contributions of, say, **King's Chapel**, built nearly 100 years *before* the Boston Tea Party, or **Park Street Church**, built 35 years after it. And despite its eventual critical role in the War of 1812, the frigate **USS Constitution** ("Old Ironsides") in Charlestown was assembled fully two decades after the Declaration of Independence.

In addition, some of the touches intended to accentuate the historic appeal of the attractions do them a disservice. The people in period costume stationed outside some of the sights can't help but grate a little, and the artificially enhanced atmosphere is exaggerated by the $1 million recently spent by the city to replace most of the painted line with bright red brick and add pseudo-old signage. The Freedom Trail remains the easiest way to orient yourself downtown, and is especially useful if you'll only be in Boston for a short time, but it's still possible, perhaps desirable, to appreciate the city's most historic sights for their individual merit.

Boston's oldest cemetery, the atmospheric **King's Chapel Burying Ground**, 58 Tremont St (daily: June–Oct 9.30am–4pm; Nov–May 10am–4pm; ☎523-1749; free), not to mention its accompanying church, is well worth a tour despite the din of nearby traffic. One of the chief pleasures of walking amongst the graves is to examine the many beautifully etched ancient tombstones, with their winged skulls and contemplative seraphim, such as that of one **Joseph Tapping**, near the Tremont Street side. King's Chapel Burying Ground was one of the favorite Boston haunts of author **Nathaniel Hawthorne**, who drew inspiration from the grave of a certain Elizabeth Pain to create the famously adulterous character of Hester Prynne for his novel *The Scarlet Letter*.

Meanwhile, the most conspicuous thing about the gray, foreboding **chapel** that stands on the grounds is its absence of a steeple (there were plans for one, just not enough money). A wooden chapel was built on the site first, amid some controversy. In 1686, King James II revoked the Massachusetts Bay Colony's charter and installed Sir Edmund Andros as governor, giving him orders to found an Anglican parish, a move that for obvious reasons didn't sit too well with Boston's Puritan population. The present chapel was completed in 1749, with the pillar-fronted portico added in 1789, and the belfry boasts the biggest bell ever cast by Paul Revere. Most visitors never go past the entrance, but it is well worth a look inside, ideally during one of the weekly chamber music concerts (Tues 12.15–12.45pm). While hardly ostentatious, the elegant Georgian interior is a marked contrast to the minimalist adornments of most other Boston churches.

Washington Street shopping district

The **Washington Street shopping district** takes up much of downtown proper, and it holds some of the city's most historic sights – the Old Corner Bookstore, Old South Meeting House and Old State House – but it tends to shut down after business hours. The stops can be seen in half a day, though you'll need to allow more time if shopping is on your agenda.

Across School Street from King's Chapel is the legendary **Omni Parker House**. It was in this hotel that **Boston Creme Pie** – really a layered cake with custard filling and chocolate frosting all around – was concocted in 1855, and the hotel reportedly still bakes 25 of them a day. On a more bizarre note, Ho Chi Minh and Malcolm X each used to wait tables at the hotel's restaurant.

Only one block long, School Street offers up some of the best in Boston charm, beginning with the antique gaslights that flank the severe western wall of King's Chapel. Just beyond is a grand French Second Empire building that served as **Boston City Hall** from 1865 to 1969. A few doors down on the left, the gambrel-roofed, red-brick former **Old Corner Bookstore** anchors the southern end of School Street as it joins Washington. The stretch of Washington from here to Old South Meeting House was nineteenth-century Boston's version of London's Fleet Street, with a convergence of booksellers, publishers and newspaper headquarters; the bookstore itself – as home to the publishing house of Ticknor & Fields – was the hottest literary salon Boston ever had, with the likes of Emerson, Longfellow, and even Dickens and Thackeray, all of whom Ticknor & Fields published.

Old South Meeting House

Washington Street's big architectural landmark is the **Old South Meeting House**, at 310 Washington St (daily 9.30am–5pm; $3), a charming brick church recognizable by its tower, a separate but attached structure, that tapers into an octagonal spire. An earlier cedarwood structure on the spot burned down in 1711, clearing the way for what is now the second oldest church building in Boston, after Old North Church in the North End. The spacious venue soon saw its share of anti-imperial rhetoric. The day after the Boston Massacre, outraged Bostonians assembled here to demand the removal of the troops that were ostensibly guarding the town. Even more telling was the meeting on December 16, 1773, when nearly seven thousand locals came to await word on whether the Crown would actually impose duty on sixty tons of tea aboard ships in Boston Harbor. When a message was received that it would, Samuel Adams rose and announced, "This meeting can do nothing more to save the country" – the signal that triggered the **Boston Tea Party** (see p.77). Today, a museum inside showcases exhibits that focus on freedom of speech.

South of the meeting house, pedestrian-friendly **Downtown Crossing**, centered on the intersection of Washington and Winter streets, brims with department stores and smaller shops that mostly cater to lower-income shoppers. Its nucleus is Filene's Basement, a magnet for bargain hunters of all socioeconomic stripes and the only thing here really worth your time. Otherwise, unless you

THE BOSTON MASSACRE

Directly in front of the State Street side of the Old State House, a circle of cobblestones embedded in a small traffic island marks the site of the **Boston Massacre**, the tragic outcome of escalating tensions between Bostonians and the British Redcoats that occupied the city. This riot of March 5, 1770, began when a young wigmaker's apprentice began heckling an army officer over a barber's bill. The officer sought refuge in the Custom House, which stood opposite the Old State House at the time, but by this time, a throng of people had gathered, including more soldiers, at whom the mob flung rocks and snowballs. When someone threw a club that knocked a Redcoat onto the ice, he rose and fired. Five Bostonians were killed in the ensuing fracas. Two other patriots, John Adams and Josiah Quincy, actually defended the offending eight soldiers in court; six were acquitted, and the two guilty were branded on their thumbs.

have the money and inclination to eat at the historic *Locke-Ober* restaurant (p.114), you may as well move on.

Old State House

That the graceful three-tiered window tower of the red-brick **Old State House**, back north of the meeting house, at the corner of Washington and State streets (daily 9.30am–5pm; $3), is dwarfed by skyscrapers amplifies, rather than diminishes, its colonial-era dignity. For years this three-story structure was the seat of the Massachusetts Bay Colony, and consequently the center of British authority in New England. Later it served as Boston's city hall, and in 1880 it was nearly demolished so that State Street traffic might flow more freely.

An impassioned speech in the second-floor Council Chamber by James Otis, a Crown appointee who resigned to take up the colonial cause, sparked the quest for independence from Britain fifteen years before it was declared. Legend has it that on certain nights you can still hear Otis hurling his anti-British barbs and the cheers of the crowd he so energized, but the current museum staff has no comment on this. The **balcony** overlooking State Street was the place from which the Declaration of Independence was first read publicly in Boston, on July 18, 1776. Ironically, Queen Elizabeth II – the first British monarch to set foot in Boston – performed the same feat from the balcony as part of the American bicentennial activities in 1976. Inside, a **museum** tracks, through images and artifacts of varying interest, the events that led up to the establishment of the Commonwealth of Massachusetts (though not, curiously, the US), along with Boston's role in the Revolutionary War. Upstairs are rotating exhibits on city history and, incongruously, a display on old Boston hotels and restaurants.

Financial District and around

Boston's **Financial District** hardly conjures the same image as those of New York or London, but it continues to wield influence in key areas (such as with mutual funds, invented here in 1925) and is not entirely devoid of historic interest – though this is generally more manifest in plaques rather than actual buildings. Like most of America's business districts, it beats to an office-hours-only schedule, and many of its little eateries and Irish pubs are closed on weekends – though some brave new restaurants are beginning to make inroads. The generally immaculate streets follow the same short, winding paths as they did three hundred years ago, only now, thirty- and forty-story skyscrapers have replaced the wooden houses and churches that used to clutter the area.

The most dramatic approach is east from Washington Street via **Milk Street**. A bust of **Benjamin Franklin** surveys the scene from a recessed Gothic niche above the doorway at 1 Milk St, across from the Old South Meeting House. The site marks Franklin's birthplace, though the building itself only dates from 1874. A bit farther down Milk Street, at its intersection with Devonshire Street, the somber 22-story **John W. McCormack federal courthouse** houses one of Boston's better post offices, with a special section for stamp collectors, though it was an earlier building on this site that gave the adjacent, triangular **Post Office Square** its name. Sneak up to the glass atrium atop the building at **One Post Office Square**; though not really open to the public, it holds jaw-dropping views of Boston Harbor and downtown that make the transgression worth it.

A prime Art Deco specimen is nearby at 185 Franklin St, the head office of **Verizon**. The step-top building was a 1947 design; more recently the phone booths outside were given a Deco makeover. **Exchange Place**, at 53 State St, is a mirrored-glass tower rising from the facade of the old Boston Stock Exchange; the *Bunch of Grapes* tavern, watering hole of choice for many of Boston's revolutionary rabble-rousers, once stood here. Behind it is tiny **Liberty Square**, once the heart of Tory Boston and now home to an improbable sculpture that commemorates the Hungarian anti-Communist uprising of 1956.

The Custom House District

The not-quite-triangular wedge of downtown between State and Broad streets and the Fitzgerald Expressway is the unfairly overlooked **Custom House District**, dotted with some excellent architectural draws, chief among which is the **Custom House Tower**, surrounded by 32 huge Doric columns. Built in 1847, the thirty-story Greek Revival tower itself was added in 1915. Not surprisingly, it is no longer the tallest skyscraper in New England, but it still has plenty of character.

Another landmark is the **Grain and Flour Exchange Building**, a block away at 177 Milk St, a fortress-like construction with a turreted, conical roof that recalls the Romanesque Revival style of prominent local architect H.H. Richardson. On **State Street**, which when it used to extend into Boston Harbor was the focal point of Boston's maritime prosperity, get a look at the elaborate cast-iron facade of the **Richards Building**, at no. 114, a clipper ship company's office in the 1850s, and the **Cunard Building**, at no. 126, its ornamental anchors a reflection of Boston's status as North American terminus of the first transatlantic steamship mail service.

Faneuil Hall, Quincy Market, and around

Located between the Financial District and the North End, the **Faneuil Hall Marketplace** is the kind of active, bustling public gathering ground that's none too common in Boston, popular with locals and tourists alike. Built as a market during colonial times to house the city's growing mercantile industry, it declined during the nineteenth century and, like the area around it, was pretty much defunct until the 1960s, when it was successfully redeveloped as a restaurant and shopping mall.

Much-hyped **Faneuil Hall** itself (daily 9am–5pm) doesn't appear particularly majestic from the outside; it's simply a small, four-story brick building topped with a Georgian spire, hardly the grandiose auditorium one might imagine would have housed the Revolutionary war meetings that earned its "Cradle of Liberty" sobriquet. But indeed this was where revolutionary firebrands such as Samuel Adams and James Otis whipped up popular support for independence by protesting British tax legislation on the second-floor meeting space. The first floor now houses a panoply of tourist shops which make for a less than dignified memorial; you'll also find an information desk and a post office. The second floor is more impressive: the auditorium has been preserved to reflect modifications made by Charles Bulfinch in 1805. Its focal point is a massive – and rather preposterous – canvas depicting an imagined scene in which Daniel Webster speaks in Faneuil Hall to a range of luminaries from Washington to de Tocqueville.

The three oblong markets just behind Faneuil Hall were built in the early eighteenth century to contain the trade that had quickly outgrown its space in the hall. The center building, known as **Quincy Market** (Mon–Sat 10am–9pm, Sun noon–6pm), holds a super-extended corridor lined with stands vending a variety of decent though pricey takeout treats – the mother of all mall food courts. To either side of Quincy Market are **North and South markets**, which hold restaurants and popular chain clothing stores, as well as specialized curiosity shops (one sells only purple objects, another nothing but vests). There's not much to distinguish it from any other shopping complex, save a few good restaurants and some surrounding bars, but sitting on a bench in the carnivalesque heart of it all on a summer day, eating scrod while the mobs of locals and tourists mill about, is a quintessential (if slightly absurd) Boston experience.

From Faneuil Hall, traverse the dim, narrow corridor known as Scott's Alley up to **Blackstone Block**, an area so far bypassed by urban renewal and as such a reasonably authentic remnant of central Boston's original architectural character. Its uneven cobblestone streets and low brick buildings have remained largely untouched since the 1650s. Nearby on Union Street jut six tall hollow glass pillars erected as a **memorial** to victims of the Holocaust. Built to resemble smokestacks, the columns are etched with quotes and facts about the Holocaust, with an unusual degree of attention to its non-Jewish victims. The brief walk makes for a sobering contrast to the self-congratulatory tone of the Freedom Trail.

Government Center

Most visitors pass through **Government Center**, west of Faneuil Hall, during their time in Boston, as it's an essential travel hub located in the midst of the city center – and passing through is just about all there is to do in this sea of towering gray government buildings which stands on the former site of **Scollay Square**, once Boston's most notorious den of porn halls and tattoo parlors. Scollay was razed in the early 1960s, eliminating all traces of its salacious past and its lively character; indeed, the only thing that remains from that time is the steaming tea kettle sign just across from the Government Center T stop. The area is now overlaid with concrete, and two monolithic edifices tower above: **Boston City Hall**, at the east side of the plaza, and the **John F. Kennedy Federal Building**, on the north.

The waterfront

A series of wharves occupying the harborside stretch below Christopher Columbus Park, Boston's **waterfront** is still a fairly active area, though no longer the city's focal point, which it was as recently as the mid-1800s. The city's decline

THE HARBORWALK

The **Harborwalk** was conceived as a way to recall Boston's history as a major port, days that seem ever more in the past, especially considering the harbor's notorious recent reputation for pollution. While the sights along the walk don't have the historical all-star quality of those on the Freedom Trail, and some of the facts would have to be spruced up to even be considered mundane, it's still a picturesque stroll, mostly running along the water, that provides a historical perspective on the waterfront not otherwise readily evident. The Harborwalk starts at the corner of State Street and Merchant's Row, proceeds along the wharves, and ends up on the Congress Street bridge at the Boston Tea Party museum. Visitors center maps can guide you along, and blue plaques along the way illustrate the relevance of the various stopping points.

as a port left the waterfront with no real function, and the construction of the elevated central artery in the 1950s physically separated it from the rest of the city. Today, the waterfront thrives, but mainly on tourism, with stands selling tacky T-shirts, furry lobsters, and the like.

Long Wharf is the best place to head for, the district's main drag since its construction in 1710. Summer is its most active season, when the wharf is dotted with stands vending kitschy souvenirs and surprisingly excellent ice cream. This is also the main point of departure for harbor cruises, whale-watching and ferries to Cape Cod. Walk out to the end of the wharf for an excellent vantage point on **Boston Harbor**. Since the city is surrounded by other land masses, you'll only see a series of peninsulas and islands, which are generally smoky and grinding with industry. It's perhaps most enjoyable – and still relatively safe – at night, when even the freighters appear graceful against the moonlit water.

Next door to Long Wharf is the **New England Aquarium**, at Central Wharf (Mon–Fri 9am–5pm, Sat & Sun 9am–6pm; $13), the waterfront's main draw and, like many of Boston's attractions, aimed at kids. It doesn't win points for atmosphere: the interior is plain, dank, and reeks vaguely, though not surprisingly, of fish. The interactive penguin exhibit on the bottom floor allows you to maneuver a point of light around the bottom of the pool; the guileless waterfowl will mistake the light for prey and follow it around hopefully. In the center of the aquarium's spiral walkway is an impressive collection of marine life: a three-story cylindrical tank with moray eels, great white sharks and other sea exotica.

South along the water to the Congress Street bridge, the **Boston Tea Party Ship and Museum** honors the brief but seminal events by combining history with a sense of irreverence (March–December, daily 9am–6pm; $8). Displays range from the expected (colonial history) to the tangential (shipbuilding, the English culture of tea), and the whole affair takes place on a replica of the original ship floating off the Congress Street bridge in Fort Point Channel. While the exhibits won't challenge your mind, they're fun in a hokey sort of way. Spirited recreations of the Tea Party are held on occasion here, but don't be taken in: the Congress Street bridge was not the real site of the Boston Tea Party. It actually took place on what is today dry land, near the intersection of Atlantic and Congress streets. Indeed, at the **Harbor Plaza**, at 470 Atlantic Ave, there's a commemorative plaque engraved with a patriotic poem expressing outrage at "King George's trivial but tyrannical tax of 3p. per pound."

Across the Congress Street bridge is the **Children's Museum**, at 300 Congress St (daily 10am–5pm; $7, kids $6, Fri 5–9pm $1), which comprises five floors of deceptively educational exhibits, designed to entice kids into learning by doing. There are plenty of buttons to push and tunnels to crawl through, and a cool shop on the second floor lets you fill a brown bag with strange objects for a couple of bucks.

Chinatown, the Combat Zone, and the Leather District

Boston's colorful and authentic **Chinatown** lies wedged into just a few square blocks between the Financial and Theater districts, but it makes up in activity what it lacks in size. Lean against a pagoda-topped pay phone on the corner of **Beach and Tyler streets** anytime and watch the way life here revolves around the food trade. By day, merchants barter in Mandarin and Cantonese over the going price of produce; by night, Bostonians arrive in droves to nosh in Chinatown's restaurants. Walk down either of those streets – the neighborhood's two liveliest thoroughfares – and you'll pass most of the restaurants, bakeries and markets, in whose windows you'll see the usual complement of roast ducks hanging from hooks and aquariums filled with future seafood dinners. There's not much else to actually see, though the impressive **Chinatown Gate**, a three-story red-and-gilt monolith guarded by four Fu dogs overlooks the intersection of Hudson and Beach streets. Chinatown is at its most vibrant during various festivals, none more so than the **Chinese New Year** in late January (sometimes early Feb); at the **Festival of the August Moon**, not surprisingly held in August, there's a bustling street fair. Call the Chinese Merchants Association for more information (☎482-3972).

Around Washington Street, between Essex and Kneeland, you can still see some vestiges of the old red-light district enigmatically called the **Combat Zone** – not quite as dangerous as it sounds. It was designated by the city as an "adult entertainment zone" in the 1960s after Scollay Square was demolished to make room for Government Center, and nowadays it keeps up a few X-rated theaters

THE BOSTON TEA PARTY

The first major act of rebellion preceding the Revolutionary War, the **Boston Tea Party** was far greater in significance than it was in duration. On December 20, 1773, a long-standing dispute between the British government and its colonial subjects, involving a tea tax, came to a dramatic head. At nightfall, an angry mob of nearly one thousand, which had been whipped into an anti-British frenzy by Samuel Adams at Old South Meeting House, converged on Griffin's Wharf. Around a hundred of them, some dressed in Indian garb, boarded three brigs and threw their cargo of tea overboard. The partiers disposed of 342 chests of tea each weighing 360 pounds – enough to make 24 million cups, and worth more than one million dollars by today's standards. While it had the semblance of spontaneity, the event was in fact planned beforehand, and the mob was careful not to damage anything but the offending cargo. In any case, the Boston Tea Party transformed protest into revolution; even Governor Hutchinson agreed that afterwards, war was the only recourse. The ensuing British sanctions, colloquially referred to as the "Intolerable Acts," and the colonists' continued resistance, further inflamed the tension between the crown and its colonies, which eventually exploded at Lexington and Concord several months later.

and bookstores, enhanced by some low-key drug dealing and prostitution. It doesn't look like the visible reminders will be around much longer, especially with Chinatown's encroachment; indeed, the former *Naked I* adult theater, at 417 Washington St, now stands as Chinatown's first *McDonald's*, decked out with green pagodas as well as golden arches.

Just east of Chinatown are six square blocks, bounded by Kneeland, Atlantic, Essex, and Lincoln streets, that designate the **Leather District**, which takes its name from the days when the shoe industry was a mainstay of the New England economy, and the leather needed to make the shoes was shipped through the warehouses here. Since then, the Financial District – with which it is frequently lumped – has horned in, and the leather industry has pretty much dried up. The distinction between the two areas is actually quite sharp, most evident where High Street transitions into South Street: gleaming modern skyscrapers are replaced by stout brick warehouses, and the place of suited bankers is taken by a melange of merchants and gallery owners, who have taken advantage of the abundance of cheap warehouse space. Some of the edifices still have their leather warehouse signs on them. Check out the **Boston Hide & Leather Co.**, 15 East St, and the **Fur and Leather Services Outlet**, at 717 Atlantic Ave – but don't expect too much going on behind the facades.

Theater District

Just south of Boston Common is the slightly seedy **Theater District**, the chief attractions of which are the flamboyant theaters that lend the area its name, such as the Wilbur, Colonial and Majestic – though not surprisingly you'll have to get play tickets in order to inspect the grand old interiors (see p.127). The Colonial anchors so-called **Piano Row**, a section of Boylston Street between Charles and Tremont that was the center of American piano manufacturing and music publishing in the nineteenth and early twentieth centuries, and still has a few piano shops. Of greater interest, though, are the trendy restaurants and clubs in the immediate vicinity, many of which are tucked into Charles and Stuart streets around the mammoth **Massachusetts Transportation Building**, and cater to the theatergoing crowd.

The North End

The **North End** is a small yet densely populated neighborhood whose narrow streets are chock-a-block with Italian bakeries and restaurants, and also hold some of Boston's most storied sights. Bordered by Boston Harbor and separated from downtown by the elevated Fitzgerald Expressway (I-93), it may seem an inaccessible district at first, and indeed the protracted dismantling of I-93 can make access a challenge, but you can avoid the hassle – and get a much better sense of the area's attractiveness – by entering from the waterfront Christopher Columbus Park, then taking Richmond Street past quiet North Square to Hanover Street, the North End's main drag, from where you can explore the must-sees fairly quickly.

The North End's detached quality goes back to colonial times, when it was actually an island, later to be joined by short bridges to the main part of town, known then as the South End. Though landfill eventually ended the district's physical isolation, the North End remained very much a place apart. Irish immigrants poured in after the potato famine of 1840; John F. Fitzgerald, J.F.K.'s grandfather, was born on Ferry Street, and the late president's mother, Rose, on nearby Garden Street. The Irish were just the first of several immigrant groups to settle in the North End, displaced by Eastern European Jews in the 1850s, and southern Italians in the early twentieth century. The latter have for the most part stayed put, and the North End is still Boston's most authentically Italian neighborhood. If you wander the winding streets on a weekday afternoon, you can watch the locals pick up their groceries from the produce and meat markets and smell the bread and pastries from the bakeries. Don't look for a supermarket around here and don't try to do your shopping after six. In recent years, however, yuppies have begun to overtake the area's waterfront side and are now making inroads into rehabilitated tenements. You can still see laundry dangling from upper-story windows and grandmothers chattering in Italian in front of their apartment buildings, but it's perhaps only a matter of time before gentrification wins out.

Hanover Street and North Square

Hanover Street has long been the main connection between the North End and the rest of Boston, and it is along here – and its small side streets like Parmenter and Richmond (actually a continuation of each other on either side of Hanover) – that many of the area's trattorias, cafés and bakeries are located. It's also where you'll find, in its first few blocks, perhaps Boston's most authentically European flavor, though when a CVS drugstore opened here in 1996, it marked the first chainstore intruder on the street – and probably not the last. The classic Italian spots remain, including *Mike's Pastry*, at no. 300, where former President Clinton has been known to enjoy their cannollis when in the area.

The little triangular wedge of cobblestones and gaslights known as **North Square**, one block east of Hanover between Prince and Richmond streets, is among the most historic and attractive pockets of Boston, although its actual center is cordoned off by a heavy chain. Here the eateries recede in deference to the **Paul Revere House**, the oldest residential address in the city, at 19 North Square (daily 9.30am–4.15pm, until 5.15pm April 15–Oct 31, closed Mondays, Jan–March; $2.50). The small two-story post-and-beam structure, which dates from about 1680, stands on the former site of the considerably grander home of Puritan heavyweight Increase Mather – that one burned down in the Great Fire of 1676. The building, in which Revere lived from 1770 to 1800, was restored in 1908 to reflect its seventeenth-century appearance; prior to that it served variously as a grocery store, tenement and cigar factory. Though the house is more impressive for its longevity than its appearance, from the outside the second-story overhang and leaded windows provide quite a contrast to the red-brick buildings around it. On the inside, the first-floor "hall," or living room, resembles a hunting lodge with its low ceiling and enormous fireplace. Examples of Revere's self-made silverwares upstairs merit a look, as does a small but evocative exhibit about the mythologizing of Revere's horseback ride to warn patriots that the British were coming.

A small courtyard, the focus of which is a glass-encased 900-pound bell that Revere cast, separates the Paul Revere House from the **Pierce-Hichborn House** (tours by appointment ☎523-2338; $2.50), a simple Georgian-style house built in 1710, making it the oldest surviving **brick house** in Boston. Moses Pierce, a glazier, built the house, and it later belonged to Paul Revere's shipbuilding cousin, Nathaniel Hichborn. The interior is typical colonial American –

sparsely furnished with some unremarkable period tables, chairs, and a few decorative lamps and cabinetry.

At Hanover's intersection with Clark Street is **St Stephen's Church**, the only still-standing church in Boston built by Charles Bulfinch and one with a striking three-story recessed brick arch entrance. Just across Hanover, the famous bronze **statue** of Paul Revere on his borrowed horse marks the edge of the **Paul Revere Mall**. Sometimes called the Prado, this much-needed urban space was carved out of a chunk of apartment blocks in 1933 and runs back to tiny **Unity Street** – home of the small red-brick **Clough House**, at no. 21, built by the mason who helped lay the brick of the Old North Church.

Old North Church

Were it not for **Old North Church**, 93 Salem St (daily 9am–5pm; Sunday services at 9am, 11am, and 5pm), as a sign affixed to a collection box just inside its entrance reads, "You Might be Making Donations in Pound Notes." Few places in Boston have as emblematic a quality as the simple yet noble Christ Church (as Old North is officially called), rising unobstructed above the monotonous blocks of red-brick apartments around it. Built in 1723, it's the oldest church in Boston, easily recognized by its gleaming 191-foot **steeple**, which is actually a replica – hurricanes toppled both the original in 1804 and its first replacement in 1954 (the weathervane, however, is the original). What secured its place in history were the two lanterns that church sexton Robert Newman is said to have hung inside it on the night of April 18, 1775, to signal the movement of British forces "by sea" from Boston Common, which then bordered the Charles River. That steeple is clearly visible from Charlestown across the water and even from the other side of the I-93, lending a certain credence to its reputation as a watch and signal tower. Still, some historians speculate that the lanterns were actually hung from another church, also called Old North, which occupied the North Square spot where the **Sacred Heart Italian Church** now stands, at no. 12; that irate Tories burned that one for firewood in 1776 adds fuel to the theory. In any case, the spotlessly white interior contains the oldest clock still ticking in an American public building, made in 1726. The timber on which the high box pews rest is supported by 37 basement level brick crypts. One of the 1100 bodies encased therein is that of John Pitcairn, the British major killed in the Battle of Bunker Hill. His remains were tagged for Westminster Abbey, but didn't quite make it.

Some of Old North's greatest charms are actually outside the church, notably the diminutive **Washington Memorial Garden**, the brick walls of which are bedecked with plaques commemorating one thing or another; more inviting and secluded is the **pocket garden** behind it. The quirky **souvenir shop** on the opposite side of the church is worth a stop if only for a look at some of its not-for-sale items, such as a vial of Boston Tea Party tea and the bellringers' contract that Paul Revere signed as a mere lad in 1750.

Copp's Hill Burying Ground

Up Hull Street from Old North Church, atmospheric **Copp's Hill Burying Ground**, with its eerily tilting slate tombstones and stunning harbor views, holds the highest ground in the North End. The most famous gravesite here is that of the Mather family, just inside the wrought-iron gates on the Charter Street side. Increase Mather and son Cotton – the latter a Salem Witch Trial judge – were big players in Boston's early days of Puritan theocracy, a fact not at all reflected in the rather diminutive, if appropriately plain, brick vault tomb. You'll notice that many gravestones have chunks missing, the consequence of British soldiers using them for target practice during the 1775 Siege of Boston. The grave of one Captain Daniel Malcolm, toward the left end of the third row of gravestones as you enter the grounds, bears particularly strong evidence of this: three musket-ball marks scar his epitaph, which refers to him as a "true son of liberty" and "enemy of oppression."

The granite **Copp's Hill Terrace**, separated from the burial ground by Charter Street, was the place from which British cannons bombarded Charlestown during the Battle of Bunker Hill. In 1919, a 2.3-million-gallon tank of molasses exploded nearby, creating a syrupy tidal wave fifteen feet high that engulfed entire build-ings and drowned 21 people along with a score of horses. Old North Enders claim you can still catch a whiff of the stuff on an exceptionally hot day.

Across the street from Copp's Hill is Boston's **narrowest house**, at 44 Hull St. It really *is* narrow – 9 1/2 feet wide – and that's about it, as it's a private residence and you can't go in.

Salem and Prince streets

While the Old North Church is **Salem Street**'s star attraction, in the lower blocks between Prince and Cross streets, Salem is arguably the North End's most col-orful artery. The change in atmosphere when venturing here from commercial-ized Quincy Market and bland Government Center couldn't be more striking – as soon as you traverse Cross Street (which snakes alongside the elevated express-way), the agreeable onslaught of Italian grocers, aromatic *pasticcerias* and cafés begins. Salem Street itself is so narrow that the red-brick buildings seem to lean into one another; light traffic makes it a common practice to walk right down the middle of the street.

Serpentine **Prince Street** cuts through the heart of the North End on an east–west axis, linking Salem and Hanover streets. At no. 76 is the 24-hour *Bova's Bakery*, which in addition to purveying a good range of sweet treats is a major sup-plier of bread to North End restaurants. Nearer Hanover Street is **St Leonard's Church**, supposedly the first Italian church in New England. The garish interior is a marked contrast to the simplicity of most other Boston churches. Its icon-strewn Peace Park, primitive stained-glass windows, and garish statues of Saints (check out St Lucia with her eyes on a tray!) may seem kitsch at first, but if you consider these as the humble attempts of New World Italians to recreate the majesty of their cathedrals, it's actually quite touching, and you can still come across young and old alike bowed intently in prayer.

Charlestown

Charlestown, across Boston Harbor via Charlestown Bridge from the North End, is a largely Irish working-class neighborhood that's quite isolated from the city, despite its annexation more than a century ago. Its historic core of quiet streets and elegant rowhouses is now all but surrounded by elevated highways and construction projects, though you won't have to worry much about the inele-gant surroundings if you arrive on one of the trolley tours – or even better, by the short $1 ferry trip from Long Wharf to the Charlestown Navy Yard.

The earliest Puritan settlers had high hopes for developing Charlestown when they arrived in 1629, but an unsuitable water supply pushed them over to the Shawmut Peninsula, which they promptly renamed Boston. Charlestown grew slowly after that, and had to be completely rebuilt after the British burned it down in 1775. The mid-1800s witnessed the arrival of the so-called "lace-curtain Irish," somewhat better off than their North End brethren, and the district remains an Irish one at heart. The longtime locals, known as "townies," have acquired a reputation for being standoffish, due to instances such as their resistance to school desegregation in the 1970s. Recent years have seen urban professionals practically take over the Federal- and Colonial-style town homes south of the **Bunker Hill Monument** – Charlestown's other big sight – much to the chagrin of the townies. The rest of the neighborhood is fairly nondescript and even somewhat dodgy in parts.

The USS Constitution ("Old Ironsides")

The sprawling **Charlestown Navy Yard** was one of the first and busiest US naval shipyards – riveting together an astounding 46 destroyer escorts in 1943 alone – though it owes most of its present-day liveliness to being home to the frigate **USS Constitution**, at Constitution Wharf. In 1974 the Yard became part of the Boston National Historical Park after President Nixon decommissioned it, and since then it has been ambitiously repurposed as marinas, upscale condos and offices. But its focal point remains the *USS Constitution*, the oldest commissioned warship afloat in the world. Launched two centuries ago to safeguard American merchant vessels from Barbary pirates and the French and British navies, she earned her nickname during the War of 1812, when cannonballs fired from the British *HMS Guerrière* bounced off the hull (the "iron sides" were actually hewn from live oak, a particularly sturdy wood from the southeastern US), leading to the first and most dramatic naval conquest of that war. The ship went on to clinch victory in more than forty battles before it was retired from service in 1830.

As tall as a twenty-story building and three hundred feet long from bowsprit to back end, she is an impressive sight from any angle, if not quite what she seems – while authentic enough in appearance, roughly ninety percent of the ship has been reconstructed. Even after extensive renovations, Old Ironsides is too frail to support sails for any extended period of time, and the only voyages it makes with any regularity are annual Fourth of July turnarounds in Boston Harbor. But it's still an active commissioned ship, meaning the guides are certified US Navy sailors. Though there's often a line, especially in the summer, it's worth the wait to get a close-up view of the elaborate rigging and to amble about the main deck – and scuttle down the nearly vertical stairways to a deck below, where you'll find two long rows of cannons.

The rest of Charlestown Navy Yard

Housed in a substantial granite building a short walk from Old Ironsides and across from Pier 1, the **USS Constitution Museum** (daily 10am–5pm; $4 suggested donation) is worth visiting before you board the ship. One especially evocative display consists of curios which sailors acquired during a two-year round-the-world diplomatic mission begun in 1844; these are creatively arranged under a forest of faux palm fronds. Among the souvenirs are wooden carved toys from Zanzibar, a chameleon from Madagascar, preserved in a glass jar, and a Malaysian model ship made of cloves. The highlight upstairs is an infectiously fun wooden "deck," replete with sail and spinning helm, that rocks back and forth according to where you throw your weight.

Berthed in between Old Ironsides and the ferry to Long Wharf is the hulking gray mass of the World War II destroyer **USS Cassin Young** (daily 10am–5pm; free). You're free to stride about the expansive main deck and check out some of the cramped chambers below, but it's mostly of interest to WWII history buffs. At the northern perimeter of the Navy Yard is the **Ropewalk building**. For years "ropewalkers" made all the cordage for the US Navy in this narrow, quarter-mile-long granite building, the only one of its kind still standing in the country; unfortunately it's not open to the public.

City Square to Bunker Hill Monument

Toward Charlestown's center, there's a wealth of eighteenth- and nineteenth-century town houses, many of which you'll pass on your way from the Navy Yard to the Bunker Hill Monument. John Harvard, the young English minister whose library and funds launched Harvard University after his death, lived in Charlestown and left a legacy of street names here: directly behind **City Square** – a traffic circle anchored by one of Boston's most popular restaurants, *Olives* (see review p.115) – Harvard Street curves through the small **Town Hill** district, site of Charlestown's first settled community. You'll also find Harvard Mall and adja-

THE BATTLE OF BUNKER HILL

The Revolutionary War was at its bloodiest on the hot June day when British and colonial forces clashed in Charlestown. In the wake of the battles at Lexington and Concord two months before, the British had assumed full control of Boston, while the patriots had the upper hand in the surrounding counties. The British, under the command of generals Thomas Gage and "Gentleman Johnny" Burgoyne, intended to sweep the countryside clean of "rebellious rascals." Americans intercepted the plans and fortified **Breed's Hill** with a thousand-plus citizen-soldiers, who streamed in on the night of June 16, 1775. The next morning, more reinforcements came to take up positions while the British, preparing for a three-day military foray in the country, set about baking bread for the journey.

Spotting the Yankee fort, the Redcoats, each carrying 125 pounds of food and supplies on their backs, rowed across the harbor to take the rebel-held town. On the patriots' side, Colonel William Prescott had issued his celebrated order to his troops that they not fire "'til you see the whites of their eyes," such was their limited store of gunpowder. When the enemy's approach was deemed near enough, the patriots opened fire; though vastly outnumbered, they successfully repelled two full-fledged assaults. Some British units lost more than ninety percent of their men, and what few officers survived had to push their men forward with their swords to make them fight on. By the third British assault, the Redcoats had shed their gear, reinforcements had arrived and the Americans' supply of gunpowder was dwindling – as were their chances of clinching victory. The rebels continued to fight with stones and musket butts; meanwhile, British cannonfire from Copp's Hill in the North End was turning Charlestown into an inferno. Despite the eventual American loss, the battle did much to persuade the patriots – and the British, who lost nearly half their men who fought in this battle – that continued armed resistance made independence inevitable.

cent Harvard Square (not to be confused with the one in Cambridge), both lined with well-preserved homes.

Just up Main Street is the atmospheric **Warren Tavern**, at no. 105, a small three-story wooden structure built soon after the British burned Charlestown in the Battle of Bunker Hill, and named for Dr. Joseph Warren, killed in combat. From the tavern, crooked Devens Street to the south and Cordis Street to the north are packed with historic, private houses; the most imposing is the Greek Revival Swallow mansion at **33 Cordis Street**. West on Main Street, the landmark **Savings Bank Building**, with its steep mansard roof and Victorian Gothic ornamentation, looms above the street-level convenience stores. Further west is the **Phipps Street Burying Ground**, which dates from 1630. While many Revolutionary soldiers are buried here, it's not part of the Freedom Trail – perhaps even more of a reason to make the detour.

Double back and head up Monument Avenue, toward the Bunker Hill Monument. The red-brick town houses that you'll pass are some of the most eagerly sought residences in town. Nearby is **Winthrop Square**, Charlestown's unofficial common, just south of the monument. The prim rowhouses overlooking it form another upscale enclave. Appropriately enough, the common started out as a military training field – a series of bronze tablets at its northeastern edge lists the men killed just up the slope in the Battle of Bunker Hill.

Bunker Hill Monument

Commemorating the Battle of Bunker Hill – and the final stop on the Freedom Trail – is the gray, dagger-like **Bunker Hill Monument** (daily 9am–4.30pm; free), a towering obelisk that probably stirs more passion for its name confusion than anything else. Around midnight on June 16, 1775, revolutionary troops began fortifying what they presumed to be Bunker Hill; at dawn they realized they were actually atop Breed's Hill, only a short distance away. Even though the battle was fought (and the memorial built) on Breed's Hill, the misnomer stuck. The tower is centrally positioned in **Monument Square** and fronted by a statue of Colonel William Prescott; at its base is a lodge that houses some decent dioramas of the battle. Inside, 294 steps wind up the 221-foot granite shaft to the top; hardy climbers will be rewarded with sweeping views of Boston, the harbor and surrounding towns – and, to the northwest, the stone spire of the **St Francis de Sales Church**, which stands atop the real Bunker Hill.

Beacon Hill and the West End

Beacon Hill, a dignified stack of red brick rising over the north side of Boston Common, is the Boston of wealth and privilege, one-time home to numerous historical and literary figures – including John Hancock, John Quincy Adams, Louisa May Alcott, and Oliver Wendell Holmes – and still the address of choice for the city's elite. Its narrow, hilly byways are lit with gaslights and lined with quaint, nineteenth-century-style town houses, all part of an enforced preservation that prohibits modern buildings, architectural innovations, or anything else to disturb the carefully cultivated atmosphere of urban gentility.

It was not always this way. In Colonial times, Beacon Hill was the most prominent of three peaks known as the Trimountain which formed Boston's geological backbone. The sunny south slope was developed into prime real estate and

quickly settled by the city's political and economic powers, while the north slope
was closer in spirit to the **West End**, a tumbledown port district populated by free
blacks and immigrants; indeed, the north slope was home to so much salacious
activity that outraged Brahmins termed it "Mount Whoredom." During the twentieth century, this social divide has been almost entirely eradicated, though it can
still be seen in the somewhat shabbier homes north of Pinckney Street and in the
tendency of members of polite society to refer to the south slope as "the good
side." Still, both sides have much to offer, if of very different character: on the
south slope, there's the grandiose **Massachusetts State House**, attractive boulevards like **Charles Street** and the **Beacon Street Promenade**, and the residences of past and present luminaries. More down-to-earth are the north slope's
Black Heritage Trail sights, such as the **African Meeting House**, and some
vestiges of the old West End.

Beacon Street

Running along the south slope of Beacon Hill above the Common, **Beacon Street**
was described as Boston's "sunny street for the sifted few" by Oliver Wendell
Holmes in the late nineteenth century. This lofty character remains today; the row
of stately brick town houses, fronted by ornate iron grillwork, presides regally
over the area. The story behind the **purple panes** in some of their windows –
most visible at nos. 63 and 64 – evinces the street's long association with Boston
wealth and privilege. When the panes were installed in some of the first Beacon
Street mansions, they turned purple upon exposure to the sun, due to an excess
of manganese in the glass. At first, their owners perceived the purple panes as
nothing more than an irritating accident, but due to their prevalence in the windows of Boston's most prestigious houses, they eventually came to be perceived
as the definitive Beacon Hill status symbol by subsequent generations – in fact,
some residents have gone so far as to shade their windows purple in imitation.

Beacon Street Promenade
Across from no. 50, on the **Beacon Street Promenade** that edges Boston
Common, is the **Founder's Monument**, commemorating Boston's first white
settler, William Blackstone. The stone bas-relief depicts an apocryphal transaction in which the peculiar loner Blackstone, who had acquired much of present-
day Boston from the Shawmut Indians, sold most of his acreage in 1630 to a group
of Puritans from Charlestown who were seeking more hospitable land.

Further up the Promenade is the majestic monument honoring **Robert Gould
Shaw and the 54th Massachusetts Regiment**. The memorial commemorates
America's first all-black company to fight in the Civil War, who were led by Shaw,
scion of a moneyed Boston Brahmin clan. Isolated from the rest of the Union army,
given the worst of the military's resources, and saddled with menial or terribly dangerous assignments, the regiment performed its service bravely; most of its members, including Shaw, were killed in a failed attempt to take Fort Wagner from the
Confederates. Augustus Saint-Gaudens' 1897 high-relief bronze sculpture depicts
the regiment's farewell march down Beacon Street, and the names of the soldiers
who died in action are listed on its reverse side (though these were belatedly added
in 1982). Robert Lowell won a Pulitzer Prize for his poem, *For the Union Dead*,
about this monument; the regiment's story was also depicted in the film *Glory*.

Massachusetts State House

Across from the Shaw Memorial rises the large gilt dome of the Charles Bulfinch-designed **Massachusetts State House**, at Beacon and Park streets (Mon–Fri 10am–4pm, last tour at 3.15pm; free), the scale and grandeur of which recall the heady spirit of the then newly independent America in which it was built. Though only three stories tall, it seems taller sitting at the confluence of the steep grade of Park and Beacon streets. Of the current structure, only the central section was part of Bulfinch's original design; the huge wings jutting out toward the street on either side and the section extending up Bowdoin Street behind the State House were all added much later. An all-star team of Revolution-era luminaries contributed to its construction: built on land donated by John Hancock, its cornerstone was laid by Samuel Adams and the copper for its dome was rolled in Paul Revere's foundry (though it was covered over with gold leaf in the 1870s).

Once inside the labyrinthine interior, make your way up one flight and proceed to the central hallway, the only section of any real interest to visitors and the easiest to navigate. The best section is the sober and impressive **Hall of Flags**, a circular room surrounded by tall columns of Siena marble, displaying original flags carried by Massachusetts soldiers into battle and lit by a vaulted stained-glass window bearing the state seal. On the third floor, the carved wooden fish known as the **Sacred Cod** hangs above the Senate chambers. The senators take this symbol of maritime prosperity so seriously that when it was stolen by Harvard pranksters in the 1930s, they shut down the government until it was recovered.

Behind the State House, on Bowdoin Street, lies pleasant, grassy **Ashburton Park**, centered on a pillar that is a replica of a 1789 Bulfinch work. The column indicates the hill's original summit, which was sixty feet higher and topped by a 65ft post with the makeshift warning light – constructed from an iron pot filled with combustibles – that gave Beacon Hill its name.

Nichols House

On the other side of the State House and up the slope of Mt Vernon Street, at no. 55, is the only Beacon Hill residence open regularly to the public, the **Nichols House** (May–Oct Tues–Sat noon–5pm; Nov–Dec & Feb–Apr Mon, Wed & Sat noon–4.15pm; $5), yet another Bulfinch design, and most recently the home of eccentric spinster Rose Standish Nichols, who counted among her allegiances Fabian Socialism and the International Society of Pen Pals. She lived in the house until her death in the early 1960s, and left it to the public as a museum rather than bequeathing it to her greedy relatives. Crowded with a patchwork of post-Victorian period pieces, the interior isn't too gripping unless you have an abiding interest in antique furnishings; best go to get some perspective on the interior life of overstuffed leisure led by Beacon Hill's moneyed elite.

Louisburg Square and around

Farther up the slope, between Mt Vernon and Pinckney streets, is **Louisburg Square**, the geographic and spiritual heart of Beacon Hill. The central lawn, surrounded by wrought-iron fencing and flanked by statues of Columbus and Aristides the Just, is owned by local residents, making it the city's only private square. On either side of this oblong green space are rows of stately brick town

THE BLACK HERITAGE TRAIIL

Massachusetts was the first state to declare slavery illegal, in 1783, partly as a result of black participation in the Revolutionary War, and a large community of free blacks and escaped slaves swiftly sprung up in the North End and Beacon Hill. Very few blacks live in either place nowadays, but the 1.6-mile **Black Heritage Trail** traces Beacon Hill's key role in local black history – and is the only major historical site in America devoted to pre-Civil War African-American history and culture. Another in the line of Boston's self-guided walking tours, the trail begins at **Smith Court,** site of the **African Meeting House** and **Abiel Smith School,** and winds around Beacon Hill, passing the memorial for the **54th Massachusetts Regiment** as well as schools, other institutions, and residences ranging from the small cream clapboard houses of Smith Court to the imposing **Lewis and Harriet Hayden House** at 66 Phillips St.

houses, though the square's distinction is due less to its architectural character than to its long history of illustrious residents and the sense of elite civic parochialism that has made this Boston's most coveted address. Among those to call the area home were novelist Louisa May Alcott and members of the illustrious Vanderbilt family; today, Senator John Kerry and his wife, ketchup heiress Teresa Heinz, own a town house here, reportedly purchased for a cool $2 million.

Just below Louisburg Square is **Acorn Street**, a narrow byway that still has the cobblestones from its construction in the early nineteenth century. Barely wide enough for a car to pass through, locals cling to it as the epitome of Beacon Hill quaint. North of the square runs **Pinckney Street**, once the sharp division between the opulent south and ramshackle north sections of Beacon Hill. The area's original developers planned it that way, arranging it so that only the back entrances and stables of estates could abut Pinckney. The distinction is no longer so sharp, and now Pinckney is merely another of Beacon Hill's picturesque streets, though its location at the crest of the hill makes for great views.

The north side of the slope, across Pinckney Street, is keyed by **Smith Court**, once the center of Boston's substantial pre-Civil War black community when the north slope was still a low-rent district, and now home to a few crucial stops on Boston's Black Heritage Trail (see above). Free blacks, who were denied access to participation in Boston's civic and religious life, worshiped and held political meetings in what became known as the **African Meeting House**, at 8 Smith Court (Mon–Fri 10am–4pm, Sat noon–4pm, Memorial Day to Labor Day, daily 10am–4pm; donations requested). Informally called the Black Faneuil Hall, the meeting house grew into a center for abolitionist activism: in 1832, William Lloyd Garrison founded the New England Anti-Slavery Society here. Today, it houses the **Museum of Afro-American History**, which, considering its site, is rather a disappointment. You won't find much in the way of displays; there's only a rotating exhibit on the first floor, usually themed on contemporary African-American art, and a meeting house on the second, restored to look like the church it once was. At the end of Smith Court, you can wander down **Holmes Alley**, a path that was part of the old Underground Railroad used to protect escaped slaves, who would duck into the doors along the narrow alley, left open by sympathizers to the cause. The **Abiel Smith School**, back on Joy Street, was the first public educational institution established for black schoolchildren in Boston. Today, it houses the Museum of Afro-American History's gift shop, which vends a decent array of literature and historical material.

The Esplanade

Back towards the river, **Charles Street** is the commercial center of Beacon Hill, lined with scores of restaurants, antique shops and pricey specialty boutiques. A jaunt just off Charles down **Mount Vernon Street** brings you past some of Beacon Hill's most beautiful buildings, none of which you can enter, including the Federal-style **Charles Street Meeting House**, at the corner of the two streets, now repurposed as an office building, and the vegetation-enshrouded Victorian Gothic **Church of the Advent**, at Mt Vernon's intersection with Brimmer Street.

Connected to Charles Street at its north end by a footbridge and spanning nine miles along the Charles River, the **Esplanade** is yet another of Boston's well-manicured public spaces, with the requisite playgrounds, landscaped hills, lakes and bridges. The stretch alongside Beacon Hill is the nicest, providing a unique and picturesque way to appreciate the Hill from a distance, while also serving as a hotspot for the city's pretty young things. On summer days the Esplanade is swarming with well-toned singles scoping and flirting during jogs and rollerblading sessions. Just below the Longfellow Bridge a **public boathouse** is the point of departure for sailing excursions on the Charles (April–Oct; two-day visitor's pass $50, 45-day membership, $95; ☎523-1038).

The white half-dome rising from the riverbank along the Esplanade is the **Hatch Shell**, a public performance space best known for its Fourth of July celebration, which features a free concert by the Boston Pops, a pared-down version of the Boston Symphony Orchestra. Free movies and jazz concerts occur almost nightly during summer (☎727-1300 for schedules and upcoming events).

The West End

North of Cambridge Street, the tidy rows of town houses give way to a more urban spread of office buildings and old brick structures, signaling the start of the **WEST END**. Once Boston's main port of entry for immigrants and transient sailors, this area has seen its lively character pretty much disappear. A vestige of the old West End manages to remain in the small tangle of byways behind the high-rise buildings of **Massachusetts General Hospital**, where you'll see urban warehouses interspersed with Irish bars, some of which swell to a fever pitch after Celtic basketball and Bruin hockey games. Those games take place at the nearby **FleetCenter**, 150 Causeway St (tours daily at 11am, 1pm, and 3pm; $5), the slick, corporate-named arena built next to the legendary Boston Garden.

Back along Cambridge Street, at no. 141, the brick **Harrison Gray Otis House** (Wed–Sun, 11am–5pm, tours hourly; $4), originally built for the wealthy Otis family in 1796, sits incongruously among mini-malls and office buildings. Its first two floors have been painstakingly restored – from the bright wallpaper right down to the silverware sets – in the often loud hues of the Federal style.

Situated on a bridge over the Charles, Boston's **Museum of Science** (daily 9am–5pm, Fri until 9pm; $10) consists of several floors of interactive, though patchy and often well-worn, exhibits illustrating basic principles of natural and physical science. The best exhibit is the Theater of Electricity in the Blue Wing, a darkened room full of optical illusions and glowing displays on the presence of electricity in everyday life. Containing the world's largest Van de Graaf generator, the theater puts on daily electricity shows in which simulated lightning bolts flash and crackle around the space. The museum also holds the **Charles Hayden Planetarium** and the **Mugar Omni Theater**, though neither has too much to recommend it, just the regular complement of laser rock shows and IMAX screenings.

Back Bay and the South End

Back Bay, a meticulously planned neighborhood where elegant, angular, tree-lined streets form a pedestrian-friendly area that looks much as it did in the nineteenth century, right down to the original gaslights and brick sidewalks, is Boston at its most cosmopolitan. A youthful population helps offset stodginess and keeps the district, which begins at the **Public Garden**, buzzing with chic eateries, trendy shops, and the aura of affluence that goes along with both. Its other main draw is its trove of Gilded Age rowhouses, specifically their exquisite architectural details; there really is no end to the fanciful bay windows and ornamental turrets. On its southern border, the sprawl of the **South End** offers another impressive, if less opulent, collection of Victorian architecture, alongside some of Boston's more inventive restaurants.

Starting with the side closest to the Charles River, the east–west thoroughfares of Back Bay are **Beacon** and **Marlborough** streets, **Commonwealth Avenue**, and **Newbury** and **Boylston** streets. These are transsected by eight shorter streets, so fastidiously laid out that not only are their names in alphabetical order, but trisyllables are deliberately intercut by disyllables: Arlington, Berkeley, Clarendon, Dartmouth, Exeter, Fairfield, Gloucester and Hereford, until you get to Massachusetts Avenue. Generally, the grandest town houses are found on Beacon Street and Commonwealth Avenue, though Marlborough, in between the two, is more atmospheric; Boylston and Newbury are the main commercial drags. In the middle of it all is a small green space, **Copley Square**, surrounded by the area's main sights: **Trinity Church**, the imposing **Boston Public Library**, and the city's classic skyscraper, the **John Hancock Tower**.

FROM SWAMP TO SWANK: THE BUILDING OF BACK BAY

The fashioning of **Back Bay** occurred in response to a shortage of living space in Boston. An increasingly cramped Beacon Hill prompted developers to revisit a failed dam project on the Charles River, which had made a swamp of much of the area. **Arthur Gilman** manned the huge landfill project, which began in 1857. Taking his cue from the grand boulevards of Paris, Gilman decided on an orderly street pattern extending east to west from the Public Garden, itself sculpted from swampland two decades before. By 1890, the cramped peninsula of old Boston was flanked by 450 new acres, on which stood a range of churches, town houses and schools. You'll notice that, with a few exceptions, the brownstones get fancier the farther from the Garden you go, a result of architects and those who employed them trying to one-up each other. The exteriors of most of the buildings remain unaltered, although visually that's as far as you usually get, unless the place has been converted into a shop, salons, or gourmet eatery; in that case, step inside and hang onto your wallet.

The Public Garden

The value of property in Boston typically goes up the closer its proximity to the lovingly maintained **Public Garden**, a 24-acre park first earmarked for public use in 1859. Of the garden's 125 types of trees, many identified by little brass placards, most impressive are the weeping willows which ring the picturesque man-made **lagoon**, around which you can take a fifteen-minute ride in one of six **Swan Boats** ($1.50). There's often a line to hop on board – instead of waiting, you can get just as good a perspective on the park from the tiny **suspension bridge** that crosses the lagoon. The park's other big family draw is the cluster of bronze bird sculptures collectively called **Mrs Mallard and Her Eight Ducklings**, installed to commemorate Robert McClosky's 1941 children's tale *Make Way for Ducklings*, which was set in the Public Garden. Of the many statues and monuments throughout the park, the oldest and oddest is the thirty-foot-tall **Good Samaritan** monument, a granite and red marble column that is a tribute to, of all things, the anesthetic qualities of ether.

Commonwealth Avenue

The garden leads easily into the tree-lined median of **Commonwealth Avenue**, the 220-foot-wide showcase street of Back Bay. The mall forms the first link in Frederick Law Olmsted's so-called **Emerald Necklace**, which begins at Boston Common and extends all the way to the Arnold Arboretum, in Jamaica Plain. "Comm Ave," as locals ignobly call it, is at its prettiest in early May, when the magnolia and dogwood trees are in full bloom.

On the street proper, the **Baylies Mansion**, at no. 5, now houses the Boston Center for Adult Education, so feel free to slip inside for a look at the opulent ballroom Baylies built expressly for his daughter's coming-out (in the old-fashioned sense) party. Rising above the avenue, at no. 110, is the landmark belfry of the **First Baptist Church of Boston** (Mon–Fri 10am–4pm), designed by architect H. H. Richardson in 1872 for a Unitarian congregation, though at bill-paying time only a Baptist congregation were able to pony up the necessary funds. The puddingstone exterior is topped off by a 176-foot **bell tower**, which is covered by four gorgeous friezes by Frederic-Auguste Bartholdi, of Statue of Liberty fame – a product of his friendship with Richardson that developed at the Ecole des Beaux Arts in Paris. Richardson's lofty plans for the interior never materialized, again for lack of money, but its high ceiling, exposed timbers and Norman-style rose windows are still worth a peek if you happen by when someone's in the church office.

Further down Commonwealth, at no. 314, is the **Burrage House**, a fanciful synthesis of Vanderbilt-style mansion and the French chateau of Chenonceaux. The exterior of this 1899 urban palace is a riot of gargoyles and sundry carved cherubim; inside it's less riotous – it serves as a retirement home.

Newbury, Boylston, Beacon, and Marlborough streets

Newbury Street takes in eight blocks of alternately traditional and eclectic boutiques, art galleries and designer spas, all tucked into Victorian-era brownstones. It's an atmospheric place to shop, though the encroachment of big chainstores like Gap and NikeTown have eroded some of its charm. Wealthy foreign students and yuppies have colonized cafes like *Stephanie's on Newbury* and *Sonsie*, and the whole street is moving decidedly upscale, but despite the occasional nod to pretentiousness, the strip's overall mood is still surprisingly inviting. And not all is shopping: Newbury and neighboring **Boylston** are home to most of the old schools and churches built in the Back Bay area.

In fact, right on the corner of Boylston and Arlington streets is Back Bay's first building, the squat **Arlington Street Church** (Mon–Fri 10am–5pm), a minor Italianesque masterpiece designed in 1861 by Arthur Gilman; its host of Tiffany stained-glass windows were added from 1895 to 1930. A block down is the prison-like **New England Mutual Life building**, with some national chainstores on the first floor that do little for its character. However, it's worth nipping inside to have a look at the **murals**, which depict such historic regional events as Paul Revere sounding his famous alarm.

Back on the first block of Newbury Street itself, the full-blown Gothic Revival **Church of the Covenant** boasts a soaring steeple and thirty-foot-high Tiffany stained-glass windows. The church's chapel houses one of Boston's biggest contemporary art spaces in the form of the Gallery NAGA. Designed as an architect's house, the medieval flight-of-fancy at **109 Newbury St** is arguably more arresting for its two donjon towers than the Cole-Haan footwear inside. A block down at **275 Dartmouth** is the Rodier Paris boutique, but again the burnt siena-colored building with mock battlements hunkered over it steals the show: originally the *Hotel Victoria* in 1886, it looks like a combination Venetian–Moorish castle, not a bad place to have your in-town condo. A block west, on the exposed side of no. 159, is the **Newbury Street Mural**, a fanciful tribute to a hodgepodge of notables from Sam Adams to Sammy Davis, Jr. A key to who's who is affixed to the parking attendant's booth in the lot next to it. Housed in a Romanesque-style police and fire station built in 1886, half of which Back Bay's firefighters still call home, the **Institute of Contemporary Art**, 955 Boylston St (Wed–Sun noon–5pm, Thurs until 9pm; $6, free Thurs 5–9pm), is Boston's main venue for modern art, with no permanent collections.

As a continuation of Beacon Hill's stately main thoroughfare, **Beacon Street** was long the province of blueblood Bostonians. It is the Back Bay street closest to the Charles River, yet its buildings turn their back to it, principally because in the nineteenth century the river was a stinking mess. On the first block of the Back Bay portion of Beacon, at no. 137, is the only house museum in the neighborhood, the **Gibson House Museum** (Wed–Sun 1–3pm, tours hourly; $5). Built in 1860, this standard-issue Back Bay town house has been more or less preserved as it was, with an almost complete lack of sunlight and a host of Victoriana that includes a still-functioning dumbwaiter, antique globes and writing paraphernalia (one of the Gibsons was apparently a travel writer), and gilt-framed photos of long-gone relatives of the long-gone Bostonian Catherine Hammond Gibson.

Sandwiched between Beacon Street and Commonwealth Avenue is quiet **Marlborough Street**, which with its brick sidewalks and vintage gaslights is one of the most prized residential locales in Boston, after Louisburg Square in Beacon Hill and the first few blocks of Commonwealth Avenue. Even though the town houses here tend to be smaller than elsewhere in Back Bay, they display a surprising range of stylistic variation, especially on the blocks between Clarendon and Fairfield streets. The final block, which links Massachusetts Avenue to Charlesgate East, is the only street in Back Bay proper that curves.

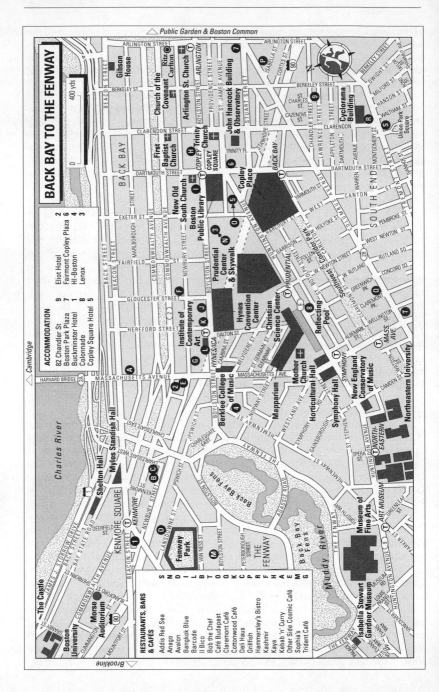

△ Public Garden & Boston Common

BACK BAY TO THE FENWAY

△ Cambridge

Charles River

Brookline △

ACCOMMODATION

82 Chandler St	9	Eliot Hotel	2
Boston Park Plaza	7	Fairmont Copley Plaza	6
Buckminster Hotel	1	HI-Boston	4
Colonnade	8	Lenox	3
Copley Square Hotel	5		

RESTAURANTS, BARS & CAFÉS

Addis Red Sea	S
Anago	N
Avalon	D
Bangkok Blue	L
Barcode	B
Il Bico	T
Bob the Chef	O
Café Budapest	Q
Claremont Café	K
Cottonwood Café	C
Deli Haus	P
Grillfish	R
Hammersley's Bistro	F
Kashmir	H
Kaya	A
Kebab 'n' Curry	E
Other Side Cosmic Café	M
Sophia's	J
Trident Café	G

Copley Square and around

Bounded by Boylston, Clarendon, Dartmouth and St James streets, **Copley Square** is the busy commercial center of Back Bay. The square itself is a relatively nondescript grassy expanse, but its periphery holds quite a bit of interest.

In his meticulous attention to detail – from the polychromatic masonry on the outside to the rather generic stained-glass windows within – Boston architect H.H. Richardson seemed to overlook the big picture for his 1877 **Trinity Church**, 206 Clarendon St (daily 8am–6pm), which as one 1923 guidebook averred "is not beautiful" – despite the reaction of the critics at the time, who dubbed it a masterpiece of Romanesque Revivalism. Skip the rather spartan interior, which feels more empty than awe-inspiring. Indeed, the most interesting aspect of Trinity Church, hulking exterior and all, is probably its juxtaposition to the John Hancock Tower, in whose mirrored panes it's reflected.

A decidedly secular building anchors the end of Copley Square opposite Trinity Church, in the form of the **Boston Public Library** (Mon–Thurs 9am–9pm, Fri–Sat 9am–5pm, Sun 1–5pm) – the largest public research library in New England, and the first one in America to actually permit the borrowing of books. Architects McKim, Mead & White built the Italian Renaissance Revival structure in 1852; the massive inner bronze doors were designed by Daniel Chester French (sculptor of the Lincoln Memorial in Washington DC). Inside, check out the imposing **Bates Reading Room**, with its barrel-vaulted ceiling and dark oak paneling.

Just opposite the Boston Public Library, on the corner of Boylston and Dartmouth streets, is one of Boston's most attractive buildings, the **New Old South Church**, 645 Boylston St (Mon–Fri 9am–5pm), a name to which there is actually some logic: the congregation in residence at downtown's Old South Meeting House (and church) outgrew it and decamped here in 1875. You need not be a student of architecture to be won over by the Italian Gothic design, most pronounced in the ornate, 220-foot bell tower – a 1937 addition – and copper-roof lantern, replete with metallic gargoyles in the shape of dragons. Its interior is an alluring assemblage of dark woods set against a forest-green backdrop, coupled with fifteenth-century English-style stained-glass windows.

At 62 stories, the **John Hancock Tower**, at 200 Clarendon St (daily 9am–11pm, Nov–April, Sun 9am–5pm; $6), is the tallest building in America north of New York City, and in a way Boston's signature skyscraper – first loathed, now loved, and taking on startlingly different appearances all depending on your vantage point. In Back Bay, the characteristically angular edifice is often barely perceptible, due to designer I.M. Pei's deft understatement in deference to adjacent Trinity Church and the old brownstones nearby. From Beacon Hill, it appears broad-shouldered and stocky; from the South End, taller than it really is; from across the Charles River, like a crisp metallic wafer. You'd never guess from any angle that soon after its 1976 construction, dozens of windowpanes popped out, showering Copley Square with glass. The sixtieth-floor **observatory** affords the expected stunning views – on a clear day you can see New Hampshire – but most interesting is the opportunity to see Boston splayed out below. Next door to the tower is the *old* Hancock Tower, which cuts a distinguished profile in the skyline with its truncated step-top pyramid roof.

Nothing can cloak the ugliness of the **Prudential Tower**, at 800 Boylston St, just west of Copley Square. This 52-story gray intruder to the Back Bay skyline is one of the more unfortunate by-products of the urban renewal craze that gripped

Boston and most other American cities in the 1960s – though it did succeed in replacing the Boston & Albany rail yards, a blighted border between Back Bay and the South End. The running joke about the "Pru Tower" is that it offers the best view of Boston – because it's the only view where you don't have to actually look at the Pru Tower. That said, the fiftieth-floor **Skywalk** (daily 10am–10pm; $4), although not quite as high as the nearby John Hancock Observatory, does offer the only 360-degree aerial view of Boston.

Christian Science buildings

People gazing down from the top of the Prudential Tower are often surprised to see a 224-foot tall Renaissance Revival basilica vying for attention amidst the urban out-croppings lapping at its base. This rather artificial-looking structure is the central feature of the world headquarters of the sprawling **First Church of Christ, Scientist**, 75 Huntington Ave, which dwarfs the earlier, prettier Romanesque **Christian Science Mother Church** just behind it, built in 1894. There may be no better place in Boston to contemplate the excesses of religion than around the cen-ter's 670-foot-long red granite-trimmed **reflecting pool**. The highlight of a visit here, though, is the unique **Mapparium** (Mon–Sat 10am–4pm; free), tucked into the grand Art Deco lobby of the Christian Science Publishing building (headquar-ters of the *Christian Science Monitor*), close to Massachusetts Avenue. This is an inverted, stained-glass globe, the thirty-foot diameter of which you can cross on a bridge of glass. The technicolor hues of the six hundred-plus glass panels, illumi-nated from the outside, reveal the geopolitical reality of the world in the early 1930s, when the globe was constructed, as evidenced by names like Siam, Baluchistan and Transjordan. Designed to symbolize the worldwide reach of the Christian Science movement, the Mapparium has perhaps a more immediate acoustical payoff, cour-tesy of its glass design: whisper something like "What's Tanganyika called today?" at one end of the bridge and someone on the opposite end will be able to hear it clear as a bell – and perhaps proffer the answer (Tanzania).

Bay Village

Back near the Public Garden is **Bay Village**, a small atmospheric satellite of Back Bay and one of the oldest sections of Boston, bounded by Arlington, Church, Fayette and Stuart streets. This warren of gaslights and tiny brick houses has managed to escape the trolley tours that make other parts of the city feel like a theme park; it's also increasingly popular with Boston's **gay population**, and is something of an extension to the nearby South End. Bay Village wakes up after the sun sets, when men of all ages zero in on spots like *Buzz* and the *Luxor*, two of the most popular gay clubs in Boston.

The area's overall resemblance to Beacon Hill is no accident; many of the arti-sans who pieced that district together built their own, smaller houses here throughout the 1820s and 1830s. A few decades later, water displaced from the fill-ing in of Back Bay threatened to turn the district back into a swamp, but Yankee practicality resulted in the lifting of hundreds of houses and shops onto wooden pilings fully eighteen feet above the water level. Backyards were raised only twelve feet, and when the water receded many building owners designed sunken gardens. You can still see some of these in the alleys behind slender Melrose and Fayette streets, but a more unusual remnant from the past is the **fortress** at the intersection of Arlington and Stuart streets and Columbus Avenue, complete with drawbridge and fake moat, that was built as an armory for the **First Corps of Cadets**, a private military organization. It's been relegated to use as an exhibition hall and convention facility for the *Park Plaza Hotel*.

Bay Village's proximity to the theater district made it a prime location for **speakeasies** in the 1920s, not to mention a natural spot for actors and impresarios to take up residence; indeed, the building at **48–50 Melrose Street** originally housed a movie studio. Around the corner from it is the site of the **Cocoanut Grove Fire** of 1942, in which 490 people perished in a nightclub because the exit doors were locked.

The South End

Though it lacks obvious tourist attractions, the **South End**, separated from Back Bay by the Copley Place shopping complex, merits a look for its wealth of Victorian architecture and its generally upbeat streetlife, which is in certain respects the most happening in town. There are large black and gay communities here, and the latter has ushered in several trendy cafés and restaurants, most clustered on **Tremont Street** and on gentrified pockets of **Columbus Avenue**. Still, despite the tendency of Boston realtors to promote the South End as the ultimate up-and-coming area, the more affluent zones here run up against some pretty destitute ones. Don't hesitate to take a cab if you're heading to and from one of the South End's many excellent restaurants at night.

Not a model of geometric precision, and definitely not to be confused with the region of Southeast Asia famed for its CIA-sponsored heroin trade, the so-called **Golden Triangle** was named by South End realtors to describe a zone, loosely bounded by Columbus Avenue and Tremont and Dartmouth streets, that is almost always modified by the term "quaint" – though for once the tag fits. Walk along quiet Chandler and Appleton streets and the appeal is obvious – refurbished bowfronted rowhouses that would be at home in London's Mayfair, and with a community feel all but absent in surrounding areas. Its heart is the intersection of Tremont Street – actually the southernmost edge of the triangle – and **Clarendon Street**, an upmarket crossing home to some of the hippest restaurants in Boston. Nearby is the domed **Cyclorama Building**, at no. 539, built in 1884 to house an enormous circular painting of the Battle of Gettysburg (since moved to Gettysburg itself), and now housing the **Boston Center for the Arts**. If the ornate kiosk in front of it looks a trifle oversized, that's because it was designed as the cupola for a building close by. Also close by is another attractive space, **Union Park Square**, that you can walk around, although not through. The elliptical park, lined by well-preserved Victorian town houses and accented with fountains and formal plantings, is fenced off.

Kenmore Square, The Fenway, and Brookline

At the western edge of Back Bay, the decorous brownstones and smart shops fade into the more casual Kenmore Square and Fenway districts, both removed from the tourist circuit but good fun nonetheless, with a studenty vibe and some of the city's more notable cultural institutions. Further west and more residential is the town of Brookline, which feels like just another sleepy part of the city, though one in which you're unlikely to find yourself spending too much time.

Kenmore Square and Boston University

Kenmore Square, at the junction of Commonwealth Avenue and Beacon Street, is the primary port of entry to Boston University and the unofficial playground for its students. Back Bay's Commonwealth Avenue Mall leads right into this lively stretch of youth-oriented bars, record stores and casual restaurants that cater to the late-night cravings of local students – as such the Square is considerably more alive when school's in session. Many of the buildings on its north side have been snapped up by BU, such as the bustling six-story Barnes & Noble mall, 660 Beacon St, on top of which is perched the monumental **Citgo Sign**, Kenmore's most noticeable landmark. This sixty-square-foot neon advertisement, a pulsing red triangle that is the oil company's logo, has been a popular symbol of Boston since it was placed here in 1965.

Boston University, one of the country's biggest private schools, has its main campus alongside the Charles River, on the narrow stretch of land between Commonwealth Avenue and Storrow Drive. The school has made inventive reuse of old buildings, such as the dormitory **Myles Standish Hall**, at 610 Beacon St, a scaled-down version of New York's Flatiron Building that was once a hotel where notables like Babe Ruth camped out. **Shelton Hall**, behind it on Bay State Road, is another hostelry-turned-dorm where playwright Eugene O'Neill undramatically made his long day's journey into night. **Bay State Road** was the westernmost extension of Back Bay, evidenced by its wealth of turn-of-the-century brownstones, most of which now house BU graduate institutes and smaller residence halls. An ornate High Georgian Revival mansion at no. 149 houses the office of the university president. The street ends at **The Castle**, an ivy-covered Tudor mansion now used for university functions. Continuing the theme back on Commonwealth is the domed **Morse Auditorium**, formerly a synagogue. One long block down is the closest thing the BU campus has to a center, **Marsh Plaza**, with its Gothic Revival chapel and memorial to Martin Luther King, Jr., a graduate here.

The Fenway

The Fenway spreads out beneath Kenmore Square like an elongated kite, taking in sights disparate enough to please most any visitor. Just past Landsdowne's clubs, the district starts in earnest with **Fenway Park**, the venerable baseball stadium where the star-crossed Boston Red Sox play, though this is quite removed from the highbrow spaces of Fenway's eastern perimeter, dotted with some of Boston's finest cultural institutions: **Symphony Hall**, the **Museum of Fine Arts** and the **Isabella Stewart Gardner Museum**. Running down the neighborhood's spine is the **Back Bay Fens**, a huge green space banking the Muddy River and designed by Frederick Law Olmsted, urban landscaper extraordinaire.

Fenway Park

Baseball is treated with reverence in Boston, so it's appropriate that it is played here in what may be the country's most storied stadium, unique **Fenway Park**, at 24 Yawkey Way (tours Apr–Oct Mon–Fri 10am, 11am, and 1pm; $5), whose giant 37-foot tall left-field wall, aka the **Green Monster**, is an enduring symbol of the quirks of early ballparks. Fenway Park was constructed in 1912 in a tiny, asymmetrical space wedge just off Brookline Avenue, resulting in its famously

THE CURSE OF THE BAMBINO

In 1903, Boston (then nicknamed the "Pilgrims") became the first team to represent the American League in baseball's World Series, upsetting the heavily favored Pittsburgh Pirates to claim the championship; their continued financial success allowed them to build a new stadium, **Fenway Park**, in 1912. During their first year there, Boston won the Series again, and repeated the feat in 1915, 1916 and 1918, led in the latter years by the young pitcher **George Herman "Babe" Ruth**, who also demonstrated an eye-opening penchant for hitting home runs.

The team was poised to become a dynasty, when its owner, Harry Frazee, began a firesale of the team to finance a Broadway play that was to star his ingenue girlfriend. Most of the players sold at bargain prices, including Ruth, went to the New York Yankees, who of course went on to become the most successful franchise in professional sports history, with the Babe and all his home run records at the forefront – indeed, Yankee Stadium is often referred to as "The House That Ruth Built." On the other hand, Frazee's play, *No, No, Nanette*, flopped. So did his Red Sox team – the 1918 World Series was the last they won. Their long periods of mediocrity have been punctuated by even more disappointing seasons in which they came agonizingly close to the championship, only to snatch defeat from the jaws of certain victory: in 1978, a late-season collapse was capped off when the Yankees' light-hitting shortstop Bucky Dent slugged a three-run homer to beat the Sox in a one-game playoff; in 1986, the Sox were one strike away from clinching the World Series against the New York Mets when a series of miscues, including the infamous grounder that rolled through the legs of first baseman Bill Buckner, brought about another crushing loss. It's become fodder for the long-suffering fans, who call it "The Curse of the Bambino" (referring back to the Babe); Boston sportswriter Dan Shaughnessy even penned a 1991 book by that same name. Today, fans will no doubt complain that the curse continues, especially with the recent spate of success by their arch rivals, the New York Yankees.

awkward dimensions – also included in which are an abnormally short right-field line (302ft) and a fence that doesn't at all approximate the smooth arc of most outfields. That the left-field wall was built so high makes up for some of the short distances in the park and also gives Red Sox' leftfielders a distinct advantage over their counterparts – it takes some time before one gets accustomed to the whimsical caroms a ball hit off there might take. You can take tours of the stadium, where greats like Ted Williams, Carl Yazstremski and even Babe Ruth roamed about, but your best bet is to come see a game, really a must for any baseball fan and still a reasonable draw for anyone remotely curious. The season runs from April to October, and tickets are quite reasonable, especially if you sit in the bleachers ($18–30; ☎267-1700 for ticket info). Sadly, the Red Sox are looking to tear it down and build a huge, more profitable stadium, and foot the bill with tax money and higher ticket prices. Among the many groups opposing the plan, Save Fenway Park (*www.savefenwaypark*) in particular is trying to gain historic landmark status for the beloved stadium.

The Back Bay Fens

The Fenway's defining element is the **Back Bay Fens**, a snakelike segment of Frederick Law Olmsted's Emerald Necklace that rather uninspiringly takes over where the prim Commonwealth Avenue Mall leaves off. The Fens were fashioned

<table>
<tr><td>

OLMSTED AND THE EMERALD NECKLACE

The string of urban parks that stretches through Boston's southern districts, known as the Emerald Necklace, grew out of a project conceived in the 1870s, when landscape architect Frederick Law Olmsted was commissioned to create for Boston a series of urban parks like those he had done in New York and Chicago. A Romantic naturalist in the tradition of Rousseau and Wordsworth, Olmsted conceived of nature as a way to escape the ills wrought by society, and considered his urban parks a means for city-dwellers to escape the clamor of their everyday life. He converted much of Boston's remaining open space, which was often disease-breeding marshland, into a series of fabulous, manicured parks beginning with the Back Bay Fens, including the Riverway along the Boston–Brookline border, and proceeding through Jamaica Pond and the Arnold Arboretum to Roxbury's Franklin Park (see "Southern Districts," p.101). While Olmsted's original skein of parks was limited to these, further development linked the Fens, via the Commonwealth Avenue Mall, to the Public Garden and Boston Common, all of which now function as part of the necklace. And which make it all the more impressive in scale, though the necklace's sense of pristine natural wonder has slipped in the century since their creation – the more southerly links in the chain, starting with Fens, have grown shaggy and are unsafe at night.

The Boston Park Rangers (9am–5pm; ☎635-7383) organize free walking tours covering each of the Necklace's segments from Boston Common to Franklin Park.

</td></tr>
</table>

from marsh and mud in 1879, a fact reflected in the name of the waterway that still runs through them today – the **Muddy River**.

Not far from the Fens' northern tip, the renowned **Berklee College of Music** makes its home on the busy stretch of Massachusetts Avenue south of Boylston Street. A few short blocks south, **Symphony Hall**, home to the Boston Symphony Orchestra, anchors the corner of Massachusetts and Huntington avenues. The inside of the 1900 McKim, Mead & White design resembles an oversized cube, apparently just the right shape to lend it its perfect acoustics. The modern campus of **Northeastern University** spreads out on both sides of Huntington further south, though it lacks any of the collegiate atmosphere and charm of other Boston schools.

Museum of Fine Arts

Rather inconveniently located in the south Fenway but well worth the trip out is New England's premier art space, the **Museum of Fine Arts**, at 465 Huntington Ave (Mon, Tues, Thurs–Fri & Sun 10am–4.45pm, Wed until 9.45pm, Sat until 5.45pm; West Wing also open Thurs & Fri until 9.45pm; $12; pay what you can after 5pm Wednesdays; West Wing only, $2 after 5pm Thurs & Fri; *www.mfa.org*). It originated in the 1850s as an adjunct of the Boston Athenaeum when that organization decided to focus more exclusively on local history rather than art, and found its permanent home here in 1906.

AMERICAN COLLECTION

On the first floor, a marvelously rich **American collection** features Gilbert Stuart's nationalistic *Washington at Dorchester Heights* and a number of John Singleton Copley portraits of revolutionary figures, plus his gruesome narrative *Watson and the Shark*. Romantic naturalist landscapes from the first half of the nineteenth century – such as Albert Bierstadt's quietly majestic *Buffalo Crossing* – dominate several rooms, and from the latter half of the century there are several seascapes by Winslow Homer, Whistler's morose *Nocturne in Blue and Silver: the Lagoon*, and works from the Boston school, notably Childe Hassan's gauzy *Boston Common at Twilight* and John Singer Sargent's spare *The Daughters of Edward Darley Boit*. Don't miss the **American Decorative Arts**, either: a gloriously nostalgic assemblage of coffee urns, elaborately styled oak furnishings and reconstructed living rooms with period furniture.

EUROPEAN COLLECTION

The second-floor **European wing** begins with Dutch paintings from the Northern Renaissance, featuring two outstanding Rembrandts, *Artist in his Studio* and *Old Man in Prayer*, and follows with several rooms of grandiose rococo and Romantic work from the eighteenth and early nineteenth centuries. The culmination of the wing is the late nineteenth-century collection, which begins with works by the Realist Jean-Francois Millet, whose *Man Turning over the Soil* and *The Sower* exhibit the stark use of color and interest in common subjects that characterized later French artists. Early Impressionists are represented by Manet and Cezanne, followed by the Impressionist room with prominent works by Monet, Degas, Renoir, and Pissarro. The room's highlight, however, is its selection of Post-Impressionist art, best of which are Van Gogh's richly hued *Enclosed Field with Ploughman* and *Houses at Auvers* and Gauguin's vibrant narrative of Tahitian life, *Where Do We Come From? What Are We? Where Are We Going?*

ANCIENT ART AND OTHER GALLERIES

A series of MFA-sponsored digs at Giza have made its **Egyptian collection** the standout of a fine collection of **ancient art**. Pieces range from prehistoric pots to artifacts from the Roman period. While rather modest by comparison, the Nubian collection is nevertheless the largest of its kind outside Africa. Most of the pieces are funerary and actually quite similar to their Egyptian contemporaries. Not nearly as well-represented, the classical section is worth a glance mostly for its numerous Grecian urns, a fine Cycladic *Female Figure*, and several Etruscan sarcophagi with elaborately wrought narrative bas-reliefs.

For those in the know, the MFA's **Asian Galleries** are a highlight. The Chinese, Indian, Southeast Asian and Islamic collections are excellent, but the standout is the Museum's **Japanese Collection**, quite simply one of the best in the world. One room is filled with striking displays of intricately decorated samurai swords and lacquer boxes, kimonos, and another has temple guardian and Buddha statues arranged in a setting designed like the great hall of a temple. There's also an astounding collection of hanging scrolls and *ukiyo-e* (woodblock prints), which, because of their fragility, are exhibited on a rotating basis.

The Isabella Stewart Gardner Museum

Less broad in its collection, but more distinctive and idiosyncratic than the MFA, is its neighbor, the **Isabella Stewart Gardner Museum**, at 280 The Fenway (Tues–Sun 11am–5pm; $10, $11 Sat & Sun). Eccentric Boston socialite Gardner collected and arranged more than 2500 objects in the four-story Fenway Court building she designed herself, making this the only major museum in the country that is entirely the creation of a single individual. It's a hodgepodge of works from around the globe, presented without much attention to period or style;

Gardner's goal was to foster the love of art rather than its study, and she wanted the setting of her pieces to "fire the imagination." Your imagination does get quite a workout – there's art everywhere you look, with many of the objects unlabeled, placed in corners or above doorways, for an effect that is occasionally chaotic, but always striking.

The Gardner is best known for its spectacular central **courtyard**, styled after a fifteenth-century Venetian palace, where flowering plants and trees bloom year-round amid statuary and fountains. However, the museum's greatest success is the **Spanish Cloister**, a long, narrow corridor which perfectly frames John Singer Sargent's ecstatic representation of Spanish dance, *El Jaleo*, and also contains fine seventeenth-century Mexican tiles and Roman statuary and sarcophagi. Gardner had an affinity for **altars**, and the collection contains several, cobbled together from various religious artifacts. Most notable of these is her **chapel**, on the third floor, which incorporates sixteenth-century Italian choirstalls and stained glass from Milan and Soissons cathedrals, as well as assorted unlabeled religious figurines, candlesticks, and crucifixes, all surrounding Paul-Cesar Helleu's moody representation of the *Interior of the Abbey Church of Saint-Denis*.

The **Titian, Veronese and Raphael rooms** comprise a strong showing of Italian Renaissance and Baroque work, including Titian's famous *Europa*, Botticelli's *Tragedy of Lucretia*, and Crivelli's mannerist *St George and the Dragon*. What was once a first-rate array of seventeenth-century Northern European works was debilitated by a 1990 art heist in which two Rembrandts and a Vermeer were among ten canvases stolen. But the majority of works in the **Dutch Room** remain, with an early *Self-Portrait* by Rembrandt and Rubens' austere *Thomas Howard, Earl of Arundel*.

Brookline

The leafy, affluent town of **BROOKLINE**, south of Boston University and west of The Fenway, appears as if it's just another well-maintained Boston neighborhood, though in fact it's a distinct municipality. It holds some vaguely diverting attractions, most oriented around bustling **Coolidge Corner**, at the intersection of Beacon and Harvard streets, though it's unlikely any of them will bring you out this way. To reach Brookline, take the Green Line's C branch to Coolidge Corner or D branch to Brookline Village.

Perhaps the biggest draw at Coolidge Corner is the **Coolidge Corner Theater**, at 290 Harvard St, a refurbished art house cinema; with plenty of students living in the area it maintains itself quite well. Close by is the **John F. Kennedy National Historic Site**, at 83 Beals St (Wed–Sun 10am–4.30pm; $2), the outwardly unremarkable house where JFK was born on May 29, 1917. The inside is rather plain, too, though a narrated voiceover by the late President's mother, Rose, adds some spice to the roped-off rooms. Brookline also happens to be where a more recent presidential aspirant, former Massachusetts governor **Michael Dukakis**, was born; strangely that, too, has yet to do much for the city's tourist appeal. Along Brookline's southern fringe is the **Frederick Law Olmsted National Historic Site**, at 99 Warren St (Fri–Sun 10am–4.30pm; free), the Olmsted family home that provides a retrospective on his life and work and is located on idyllic grounds.

Boston's southern districts

The parts of Boston that most visitors see – downtown, Beacon Hill, Back Bay, the North End – actually only cover a small proportion of the city's geography. To the south lies a vast spread of residential neighborhoods known collectively as the **southern districts**, including largely Irish **SOUTH BOSTON**, unlovely **DORCHESTER**, blighted **ROXBURY** and pleasant, trendy **JAMAICA PLAIN**, which count just a handful of highlights among them, most notably Jamaica Plain's **Arnold Arboretum** and Dorchester's **John F. Kennedy Museum and Library**. These were once rural areas dotted with the swish summer resort homes of Boston's moneyed elite, but population growth in the late nineteenth century pushed middle- and working-class families here from the increasingly crowded downtown area. Three-story rowhouses soon replaced the mansions, and the moniker "streetcar suburbs" was coined as a catch-all for the newly redefined neighborhoods. In the years immediately following World War II, each was hit to varying degrees by economic decline, and the middle class moved farther afield, leaving the districts to the mostly immigrant and blue-collar communities that remain today.

None of these areas, though fairly easily accessible on the ⓣ from downtown (if not always safe to walk around, especially after dark), will draw your attention for too long, which is one of the reasons we've gone ahead and picked out the best sights for you – as you're likely to target certain attractions rather than wandering around the rather large districts. An exception to this rule is Jamaica Plain (popularly known as "JP"), whose Centre Street has boomed into one of the hippest eating and junk shopping strips in the city – much to the distress of local residents who have seen their rents more than double in the past few years.

Castle Island and Fort Independence
South Boston narrows to an end in Boston Harbor on a strip of land called **Castle Island**, off the end of William J. Day Boulevard, a favorite leisure spot for Southie residents and, in fact, many Bostonians. The island, reachable by bus #9 or #11 from the Broadway ⓣ, is covered by parks and beaches, though you wouldn't want to swim here, since Boston Harbor's waters, while cleaner than in years past, are far from non-toxic – and they're freezing to boot. At the tip of the island is **Fort Independence** (Sat & Sun noon–3.30pm), a stout granite edifice that was one of the earliest redoubts in the Americas, originally established in 1634, though it has been rebuilt several times since. Today, what remains is a skeleton of its 1801 version, and its slate-gray walls aren't much to look at from the outside, though supposedly an incident that happened inside served as inspiration for Edgar Allan Poe's story, "The Cask of Amontillado."

John F. Kennedy Museum and Library
There's not much to see in Dorchester besides the **John F. Kennedy Museum and Library**, at Columbia Point (daily 9am–5pm; $8; JFK/Umass ⓣ), spectacularly sited in an I.M. Pei-designed building overlooking Boston Harbor. The museum's presentation opens with a well-done eighteen-minute film covering Kennedy's political career through the 1960 Democratic National Convention. The remaining displays cover the presidential campaign of 1960 and the highlights of the brief Kennedy administration. The campaign exhibits are most inter-

BUSING RIOTS

In the fall of 1974 and 1975, Boston newspapers featured front-page photographs of school buses full of African-American students, entering schools under police escort. Accompanying stories included students' testimony of being pelted with eggs and epithets, the unfortunate result of a city experiment in busing that failed to foresee the tensions being aroused.

The 1954 Supreme Court ruling **Brown v the Board of Education** that outlawed segregation in public schools had not taken effect in a number of Northern schools, something that the Massachusetts State Legislature's 1965 Racial Imbalance Act attempted to correct. In 1974, US District Court Judge W. Arthur Garrity, Jr. ruled that the city of Boston was not making an effort to integrate its schools and established a forced busing program, under which students from white neighborhoods would be required to go to schools in traditionally black neighborhoods and vice versa.

Two of the neighborhoods affected by this ruling were primarily Irish-American **South Boston** and predominately black Roxbury. Throughout the summer, parents from South Boston were extremely vocal in their opposition to the program, and candid in their reasons. Many expressed anger that they were being told where to send their children to school; they felt they had been singled out as a working-class neighborhood, while wealthy neighborhoods like Beacon Hill were unaffected. Many also expressed outright racism. All this came to a head on **September 12, 1974**, when Judge Garrity's ruling went into effect. The reaction in South Boston was striking: out of 1300 students enrolled at South Boston High, 124 showed up for classes. Whether this was primarily due to displeasure with the policy or fear of violence remains unclear. Less ambiguous was the reaction of the crowds outside South Boston High. Eggs and stones were thrown at black students arriving in buses; similar incidents occurred at junior high and even elementary schools. Although students were back in school within days, tensions remained high throughout the year and even years that followed. Twenty-three years later, the busing program was declared a success by the Boston Board of Education, and considered no longer necessary, having done its duty. Today students go to school in their own districts amidst debate over the wisdom to disable the program, which continues to flare tempers throughout the city.

esting for their television and radio ads, which illustrate the squeaky-clean self-image America possessed at that time. The section on the Kennedy administration is more serious, highlighted by a 22-minute film on the Cuban Missile Crisis that well evokes the tension of the event, if exaggerating Kennedy's heroics. The final section of the museum is perhaps its best: a roomy glass-enclosed space overlooking the harbor, with modest inscriptions bearing some of Kennedy's more memorable quotations – affecting enough to move even the most jaded JFK critic. Oddly enough, the museum is also the repository for Ernest Hemingway's original manuscripts. Call for an appointment to see them (☎929-4523).

Dorchester Heights Monument

Back at the convergence of South Boston and Dorchester rises the incline of **Dorchester Heights**, whose northernmost point, Thomas Park, is crowned by a stone obelisk **monument** commemorating George Washington's bloodless purge of the Brits from Boston. After the Continental Army had held the British under siege in the city for just over a year, Washington wanted to put an end to the whole thing. On March 4, 1776, he amassed all the artillery he could get his hands on and placed it on the towering peak of Dorchester Heights, so the tired Redcoats could get a good look at the patriots' firepower. Intimidated, they swiftly left Boston – for good. The park is generally empty, pristinely kept, and still commands the same sweeping views of Boston and its southern communities that it did during the Revolutionary War. Unfortunately, the monument is permanently closed to the public, and it's all quite a bit out of the way from any other major points of interest.

Franklin Park

Roxbury's **Franklin Park Zoo**, 1 Franklin Park Rd in Franklin Park (Apr–Oct Mon–Fri 10am–5pm, Sat–Sun until 6pm; Nov–March daily 10am–4pm; $6; Forest Hills ⓣ), the southernmost link in the Emerald Necklace, has little besides its backdrop to distinguish it from any other zoo, and is perhaps only an essential stop if you're traveling with kids. It does boast the African Tropical Forest, an impressively re-created savanna that's the largest indoor open-space zoo design in North America, and houses gorillas, monkeys, and pygmy hippos, and Bird's World, a charming relic from the days of Edwardian zoo design: a huge, ornate wrought-iron cage you can walk through while birds fly overhead.

Franklin Park itself was one of Olmsted's proudest accomplishments when it was completed, due to the sheer size of the place, and its scale is indeed astounding – 527 acres of green space, with countless trails for hikers, bikers, and walkers leading through the hills and thickly forested areas. That's about all that's still particularly impressive, as much of the park is overgrown from years of half-hearted upkeep and it borders some of Boston's more dangerous areas.

Arnold Arboretum

Jamaica Plain area has one real draw – actually the only must-see sight in all the Southern Districts – the 265-acre **Arnold Arboretum**, at 125 Arborway (daily dawn–dusk; $1 donation requested; Forest Hills ⓣ), the most spectacular link in the Emerald Necklace. Its collection of trees, vines, shrubs, and flowers has benefited from more than one hundred years of both careful grooming and ample funding, and is now one of the finest in North America. The plants are arranged along a series of paths populated by runners and dog-walkers as well as serious botanists, though it certainly doesn't require any expert knowledge to enjoy the grounds. The array of Asian species – the best in the world outside Asia – is highlighted by the **Larz Anderson Bonsai Collection** and is brilliantly concentrated along the Chinese Path, a walkway near the center of the park. Best to visit during spring, when crabapples, lilacs, and magnolias complement the greenery with dazzling chromatic schemes. "**Lilac Sunday**," the third Sunday in May, sees the Arboretum at its most vibrant (and busiest), when its collection of lilacs – the second largest in the US – is in full bloom.

Cambridge

A walk down most any street in **CAMBRIDGE** – just across the Charles River from Boston, but a world apart in atmosphere and attitude – takes you past plaques and monuments honoring literati and revolutionaries who lived and worked in the area as early as the seventeenth century. But along its colonial-period brick sidewalks and narrow, crooked roads, Cambridge vibrates with a vital

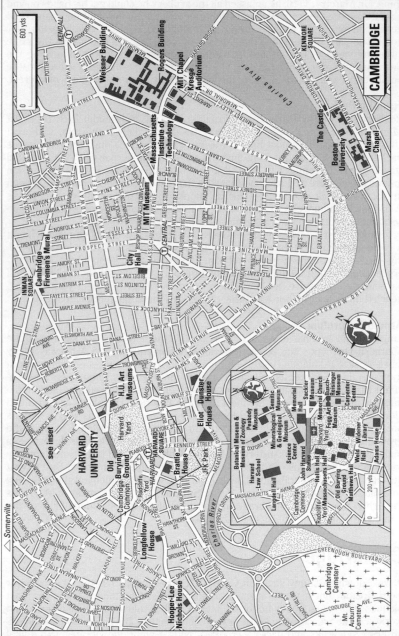

CAMBRIDGE

600 yds

0

KENDALL

Weisner Building

Rogers Building

MIT Chapel

Kresge Auditorium

Massachusetts Institute of Technology

MEMORIAL DRIVE

BROADWAY

BINNEY STREET

MAIN STREET

POTTER ST.

PORTLAND ST.

CARDINAL MEDEIROS AVE

BINNEY ST.

WINDSOR

HAMPSHIRE STREET

UNION STREET

COLUMBIA STREET

LINCOLN ST.

ELM STREET

NORFOLK ST.

TREMONT

PROSPECT STREET

BROADWAY

HARVARD STREET

CHERRY ST.

PINE STREET

HANCOCK ST.

INMAN SQUARE

Cambridge Firemen's Mural

City Hall

AMORY ST.

INMAN ST.

ANTRIM ST.

FAYETTE STREET

MAPLE AVENUE

WEST STREET

CLINTON ST.

LEE STREET

BIGELOW ST.

HARVARD STREET

MASSACHUSETTS AVENUE

MIT Museum

WORCESTER ST.

SUFFOLK ST.

ESSEX ST.

BISHOP RICHARD ALLEN DRIVE

BLANCHE

PACIFIC STREET

LANSDOWNE ST.

WAVERLY STREET

SIDNEY STREET

BROOKLINE STREET

FRANKLIN STREET

WINDSOR

ALBANY STREET

VASSAR STREET

AMHERST STREET

Charles River

HARVARD BRIDGE

MIT Chapel

Kresge Auditorium

MEMORIAL DR

AMHERST ALLEY

The Castle

Boston University

Marsh Chapel

BAY STATE ROAD

COMMONWEALTH AVENUE

MASSACHUSETTS TURNPIKE EXTENSION

KENMORE SQUARE

MEMORIAL DRIVE

CENTRAL

AUBURN STREET

WILLIAM ST.

COTTAGE ST.

PUTNAM AVENUE

RIVER STREET

GREEN STREET

FRANKLIN STREET

PEARL STREET

MAGAZINE STREET

CHESTNUT ST.

GRANITE ST.

TUFTS ST.

ALLSTON STREET

HAMILTON STREET

PRINCE STREET

PLEASANT STREET

FAIRMONT ST.

PUTNAM AVENUE

B.U. BRIDGE

STORROW DRIVE

CAMBRIDGE STREET

LEONARD AVE.

DANA ST.

ELLSWORTH AVE.

ELLERY STREET

HOVEY AVE.

ROBERTS RD.

TROWBRIDGE

LINE STREET

H.U. Art Museums

Harvard Yard

QUINCY ST.

SUMNER RD.

FRANCIS AVE.

Eliot House

Dunster House

HARVARD UNIVERSITY

Old Cambridge Common Burying Ground

HARVARD YARD

HARVARD SQUARE

Brattle House

Peabody

J.F. KENNEDY STREET

JFK Park

DIVINITY AVE.

OXFORD STREET

see inset

Radcliffe Yard

Longfellow House

BRATTLE STREET

Hooper-Lee Nichols House

MASSACHUSETTS AVENUE

Somerville

GREENOUGH BOULEVARD

Mt. Auburn Cemetery

Cambridge Cemetery

COOLIDGE

Charles River

MEMORIAL DRIVE

STORROW DRIVE

200 yds

0

Botanical Museum & Museum of Zoology

Mineralogical & Geological Museum

Semitic Museum

Peabody Museum

Sackler Museum

Busch-Reisinger Museum

Carpenter Center

Memorial Hall

Harvard Memorial Church

Fogg Arts Museum

Science Center

Harvard Law School

Harvard Yard

John Harvard Statue

Hollis Hall

Massachusetts Hall

Weld Hall

Matthews Hall

Old Burying Ground

Widener Library

Adams House

Cambridge Common

Radcliffe Yard

Langdell Hall

OXFORD ST.

MASSACHUSETTS AVE.

QUINCY ST.

A BRIEF HISTORY OF CAMBRIDGE

Cambridge began inauspiciously in 1630, when a group of English immigrants from Charlestown founded **New Towne** village on the narrow, swampy banks of the Charles River. These Puritans hoped New Towne would become an ideal religious community; to that end, they founded a college in 1636 for the purpose of training clergy. Two years later, the college took its name in honor of a local minister, **John Harvard**, who bequeathed his library and half his estate to the nascent institution. New Towne was eventually renamed Cambridge for the English university where many of its figureheads were educated, and became an enormous publishing center after the importation of the printing press in the seventeenth century. Its printing industry and university established Cambridge as a bastion of intellectual activity and political thought. This status became entrenched over the course of the United States' turbulent early history, particularly during the late eighteenth century, when the Cambridge population grew sharply divided between the numerous artisans and farmers who sympathized with the Revolution and the minority of moneyed Tories. When fighting began, the Tories were driven from their mansions on modern-day Brattle Street (then called "Tory Row"), their place taken by Cambridge intelligentsia and prominent Revolutionaries.

In 1846, the Massachusetts Legislature granted a city charter linking Old Cambridge (the Harvard Square area) and industrial East Cambridge as a single municipality. Initially, there was friction between these two very different sections; in 1855, citizens from each area unsuccessfully petitioned for the regions to be granted separate civic status. Though relations improved, the distinctive characters remain. A large immigrant population was drawn to opportunity in the industrial and commercial sectors of East Cambridge, while academics increasingly sought out Harvard, whose reputation had continued to swell, and the Massachusetts Institute of Technology, which moved here from Boston in 1916. The district's political leanings are less liberal today than in the 1960s, when Cambridge earned the name "Moscow on the Charles" due to its unabashedly Red character, but the fact that nearly half of its 93,000 residents are university affiliates insures that it will remain one of America's most opinionated cities.

present: starched businesspeople bustle past disaffected punks; clean-cut college students coexist right beside a growing homeless population; and busloads of tourists look on as street people purvey goods and perform music. In fact, many residents tend to forget the world beyond the Charles River, and the Puritan parochialism of its founders has turned into a different breed of exclusivity, touched with civic and intellectual elitism. Still, there's plenty here to make this an essential stopover on your trip.

The city is loosely organized around a series of squares – confluences of streets that are the focus of each area's commercial activity. By far the most important of these is **Harvard Square**, center of the eponymous university, and the top draw for Cambridge's visitors. The area around it is home to the city's main sights, particularly the stretch of Colonial mansions in **Old Cambridge**. The squares of **Central** and **East Cambridge** are more down-to-earth. Blue-collar **Central Square** is less touristy but no less urban than its collegiate counterpart: here you can eat at *McDonald's* (a rarity in Cambridge), and enjoy the city's best blues bars and rock music shows. Farther east along the Charles is **Kendall Square**, home to a cluster of technology companies and also the beginning of East Cambridge, a mostly Hispanic working-class district. The only part of this area that really warrants a visit is the **Massachusetts Institute of Technology** (MIT), one of the world's premier science and research institutions and home to some peculiar architecture and an excellent museum.

Harvard Square and the University

Harvard Square radiates out from the Ⓣ stop along Massachusetts Avenue, JFK Street and Brattle Street. When you exit the station, take a pass through the adjacent sunken area known as **The Pit,** a triage center for fashion victims of alternative culture. Disgruntled teens spend entire days sitting here admiring each other's green hair and body piercings while the homeless (and some of the teens) hustle for change and sell the *Spare Change*, the newspaper of the Boston homeless comunity. This is also the focal point of the **street music scene**, where folk diva Tracy Chapman (a graduate from nearby Tufts University, in Somerville) got her start. It's at its most frenetic and fascinating on Friday and Saturday nights and Sunday afternoons, when all the elements converge – crowds mill about; evangelical demonstrators engage in shouting matches with angry youths; and magicians, acrobats and bands perform on every corner.

North of Harvard Square along Massachusetts Avenue lies one of Cambridge's first cemeteries, the **Old Burying-Ground**, whose style and grounds have scarcely changed since the seventeenth century. The stone grave markers are adorned in a style somewhere between Puritan austerity and medieval superstition: inscriptions praise the simple piety of the staunchly Christian deceased, but are surrounded by death's-heads carved to ward off evil spirits. You're supposed to apply to the sexton of Christ Church for entry, but if the gate at the path behind the church is open (as it frequently is), you can enter – just be respectful of the grounds.

A triangular wedge of concrete squeezed into the intersection of Massachusetts Avenue and Garden Street, **Dawes Park** is named for the patriot who rode to alert residents that the British were marching on Lexington and Concord on April 19, 1775 – the *other* one that is, William Dawes. While Longfellow opted to commemorate Paul Revere's midnight ride instead, as have all history classes, the citizens of Cambridge and other areas north of Boston must have appreciated poor Dawes' contribution just as much. Bronze hoofmarks in the sidewalk mark the event, and several placards behind the pathway provide information on the history of the Harvard Square/Old Cambridge area.

Cambridge Common

In **Cambridge Common**, a roughly square patch of green space between Massachusetts Avenue, Garden Street and Waterhouse Street, you can retrace the old **Charlestown–Watertown path**, along which Redcoats beat a sheepish retreat during the Revolutionary War, and which still transects the park from east to west. The most prominent feature on the Common is, however, the revered **Washington Elm**, under which it's claimed George Washington took command of the Continental Army. The elm, at the southern side of the park near the intersection of Garden Street and Appian Way, is accompanied by a predictable wealth of commemorative objects: a cannon captured from the British when they evacuated Boston, a statue of Washington, and monuments to two Polish army captains hired to lead Revolutionary forces. What the memorials don't tell you is that the city of Cambridge cut down the original elm in 1946 when it began to obstruct traffic; it stood at the Common's southwest corner, near the intersection of Mason and Garden streets. The present tree is only the offspring of that tree, raised from one of its branches. To further confuse the issue, the Daughters of the American Revolution erected a monument commemorating the south*east* corner of the park as the spot where Washington did his historic thing. And recently, historians have suggested that Washington never commissioned the troops on the Common at all, but rather in Wadsworth House at Harvard Yard.

JFK Street and the Harvard Houses

The stretch of JFK Street below Harvard Square holds more of the city's many public spaces, certainly the least of which is **Winthrop Square**, site of the original New Towne marketplace and since converted into a bedraggled park. **John F. Kennedy Park**, where JFK Street meets Memorial Drive, was only finished in the late 1980s, making it an infant among Harvard Square's venerable spaces, though certainly not the first pious shrine to the university's favorite modern son. The **memorial** to Kennedy in its center is unusual and worth a look – a low granite pyramid surrounded by a moat, covered constantly but imperceptibly by a thin film of flowing water.

Harvard's fancy upperclassmen's residences, most of which are nested in the area east of JFK Street and south of Harvard Yard, are a visible remnant of the university's elite past. Nearest the Yard, at 46 Plympton St, is **Adams House**, once a haven for the Harvard avant-garde, but now with a feeble counterculture. Just south of Adams juts the graceful, blue-topped bell tower of **Lowell House**, at 2 Holyoke Place, which boasts one of Harvard's most beautiful courtyards. Further west on the banks of the Charles rises the purple spire of **Eliot House**, a community that remains a bastion of social privilege despite Harvard's attempts to shed this image. To the east along Memorial Drive lies **Dunster House**, whose red Georgian top is a favorite subject of Cambridge's tourist brochures. Alongside Adams, it has long been considered a center for radical culture, though its character is not wilting so rapidly – Dunster's riverside courtyard was once rated by *Spy* magazine as one of the top ten places in the country to have sex.

Harvard Yard

The transition between Harvard Square and **Harvard Yard** is brief and dramatic: in a matter of only several feet, the noise and crowds give way to grassy spaces and towering oaks. Its narrow, haphazard footpaths are constantly trafficked by preoccupied students and camera-clicking tour groups. The Yard is where Harvard myth and reality converge – the grandeur of Ivy League aura besieged by the visitor traffic of an amusement park.

The most common entrance is the one directly across from Harvard Square proper, which leads to the **Old Yard,** a large, rectangular area enclosed by freshman dormitories that has been around since 1636. In front of stark, symmetrical, slate-gray University Hall is the Yard's trademark icon, the **John Harvard statue**, around which chipper student guides inform tour groups of the oft-told story of the statue's three lies (it misdates the college's founding; erroneously identifies John Harvard as the college's founder; and isn't really a likeness of John Harvard at all). While it's a popular spot for visitors to take pictures, male students at the college covet the statue as a site of public urination; it's a badge of honor around here – as a result, there are about twenty surveillance cameras trained on the statue.

The architectural contrast between modest **Hollis Hall**, which dates from 1762, and its grandiose southern neighbor, **Matthews Hall**, built around a hundred years later, mirrors Harvard's transition from a quiet training ground for ministers to a wealthy, cosmopolitan university. The **indentations** in Hollis' front steps also hold some historical interest: students used to warm their rooms by heating cannonballs; come time to leave their quarters for the summer, they would dispose of the cannonballs by dropping them from their windows rather than having to carry them down the stairs.

To the east of the Old Yard lie the grander buildings of the **New Yard**, where a vast set of steps leads up to the enormous pillars of **Widener Library**. Named after Harvard grad and *Titanic* victim Harry Elkins Widener, whose mother paid for the project, it's the center of the largest private library collection in the US, which includes a first folio of Shakespeare and a Gutenberg Bible. At the opposite side of the New Yard is **Memorial Church**, whose narrow, white spire strikes a balancing note to the heavy pillared front of Widener.

North lies the main quad of the famed **Harvard Law School**, focusing on the stern gray pillars of **Langdell Hall**, the imposing edifice on its western border. Above Langdell's entrance is a Latin inscription encapsulating the Western ideal of the Rule of Law, tinctured with an unusual degree of religiosity: *"Non sub homine, sed sub deo et lege"* ("Not under man, but under God and law"). Inside is the renovated **Harvard Law Library**, where you can practically smell the stress in the air.

It's hard to miss the conspicuously modern **Carpenter Center** as you walk past down Quincy Street, a slab of slate-gray granite amidst Harvard's ever-present brick motif. Completed in 1963 as a center for the study of visual art at Harvard, the Carpenter Center is the only building in America designed by the French architect Le Corbusier. Be sure to traverse its trademark feature, a **walkway** that leads through the center of the building, meant to reflect the path worn by students on the lot on which the center was constructed. The basement of the building is the place for screenings of the Harvard Film Archives.

Harvard University Museums

Harvard's **museums** have benefited from years of scholarly attention and rich donors' ample gifts. Largely underappreciated and underattended by most visitors, not to mention the students themselves, the collections are easily some of the finest in New England. One ticket covers admission to all three of the art museums (Mon–Sat 10am–5pm, Sun 1–5pm; $5, free Sat morning and Wed all day); the more specialized science and history type museums also have a few engaging exhibits of note.

ART MUSEUMS

Housed on two floors which surround a lovely mock sixteenth-century Italian courtyard, the collections of the **William Hayes Fogg Art Museum**, at 32 Quincy St, showcase the highlights of Harvard's substantial collection of Western art. Much of the first floor is devoted to medieval and Renaissance material, mainly religious art with the usual complement of suffering Christs. This part of the collection is best for a series of capitals salvaged from the French cathedral of Moutiers-Saint-Jean, which combine a Romanesque predilection for classical design with medieval didactic narrative. The rest of the first floor is devoted to portraiture of the seventeenth and eighteenth centuries, though it's more notable for a fine display of lesser-known Neapolitan Baroque works, particularly the grotesque *Martyrdom of Saint Sebastian* by Battistello and Francesco Fracazano's robust *Drunken Silenus*. The remainder is rather stale, though Canaletto's extraordinarily precise *View of the Piazza San Marco* is not to be missed. The second floor includes several spaces for rotating exhibits, while its permanent holdings are strongest in Impressionism and modernism, especially the French contingent of Degas, Monet, Manet, Pissarro and Cezanne. But what distinguishes this upper floor is its focus on American counterparts to these largely European trends in art during the late nineteenth and early twentieth century. There is a range of fine John Singer Sargent portraits and a pair of Whistler's moody *Nocturnes*, though the standout is Sheeler's *Upper Deck*, a representation of technology that manages to combine realism and abstraction.

Secreted away at the rear of the Fogg's second floor is the entrance to Werner Otto Hall, home of the **Busch-Reisinger Museum**, concentrating exclusively on the German Expressionists and the work of the Bauhaus. The gallery starts off with *fin de siècle* art, including Klimt's *Rue de Rivoli* and *Pear Tree*, a pair of meditations on built and natural environments. The Bauhaus standouts are Moholy-Nagy's sculpture-machine *Light-Space Modulator* and Feininger's angular *Bird Cloud*. But the gallery's highlight is its Expressionist portraiture, which includes Kirchner's sardonic *Self-Portrait with a Cat* and Beckmann's nauseated *Self-Portrait in a Tuxedo*.

Right out of the Fogg and dead ahead is the five-floor Arthur M. Sackler Building, 485 Broadway, the first, second and fourth floors of which comprise the **Sackler Museum**, dedicated to the art of classical, Asian and Islamic cultures. The museum's holdings far outstrip its available space, which is why the first floor is devoted to rotating exhibits. Islamic and Asian art are the themes of the second floor, featuring illustrations from Muslim texts and Chinese landscapes from the past several centuries. The fourth floor is best for its excellent array of sensuous Buddhist sculptures from ancient China, India and Southeast Asia.

CULTURAL AND NATURAL HISTORY MUSEUMS

North past the Sackler is Divinity Avenue, on which another series of museums begins, led by the **Harvard Semitic Museum**, at no. 6 (Mon–Fri 10am–4pm, Sun 1–4pm; free), whose informative and impeccably presented displays chronicle Harvard's century-old excavations in the Near East. For some reason, the Semitic isn't officially part of the consortium known as the Harvard Museums of Cultural and Natural History; the benefit is that admission is free.

What officially begins the Harvard Museums of Cultural and Natural History, and the most prominent in that group, is the **Peabody Museum of Archeology and Ethnology**, 11 Divinity Ave (daily 9am–5pm; $6.50 covers admission to all museums below; free Sun 9am–noon year-round, and Wed 3–5pm Sept–May), which displays materials culled from Harvard's anthropological and archeological expeditions. The strength of the museum lies in its collection of pieces from Mesoamerica, ranging from digs in the pueblos of the southwestern United States to artifacts from Incan civilizations, though the wax dummies in traditional garb and the miniature dioramas can't help but seem hokey and out of place. Harvard's **Mineralogical and Geological Museum** (part of the Peabody), another of the University's very specialized museums, is, basically, a bunch of rocks. If you don't know much about geology, this probably won't do too much for you, though most of the gems are aesthetically pleasing. Right next door (you can pass through from one to the other without exiting the building), and similarly narrow in scope, is the **Botanical Museum** (also part of the Peabody) at 26 Oxford St. You might think this collection is only of interest to botanists, and much of it may well be, but it's still worth a pass to take in the stunning Ware Collection of Glass Models of Plants. This project began in 1887 and terminated almost fifty years later in 1936, leaving the museum with an absolutely unique and visually awesome collection of flower models constructed to the last detail, entirely from glass. Only seeing the display can do it justice. Housed in the same building as the Botanical Museum, but lacking a similar knockout centerpiece, the **Museum of Comparative Zoology** is really just the tip of the iceberg of the university's collection of zoological materials, most of which is inaccessible to visitors.

Old Cambridge

After the outbreak of the American Revolution, Cambridge's bourgeois majority ran the Tories out of town, leaving their sumptuous houses to be used as the quarters of the Continental Army. What was then called Tory Row is modern-day **Brattle Street**, the main drag of the **Old Cambridge** district. The area has remained a tree-lined neighborhood of stately mansions, although only two of the houses are open to the public; the rest you'll have to view from across their expansive, impeccably kept lawns.

Just off Harvard Square is the **Brattle House**, at 42 Brattle St, which fails to reflect the unabashedly extravagant lifestyle of its former resident, William Brattle. It doesn't appear nearly as grand as it once did, dwarfed as it is by surrounding office buildings, nor is it open to the public – no great loss since it now only houses offices. A sign on the corner of Brattle and Story streets commemorates the site of a tree which once stood near the **Dexter Pratt House**, home of the village blacksmith celebrated by Longfellow in the popular poem *Under a Spreading Chesnut Tree*. These days the house holds the *Blacksmith House* bakery, producers of some of the finest scones around – which may be the most exciting thing about the place.

Longfellow House

One house you can usually visit – though closed throughout 2001 – is the **Vassal-Craigie-Longfellow House**, 105 Brattle St (Wed–Sat 10am–4.30pm, tours every hour; $2), the best-known and most popular of the Brattle Street mansions, where the poet Henry Wadsworth Longfellow lived while serving as a professor at Harvard. It was erected for Royalist John Vassal in 1759, who promptly vacated it on the eve of the Revolutionary War. During the war, it was used by George Washington as his headquarters during the siege of Boston, and it wasn't until 1843 that it became home to Longfellow, who moved in as a boarder; when he married the wealthy Fanny Appleton, her father purchased the house for them as a wedding gift. Longfellow lived here until his death in 1882, and the house is preserved in an attempt to portray it as it was during his residence. The halls and walls are festooned with Longfellow's furniture and art collection: most surprising is the wealth of nineteenth-century pieces from the Far East, amassed by Longfellow's renegade son Charlie on his world travels.

Hooper-Lee-Nichols House

The second of the Brattle Street mansions open to the public, half a mile west of the Longfellow House and well worth the trip if you've got the stamina, is the **Hooper-Lee-Nichols House**, at no. 159 (Tues & Thurs 2–5pm; $5), one of the oldest residences in Cambridge and the best example of the character of life and style of housing design during Cambridge's colonial period. The house began as a stout, post-medieval farmhouse, and underwent various renovations until it became the Georgian mansion it is today. Knowledgeable tour guides open secret panels to reveal centuries-old wallpaper and original foundations; otherwise, you'll see rooms predictably restored with period writing tables, canopy beds, and rag dolls.

At the terminus of Brattle Street is the **Mount Auburn Cemetery**, an unexpected treasure. Laid out in 1831 as America's first "garden cemetery," its 170 acres of stunningly landscaped grounds, with ponds and fountains, provide a gorgeous contrast with the many spare "burying grounds" scattered all over Cambridge and Boston. Resting here are a medley of luminaries such as the painter Winslow Homer, Christian Science founder Mary Baker Eddy and many other notables. Pick up a map at the visitors' center at the entrance to find out who's where and get a sense of its scope by ascending the **tower** that lies smack in its center – from here, you can see not only the entire grounds but all the way to downtown Boston.

Central and East Cambridge

Working-class **Central Cambridge** lacks any semblance of pretension – not to mention any semblance of a reason to visit – unlike its stuffy academic neighbor. **Central Square**, as you might expect, is located roughly in the geographical center of Cambridge, and is appropriately the city's civic center as well, home to its most important government buildings. There's nothing as such to see, but it's a good place to shop and eat, and is home to some of the best nightlife in Cambridge.

Overshadowed by Cambridge's busier districts, **Inman Square** marks a quiet stretch directly north of Central Square, centered around the confluence of Cambridge, Beacon, and Prospect streets. There's little of interest here either, just a pleasant, mostly residential neighborhood where much of Cambridge's Portuguese-speaking population resides. What does make Inman worth a visit, along with its ethnic markets, is its broad range of excellent restaurants, where you can enjoy some of Cambridge's finest food without breaking the bank. If you're in the area, check out Inman's lone landmark, the charmingly inexpert **Cambridge Firemen's Mural**, at the corner of Cambridge and Antrim streets, a work of public art commissioned to honor local men in red.

Massachusetts Institute of Technology

East Cambridge is mostly taken over by the **Massachusetts Institute of Technology** (MIT), which occupies 153.8 acres alongside the Charles and provides an intellectual counterweight to the otherwise working-class character of the area. Originally established in Allston in 1865, MIT moved to this more auspicious campus across the river in 1916 and has since risen to international prominence as a major center for theoretical and practical research in the sciences.

The campus buildings and geography reflect the quirky, nerdy character of the institute, emphasizing function and peppering it with a peculiar notion of form. Everything is obsessively numbered and coded: you can go to E15 (the Weisner Building) for a lecture in 4.103 (advanced computer-assisted design), which, of course, gets you no closer towards a degree in 17 (political science). Behind the massive pillars that guard the entrance of the **Rogers Building**, at 77 Massachusetts Ave, you'll find a labyrinth of corridors through which students can traverse the entire east campus without ever going outside – known to Techies as the **Infinite Corridor**. Atop the Rogers Building is MIT's best-known architectural icon, a massive gilt hemisphere called the **Great Dome**. Just inside the entrance to Rogers, you'll find the **MIT Information Center** (Mon–Fri 9am–5pm).

MIT has drawn the attention of some of the major architects of the twentieth century, who have used the university's progressiveness as a testing ground for some of their more experimental works. Two of these are located in the courtyard across Massachusetts Avenue from the Rogers Building. The **Kresge Auditorium,** designed by Finnish architect Eero Saarinen, resembles a large tent, though its real claim to fame is that it puzzlingly rests on three, rather than four, corners. In the same courtyard is the **MIT Chapel,** also the work of Saarinen. Shaped like a stocky cylinder and topped with abstract sculpture crafted from paper-thin metals, it's undoubtedly the city's least traditional religious space. The I.M. Pei-designed Weisner Building is home to the **List Visual Art Center** (Tues–Sun noon–6pm; free), which displays student works, often more technologically impressive than visually appealing. Of perhaps more interest, down Massachusetts Avenue at no. 265, the **MIT Museum** (Tues–Fri 10am–5pm, Sat–Sun noon–5pm; $5, students and seniors $1) has two main permanent displays, the Hologram Museum and the Hall of Hacks, the latter of which provides a retrospective on the various pranks ("hacks") pulled by Techies. Among other things, the madcap funsters have placed a real MIT police car atop the Great Dome.

Eating

There is no shortage of places to **eat** in Boston. The city is loaded with bars and pubs that double as restaurants, cafés that serve full meals, and plenty of higher-end dinner-only options. There's a new level of dining adventurousness these days, too, partly in response to the traditional New England-type fare that is still the area's hallmark: hearty standbys like broiled scrod, clam chowder and Yankee pot roast, all of which owe a bit of debt to the cold-winter mentality in Boston. Most of this has shown up in the explosion of restaurants, mostly in Back Bay and the South End, serving modern, eclectic food that unfortunately doesn't always quite hit the mark.

At **lunchtime**, many places offer meals at about half the cost of dinner, a plus if you want to sample some of the food at the city's pricier and more exclusive restaurants. Pubs and taverns are also a good bet, serving sandwiches and old-fashioned grub that won't let you go hungry. **Dinner**, usually from 5pm on, is a much more exciting deal, with a wide array of **restaurants** that range from Boston's own local cuisine to ethnic foods of every stripe. You'll probably want to book ahead if you're planning to show up at a popular place (say, a bistro in the South End or on Newbury) after 6pm; places are generally open until 10 or 11pm, though in Chinatown there are numerous **late-night** spots. Also, many restaurants close on Sundays and/or Mondays, so call ahead for either of those nights, too.

As far as Boston's culinary landscape goes, there are ever-popular **Italian** restaurants, both traditional Southern and more trendy Northern, that cluster in the **North End**, mainly on Hanover and Salem streets. The city's tiny **Chinatown** packs in all types of Asian fare. **Dim sum**, where you choose selections from carts wheeled past your table, is especially big here, and you can find it anytime, though mostly at lunch – the best places are always packed on weekends, with lines down the streets. Boston's trendiest restaurants, usually of the **New American** stripe, tend to cluster in **Back Bay** and the **South End**.

Cambridge eating life centers around Harvard, Inman and Central squares, and is perhaps best distinguished for its **Indian** restaurants, forever competing against each other to offer lower prices – resulting in some of the best food values in the city.

In most places, save certain areas of downtown, you won't have a problem finding somewhere to grab a **quick bite,** whether it's a diner, deli, or some other kind of snack joint. In addition to all the spots listed below, see the bars and cafes starting on p.120, many of which offer food all day long.

Downtown, Chinatown and the waterfront

The Blue Diner, 150 Kneeland St, Downtown (☎695-0087). South Station ⊤. Campy bar and restaurant with a rare feature among retro diners: good food. It's open until 4am on weekends.

Brigham's, 50 Congress St, Downtown (☎523-9372). State ⊤. The closest thing downtown has to a coffee shop, with an excellent soda fountain.

Buddha's Delight, 5 Beach St (☎451-2395). Chinatown ⊤. Strictly vegan Chinese and Vietnamese temple cuisine, but you might not know it. Wonderful dishes, from moo shi to lemongrass, effectively imitating the flavors and textures of shrimp, pork and egg.

The Chart House, 60 Long Wharf, Waterfront (☎227-1576). Aquarium ⊤. Rich food for the rich, though worth the prices if you can afford them; the lobster and swordfish are particularly good. For a less highbrow experience, try the downstairs café.

Chau Chow, 52 Beach St, Chinatown (☎426-6266). Chinatown ⊤. One of the first Chinatown restaurants to specialize in seafood, and still one of the best. Delicious salt-and-pepper shrimp and sea cucumber. The *Grand Chau Chow*, just across Beach Street, serves basically the same food at somewhat higher prices and in fancier surroundings.

Country Life, 200 High St, Downtown (☎951-2534). Aquarium ⊤. An all-vegetarian buffet, whose cheap and quick meal options vary daily; call the menu hotline (☎951-2462) to find out what's cooking.

Dakota's, 34 Summer St in the 101 Arch Street Building, Downtown (☎737-1777). Downtown Crossing or Park ⊤. The clubby feel of this expansive American grill restaurant and great food make it the perfect place to dine after visiting nearby Filene's Basement. Closed weekends.

Durgin-Park, 340 Faneuil Hall Marketplace, Downtown (☎227-2038). Government Center ⊤. A Boston landmark in operation since 1827, *Durgin-Park* has a no-frills Yankee atmosphere and a somewhat surly waitstaff. That doesn't stop folks from coming for the pricey if sizeable pot roast and roast beef dinners in the upstairs dining room.

Ginza, 16 Hudson St, Chinatown (☎338-2261). Chinatown ⊤. Open until 4am on weekends, *Ginza* is a popular after-hours spot serving perhaps the best sushi in the city. Extensive menu covers a wide variety of Japanese dishes, from tempura to *edamame*.

Il Panino Bistro, 295 Franklin St (☎338-1000). State ⊤. Moderately priced nouveau Italian gets rave reviews for its simple, delicious food. Upstairs is one of Boston's hottest discos (see p.124).

Jimbo's Fish Shanty, 245 Northern Ave, Waterfront (☎542-5600). South Station ⊤. Operated by the proprietor's of *Jimmy's*, serving basically the same food at lower prices and in a more casual atmosphere, without the picturesque views.

Jimmy's Harborside, 242 Northern Ave, Waterfront (☎423-1000). South Station ⊤. *Jimmy's* aesthetic is totally tacky, but the harbor views and seafood are beyond reproach.

Jumbo Seafood, 7 Hudson St (☎542-2823). Chinatown ⊤. Widely regarded as one of the best restaurants in Chinatown, with fresh-from-the-tank fish and exquisite vegetable dishes as well.

Legal Seafoods, 255 State St, Waterfront (☎742-5300). Aquarium ⊤. This local chain is probably the best-known seafood restaurant in America, and for many the best as well. Its trademark is freshness: the clam chowder, Boston scrod and lobster are all top quality.

Locke-Ober Café, 3 Winter Place, Downtown (☎542-1340). Park ⊤. Don't be fooled by the name: *Locke-Ober* is very much a restaurant, and one of the most blueblooded in Boston. The fare consists of things like steak tartare and oysters on the half shell, while the setting is dark, ornate, and stuffy. There's an archaic dress code, too – jacket and tie for men.

Penang, 685–681 Washington St (☎451-6372). Chinatown ⊤. Teak décor makes this classy, fun Malaysian restaurant one of the few in Chinatown that pleases the eye as well as the palate. Delicious *satay* and noodle dishes.

Pho Republique, 1415 Washington St (☎262-0005). Chinatown ⊤. This upscale Vietnamese restaurant serves fresh and flavorful dishes in a bamboo-laden setting.

Salty Dog, Faneuil Hall Marketplace, Downtown (☎742-2094). Government Center ⊤. It's worth braving the long waits at the *Salty Dog* for the fresh seafood, such as raw oysters and clams, and a generous lobster dinner, all best in the outdoor dining area.

Seasons, Faneuil Hall Marketplace, in the *Regal Bostonian Hotel*, Downtown (☎523-3600). State ⊤. Inventive, truly excellent Modern American fare, such as stone crab with smoked corn minestrone, atop a luxurious hotel.

Sel de la Terre, 255 State St, Waterfront (☎720-1300). Aquarium ⊤. Consistently good Provencal bistro, popular with the business-lunch crowd. Everything is *prix fixe* (entrees at $21, appetizers $8, desserts $7), and well worth the cost.

Taiwan Café, 34 Oxford St (☎426-8181). Chinatown ⊤. Definitely not your standard Chinese restaurant, the specialty here is Taiwanese home-style cooking like sautéed eggplant with basil and steamed flounder. Staff are very friendly and helpful.

Union Oyster House, 41 Union St, Downtown (☎227-2750). Government Center or State ⊤. The oldest continuously serving restaurant in America has two big claims to fame: French King Louis-Philippe lived over the tavern during his youth and, perhaps apocryphally, the toothpick was first used here. The food is good too.

North End and Charlestown

Assaggio, 29 Prince St, North End (☎227-7380). Haymarket ⊤. An extensive wine list allows *Assaggio* to stand on its own as a wine bar, but it's reliable for classic Italian fare with contemporary touches, too.

Commonwealth Fish & Beer Co., 138 Portland St (☎523-8383). North Station ⊤. Boston's original brewpub has graduated from pub grub to become quite a good seafood restaurant. Good chowders and grilled selections, and the beer is still fantastic.

Ernesto's, 69 Salem St, North End (☎523-1373). Haymarket ⊤. Their cheap, oversized slices of thin-crust pizza can't be beat for a quick lunch.

Figs, 67 Main St, Charlestown (☎242-2229). Bunker Hill Community College ⊤. This noisy, popular offshoot of *Olives* (see below) has excellent thin-crust pizzas, topped with such savory items as figs and prosciutto or caramelized onions and arugula.

Gabriele's, 1 First Ave in the Charlestown Navy Yard (☎242-4040). Charles ⊤. Upscale Italian with the usual suspects – bruschetta, spinach ravioli, chicken parmigiana – but with unusually good execution. Dine on the terrace to catch the breeze on a hot summer's day.

Galleria Umberto, 289 Hanover St, North End (☎227-5709). Haymarket ⊤. When a place is open only from 11am to 2pm daily and there is a line out the door, you know something good is cooking. Here, it's pizza, cut in squares, that's cheap, greasy and delicious.

Giacomo's, 355 Hanover St, North End (☎523-9026). Haymarket ⊤. Among the handful of truly great restaurants in Boston, this small eatery, with its menu written on a chalkboard attached to a brick wall, serves fresh and flavorful seafood and pasta specialties.

Grand Canal, 57 Canal St, West End (☎523-1112). North Station ⊤. Atmospheric Irish pub and restaurant with nineteenth-century accoutrements, such as the linen tablecloths and a great mahogany bar with a mirror behind. Cheap, relatively inexpensive lobster dinners.

Il Panino, 11 Parmenter St (☎720-1336). Haymarket ⊤. Seafood, chicken, pasta and risotto, everything done well. This, plus reasonable prices, make it a local favorite.

La Famiglia Giorgio's, 112 Salem St (☎367-6711). Haymarket ⊤. Family-style Italian in a no-frills environment. No surprises here, but the prices and portion sizes are the best around.

Mama Maria, 3 North Square, North End (☎523-0077). Haymarket ⊤. A favorite special-occasion restaurant serving Northern Italian fare of consistently impeccable quality. Dinner only.

Monica's, 143 Richmond St, North End (☎227-0311). Haymarket ⊤. Some of the most intensely flavored Italian fare around, prepared and served by Monica's daughter and three sons, one of whom drew the cartoon art plastered over the walls. The family also runs an excellent pizza place at 67 Prince St, and Monica herself has a gourmet shop around the corner at 130 Salem St (see p.131).

Olives, 10 City Square, Charlestown (☎242-1999). North Station ⊤. *Olives* is consistently rated Boston's best restaurant, and it's hard to argue. Chef Todd English turns out New Mediterranean food of unforgettable flavor and sizeable portions, the cause of long lines if you show up after 6pm – and there are no reservations save for parties of six or more. Closed Sun and Mon.

Pizzeria Regina, 11 Thacher St, North End (☎227-0765). Haymarket ⊤. Tasty pizza, served in a neighborhood feed station where the wooden booths haven't budged since the 1940s. Vintage North End.

Sage, 69 Prince St (☎248-8814). Haymarket ⊤. One of the more expensive restaurants in the North End, and one of the best. Inventive, elegant food in an intimate setting.

Sorelle Bakery and Café, 1 Monument Ave, Charlestown (☎242-2125) North Station ⊤. Phenomenal muffins and cookies, plus pasta salads and other lunch fare, to be enjoyed on a delightful hidden patio.

Beacon Hill

Buzzy's Fabulous Roast Beef, 327 Cambridge St (☎242-7722). Charles ⊤. The lunch and after-hours crowds gather here for, what else, the roast beef sandwich, which really does live up to the hype. Open 24 hours.

Figs, 42 Charles St (☎742-3447). Charles ⊤. Smaller branch of the popular, groundbreaking Charlestown gourmet pizza place.

Istanbul Café, 37 Bowdoin St (☎227-3434). Charles ⊤. Basement café on a backstreet, serving excellent Turkish fare like kebabs and stuffed eggplant.

The King and I, 145 Charles St (☎227-3320). Charles ⊤. Named after a movie the Thais hate, but serving excellent soups and curries in a neighborhood that doesn't have much ethnic diversity.

Paramount, 44 Charles St, Beacon Hill (☎720-1152). Charles ⊤. The Hill's neighborhood diner serves Belgian waffles and frittatas to the brunch crowd by day, decent American standards like hamburgers and meatloaf by night.

Rebecca's, 21 Charles St, Beacon Hill (☎742-9747). Charles ⊤. This place brought New American to the area when it was still new. The nouvelle cuisine is still good, if seemingly more tame these days.

Ristorante Toscano, 41 Charles St, Beacon Hill (☎723-4090). Charles ⊤. Traditional Southern Italian food, made with classic flair and fresh ingredients.

Back Bay

Ambrosia, 116 Huntington Ave (☎247-2400). Prudential or Copley ⊤. When you get the craving for a Peruvian Purple Potato Springroll or Grilled Pulled Pig Sandwich with Indonesian BBQ Sauce Oil, this is your place. Presentation sometimes outclasses taste, though.

Anago, 65 Exeter St in the *Lenox Hotel* (☎266-6222). Copley ⊤. Hearty food like spit-roasted pork and rotisserie chicken prepared with thoughtful, not overblown, New American accents; lovely desserts, too.

Back Bay Brewing Company, 755 Boylston St (☎424-8300). Copley ⊤. Of all the brewpubs in Boston, this feels the least like a glorified bar: inventive lunch and dinner offerings.

Bangkok Blue, 651 Boylston St (☎266-1010). Copley ⊤. First-rate Thai restaurant, one of the best in town, definitely the best in the area.

Biba, 272 Boylston St (☎426-7878). Arlington ⊤. Culinary eclecticism hits absurd heights at this trendy, expensive spot; the food is description-resistant, and there's a category on the menu called "Offal"; draw your own conclusions.

Blue Cat Cafe, 94 Massachusetts Ave (☎247-9922). Hynes ⊤. This cavernous restaurant/bar has an Asian-influenced grazing menu and dark paneling designed to attract Boston's beautiful people, which to a certain extent it does.

Bombay Cafe, 175 Massachusetts Ave (☎247-0555). Hynes ⊤. Try chicken *tikka* with stuffed nan for a twist on classic Indian, although everything is done well at this casual Indian restaurant.

Cafe Budapest, 90 Exeter St in the *Copley Square Hotel* (☎266-1979). Copley ⊤. Some call it the most romantic restaurant in Boston, but elegance and inadvertent camp (like live piano-and-violin renditions of *Hello, Dolly*) are what this gaily-hued basement-level fixture does best. That and iced tart cherry soup followed by chicken paprika.

Café Jaffa, 48 Gloucester St (☎536-0230). Hynes ⊤. Boston's best falafel and other Middle Eastern staples are served in this cool, inviting space with polished-wood floors. ·

Café Marliave, 31 Broomfield St (☎423-6340). Park ⊤. Go for the first-rate ravioli and unmistakably Bostonian ambience, as it's located behind the *Omni Parker House Hotel* and next to the Province House Steps – the remains of the seventeenth-century British Government House.

Cottonwood Restaurant & Café, 222 Berkeley St (☎247-2225). Arlington ⊤. Creative, tasty Southwestern fare served in a bright setting on the ground floor of the 22-story Houghton Mifflin Building.

Gyuhama, 827 Boylston St (☎437-0188). Hynes ⊤. A very noisy basement-level sushi bar, favored by many college students for late-night Japanese snacks.

Jacob Wirth, 31 Stuart St (☎338-8586). Arlington ⊤. A German-themed Boston landmark, around since 1868; even if you don't like bratwurst washed down with a hearty lager, something is sure to please. This is a Boston must.

Kashmir, 279 Newbury St (☎536-1695). Copley ⊤. The food and decor are equally inviting at Newbury Street's only Indian restaurant. Sound bets include shrimp samosas, tandoori rack of lamb and vegetarian curries.

Kaya, 581 Boylston St (☎236-5858). Copley ⊤. This is the place to go when the craving for Japanese/Korean food kicks in; try the teriyaki salmon or steaming *shabu shabu*.

Kebab-N-Kurry, 30 Massachusetts Ave (☎536-9835). Hynes ⊤. Don't let the name put you off – this may be the best Indian restaurant in Boston. The wonderful *thali* plates are an excellent deal and while it's a little off the main drag, it is well worth seeking out.

Legal Seafoods, 26 Park Plaza (☎426-4444). Arlington ⊤. 100 Huntington Ave, Level Two Copley Place, Back Bay (☎266-7775). Copley ⊤. 800 Boylston St, Prudential Center, Back Bay (☎266-6800). Prudential ⊤. This local chain is probably the best-known seafood restaurant in America, and for many the best as well. Its trademark is freshness: the clam chowder, Boston scrod and lobster are all top quality.

Skipjack's, 500 Boylston St (☎536-3500). Arlington ⊤. A cool, South Beach-style decor and bold menu distinguish this seafood spot: you're as likely to find fresh mahimahi dipped in lemon and soy as fried scrod with tartar sauce.

Steve's Greek-American Cuisine, 316 Newbury St (☎267-1817). Hynes ⊤. Excellent Greek food makes this one of Boston's classic cheap eats. Steve's Greek salad is a favorite among the Newberry Street lunch crowd, and the grilled chicken sandwich could convert a vegetarian.

Tapeo, 266 Newbury St (☎267-4799). Hynes ⊤. Noisy tapas bar, with an excellent selection of Spanish wines and great food.

Thai Basil, 132 Newbury St (☎424-8424). Copley ⊤. Excellent seafood and vegetarian dishes, great *pad thai* and a cool, soothing decor in which to enjoy it all.

Top of the Hub, 800 Boylston St (☎536-1775). Prudential or Copley ⓣ. There are several benefits of dining atop the 50th floor of the Prudential Tower, not the least of which is enjoying the excellent city views. The New England food is worthwhile, too.

Turner Fisheries, 10 Huntington Ave (☎424-7425). Prudential or Copley ⓣ. The traditional New England seafood at this cheerful spot – from scrod and Boston clam chowder to lobster bisque – is as good as any in the city. Most nights feature live jazz, too.

South End

Addis Red Sea, 544 Tremont St (☎426-8727). Back Bay ⓣ. Ethiopian restaurant with wonderful spicy stews served on spongy sourdough pancakes. Meals are served on hand-woven tables which you eat off of with your fingers.

Anchovies, 433 Columbus Ave (☎266-5088). Back Bay ⓣ. Great local pizza place, with calzones and pasta to boot. Very popular, always crowded.

Claremont Café, 535 Columbus Ave (☎247-9001). Back Bay ⓣ. Very South End, very fresh, very good café food, soups, salads, entrees and desserts. Popular weekend brunch.

The Dish, 253 Shawmut Ave (☎426-7866). Back Bay ⓣ. Excellent, reasonable neighborhood bistro, with interesting entrees like Cajun meatloaf and pork medallions with baked apple.

Franklin Café, 278 Shawmut Ave (☎350-0010). Back Bay ⓣ. This upmarket diner has earned local fame for its tasty renditions of Yankee comfort food.

Grillfish, 162 Columbus Ave (☎357-1620). Back Bay ⓣ. No points for guessing the specialty here. Informal atmosphere and excellent seafood, of all species.

Hamersley's Bistro, 553 Tremont St (☎423-2700). Back Bay ⓣ. Widely regarded as one of the best restaurants in Boston, and with good cause. Every night star chef-owner Gordon Hamersley dons a baseball cap and takes to the open kitchen, where he dishes out unusual – and unforgettable – French-American fare that changes seasonally.

Jae's Café, 520 Columbus Ave (☎421-9405) Back Bay ⓣ. Popular, lively, and excellent "pan-Asian" restaurant, with a fantastic sushi bar.

Mike's City Diner, 1714 Washington St (☎267-9393). Back Bay ⓣ. Classic diner breakfasts and lunches (greasy but good) in an out-of-the-way setting.

On the Park, 1 Union Park (☎426-0862). Back Bay ⓣ. The French country fare here is as much of a draw here as its secluded setting on the quiet south side of Union Park. The vegetarian cassoulet is a winner.

Thai Village, 592 Tremont St (☎536-6548). Back Bay ⓣ. All your favorite Thai dishes, plus a few you may not have found yet, like mussel pancakes.

Les Zygomates, 129 South St (☎542-5108). South Station ⓣ. Modern French cuisine, accompanied by a wine selection among Boston's best.

Kenmore Square and Brookline

Audubon Circle, 838 Beacon St, Kenmore Square (☎421-1910). Kenmore ⓣ. The seemingly endless bar grabs your attention, but it's the food that's worth staying for. Any of the appetizers are good bets, as is anything grilled – from burgers with chipotle ketchup to grilled tuna with banana salsa and *fufu* (fried plantains mashed with coconut milk).

Deli-Haus, 476 Commonwealth Ave, Kenmore Square (☎247-9712). Kenmore ⓣ. This haunt is open 24 hours; try any of the breakfast fare, served all day, or the club sandwich.

Ginza, 1002 Beacon St (☎566-9688). St Mary's St ⓣ. Brookline branch of the Chinatown sushi bar; a little more elegant but equally good.

Elephant Walk, 900 Beacon St (☎247-1500). Kenmore ⓣ. Great French and Cambodian restaurant, with better ambience and better cooking than just about any other Southeast Asian restaurant in the area.

Il Bico, 468 Commonwealth Ave (☎375-0699). Kenmore ⓣ. Erratic but occasionally excellent basement trattoria, serving tasty pastas at reasonable prices.

Matt Murphy's, 14 Harvard St (☎232-0188). Brookline Village Ⓣ. If "good Irish food" sounds like an oxymoron, get on over to this popular pub in Brookline Village. Savory pies, great chips, and good pints of Guinness (which counts as a food group here).

Southern districts

Amrhein's, 80 W Broadway, South Boston (☎268-6189). JFK Ⓣ. A Southie landmark and a favorite of local politicians for generations. Good old American comfort food won't dazzle your palate, but it's reasonably priced and you get a lot of it.

Bella Luna, 405 Centre St, Jamaica Plain (☎524-6060). Forest Hills Ⓣ to #39 bus. Nouvelle pizza with a funky array of fresh toppings (you can order from their list of combinations or design your own) is available in this festive space. Jazz brunch on Sunday mornings.

Bob the Chef, 604 Columbus Ave, Roxbury (☎536-6204). Roxbury Crossing Ⓣ. The best soul food in New England, at decent prices. Good chitterlings, black-eyed peas and collard greens, and don't miss the "glori-fried chicken," the house specialty. Live jazz on weekends.

Bukhara, 701 Centre St (☎522-2195). Forest Hills Ⓣ to #39 bus. Just about the only Indian joint in this neck of the woods, with the standard selection of curries and breads, plus a menu of southern Indian specialties.

Centre Street Café, 669 Centre St (☎524-9217). Forest Hills Ⓣ to #39 bus. An old JP stand-by. Funky, creative Mexican-influenced American cuisine; best for weekend brunch, where you fight the crowds to get huge omelets, smoked salmon benedict, enormous pancakes with real maple syrup, and bottomless cups of coffee.

Cambridge

The Blue Room, 1 Kendall Square (☎494-9034). Kendall Ⓣ. One of the best restaurants in Cambridge, especially for Sunday brunch. Innovative American cuisine with a French accent. Pricey but worth it.

Boca Grande, 1728 Massachusetts Ave (☎354-7400). Porter Ⓣ. Somewhere in between a restaurant and a taco stand, crowded *Boca* vends delectable, if somewhat tempered, Mexican fare at low prices – no entree costs more than $6. Ask in Spanish, and they'll throw a little more fire onto your order.

Bombay Club, 57 JFK St, in the Galleria Mall (☎661-8100). Harvard Ⓣ. A cut above the rest of the Cambridge Indian restaurants, this spacious restaurant offers a standard menu pre-pared distinctively.

Border Cafe, 32 Church St, Cambridge (☎864-6100). Harvard Ⓣ. Cambridge's most popular (and nearly only) Tex-Mex place. It's pretty good, though not nearly so much as to justify the massive crowds that form to wait for seats on weekend nights.

Café Baraka, 80 1/2 Pearl St (☎868-3951). Central Ⓣ. Very lively Tunisian restaurant, tucked away in a residential neighborhood. Let the owner chat you up while you scoff down cous-cous, wonderfully prepared fish specials, and a stuffed eggplant to die for.

Central Kitchen, 567 Massachusetts Ave (☎491-5599). Central Ⓣ. The first hip bistro in edgy Central Square. A definite Mediterranean flair to the creative menu, from an array of deli-cious tapas to brine-cured pork chops. Gentrification should always taste this good.

Charlie's Kitchen, 10 Eliot St (☎452-9646). Harvard Ⓣ. Atmospheric townie hangout in the heart of Harvard Square, with red vinyl booths, sassy waitresses, and greasy diner food.

Chez Henri, 1 Shepard St (☎354-8980). Harvard Ⓣ. If you can get a table (no reservations, long lines), you'll enjoy what may well be Cambridge's finest cuisine. Chef Paul O'Connell's experiment in fusion brings Modern French together with Cuban influences, best in the light salads, Cuban crab cakes, and the chicken asado.

Dali, 415 Washington St, Somerville (☎661-3254). Harvard Ⓣ. Mouthwatering tapas, friendly service, above-average sangria, and wonderful desserts (particularly the *besos de amor*, "kiss-es of love," a gooey ice cream and marzipan concoction).

Darwin's Ltd, 148 Mt Auburn St (☎354-5233). Harvard Ⓣ. The rough-hewn exterior con-ceals a delightful deli that serves wonderfully inventive sandwich combinations – such as roast beef, sprouts, and apple slices – on freshly baked bread.

The Harvest, 44 Brattle St (☎868-2255). Harvard ⊤. *The* place for power brunch in Harvard Square, at a steep $35 *prix fixe*, worth every penny. The cooking focuses on New England ingredients, but with a decidedly nouveau twist. Menu changes weekly.

Henrietta's Table, 1 Bennett St, in the *Charles Hotel*, Cambridge (☎661-5005). Harvard ⊤. One of the only restaurants in Cambridge that serves classic New England fare, which it does at a price. Rich entrees such as roasted duck or pork chops work well with side dishes of wilted greens or mashed potatoes. Excellent Sunday brunch (noon–3pm; $32 per person).

Herrell's Ice Cream, 15 Dunster St (☎497-2179). Harvard ⊤. The best ice cream in Cambridge; try the chocolate pudding ice cream. Open until midnight.

House of Tibet, 235 Holland St (☎629-7567). This tiny hole-in-the-wall is the first Tibetan restaurant in New England, and as good a place as any to introduce yourself to this filling, healthy cuisine.

Jae's Cafe, 1281 Cambridge St (☎497-8380). #69 bus. Popular, lively and excellent "pan-Asian" restaurant, with a fantastic sushi bar.

Koreana, 154 Prospect St (☎576-8661). Central ⊤. Always topping the list of "best Korean restaurants," this is the place to get fiery *bibinbap* just like *ajinma* used to make.

La Groceria, 853 Main St (☎497-4214). Central ⊤. "North End food without the North End hassles" is the tag line for this establishment. Decent, straightforward Italian at reasonable prices.

Lee's Sandwich Shop, 61 Church St (☎876-4090). Harvard ⊤. An old-fashioned lunch counter, simple and unpretentious. The burgers are great – if you love beef, ask for the DBCB (double bacon cheeseburger).

Magnolias, 1193 Cambridge St (☎576-1971). #69 bus. Some of the best Cajun and Southern food in the area. Just the spot for fried green tomatoes, Cajun popcorn shrimp, and Key lime pie.

Moody's Falafel Palace, 25 Central Sq (☎864-0827). Central ⊤. With a seating capacity of five, this has to be one of the smallest "palaces" in the world. But it also has some of the best falafel in the area, plus stuffed grape leaves and other Middle Eastern specalties.

Nick's American Bar and Grill, 1688 Massachusetts Ave (☎491-9882). Porter ⊤. From the mirrored walls to tacky lighting fixtures shaped like yule logs, *Nick's* is incredibly garish and hyper-American. It also sells cheap drinks and a great double cheeseburger special.

Ole Mexican Grill, 11 Springfield St (☎492-4495). #69 bus. Just about the best Mexican food in Boston, focusing on the cooking of Oaxaca and Veracruz rather than the standard Tex-Mex.

Redbones, 55 Chester St (☎628-2200). Davis ⊤. Highly addictive barbecue and grill spot, with an all-you-can-eat ribs and chicken lunch that's likely to expand your waistline.

Roka, 1001 Massachusetts Ave (☎631-0344). Harvard ⊤. Elegant "Osaka-style" restaurant offers some of the best all-around Japanese food in the area. Try the sushi, of course, but also be sure to try the *age-dashi tofu* (deep-fried tofu), chicken wings and other great dishes.

Royal East, 782–792 Main St (☎661-1660). Kendall ⊤. Spacious Cantonese restaurant, with a strong local following. Excellent vegetables and seafood dishes.

Shalimar of India, 546 Massachusetts Ave (☎547-9280). Central ⊤. You can't throw a stone in Central Square without hitting an Indian restaurant, but this is one of the best.

Shilla, 95 Winthrop, in the basement of the Galleria Mall (☎547-7971). Harvard ⊤. Korean and Japanese restaurant, with good sushi and spicy noodle dishes.

Skewers, 92 Mt. Auburn (☎491-3079). Harvard ⊤. This basement Middle Eastern spot is one of the best places for a cheap lunch. Good kebabs, shawarma, and falafel, plus some more elaborate platters for eat-in.

Upstairs at the Pudding, 10 Holyoke St (☎864-1933). Harvard ⊤. The dining room was converted from what was originally the eating area for Harvard's ultra-elite Hasty Pudding Club, and the attitude lingers on. The food is excellent, though, falling somewhere in between New American and Old Colonial. Romantic al fresco dining in the summer. Advance reservations are essential.

Drinking

Despite – or perhaps because of – the lingering Puritan anti-fun ethic that pervades Boston, people here seem to **drink** more than in most other American cities. The most prevalent place to nurse a pint is the **Irish pub**, of which there are high concentrations in the **West End** and downtown around **Quincy Market**. More upscale are the bars and lounges of **Back Bay**, along Newbury and Boylston streets, which offer attitude as much as anything else. The rest of the city's neighborhood bars, pick-up joints, and yuppie hotspots are differentiated by their crowds: **Beacon Hill** tends to be older and a bit stuffy; **downtown**, mainly around Quincy Market and the Theater District, draws a healthy mix of tourists and locals; **Kenmore Square** and **Cambridge** are fairly student-oriented. The **café** scene is not quite as diverse, but still offers a decent range of places to hang out. The toniest spots are again those that line the Back Bay's **Newbury Street**, where you pay as much for the fancy environs as for the quality of the coffee. Value is much better in the **North End**, but the most lively cafés are across the river in **Cambridge**, and cater, unsurprisingly, to the large student population.

Bars

Bars stop serving at 2am (at the latest), and most strictly enforce the drinking-age minimum of 21. Be prepared to show either a driver's license or passport. The one potential for after-hours drinking is **Chinatown**, where some restaurants will bring you a pot of beer if you ask for the "cold tea."

Downtown

Bell in Hand Tavern, 45 Union St (☎227-2098). State or Government Center ⊤. The oldest continuously operating tavern in Boston – though it has changed locations several times – draws a fairly exuberant mix of tourists and young professionals.

The Good Life, 28 Kingston St (☎451-2622). Downtown Crossing ⊤. This trendy bar and restaurant (but more of the former) offers potent martinis, to be sipped amidst 1970s decor.

Green Dragon Tavern, 11 Marshall St (☎367-0055). Government Center ⊤. Another tavern that dates to the colonial era. Standard selection of tap beers, but a raw bar and full menu rife with twee historical humor ("One if by land, two if by seafood").

The Littlest Bar in Boston, 47 Province St (☎523-9766). Downtown Crossing T. Its tiny size is part of the charm, as are the quality pints of Guinness and free live music.

The Purple Shamrock, 1 Union St (☎227-2060). State or Government Center ⊤. A lively watering hole that draws a broad cross-section of folks, the *Shamrock* has one of Boston's better straight singles scenes, which isn't saying much; it gets very crowded on weekends.

The Rack, 24 Clinton St (☎725-1051). Government Center ⊤. Well-dressed twenty- and thirtysomethings convene at this pool hall to dine, smoke cigars, drink a bewildering variety of cocktails, and, of course, shoot a rack or two.

Charlestown

Warren Tavern, 2 Pleasant St at Main St (☎241-8142). An atmospheric place to enjoy a drink, the *Warren* is the oldest standing structure in Charlestown. They also have a generous menu of good tavern food.

Beacon Hill and the West End

21st Amendment, 150 Bowdoin St (☎227-7100). Bowdoin ⓣ. This dimly lit, down-home watering hole is a favorite haunt of legislators from the adjacent State House and students from nearby Suffolk University.

The Bull & Finch Pub, 84 Beacon St (☎227-9605). Arlington ⓣ. If you don't already know, and if the conspicuous banners outside don't tip you off, this is the bar that served as the inspiration for the TV show *Cheers*. If you've gotta go, be warned – it's packed with camera-toting tourists; the inside bears little resemblance to the NBC set; the food, though cutely named (eNORMous burgers), is pricey and mediocre, and it's quite likely that nobody will know your name.

Fours, 166 Canal St (☎720-4455). North Station ⓣ. The class of the West End's sports bars, with an army of TVs to broadcast games from around the globe, and paraphernalia from the Celtics, Bruins, and other local teams.

Irish Embassy, 234 Friend St (☎742-6618). North Station ⓣ. Up in the West End. One of the city's most authentic Irish (rather than Irish-American) pubs, with the crowd to match. Live Irish entertainment most nights, plus broadcasts of Irish soccer games.

Sevens Ale House, 77 Charles St (☎523-9074). Charles ⓣ. While all the T-shirted tourists pack into the *Bull & Finch*, you can drop by this cozy joint to get a taste of what a real neighborhood bar is like.

Back Bay and the South End

Barcode, 955 Boylston St (☎421-1818). Hynes ⓣ. The sign doesn't *say* "Barcode"—it *is* a barcode, which should give you an idea about this too-trendy for words, beautiful-people-with-cellphones hangout. Good food, if a bit overpriced.

Clery's, 113 Dartmouth St (☎262-9874). Back Bay ⓣ. Big, two-room Irish-flavored bar and restaurant on the northern cusp of the South End.

Dad's, 911 Boylston St (☎296-3237). Hynes ⓣ. Dim lights and scantily clad barmaids make this a fairly un-Back Bay drinking hole.

Daisy Buchanan's, 240A Newbury St (☎247-8516). Copley ⓣ. A real-life beer commercial: young guys wearing baseball caps, professional sports on TV, and pervasive smell of booze.

Oak Room, 138 St James Ave, in the *Fairmont Copley Plaza Hotel* (☎267-5300). Copley ⓣ. Rich wood paneling, high ceilings, swirling cigar smoke and excellent martinis make this one of the more genteel Back Bay spots to drink.

Kenmore Square, The Fenway, and Brookline

Bill's Bar, 5 Lansdowne St (☎421-9678). Kenmore ⓣ. A relaxed and homey spot with lots of beer, TV, and occasional live music – in which case, expect a cover charge of $5.

Boston Beer Works, 61 Brookline Ave (☎536-2337). Kenmore ⓣ. A brewery located right by Fenway Park – and as such a popular place for the Red Sox faithful to drink before games and drown their sorrows after.

Southern districts

Brendan Behan, 378 Centre St, Jamaica Plain (☎522-5386). Jackson Square ⓣ. A dimly lit Irish pub with a friendly staff. Catch the live music and free buffet available on most weekends.

James's Gate, 5–11 McBride St, Jamaica Plain (☎983-2000). Jackson Square ⓣ. Beat Boston's harsh winter by sipping Guinness by the blazing fireplace in this cozy pub, or trying the hearty fare in the restaurant in back. Traditional Irish music on Sundays, open mic on Thursdays.

Cambridge

The Cellar, 991 Massachusetts Ave (☎876-2580). Harvard ⓣ. If *Cheers* were set in Cambridge, this would be it. Two floors inhabited by a regular crowd of older students, faculty, and locals.

The Druid, 1357 Cambridge St (☎497-0965). #69 bus. Twee Inman Square bar featuring an old Celtic motif, with murals of druid priests and ever-present pints of Guinness. It's blessedly free of the college scene, too.

The Field, 20 Prospect St (☎354-7345). Central ⓣ. Unpretentious Irish pub with pool tables and an excellent jukebox, that attracts a diverse crowd.

Grafton Street, 1280 Massachusetts Ave (☎497-0400). Harvard ⓣ. Named after the hip pedestrian road in Dublin, this upscale pub attracts a well-heeled and thirsty crowd. Be prepared for strong mixed drinks and a packed house on the weekends.

Grendel's Den, 89 Winthrop St (☎491-1160). Harvard ⓣ. A favorite spot of locals and grad students who drink ale in these dark, conspiratorial environs. The *Den* was saved from closure by Harvard Law professor Larry Tribe, who lobbied against Puritan blue laws when a nearby church tried to get the place closed. Fantastic happy hour offers big plates of appetizers (fried calamari, nachos) for just $1.50.

Miracle of Science, 321 Massachusetts Ave (☎868-2866). Central ⓣ or #1 bus. Surprisingly hip despite its status as an MIT hangout. There's a noir decor and a trendy crowd of well-dressed professionals; quite crowded on weekend nights.

Shay's, 58 JFK St (☎354-9038). Harvard ⓣ. Relaxed bar that stands in appreciated contrast to the rowdier, student-oriented Harvard Square joints.

Cafés

Although the Starbuck's invasion has done some real damage to the eclectic café scene in Boston and Cambridge, there are still any number of independent places to work on your novel and stroke your goatee. At many cafés, you can just as easily get an excellent full meal as you can a cup of coffee. Below are the best choices for casual hanging out; there are also plenty of cafés more suited for meals listed under "Eating"(p.112).

North End

A Different Drummer Café, 135 Salem St (☎523-6263). Haymarket ⓣ. Have a grilled cheese sandwich with your coffee at this small, decidedly un-Italian café in the middle of the Italian North End.

Caffe dello Sport, 308 Hanover St (☎523-5063). Haymarket ⓣ. A continuous stream of Rai Uno soccer matches are broadcast from the ceiling-mounted TV sets, making for an agreeable din and a very local crowd.

Caffe Paradiso, 255 Hanover St (☎742-1768). Haymarket ⓣ. It's not much on atmosphere, but the pastries are hands down the best in the North End.

Caffe Vittoria, 294 Hanover St (☎227-7606). Haymarket ⓣ. A Boston institution, the *Vittoria's* atmospheric original section, with its dark wood paneling, pressed tin ceiling, murals of the Old Country, and Sinatra-blaring Wurlitzer, is a perfect setting for a fine cappuccino.

Beacon Hill and the West End

Panificio, 144 Charles St (☎227-4340). Charles ⓣ. Fine cups o' Joe, fresh tasty pastries (*biscotti* is the standout), and some of the best home-baked bread in the city.

Back Bay and the South End

29 Newbury, 29 Newbury St (☎536-0290). Arlington ⓣ. A small upscale café/bar and eatery with good, if pricey, salads and the like. In warmer weather, the self-consciously hip crowd migrates to the sidewalk terrace. Wear black and dangle sunglasses. Open until 1.30am.

Francesca's Espresso Bar, 565 Tremont St (☎482-9026). Back Bay ⓣ. This very contemporary café, situated next to Union Park, is a popular meeting spot and also a comfortable place to imbibe on one's own. There's a good selection of fresh baked goods.

The Other Side Cosmic Cafe, 407 Newbury St (☎536-9477). Hynes ⓣ. Ultra-casual spot on "the other side" of Massachusetts Avenue, cut off from the trendy part of Newbury Street, that offers gourmet sandwiches, "creative green salads," and fresh juices.

Trident Booksellers & Cafe, 338 Newbury St (☎267-8688). Hynes ⓣ. A window seat at this bookstore café (see p.130), perennially popular with the dressed-in-black student set, is the ideal vantage point from which to observe the flood of young passersby outside.

Cambridge and Somerville

1369 Coffeehouse, 1369 Cambridge St (☎576-1369). #69 bus. The *1369* mixes earnest post-graduate leftists with youthful hipsters in a laid-back environment; exquisite desserts. Another location on 757 Massachusetts Ave (☎576-4600). Central ⓣ.

Algiers, 40 Brattle St (☎492-1557). Harvard ⓣ. A fashionably cramped North African café popular with the artsy set; while the food is so-so and the service slow, there are few more atmospheric spots in which to sip first-rate coffee.

Bookcellar Café, 1971 Massachusetts Ave (☎864-9625). Porter ⓣ. Cozy, relaxed basement coffeehouse, where you can peruse a range of magazines and used books while you imbibe.

Cafe Gato Rojo, Basement of Lehman Hall (Dudley House), Harvard Yard (☎496-4658). Harvard ⓣ. One of the least-known of the Harvard Square coffeehouses, this place is hip without being overbearing, run by and for grad students, though the public is welcome.

Diesel Café, 257 Elm St, Somerville (☎629-8717). Davis ⓣ. Very cool, laid-back café with stylish décor, where you can eat good pastries and sip good latte while you sneer at the patrons of Starbuck's across the street.

Tealuxe, 0 Brattle St (☎441-0077). Harvard ⓣ. In a cool twist on the standard coffeehouse thing, what was once a curiosity shop called Loulou's Lost and Found has reincarnated itself as the only teahouse in Harvard Square. They stock over 100 varieties of tea, loose and by the cup. There's another branch on 108 Newbury St.

Nightlife

In recent years the city's **nightlife** has received something of a wake-up call, with stylish new **clubs** springing up in places such as Downtown Crossing that were once ghost towns at night. Though Boston is by no means a 24-hour city, these spots have given a bit of fresh air to a scene that lived in the shadow of the city's so-called high culture. Most of the clubs, however, tend to be geared toward – or at least chiefly attract – either moneyed students, suburbanites, or the secretarial set.

The **live music** scene plays perhaps a bigger part in the city's nightlife. Many of the bars and clubs, especially around Kenmore Square and Harvard Square, are just as likely, if not more, to have a scruffy garage band playing for only a nominal cover as they are to have a slick DJ spinning house tunes. And Boston has spawned its share of enormous **rock** acts, from the ever-enduring Aerosmith, to the Cars, pop ska-sters Mighty Mighty Bosstones, teen heartthrobs Marky Mark and the New Kids on the Block, and, more recently, a deluge of post-punk and indie groups such as the Pixies, Sebadoh and Folk Implosion. There is a bit less in the way of **jazz** and **blues**, but you can usually find something cheap and to your liking any day of the week.

For **club and music listings**, check Thursday's *Boston Globe* "Calendar" or the *Boston Phoenix*; the two best Web sites for Boston's entertainment scene are *www.boston.com* and *www.boston.sidewalk.com*.

Nightclubs

Boston's **nightclubs** are mostly clustered in downtown's Theater District and around Kenmore Square, with a few prominent ones in Back Bay and the South End. Many of the Back Bay and South End venues are **gay clubs**, often the most happening in town. For a listing of these, see "Gay and lesbian Boston," p.128. Otherwise, a number of the clubs below have special gay nights. **Cover charges** are generally in the $5–10 range, though sometimes there's no cover at all.

Avalon, 15 Lansdowne St, Kenmore Square (☎262-2424). Kenmore ⊤. A 1500-person capacity makes it the biggest dance club in Boston, and any weekend night the place is positively jamming. The cavernous central floor is flanked on either side by bars. Sunday is gay night. Sometimes live shows by underground rock acts like Patti Smith and the Charlatans.

The Big Easy, 1 Boylston Place, Back Bay (☎351-7000). Boylston ⊤. Bar and jazz club with a New Orleans theme; for the best people-watching go on a weeknight.

Club Europa/Buzz, 51 Stuart St, Downtown (☎482-3939). Boylston ⊤. On the edge of the Theater District, this is one of Boston's better dance clubs. Most of the action is on the third floor; the second tends to be louder and more crowded. On Saturday night the club becomes "Buzz," the most plugged-in gay disco in Boston.

Club at Il Panino, 295 Franklin St, Downtown (☎338-1000). State ⊤. Downstairs is a classy, reasonably-priced *trattoria*; upstairs is a three-story disco, one of the hottest in town. Latin house music on Friday and Saturday nights.

The International, 184 High St, Downtown (☎542-4747). State ⊤. Snazzy club addition to an American bistro-style restaurant, in the quiet (by night) Financial District. Live bands Friday nights.

Karma/Mambo Lounge, 9 Lansdowne St, Kenmore Square (☎421-9595). Kenmore ⊤. This multi-roomed, faux-hip dancehall aspires with limited success to a futuristic Hindu temple decor. Nightly DJs spin mostly hip-hop.

Lava Bar, 575 Commonwealth Ave, Kenmore Square (☎267-7707). Kenmore ⊤. Dance club in the heart of Kenmore Square. Saturday night is lesbian night.

Milky Way, 405 Centre St, Jamaica Plain (☎524-3740). #39 Bus. "Lanes and lounge" – that's right, bowling alley cum nightclub, right in the heart of Boston's (currently) hippest neighborhood.

Pravda 116, 116 Boylston St, Back Bay (☎482-7799). Boylston ⊤. You'll hear everything from Eurohouse and classic dance hits to world music at this dance club cum restaurant/bar.

Sophia's, 1270 Boylston St (☎351-7001). Kenmore ⊤. This great tapas restaurant is also a great spot for live salsa and Latin jazz, Tues–Sat nights. Dancing Thurs–Sat.

Live music

The strength of Boston's **live music** is its diversity, and the city serves as both a stop on the world tours of superstar performers and a hotbed of small, experimental acts. Two of the biggest venues are a ways out of town: the Great Woods Auditorium, south of the city in Mansfield (☎508/339-2333), and the Worcester Centrum, an hour or so west in Worcester (☎508/798-8888). There are still, however, plenty of adequate places to see either name bands or obscure experimental acts.

Rock

FleetBoston Pavilion, Fan Pier, Northern Ave, Downtown (☎728-1600). South Station ⊤. Formerly the Harborlights Pavilion; during the summer, concerts by well-known performers from Mel Torme to the Gipsy Kings are held here under a huge white tent at Boston Harbor's edge.

FleetCenter, 50 Causeway St (☎624-1750; tickets ☎931-2000). North Station Ⓣ. This arena, up in the West End, attracts a decent number of the big-name acts that pass through New England.

Lilli's, 608 Somerville Ave, Somerville (☎591-1661). Porter Ⓣ. A happening new live venue that attracts locally and nationally known alternative, rock and jazz acts.

Lizard Lounge, 1667 Massachusetts Ave (☎547-0759). Harvard or Porter Ⓣ. Downstairs portion of the restaurant *Cambridge Common*, it has rock and jazz acts pretty much nightly, for a fairly nominal cover charge.

Middle East, 472 Massachusetts Ave (☎354-8238). Central Ⓣ. Local and regional progressive rock acts regularly stop in at this Cambridge institution. Downstairs hosts bigger acts, smaller acts ply their experimental stuff in a tiny upstairs space. A third venue, the *Corner*, has free acts every night, with belly dancing every Wednesday.

Orpheum Theater, Hamilton Place (☎482-0630). Park or Downtown Crossing Ⓣ. Once an old-school movie house, it's now a venue for big-name music acts. The small space means you're closer to the action, but it sells out quickly and cramped seating discourages dancing.

T.T. the Bear's, 10 Brookline St (☎492-2327). Central Ⓣ. A downmarket version of the *Middle East*: lower-quality acts, but in a space with a grittiness and intimacy its neighbor lacks. All kinds of bands appear, mostly punk, rock, and electronica.

Jazz, blues and folk

Cantab Lounge, 738 Massachusetts Ave (☎354-2685). Central Ⓣ. Although from the outside, it looks like the kind of sleazy place your mother wouldn't want you to set foot in, it's actually one of the few truly bohemian spots in town, with hopping live jazz and blues, and poetry slams every Wednesday night.

The House of Blues, 96 Winthrop St, Cambridge (☎491-2583). Harvard Ⓣ. The first in the corporate monolith spawned by the same evil geniuses who started the Hard Rock Café conglomerate. The faux-roadhouse decor and stiff, middle-class patrons are painfully inauthentic, but the house still features top national blues acts.

Johnny D's Uptown, 17 Holland St, Somerville (☎776-2004). Davis Ⓣ. This is a totally mixed bag: acts include garage bands, progressive jazz sextets, traditional blues artists, and some uncategorizables.

Passim, 47 Palmer St, Harvard Square (☎492-7679). Harvard Ⓣ. Folkie hangout where Joan Baez and Suzanne Vega got their starts. There's also world music and spoken word performances.

Regattabar, 1 Bennett St, Cambridge (☎876-7777). Harvard Ⓣ. The *Regattabar* draws top national jazz acts, though as its location in the swish *Charles Hotel* might suggest, the atmosphere – and clientele – is decidedly chichi and sedate. Dress nicely and prepare to pay at least $10 cover.

Sculler's, 400 Soldier's Field Rd in *Doubletree Guest Suites Hotel*, Brighton (☎562-4111). Harvard Ⓣ. The fact that *Sculler's* is in a hotel lounge does little to dampen the enthusiasm of the first-rate jazz performers and the devoted listeners who trudge out here to see them.

Wally's Cafe, 427 Massachusetts Ave, Roxbury (☎424-1408). Massachusetts Avenue Ⓣ. This refreshingly unhewn bar hosts lively jazz and blues shows that draw a vibrant crowd. No cover.

Western Front, 343 Western Ave, Cambridge (☎492-7772). Central Ⓣ. The *Front* puts on rollicking jazz, blues, and reggae shows for a dance-crazy audience. Drinks are cheap, and the Jamaican food served on weekends is delectably authentic.

Performing arts and film

Boston's **cultural scene** is famously vibrant, and many of the city's artistic institutions are second to none. Foremost among them is the **Boston Symphony Orchestra**, which gave its first concert on October 22, 1881; in fact, Boston is arguably at its best in the **classical music** department, and there are many smaller but internationally-known chamber and choral music groups, from the Boston Symphony Chamber Players to the Handel & Hayden Society, to shore up that reputation. The **Boston Ballet** is also considered world-class, though it's probably best known in Boston itself for its annual holiday production of *The Nutcracker*.

The **theater** here is quite active too, even if it is, in a way, a shadow of its 1920s heyday. Boston remains a try-out city for Broadway productions, and smaller companies have increasingly high visibility. Still, it's a real treat to see a play or musical at one of the opulent old theaters such as the **Colonial** or **Emerson Majestic**. For current productions, check the listings in the *Boston Globe*'s Thursday "Calendar" section or the *Boston Phoenix*.

The **film** scene is dominated by the Sony conglomerate, which runs several theater multiplexes featuring major first-run movies. For foreign, independent, classic or cult cinema, you'll have to look to other municipalities – Cambridge is best, though Brookline and Somerville have their own art-movie houses.

Classical music and dance

Boston prides itself on being a sophisticated city of high culture, and nowhere does that show up more than in its proliferation of **orchestras** and **choral groups** – and the venues to house them. This is helped in no small part by the presence of three of the foremost music academies in the nation: Peabody Conservatory, New England Conservatory, and Berklee College of Music.

Chamber music ensembles

Alea III (☎353-3340). High-caliber chamber group affiliated with Boston University; they give concerts at the school's Tsai Performance Center.

Boston Baroque (☎484-9200). One of the country's oldest baroque orchestras.

The Boston Chamber Music Society (☎422-0086). Has members who are soloists of international renown; concerts at Jordan Hall and the Sanders Theater in Harvard.

Boston Symphony Chamber Players (☎266-1492). Happen to be the only permanent chamber group sponsored by a major symphony orchestra and made up of its members; concerts at Jordan Hall.

The Cantata Singers & Ensemble (☎267-6502). Boston's premier choral group; they perform oratorios and the like at Jordan Hall.

Handel & Hayden Society (☎266-3605). Around since 1815; performances at Symphony and Jordan halls.

Dance

Boston Ballet (☎695-6950). The longest-running dance company in the city, with an unparalleled reputation in America. The troupe performs at the Wang Center and the Shubert Theatre.

Dance Umbrella (☎492-7570). Modern dance group that promotes a number of contemporary acts, and most often performs at the Emerson Majestic.

Venues

Berklee Performance Center, 136 Massachusetts Ave (☎266-7455). Symphony ⊤. Berklee College of Music's main performance center, known for its contemporary repertoire.

Isabella Stewart Gardner Museum, 280 The Fenway (☎734-1369). Museum ⊤. Chamber and classical concerts, including many debuts, are regularly held on weekends at 1.30pm in the museum's Tapestry Room. The $15 ticket price includes admission to the museum.

Jordan Hall, 30 Gainsborough St (☎536-2412). Symphony ⓣ. The impressive concert hall of the New England Conservatory, just one block west from Symphony Hall, is the venue for many chamber music performances as well as those by the Boston Philharmonic (☎868-6696).

Museum of Fine Arts, 465 Huntington Ave (☎369-3306 ext 4). Museum ⓣ. During the summer, MFA "Concerts in the Courtyard" take place each Wednesday at 7.30pm; a variety of indoor performances are scheduled for the rest of the year.

Symphony Hall, 301 Massachusetts Ave (☎266-1200, *www.bso.org*). Symphony ⓣ. This is the regal venue for the Boston Symphony Orchestra; the famous Boston Pops concerts happen in May and June; in July and August the BSO retreats to Tanglewood, in the Berkshires (☎266-1492 for Tanglewood info).

Tsai Performance Center, 685 Commonwealth Ave (☎353-8724). Boston University ⓣ. Mid-sized hall that's a frequent venue for chamber music performances, prominent lecturers, and plays, all often affiliated with BU and either free or very inexpensive.

Theater

It's quite possible to pay dearly for a night at the **theater**. Tickets to the bigger shows range $25–75 depending on the seat, and there is, of course, the potential of a pre- or post-theater meal. Your best bet is to pay a visit to **Bostix** (☎482-BTIX), a half-price, day-of-show ticket outlet and Ticketmaster center with three locations: Faneuil Hall (Tues–Sat 10am–6pm, Sun 11am–4pm), Copley Square (Mon–Sat 10am–6pm, Sun 11am–4pm), and the Holyoke Center in Harvard Square (same hours as Copley Square). The half-price tickets go on sale at 11am, and only cash is accepted. You can also call **Ticketmaster** direct (☎931-2000), or call the individual theater direct or visit its box office in advance of the performance. The **smaller venues** tend to showcase more offbeat and affordable productions; shows can be under $10 – though you shouldn't bank on that.

Major venues

American Repertory Theater at the Loeb Drama Center, 64 Brattle St (☎547-8300). Harvard ⓣ. Excellent theater near Harvard Square known for staging plays by postmodern heavyweights such as Ionesco and Stoppard, as well as the works of Shaw, Wilde, and other big names.

Charles Playhouse, 74 Warrenton St (☎426-6912). Boylston ⓣ. The Charles has two stages, one of which is more or less the permanent home of *Shear Madness*, a participatory, comic murder mystery that's now the longest-running nonmusical in American theater. The other stage hosts somewhat edgier material.

Colonial Theatre, 106 Boylston St (☎426-9366). Boylston ⓣ. Built in 1900 and since refurbished, this is the glittering grande dame of Boston theaters.

Emerson Majestic Theatre, 219 Tremont St (☎824-8000). Lavish Beaux Arts beauty, with soaring rococo ceiling and Neoclassical friezes, hosts productions of Emerson Stage, the Boston Lyric Opera and Dance Umbrella.

Shubert Theatre, 265 Tremont St (☎482-9393). Boylston ⓣ. Stars from Sir Laurence Olivier to Kathleen Turner have played the Shubert at some point in their careers; today the 1680-seat theater accommodates mostly big Broadway-style productions.

Wang Center for the Performing Arts, 270 Tremont St (☎482-9393). Boylston ⓣ. The biggest performance center in Boston opened in 1925 as the Metropolitan Theater, a movie house of palatial proportions – and its 3800 seats, Italian marble and gold leaf ornamentation, and crystal chandeliers all remain.

Wilbur Theatre, 246 Tremont St (☎423-4008). Boylston ⓣ. *A Streetcar Named Desire*, starring Marlon Brando and Jessica Tandy, debuted in this small Colonial Revival theater before going to Broadway. In winter, the loud, old heating system may leave those in back straining to hear.

Small venues

Boston Center for the Arts, 539 Tremont St (☎426-0320). Back Bay Ⓣ. Several theater troupes, many of which are experimental, stage productions at the BCA, which incorporates a series of small venues on a single South End property.

Hasty Pudding Theatre, 12 Holyoke St (☎495-5205). Harvard Ⓣ. Harvard University's Hasty Pudding Theatricals troupe, one of the country's oldest, mounts one show per year here (Feb–March), then hits the road, at which time the Cambridge Theatre Company takes over.

Institute of Contemporary Art Theatre, 955 Boylston St (☎266-5152). Hynes Ⓣ. Count on the unconventional at the theater of the ICA, Boston's leading venue for all things postmodern.

Lyric Stage, 140 Clarendon St (☎437-7172). Copley Ⓣ. Both premieres and modern adaptations of classic American plays take place at this small theater in the big YWCA building.

Cinemas

If you're looking for out of the ordinary **cinematic** fare, you'll have to venture out a bit from Boston; whatever you're going to see, admission will cost you about $8, though matinees before 6pm can be considerably cheaper. Call ☎333-FILM for automated film listings.

Brattle Theater, 40 Brattle St (☎876-6837). Harvard Ⓣ. An historic cinema that pleasantly looks its age. They have the best repertory schedule in the area, with film noir Mondays and director retrospectives, plus occasional author appearances and readings. Mostly double features; $7.

Coolidge Corner Theatre, 290 Harvard St, Brookline (☎734-2500). Coolidge Corner Ⓣ. Film buffs flock to this classic theater for foreign and independent movies. The interior has balconies and is adorned with Art Deco murals.

General Cinemas Fenway, 201 Brookline Ave (☎424-6266). Kenmore Ⓣ. To check out the latest Hollywood blockbuster with all the technical fireworks, drop by this megaplex with THX sound, stadium seating and two-story high screens.

Harvard Film Archive, Carpenter Center, 24 Quincy St (☎495-4700). Harvard Ⓣ. They show a mixed bag of artsy, foreign and experimental films.

Kendall Square Cinema, 1 Kendall Square, Cambridge (☎494-9800). Kendall Ⓣ. Seemingly average multiplex, but it shows the area's widest selection of foreign and independent films.

Museum of Fine Arts Theater, 465 Huntington Ave (☎267-9300). Museum Ⓣ. Offbeat art films and documentaries, mostly by locals, and often accompanied by lectures from the filmmaker.

Somerville Theatre, 55 Davis Square, Somerville (☎625-5700). Davis Ⓣ. A newly refurbished home for camp and cult films, as well as a mixed bag of independent and foreign flicks and the occasional old classic. Tickets $5.25 at all times.

Gay and lesbian Boston

Boston is a fairly gay-friendly city and has a decent number of establishments that cater to a gay crowd. The center of the **gay scene** is the South End, a largely residential neighborhood whose businesses, mostly restaurants and cafés, are concentrated on a short stretch of Tremont Street above Union Park. Adjacent to the South End, on the other side of Arlington Street, is tiny **Bay Village**, which has most of the gay bars and clubs in the city. The **lesbian scene** is pretty well mixed-in with the gay scene, and there are very few exclusively lesbian bars or clubs.

The best sources of club **information** are the weeklies *Boston Phoenix* and *Bay Windows*. The latter, along with *in newsweekly*, are Boston's two area **gay newspapers**; both are free, and they can be found in certain bookstores, such as We Think the World of You, 540 Tremont St. Other **resources** for the gay community include the Gay and Lesbian Helpline (☎267-9001), a general information source; the AIDS Action Hotline (☎1-800/235-2331 or 536-7733); and Fenway Community Health Center, 7 Haviland St (☎267-0159), which offers HIV testing during weekdays.

Gay and lesbian bars and clubs

Axis, 13 Lansdowne St (☎262-2437). Fenway Ⓣ. Where the young, hip and pierced come to enjoy the over-the-top drag shows.

Campus/ManRay, 21 Brookline Ave (☎864-0400). Kenmore Ⓣ. One massive space – with five bars and two dance floors – with two very different theme nights. Campus, on Thursday and Sunday nights, is relatively wholesome; the other five nights, the club becomes ManRay, a fetish-and-bondage fest replete with leather and dominatrices.

Chaps, 100 Warrenton St (☎695-9500). Arlington Ⓣ. The biggest and flashiest gay disco in town features a bar and lounge area (open from 1pm daily) and a cavernous dance room, with two additional bars. Music changes nightly, and the cover varies.

Club Cafe, 209 Columbus Ave (☎536-0966). Back Bay Ⓣ. This rather understated combination restaurant/bar/lounge ("Moonshine") and club, the latter which attracts jazz acts, caters to the young professional South End crowd. Fairly mixed, though women dominate on Thursdays.

Fritz, 26 Chandler (☎482-4428). Back Bay Ⓣ. Imagine a gay "Cheers" and you have a pretty good idea about this neighborhood sports bar. They sponsor two gay softball teams.

Hideaway Pub, 20 Concord Lane, Cambridge (☎661-8828). Alewife Ⓣ. One of a very few lesbian spots in the Boston area, on Sunday and Thursday.

Jacque's, 79 Broadway (☎426-8902). Boylston Ⓣ. Past-it divas lip-synching "I Love the Nightlife," younger folks exploring their friskier sides and she-male temptresses trying very hard to indulge them. Bring the family!

Luxor, 69 Church St (☎423-6969). Arlington Ⓣ. Popular two-story, three-room gay bar upstairs from *Mario's*, an Italian restaurant. The first-floor bar is more low-key, with TVs showing sitcoms and news; upstairs is a video bar with a modern look that's standing room only on weekends.

Ramrod, 1254 Boylston St (☎266-2986). Kenmore Ⓣ. Not quite as hardcore as the name suggests, this Fenway meat market gets a pretty hungry leather-and-Levi's crowd. In the basement, a huge dance space throbs to extremes of a turbo sound system.

Uturn, 199 State St (☎685-8026). State Ⓣ. Friday is "Histurn," Saturday "Herturn," Sunday brings everybody together for tea-dancing that, if the pun continued, might be called "Ourturn" (or perhaps "Theirturn"). The restaurant serves lunch and dinner daily and Sunday brunch.

Shopping

Though Boston has its share of chainstores and typical mall fare, there are plenty of unusual and funky places to **shop** here. Best of all, Boston is an extremely pleasant place to shop, with attractive stores clustered on atmospheric streets like **Charles Street**, in Beacon Hill, and **Newbury Street**, in Back Bay. **Harvard Square** is another excellent place for such a wander, with especially good **bookstores** in the vicinity.

Otherwise, most of the action takes place in various downtown quarters, first and foremost at the **Faneuil Hall Marketplace**. This area has become more commercialized over the years, but there's still enough homespun boutiques, plus the many food stalls of **Quincy Market**, to make a trip here worthwhile. Otherwise, there's the somewhat downmarket **Downtown Crossing**, at Washington and Summer streets, centered on Filene's Basement, a bargain-hunter's delight.

Books

Boston has a history as a literary city, enhanced by its numerous universities and the authors and publishing houses that once called it home. This is well reflected in the quality and diversity of **bookstores** to be found both in Boston and neighboring Cambridge.

New books

Harvard Book Store, 1256 Massachusetts Ave (☎661-1515). Harvard ⓣ. Three huge rooms of new books upstairs, a basement for used volumes and remainders downstairs. Academic and critical work in the humanities and social sciences dominate, with plenty of fiction thrown in.

Trident Booksellers & Café, 338 Newbury St (☎267-8688). Copley ⓣ. This somewhat New-Agey hangout is a preferred lair of Back Bay Gen-Xers. If the aroma of one too many essential oils doesn't deter you, buy an obscure magazine and pretend to read it over coffee in the café (see p.123).

Wordsworth, 30 Brattle St (☎354-5201). Harvard ⓣ. The narrow aisles here overflow with a wide selection of books, many at an everyday discount.

Secondhand books

Avenue Victor Hugo Bookshop, 339 Newbury St (☎266-7746). Hynes ⓣ. One of Boston's best used bookstores, this upper Newbury fixture is the place to find recent editions at unbeatable prices. Vintage postcards and back issues of American magazines, too.

Brattle Book Shop, 9 West St (☎542-0210). Downtown Crossing ⓣ. In these fairly dingy digs is one of the oldest antiquarian bookstores in the country. Three levels, with a good selection of yellowing travel guides on the second.

House of Sarah, 1309 Cambridge St (☎547-3447). Central ⓣ. An Inman Square spot to browse used fiction and scholarly work in eccentrically stylish environs. There are often coffee and snacks, compliments of the proprietors.

Starr Bookshop, 29 Plympton St (☎547-6864). Harvard ⓣ. It's a bit like a library hit by a tornado, with books lying about or spilling over desks and tables, but if you're patient – or ask for help – you can find great discounts on literature and art criticism.

Specialist

Globe Corner Bookstore, 500 Boylston St (☎859-8008). Kenmore ⓣ. 28 Church St (☎497-6277). Harvard ⓣ. These travel specialists are well stocked with maps, travel literature and guidebooks, with an especially strong New England section.

Grolier Poetry Bookstore, 6 Plympton St (☎547-4648). Harvard ⓣ. Diminutive store specializing in in-print poetry. With 14,000 volumes of verse, it has gained an international following among poets and their fans; also hosts frequent readings.

Lucy Parsons Center, 549 Columbus Ave (☎267-6272). Central ⓣ. The radical left lives on in this shrine to socialism, with a particular bent toward women's issues, labor issues and radical economics.

New Words, 186 Hampshire St (☎876-5310). Central ⓣ. Well-organized feminist bookstore with tons of books on history criticism, lesbian studies, and the like. It also serves as a community center for women's issues and feminist events.

We Think the World of You, 540 Tremont St (☎574-5000). Back Bay ⊤. Cool music and a good selection of international magazines in bright, upscale South End gay bookstore.

Willowbee & Kent, 519 Boylston St (☎437-6700). Kenmore ⊤. The first floor of this roomy store has a good range of travel guidebooks and gear; the second is given over to a travel agency.

Food and drink

Eating out in Boston may prevail, but should you choose to cook your own **food**, or get provisions for a picnic, you won't do so badly either. There are also some excellent spots to pick up pastries, pies, and other dessert-oriented items.

Gourmet food and wine shops

Monica's Salumeria, 130 Salem St (☎742-4101). Haymarket ⊤. Lots of imported Italian cheeses, prosciuttos, cookies and pastas.

Polcari's Coffee, 105 Salem St (☎227-0786). Haymarket ⊤. Old and fusty, but brimming with coffees and every spice you could think of. Worth going inside just for the aroma.

Savenor's, 160 Charles St (☎723-6328). Charles ⊤. Known for its meats, this small gourmet food shop in Beacon Hill also has a better-than-average produce selection, in addition to pre-pared foods – ideal for taking to the nearby Charles River Esplanade for an impromptu picnic.

See Sun Co, 25 Harrison St (☎426-0954). Chinatown ⊤. The most accessible of Chinatown's markets, they've got all the basics, from huge bags of rice to a dizzying range of soy sauces; you can also get more exotic delicacies like duck's feet.

Trio's, 222 Hanover St (☎523-9636). Haymarket ⊤. The best spot in the North End for fresh ravioli and other pasta.

Health food

Bread & Circus, 15 Westland Ave (☎375-1010). Symphony ⊤. The Boston branch of this New England wholefoods chain, near Symphony Hall, has all the alternative foodstuffs you'd expect. There is a branch at 115 Prospect St, Cambridge (☎492-0070). Central Square ⊤.

Harvest Co-operative Market, 581 Massachusetts Ave (☎661-1580). Central ⊤. Salad bar, produce aisle, and plenty of bulk foods. Also in Jamaica Plain, 57 South St (☎524-1667).

Pastries and cakes

Bova's Bakery, 76 Prince St (☎523-5601). Haymarket ⊤. North End all-night bakery, with cannoli, oven-fresh cakes, and whoopie pies, that vends most items for around $5.

LMNOP Bakery, 91 Park Plaza (☎338-4220). Arlington ⊤. Excellent breads, pastries, and cookies, plus great sandwiches and pasta specials at lunchtime.

Mike's Pastry, 300 Hanover St (☎742-3050). Haymarket ⊤. The famed North End shop is one part Italian, two parts American, meaning in addition to cannoli and tiramisu, you'll find counters-full of brownies and cookies. The gelato, only served in summer, is not to be missed.

Rosie's Bakery, 243 Cambridge St (☎491-9488). #69 bus. This pastel-pink bakery features the richest, most decadent desserts in Cambridge. Their specialty is a fudge brownie called the "chocolate orgasm," though the less provocatively named lemon squares are just as good.

Malls and department stores

Boston's **malls** are well scattered about, good places if you need to pick up a number of diverse items on the same shopping trip. They often contain the city's biggest **department stores**, though a few unattached ones stand out, mostly around Downtown Crossing.

BOSTON FESTIVALS

It's always good to know ahead of time what **festivals** are scheduled to coincide with your trip to Boston, though even if you don't plan it, there's likely to be some sort of celebration or seasonal event going on. Summer is usually best for these, as the warmer weather allows for more outdoor festivals to take place. For written information, call the Boston Convention and Visitors Bureau (☎1-888/SEE-BOSTON); the City of Boston Special Events Line (☎822-0038) has recorded information on the month's festivals.

JANUARY

Late Chinese New Year. Dragon parades and firecrackers punctuate these festivities throughout Chinatown. It can occasionally fall in February, depending on the Chinese lunar calendar (☎542-2574).

FEBRUARY

First two Mondays The Beanpot. At the FleetCenter, Boston's four major college hockey teams (Boston University, Boston College, Northwestern, and Harvard) compete for bragging rights (☎624-1000).

MARCH

17 St Patrick's Day Parade and Festival. Boston's substantial Irish-American community, along with much of the rest of the city, parade through South Boston, which culminates in Irish folk music, dance and food at Faneuil Hall (☎536-4100).

APRIL

Third Monday Patriot's Day. A celebration and re-creation of Paul Revere's (and William Dawes') famous ride, from the North End to Lexington, that alerted locals that the British army had been deployed against the rebel threat (☎536-4100).

Third Monday Boston Marathon. One of America's premier running events with a world-class field (☎236-1652).

MAY

Early Blacksmith House Dulcimer Festival. In Cambridge, workshops and performances by experts of both mountain and hammer dulcimers (☎547-6789).

Mid Greater Boston Kite Festival. Franklin Park is taken over by kite-lovers during this celebration, which also has kite-makers, flying clinics, and music (☎635-4505).

JUNE

First week Boston Dairy Festival. Cows and other animals are brought back to Boston Common to graze. For a modest donation, you can indulge in unlimited samples of Boston's best ice creams.

Early to mid Boston Early Music Festival. This Renaissance fair only happens every other year, the next one scheduled for 2001. Concerts, costume shows and exhibitions take place throughout town (☎661-1812, *www.bemf.org*).

Mid to late Boston Globe Jazz Festival. The city's leading newspaper

The malls

Cambridgeside Galleria, 100 Cambridgeside Place (☎621-8666). Kendall ⓣ. This is *the* mall in Cambridge; if you think finding it is difficult, try parking.

Copley Place, 100 Huntington Ave (☎375-4400). Copley ⓣ. This ambitious, upscale office-retail-residential complex features more than 100 stores and an 11-screen multiplex. The best

sponsors a weeklong series of jazz events at various venues, usually in mid to late June. Some are free, though shows by big names can be pricey (☎929-2000).

JULY

Week leading up to 4 Harborfest hosts a series of jazz, blues and rock concerts on the waterfront. On weekend of July 4, there's the annual turnaround cruise of the *USS Constitution*, the highly competitive "Chowderfest," and tons of fireworks (☎227-1528).

4 Boston Pops Concert and Fireworks. A wildly popular yearly event at the Hatch Shell, for which people sometimes line up at dawn to get good seats for the evening concert by the scaled-down version of the Boston Symphony Orchestra (☎266-1492).

Throughout July and August Commonwealth Shakespeare Company on the Boston Common. First-rate, free Shakespeare productions, performed in the evening outside on the Tremont side of the Common (☎423-7600).

AUGUST

End of month August Moon Festival. Chinatown's merchants and restaurateurs hawk their wares on the street amid dragon parades and firecrackers (☎542-2574).

Last two weekends Italian Festas. Music, dancing, and games throughout the North End. In weekend parades, statues of the Virgin Mary are borne through the streets as locals pin dollar bills to the floats.

SEPTEMBER

Early to mid Boston Film Festival. Area theaters screen independent films, with discussions by directors and screenwriters.

Mid Cambridge River Festival. Memorial Drive is closed off from JFK Street to Western Avenue for music shows, dancing, and eclectic food offerings, all along the Charles River (☎349-4380).

OCTOBER

Second Monday Columbus Day Parade. Kicked off by a ceremony at City Hall at 1pm, the raucous, Italian-flavored parade continues into the heart of the North End.

Second to last weekend Head of the Charles Regatta. Hordes of well-off prepsters and the like descend on the Harvard Square area, ostensibly to watch the crew races, but really more to pal around with their cronies and get loaded (☎864-8415).

DECEMBER

Sunday nearest 16 Boston Tea Party Re-enactment. A lusty re-enactment of the march from Old South Meeting House to the harbor, and the subsequent tea-dumping that helped spark the American Revolution, hosted by the Boston Tea Party Museum (☎338-1773).

31 First Night. Big, though not at all wild, New Year's Eve celebration, with open galleries, performances by mimes and musicians, and other artsy happenings citywide (☎542-1399).

---

of the shops are a Rizzoli bookstore, a Nieman Marcus department store, the gift shop for the Museum of Fine Arts, and the Artful Hand Gallery, representing solely American artists.

Faneuil Hall Marketplace, Faneuil Hall (☎338-2323). Government Center Ⓣ. The city's most famous market, with a hundred or so shops, plus next door's Quincy Market. It's a bit tourist-oriented, but still worth a trip down.

The Heritage on the Garden, cnr Arlington and Boylston sts (☎423-0002). Arlington ⊤. Neither a mall nor a department store, but rather a very upscale mixed-use complex that consists of condos, restaurants, and boutiques.

The Shops at Prudential Center, 800 Boylston St (☎267-1002). Copley ⊤. This is a fairly new conglomeration of a hundred or so mid-market shops, heavily patronized by local residents and conventioneers from the adjacent Hynes Convention Center.

Department stores

Filene's, 426 Washington St (☎357-2100). Downtown Crossing ⊤. The merchandise inside downtown Boston's oldest department store is standard issue; the stunning 1912 Beaux Arts facade is not. You'll have better luck downstairs, in Filene's Basement.

Filene's Basement, 426 Washington St (☎542-2011). Downtown Crossing ⊤. Established in 1908, Filene's Basement is now a separate business from Filene's; though it has become a chain, nothing beats the original. Heavily discounted merchandise from not only Filene's, but other big-name department stores and a few Boston boutiques. Be warned: dressing rooms are communal.

The Harvard Coop, 1400 Massachusetts Ave (☎499-2000). Harvard ⊤. Harvard's local department store, with a wide selection of fairly expensive insignia clothing and the like.

Loehmann's, 385 Washington St (☎338-7177). Downtown Crossing ⊤. Well-known chain that specialized in dramatically discounted designer-label womenswear.

Music

The best places for new and used **music** in Boston are on Newbury Street in Back Bay, around Massachusetts Avenue near Kenmore Square, and up in Harvard Square, basically all the places students can be found hanging about.

New

Newbury Comics, 332 Newbury St (☎236-4930). Hynes ⊤. Boston's biggest alternative record store carries lots of independent labels you won't find at the national chains, and there's a substantial array of vinyl 12-inches and singles as well as posters, zines, and kitschy T-shirts. There's also a branch in Harvard Square (☎491-0337), in the Garage shopping mall, 36 JFK St.

Nuggets, 486 Commonwealth Ave (☎536-0679). Kenmore ⊤. American jazz, rock, and R&B are the strong suits at this venerable new and used record store.

Satellite, 49 Massachusetts Ave (☎536-5482). Hynes ⊤. This storefront hideaway has a great selection of imported techno and trance, in both CD and vinyl format.

Tower Records, 360 Newbury St (☎247-5900). Hynes ⊤. Typically vast representative of this music superstore chain, with a standard selection of all types of music.

Used and vintage

Disc Diggers, 401 Highland Ave, Somerville (☎776-7560). Davis ⊤. The largest selection of used CDs in New England, though not equal quality. Forgotten albums by one-hit wonders abound.

In Your Ear, 72 Mt Auburn (☎491-5035). Harvard ⊤. Downstairs shop heavy on the vinyl, especially good for rock albums.

Pipeline, 1110 Massachusetts Ave (☎661-6369). Harvard ⊤. Mainly used CDs and vinyl, but also new music, kitsch Americana, and videos of the Russ Meyer ilk.

Planet Records, 54B JFK St (☎492-0693). Harvard ⊤. Where to buy that Duran Duran or Styx LP missing from your collection – or to sell the one you're tired of.

Skippy White's, 538 Massachusetts Ave (☎491-3335). Central ⓣ. Excellent collection of jazz, blues, R&B, gospel, funk, and hip-hop.

Stereo Jack's, 1686 Massachusetts Ave (☎497-9447). Harvard ⓣ. Probably the best shop for jazz in Boston, with some incredible bargains on vinyl.

Twisted Village, 12 Eliot St (☎354-6898). Harvard ⓣ. A really weird mix of fringe styles, among them avant-garde, beat, spoken word and psychedelic rock.

Specialty shops

Black Ink, 101 Charles St (☎723-3883). Charles ⓣ. Eclectic assortment of things you don't need but are still cool: rubber stamps, campy refrigerator magnets, and a panoply of Tintin paraphernalia.

The Garment District/Dollar-A-Pound, 200 Broadway (☎876-9795). Kendall ⓣ. If you are willing to wade through the mounds of clothing alongside the scores of pierced teenagers, you are likely to find something worth the price ($1 per pound, as the name says). The items one flight up, in *The Garment District*, are pricier, though not necessarily better.

International Poster Gallery, 205 Newbury St (☎375-0076). Copley ⓣ. Hours are easily lost here while sifting through the impressive collection of vintage posters including travel, army recruiting, war propaganda (from all sides) and classic advertisements.

Justin Tyme Emporium, 91 River St (☎491-1088). Central ⓣ. Justin's is all about pop culture artifacts, featuring boffo American detritus like lava lamps, Donny and Marie Osmond pin-ups and campy T-shirts with iron-ons.

Leavitt and Pierce, 1316 Massachusetts Ave (☎547-0576). Harvard ⓣ. Old-school tobacconists have been around almost as long as Harvard. An outstanding selection of cigars, imported cigarettes and smoking paraphernalia (lighters, rolling papers, ashtrays), plus an upstairs smoking loft right out of the carefree past.

The London Harness Company, 60 Franklin St (☎543-9234). Downtown Crossing ⓣ. Chiefly known for its quality luggage goods, this atmospheric shop reeks of traditional Boston – indeed, Ben Franklin used to shop here. Chess sets, clocks, candlesticks, and decorative boxes, too.

Tokai Pottery, 207 Newbury St (☎578-0976). Copley ⓣ. Excellent collection of high-quality Japanese pottery and other crafts.

Listings

Airlines American Airlines ☎1-800/433-7300; British Airways ☎1-800/247-9297; United Airlines ☎1-800/241-6522; US Airways ☎1-800/428-4322; Virgin Atlantic ☎1-800/862-8621. American and United have offices in the *Park Plaza Hotel* (in addition to one at Logan Airport); British Airways' office is across from the Government Center ⓣ station.

Banks and currency exchange Fleet Bank is the biggest bank, with branches and ATMs throughout the city. Bureaux de change are not very prevalent. You can find locations at Logan Airport Terminal E (International); Thomas Cook, 399 Boylston St; and many Fleet Bank branches.

Bowling Boston's variation on tenpin bowling is "candlepin" bowling, in which the ball is smaller, the pins narrower and lighter, and you have three rather than two chances to knock the pins down. Try the Ryan Family Amusement Center, 82 Landsdowne St (Sun, Mon, Wed & Thurs noon–11pm, Tues 9am–11pm, Fri & Sat noon–midnight; ☎267-8495).

Consulates Canada, 3 Copley Place (☎262-3760, *www.dfait-maeci.gc.ca*); France, 31 St James Ave (☎542-7374, *www.franceboston.org*); UK, 600 Atlantic Ave (☎248-9555, *www.britainusa /boston*).

Emergencies Dial ☎911 for emergency assistance.

Film and processing Almost any kind of film can be found at pharmacies and camera specialty shops around town. For one-hour developing service, try Moto Photo, with locations in the Financial District, 101 Summer St (☎423-6848); Back Bay, 657 Boylston St (☎266-6560); and Harvard Square, 19 Dunster St (☎497-0731).

Hospitals Boston is home to some of the world's best hospitals, including Massachusetts General Hospital, 55 Fruit St (☎726-2000); Beth Israel Deaconess Medical Center, 330 Brookline Ave (☎667-7000); Brigham and Women's Hospital, 75 Francis St (☎732-5500); Mount Auburn Hospital, 330 Mt Auburn St, Cambridge (492-3500); and Children's Hospital, 300 Longwood Ave (☎355-6000).

Internet The Boston Public Library has free Internet access for library card holders. Others should head to the nearest Kinko's: Harvard Square, 1 Mifflin Place (☎497-0125); Back Bay, 187 Dartmouth (☎262-6188); Downtown, 10 Post Office Square (☎482-4400); and various other locations throughout the region.

Laundries Back Bay Laundry Emporium, 409A Marlborough St (daily 7.30am–11pm, last wash at 9pm), is a good, clean bet; drop-off service is 90¢ per pound of clothing.

Libraries The biggest and best library is the main branch of the Boston Public Library, at Copley Square (Mon–Thurs 9am–9pm, Fri–Sat 9am–5pm, Sun 1–5pm; ☎536-5400).

Parking A nightmare. Garages can cost $15–20 per evening, more overnight. There are metered spots on main streets like Newbury, Boylston, and Charles, but the chances of finding one on any given evening is slim at best. In Cambridge, most parking is residential only, but there are a few metered spots, mostly on and right off Mass Ave, which are not enforced 6pm–8am. Still, the smartest thing to do is park your car at Newton Ⓣ (exit 16 off the Mass Turnpike) and take the Ⓣ into and around the city.

Pharmacies The CVS drugstore chain has locations all over the city, though not all have pharmacies. For those, try the branches at 155–157 Charles St, in Beacon Hill (open 24 hours; ☎227-0437, pharmacy ☎523-1028), and 35 White St, in Cambridge's Porter Square (☎876-4037, pharmacy ☎876-5519).

Police In case of emergency, get to a phone and dial ☎911. For nonemergency situations, contact the Boston Police, headquartered at 154 Berkeley St, in Back Bay (☎343-4200).

Post office The biggest post office downtown is J.W. McCormack Station in Post Office Square, at 90 Devonshire St (Mon–Fri 7.30am–6pm, Sat 7.30am–3pm; ☎720-4754); other central branches are at 125 Mt Auburn St, in Harvard Square (same hours; ☎876-6483) and 77 Massachusetts Ave, in Central Square (☎876-0620). The General Post Office, at 25 Dorchester Ave, by Fort Point Channel, is open 24 hours (☎654-5326).

Sports Baseball: Boston Red Sox (☎267-1700) play at Fenway Park, seats $18–40; Basketball: Boston Celtics (☎523-3030) play at the FleetCenter, 150 Causeway St, in the West End, seats $10–85; Hockey: Boston Bruins (☎931-2222) also play at the FleetCenter, seats $20–75.

Travel agents Council Travel, 12 Eliot St, 2nd Floor, Harvard Square, Cambridge (☎497-1497), specializes in student and youth travel; American Express Travel, 170 Federal St (☎439-4400), provides general services.

CHAPTER TWO

EASTERN MASSACHUSETTS

The vast majority of Massachusetts' six million residents live within a few miles of its eastern coast, many of them direct descendants of successive waves of Europeans, going all the way back to the Mayflower Pilgrims, who arrived here, miles off course, in 1620. They were heading, in fact, for Jamestown, Virginia, though after the initial disappointment wore off they must have been impressed by what they had found: natural harbors to facilitate trade and commerce, waters teeming with fish for food, virgin forests providing endless supplies of wood for fuel and for building, even creeks and salt marshes that reminded them of their native England. Heartened by their initially friendly contact with indigenous Native Americans who were willing to share their agricultural knowledge of the terrain, the Pilgrims stayed put. The rest, as they say, is history.

That's apt, considering that **Eastern Massachusetts** has quite a bit to offer in the way of history, cradle as it is of much early American development. The coast itself can hardly be said to be spectacular, like that of California, or even nearby Maine (though for stupendous geological formations, you can't get much more impressive than Cape Cod); rather, the shoreline draws its charm from the diversity it offers – surf-lashed promontories, windswept offshore islands, pristine beaches, and the laid-back towns that surround them along the way. Wherever you happen to take a short stay – there's no overwhelming need to spend more than a few days, if that, in any one area – you likely won't be more than a stone's throw away from a vast number of historical sights, even at the very end of the Cape, where you probably thought you could escape from it all.

Just inland from Boston, and easily done as a day-trip, are the towns of **Lexington** and **Concord**, major players during the Revolutionary War. Otherwise, Massachusetts' long coast can be divided into four sections, all linked by the major highways which radiate from Boston: the **North Shore**, which stretches from

ACCOMMODATION PRICE CODES

All accommodation prices in this book have been coded using the symbols below; prices are for the least expensive **double rooms** in each establishment. For a full explanation see p.28 in Basics. Individual rates rather than price codes are given for **hostels**.

① up to $30	④ $60–80	⑦ $130–175
② $30–45	⑤ $80–100	⑧ $175–250
③ $45–60	⑥ $100–130	⑨ $250+

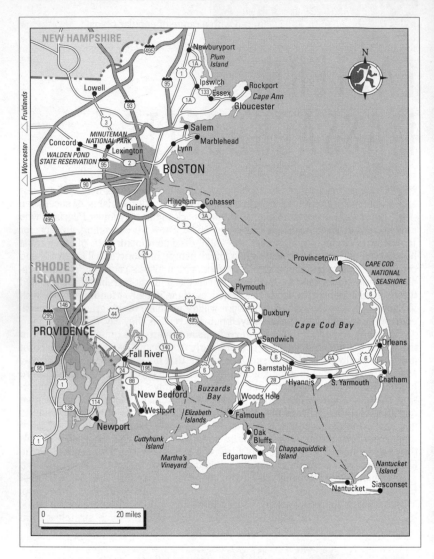

Boston's unsalubrious northern suburbs to the New Hampshire border, including the famous Witch Trial town of **Salem** and the rocky **Cape Ann** peninsula with the salty old fishing ports of **Gloucester** and **Rockport**; the **South Shore**, extending from the southern outskirts of Boston towards **Plymouth**, with its Pilgrim-related sights, all the way to the Rhode Island border, passing the partially restored whaling port of **New Bedford**, among more dreary outposts, in its course; the outstretched arm of **Cape Cod**, a vast glacial deposit reaching more than seventy miles into the Atlantic, and splattered with a range of popular resorts, none better than bohemian **Provincetown**; and the relaxed, upmarket holiday islands of **Martha's Vineyard** and **Nantucket**, playgrounds of the rich and famous.

LEXINGTON AND CONCORD

The sedate towns of **Lexington** and **Concord**, almost always mentioned in the same breath, cash in on their fame as the locations of the Americans' first armed confrontation with the British. Lexington is mostly suburban today, while Concord, five miles east, still has the flavor of a genteel country town. Most of the area's historical sights have been incorporated into the **Minute Man National Park**, which takes in the Lexington Battle Green, the North Bridge area in Concord, and much of Battle Road, the route the British followed on their retreat from Concord to Boston. The battles of Lexington and Concord are evoked in a piecemeal but relentless fashion throughout, with visitors' centers full of scale models and remnant musketry, and old colonial houses boasting the odd preserved bullet hole, though only a few of these spots are worth any more than a quick look. The whole affair tends to be overly structured – in many instances you must take hour-long tours of tiny houses you could walk through in two minutes. The Park also includes the **Old Manse** and **The Wayside**, two rambling old Concord houses with bookish pasts, though some other "literary" sites, such as **Walden Pond** in Concord, are just beyond its boundaries.

Some history

What finally precipitated the celebrated battle of April 19, 1775 was the march of British troops to Concord to seize the munitions that the Americans had squirrelled away there. Such plans were hardly a secret; the "Minute Men" were so called because they knew they might have to fight at a moment's notice. When the British troops disembarked from Boston Common, Paul Revere and William Dawes set out on separate routes to sound the alarm. Within minutes, church bells were clanging and cannon roaring throughout the countryside, signalling the rebels to head for Lexington Green; hundreds more converged around the North Bridge area of Concord. Revere, who was questioned at gunpoint en route to Lexington but managed to escape, gave the final alarm to John Hancock and Samuel Adams (who were in town to attend a provincial congress) at the Hancock-Clarke House.

GETTING TO LEXINGTON AND CONCORD

Despite their rural setting, Concord and Lexington are only about a dozen miles from downtown Boston, and therefore readily accessible from the city. The MBTA (☎617/722-3200) operates trains to Concord from **North Station** and also operates buses to Lexington from Cambridge's **Alewife Station**. Journey time is again around one hour. If you are coming from Boston by **car**, take Route 2 (Mass Ave) out of the city to Arlington Center, then follow the signs to Lexington. If you're in shape and the weather permits, the **Minuteman bike path** goes from Cambridge to Lexington Green. The easiest places to pick up the bike path are behind Davis or Alewife Ⓣ stations on the red line.

John Parker, the colonial captain, was down the street at the Buckman Tavern, when he received word that the British were closing in on the Green. "Don't fire unless fired upon," he ordered the men, "but if they mean to have a war, let it begin here." With only 77 Americans pitted against 700 British regulars, it was more a show of resolve than a hope for victory. Who fired the first shot remains a mystery, but in the fracas that followed, eight Americans were killed, including Parker. The British suffered no casualties, and marched three miles west to Concord.

By the time they arrived, it was already after sunrise on April 19, and hundreds more Minute Men had amassed on a farm behind North Bridge near where the lion's share of munitions were stored. When a British officer accidentally set fire to a building the Americans believed that the town was going up in smoke. They fired on the British guarding the other side of the bridge: the "shots heard round the world," as history books have it. The British were now outnumbered four to one, and suffered heavily in the ensuing battle, which continued all the way back to Boston.

Lexington

The main thing to see in **LEXINGTON** itself is the grassy, meticulously manicured **Battle Green**, the only site where the American flag is flown 24 hours a day. The land serves as Lexington's town common and is fronted by Henry Kitson's diminutive but dignified statue of *The Minute Man*. Though this musket-bearing figure of **Captain John Parker** was not dedicated until 1900, it stands on boulders dislodged from the stone walls behind which the colonial militia fired at British troops on April 19, 1775. The **Lexington Visitor Center**, 1875 Massachusetts Ave, on the eastern periphery of the Green (daily 10am–4pm; ☎781/862-1450, *www .lexingtonchamber.org*), has a diorama that shows the detail of the battle, while in the **Buckman Tavern**, facing the Green, 1 Bedford St, a bullet hole from a British gun has been preserved in an inner door near the restored first-floor tap room. A couple of blocks north, an old plaque affixed to the **Hancock-Clarke House**, 35 Hancock St (mid-March to late Oct Mon–Sat 9am–5pm, Sun 1–5pm; $4), solemnly reminds that this is where "Samuel Adams and John Hancock were sleeping when aroused by Paul Revere." If you don't want to pay for the grand tour, check out the free exhibits on the first floor, which include the drum on which William Diamond beat the signal for the Minute Men and the pistols that British Major John Pitcairn lost on the retreat from Concord. The small, wooden **Munroe Tavern**, 1332 Massachusetts Ave (same details as Hancock-Clarke House), a bit removed from the town center, served as a field hospital for British soldiers, but for a mere ninety minutes. Just outside of Lexington town, a contemporary brick-and-glass building houses the **Museum of Our National Heritage**, 33 Marrett Rd (Mon–Sat 10am–5pm, Sun noon–5pm; free), which tries to be just that, with rotating displays on all facets of American history, daily life, and culture, plus a permanent exhibit on the battle events of Lexington.

Practicalities

Accommodation in Lexington includes the *Battle Green Motor Inn*, 1720 Massachusetts Ave (☎781/862-6100 or 1-800/343-0235; ④–⑤), with 96 comfortable, basic rooms. The *Desiderata Bed & Breakfast,* 189 Wood St (☎781/862-2824; ④–⑤), is quieter, a Victorian farmhouse with three guest rooms, all non-smoking, with private baths; *Pacem*, 62 Sherburne Rd (☎781/862-3337; ③–④), is another small family-run establishment. For something to **eat**, *Versailles*, 1777 Massachusetts Ave (☎781/861-1711), serves fine French fare in an intimate setting.

Concord

CONCORD was one of the few sizeable inland towns of New England at the time of the Revolution, but it hasn't grown much since and you can see the major sights in a matter of minutes. It's a good spot to explore by bike; the countryside around town is some of the most pristine in this part of the state, filled with bucolic fields and historic colonial houses. The business district hugs **Main Street**, which intersects Monument Street right by the historic **Colonial Inn**, where many of the wounded from the battles of Lexington and Concord were tended; today it is an atmospheric place to stay or just to eat a tavern lunch of fish cakes and chips. Main Street crosses Lexington Road at the **Hill Burying Ground**, from the top of which you can survey much of Concord. A few blocks behind the grounds, off Route 62, lies **Sleepy Hollow Cemetery**, where Concord literati Ralph Waldo Emerson, Nathaniel Hawthorne, Henry David Thoreau, and Louisa May Alcott are interred atop "Authors' Ridge," a centrally located crest.

The most vaunted spot in Concord is the **North Bridge Area**, slightly removed from the town center and site of the first effective armed resistance to British rule in America. If you approach from Monument Street, as most tourists do, you'll be following the route the British took, as a plaque on a group grave of some British regulars reminds: "They came 3000 miles and died to keep the past upon its throne." The focal point, of course, is the bridge, which, though photogenic enough, looks a bit too groomed to provoke much patriotic sentiment – indeed, it's a 1954 replica of an earlier replacement. On the far side of the bridge is another Minute Man statue, this one sculpted by Daniel Chester French, of Lincoln Memorial fame. A short walk takes you to a **visitor's kiosk**, 2 Heywood St (May–Oct daily 9.30am–4.30pm).

Literally a stone's throw from North Bridge is the **Old Manse**, 269 Monument St (mid-Apr–Oct Mon–Sat 10am–4.30pm, Sun noon–5pm; $5.50), a grey clapboard house built for Ralph Waldo Emerson's grandfather, the Reverend William Emerson, who was able to witness the nearby hostilities from his window. Of the numerous rooms in the house, all with period furnishings intact, the most interesting is the small upstairs study, which is where Nathaniel Hawthorne, who rented the house in the early 1840s, wrote *Mosses from an Old Manse*, a rather obscure book that endowed the place with its name. On the first floor, a framed swath of original English wallpaper features the British "paper" stamp tax mark on the reverse side.

Another Concord literary landmark is the seventeenth-century **Wayside**, 455 Lexington Rd (April–Oct Tues–Sun 10am–5.30pm; $2), a three-hundred-year-old yellow wooden house where the Alcotts and Hawthornes lived and wrote, albeit at different times. Louisa May Alcott's girlhood experiences in the house are said to have inspired *Little Women*, by far her best-known novel. Amongst the many antique furnishings, including an original Franklin stove in the kitchen, the most evocative is in the fourth-floor "tower" that Hawthorne had added on: the slanted writing desk at which the author toiled, standing up. If you don't feel like taking a guided tour, you can stop in at the small but very well-done **museum** at the admissions area to get a flavor of the personalities behind the famous bylines.

Alcott actually penned *Little Women* next door at the gloomy, brown-clapboard **Orchard House**, 399 Lexington Road (April–Oct Mon–Sat 10am–4.30pm, Sun 1–4.30pm; Nov–March Mon–Fri 11am–3pm, Sat 10am–4.30pm, Sun 1–4.30pm; closed Jan 1–15; $7), where the family lived from 1858 to 1877. Next door to the Wayside is the **Concord Grape Cottage**, where in 1849 Ephraim Bull developed the Concord grape, one of only three fruits native to North America (the others are the cranberry and blueberry). You can see the vines that stemmed from the first successful fruit, but that's about it – it's a private home and not open to the public.

Just past the Orchard House, at the intersection of the Cambridge Turnpike and Lexington Road, is what has become known as the **Ralph Waldo Emerson House**, 28 Cambridge Turnpike (mid-April to Oct Thurs–Sat 10am–4.30pm, Sun 2–4.30pm; $2.50), where the essayist and poet lived from 1835 until his death in 1882. Emerson's study has been reconstructed across the street at the excellent **Concord Museum**, 200 Lexington Rd (Jan–March Mon–Sat 11am–4pm, Sun 1–4pm; April–Dec Mon–Sat 9am–5pm, Sun noon–5pm; $7), where his apple orchard once stood. The museum has more than a dozen galleries which display period furnishings from eighteenth- and nineteenth-century Concord, including a sizeable collection of Thoreau's personal effects, such as the simple bed from his Walden Pond hut. More interesting, however, are the Revolutionary War artifacts, including one of the signal lanterns hung from the Old North Church in Boston.

Practicalities

For somewhere to **stay**, the *Amerscot House B&B,* 61 West Acton Rd, Stow (☎978/897-0666; ⑥–⑦), offers attentive hospitality in a restored 1734 farmhouse, while the *Concordian Motel*, a few miles west of downtown Concord on Route 2 at Hosmer Street, Acton (☎978/263-7765; ④–⑤), has 52 comfortable and inexpensive air-conditioned rooms. There are a few nice places to **eat**, including the *Walden Grille*, 24 Walden St (☎978/371-2233), which serves fresh fish, grilled meats and pasta in a relaxed atmosphere, and the *Ninety-Nine Restaurant & Pub*, 13 Commonwealth Ave (☎978/369-0300), a neighborhood restaurant specializing in steaks, seafood, pasta, and chicken. For a gourmet sandwich or picnic basket, try *The Cheese Shop*, 25–31 Walden St (☎978/369-5778).

Walden Pond State Reservation

The tranquility which Thoreau sought and savored at **Walden Pond**, just south of Concord proper off Route 126 (daily 7am–4.30pm, until sundown in summer; $2), is for the most part gone, thanks mainly to the masses of tourists who pour in to retrace his footsteps. The place itself, however, unremarkable but for its literary connection, has remained much the same since the author's famed exercise in independence from 1845 to 1847. Thoreau described his experiment in solitude and self-sufficiency in his 1854 book *Walden*, where he concluded, "A man is rich in proportion to the number of things which he can afford to let alone." Of his life in the simple log cabin, he wrote, "I did not feel crowded or confined in the least." A reconstructed single-room hut, replete with a journal open on its rustic desk, is situated near the car park (you'll have to be content with peering through the windows), while the site of the original cabin, closer to the shores of the pond, is marked out with stones. The pond, popular with long-

CONCORD AND TRANSCENDENTALISM

A half-century after the social tumult that precipitated independence, Concord became the center of a revolution in American thinking known as **transcendentalism**, a cerebral mix of religion, philosophy, mysticism and ethics. Heavily influenced by Unitarianism and the teachings of **Reverend Ellery Channing**, the transcendentalists, many of them Harvard-educated Unitarian ministers unhappy with their church's conservatism, denied the existence of miracles, and stressed the conviction that insight and intuitive knowledge were the ways to enhance the relationship between man, nature and the "over-soul." These beliefs, originating in the Platonic belief of a higher reality not validated by sense, experience, or pure reason, were borne of a passion for rural life, liberty and intellectual freedom. Indeed, the free thinking that transcendentalism unleashed put area writers at the vanguard of American literary expression.

In 1834, **Ralph Waldo Emerson** moved into the Old Manse, the house his grandfather had built near the North Bridge; there, in 1836, he wrote the book that would signal the birth of the movement, *Nature*, which argued for the organicism of all life, and the function of nature as a visible manifestation of invisible spiritual truths. His stature as an intensely pensive, learned scribe drew other intellectuals to Concord, notably Thoreau, Hawthorne, and the Alcotts, and in 1840 he co-founded *The Dial*, the literary magazine which became the movement's semi-official journal, with Margaret Fuller. The Concord authors formed a close-knit group. Nathaniel Hawthorne, a native of Salem, rented out the Old Manse for three happy years, returned to his hometown, then moved back to Concord permanently in 1852. Meanwhile, Emerson financed Thoreau's Walden Pond sojourn and the Alcotts lived in Orchard House, on Lexington Road. It was a largely wholesome literary movement and the short-lived utopian farming communities it spawned – Hawthorne's Brook Farm and Bronson Alcott's Fruitlands – seem almost quaint in retrospect. Its effect was longer lasting than these communities, however, as its proponents were to play an important role in supporting educational innovation, abolitionism and the feminist movement.

distance swimmers, was spared from development by a band of celebrities led by ex-Eagle Don Henley. It looks best at dawn, when the pond still "throws off its nightly clothing mist"; late risers should plan an off-season visit to maximize their transcendental experience of it all.

DeCordova Museum, Codman House, and Fruitlands

Though technically a part of the town of Lincoln, the **DeCordova Museum and Sculpture Park**, 51 Sandy Pond Rd (Tues–Sun 11am–5pm; museum $6), is only a few miles south of downtown Concord and worth a visit. All manner of contemporary sculpture peppers the museum's expansive 35-acre grounds, but most fascinating are the bigger works, like John Buck's *Dream World* and Paul Matisse's *Musical Fence*, which look like they busted the walls of a museum and tumbled into their present positions. Most of the sculptures are by American (and in particular New England) artists, and are sufficiently impressive to make the small on-site museum an afterthought.

Also in Lincoln, the three-story, gray-shingled **Codman House**, Codman Road (June to mid-Oct Wed–Sun noon–4pm; $3), which dates from 1735, and was home to five generations of the Codman family, contains eclectic architectural features from every period, from Georgian paneling through to a Victorian dining room. The grounds resemble those of an English country estate.

Thirty miles west of Boston, the small town of **Harvard** is home to the collection of museums known as **Fruitlands**, 102 Prospect Hill Rd (museums open mid-May through Oct Tues–Sun 10am–5pm; grounds and trails open daily year-round 10am–5pm; $8), which tell the story of the daily life, art and beliefs of a high-minded group, headed by **Bronson Alcott**, that aimed to create a "New Eden." Alcott started the idealistic but short-lived commune here with his English friend Charles Lane in 1843, espousing vegetarianism, freedom of expression, and celibacy (the latter after siring four daughters, including Louisa May), but talk of living off the "fruits of the land" proved much easier than actually doing it. True to Alcott's pastoral proclivities, today there are two hundred acres of woodlands and meadows on the site, which you can explore on four well-marked nature trails. The original farmhouse now houses a **museum** with exhibits on the transcendentalist movement, including letters and memorabilia of Alcott, Emerson and Thoreau. The **Shaker Museum** has displays of furniture, crafts and artifacts retrieved from a Shaker community that once existed here; the **Picture Gallery** features a collection of American art, including New England landscape paintings by Hudson River School artists Thomas Cole and Frederick Edwin Church; and an **Indian Museum** highlights Native American handicrafts and design including richly decorated clothing, headdresses, pottery, dolls and carved wood.

THE NORTH SHORE

The mainly rocky **North Shore**, which extends north of Boston to the New Hampshire border, takes in some of Massachusetts' most disparate geography and culture. Outside Boston a series of glum working-class suburbs – Revere, Saugus and Lynn – gradually yield to such bedroom communities as Swampscott and Beverly Farms, then to the charming waterfront towns of **Marblehead** and **Salem**, the first real places of any interest, and the latter synonymous with the infamous Witch Trials which took place there in 1692. Just north juts the promontory of scenic **Cape Ann**, the so-called "other Cape"; with its lighthouses, seafood shanties and rocky shores pummeled by the cold Atlantic, it's a scaled-down version of the Maine coast. Highlights include the fishing port of **Gloucester** and the laid-back oceanfront village of **Rockport**. Further up the Cape, the land becomes flatter, with acres of salt marshes and white sands, some of the finest in New England, particularly on **Plum Island**. If the beach is not your thing, here, too, are sleepy villages like **Essex** and **Ipswich**. Closer to the New Hampshire border, the elegant old fishing burg **Newburyport** is of some historical interest, with scores of Federal mansions and a red-brick commercial district built in the early 1800s. Any of these North Shore towns can be reached in an easy day-trip from Boston, and none should take more than a day to explore anyway, with the possible exception of Salem.

The quickest route north from Boston is **Route 1**, but the more scenic (and closer to the coast) is **Route 1A**, which also traverses the bucolic horse country of Hamilton and Ipswich between Salem and Newburyport. From Route 1, **Route 127** branches off to loop around Cape Ann.

Salem

The Witch Trials of 1692 put it on the map for all the wrong reasons, but the unpretentious coastal town of **SALEM**, sixteen miles north of Boston, has done little since to distance itself from such macabre associations; indeed, a number of its attractions focus on the witch-related activity. It's all a bit misleading, considering Salem was the site where the Massachusetts Colony was first established – with the most elevated of intentions – and also for years an immensely prosperous port, the history of which has been largely forgotten. A walk around downtown, however, does much to demonstrate this other legacy: the stately sea captains' houses in the square-mile **McIntire District**; the **Essex Street Mall**, a pedestrian area with shops, cafés, and the **Peabody Essex Museum** – a treasure-trove of merchandise brought home by sea captains on their travels round the world; and the **harbor** area, which includes the famed **House of the Seven Gables** and the **Salem Maritime National Historic Site**, recalling the period of prosperity immediately after the Revolution when Salem boasted no fewer than 185 vessels in its merchant fleet.

Indeed, Salem had such a maritime empire that at one time many Asian merchants were under the impression that the town was the capital of the United States. A deep, well-protected harbor lured a handful of English settlers from Cape Ann to the spot they first called **Naumkeag**, and the Massachusetts Bay Colony was born. By 1683, Salem was one of the few lawful ports of entry for foreign cargos in British America, and by the time the Revolutionary War broke out, good fortune on the high seas had turned Salem into an unrivaled commercial dynamo. **Elias Derby**, said to be America's first millionaire, built his fortune by

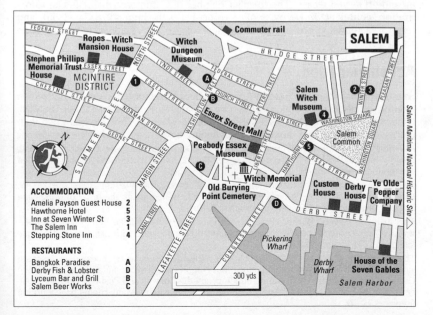

SALEM

Salem Maritime National Historic Site

ACCOMMODATION

Amelia Payson Guest House	2
Hawthorne Hotel	5
Inn at Seven Winter St	3
The Salem Inn	1
Stepping Stone Inn	4

RESTAURANTS

Bangkok Paradise	A
Derby Fish & Lobster	D
Lyceum Bar and Grill	B
Salem Beer Works	C

0   300 yds

running privateers from Salem during the war; afterwards, when British ports barred American vessels, he simply had his ships sail farther afield, most gainfully to China and the East Indies.

Of the many goods on the outbound ships of Salem traders, the most lucrative by far was **cod**, which found a huge market in Catholic Europe. Salem's "merchant princes" brought back everything from spices to olive oil to fine china, for a while fairly monopolizing the luxury goods trade in America. At a time when most of the federal government's income came from customs duties, millions of dollars poured in by way of Salem's **Federal Customs House**. But the California Gold Rush, Civil War and silting up of the harbor all conspired to rob Salem of its generations of prosperity. Today the harbor is still home to hundreds of boats, though mostly pleasure craft.

Arrival, information and getting around

MBTA (☎617/722-3200) commuter **trains** run hourly (every two hours at weekends) between Salem and Boston's **North Station**, and there's a regular **bus service**, also run by MBTA, from Haymarket Square in Boston. If you are traveling by **car** from Boston, you can choose between the slow but more interesting Route 1A, or the much faster Route 128. Take exit 25A for Salem. Once you've arrived, downtown Salem is so compact you're unlikely to need anything more than a pair of feet to get around; the **Salem Heritage Trail**, a painted red line on Salem's sidewalks, links some of the key sights, similar to Boston's more well-known Freedom Trail. The **Salem Trolley** (☎978/744-5469), which operates between July and October, also links the main sights. The $8 tickets are valid for a whole day, so you can jump on and off as you please. The town's Chamber of Commerce maintains an **information center** at 32 Derby Square (Mon–Fri 9am–5pm; ☎978/745-3855), and there is a tourist office on the third floor of the City Hall, 95 Washington St (Mon–Fri 8am–4pm; ☎1-800/777-6848).

Accommodation

Salem is perhaps the only town in America where **hotels** are booked for Halloween months in advance; if you plan on coming any time in late October, beware. Otherwise, apart from the peak summer period when the town is crammed with tourists, you should have no difficulty in finding a room, although none are cheap.

Amelia Payson House, 16 Winter St (☎978/744-8304, *www.ameliapaysonhouse.com*). Small, friendly, historic B&B in a restored 1845 Greek Revival home, where each room is furnished with period antiques. [5]–[6].

Hawthorne Hotel, 18 Washington Square W (☎978/744-4080 or 1-800/SAY-STAY, *www.hawthornehotel.com*). Salem's only full-service hotel is right in the heart of things and home to two of the town's better restaurants. [5]–[6].

The Inn at Seven Winter Street, 7 Winter St (☎978/745-9520 or 1-800/932-5547, *www.inn7winter.com*). Ten elegant air-conditioned rooms, some with fireplace and antique bed in an 1871 Victorian house. [6]–[7].

The Salem Inn, 7 Summer St (☎978/741-0680, *www.saleminnma.com*). Located on the south side of the McIntire District, this historic inn comprises 38 well-maintained rooms in the Captain West House, the main central building, and the Curwen and Peabody Houses, smaller ones on either side of the West with all non-smoking rooms. Many rooms have working fireplaces. [6]–[7].

THE SALEM WITCH TRIALS

By their quantity alone, Salem's witch memorials and "attractions" speak of the magnitude of the hysteria that gripped the town for much of 1692 and 1693. Bostonians had overthrown the Massachusetts Bay Colony's first royally-appointed governor, Sir Edmund Andros, in 1689, plunging the region, already under constant threat of French and Indian attack, into political instability. That same year, Boston minister and eventual Witch Trial judge **Cotton Mather** published his popular book *The Wonders of the Invisible World*, a sort of Rough Guide to the supernatural that would help feed the imagination of the town's gullible inhabitants later on. Salem itself was experiencing identity trouble: Salem Village, slightly inland, was a struggling community of farmers mired in property disputes and personality clashes, while Salem Town was an increasingly affluent port. Those caught up in the intrigue lived in Salem Village (which separated to form the town of Danvers in 1752), while the actual trials took place in Salem Town, which is known today simply as Salem.

The first casualties of the villagers' Calvinist lifestyle were their young and supremely bored teenage daughters, who reported as truth fireside tales of the occult as told by **Tituba**, a West Indian slave woman. The children ate up the stories and washed them down with hard cider and various potions, also proffered by Tituba. The fun and games took a sinister turn when the daughter of a new clergyman, Samuel Parris, and his niece experienced convulsive fits and started barking. Whether it was epilepsy or the adverse effects of eating mold-contaminated bread – or witchcraft – other girls started to copy them, and when the village doctor failed to diagnose the problem, the girls' accusations of witchcraft began to be taken seriously.

The trials that ensued pitted neighbor against neighbor, even husband against wife. Confessing to witchcraft spared you the gallows but meant castigation and the confiscation of your land. Mary Lacy of Andover, for instance, "confessed" that "me and Martha Carrier did both ride on a stick when we went to a witch meeting in Salem Village." Another accused, Giles Cory, first testified that his wife was a witch, then refused to agree that the court had the right to try him. To coerce him into acknowledging the court's authority, he was staked on ground under planks while heavy stones were pressed on top of him. He lasted two days, and died without confessing.

The trials were also marked by the girls' crazed ravings: in a scene re-enacted at the Witch Dungeon Museum, Ann Putnam claimed that Sarah Good, a pipe-smoking beggar woman, was biting her, right in front of the judge. Such **"spectral evidence"** was accepted as fact, and the trials soon degenerated into the definitive case study of guilt by association. More than 150 villagers were accused and imprisoned (this in a village of 500), nineteen were hanged and four died in jail. Tituba, who readily confessed to sorcery, was not among them. Two dogs were even hanged after some girls claimed they had given them "the evil eye."

The most grisly day in Salem's history came on **September 22, 1692**, when on the final day of execution eight villagers were hanged on **Gallow's Hill**, the precise location of which is not known. Though the hysteria continued for a while unabated, with another 21 people tried in January 1693, the court's legitimacy, shaky from the start (it was formed in direct response to the accusations), was starting to wear thin. One of the judges, Jonathan Corwin, and his family, stood to gain heavily from the proceedings; indeed, much purloined land fell into the hands of his son George. The new royal governor, **William Phipps**, appalled by the sordid state of affairs, finally intervened after his wife was accused. He responded by forbidding the use of spectral evidence as proof, and all of the accused were acquitted that May, with families of the victims eventually awarded damages.

The Stepping Stone Inn, 19 Washington Square N (☎978/741-8900, *www.steppingstoneinn .com*). An unassuming B&B in an 1846 building across from Salem Common and next to the Witch Museum. [5]–[6].

The Town

You're never very far from the Puritans' woeful legacy in Salem, with its plethora of witch-related museums, exhibits and memorials – most child-oriented and some frighteningly tacky, but others unexpectedly enlightening. There's no shortage of witches, either, as a sizeable and highly visible contingent of latter-day sorceresses has staked Salem out as their turf. Many of the so-called witches keep storefronts, and are more than willing to read your palm or otherwise prognosticate your future for a modest fee. Indulge if you must, but bear in mind they're as much a part of the tourist industry as everything else in Salem. Ironically, Salem's witch heritage has proved to be its ultimate salvation, because were it not for the spruced-up center that capitalizes on it, all of the once-proud port might look as industrial and unsightly as some neighboring North Shore towns.

Essex Street Mall

The **Essex Street Mall** is the closest thing Salem has to a main drag, a car-free, boutique-filled stretch of Essex Street that is convenient to many of the city's best sights. At its northern end, the **Salem Witch Museum**, Washington Square, (daily: July–Aug 10am–7pm; Sept–June 10am–5pm; $6; ☎978/744-1692), provides some entertaining, if kitschy, orientation on the Witch Trials. It's really just a sound-and-light show that makes ample use of wax figures to depict the events of 1692, housed in a suitably spooky Romanesque building that once served as a church. In front of it is the imposing statue of **Roger Conant**, founder of Salem's first Puritan settlement. More hokey but actually far more evocative of Salem's darker hours is the **Witch Dungeon Museum**, 16 Lynde St (daily 10am–5pm; $5; ☎978/741-3570), on the west side of town. The theater-cum-museum is situated on the site of the prison where the accused witches were locked up, uncovered during preliminary construction by the local phone company. Inside you're again treated to reconstructions of key events, this time by real people: upstairs are surprisingly well-done re-enactments of the farcical trial of Sarah Good, a beggar falsely accused of witchcraft, based on actual transcripts. Afterwards the actors escort you to a re-created "dungeon," where you see that some of the prison cells were no bigger than a telephone booth. Dank and supremely eerie, it's not hard to believe claims that the place is haunted. If it's all a bit too theatrical, head to the simple and moving **Witch Memorial**, at Charter and Liberty streets, a series of stone blocks etched with the names of the hanged. It's wedged into a corner of the **Old Burying Point Cemetery**, where one of the witch judges, **John Hathorne**, forebear of Salem's most famous son, Nathaniel Hawthorne, is buried. The author of *The Scarlet Letter* added a "w" to his name in an attempt to exorcise the shame.

Peabody Essex Museum

The best thing going in Salem, and a good primer before heading down to the harbor area, is the **Peabody Essex Museum**, right off the mall at East India Square (April–Oct Mon–Sat 10am–5pm, Sun noon–5pm; Nov–Mar Tues–Sat

10am–5pm, Sun noon–5pm; $10; *www.pem.org*), an assemblage of more than thirty galleries that hold an overwhelming mishmash of art and artifacts from around the world. Founded by ship captains in 1799 to exhibit their exotic *objets de voyage*, it houses the biggest collection of nautical paintings in the world. Other galleries display Chinese and Japanese, Asian, Oceanic, and African ethnological artifacts (there are some thirty thousand Japanese artifacts alone), American decorative arts and, in one of the preserved houses in the grounds, court documents from the Salem Witch Trials.

The first floor is home to the core museum displays, with creatively curated whaling exhibits that feature not only the requisite scrimshaw but Ambrose Garneray's famous 1835 painting *Attacking the Right Whale* and the gaping lower jaw of a sperm whale. There are also intelligent exhibits on the elite traders, dubbed "merchant princes," of Salem's seafaring golden age, and *Lady with a Medallion*, a ship's figurehead said to be by Samuel McIntire. Upstairs highlights include a cavernous central gallery with more fanciful figureheads from otherwise demolished ships hung from the walls and the reconstructed salon from America's first yacht, *Cleopatra's Barge*, which took to the seas in 1816.

Salem Harbor

Salem's once-bustling **Custom House** stands like a red-brick ghost in front of the defunct, 2000-foot long **Derby Wharf**, and the two are the rather melancholic central features of the **Salem Maritime National Historic Site** (orientation center at 193 Derby St; site open daily 9am–6pm; ranger-led tours $3), a federally run area of disused buildings, wharves, warehouses and lighthouse. Nathaniel Hawthorne had a miserable three-year stint at the Custom House that he later described as "slavery." You can take tours of the interior at irregular hours, but the warehouse in the rear, with displays of tea chests and such, is usually open during the day for casual inspection. Park rangers also give tours of the **Derby House**, an elegant brick mansion built in 1762 by millionaire Elias Hasket Derby to monitor the shipping empire over which he presided. Next door, the **West India Goods Store** sells the kinds of spices and knick-knacks common to Salem's nineteenth-century shops, such as molasses candy.

The most famous sight in this part of Salem is the **House of the Seven Gables**, 54 Turner St (open for guided tours daily 10am–5pm; Jan–March Mon–Sat 10am–5pm, Sun noon–5pm; $8), the inspiration for Hawthorne's gloomy 1851 novel of the same name. The "rusty wooden house with seven acutely peaked gables" that Hawthorne described, a three-story dark-clapboard house originally built in 1668 by local merchant John Turner and restored in 1910, is not as sinister as its reputation might imply, with the possible exception of a bricked-off "secret stairway" that leads to a small bedroom. The house was inhabited in the 1840s by Susan Ingersoll, a cousin of Hawthorne's whom he often visited. Also on the grounds are a small cottage that was the author's birthplace (actually built before 1750 and later moved onto the grounds), and lovely gardens that overlook Salem Harbor and feature a wishing well. They are a great place to nibble candies from **Ye Olde Pepper Company** nearby at 122 Derby St (☎978/745-2744), which claims (with some justification) to be the country's oldest candy store.

The McIntire District

The witch attractions pick up again at the so-called **Witch House**, 310 Essex St, west of the Essex Mall (daily: March–June 10am–4.30pm; July–Aug 10am–6pm;

Sept–Dec 10am–4pm; $5), the well-preserved former home of Judge Jonathan Corwin where the preliminary examinations of those accused of witchcraft took place. It's a good point of departure for exploring the **McIntire District**, a square mile of sea captains' homes west of downtown between Federal and Essex streets, named after a prominent local architect of the late eighteenth century, Samuel McIntire. The most picturesque stretch of these mansions, built after the Revolutionary War for sea captains who wanted to escape the congested waterfront, is along **Chestnut Street**. Of these, the **Stephen Phillips Memorial Trust House**, at no. 34 (Memorial Day to mid-Oct Mon–Sat 10am–4.30pm; $3), is the one to tour, for its trove of bric-a-brac from around the world, including Chinese porcelain and Oriental rugs. The **Ropes Mansion**, at 318 Essex St, is run by the Peabody Essex Museum (you'll have to request entrance permission there), but you can skip the inside anyway – there's little to distinguish it from similar ones – and instead check out its delightful formal garden, admission to which is free.

A bit outside of town (too far to walk, but feasible by bike or car), off of Rte-1A South, is the **Salem 1630 Pioneer Village** (Apr–Nov Mon–Sat 10am–5pm, Sun noon–5pm; $7), yet another of New England's colonial village staffed with period-costumed interpreters. It was, in its defense, one of the first of its kind, built in 1930 to celebrate the 300th anniversary of the Naumkeag settlement (and perhaps in a vain attempt to give colonial Salem a reputation as something other than "that place where they hanged all those witches"). The twelve buildings, primarily thatch-roofed cottages, represent a seventeenth-century fishing village, and, while it's no Sturbridge Village, it is a pleasant enough place to spend an hour or two. The most notable building is the Governor's Faire House, a rare example of a grand early colonial mansion.

Eating and drinking

It's inevitable that a town as geared to the tourist as Salem will have a range of places to **eat and drink**, though there's nothing too out of the ordinary here. Most of the top seafood spots are situated near the harbor.

Bangkok Paradise, 90 Washington St (☎978/825-9202). This cavernous Thai eatery is easily as good as any counterpart in Boston and well worth dropping by.

Bella Luna Café, 62 Wharf St (☎978/744-5555). A bistro-style restaurant where you will find blackened seafood, pastas with sun-dried tomatoes, and other trendy fare at reasonable prices (lunch usually under $10).

Café Bagel Company, 122 Washington St (☎978/740-3180). Clean, Starbucks-style place for a bagel sandwich and gourmet coffee.

Derby Fish & Lobster, 215 Derby St (☎978/745-2064). You'll get no prizes for guessing what's best at this inexpensive fixture near the harbor.

Lyceum Bar and Grill, 43 Church St (☎978/745-7665). Yankee cooking with modern updates at this popular eatery. Try their grilled pork tenderloin with garlic mashed potatoes.

The Museum Café, East India Square (☎978/740-4551). Though it's part of the Peabody Essex Museum, this elegant indoor/outdoor eatery is worth a visit in its own right – and you don't have to pay the museum admission to get in.

Nathaniel's, at the *Hawthorne Hotel*, 18 Washington Square W (☎978/744-4080). One of two restaurants in the hotel, and the fancier by far, creating concoctions like rope-grown mussels steamed in ale with roasted shallots.

Rockmore Drydock, 94 Wharf St (☎978/740-1001). Fresh seafood, steaks and chowders, in a choice of formal or informal settings at this waterfront restaurant.

Salem Beer Works, 278 Derby St (☎978/745-2337). The microbrew phenomenon hits Salem, with all the requisite nouveau pub grub to wash it down.

Salem Diner, 70 Loring Ave (☎978/741-7918). Your basic diner fare in an original Sterling Streamliner diner car, one of only four remaining in the US.

Marblehead

Just a few miles on from Salem, **MARBLEHEAD** sits on a peninsula thrusting out into Massachusetts Bay, its rocky shoreline cliffs overlooking a wide natural harbor – which has helped to make it one of the East Coast's biggest yachting centers. Thanks to its occupants' affluence, though, and, strangely, a severe shortage of parking, Marblehead has managed to escape the ravages of rampant commercialism typical of such playpens.

Founded by hardy fishermen from Devon and the English West Country in 1629, Marblehead prides itself on being the birthplace of the US Navy. Originally part of Salem, whose harbor it sits opposite, Marblehead gained its **independence** in 1648 and was incorporated as a town the following year. It became a thriving **fishing and trading port**, especially in the years leading up to the Revolution, and by 1760 was the sixth largest town in the colonies, with a population in excess of five thousand. Any aspirations of becoming one of the nation's great cities were soon dashed, however: Marblehead sent an entire regiment to fight in the Revolution; later, George Washington commissioned the schooner *Hannah*, owned and manned by Marbleheaders, and four subsequent vessels built here, wiping out the town's prospering commercial trade. Though fishing made a brief comeback, followed by shoemaking, it's boating that the town has become known for. In fact, Marblehead is at its most animated during the annual **Race Week** (the last week of July).

Winding streets lined with old clapboard houses trail down to the waterfront in testimony to the thriving early colonial community, most of them quite modest, their tiny gardens witness to the fact that only fishermen, not farmers, lived downtown. A bit further back from the oceanfront, along **Washington Street**, are the much larger and more sumptuous homes of the wealthy merchants who prospered during the pre-Revolutionary period. Among them is the 1768 **Jeremiah Lee Mansion** (June through mid-Oct Tues–Sat 10am–4pm, Sun 1–4pm; $5; ☎781/631-1069), the Georgian home of former shipping magnate Jeremiah Lee, who imported the decorative materials, including English wallpaper and South American mahogany, for his magnificent home. In fact, Lee's wallpaper is the only eighteenth-century hand-painted paper in existence today. Nearby, at the early eighteenth-century **King Hooper Mansion**, 8 Hooper St (Mon–Sat 10am–4pm, Sun 1–5pm; free; ☎781/631-2608), you can contrast the slave quarters with a lavish third-floor ballroom. While you're in the area, check out **Abbot Hall**, Washington Square (Memorial Day–Oct, Mon, Thurs & Fri 8am–5pm, Tues & Wed 8am–9pm, Sat 9am–6pm, Sun 11am–6pm; Nov–May, Mon–Thurs 8am–5pm, Fri 8am–1pm; free; ☎781/631-0000), Marblehead's uninspiring red-brick town hall, which houses Archibald Willard's famous patriotic painting *The Spirit of '76*.

Abbot Hall can actually be seen from far out at sea, but to get a sweeping view of the port, head to **Fort Sewall**, at the end of Front Street, the remnants of fortifications the British built in 1644, then enlarged in 1742 to protect the harbor from French cruisers (and that later protected the frigate *USS Constitution* in the War of 1812). Closer to the center of town, but with similar panoramic views, is **Old Burial Hill**, Orne Street, which holds the graves of more than six hundred Revolutionary War soldiers.

Practicalities

The Marblehead Chamber of Commerce maintains an **information booth** at the corner of Pleasant and Essex streets (Memorial Day to Labor Day 9am–5pm) and an **office** at 62 Pleasant St (Mon–Fri 9am–5pm; ☎781/631-2868).

Of the posh places to **stay** in Marblehead, most of which are **B&Bs**, best is *Spray Cliff on the Ocean*, 25 Spray Ave (☎781/631-6789 or 1-800/626-1530; ⑦–⑧), a restored 1919 mock-Tudor mansion with large rooms that afford sweeping ocean vistas. For lunch or **dinner**, try *Flynnie's*, 5 Haley Rd (☎781/639-2100), or *Flynnie's on the Beach*, Devereaux Beach, off Ocean Avenue, two casual eateries with inexpensive seafood; *Maddie's Sail Loft*, 15 State St (☎781/631-9824), is a neighborhood bar with great chowder and fish 'n' chips.

Cape Ann

Gloucester and **Rockport** are the two principal, but quite different, towns on low-key **Cape Ann**, which reaches into the Atlantic some forty miles north of Boston. The area draws plenty of visitors mainly on account of its salty air and seafood restaurants, but there aren't many sights per se, and in fact the best thing about the place is its unspoiled scenery, the kind of setting that inspired T.S. Eliot, who came here for his family holidays – The Dry Salvages of the third of his *Four Quartets* are a group of offshore rocks. Rocky headlands, lighthouses and sea spray define Cape Ann more than the little towns and villages do, and it's quite easy to feel very far from civilization here, if only for an afternoon. From I-95, Route 128 East will take you all the way to Gloucester, then it's either Route 127 or scenic Route 127A to Rockport.

Gloucester

Founded in 1623, gritty **GLOUCESTER** is the oldest fishing port in Massachusetts, though years of over-fishing the once cod-rich waters have robbed the town of any aura of affluence it may have had in the past, and federal regulations threaten to reduce the current fleet of fishing boats still further. It has long had an artistic identity as well, initially established by the painter **Winslow Homer**, who summered out in the harbor on Ten Pound Island in 1880. Homer was followed by a bevy of other artists who set up a colony on **Rocky Neck**, just east of downtown, where they converted fishermen's shacks into studios. The now-run-down district whose modern galleries are salt-box shacks selling the kinds of tacky nautical prints that end up in motel bathrooms, was also once the temporary home of Rudyard Kipling, whose 1897 novel *Captains Courageous* involved a Gloucester ship. Recently Gloucester has seen a bit of a tourist boom, triggered by the popular film version of Sebastian Junger's 1997 book *The Perfect Storm* (see p.553 for an excerpt); the **Crows Nest**, a bar and lodge depicted in the film, is the object of most visitors' affections (see review under "Practicalities" below). The friendly people in the **visitors' center**, located down by the harbor, at Stage Fort Park, Route 127 (June to mid-Oct daily 9am–5pm; ☎978/281-8865),

WHALE-WATCHING AND SAILING ON CAPE ANN

One of the most popular and exhilarating activities along this stretch of coast is **whale-watching**; trips depart from Gloucester, Salem, and Newburyport to the important whale feeding grounds of **Stellwagen Bank** and **Jeffreys Ledge**, where an abundance of plankton and small fish provide sufficient calories (around one million a day) to keep a 50ft, 25-ton humpback happy. Ongoing narration throughout the trip from a marine scientist interprets the sightings and behavior of all whales and marine life encountered, and researchers are available to answer questions on the return journey. Several of the companies rely on reports from deep sea fishing boats which radio back the location of the feeding whales, so the whale-watch boats know where to go before they even leave the docks. Most claim a 99 percent or higher sighting record, though this does not necessarily mean that you're going to see a whale performing a photogenic pirouette just a few feet away – sometimes you may catch no more than a glimpse of a tail. Even on a hot day, it can be quite cool twenty miles offshore, so bring a jacket or sweater, sunglasses, rubber-soled shoes, and a hat to protect you from the powerful sun. Two of the leading companies operate out of Gloucester Harbor. The Yankee Fleet is at 75 Essex Ave (☎978/283-0313 or 1-800/WHALING), and Captain Bill's (☎978/283-4253 or 1-800/33WHALE) is next to **Captain Carlo's** restaurant on the Harbor Loop. Both offer two four-hour trips a day during the summer season, probably the best time to see the whales, for around $24.

From Gloucester, a worthwhile alternative to whale-watching is a **schooner trip** aboard the *Thomas E. Lannon*. Built in 1997, but modelled after a 1903 sword-fishing schooner, the 65-foot vessel takes up to 49 passengers on two-hour sailing tours of the Gloucester coast. The *Lannon* sails daily from Seven Seas Wharf at the Gloucester House Restaurant, 10am to 8pm in July and August; weekends only, Labor Day–Oct 15. Call ☎978/281-6634 for booking information.

can give you a map of locations used in the film, and it seems nearly everyone has a story about how nice George Clooney was during his stay.

Coming into town, which you can do either via Route 128 or 127, both of which feed into Main Street, you'll likely be drawn toward one of Gloucester's sources of pride, the *Gloucester Fisherman*, right on the waterfront near the drawbridge, an overhyped statue of an angler at the wheel of a ship. To learn a bit more about the port's fishing past, head to the excellent **Cape Ann Historical Association**, 27 Pleasant St, near the docks (Tues–Sat 10am–5pm; $3.50), where the history of Gloucester and Cape Ann is well documented through old photographs, fishing implements, and paintings of mostly local scenes by a variety of artists including Winslow Homer, Milton Avery, Augustus Buhler and Gloucester-born marine artist Fitz Hugh Lane. Over in East Gloucester, at Eastern Point off Route 127A, **Beauport** (tours hourly, mid-May to mid-Sept Mon–Fri 10am–4pm; mid-Sept to mid-Oct daily 10am–4pm; $6; ☎508/283-0800) is a 45-room mansion perched on the rocks overlooking Gloucester Harbor. Started in 1907 as a simple summer retreat for the collector and interior designer Henry Davis Sleeper, the house evolved over the following 27 years into a gabled, turreted villa filled with vast collections of European, American and Asian objects. Sleeper wasn't interested in the historical integrity of his aggregation so much as the aesthetic balance, and the house is an intriguing mixture of styles and themes, each room strikingly different from the next, with cozy, dark colonial rooms leading directly into bright, open Mediterranean-style rooms with jaw-dropping ocean views. The tour, which meanders through these rooms, provides a fascinating view of the lifestyles of the rich and famous in the early part of the twentieth century.

Hammond Castle Museum

On the southwestern corner of Gloucester's harbor is the imposing **Hammond Castle Museum**, 80 Hesperus Ave (June–Oct daily 10am–5pm; Nov–May weekends only 10am–4pm, $6; ☎978/283-7673), once the home of the eccentric financier and amateur inventor John Hays Hammond, Jr. (he made some advances in guided missile and radio communications technology), who wanted to bring medieval European relics back to the US. By all accounts, he succeeded: the austere fortress, which overlooks the ocean and site of the spot that inspired Longfellow's poem *The Wreck of the Hesperus*, is brimming with them, from armor and tapestries to the elaborately carved wooden facade of a fifteenth-century French bakery. Also among the artifacts is the partially crushed skull of one of Columbus' shipmates. A murky 30,000-gallon pool inside the castle can, at the switch of a lever, change from fresh to sea water.

Practicalities

The **train station** is only about half a mile from Gloucester harbor, but to get the most out of the town's spread-out sights and the area in general, you should probably count on some other means of transportation – either a car or a bike. **Accommodation** options range from fairly inexpensive bed-and-breakfasts like *Julieta*, 84 Prospect St (☎978/281-2300; ⑥), and *The Harborview Inn*, 71 Western Ave (☎978/283-2277; ⑤–⑥), both quiet, friendly establishments minutes from all of Gloucester's attractions, to five or six motels, several with impressive water views, like the *Cape Ann Motor Inn*, 33 Rockport Rd (☎978/281-2900; ④–⑤), a three-story establishment right on Long Beach.

As is to be expected, many of the city's **restaurants** specialize in fresh seafood, like *Captain Carlo's* at Harbor Loop (☎978/283-6342), which has the added bonus of being right where the fishing action is (the professionals, not participatory); *Halibut Point*, 289 Main St (☎978/281-1900), with a pubby atmosphere and lots of spicy seafood dishes as well as burgers and sandwiches; and *Mad Fish Grill*, 77 Rocky Neck Ave (☎978/281-4554; closed winters), its airy, waterfront setting perfect for downing creatures of the sea – don't miss the tuna carpaccio with wasabi. More upscale is the *Franklin Café*, 118 Main St (☎978/283-7888), a New American bistro that's about as close to hip as Gloucester gets. If you're looking for action at night, **bars** like *The Crows Nest*, 334 Main St (☎978/281-2965), long a fisherman's hangout (and with great clam chowder), though it has lost some of its rough-and-tumble feel in the wake of its *The Perfect Storm* success, and the *Blackburn Tavern*, 2 Main St (☎978/282-1919), a cozy neighborhood pub with live music, are the likeliest places to start.

Rockport

ROCKPORT, about five miles north of Gloucester, is the more scenically situated of the two towns, and also the more self-consciously quaint, though only oppressively so on crowded summer weekends. It, too, started life as a fishing village, then became an important granite-quarrying center, a business that fizzled out here during the 1920s and 1930s and hasn't found much of a replacement since.

From early on, Rockport attracted summer vacationers and artists, drawn by the picturesque harbor and the surrounding shingled shacks and has some renown as a one-time artists' colony: a red lobster shed near the harbor's edge has been christened "Motif #1" because it's been painted so many times. Works by contemporary local artists, some of them terribly kitsch, can be seen at the **Rockport Art Association**, 12 Main St (Memorial Day to Columbus Day, Mon–Sat 10am–5pm, Sun noon–5pm; winter, Tues–Fri 10am–4pm, Sat 10am–5pm, Sun noon–5pm; ☎978/546-6604), and at a number of small shops and galleries throughout town. The main drag is a thin peninsula called **Bearskin Neck**, lined with old saltbox fishermen's cottages transformed into art galleries and restaurants. The neck rises as it reaches the sea, and there's a nice view of the rocky harbor from the end of it. Otherwise, aside from shopping and strolling, there isn't much doing here. Inside the aptly named **Paper House**, just outside Rockport in Pigeon Cove, Pigeon Hill Street (July & Aug daily 10am–5pm; $1), everything is made of paper, from chairs and a piano (keys excepted) to a desk fashioned from copies of the *Christian Science Monitor*. It's the end result of a twenty-year project undertaken in 1922 by a local mechanical engineer who "always resented the daily waste of newspaper." He hasn't really helped the cause.

Practicalities

There's plenty of **accommodation** in Rockport, mostly in a score of inns and B&Bs situated near the center of town. Among these, the *Pleasant Street Inn*, 17 Pleasant St (☎978/546-3916 or 1-800/541-3915; [5]–[6]), is a gracious eight-room Victorian inn perched on a knoll overlooking the village; a separate carriage house contains a two-bedroom apartment. There's also the delightful *Addison Choate Inn*, 49 Broadway (☎978/546-7543 or 1-800/245-7543; [5]–[6]), a Greek Revival house with a lovely shaded porch, pool, and complimentary breakfast buffet. Like Gloucester, Rockport's **restaurants** mainly focus on fresh seafood dishes. With little to choose between many of them, the added incentive of a view often makes for the biggest draw. The *Greenery*, 15 Dock Square (☎978/546-9593), has lovely views over the harbor, serving lobster and superb grilled swordfish, plus gourmet sandwiches at lunchtime, and *Ellen's Harborside* at T Wharf (☎978/546-2512), also right on the harbor, dishes up seafood specials and burgers in a casual atmosphere.

Ipswich and Essex

Though it was founded in 1633, little **IPSWICH,** a few miles northwest of Gloucester along Rte-133, isn't much of a town, its dubious claim to fame being that it has more houses built before 1725 than any other community in the country. One of these, the double-gabled **John Whipple House**, 53 S Main St (May–Oct

ROUTE 127'S COASTAL TRAIL

Route 127A ends shortly after Rockport, after which you can catch 127 South back inland, or continue along scenic 127 North to **Halibut Point State Park**, a beautiful stretch of rocky, wooded coast with **hiking trails** to the northernmost tip of Cape Ann. From there, 127 turns back in toward Gloucester and Essex, but stays close to the coast all the way, yielding majestic views of ocean and coves. It's one of the most **scenic drives** you'll find along the Massachusetts coast.

Wed–Sat 10am–4pm, Sun 1–4pm; $7), built in 1640 and one of the nation's first homes to be restored – in 1898 – is filled with a variety of antiques and Arthur Wesley Dow paintings, and an outside herb garden contains some fifty varieties of medicinal plants. The price of admission includes entry to the nearby **John Heard House**, 40 S Main St (same hours as Whipple House), a 1795 sea captain's home built in the Federal style, with Chinese and early American furnishings and a collection of carriages. Most people come to Ipswich, however, to visit **Crane's Beach**, part of the Crane Memorial Reservations, Argilla Road (daily 8am–sunset), four miles of beautiful sand lining Ipswich Bay. There's a large parking lot which fills on summer weekends, despite a $15 per-car parking fee. You can get a better vantage on the oceanside by ascending to **Castle Hill**, 290 Argilla Rd (May–Oct 10am–4pm, $7; tours: July–Aug 11am & 1.30pm free with admission; grounds open year-round, free; ☎978/356-4351), a reproduction 59-room English-style mansion built by plumbing tycoon Richard Crane in the 1920s. Unfortunately it's often rented out for private events, so call ahead.

To best soak up the pristine tidal flats, take a boat out to the **Crane Wildlife Refuge** (Memorial Day to late Oct 9am–3.30pm; $2; ☎978/356-4351), a spectacular, 650-acre expanse of dunes, woodlands and five islands, all maintained by the Trustees of Reservations, a historical conservation group that runs seasonal twice-a-day (10am and 2pm) tours of the refuge aboard the *Osprey*, a 22-seater pontoon. The trip includes a stop at **Hog Island**, where the film of *The Crucible* was filmed, and a hay wagon ride to an elevated spot on the island that affords great tri-state views (tours Memorial Day to Columbus Day at 10am, 2pm and 5pm; $12; ☎508/356-4351).

The former shipbuilding town of **ESSEX**, off Route 1A, though somewhat of a noted antiques center, should be visited primarily for the splendid **Essex Shipbuilding Museum**, 29 Main St (May–Sept Wed–Mon 10am–5pm; Oct–Apr Thurs–Sun 10am–5pm; $5; ☎978/768-7541), right in the center of the village, where more than four thousand ships have been constructed over the years, including schooners, steamers, and yachts. The museum traces their fascinating history through models of ships, tools, and old photographs. At the **Story Shipyard**, 66 Main St, also part of the museum, you can see restoration work on the *Evelina M. Goulart*, one of five surviving Essex-built schooners.

Practicalities

Most of the best **restaurants** in the area are in Essex. *Jerry Pelonzi's Hearthside*, Rte-133 (☎978/768-6002), is a lovely old farmhouse with views over the marshes where you can tuck into marine delights like finnan haddock, done the traditional Scottish way with eggs, as well as steaks and a range of sandwiches. *Woodman's*, 121 Main St (☎978/768-6451), lays claim to being the first restaurant to serve fried clams; less famous, but certainly no less good, is *J.T. Farnhams Seafood and Grill*, Rte-133 (978/768-6643). Over in Ipswich, try the *White Cap Restaurant and Tavern*, 141 High St (☎978/356-5276), which also specializes in fried clams, shucked daily on the premises. Among the few places to **stay** in these parts is the *Essex River House Motel*, Rte-133 (☎978/768-6800; [4]–[5]), right on the river, with comfortable, air-conditioned rooms and efficiencies and the *George Fuller House*, 148 Main St, also in Essex (☎978/768-7766; [6]–[7]), a rambling old Federal home with Victorian additions with attractive, air-conditioned rooms, some with views over the marshes, and a full breakfast. Cheaper is the *Whittier Motel*, 120 County Rd, Ipswich (☎978/356-5205; [4]–[5]), fairly standard but at least close to the local attractions.

Newburyport

Further up I-95, just south of the New Hampshire border, **NEWBURYPORT** is Massachusetts' smallest city and one of its most appealing, a pleasant and unsullied mix of upscale boutiques and historic homes that still functions as a fishing port. Its location at the mouth of the Merrimack River proved convenient to the English fishermen who settled here as early as 1635, and to shipbuilders in the two centuries that followed, resulting in the accumulation of an enormous amount of shipbuilding wealth, attested to by the imposing mansions on **High Street**, on the northern rim of town. Today Newburyport exudes a real flavor of the past, but the **Market Square Historic District**, with its bricked sidewalks, old lampposts and upscale shops and eateries, is not quite as historic as you'd think – a fire destroyed the area in 1811, and everything had to be rebuilt.

Your best bet is to simply stroll the streets of the city center, especially **State Street**, sample some incredibly fresh seafood, and watch the boats from the two-acre Waterfront Park and Promenade, which faces the Merrimack River as it spills into the ocean. Near the waterfront, the **Custom House Maritime Museum**, 25 Water St (Mon–Sat 10am–4pm, Sun 1–4pm; $4), is a one-time custom house that seems to have far more empty space than exhibits. What little there is consists of old model ships and a rather dreary re-created tidepool. On the other side of downtown, the handsome 22-room Federal-style **Cushing House**, 98 High St (Tues–Fri

---

LOWELL NATIONAL HISTORIC PARK

Perhaps more properly a part of New Hampshire's Merrimack River Valley than the North Shore, **LOWELL** is filled with grim and derelict factories that make it appear more like a midwestern Rust Belt town than a New England village. The one portion that remains intact and attracts visitors is the **Lowell National Historic Park**, in the center of downtown, a preserved factory city founded in the 1820s by Boston industrialist and anthropologist Francis Cabot Lowell. The modern housing was considered a humane alternative to the smog-choked slums of England's industrial cities and for a while it was; workers were not only well paid but also encouraged to attend literacy classes in their spare time. Charles Dickens was one of many British visitors favorably impressed by the place. With the advent of cheap Indian cotton, however, the textile mill fell on hard times, and never recovered. Of the many factories and buildings that have been preserved, the mill at 246 Market St, also the site of the visitor center, functions as a gloomy but interesting open-air **museum** (daily 9.30am–5pm; $4), its web of streets and industrial canals still intact. The city grew up around the manufacturing site, attracting immigrant workers from all over the world; French-Canadians at first, through to the Cambodian immigrants of today – but driving around its depressing streets, it's no wonder that Lowell native **Jack Kerouac** hit the road at the earliest opportunity. A guide to the sights associated with Kerouac, including the **Patrick J. Mogan Cultural Center**, 40 French St (noon–5pm; free), where you can see his Underwood typewriter and copies of some of his better-known works, can be picked up at the park's visitor center. Kerouac is buried in the **Edson Cemetery**, at the corner of Gorham Street and the Lowell Connector, which links Lowell to I-95. If hunger strikes along the way, head to the *Southeast Asian Restaurant,* 343 Market St (☎978/452-3182), which offers an excellent $5 lunch buffet incorporating dishes from all over Southeast Asia.

10am–4pm, Sat 11am–2pm; guided tours only, $4), once home to Caleb Cushing, the nation's first ambassador to China, has among its rather musty antique furnishings a lovely hand-painted Dutch baby cradle in the canopy bedroom. You're better off milling about the eerie **Old Hill Burying Ground**, adjacent to the beautiful Bartlett Mall on High Street, where many Revolutionary War veterans and prominent sea captains are interred.

Newburyport is also accessible by **commuter rail** from Boston's North Station. When you get to the train station, you may find a touristy trolley bus offering to take you to the center of Newburyport for a mere $5 – be advised that it's less than a mile walk.

Plum Island

Plum Island, a nine-mile barrier beach just south of Newburyport on Route 1A, is mostly occupied by the **Parker River National Wildlife Refuge** (daily dawn–dusk; $5 per car, $2 walk-in), a bird-watching sanctuary located on the migratory route of a vast number of different species. As such it is populated in summer by great blue herons, glossy ibises, and snowy egrets, though a less impressive array year-round. The beach itself here gets better, and less developed, the further south you go. Outside of the refuge, the beach is free save for a small fee for parking ($3–5).

Practicalities

Newburyport is an ideal place to spend an afternoon or stopover for **dinner**. Some of the more reliable spots in town are *Scandia*, 25 State St (☎978/462-6271), good for soups and salads at lunchtime and bistro fare in the evenings; *Glenn's*, 44 Merrimac St (☎508/465-3811), where you can tuck into big portions of grilled seafood; and *The Bayou*, 50 State St (☎978/499-0428), an excellent Cajun restaurant. For **accommodation**, try *The Windsor House*, 38 Federal St (☎978/462-3778; ⑤), an eighteenth-century Federal mansion where you can enjoy delicious English breakfasts and afternoon tea. Just slightly more modern, *The Clark Currier Inn*, 45 Green St (☎978/465-8363 or 1-800/360-6582; ⑤–⑥), dates from 1803, and has plenty of spaces in which to relax, including an outdoor garden with gazebo and pond. *The Essex Street Inn*, 7 Essex St (☎978/465-3148; ⑤–⑥), is an attractive Colonial-style house right off the main drag, State Street, with beautiful large rooms and private baths.

THE SOUTH SHORE

The **South Shore** makes a clean sweep of the Massachusetts coast from suburban Quincy, just south of Boston, to the former whaling port of **New Bedford**, west of Cape Cod. **Plymouth** is the only really tourist-driven place along this stretch, on account of the **pilgrim** associations; if you're not interested in reliving the coming of the *Mayflower*, the town, while pleasant enough, will probably not merit more than a few hours' exploration. **New Bedford** has fewer sights, one of which is a well-conceived whaling museum, but its historic associations feel a bit more authentic than those of Plymouth. Still, the South Shore's biggest draw may be its unclogged seaside villages and miles of coastal scenery that in other parts of the country would doubtless have already succumbed to strip mall mania; likely the only reason this hasn't happened is because everybody is too geared up for Cape Cod and the islands beyond to stop off.

Route 3A: Quincy to Duxbury

Although Route 3 is the most direct route from Boston to Cape Cod, you'll hardly catch a glimpse of the coast from it. A better alternative is to take **Route 3A,** which splits off from I-93 just south of Boston. Although not by any means a "scenic drive," the road does go through some pretty residential neighborhoods and gives up occasional harbor and beach views. The first town you hit on this route is **QUINCY**, not much more than part of the urban sprawl of metropolitan Boston, but which bills itself rather imperiously as the "City of Presidents" – it was the birthplace of John Adams and his son John Quincy Adams, the second and sixth presidents of the United States. This grasp at heritage is preserved at the **Adams National Historic Site**, 1250 Hancock St (mid-April–Nov daily 9am–5pm; tours $2; ☎617/770-1175), highlighted by the Adams Mansion, residence of the family for four generations and boasting, out in the garden, the magnificent cathedral-ceilinged **Stone Library**, which houses presidential books and manuscripts. Just a short walk away on the grounds stands the modest 1681 saltbox where the elder Adams entered the world, and adjacent to that, the 1663 house where his son was born.

If for some reason you find yourself **staying** here, there are a few large, insipid chain hotels and motels which straddle the expressway to Boston and the surrounding roads. There are, however, some decent places for a bite to **eat**: *Tullio's*, 150 Hancock St (☎617/471-3400), does admirable pastas, and *Gina's On the Boardwalk*, 307 Victory Rd (☎617/770-9355), set on a boardwalk with ocean views, is a nice spot to sip an espresso and munch on pastries or sandwiches.

Hingham

After a few twists and turns through heavy industrial areas, Route 3A opens up to picturesque **HINGHAM**. Founded in 1635, it's the kind of affluent place you would more expect to find on Cape Cod, though considerably quieter and less visited, of course. **Main Street** is lined with small, black-shuttered eighteenth- and nineteenth-century houses, none of which are open to the public; in fact, the only house in Hingham you can visit is the **Old Ordinary**, 21 Lincoln St (mid-June to mid-Sept Tues–Sat 1.30–4.30pm; $2), its name a reference to "ordinary" meals at fixed prices that used to be served at this former stagecoach stop between Boston and Plymouth. Today it's the house museum of the Hingham Historical Society, with a tap room set up as it would have been when the house was a tavern, and a dining room with various Hepplewhite and Chippendale furnishings. Back on Main Street, at no. 107, the **Old Ship Church**, whose roof resembles an inverted ship's hull (it was built by ship carpenters), claims to be the oldest building in continuous ecclesiastical service in the United States – since 1681. Behind the church an attractive garden-style cemetery affords good views of the harbor. If you want to get a bit closer to the water, head to the peninsula of parkland known as **World's End** (daily 9am–5pm), not quite the end of the world, but a sufficiently nice place for a walk or picnic, with impressive views of the distant Boston skyline.

Cohasset and Duxbury

Further south is the quiet, moneyed town of **COHASSET**, where according to maritime historian Samuel Eliot, "the granite skeleton of Massachusetts protrudes for the last time." Captain John Smith, who in 1607 had helped establish the first permanent English colony in North America at Jamestown, Virginia, disembarked briefly here in 1614 in his initial exploration of New England. Make your detour at the enclave of **Cohasset Village**, slightly east of Route 3A, a pristine blink-and-miss-it town featuring a wide town green perhaps recognizable from the movie *The Witches of Eastwick*. From here, a drive along **Jerusalem Road** reveals stunning views of the coast and rambling (private) mansions.

Another fifteen miles down 3A is affluent **DUXBURY**, settled in 1627 by Myles Standish and other Plymouth Pilgrims who needed more land for their cows. It has a beautiful five-mile barrier **beach** on Route 139, access to which is nearly impossible due to residents-only parking. You can, however, get to isolated smaller beaches by parking along the residential streets. The only historical sight of note is the **John Alden House**, 105 Alden St (mid-May to mid-Oct Mon–Sat 10am–5pm, Sun noon–5pm; $1), originally built in 1653 for John and Priscilla Alden, passengers on the *Mayflower*, and just having undergone minimal structural change since. Check out the East Chamber, or master bedroom, with its post-and-beam construction clearly visible and canopy bed with trundle bed underneath, and the Great Room (living room), centered on an eighteenth century gate-leg table. South of town, the **Myles Standish State Forest**, 14,000 hilly acres of mostly pine woodlands and meadows, is a good place to stretch, traversed by hiking trails and bicycle paths and dotted with fifteen ponds.

You probably won't have much need to linger in Duxbury, especially with Plymouth just down the road, but if you're looking for a place to **eat** *and* **stay**, the *Windsor House Inn*, 390 Washington St (☎781/934-0991; ⑦–⑧), is an 1803 inn with two guest rooms and two suites done out with reproduction antique furniture. The elegant main dining room is open weekends only, though there's a carriage room restaurant open daily; both specialize in seafood (especially lobster) and meat dishes.

Plymouth

PLYMOUTH, dubbed "America's hometown," is one of the largest towns in area in the United States, about the same size as Boston, though its population is largely clustered round the waterfront area where the Pilgrims landed in December 1620 (they had landed prior to this near Provincetown, on Cape Cod). Much of the town is given over to commemorating, in various degrees of taste and tact, this event: apart from the expected crop of Pilgrim-related monuments and museums, there would be little to distinguish Plymouth's concentration of fast-food restaurants, gas stations and mini-malls from any of America's other hometowns.

The Town

The proceedings start off with a solemn pseudo-Greek temple by the sea that encloses the nondescript **Plymouth Rock**, where the Pilgrims are said to have

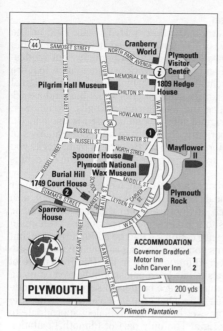

PLYMOUTH

ACCOMMODATION
Governor Bradford
Motor Inn   1
John Carver Inn   2

0   200 yds

▽ *Plimoth Plantation*

touched land; as they had already spent several weeks on Cape Cod, and there are no contemporary references to the rock, its importance is purely symbolic. On the hill behind the rock, **The Plymouth National Wax Museum**, 16 Carver St (daily: March–May & Nov 9am–5pm; July–Aug 9am–9pm; June, Sept & Oct 9am–7pm; $5), disguises a series of inadvertently kitschy sound-and-light tableaux of the early days of settlement, vaguely educational but well past their expiration date. Down the street, the **Pilgrim Hall Museum**, 75 Court St (Feb–Dec daily 9.30am–4.30pm; $5.50), in operation since 1824, is still just essentially a room filled with furniture that may or may not have come over on the *Mayflower* and numerous pairs of tattered shoes, which the Pilgrims may or may not have worn. Other artifacts assembled include the skeletal hull of the *Sparrow-Hawk*, one of the many ships that brought the early colonists here, a painting of Edward Winslow, the only known painting of a *Mayflower* passenger, and Bibles which belonged to John Alden and William Bradford.

Closer to the waterfront are a couple of historic homes which were indeed inhabited by early settlers of the area. The **1809 Hedge House**, 126 Water St (tours hourly, June 1–Oct 7 Thurs–Sat 10am–4pm; $3), is an impressive Federal-style mansion built by a wealthy shipping family filled with stylish period furnishings that include a remarkable collection of Chinese import porcelain. The older, **Spooner House** at 27 North Street (tours hourly, June 1–Oct 7 Thurs–Sat 10am–4pm; $3) was home to five generations of Spooners, a noted mercantile family, and is decorated with their family heirlooms. However, the most interesting feature is the secret garden out back, though the tours are pretty tight affairs and you can't simply stroll the gardens at your own leisure.

Since "how old is it?" is a question that seems to thread itself throughout a tour of Plymouth, it is worth heading over to two of the oldest structures in the town. The **1749 Court House and Museum**, 12 Market St (Memorial Day to Labor Day daily; free), is distinguishable as America's oldest wooden courthouse. The courthouse almost went the way of every other wooden courthouse in the country in the early 1950s when it was slated for demolition, but was saved as an historical site and still stands as it always has for the past two hundred years. The museum attached is little more than a collection of tools, housewares and the usual assorted artifacts, but it's fun anyway. Just a little further south on Market Street is the **Sparrow House**, 42 Summer St (daily 9am–5pm except Wednesday; $5.50), the oldest house in Plymouth, built in 1640 by one of the Mayflower's brave passengers.

Mayflower II and Plimoth Plantation

You're better off spending your time at the **Mayflower II**, 11 State Pier, on the harbor (April–Nov daily 9am–5pm; $7, or $17 for combined ticket with Plimoth Plantation; ☎508/746-1622), which makes no claim to authenticity, but meticulously reproduces the buff brown hull and red strapwork ornamentation that are typical of a seventeenth-century merchant vessel – which is what the original *Mayflower* was, before being outfitted for passengers prior to its horrendous 66-day journey across the Atlantic. Notice the hawthorn, or English mayflower, carved into the stern; whether the original ship was so adorned is unclear. On board, role-playing "interpreters" in period garb, meant to be representatives of the 102 Pilgrim passengers, field visitors' questions. Below the main deck, you can have a look at the "tween decks" area, where the Pilgrims' cramped cabins would have been.

South of town off Route 3 is somewhat of a companion piece to the Mayflower replica, the **Plimoth Plantation** (same days and hours as above, $15 alone), also staffed by costumed interpreters, each of whom acts out the part of a specific Pilgrim or Indian. The charade that visitors are expected to perform – pretending to have stepped back into the seventeenth century – can be a little tiresome, but the sheer depth of detail ultimately wins you over, so long as you are not too critical of the villagers' taste in decor. Everything you see in the Pilgrim Village of 1627 and the Wampanoag Indian Homesite has been painstakingly created using traditional techniques; even the farm animals were bred from seventeenth-century gene pools. Ask one of the pseudo-farmers what crop he's planting, or his wife what she's cooking, and you'll get an answer in an English dialect appropriate to the era and the individual's place of origin. The only part of Plimoth Plantation that makes concessions to the modern age is the crafts center, where interpreters not only weave baskets, which is historically accurate, but make pottery and ceramics, which is not (the Pilgrims had to import that stuff from England). Even the name, "Plimoth," is spelled thusly in deference to an antique map and to distinguish the Plantation from modern-day Plymouth.

A reasonably interesting way to pass time for free, and only about ten minutes north of Plymouth Rock on foot, is **Cranberry World**, 158 Water St (May–Nov

---

THE WORLD'S CRANBERRY CAPITAL

If you're fortunate enough to visit Plymouth during the first half of October, you'll coincide with cranberry country's **annual wet harvest**. Nearly half the country's crop of cranberries come from Plymouth County, its boggy terrain and acidic soil just perfect for this creeping evergreen of the heath family, as the Native Americans discovered centuries before the first colonists arrived. Cultivation involves planting cuttings in about three or four inches of sand laid over the soil. The planting area is then flooded for a day or two to secure the cuttings in the ground, a ploy that is also used in the winter to protect the plants from frost. After four or five years, they are ready to be harvested. The farmers flood the bogs, which are surrounded by forest, with about a half-meter of water and the berries float to the surface in an explosion of glittering crimson. Most of the bogs are situated around **Carver** and **South Carver**, in particular the stretch of Route 58 between routes 44 and 28. Every Columbus Day weekend, South Carver plays host to the **Cranberry Harvest Festival**, at the Edaville Cranberry Bogs off Route 58. There are parades, baked goods, and helicopter rides over the bogs.

daily 9.30am–5pm; free; ☎508/747-2350), a slick little museum sponsored by juice giant Ocean Spray. Exhibits show how the tart crimson berries are harvested from local bogs and processed, and the frequent tours conclude with free juice samples.

Practicalities

Plymouth's **visitor center** is in a park on North Park Avenue (☎508/747-7525). Plymouth & Brockton buses (☎508/746-0378) run back and forth to Boston, stopping at various points in downtown Plymouth. The best **accommodation** in Plymouth is the *John Carver Inn*, 25 Summer St (☎508/746-7100 or 1-800/274-1620; [4]–[5]), a modern, 79-room inn close to the waterfront and all the downtown attractions. Less expensive options include the *Pilgrim Sands Motel*, 150 Warren Ave/Rte-3A (☎508/747-0900 or 1-800/729-SANDS; [4]–[6]), and the *Governor Bradford Motor Inn*, 98 Water St (☎508/746-6200 or 1-800/332-1620; [5]). America's hometown isn't much of a **restaurant** town, but the casual *Hearth 'n' Kettle*, in the *John Carver Inn*, is a safe bet for New England specialties, as is *Isaac's on the Waterfront*, 114 Water St (☎508/830-0001), a favorite with locals who also come for the ocean views. Outside of town, the *Crane Brook Restaurant* at 229 Tremont St, South Carver (☎508/866-3235), which serves superb French and American dishes in a dining room overlooking a pond, was rumored to be a favorite of the late King Hussein of Jordan – reservations are essential.

New Bedford

Don't be put off by **NEW BEDFORD**'s grimy appearance. This once-prosperous whaling port, 45 miles south of Boston, is still home to one of the nation's largest fishing fleets and although new development and a waterfront highway have hardly contributed to the aesthetic appeal of the place, the old mercantile buildings, nineteenth century houses and cobblestone streets in the city center still manage to conjure up the atmosphere that inspired Herman Melville to set the beginning of *Moby Dick* here. These four square blocks are assembled as the recently christened New Bedford Whaling National Historic Park, whose centerpiece is the uncluttered **New Bedford Whaling Museum** at 18 Johnny Cake Hill (Mon–Wed, Fri–Sun 9am–5pm, Thurs 9am–8pm; $6). Scrimshaw and whale jaws abound, but more stimulating is the half-scale model of the whaling vessel *Lagoda*, housed in a necessarily immense building – formerly a church – that also contains harpoons, artifacts whalemen retrieved from the Arctic and Pacific, and fascinating black-and-white photos of whaling journeys from the 1880s. A smaller section of the museum has the roster of the whaling ship *Acushnet*, which shows Melville as one of its crew. Here you'll also see "tally pages" from the whalemen's logbooks, with rubber stamps depicting sperm whales to indicate the ones killed (a vertical stamp meant the whale was harpooned but lost to the sea). A recent addition is a modern building housing the 66-foot skeleton of a blue whale that had the bad fortune to be washed up on the South Shore. Immediately opposite the museum stands the **Seamen's Bethel**, the famous "Whaleman's Chapel" built in 1832 and described in *Moby Dick* (May–Oct Mon–Sat 10am–4pm, Sun noon–4pm; Nov–April Mon–Fri 11am–1pm, Sat 10am–4pm, Sun 1–4pm; donation requested). It features a rather disappointingly small replica of the ship-shaped pulpit described in Melville's book. More evocative are the memorials to those who died at sea that line the walls of the chapel.

There are a few other remnants of New Bedford's whale-derived wealth, chief among which are the old Federalist and Victorian mansions around **County Street**, of which Melville commented:

> *Had it not been for us whalemen, that tract of land would this day perhaps have been in as howling condition as the coast of Labrador . . . all these brave houses and flowery gardens came up from the Atlantic, Pacific and Indian oceans. One and all, they were harpooned and dragged hither from the bottom of the sea.*

Generally speaking, the mansions did not belong to working ship captains, but rather to those who had turned to international trade and investment in the whaling industry. The Greek Revival **Rotch-Jones-Duff House & Garden Museum,** 396 County St (Jan–May Tues–Sat 10am–4pm, Sun 12.30pm–4pm; June–Dec Mon–Sat same hours Sun same hours; $4), built by a Quaker whaling captain in 1834, retains many of its original decorations and furnishings. The formal gardens, laid out in their original style, with boxwood hedges, roses, and wildflowers, occupy an entire city block. Neighboring **Madison, Maple**, and **Orchard streets** also contain a number of fanciful, brightly repainted mansions. It's worth driving by – about all you can do, as they're all private – before heading out of town.

Practicalities

If you want to **stay** in New Bedford, the town's **visitor centers** at 47 N Second St (☎508/991-6200) and at Pier 3 (☎508/979-1745) can pre-book accommodation, but in reality a couple of hours of wandering about the town should be enough before moving on. Still, the *1875 House* is an atmospheric B&B at 36 Seventh St (☎508/997-6433; ④). *Spearfield's*, 1 Johnny Cake Hill (☎508/993-4848), is as good as any place for a quick bite to **eat**, serving omelettes and salads in a cottage across from the whaling museum. For a more substantial meal, try the authentic Portuguese dishes at *Antonio's*, 267 Coggeshall St (☎508/990-3636). New Bedford also has a great find of a **bookstore**, Upstairs Used Books, 528 Pleasant St (☎508/990-0649), which is, as its name suggests, two second-floor rooms crammed with an esoteric collection of books, primarily literature, biography and philosophy, with nearly everything priced at under $3. Be prepared to browse; beyond category separation, books are organized, in the owner's words, "by size."

Westport

On either side of New Bedford, fronting Buzzards Bay and Rhode Island Sound, run a series of coastal villages usually consisting of no more than a post office and a general store. By far the most attractive is **WESTPORT**, on the Rhode Island state line, where the Westport River spills into the ocean, forming a natural harbor. Positioned here is **Horseneck Beach**, a two-mile long stretch of sand that is a favorite with students from the nearby University of Massachusetts at Dartmouth, but never overcrowded because of its vast size. There's ample parking, which costs $10 per car on summer weekends. For a much starker seascape, head east along Route 88 to **East Beach**, a half-mile of pebbly shoreline once the site of dozens of homes until the hurricane of 1938 (and the subsequent hurricane of 1954) swept them all away. What's left are dozens of telephone and power poles and lines, but no homes to attach themselves to.

In the small cluster of cottages that was just far enough away from the ocean to survive the devastation is *The Bayside*, 1253 Horseneck Rd (☎508/636-5882), a family-owned **restaurant** that serves excellent seafood. **Westport Point**, just off Route 88, is a village built on a neck of land leading down to a quay, its main street lined with the white-clapboard eighteenth- and nineteenth-century homes of sea captains. At the foot of the street, nearest the water, the charming *Paquachuck Inn* (☎508/636-4398; [5]–[7]) occupies an 1827 building with lovely views over the water.

Fall River

The fate of **FALL RIVER**, a glum-looking town about fifteen miles west of New Bedford, will forever be linked to the sensational trial of **Lizzie Borden**, a spinster Sunday school teacher accused of the axe murders of her wealthy father and stepmother in August 1892; in many ways, the town plays up the associations. Borden was at home when the murders took place, but the prevailing notion that such brutal crimes were beyond a woman's capability bolstered her case. Her lawyer even made her wear antiquated Victorian dresses to the thirteen-day trial to help conceal her sizeable wrists. It must have worked – she was acquitted, though perhaps not in the public's opinion: as the popular rhyme goes, "Lizzie Borden took an axe and gave her mother forty whacks/When she saw what she had done, she gave her father forty-one." The **Fall River Historical Society**, 451 Rock St (April–Dec Tues–Fri 9am–4.30pm, summer weekends also 1–5pm; $5), contains the inevitable exhibits of the affair, including some vintage photographs of Lizzie and her family, as well as more general information about the city, particularly its industrial heritage. There's also a **museum** at the **Lizzie Borden B&B**, 92 Second St (daily 11.30am–2.30pm, tours on the hour; $7), where the awful deeds were done.

Aside from Lizzie-mania, Fall River is better known as a mill town. Though its prosperity from wool manufacture unravelled ages ago, dozens of huge old mills remain, many of which have been transformed into **factory outlets**, the greatest concentration of which is at the confluence of I-195 and Route 24. Though the stores are far from original, you can still find some decent bargains in shoes, designer clothing, jewelry, and household goods, all tax-free. The town's other attraction, as it were, is **Battleship Cove**, I-195 to exit 5 at the Braga Bridge (daily 9am–5pm; $9), site of an impressive assemblage of World War II naval craft), most intriguing of which are the enormous *USS Massachusetts* and the submarine *USS Lionfish*.

Practicalities

Fall River's Chamber of Commerce provides **tourist information** at its office at 200 Pocasset St (☎508/676-8226), but a safer bet (if you're driving) might be the **Bristol County Visitors' Bureau** located between exits 1 and 2 on I-195 eastbound in neighbouring Swansea. One of the few places to **stay** in Fall River is the suitably gloomy *Lizzie Borden B&B*, 92 Second St (☎508/675-7333; [6]–[7]). You can stay in the rooms where Lizzie's parents were found, savor the same kind of breakfast enjoyed by the family on the day of the murders and load up on Lizzie memorabilia in the gift shop. More mundane is the *Best Western*, 360 Airport Rd (☎508/672-0011; [4]–[6]), just up the hill from Battleship Cove, the only motel within the city boundaries. New Bedford supports a large Portuguese population, a fact reflected in its proliferation of Portuguese **restaurants**. Two of the better entries are *Sagres*,

181 Columbia St (☎508/675-7018), which adds folk singing to the mix on weekends, and *T.A. Restaurant*, 408 S Main St (☎508/673-5890), with lots of fresh local seafood done the spicy Portuguese (Azores) way, with tomatoes, peppers and Tabasco.

Cuttyhunk Island

If you're really desperate to get away from the crowds, take a one-hour boat trip from Pier 3 in New Bedford out to minuscule **CUTTYHUNK ISLAND**, an entirely uncommercialized chunk of land, with unpaved roads and beaches lined with glorious wildflowers, such as **Channel Beach**, just a short walk from the ferry dock, and **Church's Beach** on the other side of the island, ideal for swimming or a peaceful walk. The outermost of the **Elizabeth Islands,** which stretch for sixteen miles from Buzzards Bay, and one of the few not privately owned, Cuttyhunk was the site of the first English settlement in the Bay State: a short, 22-day sojourn which resulted in the building of a stockade and the planting of a medicinal garden. A small stone tower on an island in **Gosnold Pond**, at Cuttyhunk's western end, honors the event.

The **ferry**, run by Cuttyhunk Boat Lines (☎508/992-1432, *www.cuttyhunk.com*), runs daily from mid-May to mid-October, with same-day round-trip prices at $17, one way $12, plus $1 per unit baggage charge; services run on Fridays only for the rest of the year. The ride can be an experience in its own right: it's the only means of transporting goods back and forth, meaning you may find yourself squeezed into a corner surrounded by towers of six packs – or blocked in by a car.

The island has a year-round population of just thirty and **bicycles** are really the best way to get around; rent one in New Bedford and take it over with you on the ferry. There are only a couple of **restaurants** on the island, too, so you're best off bringing your own lunch; again, the main reason you're here is to get away from it all. A few commercial establishments are located at **Four Corners**, the island's hub, such as gift shops and markets. Also nearby is the tiny **Historical Society Museum**, which traces the history of the island through an assortment of artifacts.

If you want to **stay**, the *Cuttyhunk Bed & Breakfast Inn* (☎508/993-6490; ⑥–⑦) offers superb views from its front porch; close to the ferry, the *Cuttyhunk Fishing Club* has an inn which offers clean and comfortable rooms in an idyllic setting (☎508/992-5585; ⑥–⑦).

CAPE COD

CAPE COD, one of the most celebrated slices of real estate in America, boasts a consistently stunning quality of light that mostly compensates for its flat, lackluster landscape and sometimes suffocating quaintness. The slender, crooked Cape gives Massachusetts an extra three hundred miles of coastline, access to much of which is hampered by shore-hugging upper middle-class homes. Those parts of the Cape that haven't fallen prey to suburban overdevelopment have been preserved as the snug, rather humorless villages they were a hundred or more years ago, replete with town green, white steeple church and the odd lighthouse. Only **Provincetown**, at the very tip, manages to successfully mesh the past with the present; its unique art galleries, shops and restaurants make it far and away the destination of choice here. It's also perched on the best stretch of the extensive **Cape Cod National Seashore**, so there's no overwhelming need to go elsewhere, though tiny upscale towns like

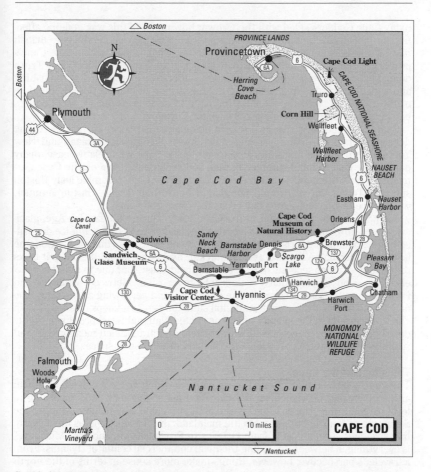

Boston

PROVINCE LANDS

Provincetown

Cape Cod Light

N

Herring
Cove
Beach

Truro

Boston

Corn Hill

Plymouth

Wellfleet

CAPE COD NATIONAL SEASHORE

Wellfleet
Harbor

C a p e   C o d   B a y

NAUSET
BEACH

Cape Cod
Canal

Sandwich

Sandy
Neck
Beach

Cape Cod
Museum of
Natural History

Eastham

Nauset
Harbor

Orleans

Brewster

Sandwich
Glass Museum

Barnstable
Harbor

Dennis

Scargo
Lake

Pleasant
Bay

Barnstable

Yarmouth Port

Cape Cod
Visitor Center

Yarmouth

Harwich

Hyannis

Chatham

Harwich
Port

MONOMOY
NATIONAL
WILDLIFE
REFUGE

Falmouth

Woods
Hole

N a n t u c k e t   S o u n d

0   10 miles

CAPE COD

Martha's
Vineyard

Nantucket

Sandwich, **Brewster** and **Chatham** make for scenic stops along the way. In recent years local chambers of commerce have been trying to lure tourists in the off-season by touting the region's "historical attractions" – the museums, the Kennedy associations, and so on – in lieu of its more typical shore-oriented ones, but the reality is that for most visitors the beach reigns supreme. It's also worth noting that sights and beaches are heavily geared toward families, not independent travelers.

Some history

In all the hype about Plymouth and its associations with the Pilgrims, it's often forgotten that they first set foot on North American soil at Provincetown – despite the presence of an enormous monument there to commemorate the event. Immigration to the Cape up to 1700 was almost exclusively made up of homesick Englishmen who crossed the Atlantic to take advantage of the burgeoning markets of the New World, and who named the places after towns back home, such as Sandwich, Falmouth and Barnstable. Indeed, during the Revolutionary War many Cape Codders sided with the Crown; how much of this was genuine affection for British rule and how much was prompted by their vulnerability to British naval strength is debatable. By the early 1800s, whaling had become the Cape's primary industry, the ports of Provincetown, Barnstable, Wellfleet, and Truro doing particularly well, while other Cape Codders were employed in the fishing and agricultural industries, including the harvesting of cranberries. By the time of the Civil War, with the whaling industry in serious decline, Cape Codders began to look to the burgeoning railways for salvation.

Cape Cod's meteoric rise as a tourist destination is mainly attributable to the development of the motor car and the railway. Wealthy Bostonians and New Yorkers were, for the first time, able to get to the Cape with relative ease, many purchasing land to build summer homes and returning to live on the Cape permanently on retirement, so much so that parts of the Cape resemble leafy Boston suburbs. Today, the year-round population more than doubles in the summer, when more than 80,000 cars a day cross the Cape Cod Canal.

But nature is the real arbiter of the Cape's fate. During the last Ice Age, glaciers moved down across Canada and New England. The vast sheet of ice deposited huge amounts of debris as it began to melt and retreat, forming Cape Cod, the islands of Martha's Vineyard and Nantucket, and Long Island. Because it lacks the solidity of other sections of the New England coast, and due to rising sea levels, Cape Cod is particularly vulnerable to erosion. Between Wellfleet and Provincetown the land is scarcely one mile wide, and narrowing all the time. The one benefit of the adverse environmental situation is that it keeps development in check, especially in the vicinity of the protected National Seashore. Even highly developed areas are interspersed with pockets of untrammeled meadowland and seagrass, lending the Cape at least the illusion of wide open spaces.

The shape of the Cape

The Cape is shaped like a **flexed arm**, with Sandwich at the shoulder, Chatham at the elbow and Provincetown the clenched fist at the very end. According to local parlance, the "Upper Cape" is the area you come across after crossing the Sagamore or Bourne bridges from the mainland, the "Lower Cape" is the forearm that stretches approximately from Orleans to Provincetown, and the "Mid-Cape" is everything in between, including the main commercial center of Hyannis. From a traveler's perspective, however, things make more sense in terms of the **north coast** of the Cape from Sandwich to Brewster, the **south coast** from Falmouth to Chatham, and the **outer Cape**. The best plan of attack is Route 6A, the Old King's Highway, from Sandwich to Brewster. At Orleans, just past Brewster, Route 6A joins Route 6, the Mid-Cape Highway, an exceedingly dull road that does little else than get you to Provincetown in a hurry. With a very few exceptions, Route 28, the main thoroughfare on the south coast, wends past baleful outcroppings of suburbia – even Cape Codders will tell you that it's a byway best avoided in favor of its scenic northern cousin.

Getting to the Cape

The main way of reaching the Cape is by **car**, though if you're heading there on a summer weekend, you may well regret this choice. On a fairly quiet day it takes about two hours to get from downtown Boston to the Sagamore Bridge, but expect this to double on summer weekends and holidays. Bonanza Buses (☎1-800/556-3815) operate a **bus** service in summer from Boston to Woods Hole and Falmouth,

THE CAPE COD CANAL

Between 1909 and 1914 a **canal** was dug across the westernmost portion of Cape Cod, effectively making the Cape an island. It was an old idea – the Pilgrims who landed on the Cape some three hundred years earlier had talked about building a canal as a means of avoiding the shipwreck-prone 135-mile trip around the Cape, thus facilitating trade between the Plymouth colony and the Dutch colony of New Amsterdam (New York), but they lacked the manpower to get the work done. Later on, George Washington, contemplating the advantages a canal would have in protecting naval ships and commercial vessels during war, resurrected the idea, but it was not until 1880 that work finally started on building a canal. The Cape Cod Canal Company employed more than five hundred immigrant workers to begin the laborious process – hand shovels were used, and the debris carted away in wheelbarrows. In 1899 wealthy New York businessman Augustus Belmont took over the project; ten years later, state-of-the-art earthmoving equipment was introduced, and the canal was completed in 1914, though at the time it was too shallow and narrow to allow anything but one-way traffic. In 1928 the canal was bought by the federal government, which subsidized the modifications necessary to permit larger vessels to trawl the waters. Hundreds of boats now use the canal every day, many of them leisure craft that have to contend with dramatic shifts in water currents and tides. You can join them on a **boat trip** with Cape Cod Canal Tours, Onset Bay Town Pier off Routes 6 and 28 ($6.50–8; ☎508/295-3883). Still, you don't have to be on the canal to enjoy it; the view of the canal and its verdant shores from the Sagamore and Bourne bridges is one of the most dramatic on the East Coast. There is also a **bike trail** on either side of the canal.

while the Plymouth & Brockton Bus Company (☎617/773-9401) plies the route from various points in Boston to Hyannis. You can also take the **boat** from Boston to Provincetown: Bay State Cruise Company (☎617/748-1428, *www.baystatecruise company.com*) runs daily from mid-June to Columbus Day from Boston's Commonwealth Pier; an adult round-trip fare costs $30, and the express (which cuts travel time in half) is $49 round-trip. Boston Harbor Cruises (☎781/749-8009, *www.bostonboats.com*) also runs an express service, leaving Long Wharf twice a day and reaching Provincetown ninety minutes later for $45. A Plymouth to Provincetown ferry service is run by Captain John's Boats (☎508/746-2643 or 1-800/242-2469). Finally, a number of **airlines** fly direct to Cape Cod – perhaps the best way to dodge traffic – including Continental (☎1-800/525-0280) and US Airways (☎1-800/428-4322), which go to Hyannis from Boston, and Cape Air (☎1-800/352-0714), which heads to Provincetown from Boston several times a day, even in winter. The main Cape Cod **visitor center**, annoyingly hidden behind a clump of trees at the junction of Routes 6 and 132 in Hyannis, has information about all the towns on the Cape (Mon–Fri 8.30am–5pm; summer weekends also 10am–4pm).

Cape Cod's south coast

Route 28, which hugs the Nantucket Sound coast of the Cape until it merges with Routes 6 and 6A at Orleans, is certainly not the most attractive or scenic route on the Cape; much of it is lined with motels and commercial premises, and it can get seriously clogged up with traffic during the summer. Nonetheless, it runs through a number of important hubs along the south coast, notably **Falmouth** and **Hyannis**, that many find themselves visiting for one reason or other. At its culmination are the two best reasons for hitting this path, the quiet town of **Chatham** and the even quieter **Monomoy National Wildlife Refuge**, reachable only by ferry.

Falmouth and Woods Hole

FALMOUTH boasts more coastline than any other Cape Cod town and no fewer than fourteen harbors among its eight villages, at the center of which is **Falmouth Village**, with its prim, picket-fence-encircled central green surrounded by Colonial, Federal, and Greek Revival homes. Typical of New England, a number of these old sea captains' houses now serve as B&Bs, and are complemented by a touristy mixture of clothes shops, ice-cream parlors and real estate agents. The **First Congregational Church**, right on the green at 68 Main St, is also picture-perfect New England, a white-steepled church with a bell commissioned from Paul Revere. Nearby, at 55–65 Palmer Ave, the 1794 **Conant House** (mid-June to mid-Sept Mon–Fri 2–5pm; $2), run by the Falmouth Historical Society, contains scrimshaw, rare glass and china, and sailors' memorabilia. There's also a room dedicated to local girl **Katherine Lee Bates**, who composed **America the Beautiful**; she was born in 1859 down the road at 16 Main St, where a plaque commemorates the event. The Historical Society also maintains the **Julia Wood House**, next door to the Conant House (same hours and price), an early nineteenth-century doctor's home, one room of which is set up as a clinic, with a horrifying display of primitive dental utensils – doctors doubled up as dentists in those days.

The salty drop of a town that is **WOODS HOLE** owes its name to the water passage, or "hole" between Penzance Point and Nonamesset Island, linking Vineyard Sound and Buzzards Bay. It's little more than a clump of casual restaurants and convenience stores clustered around the harbor and the **Woods Hole Oceanographic Institute**, 15 School St (May–Oct Tues–Sat 10am–4.30pm, Sun noon–4.30pm; Nov, Dec, March & April Fri & Sat 10am–4.30pm, Sun noon–4.30pm; free). OceanQuest, a private non-profit, runs research-based ocean cruises out of Woods Hole; they are open to the public in the months of July and August, and by reservation for groups of thirty year-round (☎1-800-37-OCEAN; $19 individuals, $15 groups). Apart from that, and a small building that houses an exhibit on the rediscovery of the *Titanic* in 1986, a project the institute spearheaded, there's little for the visitor to see. The National Marine Fisheries Service in Woods Hole is not public-oriented, though it does maintain America's oldest **aquarium** at the corner of Albatross and Water streets (April, May and Oct Mon–Fri 10am–4pm; June–Sept daily 10am–4pm; free; ☎508/495-2000). With a mission to preserve local marine life, its displays are limited to the likes of codfish, lobster and other piscine creatures that are more appealing on a plate.

Practicalities

Regardless of what you may find in the area to divert you, it doesn't make much sense to **stay** unless you're catching the **ferry** from Woods Hole to Martha's Vineyard. Of the central motels in Falmouth, the best may be *Best Western Marina Tradewinds*, 26 Robbin Rd, Falmouth (☎508/548-4300 or 1-800/341-5700; [5]), a comfortably modern motel with magnificent views over Falmouth Harbor. Otherwise, bed and breakfasts abound, including *The Beach House at Falmouth Heights*, 10 Worcester Court, Falmouth Heights (☎508/457-0310 or 1-800/351-3426, *www.capecodbeachhouse.com*; [6]; open May–Oct), where the whimsically decorated rooms come as a cheerful antidote to the country quaint that normally reigns supreme. Other choice options are *Mostly Hall*, 27 Main St, Falmouth (☎508/548-3786 or 1-800/682-0565; [5]–[6]; closed Jan), an amiably run 1849 mansion and, down in Woods Hole, *Woods Hole Passage*, 186 Woods Hole Rd (☎508/548-9575; [6]–[7]), a refurbished red-shingled carriage house set on spacious grounds.

Most of the choices for **eating** are in Falmouth, too, including popular local institution *The Clam Shack*, 227 Clinton Ave (☎508/540-7758), which has both indoor and outdoor seating. Also worth stopping for is *Betsy's Diner*, 457 Main St (☎508/540-0060), an authentic Fifties diner serving no-nonsense food and beckoning you to "Eat Heavy." Another diner option is *My Tinman*, outside town in Pocasset (☎508/564-5518), that works a *Wizard of Oz* theme and has cheap home-style fare. Still, you may be better off going to the waterfront in Woods Hole for moderately priced seafood; highly recommended is *Fishmonger's Cafe*, 56 Water St, Woods Hole (☎508/548-9148), a laid-back eatery with a surprising number of vegetarian dishes.

Hyannis

The largest town on the Cape, and its main commercial hive, **HYANNIS** somewhat desperately clings to its JFK heritage; the so-called **Kennedy Compound**, the family's best-known summer home, is located in **Hyannis Port**, an upscale residential district a couple of miles southwest of the town's business district. This connection is by far the most glamorous bit in Hyannis' long history. Settled by Eastern Algonquian Indians over one thousand years ago, the first documented exploration by a European came from Captain **Bartholomew Gosnold** in 1602. Shortly after that, settlers persuaded the local Native American chief **Ianno** to sell them what is now Hyannis and Centerville for about $30 and two pairs of trousers; it's from the name Ianno that Hyannis derives. When the first railway trains reached the place in 1854, the economy skyrocketed, further boosted by the development of transportation links to Martha's Vineyard and Nantucket. Today, Hyannis is not surprisingly clogged up with traffic in summertime, which at least means there's some semblance of shopping and nightlife, even if they are playgrounds for the over-privileged young.

If it's Kennedy memorabilia you've come to see, probably the best place to start is the **John F. Kennedy Hyannis Museum**, 397 Main St (Mon–Sat 10am–4pm,

MOVING ON FROM HYANNIS

Hyannis is just about the nearest thing to a big city on the Cape; fortunately, because it's also the transportation center of Cape Cod, it's easy to escape for quieter pastures, like Nantucket, or Martha's Vineyard, both of which can be reached by **ferry** from Steamship Authority (☎508/477-8600) or Hy-Line (☎508/778-2600). On the ground, the **Cape Cod Scenic Railroad** (May–Oct; ☎508/771-3800; $13) runs from Center Street along a meandering two-hour circuit west through cranberry bogs to the Cape Cod Canal and Sandwich. The bogs are at their most colorful at harvest time, usually in mid-October.

Sun 1–4pm; $3), which displays the expected Kennedy nostalgia, mainly in the form of old black-and-white photographs. Visitors who come to Hyannis expecting to take a guided tour round the **Kennedy Compound** will be disappointed: this group of houses is concealed by tall fences, and it's best glimpsed, if you must, out on the water – Hy-Line Cruises, Ocean Street Docks (☎508/778-2600; $8), runs hour-long cruises that peek in on the compound. Joe and Rose Kennedy bought their house here in 1929, and immediately set about remodeling it to accommodate their burgeoning family; Jack and Bobby Kennedy bought neighboring houses in the 1950s.

For a welcome non-Kennedy diversion, you might take a free tour round the **Cape Cod Potato Chip Factory**, on Breed's Hill Road near the Cape Cod Mall (Mon–Fri 9am–5pm; also July–Aug Sat 10am–4pm; ☎508/775-7253). The tasty chips, once a local phenomenon but now successful nationwide, are made with natural ingredients hand-cooked in kettles; it's hard to resist the free samples, in any case.

Practicalities

The local Chamber of Commerce maintains an **information center** at 1481 Route 132 (Mon–Sat 9am–5pm; also summer Sun 9am–5pm), not to be confused with the Cape Cod Visitor Centre just up the road (see p.169). If you have a boat to catch and need to **stay** in Hyannis, options include the *Anchor-In Motel*, at the harbor's edge, 1 South St (☎508/775-0357; ④–⑥); *The Inn at Fernbrook*, 481 Main St (☎508/775-4334; ⑥–⑨), an appealing wood-shingled Victorian building set on eighteen acres in neighboring Centerville; and the *Simmons Homestead Inn*, 288 Scudder Ave (☎508/778-4999 or 1-800/637-1649; ⑥), the only B&B in Hyannis Port, thirteen rooms with private baths in an 1820 sea captain's home. To access many of the **restaurants**, it's helpful to have a car. Recommended are *Alberto's*, 360 Main St (☎508/778-1770), for Northern Italian dishes; *Cooke's Seafood*, 1120 Iyanough Rd/Rte-132 (☎508/775-0450), where it's hard to go wrong with the fresh broiled and fried seafood – especially the clams; *The Egg & I*, 521 Main St (☎508/771-1596), a great spot for big breakfasts; *Sam Diego's*, 950 Route 132 (☎508/771-8816), a dependable, casual restaurant serving Mexican, Southwestern, and barbecue fare; and *Steamer's Grill and Bar*, 235 Ocean Street (☎508/778-0818), for fresh, inexpensive surf-and-turf across from the ferry docks.

Harwich

Sleepy **HARWICH**, about ten miles east of Hyannis on Route 28, is not a bad place to get close to the ocean, boasting three scenic harbors – including man-made **Wychmere Harbor**, once a landlocked salt pond, and the naturally formed **Saquatucket Harbor**, the largest municipal marina on the Cape – and some excellent beaches. At the latter, parking tends to be restricted to residents and visitors with stickers, but a free bus service can drop you off at **Red River Beach**, Uncle Venies Road, off Route 28, which offers a full range of facilities.

Harwich Port, the central village in Harwich, has a fairly active main street that boasts some well-preserved nineteenth-century architecture, including the **Brooks Academy Museum**, 80 Parallel St (mid-May to mid-Oct Thurs–Sun 1–4pm; free), an 1844 Greek Revival school building which housed one of the nation's first schools of navigation; inside are exhibits on local history. The town springs to life for ten days every September during the **Harwich Cranberry Festival**, a small-town extravaganza marked by crafts fairs, a parade, and fireworks.

Practicalities

You likely won't be **staying** here, though *Handkerchief Shoals Motel*, Route 28 at Deep Hole Road (☎508/432-2200; ③–⑤), is a good budget option, located halfway between Harwich Port and Chatham. Also worthwhile are the *Augustus Snow House*, 528 Main St (☎508/430-0528; ⑥–⑦), five impeccably decorated rooms in a Queen Anne Victorian, and *Harbor Walk*, 6 Freeman St (☎508/432-1675; ④–⑤), a moderately priced B&B, close to scenic Wychmere Harbor; two of the six guestrooms have shared baths. If you're looking to **eat**, sample the French take on local seafood at *L'Alouette*, 787 Main St/Rte-28 (☎508/430-0405), or check out the fresh seafood, burgers, and pizza at *400 East*, Rte-137/Rte-39, East Harwich (☎508/432-1800).

Chatham

Few of the pocket-sized towns on the southern flank of the Cape are as genteel as **CHATHAM**, six miles east of Harwich Port and one of the few Cape destinations worth an overnight stay. The quiet and posh small-town atmosphere is largely attributable to some strictly enforced zoning laws, which have prevented the kind of indiscriminate attract-tourists-at-all-costs mentality evident in so many other Cape communities. The focal point is **Chatham Village**, whose **Main Street** is home to a variety of upscale boutiques, provisions stores, and some sophisticated restaurants and charming inns. Just off Main Street is one of the town's best historical attractions, the gambrel-roofed **Atwood House and Museum**, 347 Stage Harbor Rd (mid-June to Sept Tues–Fri 1–4pm; $3), built in 1752 as a sea captain's home, with a variety of seafaring artifacts, antique dolls, seashells, toys and a herb garden. The adjacent Mural Barn houses the rather gaudy Stallknecht Murals, a triptych painted in 1931 by Alice Stallknecht Wight that depicts recognizable

---

MONOMOY NATIONAL WILDLIFE RESERVE

Stretching out to sea for nine miles south of Chatham, desolate **Monomoy National Wildlife Refuge** is a fragile barrier beach that was attached to the mainland until breached by a storm in 1958. A subsequent storm in 1978 divided the island in half, and today the islands are accessible by boat only – when weather conditions permit. The refuge spreads across 2750 acres of sand and dunes, tidal flats and marshes, with no roads, no electricity and, best of all, no human residents, though a small fishing community once existed here. Indeed, the only man-made buildings on the islands are the South Monomoy Lighthouse and lightkeeper's house.

It's a perfect stopover point along the North Atlantic Flyway for almost three hundred species of shorebirds and migratory waterfowl, including many varieties of gull and the endangered piping plovers, for whose protection several sections of the refuge have been fenced off. In addition, the islands are home to white-tailed deer and harbor and gray seals are frequent visitors in winter. Several organizations conduct island tours, among them The Cape Cod Museum of Natural History (☎508/349-2615) and the Wellfleet Bay Wildlife Sanctuary (☎508/349-2615); prices vary, depending, among other things, on the number of people in your group. In any case, if there are six or more of you, you'll need to get a special permit from the headquarters of the Wildlife Refuge, located on Morris Island (☎508/945-0594), which also has a visitor center offering leaflets on Monomoy. Morris Island is accessible from Morris Island Road, south of the Chatham Light.

Chatham townsfolk listening in awe to a contemporarily-dressed Christ. Tour **maps** of Chatham are available from the information booth at 533 Main St (☎508/945-5199 or 1-800/715-5567).

A few minutes' drive outside the village, the 1877 **Chatham Light** stands guard over a windswept bluff beyond which many a ship had met its doom on the "Chatham bars," a series of sandbars that served to protect the town from the worst of the Atlantic storms – until in January 1987, when a fierce nor'easter broke through the barrier beach to form the **Chatham Break**, leaving Chatham exposed to the vagaries of the ocean. Right below the lighthouse is a nice beach, but with parking limited to half an hour, you're better off biking there from town if you want to do anything other than take a brief walk along the shore. A mile north on Route 28, the **Fish Pier** on Shore Road provides a spot to wait for the fleet to come in mid-afternoon. From here you can also take a $10 water taxi to Monomoy Island, a 2700-acre wildlife refuge (see box p.173).

Accommodation

Chatham is well endowed with tasteful **accommodation**, mostly the kind of romantic **B&Bs** found throughout the Cape. Despite the ample selection, reservations are strongly advised, even outside of high season.

The Captain's House Inn, 369–371 Old Harbor Rd (☎508/945-0127 or 1-800/315-0728, *www.captainshouseinn.com*). Easy elegance prevails at this sumptuously renovated 1839 Greek Revival whaling captain's home; most rooms have fireplaces, the staff are English, and prices include gourmet breakfasts and afternoon tea with freshly baked scones. [7].

Chatham Bars Inn, 297 Shore Rd (☎508/945-0096 or 1-800/527-4884; *www.chathambarsinn.com*). The grande dame of Cape Cod's seaside resorts has a total of 205 rooms; forty rooms in the main inn building and 26 comfortably appointed cottages spread about the 22-acre oceanfront property. [6]–[8].

Chatham Tides Waterfront Motel, 394 Pleasant St, South Chatham (☎508/432-0379, *www.allcapecod.com/chathamtides*). Choose between standard hotel rooms or self-catering town-house suites at this relative bargain directly on Nantucket Sound. Closed October–May [5]–[6].

Chatham Wayside Inn, 512 Main St (☎508/945-5550 or 1-800/391-5734). This 56-room refurbished 1860 sea captain's home is one of the finer inns in the area, though at a price. [6]–[7].

Cyrus Kent House, 63 Cross St (☎508/945-9104 or 1-800/338-5368; *www.capecodtravel.com/cyruskent*). Ten graciously appointed guest rooms, all with private baths, in a stately 1877 home one block from the center of town. [5]–[8].

Eating

Not surprisingly, given its status as one of the more sophisticated destinations on Cape Cod, Chatham abounds in upmarket **restaurants**, as well as the more casual eateries typical in these parts.

Chatham Bars Inn, 297 Shore Rd (☎508/945-0096 or 1-800/527-4884). The hostelry's formal dining room offers New England cuisine with wonderful ocean views. Expensive.

Chatham Squire, 487 Main St (☎508/945-0945). This informal lunch spot with a raw bar and an eclectic menu incorporating elements of Mexican and Asian cuisine often has live acoustic bands at night.

Christian's, 443 Main St (☎508/945-3362). The movie posters upstairs are fitting, considering that the menu items are named after films; hard to go wrong with a Roman Holiday (Caesar salad) followed by A Fish Called Wanda (salmon sautéed with mushrooms).

The Impudent Oyster, 15 Chatham Bars Ave (☎508/945-3545). Popular upscale bistro with generous portions of inventively prepared fresh seafood.

Vining's Bistro, 595 Main St (☎508/945-5033). Imaginative offerings at this appealing dinner spot range from Thai Street Vendor's Beef Salad to a warm lobster taco.

Cape Cod's north coast

The meandering stretch of highway that parallels the Cape Cod Bay shoreline between Sandwich and Orleans is among the most scenic in New England, affording glimpses of the Cape Cod of popular imagination: salt marshes, crystal clear ponds, ocean views and tiny villages. What began as a Native American pathway from Plymouth to Provincetown became the Cape's main road in the seventeenth and eighteenth centuries. There are hundreds of historic buildings along the 34-mile stretch, a frightening number of which have been turned into antiques shops or bed-and-breakfasts, and the towns that hold them are pleasant enough, though **Sandwich** and **Brewster** have the highest concentration of well-preserved historical homes. Even if you're traveling by car, it's worth it to temporarily ditch the wheels in favor of a bike to take the **Cape Cod Rail Trail**, a totally flat but popular bike path on the site of the former Old Colony Railroad track, running from **Dennis**, about fifteen miles past Sandwich, through Brewster to **Wellfleet**, a distance of twenty miles up the Cape.

Sandwich

Overlooked **SANDWICH** kicks off Route 6A with little of the crass commercialization common to so many Cape towns, thanks in part to its position so close to the mainland. The first permanent settlement on Cape Cod, Sandwich traces its roots to Pilgrim traders in the late 1620s who appreciated its proximity to the **Manomet Trading Post**, where they could barter goods and knowledge with the local Native Americans. The salt marshes in the area also provided an abundant supply of hay for their animals. Unsurprisingly, agriculture was Sandwich's main industry until the 1820s, when Bostonian Deming Jarves established a glassmaking factory here. Though the dense woodlands provided plenty of fuel for the furnaces, by the 1880s the Sandwich factory was no longer able to compete with the coal-fired glassworks of the Midwest. Today, tourism plays a role in the local economy, but, unlike so many other Cape communities, Sandwich is not totally dependent on it.

The Town

A stroll around Sandwich's old **village center** gives you a good taste of things to come along Route 6A: a little village green, white steepled church, a smattering of bed-and-breakfasts, antiques shops, and a general store. Near Main and River streets, the **Shawme Duck Pond** and adjacent **Dexter Grist Mill**, a replica of one built in 1654, make for a pleasant, peaceful stop, especially if you want to hear about the milling process (mid-June to mid-Sept Mon–Sat 10am–4.45pm, Sun 1–4.45pm; mid-May to mid-June & mid-Sept to mid-Oct Sat 10am–4.45pm, Sun 1–4.45pm; $1.50). On Water Street, overlooking the pond, and well worth a visit, the **Hoxie House** (mid-June to mid-Oct Mon–Sat 10am–5pm, Sun 1–5pm; $1.50, combination ticket with Dexter Grist Mill $2.50) is a seventeenth-century shingled saltbox house claimed by some to be the oldest on the Cape. It showcases authentic colonial furniture on loan from the Museum of Fine Arts in Boston, rare diamond-shaped lead-glass windows and antique textile machines. Close to the shore, at 129 Main St, the **Sandwich Glass Museum** (April–Oct daily 9.30am–4.30pm; Nov–Dec & Feb–March Wed–Sun 9.30am–4pm; $3.50) contains fourteen galleries that house artifacts from the Boston & Sandwich Glass Company, which set up shop here in 1825. Besides thousands of functional and decorative pieces, a diorama re-creates the factory interior, a video describes the demise of the industry, and glassmaking demonstrations are routinely held.

The other museums dotted around town are only really recommended for those with an abiding passion for Americana, primarily the **Heritage Plantation of Sandwich** at Grove and Pine streets (mid-May to late Oct daily 10am–5pm; $8), which features a mega-attic of Currier and Ives prints, old American firearms, a working 1912 carousel, replicas of American flags and, inexplicably, a collection of polished old cars housed in a reproduction of the Shaker round barn in Pittsfield, a western Massachusetts town. The seventy-plus-acre gardens on the grounds are beautiful in season, especially July when the rhododendrons typically bloom. A couple of miles to the east, on Route 6A in East Sandwich, the **Green Briar Nature Center & Jam Kitchen**, 6 Discovery Hill Rd (April–Dec Mon–Sat 10am–4pm, Sun 1–4pm; free), run by the Thornton W. Burgess (of *Peter Rabbit* fame) Society, seems mainly geared for toddlers, housing such wonders as a stuffed beaver, a live garden snake, a box turtle, and assorted snapshots of the turtle.

Sandwich's attractions also include several miles of **beach** on Cape Cod Bay, but, like all the Cape's bayside beaches, the water is several degrees cooler than over on the Nantucket Sound side (cut off from the warming influence of the Gulf Stream). It will cost you $5 to park at **Town Neck Beach**, Town Neck Road, off Route 6A.

Practicalities

The place to **stay** in Sandwich is the *Dan'l Webster Inn* at 149 Main St (☎508/888-3622; ⑥–⑦), a rambling colonial-style hostelry, modeled on an earlier building that was a haunt of Revolutionary patriots, with first-rate rooms and charming courtyards. Nearby, the *Captain Ezra Nye House*, 152 Main St (☎508/888-6142 or 1-800/388-2278; ⑤–⑥), has six rooms and private baths in an 1829 sea captain's home. The best **meals** are also served at the *Dan'l Webster Inn:* top-notch, classic American dishes every evening, with the compelling opportunity to nibble edible flowers (among other things) from the inn's aquafarm; they also serve breakfast and lunch in a sunlit conservatory.

Barnstable

BARNSTABLE, ten miles east of Sandwich on Route 6A, was, after Sandwich, the second town to be founded on Cape Cod, in 1639. Early prosperity was attained thanks to its trade in whale products, and Barnstable's harbor was the busiest port on the Cape until it silted up earlier this century. Wayward cetaceans would frequently wash ashore at **Sandy Neck**, a beautiful eight-mile barrier beach, the best on Cape Cod Bay that protects Barnstable's harbor. No longer used as a site for burning blubber, the beach is probably your main reason for checking out the town, though parking will set you back $8. Follow Sandy Neck Road, just over the Sandwich line.

Evidence of Barnstable's earlier prosperity can be seen in several imposing domestic and civic buildings in the leafy village center, among them the impressive granite mass of the **Barnstable County Superior Courthouse** at 3195 Route 6A, a reminder that Barnstable is also the county seat for the whole of the Cape. Nearby, the dignified red-brick **Donald G. Trayser Memorial Museum**, 3353 Route 6A (July & Aug Tues–Sat 1.30–4.30pm; free), was built in 1855 as the town's Customs House. Inside is an eclectic range of Americana, from vintage clothes to Sandwich glass and, on the grounds, an eighteenth-century jail cell.

Many former residences of Barnstable's hundreds of sea captains survive to this day, including that which belonged to **William Sturgis**, who set out to sea at the age of fifteen after the death of his father and returned four years later as a captain. Sturgis, uneducated, but an avid reader, bequeathed his house to the town for use as a library; the resultant **Sturgis Library**, 3090 Route 6A (Mon, Wed, Fri 10am–5pm, Tues & Thurs 1–8pm, Sat 10am–4pm, Sun 1–5pm; free), contains genealogical records dating back to the area's first European settlers, an original 1605 Lothrop Bible and an extensive collection of maritime maps, charts, and archival material. A few miles away, in West Barnstable, the majestic Neoclassical **West Parish Meetinghouse**, Route 149 at Meetinghouse Way, is the oldest surviving Congregationalist building in the US, constructed in 1717. The bell tower contains a bell cast by Paul Revere in 1806.

Practicalities

For something to **eat** in Barnstable, try the *Barnstable Tavern* at 3176 Route 6A (☎508/362-2355), for casual American food with an unusual Lebanese touch. Waterfront views and classic American seafood can be had at the *Mattakeese Wharf*, 271 Mill Way, Barnstable Harbor (☎508/362-4511; May–Oct). If you want to **stay** overnight, *Beechwood*, 2839 Route 6A (☎508/362-6618; ⑥), an 1853 Queen Anne-style house, has six romantic rooms decorated Victorian style. Another lovely option is the *Honeysuckle Hill B & B,* 591 Old King's Highway/Rte-6A (☎508/362-8418; ⑥), three rooms and one suite in a quintessential Cape Cod 1810 National Register home. In addition to the full breakfast, you can enjoy sitting by the fireplace in the living room, perhaps accompanied by the owners' friendly black Labrador.

Yarmouth Port

YARMOUTH PORT, part of the much larger town of Yarmouth, is the next hamlet eastward on Route 6A, marked by a series of old sea captains' houses that have been converted into bed-and-breakfasts. Indeed, along one two-mile stretch, no building was constructed later than the turn of this century, creating somewhat of a time-warp effect, augmented all the more by a visit to **Hallet's**, at 139 Route 6A, a general store that started out as a pharmacy in 1889 – later serving as a post office and town meeting hall – and still has an original oak counter and old-fashioned soda fountain. Upstairs, a memorabilia-filled museum traces local history. Nearby, on the town green off Route 6A at 11 Strawberry Lane, the **Captain Bangs Hallet House** (tours hourly, June–Oct Sun 1–3pm; July & Aug also Thurs 1–3pm; $3) is a Greek Revival mansion built in 1740 by one of the town's founders, though its name comes from the successful sea captain who lived here in the late 1800s. The original kitchen comes complete with beehive oven, and a glorious weeping beech tree enhances the view from the back of the house. The 1780 **Winslow Crocker House**, 250 Route 6A (June–Oct Tues–Thurs & weekends noon–4pm; $4; ☎508/362-4385), is a two-story Georgian home moved from West Barnstable to its present site in 1936 by Mary Thacher, a descendant of one of the original town founders, Thomas Thacher. The dwelling holds a range of seventeenth- to nine-teenth-century furniture, rugs, and ceramics collected by Mrs. Thacher.

In decent weather, you might walk amongst the 53 acres of the **Botanic Trails of Yarmouth**, entered right behind the post office, on Route 6A (trails open year-round during daylight hours; suggested donation $1). This peaceful park contains oak and pine woods, and a wealth of flora, including rhododen-drons, blueberries, hollies, and lady's slippers. An extension of the trail leads to **Kelley's Chapel**, a seaman's bethel built in 1873 by a father for his daughter who was grieving the death of her son; Kelley is not a surname but the first name of the daughter.

Practicalities

For quintessential country inn ambience, **stay** at the *Wedgewood Inn*, 83 Main St, Yarmouth Port (☎508/362-5157; ⑥), whose six rooms each have canopy beds and fireplaces. You can **eat** decent Italian fare year-round at *Abbicci*, 43 Main St/Rte-6A (☎508/362-3501), which serves excellent local seafood as well as more tradi-tional meat and pasta dishes; another option, *Jack's Outback*, 161 Route 6A (☎508/362-6690), a local institution with the motto "Good food, lousy service," is not for the fainthearted, but the down-home American grub *is* good.

Dennis

In **DENNIS**, just down the road from Yarmouth, detour onto Old Bass River Road to pristine **Scargo Lake** for sweeping views from a thirty-foot **stone observation tower** built on a bluff overlooking it. The town itself, named after its founder, the Rev Josiah Dennis, retains much of its colonial feel, notably in places like the clergyman's home, the **Josiah Dennis Manse** at 77 Nobscusset Rd (July & Aug Tues 10am–noon, Thurs 2–4pm; small donation requested), a saltbox built in 1736 and set up to reflect life in the Reverend's day, filled with antique toys and furniture, china and pewter, plus the inevitable portraits of sea captains. There's also an attic containing spinning and weaving equipment, and, on the grounds, a one-room schoolhouse dating from 1770. One of the most famous summer theaters in the States, the **Cape Playhouse**, Rte-6A between Nobscusset and Corporation roads (late June to mid-Sept daily except Sun; ☎508/385-3838 for ticket info), was a Unitarian Meeting House until its pur-chase in 1927 by Raymond Moore, a Californian who had intended to start a theater company in Provincetown but found it too remote. Famous names who have trod the boards here include Basil Rathbone (who starred in the first per-formance, *The Guardsman*), Lana Turner, Gregory Peck, Humphrey Bogart and Bette Davis, who also worked here as an usherette. There's also an art cin-ema, open year-round, modeled after a congregational church. On the ceiling is a 6400-square-foot mural designed by Rockwell Kent and Jo Mielziner. In the same complex, the **Cape Museum of Fine Arts** (May to mid-Oct Mon–Sat 10am–5pm, Sun 1–5pm; mid-Oct to April Tues–Sat 10am–5pm, Sun 1–5pm; $5) showcases more than 850 works of local artists in a former barn. For cycling enthusiasts, the **Cape Cod Rail Trail**, a tarred bicycle path that was formerly the Old Colony Railroad, extends 26 miles from Dennis to Wellfleet (beginning in South Dennis, on Rte-134 south of Rte-6); All Right Bikes, 118 Route 28 (☎508/790-3191), rent bikes at reasonable prices.

MICHELLE WOODWARD

MAURICE JOSEPH/ROBERT HARDING

S. GRANT/TRIP

John Hancock building, Boston, MA

Tall Ships race, Boston, MA

Boston skyline, MA

Replica of the *Mayflower*, Plymouth, MA

Lobster weathervane, Boston, MA

Oak Bluffs, Martha's Vineyard, MA

Salem Witch Museum, MA

Beacon Hill houses, Boston, MA

Hail to the Sunrise statue, Mohawk Trail, MA

Gay Head Cliffs, Martha's Vineyard, MA

M. STEVENSON/TRIP

The Breakers, Newport, RI

ROBERT FRANCIS/ROBERT HARDING

School marching band, Fourth of July Parade, Bristol, RI

Practicalities

If you're looking to **stay** in Dennis, the *Four Chimneys Inn,* 946 Main St/Rte-6A (☎508/385-6317 or 1-800/874-5502; ④), is an appealing B&B with high ceilings and marble fireplaces in most rooms, while the *Isaiah Hall B&B Inn,* 152 Whig St (☎508/385-9928 or 1-800/736-0160; ⑤; closed Nov–May), is an 1857 Greek Revival farmhouse within walking distance of village and beach. For somewhere really peaceful, *Lane's End Cottage,* 268 Route 6A (☎508/362-5298; ⑤), with just three guest rooms, is located in an idyllic setting at the end of a dirt track. You can **eat** generous portions of a tried-and-true New England staple at *Captain Frosty's Fish & Chips,* Route 6A, Dennis (☎508/385-8548). Off Route 28 south of Dennis proper, the *Sundae School Ice Cream Parlor,* 387 Lower County Rd, Dennisport (☎508/394-9122), vends home-made ice cream, topped with real whipped cream, from an antique marble soda fountain.

Brewster

BREWSTER is yet another agreeable, if anodyne, Cape Cod town, known as a leading antiques center and popular with young couples who choose to tie the knot here, usually in one of the many bed-and-breakfasts that line Route 6A. The town, as ever, traces its affluence to the sea captains who settled here – even though Brewster doesn't have a harbor. The **cemetery** in which many of these seamen are buried is adjacent to the 1834 **First Parish Church**, at 1969 Route 6A; it has one of New England's more fascinating legends attached to (or buried in) it. One of the gravestones bears the names of two men lost at sea: Captain David Nickerson and his adopted son, Captain René Rousseau. Nickerson was in Paris during the French Revolution when a veiled woman handed him the infant René; longtime locals maintain he was the son of Louis XVI and Marie Antoinette. More picturesque, the still-functioning **Stony Brook Mill**, 830 Stony Brook Rd, just off Rte-6A (May & June Thurs–Sat 2–5pm, July & Aug Fri 2–5pm; $1), was built in 1873 on the site of an earlier mill.

Brewster also boasts the **New England Fire & History Museum**, 1439 Rte-6A (late May to early Sept Mon–Fri 10am–4pm, Sat & Sun noon–4pm; early Sept to mid-Oct Sat & Sun noon–4pm; $4.50), which lures visitors with the tantalizing invitation to "see the fire fighting apparatus of yesteryear." That includes more than thirty buffed and polished fire engines, one of which is a one-and-only 1929 Mercedes-Benz Nurburg 460. There is also an extensive collection of fire helmets and a sizeable diorama of the Chicago Fire of 1871. Further down the road, at 869 Route 6A, the **Cape Cod Museum of Natural History** (Mon–Sat 9.30am–4.30pm, Sun 12.30–4.30pm; $5) makes for a somewhat more enlightening alternative – especially for kids – with its exhibits on the fragile Cape environment, aquaria and short nature trails that straddle cranberry bogs and salt marshes.

Accommodation

Brewster is well equipped with typical Cape **B&Bs**, including the *Brewster Farmhouse Inn,* 716 Main St/Rte-6A (☎508/896-3910 or 1-800/892-3910; ⑥–⑧), where you're likely to get a personalized experience (there are only eight rooms) and a delicious breakfast. *The Captain Freeman Inn,* 15 Breakwater Rd (☎508/896-7481 or 1-800/843-4664; ④–⑤), is an 1866 post-and-beam structure, with high-ceilinged rooms and a delightful wraparound porch with rocking chairs. *Bramble Inn,* 2019 Main St (open May–October; ☎508/896-7644; ⑥–⑧), takes in three rustic homes, and its gourmet restaurant is among the Cape's finest.

Eating

Bramble Inn Restaurant, 2019 Main St (☎508/896-7644). Romantic setting for daring seafood dishes, such as lobster in an open shell, filled with scallops, shrimp and cod covered in toasted almonds and coconut.

Brewster Coffee Shop, Route 6A (☎508/896-8224). If you want American chow – from a turkey sandwich to scrambled eggs – and you want it cheap, look no further.

Brewster Fish House, 2208 Route 6A (☎508/896-7867). Creatively prepared and moderately priced seafood pulls the crowds in, so arrive early to avoid a wait.

Café Alfresco, 1097 Main St (☎508/896-1741). Tasty pastries, sandwiches and other informal fare in often times stuffy Brewster.

Chillingsworth, 2449 Route 6A (☎508/896-3640 or 1-800/430-3640). Contemporary French cuisine in one of the Cape's most celebrated and highly recommended restaurants. If you're going to splurge, you may as well go for the seven-course *table d'hôte* menu. At around $50 per person, it's not cheap, but the setting is sumptuous and the food superb.

High Brewster, 964 Satucket Rd (☎508/896-3636 or 1-800/203-2634). Romantic and expensive place serving the kind of food Americans think English aristocrats still eat (pheasant breast, rabbit sausage pie, tea-smoked salmon, etc).

Outer Cape: Orleans to Wellfleet

ORLEANS, at the southernmost portion of the Outer Cape, was named after Louis-Philippe de Bourbon, duc d'Orleans, who is said to have visited the area at the time of his exile from France in the 1790s. Such grasps at royalty are long forgotten, as modern Orleans is basically a series of strip malls on either side of Route 6A, a place to stock up on snacks for a trip to the beach or to fuel up for the ride onward to Provincetown. In the "town," which is a generous designation, the **Bird Watcher's General Store**, 36 Route 6A (☎508/255-6974), is worth a stop, just to partake of the store tradition of telling the cashier a joke. If he likes it, he'll ring a little bell and reward you with a gift. On Route 6A at Town Cove Park, the well-traveled **Jonathan Young Windmill** (July & Aug daily 11am–4pm; free) started life in the 1720s in East Orleans, was subsequently moved to the center of town, then to Hyannisport, and finally, in 1983, moved back to Orleans. Although no longer in operation, this gristmill does have its machinery intact, and there's a resident miller who will explain how it all works. A much better diversion is a visit to atmospheric **Rock Harbor**, at the end of Rock Harbor Road off Main Street, a former landing place for packet ships until it silted up, and now a small fishing port and a departure point for charter fishing trips. Over in East Orleans is one of the Cape's better beaches, the nine-mile-long oceanside **Nauset Beach**, off Beach Road ($8 parking fee). You can also hook up with the **Cape Cod Rail Trail** here; find it just past the Mid-Cape Home Center. Rent bikes in town at Orleans Cycle, 26 Main St (☎508/255-9115).

There are a few surprisingly good **restaurants** in Orleans, notably the *Captain Linnell House*, 137 Skaket Beach Rd (☎508/255-3400), serving New England fare in a candelit 1840 clipper captain's mansion; *Land Ho!*, Route 6A and Cove Road (☎508/255-5165), with its generous portions of burgers and fried seafood; and *Mahoney's Atlantic Tavern*, 28 Main St (☎508/255-5505), a great place for pasta and seafood. **Accommodation** in Orleans is plentiful, with a combination of modestly priced motels along Route 28 and close to Nauset Beach, and several comfortable bed-and-breakfasts. *The Cove*, 13 Route 28 (☎508/255-1203 or 1-800/343-2233; ③), is a 47-room motor inn on Town Cove with an outdoor pool,

CAPE COD NATIONAL SEASHORE

The protected **Cape Cod National Seashore**, which President Kennedy saved from development because of his fondness for it, extends along much of the Cape's Atlantic side, stretching forty miles from Chatham north to Provincetown. It's a fragile environment: three feet of the lower Cape is washed away each year, and much of it ends up as extra sand on the beach before the sea takes that away, too. Environmentalists are hoping that an extensive program of grass-planting will help prevent further erosion.

It was on these shifting sands of the outer Cape that the **Pilgrims** made their first home in the New World. They obtained their water from Pilgrim Spring near Truro; at Corn Hill Beach they uncovered a cache of corn buried by the Wampanoag Indians who had been living on the Cape for centuries – a discovery which kept them alive their first winter, before moving on to Plymouth.

Displays and films at the **Salt Pond Visitor Center**, on Route 6 just north of Eastham (summer daily 9am–5pm; winter daily 9am–4.30pm; ☎508/255-3421), trace the geology and history of the Cape. A pretty road and hiking/cycling trail head east to the sands of **Coast Guard Beach** and **Nauset Light Beach**, both of which offer excellent swimming. You can also catch a free shuttle ride there from the visitor center in summer. Another fine beach is **Head of the Meadow**, halfway between Truro and Provincetown. In several areas parking is restricted to residents only, but you can often park by the road and strike off across the dunes to the shore.

while *Parsonage Inn*, 202 Main St, East Orleans (☎508/255-8217; [5]–[7]), is an eighteenth-century house with eight antique-furnished rooms. *Nauset Knoll Motor Lodge*, Nauset Beach, East Orleans (☎508/255-2364; [6]–[7]), stands just steps from the ocean, and has the requisite accompanying views.

Eastham

Largely undiscovered **EASTHAM**, up Rte-6 past Orleans as the Cape begins to curve up toward Provincetown, is home to fewer than five thousand residents, most of whom are quite content to sit and watch the heavy summer traffic pass by on its way to Provincetown. Though the sum of Eastham's commercial facilities is little more than a small strip of shopping malls and gas stations along Route 6, if you veer off the highway in either direction you will capture some authentic Cape flavor.

The first detour is the **Fort Hill area**, part of the Cape Cod National Seashore, with a scenic overlook for sweeping views of **Nauset Marsh**, originally a bay, but which became a marsh when **Coast Guard Beach** was formed. Along the way, you'll pass the **Captain Edward Penniman House**, Fort Hill Road (☎508/255-3421), a partly restored Second Empire-style house with an octagonal roof that looks straight out of the movie *Psycho*. Unfortunately, it's only open to the public sporadically – but worth it if you can get in. North of Coast Guard Beach, at the corner of Ocean View Drive and Cable Road, is the red and white **Nauset Light**, orginally located in Chatham, but installed here in 1923 and moved back 350 feet in 1996 when it was in danger of crumbling into the sea. In 1838, this spot was home to no fewer than three brick lighthouses, known as the "Three Sisters," and built 150ft apart to protect ships from dangerous shoals off the coast. In 1892, serious erosion necessitated their replacement by three wooden towers; two were eventually moved away in 1918 and the third in 1923. Having been acquired by the National Park service, they now stand in the woods well away from today's coastline. **First Encounter Beach**, off Samoset Road on the town's bayside, refers to the first meeting of Pilgrims and Native Americans in 1620. It was hardly a cordial rendezvous; with the *Mayflower* anchored in Provincetown, an exploration party led by Myles Standish came ashore only to meet a barrage of arrows. Things settled down after a few gunshots were returned, and since then the beach has been utterly tranquil. A plaque set back in the dunes describes the encounter in detail.

Practicalities

The place to **stay** in Eastham is the *Whalewalk Inn*, 220 Bridge Rd (☎508/255-0617; [8]). Immaculate guest rooms and tasty breakfasts are the big draws; the cottages are more spacious than the rooms in the main inn building. For something to **eat**, *Arnold's Lobster & Clam Bar*, 3580 Route 6 (☎508/255-2575), provides generous portions of fried New England seafood, while for something more exotic, *Mitchel's Bistro*, Main Street Mercantile, Route 6 (☎508/255-4803), features Indian and West Indian buffets as well as traditional American seafood and meat dishes.

Wellfleet

WELLFLEET, with a year-round population of just 2500, is, like Eastham 8 miles to the south, one of the least developed towns on Cape Cod. Once the focus of a thriving oyster fishing industry, today it is a favorite haunt of writers and artists who come here to seek inspiration from the unsullied landscapes and the constantly heaving ocean. Despite the fact that a number of art galleries have surfaced, most of them along **Main Street** or **Commercial Street**, the town remains a remarkably unpretentious place, with many of the galleries themselves resembling fishing shacks and selling highly distinctive original work aimed at the serious collector, alongside mass-market souvenirs. The **Art Gallery Association** produces a guide to the galleries which can be picked up at the information booth at the corner of Route 6 and LeCount Hollow Road (☎508/349-2510).

The **Wellfleet Historical Society Museum**, 266 Main St (late June to Sept Tues–Sun 2–5pm; $1), has an interesting collection of furniture, items salvaged from shipwrecks, nautical artifacts, and photographs as well as exhibits on the local oyster industry. Close by at no. 200, the **First Congregational Church** is worth a peek inside for its curved pews and restored Hook and Hastings organ.

As in Eastham, however, the most scenic part of Wellfleet is actually outside the town proper, here in the form of the **Marconi Area**, east off Route 6 in South Wellfleet. It was on this beach that Guglielmo Marconi issued that first transatlantic radio signal on January 18, 1903. Nothing remains of the tall radio towers built for that purpose, but there are some scale models beneath a gazebo-type structure overlooking the ocean. A short trail leads to a vantage point from which you can see horizontally across the entire Cape, at this point just a mile wide.

Practicalities

If you want to **stay** the night in Wellfleet, try the laid-back *Holden Inn*, Commercial Street (☎508/349-3450; closed Oct-May; [3]), a farmhouse-style structure with 27 rooms, some with shared baths, or the charming *Inn at Duck Creek*, 70 Main St (☎508/349-9333; [4]–[5]), a cozy country inn situated on five woodland acres. Tiny though Wellfleet is, there are a number of casual seafood **restaurants** worth checking out, such as the *Bayside Lobster Hutt*, 91 Commercial St (☎508/349-6333), an old oyster shack, and *Aesop's Tables*, 316 Main St (☎508/349-6450), which also boasts terrific homebaked desserts. Continuing the theme, *Moby Dick's*, Route 6, across from Gull Pond Rd (☎508/349-9795), offers family seafood dining. For something a bit different, there's *Painter's Restaurant & Studio Bar*, 50 Main St (☎508/349-3003), a former tavern that doesn't look like much from the outside, but has funky American fusion food and a festive atmosphere.

Truro

Most of **TRURO**, a sprawling town that continues on Rte-6 right up to Provincetown, falls within the boundaries of the Cape Cod National Seashore, allowing it to keep preserved the kind of natural beauty that has attracted the likes of artists, writers, even politicians – Edward Hopper built a summer house here which he used from 1930 to 1967 and Vice President Al Gore and his family vacationed here in 1997. Although at over 43 square miles, it's one of the largest towns on the Cape in area, it's the smallest in population – no surprise, then, that downtown is little more than a strip mall with just a few shops, a post office, town hall, and police station.

It was in windswept Truro that Pilgrim leader Myles Standish and his companions from the *Mayflower* found the cache of Indian corn that helped them survive their first New England winter in 1620; a plaque at **Corn Hill** marks the exact spot. It wasn't until 1697, however, that the first permanent settlement was established. Originally called Pamet, after the Native American tribe that once lived here, it was changed in 1705 to Dangerfield due to the particularly treacherous offshore currents, and finally to Truro, after the town in Cornwall, England. In its early days, Truro depended on the sea for its economic well-being, even becoming the site of Cape Cod's first lighthouse in 1797, powered by whale oil. A golf course unappealingly sidles up to the lighthouse's 1857 replacement, the **Cape Cod Light** on Lighthouse Road. Also known as the Highland Light, it was automated as recently as 1986, and even more recently moved back 450 feet from the eroding shoreline where it was in danger of collapsing into the ocean. Thoreau stayed at the old lighthouse during his travels around the Outer Cape, a place where he said he could "put all America behind him." Also dwarfed by the golf course is the **Truro Historical Museum**, Lighthouse Road (Memorial Day–Sept daily 10am–5pm; $2; ☎508/487-3397), home to some rather prosaic remnants of yesteryear like fishing and whaling equipment, old photographs and seventeenth-century firearms; better are the objects obtained from the many shipwrecks that have occurred offshore.

Practicalities

Other than privately owned summer homes, which can be rented by the week from Duarte/Downey Real Estate, 12 Truro Center Rd (☎508/349-7588), **places to stay** in Truro are mainly confined to a strip of sandy terrain which hugs the bay shoreline west of Shore Road (Route 6A) in North Truro. Here *Kalmar Village* (☎508/487-0585; ⑥–⑦) consists of 45 spacious and well-kept one- and two-bedroom cottages in an oceanfront community. In July and August, these can only be rented by the week; at other times, nightly rentals are possible. The *Top Mast*

Motel, 209 Shore Rd (Route 6A), North Truro (☎508/487-1189, *www .capecodtours.com/topmast*; ④–⑥; closed Oct–May), has beachfront rooms rented on a weekly basis, and non-beachfront rooms rented by the night. There's a pool and a restaurant on the premises. For something to **eat**, *Adrian's*, Route 6, North Truro (☎508/487-4360), serves breakfasts and dinners with an Italian touch, while the *Blacksmith Shop*, Truro Center Road off Route 6A (☎508/349-6554), is a local institution, mainly for its hefty portions of prime rib and shrimp.

Provincetown

> *"Far from being out of the way, Provincetown is directly in the way of the navigator...*
> *It is situated on one of the highways of commerce, and men from all parts of the globe*
> *touch there in the course of a year."*
>
> from *Cape Cod* by Henry David Thoreau

PROVINCETOWN, or "P-Town," the ebullient fishing hamlet at land's end on the tip of Cape Cod, is an incredibly popular summer destination for bohemians, artists, and fun-seekers in general, lured by the excellent beaches, art galleries, and welcoming atmosphere. The year-round population of five thousand, largely comprised of gays, lesbians, and various artsy types, swells from Memorial Day to Labor Day by up to 50,000 visitors, adding to the carnival mood on the bustling streets. Though undeniably a premier **gay** vacation spot, Provincetown should really be a must-see for everyone, worth skipping over much of the rest of the Cape for, especially as it can be visited directly from Boston by **ferry**, at least during summer.

Some history

Provincetown has a number of Pilgrim-related monuments – after all, they landed here before heading to Plymouth – but the Pilgrims were not the first European visitors to arrive at Provincetown. Way back in 1004, Leif Erikson's brother, **Thorvald**, disembarked here to repair the broken keel of his ship and named the place "Cape of the Keel," and in 1602 the area was visited by explorer **Bartholomew Gosnold**, the first European to visit southeastern New England, who dubbed it "Cape Cod" on account of the profusion of cod in the local waters. The Pilgrims came ashore here and stayed for five weeks in 1620, signing the **Mayflower Compact**, one long and rather vaguely worded sentence espousing a democratic form of self-government, before sailing across Cape Cod Bay.

The town was incorporated in 1727, and soon became a thriving fishing, salt-processing and whaling port; indeed, by 1880, the town was the richest per capita in Massachusetts. Fishing retains its importance here, and many of the fishermen working today are direct descendants of the Portuguese from the Azores who settled here in the 1800s. Its destiny to become one of the east coast's leading **art colonies** was assured in 1899, when painter Charles W. Hawthorne founded the **Cape Cod School of Art**, which encouraged artists to explore the outdoors and exploit the Mediterranean-like quality of the light. So many of his friends came to investigate the place that it became known as the "Greenwich Village of the North." By the early 1900s, many painters had begun to ply their highbrow trades in abandoned "dune shacks" by the sea, and by 1916 there were no fewer than six art schools here. The natural beauty and laid-back atmosphere also began to

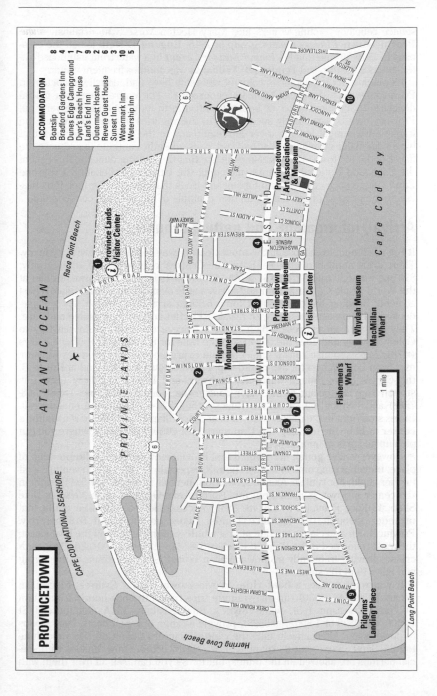

PROVINCETOWN

ACCOMMODATION
Boatslip 8
Bradford Gardens Inn 4
Dunes Edge Campground 1
Dyer's Beach House 7
Land's End Inn 9
Outermost Hostel 2
Revere Guest House 6
Sunset Inn 3
Watermark Inn 10
Watership Inn 5

ATLANTIC OCEAN

CAPE COD NATIONAL SEASHORE

Race Point Beach

PROVINCE LANDS

Province Lands Visitor Center

Pilgrim Monument

TOWN HILL

WEST END

EAST END

Provincetown Art Association & Museum

Provincetown Heritage Museum

Visitors' Center

Fishermen's Wharf

MacMillan Wharf

Whydah Museum

Cape Cod Bay

Pilgrims' Landing Place

Herring Cove Beach

Long Point Beach

0   1 mile

seduce rebellious young writers like Mary Heaton Vorse, who established the **Provincetown Players** theater group in 1915. **Eugene O'Neill** joined the company in 1916, premiering his *Bound East for Cardiff* in a waterfront fish house kitted out as a theater, and **Tennessee Williams** was another frequent visitor.

As much of an impact as its colorful residents have had, equally important in Provincetown's history has been its **geography**. The entire Cape is a glacial deposit on a crooked sliver of bedrock, but due to its position at the very tip, Provincetown is particularly susceptible to the vagaries of wind and water, the fragile environment lending a certain legitimacy to the strict **zoning laws** that have kept major development at bay and, consequently, continue to preserve the flavor of the old town. There's also evidence that the shifting dunes of this part of the Cape Cod National Seashore, including the barren but beautiful **Province Lands**, were once covered with topsoil and trees that were cut for fuel, thus hastening the process of erosion – a further example of the need for conservation.

Arrival, information, and getting around

If you're coming from Boston, the most pleasant way to get to P-town is by **ferry**. There are a number of choices. Bay State Cruises' regular ferry (summer only; $18 one-way, $30 round-trip; ☎617/748-1428)departs from Commonwealth Pier at the World Trade Center at 9am and arrives at Provincetown's MacMillan Wharf at noon, heading back at 3.30pm for a 6.30pm arrival in Boston. It's a triple-decked, 1100-passenger ship, with breakfast buffet and lunch available on board. They also run an **express** which departs twice a day from Memorial Day to Columbus Day and does the trip in half the time for $49. Boston Harbor Cruises (☎781/749-8009) also runs a ninety-minute express service twice a day all summer from Long Wharf for $45 round-trip. Provincetown is at the end of **Route 6**, the Cape's main, though unscenic, highway, and **buses** regularly trawl this stretch from Boston and all the major Cape towns; Bonanza Bus Lines (☎508/548-7588) and Plymouth & Brockton Buses (☎508/771-6191) are the ones to call. Buses stop right in the middle of town near MacMillan Wharf. There is a **visitor's center** right by the bus stop, 307 Commercial St (☎508/487-3424), where you can pick up all sorts of information.

However you've gotten here, you'll find Provincetown a very **walkable** kind of place; **bicycles** can come in handy, though, especially if you want to venture a bit further afield. For rentals, Arnold's, 329 Commercial St (☎508/487-0844), right in the center of town, is open from mid-April to mid-October, as is Nelson's Bike Shop, 43 Race Point Rd (☎508/487-8849), located close to the **bike trails** that meander through the Province Lands. Bikes go for about $16 per day. Provincetown also claims the title of first **whale-watching** spot on the East Coast; the most renowned is the Dolphin Fleet (☎508/349-1900 or 1-800/826-9300), with cruises leaving frequently from MacMillan Wharf; $18 per person in the spring and fall, $19 in the summer.

If you want to take a **boat ride**, Provincetown Harbor Cruises, MacMillan Wharf (☎508/487-4330) run forty-minute trips round the bay hourly from 11am to 7pm in season ($5), while Flyer's Boat Rentals, 131A Commercial St (☎508/487-0898 or 1-800/750-0898), provide a range of rental boats, from sloops to powerboats. Alternatively, take their **shuttle** across Cape Cod Bay (mid–June to mid–Sept; $5 one-way, $8 round-trip; ☎508/487-0898). Only vehicles with special permits are allowed on the dunes, but for $9 you can trek all over them with

Art's Dune Tours (Art's sport-utility vehicles are parked across from MacMillan Wharf; ☎508/487-1950). You can also **fly** over them in a replica 1938 biplane (☎1-888/BIPLANE or 508/428-8732). Twenty-minute flights take off from the Cape Cod Airport, near the intersection of Race Lane and Route 149.

Accommodation

Many of the most picturesque cottages in town are **guesthouses**, some with spectacular views over Cape Cod Bay. The best place to be is the quieter West End (the lower the address on Commercial Street, the deeper into the West End), though anything on Bradford Street will also be removed from the summertime racket. Prices are generally very reasonable until mid-June, and off-season you can find real bargains. In addition, there are a few **motels**, mostly confined to the outskirts of town, towards the Truro line.

Provincetown Reservations (☎508/487-2400 or 1-800/648-0364) and the gay-oriented Intown Reservations (☎508/487-1883 or 1-800/67P-TOWN) can usually rustle up lodgings at busy times. The welcoming **Dune's Edge Campground**, on Route 6 just east of the central stop lights (☎508/487-9815), charges $22 for use of one of its wooded sites.

Boatslip, 161 Commercial St (☎508/487-1669 or 1-800/451-7547, *www.boatslipbeachclub.com*). Famous gay in-town motel right on the water with pool and huge deck – a venue for a daily afternoon tea-dance in season. ⑦–⑨.

Dyer's Beach House, 173 Commercial St (☎508/487-2061). Motel-style rooms in this centrally located inn have sliding doors which open to a common deck with ocean views. ⑥–⑦.

Land's End Inn, 22 Commercial St (☎508/487-0706 or 1-800/276-7088, *www.sunsol.com/landsend*). Sixteen meticulously decorated rooms and suites, many with sweeping ocean views, and simply stunning gardens. Highly recommended. ⑨–⑦.

Outermost Hostel, 28 Winslow St (☎508/487-4378). Hostel with $15 beds in five dorm cabins. ①.

Revere Guest House, 14 Court St (☎508/487-2292, *www.reverehouse.com*). A pleasant B&B with garden patio and antiques-accented rooms, some with shared baths. ③–④.

Snug Cottage, 178 Bradford St (☎508/487-1616 or 1-800/432-2334, *www.snugcottage.com*). Comfortably appointed B&B rooms and cottages in surprisingly calm location close to the city center. ④–⑥.

Sunset Inn, 142 Bradford St (☎508/487-9810 or 1-800/965-1801). Clean, quiet rooms in an 1850 captain's house close to the center of town. Clothing-optional deck out back. ④.

Watermark Inn, 603 Commercial St (☎508/487-0165, *www.watermarkinn.com*). Ten immaculate, contemporary suites, several of which have private decks with ocean views. ⑨–⑦.

Watership Inn, 7 Winthrop St (☎508/487-0094 or 1-800/330-9413, *www.capecod*.net /watershipinn*). Fifteen rooms with private bath in an 1820 sea captain's home; rates include a good continental breakfast. ④.

The Town and around

The town center is essentially two three-mile-long streets, **Commercial** and **Bradford,** connected by about forty tiny lanes of no more than two short blocks each. Though much diluted by tourism, the beatnik spirit is still in evidence, most pronounced in regular Friday-night expositions in the many art galleries along Commercial Street. On summer evenings the narrow street fills with hordes of sightseers, locals, and, amazingly, cars, even though they can do little more than crawl along. **Fisherman's Wharf** and the more touristy **MacMillan Wharf**, busy with whale-watching boats, yachts and colorful old Portuguese fishing vessels, split the town in half. MacMillan Wharf also houses the **Whydah Museum** (April–October daily 10am–5pm; $5; free with ferry or whale watch ticket), which displays some of the bounty from a famous pirate shipwreck off the coast of Wellfleet in 1717. The lifelong quest of native Cape Codder Barry Clifford to recover the treasure from the one-time slave ship *Whydah* – repository of loot from more than fifty ships when it sank – paid off royally with his discovery of the ship in summer 1983. Thousands of coins, gold bars, pieces of jewelry and weapons were retrieved, and the process continues. The most evocative display in the museum, glimmering gold coins notwithstanding, is the ship's **bell**, a little rusty but not so corroded that you can't read "The Whydah Galley – 1716" clear as day.

Two blocks north of the piers, atop aptly named Town Hill, is the 252-foot granite tower of the **Pilgrim Monument** (July & Aug daily 9am–7pm; May, June, Sept–Nov daily 9am–5pm; $6), modeled on a bell tower in Siena, Italy. It commemorates the Pilgrims' landing and their signing of the Mayflower Compact. From the observation deck, the whole Cape (and, on a clear day, Boston) can be discerned. Not far away in the lively East End, the **Provincetown Heritage Museum**, 356 Commercial St (daily: summer 10am–6pm; rest of year 10am–5pm; $3), is housed in an 1860 Methodist church. This comprehensive collection of Provincetown memorabilia includes a 68-inch striped bass, a Portuguese altar, and a reconstruction of the "dune shack" of Harry Kemp, beach-bum poet and crony of Eugene O'Neill. The second floor houses an impressive half-scale model of the *Rose Dorothea*, a much-loved old Provincetown fishing schooner. Further out, the delightful **Provincetown Art Association and Museum**, 460 Commercial St (April–Oct daily noon–5pm & 8–10pm; Nov–March Sat & Sun noon–4pm; $3), rotates works from its collection of nearly two thousand, with equal prominence given to local artists as well as established figures. Do your best to come on a Friday night, when openings by new artists frequently take place.

On the other side of the wharves is the quieter and slightly less cramped **West End**, where many of the weathered clapboard houses are cheerfully decorated with colored blinds, white picket fences, and wildflowers spilling out of every possible orifice. At Commercial Street's western end, the actual **landing place** of the Pilgrims is marked by a modest bronze plaque on a boulder.

The beaches

A little ways beyond the town's narrow strip of sand, a string of **undeveloped beaches** are marked only by dunes and a few shabby beach huts. You can swim in the clear cool water from the uneven rocks of the two-mile breakwater at the western end of Commercial Street, where the seabed crunches with soft-shell clams, or head down a trail of scented wild roses and beach plums toward **Long Point Beach**, to find blissful solitude. Due west of town, at the end of Route 6, **Herring Cove Beach**, easily reached by bike or through the dunes and famous for sunset-watching, is actually more crowded than the beaches nearer town, though never unbearably so.

At the Cape's northern tip, off Race Point Road, **Race Point Beach** has a wide swath of white sand backed by beautiful, tall dunes – the archetypal Cape Cod beach. Race Point abuts the beautiful **Province Lands**, where vast sweeping moors and bushy dunes are buffeted by a crashing surf, site of some three thousand known shipwrecks. The **visitor center** (summer daily 9am–5pm; spring and fall daily 9am–4.30pm; ☎508/487-1256), in the middle of the dunes off Race Point Road, has an observation deck from which you might spot a whale – or even, when the tide is right, the ruins of the **HMS Somerset**, a sunken British battleship from the Revolutionary War.

Eating

Food in Provincetown can be expensive: the snack bars around MacMillan Wharf are generally extortionate, and the eclectic cuisine in the predominantly gay restaurants can hit $10 for a salad and a coffee. Still, there are some real discoveries to be made, and they need not break your budget – look out in particular for the Portuguese restaurants that can be found throughout the town. Whenever possible, especially in the few restaurants where it's possible to eat al fresco (mosquitos can be a big problem), arrive early or call ahead to make a reservation; many restaurants are packed in season, and just as many close for the winter.

Cafés and bakeries

Café Blasé, 328 Commercial St (☎508/487-9465). Touristy pastel café, one of the few places with outdoor seating for great people-watching. Pricey for dinner, but delicious $6 fresh fruit and waffle breakfasts.

Café Crudité, 336 Commercial St (☎508/487-6237). Casual upstairs eatery serving exclusively vegetarian fare, like delicious tofu salad.

Café Edwidge, 333 Commercial St (☎508/487-2008). Breakfast's the thing at this popular second-floor spot; try the home-made Danish pastries and fresh fruit pancakes. Creative bistro fare at dinner time.

Café Heaven, 199 Commercial St (☎508/487-9639). Light and airy upmarket café serving all-day breakfasts, cappuccino and creative salads from $5. Closed 3–6.30pm, then reopens until 10pm.

Fat Jack's Café, 335 Commercial St (☎508/487-4822). Low-priced, no-nonsense breakfasts, and lunch and dinner specials.

Portuguese Bakery, 299 Commercial St (☎508/487-1803). This old standby is the place to come for cheap baked goods, particularly the tasty fried *rabanada*, akin to portable French Toast.

Post Office Café, 303 Commercial St (☎508/487-3892). Small restaurant serving healthy lunches and dinners for $5–10.

No Ordinary Joe, 148A Commercial St (☎508/487-6656). Coffee shop serving delicious pastries and *biscotti*.

Restaurants

Bubala's by the Bay, 183 Commercial St (☎508/487-0773). Snappy seafood with international influences is the signature of the brightly painted West End eatery, where the service is not quite so snappy; additional seating on a big outdoor deck.

Chester, 404 Commercial St (☎508/487-8200). Preciously chic spot with an award-winning wine list. Menu changes weekly, emphasizing fresh ingredients, unusual combinations like sea scallops with apples and sage, and high prices.

Ciro & Sal's, 4 Kiley Court (☎508/487-0049). Traditional Northern Italian cooking with plenty of veal and seafood choices; a bit on the pricey side, but worth it.

The Commons, 386 Commercial St (☎508/487-7800). French bistro food and tasty pizzas from a wood-fired oven make this a popular spot.

Dancing Lobster, 9 Ryder Street (☎508/487-0900). The Tuscan-prepared seafood and sunset views pack them in here, so arrive early to avoid a wait.

Grand Central, 5 Masonic Place (☎508/487-7599). Romantic, pricey bistro directly across from the *Atlantic House* bar.

Lobster Pot, 321 Commercial St (☎508/487-0842). Its landmark neon sign is like a welcome mat for those who come from far and wide for the ultra-fresh crustaceans. Affordable and family-oriented.

The Moors, 5 Bradford St (☎508/487-0840). Classic Portuguese – meaning hearty seafood and pork dishes – in an appropriately nautical setting.

Napi's, 7 Freeman St (☎508/487-1145). Popular dishes at this art-strewn spot include pastas and seafood items, notably a thick Portuguese fish stew.

Pucci's Harborside, 539 Commercial St (☎508/487-1964). Casual American away from the madding crowds in the East End of town.

Spiritus, 190 Commercial St (☎508/487-2808). Combination pizza place and coffee bar with an especially lively after-hours scene.

Stormy Harbor, 277 Commercial St (☎508/487-1680). Inexpensive dishes with a focus on Italian and seafood.

Nightlife and entertainment

Each in-season weekend, boatloads of revelers seek out P-town's notoriously wild **nightlife**. Most of the action, which ranges from house music raves to drag cabarets, all of course very gay-friendly, takes place along Commercial Street.

The Atlantic House, 6 Masonic Place, behind Commercial St (☎508/487-3821). The "A-House" – a dark drinking hole that was a favorite of Tennessee Williams and Eugene O'Neill – is now a trendy (and still dark) gay dance club and bar.

Chaser's, 293 Commercial St (☎508/487-7200). Subterranean disco for women, with occasional live music, right in the heart of the action.

Club Euro, 258 Commercial St (☎508/487-2505). Music videos, world-beat sounds, and a good buzz in an 1843 former Congregational church with 3-D mermaid emerging from the wall.

Crown & Anchor, 247 Commercial St (☎508/487-1430). Noisy, popular pub with nightly drag shows and cabaret.

Governor Bradford, 312 Commercial St (☎508/487-2781). Popular bar where you can enjoy live jazz, reggae and R&B, or just sit and watch the world go by.

Pied Piper, 193A Commercial St (☎508/487-1527). This is the lesbian counterpart to the *Atlantic House*.

Vixen, 336 Commercial St (☎508/487-6424). High-energy lesbian disco featuring national and local entertainers.

Shopping

Like most coastal New England towns dependent on tourism, there are more T-shirt **shops** in Provincetown than you can count. However, there is also a wealth of trendy boutiques and unusual galleries – many cooler than those you'll find in Boston – with an unmistakable air of buccaneer chic.

Himalayan Handicrafts, 368 Commercial St (☎508/487-6542). Meditation singing bowls, antiques, clothing, incense, music, and masks in this Eastern-oriented shop.

La Spiaggia, 364 Commercial St (☎508/487-7245). Let your nose take a wander through the extensive selection of scented candles and hand-cut soaps. Jewelry and other gifts dazzle the eye as well.

Marine Specialties, 235 Commercial St (☎508/487-1730). Cavernous emporium brimming with inexpensive knick-knacks, not exclusively ocean-related.

Shop Therapy, 346 Commercial St (☎508/487-9392). Outlandish only begins to describe the painted exterior of this singular store, where inside you'll find "retail nirvana for alternative lifestyles."

Toys of Eros, 200 Commercial St (☎508/487-0056). "Quality erotica and fetish wear" to add a little spice to the holidays of boys and girls of all proclivities.

MARTHA'S VINEYARD AND NANTUCKET

Just five miles south of Cape Cod, the sedate, forested island of **Martha's Vineyard** has long been one of the most popular and prestigious vacation destinations in the US, a status that has only grown in recent years, as a gaggle of celebrities from Carly Simon to President Clinton have come for its mannerly New England towns, untouched beaches, and above all, peace and quiet. Like its slightly further afield cousin, **Nantucket,** it mingles an easygoing cosmopolitan atmosphere, assured by some of the best restaurants and bed-and-breakfasts on the East Coast, with a taste of remoteness, even though Boston and New York are just short flights away. Neither island boasts much in the way of traditional sights, and almost all locals are more than happy to keep it that way.

Martha's Vineyard

Bigger than Nantucket, **MARTHA'S VINEYARD** encompasses more physical variety too, with hills and pasturelands providing scenic counterpoints to the beaches and wild, windswept moors on the separate island of **Chappaquiddick**. Roads throughout the Vineyard are framed by knotty oak trees, which lend a romantic aura to an already pretty landscape. The most genteel town on the island is **Edgartown**, all prim and proper with its freshly painted, white-clapboard colonial homes and manicured gardens. The other main town, **Vineyard Haven,** has a more commercial atmosphere, not surprising considering that it is one of the main places where the ferries come in. **Oak Bluffs,** in between the two (and the other docking point for ferries), has an array of wooden gingerbread cottages and inviting eateries. Regardless of where you visit, watch out for the terminology: heading "Up-Island" takes you, improbably, southwest to the wondrous cliffs at **Gay Head**; conversely, "Down-Island" refers to the easterly towns of Vineyard Haven, Oak Bluffs, and Edgartown.

Some history

Martha's Vineyard was reputedly named by the British explorer who discovered it in 1602, **Bartholomew Gosnold,** for his daughter, **Martha**. The "Vineyard" part was for its fertile store of vines – back then the triangular-shaped island was virtually covered with wild grapes, none of which remain. While Gosnold spent only three days on the island, **Wampanoag Indians** had been calling it home for at least ten thousand years, and a small community of around three hundred remains at **Aquinnah**, near the multicolored limestone cliffs of Gay Head. They

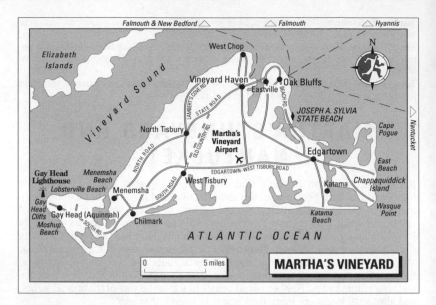

claimed that in order to separate his tribe from enemies on the mainland, the Indian chief **Moshup** placed his cape on the ground and created Vineyard Sound, though geological records put that event as happening about 50,000 years ago.

For a few decades after Gosnold's departure the island was once again the exclusive province of the natives, but in 1642 one **Thomas Mayhew** bought it from the earl of Stirling for forty pounds and a beaver hat, paving the way for other English Puritan farmers to settle here. They learned tricks of the whaling industry from the natives, and the economy flourished: while Martha's Vineyard never ousted Nantucket or New Bedford as whaling capital of the east, many of its captains did very nicely out of the industry, evidenced by the gracious sea captains' houses that remain in Edgartown and Vineyard Haven. By the time of the Civil War in the 1860s, however, whaling was in serious decline, and had it not been for the **Methodist Camp Meetings** that started here in 1835, the island's tourist industry might never have taken root. Dozens of Methodist families from churches all over the nation started gathering in tents at sparsely populated Oak Bluffs for two weeks of vigorous preaching and recreation; they were looking for an isolated location far away from the temptations of the flesh. As the movement grew, so did the desire of many families to return, some building permanent platforms, arranged around the preachers' tent, and later constructing small cottages with extraordinarily fancy facades, now familiar as "gingerbread" style – more than half of which remain clustered round the village green. In 1867, recognizing the island's potential as a resort, developers constructed a separate secular community next to the original campground, and large hotels were soon constructed around the harbor.

Though the tourism has never abated, today, strictly enforced **zoning** laws insure that major development is kept to a minimum; billboards, neon signs, even parking meters, are outlawed. Concerned residents come out in force at the slightest whiff of change; a car sticker campaign a few years ago urged "Mac to Keep Off Martha," in response to an application by McDonald's to open a franchise here – they were successful.

Arrival, orientation, and getting around

Most people come to Martha's Vineyard by **ferry**, arriving at either Oak Bluffs or Vineyard Haven (see box overleaf for schedules and fares). You can also **fly** via Cape Air (☎508/771-6944 or 1-800/352-0714) from Boston (from which there's an hourly shuttle in the summer), Hyannis, Nantucket, or New Bedford. The Vineyard's **airport** (☎508/693-7022) is in West Tisbury. **Taxis** greet all arriving ferries and flights; reputable companies include Martha's Vineyard Taxi (☎508/693-8660) and All Island Taxi (☎508/693-3705).

In summer a shuttle **bus** service connects the main towns on the island, operating from 7am to 12.45am daily (☎508/693-1589 for schedule information). Tickets cost $1.50–3 each way, and an unlimited pass is $5 per day. Two-hour pithily narrated **bus tours,** which are a good way of getting oriented, operate from spring to autumn from all ferry arrival points; expect to pay around $15. Still, it's best to explore the island for yourself. Bringing a **car** over is expensive and rather pointless, but as soon as you get off the ferry you encounter rows of **bike** rental places; other rental options are Anderson Bike Rentals on Circuit Avenue in Oak Bluffs (☎508/693-9346), or R.W. Cutler Bikes at 1 Main St, Edgartown (☎508/627-4052). Wherever you get it from, expect to spend from $10 to $17 a day. If you just can't do without a car, you can rent one from Budget, in both Vineyard Haven and Edgartown (☎508/693-1911 or 1-800/527-0700), or, a bit more upscale, Vineyard Classic Cars, Lake Avenue, Oak Bluffs (☎508/693-5551). **Mopeds** can be somewhat useful, but they are frowned on by many residents because of the resultant noise and accidents. Should you want to rent one, Ride On Mopeds, Circuit Ave Extension, Oak Bluffs (☎508/693-2076), will be able to help.

NAME CONFUSION ON THE VINEYARD

There's no way around the **name confusion** of Martha's Vineyard towns other than acquainting yourself with a bit of island history. Most muddled of all are Vineyard Haven and West Tisbury. Where, you might wonder, is Tisbury? The answer is, nowhere. Well, officially, but not really. Vineyard Haven, north of West Tisbury, is incorporated as Tisbury, but no one ever calls it that. Name changing on the island began in 1642, when the settlement of Nunnepog was renamed Great Harbor. But in 1673, Governor Thomas Mayhew opted for another name, Edgar Towne, a nod to the son of the Duke of York and heir presumptive of Charles II, the reigning monarch at the time. The habit has proven hard to break. Oak Bluffs was called Cottage City until 1907. Gay Head, home of the famous cliffs, recently reverted, officially, to its Wampanoag Indian name of Aquinnah, though people still refer to it as Gay Head. Then there is the matter of Chilmark, which, though endowed with a town hall, is not endowed with a town. It's all very fitting for a place that, after all, neither belongs to "Martha" nor is a vineyard.

FERRIES TO MARTHA'S VINEYARD

Unless otherwise specified, the ferries listed below run several times daily in the peak mid-June to mid-September holiday periods. Most have fewer services from mid-May to mid-June, and between mid-September and October. There is at least a skeleton service to each island, though not on all routes, year-round. Round-trip passenger fares from **Woods Hole** and **Falmouth** to Martha's Vineyard are around $12; from **Hyannis**, $24; from **New Bedford**, $20; and from **Montauk**, Long Island, $40. Round-trip costs for cars (mid-May to mid-Sept) are around $104, not including passengers ($48-60 off-season). You *must* have a reservation for cars; book early if possible. Large car parks are provided for day-trippers and for those who want to stay overnight, costing $6–10 per car.

From Cape Cod

Falmouth to Oak Bluffs (about 35 minutes). Passengers only. The *Island Queen* (☎508/548-4800).

Falmouth to Edgartown (1 hour). Passengers only. Falmouth Ferry Service (☎508/548-9400).

Woods Hole to both Vineyard Haven and Oak Bluffs (about 45 minutes). Car ferry. Steamship Authority (☎508/447-8600).

Hyannis to Oak Bluffs (about 100 minutes). Passengers only. Hy-Line (☎508/778-2600 in Hyannis; ☎508/693-0112 on Martha's Vineyard).

From elsewhere in Massachusetts (and New York)

New Bedford to Vineyard Haven (90 minutes). Passengers only. Cape Island Express (☎508/997-1688).

Montauk, Long Island, NY to Oak Bluffs (about 6 hours). Passengers only, summer Thursdays only. Viking Ferry (☎631/668-5709).

Accommodation

There's a tremendous variety of **accommodation** on the island, ranging from resort hotels with every conceivable creature comfort, to old sea captains' homes oozing with charm and personality, and rental cottages, usually booked on a weekly basis. Remember that, whatever type of lodging you decide on, summer accommodation in Martha's Vineyard gets booked up very early, so reserve well in advance. If you do get stuck with nowhere to stay, the main **Chamber of Commerce** office at 24 Beach Road, Vineyard Haven (☎508/693-0085), will always do their best to help. Remember too, that in-season and off-season prices can vary dramatically, hence the big range in some of the prices listed below. If you want (or need) to save money, check out the **campgrounds** in Vineyard Haven (☎508/693-3772) and Oak Bluffs (☎508/693-0233).

Oak Bluffs

Admiral Benbow Inn, 520 New York Ave (☎508/693-6825). Seven pleasant, non-smoking rooms in this newly restored turn-of-the-century landmark inn close to the harbor. ⑥–⑦.

Attleboro House, 11 Lake Ave (☎508/693-0085). Charming, old-fashioned guesthouse with a distinguished harbor-view terrace – no private bathrooms. ⑤–⑥.

Nashua House B&B, Kennebec and Park aves (☎508/693-0043). Small rooms, shared baths, but one of the less expensive choices in these parts. ④–⑤.

Wesley Hotel, 1 Lake Ave (☎508/693-6611 or 1-800/638-9027). The last of Oak Bluff's grand hotels, with plenty of character intact. Most rooms are $130-plus, but a few with shared bathroom cost less. ⑦–⑨.

Edgartown

Colonial Inn, 38 N Water St (☎508/627-4711 or 1-800/627-4701). Extremely central white-clapboard inn that's part of a largish mall. Some off-season bargains, but midsummer rates are high. ⑧.

Edgartown Commons, Pease's Point Way (☎508/627-4671). Adequate and inexpensive one- and two-bedroom efficiencies in Edgartown's historic district. ⑦.

Harborside Inn, 3 S Water St (☎508/627-4321 or 1-800/627-4009). Comfortable rooms on the waterfront with heated pool and sauna. ⑦–⑨.

Shiretown Inn, 21 N Water St (☎508/627-3353 or 1-800/541-0090). Variety of different-styled B&B rooms, including some very costly ones, slap bang in the center of town. ⑥–⑦.

Tuscany Inn, 22 N Water St (☎508/627-4784). Savor an unexpected slice of Italy in the center of (somewhat stuffy) Edgartown, reflected mainly in the food and decor. ⑦.

Elsewhere on the island

HI-Martha's Vineyard, Edgartown–West Tisbury Rd (☎508/693-2665). A nice setting, but a bit off the beaten track. April to mid-Nov; $16 members, $19 nonmembers.

Lambert's Cove Country Inn, Lambert's Cove Rd, West Tisbury (☎508/693-2298). Quiet, secluded country inn on idyllic grounds that include access to a private beach. ⑥–⑦.

Menemsha Inn & Cottages, North Road, Menemsha (☎508/645-2521). Suites in the carriage house, rooms in the main building and 12 cottages in the grounds. Open May–Nov; book early. ⑦.

The island

The Vineyard is basically divided in two sections, the far busier of which is "Down-Island," which includes the ferry terminals of **Vineyard Haven** and **Oak Bluffs**, and smart **Edgartown**. The largely undeveloped western half of the island, known as "Up-Island," comprises woods, agricultural land, ponds, and nature reserves, with a smattering of tiny villages thrown in between, including **West Tisbury**, **Chilmark** and **Gay Head**. Although there are plenty of trails to explore, much of the land belongs to strictly private estates and as such is out of bounds to the public.

Vineyard Haven

Most visitors by boat arrive at **VINEYARD HAVEN** (officially named Tisbury), at the northern tip of the island. Founded by islanders from Edgartown disillusioned with the iron-fist Puritan rule of the Mayhew family, Vineyard Haven supplanted Edgartown as the island's main commercial center in the mid-1800s, because ferries preferred the shorter run to the mainland; today, the town, which may well be the least attractive on the island, retains its distinctively business-like ambiance, its late-Victorian main street lined with a mix of shops, banks, law and real estate offices, and ice-cream parlors.

The brand-new **bus terminal** visible as you get off the ferry is also home to a small visitor's kiosk, but for more detailed information and help in finding accommodation, walk up Beach Road to the **Martha's Vineyard Chamber of Commerce**, 24 Beach Rd (Memorial Day to Labor Day Mon–Fri 9am–5pm, Sat 10am–2pm). Along the way, you'll pass the legendary **Black Dog Tavern**, as famous for its souvenirs – like the bag that President Clinton gave to Monica Lewinsky – as for its food and drink. From here, it's just a few yards up to **Main Street**, many of whose original buildings were destroyed in the Great Fire of 1883, though it's rebuilt and thriving now. One which escaped the blaze is the 1829 **Old Schoolhouse Museum**, no. 110 (mid-June to mid-Sept Tues–Fri & Sun noon–4pm; $2), the town's first school, which contains items brought back from whaling expeditions, along with antique musical instruments and school reports from the Victorian era. A **liberty pole** out front honors three young island girls who crept out of their homes and risked their lives one night in 1776 to blow up the town's captured liberty pole, rather than allow the British sea captain who had seized it to keep it. Close by, **William Street** also escaped the ravages of fire and is now a historical district brimming with elegant Greek Revival sea captains' houses from the prosperous whaling days. Just round the corner, at 51 Spring St, the 1844 Association Hall houses both the **Tisbury Town Hall** and the **Katharine Cornell Theatre**, the latter partly created with funds donated by the famous actress, a long-time summer resident, in her will. Miss Cornell is buried close by in the pine-shaded **Center Street Cemetery**, which dates back to 1817, with simple gray slate slabs marking the resting places of early nineteenth-century islanders.

Oak Bluffs

OAK BLUFFS, just across Lagoon Pond from Vineyard Haven, is the newest of the island's six towns, a quiet farming community until the Methodists established their campground, known as "Wesleyan Grove," here in the 1850s. This section of Oak Bluffs remains a relatively tranquil haven filled with the brightly colored "carpenter Gothic" or "gingerbread" cottages they built. Family-oriented events and Sunday morning services are still held in the iron and wood-constructed **tabernacle** during summer. At one end of the Tabernacle circle, the 1867 **Cottage Museum** at 1 Trinity Park (mid-June to Sept Mon–Sat 10am–4pm; $1 donation) offers a charming collection of photographs, old Bibles, and other artifacts from the campground's history. In a frenzy of post-Civil War construction, speculators built up the area near the waterfront with dance halls, a skating rink, a railway linking "Cottage City" to Edgartown, and resort hotels, of which only the 1879 **Wesley Hotel**, on Lake Avenue, survives. Most of the current action focuses on **Circuit Avenue**, where the shops and bars attract a predominantly young crowd. The recently restored **Flying Horses Carousel**, at Circuit and Lake avenues (mid-April to mid-Oct daily 10am–10pm; $1 a ride), is reputedly the oldest operating carousel in the country, hand-carved in 1876.

Oak Bluffs also has a few beaches worth checking out, though the **town beach**, Sea View Avenue, can get very noisy and crowded in season. Further south, the **Joseph A. Sylvia State Beach**, a sandy six-mile stretch of shore, is more appealing, and it parallels an undemanding pedestrian/cycle path that leads all the way to Edgartown, with pleasant views to accompany you.

Edgartown

Six miles southeast of Oak Bluffs, **EDGARTOWN**, originally known as Great Harbor, is the oldest and swankiest settlement on the island, and has been extravagantly dolled up for visitors, its elegant colonial residences glistening white and surrounded by exquisitely maintained gardens and trimmed hedges. It doesn't end there, of course; downtown brims with upmarket boutiques, smart restaurants, and artsy galleries. You may recognize the place as the location for the *Jaws* films – rumor has it that filming for Steven Spielberg's blockbuster movie was delayed when the Californian-built monster shark began to disintegrate in the salty New England brine.

Once you've got your bearings at the **Edgartown Visitors' Center**, Church Street, which has a full range of facilities, but no phone, it's a short walk to the **Vineyard Museum**, Cooke Street at School Street (mid-June to mid-October Tues–Sat 10am–5pm; rest of year, Wed–Fri 1–4pm, Sat 10am–4pm; $6), a complex of buildings maintained by the Dukes County Historical Society, including a pre-Revolutionary War house full of whaling relics and, best of all, an Oral History Center, which traces the history of the island through more than 250 recorded narratives of older islanders. A couple of blocks to the east, on Main Street, the massive **Old Whaling Church**, whose 92ft-high clock tower is visible for miles around, started life in 1843 as a Methodist church and is now used as a performing arts center, among other things. Its impressive six-column portico leads into a simple, elegant interior, where the original box pews are still in place. If you're not attending a show, you'll have to see it on one of the Liz Villard's **Ghosts, Gossip, and Downright Scandal walking tours** (May–Dec, call for times; $10; ☎508/627-8619). Just behind the church, the 1672 **Vincent House Museum** (May to mid-Oct daily noon–3pm; $3; $6 combo admission includes tours of Fisher House and Whaling Church) is the oldest house on the island, and has the furniture to prove it. Also on Main Street, the Federal-style **Dr. Daniel Fisher House** was built in 1840 for the entrepreneurial Fisher (who besides serving as a doctor, owned a whale-oil factory, and founded the Martha's Vineyard National Bank); exquisitely preserved features include an enclosed cupola and roof and porch balustrades. A short walk along North Water Street leads past more charming sea captains' houses to the white cast-iron **Edgartown Lighthouse** – it's a replacement of the 1828 original, destroyed in the hurricane of 1938. There's a pleasant **public beach** here, though if you want to swim, you'll have to deal with an abundance of smelly seaweed.

Chappaquiddick

Though in truth inordinately peaceful, **Chappaquiddick Island** instantly conjures up the political strife of Senator Edward J. Kennedy, in whose car 28-year-old Mary Jo Kopechne drowned in the summer of 1969 at **Dike Bridge**, circumstances that conspiracy theorists still debate. The island is easily accessible from Edgartown via the *On Time* ferry (so called because it has no regular schedule and is thus always "on time"; $2.50), which departs from a ramp at the corner of Dock and Daggett streets, or by walking along the long sandy spit from South Beach in **Katama**. This latter entrance leads to the **Wasque Reservation**, largely a continuation of the beach on the Vineyard's "mainland." Indeed, most of Chappaquiddick's space is given over to beautiful beaches and wildlife reservations, such as the **Cape Pogue Wildlife Refuge**, on the island's eastern side, five hundred acres of dunes, salt marshes, ponds, scrubland, and barrier beach, and an important habitat and migration stopover for thousands of birds. Half the state's scallops are harvested here, too. The best way to see it is to take one of the three-hour guided **natural history tours** that run at 8.30am and 4pm during the summer (Memorial Day to Columbus Day; $30; ☎508/627-3599).

West Tisbury

There's little to bring you to the largest of Up-Island communities, **WEST TIS-BURY**, although if you fly into town, this is where you'll land. In July of 1999, West Tisbury joined Chappaquiddick in the lore of the Kennedy curse, when John Kennedy, Jr's plane crashed in the water less than twenty miles from the landing field. A relatively inexperienced pilot, Kennedy apparently became disoriented and put himself into a fatal dive, killing himself, his wife and sister-in-law.

Most of West Tisbury's history has been considerably more peaceful. The town was founded in the 1670s by settlers from Edgartown, who happened upon a fast-flowing stream here. As the community developed, sheep farming became the main industry; although few sheep are left today, West Tisbury residents dote on its rural atmosphere, and there are several flourishing horse and agricultural produce farms. Indeed, the **Farmers' Market**, held at the 1859 **Agricultural Hall** on South Road every Saturday morning (and sometimes Wednesday mornings in the summer), attracts visitors from all over the island for its colorful displays of locally grown produce. Recently an additional Agricultural Hall was built to complement the old one – to be used as a setting for shows, dances, pot-luck suppers, and an annual country fair that takes place at the end of August. Across the street from the old hall is the **Field Gallery**, State Road (☎508/693-5595), locally famous for Tom Maley's larger-than-life sculptures of ladies dancing on the grass. Also on State Road, check out **Alley's Store** (☎508/693-0088), an island institution since 1858, selling everything from cans of baked beans to mini ouija boards, and with a wide front porch where locals often meet for a chat. There's a place behind the store, appropriately enough *Back Alley's*, to get good sandwiches. North of West Tisbury village tiny **Mayhew Chapel**, on Christiantown Road, off Indian Hill Road, was dedicated to Rev Thomas Mayhew, Jr, who converted members of the Wampanoag tribe to Christianity in the mid-1600s. These "Praying Indians," as they became known, established a community here called Christiantown; many of them are buried in the neighboring **Burial Ground**.

West Tisbury has a bountiful supply of conservation areas, including the **Cedar Tree Neck Wildlife Sanctuary**, Indian Hill Road (daily 8.30am–5.30pm; free), in which bayberry bushes, swamp azaleas, tupelos, and pygmy beech trees can be spotted. The trails lead to a pretty but stony beach and a bluff with views to Gay Head and the Elizabeth Islands. Meanwhile, the **Sepiessa Point Reservation**, New Lane, off West Tisbury Road (daily sunrise–sunset; free), surrounds West Tisbury Pond, with ideal trails for bird-watching.

Chilmark

Five miles west, unspoiled **CHILMARK**, with just 821 year-round residents, is the land that time almost forgot, full of pastures separated by stone walls, dense woodlands and rugged roads. That's not to say that the twentieth century hasn't arrived: **Beetlebung Corner**, where Middle, State, South, and Menemsha Cross roads meet, is the village's center, heralded by a small grocery-deli, a boutique, and some other modern commercial concerns, though also there is an old schoolhouse, the last one-room version on the island.

On South Road the tranquil **Chilmark Cemetery** holds the final resting places of writer Lillian Helman and wild funnyman John Belushi, who claimed that the island was the only place in the world where he could get a good night's sleep. Near the entrance, a boulder engraved with the comedian's name, a decoy to

ISLAND BEACHES

The Vineyard's **beaches** vary from calm, shallow waters, predominantly on the northern and eastern sides, to long stretches of pounding surf on the southern side, where the water also tends to be slightly warmer. Unfortunately, many of the best beaches are off-limits to nonresidents, but there are some notable exceptions.

Vineyard Haven

Lake Tashmoo Town Beach, Herring Creek Rd. Swim in the warm, brackish water of the lake, or in the cooler Vineyard Sound.

Owen Park Beach, off Main St. A harbor beach, close to the center of town.

Oak Bluffs

Joseph A. Sylvia State Beach, along Beach Rd between Oak Bluffs and Edgartown. A six-mile strand of sandy beach with clear, gentle waters and plenty of roadside parking.

Oak Bluffs Town Beach, between the Steamship Authority Dock and the State Beach. Narrow sliver of beach on Vineyard Sound that gets very crowded in season.

Edgartown

Bend-in-the-Road Beach, Beach Rd. Really an extension of the Joseph A. Sylvia State Beach, with similar facilities and access.

East Beach (Cape Pogue Wildlife Refuge and Wasque Reservation), on Chappaquiddick Island. Lovely, isolated setting with strong surf, but difficult to get to (access by boat or jeep from the Wasque Reservation).

Katama Beach (South Beach), end of Katama Rd. Beautiful barrier beach backed by protected salt pond. Strong surf and currents.

Lighthouse Beach, Starbuck's Neck, off North Water St. Close to town, this harbor beach can get a bit too mucked with seaweed.

West Tisbury

Lambert's Cove Beach, Lambert's Cove Rd. One of the island's prettiest beaches, but open only to residents during the season.

West Tisbury South Shore Town Beach, off Edgartown–West Tisbury Rd. Beautiful, deserted beach with good surf but the same access limitations as Lambert's Cove.

Chilmark

Lucy Vincent Beach, off South Rd. Wide sandy beach restricted in season to Chilmark residents and visitors with passes.

Menemsha Public Beach, next to Menemsha Harbor. The only Chilmark beach open to the public, with sparkling waters and a picturesque setting.

Gay Head

Lobsterville Beach, Lobsterville Rd. Two miles of prime Vineyard Sound beach backed by dunes. Parking on Lobsterville Road is prohibited, so bike or taxi here.

Moshup Beach (Gay Head Public Beach), State Rd/Moshup Drive. Gorgeous setting at the foot of Gay Head Cliffs, best reached by bicycle, shuttle bus, or taxi. Parking costs $15 a day in season.

prevent fans from finding his actual unmarked grave, is where legions leave their rather unceremonious "offerings," like beer cans and condoms. Off South Road, a dirt track leads to **Lucy Vincent Beach**, named after the town's prim and proper librarian, who saw it as her mission to protect Chilmark residents from corruption by cutting out from her library books all pictures she deemed to be immoral. Rather ironically, the beach, which is open only to residents and their guests in the summer, today doubles up as a **nudists'** spot. Off North Road, pick up a map at the trailhead of **Waskosim's Rock Reservation** for a fascinating three-mile hike through a variety of habitats including wetlands and black gum and oak woods. The rock itself was dumped here by retreating glaciers ten thousand years ago.

Menemsha

In the northern part of Chilmark, another tiny village, **MENEMSHA**, is a picturesque but hotchpotch collection of gray-shingled fishing shacks with a man-made harbor used for location shots in the making of *Jaws*. The harbor also serves as an important commercial and sports-fishing port, much of the catch ending up at restaurants all over the island. Stroll past the fish markets of **Dutcher's Dock** for a real sense of the island's maritime heritage, or bring an early-evening picnic to pebbly **Menemsha Beach** to enjoy the spectacular sunsets. The **Menemsha Hills Reservation**, just north of the beach, is also well worth a visit, its mile-long rocky shoreline and sand bluffs along Vineyard Sound peaking at **Prospect Hill**, the highest point on the Vineyard, with wonderful views of the Elizabeth Islands.

Gay Head (Aquinnah)

In 1997, the people of **GAY HEAD** voted to revert the town's name back to its original Wampanoag Indian name of **Aquinnah**, the culmination of a ten-year-plus court battle in which the Wampanoags won guardianship of 420 acres of land, to be held in perpetuity by the Federal Government and known as the **Gay Head Native American Reservation**. Gay Head is also the location of the estate of the late **Jacqueline Onassis**, though it's strictly private and hidden by trees.

Most people come to this part of the island, its westernmost point, to see the multicolored clay **Gay Head Cliffs**, whose brilliant hues are the result of millions of years of geological work. When the oceans were high, and the Vineyard was underwater, small creatures died and left their shells behind to form the white layers. At other times, the area was a rainforest and vegetation compressed to form the darker colors. The weight of the glaciers thrust the many layers of stone up at an angle to create the cliffs, dubbed "Gay Head" by passing English sailors in the seventeenth century, on account of their bright colors. The clay was once the main source of paint for the island's houses, but now anyone removing any (unless you're a Wampanoag Indian) faces a substantial fine; in any case, the cliffs are eroding so fast that it's not safe to approach them too closely anyway. A short steep path lined with seafood shacks and craft stalls leads the way from the car park to the **overlook**, which affords stunning views to the Elizabeth Islands, and, on a clear day, as far as the entrance to Rhode Island's Narragansett Bay. The imposing red-brick **Gay Head Lighthouse** (July to mid-Sept Fri & Sat eves only; $2), built in 1854 to replace a wooden structure that dated from 1799, is well situated for sunset views, on the edge of the cliffs. Below the lighthouse, though not accessible from it, a **public beach** provides an equally impressive view of the cliffs from a different angle. To reach it, take the wooden boardwalk from the **Moshup Beach** car park to the shore, then walk round towards the lighthouse.

Martha's Vineyard eating and drinking

It's easy enough to find something to **eat** on Martha's Vineyard. The ports in particular have rows of places to tempt tourists who've just disembarked the ferries. With four of the island's six towns dry, only in Edgartown and Oak Bluffs can you order booze with meals, but you can bring your own bottle(s) elsewhere. Many pubs, too, serve inexpensive food, though the people partaking of it often look as if they've just stepped out of a Ralph Lauren catalog.

Vineyard Haven

The Black Dog Bakery, Water St (☎508/693-4786). You'll see these T-shirts all over the island and the mainland but it's best to skip the touristy and overrated *Black Dog Tavern* next door (☎508/693-9223), which serves full (and somewhat expensive) dinner, and stock up on delicious muffins or bagels here for the return ferry ride. Either way, both spots feel like pretty unavoidable places, especially located as they are right near the terminal.
Café Moxie, 70 Main St (☎508/693-4480). A trendy neighborhood seafood and pasta joint with surprisingly fair prices.

Oak Bluffs

Giordano's, 107 Circuit Ave (☎508/693-0184). Popular and reasonably priced Italian family restaurant. Their chicken cacciatore is particularly good.
Jimmy Sea's Pan Pasta, 32 Kennebec Ave (☎508/696-8550). Huge portions of tasty pasta in this small, casual eatery favored by locals. Not especially inexpensive, but on the whole worth the price, especially considering where you are.
Zapotec, 10 Kennebec Ave (☎508/693-6800). Exciting seafood variations on Mexican cuisine, like swordfish fajitas.

Edgartown

Main Street Diner, 65 Main St, Old Post Office Square (☎508/627-9337). Down-to-earth 1950s-style diner offering good-value traditional home cooking. Open for breakfast, lunch, and dinner.
The Newes from America, 23 Kelley St (☎508/627-7000). Swill five hundred beers in this atmospheric pub (not necessarily all the same night) and they'll name a stool after you. Decent and filling food, on the relatively affordable side, to help prevent the alcohol from going to your head.
The Wharf, Lower Main St (☎508/627-9966). One of the better-priced seafood joints on the island, on the east side of town.

Elsewhere on the island

Home Port, North Rd, Menemsha (☎508/645-2679). Unpretentious place serving lobster, swordfish and steaks, with lovely views of Menemsha Creek.
Lambert's Cove Inn, Lambert's Cove Rd, West Tisbury (☎508/693-2298). The restaurant at this hideaway inn – surrounded by forest and apple orchards – is a gem; try the delectable soups.

Nantucket

The thirty-mile, two-hour sea crossing to **NANTUCKET** may not be an oceangoing odyssey, but it does set the "Little Gray Lady" apart from her larger, shore-hugging sister, Martha. Just halfway out from Hyannis, neither mainland nor island is in sight, and you realize why the Native Americans dubbed it "distant land." Once

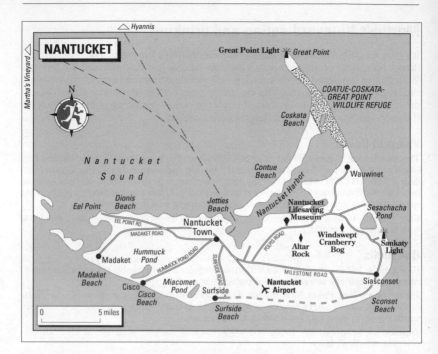

you've landed, you can avert your eyes from the smart-money double-deck cruisers with names like *Pier Pressure* and *Loan Star* and let the place remind you that it hasn't always been a rich folks' playground. Indeed, despite the formidable prowess of its seamen, survival for settlers on the island's barren soil was always a struggle.

The tiny, cobbled carriageways of **Nantucket Town** itself, once one of the largest cities in Massachusetts, were frozen in time by economic decline 150 years ago. Today, this area of delightful old restored houses is very much the center of activity, while, seven flat easily cyclable miles to the east, the pretty, rose-covered cottages of **Siasconset** (always abbreviated to 'Sconset) give another glimpse of days gone by. But however appealing the island's man-made attractions are, it's Nantucket's gentle natural beauty that's the real draw, with heaths and moorlands, mile after mile of fabulous beaches, and a network of bicycle paths that connect the many spots maintained by conservation trusts.

Some history

European settlement on Nantucket dates from 1659, when **Thomas Mayhew**, who had originally purchased the island sight unseen, sold it on the cheap to a group of nine shareholders from Massachusetts who were anxious to escape the repressive policies of the Massachusetts Bay Colony. Those nine then sold half-shares to people whose skills they thought would be needed to expand the new settlement. Even this wasn't enough; the settlers, who landed at **Madaket**, were only able to survive their first winter thanks to assistance from the Wampanoag natives living on the island at the time. In time the number of settlers began to rival that of the natives, who were decimated by disease, and they maintained themselves by developing the business of **whaling**. Though they had learned to spear whales from the shore, where they basically waited at home for the whales to pass by, they began to sail the neighboring ocean to pursue their prey. It paid off in 1712, when one of the ships was blown far out to sea and managed to harpoon a sperm whale, whose highly sought-after oil would fetch very high prices. For the next 150 years, the trade flourished, as did the island; the population grew to more than 10,000, and Nantucket became synonymous with whaling – at its peak, the harbor was base to some one hundred whaling boats plying their trade.

The beginning of the end came when larger ships were needed to cater for the longer (up to five-year) periods at sea. These ships were unable to cross the shallows, and much of Nantucket's whaling activity transferred to the deep-water harbors at New Bedford and Edgartown. Then, a major **fire** in 1846, which started in a hat shop on Main Street, spread to the harbor, where it set light to barrels of whale oil. The harbor was virtually destroyed, along with up to a third of Nantucket Town. The final blow was whale oil's replacement as the fuel of choice by the much-cheaper kerosene. Nantucket declined for the next century, until a local entrepreneur revamped the waterfront in the 1950s; suddenly people began work to preserve the old buildings and salt-encrusted cottages that still stood. There's little doubt that visitors from all over have taken notice once again.

Arrival, information and getting around

Most people arrive in Nantucket by **ferry**. Both the Steamship Authority (☎508/477-8600) and Hy-Line (☎508/778-2600) run year-round passenger services to the island from Hyannis, but only the Steamship Authority's service takes cars. Both charge around $13 each way for passengers, with a fare of $110 per vehicle on the Steamship Authority. Passenger ferries from Harwich Port to

THE WHALERS OF NANTUCKET

The whalers of Nantucket commanded the attention of many with their whaling skill and resultant domination of such a treacherous trade. The early chronicler Crèvecoeur provided an extensive account of Nantucket as it was in 1782 in his *Letters from an American Farmer*. Although perturbed by the islanders' universal habit of taking a dose of opium every morning, he held them up as a model of diligence and good self-government. Whaling was a disciplined profession, unmarred by the stereotyped debauchery of sailors elsewhere, and to feed themselves and equip their ships the islanders kept up a shrewd and extensive trade with the mainland. At that time there were already more than a hundred ships. The whalemen were not paid; instead each had a share (a *lay*) of the final proceeds of the voyage. Crèvecoeur was impressed by the Nantucketers' ambition: "Would you believe that they have already gone to the Falkland Islands and I have heard several of them talk of going to the South Sea."

They did indeed reach the Pacific, though Nantucket will always be the locale most closely associated with the whaling industry. Read about the whalers in Herman Melville's *Moby Dick*, a valediction of sorts; by the time it was published in 1851, Nantucket's fortunes had gone into an abrupt decline. As a magazine article of 1873 reported, "Let no traveler visit Nantucket with the expectation of witnessing the marks of a flourishing trade . . . of the great fleet of ships which dotted every sea, scarcely a vestige remains."

Nantucket are operated by Freedom Cruise Line (☎508/432-8999), but only from June to October. Fares are around $16 each way. A much quicker way to get to the island is by **air**. Both Nantucket Airlines (☎1-800/635-8787) and Island Airlines (☎1-800/248-7779) run year-round daily services from Hyannis to Nantucket, with Cape Air (☎1-800/352-0714) also offering daily services to Boston. The **airport** (☎508/325-5300) is about three miles southeast of Nantucket Town.

Once you've arrived, **getting around** should pose no problem. From the moment you get off the ferry you're besieged by **bike** rental places and tour companies. Try Young's Bicycle Shop (☎508/228-1151), conveniently located on Steamboat Wharf; it should cost $15–20 per day. Driving a **car** makes little sense, especially in peak season, when island arteries can easily get clogged, and it won't endear you to the locals. If you didn't bring one with you on the ferry, there is a limited on-island supply available from Nantucket Windmill (☎508/228-1227), Budget (☎508/228-5666) or Hertz (☎508/228-9421), though none will come cheap. A better way to get around is by **bus**: five shuttle routes round the island are operated between June and September by the Nantucket Regional Transit Authority (☎508/228-7025), with fares starting at just 50¢ per journey for in-town travel; you can get unlimited travel for a week ($15) or a month ($30). There are also shuttle buses to the beaches from Nantucket Town available on Barrett's Tours (☎508/228-0174 or 1-800/773-0174). You probably won't need the aid of **taxis** while here, but they are usually available at the airport or by the ferry terminal; A-1 Taxi (☎508/228-3330) and All Points Taxi (☎508/228-5779) are both reliable.

Visitor information is available from the Nantucket **Chamber of Commerce**, 48 Main St (Mon–Fri 9am–5pm; ☎508/228-1700), or from the helpful **Nantucket Information Bureau**, 25 Federal St (July to Labor Day 9am–9pm, rest of year 9am–6pm; ☎508/228-0925). The **Nantucket Historical Association**, 15 Broad St (Mon–Fri 9am–5pm; ☎508/228-1894, *www.nha.org*), which maintains fourteen historical properties on the island, offers a $10 combination ticket for entrance to all its buildings. The sights are generally open daily from Memorial Day to Labor Day, 10am until 5pm; from Labor Day to Columbus Day, daily from 11am to 3pm; closed the rest of the year.

Accommodation

There's a wide range of accommodation on the island, from resorts with pools, health clubs and sophisticated restaurants to cozy inns and B&Bs, and private homes that can be rented by the week. Be sure to book well in advance, especially for stays during the hectic summer season, when the island gets full up. For hassle-free booking, **Martha's Vineyard and Nantucket Reservations**, Box 1322, Lagoon Pond Rd, Vineyard Haven, MA 02568 (☎508/693-7200 or 1-800/649-5671), or **Heaven Can Wait Accommodations,** Box 622, Siasconset, MA 02564 (☎508/257-4000), should be able to help. If you're stuck at the last minute with nowhere to stay, try the **Nantucket Information Bureau** (☎508/228-0925), which maintains a list of vacancies during the season.

All of the places listed below are in **Nantucket Town**, unless other indicated in the address.

Anchor Inn, 66 Center St (☎508/228-0072). Period-style furnishings and queen-size canopy beds in this inn in the heart of the historic residential district. [4]–[5].

Century House, 10 Cliff Rd (☎508/228-0530). Elegant rooms with private baths and country-house ambiance in this 1833 late Federal home. [6]–[7].

Cliff Lodge, 9 Cliff Rd (☎508/228-9480). Quiet B&B in residential area with some low-priced singles in the off-season. ④–⑤.

Hawthorn House, 2 Chestnut St (☎508/228-1468). Central, well-appointed guesthouse. ④–⑥.

HI-Nantucket, Surfside Beach (☎508/228-0433). Dorm beds at Surfside Beach, just over three miles south of Nantucket Town. $17 members, $20 nonmembers. Lockout 10am–5pm, curfew 11pm. April–Oct 15 only.

Hungry Whale, 8 Derrymore Rd (☎508/228-0793). Good-value, friendly B&B, a short walk from the center. Five rooms, one with private bath. ④.

Jared Coffin House, 29 Broad St (☎508/228-2400 or 1-800/248-2405). Sixty rooms, all with period furniture in four adjacent buildings in the town center. Superb restaurant and pleasant bar. ⑥–⑦.

Martin House Inn, 61 Center St (☎508/228-0678). Thirteen lovely rooms offer good value in this 1803 seaman's house. ④–⑤.

The Nesbitt Inn, 21 Broad St (☎508/228-0156). The central location and affordable rooms, most with original furniture, compensate for the shared baths in this Victorian inn, built in 1872. ③–⑤.

Ship's Inn, 13 Fair St (☎508/228-0040). Three-story whaling captain's home with ten biggish rooms, all with private bath. ④–⑦.

The Wauwinet, Wauwinet Rd, Wauwinet (☎508/228-0145 or 1-800/426-8718). For many, *the* place to stay on the island, and out a bit from the main town. Luxury historic resort hotel restored in 1986 with full range of leisure facilities, beautifully appointed rooms, excellent dining, and great views. ⑨.

Nantucket Town

The tiny cobbled carriageways of **NANTUCKET TOWN** were frozen in time by economic decline 150 years ago. Today, this area of delightful eighteenth- and nineteenth-century homes, concentrated around **Main Street**, is very much the center of activity on the island. Before arriving there, though, you can get the salty feel of the half-dozen **wharves** around Nantucket's harbor when arriving on the ferry, which docks at **Steamboat Wharf**. A number of private summer homes are perched on Old North Wharf just south of that, while lively **Straight Wharf**, which dates to 1723, contains souvenir shops, restaurants, and the restored red-brick building of the **Museum of Nantucket History** (hours vary; ☎508/228-3899), originally a warehouse for whaling supplies. Exhibits include early fire-fighting apparatus, old photographs, and a diorama depicting the waterfront's busy goings-on before the fire. Straight Wharf leads directly onto Main Street, where at its junction with South Water Street, the **Pacific Club**, a three-story Georgian edifice built as a country house for William Rotch, owner of two of the three ships involved in the Boston Tea Party, once served as a US customs house; since 1861 it has been used as an elite private club (meaning you can't go in), where retired whaling captains could exchange the latest gossip over a game of cribbage. A short walk north along Federal Street leads to the **Athenaeum**, 1 Lower India St (hours vary; ☎508/228-1110), the town library and repository for various antiques, scrimshaw, and old island newspapers.

Continue up Federal Street to Broad Street, where the **Nantucket Whaling Museum** (late April to Oct 11am–3pm; $5) is housed in an old candlemaking factory built just before the big fire. Among its intriguing collection of exhibits, look out especially for such scrimshaw artifacts as a set of 21 whale types carved from whales' teeth, the astonishing harpoon corkscrewed in the "flurry" or last struggle of a dying whale, and the original 16ft high prism from the Sankaty Lighthouse. Just steps away, the **Peter Foulger Museum**, 15 Broad St (Mon–Fri 10am–4pm; $4), dedicated to one of the island's first settlers, displays an extensive collection of portraits, textiles, and furniture, plus the fascinating "Away from the Shore" exhibit, which traces the island's geological origins. More history can be found in the Nantucket Historical Association's Research Center, in the same building, though the ships' logs and genealogical records there are only available for those doing research.

Back on Main Street, at nos. 75 and 78, the **Henry Coffin House** and the **Charles Coffin House** belonged to two brothers who inherited a fortune from their father's candlemaking business. Their houses were built opposite each other, employing the same carpenters and masons, but in completely different styles: Charles' house a simple yet dignified Greek Revival, Henry's a late-Federal style home with ornate marble tower and cupola. Another grand house nearby, the Greek Revival **Hadwen House**, 96 Main St (April–May & Sept–Oct Sat–Sun 11am–3pm; June–Aug daily 10am–5pm; $3), contains gas chandeliers, a circular staircase, and silver doorknobs, with a lovely period garden out back.

Built in 1834, the **First Congregational Church**, 62 Center St (mid-June to Sept Mon–Sat 10am–4pm; $1.50 donation to climb tower), is famous for its 120ft steeple, from which you can get a spectacular bird's-eye view of the island. The inside is worth a peek, too, for its restored trompe l'oeil ceiling, 600-pound brass chandelier and rows of old box pews. Follow Center Street and West Chester Street past Lily Pond Park to the aptly named **Oldest House** (the Jethro Coffin House), Sunset Hill Road ($3 or NHA pass; ☎508/228-1894), though there's not much to see other than the central brick chimney; the house is spartanly decorated, with the most prominent feature inside an antique loom.

Polpis Road

Polpis Road, an indirect and arcing track from Nantucket Town to 'Sconset, holds a number of natural attractions both on and off its main course, though the first stop-off should be the less wild **Nantucket Life Saving Museum**, off the northern side of the road (mid-June to mid-Oct daily 9.30am–4pm; $3), filled with two lifesaving surfboats, buoys, rescue equipment, photographs, artifacts from the *Andrea Doria*, which sunk off Nantucket forty years ago, and a horse-drawn carriage from the Henry Ford Museum. Further on, an unmarked track leads south to **Altar Rock**, where you'll want to walk around for views of the surrounding bogs. One of these, the 200-acre **Windswept Cranberry Bog**, east on Polpis Road, is a feast of color at most times of the year, especially so in mid-October, when the ripened berries, loosened from the plants by machines, float to the top of the water.

Siasconset, Great Point and Coatue

Seven flat miles east of Nantucket Town, the village of **SIASCONSET**, or 'Sconset as it's known, is filled with venerable cottages literally encrusted with salt and covered over with roses. Once solely a fishing village, it began to attract visitors eager to get away from the foul smells of Nantucket Town's whale-oil refineries, and in the late 1800s, enough writers and actors came from big cities to give 'Sconset some modicum of artistic renown.

There's not too much to see, other than the houses themselves along Broadway and Center streets – certainly picture-pretty enough – and the year-round

NANTUCKET BEACHES

With fifty miles of beaches, most of which are open to the public, Nantucket is more accessible than Martha's Vineyard for water enthusiasts. The island's southern and eastern flanks, where the water tends to have rougher surf, is ideal for surfers, while the more sheltered northern beaches are good for swimming. With limited parking, it makes sense to walk or cycle to all but the most far-flung of the strands.

Nantucket Town

Brant Point, off Easton St. Strong currents at the harbor entrance mean this beach is better equipped for tanning and watching the comings and goings of boats in the harbor.

Childrens' Beach, off South Beach St. Just minutes from Steamboat Wharf, this calm harbor beach is perfect for children, and has a full range of facilities.

Dionis Beach, Eel Point Rd. A quiet beach with high dunes and calm waters.

Jetties Beach, off Bathing Beach Rd. Catch the shuttle bus or leg it to this popular beach whose facilities include lifeguards, changing rooms, and a snack bar.

East of Town

Sconset Beach (known as Codfish Park). Sandy beach with moderate surf and a full range of facilities. Just a short walk to several eating places.

South Shore

Cisco Beach, Hummock Point Rd. Long, sandy beach with lifeguards and restrooms; again, ideal for surfing.

Madaket Beach, at the end of the Madaket Bike Path. Another long beach with strong surf and gorgeous sunsets. portable restrooms (not for the squeamish), lifeguards and shuttle bus.

Surfside Beach, off Surfside Rd. Wide sands attract a youthful crowd of surfers; there's a large parking lot, but you'd do better to take the shuttle bus from town.

population of 150 only supports a few commercial establishments, located close to one another in the center of town. A few miles north, the red-and-white striped **Sankaty Light**, an 1849 lighthouse, stands on a 90ft bluff, though it seems only a matter of time until it falls victim to the crashing waves below.

North of here, and also accessible heading east on Polpis Road from Nantucket Town, **Wauwinet** is largely notable for holding the inn of choice on the island, simply titled *The Wauwinet* (see p.205 for review, p.209 for details on its restaurant, *Toppers*).

Further north, **Coatue-Coskata-Great Point**, a five-mile-long, razor-thin slice of sand, takes in three separate wildlife refuges, and is accessible only by four-wheel drive (for which you'll need a special permit; call ☎508/228-2884) or on foot. If you don't feel like walking (the sand is very soft and taxing on the feet), you could take one of the tours offered by Ara's Tours, 25 Federal St (90min tours cost $11; ☎508/228-1951). In the Coskata section, the somewhat wider beaches are backed by salt marshes, and even some trees: with binoculars, you may catch sight of plovers, egrets, oystercatchers, terns, and even osprey. The beach narrows again as you approach the 70ft **Great Light**, at the end of the spit, put up in 1986 after an earlier light was destroyed during a 1984 storm; the new one is said to be able to withstand 240mph winds and 20ft waves. Unsurprisingly, this is not the safest place to swim, even on a calm day. Coatue, the last leg of the journey, is the narrow stretch that separates Nantucket harbor from the ocean; so narrow, in fact, that stormy seas frequently crash over it, turning Great Point into an island.

Madaket and the South Shore

At the western tip of Nantucket, rural **MADAKET** is the small settlement located on the spot where Thomas Macy landed in 1659. There's little in the way of visitor attractions, but the area's peacefulness and natural beauty makes up for that. Unspoilt **Eel Point**, a couple of miles north, sits on a spit of sand covered with all manner of wild plants and flowers, including wild roses and bayberries, which attract an array of birds, including the graceful egrets which can be seen in late spring and summer stalking the shallow offshore sandbars. Maps and self-guided tours are available at $4.50 from the Maria Mitchell Association, 2 Vestal St (☎508/228-9198), and for $4 from the Nantucket Conservation Foundation, 118 Cliff Rd (☎508/228-2884). East of Madaket, and only about three miles from Nantucket Town, **Cisco** manages a beach that bears the brunt of winter storms; several homes have been lost to erosion in recent years. Not surprisingly, it's a popular beach with surfers. Two miles east of Cisco, freshwater **Miacomet Pond**, surrounded by reeds and grasses and a favorite haunt of swans and ducks, is a prime spot for a picnic.

Nantucket eating and drinking

The early chronicler Crèvecoeur, in an extensive account on Nantucket published in 1782, stated that on Nantucket "music, singing and dancing are holden in equal detestation." Thankfully, **eating** is not: Nantucket abounds in first-rate restaurants, most of which specialize in seafood. Be prepared, however, for the shock of the bill; it's often Manhattan prices, and then some. As far as **drinking** goes, many of the restaurants have bars attached to them, though there are also a few pubby places to get boozed up. All of the places below, unless otherwise indicated, are in **Nantucket Town**.

Arno's, 41 Main St (☎508/228-7001). Good-value breakfasts, lunches and dinners in this atmospheric eatery.

Boarding House, 12 Federal St (☎508/228-9622). Downstairs dining room with contemporary American cuisine; lively bar upstairs with lighter (and cheaper) bistro fare.

Brandt Point Grill, at the *White Elephant Hotel*, Easton St (☎508/228-2500 or 1-800/475-2637). Enjoy spectacular harbor views while dining on local Nantucket specialties with a Tuscan influence – like Tuscan Oricchioni with crab, artichokes, olive oil, and lemon thyme.

Centre Street Bistro, 29 Centre St (☎508/228-8470). Intimate (seven tables) café specializing in seafood, with wonderful home-made desserts to top it off. Serves a mean weekend brunch, too.

Cioppino's, 20 Broad St (☎508/228-4622). Stylish Mediterranean and New American cuisine in the center of town. Try their grilled lobster tails and fresh shrimp on a bed of pesto pasta.

Espresso Cafe, 40 Main St (☎508/228-6930). Inexpensive, mostly healthy lunches, including some vegetarian dishes.

The Muse, 44 Surfside Rd (☎508/228-6873). Popular, happening bar that features live bands on weekends.

Nantucket Lobster Trap, 23 Washington St (☎508/228-4041) Dinner-only establishment specializing, as its name indicates, in lobster.

Nantucket Tapas, 5 S Beach St (☎508/228-2033). Globally inclined menu takes the Spanish idea of tapas, throws in things like "spicy fried Thai calamari" and "Sechwan (*sic*) style grilled filet of beef," and takes advantage of the location to throw in a very fresh sushi bar.

Rose & Crown, 23 S Water St (☎508/228-2595). Traditional pub-style saloon that offers sandwiches, chicken wings, and the like. Music and comedy in the evenings.

Sea Grille, 45 Sparks Ave (☎508/325-5700). One of the best places for seafood, whether grilled, blackened, steamed, or fried, and not badly priced at that.

Ships Inn, 13 Fair St (☎508/228-0040). Choose from California-French style dishes, such as pan-roasted striped bass, served in a bright and airy space.

Topper's, 120 Wauwinet Rd, Wauwinet (☎508/228-8768). Pricey but outstanding New American cuisine in this quiet, upscale restaurant at the *Wauwinet* hotel and resort a few miles outside Nantucket Town.

Vincent's, 21 S Water St (☎508/228-0189). Moderately priced Italian dishes in a casual, relaxed atmosphere.

Entertainment and nightlife

There are two **movie theaters** on Nantucket; the Dreamland Theater, 19 S Water St (☎508/228-5356), which shows first-run movies from June to September, and the Gaslight Theatre, 1 N Union St (☎508/228-4435), for more arty fare. The Theatre Workshop of Nantucket puts on **plays** and musicals at Bennett Hall, 62 Centre St (☎508/228-4305), while Actors Theatre of Nantucket produces Broadway-type plays, comedy nights and children's matinees at the Methodist Church, 2 Centre St.

    Music venues include the *Brotherhood of Thieves*, 23 Broad St (no phone) for year-round live folk music; *The Muse*, 44 Surfside Rd (☎508/228-6873), for a mixture of rock, reggae, and just about anything else you can dance to; and *The Tap Room*, Jared Coffin House, 29 Broad St (☎508/228-2400), for live guitar music – but only during the season. Meanwhile the Nantucket Musical Arts Society, 62 Centre St, at the First Congregational Church (☎508/228-1287), organizes concerts in July and August with renowned **classical** musicians. Current **listings** can be found in the free weekly *Nantucket Map & Legend* and *Yesterday's Island*, another freebie.

CHAPTER THREE

CENTRAL AND WESTERN MASSACHUSETTS

Moving west from the coast, Massachusetts' well-preserved and cultivated charm quickly dissolves amid the strip malls, franchises and faded storefronts of the area loosely known as Central Massachusetts. Compromised mostly of semi-industrial towns still struggling to redefine their identity in the shadow of labor migrations, recessions, and Boston's thriving tourist industry, these towns are not going to be the focal point of your itinerary, and they have little to detain you for too long. But there are exceptions. Worcester, the first town you reach traveling west from Boston, has one of the state's best collections of art, and Springfield, a little further west, is home to the Basketball Hall of Fame, and where the game was invented. Springfield is also the most sensible jumping-off point for the **Pioneer Valley**, which stretches north from here, where small-town charisma and New England gentility begin to reassert themselves. Home to four separate colleges and a major university, the "Valley" supports a year-round population of down-to-earth academics, artists and community activists who, in turn, patronize a bevy of restaurants, cafes and bookstores – giving the area a continuous, if low-key, buzz. You can base yourself in any one of three or four locations to explore this region, but **Northampton** is probably the liveliest, with a good range of places to stay and most of the area's nightlife.

From the Pioneer Valley, most roads lead west to **the Berkshires** – as the smattering of tiny towns nestled in among the Berkshire Mountains, dividing Massachusetts from New York state, are collectively known. This area holds some of the Northeast's most desirable vacation spots for local city-dwellers, and is the adopted summer stage of many Boston and New York dance companies, orchestras and theater troupes. With its tony spas, pricey inns and sophisticated cultural happenings, it's a lovely spot – if you can afford it. And even if

ACCOMMODATION PRICE CODES

All accommodation prices in this book have been coded using the symbols below; prices are for the least expensive double rooms in each establishment. For a full explanation see p.28 in Basics. Individual rates rather than price codes are given for hostels.

① up to $30	④ $60–80	⑦ $130–175
② $30–45	⑤ $80–100	⑧ $175–250
③ $45–60	⑥ $100–130	⑨ $250+

you can't, the region's simpler pleasures – such as camping, hiking and biking – are all available in abundance. You can either base yourself in the slightly precious small towns of **Lenox** or **Stockbridge** in the southern Berkshires, or **Williamstown** in the north, which has a good selection of museums and galleries to explore – not least the Massachusetts Museum of Contemporary Art, or MASS MoCA.

CENTRAL MASSACHUSETTS

What **Central Massachusetts** has to offer is more by way of scenic driving routes than as a destination in its own right. This is how most people experience the region, as it isn't by any stretch of the imagination the highlight of the state. However, it is close to Boston, and it does have one or two spots worth stopping over at on your way west, most notably Worcester's Art Museum and Springfield's Basketball Hall of Fame.

Worcester

Forty miles west of Boston on I-90, **WORCESTER** is Massachusetts' second largest city, and the only industrial city in the US beside neither sea, lake nor river. Incorporated in 1722, the city enjoyed a century and a half of unbridled prosperity and was a thriving multiethnic town of Greek, Yiddish and Italian bakeries, textile mills, and close-knit immigrant communities before lapsing into recession during the 1970s and 1980s. Famous as the birthplace of such American icons as the Valentine's Day card (the card's creator made and marketed them here), the birth control pill, and Abbie Hoffman, the spiritual father of the rabble-rousing Yippies of the Sixties, it's only now beginning to pick itself up – which means that for the moment its downtown area doesn't have much to lure you beyond a good museum.

The Town

Worcester's solution to its defunct business district has been to park the enormous **Worcester Common Fashion Outlet Mall**, just off I-290 (exit 14 or 16), smack in the center of town. With almost a hundred designer and designer-like stores under one roof, the outlet mall has brought a bit of vitality and a much-needed influx of cash back into the city, although – sadly – smaller independent businesses haven't succeeded, and this part of Worcester is dotted with "For Rent" signs and empty storefronts.

Ironically, what charm Worcester does possess rests not on its attempts at rejuvenation but in its preservation of the past. The **Worcester Art Museum**, 55 Salisbury St (Wed–Fri 11am–5pm, Sat 10am–5pm; $8; free Saturday), located in a leafy, manicured part of town about two miles north of downtown, dominated by brick terraces, is the city's major thing to see – and is an absolute gem. Its vast holdings include a Romanesque Chapter House from the twelfth century, shipped from Europe and reassembled in Worcester, a permanent gallery of American portrait miniatures and an impressive collection of mosaics from

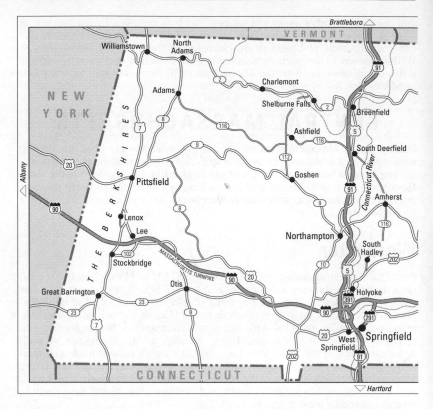

Antioch. In addition, there are lesser-known paintings by Braque, Cezanne, Gainsborough, Gauguin, Goya, Kandinsky, Matisse, Turner and Renoir, and the museum is blessed with an expansive photography collection, with works from the Civil War to the present, including recognizable images from Cartier-Bresson, Stieglitz, and Weston, and stages frequent exhibitions that draw from its holdings of over 2000 prints.

Just outside the downtown area is the **American Antiquarian Society**, 185 Salisbury St (Mon–Fri 9am–5pm, tours Wed 2pm; free; *www.americanantiquarian .org*), which holds copies of two-thirds of all the material published in America before 1821, more even than the Library of Congress in Washington DC. Among the highlights are impressions of nearly all the prints of Paul Revere and an excellent collection of the works and private papers of James Fenimore Cooper. Further down the road, off of Rte-122A, the remarkable castle-like **Higgins Armory Museum**, 100 Barber Ave (Tues–Sat 10am–4pm, Sun noon–4pm; $5.75), is also worth a visit, with a collection that represents years of careful collecting in post-World War I Europe by John Woodman Higgins, the founder of the Worcester Pressed Steel Company. It's chock-full of armor, swords, knives, chain mail, and helmets from ancient Greece and Rome, medieval and renaissance Europe, and feudal Japan.

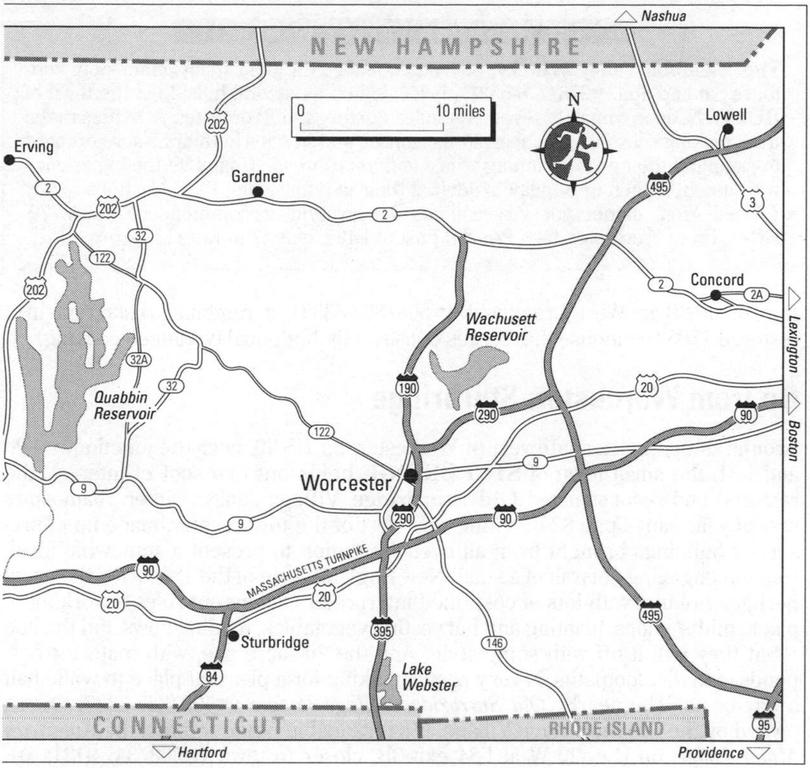

Practicalities

There are two **train stations**, **Amtrak** and **MBTA**; if you're coming from Boston, the [T] is $3.50 to Amtrak's $14, but either way, you'll have to navigate across four lanes of traffic, with nary a crossing signal or sidewalk in sight to get into town. It's not deadly, just annoying.

Worcester works best as a day-trip from Boston or Northampton. However, if you need to **stay over**, you'll find the *Hampton Inn*, 110 Summer St (☎508/757-0400 or 1-800/426-7866; [5]), centrally located, and with good, clean rooms. For **food**, the *Sole Proprietor*, 118 Highland St (☎508/798-3474), is a reliable fish restaurant, not especially cheap but well worth the price. *Living Earth*, 232–234 Chandler St at the corner of Park Ave (☎508/753-1896), is a friendly health-food store with an attached sun-drenched café that is a welcome oasis in an otherwise impersonal area of gas stations and convenience stores. For good Italian, head to *Anthony*'s, 172 Shrewsbury St (☎508/575-6864), where the appetizer of choice is the "172 ravioli," a single gargantuan pasta shell enfolding a center of artichoke and roasted garlic. *El Basha*, 424 Belmont St (☎508/797-0884), is a popular Lebanese spot near the Umass Medical Center, where nothing on the menu will set you back more than $10. About twenty miles west of Worcester, but worth the detour, is the *Salem Cross*

THE NASHOBA VALLEY WINERY

The Nashoba Valley Winery, on Wattaquadoc Hill Road (daily 11am–5pm with tours Sat and Sun; ☎978/779-5521), is located on a pastoral hillside in the town of **BOLTON**, approximately seventeen miles northeast of Worcester. Activities range from picking seasonal peaches, plums, apples, and berries in their 55-acre orchard to sampling their award-winning wines and microbrews. Complete the experience with lunch, dinner, or Sunday brunch at their in-house café, J's at Nashoba Valley (closed Mon, dinner not served Tues, reservations recommended; ☎978/779-9816). From Worcester, take Rte-290 East to I-495, exit 27 to Rte-117.

Inn, on Rte-9 in West Brookfield (☎508/867-8337), a rambling restaurant in a restored 1705 farmhouse that serves consistently high-quality Yankee cooking.

On from Worcester: Sturbridge

Around fifteen miles southwest of Worcester, on US-20, near the junction of I-90 and I-84, the small town of **STURBRIDGE** holds but one spot of interest, the restored and reconstructed **Old Sturbridge Village** (daily: winter 10am–4pm; rest of year 9am–5pm; $20), a little way west of the town center, made up of preserved buildings brought from all over the region to present a somewhat idealized but engaging portrait of a small New England town of the 1830s. It's the usual heritage hokum, with lots of costumed interpreters acting out roles – working in blacksmiths' shops, planting and harvesting vegetables, tending cows and the like – but they pull it off with some style. And the 200-acre site, with mature trees, ponds, and dirt footpaths, is very pretty, making for a pleasant place to while half a day or so. The nearby *Old Sturbridge Village Lodges* (☎508/347-3327; [5]–[6]), owned by the Old Sturbridge Village, is a reasonable **place to stay**; the *American Motor Lodge*, on Hwy-20 W at I-84 exit 3B, closer to town (☎508/347-9121; [4]), costs a bit less.

Springfield

SPRINGFIELD, situated at the point where I-90 crosses I-91, ninety miles from Boston at the southern end of the Pioneer Valley (see p.217), sprang up along the banks of the Connecticut River, and was once the industrial hub of central Massachusetts. America's first frozen foods were made in Springfield; it was the home of the Springfield rifle, and the late children's author **Dr Seuss**, née Theodore Geisel. But, like so many places in this part of the state, the city was soon hit by recession and became rapidly depopulated. Nowadays, blessed with a central location and the optimistic nickname "The Comeback City of America," it's slowly restoring its fortunes. Most importantly, Springfield is the town where the sport of **basketball** was invented, and therein lies the main reason for any visit.

The Town

Springfield's unwieldy and unattractive city center is split by the wide Connecticut River. There's not much to see here beyond a handful of museums (see below), and most signs point you in the direction of the **Basketball Hall of Fame** at 1150 W Columbus Ave, next to the river just south of Memorial Bridge (daily 10am–5pm; $10; *www.hoophall.com*), which commemorates the 1890s invention of Dr James Naismith. Naismith designed the game as a way of providing exercise for athletes at the YMCA, and its popularity spread with amazing rapidity. After Naismith took a trip to the Berlin Olympics in 1936, the National Association of Basketball Coaches started to discuss the idea of establishing a museum, finally realized in 1959. With the growth of the game, the hall has become a major attraction for everyone who's dreamed of stepping in Michael Jordan's shoes. There's plenty here: movies, videos, memorabilia, and some high-tech interactive gadgets, like a computer that lets you challenge Bill Walton to a virtual one-on-one, and an activity center which allows you to clock and measure all the vital statistics, such as how high you can jump, wing-span, and hang time, and compare them with the greats.

Back in the center of town, Springfield's other museums are located at **The Quadrangle**, a tree-lined square at the corner of State and Chestnut streets (all museums Wed–Fri noon–5pm, Sat–Sun 11am–4pm, Tues noon–5pm July–Aug; $6; *www.quadrangle.org*). They're not all that interesting individually, but taken together can make for a decent afternoon diversion. The **Smith Art Museum**,

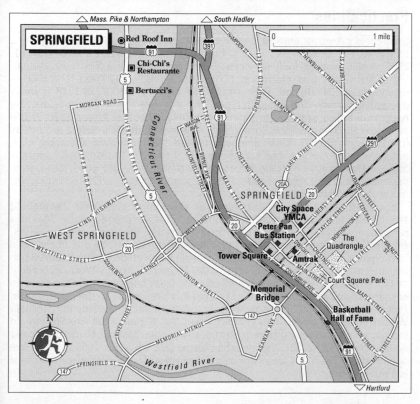

housed in an airy Italian palazzo-styled building blessed with Tiffany stained-glass windows, displays the eclectic collection of George Walter Vincent and Belle Smith (local art collectors), which focuses on Asian decorative arts, including the largest collection of Chinese cloisonné pottery outside of Asia, but also takes in nineteenth-century American painting and rugs from the Middle East. **The Museum of Fine Art** is slightly more coherent, proudly displaying Winslow Homer's *The New Novel* and Frederic Church's *New England Scenery* alongside lesser-known pieces by Monet, Calder, and Georgia O'Keefe. Also of local interest, the **Connecticut Valley Historical Museum** has an interactive exhibit on "The World of Doctor Seuss" to keep the kids busy while you check out their collection of furniture, toys, paintings, games, and artifacts that were once the possessions of settlers in the region. This museum also houses a **Genealogy and Local History Library**, which showcases its new database, Project Shamrock, which allows the descendants of Irish immigrants to search for relatives who may have been living in the greater Springfield area between 1840 and 1900. Finally the **Springfield Science Museum** has a crowd-pleasing life-sized replica of Tyrannosaurus Rex, an exhibit on life under the Connecticut River, lots of hands-on displays, and a **planetarium** with daily shows – though these cost extra.

Practicalities

Springfield's **Amtrak station** is very centrally situated, at 66 Lyman St, about a mile from The Quadrangle. Several bus lines, including Peter Pan (☎413/781-2900), which provides daily services to and from Boston and New York, operate out of the nearby **bus station** at 1776 Main St (☎413/781-7882). The **CVB** is downtown at 34 Boland Way (☎413/787-1548 or 1-800/723-1548, *www.ci .springfield.ma.us*). You shouldn't need to stay, but if you do, consider the **accommodation options** sprinkled along Rte-5, otherwise known as Riverdale St, across the river in West Springfield, with most hotels clustering around its intersection with I-91. Geared mostly toward the convention-attending businessperson, the *Red Roof Inn*, 1254 Riverdale St (☎413/731-1010; ③–④), and the *Super 8 Motel*, 1500 Riverdale St (☎413/736-8080; ④–⑤), are good, clean, standard choices. The *Cityspace YMCA*, 275 Chestnut St (☎413/739-6951x130; ③), has rooms for men and women.

For **food**, *Chi-Chi's Restaurante*, 955 Riverdale St in West Springfield (☎413/781-0442), is a local institution, a massive pseudo-adobe Mexican restaurant on Hwy-5, just south of the I-91 bridge. Further down the street, *Bertucci's*, 847 Riverdale Rd (☎413/788-9900), despite being a chain, is a crowd-pleasing, quality establishment serving pasta dishes and brick-oven pizzas at reasonable prices. *Caffeine's*, 1338 Memorial Ave in West Springfield (☎413/731-5282), serves a range of entrees, from barbecue chicken pizza to soyburgers and *foccaccia*. Tiny Fort Street has been home to the *Fort/Student Prince* (☎413/734-7475) for over sixty years, a local favorite for German Wiener schnitzel, goulash and sauerbraten. *Gus & Paul's* has two Springfield locations with distinctly different attitudes. The 1500 Main St branch, at Tower Square (☎413/781-2253), has an urban bistro feel, while the 1209 Sumner Ave option (☎413/782-5710) leans towards old-world-style deli. Either way, the food is fresh and tasty.

THE PIONEER VALLEY

The Pioneer Valley, a verdant corridor created by the Connecticut River and centuries of glacial activity, is the epicenter of recreational and cultural activity in Central Massachusetts. The towns of **Northampton, South Hadley,** and **Amherst** are hosts to Smith College, Mount Holyoke College and Amherst College, the University of Massachusetts, and Hampshire College respectively – schools that have formalized their relationship through the creation of the co-operative "Five College Consortium," which links the communities academically, economically, and culturally. One and a half hours from Boston and just three hours from New York City, the Valley is a good, and much less popular, alternative to the busier Cape or the Berkshires – an excellent choice for those who like to hike, bike, hang out in cafés, browse bookstores, and pretend, if only for a weekend, that they actually live in this idyllic little spot.

Practicalities

By **car**, Northampton is off of I-91 approximately fifteen miles north of the Massachusetts Turnpike (I-90). All exits marked "Northampton" lead to the center of town. During leaf season, those coming from Boston should consider taking the less traveled and more scenic Rte-2 from Concord west to Rte-202 through the woods skirting the Quabbin Reservoir and picking up Rte-9 into Amherst. The closest commercial airport is **Bradley International Airport** (☎203/627-3000) in Windsor Locks, CT, roughly 45 minutes south of Northampton on I-91. A more popular mode of transportation is the **Peter Pan Bus Lines** (☎1-800/237-8747), which make the connection to New York, Boston, Hartford and Albany. Purchase tickets and catch the bus at 1 Roundhouse Plaza in Northampton and at 79 South Pleasant St in Amherst.

The **Northampton Chamber of Commerce**, 99 Pleasant St (Mon–Fri 9am–5pm; ☎413/584-1900), and the **Amherst Chamber of Commerce**, 11 Spring St (Mon–Fri 9am–5pm; ☎413/253-0770), both offer the usual array of maps and recommendations. **Bookstores** in both towns are a significant source of local maps and advice. *The Valley Advocate*, a free weekly newspaper available in any café, prints a complete listing of area happenings, movie listings and restaurant reviews. Contact the **Northampton Conservation Commission** (☎413/586-6950) or the **Amherst Conservation Commission** (☎413/256-4045), which between them oversee the maintenance of 37 distinctly different nature preserves, for suggestions and listings of nature hikes and recreation areas.

Shuttling between Northampton, Amherst, and South Hadley and stopping at points in between is the **Pioneer Valley Transit Authority (PVTA)** (☎413/781-7882). Financed and operated by the area colleges and driven by UMass students, the PVTA is a free service available to anyone who wants to use it. Generally, buses begin circulating at 6am and head home at 12.30am, passing each stop every thirty minutes or so. Schedules are available on each bus and posted at the sidewalk stops. The paved **Norwottuck Trail Bike Path** weaves its way for around eight miles between Northampton and Amherst in the footprint of a former railroad bed. Used for biking, walking, and rollerblading, the path, though crowded in nice weather, offers an attractive alternative to driving the very developed Rte-9.

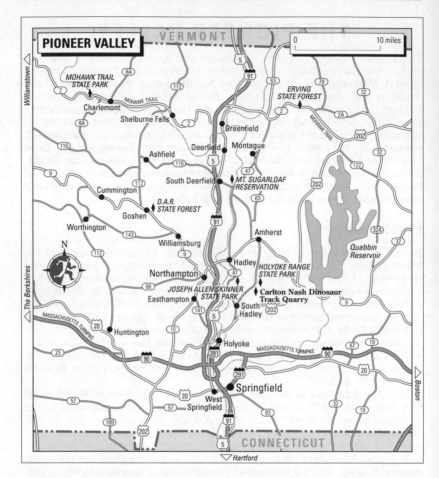

Though cheaper than Boston and the Berkshires, the Pioneer Valley still isn't a cheap **place to stay**. Like other parts of New England, the Valley fully understands the market value of its quaintness and charges for anything vaguely approaching it. Offerings range from stately inns to the easily recognizable national chains, with most options in between having the look and feel of a roadside dive in a Stephen King novel. Reservations are required at most hotels and many of the bed-and-breakfasts in the area mandate a two-night minimum stay most weekends, so calling ahead is advisable. A vibrant **fall foliage** season usually means higher rates.

In an effort to feed and please everyone, from students to professors to artists, musicians, activists, writers, and children, the chefs in the Pioneer Valley have had to be quite creative. The results are enough choice in price, style, atmosphere, and taste, to cater to just about every craving and budget. Conveniently, most **eating establishments** cluster along the main streets of both Northampton and Amherst. The adventurous will, however, find some real culinary gems hiding somewhat unexpectedly in the surrounding hill towns.

Northampton

In 1654 the Puritans purchased what is easily some of the most fertile farmland in the densely wooded hills of Central Massachusetts from the Nonotuck Indians for ten coats, several trinkets, and 100 fathom of wampum and christened it **NORTHAMPTON**. Ironically, these vast land holdings became a liability, when, after the Revolutionary War, depressed and indebted farmers were in danger of losing their property to creditors looking to recover the war debt. Rising to meet this injustice in 1786 was farmer Daniel Shays, who rustled up hundreds of his compatriots and marched to the county courthouse in Northampton, and soon after attacked the federal arsenal in Springfield in what would later come to be known as **Shays' Rebellion**. In another example of bad timing, Northampton's canal connection to New Haven, CT and the Atlantic was completed in 1835, only to be overshadowed by the 1845 arrival of the railroad. Transportation, in turn, encouraged the development of industry, which by the early to mid-twentieth century was undermined by the rush to use cheaper southern and international labor. In retrospect, Northampton's saving grace has been its investment in education and the intellectual environment it has fostered. Smith College, founded in 1871 by Sophia Smith and financed with her personal inheritance, survives as a prestigious women's college.

Today, liberal, progressive, and content to march to a different drummer, Northampton (population 30,000 or so), fondly nicknamed NoHo, has settled into its role as a tolerant town of artists, writers, students, teachers, and activists. Oddly enough, it was cited in *Parents' Magazine* as one of the best small towns in America to raise a family, and in *Newsweek* as the "lesbian capital of the Northeast" – both distinctions it accepted with pride.

Accommodation

You shouldn't have a terrible time finding somewhere reasonable to stay in town, though, that said, many of the places tend to be of the stylish inn variety, similar to the way things are over in Amherst (see p.222).

Autumn Inn, 259 Elm St (☎413/584-7660). A locally owned and operated establishment. Clean, comfortable, and close to the action. Reservations required. ⑥–⑦.

Hotel Northampton, 36 King St (☎413/584-3100, *www.hotelnorthhampton.com*). Copious flower arrangements in the entryway of this over-sized historic 1927 hotel give an immediate sense of its inflated – though entirely deserved – self-importance. The attention to detail and charm make up for the smallish rooms. ⑥–⑧.

The Inn at Northampton, 1 Atwood Drive (☎413/586-1211 or 1-800/582-2929). Exit 18 off of I-91. Formerly part of the Hilton chain, this place is now independently owned. Wood paneling, roaring fireplace, and an indoor pool topped with a glass dome combine to make for a pleasant, calming atmosphere. The smallest bed is a queen-size. Friendly staff. ⑤–⑥.

Lupine House, 185 N Main St (☎413/586-9766). Three antique-furnished rooms with private bath in a lovely colonial house a short drive from downtown Northampton. Continental breakfast included. ④.

North King Street Motel, 504 N King St (☎413/584-8847). Fifteen clean and basic rooms in a well-worn 1950s style roadside motel. The chatty owners give this otherwise slightly dreary place a comfortable, lived-in feel. ③.

The Saltbox, 153 Elm St (☎413/584-1790). A lovely B&B near Smith College, housed in a 1780s house, offering three cozy sunlit rooms complete with quilts and overstuffed armchairs. Breakfast included. ⑥.

The Town

Although Northampton doesn't have much in the way of tourist attractions per se, the town itself has a well-earned reputation as one of the most livable places in the U.S. Walk down Main Street, and you could be in a major city, not a small college town, from the wealth of shops, restaurants and cafes, as well as the diversity of the population. But the traffic remains relatively light (except for the snail's pace rush hour commutes to and from Amherst), the streets clean and safe. For now, it's the best of both worlds – until the rest of the world finds out, which may not be long.

Typically, the principal thing to see in Northampton is on the grounds of the institution that most defines the town – Smith College – where the **Smith College Museum of Art** (closed for renovations until 2003; call ☎413/585-2760 for information) has a well-earned reputation as a superb small-college art museum. What you can expect when they reopen the doors is a focus on nineteenth- and twentieth-century art, with works by Monet (*Field of Poppies*), Georgia O'Keefe (the nearly translucent *Squash Flowers, #1*), Jean Arp (a languid *Torso*), and Frank Stella, who is represented by the enormous *Damascus Gate (Variation III)*. There's also an 8000-strong print collection, which contains a startling number of prints and engravings from Daumier, Delacroix, Durer, Munch, Picasso, and Toulouse-Lautrec, as well as odd items like an exquisite Luba ceremonial axe from Zaire.

You may want to call in at other areas on the attractive campus (*www.smith.edu*), such as the **botanic garden**; tours can be made from the admissions office, pretty much on the hour during weekday mornings and early afternoons. Besides exploring Smith College and taking in the laid-back vibe of Northampton's student community, the biggest attraction is the city's nightlife and coffee culture. It's worth slowing down the pace of your travels here and taking in some music at the legendary *Iron Horse* or a couple pints at the *Brewery*.

Eating and drinking

Northampton is the top place in the Pioneer Valley for eating, and establishments are typically a lot less precious here than they are over in the Berkshires.

Bart's Homemade, 235 Main St (☎413/584-0721). From cow to cone, *Bart's* reputation for using quality local ingredients to create melt-in-your-mouth indulgences is well earned. A great place to nurse a novel and a latte. Also one in Amherst at 103 N Pleasant St (see p.224).

Del Raye, 1 Bridge St (☎413/586-2664). A sophisticated urban-style bistro serving French inspired steaks and seafood. Chic and rather pricey.

Eastside Grill, 19 Strong Ave (☎413/586-3347). A well-established steakhouse serving steaks, chicken, and seafood with a Cajun bite. Extensive menu, attentive service, but often crowded.

Haymarket Café & Juice Joint, 185 Main St (☎413/586-9969). Popular hangout for people looking for a cheap fix of the healthy variety. Soups, salads, and sandwiches for around $5.

Java Net Café, 241 Main St (☎413/587-3400). A comfortable cybercafé serving up just what you'd expect – coffee, tea, croissants, and muffins – all at reasonable prices.

La Veracruzana, 31 Main St (☎413/586-7181). Bright, cheerful, and informal, the folks at *La Veracruzana* are credited with bringing the take-out burrito to the Valley. There's another branch in Amherst; see p.224.

Paul and Elizabeth's, 150 Main St, in Thorne's Marketplace (☎413/584-4832). Vegetarian and seafood entrees, home-made breads, and desserts served in a serenely airy dining room.

Pizzeria Paradiso, 12 Crafts St (☎413/586-1468). A cozy pizza place kept warm with wood-fired ovens imported from Italy. The extensive choice of toppings, drinks, and desserts make this much more than just another pizza joint.

Spoleto, 50 Main St (☎413/586-6313). Fabulous pasta creations, an extensive wine list, and wonderful desserts. Always busy – and deservedly so.

Sylvester's, 111 Pleasant St (☎413/586-5343). Housed in the former home of Sylvester Graham, the inventor of the Graham Cracker, *Sylvester's* serve up tasty fare, including delightful breakfast treats like banana bread French toast. Very child-friendly.

Nightlife and entertainment

The Pioneer Valley's most active **nightlife** is in Northampton, though most cafés are open late in Amherst, which gives it too a bit of a nocturnal buzz. Thanks to its relatively close proximity to New York and Boston, and energetic local promoters like "The Iron Horse Entertainment Group," Northampton attracts some of the biggest names in most branches of the performing arts. This being college student country, expect your ID to be checked if you look a day under 60.

The Calvin Theatre and Performing Arts Center, 19 King St (☎413/584-0610). The folks responsible for *The Iron Horse* (below) have lovingly transformed the 75-year-old movie house into a beacon of the performing arts. Live theater, music and dance performance for all ages and tastes.

FitzWilly's, 23 Main St (☎413/584-8666). Smack in the middle of it all, this established local bar is a relaxing place to knock a few back and soak up the atmosphere.

The Grotto, 25 West St (☎413/586-6900). Popular restaurant, bar and nightclub catering to gay men and women. Upstairs lounge, outside patio and pool tables. Look for the awning with the white "G" across from Smith College.

The Iron Horse, 20 Center St (☎413/584-0610). An institution in the world of folk music, *The Iron Horse* has been cheering on emerging artists for twenty years. One of the few small coffeehouse-style venues left in the country, and with a knack of booking the big names of folk, bluegrass, jazz and blues. Call ☎413/586-8686 or 1-800/THE-TICK for information and reservations.

Northampton Brewery, 11 Brewster Court, behind Thorne's Marketplace (☎413/584-9903). With a solid selection of high-quality microbrews on tap, an extensive munchies menu, and relaxing outdoor patio, this is a great place to while away a summertime happy hour or a snowy winter night.

Packards's, 14 Masonic St (☎413/584-5957). A good watering hole with great billiards table upstairs.

Pearl Street Night Club, 10 Pearl St (☎413/586-8686 or 1-800/THE-TICK). Two-story live music and dance club. Reggae, alternative, hip-hop and Grateful Dead tribute acts abound.

Pleasant Street Theater, 27 Pleasant St (☎413/586-0935). Independent, classic, and foreign films are screened in this intimate movie theater – a worthy leftover from the pre-multiplex era.

Amherst

Settled in 1727, incorporated in 1759, and named for General Jeffrey Amherst, **AMHERST** developed for the most part like its neighbor, Northampton, as a college town. In 1821, the citizens of Amherst financed and opened the Collegiate Charitable Institution to educate the town's young men, and by 1825 this had become Amherst College. In 1866, the Massachusetts Agricultural College opened in Amherst to teach military, agricultural and technical skills, and today, as the renamed University of Massachusetts at Amherst, it is the main cog in the Massachusetts public university system. Hampshire College, just outside town on the road to South Hadley, was founded in the idealistic days of the 1970s, by the presidents of four local colleges, as an experiment in true liberal arts study, one that emphasized the individual and inter-disciplinary nature of education.

Today, Hampshire College has only recently begun to outgrow its reputation as a flaky hippie haven, but the town as a whole maintains the feel of a small, bookish community, a bit larger but in fact less hurried than Northampton, with a healthy mix of college students, hippies, young families and professionals – all in all a good place to kick back for a day or two and explore the surrounding countryside.

Accommodation

Amherst's **accommodation** options range from expensive inns and intimate bed-and-breakfasts with an ecological bent to predictable branches of the national chains. The best bet for inexpensive lodging is to drive the length of Route 9 and check out some of the smaller, slightly rumpled-looking motels along here. Many of them are safe and clean, if visually unappealing. Remember, wherever you stay you can expect to pay more during foliage season.

Allen House Victorian Inn, 599 Main St (☎413/253-5000). A charming and award-winning Victorian B&B, across the street from the Emily Dickinson Homestead, that also serves full breakfasts and afternoon tea. ④–⑥.

Delta Organic Farm, 352 E Hadley Rd (☎413/253-1893). An organic Nirvana for health-conscious travelers. Special needs and requests are welcomed by the concerned and accommodating owners. Organic breakfast. ④–⑥.

Howard Johnson Motor Lodge, 401 Russell St (Rte-9), Hadley (☎413/586-0114). Despite looking like little more than a cement block airlifted into place along the highway between Amherst and Northampton, this motor lodge is clean, comfortable, and everything you have come to expect from HoJo. ④–⑥.

Lord Jeffrey Inn, 30 Boltwood Ave (☎413/253-2576 or 1-800/742-0358). Situated on Amherst Common, this is a quintessential rambling and richly decorated New England inn – so much so that it is often used for weddings. The rooms are a luxurious treat. ⑤–⑥.

The Town

Just about everybody who comes to Amherst visits the **Dickinson Homestead**, 280 Main St (guided tours March, November and December, Wed & Sat 1–4 on the hour, April–Oct Wed–Sat 1–4 hourly, June–Aug every half hour; $5, reservations advised; ☎413/542-8161), where the celebrated

American poet Emily Dickinson lived all her life. Born in Amherst in 1830, Emily Dickinson attended nearby Mount Holyoke College, but loneliness drove her back home without finishing her studies, and she shortly afterwards began a life of self-imposed exile in the family home here on Main Street. Emily Dickinson read voraciously, wrote incessantly, corresponded with friends, and over the course of her life penned some 1800 poems most of which mirrored her lifelong struggle between isolation and an intense search for inspiration. Despite this literary hyperactivity, she published less than a dozen poems during her life, and was a completely unknown woman, much less poet, when she died in 1886. Her work was collected and published four years later by her sister, and she has since been recognized as influential in giving American poetry its own resounding voice.

The world Dickinson wrote of from her house no longer exists, but her room here is frozen in time, with an array of personal effects, such as the desk where Dickinson's poems were found after her death. It's a pretty low-key display on the whole, but for most visitors – especially those who also visit **Dickinson's grave** in the nearby West Cemetery, off Pleasant Street – this seems to be just enough. Also of notable literary interest, the original copy of *Stopping by Woods on a Snowy Evening* written by the American poet Robert Frost, who was a professor at Amherst College for thirty years, sits under glass in the **Jones Library** on Amity Street.

There's further cultural interest in the **Mead Art Museum**, on the lovely campus of **Amherst College** (academic year Mon–Fri 10am–4.30pm, Sat & Sun 1–5pm; summer Tues–Sun 1–4pm; free), where works by Frederic Church, Thomas Cole, John Singleton Copley, Thomas Eakins, and Winslow Homer dominate a collection strong on early twentieth-century American art. There's also a sprinkling of Renaissance European works, notably a seductive *Salome* by Robert Henri and a gory *Still Life with Dead Game* by Frans Synders.

There's a small **Museum of Natural History** in the Amherst precincts (same times), but you might be better off heading on to Hampshire College, where the campus is home to the **National Yiddish Book Center** (Sun–Fri 10am–3.30pm; closed on Jewish holidays; free), which houses one of the world's largest collections of Yiddish books – many culled from New York City dumpsters – in a sprawling building designed to emulate an Eastern European *shtetl*.

Eating and drinking

Though Amherst doesn't have as many **restaurants** as Northampton, you surely won't go hungry. The high student population has led to a large percentage of sandwich places, pizza joints, chain coffee shops, and casual eateries. A stroll along either Main Street or North Pleasant Street pretty much sums up the choices.

Amber Waves, 63 Main St (☎413/253-9200). Southeast Asian noodle soups and stir fries designed to please carnivores, vegetarians and vegans alike.

Amherst Brewing Company, 24–36 N Pleasant St (☎413/253-4400). The brass bar and exposed brick add a touch of upscale yearning to this prime drinking spot.

Amherst Chinese Food, 62 Main St (☎413/253-7835). Believe it or not, the owners of this restaurant grow the organic vegetables they use in their dishes and add nothing artificial as they pick, steam, sauté, fry and deliver them piping hot to your table. Unsurprisingly popular with a health-conscious crowd.

A FORGETTABLE LEGACY

The town of Amherst takes pride in its scholars at Amherst College and the University of Massachusetts, as well as its famous poet-in-one-time residence, Emily Dickinson. Less attention is given to the achievements of **General Jeffrey Amherst** – perhaps for good reason.

Amherst was a popular British general when the town was named after him in 1759, best known for his many victories during the French and Indian War. After the French surrendered, Amherst was fairly charitable to the defeated French troops; however, continuing a well-established practice in colonial American times, he was allegedly brutal and cruel to the Native Americans.

Although it is uncertain with whom the idea originated, a series of correspondences between Amherst and Colonel Henry Bouquet in the summer of 1763 refer to "innoculat[ing]" the Native Americans by means of blankets," some historians believing that the idea was to spread the disease of smallpox by distritributing infected blankets to the natives. Smallpox is not specifically mentioned, although other documents do confirm its presence among the British in the area. General Jeffrey's intentions are made clearer by his urging of Colonel Bouquet to "try Every other method that can serve to Extirpate this Execrable race." Although no follow-up to this plan has been discovered in the correspondences, and debate rages on over Amherst's burden of responsibility, smallpox did appear among the native peoples at about this time – perhaps one of the earliest instances of biological warfare.

Antonio's, 31 N Pleasant St (☎413/253-0808). This is *the* pizza place in town where the slices are always just out of the oven and good.

Bart's Homemade, 103 N Pleasant St (☎413/253-9371). Amherst branch of a Northampton favorite (see p.220).

The Black Sheep, 79 Main St (☎413/253-3442). Stacked sandwiches, pastries, coffee and desserts served in a down-to-earth café. Open late for coffee and occasional music including open-mic nights. Highly recommended.

Boltwood Tavern, 30 Boltwood Ave (☎413/253-2576). Part of the *Lord Jeffrey Inn*, this is a popular spot for good beers and pub grub. Upstairs is the *Windowed Hearth*, a more expensive and upscale counterpart where you're likely to find professors rather than students.

Bub's BBQ, Rte-116, Sunderland (☎413/259-1254). Despite the address, this is only minutes by car from Amherst. From Rte-9, take Rte-116 N, look for the fluorescent pink porker on the right inviting you to "Pig out in style." Smokin' barbecue and homestyle sides.

Judie's, 51 N Pleasant St (☎413/253-3491). Famous for meal-sized salads and home-made popovers served with apple butter.

La Veracruzana, 63 S Pleasant St (☎413/253-6900). Burrito joint that's the sister restaurant of the Northampton place of the same name.

South Hadley

Located at the intersection of Routes 116 and 67, the small town of **SOUTH HADLEY** completes the circle of towns in the Five College Consortium and is known solely as the home of bucolic Mount Holyoke College. Founded in 1836 by education pioneer Mary Lyon, Mount Holyoke is the oldest college for women in America and is one of the prestigious "Seven Sisters" group, along with its neighbor, Smith College.

The Town

Though the smallest of the area's towns, South Hadley is a worthwhile destination in its own right, mainly due to the presence of the **Mount Holyoke College Art Museum** (closed at the time of writing until 2002), Mount Holyoke College, Rte-116 (Tues–Fri 11am–5pm, Sat & Sun 1–5pm; free); which has an impressive permanent collection of Asian, Egyptian and Mediterranean paintings, drawings and sculpture, as well as mounting regular high-quality special exhibitions. The museum has acquired a *Head of Faustina the Elder*, a marble Roman sculpture of the second-century Empress Faustina, whose likeness was reproduced on coins and statues of the period, and whose elaborate braided hairstyle is a feat of both the art of sculpting and hairdressing.

There's also the **Joseph Allen Skinner Museum**, 35 Woodbridge St/Rte-116 (May–Oct Wed–Sun 2–5pm; free), the fantastic exhibits of period glassware, musical instruments, housewares, antique furniture and weaponry. The museum, a Congregational church built in 1846 and moved to this site from its original resting place – now under the placid waters of the nearby Quabbin Reservoir – houses this eclectic collection of Mr. Skinner, a wealthy mill owner and world traveler. There's very little organization to speak of, and those who have tried to trace and label the various bows and arrows, pistols, knickknacks, harpoons and farm implements were obviously defeated by the Sisyphean futility of their task.

Just outside town, **Carlton Nash Dinosaur Track Quarry**, Amherst Rd/Rte-116, is one of the more surreal local sights (Memorial Day–Labor Day Mon–Fri 10am–4pm, Sat–Sun noon–4pm; ☎413/467-9566; $2 adults, $1 children), a roadside collection of locally excavated dinosaur bones and footprints. In its previous incarnation as Nash Dinosaur Land, it was something of a roadside legend, as its elderly proprietor would not only show you the dinosaur bones but also spin animated tales about the property to all that would listen. Carlton has since passed away, and the place is a bit more low-key.

For **something to eat**, your only sure bet for several miles is Tailgate, in the shopping area across the street from Mount Holyoke (☎413/532-7597), which has a large selection of bagels, pasta salads and gourmet treats. If you need a snack before heading to one of the nearby parks, be sure to stop here first as you won't pass any other options en route.

Around South Hadley

Further along Rte-116 between South Hadley and Amherst, **The Notch**, an impasse between Bare Mountain and Mount Norwottuck, is the location of the entrance and visitors' center of the **Holyoke Range State Park** (information available through the "Friends of the Holyoke Range," 1500 West St, Amherst; ☎413/253-2883), which consists of 2936 acres spread out over nine miles and rising to heights of over 1000 feet with marked hiking trails throughout. On Rte-47, about halfway between South Hadley and Northampton, is the entrance to **Skinner State Park** (☎413/586-0350), which sits proudly perched atop Mount Holyoke. Head up to the aptly named **Summit House** (weekends April–Nov), where the park's visitors' center has wide and stunning views of the river valley, particularly the bend referred to as the "Ox Bow" – immortalized in Thomas Cole's famous painting.

The Upper Pioneer Valley

If you have a car and the desire to hit the back roads, exploring the area known as the **Upper Pioneer Valley** can yield many pleasant surprises. In sharp contrast with the relative economic and cultural stability of the college towns of Northampton and Amherst, the smaller rural towns surrounding them embrace an entirely different lifestyle. With the harsh weather, instability of the family farm, and the loss of industrial dollars, life in these hills can be grueling – and the picturesque scenery sometimes masks a rural poverty uncharacteristic of this part of New England. The hills in these parts yield simple pleasures: the odd roadside vegetable stand, good local diners, disarming vistas, eclectic yard sales, maple syrup farms and, especially in the summer, numerous festivals ranging from the Riverfest in Shelburne Falls (June) to the Turn of the Century Ice Cream Social in Deerfield (July).

Quabbin Reservoir, Mount Sugarloaf, and beyond

Leaving the Five College area, the Pioneer Valley becomes quite rural quite quickly. The beauty of **Quabbin Reservoir** (entrance on Rte-9 between Ware and Belchertown) belies its origins: in 1939, in a bureaucratic decision designed to benefit the eastern part of the state, the Swift River was dammed and the towns of Dana, Greenwich, Enfield, and Prescott were evacuated and flooded with some 39 square miles of water, since which time the metropolitan Boston area has had to give little thought to the source and availability of its water. And while you cannot swim, camp, or barbecue at Quabbin, its 81,000 acres of protected wildlife reservation land provide a fair degree of serenity.

Just outside South Deerfield (see below), the **Mount Sugarloaf Reservation** (Rte-116) consists of North and South Sugarloaf mountains, the latter of which has a paved road allowing cars to climb to the summit. Scenic views and good picnicking make this a popular spot, and there are opportunities for camping, too – though reservations are advised. On the other side of Deerfield, the **Daughters of the American Revolution (D.A.R.) State Forest** (Rte-112, Goshen) is also

---

MAPLE SYRUP

Though the raw, muddy, unpredictable and seemingly endless weeks of March in New England have few virtues, one is the proximity of spring and the other is **maple syrup**. The sugar shacks of the Upper Pioneer Valley are responsible for producing most of the maple syrup made in Massachusetts. Surrounded by ancient maples and using time-honored methods, these tiny, often family-owned and -run, sugar houses welcome visitors, give tours, and even offer weekend brunches where the maple syrup flows generously. The season usually begins the first weekend of March and continues for six weekends afterward. Calling ahead is wise and arriving early is even wiser, as the farms are quite popular. Try **South Face Farm**, Watson-Spruce Corner Road, off Rte-116 in Ashfield (March–mid-April Sat & Sun 8.30am–3.30pm; ☎413/628-3268), where they make pancakes, waffles, and fried corn fritters and dare you to top them with both syrup and ice cream.

a good place for camping, with tent and RV sites available May 1 through Labor Day ($12, two-night stay minimum). The **Mohawk Trail State Forest** (Rte-2, Charlemont; ☎413/339-4470) offers 56 campsites and 6 cabins (tent sites available mid-May–Columbus Day, cabins all year-round; $8). **Erving State Forest** (Wendell Depot Road, off Rte-2A at Erving Center) is a bit more rough-and-ready, with no showers or flush toilets, but makes up for it by allowing almost every outdoor activity you could think of, from snowshoeing to fishing.

South Deerfield

Despite the sedate appearance of present-day **SOUTH DEERFIELD**, its history is punctuated with violent episodes of unusual intensity, even for America. The town was first settled in 1669 as a frontier outpost of British North America. Its position in the woods far away from established colonial centers on the coast left it vulnerable to attack, which local Indians did on September 18, 1675. One of the bloodiest clashes of King Philip's War (see p.537), this culminated in the death of 64 men at "Bloody Brook" in South Deerfield. But it was in February 1704, in a colonial extension of Queen Anne's War, that Deerfield earned its notoriety. In a raid that began at dawn and lasted five hours, some 350 Indians – led by the French – killed 49 settlers and set fire to the town. More than a hundred prisoners were promptly marched 300 miles to Canada; a fifth perished en route. Deerfield was abandoned afterward, but it eventually became a prosperous farming town. Today South Deerfield, basically a developed spot along Routes 5 and 10 (exit 24 off of Rte-91), is home to both Historic Deerfield and the Yankee Candle-Making Museum.

Accommodation

Charlemont Inn, Rte-2, Charlemont (☎413/339-5796). Travelers from Benedict Arnold to Mark Twain have homed in on this Mohawk Trail inn since 1787. Full of character and comfort, it drips with New England charm. ⑨.

Deerfield Inn, The Street (☎413/774-5587 or 1-800/926-3865). The one and only place to stay in Historic Deerfield itself, this commodious country inn has good dining, too. ⑦.

Motel 6, Rte-5, South Deerfield (☎413/665-7161). Completely lacking in rustic charm, but offering clean rooms, friendly service, and reasonable rates. Located in a conifer grove off of I-91 at exit 24. ③.

The Town

Historic Deerfield, with dutifully preserved old houses girdled by a thousand acres of lush meadows and farmland, is a destination frozen in time. The town considers itself the home of the preservation movement in New England, and also one of the first to milk the appeal of Olde New England. Restoration began here as early as in 1890, when Alice Baker purchased the Frery House, restored it and opened the doors to the public. This was something of a first back then, and today, of the 65 or so eighteenth- and nineteenth-century structures on either side of **The Street** (the main drag), fourteen house museums open for guided tours. These small-scale studies in simple elegance are filled with over 20,000 objects, from furniture and fabrics to silver and glass, either made or used in America between 1650 and 1850. About the only thing that infuses the strip with a touch of modernity (other than the tourists) is the presence of the 1797 **Deerfield Academy**, an American answer to Eton. If you don't have the patience for guided tours – and unless you have an overriding interest in antique home decor you probably need not go on more than one or two – the best thing is to peruse the new Flynt Center for Early American Life and take in the excellent Memorial Hall Museum, both of which are self-guiding.

Housed around the corner from The Street in the original building of the Deerfield Academy, the three-story **Memorial Hall Museum**, 8 Memorial St (daily 9.30am–4.30pm; $5), houses a superb collection of New England antiquities, and, on the second floor a door destroyed during a 1704 raid by Native Americans. Judging by the hole in the center left by a battering axe, the wielder of the weapon didn't quite make it inside, but to get a sense of that moment of terror all you have to do is walk behind the door, preserved in a glass case. The door was pried off the 1698 John Sheldon House, itself demolished in the 1840s. Other exhibits include Native American artifacts, New England quilts and well-curated period rooms with ceramics, glassware, paintings and similar accoutrements of a generally placid past.

The best way to orient yourself is to check in at the **Hall Tavern Information Center**, across from the *Deerfield Inn*, and where you have to purchase house tickets anyway (daily 9.30am–4.30pm; $6 single house admission, $12 unlimited admission ticket good for one week; ☎413/774-5581). There's a small museum inside, but the main thing is to check to see which of the houses are open for touring on the day you happen to be there. Next to Hall Tavern is the 1799 **Stebbins House**, one of the most interesting of the houses for its spiral staircase, stately New England furniture and ornate French wallpaper. Tackling The Street top to bottom, the 1825 brick **Wright House** is noted for Federal-style furniture and clocks and Chinese export porcelain. A few doors down, The **Henry N. Flynt Silver & Metalware Collection** has on display both English and American silver and pewterware, some crafted by Paul Revere. Across the way is the **Ashley House**, with the upscale furnishings of the eighteenth-century Connecticut River Valley elite. Four doors down from the latter is the **Indian House Memorial**, a reconstruction of the Sheldon House, the earliest-known Deerfield house. From here you can take the short but enchanting **Channing Blake Meadow Walk** down to the Deerfield River.

The **Wells-Thorn House**, at the corner of The Street and Memorial Street, has period rooms that depict the lifestyle of Deerfield residents from 1725 to 1850. One short block south is the **Dwight House**, a circa-1725 merchant's home that was moved here from Springfield. Behind the Dwight House is the new **Flynt Center for Early American Life**, which houses some 10,000 objects of interest, and is the only place in Historic Deerfield with rotating exhibits. Allow an hour or more to take it all in, including the Helen G. Flynt Textile Collection.

There's not much to the rest of Deerfield, although if you have the energy, the **Yankee Candle-Making Company and Car Museum** (daily 9.30am–6pm; $5 admission to car museum), and the shopping complex it shares with the tourist-targeted Bavarian Christmas Village and Kringle Market, is worth a brief stop-off for its regular demonstrations of traditional candlemaking techniques using 200-year-old equipment, and the assortment of collectors' cars on display.

Eating

As you exit I-91 and turn north onto Routes 5 and 10 (which are, at this point, one road), you will pass the Sugarloaf Shoppes and *Motel 6* and arrive at a stop light. Take a right at the light onto Elm Street, cross the railroad tracks, and the small business district you see represents the extent of the South Deerfield area's offerings. If you're giving Historic Deerfield a few days and looking for dinner (not to mention something to *do* at night), you may have more luck in neighboring Greenfield, ten minutes to the north on Rte-5.

The Deli and Bakery, The Sugarloaf Shoppes. Bagels, sandwiches, and coffee for hungry picnickers heading up Mount Sugarloaf (see below).

The People's Pint, 24 Federal St, Greenfield (☎413/773-0333). Local brewpub even makes its own sodas, as well as serving well-prepared dishes using local and organic ingredients.

Sienna, 6 Elm St (☎413/665-0215; closed Mon & Tues). It may be the fact that it is only open for dinner or possibly that its storefront, when not lit, has the look of an abandoned dime store, but it is easy to miss *Sienna*. Whatever the reason, its unassuming nature undoubtedly contributes to its status as one of the area's best-kept secrets. A warm terracotta colored interior, candles, and dishes ranging from chile rellenos with Vermont goat cheese to steamed mussels in a Thai-inspired lime-coconut, this is a dining experience you will not quickly forget. Entrees in the $18–21 range, desserts and appetizers $6–9.

Shelburne Falls

Nestled in the Berkshire foothills and straddling the Deerfield River approximately two miles from Rte-2 is the tiny town of **SHELBURNE FALLS**, a community whose buzz of artistic activity and scenic surroundings give a taste of modern New England small-town life. You wouldn't make a special trip to Shelburne Falls, but the scenic drive you have to make to get here and its eminently strollable Main Street, dotted with antique shops and glass-blowing galleries, make it a pleasant enough if low-key spot. Be warned, though, that what one would logically consider Shelburne Falls are actually the two towns of Shelburne Falls and Buckland, each on its respective side of the river. This fact, though largely arbitrary, is momentarily confusing when you drive into what you expect to be Shelburne Falls and are greeted by the Buckland Town Hall.

The Town

The most prominent – and most touted – thing to see in Shelburne Falls is the so-called **Bridge of Flowers**, an old trolley bridge festooned with flowering foliage each spring by the Shelburne Falls Women's Club that's talked up by the local authorities as "internationally known" – an exaggerated claim that doesn't detract from the bridge's appeal, though it's basically a well-executed show of civic pride rather than a botanical wonder. The town's other attraction is a naturally occurring one, a series of geologically bizarre glacial **potholes**, east of Bridge Street, formed by several hundred million years of erosion and pitted by the splashing from the waterfalls upstream. Worth a quick look, they resemble an enormous solid mass of once-molten stone that has now been whittled into a svelte sculpture along the riverbed.

Practicalities

Shelburne Falls is located approximately two miles south of Rte-2 and 10 miles west of the intersection of Rte-2 and I-91 at Greenfield. If you are coming from Northampton, consider taking the more scenic Rte-9 N to Goshen and climbing Rte-112 north to Shelburne Falls. If you are coming from Amherst or South Deerfield, you can take the equally scenic Rte-116 north to Rte-112 N (Ashfield is a worthwhile stop, but mostly closed on Sundays). Antique shops, two grocery

---

A ROAD LESS TAKEN

Lovers of books will feel right at home at the **Book Mill**, 440 Greenfield Rd, off Rte-63 in Montague (daily 10am–6pm; ☎413/367-9206), which accurately bills itself as offering "books you don't need in a place you can't find." With 40,000 used and discount books, well-seasoned armchairs, and large windows overlooking the river, the Book Mill is a pleasant place to spend a couple of lazy hours. Consider having Sunday brunch in their newly opened *Blue Heron Restaurant* (☎413/367-2101).

---

stores, restaurants, and a **Village Information Center** (☎413/625-2544) line State Street in Buckland and Bridge Street in Shelburne Falls.

Accommodation options are spread out, but the *Bear Haven Bed & Breakfast*, 22 Mechanic St (☎413/625-9281; ④–⑤), is centrally located, home to the large collection of teddy bears of its owners, Chris and Deane Merrill, and a nice resting-place for humans as well. You can't miss its rambling blue and lavender exterior. It is hard to go wrong stopping for a **bite to eat** in Shelburne Falls; the town's culinary offerings are packed into the little commercial center and the quality is surprisingly good for a town this small. *Margo's Bistro* (☎413/625-0200) offers innovative fare with trendy ingredients like gorgonzola and Thai peanut sauce, wooing clients with their terrific brunch served with a complimentary tea tray of fruit and home-made biscuits. Another option, *Mother's* (☎413/625-6300), offers sandwiches galore plus hearty breakfasts, in a welcoming environment. Finally the *Copper Angel* (☎413/625-2727) offers resourceful vegetarian and non-red-meat cuisine on its summertime outdoor terrace above the Bridge of Flowers.

THE BERKSHIRES

A rich cultural history, world-class summer arts festivals and a bucolic landscape of forests and verdant hills – reminiscent of the English Lake District – make **the Berkshires**, at the extreme western edge of Massachusetts, an unusually civilized region. Since the mid-nineteenth century, the beauty and tranquility of this region have attracted a moneyed crowd, the most visible manifestations of which are sumptuous Newport-style summer "cottages" nestled in the woods around the sedate villages of **Stockbridge** and **Lenox**. The latter is also home to **Tanglewood**, summer quarters of the Boston Symphony Orchestra and symbol of putative East Coast cultural superiority. But venture beyond these bastions of gentility and the more typical aspects of New England quickly reemerge, from the economically battered old mill town of **Pittsfield** to dignified **Williamstown** and time-warp hill towns as remote as any in Vermont or New Hampshire.

Navigating the region is not difficult, as long as you have a car and a good map – road signage is decidedly geared for residents, not visitors. The main highway, **Rte-7**, runs the length of the region (and the state) from north to south, following the cleft between the Taconic mountains on the New York border and Hoosic ranges to the east. Because the Berkshires are at the end of the end of the state, the biggest decision you have to make in terms of driving – assuming you are coming from points east – may well be how you want to arrive. The **Mass Turnpike** takes you from Boston to West Stockbridge in a stupendously dull three hours; a more appealing option might be to pick up I-91 south from Rte-2,

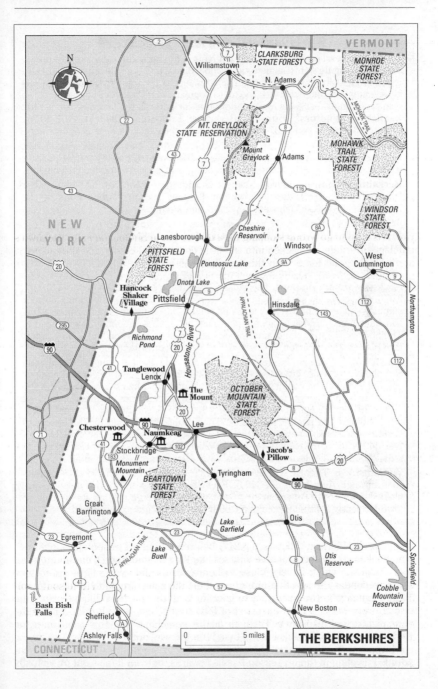

N

VERMONT

Williamstown
CLARKSBURG
STATE FOREST
N. Adams
MONROE
STATE
FOREST

MT. GREYLOCK
STATE RESERVATION
▲ Mount
Greylock
Adams

MOHAWK
TRAIL
STATE
FOREST

NEW
YORK

Cheshire
Reservoir

WINDSOR
STATE
FOREST

Lanesborough
PITTSFIELD
STATE
FOREST
Pontoosuc Lake
Windsor
West
Cummington

Onota Lake
Hancock
Shaker
Village ▲
Pittsfield
Hinsdale

APPALACHIAN TRAIL

Richmond
Pond

Northampton

Tanglewood
Lenox
The
Mount

OCTOBER
MOUNTAIN
STATE
FOREST

Chesterwood
Naumkeag
Lee
Stockbridge
Monument
Mountain ▲
BEARTOWN
STATE
FOREST
Jacob's
Pillow

Tyringham

Springfield

Great
Barrington
Lake
Garfield
Otis

Egremont
Lake
Buell
Otis
Reservoir

APPALACHIAN TRAIL

Cobble
Mountain
Reservoir

Bash Bish
Falls
New Boston

Sheffield

Ashley Falls

CONNECTICUT

0   5 miles

THE BERKSHIRES

Housatonic River

CULTURE IN THE BERKSHIRES

There are several **summer cultural festivals** in the Berkshires, but none so prominent as the big three of Tanglewood, Jacob's Pillow, and the Williamstown Theatre Festival. Virtually every concert and performance at the more established festivals is well-attended, and tickets for the more popular events sell out far in advance, so plan accordingly. For a current calendar that includes all the festivals, contact the **Berkshire Visitors' Bureau**, Berkshire Common, Pittsfield, MA 01201 (☎413/443-9186 or 1-800/237-5747). Also ask for the excellent *Four Seasons Guide*.

Aston Magna Festival, St. James Church, Rte-7 and Taconic Ave, Great Barrington (July & Aug Sat; ☎413/528-3595). The country's oldest annual summer festival, devoted to performances of Baroque music, played on period instruments.

Berkshire Theatre Festival, Main St, Stockbridge (Mon–Sat, late June–Labor Day; ☎413/298-5576). Best known for its four summer productions at the Berkshire Playhouse Mainstage, but also noteworthy for Unicorn Theatre readings of plays in progress.

Jacob's Pillow, Rte-20 between Becket and Lee (Tues–Sat, late June through Aug; ☎413/243-0745). Perhaps the most famous contemporary dance festival in the country, improbably located in the middle of (an admittedly lovely) nowhere. Artists-in-residence give free performances of works in progress before the main programs.

Shakespeare & Company, The Mount, Plunkett St, Lenox (May–Nov; ☎413/637-3353). One of the country's biggest Shakespeare festivals uses The Mount, former summer estate of Edith Wharton, as its venue. One comedy is performed in July and August on the Mainstage; ten plays, not all Shakespearean, are performed in The Stables Theatre, and dramatizations of stories by Wharton and Henry James take place at the Wharton Theatre, in The Mount's drawing room.

Tanglewood, West St/Rte-183, Lenox. From July to late August the Boston Symphony Orchestra gives concerts at this, perhaps the most celebrated outdoor cultural venue in the country. Full-orchestral concerts take place weekends at the Shed; the newer Ozawa Hall is used on other days, mainly for chamber-music concerts. The musical options include open rehearsals for the BSO on Saturday mornings, and jazz and pop performances. Though tickets are sold for the Shed and Ozawa Hall, it is cheaper and arguably more enjoyable to sit on the grass – but if you do, bring a towel or lawn chair. When ordering tickets in advance, call ☎617/266-1492 September through May; otherwise ☎413/637-1600.

Williamstown Theatre Festival, 84 Spring St, Williamstown (Tues–Sun, mid-June through Aug; ☎413/597-3400). Every summer several of the most accomplished actors from American stage and screen converge on this stately college town for nearly a dozen productions, both time-tested and experimental.

sampling the Pioneer Valley (see p.217) before striking off west on pristine Rte-9, which takes you past tourist-free villages like Williamsburg and Cummington and into Pittsfield, which is very close to Lenox. In the fall, you might opt to take scenic secondary routes that branch west off Rte-9 itself, notably routes 112 and 143. Alternatively, you may want to take Rte-2 all the way to Williamstown – the stretch from Miller's Falls (just east of I-91) to the New York border follows the very picturesque **Mohawk Trail**; in fact, if you don't take this route into the Berkshires, you'd be remiss not to take it on the way out.

More so than other parts of New England, tourism in the Berkshires is **seasonal**. Traveling in the off-season has its rewards, but you'll miss out on virtually all the big cultural festivals and find most of the museums either closed or on skeleton winter schedules. On the other hand, in the summer you're competing with East Coasters who have been coming here for years, which makes planning far in advance to secure accommodations and/or tickets less a good idea than a requirement. Perhaps the best times to visit are late May – spring is delightful in the Berkshires – or September, when the leaves are changing but before the October "leaf peepers" arrive in force.

STOCKBRIDGE

Strolling the spotless main street of **STOCKBRIDGE** either entices or unsettles, depending on whether you see it as the picture-postcard New England village it touts itself as or the essence of prefabricated quaint. Accordingly, you can either credit or curse Norman Rockwell, who lived and painted here for 25 years, for your reaction to the place. His Stockbridge paintings, like all the rest, capture a small-town American charm that may have only ever existed on the surface; regardless, his illustrations pass for great art in these parts (especially at his eponymous museum), and buying into the illusion of all-pervasive gaiety – the legacy of his work – for the length of your visit will at least increase your enjoyment. The social reality of Stockbridge is not quite Rockwell: the majority of the residences in town are summer homes for wealthy New Yorkers. Ironically, Stockbridge's other, uncelebrated, claim to fame is at quite the other end of the socio-cultural spectrum: the town is the setting for Arlo Guthrie's classic anti-draft song/monologue "Alice's Restaurant." White-clapboard schmaltz aside, there's actually quite a bit to see and do in and around Stockbridge, from the sprawling Newport-style estates of Naumkeag and Chesterwood outside town to other historical houses and relics within easy reach of the town.

Stockbridge has the bulk of weighty historical associations in a region that has relatively few, especially compared to eastern Massachusetts. When in 1722 pioneers wrested a chunk of land along the Housatonic River from local Indians, they set aside a bit as "Indian Town," where they attempted to "English" them – with limited success. Indian Town was soon renamed Stockbridge, and, in the days before it attracted a wealthy summer population, owed its sustained existence to farming and its location on the stagecoach route between Boston and Albany, New York. On February 26, 1787, disenfranchised Revolutionary War veterans plundered Stockbridge houses and holed up for the night in the *Red Lion Inn*; the ill-fated Shay's Rebellion ended the next day with a shoot-out in Great Barrington, the next town south on Rte-7. *The Red Lion Inn* depicted in Norman Rockwell's *Main Street Stockbridge at Christmastime*, incidentally, was built on the site of the original, which burned in 1896.

Accommodation

The Stockbridge Chamber of Commerce (☎413/298-5200; *www.stockbridgechamber.org*) can help you with accommodation and other information.

Berkshire Thistle Bed and Breakfast, 19 East Street/Rte-7, Stockbridge (☎413/298-3188, *www.berkshirethistle.com*). This oversized residence resting confidently on five forested acres has five beautifully furnished rooms waiting to comfort tired travelers.. Full breakfast on weekends, generous continental breakfast buffet during the week. [5].

234/CENTRAL AND WESTERN MASSACHUSETTS

Meadowlark, Chesterwood (☎413/298-5545). The second, smaller studio Daniel Chester French built on his large estate is rented out in season; staying in this unusual spot grants you free admission to the rest of Chesterwood. ⑦–⑧.

Red Lion Inn, Main St, Stockbridge (☎413/298-5545). Brimming with the kind of bric-a-brac you wish your grandmother would toss, what for many is the quintessential New England hostelry – and therefore popular with tour groups – is for others a case study in quaintness run amok. The gift shop is called The Pink Kitty. Draw your own conclusions. ④–⑤.

The Town and around

The actual town of Stockbridge is tiny, basically consisting of a few nineteenth-century buildings on Main Street and those around the corner on Elm Street. Unless they're staying at the grandmotherly **Red Lion Inn**, most people tend to park their car near it and and wander from there, either having iced tea on the inn's venerable front porch, or else stocking up on provisions at one of the numerous good country markets such as Williams and Sons.

There are few specific sights in the town center. The Historical Room of the **Stockbridge Library**, at the corner of Main and Elm streets (Mon–Fri 9am–5pm, Sat 9am–4pm), contains artifacts from the Mahican Indians, who first lived in the area. The small **Mission House**, at the corner of Main and Sergeant streets (daily mid-May to end October; $5), is where the Reverend John Sergeant planned his missionary work, under the auspices of the London Society for the Propagation of the Gospel in Foreign Lands. Though built in 1739, it was relocated here from a nearby site in 1928. The exterior has a pretty arched Connecticut River Valley-style doorway, while the inside is noteworthy mainly for the eighteenth-century chairs on which Sergeant is said to have sat. Opposite the Mission House, the **Merwin House** is another period residence (Sat & Sun 11am–4pm; $4), and open to public viewing by way of regular guided tours. The elegant Federal-style building exemplifies gracious Stockbridge living in the early part of the 1800s, and is stocked with an interesting selection of paintings and antiques.

Most people skip all this, however, in favor of the **Norman Rockwell Museum** (May–Oct daily 10am–5pm; Nov–April Mon–Fri 11am–4pm, Sat–Sun 10am–5pm; $9), just outside the town center off Rte-183. Given the steep admission, the selection is more limited than one might expect, but the two floors of Rockwell originals and reproductions are well displayed in a $10 million facility built in part with a donation from Steven Spielberg. Even the biggest fan of his work may have the limits of their admiration tested by the gallery of Rockwell's advertising endorsements, for everything from cereal to cars, which make it seem like he would have given his name to just about anything. The facility itself is rather sterile, looking like nothing so much as a nursing home from the outside, but the grounds include the little red studio that was Rockwell's own studio.

Beyond the Rockwell Museum, the **Berkshire Botanical Garden**, at the junction of routes 102 and 183 (May–Oct daily 10am–5pm; $5), is home to around fifteen acres of landscaped gardens, with wildflowers on display in spring and roses during summer. You can also make a fragrant loop through the woods.

There's another, also rather overrated, attraction just down the road in the form of **Chesterwood**, at 4 Williamsville Rd (May–Oct daily 10am–5pm; $7, grounds only $5), the former summer home of sculptor Daniel Chester French, best

NORMAN ROCKWELL

Love him or hate him, if you spend any time in Western New England, it's hard to avoid the work of **Norman Rockwell**. The man dubbed "America's best-loved artist" lived and painted in Arlington, VT, and, more famously, in Stockbridge, MA, and there are no fewer than three museums in his honor. For more than half a century, Rockwell was a fixture on the landscape of American popular culture, known as much for his product endorsements as for his *Saturday Evening Post* covers. Of American artists, perhaps only Warhol, in many ways his spiritual opposite, is so easily recognizable.

Born in 1894 in New York City, Rockwell dropped out of high school to attend classes at the National Academy of Design and at the age of 22 sold his first painting to the **Saturday Evening Post**; in the forty years that followed, he contributed more than 300 paintings to that publication alone. His work presented, in the artist's own words, "life as it should be": children playing, adults relaxing, doctors examining healthy patients, family struggles that seemed certain to have a happy ending. His work stands in dramatic contrast to the "serious artists" of the twentieth century, the surrealists, dadaists, cubists and abstract expressionists, much as his idyllic images stand in contrast to the often turbulent times in which he lived.

Many have questioned the veracity of these images, yet it seems doubtful that Rockwell saw much in the way of war, riots or lynchings during his placid suburban life. However, later in his career, working for *Look* magazine, Rockwell did take on such issues as integration of schools and neighborhoods, and did so with the same gentle dignity that he had devoted to more insular concerns.

known for his oversized rendition of President Lincoln that sits in his eponymous memorial in Washington, DC. The humdrum plaster models in the artist's studio perhaps betray the fact that he had no formal training. His 130-acre estate is idyllic, though; as he averred, "I live here six months of the year – in heaven. The other six months I live, well – in New York."

With its spectacular views of the Stockbridge hills, distinctive gardens and aesthetically balanced interiors, the Gilded Age estate of **Naumkeag**, on Prospect Hill Road (Memorial Day–Columbus Day Tues–Sun 10am–5pm; $7, gardens only $5), nestled amongst several other sumptuous private estates (including the nearby Oronoque, a stylized royal hunting lodge built the same year as Naumkeag), is like a Newport mansion without the forced opulence. It was built by Stanford White in 1886 as a family home for the prosperous attorney Joseph Hodges Choate, later made ambassador to the Court of St James (the estate's name, pronounced "Nómkeg," derives from the Native American word for Salem, Choate's birthplace). The touches of a master architect are evident everywhere, from the synthesis of American elements such as a shingle roof with European-style brick and stone towers to understated flourishes throughout the 26 rooms of the house, including a combination of cherry, oak, and mahogany paneling and a three-story handcarved oak staircase. Original furnishings and domestic appointments from European tapestries to Asian ceramics, give the impression the Choates have just slipped out for a ride in the country; indeed there are even coats left hanging in the closet. Although only guided tours of the inside are available, this is one of the few places where taking one is actually worthwhile.

As impressive as the house is, the real attraction here is the eight acres of meticulously planned and tended **gardens**, subtly studded with contemporary sculpture. To fully appreciate them, you need to take your time, perhaps even pack a picnic. The first green space of note, more like an adjunct to the house, is the Afternoon Garden, a 1928 addition remarkable for its vividly painted Venetian-style oak posts. The Perugino View, named for a sixteenth-century landscape painter, adjoins the Top Lawn and affords intoxicating views over the grounds and across to Monument Mountain. From here it's a short walk to the Blue Steps, named for a succession of blue-colored fountains flanked by stairs that lead to yet more gardens. The atmospheric Linden Walk ends with a statue of the Roman goddess Diana.

Eating

Boiler Room Café, 405 Stockbridge Rd/Rte-7, Great Barrington (☎413/528-4280). It comes as a pleasant surprise to find such toothsome Mediterranean cooking, with an emphasis on Provençal and Catalan dishes, just outside of Stockbridge. Recommended.

Glendale River Grille, Rte-183, Stockbridge (☎413/298-4711). Elegant, spacious grill and tavern, about five miles south of the Rockwell museum. Some adventurous entrees – such as roast duckling Cantonese with hoisin sauce – in addition to the standard grill fare like steaks and swordfish.

The Red Lion Inn, Main St, Stockbridge (☎413/298-5545). Repair to the old inn's atmospheric tavern room for big portions of reliable Yankee fare, from prime rib to *sole meunière*.

Lenox

From Stockbridge, a slight detour off Rte-7 takes you onto Rte-7A and into the genteel village of **LENOX**, the cultural nucleus of the Berkshires by virtue of its proximity to Tanglewood, the summer home of the Boston Symphony Orchestra. It's a quiet place for most of the year, but on summer weekends, during its summer music festival, traffic jams are not uncommon – summering in Lenox has been a New York (rather than Boston) tradition since the mid-nineteenth century, and, not surprisingly, although the number of shops and restaurants is necessarily limited by the town's small size, in terms of both price and attitude their atmosphere is more Manhattan than New England.

Accommodation

The friendly folks at the **Lenox Chamber of Commerce** (☎413/637-3646, *www.lenox.org*) will gladly help you find a place to stay. Don't expect to stroll into town and find a room while Tanglewood is in session.

Amadeus House Bed & Breakfast, 15 Cliffwood St (☎413/637-4770 or 1-800/205-4770). This altogether cheerful B&B, with an impressive variety of guest rooms – named after composers – is located right in Lenox village, on the side closest to Tanglewood. For a longer or group stay, consider the two-bedroom Beethoven Suite. ④–⑥.

Blantyre, Blantyre Rd (☎413/637-3556 or 1-800/860-4930). A roomy Scottish Tudor mansion with Gothic flourishes – a former summer "cottage" – that has been purposed as one of the country's most luxurious resorts, and as such is almost a destination in itself. ⑦–⑨.

Brook Farm Inn, 15 Hawthorne St (☎413/637-3013 or 1-800/285-POET). The innkeepers at this 1870 Victorian B&B with twelve guest rooms are poetry aficionados, so in summer you can borrow a tape recorder and listen to the bard of your choice, on the porch or by the pool, and in winter curl up with a book of verse in front of a fireplace, either in the common area or in your room. ⑤.

The Village Inn, 16 Church St (☎413/637-0020 or 1-800/253-0917). A country-inn-style hotel – meaning 32 rooms with antiques, bountiful breakfasts and afternoon English tea – in the center of Lenox. ⑥–⑧.

Walker House, 74 Walker St (☎413/637-1271 or 1-800/235-3098). This informal eight-room B&B is pet-friendly – the innkeepers have eight cats. ⑥.

Wheatleigh, Hawthorne Rd (☎413/637-0610). Built by a New York financier in 1893 as a wedding present for his daughter, who married a Spanish count, today this Florentine palazzo-style estate-cum-resort combines antique and contemporary decor to sumptuous, successful effect. The lush grounds were landscaped by Frederick Law Olmsted, designer of New York's Central Park, and to stay any closer to Tanglewood you'd have to camp on its lawn. ⑧–⑨.

The Town and around

Even if you're visiting after Labor Day, it's well worth making a stop off West Street (Rte-183), about a mile outside town, to walk around **Tanglewood**. Though its lush grounds were formerly part of the estate of a wealthy Boston banker, it was Nathaniel Hawthorne who coined the name – today musicians practice in a reconstruction of the little red farmhouse where he lived with his wife Sophia in 1850 and 1851, penning *The House of the Seven Gables* on the premises. On summer weekends, concerts are given in the aptly named "Shed," a barebones, indoor/outdoor hall, as well as the newer Ozawa Hall. From the edge of sprawling lawn there is a good view of the Stockbridge Bowl, a mile-wide pond – a view which is even better from the more elevated **Kripalu Center for Yoga and Health**, across the street from Tanglewood's main entrance (just drive through the parking lot and pretend to be in meditation if questioned). Another way to appreciate the countryside around here is on horseback; **Undermountain Farm** (☎413/637-3365) offers guided trail rides and is a very scenic place for a ride.

While most of the expansive "cottages" that transformed Lenox and vicinity into "the inland Newport" at the turn of the century remain in private hands (as homes, hotels, and even medical facilities), **The Mount**, at the southern junction of routes 7 and 7A, at the corner of Plunkett Street and Rte-7 (Memorial Day–Nov 2, tours daily 9am–3pm; last tour at 2pm; $6; ☎413/637-1899), the summer home of novelist Edith Wharton from 1902 until 1911, is open to the public, even in the midst of its current major restoration. Its order, scale, and harmony are a reflection of the principles Wharton promoted in her first successful book, *The Decoration of Houses*, published a few years before she moved in. One of her precepts was to ease the transition from outdoors to inside – an example of which is the indoor wrought-iron stair rails, a material typically associated with exterior ornamentation. Though Wharton's years at The Mount were productive – among other things, she wrote *Ethan Frome* here – they were not entirely happy; boredom with her husband and unapologetic disgust for the turpitude of American culture sent her packing for France, where she lived out her final years. The Mount is these days another performance space, with four stages, the main one of which is open-air; adaptations of stories by Wharton and her soulmate Henry James also take place in season in the drawing room.

Eating

Bistro Zinc, 56 Church St (☎413/637-8800). Popular power-lunch spot filled with diners on cell phones taking down flavorful French fare at reasonable prices – though dinner is considerably more expensive.

Café Lucia, 90 Church St (☎413/637-2640). It may not be on the menu, but you're likely to get a serving of attitude along with your pricey but tasty Italian entrees at this popular, noisy spot where a Manhattan ambiance prevails.

Church Street Café, 69 Church St (☎413/637-2745). Updated New England fare, from sautéed Maine crab cakes to parsley fettucine with Gulf shrimp, oven-roasted tomatoes and pesto, wins accolades for this eatery – more restaurant than café – in the center of Lenox.

Wheatleigh, Hawthorne Rd (☎413/637-0610). Very highly priced, but you get what you pay for – outstanding flavors of contemporary continental cuisine, including low-fat and vegetarian menus, ambrosial, artfully prepared desserts and impeccable service. The decor, from crystal chandeliers to Italianate paintings, is deliberately soothing.

Lee and Tyringham

During the busy summer cultural season, many last-minute travelers who think they'll find a room in Lenox end up staying in nearby **LEE**, which is just as well, for there is a genuine aspect to the place altogether lacking in its ritzier neighbor. Plus, there are many small inns and B&Bs, all of which have the advantage of being near the thick of things yet removed from the commotion. Like other Berkshire towns, Lee was once a papermaking center, but it was better known for its unusually strong marble – which found its way to the US Capitol, the Empire State Building, St Patrick's Cathedral and other East Coast landmarks. It's also in evidence in Lee itself, for example in certain buildings along the archetypal **Main Street**. McClelland's Drug Store here at no. 43, replete with vintage soda fountain (which unfortunately uses Ben & Jerry's instead of home-made ice cream) is a big draw as is the perenially busy *Joe's Diner*, at Main and Center streets (see opposite), where quality eats from omelettes to club sandwiches come at ridiculously low prices.

One of the better-kept secrets in Massachusetts is the incredibly scenic Tyringham Valley (see below), practically hidden between Routes 102 and 23. **TYRINGHAM** itself, which basically consists of a post office and a church, was settled as a hinterland community in the eighteenth century and hasn't perceivably changed since. The only tangible sight is an unusual museum called **Santarella** at 75 Main Rd (May–Oct daily 10am–5pm; $4), designed and built by Englishman Sir Henry Hudson Kitson – the sculptor of the *Minute Man* in Lexington – as his sculpture studio in the 1930s. Its signature feature is the eighty-ton roof, a sculpted simulation of thatching that succeeds in conveying the image of the undulating Berkshire Hills in autumn. Despite a few noteworthy works, Kitson was a minor figure on the American artistic landscape, however, and the "museum" in his honor isn't all that impressive. What makes Santarella worth a stop, however (other than getting a look at its fantastic roof), is the contemporary art gallery inside, which spills onto the serene gardens and around a lily pond behind the house.

Just south of Santarella, the Tyringham Road opens onto the **Tyringham Valley**, which is more reminiscent of an unsullied Irish glade than any part of New England proper. The highest spot, on the right, is the **Tyringham Cobble**, a forest-covered outcropping of limestone and quartzite that rises 400 feet over the valley: to hike it, make a right on Jerusalem Road, after the village, and proceed for a quarter of a mile. The reward for your two-mile endeavour will be views that are breathtaking, and on a clear spring or fall day, positively immobilizing. A right turn on Art School Road, the next street down, takes you to the highly regarded Joyous Spring Pottery. A couple of miles further south, the road intersects Rte-23, heading west on which takes you through equally tiny Monterey and back to Rte-7.

Accommodation

Applegate, 279 W Park St, Lee (☎413/243-4451). A calm, ship-shape B&B, in a Southern-style Georgian colonial home, whose six guest rooms have old-fashioned character but a contemporary feel; fresh baked goods contribute to great breakfasts. ⑥–⑧.

Chambéry Inn, 199 Main St, Lee (☎413/243-2221 or 1-800/537-4321). Six meticulously refurbished suites with high ceilings and big windows – and modern touches like in-room phones and cable TV – in an 1885 French country house, built as the country's first parochial school. ⑥–⑧.

Historic Merrell Inn, 1565 Pleasant St/Rte-102, South Lee (☎413/243-1794 or 1-800/243-1794). This atmospheric old nine-room inn, well-situated between Stockbridge and Lee, has some interesting relics from its days as a stagecoach stop, such as a vintage birdcage bar in the Tavern Room, where breakfast is served. Ask for a room overlooking the meandering Housatonic River. ⑤–⑥.

Sunset Farm Bed & Breakfast, 74 Main Rd, Ty (☎413/243-3229). Old New England lives on at this blissfully isolated farmhouse on a hillock in the gorgeous Tyringham Valley. Four rooms, of which three have private baths, are a bit frayed at the edges, but the feel is very authentic without being twee. The owners are warm, the food good, and there's a nice place to hike out back. ⑤.

Eating

Joe's Diner, 63 Center St, South Lee (☎413/243-9756). Whether you want a weighty corned beef sandwich, tuna salad on rye, or scrambled eggs and waffles, it's hard to go wrong at this popular spot with extremely low prices and attendant lines at peak grazing times.

Salmon Run Fish House, 78 Main St, Lee (☎413/243-3900). Reasonable prices and informal atmosphere for a variety of seafood and pasta dishes.

Great Barrington, Monument Mountain, and Ashley Falls

South of Stockbridge, the landscape takes on a more rusticated flavor, even infiltrating the only town of any size, **GREAT BARRINGTON**. It was the site of the last attempt of the British to hold court in America: Shay's Rebellion ended with five casualties here on February 27, 1787, when the Sheffield militia confronted one hundred anti-government insurgents and the hostages they had taken from Stockbridge. Another claim to fame is **Monument Mountain**, on US-7, five miles north of the town center, a picturesque peak known in literary lore as the place where Nathaniel Hawthorne and Herman Melville met during an afternoon hike in August 1850. In a thunderstorm-induced interlude, they and some other climbers drank champagne and recited poetry; the two authors became fast friends. Yet Great Barrington is perhaps most notable as the unlikely birthplace of one of the greatest civil rights leaders in U.S. history, Dr. **W.E.B. Dubois**, a well-regarded writer and one of the founders of the National Association for the Advancement of Colored People (NAACP).

Today **Great Barrington** is still a modest country town, though one with alternately hip and hippie touches. What buzz there is centers on **Main Street** near Railroad and Castle streets, where upmarket home decor shops bestride a number of good eateries, such as *20 Railroad Street* for casual American food and *Bev's* for even more casual American dining, including home-made ice cream. If it's raining, you might take in a movie at the old fashioned **Mahaiwe Theater** on Castle Street. If it's the season, you may want to pick apples at **Windy Hill Farm** at 686 Stockbridge Rd (☎413/298-3217) or pumpkins at **Taft Farms** on Rte-183 (☎413/528-1515). Just south of town on Rte-7, Guido's is a popular gourmet food market. Rte-23 east from town takes you to tiny **SOUTH EGREMONT**, near which are the **Bash Bish Falls**, named for the Indian girl whose amorous woes prompted her to plunge fifty feet to her demise in a rock-bottom pool. Heading west on Rte-23 from Great Barrington takes you on a more serene trajectory to Monterey, from where you can head back to Tyringham and Lee.

There's little need to proceed much further south on Rte-7 unless you want to go antique shopping or hiking. **SHEFFIELD**, the next town down, is the antique capital of the region. There's not much of a town center, however; if you see an antiques store that grabs your fancy, just pull over by the side of the road and check out the merchandise. **ASHLEY FALLS**, practically straddling the Connecticut border, is the site of **Bartholomew's Cobble**, a mineral outcropping that rises above the placid Housatonic River. A contiguous **nature reserve**, known for its abundant ferns, has a series of easy walking trails that are heavily trodden in summer and fall. Very nearby, on Cooper Hill Road, is the white-clapboard **Ashley House**, a rather unremarkable colonial abode. Built in 1735, this is said to be the oldest house in Berkshire County but is more interesting for its historical associations than anything inside. In 1773, townsmen here drafted the "Sheffield Declaration," a statement of grievances against English rule; in 1781 Ashley's slave Mum Bet sued for freedom – which she won two years later.

Accommodation

The Great Barrington **Chamber of Commerce** can arrange for accommodation via their lodging hotline (☎413/528-4006 or 800/269-4825).

Manor Lane B&B, 145 Hurlburt Rd (☎413/528-8222). Sitting quietly five minutes outside of town, this inviting house offers all the amenities you can ask for at a reasonable price. Make sure to reserve one of the three large rooms ahead of time, and be sure to take advantage of the outside pool, tennis courts, and walking trails. ⑥.

Wainwright Inn, 518 S Main St (☎413/528-2062, *www.wainwrightinn.com*). Huge 1766 mansion right outside the center of town. All rooms have private bath, and full breakfast included. ⑤–⑦.

Windflower, 684 South Egremont Rd/Rte-23, Great Barrington (☎413/528-2720 or 1-800/992-1993). A relaxed country inn with thirteen guest rooms, most with fireplaces – the biggest of which is in room 12. ⑤–⑦.

Eating

Baba Louie's, Main St, Great Barrington (☎413/528-8100). Excellent wood-fired sourdough pizzas, made with local organic produce.

Bizen, 17 Railroad St, Great Barrington (☎413/528-4343). Just about the only place to fill a sushi craving in the Berkshire region. Japanese chefs and energetic atmosphere.

Jack's Grill, Main St, Housatonic (☎413/274-1000). What the owners of *Jack's* saved on rent – this town is in the middle of nowhere – they lavished on romper-room decor, which features a model train that chugs around a track suspended from the ceiling, lunch boxes and tube radios from the 1950s, very funky bathrooms, and more. If only they paid as much attention to the food – which aspires to updated American comfort – it might be worth the detour. A few miles north of Great Barrington, towards Stockbridge.

John Andrew's, Rte-23, South Egremont (☎413/528-34690). Roundly praised contemporary American fare with tasteful decor to match – a double surprise for what appears from the outside to be just another building at the edge of a forest.

La Tomate, 293 Main St/Rte-7, Great Barrington (☎413/528-3003). Great, easy-to-find French bistro with an emphasis on Provençal dishes and simple but delicious desserts.

The Old Mill, Rte-23, South Egremont (☎413/528-1421). Reliably good-tasting New England fare, and sizeable portions of it, in a cozy riverside building that – you guessed it – used to be an old mill.

Pittsfield and around

PITTSFIELD, once a prosperous center for paper milling, is now the grim epitome of a town that has failed to reinvent itself. Worse, it doesn't even appear to be trying. One paper manufacturer in the vicinity, Crane and Company, carries on, in part due to its having cornered the niche market of all-rag papers – used in upscale stationery products, and, perhaps more lucratively, US dollar bills.

The company maintains the **Crane Museum** off Routes 8 and 9 (June–mid-Oct Mon–Fri 2–5pm; free), housed in a old stone mill in nearby Dalton, where the exhibits focus on American paper manufacture since the Revolutionary years. The only other sight that might keep you in Pittsfield is **Arrowhead**, just south of the town center on Holmes Street (May–Oct daily 9am–5pm; $5), the eighteenth-century farmhouse where Herman Melville lived for thirteen years and wrote *Moby Dick*. In Pittsfield itself, the generic art-and-science **Berkshire Museum** (Tues–Sun 9am–5pm; $3) has little that can't be found at similar smaller collections around the country. Otherwise you'd be best off heading out to the Hancock Shaker Village (see below).

Heading north on Rte-7 toward Williamstown, *Bob's Country Kitchen* (☎413/499-3934) in not unlovely Lanesborough is a good place to stop for a cheap, bountiful coffee shop-style breakfast or lunch – especially if you plan a hike at nearby Mount Greylock, Massachusetts' highest peak (see below). Back in Pittsfield, *Dakota*, 1035 South St/Rte-7 (☎413/499-7900), is a capacious place with updated hunting lodge decor, a bit of a relief from the faux hipness of so many Berkshire restaurants. Big portions of American staples like Maine lobster and mesquite-grilled chicken are the draws, as is the large salad bar.

Hancock Shaker Village

Our tools are kind and gentle words, our shop is in the heart, And here we manufacture peace, that we may such impart.

from a Shaker song

From 1790 until 1960, **Hancock Shaker Village**, at the junction of routes 20 and 41 (daily 10am–3pm; $10; ☎413/443-0188), five miles west of Pittsfield, was an active community of the famous offshoot of Quakers from Manchester, England, so named for their convulsive fits of glee experienced when worshipping. The pacifist cult, which was renowned for its vegetable seeds and simply but elegantly crafted furniture, didn't survive, partly due to its members' vows of celibacy, although one community shakes on at Sabbathday Lake in Maine. Hancock was the third Shaker village established, and retains one of the biggest collections of Shaker furniture and objects. Its twenty preserved buildings, located in fairly close proximity amid 1200 acres, are well worth poking about. The most interesting, and most photographed, is **the Round Stone Barn**, built in 1826 and the only one of its kind. Its circular shape allowed a single man to feed 54 cows at the same time from the center. In another unsung instance of Shaker ingenuity, manure was dropped through trap doors to the barn's cellar, where it was stored until needed as fertilizer. Other structures include a schoolhouse, meetinghouse, privies and a two-car garage added in 1914.

Much of the fun to be had at Hancock Shaker Village is of the pastoral variety. In the Barn Complex you can try your hand at a spinning wheel or quill pen, or try on a range of Shaker fashions. You can also milk a plastic cow – if the teats seem spent, ask a guide to turn the heifer on – or chat with a guide tending one of the gardens, where heirloom vegetables are raised. Other activities and demonstrations vary day to day, but could include anything from a plowing match to sheep shearing. The highlight of a visit, however, may well be lunch or a snack in the on-site *Village Café*, which serves inexpensive and surprisingly tasty Shaker specialties and devilishly savory baked goods.

Mount Greylock

To Americans from the western states it will never be more than a sizeable hill, but those from Massachusetts take no small amount of pride in **Mount Greylock**, the tallest peak in the state. Though somewhat short of spectacular, it does make for a scenic hike or drive, especially in the fall. From the peak, at 3491 feet, you can sometimes see five states, though admittedly they all look pretty much the same from here. The ninety-foot-tall **War Memorial Tower**, erected to honor the Massachusetts casualties of all wars, stands near the top. Access to Mount Greylock is easy enough: from Rte-7 one mile north of Lanesborough, turn right (east) onto Rockwell Road, where in two miles there's a **visitor's center** with trail maps and such; the summit is eight miles further.

Williamstown and around

Pretty **WILLIAMSTOWN**, right at the very northwesternmost corner of the state, may seem a bit remote to be one of the region's premier art destinations, but the presence of the **Clark Institute**, with its excellent Impressionist collections, the **Williams College Museum of Art** and the new **Massachusetts Museum of Contemporary Art** a few miles east, in North Adams, has put it on the map. These three, plus the beautiful campus of Williams College and its prime location at the terminus of the Mohawk Trail, make Williamstown a choice spot to spend a few days. Most of the action, of which there is actually little save for during the famous summertime Williamstown Theatre Festival (see box, p.232), centers on block-long **Spring Street**, with the requisite range of shops and restaurants, most infused with an unmistakable upscale-collegiate atmosphere.

> ### THE MOHAWK TRAIL
>
> The best-known scenic route in the Berkshires is the **Mohawk Trail**, otherwise known as Rte-2 from the town of Millers Falls to the Massachusetts–New York border. Originally the 63-mile stretch was a trail that Native Americans of the Five Nations used to travel between the Hudson and Connecticut river valleys. During the French and Indian War, they put it to use as an invasion route. Today the chief attraction of the trail is simply taking in the bucolic vistas it affords on either side.

Accommodation

The 1896 House, Rte-7 (☎413/458-8125, *www.1896house.com*). Close to the center of Williamstown, this easily found hostelry proffers spotless "brookside" and "pondside" accommodations and a good restaurant with traditional and updated Yankee cooking. ④–⑥.

Bed & Breakfast at Field Farm Guest House, 55 Sloan Rd (☎413/458-3135). Five bedrooms, each with private bath, in a 1948 country estate surrounded by nearly 300 acres of meadows and woodlands. ⑥–⑦.

The Maple Terrace Motel, 555 Main St/Rte-2 (☎413/458-9677). Reliable motel set off from the street from which you can walk to the Williamstown Theatre Festival. ④.

The Orchards, 222 Adams Rd (☎413/458-9611 or 1-800/225-1517). This is a modern hotel with a country-inn theme, meaning English antiques, afternoon tea, and several rooms with fireplaces, but twentieth-century touches like TVs and VCRs in the (very spacious) rooms. ⑧.

Steep Acres Farm B&B, 520 White Oaks Rd (☎413/458-3774). Four rooms with shared baths in a 1900 cottage on fifty very scenic acres with an orchard and spring-fed pond; the breakfast is as filling as the environs are relaxing. ③–④.

The Town

What makes Williamstown an essential ingredient of any Berkshires tour is not the college itself – attractive as it is – but rather two superb museums, one of which, the **Sterling and Francine Clark Art Institute** at 225 South St (Tues–Sun 10am–5pm; free), is known far and wide for its extensive collection of French Impressionist paintings – including thirty by Renoir – and it comes as a surprise to see them displayed in so seemingly remote a location. There are also paintings by Fragonard, Géricault, Rembrandt and Alma-Tadema, and a sizeable collection of American works by Homer, Sargent, and Remington. You should allow two hours or so to take it all in, longer if you have a snack or light lunch at the excellent museum café.

Located on the Williams campus, the **Williams College Museum of Art** on Main Street (Tues–Sat 10am–5pm, Sun 1–5pm; free) is ravishing on two counts: its facility and its collections. Part of it is housed in an 1846 two-story brick octagon, capped by a Neoclassical rotunda; a three-story entrance atrium connects it to a contemporary addition, and from the polished floors to lighting and crisply painted walls, the place could not be more immaculately maintained. The thrust of the exceedingly well-curated collection is American visual art from the late eighteenth century to the present day, and some of the best exhibits are those by contemporary artists. The non-Western collections include Asian art and a small but stunning selection of Mesopotamian and ancient Greek antiquities.

Music junkies will want to stop at the **Toonerville Trolley**, 131 Water St (☎413/458-5229), one of the best record stores in the region. There's a cheap selection of used vinyl in the back, an excellent selection of jazz, rock, blues and world music, and a staggering, if pricey, selection of concert recordings. A must for serious collectors.

Around Williamstown

Settled in the 1730s and once a fairly prosperous factory town, the small town of North Adams, on the Mohawk Trail, might be just another post-industrial eyesore save for the **Massachusetts Museum of Contemporary Art** (MASS MoCA), 87 Marshall St, North Adams (daily 10am–6pm; $8), a huge arts center housed in a resurrected old mill site. Poised to become one of the country's leading centers for visual, performing and media arts, MASS MoCA mounts an extensive range of exhibits and performances by international artists. The site comprises 27 refurbished red-brick buildings, linked by a web of bridges, passageways, viaducts, and courtyards. One of the museum's objectives is to showcase works-in-progress, in a variety of media. Most of the work is installation-oriented, and although much of the content may provoke even the most open-minded to wonder aloud, "Can you really call this *art*?," there's an undeniable neo-funhouse pleasure in wandering through the configurations of materials, collages, video monitors, found objects, oversized photographs, flashing lights, and anything else you could imagine (as well as much you probably couldn't). The space also hosts modern dance performances and concerts by such internationally known artists as Patti Smith and Merce Cunningham, and, as if that weren't enough, there's also a film series. Definitely worth a stop, even if you thought you'd had your fill of art in Williamstown.

Eating

Chopsticks Chinese Restaurant, 412 Main St (☎413/458-5750). This minimal Chinese probably won't win any awards, but can be a welcome find in an area with very few non-American restaurants.

Clarksburg Bread Company, 37 Spring St (☎413/458-2251). Sure, they have bread galore, but the coffee cakes and cookies – especially the peanut butter chocolate chip – are what you'll want to fill up on.

Cobble Café, 27 Spring St (☎413/458-5930). Whether the menu is infused with attitude or innovation is up to you, but stick to the quesadillas, salads and such and you'll be fine.

Miss Adams Diner, 53 Park St, Adams (☎413/743-5300). A few miles south of Williamstown, you can order all manner of classic diner fare at this 1949 institution, but what makes it worth braving even the nastiest of weather to get to are the great diner breakfasts and home-made cream pies.

CHAPTER FOUR

RHODE ISLAND

Just 48 miles long by 37 miles wide, tiny **Rhode Island** is easily the smallest state in the Union, barely even noticeable on a map of the country. For that reason alone, it often tends to be overlooked as a tourist destination, even if it is home to more than twenty percent of the nation's historical landmarks. Indeed, locals take great satisfaction in pointing out the state's disproportionately large influence on national life: it enacted the first law against slavery in North America on May 18, 1652, and was one of the first of the thirteen original colonies to declare independence from Great Britain. Rhode Island also claims the city of Newport as the birthplace of the US Navy (though Marblehead, Massachusetts, has a rival claim), and the Blackstone River Valley, which runs northwest from Providence, as the cradle of the Industrial Revolution, an event that followed the 1793 construction of America's first water-powered cotton mill in Pawtucket.

Despite its size, Rhode Island has more than four hundred miles of impressive, sometimes spectacular, coastline with more than one hundred public and private beaches, not to mention thousands of acres of pristine woodlands within a surprisingly diverse geography. Most of this coastline is hacked out of the state's most conspicuous feature, **Narragansett Bay**, a vast expanse of water that has long been a determining factor in Rhode Island's economic development and strategic-military importance. In fact, more than thirty tiny islands make up the state, including Hope, Despair, and the bay's largest island, Rhode Island, which gives the state its name – though it's more often referred to by its Native American name, "Aquidneck."

Rhode Island's size and compactness is, ultimately, one of its most endearing features, and means that you are rarely more than an hour's drive or bus ride away from any other point in the state. The prime destinations are the colonial college town of **Providence**, right on I-95, the main highway that runs through the state (and indeed, the east coast), and well-heeled **Newport**, yachting capital of the world, with good beaches and outrageously extravagant mansions. More scenic than I-95, US-1 hugs the coast of Narragansett Bay – which presents endless opportunities for swimming, boating, and other water-related leisure activities – and parallels the Atlantic coast through **South County** into Connecticut.

ACCOMMODATION PRICE CODES

All accommodation prices in this book have been coded using the symbols below; prices are for the least expensive **double rooms** in each establishment. For a full explanation see p.28 in Basics. Individual rates rather than price codes are given for **hostels**.

① up to $30	④ $60–80	⑦ $130–175
② $30–45	⑤ $80–100	⑧ $175–250
③ $45–60	⑥ $100–130	⑨ $250+

> The area code for all of Rhode Island is ☎401

Along the coast are plenty of sleepy small towns and ports worth a look, most notably **Watch Hill** and **Galilee**. The latter also happens to be the main point of departure for ferries to **Block Island**, a popular excursion for visitors seeking a pleasant stretch of sand.

Some history

The first European to explore the shores of Rhode Island may have been Portuguese navigator **Miguel de Cortereal** who sailed along the coast in 1511, but it was **Giovanni da Verrezano**, an Italian explorer working for France, who arrived in 1524 and remarked on its striking resemblance to the Greek island of Rhodes. One can only surmise either that the weather was foggy, or that the summer heat (and a bottle or two of rum) had gone to his head. Others claim that the name is down to Dutch explorer **Adrian Block**, who in 1614 named an island in Narragansett Bay *Roodt Eylandt* (Red Island) because of its prominent red clay and rocks.

In 1636, dissent among the ranks of the Plymouth colonists prompted the **Reverend Roger Williams** to establish a new colony as a "lively experiment" in religious freedom. Williams did not leave fully of his own accord, though – his radical ideas (including the notions that Indians should be paid for their land and that there should be a total separation of church and state) had incurred the wrath of the Puritan zealots, and they covertly arranged to ship the turbulent cleric back to England. He got word of the plan and managed to escape to present-day Providence, safely out of the jurisdiction of the Massachusetts authorities, where he declared the place a refuge for the oppressed and sent word to his freethinking colleagues in Massachusetts to join him. Relations with local Native Americans – longtime settlers in the region – which had been good up to this point, soured in 1675, when Wampanoag chief King Philip (Metacomet) attacked New England colonists to protect tribal lands in Massachusetts, resulting in what became known as **King Philip's War**. A series of battles culminated in the **Great Swamp Fight** in what is now South Kingstown, where the Wampanoags were virtually wiped out.

By 1680 the first wharf was built, encouraging maritime trade and commerce, especially whaling; a good deal of smuggling occurred, too, helping earn the state the unflattering nickname of "**Rogues' Island.**" Bolstered by economic power and prosperity, self-assured Rhode Islanders were at the forefront of Revolutionary feeling, resenting the stringent economic pressures placed on them from England and declaring independence from the Old Country prior to the other twelve states. However, no Revolutionary battles were ever fought on Rhode Island soil, and the state, apprehensive at the prospect of yielding power to a federal government, was the last to ratify the Constitution.

Between the Revolution and the Civil War, the economic focus shifted from maritime trade to manufacturing, and Rhode Island became the birthplace of the American **Industrial Revolution**, when, in 1790, Pawtucket became the site of the nation's first water-powered **textile mill**, the brainchild of local entrepreneur Samuel Slater. The textile industry lured thousands of immigrant workers, including Russians, French-Canadians and English, into Rhode Island, resulting in the ethnic mix that exists today. Manufacturing still plays an important role in the life of the state, though not in the places that people come to see: Providence and Newport both originated as port cities.

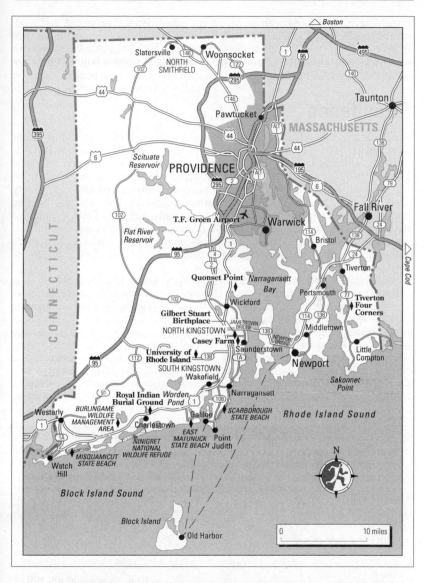

In recent years, Rhode Island's economic fortunes have fluctuated, but confidence took a major nosedive in 1990, in a disastrous **banking crisis** which closed many of the state's credit unions and resulted in the loss of millions of dollars from the savings accounts of thousands of ordinary Rhode Islanders. A tightening of regulations has helped put the state on a more secure financial footing, prompting improvements to the state's infrastructure – including repairs to its crumbling roads – along with some decent urban renewal programs and modernization of the state's main airport, T. F. Green, at Warwick. Meanwhile the vastly improved east coast rail link to Boston and New York has made the state more easily accessible; whether folks will stop by in tangibly greater numbers to investigate is another matter.

Providence

Until recently, the millions who whizzed toward New York or Boston in either direction on I-95 had little incentive, or so they thought, to stop in **PROVIDENCE**, which had always languished in the shadow of its larger and more self-assured neighbors. Put off by the towering chimneys of the elephantine Narragansett Power Station, drab office buildings, and ugly oil tanks and empty shop-fronts along once-prosperous Westminster Street, few took the time to notice that the city center holds more intact colonial and early Federal buildings than any other community in the nation. After an aggressive urban renewal program throughout the late 1990s, the city has emerged with a new sense of pride and vigor reflected by *Money* magazine's naming it the "Best Place to live in the Northeast 2000."

Stretching across seven hills on the Providence and Seekonk Rivers, Providence was Rhode Island's first settlement, established "in commemoration of God's Providence" on land given to **Roger Williams** by the Narragansett Indians. The city flourished as one of the most important ports of call in the notorious "**triangle trade**," where New England rum was exchanged for African slaves to be exchanged in turn for West Indian molasses. Many lavish homes were constructed during this period, some of which can still be seen in the Benefit Street district. Among those who prospered was **James Brown**, who opened a lucrative distillery and slaughterhouse, while also entering the shipping trade. His four sons found success, too: Joseph, an architect responsible for many

---

URBAN REGENERATION IN PROVIDENCE

The 1990s saw an ambitious multi-million-dollar urban regeneration program spearheaded by charismatic mayor **Vincent "Buddy" Cianci**, a last-ditch effort to reverse years of decline and decay. One of the main aims was to open up entire sections of the **Providence River**, which for most of the twentieth century had been buried beneath concrete and steel; a prime beneficiary of this has been the newly established **Waterplace Park**, a four-acre green space surrounding a tidal basin that is afloat with kayaks, canoes, and – in tribute to the Italian heritage of Providence (and its mayor) – gondola rides. The renovation has also involved scores of Providence's historic buildings; meanwhile, a major surge in construction has seen the building of new hotels, a convention center, and a state-of-the-art train station to replace the rotting Union Station. Even the city's airport got a major (and much-needed) facelift. The *pièce de résistance* – though also the work that feels most out of place with the historic atmosphere – is the Providence Place Mall, a massive new downtown shopping facility costing nearly $500 million, with department stores and a hundred fifty or so smaller outlets, a fourteen-screen stadium theater, and plenty of restaurants. Thus far, it all seems to be having the desired knock-on effect, and Providence is buzzing once again.

of the city's most elegant buildings; John, a somewhat ruthless merchant; Nicholas, who donated land for the university that bears his name; and Moses, who helped Samuel Slater introduce the nation's first water-powered cotton mill in nearby Pawtucket, insuring that the textile industry was to become a mainstay of the local economy.

Rhode Island's **capital** since 1901, the city proper, with a population of 160,000, is the third largest in New England (after Boston and Worcester) – and the second largest conurbation, with a population of around 900,000. The compactness of its **downtown** area, bounded on the south by I-195, to the west by I-95, to the east by College Hill and to the north by Constitution Hill – bursting with energy and full of cafes, restaurants, shops and nightclubs – means that you can see most of the main attractions on foot. The city's **ethnic diversity**, one of its greatest strengths, is reflected in the large Italian community on **Federal Hill**, west of the river, and by fairly voluble Greek and Portuguese – especially Cape Verdean – communities elsewhere in the city.

The oldest and most interesting section of Providence, where founder Roger Williams and his followers first settled, lies on the eastern side of the riverfront area along North and South Main streets and Benefit Street. Known as the **East Side**, it's crowned by **College Hill**, a showcase of architectural preservation, and home to Ivy League **Brown University** and the **Rhode Island School of Design** (RISD or "Rizdee"), both of which give the place a certain cultural verve, at least in their immediate vicinities.

Arrival, information, and getting around

T.F. Green Airport is on Post Road, just off I-95 in **Warwick** (☎401/737-4000), nine miles south of downtown Providence. It's not an international airport (unless flights to Canada count), but there are connections to all main US cities. The Amtrak **train station**, 100 Gaspar St (☎1-800/USA-RAIL), is housed in a domed building a short walk southwest of the capitol building. Greyhound and Bonanza **buses** stop downtown at Kennedy Plaza; Bonanza's main terminus is considerably further out at 1 Bonanza Way, off I-95 (☎401/751-8800). Local bus transportation is provided by RIPTA (Rhode Island Passenger Transport Association; Mon–Sat 7am–7pm; ☎401/781-9400), with most city and statewide services operating from Kennedy Plaza. Particularly useful for getting round downtown are RIPTA's Gold Line – which runs from north to south across the central area – and its Green Line, running from east to west. Services run every eleven minutes, and cost $1.25, however many stops you're traveling. There's a transport **information booth** in Kennedy Plaza (Mon–Fri 7am–6pm), and bus schedules are available, but despite the advertised hours, don't count on it being staffed. You don't really need a **car** to get around – Providence is a very walkable city and sightseeing best done on foot – but just in case, most major **car rental** companies have offices around town; if you don't mind an older car, Rent-a-Wreck, 1078 Douglas Ave (☎401/454-1234, *www.rent-a-wreck.com*), will do the trick at about half the cost of renting a new car.

The **CVB**, 1 W Exchange St (Mon–Fri 10am–5pm; ☎401/751-1177 or 1-800/233-1636), provides maps and brochures, as does the **Providence Preservation Society** located in the 1772 Shakespeare's Head, 21 Meeting St (Mon–Fri 9am–5pm; ☎401/831-7440), a pre-Revolutionary wood frame dwelling which once housed the family and printing press of John Carter, a prominent local worthy and publisher of the *Providence Gazette*. Information on self-guided historic tours is available here, including the innovative **Banner Trail**, which takes in the city's main cultural, historic, and architectural sights through a system of banners, information centers, indoor galleries, outdoor murals, and art exhibitions. There's yet another **information center** in the Roger Williams National Memorial Park, 282 N Main St (daily: summer 9am–5pm; rest of the year 9am–4.30pm; ☎401/785-3510).

Accommodation

Providence is not exactly brimming with **places to stay**, though the city's recent redevelopment included the building of a 350-room hotel, the *Westin* (see review below); the hopes are – among city officials at least – that this will be the first of many such new constructions in the future. There are fairly few **budget rooms** available around town, and no **hostels**, although **B&Bs** are a viable option – Anna's Victorian Connection, (☎1-800/884-4288) can book these type of rooms for a $5 commission. Motorists can take advantage of the swath of mid-priced **motels** along I-95 towards Pawtucket, north of the city, and to the south near the airport in Warwick. **Camping** is not much of an option, with the closest sites fifteen miles away in Coventry.

Annie Brownell House B&B, 400 Angell St (☎401/454-2934, *www.members.home.net /satunder*). Nice and spacious Colonial Revival house built in 1899, within walking distance of the city's main attractions. The newly refurbished guest rooms are bright and airy and are decorated in period style; friendly owner, too. ⑤.

C.C. Ledbetter Bed & Breakfast, 326 Benefit St (☎401/351-4699). Clean rooms in a 200-year-old house, with harbor views. ④.

The Cady House, 127 Power St (☎401/273-2934). An elegant, classical revival house set on College Hill, adorned with antiques and folk art. A good location for Brown, RISD and downtown. ④–⑤.

Comfort Inn, 1940 Post Rd, Warwick (☎401/732-0470). Adequate lodging in this chain motel, located right by the airport. Also a branch at 2 George St, in nearby Pawtucket (see p.000; ☎401/723-6700). ④–⑤.

Day's Hotel on the Harbor, 220 India Point (☎401/272-5577). Reasonably priced entry overlooking India Point Park on the east side of town, next to I-195. ③–④.

Holiday Inn Downtown, 21 Atwells Ave (☎401/831-3900). Standard chain hotel offering next to the Civic Center and close to the restaurants of Little Italy. ⑥.

The Old Court, 144 Benefit St (☎401/831-3900, *www.oldcourt.com*). Charming B&B in an old red-brick rectory near RISD, featuring ten rooms done up with Victorian trimmings. ⑥.

The Providence Biltmore, Kennedy Plaza (☎401/421-0700, *www.grandheritage.com*). A Providence landmark since 1922, the *Biltmore* may be the prime place to stay here, if you can afford it: elegant, newly restored city-view rooms in a convenient downtown location. ⑧.

The Providence Marriott, Charles & Orme streets (☎401/272-2400, *www.marriott.com*). Large luxury hotel with a convenient downtown location. ⑧.

State House Inn, 43 Jewitt St (☎401/785-1235, *www.providence-inn.com*). Pleasant, central B&B in a restored former tenement near the state capitol; rooms are outfitted with antique furnishings. ④.

Susse Chalet Warwick, 36 Jefferson Blvd, Warwick (☎401/941-6600, *www.sussechalet.com*). Comfortable rooms in a chain noted for its exceptional value. Outside the city, but still close to I-95 for easy access. ④–⑥.

The Westin, 1 W Exchange St (☎401/598-8021, *www.westin.com*). Deluxe modern accommodation, which shows in the prices, in this newish multistory hotel; close to all the city sights. ⑧.

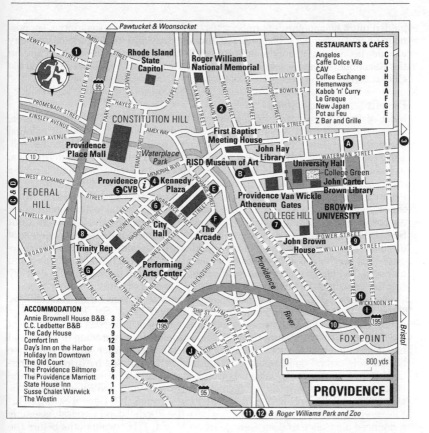

RESTAURANTS & CAFÉS

Angelos	C
Caffe Dolce Vila	D
CAV	J
Coffee Exchange	H
Hemenways	B
Kabob 'n' Curry	A
Le Greque	F
New Japan	G
Pot au Feu	E
Z Bar and Grille	I

ACCOMMODATION

Annie Brownell House B&B	3
C.C. Ledbetter B&B	7
The Cady House	9
Comfort Inn	12
Day's Inn on the Harbor	10
Holiday Inn Downtown	8
The Old Court	2
The Providence Biltmore	6
The Providence Marriott	4
State House Inn	1
Susse Chalet Warwick	11
The Westin	5

PROVIDENCE

The City

Providence's main attractions focus around three of its seven hills. Downtown, which centers on **Kennedy Plaza**, is sited just below **Constitution Hill**. **City Hall**, at the western end of the Plaza, is mostly notable for a star-spangled midnight blue ceiling in the Alderman's Chamber; though designed in the style of the Louvre and the Tuileries palaces in Paris, you'll find nothing to compare with the *Mona Lisa* here. The nearby Beaux Arts **Union Station**, built in 1898 but no longer in use as a train terminal, is a fine example of the kind of historic restoration at which the city excels. To the southeast of the Plaza, in Westminster Mall, is the 1828 **Arcade**, the sole survivor of many such "temples of trade" built in America during the Greek Revival period and America's oldest indoor shopping mall. Now it's a lively marketplace, with plenty of trendy places to eat, drink, and buy expensive designer clothes. The state's only national park, the **Roger Williams National Memorial**, at the corner of North Main and Smith streets, was the site of the original settlement of Providence in 1636, and includes an original well said to have been used by Williams and his followers. At the top of the hill, the white marble **State Capitol** (Mon–Fri 8.30am–4.30pm;

guided tours by appointment only; ☎401/277-2357) sports a vast dome, supposedly the fourth largest self-supported dome in the world, that dominates the city skyline. Inside, you can view the original Rhode Island Charter of 1663 and, in the Reception Room, a portrait of George Washington by Rhode Island artist Gilbert Stuart.

Benefit Street and around

Most of Providence's historic legacy can be found in the **College Hill** area, across the river from downtown – an attractive tree-lined district of colonial buildings, museums, and **Brown University** facilities. Part of Williams' religious experiment was the establishment of a Baptist church, the first in America, in 1638: the white-clapboard **First Baptist Meeting House**, 75 N Main St, is the third such church building on the site, built in 1775 and topped by a tall steeple inspired by St Martin-in-the-Fields in London. The street leads into **South Main Street**, once bustling with waterfront activity and now home to a number of new upmarket restaurants, though the real action is a block up the hill, on **Benefit Street**. This is Providence's "mile of history" – the most impressive collection of original colonial homes in America. Lined with the beautifully restored white-clapboard residences of Providence's merchants and sea captains, it was just a dirt track leading to graveyards until it was improved in the eighteenth century "for the benefit of the people of Providence," hence its name.

The elegant **John Brown House**, 52 Power St at Benefit Street (March–Dec Tues–Sat 10am–5pm, Sun noon–4pm; Jan & Feb Fri & Sat 10am–5pm, Sun noon–4pm; $5), a three-story residence constructed in 1786, was home to one of the city's most aggressive merchants, who made his money trading in slaves and building commercial links with China. Designed by his brother Joseph, the house has a lovely central hall flanked by large formal rooms used by Brown to entertain his illustrious guests; it also retains much original furnishing, silverware, and china, and holds displays on the formidable Brown family and Rhode Island history in general. The plain, dignified **Old State House**, 150 Benefit St (Mon–Fri 8.30am–4.30pm; free), built in 1762, is where the Rhode Island General Assembly renounced allegiance to King George III on May 4, 1776, two months before the Declaration of Independence.

Further up the street, the small but excellent collection of the **RISD Museum of Art**, 224 Benefit St (July to Labor Day Wed–Sat noon–5pm; Labor Day to June Tues–Thurs & Sat 10.30am–5pm, Fri noon–8pm, Sun 2–5pm; $5, free Sat), Rhode Island's leading museum of fine and decorative arts, is worthy of its association with one of the foremost art schools in the country. The antiquities section contains a Ptolemaic Egyptian mummy, Roman frescoes, and fabulous array of Greek coins, while the Asian art collection includes more than six hundred Japanese bird-and-flower woodblock prints and a Heian Buddha – the largest historic Japanese wooden sculpture in the States. Other wings are devoted to textiles and costumes, paintings and prints, and multimedia contemporary art. Across the road, the Greek Revival **Providence Atheneum**, 251 Benefit St (year-round Mon–Thurs 10am–8pm, Fri & Sat 10am–5pm, Sun 1–5pm; closed Sun in summer; free), is where Edgar Allan Poe and Sarah Whitman carried on their courtship among the stacks. The library, one of America's oldest, holds original Audubon prints and rare books, and the piano and hand-painted chairs in the cozy reading rooms give it the feel of someone's living room.

Brown University

The extensive campus of Ivy League **Brown University**, a short walk up Waterman Street from RISD, occupies 133 acres of College Hill, giving the whole neighborhood a relaxed, intellectual feel. The third oldest college in New England, and seventh oldest in the nation, it was founded in 1764 in Warren as Rhode Island College before it moved forty years later to Providence, where it was renamed after Nicholas Brown II, who donated substantial funds and extensive land. The wrought-iron **Van Wickle Gates**, on Prospect Street, lead on to the historic core of the university, pleasant **College Green**, skirted by a collection of mostly colonial and Greek Revival buildings, among which stands the 1904 Beaux Arts **John Carter Brown Library** (Mon–Fri 8.30am–5pm, Sat 9am–noon; free), with an extensive collection of Americana, including the first printed accounts of Columbus's arrival in the New World. Nearby, the school's oldest building – dating from 1770 – **University Hall**, which stood alone on College Hill for its first fifty years, was used as a barracks for the Revolutionary troops and their French allies.

Of the other 150 or so buildings that constitute the university, don't miss the **John Hay Library**, just down the road from University Hall, home to Brown University's special collections, where you can see hundreds of Abe Lincoln manuscripts and a vast display of miniature soldiers (Mon–Fri 9am–5pm; free). For **free tours** of the Brown University campus, contact the admissions office, 45 Prospect St (Mon–Fri 8am–4pm; tours 10am, 11am, 1pm, 3pm & 4pm; 11am & 3pm only during Christmas and Spring Break. Mid-Sept–mid-Nov Sat tours only 10am, 11am, noon).

Behind College Hill, happening **Thayer Street** and neighboring streets are home to the half dozen or so best bookstores in the area, while at the eastern end of the hill, studenty **Wickenden Street** buzzes with an assortment of thrift stores, cafés, galleries and restaurants. Further towards Gano Street lies the increasingly gentrified **Fox Point** district, once Providence's main Portuguese neighborhood, with many pastel-shaded dwellings redolent of Cape Verde and bakeries selling Portuguese delicacies.

Federal Hill and Roger Williams Zoo

Back west of downtown, **Federal Hill**, Providence's **Little Italy**, can be entered through a large arch topped with a bronze pinecone at Atwells Avenue. Long a powerful Mafia stronghold, this area is one of the safest and friendliest in the city, where you can savor the nuances of Italian culture and cuisine in dozens of restaurants, bakeries and grocery stores. If it's just a drink you want, head to the bars and cafés around the **Piazza DePasquale**, where there's even a large Italianate fountain, reminiscent of the kind found in Naples. Meanwhile south of Federal Hill, at 100 South Street, accessed by bus #1 or #3 from Kennedy Plaza, or from I-95 exit 20, is the excellent **Providence Children's Museum** (year-round Tues–Sun 9.30am–5pm; $4.50), where the range of interactive displays includes a fun look at teeth in a giant mouth, a walk-in kaleidoscope, a time-traveling adventure through Rhode Island's history and a chance to climb down a manhole and explore the world below street level.

A few miles southwest of downtown, off exit 17 of I-95, the 430-acre **Roger Williams Park** spills with serpentine paths, rolling hills, and peaceful ponds. Aside from a **carousel** and a **Museum of Natural History**, there's the **Roger**

Williams Zoo, with nearly a thousand animals, including giraffes, cheetah and zebra in a "Plains of Africa" area, a tropical rainforest, a Madagascar exhibit of endangered lemurs, and an Australasian section with an open-air aviary and clouded leopard exhibit. Even if zoos aren't normally your thing, you can't help but admire the imaginative way this one has been laid out, with its close attention to culture and history, alongside zoology (daily: Memorial Day to Labor Day 9am–5pm (6pm weekends); rest of year 9am–4pm; $6, children $3.50).

Eating

Providence's ethnic diversity means that it's never difficult to find good food here. **Thayer Street** is lined with inexpensive lunch places, almost all of which stay open until late. Nearby **Wickenden Street** is more alternative, and more expensive, while the family-run Italian restaurants on **Federal Hill** offer superb value; **downtown** is home to a burgeoning bevy of up-and-coming establishments.

Cafes

Caffe Dolce Vita, 59 DePasquale Square (☎401/331-8240). Sandwiches, salads and desserts made with fresh and imported Italian ingredients.

Coffee Exchange, 207 Wickenden St (☎401/273-1198). This happening coffee bar is a popular meeting place for would-be intellectuals; deck chairs and barrels act as pavement seating and tables.

Restaurants

Al Forno and **Provincia at Al Forno**, 577 S Main St (☎401/273-9760). Upstairs, at *Al Forno*, you can try the wood-grilled pizzas, pasta, and interesting twists on steak and seafood at what has been called one of the five best restaurants in America; downstairs, the newer *Provincia* features a mix of Italian and Provençal dishes. Whichever spot – or cuisine – you choose, expect to pay upwards of $20 a dish.

Angelo's, 141 Atwells Ave (☎401/621-8171). Family-style restaurant offering affordable Italian standards.

Anthony's, 1065 Chalkstone Ave (☎401/331-6401). Established over sixty years in the same location, this moderately priced restaurant is one of Providence's best Italian joints.

Atomic Grill, 99 Chestnut St (☎401/621-8888). Lively, hip, off-beat restaurant, with a wide range of choices from steaks to quesadillas. Live jazz on Monday.

CAV Restaurant, Antiques and Gifts, 14 Imperial Pl (☎401/751-9164). Trendy eating place in an atmospheric historic loft; live jazz after 9.30pm from Thurs to Mon. Stop by next door at 18 Imperial Pl to check out the working studio and glass gallery featuring art and jewelry by local stand-out David Van Noppen and other glass artists.

Hemenways, 1 Old Stone Square, S Main St (☎401/351-8570). Classic international seafood like Norwegian salmon and Alaskan king crab, to be eaten in an attractive glass atrium setting.

Intermezzo, 220 Weybosset St (☎401/331-5100). Conveniently located next to the Providence Performing Arts center, this cozy bistro-style restaurant is a great place for a pre- or post-theater meal.

Kabob 'n' Curry, 261 Thayer St (☎401/273-8844). Above-average Indian meals on lively Thayer Street.

Le Greque, 24 Arcade Mall (☎401/351-4354). The cheapest yet most interesting food of all the shops in the mall. Greek specialties include marinated chickpeas and rice and spinach pies.

New Japan, 145 Washington St (☎401/351-0300). Reasonably priced Japanese place, with excellent tempura and teriyaki; sushi only served on Sundays.

Pot au Feu, 44 Custom House St (☎401/273-8953). Salon dining upstairs, moderately priced bistro downstairs, but a cozy, romantic atmosphere in both. Try the bouillabaisse.

Z Bar and Grille, 244 Wickenden St (☎401/831-1566). Boxing matches once took place in this spot, the former *Ringside Café*. It retains that boisterous environment while serving up decent salads, burgers, steaks and the like.

Nightlife and entertainment

Providence's **nightlife**, concentrated mainly in the city's commercial core off Kennedy Plaza, is largely student-generated, which means things can get a bit quiet during the vacations, though **Thayer Street** is always throbbing. On summer evenings, a **party trolley** with balloons and noisy music rumbles through downtown, offering entrance to six nightclubs on its route (Fri & Sat 8.30pm–2am; $6; ☎401/861-1385).

For those less inclined towards drink, the Cable Car Cinema, 204 S Main St (☎401/272-3970), and the Avon Rep Cinema, 250 Thayer St (☎401/421-3315), show good independent and art **films**, while the Tony Award-winning Trinity Rep, 201 Washington St (☎401/351-4242), one of America's foremost regional theaters, puts on innovative productions of contemporary and classic **plays** in two different theater spaces year-round. The Providence Performing Arts Center, 220 Weybosset St (☎401/421-2787), hosts **musicals** and other lavish productions in a grand old (recently restored) Art Deco movie house. Complete entertainment listings can be found in the free weekly *Providence Phoenix* and the *Providence Journal*'s Thursday edition.

Bars

AS220, 115 Empire St (☎401/831-9327). Unabashedly artsy café-bar hangout for locals and students. Also a music venue featuring everything from mellow jazz to performance art; there's a gallery on the second floor. Cover $2–5.

Finnegan's Wake, 397 Westminster St (☎401/751-0290). Authentic Irish pub, right down to the corned beef and cabbage.

Snooker's Café, 145 Clifford St (☎401/351-7665). Lively pool hall with a variety of table games. Its green room features alternative DJs and is one of the city's most sociable spots. No cover.

Trinity Brewhouse, 186 Fountain St (☎401/453-2337). Hang out here after a Providence Bruins (minor league hockey) or Friars (college basketball) game to quaff microbrews in either celebration or despair.

Union Street Station, 69 Union St (☎401/331-2291). Lively gay bar attracts a fairly mixed crowd for nightly boogeying.

Clubs and live music

Club Oxygen, 235 Promenade St (☎401/521-7110). The latest dance sounds in countercultural surroundings. Thurs–Sat only.

G Clef, 40 Tockwotten St (☎401/273-0095). Club offering jazz to a mainly collegiate set.

Lupo's Heartbreak Hotel, 239 Westminster St (☎401/272-5876). This is *the* spot in town to see nationally recognized bands rock Providence.

Metropolis, 172 Pine St (☎401/454-5483). Downtown hotspot, offering international DJs and a spectacular light show.

Sh-Booms, 108 N Main St (☎401/751-1200). Car-hopping dance club featuring music from the 1950s to the 1980s, plus today's Top 40, all by request.

Strand Theater, 79 Washington St (☎401/272-8900). The place in town for heavy metal and rock music, with a large space for dancing.

Around Providence: Pawtucket, Woonsocket, and Bristol

Northwest of Providence, the **Blackstone River Valley** has been given special status by the Department of the Interior for its role in America's development as the world's leading industrial power. It's a gritty strip, really, with not much of a future, but clearly plenty of past, beginning with **PAWTUCKET**, just a few short miles up I-95 from downtown Providence. Here you can start your explorations back through time at the **Slater Mill Historic Site**, where the **Old Slater Mill** was built to house the innovative machinery Samuel Slater developed (see box below). Today, the mill contains a copy of an original carding engine, a spinning frame and mule, and some very rare textile machines that date from 1838 up to the 1960s, all conspiring to illustrate the process of transforming raw cotton to yarn. Also included in this living museum is the 1810 **Wilkinson Mill**, where a nineteenth-century machine shop, complete with belt-driven machine tools, still operates, and the 1758 **Sylvanus Brown House**, 67 Roosevelt Ave, an early skilled worker's home furnished as it was in the early 1800s. (Historic site open May–Nov Mon–Sat 10am–5pm, Sun noon–5pm; Dec–Apr Sat 10am–5pm, Sun noon–5pm; $6).

Slater and a group of business partners, including his brother John, pioneered the building of **Slatersville**, off Route 146 in North Smithfield, a model village constructed in 1808 to accommodate the workers who labored in the two mills they had built nearby. The village remains intact, restored earlier this cen-

---

THE BIRTHPLACE OF THE INDUSTRIAL REVOLUTION

The Blackstone River cuts through the northeastern portion of Rhode Island, not much of a landmark in and of itself – but it was largely along these riverbanks that the Industrial Revolution had its seeds in America. Dubbed the **Blackstone River National Heritage Corridor** and stretching from Providence to Worcester, Massachusetts, it encompasses two dozen of the original manufacturing communities where thousands of Americans and immigrants came to work and live, at least until the valley's demise.

The area was a desolate wilderness when its first white settler, **Reverend William Blackstone**, arrived here in 1635 after fleeing the intolerant Puritan regime in Boston. More settlers arrived, of whom one Joseph Jencks, Jr, a blacksmith by trade, realized that the vast forests of **Pawtucket** would provide a virtually inexhaustible supply of timber to fire a forge. His new smithy boomed, and soon other blacksmiths began to settle here, setting the stage for future development.

The industrial expansion received a huge boost in 1793, when **Samuel Slater**, a manufacturer's apprentice originally hailing from Derbyshire, England, with the help of entrepreneur Moses Brown, of the wealthy Providence family, used new technology surreptitiously imported from his native land to produce cotton yarn. The resultant success fueled another century of high prosperity, but as you'll find touring the preserved mills, much of the machinery has not been spinning for some time, most of the companies having relocated to the south, where overhead and labor were much cheaper.

For an unusual perspective of the Blackstone River Valley's history and environment, a narrated **riverboat tour** departs from various locations, run by Blackstone Valley Explorer (Apr–Oct; ☎401/724-1500 or 1-800/619-BOAT).

tury, its small, white-clapboard homes, churches, schools, and meeting house still visible round a pretty village green.

A few miles east in **WOONSOCKET**, another major manufacturing center, the fascinating new **Museum of Work and Culture**, at 42 S Main St (Mon–Fri 9.30am–4.30pm, Sat 10am–5pm, Sun 1–5pm; $5), traces the story of mill workers who came from the farms of Quebec in the last third of the eighteenth century to work in the shoe and textile factories of New England. A self-guided journey through the workaday world of Woonsocket's residents and immigrant arrivals takes you from the shop floor of a textile mill to the porch of a three-story tenement house and lets you out on the real-life city streets.

Bristol

Fifteen miles southeast of Providence on Ferry Route Road (Route 114), the town of **BRISTOL** holds, unexpectedly, the oldest and largest **Fourth of July** celebration in the nation, a parade and fireworks spectacular that attracts hundreds of thousands of spectators. Otherwise, the only thing to bring you here is the **Blithewold Mansion and Gardens** (grounds open year-round Tues–Sun 10am–5pm; mansion open mid-Apr–mid-Oct Wed–Sun 11am–3.30pm; $8), one-time summer residence of Pennsylvania coal magnate Augustus Van Wickle and his wife Bessie, who filled the 45-room manor house with knick-knacks from her globetrotting adventures. The arboretum merits a wander too; seek out the 83-foot giant redwood, an anomaly in these parts, for a good photo opportunity.

Newport

NEWPORT, cheekily named "America's First Resort," is probably best known for its summer "cottages" – more like huge palaces – which were built by nineteenth-century industrial magnates and business tycoons each trying to outdo one another. These monuments to opulence and greed, like **Rosecliff** and **Beechwood** on **Bellevue Avenue**, offer a glimpse into the ostentatious lives behind such names as the **Astors** and **Vanderbilts**, but even before those families arrived on the scene, Newport had established itself as a major port, rivaling New York and Boston in size and importance.

First settled in 1639 by refugees from neighboring Massachusetts seeking **religious freedom**, the area was soon recognized for its excellent **trade location** and quickly developed into a bustling seaport. Although the city became renowned for its liberal approach in matters of religion, which brought an influx of Jews, Quakers, and Baptists to the city, such charity did not extend to the slave trade; in the eighteenth century, the local fleet was heavily involved in trading African **slaves** for West Indian sugar and molasses and the city was a haven for privateers, often barely distinguishable from pirates.

The prosperity that international trade had brought suffered a severe setback when British and Hessian troops occupied Newport in 1776, blockading the harbor and forcing residents to use the city's timber wharves as firewood during the brutally cold winter. During the next three years, many locals fled, buildings were either destroyed or left to decay, and the city floundered. By the end of the war, so poor was the city that townsfolk wanting to expand their properties could not even afford to tear down their own homes, let alone rebuild. The wealth of fine **colonial buildings** seen today is largely the result of this.

In the 1850s, the town became fashionable again as a resort for wealthy Southern merchants, and very soon nouveau riche industrialists such as the Astors, Belmonts, and Vanderbilts were building the mansions along the coastline for which the city has become known. Despite an end to the decadence, the city kept on as a major naval town, home to the **United States Naval War College**, and is a prime playpen for the yachting set: in 1980 and 1983 the **America's Cup Race** was held off Newport, and every summer the harbor is lined with majestic sailboats, pleasure boats, and touring vessels. There's no question that today's Newport is unashamedly geared to the tourist, as a stroll around the tacky harbor area will testify. Somehow, though, the rough old port still manages to linger, with beer and R&B clubs as evident as cocktails and cruises, making this an essential urban stop, especially during the summer **festival season**. Additionally, Newport is a good base for exploring the more peaceful neighboring towns of **Portsmouth** and **Middletown**, and, across the bay, the appealing villages of **Tiverton Four Corners** and **Little Compton**, full of stone-walled country lanes, rocky shorelines, and idyllic beaches.

Arrival, information, and getting around

Newport, Middletown and Portsmouth are all located on **Aquidneck**, also known as Rhode Island. The island is connected to the mainland from I-95 and the west by Route 138, which crosses the impressive **Newport Bridge** ($2 toll). The nearest Amtrak (☎1-800/USA-RAIL) **station** is on Route 138 at South Kingstown, some nineteen miles away.

Newport itself, spanning only ten miles, is eminently walkable. **Thames** (pronounced *Thaymz*) **Street** is the main drag; it's separated from the shops and restaurants of the harbor district by **Admiral's Cup Avenue**, a wide, ugly road that doesn't even succeed in speeding up traffic through the town, especially in the summer. It's here, at no. 23, that you will find Newport's main **visitor center**, a vast, glitzy operation with plenty of maps, guides and advice to keep you busy (daily: summer 8am–8pm; rest of year 9am–5pm; ☎401/849-8048 or 1-800/326-6030). Parking in the adjacent Gateway Center's parking lot is free for the first hour.

The **Gateway Center** is in fact the terminal for Bonanza Buses (☎401/846-1820) and RIPTA buses, which run through town and out to the beaches and Providence ($1–3; ☎401/781-9400 or 1-800/244-0444). Also based here are free summer **shuttle buses** which connect the main sights and shopping areas (daily 10am–7pm); Viking Tours, whose bus and harbor excursions include admission to one or more mansions ($12.50–25; ☎401/847-6921); and Newport Trolley Tours ($7.50; ☎401/849-8005), whose all-day tickets allow you to hop on and off the **trolleys** that make continuous loops through downtown and to the mansions. Rental **bikes** are good for getting around, especially if you're heading to one of the beaches; it's $5 per hour ($25 per day, $70 per week) from Ten Speed Spokes, 18 Elm St (☎401/847-5609).

The Newport Historical Society, 82 Touro St (Tues–Fri 9.30am–4.30pm; ☎401/846-0813), organizes **walking tours** through colonial Newport on summer Fridays and Saturdays at 10am, with a $5 fee. Other walking tours are provided on a daily basis between April and November by **Newport On Foot** (☎401/846-5391; $7). If you must rent a **car**, International Car Rental, 6 Valley Rd, Middletown (☎401/847-4600), will deliver the vehicle to your hotel, but be warned: parking is a major problem on the city's narrow streets. Easily the best and most relaxing way of getting a good overview of the mansions and town is on the beautiful 72-foot **schooner** ***Madeleine*** (☎401/849-3033), which departs four times a day from Bannister's Wharf; the two-hour tour costs $20.

Accommodation

Newport has plenty of reasonably priced **guesthouses**, but it's always a good idea to **book ahead**, especially on summer weekends when prices can skyrocket. The visitor center (see above) has free phone links to inns and motels in all price ranges. Due in part to the abundance of Victorian mansions, the most common form of accommodation here is the **B&B**. Large rooms often with fireplaces and ocean views can be expected; however, prices can get a little steep. To find something a bit more stripped down and for a better price there are three established agencies: Bed and Breakfast of Rhode Island (☎401/849-1298 or 1-800/828-0000), which can find rooms from around $75, Anna's Victorian Connection, 5 Fowler Ave, Newport (☎401/849-2489 or 1-800/884-4288), whose range starts at about $45, and Bed & Breakfast of Newport, 33 Russell Ave (☎401/846-5408), which specializes in smaller bed-and-breakfasts (see p.62) you might otherwise find difficult to locate. One problem you might run into throughout Newport is accommodation options for travelers with children under twelve – make sure to call ahead and confirm individual policies.

1885 Marshall Slocum Guest House, 29 Kay St (☎401/841-5120, *www.marshallslocuminn.com*). Close to Bellevue Ave, this unpretentious inn is located in a former parsonage. [4]–[5].

Admiral Fitzroy Inn, 398 Thames St (☎401/848-8000 or 1-800/343 2863, *www.admiralsonns.com*). Cheerfully decorated B&B in the heart of the action, with a roof deck overlooking the harbor and excellent breakfasts. [7].

The Clarkeston, 28 Clarke St (☎401/849-7397 or 1-800/524-1386, *www.innsofnewport.com*). Sumptuous circa 1705 colonial inn with working fireplaces, jacuzzi tubs, canopy and feather beds. [7].

Chase Farm B&B, 308 Chases Lane, Middletown (☎401/849-9223). Romantic Victorian farmhouse with wonderful waterview sunsets and just a few minutes to Newport's main attractions. [6].

Cliffside Inn, 2 Seaview Ave (☎401/847-1811, *www.cliffsideinn.com*). Gorgeous 1876 Victorian manor house, one minute from the Cliff Walk and First Beach. All rooms have fireplaces, private baths, telephones, air-conditioning and cable TV plus full breakfast and afternoon tea. [8]

Commodore Perry Inn, 348 Thames St (☎401/846-4256 or 1-800/343-2863). Clean and comfortable rooms in a prime position above a restaurant. [3].

Elm Tree Cottage, 336 Gibbs Ave (☎401/849-1610, *www.elm-tree.com*). A former summer house with antique-filled rooms, tucked away in a quiet neighborhood overlooking Easton Pond and First Beach. [7].

Howard Johnson Lodge, 351 E Main Rd, Middletown (☎401/849-2000 or 1-800/446-4656, *www.hojo.com*). Two miles north of downtown Newport, this represents the best hotel value in the area. Much-reduced rates outside of peak season in July & August. [5].

Jailhouse Inn, 13 Marlborough St (☎401/847-4638 or 1-800/427-9444). Spacious modern rooms with jailhouse trimmings in this restored 1772 clink, right in the heart of town. [6]–[7].

Las Palmas Inn, 12 Collins St (☎401/848-0708). Unusual inn done out in "Key West Victorian" style and close to all the main attractions. [7].

Melville House, 39 Clarke St (☎401/847-0640, *www.melvillehouse.com*). Colonial B&B in a peaceful location two blocks from the harbor; the rooms are small, but pleasant. [7].

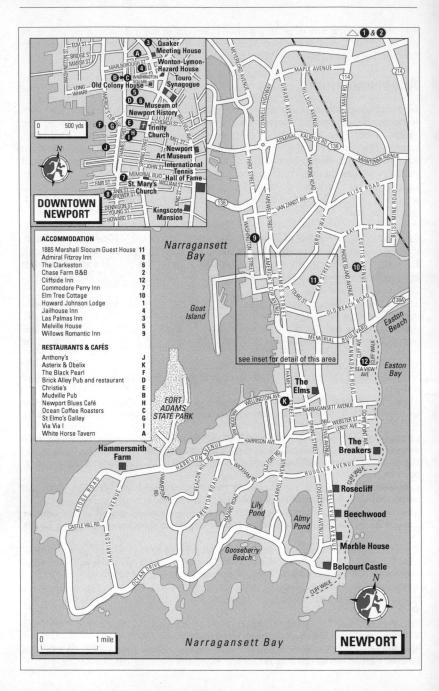

DOWNTOWN NEWPORT

A. Quaker Meeting House
Wonton-Lymon-Hazard House
Old Colony House
Touro Synagogue
Museum of Newport History
Trinity Church
Newport Art Museum
International Tennis Hall of Fame
St. Mary's Church
Kingscote Mansion

0   500 yds

Narragansett Bay

Goat Island

ACCOMMODATION

1885 Marshall Slocum Guest House	11
Admiral Fitzroy Inn	8
The Clarkeston	6
Chase Farm B&B	2
Cliffside Inn	12
Commodore Perry Inn	7
Elm Tree Cottage	10
Howard Johnson Lodge	1
Jailhouse Inn	4
Las Palmas Inn	3
Melville House	5
Willows Romantic Inn	9

RESTAURANTS & CAFÉS

Anthony's	J
Asterix & Obelix	K
The Black Pearl	F
Brick Alley Pub and restaurant	D
Christie's	E
Mudville Pub	B
Newport Blues Café	H
Ocean Coffee Roasters	C
St Elmo's Galley	G
Via Via I	I
White Horse Tavern	A

see inset for detail of this area

Easton Beach

Easton Bay

The Elms

FORT ADAMS STATE PARK

Hammersmith Farm

The Breakers

Rosecliff

Beechwood

Lily Pond

Almy Pond

Marble House

Gooseberry Beach

Belcourt Castle

N

CASTLE HILL RD

0   1 mile

Narragansett Bay

NEWPORT

The Old Beach Inn, 19 Old Beach Rd (☎401/849-3479 or 1-888/303-5033, *www.oldbeachinn.com*). A romantic and handsome B&B boasting seven rooms each decorated in a floral theme (rose room, morning glory room etc), all with private bath, some with fireplaces and air-conditioning. Generous continental breakfasts and private parking. [5].
Willows Romantic Inn, 8–10 Willow St (☎401/846-5486, *www.newportri.com/users/willows*). If you liked Beechwood (see below) you'll feel right at home with the daily "living history lesson" that comes with your breakfast in bed. [4].

The Town

Newport's main attractions are obviously its **mansions**, but there is nothing to be gained by attempting to tour them all, and although it is pleasant enough to stroll around the predominantly colonial **downtown**, the ever-growing profusion of souvenir shops is somewhat off-putting. Otherwise, if you don't fancy beautiful-people-spotting on the harbor, you'll do better following the crowds to one of Newport's fine **beaches**.

The mansions

When horrified sociologist Thorstein Veblen visited Newport at the turn of the twentieth century and coined the phrase "**conspicuous consumption**" he was criticising the desperate need felt by some of the new entrepreneurial **millionaires** of the time to define their fragile identities and perhaps establish an instant American aristocracy by flaunting their newly acquired wealth. More than just a summer resort, Newport became an arena in which families competed with increasing mania to outdo each other – though the "**season**" of wild and decadent parties lasted only a few weeks and many of the multi-million dollar homes remained empty for months, even years at a time. The results of their efforts, described as "white elephants" by Henry James, are the sumptuous mansions of Bellevue Avenue and Ocean Drive.

BEECHWOOD

It's difficult to take in the sheer wealth involved by merely gawking at the mansions' facades, but after being herded in and rushed through more than a couple, the opulence rapidly begins to pall. The most important mansions stand on **Bellevue Avenue**, **Ocean Drive**, and **Harrison Avenue**. The Astors' **Beechwood**, 580 Bellevue Ave (Feb–May Fri, Sat & Sun 10am–4pm; mid-May–Nov daily 10am–5pm; Nov & Dec daily 10am–4pm; $9), is an entertaining antidote to the drier historical drills given on other tours. Inside the stucco house, costumed actors welcome visitors as houseguests who have arrived for a party to be given by Mrs Caroline Astor, the self-proclaimed queen of American society, known for her attempts to stave off the advances of "new money" families into society's inner circles. Anecdotes, bitchy asides and a constant stream of activity – as well as strawberry tea in the servants' kitchen – make it all a great deal of fun.

MARBLE HOUSE, ROSECLIFF, KINGSCOTE AND THE BREAKERS

Also on Bellevue Avenue, the **Marble House** is the most over-the-top example of Gilded Age excess, with a golden ballroom and a Chinese teahouse in the grounds; both this and **Rosecliff**, with its colorful rose garden and heart-shaped staircase, were used as sets during the filming of *The Great Gatsby*. **Kingscote**, further up the avenue, is a quirky Arts and Crafts cottage with a lovely interior that features mahogany paneling and a Tiffany glass wall in the dining room. The biggest and best of the lot, however, is Cornelius Vanderbilt's four-story **The Breakers**, on Ochre Point Avenue, a sumptuous Italian Renaissance palace built for President and Chairman of the New York Central Railroad Cornelius Vanderbilt II by renowned architect Richard Morris. Located on a 13-acre ocean-front estate, the imposing "cottage" was completed in 1895 and includes a 45-foot high central Great Hall, and seventy additional rooms, many of which were constructed overseas by European craftsmen then shipped to Newport. The waves crashing on the rocks below give the house its name.

These houses are all run by the **Preservation Society of Newport County**, 424 Bellevue Ave, whose combination tickets slightly help to beat the hefty admission prices (April–Oct daily 10am–5pm, rest of year schedule varies; The Breakers costs $15, all others $9; any seven Society properties $38; ☎401/847-1000, *www.newportmansions.org*).

BELCOURT CASTLE, THE CLIFFWALK AND HAMMERSMITH FARM

Standing slightly apart from this parade, but a competitor nonetheless, **Belcourt Castle**, at Bellevue Avenue and Lakeview (late May–Nov 9am–5pm; rest of year except January 10am–3pm; $9), was built to echo a hunting lodge, and guides are indeed decked out in medieval costume when you enter. As yet another Newport example of excess, former resident Oliver Belmont's horses slept in white linen sheets in a specially designed stable.

You can peek at the Bellevue Avenue mansions on the cheap by taking the invigorating **Cliff Walk**, which begins on Memorial Avenue where it meets First Beach. This three-and-a-half-mile oceanside path alternates from pretty sections meandering among jasmine and wild roses to ugly concrete underpasses and dangerous stretches across perilous rocks. For those with a car, Ocean Drive continues from Bellevue Avenue where the Cliff Walk ends, following the coast eastwards and passing the shingle-sided **Hammersmith Farm**, John and Jackie Kennedy's 28-room summer home, originally owned by Jackie's mother, Mrs Hugh Auchinloss. The newly married Kennedys' wedding reception was held here in 1953, and the couple were such frequent visitors that it became known as the "**summer White House**." The interior, built on the site of an earlier farmhouse, is English country-style and includes Jackie's childhood bedroom and a smattering of mementos from the JFK years. The selling of the estate a few years ago means that the farm is no longer open to the public.

Downtown Newport

Colonial Newport's political and commercial center, **Washington Square**, starts just south of the Gateway Center, where Thames Street meets the **Brick Market**. The 1762 market, off **Long Wharf** (the most important of Newport's colonial wharves), has been reconstructed to include a mixture of galleries and pricey souvenir shops. Also inside, the **Museum of Newport History** (Mon & Wed–Sat 10am–5pm, Sun 1–5pm; $5) gives a good overview of Newport's past through interactive exhibits, photographs and pithy oral histories. Across the square stands the **Old Colony House** (Mon–Fri 9.30am–noon & 1–4pm, Sat & Sun 9.30am–noon; free), one of Rhode Island's few pre-Revolutionary brick buildings and seat of government from 1739 to 1900 – the second oldest capitol building in the United States. It was here that in May 1776, Rhode Island became the first state to declare its independence from Britain – two months before the official

THE MYTH OF THE MILL

The construction of the circular **Old Stone Mill**, located at the top of a hill in Touro Park, at the corner of Mill Street and Bellevue Avenue, has been alternately attributed to Vikings, Native Americans, Portuguese explorers, even as late as English colonists – leaving its vintage, and original intent, in doubt. Some archeologists have suggested that it was built as a windmill by Governor Benedict Arnold, and fortified because of the perceived threat from local Native American tribes. Locals hang close to the idea that it was left by the Vikings – implausible on the surface, though given some credibility by the fact a suit of Viking armor was found further up the coast (and immortalized in Longfellow's *The Skeleton in Armor*). If this were so, of course, it would mean the Providence area would usurp Plymouth's place as the site of the first European settlement in these parts.

proclamation. Just up from Washington Square, at 17 Broadway, the **Wanton-Lyman-Hazard House** (mid-June to Labor Day Thurs–Sun 1–5pm; $3) appears uncomfortably hemmed in among surrounding commercial buildings for good reason: it is one of the oldest dwellings in Newport, built sometime between 1650 and 1700. The central chimney and pitched roof are typical of the early settlers' homes; inside, the surviving original plasterwork is made from ground shells and molasses. To the north, the **Easton's Point** district, between Washington Square and Spring Street, is lined with the eighteenth-century homes of ships' captains. Of these, the 1748 **Hunter House**, 54 Washington St (March–Oct daily 10am–5pm; $9), the only one open to the public, has been carefully restored to reflect its original state.

The oldest religious building in town is the 1699 **Quaker Meeting House**, at the corner of Farewell and Marlborough streets (free tours by appointment; ☎401/846-0813), restored to its nineteenth-century state and completely free of adornment. The Quakers, like other religious sects, received a warm welcome in Rhode Island; indeed, the state's penchant for religious tolerance is echoed by the presence of the elegant **Touro Synagogue**, at 85 Touro St, the oldest house of Jewish worship in America. Built in 1763 and modeled on Sephardic Jewish temples in Portugal and Holland, the synagogue displays a letter to the Jewish community written by George Washington himself, advocating religious freedom (July 4 to Labor Day Sun–Fri 10am–5pm; Labor Day to mid-Oct Mon–Fri 1–3pm, Sun 11am–3pm; rest of year Mon–Fri 2pm by appointment only, Sun 1–3pm; free). Rhode Island's tolerance even extended to the much-despised Anglicans, who were the main reason for the Puritan exodus from England. Their 1726 **Trinity Church** on Queen Anne Square (mid-June–July 4 Mon–Fri 10am–4pm, July 4 to Labor Day daily 10am–4pm; rest of year 10am–1pm; free) was based on the Old North Church in Boston and the designs of Sir Christopher Wren, with a bleach-white 150-foot tower which acts as a beacon for ships as well as worshippers. Inside the only triple-decked, freestanding pulpit left in America stands in its original position in front of the altar, evidence of the emphasis at the time on preaching rather than communion. The Roman Catholic **St Mary's Church**, Spring Street and Memorial Boulevard (Mon–Fri 7–11.30am; free), completed in 1848, witnessed the union of Jacqueline Bouvier and John Kennedy on September 12, 1953.

Bellevue Avenue, the street of Newport's mansions, is also home to two noteworthy museums not far from downtown. The **Newport Art Museum**, at no. 76

(Memorial Day to Labor Day Mon–Sat 10am–5pm, Sun noon–5pm; rest of year Mon–Sat 10am–4pm, Sun 10am–4pm; $4), exhibits New England art from the last two centuries in the 1864 mock-medieval Griswold House; the grand **Newport Casino**, no. 194, was an early country club which held the nation's first tennis championships in 1881. It now houses the **International Tennis Hall of Fame** (daily 10am–5pm; $8), and still keeps its grass courts open to the public. Exhibits include the original patent for the game granted by Queen Victoria in 1874, displays on tennis fashion, a portrait of Chris Evert by Andy Warhol and a video theater where you can watch classic matches.

The beaches

The indubitable attraction of Newport's shoreline, with its rocky coves and gently sloping sandy beaches, is slightly marred by the fact that several are strictly private; still, some of the best strands remain within the public domain. The calm waters of **Gooseberry Beach**, nestled among the rocks in an attractive inlet off Ocean Avenue, appeals to families and charges a $1 admission for parking. The town beach, also known as **First** or **Easton's Beach**, is a wide stretch at the east end of Memorial Boulevard that gets very busy despite the relatively high $8 parking fee ($10 on weekends). There's also an aquarium with a tidepool and tanks of local sea life. The most attractive of all the Aquidneck Island beaches is further east in neighboring Middletown, pleasant **Second Beach**, with acres of soft gray sand and good surf ($10 weekdays; $15 weekends). You can combine a few hours on the beach with a visit to the nearby **Norman Bird Sanctuary**, 583 Third Beach Rd (Tues–Sun 9am–5pm; $4), more than ten miles of trails with a nature museum and education building. Peaceful **Third Beach**, further on, is not technically an ocean beach as it's on the inner side of Narragansett Bay; parking is $10 weekdays, $15 at weekends.

Eating

Many of Newport's **restaurants** are smug and overpriced, with the result that visitors on strict budgets have to make do with snacks. However, there are some notable exceptions and the seafood here is worth the blowout if you have the extra cash.

Anthony's Shore Dinner Hall, Waite's Wharf (☎401/848-5058). Inexpensive, family-style fried clams, fresh lobster and other seafood dishes. Outdoor tables.

Asterix & Obelix, 599 Thames St (☎401/841-8833). Happening, moderately priced eatery in a former garage, with abstract paintings on the walls and Oriental rugs covering an orange cement floor. The food is eclectic, with Asian flourishes.

The Black Pearl, Bannister's Wharf (☎401/846-5264). This Newport institution is famed for its chunky clam chowder; repair to the Commodore Room for more formal (and more expensive) dining.

Brick Alley Pub & Restaurant, 140 Thames St (☎401/849-6334). Attracts a good mix of locals and tourists for lunch, dinner, and cocktails; Sunday brunch is especially popular. The food's fairly straightforward: burgers, some seafood options and the like.

Christie's, 351 Thames St (☎401/847-5400). Very popular waterfront restaurant specializing in seafood. Try their scrumptious house specialty, Narragansett fish pie.

Grappa, 109 Long Wharf (☎401/849-0011). Spectacular views over Newport Harbor and contemporary Italian cooking provide an irresistable combination – particularly so in the summer when you can dine al fresco.

Mudville Pub, 8 W Marlborough St, adjacent to the Cardine's Field Baseball Stadium (☎401/849-1408). Lively sports bar serving sandwiches and burgers, and packed out especially after a home game.

Newport Blues Café, 286 Thames St (☎401/841-5510). Elegant dining in an old bank building overlooking the harbor. Live blues and jazz from 10pm nightly.

Ocean Coffee Roasters, 22 Washington Square (☎401/846-6060). Hip, upbeat café serving aspiring artists and poets rather than yacht club types. Crepes from $4, lunch specials with an international twist from $5.50, flavored coffees and teas. Occasional poetry readings and exhibitions.

Puerini's, 24 Memorial Boulevard (☎401/ 847-5506). Classic and innovative Italian fare make this a firm favorite with locals and visitors alike.

St. Elmo's Galley, 18 Market Square (☎401/849-1340). Inexpensive sandwiches and salads in a small café inside the Seamen's Institute.

Via Via I, 112 William St (☎401/846-4074). Specialty oven-fired pizza – shrimp pesto or chicken and goat's cheese, for example – that can also be delivered until 2am. The slightly better-situated *Via Via II* is nearby at 372 Thames St (☎401/848-0880).

White Horse Tavern, Marlborough and Farewell streets (☎401/849-3600). Intensely atmospheric restaurant (the building dates from 1687) serving hearty American fare such as New York sirloin, sautéed lobster and baked Atlantic salmon. Expensive, but more affordable at lunchtime.

Nightlife and entertainment

Newport has a reputation for being a lively party town, with fairly unrefined **nightlife**, which irks many of its residents – to the point that the town council has tried to tone things down through various regulations and restrictions. Most, but by no means all, of the noisiest **bars** and **clubs** are found in the waterfront area.

The Daisy, downstairs at the Clarke Cooke House, Bannister's Wharf (☎401/849-2900). One of the most popular discos in town, the *Daisy* attracts a fairly mixed crowd.

David's, 21 Prospect Hill St (☎401/847-9698). Aquidneck Island's only gay bar, just a short walk from the waterfront, has a friendly, neighborhood atmosphere and a pleasant patio to sit on.

One Pelham East, cnr of Thames and Pelham sts (☎401/847-9640). Long-established and still popular venue that has been hosting live bands for over twenty years.

NEWPORT'S MUSIC FESTIVALS

Newport is nearly famous for the plethora of prominent annual music festivals that take place here in the summer months, the two most popular of which are **Ben & Jerry's Folk Festival**, in late July or early August, followed by the **August Jazz Festival**, in the middle of the month. Both feature big-name performers in their respective fields; call ☎401/847-3700 for details. Later in August, two more gatherings, the **Rhythm & Blues Festival** (same number) and the **Newport Irish Music Festival** (☎1-800/651-3990), which includes a bagpipe band competition and exhibits of Irish and Celtic literature, art and dance, are based in **Fort Adams State Park,** originally built to guard the entrance to Narragansett Bay and now a state park with sweeping views of the harbor, Newport Bridge, and the downtown area. The lesser-known but arguably more memorable Newport Music Festival (☎401/846-1133) emphasizes international classical music and takes place during July in a number of Newport's mansions. The program features world-class artists performing everything from chamber and orchestral music to sea shanties.

The Red Parrot, 348 Thames St (☎401/848-9920). This is the place for live jazz and world music nightly.

The Rock, 162 Connell Highway, at the Rotary (☎401/849-5159). Newport's primary rock club offering local and regional talent plus the occasional "big name."

Senor Frogg's, 108 William St (☎401/847-4747). Largest dance and rock club in the area, featuring alternative, progressive, and dance music.

Sports Ticket, 15 Aquidneck Ave, Middletown (☎401/847-7678). Sports bar with 32 TV screens and an outdoor deck overlooking First Beach.

The Wharf Deli & Pub, 37 Bowen's Wharf (☎401/846-9233). Somewhat touristy microbrewery in the heart of it all that puts on R&B and jazz.

Around Newport

Newport has plenty to keep you occupied, no matter what your proclivities, but if you are interested in getting out of town for a while, there are some worthwhile detours nearby, the best of which are on the **Sakonnet Peninsula**, a remote area that was once part of Massachusetts, and bears little of the development characteristic of other coastal sections of the state. Sakonnet is basically an island, with virtually no public transport; **cars** and **bicycles** can be rented in Fall River, a couple of miles across the border in Massachusetts. If you are driving from Newport, just take Route 77 south off I-24 and follow it down the length of the land.

Portsmouth

Founded in 1638 by Anne Hutchinson, another refugee from Massachusetts, **PORTSMOUTH**, about ten miles north of Newport on Route 138, was until recently a small rural community; now it's little more than a bedroom suburb of Newport.

The **Portsmouth Historical Society**, based in the Old Union Church, corner of East Main Road and Union Street, comprises several interesting buildings, including what may be the oldest one-room schoolhouse in the country, completed in 1723; the original Portsmouth Town Hall; and the church itself, once home to a nineteenth-century religious sect with connections to the abolitionist movement, that currently displays local artifacts like coal fossils from the town's now-derelict coal mines and various Native American tools (Memorial Day to Oct Sat & Sun 1–4pm; free). The **Green Animals Topiary Gardens**, Cory's Lane, off Route 114, has more than eighty sculpted trees and animal-shaped shrubs set on an idyllic lawn that slopes down to Narragansett Bay. There are espaliered fruit trees, a rose arbor, formal flower beds and a small Victorian **toy museum** (May–Oct daily 10am–5pm; $9).

Those that choose to **stay** – not a bad option, as it is little more than a twenty-minute drive from downtown Newport – typically do so at the *Founder's Brook Motel*, 318 Boyd's Lane, at the junction of routes 138 and 24 (☎401/683-1244, [4]–[6]), or the 85-room *Ramada Inn*, 144 Anthony Rd (☎401/683-3600; [4]–[5]), with an indoor pool and health club. **Eating** options revolve around Portsmouth's star contender: the **Seafare Inn**, 3352 East Main Road, Portsmouth (☎401/683-0577). It would be a shame to miss this excellent fish venue which has been voted one of the top ten seafood restaurants in the US year after year.

The Sakonnet Peninsula: Tiverton and Little Compton

The rather nondescript and tatty northern section of **TIVERTON** that you imme-
diately encounter after crossing Route 24 is redeemed only by some delightful
views of the **Sakonnet River**, which parallels Route 77 the length of Sakonnet
Peninsula. Heading south, the first spot of interest is **Fort Barton**, on Highland
Street, an original redoubt built during the American Revolution and named after
Colonel William Barton, who captured Newport's British commander during the
War. A climb of the observation tower affords a spectacular view of neighboring
Aquidneck Island. Two miles south, Seapowet Avenue leads to the **Ruecker
Wildlife Refuge**, forty acres of shallow marshes and upland woodlots donated to
the Rhode Island Audubon Society in 1965. Trails are well marked, and all kinds
of birdlife can be seen, including herons and egrets, catbirds and cardinals.

Further south on Route 77, **Tiverton Four Corners** is a motley collection of
specialist stores, art galleries, and historic homes, several of which date from the
eighteenth century, among them the 1730 gambrel-roofed **Chase Cory House**,
3980 Main Rd (June–Sept Sun 2–4.30pm; free), now the base for the Tiverton
Historical Society. The home retains many features indigenous to Colonial village
farms, such as an eight-foot-tall kitchen fireplace with beaded chimney. **Pond
Bridge Road**, a mile south of Four Corners, a pretty country lane bordered by
lush hedges and rugged stone walls, traverses gentle farmland to reach **Fogland
Beach** (parking $5), Tiverton's shingly but safe town beach which skirts the
southern edge of a comma-shaped peninsula jutting out into the Sakonnet River.
There are splendid views down the river, with the Sakonnet Lighthouse and the
various elephantine rocks that surround it looming in the distance.

A couple of miles on, the **Sakonnet Vineyard**, 162 Main Rd/Rte-177 (daily:
June–Sept 10am–6pm; Oct–May 11am–5pm; tours Wed–Sun; free), is New
England's largest winery, at which you can take a guided or unguided tour that
includes free samples. Local shrine **Walker's Farm Stand**, 251 W Main Rd
(☎401/635-4719), is a veritable kaleidoscope of color, especially in the late summer and autumn when bright orange pumpkins bask seductively in the golden
autumnal glow.

Little Compton

The 4500 year-round residents of tiny but wealthy **LITTLE COMPTON** are ultra-
protective of their environment, evidenced by car stickers that bluntly demand
"Keep Little Compton Little," the conspicuous absence of places to stay and a lack
of what nearly every other tiny New England town has – a visitor center. Rumor
has it that its classic village center, **Little Compton Commons**, was the favored
location for the film *The Witches of Eastwick* (eventually filmed in Cohasset,
Massachusetts; see p.160), but that the residents turned down the opportunity for
fear that it would put the town rather too firmly on the tourist map. Though its
population does increase during the summer, it manages to retain its composed
self – thanks to a planning code that prohibits the construction of fast-food joints
and glitzy malls.

You can check out that town square yourself on Meetinghouse Lane, where the
commons is dominated by the lofty, brilliant-white spire of its 1832 **Congregational
Church**, with an adjacent burial ground that predates the building by 150 years. It
contains the grave of one **Benjamin Church**, an Indian fighter who took part in the

execution of King Philip back in the 1600s. Opposite the church, the meandering maze of rooms that is **Wilbur's Store**, established more than two hundred years ago, is Little Compton's own Lilliputian department store, selling everything from food to hardware.

At 548 W Main Rd, the **Wilbor House** (June–Sept Tues–Sat 2–4pm; $5) is a restored 1690 structure with low ceilings and exposed wooden beams that contains numerous examples of eighteenth- and nineteenth-century domestic furniture. Far more interesting than the house is the accompanying barn, where old farm implements and vehicles are on display, along with photographs and items celebrating Little Compton's Portuguese heritage and a replica of a one-room schoolhouse. Nearby, evocatively named Swamp Road leads to the town-owned **Wilbour Woods**, which contain, among all the maples, hollies and ferns, a monument to **Queen Ashawonk**, a Native American woman who chose to side with the new settlers rather than the Wampanoag tribe during King Philip's War. In case you're wondering, the many variations on the Wilbur name derive from one **Samuel Wilbore**, an early settler of the Little Compton area. It was he who built the Wilbor House and so established the legacy of Little Compton's would-be first family, which as it branched out geographically began to utilize different spellings.

Main Road struggles south toward the Atlantic to **Sakonnet Point**, where a broad, sweeping vista of an often angry seascape is framed on one side by a newly restored **lighthouse** and on the other by the rocky crags and promontories of Newport and Middletown. In between, the graceful mock-English Gothic tower of St George's School punctuates the horizon. It's far too dangerous to swim at the nearby harbor; instead, park at the **Little Compton Town Beach**, at the end of South Shore Road ($9 weekdays, $13 weekends), and walk on to pretty **Goosewing Beach**, sandier and quieter than the town beach, at least for the moment – the question of better access, meaning in turn, more visitors, is perennially up in the air.

Tiverton and Little Compton practicalities

Just about the only **place to stay** in either Little Compton or Tiverton (save a few small B&Bs) is the *Stone House Club*, 122 Sakonnet Point Rd (☎401/635-2222; [6]), housed in a rugged three-story granite building overlooking the Atlantic. This local gathering spot is technically a private club, but you can book a room as long as you pay the $20 membership fee; there's also a restaurant and cellar bar on the premises. If you really want to relax, your best bet is to rent a **cottage** way down in Sakonnet, a pricey option (starting at $600 per week) – try local agents T.L. Holland (☎401/624-8469).

Places to eat are few and far between as well. The *Provender*, 3883 Main Rd, Tiverton (☎401/624-8096), is a delightful gourmet food store where you can choose from an exotic array of designer sandwiches and freshly baked desserts, while tiny *Olga's Cup and Saucer*, 261 W Main Rd, Little Compton (☎401/635-8650), a café with a loyal following of locals and tourists, has good *caffè latte* and black bean burritos. Local no-frills institution the *Commons Lunch*, East Side, Little Compton Commons (☎401/635-4388), serves luscious lobster rolls, stuffed quahogs and prize-winning johnnycakes, while *Gray's Ice Cream*, at the intersection of Routes 77 and 177 (☎401/ 624-4500), vends numerous home-made flavors of the sweet stuff.

South County: Rhode Island's Southern Coast

SOUTH COUNTY is the unofficial name given to Rhode Island's southernmost towns, a coastal stretch that begins with North Kingstown in the east and runs past gently rolling hills, quaint villages and gray sandy beaches to Westerly, just this side of the Connecticut border. Further inland the geography is a bit more diverse, full of dense woodlands, wildlife reserves and oversize ponds, but somewhat lacking in must-see sights that would make you stray very far off the coastal highway of **US-1**, actually once the main connecting route between New York and New England. In any case, the construction of I-95 some miles north has insured that this chunk of Rhode Island remains relatively unscathed by the kind of overdevelopment seen in other parts of the state. Indeed, many visitors bypass entirely this area while wending their way over to Cape Cod or up into northern New England – which makes it all the more appealing.

The place is alive with reflections of its colonial and Native American heritage, the latter attested to by such place names as Misquamicut and Quoquonset. Historic points of interest include **Smith's Castle**, America's oldest plantation house, and, in North Kingstown, the **birthplace of Gilbert Stuart**, the portraitist, whose painting of George Washington is seen on all US dollar bills. **Watch Hill** and **Narragansett**, on the coast, are – like Newport – known for their massive summer "cottages" and resort facilities, while **Galilee** is the point of departure for ferries to unspoilt Block Island, as well as being one of the busiest fishing ports in New England, a great place to enjoy a seafood meal while watching the boats come in.

North Kingstown

NORTH KINGSTOWN, known as "plantation country" for its many longstanding farms, is less a town than a collection of rural communities straddling Route 1A on the eastern shore of Narragansett Bay. The best-known of these is the harborside village of **Wickford**, full of shady tree-lined lanes, handsomely preserved eighteenth- and nineteenth-century homes. Wickford is also home to the oldest Episcopal (Anglican) church north of Virginia, **Old Narragansett Church**, at 60 Church Lane (July to Labor Day Thurs–Mon 10am–4pm; free), built in 1707 in the square "preaching box" style which makes it look more like a congregational meetinghouse from the outside. Among its treasures are a Queen Anne communion set and reputedly the oldest organ in America, dating back to 1680. Box pews and a slave gallery are reminders of a grim and turbulent past. The **Wickford Town Dock**, at the end of Main Street, was a bustling waterfront for years, especially when it was trading with the West Indies; today it's a peaceful, relaxing place where local quahog skiffs rub shoulders with posh yachts and the only bustle of any kind comes when an annual Arts Festival is held here in July. Just north of town off Route 1, **Smith's Castle**, 55 Richard Smith Drive (May & Sept Fri–Sun noon–4pm; Jun–Aug Thurs–Mon noon–4pm; other times by appointment; $3; ☎401/294-3321), a red-clapboard plantation house that dates back to 1678, was the site of much of Roger Williams' preaching activity. It replaced an earlier trading post that was destroyed by Native Americans in 1676, having been used to plan the attack against King Philip of the Wampanoags. The castle was recently restored to resemble how it appeared in 1740. Also north of town, the only brick hangar on the east coast houses the **Quonset Air Museum**, 488 Eccleston Ave, Quonset Naval Air Base, North Kingstown (Fri–Sun 10am–3pm; $4), which displays vintage aircraft, both military and commercial, such as a Russian MIF-17 and an A-4 Skyhawk.

Most of North Kingstown's other points of interest are further south, in and around **Saunderstown**, including the three-hundred-acre **Casey Farm**, 2325 Boston Neck Rd, also known as Rte-1A (June–mid-Oct Tue, Thurs & Sat 1–5pm; $3), constructed in 1750 and one of the oldest working farms in the United States. It was originally the center of a plantation that produced food for local and foreign markets, and today, resident farmers raise organically grown vegetables, herbs and flowers for subscribing households in a Community Supported Agriculture Program. The farmhouse contains original furniture and family memorabilia; in the parlor door, a musket hole bears witness to a British attack on the property when it was used as a garrison by American military during the Revolutionary War. The **Gilbert Stuart Birthplace and Museum**, 815 Gilbert Stuart Rd (April–Oct Thurs–Mon 11am–4pm; $3), childhood home of the celebrated eighteenth-century portraitist, disappoints in that it only contains one reproduction of the 111 portraits of George Washington that Stuart painted during his lifetime.

Few people should have the need to **stay** or **eat** in North Kingstown, and should in any case opt for such practicalities in **Narragansett** and **Galilee**, described below.

Narragansett

NARRAGANSETT, the Native American word for "little spit of land," occupies a narrow patch snaking out into the Atlantic, its long coastline of rocks interspersed by broad expanses of sand – a major attraction for swimmers, watersports enthusiasts, bird watchers and fishermen. The center, **Narragansett Pier**, had its heyday during the Victorian era, when the town competed with Newport as a major resort destination. It succeeded to some extent, luring visitors especially with the **Narragansett Casino Resort**, designed by the architectural firm of McKim, Mead & White in 1884. Hopes of lasting fame and prosperity came to an abrupt end in 1900, however, when fire swept through the casino complex, destroying all but its turreted towers, which today remain the most striking feature of the town center, and house the Narragansett Historical Society and the **visitor information center**, Ocean Road (Mon–Fri 9am–4pm; ☎401/783-7121). For additional explication of Narragansett's role over the years, visit the **South County Museum**, Rte-1A, opposite Narragansett Beach Pavilion (May–Oct daily except Tues 10am–5pm; $3.50), which contains thousands of local artifacts, not to mention a replicated print shop, smithy, general store, and one-room schoolhouse.

Narragansett's long coastline boasts several outstanding **beaches** (see box p.272) and the charmingly chaotic fishing port of **Galilee**, four miles south of the town center. The potholed main drag, where the fishy whiff can at times be overwhelming, is home to a large commercial fishing fleet, half a dozen fish markets, two or three fish-processing works, beach accessory stores and the **Block Island Ferry** (see p.275 for details). If you want to go on a guided **whale-watch**, the boats of Francis Fleet ($30 adults, $20 children under 12; ☎401/783-4988 or 1-800/662-2824) depart from a point just behind *Finback's* restaurant. A mile east, the **Point Judith Lighthouse**, at the end of Ocean Road, has been warning ships off the rocky coast since the early 1800s. The present lighthouse, built in 1857, is closed to the public, but the view from the adjacent parking lot is breathtaking, especially on a stormy day.

Practicalities

Galilee is home to a number of excellent **seafood restaurants**, the most popular of which are *George's*, 250 Sand Hill Cove Rd (☎401/783-2306), and *Champlin's*, 256 Great Island Rd (☎401/783-3152), which has nice views of the fishing boats from an upstairs covered deck. Not far away, *Aunt Carrie's*, 1240 Ocean Rd (☎401/783-7930), is a Rhode Island institution, the place for traditional shore dinners in an unpretentious, relaxed atmosphere, while *Spain*, 1144 Ocean Rd (☎401/783-9770), serves a variety of Spanish, American, and seafood dishes in a contemporary setting. Downtown Narragansett boasts several upmarket restaurants, including the *Coast Guard House*, 40 Ocean Rd (☎401/789-0700), where the view, if not the food, is spectacular; *Basil's*, at 22 Kingstown Rd, on the pier (☎401/789-3743), has established a strong local following for its fine French cuisine.

Accommodation is never hard to come by in Narragansett, except at the height of the season, when it's advisable to book well in advance. In Galilee, opposite the Block Island ferry at Great Island Road, is the *Lighthouse Inn* (☎401/789-9341 or 1-800/336-6662; ⑥–⑦), a comfortable 100-room hotel near all the beach and boating activities. More atmospheric digs are available in the Narragansett Pier area, where, at 113 Ocean Rd, the *Pier House Inn* (☎401/783-4704; ⑥–⑦) is a remnant of Narragansett's glory days with a three-story Victorian house and an adjacent structure resembling a motel and you can't get much closer to the beach than *The Galilean*, 225 Sand Hill Cove Road, Galilee (☎401/783-8159; ④–⑤). If you prefer to rent a cottage, Durkin Cottage Realty (☎401/789-6659) has the largest selection in the area, starting at around $600 a week.

South Kingstown

SOUTH KINGSTOWN's 62 square miles – in area, Rhode Island's largest town – takes in fourteen separate villages covering both sides of Route 1, quite different in nature depending on which side of the highway you're traversing. Inland, dense woods hide well-preserved colonial villages, potato farms and wildlife refuges; the most logical first stop here is **Kingston**, founded in 1674, and a seat of Rhode Island government until it was centralized in Providence. Many well-preserved examples of Federal-style architecture can still be seen, including the 1775 **Kingston Free Library**, Kingstown Road, originally the Washington County Courthouse, where the state's General Assembly, Supreme Court, and local town council all shared their sessions. Nearby, in the **Old Washington County Jail**, at 2636 Kingstown Rd (May–Oct Tues, Thurs & Sat 1–4pm; free), you can see old jail cells which have been around since 1792, along with a decent museum containing changing exhibits on South County life over the past three hundred years. Rural Kingston is also the unlikely location of the **University of Rhode Island**, North Road, whose leafy 1200-acre campus once centered on a small farmhouse – fitting, as this was started as an agricultural school. On Route 2, a mile south of the junction with Route 138, a dilapidated sign points the way to the **Great Swamp Fight Monument**, which commemorates the bloody 1675 battle in which King Philip's Wampanoag tribe was decimated by colonial forces. Route 108 leads south from here to the village of

SOUTH COUNTY BEACHES

Many of Rhode Island's best **saltwater beaches** can be found in South County, and are generally open to the public, although access to some of them is virtually impossible without a car, and there is usually a hefty parking fee, especially on summer weekends. Outside of season, parking is often free and the beaches, on weekdays at least, are deserted. Ocean temperatures peak at a refreshing 70–75 degrees during the dog days of August.

Charlestown Town Beach, Charlestown Beach Road, Charlestown. This beach looks like it belongs in California: lots of volleyball players, surfers, and bronzed bodies. $5 weekdays, $10 weekends.

East Matunuck State Beach, Succotash Road, South Kingstown. Another beach popular with the young. $4 weekdays, $5 weekends.

Misquamicut State Beach, Misquamicut. Only half a mile long, but incredibly crowded. Amusements and fast food are close at hand. $4 weekdays, $5 weekends.

Moonstone Beach, Moonstone Beach Road, South Kingstown. Naturalists used to flock to this beach but have been discouraged since it became a wildlife refuge. No parking.

Napatree Point, Watch Hill. A complete contrast to Misquamicut; limited access only to this pretty, ecologically fragile beach. No parking.

Narragansett Town Beach, Route 1A, Narragansett. A half-mile-long beach popular with families. $5.

Roger Wheeler Beach, Cove Wood Drive, Narragansett. A mile of gray sand with excellent facilities and expansive parking. $4 weekdays, $5 weekends.

Scarborough State Beach, Ocean Drive, Narragansett. Popular with students from the nearby University of Rhode Island. $4 weekdays, $5 weekends.

South Kingstown Town Beach, South Kingstown. Beautiful beach backed by dunes. $10.

Wakefield, whose Main Street holds a pleasant mix of antique shops, restaurants, and historic buildings, though nothing of particular interest.

Meanwhile, to the south of Route 1, a succession of laid-back coastal communities are separated by a series of saltwater ponds protected by fragile barrier beaches; seaside villages worth stopping by include **Jerusalem** and **Snug Harbor**, with their hotchpotch of summer cottages and executive homes. Otherwise, the main reason for coming down here is to join the crowds at the beaches, namely **East Matunuck**, a favorite with URI students, **Green Hill**, and **Moonstone** – once favored by naturists and now a nature preserve. Summer crowds are entertained at the barn-like **Theatre-by-the-Sea**, 364 Cards Pond Rd (shows nightly except Mon; matinees Thurs; tickets $25–35; ☎401/782-8587) – an absolute must if you enjoy jolly musicals of the *South Pacific* variety.

Practicalities

Places to stay in the area include the *Admiral Dewey Inn*, 668 Matunuck Beach Rd, Matanuck (☎401/783-2090 or 1-800/457-2090; ④–⑥), a traditional beach lodging house where you can relax and unwind on the wraparound porch. In Wakefield, the 160-year-old family-run *Larchwood Inn*, 521 Main St (☎401/783-5454; ⑥), offers twelve cozy rooms, a nice complement to the elegant **restaurant** on the premises, which serves classic American fare with a Scottish twist. In Jerusalem, *Cap'n Jack's*, 584 Succotash Rd (☎401/789-4556), serves generous portions of fresh seafood.

Charlestown

Laid-back **CHARLESTOWN**, South Kingstown's western neighbor along Route 1, is one of the fastest-growing communities in the state, its recent arrivals having been seduced by an attractive coastline – miles of barrier beach backed by pristine salt ponds. First settled by the Narragansett Indians, Charlestown received its charter from King Charles II in 1663, and was thus named for him. The Narragansetts, however, still own plenty of land in town, and maintain a significant cultural impact, best observed during the **Annual Inter-Tribal Pow-Wow**, held the second weekend of August on tribal lands just off Route 2 and featuring Native American dancing, crafts, food, and storytelling. Also located on these lands are the **Royal Indian Burial Grounds**, used for centuries as the resting place for tribal chiefs, and the **Narragansett Indian Church**, a reconstruction of an 1859 granite Greek Revival building reopened in 1998 after a disastrous fire. The church is not generally open to the public, though you can try to check it out during Sunday services.

The **Ninigret National Wildlife Refuge** highlights Charlestown's protected coastline and consists of four hundred acres of diverse upland and wetland habitats. Nine miles of trails offer plenty of opportunity for bird-watching or just for a simple stretch of the legs. It's merely one of a number of recreational areas that surround **Ninigret Pond**.

Inland, on Buckeye Brook Road, off Route 216, the **Burlingame Wildlife Management Area** (☎401/322-7994) is crossed by trails through a variety of habitats, where foxes and deer, wild turkeys, coyotes, and ruffed grouse can be seen. Further in, a number of tiny communities provide a glimpse into rural Rhode Island life, especially **Shannock**, on Route 112, a disarmingly pretty New England mill village of white-clapboard houses near the Pawcatuck River. Once virtually abandoned, the whole place was purchased and restored by a local developer, with the express intention of turning upwardly mobile young couples on to the charms of country living, to date a partly successful venture.

Practicalities

Many of Charlestown's **hotels** and **motels** line the main US-1 road, including the *General Stanton Inn*, 4115 Old Post Rd (☎401/364-8888; ③–⑤), which has been a resting place for travelers on the Providence–New London run since Revolutionary days. An adjacent flea market keeps guests busy at weekends. *One Willow By the Sea*, 1 Willow Rd (☎401/364-0802; ④–⑤), is a peaceful hostelry near the wildlife refuges. The bulk of the town's **restaurants** specialize in seafood, unsurprisingly, like the casual *Charlestown Lobster Pot*, Old Post Rd (☎401/322-7686), and *West Winds Bistro by the Sea*, 4605 Old Post Rd (☎401/364-0700), a great place to stop for a lobster pie.

Westerly and Watch Hill

WESTERLY, as its name implies, occupies the most westerly point of Rhode Island, sharing the Pawcatuck River with the town of Pawcatuck, Connecticut. Once a prosperous manufacturer of textiles and fine-grained granite, its downtown area holds few reminders of those days. The most impressive specimen left is the **Babcock-Smith House**, 124 Granite St (May–June & Sept–Oct Sun 2–5pm; July–Aug Sun & Wed 2–5pm; $3), built in 1734 for Dr Joshua Babcock, Westerly's first physician, who moonlighted as the town's postmaster, the chief justice for Rhode Island, and major-general in the Revolutionary army. The handsome two-story gambrel-roofed building contains much of its original trimmings, including the wooden paneling, the open fireplace in the kitchen, a Queen Anne daybed, and, above the mantelpiece in the dining room, an engraving that depicts Babcock engaged in an act of diplomacy at the French court.

Most visitors, however, forsake Westerly's downtown in lieu of the **Watch Hill** area a few miles south, which, after Newport, is Rhode Island's most select resort, with salty seaside shops and turn-of-the-century **cottages** overlooking the Atlantic. One holdover from its birth as a resort is the **Flying Horse Carousel** at the end of Bay Street, which, like several others in New England, is claimed to be the nation's oldest (1879). The twenty horses are not attached to the floor but instead suspended from a central frame, swinging out or "flying" when in motion. The other highlight in town, the granite **lighthouse** on Lighthouse Road, built in 1856 to replace an earlier wooden edifice, houses a small **museum** containing the usual bits on lighthouse history (July & Aug Tues & Thurs 1–3pm; free). To the west, accessible from Watch Hill Beach, the two-mile-long barrier beach of **Napatree Point** once supported a number of homes before they were destroyed by the devastating hurricane of 1938. Today it is a peaceful conservation area filled with myriad bird species and affording stunning ocean views.

Practicalities

For somewhere to **stay** in Westerly, try the *Shelter Harbor Inn*, 10 Wagner Rd (☎401/322-8883; [4]–[5]), a 23-room country inn done out in early American fittings, with an excellent restaurant to boot. The *Winnepaug Inn*, 169 Shore Rd (☎401/348-0350 or 1-800/288-9906; [4]–[5]), is a well-appointed three-story motor hotel set on beautifully manicured grounds overlooking a golf course.

Of the best places to **eat**, the spacious *Mary's Italian Restaurant*, Post Road (☎401/322-0044), doles out Italian home-cooking in unpretentious surroundings; closer to downtown, the *China Pavilion*, 148 Granite St (☎401/596-9888), is good for authentic Cantonese and spicy Szechuan food. At the other end of the town, the *Weekapaug Inn*, 15 Spring St, Weekapaug (☎401/322-0301), offers classic American fare in a bright and airy dining room. Down in Watch Hill, *St Clair Annex*, 141 Bay St (☎401/348-8211), run by the same family for over 100 years, serves wonderful breakfasts and home-made ice cream in thirty flavors. For something more substantial, the *Olympia Tea Room*, 74 Bay St (☎401/348-8211), has a variety of seafood dishes and mouth-watering desserts.

Entertainment in Westerly centers on the Greek Revival Colonial Theater, 1 Granite St (☎401/596-0810), a former church building. The theater presents drama, comedy, and every August, a classic American musical. Since 1991, the Colonial's free Shakespeare-in-the-Park productions in Wilcox Park have been a highlight of the summer. The park is also the venue for the renowned **Westerly Chorus**' Summer Pops concerts, which draw up to 25,000 people. Throughout the year the ensemble puts on classical concerts at the **Westerly Performance Hall**, 119 High St (☎401/596-8663), formerly the Immaculate Conception Church.

Block Island

It may not be the "Bermuda of the North," or "one of the last great places on earth," as it is also sometimes described, but small, nearly treeless **BLOCK ISLAND**, twelve miles off the coast of southern Rhode Island, has managed to preserve its melancholy, seductive charm even in the face of growing hordes of visitors and the rampant construction of summer homes in the 1970s and 1980s, which threatened to disfigure the landscape's simple beauty as well as destroy many of its unique natural habitats. Inhabited by 800 year-round residents, who scatter themselves around the gently rolling hills and broad expanses of moorland, Block Island still exudes an air of desolation, at least off-season, a mood exacerbated when the ferry between it and Point Judith (there are summer ferries available from Providence and New London, CT) is incapacitated due to bad weather. There's not much to see once you get over, just lovely coves and sandy beaches, but, like its Massachusetts cousins Martha's Vineyard and Nantucket, the island gets chock-a-block between July 4 and Labor Day, when tourists, part-time residents and day-trippers all seem to take to the island's scant network of roads at once.

Some history

Native Americans, who called it "Manisses" or "Island of the Little God," had inhabited Block Island for centuries before **Giovanni de Verrezano**, he of the famous bridge in New York City, spotted it in 1524. With the prospect of a substantial bonus in sight, he cannily named it **Claudia**, after the mother of the French King, Francis I, who had commissioned him. Later on, in 1614, the intrepid Dutch explorer, Adrian Block, stopped for a time on the island and gave it the name "**Adrian's Eyelandt**" which eventually became **Block Island**.

A group of English settlers seeking religious freedom arrived here in 1661 and established a small farming and fishing community that still exists today. A relatively quiet couple of hundred years followed until 1842, when the island's first hotel was built and visitors began to recognize Block Island's many charms; thirty years later a new breakwater was built, meaning that larger ships could dock – and more people could come over on them. Things took a turn for the worse with the 1938 hurricane that devastated much of the New England coast: it destroyed nearly all of Block Island's fishing fleet and caused considerable structural damage to the hotels and other buildings around Old Harbor, the island's commercial center.

There's little remnant of hard times today: Block Island has only become increasingly fashionable, a highly sought-after real estate destination with many properties surpassing the million-dollar mark. In recent years residents of **New Shoreham**, the island's official title, passed a number of measures designed to preserve the relative tranquility and natural environment they had so expensively become privy to: camping and tenting were banned, the operation of mopeds and motorcycles between midnight and 6am prohibited, and shell-fishing without a license no longer tolerated.

Arrival, information, and getting around

Most people arrive on Block Island by **ferry**. From the Galilee State Pier in Narragansett, the Interstate Navigation Co. (☎401/783-4613) runs six or seven ferries a day during the summer months and two or three a day during the winter. The seventy-minute trip costs $8.40 one way, $13.50 for same-day return.

Passengers taking cars need to make reservations in advance; foot passengers just need to arrive 45 minutes early. The same company runs daily ferries from Providence's India Street Pier between Memorial Day and October (with a stop first at Newport's Fort Adams State Park), as well as from New London, Connecticut, leaving at 9am daily from June to September. If you'd rather fly, **New England Airlines** (☎401/596-2460) provide hourly flights from Westerly during the summer season.

The Block Island Chamber of Trade operates an **information center** right where you come off the ferry, set to open and shut with ferry times. The other thing you'll see as you disembark is a bewildering array of **bike**, **moped**, and **car rental** agencies, with still more lurking behind the shops. Prices vary, so do not be afraid to shop around. Two good options are the Old Harbor Bike Shop (☎401/466-2029), a dockside shack just left as you disembark the ferry, and Island Bike and Moped, Chapel Street (☎401/466-2700), just behind the *Harborside Inn*. There are plenty of **taxis** lined up too, at least on summer days, useful if you're weighed down with luggage or if your accommodation is located at some far-flung corner of the island. Some of the more ambitious cabs provide narrated (and fairly pithy) **island tours**, at $30 for up to two people and a further $5 for each additional person; in the absence of tour buses, this can be a good way to get oriented. Kirb's Cab (☎401/466-2928) is your best bet for these.

Still, you'll mostly want to get around **on foot**. There are around 25 miles of walking trails, a system known as **The Greenway** and maintained by the Nature Conservancy (☎410/466-2129), which offers guided nature walks during the summer. If your wanderings take you through grassy terrain, be especially wary of ticks, which delight in attaching themselves to your socks before they proceed to other parts of your anatomy.

Accommodation

If you want to **stay** in Block Island during the summer, it's advisable to book well in advance; even with more than seventy hotels, inns, B&Bs, and studio rentals, accommodation fills up rapidly, especially at weekends. Expect to pay anything from $80 to $350 per night for a room, and $750 a week up to an incredible $4000 for a cottage rental. Because the island is so small, numbers are rarely, if ever, used in addresses; fortunately, it's virtually impossible to get lost. Most hotels are located in any case on **Old Harbor**; the only one listed below that's not is the *Samuel Peckham Inn*. The **Block Island Reservation Center** on Water Street (☎1-800/825-6254), next to the *Mohegan Café*, will help you to choose rooms and supply other general information.

1661 Inn & Guest House, Spring St, Old Harbor (☎401/466-2063). Opposite the *Manisses*, set on a hill overlooking the sea. Nine pleasant rooms, great views. ⑥–⑧.

Atlantic Inn, High St, Old Harbor (☎401/466-5678). Laden with (mainly Victorian) antiques and set on six acres, *The Atlantic* offers superior rooms, many with superb views. Guests who feel so inclined can enjoy a game of tennis at the Inn's two courts, or a game of croquet on the lawn. Good restaurant, too – see p.279 for review. ⑦–⑧.

Blue Dory, Dodge St, Old Harbor (☎401/466-5891 or 1-800/992-7290). A guesthouse since it was constructed in 1898, all rooms here have either ocean or harbor views. ⑥–⑦.

The Gothic Inn, Dodge St, Old Harbor (☎401/466-2918). Perched high above Crescent Beach, this Victorian, family-run inn has oodles of character; unusually steep gables complete with gingerbread trimmings and a wide, relaxing porch overlooking Dodge Street. It's just three minutes from the ferry. ⑤–⑥.

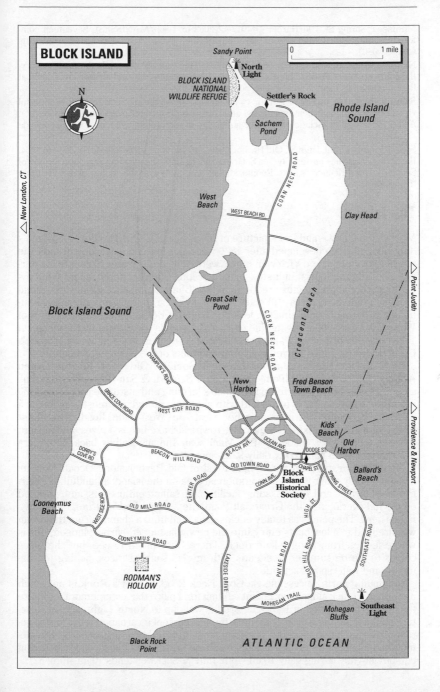

Manisses, Spring St, Old Harbor (☎401/466-2063 or 1-800/MANISSES). Seventeen comfortable antique-filled rooms, some overlooking the ocean, each named after local shipwrecks. ⑥–⑦.

National, Water St, Old Harbor (☎401/466-557). This vast Victorian pile dominates everything else on Water Street. There's a delightful wraparound porch and all mod cons, none at the expense of its charm. Fills up fast, so book early. ⑤–⑥.

Samuel Peckham Inn, New Harbor (☎401/466-2439). All the rooms come with wonderful views (some even have their own decks) at this large hotel on a hill overlooking New Harbor. Additional amenities include microwave and fridge in each room, and a pool with a poolside bar. ⑥–⑦.

Spring House Hotel, High St, Old Harbor (☎401/466-5844 or 1-800/234-9263). Built in 1854, the *Spring House* has hosted Ulysses S. Grant, and, in 1993, the wedding reception for one of Senator Edward Kennedy's sons. Rooms, studios and suites available, done out in a Victorian theme. ⑥–⑧.

The Island

Most visitors' first – and last – picture of Block Island is **Old Harbor**, the island's only village, which developed after 1870 when the Federal Government built the two breakwaters. Huge Victorian hotels were built along **Water Street** to encourage the fledgling tourist industry, many boasting cupolas, porches and flamboyant gingerbread architecture redolent of Oak Bluffs on Martha's Vineyard. Some of these grand structures still stand, albeit amidst a touristy mix of shops, boutiques, restaurants, and smaller, less atmospheric B&Bs. At the western end of Water Street, smack in the middle of the road, stands the **Statue of Rebecca**, an 1896 recasting of a biblical allegory, Rebecca at the well, erected by the Women's Christian Temperance Movement to remind folks of the dangers of alcohol.

Close by, the **Block Island Historical Society**, Old Town Road at Ocean Avenue (July & Aug daily 10am–5pm; June & Sept Sat & Sun 10am–5pm; $2), has a number of exhibits describing the island's farming and maritime past. This 1850 structure, once an inn, is furnished with antiques, though it's mostly useful as a place to get your bearings. Further west, on West Side Road, **The Lost Manissean Indian Exhibit** features arrowheads, axe heads, knives, and ancient mortars and pestles made by the Manissean Indians dating back 450 years (Memorial Day to Labor Day daily 9am–5pm; $1).

New Harbor, perhaps a mile northwest of Old Harbor along Ocean Avenue, boasts the only other would-be commercial area on the island: a handful of waterfront restaurants and shacks, some facilities for sailing enthusiasts, and, perched on the hill overlooking the Great Salt Pond, the *Samuel Peckham Inn*, one of two hotels here. The pond was totally enclosed by land until a channel from the ocean was dredged to allow boats entry into the newly fashioned harbor; indeed, this is where ferries from Long Island dock. There's not much to see, but the place comes to life on summer weekends with myriad sailboat races, fishing tournaments, and watersports activities.

Continuing north, accessible via Corn Neck Road, **Settler's Rock** is not much more than a quick stopping-off point – fitting for a place that commemorates where the settlers first landed in 1661 – before the walk up to **North Light**, a grim structure at Block Island's isolated northern tip. The current incarnation is the fourth go-round for this lighthouse, the previous three having been destroyed by the elements. A museum traces the island's maritime history and displays old life-saving equipment (July & Aug daily 10am–4pm; June & Sept weekends 10am–4pm; $2).

BLOCK ISLAND'S BEACHES

Block Island has some fine **beaches**, and even in the peak of the summer season it's possible to get far from the madding crowd and find the bliss of solitude. The main "family" beach is the **Fred Benson Town Beach**, a two-mile-long swath of sand with showers, lockers and chairs, umbrellas and kayaks to rent and lifeguards to keep an eye on things. There's ample free parking and extensive bicycle racks. At its sheltered southern tip, **Kids' Beach**, children can play in relatively shallow water, and look for small crabs, mussels and the like. **Ballard's Beach**, just south of Old Harbor, is the island's only other lifeguard-staffed beach. Quiet **West Beach**, on the northwestern coast, is backed by dunes that you must keep off: they are part of a bird sanctuary. **Cooneymus Beach**, at the southwest corner of the island, may look like a lovely sandy stretch, but the water is somewhat dangerous due to strong currents. Last, a venture to beautiful **Black Rock**, on the island's southern shore, rewards not with swimming opportunities but with a dramatic seascape at which many ships have met their untimely end.

Back from Old Harbor, Spring Street trails to the southernmost tip of the island, where **Mohegan Bluffs**, the spectacular 150-foot cliffs named for an Indian battle that occurred at their base, tower over the Atlantic. Positioned atop is the redbrick **Southeast Light**, built in 1873 but not moved to its present position until 1993 after erosion threatened its survival. It, too, hosts a small museum (Memorial Day to Labor Day daily 10am–4pm; $5 donation); better yet are the stunning **ocean views** to be glimpsed.

Further west, a dirt track (Black Rock Road) leads from Cooneymus Road to the preserved sanctuary of **Rodman's Hollow**, a deep glacial depression offering more panoramic views of the Atlantic.

Eating

For such a small island, there is a remarkable variety of good **places to eat**, a result of the high number of visitors expected. Not surprisingly, **fresh seafood** tops the bill at many of the establishments, with lobster a firm favorite. Remember that all of them reduce their hours drastically for the spring and autumn and all but one or two close for the entire winter. Summer weekends in particular can be very crowded, and not all restaurants take reservations.

Atlantic Inn, High St, Old Harbor (☎401/466-5883). This restaurant's main claim to fame is that President Clinton dined here in the summer of 1997 – whether or not he partook of the excellent $39 four-course prix-fixe menu is uncertain. Contemporary American cuisine – the grilled shark on a bed of spinach is particularly good – is complemented by fantastic ocean views, best enjoyed accompanied by a cocktail or two on the verandah.

Ballard's Restaurant, Water St, Old Harbor (☎401/466-2231). Overlooking the beach, this casual standby offers seafood classics like fish and chips, clam cakes, and fried clams.

Bethany's Airport Diner, State Airport, Center Rd (☎401/466-3100). Breakfast, lunch, and dinner in an informal atmosphere, plus daily homecooked specials, like meatloaf and London broil.

Ernie's Old Harbor Restaurant, Water St, Old Harbor (☎401/466-2473). Block Island's favorite breakfast destination for forty or so years. Arrive early (opens 6.30am) to get a seat on the deck overlooking the harbor.

Hotel Manisses, Spring St, Old Harbor (☎401/466-2421). Elegant dining in a Victorian inn (see p.278) featuring an innovative menu with tasty twists on local seafood.

Juice 'n' Java Caffe, Dodge St, Old Harbor (☎401/466-5108). Award-winning coffees, espressos and teas to accompany a choice of eighty desserts.

The Oar, West Side Road, New Harbor (☎401/466-8820). Island landmark famous for the scores of painted oars that hang from the ceiling. The seafood bar offers chowder, peel-and-eat shrimp, lobster rolls and the like; you can take your food outside and enjoy superb views of the Old Harbor from the porch.

Old Post Office Bagel Shop, Corn Neck Rd and Ocean Ave, Old Harbor (☎401/466-5959). Fresh bagels baked daily. Eat inside or al fresco.

Samuel Peckham Tavern, West Side Rd, New Harbor (☎401/466-2231). Unpretentious restaurant and bar serving down-to-earth steaks, ribs, chicken, and, of course, fish.

Nightlife and entertainment

Although Block Island is so quiet for most of the year you can hear the grass grow, on summer nights the **nightlife** picks up, mostly centering on the ample selection of **bars**. Some of these are staid and courtly; others are renowned for their boisterous weekend parties. In recent years, the **Spring House Music Festivals** (three per summer) have even brought full-blown rock concerts to the island. More "wholesome" entertainment is provided by two **cinemas**: the Empire Theater, Water Street (☎401/466-2555), shows first-run movies and midnight cult films, while the Oceanwest Theater, Champlin's Marina, New Harbor (☎401/466-2971), offers more first-runs and childrens' matinees.

Captain Nick's Rock & Roll Bar, Ocean Ave, Old Harbor (☎401/466-5670). The island's biggest nightclub, featuring live music at weekends that ranges from national headliners to locals eager to strut their stuff.

Club Soda, Connecticut Ave, Old Harbor (☎401/466-5397). Drinks and music amidst strange, sort of kitsch, decor.

McGovern's Yellow Kittens Tavern, Corn Neck Rd, Old Harbor (☎401/466-5855). This 126-year-old institution has no shortage of activities in which to engage – pool, ping-pong, darts, pinball – while imbibing. Live music throughout the summer, too.

Mohegan Café & Brewery, Water St, across from the ferry on Old Harbor (☎401/466-5911). Microbrews direct from an in-house brewery, plus nightly entertainment in season.

Payne's Dock, New Harbor (☎401/466-5572). Dockside bar featuring live entertainment Wednesdays and weekends during the summer.

CHAPTER FIVE

CONNECTICUT

N ew England's southernmost state, **CONNECTICUT**, a rectangle about 90 miles long by 55 miles wide, was named *Quinnehtukqut* ("great tidal river") by the Native Americans after the river that bisects it and spills into Long Island Sound. It's a small and densely populated state, despite being predominantly rural: the vast majority of residents live in the large coastal cities, in and around the state capital **Hartford**, or in the southwestern corner of the state, which is little more than a conservative, high-rent suburb of New York City where canny commuters can earn huge Big Apple salaries while avoiding its high taxes.

Connecticut's first white settlers came in the 1630s when **English** refugees from Massachusetts seeking political and religious freedom arrived at the town of Windsor. Settlements followed in Wethersfield and Hartford, and in 1636 the three united to form the **Connecticut Colony**, adopting the **"Fundamental Orders,"** a charter which was later used as a model for the American Constitution; indeed, Connecticut is still sometimes referred to as the **"Constitution State."** After the Pequot War of 1637, which effectively displaced the Native Americans from their home of several thousand years, more communities were established, and a **second colony**, composed of the coastal towns surrounding New Haven, was formed in 1643, only to unite with the first around twenty years later.

Connecticut soon became a center for **"Yankee ingenuity,"** principally the invention and marketing (often by notorious and not always honorable Yankee peddlers) of many a useful household object. Meanwhile, on the coast, locals were turning to the sea for their livelihood; shipbuilding and whaling were both big business. The Puritan infatuation with education resulted in the establishment of **Yale University**, founded in 1701 as the Collegiate School in Killingsworth before moving to Saybrook, and eventually New Haven in 1716. Among its earliest students was **Noah Webster**, whose *American Dictionary of the English Language*, published in 1828, became the definitive dictionary for American English and helped standardize spelling and pronunciation.

Although the colony was hit very badly by English raids during the **Revolutionary War**, its role in providing the war effort with crucial supplies earned it the nickname of the **"Provisions State."** This period also produced one of Connecticut's great folk heroes, **Nathan Hale**, hanged by the British for spying.

Connecticut continued to prosper during the late eighteenth and nineteenth centuries, with steady industrialization helped along by **Eli Whitney**, developer of efficient machine tools, and entrepreneurs like Hartford's **Samuel Colt**, inventor of the repeating pistol. While it was producing some of the nation's great businessmen, the state was also having a cultural impact – during a long sojourn in Hartford, **Mark Twain** wrote *The Adventures of Tom Sawyer* and *The Adventures of Huckleberry Finn*, while **John Brown**, perhaps the nation's greatest abolitionist, was a native of Torrington. The state has produced a fair number of eminent politicians, most recently Al Gore's vice-presidential running-mate in 2000, Senator **Joseph I. Lieberman**, who hails from New Haven.

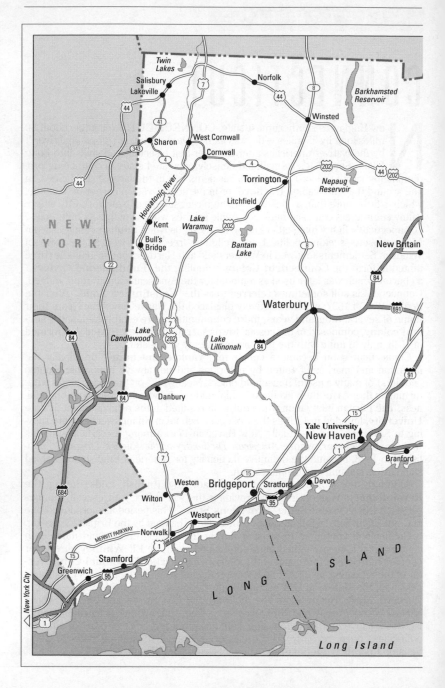

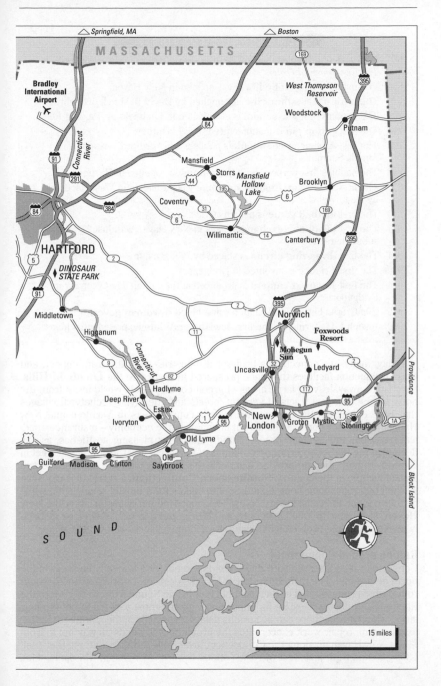

0   15 miles

SOME CONNECTICUT FIRSTS

1639   Connecticut produces the first **written constitution** in the colonies, *The Fundamental Orders.*

1656   The nation's first **public library** is opened in New Haven.

1775   The world's first **submarine** is launched by David Bushnell of Saybrook.

1784   The nation's first **law school** is established in Litchfield by Tapping Reeve.

1794   The first **cotton gin** is manufactured by Eli Whitney.

1796   The first **American cookbook** is published in Hartford, written by Amelia Simmons.

1796   The nation's first purpose-built **state house** is opened in Hartford.

1806   The first **American/English dictionary** is published in West Hartford by Noah Webster.

1873   The first **football game** is played at Yale.

1878   The first **telephone exchange** opens in New Haven with just 21 subscribers.

1881   The first **three-ring circus** is staged by P. T. Barnum.

1920   The first **Frisbee** is invented in Bridgeport.

1934   The first **Polaroid camera** is produced at the Frisbie Pie Company in Bridgeport.

1975   Ella Grasso becomes the nation's first **elected woman governor.**

2000   Joseph I. Lieberman is the first **Jewish candidate** on presidential ticket.

Today, many of Connecticut's traditional industries, like the iron, copper, and brass production facilities that once prospered in areas like the **Litchfield Hills**, have faded away, leaving large areas of green countryside a world away from the noisy Interstates, vast tracts of verdant forests and the idyllic archetypal villages that have everything in common with their counterparts in Vermont and New Hampshire further north. The current linchpins of the economy – insurance, medical research, and military bases – hardly make for pleasing aesthetics, as evidenced in the high-rise corporate buildings of **Hartford** and the submarine fleet in **Groton**, though they do provide Connecticut's citizens with the highest average annual income in the country. **Southeastern Connecticut**, a series of rocky surf-washed outcrops along Long Island Sound, makes for a mostly scenic trek, while further west on the coast towards New York, more industrial-based cities like **New Haven**, also home to Yale University, and **Bridgeport**, in particular, face distinctly un-New England problems like drug wars, homelessness and violent crime.

Getting around Connecticut

Connecticut is well served with major **roads**, except for a few isolated areas in the north of the state. The main Interstate is I-95, the east coast's primary north–south route, which runs parallel to the coast of Long Island Sound from New York to the Rhode Island border. Despite its importance, for the most part it's limited to four lanes, which means there can be serious delays, especially in the summer months; longstanding repair work exacerbates the problem. I-91 wends its way north from I-95 at New Haven up along the Connecticut River Valley to Vermont. Further east, I-395 extends from just west of New London towards Worcester, Massachusetts,

ACCOMMODATION PRICE CODES

All accommodation prices in this book have been coded using the symbols below. Note that prices are for the least expensive **double rooms** in each establishment. For a full explanation see p.28 in Basics.

[1] up to $30	[4] $60–80	[7] $130–175
[2] $30–45	[5] $80–100	[8] $175–250
[3] $45–60	[6] $100–130	[9] $250+

and I-84 links Danbury, near the New York state line, with Hartford. As with all New England states, it's more fun to get off the highways and on to the side roads where you have more time to appreciate the attractive rural scenery and pretty colonial villages for which Connecticut is famous. Even getting lost can be fun; distances are so small that you'll find your way back sooner rather than later.

If you want to **fly** to or from Connecticut, the state's major airport, **Bradley International** (☎1-888/624-1533), twelve miles north of Hartford, has connections to most of the nation's principal cities. Amtrak **trains** (☎1-800/USA-RAIL) ply the main northeast corridor route between Washington DC, New York City, and Boston, with most trains stopping at Stamford, Bridgeport, New Haven, New London, and Mystic. Metro North (☎1-800/638-7646) provides a commuter service between New Haven and New York City, with connecting services to many other towns. Greyhound (☎1-800/231-2222), Bonanza (☎1-800/556-3815) and Peter Pan (☎1-800/343-9999) provide **bus** services to most of Connecticut's major towns; Connecticut Transit (☎203/327-7433) serves the inland area around Hartford.

SOUTHEASTERN CONNECTICUT

The much-visited **southeastern coast** of Connecticut stretches fifty miles from Stonington in the east to Branford in the west, bisected by the Thames (pronounced *Thaymz*) River. A succession of picturesque colonial communities, old whaling towns and unattractive industrial cities characterize this section of Long Island Sound. No longer are they the iniquitous and rumbustious ports that so inspired Melville, but they're still keen to preserve, with varying degrees of success, a sense of their history. Among the highlights is **Mystic Seaport**, a reconstructed nineteenth-century maritime village with a fine collection of restored ships, including a replica of the *Amistad* (see box, p.299) the salty old whaling city of **New London** is struggling to come to terms with the economic realities brought about by the defense cutbacks at neighboring **Groton**, but with a cluster of halfway decent galleries and museums as well as some fine old sea captains' houses; further west, the prosperous towns of **Old Lyme** and **Old Saybrook** are home to a cluster of beguiling art galleries and museums, while **Guilford** has one of the largest collections of seventeenth- and eighteenth-century homes in the northeast, several of which are open to the public. A bit inland, the massive casinos opened by Native Americans at **Foxwoods** and **Mohegun Sun** attract millions of visitors annually; if you're looking to get well away from such bustle, there's no better place than off the coast of **Branford**, where a series of rocky outcrops, some inhabited, some not, is better known as the **Thimble Islands**.

Mystic

The old whaling port and shipbuilding center of **MYSTIC**, right on I-95, purists will tell you, does not really exist; it's an area governed partly by Groton and partly by Stonington. Nonetheless, it does have a small, well-kept and rather touristy **downtown**, lined with typical New England-quaint clapboard galleries and antique shops. Before going on to see Mystic's main attractions, you might first want to take a look at the **Mystic Art Association Gallery**, 9 Water St (Mon–Fri 11am–5pm; donation; ☎860/536-7601), with changing exhibits and a section devoted to the works of modern impressionist William North, many of which depict local landscapes. Not far away, the **Portersville Academy**, 74 High St (late May–Oct Tues, Thurs & Sat, hours vary; ☎860/536-4779), contains a restored classroom where you can enjoy the thrill of sitting at a school desk more than a hundred years old. The old drawbridge across the **Mystic River**, which divides the town down the middle, still opens hourly, and self-guided walking tours take in the many old sea captains' houses. Along the western bank of the river is River Road, a four-mile stretch ideal for walking or cycling, which passes **Downes Marsh**, a sanctuary where you may catch a glimpse of osprey.

Mystic Seaport and around

What tourists come to Mystic to see is on the other side of the bridge, the meticulously constructed waterfront village of **Mystic Seaport**, at the mouth of the river (daily: summer 9am–5pm; rest of year 10am–4pm; $16, late-afternoon arrivals are granted free entrance on the next day), where more than sixty weathered buildings house old-style workshops and stores, including an apothecary and a printing press. The **Stillman Building** contains beautifully carved scrimshaw, ornate figureheads and vast numbers of objects made from whales' wax-like spermaceti, as well as disturbing video footage of a bloody whale hunt. Demonstrations of sea-shanty singing, fish-splitting, sail-setting and knot-tying vie with storytelling and theater, and state-of-the-art interactive computers enable visitors to track hurricanes and encourage children to become sailors. In the **shipyard**, you can watch the building, restoration and maintenance of a vast collection of wooden ships, among them the *Joseph Conrad*, an 1882 training ship, the *L.A. Dunton*, a 1921 fishing schooner and the restored *Charles W. Morgan*, a three-masted wooden Yankee **whaling ship** built in 1841, and the last of its kind. Done up as if ready to embark on a two-year voyage, the ship is filled with whaling memorabilia; below deck, accessed by perilously narrow stairs, the blubber room is crowded with huge iron try-pots for melting down the stinking stuff. The seaport's *piece de resistance*, however, is an evocative new reproduction of the 77-foot *Amistad*, a vessel which carried 53 Africans who had been illegally sold into slavery – and the subject of a 1997 Spielberg historical drama of the same name. The Seaport also boasts the nation's largest maritime bookstore and the **Mystic Maritime Gallery**, a center for contemporary marine art with a display of model ships.

About a mile north of the Seaport, adjacent to I-95, the **Marinelife Aquarium** is Mystic's other major draw (daily: July–Labor Day 9am–6pm; rest of year 9am–5pm; $14), where more than six thousand weird and wonderful marine specimens glug about. Beyond the striking glass entrance, visitors are confronted with bonnet head sharks, mudskippers (slippery critters that can live half in the mud

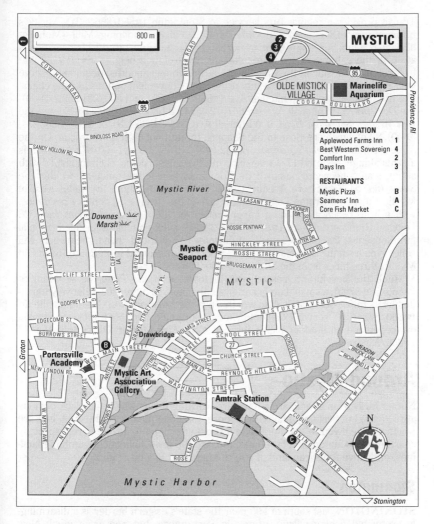

and half on dry land), and a thirty-thousand-gallon reef display with thirty types of artificial coral. Also good is the California Coast exhibit, which features leopard sharks and garibaldis. Nearby, not-so-quaint factory outlets occupy the overdone **Olde Misticke Village**, at the intersection of I-97 and Route 27, an outdoor mall with more than sixty upmarket shops in mock-Colonial buildings.

Practicalities

There's a **train station** in Mystic where Amtrak calls in on its Boston to Washington route (for schedule information, call ☎1-800/872-7245), and South East Area

Transit provides a regular **bus** service to Stonington (☎860/886-2631). Mystic's **information office** is in the Olde Mistick Village Shopping Mall (Mon–Sat 9.30am–6.30pm, Sun 10am–6pm; ☎860/536-1641); **accommodation** information is available there. It may be useful to take advantage of their help, as it's very difficult to find a place to stay in the town in the peak summer months; definitely reserve your room well in advance if it's July or August. Convenient options include chains like the *Comfort Inn*, 48 Whitehall Ave (☎860/572-8531 or 1-800/221-2222; [5]–[6]), the *Days Inn*, 55 Whitehall Ave (☎860/572-0574 or 1-800/572-3993; [5]–[6]) and the *Best Western Sovereign Hotel*, 9 Whitehall Ave (☎860/536-4281 or 1-800/528-1234; [5]–[6]), all of which are close to the Seaport, though not high on character. On the same road, the *Whitehall Mansion*, no. 42 (☎860/572-7280 or 1-800/572-3993; [7]), is a painstakingly restored 1771 mansion with five guest rooms, each furnished with antiques and queen-size canopy beds. For somewhere a little quieter, try either the *Shore Inn*, 54 East Shore Avenue (☎860/536-1180; [7]), about five miles west of Mystic Village on Groton Long Point, a turn-of-the-(twentieth)-century residence, with private beach and fishing opportunities, or the *Applewood Farms Inn*, 528 Ledyard Highway, Ledyard (☎860/536-2022; [5]), a delightful antique-filled colonial farmhouse just five minutes north of downtown; if you call ahead, the owners will collect you from the train station. The Seaport **campground** is on Route 184 in Old Mystic, three miles from the Seaport (☎860/536-4044).

Much the best-known **restaurant** in town is *Mystic Pizza*, 56 W Main St (☎860/536-5700), a small, family-run place that serves huge pies, relatively unruffled by its movie-star status. Also worth a try, the *Seamen's Inn*, Greenmanville Rd (☎860/572-5303), serves excellent prime rib, or you can grab a fried seafood take-out order and an outdoor picnic table at *Cove Fish Market*, Old Stonington Rd (☎860/536-0061).

Around Mystic

Not far away from Mystic are a few hard-working towns which may lack obvious attractions, but certainly make for a more complete picture of the area, and are worth a poke if you've got more than a short afternoon to devote here, especially charming Stonington. Not far inland, too, are the few Connecticut gambling facilities, on Native American land, if you're interested in a bit of glitz.

Stonington

STONINGTON, just south of I-95 near the state's eastern border, is a disarmingly pretty old fishing village, originally Portuguese, but now very much New England with its attractive whitewashed cottages, white picket fences, colorful gardens and peaceful waterfront. Its main street, **Water Street**, is brimming with antique shops and upmarket thrift stores, packed with well-to-do bargain hunters on weekends. At no. 7, the **Lighthouse Museum** (July–Aug daily 10am–5pm; May–June & Sept–Oct Tues–Sun 10am–5pm; $4), moved back a bit from its original position due to the dangers of erosion, dates from 1823 and is full of local memorabilia, maps, drawings, and whaling and fishing gear. You can climb the stone steps and iron staircase for views over Long Island Sound. Close to Lambert's Cove Bridge, the Italianate **Captain Nathaniel B. Palmer House**, 40 Palmer St (May–Oct Tues–Sun 10am–4pm, last tour 3pm; $4), celebrates the life of Palmer, whose main claim to fame was the discovery of the Antarctic landmass in 1820. The mansion, topped by an octagonal cupola from which Palmer and his family could identify ships arriving from far-off ports, contains exhibits about his work.

A few miles out of the village center, at Exit 91 off I-95, follow the "wine trail" signs to the **Stonington Vineyards**, 523 Taugwonk Rd (daily 11am–5pm; tour at 2pm), for a look around a local wine producer, and some free tastings of their concoctions like Seaport White and Seaport Blush.

Practicalities

If you'd like to **stay** in Stonington, *Lasbury's Guest House*, 24 Orchard St (☎860/535-2681; [5]), offers three pleasant rooms decorated with a nautical theme in a secluded cottage at the rear of a much larger house. Alternatively, for a little less money, try the *Cove Ledge Motel*, Whewell Circle (☎860/599-4130; [4]), where you'll find simple, uncluttered rooms close to the water. Authentic clam chowder, as well as full meals, can be had at *Noah's*, 115 Water St (☎860/535-3925), an old Portuguese **restaurant** with a friendly atmosphere. Two seafood restaurants, *Water St Café* and *Skipper's Dock,* share premises at 60 Water St (☎860/535-8544); the former is for elegant dining, the latter less expensive and rowdier, with a deck offering fantastic ocean views.

Groton

Seven miles west of Mystic Seaport, **GROTON** is a suitably unpleasant name for the home town of the hideous **US Naval Submarine Base**, Crystal Lake Road, off Rte-12 (mid-May–Oct Wed–Mon 10am–5pm, Tues 1–5pm; Nov–mid-May Wed–Mon 9am–4pm; free), headquarters for the North Atlantic Fleet, and the place where the **USS Nautilus**, America's first nuclear-powered submarine, was built. You can tour the submarine, winding your way through narrow, claustrophobic passages past the wardroom and officers' berthing area and the attack center, down a short, steep staircase to the control room, the radio room and the crew's quarters, with bunks stacked three and four high, complete with pin-ups of Marilyn Monroe. The **Submarine Force Museum** next door traces the history of submersibles from Bushnell's *Turtle,* used in the Revolutionary War, to the powerful *Trident.* The main hall features a re-created World War II attack center, where you can look through one of three periscopes and take aim on cars in the parking lot. For a different perspective, the tour boat *Patriot* makes excursions up and down the Thames, including one called "See Subs by Boat," departing from City Pier at the end of State Street in New London (☎860/444-7827). Proces for the various tours range from about $12 to $16.

New London

On the opposite bank of the Thames from Groton, **NEW LONDON**, with 26,000 residents, is the largest city along this stretch of the coast, though it's hardly a metropolis and spreads over but six square miles. It was a wealthy whaling port in the nineteenth century, and by the 1850s was second only to New Bedford, Massachusetts, for the size of its whaling fleet. Today, the city is struggling to come to terms with the economic realities brought about by cuts in military spending, though it is trying very hard to liven up the downtown area, still shabby in parts, but with enough historical interest to warrant perhaps a half-day detour.

Its most popular attraction, the **US Coast Guard Academy**, Mohegan Avenue off I-95, spreads out on an attractive sloping campus overlooking the Thames. Visitors can tour the *USS Eagle*, the only tall ship on active duty, and now used as a training ship. The **US Coast Guard Museum** explores two centuries of coast-guard history and includes ships' portraits and the figurehead from the *Eagle* (Mon & Wed–Fri 9am–4.30pm, Tues 9am–8pm, Sat 10am–5pm, Sun noon–5pm; free). Just opposite the Academy entrance, the **Lyman Allyn Art Museum**, 625 Williams St (Tues–Sat 10am–5pm, Sun 1–5pm; $4), contains all varieties of American fine arts and crafts, including a silver tankard by, whom else, Paul Revere, and a superior collection of dolls, dollhouses and toys from the eighteenth and nineteenth centuries. At 33 Gallows Lane, just off Williams Street, the **Science Center of Eastern Connecticut** (Tues–Sat 10am–6pm, Sun 1–5pm; $6), tucked in the woods, has a sound room where you can create long and short sound waves on an oscilloscope or freeze a wave on a contraption made of membrane, a strobe light and a speaker.

A self-guided walking tour of New London's downtown takes you past **Whale Oil Row**, a short line of 1832 Greek Revival houses once owned by leaders in the whale-oil business, though none is open to the public. Just round the corner, salty **Captain's Walk** is New London's main street, lined with a variety of shops and restaurants. Not too far away, on Eugene O'Neill Drive, the **Nathan Hale Schoolhouse**, first called Union Schoolhouse, is where Nathan Hale, the Revolutionary War hero famed for his last words, "I only regret that I have one life to lose for my country," taught for sixteen months before starting military service. A bit west, the **Shaw Mansion**, 11 Blinman St (Wed–Fri 1–4pm, Sat 10am–4pm; $4), a stone house built in 1756 for wealthy shipowner and trader Nathaniel Shaw, has unusual paneled-cement fireplace walls and some period furnishings and portraits. Meanwhile, New London's oldest house, the 1678 **Joshua Hempstead House**, 11 Hempstead St at Jay St (mid-May–mid-Oct Thurs–Sun 1–5pm; $4), was said to have been used as a safe haven on the Underground Railroad, though you'll find nothing too special here to mark it as such. Admission gets you into the **Nathaniel Hempstead House** – Nathaniel was Joshua's grandson – across the lawn, which stands out for its two-foot-thick stone walls and outdoor stone beehive oven.

New London is also renowned as the birthplace of boozy playwright **Eugene O'Neill**, whose childhood home, the **Monte Cristo Cottage**, 325 Pequout Ave (Memorial Day–Labor Day Tues–Sat 10am–5pm, Sun 1–5pm; tours 10am, noon, 2pm & 4pm; $4), can be toured complete with juicy details of his trauma-ridden early life – though they may already be familiar to you from his *Long Day's Journey into Night*. The author's influence is felt further at the O'Neill Memorial Theater Center at 305 Great Neck Rd in nearby **Waterford** (I-95 exit 82), an acclaimed testing-ground for playwrights and actors, where audiences can take pot luck and watch new, often experimental shows in rehearsal (performances held sporadically May–Aug; ☎860/443-5378). Just beyond the Monte Cristo Cottage, **Ocean Beach Park**, Ocean Avenue (summer daily 9am–11pm; $2), holds a beach with a wooden boardwalk and a massive saltwater pool.

Groton and New London practicalities

You could be forgiven for thinking that, thanks to New London's proximity to I-95, everyone arrives by road. Not so. There's a **car ferry** from Orient Point on Long

GAMBLING ON CONNECTICUT'S NATIVE AMERICAN RESERVATIONS

Until the late 1980s, the $400 billion-a-year gambling business was confined to just two states, Nevada and New Jersey, but a lobbying push from Native American tribes, eager for greater self-determination to manage their own affairs, moved Congress to pass the Indian Gambling Regulatory Act. This reform recognized the rights of Native American tribes in the US to establish gambling and gaming facilities on their reservations, so long as the states in which they are located have some form of legalized gambling, and, indeed, today gambling is only *not* legal in the two states of Hawaii and Utah.

Connecticut has become home to three major Indian casinos, over objections from environmentalists, anti-gambling agencies and residents. The most successful such venture, the massive **Foxwoods Casino and Resort**, Rte-2, Ledyard (☎1-800/752-9244, *www.foxwoods.com*), which rises dramatically above the virgin pine forests north of New London, draws millions of visitors annually to what is now the world's largest purpose-built gambling facility. Built by the Mashantucket Indians, the resort boasts no fewer than eleven restaurants, shops, a theater, dance club, and an amusement park, with an Amtrak station to follow. Three huge hotels accommodate visitors, who can play all manner of slots, table games and bingo. Just a few miles away, the **Mohegan Sun Casino**, Rte-2A, Uncasville (☎1-888/226-7771, *www.mohegansun.com*), opened its doors in 1996. About half the size of Foxwoods (indeed, the bingo hall here only seats 1500, as compared to Foxwoods' 3200-seater), the atmosphere is far less frantic.

Island (Cross Sound Ferry; ☎860/443-5281), and even an **airport**, with a limited service to the rest of New England (and several car rental outfits). Amtrak runs a regular service to New London from New York, Boston and other points along the main east coast line. Greyhound and Bonanza **buses** both serve the city, and there's a less than comprehensive **local bus** network, too (☎860/886-2631). New London is generally a less expensive place to stay than touristy Mystic, with several reasonably priced **motels** along I-95, including the *Holiday Inn*, I-95 and Frontage Rd (☎860/442-0631; [5]–[6]), and the *Red Roof Inn*, 707 Colman St (☎860/444-0001 or 1-800/843-7663; [3]–[4]). **B&Bs** in the area can be booked via Seacoast Landings B&B Registry, 133 Neptune Drive, Groton (☎860/442-1940), while in Groton there are also plenty of budget motels off I-95 exit 86, including a *Super 8* (☎860/448-2818 or 1-800/800-8000; [3]).

New London has a few good **restaurants** worth stopping into, including *Lorelei*, 158 State St (☎860/442-3375), serving seafood and steaks in a casual atmosphere; for Continental-style cuisine, *Timothy's*, 181 Bank St (☎860/437-0526), is hard to beat. On the cheaper side is the *Recovery Room*, 445 Ocean Ave (☎860/443-2619), an award-winning pizzeria. Over the water in Groton, *G. Williker's*, 156 King's Highway (☎860/445-8043), with an enormous menu, is a good place for steaks, seafood and sandwiches, while the *Fun 'n' Food Clam Bar*, 283 Rte-12 (☎860/445-6186), serves foot-long hot dogs, clam fritters, gigantic grinders and the like. For more eating and accommodation information, the Southeastern Connecticut Chamber of Commerce has offices at 470 Bank St (☎860/444-2206 or 1-800/TOENJOY) and at 1 Whale Oil Row (☎860/443-8332 or 1-800/222-6783).

West to New Haven

Fifteen miles west of New London, at the mouth of the Connecticut River, sits **OLD LYME**, the site of an Impressionist art colony dating from the end of the nineteenth century. It was started when three sisters and their mother began to attract a regular clientele of artists to their boarding house each summer. The **Florence Griswold Museum**, 96 Lyme St (Jan–Apr Wed–Sun 1–5pm, May–Dec Tues–Sat 10am–5pm, Sun 1–5pm; $5), named after the sister – "Miss Florence" – most involved in developing the colony, is located in the very boarding house that the family managed. Guided tours of the 1817 house cover its history, Griswold's life and the work of the various artists who stayed there, including Willard Metcalfe, Childe Hassam and William Chadwick, whose studio is set up just as it was during his lifetime. A few doors away, the **Lyme Academy of Fine Arts**, at 84 Lyme St (Tues–Sat 10am–4pm; donation), founded in 1976, features drawing, painting and sculpture by contemporary artists housed in a Federal-style John Sill house also dating from 1817.

Old Saybrook

The former shipbuilding center of **OLD SAYBROOK**, opposite Old Lyme on the western bank of the Connecticut River, claims a few historic houses along its main road, though little else to draw your attention. Puritan settlers arrived in 1635 and soon erected a fort to guard the river entrance to the town, an act remembered in **Fort Saybrook Monument Park**, at the stronghold's former site, though nothing of the fort remains today. In 1701 the town became the venue for the **Collegiate School**, later to move to New Haven and rename itself **Yale University**. Commercial activity centers on Boston Post Road, while the unusually wide **Main Street** becomes progressively more interesting the further south you get toward Saybrook Point, showcasing architectural styles from seventeenth-century saltboxes to nineteenth-century Federal buildings. Of these, the 1767 **General William Hart House**, 350 Main St (late May to Sept Fri–Sun 12.30–4pm; suggested donation $2.50), once the residence of a prosperous merchant who owned a fleet of sailing ships and served in the Revolutionary War, has been restored to its original elegance. It contains eight corner fireplaces, one decorated with Sadler and Green transfer print tiles illustrating scenes from Aesop's fables, as well as local history exhibits and a reference library. The **James Gallery**, 2 Pennywise Lane at Main St (Mon–Fri 3–9pm, weekends 10am–9pm; ☎860/395-1406), is an unusual art gallery-cum-soda fountain, housed in a former general store and pharmacy.

Practicalities

Local **bus** services are provided by the Estuary Transit District (☎860/388-3497), and some Amtrak **trains** stop at Old Saybrook (☎1-800/872-7245), with a local commuter service between New Haven and New London provided by Shore Line East (☎1-800/255-7433). The **Old Saybrook Chamber of Commerce** maintains an information booth on the Old Saybrook Town Green (Memorial Day–Labor Day Mon–Fri 10am–3pm) and an office at 146 Main St (year-round Mon–Fri 10am–3pm; ☎860/388-3266). They'll have info on the wide variety of **accommodation** in the area, ranging from historic **B&Bs** like the 1746 *Deacon Timothy Pratt House B&B*, 325 Main St, Old Saybrook (☎860/395-1229; ⑥), with rooms furnished in period (ie 1746) style, with working fireplaces and four-poster beds, and the luxurious

Saybrook Point Inn, 2 Bridge St, Old Saybrook (☎860/395-2000 or 1-800/243-0212, *www.saybrook.com*; ⑥–⑨), where most rooms have water views and balconies, to a number of motels and inns all located along Boston Post Road (Rte-1). These include the friendly, 45-room *Sandpiper Motor Inn*, no. 1750 (☎860/399-7973 or 1-800/323-7973, *www.thesandpiper.com*; ⑥–⑦), the smaller but equally comfortable *Heritage Motor Inn*, no. 1500 (☎860/388-3743; ④–⑤) and the *Water's Edge Inn & Resort*, no. 1525 (☎860/399-5901; ⑥–⑨), on a lovely setting overlooking the Sound.

Many of Old Saybrook's **restaurants** are also to be found on Boston Post Road: the *Old Saybrook Diner*, at no. 809 (☎860/395-1079), a town fixture, serves great spinach pie, while *Cuckoo's Nest*, at no. 1712 (☎860/399-9060), offers Mexican, southwestern and Cajun dishes. Away from Boston Post Road, *Dock & Dine*, College St, Saybrook Point (☎860/388-4665 or 1-800/362-3625), has lovely views over the Connecticut River to go with its classic American steak and seafood dishes – though you'll pay for it.

Clinton

CLINTON, eight miles west of Old Saybrook, pushes itself as one of the most visited leisure ports on Long Island Sound, thanks to the abundance of well-equipped marinas. Its historic district includes the **John Stanton House**, 63 East Main St (June–Sept Tues–Sat 2–5pm; donation requested), built around 1790 and where the Marquis de Lafayette stayed in 1824; the bed in which he slept is still displayed in its original surroundings. The house served as a general store for many years, supplying goods and services to the sailors whose boats docked nearby; on display are items sold back in those days, together with a collection of antique American and Staffordshire dinnerware. Still, Clinton is better known for its **Clinton Crossing Premium Outlets**, just off I-95 (Mon–Sat 10am–9pm, Sun 10am–8pm), with more than seventy upmarket stores that offer savings on designer goods like Calvin Klein, Liz Claiborne and Polo. You're unlikely to **stay** here, though the town is pleasant enough; if you do, consider the *Captain Dibbell House*, at 21 Commerce St (☎860/669-1646; ④–⑤), an excellent-value B&B, or, for something a bit different, *A Victorian Village – Marina Cottages*, 345 East Main St (☎860/669-3009; ⑦–⑧) – a cluster of comfortable, antique-filled cottages around a landscaped garden.

Madison

Just a few miles west on Route 1, posh **MADISON** sits on the waterfront with an attractive shady green overlooked by a white-spired church and a broad main street lined with upmarket boutiques and trendy cafés. There's not much to distinguish it from nearby Clinton, though it does contain two historic buildings of note. The **Deacon John Grave House**, 581 Boston Post Rd (mid-June–Labor Day Wed–Sat 1–4pm; Labor Day–mid-Oct Sat & Sun 10am–4pm; $2), Madison's oldest residence, built in 1685 and used over the years as a school, a wartime infirmary and weapons depot, an inn, a tavern and a courtroom, has nevertheless remained all this time under the auspices of the Grave family. Indeed, there's even a surviving ledger of their household expenditures from 1678 to 1895. Further down the road, the white-clapboard saltbox **Allis-Bushnell House**, at no. 853 (Wed, Fri & Sat 1–4pm; donation), dates from about the same period, and contains original paneling and unusual corner fireplaces. One room has been restored as a turn-of-the-century doctor's office in memory of **Dr Milo Rindye**, a popular physician who lived and worked in the house. There's also an interesting collection of artifacts, from costumes and kitchenware to a Victorian hearing aid and working looms.

About two miles east of downtown Madison, off Route 1, **Hammonasset Beach State Park** (daily 8am–sunset; parking $8 weekdays, $12 summer weekends) maintains two miles of prime sandy beach, backed by dunes and a salt marsh. If you don't want to face the briny deep, there's a **nature center** in the park that contains exhibits about the wildlife and history of the area.

Good **accommodation** choices are *The Inn at Café Lafayette*, 725 Boston Post Rd (☎203/245-7773 or 1-800/660-8984; [6]–[7]), a smart downtown establishment with antique furnishings, the *Dolly Madison Inn*, 73 West Wharf Rd (☎203/245-7377; [4]–[6]), just two minutes from the water, with access to one of the town beaches and the *Honeysuckle Hill B&B*, 116 Yankee Peddlar Path (I-95 exit 61), a cozy, quiet, country-style retreat (☎203/245-4574; [4]). **Places to eat** include the casual *Perfect Parties*, 885 Boston Post Rd (☎203/245-0250), with good salads, soups, sandwiches for eat-in or take-out, and *The Wharf*, 94 West Wharf Rd at the *Madison Beach Hotel* (☎203/245-1404), where seafood – baked, grilled, fried or stuffed – is the thing.

Guilford

First settled by English vicar Reverend Henry Whitfield in 1639, **GUILFORD** has one of the largest collections of seventeenth- and eighteenth-century homes in New England, only three, unfortunately, are open to the public. Among them, Whitfield's own home at 248 Old Whitfield St, the oldest surviving stone house in New England, has been transformed into the **Henry Whitfield State Museum** (Wed–Sun 10am–4.30pm; closed Dec 15–Jan 31; $3.50). The fortress-like dwelling also served as a church and meeting hall for the village community, and currently contains a collection of antique furniture, weaving and textile equipment, and the first tower clock made in the colonies, dating from 1726. Nearby, at 84 Boston St, the **Hyland House** (June–Labor Day Tues–Sun 10am–4pm; Sept–mid-Oct Sat & Sun 10am–4pm; $3.50), a saltbox built in the 1660s, belonged to esteemed clockmaker Ebenezer Parmelee. Little refurbishment has gone on since; the house is held together by the same old nails and bolts, and has its original casement window and hand-hewn floorboards. The last of the three houses open to the public is a short walk away at 171 Boston St, the **Thomas Griswold House** (mid-June–Sept Tues–Sun 11am–4pm; Oct Sat & Sun 11am–4pm; $2), another saltbox, built in 1774, and full of period furniture and clothing, photographs, and changing local history exhibits. Outside, there's a working blacksmith's shop and colonial-style garden. Guilford's large **village green** is the attractive location for summer concerts and recitals, lined on two sides with boutiques and restaurants.

Practicalities

For pleasant **accommodation** in Guilford, try the Georgian-style *Guilford Corners Bed & Breakfast*, 133 State St (☎203/452-4129; [5]–[6]); slightly less charm can be had at the *Guilford Suites Hotel*, 2300 Boston Post Rd (☎203/452-0123 or 1-800/626-8604; [6]–[7]). There's no shortage of excellent **restaurants** along this stretch of the coast. A good stop is *Steamers*, 505 Whitfield St (☎203/458-1757), where not surprisingly, the focus is on seafood. For a more unusual dining experience, *The Place*, Boston Post Rd (☎203/453-9276), does grilled seafood outdoors, where diners sit on logs and toss their shells onto the gravel.

Branford and the Thimble Islands

You'll have little reason to stop in **BRANFORD**, despite its surprisingly good collection of restaurants, other than perhaps its proximity to the **Thimble Islands**. If you do find yourself with a couple of hours to kill in town, stop by the **Harrison House**, 124 Main St (June–Sept Thurs–Sat 2–5pm; donation requested), built in 1724 but altered many times since, and containing an interesting display of farm implements in its barn. Further down the road, the **Branford Craft Village**, on 85-acre Bittersweet Farm (Tues–Sat 11am–5pm, Sun noon–5pm; free), collects twenty craft shops and studios in a village setting, with frequent "live" displays by glassblowers, potters, and sculptors.

Branford's main attraction is unquestionably the **THIMBLE ISLANDS**, a group of 365 tiny islands off the village of **Stony Creek**, best accessed by exit 56 off I-95. The so-called chain of islands is in reality a cluster of granite rocks within a three-mile radius of shore, ranging in size from one large enough to support a small community of 24 homes, to some that actually disappear at high tide. Years ago, they provided a perfect hiding place for pirate ships waiting to attack passing boats in Long Island Sound; one of the individuals who purportedly used these waters to this end was **Captain Kidd**, who is said to have hidden treasure here (he could hardly have buried it) when being chased by the British. You can hear the colorful narratives spun about the islands by taking a tour on either the *Islander* ($7; ☎203/397-3921) or the *Volsunga IV* ($7; ☎203/481-3345), two boats that offer 45-minute daily trips from mid-May until Columbus Day, departing from the Town Dock at the end of Thimble Island Road.

Practicalities

Branford's many fine **restaurants** are primarily located around the Branford Green, like the *Café Bella Vita*, 2 East Main St (☎203/483-5639), with Northern Italian specialities, and *Le Petit Café*, Branford Green, opposite Trinity Church (☎203/483-9791), one of the best restaurants around for French bistro cuisine. Much more casual is *Lenny's*, Route 146 (☎203/488-1500), a seafood shack teeming with noisy kids and their parents; dinner specials start at $9.95. Near the dock in Stony Creek, the *Stony Creek Market*, 178 Thimble Islands Rd (☎203/488-0145), sports a combined restaurant, bakery, deli, and (in the evenings) pizzeria, with stunning views of the Thimbles from its deck. Branford's absence of inns and B&Bs is compensated for by the abundance of inexpensive **hotels** and **motels**, most of which are located on East Main Street, such as the *Motel 6*, no. 320 (☎203/483-5828; ③), and the *Branford Motel*, no. 470 (☎203/488-5442; ③).

NEW HAVEN AND SOUTHWESTERN CONNECTICUT

An essential stop on any tour of Connecticut, **New Haven** is one of the state's more bearable bigger cities, given life by its intriguing mix of downbeat industrial center and college town. It practically divides the shoreline in half, and can really be visited in conjunction with the coastal stretch on either side, or even Hartford, its urban rival just over thirty miles away. Still, it's most similar in character to the built-up coast in the **southwestern** portion of the state, which leads all the way to the outskirts of New York City. Indeed, the southwest is by far the most developed part of Connecticut, and the former hub of its manufacturing base. It's an unattractive region on the whole, a result of the decline in industry, alleviated only in parts by the odd historic building and the grassy sights on **Merritt Parkway**, a good alternative to the parallel – and much busier – Route 95, which runs directly along the coast throughout the region. The state's largest city, **Bridgeport**, despite valiant attempts to reverse its urban decline, is still a depressing place to visit, while **Stamford**, marginally less ugly, has been quite successful in managing to entice leading business corporations away from New York City. **Norwalk** is another city which had fallen on bad times and is now working hard to improve things, while, inland, predominantly residential **Danbury**, the city once known as the nation's "hat capital," sits in the **Housatonic Valley**, a pleasant, hilly landscape dotted with rivers and lakes.

New Haven

Don't be put off by the grubby initial impression you get when you arrive in **NEW HAVEN** on I-95 or by train: the grimy factories, the tall chimneys, and architecturally nondescript office blocks. Tucked away, in fact, are some of the best restaurants, most exciting nightspots and diverting cultural activities in all of New England – not to mention, of course, the idyllic, leafy Ivy League campus of **Yale University**. The resultant tensions between these two very different facets make it a somewhat uneasy place, to be sure. Town-versus-gown conflicts are so marked as to give the city a crackling energy, and New Haven is certainly less WASPish and smug than many other Ivy League towns. Drug pushing, homelessness, and gang warfare notwithstanding, blacks and whites – and Italians, Irish, and Asians – coexist ambivalently in New Haven in a way unseen in the rest of New England. Even the students themselves seem a less snooty, less smug breed than their counterparts at Princeton or Harvard.

Some history

Founded in 1638 by a group of wealthy Puritans on a large natural harbor at the mouth of the Quinnipiac River, New Haven started life as an independent colony, the early settlers living in relative harmony with the native Quinnipiac Indians. Very early on, the town was laid out in nine "**squares**" that can still be seen today in the downtown area's grid pattern. The efforts of the community's leaders to create a prosperous economy foundered, however, and in 1662 New Haven became part of the Connecticut Colony, based in Hartford. In 1701 Connecticut's first university, the Collegiate School, was founded, and classes met in a variety of towns, until, in 1716, the school established a permanent home in New Haven, eventually becoming Yale University as a sign of respect to **Elihu Yale**, a wealthy Anglican who made generous donations. Meanwhile, New Haven's shipping industry was finally beginning to flourish, the result of a fine deepwater harbor.

Still, it was manufacturing that would lead the city forward. During the Revolutionary War, the city produced gunpowder and cannonballs, and towards the end of the eighteenth century, Yale-educated **Eli Whitney** started manufac-

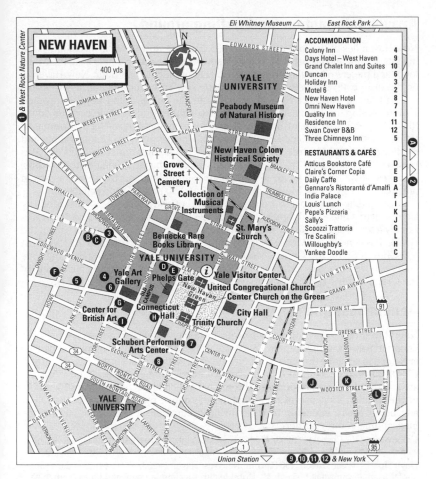

NEW HAVEN

0 ——— 400 yds

N

Eli Whitney Museum △   East Rock Park △

YALE UNIVERSITY

Peabody Museum of Natural History

New Haven Colony Historical Society

Grove Street Cemetery †

Collection of Musical Instruments

St. Mary's Church

Beinecke Rare Books Library

YALE UNIVERSITY

Yale Art Gallery   Phelps Gate   (i) Yale Visitor Center

United Congregational Church
Center Church on the Green

Center for British Art   Connecticut Hall   City Hall

Trinity Church

Schubert Performing Arts Center

YALE UNIVERSITY

ACCOMMODATION

Colony Inn ... 4
Days Hotel – West Haven ... 9
Grand Chalet Inn and Suites ... 10
Duncan ... 6
Holiday Inn ... 3
Motel 6 ... 2
New Haven Hotel ... 8
Omni New Haven ... 7
Quality Inn ... 1
Residence Inn ... 11
Swan Cove B&B ... 12
Three Chimneys Inn ... 5

RESTAURANTS & CAFÉS

Atticus Bookstore Café ... D
Claire's Corner Copia ... E
Daily Caffe ... B
Gennaro's Ristoranté d'Amalfi ... A
India Palace ... F
Louis' Lunch ... I
Pepe's Pizzeria ... K
Sally's ... J
Scoozzi Trattoria ... G
Tre Scalini ... L
Willoughby's ... H
Yankee Doodle ... C

Union Station ▽   ⑨ ⑩ ⑪ ⑫ & New York ▽

turing mass-produced firearms, the result of using standardized parts as the basis of the assembly line in his factory outside of town, dubbed Whitneyville. New Haven also churned out Winchester rifles, musical instruments, tools, carriages, and corsets. Local entrepreneurs, realizing that the city could do better still if it had access to interior New England, decided to build an eighty-mile canal which would extend as far as Northampton, Massachusetts. The canal, however, was a financial flop. Nevertheless, New Haven continued to progress until the middle of this century, when the problems of unplanned urban growth and increasing economic competition from the suburbs began to take their toll. Millions of dollars in federal funds were then pumped into the city to begin the process of urban renewal, but unemployment continued to grow and, today, there is little manufacturing activity left in New Haven. Despite more progressive programs, the air of depression remains – except, of course, on the hallowed grounds of the university itself.

Arrival, information, and getting around

New Haven lies at the fork of I-91 and I-95. Parking downtown is atrocious: parking lots are few and far between (though several of the major hotels have their own lots), and meters often allow a maximum stay of only half an hour. New Haven is on the main **train** line between Washington, New York, and Boston; services also run to Canada. Amtrak's main terminal is in the colossal and newly renovated **Union Station**, on Union Avenue six blocks southeast of the Yale campus downtown. You can also get to or from New York on the Metro-North Commuter Railroad (☎203/497-2089 or 1-800/638-7646), which runs from Union Station, and is a better deal than Amtrak. The terminal for Greyhound, Bonanza, and Peter Pan **buses** is at 45 George St (☎203/772-2470); whether you're arriving by train or bus, it makes sense to grab a **cab** to your hotel, as the bus and train stations are in potentially dodgy areas. Metro Taxi (☎203/777-7777) has a good reputation.

Local public transport to outlying parts of New Haven is provided by Connecticut Transit, 470 James St (☎203/624-0151), but the service deteriorates rapidly after 6pm. An **information booth** at 200 Orange St, two blocks east of the Green, has schedules (Mon–Fri 9am–5pm). The **Greater New Haven CVB** is at 195 Church St, on the Green (Mon–Fri 8.30am–5pm; ☎203/787-8822), and Yale University runs its own **information center** at 149 Elm St, on the north side of the Green (Mon–Fri 9am–4.45pm, weekends 10am–4pm; ☎203/432-8469).

Accommodation

New Haven has surprisingly few **hotels** for a city of its size; not even expensive ones for parents visiting their Yalie offspring. **B&Bs** from around $50 can be arranged in advance through Nutmeg Bed & Breakfast, 222 Girard Ave, Hartford, CT 06105 (☎203/236-6698). The downtown hotels, though somewhat overpriced, are worth it for their proximity to the main sights and for the comparative safety of the location. Because of the shortage of rooms, make sure to book well in advance if you're intending to visit during graduation in early June, always the busiest time of the year here.

Colony Inn, 1157 Chapel St (☎203/776-1234, *www.colonyatyale.com*). Intimate full-service hotel with colonial trimmings. Adjacent to the Yale campus and main downtown attractions. ④.

Days Hotel – West Haven, 490 Sawmill Rd, West Haven (☎203/933-0344). Standard rooms not far from downtown at I-95 exit 42. Hotel features swimming pool and fitness center. ④.

Grand Chalet Inn & Suites, 400 Sargent Drive (☎203/562-1111 or 1-800/5-CHALET). Good-value hotel with 152 rooms overlooking the harbor. ④–⑥.

Holiday Inn, 30 Whalley Ave (☎203/777-6221). Generic rooms in a good central location adjacent to Yale. ④–⑤.

Hotel Duncan, 1151 Chapel St (☎203/787-1273). Comfortable rooms in an old-fashioned hotel, a few steps away from Yale, with singles in the $40 range. ③.

Motel 6, 270 Foxon Boulevard (☎203/469-0343). Inexpensive but comfortable motel located just off I-91 north of town. ③–④.

New Haven Hotel, 229 George St (☎203/498-3100, *www.newhavenhotel.com*). Small, quiet, central hotel with better-than-adequate rooms, a health club and indoor pool. ⑤.

Omni New Haven Hotel at Yale, 155 Temple St (☎203/772-6664 or 1-800/THEOMNI. *www.omnihotels.com*). Recently refurbished, New Haven's plushest hotel has 306 luxury rooms, health club, and a superb (though expensive) restaurant with spectacular city views. It's adjacent to the Yale campus. ⑥–⑦.

Quality Inn, 100 Pond Lily Ave (☎203/387-6651, *www.schafferhotels.com*). More than one-hundred good-value standard rooms, all with queen-size beds; there's also an indoor pool and jacuzzi. Located at exit 59 off Route 15. ④.

Residence Inn, 3 Long Wharf Drive (☎203/777-5337 or 1-800/331-3131, *www.residenceinn .com*). Luxurious, all-suite waterfront hotel that's part of the Marriott empire. ⑥–⑦.

Swan Cove B&B, 115 Sea Street, exit 44N off I-95 (☎203/776-3240,*www.swancove.com*). Pleasant 1890s historic district house with views over Long Island Sound. ⑥–⑦.

Three Chimneys Inn, 1201 Chapel St (☎203/789-1201, *www.threechimneysinn.com*). Just a few blocks from the Green, this elegant Victorian B&B is central to Yale, theater, and museums. Formal parlor with Queen Anne chairs, and porch overlooking landscaped courtyard. ⑥–⑦.

The City

A succession of remarkably ugly buildings put up during the 1950s rather blighted New Haven, but its **downtown**, centered on the **Green**, remains both attractive and walkable, thanks in part to some sensitive restoration. The Green, laid out in 1638 and originally called "**The Marketplace**," was the site of the city's original settlement, and also functioned as a meeting area and a burial ground. Around it are three churches, a grand library, and a number of stately government buildings; the park itself is now home to a handful of harmless itinerants, and borders the student-filled College and Chapel Street district.

The Green
Standing in the middle of the Green, and flanked by two other churches, the **Center Church on the Green**, built in 1812, is the successor to New Haven's first religious building, the First Church of Christ. Though it once held nearly a dozen Tiffany windows, all but one were given away during a renovation in the 1960s (some of which can be viewed at the Southern Connecticut State University, 501 Crescent St); the remaining window sits in a place of honor over the pulpit, and depicts John Davenport, the first minister, preaching the first service in New Haven colony. Below the church, a fascinating **crypt** holds tombs from as far back as 1687. (Tours of church and crypt Tues, Thurs & Sat 11am–1pm & Sun after

---

THE AMISTAD

In the spring of 1839, more than 500 Mendi tribesmen were illegally kidnapped from their Sierra Leone homes and brought to Havana, Cuba. Fifty-three of them were placed on a smaller ship, the *Amistad*, for delivery to another Cuban port. Three days after setting sail, the Africans, led by Joseph Cinque, revolted and took control of the ship with the intent to return home, killing several crew members in the process. After 63 days the ship arrived off Long Island, where it was intercepted by the US Navy. The Africans were taken into custody and charged as pirates and murderers, despite the protests of abolitionists. A series of trials in both Hartford and New Haven followed; after two years of legal wrangling, the case went all the way to the US Supreme Court. Having received the powerful backing by that time of none other than the president himself, John Quincy Adams, they were eventually acquitted and released. In 1842, the 35 survivors were able to return home, though slavery was not to be abolished for another twenty years. Steven Spielberg dramatized the incident in the 1997 film of the same name.

11am service; donation.) Close by, fronting Temple Street, the Gothic Revival **Trinity Episcopal Church**, built in 1816, holds even more Tiffany windows; the **United Congregational Church**, also known as the **North Church**, is based on a design copied from a French book on English architecture. At the southern end of the Green is the recently restored High-Victorian **City Hall**, built in 1861. Behind the unusual, wrought-iron staircase in the building's graceful, spacious lobby you can see a scale model of the city. City Hall overlooks the 1992 **Amistad Memorial**, a three-sided bronze relief monument on the site of the former New Haven Jail.

Yale University and around

At the opposite end of the Green, Yale University's **Connecticut Hall**, built in 1750 and based on Harvard's Massachusetts Hall, is notable for being the oldest surviving building in New Haven and the only remaining structure from Yale's Old Brick Row. Just outside of Connecticut Hall stands a statue of Revolutionary War hero **Nathan Hale**, a Yale graduate. A short way down College Street, the 1895 **Phelps Gate** is known as "Yale's front door" and allows access to the Old Campus of **Yale University**, New Haven's prime attraction. You can wander at will, though free hour-long student-led **tours** set off daily from the Yale Visitor Information Center at 149 Elm St (☎203/432-2300); the center also provides maps for self-guided tours. Whatever you decide, expect a good deal of trooping to and fro, as the University's buildings are strewn out over several blocks.

It makes sense to start with the cobbled courtyards of the Old Campus (mostly built in the 1930s but painstakingly manicured to look suitably ancient) and ending up at the remarkable **Beinecke Rare Books Library**, 121 Wall St (Mon–Fri 8.30am–5pm, Sat 10am–5pm; free), where priceless ancient manuscripts and hand-printed books are viewed with the aid of natural light seeping through the translucent Vermont marble walls – the marble also has the effect of blocking out the harmful solar radiation that would otherwise cause them to deteriorate. There's a 1455 Gutenberg Bible, along with some original Audubon prints in the collection. Other buildings of interest include the modernist, Louis Kahn-designed **Yale Center for British Art**, 1080 Chapel St (Tues–Sat 10am–5pm, Sun noon–5pm; free), which prides itself on having the most comprehensive collection of British art outside the UK. The collection traces the development of British art, beginning with paintings from the sixteenth and seventeenth centuries, highlighting the period from William Hogarth in the early eighteenth century to J.M.W. Turner in the mid-nineteenth and moving through to the twentieth century boasting works by Walter Sickert and the Bloomsbury Group, with a special emphasis on Alfred Munnings and Ben Nicholson – favorites of the center's founder, Paul Mellon. The Center's large collection of portraits contains full-lengths by Van Dyck, Gainsborough and Reynolds and some fine landscapes including J.M.W Turner's *Dort and Staff, Fingal's Cave* and John Constable's *Hadleigh Castle*. The modern building opposite houses the **Yale University Art Gallery**, 1111 Chapel St (Tues–Sat 10–5pm Sun 1–6pm; free), the nation's most venerable university art collection. Founded in 1832 with John Trumbull's original donation of 100 paintings to Yale, the collection now boasts more than 100,000 objects from around the world, dating from ancient Egyptian times to the present, and features American decorative arts, Etruscan vases, regional design and furniture, and African and pre-Columbian works. Among the highlights are Vincent Van Gogh's famous 1888 composition *Night Café*, which the artist complained was "one of the ugliest pictures I have done," and works by Manet, Monet, Picasso and Homer. The surrounding five blocks are a genuinely lively place in which to hang out, filled with bookstores, cafés, clubs, and hip clothes shops; the **Neon Garage**, an art exhibit in a real parking lot on Crown Street, is particularly notable. There are some rough pockets, but generally speaking, New Haven is reasonably safe to wander around, especially during term-time, when the streets are brimming with students.

A short walk two blocks east of the Green, **Hillhouse Avenue**, designed by James Hillhouse in the 1790s and completed by his son in 1837, is one of New Haven's most attractive thoroughfares – so attractive that when Charles Dickens visited he proclaimed it to be the most beautiful street in America. Once the domain of New Haven's rich and famous, much of it is now taken up with Yale University's administrative offices. A quirky, 800-strong **Collection of Musical Instruments**, some dating back as far as the sixteenth century, can be seen at no. 15 (Tues–Thurs 1–4pm; closed summer), while at the street's lower end, Gothic **St Mary's Roman Catholic Church**, the first Roman Catholic parish in New Haven, is the place where Friar Michael McGivney founded the Knights of Columbus charitable order in 1882.

Just beyond Crown Street, southeast of the Green, New Haven's close-knit **Italian District** is based among the well-kept brownstones and colorful window boxes of **Wooster Street**, where the city's original Italian immigrants settled when they came to work on the railway. There's little to see here, but there are some incredibly popular restaurants, and it's well worth stopping by when there's a festival on.

Whitney Avenue

Whitney Avenue leads north from the Green, with several worthy stops along the way. The **Peabody Museum of Natural History**, 170 Whitney Ave (Mon–Sat 10am–5pm, Sun noon–5pm; $5), one of the largest museums in New England, hosts exhibits of dinosaur skeletons, including a 67foot brontosaurus, a 75-million-year-old turtle and a vast section on America's ancient civilizations, in particular the Native Americans of Connecticut. On the same street, the **New Haven Colony Historical Society**, at no. 114 (Tues–Fri 10am–5pm, Sat & Sun 2–5pm; $2; ☎203/562-4183), housed in a handsome 1930s Georgian Revival building, traces New Haven's history through a series of fine art displays, industrial artifacts, maps, and genealogical records. One of the galleries is dedicated to the maritime history of the city and the much-reproduced Nathaniel Jocelyn portrait of the leader of the *Amistad* slaves, Cinque; you can also see Eli Whitney's original cotton gin and Charles Goodyear's rubber inkwell. More Whitney-related exhibits can be seen at the **Eli Whitney Museum**, two miles further out at 915 Whitney Ave (Wed–Fri & Sun noon–5pm, Sat 10am–3pm; $2), housed in the original gun factory where mass production originated. The museum includes an 1816 barn that was part of Whitney's factory town and a glut of hands-on experiments, mostly designed for children.

The city outskirts

When you've had enough traipsing around museums and galleries, head for **East Rock Park**, East Rock Road (April–Nov daily sunrise–sunset), named for the huge outcrop of reddish rock that dominates the skyline for miles around, and from which there are spectacular views of New Haven, Long Island Sound and beyond. On the other side of town, at the **West Rock Nature Center**, Wintergreen Avenue at Baldwin Drive (Mon–Fri 10am–4pm), the Regicides Trail leads to Judges' Cave, where two of the men who signed Charles I of England's death warrant fled after the restoration of the monarchy.

At the extreme southeastern tip of the city, follow Lighthouse Road off I-95 to the **Pardee-Morris House**, 325 Lighthouse Rd (late April to Labor Day Sat & Sun 11am–4pm; $2), a small but worthwhile museum housed in a 1750s Georgian farmhouse rebuilt after an earlier one was burnt to the ground by the British. It's furnished with period antiques, some of them original to the house, and there are demonstrations of butter- and ice cream-making. At the end of Lighthouse Road, **Lighthouse Point Park** (daily 10am–6pm; cars $2 weekdays, $5 weekends), an eighty-acre park with a sandy public beach, nature trails, and a restored antique carousel, is a stopover point for hawks, eagles, and falcons on their winter migration. Here, too, are the **Black Rock Fort** and **Fort Nathan Hale**, remains of two forts from the Revolutionary and Civil Wars, both offering spectacular views of New Haven Harbor, though there's not enough left of either to warrant anything more than a quick poke round.

Eating

Don't leave New Haven without trying the local **pizza** (known by the cognoscenti as tomato pies). The *New York Times* discovered New Haven's pizzas a number of years ago, and since then there have been queues down the street at all the family Italian restaurants in Wooster Square. There are plenty of other ethnic cuisines to savor in New Haven as well, with many of the best places to eat located around the Green and on Chapel and College streets.

Cafés and bakeries

Atticus Bookstore Café, 1082 Chapel St, next to the Yale Center for British Art (☎203/776-4040). Salads, soups, sandwiches, brioches, and great coffee in a relaxed bookstore open until midnight.

Daily Caffe, 316 Elm St (☎203/766-5062). Laid-back, artsy café, sometimes open until 1am, catering to the cappuccino and *New York Times* set. Sandwiches and cakes from $2.

Willoughby's, 1006 Chapel St (☎203/789-8400). Self-consciously trendy gourmet coffee bar frequented by hip intellectuals and fashionable townies. Superb coffee and sticky cakes.

Yankee Doodle, 260 Elm St (☎203/865-1074). Yalies' favorite low-cost caff, with original Fifties fittings and shop sign.

Restaurants

Claire's Corner Copia, 1000 Chapel St (☎203/562-3888). Corny name, but excellent Mexican and Middle Eastern food at moderate prices. Vegetarian-friendly.

Gennaro's Ristorante d'Amalfi, 937 State St (☎203/777-5490). Excellent Italian restaurant serving specialities including traditional Amalfian dishes. For around $25 or so, sample their *linguini in cartoccio* – clams, anchovies, olives, white wine, and tomatoes served in a brown bag.

India Palace, 65 Howe St (☎203/776-9010). Serviceable Indian restaurant, most noteworthy for its $6 buffet lunch.

Louis' Lunch, 261–263 Crown St (☎203/562-5507). Small, dark and ancient burger institution which claims to have served the first hamburger in the US in 1900. The meat, cooked in an upright broiler, thus reducing the fat, is presented between two slices of toast, accompanied by onions and tomato. It's very popular, so expect queues, and don't ask for ketchup either.

Pepe's Pizzeria, 157 Wooster St (☎203/865-5762). Most popular of the Wooster St establishments; plain, functional, and friendly, with huge "combination pies" starting at $6. The secret, allegedly, is in the coal-fired ovens and genuine Italian tomatoes.

Sally's, 237 Wooster St (☎203/624-5271). Another Wooster St pizzeria, and a good alternative to *Pepe's*.

Scoozzi Trattoria, 1104 Chapel St (☎203/776-8268). Northern Italian restaurant specializing in pasta – eighteen varieties – gourmet pizza and fish.

Tre Scalini, 100 Wooster St (☎203/777-3373). Upmarket Italian restaurant in an elegant setting, with entrees like chicken breast with olives, sun-dried tomatoes, wild mushrooms and fresh sage.

Nightlife and entertainment

New Haven has an undeniably rich **cultural scene**, especially strong on **theater**. The Yale Rep Company, 1120 Chapel St (☎203/432-1234), which boasts among its eminent past members Jodie Foster and Meryl Streep, turns out consistently good shows during term-time. The Long Wharf Theater (☎203/787-4282), 222 Sargent Drive, just off I-95, has a nationwide reputation for quality performances, as does the refurbished Shubert Performing Arts Center, 247 College St (☎203/562-5666).

As you'd expect with such a large student population, there are plenty of excellent **bars** and **clubs**, mostly concentrated around Chapel and College streets. The *New Haven Advocate*, a free weekly news and arts paper, has detailed listings of what's on in and around the city, while a free biweekly, *Hip*, available from the clothes shops along Chapel Street, lists trendy goings-on.

168 York Street Café, 168 York St (☎203/789-1915). New Haven's oldest gay joint has two downstairs bars, and a quieter upstairs bar with lots of TV screens. Busy, especially at weekends.

Anchor Bar, 272 College St (☎203/865-1512). Authentic Fifties bar, one of the best spots in town. Snug plastic booths, dim orange lighting, frosted windows and a formidable matronly hostess.

Bar, 254 Crown St (☎203/495-8924). Simple name, outrageous place – this is where the New Haven gay community lets its collective hair down on Tuesday nights.

The Bash, 239 Crown St (☎203/562-1469). Pseudo-Fifties club with various nightly specials.

Cafe Nine, 250 State St (☎203/789-8281). Intimate club with live jazz Saturday and Sunday nights.

GETTING AROUND SOUTHWESTERN CONNECTICUT

I-95 and the Merritt Parkway parallel each other along the southwestern coast, connecting all the major towns and cities. Amtrak (☎1-800/872-7245) **trains** stop at Bridgeport; commuter trains run by Metro-North (☎1-800/638-7646) link most of the towns along the coast. Interstate **bus** services to the main cities are provided by Greyhound (☎1-800/231-2222) and Peter Pan (☎1-800/343-9999), while for local services, Bridgeport Transit District (☎203/735-6824) and Milford Transit District (☎203/783-3258) provide limited services. A year-round **ferry** service operated by the Bridgeport & Port Jefferson Steamboat Co (☎203/367-3043) links Bridgeport with Port Jefferson, on Long Island, and there are year-round **visitor centers** at 5 N Broad St, Milford (Mon–Fri 8.30am–4.30pm; ☎203/878-0681) and 297 West Ave, Norwalk (☎1-800/866-7925 or 203/854-7825).

Gotham Citi, 130 Crown Street (☎203/498-2484). Large, steamy club where those "in-the-know" head for a late night of drinking, dancing and simply looking good. Gay on Mondays and Saturdays.

GYPSCY Bar, 204 York St (☎203/432-2638). On-campus bar, open to the general public; live music at weekends.

New Haven Athletic Club, 806 State St (☎203/777-6670). Open to the public Sunday nights for live blues or jazz.

Toad's, 300 York St (☎203/624-8623). Mid-sized nationally renowned live-music venue, where the likes of Dylan and the Stones "pop in" occasionally to play impromptu gigs. Tickets $15–25.

Bridgeport and around

Long the state's leading industrial center, **BRIDGEPORT**, not quite twenty miles southwest from New Haven, suffered greatly during the economic decline of the 1960s and 1970s, when dozens of factories and businesses closed down, giving rise to some serious social and environmental problems. Now littered with redundant factories, boarded-up stores and run-down neighborhoods, the city is gloomy at best, though it does contain some diverting attractions, especially if you're traveling with kids. The **Beardsley Zoo**, the largest in the state, is still small enough to appear intimate by big city standards, while the entertaining, hands-on **Discovery Museum** is one of the better children's museums on the east coast. On top of that, the city has close ties to showman **P.T. Barnum**, a one-time mayor of Bridgeport; there's a downtown museum in his honor.

The City

The **Barnum Museum**, 820 Main St (Tues–Sat 10am–4.30pm, Sun noon–4.30pm; $5; *www.barnum-museum.org*), Bridgeport's most endearing visitor attraction, gets off to an uninspiring start on its first two floors, which are devoted to the city's industrial history. The third level, however, is entirely dedicated to Barnum, with exhibits on General Tom Thumb and Jenny Lind, the "Swedish Nightingale," various props and memorabilia, and, most impressive of all, a complete scale model of his best-known creation, the "Three Ring Circus." A block away, the **Housatonic Museum of Art**, 900 Lafayette Blvd (Sept–May Mon–Fri 8.30am–5.30pm; free; ☎203/332-5000), holds works by Picasso, Matisse, and Warhol, plus African and Asian ethnographic collections, contemporary Latin American art, and decent local pieces. Located at Black Rock Harbor, at the end of Bostwick Avenue, **Captain's Cove Seaport** consists of a boardwalk, craft shops, a restaurant, and a replica of the British frigate the *HMS Rose*, supposedly the largest wooden square-rigger in the world. When the *Rose* is off gallivanting round the world representing the US in tall ships festivals, you can take instead a guided tour of the lightship *Nantucket*, the largest ship of its kind ever built, and a permanent fixture here (☎203/335-1433).

A little way out of the city center, the **Discovery Museum**, 4450 Park Ave (July & Aug Mon–Sat 10am–5pm, Sun noon–5pm; closed Mon rest of year; adults $7, children $5.50; *www.discoverymuseum.org*), is an interactive art and science museum with more than a hundred hands-on exhibits, including an eye-hand co-ordination game with a space exploration theme, a planetarium, exhibits on nuclear energy,

P.T. BARNUM

Phineas Taylor Barnum, world's greatest showman (and huckster), was born in Bethel, Connecticut, in July 1810, and worked as a lottery ticket salesman before venturing into the world of showbusiness – and forever altered history – in 1835. With an eye for the bizarre, he purchased a frail hymn-warbling old black woman, who he claimed was 161 years old, and exhibited her as George Washington's nurse. Further "success" followed with the "Feejee mermaid," in reality the upper half of a monkey sewn to the body of a fish. Barnum made his fortune out of the midget Tom Thumb – actually a native of Bridgeport – and the Swedish singer Jenny Lind, both of whom drew massive crowds thanks to Barnum's publicity efforts. Barnum plowed much of the profits from these efforts into the American Museum in New York City, which he acquired in 1841 and where dozens of curiosities, both of the human and animal variety, were put on show. Part of the complex, a large, well-equipped theater known as the "lecture room," became the venue for a variety of popular dramatic productions such as "The Drunkard." Buoyed by this venture, which soon became one of New York's most popular places of entertainment, in 1871 Barnum fulfilled a personal dream by launching a huge traveling circus and museum. Attracting vast crowds wherever it performed, it eventually merged with James A. Bailey's London Circus and became known as the Barnum & Bailey Show, until it was bought out by the Ringling Brothers. Throughout his life, Barnum maintained strong links with his home city and state, serving in the Connecticut state legislature, and as one of Bridgeport's most popular mayors. Today, a statue commemorating Barnum's contribution to the city stares out to Long Island Sound from a plinth in Bridgeport's Seaside Park, which he himself gave to the city; three showpiece homes Barnum owned in the city, including Iranistan, a typically eccentric model of a Persian mosque, no longer exist.

electricity, sound and light, an art gallery and, best of all, the Challenger Learning Center, honoring the memory of the ill-fated *Challenger* crew. Another top-drawer destination for kids, the forty-acre **Beardsley Zoological Gardens**, 1875 Noble Ave (daily 9am–4pm; $6 (children 3–11 $4); *www.beardsleyzoo.org*), has exhibits ranging from North American mammals like timber wolves, pronghorn antelope, and bison to exotic animals from the South American rainforests. There's also a farmyard-like children's zoo and a splendid working carousel on the grounds.

Around Bridgeport: Stratford and Putney

Adjacent to Bridgeport, **STRATFORD**, named after its English counterpart Stratford-upon-Avon, shares a connection with that city's most famous son as the longtime home to the prestigious **American Shakespeare Theatre**. Although it closed down in 1982, plans are apace to renovate the existing theater (call ☎203/378-1200 for updated information). Also in town is the **Catharine B. Mitchell Museum**, 967 Academy Hill (mid-May–Oct Wed, Sat & Sun 11am–4pm; $2), with displays on local Indian and African-American history.

One of New England's most bizarre museums can be found nearby in **PUTNEY**. The **Boothe Memorial Park & Museum**, Main Street (park open daily June–Sept 9am–5pm; museum Tues–Fri 11am–1pm, Sun 1–4pm; free), for almost three hundred years the estate of the wealthy Boothe family, comprises an assortment of some twenty buildings bequeathed to the community by the last surviving members of the family – two eccentric, globetrotting brothers. Among the highlights are a 44-sided blacksmith's shop, a redwood "cathedral" with an organ, an Americana Museum focusing on nineteenth-century farming techniques and domestic life, and a collection of odds and ends collected by the brothers on their travels.

Bridgeport area practicalities

With very few B&Bs in the area, most of the **accommodation** on offer is in larger chain hotels and motels. Since most of their clientele are business travelers, rates will be substantially lower at weekends. The exception to the B&B rule is the *Nathan Booth House*, 6080 Main St, Putney (☎203/378-6489; [5]–[7]), a restored Greek Revival farmhouse near the Booth Museum. There's a conveniently located *HoJo Inn* at 360 Honeyspot Rd, off I-95, Stratford (☎203/375-5666; [5]–[6]), while the *Holiday Inn*, 1070 Main St (☎203/334-1234; [6]–[7]), is the only major hotel in downtown Bridgeport. If you're stuck, the Coastal Fairfield County Tourism District (☎203/854-7825 or 1-800/866-7925) can provide extensive listings.

There's no shortage of places to **eat** in the area: *Scribner's*, 31 Village Rd, Milford (☎1-800/828-7019), is *the* place for seafood; in downtown Bridgeport, *Ralph & Rich's*, 121 Wall St (☎203/366-3597), has excellent pasta, and the *King & I*, 545 Broadbridge Rd (☎203/374-2081), serves good-value Thai dishes. Over in Stratford, try the prime rib at the *Blue Goose*, 326 Ferry Blvd (☎203/375-9130), or, slightly more exotic, Japanese food at *Sapporo*, 520 Sniffens Lane (☎203/375-3986), in a pleasant setting overlooking the Housatonic River.

Westport and around

Artsy **WESTPORT**, another fourteen miles down the road, has spent this century shedding its industrial image, and in place of its mills and tannery now sit the designer boutiques and upmarket galleries of a chic downtown. Lending to the proceedings is the prestigious **Westport Country Playhouse**, 25 Powers Court (☎203/227-4177), one of the oldest repertory theaters in the country, housed in a rustic rural barn, where stars like Henry Fonda, Gene Kelly, Liza Minnelli and Stephen Sondheim first strutted their stuff. One of the few sights, the 1795 **Wheeler House**, 25 Avery Place (Tues–Fri 10am–3pm, Sat noon–3pm; donation requested), sports beautifully restored Victorian rooms and a Victorian costume and textile collection. The adjacent Bradley-Wheeler Barn, the only documented octagonal cobblestone barn in the state, contains local historical archives and genealogical information. The lone public beach in the county, the **Sherwood Island State Park**, Sherwood Connector Road, exit 18 off I-95 (8am–sunset; May–Sept $5 weekdays for Connecticut-registered vehicles, $8 out-of-state; weekends, $7 CT vehicles, $12 out-of-state; rest of year free), also happens to be one of the best in the state, with miles of sandy shoreline and a small nature center with hiking trails.

If you fancy a splurge, there's nowhere better in the area to **stay** than *The Inn at National Hall*, 2 Post Rd (☎203/221-1351 or 1-800/NAT-HALL; [8]–[9]), a lavish hotel with eighteen-foot-high ceilings, and individually decorated rooms and suites, some with sweeping river views. By contrast, the simple *Westport Inn*, 1595 Post Rd East (☎203/259-5236; [4]–[5]), offers 116 reasonably priced units, with a smart lounge and fitness center. There are some fine **restaurants** in downtown Westport, too, among them the *Sole e Luna Ristorante Toscana*, 25 Powers Court (☎203/222-3837), for excellent *osso buco* and Tuscan specialties, and the surprisingly reasonably priced *Restaurant Zanghi* at *The Inn at National Hall* (☎203/221-7572), where you can dine on seared sesame-and-peppercorn-crusted tuna while you gaze out past tasseled drapes across the Saugatuck River.

Weston and Wilton

A few miles inland from Westport, in the town of **WESTON**, the 1746-acre **Devil's Den Preserve**, 33 Pent Rd, is so named for the strange hoof-like rock formations which charcoal makers who once worked here believed were the footprints of the devil. Several rare species of plant can be found in this nature conservancy, including the hog peanut and Indian cucumber root. In nearby **WILTON**, don't miss the **Weir Farm National Historic Site**, 735 Nod Hill Rd (grounds open daily, dawn–dusk; visitors' center open April–Oct Wed–Sun 8.30am–5pm; Nov–March Wed–Fri 8.30am–5pm; ☎203/834-1896), Connecticut's only national park, which once served as the summer home and studio of prominent Impressionist **J. Alden Weir**, who acquired the 150-acre site in 1882 in exchange for a painting (not one of his own) and a measly $6. Its proximity to New York City enticed a group of artists including John Twachtman, Albert Pinkham Ryder and Childe Hassam to visit and subsequently form an informal art colony that became known as the "School of Ten." The Weir House remains a private artists' residence, and is not generally open to the public, but a visitors' center in the **Burlingham House** contains historical background – though don't expect to see any of the original canvases. You can combine a visit to Weir Farm with a look around the enchanting **Wilton Heritage Museum**, 249 Danbury Rd (Tues–Thurs 10am–4pm; $2), a 1756 center-chimney farmhouse with a heavy concentration of dolls and dollhouses.

Norwalk

It was in 1651 that **NORWALK** was first settled by Europeans, soon becoming the largest population along this stretch of the coast, thanks to the economic prosperity brought about by a thriving oyster-fishing industry, and, later, by the prolific output of the Silvermine River mills, which produced among other things, shoes and boots, hats, earthenware, candles, and ships. The arrival of the railway in 1840 provided another major boost to the city, but many of the factories closed down in the 1960s and 1970s. Today the area is thriving, thanks to large companies like retail giant Caldor and world-renowned accounting firm Deloitte and Touche that are headquartered here, and to the vision of city officials and private individuals who initiated a massive renovation of **South Norwalk**, affectionately known as "SoNo," full of restaurants, clubs, and galleries.

The Town

South Norwalk is anchored by the fabulous **Maritime Aquarium**, 10 N Water St (July–Aug 10am–6pm; Sept–June 10am–5pm; $8.25), which presents a graded look at the marine life and culture of Long Island Sound, taking you from the creatures at the surface level of salt marshes down through to those of the deep – culminating in a 110,000-gallon tank filled with sharks. Seals, jellyfish, river otters, and 125 other species of marine life are also on display, and you can even take a boat study cruise out into the Sound and get a firsthand look at the catch of the day and see how lobsters are tagged. A boat ride of a different sort is available from adjacent Hope Dock out to the 1868 **Sheffield Island Lighthouse**, whose function was to keep boats off the Norwalk Islands, a chain of thirteen islets across the mouth of the Norwalk River. Visitors can take a brief tour of the ten-room lighthouse, abandoned since 1902, and then spend a bit of time on the island, depending on ferry times (June–Labor Day; 45-minute; $9; call ☎203/838-9444 for schedule information). Back on the mainland, head to the Second Empire-style **Lockwood-Mathews Mansion Museum**, 295 West Ave (mid-March to mid-Jan Tues–Fri 11am–3pm, Sun 1–4pm; $5), built in 1864 as the summer home of Norwalk resident LeGrand Lockwood, who made his immense fortune in the insurance and railway industries. Nicknamed "America's first chateau," it would seem more at home with Newport's grand palaces (see p.261). Of the mansion's 52 rooms, best is the drawing room, in the rear, where above all the stenciling and grand inlaid woodwork, the ceiling boasts a spectacular gilt chandelier and an oil painting, *Venus at Play with her Cupids*, by Pierre-Victor Galland. It's a short walk to **Norwalk City Hall**, 125 East Ave (Mon–Fri 8.30am–5pm; free; tours by arrangement, $3 ☎203/866-0202), which contains a rare collection of WPA murals commissioned during the Great Depression.

Practicalities

Pleasant **accommodation**, in a refined Yankee kind of way, is available at the *Silvermine Tavern*, 194 Perry Ave (☎203/847-4558; ⑥–⑦), which boasts ten delightful rooms in a 1758 Colonial next to a waterfall. **Budget options** abound on Westport Avenue, where the *Round Tree Inn*, no. 469 (☎203/847-5827 or 1-800/275-2290; ③–④), the *Garden Park Motel*, no. 351 (☎203/847-7303; ③–④), and the *Norwalk-Westport Motel*, no. 344 (☎203/847-0665; ③), all provide perfectly adequate accommodation.

The best **restaurants** are in South Norwalk around Washington Street, where *Siam Rialto*, 128 Washington St (☎203/852-7000), is good for Thai curries, and *New England Brewery Company*, 13 Marshall St (☎203/853-9110), offers standard American fare alongside microbrewed beer. For **nightlife**, again explore the SoNo district, full of lively bars and clubs, some of which, like *Shenanigans*, 80 Washington St (☎203/853-0142), and *Tra-peze*, 18 S Main St (☎203/853-2123), offer live music.

Stamford

While for many years **STAMFORD** had benefited from its proximity to New York, it's only in the last twenty or thirty years that businesses have moved to make it their home, attracted by the lower taxes. The results have not been entirely welcome for the city: the upswing in the local economy has been accompanied by the kinds of modern corporate office buildings and chain hotels that fairly taint its downtown area.

The Town

Most of the action is centered on **Atlantic Street** and the side streets off it. On the corner of Atlantic Street and Tresser Boulevard, the impressive **Whitney Museum of American Art at Champion**, One Champion Plaza (Tues–Sat 11am–5pm; free; ☎203/358-7630, *www.whitney.org*), is a satellite of the esteemed Whitney Museum of New York City, dedicated to works from the first half of the twentieth century. Housed in the headquarters of the Champion International Corporation, the museum mounts six major exhibits per year and now has a permanent collection of around 130 works reflecting the principal areas of the Whitney's holdings – paintings, sculpture, prints, photographs, and drawings. There are also galleries devoted to three of the artists most closely associated with the Whitney: Edward Hopper, whose 1930 *Early Sunday Morning* is on display, Georgia O'Keeffe, with her evocative *Summer Days, 1936* and Alexander Calder. Also in the building is the **Champion Greenhouse**, on one of the upper floors, a showcase for horticultural shows and environmental displays, with the stated goal of demonstrating the roles that trees and other plants play in people's lives – apt for a company that is a major paper product supplier.

On your way out of town, check out the 1958 **First Presbyterian Church**, 1101 Bedford St (July & Aug Mon–Fri 9am–5pm; Sept–June Mon–Fri 9am–5pm; free), a unique fish-shaped building, designed by architect Wallace K. Harrison, that contains the largest mechanical pipe organ in Connecticut. North of downtown, off Route 15, the **Stamford Historical Society Museum**, 1508 High Ridge Rd (Tues–Sat noon–4pm; $2), gives a good insight into local history and is worth a quick visit, mostly for the admission it provides to the Hoyt-Barnum House, a restored blacksmith's home at 713 Bedford St. Nearby, the **Stamford Museum & Nature Center**, 39 Schofield Rd (Mon–Sat 9am–5pm, Sun 1–5pm; $5), a nineteenth-century working farm and country store, was once the home of a prosperous New York clothier Henri Bendel. Its seven galleries display an array of farm tools, Americana and fine art.

Practicalities

Many of Stamford's often huge chain **hotels** are located downtown and are geared primarily to corporate travelers. Both the *Stamford Marriott*, 2 Stamford Forum (☎203/357-9555; ⑥–⑧), and the *Sheraton Stamford*, 1 First Stamford Place (☎203/967-2222 or 1-800/338-9115; ⑥–⑧), are particularly good places to take advantage of weekend deals; they also offer nicer than average rooms. **Budget accommodation** is scarce in Stamford; try either the *Stamford Suites*, 720 Bedford St (☎203/359-7300; ④), with health-club privileges, or the *Stamford Super 8*, 32 Grenhart Rd (☎203/324-8887 or 1-800/800-8000; ④).

There's no shortage of **restaurants** in Stamford, one of the few benefits of its development as a business center. For generous portions of steaks and seafood try *Giovanni's*, Long Ridge Rd (☎203/322-8870); Italian standards can be had at *Il Falco*, 59 Broad St (☎203/327-0002). If you're in the mood for something different, two interesting options are *Amadeus*, 201 Summer St (☎203/348-7775), which serves Austrian dishes like schnitzel and strudel, and *Lacaye Restaurant*, 410 Elm St (☎203/358-8008), a no-frills Haitian restaurant, where, for around $11, you can try such delectable entrees as conch with eggplant or goat meat with gravy.

After dark, check what's on at the two **theaters** maintained by the Stamford Center for the Arts (☎203/325-4466) – the Rich Forum, 307 Atlantic St, mainly plays, and The Palace, 61 Atlantic St, a wonderfully restored music hall hosting mainly musical events. If you want to dance the night away at one of Stamford's many **nightclubs**, best thing to do is to check the listings in the freebie *Fairfield County Weekly*, widely available throughout the area.

Greenwich

GREENWICH, nearly as populated as Stamford, has a much more casual feel, with a main thoroughfare, Greenwich Avenue, that's eminently walkable and lined with fine shops, boutiques, and restaurants. Originally a sleepy farming community, the arrival of the railroad in the 1840s benefited the town by facilitating its development as both an industrial power and choice resort for New Yorkers. Indeed, Greenwich remains home to a host of media celebrities as well as the CEOs of several multinational corporations – its private beaches are backed by luxurious homes and fronted by marinas stocked with lavish yachts.

The Town

No visitor should miss the **Bruce Museum**, 1 Museum Drive (Tues–Sat 10am–5pm, Sun 1–5pm; $3.50, Tues free; ☎203/869-0376), which originated in a private home that looks like something out of a Hitchcock movie, and has now developed into a major museum with collections on American cultural history and the environmental sciences. Exhibits include a small collection of nineteenth- and early twentieth-century paintings by the noted Cos Cob School of American Impressionism, and a new science and environment wing features a mine shaft, woodland habitat, minerals, fossils, and a marine touch tank. Greenwich's other star attraction is the **Bush-Holley Historic Site & Visitor Center**, 39 Strickland Rd (Jan–March Wed noon–4pm, Sat 11am–4pm, Sun 1–4pm; April–Dec Wed–Fri noon–4pm, Sat 11am–4pm, Sun 1–4pm; $6; ☎203/869-6899), a two-story white-clapboard house turned into a boarding house by the Holley family in the late 1800s. Like the Griswold home in Old Lyme (see p.292), the Holley residence began to attract artists eager to escape the summer heat and humidity of the big city – among them, Childe Hassam, John Henry Twachtman and J. Alden Weir, some of whose original works hang today in the house. In addition, there is the fine late-eighteenth-century Connecticut furniture and the ornate woodwork of the house itself, not to mention the studio of Elmer Livingston McRae, the husband of a subsequent owner and himself an artist, which has been left virtually intact. Look out, too, for pottery by Leon Volkmar. For history buffs, the scalloped, shingle-sided **Putnam Cottage**, 243 E Putnam Ave (Wed, Fri & Sun 1–4pm; $2), built in 1690 and licensed as the *Knapp Tavern* from 1732, has a bit of romantic history to it: legend goes that one day in 1779, local patriot General Israel Putnam, a regular here, was busy shaving when he noticed advancing British troops in his mirror. Forced to flee, he jumped on a horse and managed to escape down a steep cliff, returning later with reinforcements to rout the enemy. The cottage contains original fieldstone fireplaces, antique furniture, and Putnam's uniform.

Practicalities

Accommodation in Greenwich tends to be of the B&B variety. Of these, the 1799 *Homestead Inn*, 420 Fieldstone Point Rd (☎203/869-7500; ⑧–⑨), is perched on a hill in a peaceful residential area, while the *Harbor House Inn*, 165 Shore Rd (☎203/637-0145; ⑦), is close to the water in Old Greenwich, as is the *Cos Cob Inn*, 50 River Road (☎203/661-5845; ⑦), an 1870s federal-style mansion with oodles of "olde worlde" charm. You're spoiled for choice in Greenwich as far as **eating** is concerned – though, not surprisingly, in such an affluent place, restaurants can be expensive. If you're up for a splurge, try *La Maison Indochine*, 107 Greenwich Ave (☎203/869-2689), for excellent Vietnamese cuisine, or *The Homestead Inn*, 420 Field Point Rd (☎203/869-7500), for top-notch French food. Less expensive options include the *Stationhouse*, with its pubby atmosphere; *Panda Pavilion*, 137 W Putnam Ave (☎203/869-1111), a better than average Chinese restaurant; and *Atlantis*, 500 Steamboat Rd, in the *Greenwich Harbor Inn* (☎203/861-1111), where you can chow on steaks and chops while gazing at the posh yachts in Greenwich Harbor.

Danbury and the Housatonic Valley

The company town of **DANBURY**, 25 miles north of Norwalk on Route 7, became famous as the "hat capital" of America; the ten-gallon Stetson was first fashioned here, and at one point, there were more than three dozen factories engaged in the hatmaking industry. When that industry declined in the 1960s and 1970s, Danbury's savior became **Union Carbide**, whose headquarters are still located here.

There's little of interest in the drab downtown area, where Danbury Green is the focus of an ambitious series of festivals and concerts. Nearby, the **Scott-Fanton Museum**, 43 Main St (Wed–Sun 2–5pm; donation; ☎203/743-5200), housed in the 1785 John and Mary Rider House, is mostly of note for its cool exhibits relating to the city's hat industry. The hatmaking industry developed in Danbury during the colonial period, thanks to an abundant supply of natural resources, especially water. The museum's hatting exhibit is displayed in a replica of an eighteenth-century shop, and interprets the impact of the industry on Danbury and surrounds. The Scott-Fanton Museum also maintains, at 5 Mountainville Ave, the birthplace of Charles Ives, the local boy who went on to win a Pulitzer in 1947 for his *Third Symphony*, forty years after it was written. The house, built in 1780 by New York silversmith Thomas Tucker, is open by appointment only; call the museum for details. The **Military Museum of Southern New England**, 125 Park Ave, I-84 exit 3 (Tues–Sat 10am–5pm, Sun noon–5pm; $4; ☎203/790-9277), contains enough life-size dioramas of World War II scenes to sate most any military buff. There's also a 1917 Renault, the first tank ever made in the US, and one of the original self-propelled Howitzers. Danbury's other main visitor attraction is the **Danbury Railway Museum**, 120 White St (Apr–Dec Tues–Sat 10am–5pm, Sun noon–5pm; Jan–March Thurs–Sat 10am–5pm, Sun noon–5pm; $3), with a station and accompanying railroad yard.

About ten miles south of Danbury, picturesque **RIDGEFIELD** nearly seems an extension of the Litchfield Hills, its early buildings having escaped the rampant development so typical in Connecticut. If you make it over, check out the **Keeler Tavern Museum**, 132 Main St (Feb–Dec Wed, Sat & Sun 1–4pm; $4; ☎203/438-5485), which was a popular drinking place even before the Revolutionary War, but a hotbed of patriotic fervor during, especially after it was hit by British cannon. The offending cannonball is still embedded in the building. Down the street, the **Aldrich Museum of Contemporary Art**, 258 Main St (Thurs–Sun 1–5pm; $3), was the first museum in America devoted solely to contemporary art. Its nine galleries hold a series of rotating exhibitions, and there's a lovely two-acre sculpture garden out back.

Apart from Danbury and Ridgefield, the Housatonic Valley offers a few natural attractions, with much of its landscape set aside as nature reserves and sanctuaries. **Candlewood Lake**, just north of Danbury, is Connecticut's largest freshwater lake, with opportunities for swimming, boating and fishing. Further south, **Saugatuck Reservoir**, near Redding, is so peaceful and undeveloped you'd swear you were in northern Maine, while **Huntingdon State Park** is a great place for mountain biking. For avid hikers, east of Danbury, in Newtown, you can walk along the banks of the Housatonic River in the **Paugussett State Forest**.

Practicalities

A detailed brochure and map, available from the **Housatonic Valley Tourism Commission**, 30 Main St, Danbury (☎203/743-0546 or 1-800/841-4488), outlines the architectural or historic interest of many of the structures along Ridgefield's Main Street, and the side streets off of it. If you're interested in **staying** in the area, Danbury's *Ethan Allen Inn*, exit 4 off I-84 (☎203/744-1776 or 1-800/742-1776; ⑥), is a large, modern hotel, though rooms are stocked with authentic Ethan Allen furniture. Quieter Ridgefield's *Stonehenge Inn*, Rte-7, Stonehenge Rd (☎203/438-6511; ⑥), is an 1827 colonial inn in an idyllic garden setting next to a duck pond. Also in Ridgefield, the peaceful *West Lane Inn*, 22 West Lane (☎203/438-7323; ⑥), contains twenty antique-stuffed rooms. For something to **eat**, try *Ondine*, 69 Pembroke Rd (☎203/746-4900), for contemporary French cuisine, though it's a bit pricey; by contrast, *Ernie's Roadhouse*, 30 Padanaram Rd (☎203/790-0671), is the place for American staples – barbecued ribs, prime rib, and so on, at moderate prices. In Ridgefield, the *Stonehenge Inn* (see above) serves classic French cuisine, though at more than $40 for a Saturday night prix-fixe meal, it's a bit of a splash.

HARTFORD AND THE CONNECTICUT RIVER VALLEY

The **Connecticut River**, New England's largest, rises in the mountains of New Hampshire close to the Canadian border and runs all the way down to Long Island Sound. Growing up along either side of it, at least in Connecticut, has been a stretch of relatively peaceful towns, unable to make much industrial use of the river due to its shallowness. The one exception to the slow picturesqueness is **Hartford**, the state capital, an unattractive and largely dull city of some importance as a stronghold of the Connecticut economy. A mile west of the city, **Nook Farm** was home in the late nineteenth century to some of the greatest literary figures of the age, including such as Mark Twain and Harriet Beecher Stowe, while

West Hartford is where Noah Webster published his *American Dictionary* in 1828. Further west, gentle countryside leads to the pleasant town of **Farmington**, and the less attractive, but stimulating industrial city of **New Britain**, one of the nation's main producers of hardware. South of Hartford, the Connecticut River wends its way past **Wethersfield**, where Washington planned the final stages of the Revolutionary War, **Rocky Hill**, whose 185-million-year-old dinosaur tracks can be seen in Dinosaur State Park, **East Haddam**, site of the Goodspeed Opera House and **Hadlyme**, whose unusual hilltop Gillette Castle is one of the state's leading peculiarities. **Ivoryton**, famed for its summer theater, and **Essex**, with the excellent Connecticut River Museum, complete the picture, as the river widens and nears the sea.

Hartford

The town that Mark Twain once described as "the best built and handsomest town I have ever seen" is today hardly recognizable as such – a hotchpotch of ugly office buildings, multistory parking garages, factories and sprawling suburbs. Indeed, the modern capital of Connecticut, **HARTFORD**, on the Connecticut River, is actually best known as the insurance center of the United States, and will probably not take more than a day or so of your time to explore – although the longer you stay, the more unexpected charms you are likely to find. Highlights include the 1878 **State House** with its golden dome and verdant grounds, the superb **Wadsworth Atheneum**, the nation's oldest continuously operating public museum, and the whimsical mansion **Mark Twain** built.

Some history

Originally known by the Indian name of *Suckiaug* ("black earth"), Hartford was dubbed "House of Good Hope" by Dutch merchants who established a trading post here in 1633. When a group of Puritans from Massachusetts arrived in 1635, they named the place "Newtown" after their Massachusetts home, then renamed it Hartford after the town of Hertford (pronounced "Hartford"), England. From its earliest days, it was an important center for government: Connecticut's governor John Winthrop, Jr., set out from here in 1661 on a mission to seek from King Charles II a charter guaranteeing the colony certain rights. Charles' more authoritarian successor, James II, attempted to rescind those rights and establish his own authority over the colony by dispatching his emissary Sir Edmund Andros to the city in 1687. The charter was whisked away by stealth and hidden in the hollow bark of an oak tree on land belonging to Samuel Wyllys. The "Charter Oak" was destroyed during a violent storm in 1856, but the legend lives on in the names Charter Oak Avenue and Charter Oak Place, at whose corner it stood.

Leading the manufacturing charge, the Hartford Woollen Company became the first in the country to devote itself to producing woollen cloth; other goods manufactured locally included Colt revolvers, Sharps rifles, and the Pope motor car, and the pioneering city was the first in the nation to be lit by electricity. Hartford's greatest claim to fame, though, has been its position as the nation's insurance capital, a status begun with a policy issued in 1794 by the Hartford Fire Insurance Company. By the middle of this century, there were up to fifty insurance companies based in the city, providing twenty percent of the nation's cover on certain types of policies; today the downtown Travelers Tower, which, until the Eighties, was the third tallest building in New England behind Boston's John Hancock Tower and Prudential Tower, still dominates for miles around, while Phoenix Home Life and Aetna and a host of other insurers maintain headquarters here.

Arrival, information, and getting around

Hartford lies at the junction of the north–south highway I-91 and I-84 (east–west) so the city is easily accessible by **car**. It's also well served by long-distance **buses**: Greyhound (☎1-800/247-3524), Peter Pan (☎1-800/343-9999) and Bonanza (☎1-800/556-3815) all pull in to the Union Station terminal at Union Place. The **local bus** system is operated by Connecticut Transit (☎860/525-9181), which maintains an information bureau at State House Square and Market Street (weekdays 10am–6pm; ☎680/525-9181). If you're coming by **train**, the main Amtrak (☎1-800/872-7245) services also pull in to Union Station. In the unlikely event that you're traveling to Hartford by **air**, Bradley International Airport is Connecticut's main airport, with connections to most major US cities and into Canada. Several reliable cab companies serve the city, among them Yellow Cabs (☎860/666-6666) and Greater Hartford Cab Company (☎860/953-7433). Hartford's downtown is also "patrolled" by the **Hartford Guides**, who can help with directions and information (☎860/293-8105). The **Greater Hartford Tourism District**, Civic Center Plaza (☎860/244-8181 or 1-800/793-4480), can help you find accommodation and doles out information on attractions and current events.

Accommodation

Hartford has a limited range of **accommodation** possibilities, from a few budget motels and a couple of hostels, to three or four large (and usually pricey) downtown hotels which cater mainly for business visitors and where, consequently, big reductions can be had at weekends. For something a little quieter check out the accommodation options in nearby Farmington (p.320), a charming and convenient spot just south and west of the city center.

1895 House B&B, 97 Girard Ave, off I-84 exit 46 (☎860/232-0014). Inexpensive rooms with shared bathrooms located in a pleasant residential district near the Mark Twain House. ④.

Crowne Plaza Downtown, 50 Morgan St (☎860/549-2400). Large, 350-room hotel right in the center of town, close to all the main attractions. ⑥–⑦.

Goodwin Hotel, Goodwin Square, 1 Haynes St (☎860/246-7500 or 1-800/922-5006. *www.goodwinhotel.com*). Elaborately restored luxury hotel opposite the Civic Center in downtown Hartford, with a full range of facilities, including an excellent restaurant. ④–⑦.

The Hastings, 85 Sigourney St (☎860/727-4200). Originally a conference center for employees of Aetna Insurance, and now a comfortable 270-room hotel. ⑥.

Mark Twain Hostel, 131 Tremont St (☎860/523-7255). A 25-bed facility with some private rooms; otherwise, it's just $13 a night. Reservations are advisable, as the place gets full.

Sheraton, 315 Trumbull St (☎860/728-5151 or 1-800/325-3535, *www.sheraton.com/hartford*). Large, conveniently located downtown hotel with health club and indoor pool. ⑥–⑦.

Super 8, I-91 exit 33 (☎860/246-8888 or 1-800/800-8000, *www.super8.com*). Another budget motel offering basic, inexpensive accommodation, close to the Meadows Music Theatre. ③.

Susse Chalet, I-91 exit 27 (☎860/525-9306 or 1-800/258-1980, *www.susschalet.com*). Comfortable, good-value motel that is part of a better-than-average chain. ④.

YMCA, 160 Jewell St (☎860/522-4183). Economy rooms with shared bath start at around $18; with private bath, from $22.

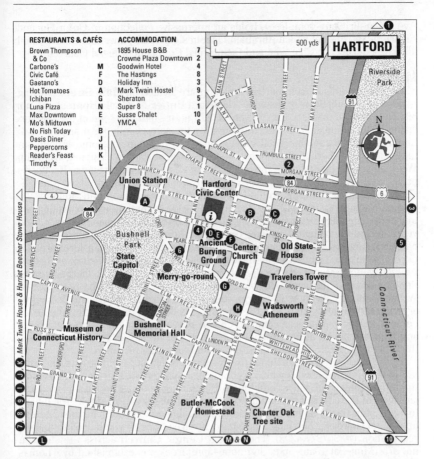

RESTAURANTS & CAFÉS		ACCOMMODATION	
Brown Thompson & Co	C	1895 House B&B	7
Carbone's	M	Crowne Plaza Downtown	2
Civic Café	F	Goodwin Hotel	4
Gaetano's	D	The Hastings	8
Hot Tomatoes	A	Holiday Inn	3
Ichiban	G	Mark Twain Hostel	9
Luna Pizza	N	Sheraton	5
Max Downtown	E	Super 8	1
Mo's Midtown	I	Susse Chalet	10
No Fish Today	B	YMCA	6
Oasis Diner	J		
Peppercorns	H		
Reader's Feast	K		
Timothy's	L		

The City

Bleak insurance towers dominate the skyline of downtown Hartford, but despite
that it's a surprisingly open city, with wide streets and plenty of greenery to break
up the concrete and steel. The broad lawns and plantings of **Bushnell Park**,
designed by eminent landscape architect Frederick Law Olmsted, surround the
golden-domed **State Capitol** (Mon–Fri 9am–3pm, free tours on the hour,
9.15am–2.15pm; Sat 10.15am–2.15pm), an 1878 mixture of Gothic, classical, and
Second Empire styles. Its ornate exterior, with niches containing statues of
Connecticut political worthies, looks more like a church; inside, massive granite
columns, stained-glass windows, and lofty ceilings continue the ecclesiastical
ambiance. The Hall of Flags contains some fascinating relics of Connecticut's history, including bullet-ridden flags and the camp bed Lafayette slept on when he
visited the city. After you have traipsed round the Capitol you can take a ride on
the antique **merry-go-round** in the park, which gives jangling rides for a mere
quarter. The **Museum of Connecticut History**, across the road at 231 Capitol

Ave (Mon–Fri 9am–4pm; free), holds an impressive collection of Colt rifles and revolvers, the desk at which Abraham Lincoln signed the paper that emancipated all slaves during the Civil War, and the original Connecticut Royal Charter.

Main Street

Many of Hartford's most important buildings are located on **Main Street**, starting (from south to north) with the white-clapboard **Butler-McCook Homestead**, no. 396 (mid-May to mid-Oct Tues, Thurs & Sun noon–4pm; $4), one of the few surviving historic homes in Hartford. Owned by the same family for more than two hundred years, it contains a collection of armor from Japan and some antique furniture and toys; behind the house, an 1860s formal garden designed by Jacob Weidenmann is reputed to be the oldest domestic garden in the States. Hartford's pride and joy is the Greek Revival **Wadsworth Atheneum**, 600 Main St (Tues–Sun 11am–5pm; $7; free all day Thurs & before noon Sat), founded by Daniel Wadsworth in 1842 and the nation's oldest continuously operating art museum. The Atheneum houses more than 50,000 pieces, spanning over 5000 years, including ancient Egyptian, Greek and Roman bronzes; renaissance and baroque paintings; seventeenth- and eighteenth-century American furniture and decorative arts and a host of Old Masters, including Rubens' *The Return of the Holy Family from Egypt* and, in the French Impressionists collection, Pierre-Auguste Renoir's *Monet Painting in His Garden at Argenteuil*. Of particular note are the Wallace Nutting collection of "Pilgrim-century" American furniture and decorative arts, the largest of its kind, and the "*Amistad*" collection, documenting the development of African-American culture from the slave period to the present. Lectures and films are put on at the Atheneum Theater, and there's an excellent café, too, that's open for lunch Tuesday to Saturday, and for Sunday brunch.

A few hundred yards north, on the corner of Main and Gold streets, the lofty 527-foot-high **Travelers Tower**, corporate headquarters of Traveler's Assurance, though no longer the tallest building in Hartford, can be ascended for spectacular views of the city and beyond from an open-air **observation deck**. You'll have to be fit: after the 24-floor climb or ride up, you'll need to climb a further 72 steps up a spiral staircase. The half-hourly tours are free, though you'll need to make a reservation (☎860/277-4208). The elegant **Center Church** across the street at no. 675 (Mon–Sat 10am–5pm, Sun noon–5pm; free) was established by Thomas Hooker, the leader of the band of dissenters from Newtown, Massachusetts. Modeled, like so many others, on London's St Martin-in-the-Fields, the church holds no fewer than six Tiffany windows and a barrel-vaulted ceiling. It overlooks the tranquil **Ancient Burying Ground**, established in 1640, and the final resting-place for many of the city's first settlers, including Hooker, who died in 1647.

At 800 Main St, the red-brick **Old State House** (Mon–Fri 10am–4pm, Sat 11am–4pm; free), a 1796 Federal-style building designed by Boston architect Charles Bulfinch – his first public commission – provides a dignified contrast to the drab modern office buildings that surround it, especially since its renovation in 1996, when the early nineteenth-century ornamental iron fencing and gaslights were restored. Inside, the Court Room, which witnessed, among others, the *Amistad* and Prudence Hill trials, has been restored to its initial appearance; downstairs, a new, imaginative museum traces the state's history through various interactive displays and hands-on exhibits. The Connecticut Historical Society, which maintains the museum in the Old State House, is also obviously the force behind the **Connecticut Historical Society Museum**, 1 Elizabeth St

(Tues–Sun noon–5pm; $5), with its large collection of eighteenth- and nineteenth-century Connecticut furniture, and Connecticut landscape paintings.

Trinity College
South of downtown, at 300 Summit St, the beautiful and compact campus of **Trinity College** is located at the highest point in the city and is a pleasant place to spend an hour or two. Founded in 1823, it hosts an array of stunning architecture, particularly on the main square, the Long Walk, notable for its three very impressive brownstone Victorian Gothic buildings. Also notable is the college chapel, purported by some to be the best example of Victorian Gothic in the nation. Organ and chamber concerts are held here regularly while across the green the college's CineStudio hosts independent movies nightly. The campus is also home to the excellent Gallows Bookstore, which presents weekly readings with visiting authors. For details on current events at the College, call ☎860/297-2000.

Mark Twain House and Harriet Beecher Stowe House
About a mile west of downtown Hartford on Route 4, a hilltop community known as Nook Farm was home in the 1880s to next-door neighbors **Mark Twain** and **Harriet Beecher Stowe**. Today their Victorian homes, furnished much as they were then, are open for tours. The bizarre **Mark Twain House**, 351 Farmington Ave (May–Oct Mon–Sat 9.30am–5pm, Sun noon–5pm; Jan–Apr & Nov Mon, Wed–Sat 9.30am–5pm, Sun noon–5pm; $9), which the author built in 1874 and lived in with his family until 1891, saw him write many of his classic works, such as *The Adventures of Huckleberry Finn*. Looking at the newly restored house, it's easy to see where the author spent the publishing royalties from those books: designed by Edward Tuckerman Potter, the place is outrageously ornate, with black and orange brickwork, decorative work by the Associated Artists, an important collection of fine and decorative arts and the only remaining domestic interior by Louis Comfort Tiffany. Check especially the elaborate woodwork and furnishing in the library, where guests were regaled with readings of Twain's own works in progress, and the dining room, where Twain and his wife Livy entertained such luminaries as William Dean Howells and General Sherman.

The much less flamboyant **Harriet Beecher Stowe House**, 73 Forest St (summer Mon–Sat 9.30am–4.30pm, Sun noon–4.30pm; rest of year closed Mon; $6.50), celebrates the life of the author of *Uncle Tom's Cabin*, one of the most important American literary works of the nineteenth century. Stowe, who lived here from 1873 until her death in 1896, was an ardent abolitionist, but also found time to write about housekeeping ideals in the book she penned with her sister, Catherine Beecher, *The American Woman's Home*. The house, built in 1871, is a fine example of a nineteenth-century "cottage" with a hint of the romantic villas made popular by Andrew Jackson Downing and Calvert Vaux. Inside you can see Stowe's writing table and some of her paintings.

West Hartford
Farmington Avenue, a long strip with a mix of cheap diners, fast-food joints and a few quaint gourmet shops and bookstores, continues out of the capital to **WEST HARTFORD**, home to a few scattered highlights, namely the **Noah Webster House**, 227 S Main St (Oct–mid-June Thurs–Tues 1–4pm; mid June–Sept Mon, Tues, Thurs & Fri 10am–4pm, Sat & Sun 1–4pm; $5), an eighteenth-century farmhouse that was home to Noah Webster, compiler of the pioneering *American*

HARTFORD'S DEFINING RESIDENT

Noah Webster was born in West Hartford on October 16, 1758. A lexicographer and author, he wrote educational textbooks before eventually compiling the **first dictionary** to distinguish American usage of the English language from British usage. His spelling book – *The Blue-backed Speller* – helped standardize American spelling and greatly contributed to the country's growing national identity. Encouraged by the enormous success of the first book, he compiled and edited a series of dictionaries culminating in the extensive, two-volume *American Dictionary of the English Language*, which went on to become the nation's most trusted and well-known dictionary. Webster later co-founded Amherst College in Massachusetts (see p.222) and *Webster's Dictionary* keeps his name synonymous with the development of the English language in America.

Dictionary, published in 1828. Also in town is the **Museum of American Political Life**, University of Hartford, 200 Bloomfield Ave (Sept–May Tues–Fri 11am–4pm, Sat & Sun noon–4pm; June–Aug Tues–Fri 11am–4pm, Sat noon–4pm; donation), which holds all sorts of political memorabilia and thematic exhibits on political movements. Particularly topical to these days, "The Presidency and the Press" surveys the use of newspapers in political campaigns and examines the relationship between television and presidential politics.

Back closer to town, north of off Farmington Avenue, on Prospect Avenue, **Elizabeth Park** was the first municipal rose garden in the nation. In addition to the more than 800 varieties of roses, including rarities such as Earth Song and Grenada, there are rock gardens, greenhouses (daily 10am–4pm; free) and miles of tranquil walking paths.

Eating

To take advantage of the surprisingly good eating options Hartford has to offer, you'll probably end up touring a few different neighborhoods, depending on what you're looking for. For good home-cooking, head for Farmington Avenue, which offers the city's most laid-back and tasty diners and cafés by far. Many of downtown Hartford's choice Italian **eateries** can be found along Franklin Avenue, the heart of the city's Italian district, while more sophisticated and expensive French, Italian and American restaurants predominate downtown serving the city's busy business work force. While you should not have a problem during the week getting a table, reservations are always a good idea at the upper-echelon eateries – and a must on weekends.

Brown, Thompson & Co, 924 Main St (☎860/525-1600). Popular downtown restaurant with dinner dishes starting at around $7 and live comedy at weekends.

Carbone's, 588 Franklin Ave (☎860/296-9646). Excellent Italian restaurant – probably the best in town – opened in 1938. Lots of veal and poultry, good pastas, and a winning lobster *fra diavolo*.

Civic Café, 150 Trumbull St (☎860/493-7412). Popular, trendy eatery with an eclectic menu that features innovative slants on a variety of traditional dishes. Notable as one of the city's latest up-and-coming hot spots.

Gaetano's, One Civic Center Plaza (☎860/249-1629). Stylish Italian restaurant located among the shops in the Civic Center, with an attached bistro.

Hot Tomato's, 1 Union Pl (860/249-5100). A relaxed, energetic Italian spot, popular for its huge garlicky portions and fair bill.

Ichiban, 1 Gold St (☎860/560-1414). *The* place for sushi in downtown Hartford, but check out the Korean menu, too, where fish broths, stews, and fried meat dishes offer a welcome alternative for those who can't cope with raw fish.

Luna Pizza, 341 Franklin Ave (☎860/296-0353). Brick-oven thin-crust pizza with a somewhat unusual variety of tasty toppings, such as salmon and capers.

Max Downtown, 185 Asylum St (☎860/522-2530). Considered Hartford's best restaurant, this dynamic spot, brimming with creative flair, prepares impeccable American-nouveau dishes at a considerable (but worthwhile) cost.

Mo's Midtown, 25 Whitney St (☎860/236-7741). You get the greatest breakfast to cure all hangovers at this friendly and hugely popular diner right off Farmington Ave. Recommended is the "Papa Mo" breakfast – a classic "fry-up" – and for those with smaller stomachs, the "Momma Mo" and "Baby Mo" still get the job done. Beware of daunting lines on weekends, however they move along fairly fast.

No Fish Today, 80 Pratt St (☎860/244-2100). Despite its name, seafood – Italian-style – is the thing in this relaxed downtown restaurant.

Oasis Diner, 267 Farmington Ave (☎860/241-8200). Original 1948 dining car with hearty, down-to-earth home-cooking, like meat loaf, pot roast and mashed potatoes.

Peppercorn's Grill, 357 Main St (☎860/547-1714). One of the better eateries in Hartford, rivalling *Max Downtown,* is this minimalist American-Nouveau standout. The menu is sophisticated and creative and the staff attentive without being overbearing. The bill can get pricey, however, with an appetizer and entree running to about $30 – worth it nonetheless.

Reader's Feast, 529 Farmington Ave (☎860/232-3710). Wonderful soups and sandwiches in an unassuming bookstore and café. The relaxed atmosphere can pull you in for entire afternoons.

Timothy's, 243 Zion St (☎860/728-9822). Super little restaurant serving a melange of the twenty most popular classic American dishes in the northeast.

Nightlife and entertainment

There's no shortage of **nightlife** in Hartford, whether you want to see a play, listen to a symphony concert or bop till the wee hours in a nightclub. Among the main music venues are the **Bushnell** Memorial Hall, 166 Capitol Ave (☎860/246-6807), home to the Hartford Symphony Orchestra, the Hartford Ballet, and the Connecticut Opera, the new **Meadows Music Theatre**, 92 Weston St (☎860/548-7370), venue for rock, pop, country, blues, and jazz and the **Hartford** Civic Center Coliseum, Trumbull and Asylum streets (☎860/727-8010), home of the Hartford Whalers hockey team and host to a variety of sports competitions and rock and pop concerts. Meanwhile, the award-winning **Hartford Stage Company,** 50 Church St (☎860/527-5151), holds classic plays and bold experimental productions, while **Theaterworks**, 233 Pearl St (☎860/527-7838), is a local professional company presenting contemporary pieces.

Hartford's **bars** and **nightclubs** are mainly confined to the downtown area. For current listings, check out the free arts and entertainment weekly the *Hartford Advocate* or the city's daily newspaper, the *Courant.*

Bar With No Name, 115 Asylum St (☎860/522-4646). A stylish bar with a good-looking and loyal clientele. Cover charge $4 when live bands perform. Thursday night drink specials.

Black-eyed Sally's, 350 Asylum St (☎860/278-7427). Live blues music Thurs to Sun and hearty Cajun cooking in this atmospheric restaurant/club.

The Brickyard, 113 Allyn St (☎860/249-2112). Casual sports bar with pool tables and plenty of TV screens.

Coach's, 187 Allyn St (☎860/522-6224). As the name implies, this bar/restaurant has a sports theme, with the typical memorabilia to show for it.

Hartford Brewery, 35 Pearl St (☎860/246-2337). Beer brewed on the premises at this friendly, unpretentious spot.

Jazz & Blues Café, 88 Pratt St (☎860/522-7623). Live music Thurs to Sat at this club, which doubles up as a coffee bar by day.

Mad Murphy's, 22 Union Place (☎860/549-1722). Take a chance on the evening's entertainment – it could be live jazz, rock, or karaoke sing-song.

Russian Lady Café, 191 Ann St (☎860/525-3003). Busy nightclub with live music Thursdays and weekends. The rooftop patio has great views.

Around Hartford

A cluster of towns to the **south and west of Hartford** have managed to retain much of their traditional New England atmosphere, even in the face of Hartford's growing suburban sprawl. None exactly overwhelm with things to do, but they make a decent alternative if you tire of spending time in the city.

Farmington

Lush **FARMINGTON**, about ten miles southwest of Hartford, had its heyday in the 1830s and 1840s, when the Farmington Canal operated between New Haven and Northampton, Massachusetts. Though today a more mundane suburb, it still merits a visit in order to see the **Hill-Stead Museum**, 35 Mountain Rd (May–Oct Tues–Sun 10am–5pm, rest of year Tues–Sun 11am–4pm; $6), an impressive turn-of-the-century Colonial Revival house that belonged to industrial magnate Alfred A. Pope. Designed by his daughter, Theodate – one of the nation's first female architects, whose illustrious career nearly ended while aboard the ill-fated *Lusitania* (she escaped by hanging on to an oar) – it now holds an outstanding assortment of American and European furniture and a collection of Impressionist paintings, including works by Monet, Manet, Degas and Whistler. Also in Farmington, the **Stanley-Whitman House**, 37 High St (May–Oct Wed–Sun noon–4pm; Nov–Apr Sun noon–4pm: $5), is a colonial homestead dating from 1720, with some interesting architectural features, such as its narrow casement windows with small diamond panes.

Practicalities

If you prefer to **stay** here rather than downtown Hartford, options include the *Farmington Inn*, 827 Farmington Ave (☎860/677-2821 or 1-800/648-9804; ⑦), a large, luxury facility whose comfortable rooms and suites contain paintings by local artists, while the *Hartford Marriott*, 15 Farm Springs Rd (☎860/678-1000; ⑦), has just what you expect from a large chain – and with big weekend bargains. For something to **eat**, *Apricots*, 1593 Farmington Ave (☎860/673-5405), is a true gem with an English-style pub downstairs, and two formal dining rooms offering Continental cuisine upstairs. The *Connecticut Culinary Institute*, 230 Farmington Ave (☎860/677-7869), is a training school for future chefs, with a varied, good-value menu.

New Britain

Industrial **NEW BRITAIN**, ten miles southeast of Farmington, once one of the country's leading producers of locks, tools, ball bearings, and other hardware items, is the unlikely location for one of the northeast's best collections of American art, with nineteenth galleries housing more than over 5,000 exhibits including oils, watercolors, drawings and sculpture spanning 250 years. The **New Britain Museum of American Art**, 56 Lexington St (Tues–Sun 1–5pm; free), boasts representative works by Whistler, Copley, Sargent and Church, and murals by Thomas Hart Benton, all housed in an attractive nineteenth-century mansion. The town's manufacturing past and present is the focus of the **New Britain Industrial Museum**, 185 Main St (Mon–Fri 2–5pm; free), with exhibits devoted to the large manufacturing companies, such as Stanley Tools and Fafnir Bearings, that brought the city prosperity (and employment). Items on display include everything from tools to Art Deco kitchenware. If you're looking for something to **eat** while in town, good-value Chinese food can be had at *Great Taste*, 597 W Main St (☎860/827-8988).

Wethersfield

Just six miles south of downtown Hartford, **WETHERSFIELD** had its own harbor on the Connecticut River until a major flood in 1692 rerouted the water and so stripped much of the town's prosperity; indeed, by the late 1700s, farming had overtaken trade as the main economic activity. Still, a few well-preserved homes lend the place a certain picturesqueness. Much of the historical interest focuses on the **Webb-Deane-Stevens Museum**, 211 Main St (May–Oct Wed–Mon 10am–4pm; Nov–Apr Sat & Sun 10am–4pm; $8 includes entry to all three houses), made up of three eighteenth-century houses. The **Webb House**, built in 1752 by a prosperous merchant, Joseph Webb, Sr, and notable for its wide, central hall and well-proportioned rooms, contains period furnishings and decorative arts in its rooms, one of which was a bedroom especially designed for the arrival of George Washington, who came here to plan the Yorktown campaign with Jean-Baptiste Rochambeau. The 1766 **Silas Deane House** was home to a lawyer-diplomat who played an important role in the First Continental Congress and traveled to Paris to seek French assistance for the forces of the Revolution. In an all-too-familiar story, Deane became involved in some dubious business deals while abroad that led him to be accused of treason, and spent much of the rest of his life in an unsuccessful attempt to clear his name. The more modest **Stevens House** was built in 1788 by a local leatherworker for his bride, its simple decor and lack of embellishments proving that not everyone here was a member of the aristocracy. Down the road, at 150 Main St, **The Old Academy** (Tues–Fri 10am–4pm, Sat 1–4pm; $2) is a handsome brick building which has served as a town hall, library, women's seminary, and now as the unexciting headquarters of the Wethersfield Historical Society. Just behind it, at 249 Broad St, the charming **Buttolph-Williams House** (May–Oct Wed–Mon 10am–4pm; $2), built in 1700, is one of the oldest surviving homes in the town, with the dark clapboards and small windows that were characteristic of the earliest homes. A massive fireplace dominates the main living room, and the whole place is done out with period furniture. Not far away, the 1764 **First Church of Christ, Congregational**, at 250

Main St, boasts a cupola that's an exact replica of the one at Old North Church in Boston. Main Street ends at the **Wethersfield Cove**, where the lone survivor of the flood stands – the **Cove Warehouse** (opening times vary; call the Historical Society ☎860/529-7656; $1).

Dinosaur State Park

In 1966, the discovery of hundreds of dinosaur tracks in Rocky Hill, south of Wethersfield, led to the foundation of the **Dinosaur State Park**, a mile east of exit 23 off I-91 (park open daily, parking free; exhibition center open Tues–Sun 9am–4.30pm; $2, *www.dinosaurstatepark.org*), where you can see hundreds of dinosaur prints and explore the park's nature trails. The trails take you through a variety of natural environments, including a prehistoric swamp. You can even make your own dinosaur print if you so care; you just need ten pounds of plaster of Paris, one cup of cooking oil and a five-gallon plastic bucket. If you don't happen to have these upon your person at the time, the museum will point you in the direction of local stores that can provide them.

Practicalities

Recommended **restaurants** in Wethersfield include the fairly pricey *Standish House*, 222 Wethersfield Ave (☎860/257-1151), which serves classic French food with a Swiss/German twist – like seafood strudel – in an elegant eighteenth-century colonial. By contrast, *City Limits*, 70 Wolcott Hill Rd (☎860/257-7100), is a family restaurant which serves inexpensive Southern Italian dishes. In the event that you want to **stay** in Wethersfield, the *Chester Bulkley House*, 184 Main St (☎860/563-1651; [4]–[5]), has elegant and fairly inexpensive rooms in an 1830 Greek Revival home right in the center of things.

The Connecticut River Valley

The suburbs end and the valley starts in earnest again with **MIDDLETOWN**, once the busiest port on the Connecticut River, which retains a number of gracious nineteenth-century merchants' homes, to be found on the campus of prestigious **Wesleyan University**. Of these, the most prominent is the brick Federal-style **General Mansfield House**, 151 Main St (Sun 2–4.30pm, Mon 10am–4pm; $2), constructed in 1810. Also on campus, the **Zilkha Gallery**, Washington Terrace/Wyllys Avenue (Tues–Fri noon–4pm, Sat & Sun 2–5pm; free; ☎860/685-2695), showcases a rotating display of modern works in various media. Middletown's **Harbor Park** is the departure point for narrated **river cruises** aboard the Deep River Navigation Company's *Aunt Polly* (mid-June to Labor Day daily; Sept & Oct Wed–Sun; ☎860/526-4954).

South on Route 154, **HIGGANUM** contains little save the yellow-clapboard **Thankful Arnold House**, corner of Hayden Hill and Walkley Hill roads (open year-round by appointment; ☎860/345-2400), a three-story gambrel built between 1794 and 1810, with entrances on two levels and tours given by a resident "ghost." The magnificent **herb and vegetable garden** has been carefully researched to reflect the plantings of the period. Another horticultural treat nearby, the **Sundial Herb Garden**, Brault Hill Road (gardens: mid-May–mid-Oct Sat & Sun 10am–5pm; $1; shop: Jan–mid-Oct Sat & Sun 10am–5pm; tea: April–Sept Sun afternoons; ☎860/345-4290), contains a series of interrelated formal gardens based on seventeenth- and eighteenth-century principles, with topiary, avenues, knots, statuary, and sundials. Even more enticing are the **afternoon teas** put on by the husband and wife proprietors.

East Haddam and Hadlyme

About seven miles south, on the opposite side of the river, the village of **EAST HADDAM** is the unlikely location for the amazing **Goodspeed Opera House**, Goodspeed Landing, off Route 82 (tours June–Oct Sat 11am–1.30pm; Mon 1–3pm; $2; performances April–Dec; ☎860/873-8668), which rises above the water like a giant wedding cake. Built in 1876 by shipping and banking magnate William Goodspeed to provide a venue for his love of theater, the Opera House later served as a military base and as a storage depot for the Connecticut Highway Department, until, in the late 1950s, restoration work on the run-down structure was initiated by a group of local preservationists. East Haddam's other notable feature is the **Nathan Hale Schoolhouse**, Main Street behind St Stephen's Church (Memorial Day–Labor Day weekends & holidays 2–4pm; donation requested), where Hale taught from 1773 to 1774. The one-room schoolhouse contains a small collection of his possessions as well as items of local historical interest.

Five miles south, on the east bank of the river, **HADLYME** is home to the **Gillette Castle** (daily: Memorial Day – Columbus Day 10am–5pm; Columbus Day – Christmas 10am–4pm; $4), the centerpiece of **Gillette Castle State Park**, a prime hiking and picnicking venue. This 24-room granite castle-at-the-top-of-a-hill was built between 1914 and 1919 by actor/playwright William Hooker Gillette, known for his portrayal of cool, unruffled men of action in plays like *Held by the Enemy* and *Secret Service*, and, more famously, in the title role of *Sherlock Holmes*, first produced in New York in 1899. Gillette's performances must have been good; not only did he play the part until five years before his death in 1937, but the result of his fortune was this mansion, into which he built incredible features: a dining table on tracks; a grand hall with balconies on three sides and a mirror which allowed Mr Gillette to seize the correct moment for his grand entrance; and a replica of the sitting room at 221B Baker St, complete with violin, chemistry set, scattered copies of the *London Times* and *Illustrated London News*, and pipe.

Practicalities

Among the **places to stay** in East Haddam are *Gelston House*, 8 Main St (☎860/873-1411; ⑦), providing luxurious and spacious accommodation adjacent to the Goodspeed Opera House, and the *Bishopsgate Inn*, Rte-82 (☎860/873-1677; ⑥), a charming colonial house built in 1818 with six cozy rooms, each provided with a wood-burning stove. *Gelston House* has an elegant **restaurant** serving American and French dishes, or you could opt for *Hale 'n' Hearty*, 381 Town St (☎860/873-2640), for casual American dining of the broiled seafood, steak and pot roast variety.

Ivoryton and Essex

Back across the river on Route 9 is the village of **IVORYTON**, formerly known as Centerbrook until it became a hub, along with the nearby towns of Chester, Deep River and Essex, for the production of ivory. Beginning in 1789, when Phineas Pratt first manufactured ivory combs here, the industry grew to include piano keys, crochet needles, brushes and organ stops. It is estimated that more than three-quarters of all the ivory exported from Zanzibar in 1884 found its way to Ivoryton and Deep River. However, these days the hamlet is best known for its summer theater, the **Ivoryton Playhouse**, 103 Main St (☎860/767-8348). Many a showbiz career has been launched from this fairly insignificant-looking dark brown wooden structure, including that of local girl Katharine Hepburn. For more pomp and circumstance, head to the **Museum of Fife and Drum**, 62 N Main St (June–Sept Sat & Sun 1–5pm; $2), where the history of military music is traced through costumes, photographs, sheet music and instruments from early colonial days through the Revolutionary period to the present. The museum sponsors occasional concerts in the summer.

The river begins widening noticeably as you head further south towards little **ESSEX**, everyone's idea of how a quaint New England town should look, with some lovely colonial homes, a main street brimming with inviting stores and boutiques, and a riverfront marina lined with posh boats. At the end of Main Street, in an 1878 waterfront dockhouse, the **Connecticut River Museum** (daily 10am–5pm; $4) traces local history through paintings, photographs, models and artifacts. The chief item of interest is a full-size reproduction of the *American Turtle*, the world's first submarine, powered by foot pedals. The **waterfront park** outside is a great place to watch the boats coming and going. Just south of downtown, the 1701 **Pratt House**, at 19 West Ave (June to mid-Sept Sat & Sun 1–4pm; $3) is the oldest house in the area, and belonged to the town founders. Besides the usual period furnishings, there's ironwork created by the former Pratt smithy, and a reproduction post-and-beam barn at the back, containing exhibits on Essex's agricultural and domestic history. For something completely different, the restored steam trains of the **Valley Railroad**, Railroad Avenue (May–Dec; ☎860/767-0103), can take you an hour upriver; you can return either by boat or train.

Practicalities

Accommodation options in Ivoryton and Essex include the *Griswold Inn*, 36 Main St, Essex (☎860/767-1776; ⑧), open since 1776, with luxurious suites complete with four-poster beds and wood-burning stoves, or the *Copper Beech Inn*, 46 Main St, Ivoryton (☎860/767-0330; ⑥–⑨), a restored carriage house with spacious, well-appointed guest rooms and a fine French **restaurant** spread out over three elegant rooms. If, by contrast, it's just a snack you want, try *Sweet Martha's*, Main St, Essex (☎860/767-0632) for soups, sandwiches and excellent coffee.

THE LITCHFIELD HILLS

The rolling, tree-clad **LITCHFIELD HILLS**, tucked away in Connecticut's tranquil northwestern corner, provide a vivid contrast to the hustle and bustle of the coastal stretch, not to mention the industrial centers of New Haven and Hartford. Lakes, rivers, clear rushing brooks, and dense pine-scented forests permeate the area, interrupted by picturesque villages of mostly similar pedigree. Right at the center, the small town of **Litchfield** is prototypical New England: a wide, maple-dotted village green surrounded by elegant clapboard homes, all overlooked by a dazzling white church steeple. North of Litchfield are equally attractive but much smaller locales, like the peaceful rural community of **Winsted**, and pretty **Norfolk**, home of the Yale Summer School of Music. In the far northwestern cor-

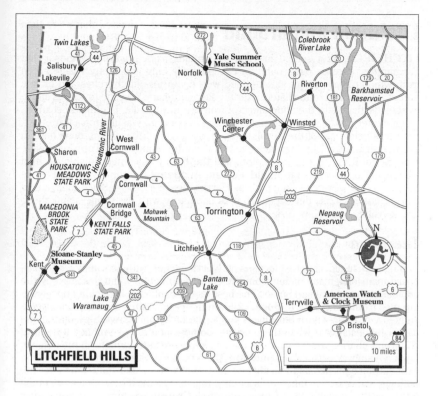

LITCHFIELD HILLS

ner, **Salisbury** and **Lakeville** are close to Connecticut's tallest peaks, **Bear Mountain** and **Bald Peak**, while further south are **West Cornwall**, with its famous covered bridge, **Cornwall** and **Kent**, virtually unheard of until it was "discovered" by artists, craftspeople, and designers from New York City in the 1980s. All these places abound with traditional country inns, some surprisingly inexpensive. The area's commercial center, **Torrington**, about seven miles northeast of Litchfield, is insignificant save for being the birthplace of abolitionist John Brown.

Getting there

The nearest **train** station to the Litchfield Hills is in Brewster, New York. Metro North (☎1-800/METRO-INFO) runs a daily train service there from Grand Central Station, New York City, with a connecting bus service to Litchfield and Torrington provided by Kelly Transit (☎860/489-9243). By far the best way both to get to the region, and to explore it fully, is by **car**. From New York City, I-84 heads northeast past Danbury, then passes along the southern fringe of the region on its way to Hartford. From I-84, take Rte-7 north for Kent, Rte-202 for Litchfield. From Boston, take the Massachusetts Turnpike (I-90) west to Sturbridge, then join I-84 west past Hartford to Rte-8 north, as far as Rte-202 west to Litchfield. Although Litchfield, the center of the region, is only thirty miles west of Hartford, even with such short distances, journeys can often take well over an hour.

Litchfield and around

LITCHFIELD, first settled in 1720 by families from Hartford, Windsor and Farmington, spreads out around an exceptionally long and pretty village green from which radiate quaint streets lined with centuries-old churches and private homes. During and immediately after the Revolutionary War, the town was a hive of activity: thanks to the abundance of iron ore in the hills, Litchfield became a major center for the manufacture of supplies for George Washington's war effort, even producing one of the Revolution's great heroes, Ethan Allen, born here in 1738. After the war, the town achieved fame as the home of the **Tapping Reeve Law School**, the first in the nation, and the highly esteemed finishing school which later became the **Litchfield Female Academy** and the Litchfield Female Seminary, one of whose students was Harriet Beecher Stowe. Since then, a new kind of notoriety has developed from its popularity with day-trippers and short-break visitors from New York.

The Town

Much of Litchfield's interest focuses on **North Street**, with its stately white-clapboard mansions, many dating from the eighteenth century and designed by the popular architect William Spratt. The best way to explore is by picking up a walking map from the **visitor's kiosk**, right on the Green (June–mid-Sept and weekends in Oct 10am–4pm), but unless you strike lucky and arrive here on the one day in July each year when these private homes open to raise money for a local children's charity, you'll have to be content simply to view them from the outside. Look out anyway for the 1760 **Sheldon Tavern**, North Street, a graceful mansion with entrance portico and Palladian window that were added some time after the building had ceased to function as a public house. The most striking feature of the Green is the graceful 1829 **Congregational Church**, restored a century later after being used as an armory, hall, and theater. One of the early pastors here was Reverend Lyman Beecher, father of locals Henry Ward Beecher and Harriet Beecher Stowe. The **Litchfield Historical Society Museum**, also on the Green, at the corner of South Street and South Main Street (April–mid-Nov Tues–Sat 11am–5pm, Sun 1–5pm; $3), traces the development of northwestern Connecticut with special emphasis on the so-called "golden age" of the late 1700s and early 1800s, when the area was expanding rapidly.

The Historical Society also maintains the **Tapping Reeve House & Law School** (mid-May to mid-Oct Tues–Sat 11am–5pm, Sun 1–5pm; $2), former home of the College of New Jersey (now Princeton) graduate who started practicing law in Litchfield in 1772 and opened his Litchfield Law School in 1774, the first such school in the United States. Among many of his notable achievements was his instigation of the movement to allow married women to control their own property. Under his guidance, later students of the school were Aaron Burr, John C. Calhoun and Horace Mann. As the size of the student body grew, Reeve required more room and eventually built the adjacent one-room schoolhouse, which now contains exhibits on the life and work of Reeve, his influence on legal education in America, and the achievements of some of his students after graduation.

About two miles south of the Green, on Route 202 West, the **White Memorial Foundation** (daily dawn–dusk; free), at four thousand acres the largest wildlife sanctuary in the state, has miles of trails for hiking and horse riding; there are also plenty of bird-watching, fishing, and picnicking opportunities. For a complete contrast, the **Lourdes of Litchfield Shrine**, east of Litchfield Green on Route 118, liberally re-creates the famous shrine of Our Lady of Lourdes, France, by means of a grotto built into the natural rock, where services are held regularly. Even if you don't subscribe to the faith, it's a fine place for a bit of quiet reflection.

Practicalities

This is a great area for hiking and cycling, with miles of trails, including a stretch of the Appalachian Trail. For **bike rental**, try the Wilderness Shop, 85 West St (☎860/567-5905), which also rents out skis and snowshoes. A useful **information booth** is right on the Green (June–Sept daily 10am–4pm).

There are plenty of charming **places to stay** in Litchfield, starting with the *Abel Darling B&B*, 102 West St (☎860/567-0384; [5]), a 1782 colonial building close to Litchfield's main attractions. South of the Green, *The Litchfield Inn*, Rte-202 (☎860/567-4503; [6]–[7]), is a modern hotel built in the Colonial style, with spacious, elegant rooms, and the *Tollgate Hill Inn*, Rte-202 and Tollgate Rd (☎860/567-4545; [6]–[8]), an eighteenth-century inn with twenty gracious rooms containing antique reproduction furniture.

Many of Litchfield's **restaurants** line the Green along West Street. Casual *Aspen Garden*, 51 West St (☎860/567-9477), has a large outdoor patio and Mediterranean-influenced dishes. Close by, you can hobnob with the rich and famous at the excellent but expensive *West Street Grill*, West St (☎860/567-3885). For a cheaper alternative, *The Village*, 25 West St (☎860/567-8307), offers inexpensive, homestyle cooking, while *Spinell's Litchfield Food Company*, West St (☎860/567-3113), is an upmarket café, bakery, and gourmet food store serving home-made soups, sandwiches, pastries and desserts. Slightly further afield, *The Bistro East*, Rte-202, inside the *Litchfield Inn* (☎860/567-9040), does contemporary American cuisine in a relaxed, torch-lit bistro setting.

Around Litchfield: Terryville and Bristol

An unusual opportunity avails itself in the village of **TERRYVILLE**, once an important lock and key manufacturing town, about twelve miles south of Litchfield on Route 6: the **Lock Museum of America**, 130 Main St (May–Oct Tues–Sun 1.30–4.30pm; $3), standing on the site of the old Eagle Lock company factory, holds the largest collection of locks and keys and ornate Victorian hardware in the United States. Key items, so to speak, include a combination padlock dating back to 1846, a 4000-year-old Egyptian-made pin tumbler lock, and the original patent model of the mortise cylinder pin lock designed by Linus Yale, Jr., in 1865.

In neighboring **BRISTOL**, once the largest clock manufacturing center in the world, make time for the **American Watch & Clock Museum**, 100 Maple St (April–Nov daily 10am–5pm; $3.50), reputed to be the finest collection of American clocks in existence – more than three thousand of them, including "Dewey," one of a series of six clocks introduced in 1899 to commemorate the Spanish–American war, with a likeness of Admiral Dewey at the top. Be prepared to cover your ears at the top of the hour, when hundreds of chimes resonate round the house.

Torrington and around

It's no coincidence that **TORRINGTON**, the largest and least attractive town in northwest Connecticut, is also the area's business center. Even its main claim to fame – being the birthplace, in 1800, of abolitionist **John Brown** – fails to provide a reason for visiting, as the house in which he was born no longer stands. One house that does, the **Hotchkiss Fyler House**, 192 Main St (mid-April–Oct Tues–Fri 10am–4pm, Sat & Sun noon–4pm; $3), a grand Victorian mansion constructed in 1900 by one of the town's industrial magnates, holds some interest in its original family furnishings and rare paintings by artists Winfield S. Clime and Ammi Philips. Nearby, the **Warner Theatre**, 68 Main St (☎860/489-7180), is a huge restored Art Deco movie palace that hosts musicals, concerts, comedy and ballet.

At the very least, Torrington does provide plenty of **budget accommodation**, considering the region. Particularly good value is the *Super 8 Motel*, 492 E Main St (☎860/496-0811; [3]–[4]). More expensive, but full of character is the *Yankee Pedlar Inn*, 93 Main St (☎860/489-9226 or 1-800/777-1891; [5]–[6]), located downtown, opposite the Warner Theatre. Its sixty rooms come complete with Hitchcock furnishings (see below). For something to **eat**, *Marino's*, 12 Pinewoods Rd (☎860/482-6864), serves Italian-American cuisine in a casual, laid-back atmosphere, while *The Venetian Restaurant*, 52 E Main St (☎860/489-8592), is one of the best Italian restaurants around, and not overly expensive; try the *osso buco*.

North from Torrington

From Torrington, Route 8 leads north to the tranquil rural village of **WINSTED**, which hosts an annual summer festival in honor of the mountain laurel, Connecticut's state flower, which grows in profusion around here. On the corner of Lake and Prospect streets, the **Solomon Rockwell House** (June–Sept Thurs–Sun 2–4pm; free), a Greek Revival mansion built in 1813 by a prosperous iron manufacturer, displays period furnishings, rare nineteenth-century portraits, clocks, toys, war memorabilia, and a collection of wedding gowns.

Four miles west, **WINCHESTER CENTER** maintains a post-colonial charm, its village green an intersection of narrow roads and open fields populated by maples, and a cluster of pristine early nineteenth-century buildings, including several traditional farmhouses and a classic New England church, complete with Doric portico. Near the church is an early nineteenth-century post office, where you can glimpse a remarkable private collection of more than five hundred antique kerosene lamps in the **Kerosene Lamp Museum**, 100 Waterbury Turnpike (daily 9.30am–4pm; free). North of Winsted on Route 20, **Riverton** was once known as Hitchcocksville thanks to its **Hitchcock Chair Factory**, where Lambert Hitchcock began manufacturing the elaborately stenciled chairs and cabinets that became famous throughout America. The factory is still in operation, but to see the work on display, head for the **Hitchcock Museum**, housed in the sturdy 1826 **Old Union Church** (April–Dec Fri–Sun noon–4pm; free), which contains an extensive and rare collection of original hand-painted and decorated antique furnishings.

Norfolk

Route 44 leads west from Winsted through dairy farming country to **NORFOLK**, a relatively undeveloped spot whose tall church steeple stands sentinel over a lush village **Green**. Note the elaborate **Eldridge Fountain**, designed by Stanford White, that has been quenching people's thirst for years; also on the Green, the so-called **White House** was once part of the estate of music-loving local resident Ellen Battell Stoeckel, who here entertained such luminaries of the music world as Fritz Kreisler, Rachmaninov, and Sibelius. The estate was left to the **Yale Music School**, which organizes each July and August the Norfolk Chamber Music Festival. Concerts take place in the 950-seat "Music Shed," Ellen Battell Stoeckel Estate, at the intersection of Routes 44 and 272 (☎860/542-3000). Also in town, the **Norfolk Historical** Society Museum, 13 The Green (Memorial Day to mid-Oct Sat & Sun 1–4pm; free), housed in the former Norfolk Academy, has on permanent display a traditional Norfolk country store and post office.

Practicalities

If you want to **stay** in Norfolk, the *Loon Meadow Farm B&B*, 41 Loon Meadow Drive (☎860/542-6085; ⑤), offers peace and quiet in a nineteenth-century country farmhouse, and *Manor House*, 69 Maple Ave (☎860/542-5690; ⑤–⑧), was built by the architect of the London Underground system. Another accommodation option is the *Mountain View Inn*, 67 Litchfield Rd (☎860/542-6991; ④–⑥), a beautifully restored 1875 house overlooking Norfolk that's particularly noted for its excellent breakfasts. For something to **eat**, the *Pub & Restaurant*, Rte-44 (☎860/542-5716), with English pub decor, if not atmosphere, offers good-value American fare. If you're really hungry, you can even order a roast suckling pig – just give them six days' advance notice.

The northwest corner: Routes 41 and 7

Further west, **LAKEVILLE** and neighboring **SALISBURY** are situated amid some of the state's most attractive scenery and an abundance of quaint guest-houses and inns. Lakeville's chief attraction, the **Holley Willams House**, routes 44 and 41 (July–Sept Sat & Sun 1–4pm; $3), was built in 1808 by a local "iron baron" and is now a museum containing items collected by the Holley family during the 170 years they lived here. The **Salisbury Cannon Museum**, housed in the adjacent Carriage House (Memorial Day–Labor Day Sat & Sun; 10am–5pm; free), tells the story of the Revolutionary War Cannon Factory that provided ammunition for Washington's army. There's also a scale model of an iron furnace and a display of tools. Also on routes 41 and 44, *The American Grill*, Salisbury (☎860/435-9844), is an intimate **restaurant** specializing in inventive fresh seafood and poultry fishes.

South of Lakeville on Route 41, **SHARON** is yet another quintessential New England village with a long narrow green, some pristine nineteenth-century homes and a white-steepled church. At the **Sharon Audubon Center** on Route 4, you can explore seven hundred acres of nature trails where you may see beavers, muskrats, and even otters, and an interpretive center (trails open daily, dawn–dusk; interpretive center Mon–Sat 9am–5pm, Sun 1–5pm; $3; ☎860/364-0520).

West Cornwall, Cornwall, and Mohawk Mountain

Due east of Sharon, on Route 7, the minuscule village of **WEST CORNWALL** has a number of craft shops and restaurants, but is mainly known for its bright-red, much-photographed **covered bridge**, built in 1837 of native oak and restored a few years ago. **CORNWALL**, a quite separate village three miles east on Route 4, is where the **Cornwall Foreign Mission School** was located from 1817 to 1827. Henry Obookiah, a young Hawaiian who managed to stow away on a New Haven-bound ship after his family was killed in a tribal war, converted to the Christian faith and spent several years preaching in and around the Litchfield hills until dying of typhoid at the age of 26. His enthusiasm for the faith inspired the American Missionary Board to send a group of missionaries to Hawaii, a story fictionalized in James Michener's *Hawaii*. Close by, the **Mohawk Mountain Ski Area**, Great Hollow Road (☎860/672-6464), is the largest in the state; a full day pass costs $29.

There's very little in the way of **lodgings** around here, but you could try *The Hitching Post Country Motel*, Rte-7, Cornwall (☎860/672-6219; [5]–[6]), a small, recently remodelled motel with slightly better-than-average rooms. For **food**, there's the *Brookside Bistro*, Rte-128, West Cornwall (☎860/672-6601), as its name implies, next to a gurgling stream, specializing in French cuisine, and *West Main Café*, 13 West Main St, Sharon (☎860/364-9888), for soups, sandwiches and the like.

Kent

Locals wax lyrical about **KENT**, nestled on a flat alluvial plain among the hills which border the Housatonic Valley, though in truth it's hard to understand why. This relatively nondescript town was virtually unknown, other than to members of the famous Kent School, until the 1980s, when it became a choice spot for country homes of various New York artists, designers and craftspeople. As a result, **Main Street**, which straddles busy Route 7, is lined with a weird hotchpotch of art galleries, trendy boutiques, coffee shops and bookstores – perhaps a pleasant enough place for a swig of *caffè latte* or a quick shopping spree, but little else.

The Town

Chief among the town's sights is the **Sloane-Stanley Museum**, Rte-7, one mile north of downtown (mid-May–Oct Wed–Sun 10am–4pm; $3.50), which houses a unique assortment of hand tools and implements made by early settlers and collected by noted Connecticut writer, artist, and tool collector Eric Sloane. One of the items on display, a leather-bound 1805 diary of one Noah Blake, was discovered by Sloane in a nearby house; Blake describes his austere house in great detail, parameters Sloane used to build a replica small wood cabin next to the museum. The museum stands on the site of the once-thriving **Kent Iron Furnace**, which began production of pig iron in 1826 – ceasing seventy years later – and whose ruins can be seen below the museum. More local history can be spotted at the **Seven Hearths Museum**, 4 Studio Hill Rd (May–mid-Oct Sat & Sun 2–4.30pm; donation requested), built in the 1750s to accommodate both a family and a general store. Period furnishings and local ironwork are on display, along with a collection of paintings by local artist George Laurence Nelson, who lived here until his death in 1978.

Kent combines opportunities to browse local galleries and bookstores with a chance to explore the countryside, namely in the three state parks that lie within the town's 49-square-mile administrative district. About seven miles north of downtown Kent, the **Kent Falls State Park** has a cascading 200-foot waterfall with trails on either side that allow you to climb to the top, where you are rewarded with a spectacular view (daily 8am–dusk; free weekday parking; $5 CT, $8 out-of-state parking fee on summer weekends). A couple of miles further north on Route 7, the **Housatonic Meadows State Park**, a densely forested area which stretches for two miles along the Housatonic River, is popular with hikers and picnickers. Two miles west of downtown Kent, on Macedonia Brook Road, beautiful **Macedonia Brook State Park** holds deep gorges, falls, and the 1350-foot summit of Cobble Mountain, which commands views as far as the Catskills in New York State. At the southern end of town, five miles south of downtown, a right turn at Bulls Bridge Road leads to **Bulls Bridge**, one of only two original covered bridges in the state which is open to vehicular traffic. Restored a few years back, it's certainly in better condition today than when George Washington crossed it on horseback. The horse stumbled on a broken plank, so the story goes, forcing its illustrious rider into an overnight stay.

Practicalities
There are several nice places to **stay** in Kent. Located at the top end of Kent's shopping district, *Fife 'n' Drum*, 42 N Main St (☎860/927-3509; ③–⑤), is an above-average small motel that also contains a rustic restaurant; also within walking distance of the center, *Chaucer House*, 88 N Main St (☎860/927-4858; ④–⑤), is a small, pleasant B&B. Just north of the town, and offering excellent value, *The Country Goose*, 211 Kent-Cornwall Rd (☎860/927-4746; ⑤–⑥), is a 1740 colonial set on five acres with gorgeous rooms, antique furnishings, and a garden with gazebo. The *Bulls Bridge Inn*, 333 Kent Rd (☎860/927-1617), is an inexpensive dinner and Sunday brunch-only **restaurant** serving classic American fare. Good for soups, burgers, sandwiches and huge milkshakes is the *Villager Restaurant*, 28 N Main St (☎860/927-3945), but it's only open for breakfast and lunch.

Waterbury

At the very southern edge of Litchfield Hills, and certainly no part of them in spirit, **WATERBURY** – known to the Indians as "the place where no trees will grow" because of persistent flooding – valiantly celebrates its glorious past of brass and coppermaking. That's not necessarily a reason to come, though if you do, you'll find the requisite history in the **Mattatuck Museum**, 144 W Main St (Tues–Sat 10am–5pm, Sun noon–5pm; free), which also includes a permanent collection of nineteenth- and twentieth-century art such as *Adirondack Landscape: Mount McIntire* by John Frederick Kennsett and Frederic Edwin Church's *Icebergs*. The rest of the downtown is pleasing enough, with red-brick and white marble municipal buildings, including the **Chase Building** and the **Waterbury National Bank**, designed by Cass Gilbert, architect of the Woolworth Building and the George Washington Bridge in New York. Look, too, for the Waterbury Republican building, once the town's **main railroad station**, and modeled on City Hall in Siena, Italy, with a tall campanile-style tower that is the city's most notable landmark.

If you need to **stay** in Waterbury, *The House on the Hill*, 92 Woodlawn Terrace (☎203/757-9901; ⑥), is a large 1888 home containing guest rooms and suites filled with antiques and boasting fireplaces and an attractive wraparound porch, while the turn-of-the-century *Seventy Hillside,* 70 Hillside Ave (☎203/596-7070; ⑦), an elegant mansion with cozy rooms, fireplaces, and a sweeping staircase, is situated in a glorious park setting. *Dreschler's,* 25 Leavenworth St (☎203/573-1743), a **restaurant** open since 1868, offers a variety of Continental and American dishes in a delightful antique-filled dining room.

NORTHEASTERN CONNECTICUT

Once a prosperous textile-manufacturing region which spewed out cotton and silk, the predominantly rural **northeastern corner** of Connecticut, bordering the Rhode Island and Massachusetts state lines, has remained almost entirely devoid of major development and large-scale tourism. Its rolling hills and blossoming orchards are best viewed by driving along the 32-mile stretch of scenic **Route 169**, from Canterbury to Woodstock – along the way, you'll also spot some of the redundant old mills and warehouses, many of which have been carefully restored or converted into businesses. The best detours are in **Coventry**, home of revolutionary hero Nathan Hale; **Lebanon**, whose historic village green stretches a mile along Route 87; and **Putnam**, named after the famous revolutionary General Israel Putnam, alleged to have made the famous "whites of their eyes" command at the Battle of Bunker Hill (see p.83).

Bonanza **buses** (☎401/331-7500) run through the region, with stops at Willimantic and Danielson; local transportation, save for taxis, however, is virtually non-existent – try either Pomfret Livery and Community Cabs of Putnam (☎860/963-0690), or Red City Cabs, Willimantic (☎860/423-5700). The Northeast Connecticut Visitors' District, PO Box 598, Putnam, CT 06260 (☎860/928-1228 or 1-888/628-1228), publishes several guides for visitors, including an **accommodation** list and very useful bicycle guide and a guide to the waters of the region. Alternatively, you can drop in to the Coventry **visitor center**, 1195 Main St (☎860/742-1085).

Scenic Route 169: Woodstock to Canterbury

PUTNAM, just off I-395 in the northeast corner of the region, has a bit of history to it, having been named for Revolutionary War General Israel Putnam, and having been an important stop on the Underground Railroad prior to the Civil War. Though the town achieved economic prosperity as a result of the textile mills that developed along the fast-flowing **Quinebaug River** and the **Cargill Falls**, little evidence of its industrial past remains today. After years in the doldrums, revitalized Putnam is now one of the hottest antique shopping areas in the Northeast. Most of the shops are on or around Main Street, where the highlight is a former Victorian department store that has been renovated to form the **Antiques Marketplace**, with more than 300 dealers plying their trade. Apart from browsing the shops, there's little else of interest in Putnam. North of the town, on East Putnam Road, the 120-acre **Quaddick State Park** is a good place to relax, with a vast, 466-acre reservoir and a separate swimming pond, with ample opportunities for hiking, boating and fishing.

Just north on Route 169, peaceful **WOODSTOCK** is notable as the site of the 1846 **Roseland Cottage** (June–mid-Oct Wed–Sun 11am–5pm; $4), the former summer retreat of Henry C. Bowen, publisher of abolitionist weekly paper the *Independent*. The striking salmon-colored Gothic Revival residence, designed by English architect Joseph Wells, is notable for its steep gables, profuse Gothic tracery, stained-glass windows, and opulent interior – a suitable setting for Bowen to entertain four US presidents (Grant, Hayes, Harrison, and McKinley) at his lavish Fourth of July parties. The house, which contains its original furnishings, also includes an antique bowling alley.

Canterbury: the Prudence Crandall Museum

A small community at the junction of routes 14 and 169, **CANTERBURY** is home to the **Prudence Crandall Museum** housed in an attractive 1805 home that became New England's first academy to admit black women (Feb–mid-Dec Wed–Sun 10am–4.30pm; $2). From 1834 to 1844 the academy was run by Baptist schoolmistress Crandall, who gained notoriety when she accepted a young African-American girl in her school. The residents' violent response – the building was stoned – led to the school's closure, and Crandall was taken to court, though later exonerated. There is a permanent display devoted to Crandall's life and work, and others on black history, abolitionism and women's rights.

Practicalities

Places to stay in the area include the *King's Inn*, 5 Heritage Rd, Putnam (☎860/928-7961 or 1-800/541-7304; ④–⑤), a friendly hotel with well-appointed rooms plus its own steakhouse, and the *Inn at Woodstock Hill*, 94 Plaine Hill Rd, Woodstock (☎860/928-0528; ④–⑥), with spacious, yet cozy rooms. The *Inn* also boasts an excellent **restaurant**, which features a sumptuous French-influenced American menu, with entrees like poached salmon tarragon. Back in Putnam, *Mrs. Bridge's Pantry*, 136 Main St (☎860/963-70040), is a British style tearoom, serving Lapsang Soochong, Oolong and everything in between. South towards Canterbury, in **Brooklyn**, the *Golden Lamb Buttery*, 499 Wolf Den Rd (☎860/774-4423), offers a somewhat more daring experience, where diners meet at a set time in the barn, then are invited to take a hayride to view the pastoral setting. Dinner, accompanied by a singing guitarist (whom you met before on the hayride), includes entrees like roast pork with apricots, garlic, and mushroom.

Storrs, Mansfield and Coventry

West on Route 44, **STORRS** is home to the campus of the **University of Connecticut**, site of a few decent museums. The **Connecticut State Museum of Natural History**, Wilbur Cross Building, Rte-195 (Thur–Mon noon–4pm; suggested donation $1), with exhibits on Connecticut Indians including a life-sized wigwam, mounted hawks and owls, insects, minerals, and mammals. Also on campus is the **William Benton Museum of Art** (Tues–Fri 10am–4.30pm, weekends 1–4.30pm; free; ☎860/486-4520), with a program of changing exhibits, and a permanent collection which includes European and American paintings, among them works by Henry Ward Ranger, Ernest Lawson, Gustav Klimt, and Edward Burne-

Jones; drawings, prints, and sculptures from the sixteenth century to the present day, and a large collection of theater drawings by Reginald Marsh. If you're green-fingered, be sure not to miss the **University of Connecticut Greenhouses,** 75 N Eagleville Rd, Storrs (Mon–Thur 9am–4pm, Fri 9am–3pm), a complex by the university's department of ecology and evolutionary biology, containing more than 3000 species of plants, including orchids, cacti, palm trees, a redwood, and even carnivorous aquatic plants, while on Stone Mill Road, the **Gurleyville Grist Mill** (June–mid-Oct Sun noon–4pm; free), on the Fenton River, built in 1830 to replace an earlier construction, contains a miller's house that was once the home of Governor Wilbur Cross, and now houses a small museum.

Just north, **Mansfield** has some of the area's better spots for **eating** and **accommodation**. The *Fitch House B&B*, 563 Storrs Rd (☎860/456-0922; [4]–[5]), an elegant Greek Revival mansion, has two large, tastefully decorated rooms. Down the road, you can enjoy Continental cuisine at the *Altnaveigh Inn,* 957 Storrs Rd (☎860/429-4490), an atmospheric country farmhouse, or dine more casually at *The Depot*, 57 Middle Turnpike/Rte-44 (☎860/429-3663), in an original train depot setting popular with students from UConn.

Coventry

COVENTRY, west of Storrs, is another quiet former mill community, though with a decent selection of restaurants and shops, plus the **Nathan Hale Homestead**, 2299 South St (mid-May to mid-Oct daily 1–4pm; $4), a three-story farmhouse rebuilt in 1776 by his father, Deacon Richard Hale, just after Hale was hanged by the British as an American spy. More Hale memorabilia can be viewed close by at the **Strong-Porter House**, 2382 South St (mid-May to mid-Oct Sat & Sun 1–5pm; $1), one-time home to Hale's maternal ancestors.

Coventry makes for a nice **place to stay**, with inns like the *Bird-in-Hand*, 2011 Main St (☎860/742-0032; [5]), an attractive antique-filled colonial house. Its **restaurants**, too, are good, including the *Bidwell Tavern*, 1260 Main St, South Coventry (☎860/742-6978), with all-American food in an historic tavern that dates back to 1822.

Willimantic and Lebanon

South of Coventry, on the Willimantic River, lies **WILLIMANTIC** (in Native American language, "land of the swift running waters"), yet another mill village, once home to the Willimantic Thread Company. The company's former complex contains the **Windham Textile and History Museum**, 157 Union St (May–mid-Oct Thurs–Sun 1–5pm; rest of year Fri–Sun 1–4pm; $4), which preserves the thread-making machinery and workers' quarters typical of the time.

Straddling a village green that stretches more than a mile along Route 87, **LEBANON** was home to one **Jonathan Trumbull**, ardent patriot and the only crown-appointed governor to side with the Revolutionaries. It was his presence that encouraged a battalion of hussars under the leadership of the duc de Lauzun to camp here in 1780, awaiting Rochambeau and his men for the final push of the Revolutionary War. Two Trumbull homes are open to the public: the **Jonathan Trumbull House**, 169 W Town St (mid-May to mid-Oct Tues–Sat 1–5pm; $2), built in 1735 and furnished with period pieces; and the Georgian **Jonathan Trumbull Jr House** (mid-May to mid-Oct Sat & Sun 1–5pm; $1), built in 1769 by his son, a noted painter who was commissioned by Congress in 1816 to paint the famous historical scenes that decorate the capitol's rotunda. Close by on West Town Street, you can see Trumbull Sr's **Revolutionary War Office** (June–Sept Sat & Sun 11.30am–4.30pm; free), Trumbull's two-room office and store which became the headquarters of the Council of Safety, who plotted strategy and coordinated supplies during the war.

CHAPTER SIX

VERMONT

I n many ways, **Vermont** comes closer than any other New England state to fulfilling the quintessential image of small-town Yankee America, with its white churches and red barns, covered bridges and clapboard houses, snowy woods and maple syrup. No city manages a population of forty thousand (only Burlington even comes close) and the chief tourist attraction is none other than Ben and Jerry's ice-cream factory in Waterbury. Though rural, the landscape is not all that agricultural, and much is covered by verdant, mountainous forests (the state's name supposedly comes from the French *vert mont*, or green mountain). True, in certain areas, the bucolic image proffered forth can seem a bit packaged, but you probably won't tire of trawling its many scenic byways and village greens.

The people who choose to live here represent a number of seemingly disparate groups – hippies, diehard conservatives, taciturn codgers who have never left the state – who tend to band together to preserve their environment and lament the advent of yet another ski resort. However, their political philosophies remain fiercely in contrast, which became all too clear when Governor Howard Dean signed Vermont's **civil union** bill into law in 1999, making Vermont the first state in the US to sanction same-sex marriage. While the governor and the action were widely praised, giving proof to those who proudly proclaimed Vermont "the most progressive state in the nation," another, more conservative, contingent condemned Dean as a "coward" giving in to pressure from "flatlanders" – a derogatory term for Vermont residents transplanted from other parts. Although Dean narrowly won re-election in 2000, the debate rages on, and in front of many a dilapidated farmhouse it's possible to see signs reading "take back Vermont."

Its liberal voice could be traced to it being the youngest of New England's states, settled last, early in the eighteenth century. As French explorers worked their way down from Canada, American colonists began to spread north; but even as that rivalry died down, a further antipathy developed between settlers from New Hampshire and those from New York. The wealthy New York merchants who built fine homes along the Connecticut River Valley thought of themselves as "River Gods," but the hardy settlers of the lakes and mountains to the west had little time for their patrician ways. Their leader was the now-legendary Ethan Allen, who formed his Green Mountain Boys in 1770, proclaiming that "the gods of the hills are not the gods of the valley." When the Revolutionary War superseded such conflicts, this all-but-autonomous force captured Fort Ticonderoga from the British and helped to win the decisive Battle of Bennington. For fourteen years, Vermont was an independent republic (it was not one of the original thirteen states), with the first constitution in the world to explicitly forbid slavery and grant universal (male) suffrage, but once its boundaries with New York were agreed, it joined the Union in 1791. Strangely, the two seminal figures of the **Mormon** religion were born in Vermont shortly thereafter – Joseph Smith in 1805 and his lieutenant and successor Brigham Young in 1801.

With the occasional exception, such as the extraordinary assortment of Americana at the **Shelburne Museum** near Burlington (a lively city worth visiting in any case), there are few specific sights as such to seek out; indeed, tourism here is more activity-oriented, with most visitors coming during two well-defined seasons: to see the **fall foliage** in the first two weeks of October, and to **ski** in the depths of winter, when the resorts of **Killington** and **Stowe**, further north (home of *The Sound of Music*'s Von Trapp family), spring to life. For the rest of the year, you might just as well explore any of the state's minor roads that strike your fancy, confident that some impressive village will be around the corner, doubtless surrounded by lakes and mountains and punctuated by lovely country inns in which to lodge overnight.

Getting around Vermont

Vermont's only sizeable commercial **airport** is in Burlington, a few miles east of town along US-2; the two carriers with the most flights are Continental Airlines (☎1-800/525-0280) and USAir (☎1-800/428-4322), each of which have flights to and from Boston and New York City. Other gateways to Vermont include Albany, Hartford and Montréal. Amtrak-affiliated Vermonter **trains** between Montréal and Washington, DC, stop at Brattleboro, Bellows Falls, White River Junction, Montpelier, Waterbury, Stowe, Burlington, and St Albans in the early morning southbound and mid-evening heading north. The *Vermonter* has a special car for bikes, skis and snowboards. Amtrak's *Ethan Allen Express* travels from New York City to Rutland, VT, where during ski season you can get direct motorcoach service to Killington Resort. Greyhound-affiliated Vermont Transit lines **buses** (☎1-800/642-3133 in Vermont; ☎1-800/451-3292 elsewhere in New England) connect Montréal with Boston and New York, passing through Burlington, Montpelier, Rutland, White River Junction, and Brattleboro. Local bus services link Stowe with Burlington, cross the north from Newport to Portland, Maine, and traverse the Green Mountains.

Lake Champlain Ferries (☎802/864-9804) carry cars to New York from Burlington, Charlotte and Grand Isle, and a six-minute ferry journey links Larrabee's Point with Ticonderoga farther south. Bike Vermont, Inc, PO Box 207, Woodstock, VT 05091 (☎1-800/257-2226, *www.bikevt.com*), Vermont Mountain Bike Tours, PO Box 541, Pittsfield, VT 05762 (☎802/746-8580), and Vermont Bicycle Touring, PO Box 711, Bristol, VT 05443 (☎802/453-4811 or 1-800/245-3868, *www.vbt.com*), can organize **cycling tours** around the state.

SOUTHERN VERMONT

Of the two towns located at either end of Vermont's southern corridor – a mere forty miles from east to west linked by Hwy-9 – **Brattleboro**, probably your best bet around these parts, has the atmosphere of a college town, but not the college, while **Bennington** has the college but not the atmosphere. In between, the Green Mountain National Forest is dotted with traditional resort villages like **Newfane** and **Mount Snow**, worth investigating though not for any extended period of time. Nearer to Bennington, hikers can pick up the **Long Trail** close to its southern terminus.

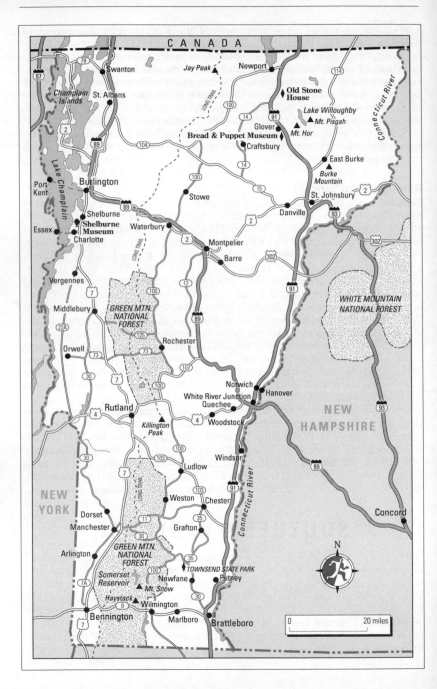

Brattleboro

If **BRATTLEBORO**, in the southeastern corner of the state, just off I-91, is your first taste of Vermont, it may come as a surprise. Not the quaint, 1950s-throwback village you might expect, its style owes more to the central and northern Massachusetts college towns, with numerous little stores and coffeehouses, not to mention the liveliest nightlife scene in the state outside of Burlington, all catering to the youthful and vaguely "alternative" population that has moved into the surrounding hills the past few decades. Sitting beside the Connecticut River, the city lies near the site of **Fort Dummer**, the first English settlement in the state, which was built to protect neighboring Massachusetts from Indian raids. Gradually businesses and farms sprang up alongside the river and the fort, and in the 1800s Brattleboro enjoyed a modest reputation as a railroad town and a mill town, even briefly as a health care center, after pure springs were discovered along the Whetstone Brook. Rudyard Kipling penned his two *Jungle Books* here, giving the town its lone claim to fame, though one you can't really experience – the only site related to him is his former home **Naulakha**, used only for private parties.

Arrival, information and getting around

If you're flying in, the closest major **airport** is in Hartford, Connecticut, approximately ninety minutes south of the Vermont border. Brattleboro is more easily reached by **train**; two Amtrak lines pass through daily, and the station is centrally located on Vernon Street. Meanwhile, Vermont Transit interlines with Greyhound **bus service** in these parts, and their terminal is conveniently located at the junction of US-5 and I-91. Brattleboro's **town bus** is a bargain at only 75¢, although in a town of this size, you won't need it much.

The **Chamber of Commerce**, 182 Main St (☎802/254-4565), has a standard selection of brochures on area attractions, and operates an information **kiosk** on the Brattleboro Town Common, just north of town on Putney Road. The official town Web site, *www.sover.net/~bratchmb*, provides copious information of the same ilk, as does *www.brattleboro.com*.

If you're interested in seeing the town from the **water** nearby, Connecticut River Safaris, north of town on Putney Road (☎802/257-5008), rents motorboats, canoes, and kayaks. The *Belle of Brattleboro*, also on Putney Road (June–Oct, plus special foliage cruises; ☎802/254-1263; $8), seats about fifty people and runs cruises on the Connecticut with a narrative outlining its history, folklore, and wildlife. Sunset cruises are a bit lower key, with cruise guides letting the view speak for itself.

ACCOMMODATION PRICE CODES

All accommodation prices in this book have been coded using the symbols below; prices are for the least expensive **double rooms** in each establishment. For a full explanation see p.28 in Basics. Individual rates rather than price codes are given for **hostels**.

① up to $30	④ $60–80	⑦ $130–175
② $30–45	⑤ $80–100	⑧ $175–250
③ $45–60	⑥ $100–130	⑨ $250+

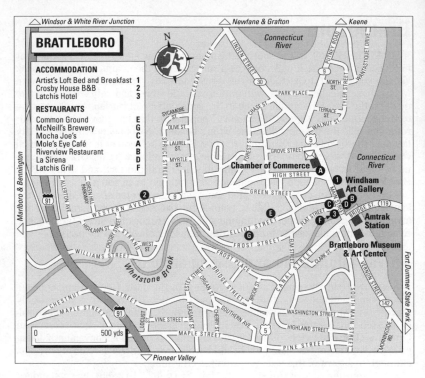

Accommodation

A number of chain and independently owned **motels** line Putney Road (US-5) north of town, though the independent ones are cheaper and have a bit more character. The best **camping** in the area is at Hidden Acres Campground (☎802/254-2098), two miles north along Putney Road after its intersection with Rte-9.

40 Putney Road, 40 Putney Rd (☎802/254-6268 or 1-800/941-2413, *www.Putney.net/40putneyrd*). Luxurious bed and breakfast in a French Baronial house decorated with antique furnishings. ⑥.

The Artist's Loft B&B and Gallery, 103 Main St (☎802/257-5181, *www.theartistsloft.com*). Tiny B&B above art gallery offers only one suite, but it's a luxurious two-room that overlooks the Connecticut River. Private entrance, video and book libraries available. ⑥.

Colonial Motel & Spa, Putney Rd, US-5 and Rte-9 (☎802/257-7733 or 1-800/239-0032, *www.colonialmotel.com*). This family owned and operated lodge has quality rooms with indoor pool, sauna, health club, and Redwood hot tub. Their in-house restaurant serves fine breakfasts (available at a discount for guests). ②–③.

Crosby House B&B, 45 Western Ave (☎802/257-4914 or 1-800/528-1868, *www.sover.net/~tomlynn*). Restored Italianate Victorian home with luxurious accommodations: queen-sized beds, fireplaces, jacuzzi, book and video library, and elegant breakfast settings. Geared more toward couples than families. ⑥.

Lamplighter Motel, 1336 Putney Rd (☎802/254-8025). The basic rooms look like they haven't been redecorated since the 1960s, but they're clean and very cheap. ②.

Latchis Hotel, 50 Main St (☎802/254-6300, *www.brattleboro.com/latchis*). Small and centrally located thirty-room Art Deco hotel is definitely the best place to stay if you can afford it. Guests staying in pricier rooms and suites receive free passes to the movie theater next door, which shows both studio and indie flicks in an elaborate interior of balconies and a ceiling painted with golden zodiac signs. The hotel shares a roof with a microbrewery and a good restaurant, the *Latchis Grille* (see p.000). [4]–[5].

The Town

Main Street spans the length of Brattleboro's diminutive downtown, lined with hip coffeehouses, art galleries, holistic apothecaries, and used-CD shops. You could spend time browsing in any of them, including the funky **Windham Art Gallery**, 69 Main St, an artists' cooperative, exhibiting an eclectic array of fine arts; the featured artists can occasionally be seen prowling the halls.

Just west off the southern end of Main Street is the center of Brattleboro's concentration of **bookstores**. Brattleboro Books, 36 Elliot St, purveys a staggering array of used volumes at incredibly cheap prices. Across the street, at 25 Elliot, Everyone's Books is part leftist bookstore, with special sections for indie zines and anarchic political tracts, and part community center for the local counterculture (it's located right downstairs from the *Common Ground* restaurant, see p.342).

At the foot of Main Street, just before it intersects with Bridge Street, the 1930s Art Deco **Latchis Hotel** is worth a look for its old sign, a sleek chrome example of high Deco style, and interior trimmings, including a series of faux-Greek friezes, even if you have no intention of staying the night. Across the bridge, the **Brattleboro Museum and Art Center** (mid-May–Oct Tues–Sun noon–6pm; $3) occupies the old railroad station building. It features changing – and usually rather nondescript – exhibits on contemporary art and regional history, as well as several locally made Estey organs, which the town produced and shipped to churches throughout the world during the early part of the twentieth century.

A couple of miles north of town off I-91 in the village of Dummerston is **Naulakha**, the home of Rudyard Kipling. Kipling lived there from 1891 to 1896, writing some of his most celebrated work, including *Captains Courageous* and *The First and Second Jungle Books*. Named after a temple in Janakpur, Nepal, the two and a half story shingle-clad house sits atop a hill, with views of the Connecticut River valley and Mount Monadnock, across the border in New Hampshire. At present, Naulakha, though maintained by the Vermont Heritage Network, is not open to casual visitors. But hardcore Kipling fans can arrange to stay there for a paltry $2000 a week ($250 a night in winter). Inquiries must be directed to Landmark Trust, Shottesbrooke, Maidenhead, Berkshire SL6 3SW, UK; fax 011-44-1628-825417.

Eating, drinking and entertainment

Brattleboro's **restaurants** cater to the youthful counterculture with a variety of cuisines rarely duplicated in Vermont. Most of the best options are located on or just off Main Street, and the same goes for **bars** in the town. A good place to stock up for a camping trip is the Brattleboro Food Co-op, 2 Main St (☎802/257-0236), in the Brookside Plaza at the intersection of Canal and Main streets, which stocks a wide selection of wholefood. The local **music scene** bops with pretty good local acts on a nearly nightly basis; pick up a Thursday edition of the *Brattleboro Reformer* for an exhaustive listing of the week's events.

Back Side Café, 24 High St (☎802/257-5056). Good omelettes and burgers at bargain prices.

The Café Beyond at Collected Works Bookstore, 29 High St (☎802/254-2920). Above average Euro-style sandwiches, espresso drinks, soups, and desserts served in a bright industrial-chic setting surrounded by windows, books, and art. Take-out available. Closed Sundays.

Carol's Main Street Café, 71 Main St (☎802/254-8380). Chow on soups and fresh bagels while jawing with crusty locals at the old-fashioned lunch counter.

Common Ground, 25 Elliot St (☎802/257-0855). A variety of vegetarian wholefoods and inventive daily specials like Jamaican tofu jerk-adilla are served at this long-established vegetarian collective wholefood restaurant, organic wherever possible, a gathering ground for the crunchiest of the crunchy. Free dinners on Thanksgiving and work-for-food trade.

Juice Bar Cafe, 127 Main St (☎802/257-7412). Juice beverages and smoothies in a psychedelic setting. Closed Sun & Mon.

La Sirena, 39 Main St (☎802/257-5234). By New England standards, this is really good Tex-Mex, which of course is not saying all that much. Wide selection of local microbrews and tangy margaritas as well. Lunch specials are a great deal.

Latchis Grille, 6 Flat St (☎802/254-4747). An eclectic mix of enticing New American dishes, such as savory grits with Andouille sausage and shrimp, and old filling standards, like knockwurst & bratwurst, and fish & chips. Quality beer available from the on-site Windham Brewery. Some of the entrees are on the expensive side, but well worth the price. Closed Mon.

McNeill's Brewery, 90 Elliot St (☎802/254-2553). Rough-hewn bar where you can sample eleven different varieties of local microbrews, including Apocalypse Now and Old Ringworm.

Mocha Joe's, 82 Main St (☎802/257-7794). Good caffeine-filled beverages in a stylish basement below Main St.

Mole's Eye Cafe, 4 High St (☎802/257-0071). Brattleboro's most happening nightspot, bar, and dance floor with a wide range of live music most nights – blues, Latin, R&B, jazz, calypso – for about a $5 cover.

Riverview Restaurant, 3 Bridge St (☎802/254-9841). The tasty, cheap seafood makes for an ample meal, but the real treat is the outdoor dining available on the deck, accompanied by great views of the Connecticut River.

North from Brattleboro: Newfane, Grafton and Chester

Slightly inland and north from Brattleboro, **NEWFANE** and **GRAFTON** are two beautifully restored villages offering the best of small-town Vermont with their white churches and romantic inns. There's nothing of real note to see in the former, but it boasts a town green flanked by no less than three white-steepled buildings, the union hall, the Congregational church, and the county courthouse – pretty enough if you're stopping through. If you're looking for a **place to stay**, try the *Inn at South Newfane*, 369 Dover Rd, South Newfane (☎802/348-7191 or 1-877/548-7191; ⑤–⑥), a turn-of-the-century manor house filled with antiques and a cluttered decor that can best be described as eclectic.

There's marginally more to do in Grafton, though still, the biggest draw here is a cheese shop, the **Grafton Village Cheese Company**, on Townsend Road a half mile south of the village (Mon–Fri 8am–4pm, Sat–Sun 10am–4pm; ☎802/843-2221 or 1-800/GRAFTON). Take some of their excellent cheddar with you on a picnic to nearby Townsend State Park (see below). A little closer to town, the **Nature Museum**, 186 Townshend Rd (Memorial Day–mid-October Sat & Sun by appointment; rest of year Sat 10am–4pm; $5; ☎802/843-2111), is a somewhat haphazard taxidermical and geological collection crammed into a former hall. If you've got time to kill and an abiding interest in local history, the Grafton Historical Society runs the **History Museum** at 147 Main St (June–mid-Oct Sat, Sun & holidays 10am–noon &

2pm–4pm; $3), a collection of relics from Grafton homesteads, such as soapstones from the local quarries, textiles, and photos. They can also provide you with a helpful **walking tour** map. The *Old Tavern*, 92 Main St (☎1-800/843-1801, *www.old-tavern.com*; 8), is a combination **B&B/restaurant** that sits in the heart of the tiny village and has been around since 1801, having accommodated such luminaries as Ulysses S. Grant, Nathaniel Hawthorne, and Henry David Thoreau.

Just a few miles north of Newfane, **Townsend State Park** (☎802/365-7500) provides excellent opportunities for both casual and serious hikers. Its trails, open May through mid-October, include the steep, rocky, 1680-foot climb to the summit of **Bald Mountain**; other trails are not quite as challenging. There's swimming, tubing, and canoeing at the nearby Townsend Dam.

Chester

It's easy enough to miss tiny **CHESTER**, at the junction of Rte-103, Rte-11 and Rte-35, seven miles north of Grafton, though its prototypical Vermont charm may well draw you in. If so, drop by the talkative folks at the **Historical Society** on Main Street and Chester Green who can give you a walking-tour brochure to the historic houses scattered about town. Besides wandering through, you can jump aboard the **Green Mountain Flyer** (June 24–Sept 4 Tues–Sun, Sept 16–Oct 22 daily; 1 departure at 12.10pm; $12; *www.rails-vt.com*), a sightseeing train that runs two-hour round-trips down to Bellows Falls, right at the New Hampshire border. The engine chugs slowly down, crossing rivers and passing covered bridges at a leisurely pace, leaving lots of time to take in the scenery, which is spectacular in the fall.

The **bed-and-breakfasts** and inns are much the best reason for staying: try the *Chester House Inn*, 166 Main St (☎888/875-2205; 5–7), which has seven rooms with private baths, each decorated in a different style and color; the *Hugging Bear Inn and Shoppe*, 244 Main St (☎802/875-2412, *www.huggingbear.com*; 4–6), claims "the finest selection of teddy bears in the Northeast"; while just off the Chester Green, *Rose Arbour* (☎802/875-4766; 4–5) is a pretty B&B with an attached tea-room; the top floor is a five-room suite, complete with kitchen. The best place to **eat** in town is *Raspberries and Tyme*, on the Green (☎802/875-4486), serving creative salads, burgers and sandwiches.

West to Bennington

Route 9 heads west from Brattleboro not forty miles to Bennington; the first town of any size along the way is uninspiring **MARLBORO**, just a few miles along. In midsummer, the town is besieged by chamber music fanatics, as it plays host to the **Marlboro Music Fest** (☎802/254-2394, *www.marlboromusic.org*). South along Hwy-100, the birthplace of Mormon prophet Brigham Young is marked by a granite monument at **WHITINGHAM**'s town common.

Further on, **MOUNT SNOW** and **HAYSTACK MOUNTAIN** provide perfectly fine places to ski, both officially part of the **Green Mountain National Forest**, though not getting quite as much press as the mountains' other major snowbound havens such as Killington. Still, that may be reason enough to opt for it, if you're looking to avoid the crowds while having your choice of types of run. Mount Snow is the larger, and more popular, of the two, offering some 130 trails; Haystack, by contrast, has less than fifty. You'll also find plenty of outdoorsy stuff to occupy you here in the summer, too. For more info, contact the **Mount Snow-Haystack Chamber of Commerce**, PO Box 3, Wilmington, VT 05363 (☎802/464-8092).

Bennington

Little has happened in **BENNINGTON** in the past two hundred years to match the excitement of the days when Ethan Allen's Green Mountain Boys were based here and known as the "Bennington Mob." Today, despite the presence of the exclusive, arts-oriented **Bennington College** – which has seen the likes of hot young authors Bret Easton Ellis and Donna Tartt pass through its halls – the city is a sleepy town most notable for its rich Revolutionary history and one fine museum of American folk art.

Settled in 1761 on a rise by the Walloomsac River, overlooking the valley between the Green and Taconic mountains, the town became a leading nineteenth-century industrial outpost for paper mills, potteries, gristmills, and the largest cotton-batting mill in the US. That heritage is preserved today in **Old Bennington**, just up the hill from the center of town, and the one obvious spot to explore.

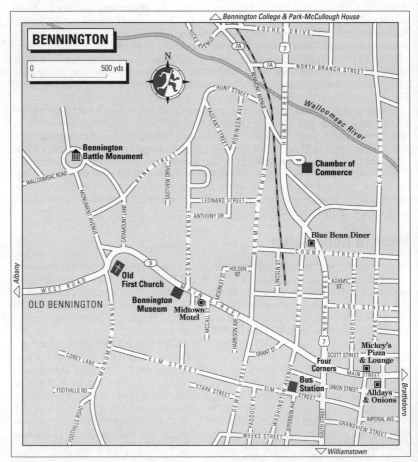

Arrival and information

Bennington is centered on the intersection of US-7 and Hwy-9, an intersection known locally as the "Four Corners." In town, Hwy-9 is referred to as Main Street, while the local stretches of US-7 above and below the Corners are called North and South streets. The nearest commercial **airport** is forty miles away in Albany, New York.

The **Bennington Area Chamber of Commerce**, Veterans Memorial Drive (Mon–Fri 9am–5pm; ☎802/447-3311, *www.bennington.com*), should likely be your first stop for info on nearby and surrounding attractions; it has clean public restrooms to boot. There's also a **kiosk** with basic practical information at the Four Corners.

Accommodation

Cookie-cutter **budget motels** line South Street and West Main Street, and there are a few other options scattered about. Those who might prefer "name brand" chain motels will be disappointed in what the Bennington area has to offer (namely just a *Best Western* on Northside Drive), but its independent motels and hotels are generally clean and far less expensive than those found in other Vermont cities and towns.

Alexandra Inn, Rte-7A and Orchard Rd (☎802/442-5619, *alexandr@sover.net*). Clean restored colonial with thirteen luxurious rooms and baths, fireplaces, TV, hearty gourmet breakfasts, and beautiful views of Mount Anthony and the Battle Monument. ⑥– ⑦.

Catamount Motel, 500 South St (☎802/442-5977). Immaculate quarters, featuring a pool and a picnic area in which to barbecue. ③.

Fife 'n' Drum Motel, US-7 South, 1.5 miles south of Bennington (☎802/442-4074 or 442-4730, fax: 442-8471). Pleasant, well-appointed rooms with color cable TV, coffee makers, and air-conditioning. Pool, spa, and spacious lawn with grills. ③.

Greenwood Lodge Hostel and Campground (HI/AYH), on Prospect Mountain off Rte-9 (☎802/442-2547). Clean dorm beds with access to kitchen and recreation areas. $14, non-members $17. Twenty wooded campsites nearby do not include access to lodge facilities. Best to call before going.

Mid-Town Motel, 107 W Main St (☎802/447-0189). Extremely basic efficiencies, somewhat less expensive and much less appealing than its numerous neighbors. ③.

Molly Stark Inn, 1067 Main St (☎802/442-9631 or 1-800/356-3076, *www.mollystarkinn.com*). Nine double-occupancy guest rooms with quilts and claw-footed tubs in a cozy Queen Anne-style cottage. Full breakfast and friendly owners. ④–⑤.

The Town

There's nothing much doing in the center of Bennington, and the best place to begin your wanderings is around the western end of Main Street, in historic **Old Bennington**, an assortment of public and residential buildings done in all manner of architectural styles. The town's most prominent icon is nearby at the **Bennington Battle Monument**, 15 Monument Circle (mid-April–Oct daily 9am–5pm; $1.50), a 306-foot hilltop obelisk that commemorates the August 1777 Battle of Bennington. This pivotal conflict pitted the Continental Army against the superior forces of General Burgoyne, who had made it an objective to seize the arsenal depot at Bennington. The unexpected victory of the Revolutionaries bolstered their morale and debilitated Burgoyne's troops, contributing to their ultimate defeat at the subsequent Battle of Saratoga, the major turning point of the war. The monument is located on the hilltop that was the site of Burgoyne's objective (though the battle actually took place just over the Walloomsac River, in New York State). Just down Monument Avenue, **Old First Church**, Monument Circle, erected in 1805, abuts a well-preserved cemetery holding the grave of poet and adoptive Vermonter Robert Frost. His tombstone, well-marked by directional signs, reads simply, "I had a lover's quarrel with the world," an epitaph that never ceases to amuse the church's many visitors.

East of here, the **Bennington Museum and Grandma Moses Gallery**, West Main Street (daily: June–Oct 9am–6pm; rest of year 9am–5pm; $6), contains a fine array of Americana, including several Tiffany lamps, what may be the oldest American flag in existence, and the "Wasp," a 1925 luxury touring car, built in Bennington and the only surviving example of its kind. The highlight of the collection, however, is its exhibit on American folk artist Anna Mary Robertson Moses, known popularly as **Grandma Moses**. Moses, who first exhibited her simple, pleasing representations of rural life at the age of 80, experienced a meteoric rise to fame in the worlds of high art and popular culture, and eventually lived to enjoy national adulation upon reaching her 100th birthday. In addition to the largest public collection of her work, the museum has a reconstruction of the schoolhouse she attended as a youngster, which displays many of her personal belongings, photographs, painting equipment, and awards.

Rte-67A splits off from US-7 and continues on to North Bennington, where three **covered bridges** – the Silk Road, Paper Mill Village, and the Burt Henry – span the Walloomsac River. This area is marked by reminders of late eighteenth-century industrial activity, notably the mill housing along Sage Street. Also here is the elaborate Greek Revival **Park-McCullough House**, Park and West streets (mid-May to mid-Oct Mon & Thurs–Sun 10am–3pm, tours hourly; $5), a sumptuous 1864 mansion filled with most of its original period furnishings, including horse-drawn carriages and children's toys.

Eating, drinking and entertainment

There's not an overwhelming variety when it comes to **restaurants** in Bennington, most seeming to serve the simple omelettes and burgers-type fare found in most diners. Nights are fairly quiet in Bennington, too, as the college population rarely gets too rowdy.

Alldays and Onions, 519 Main St (☎802/447-0043). Creative seafood and pasta dishes at reasonable prices.

Blue Benn Diner, 102 Hunt St (☎802/442-5140). Authentic, 1940s-era diner draws a diverse crowd of hard-boiled locals and artsy students. Open from 6am daily.

Madison Brewing Co, 428 Main St (☎1-800/44BREWS). Fun, stylish brewpub with hearty burgers and six varieties of in-house beer. Live blues most nights of the week. Open daily until 2am.

Mickey's Pizza and Lounge, 510 Main St (☎802/447-1555). Pizza joint on one level; above that is an unselfconsciously tacky townie dive with live music, cheap beer, and rowdy company.

The Publyk House, near the intersection of US-7 and Historic Rte-7A (☎802/442-8301). Remodeled barn turned gourmet restaurant, located on a hill with excellent views of New York, New Hampshire, and Massachusetts. Excellent – though expensive – steaks and seafood.

Rattlesnake, 230 North St (☎802/447-7018). A popular Mexican joint – about the closest you'll come to exotic cuisine in Bennington.

Suzy Q's, 108 School St (☎802/447-8558). This noisy pool hall/video game room caters to the younger crowd, but also serves decent soups and sandwiches and excellent microbrews and espresso drinks.

THE GREEN MOUNTAINS

The **Green Mountains** that form the backbone of Vermont are not as harsh as New Hampshire's White Mountains, though the forests for which they are named are invariably buried in snow for most of the winter, and the higher roads are liable to be blocked for long periods. For the most part, the sides and the summits are covered with evergreens such as spruces, hemlocks, and firs, the inspiration to the French colonialists for the state's name (and, more obviously, the name of the range). Here and there, denuded patches mark where trees have been shaved away to create ski-runs, but otherwise the usually peaceful Rte-100 and US-7, which run along the base of the mountains to the east and west, respectively, offer unspoiled mountain views as well as a few charming towns along the way. When accessible (mostly in summer), the mountains are excellent opportunities for hiking, camping, fishing, canoeing, and swimming.

The Green Mountain National Forest runs from the southern border of Vermont nearly up to the state capital, Montpelier, only interrupted around the city of **Rutland**, notably for a nearby museum devoted to the work of **Norman Rockwell**. In that first stretch, outside of the expected quaint towns, there's not much to divert you other than **Manchester**, the outlet shopping center of Vermont, fairly tacky but with an authentic enough historic core. Probably the most interesting, and certainly the most cosmopolitan, village in the area is **Middlebury**, home to a noted university of the same name. Past that, the obvious highlights are genteel **Woodstock**, east of Rutland, and unpretentious **Montpelier**, another fifty miles north. In addition, there are the ever-popular ski resorts of **Stowe** and **Killington**, and to top it all off, the **Ben and Jerry's Ice Cream Factory** in Waterbury, perhaps the apotheosis of Vermont activism-cum-tourist attraction.

Hwy-100 scenic drive: Weston

Hwy-100 continues north of Mount Snow, snaking along the east of the Green Mountains, and continues, through the center of the state, to Killington (see p.354) and beyond. If you choose to head through this way, consider stopping in **WESTON**. One of the prettier villages along scenic Hwy-100, Weston spreads beside a little river and centered on an idyllic green, where a stone slab commemorates the seventeen local soldiers who were killed on the same day during the Civil War, at Alexandria in Virginia. This is one of the few Vermont towns that tries to cater to a summer crowd, through various art-related and outdoor activities, but things never get so busy that you would mistake it for any sort of tourist haven.

In town, Hwy-100 turns into Main Street, and is lined with stores selling antiques, toys and fudge. The spell is slightly broken when you realize that the **Vermont Country Store**, for all its seeming quaintness, is actually part of a heartless corporate chain of superstores that relentlessly package and market the state's bucolic image. The **Weston Village Store** opposite contains a much more authentic, if not as vast, range of vaguely rural and domestic articles, such as gallon tins of real maple syrup and local cheeses. The **Weston Bowl Mill**, on the north side of town, carries the expected bowls as well as a range of artfully crafted woodwork.

THE LONG TRAIL

Spanning the entirety of Vermont – 265 miles from the Massachusetts border to Quebec – the Long Trail is one of America's premier hiking trails, popular with seasoned outdoorsmen but accessible for amateurs as well. It runs along the crest of the Green Mountains, affording fabulous views of small towns and vast stretches of countryside. The terrain is varied, to put it mildly, and close attention should be paid to boulders, errant rocks, mud masquerading as dry land, ledges, wooden ladders, and more, all of which becomes more rugged the further north you go. If you're heading out here to attempt the entire length, make sure to bring a map, compass, plenty of water and supplies, and so on; note, too, that along the way are seventy shelters maintained during the summer. The essential tome for interested parties is the *Guide Book of the Long Trail* ($10), published by the caretakers of the trail, the **Green Mountain Club**, RR 1, Box 650, Rte-100, Waterbury Center, VT 05677 (☎802/244-7037). The club also organizes group tours and distributes a series of free pamphlets about hiking and outdoor recreation in Vermont, among them *A Day Hiker's Vermont Sampler* and *The Long Trail*.

Right on the town green, the 1797 **Farrar-Mansur House** (July & Aug Wed–Sun 1–4pm; May, June, Sept & Oct Sat–Sun 1—4pm; $3 donation requested), an early tavern that has been restored to depict lives of early Vermont settlers, presents an array of antique housewares and some decent American folk art. Next door, the **Old Mill Museum** (May–Aug daily 1–4pm; $3 donation requested) occupies a converted sawmill and possesses an impressive historical assortment of tinsmith, woodworking, and farm and dairy tools. The nearby **Weston Playhouse**, which spawned the career of the late Lloyd Bridges, is a typical small-town Vermont theater, putting on a mixture of standard summer-stock musicals with occasionally more daring offerings, such as works by Brian Friel and Moliere (Tues–Sun; ☎802/824-5288).

Practicalities

The best **accommodation** in town is the lovely, centrally located *Inn at Weston* near the village green (☎802/824-6789, *www.innweston.com*; [6]), which also features a first-class restaurant serving divine steak *au poivre*, and a snug pub to boot. *The Wilder Homestead Inn*, 25 Lawrence Hill Rd (☎802/824-8172, *www.wilderhomestead.com*; [5]–[6]), is another nice bed-and-breakfast, set alongside a pleasant brook. Decent alternatives away from the town center include the *Colonial House Inn & Motel*, south on Hwy-100 (☎802/824-6286 or 1-800/639-5033; [4]), and the *Friendly Acres Motel & Inn*, 913 Rte-100 (☎802/824-5851; [4]), a little closer to town on the same road, each of which provide breakfast, though the *Colonial House* has the edge with its offer of fresh home-made cookies to all visitors.

If you're looking to **eat** more than cookies, a magnificent soda fountain dominates the 1887 mahogany bar of the lunch-only *Bryant House* restaurant (☎802/824-6287; closed Sun), two doors down from the Vermont Country Store. The menu includes such classic New England fare as "johnny cakes" of cornbread with molasses. For a quicker and less expensive snack, design your own sandwich at *Country Picnic* (☎802/824-6909), at the other end of Main Street.

US-7 scenic drive: Arlington and Historic 7A

US-7 and **Historic Route 7A** parallel each other as they run from Bennington north to Manchester, though the latter is the preferable path to take, not only a more scenic drive but with a few notable stop-offs along the way. The great spine of Green Mountains rises up to its east, with the Taconics somewhat more irregularly splayed out along the west, putting it smack in the so-called "Valley of Vermont."

About halfway up Rte-7A, the small town of **ARLINGTON** is the former home of illustrator Norman Rockwell, who created some of his most memorable *Saturday Evening Post* covers while living here between 1939 and 1954. Though there is an **exhibit** in his honor here (daily: May–Oct 9am–5pm; Nov–Apr 10am–4pm; ☎802/375-6423), it only contains models of what he painted rather than actual paintings, and is easily missed. Four miles north, the **Equinox Sky Line Drive** (May–Oct; $8 toll per car and driver, $2 per each additional passenger; ☎802/362-1114) branches off the highway, a six-mile stretch that winds and elbows its way around Mount Equinox, eventually reaching the 3816-foot summit, which offers views clear across to New Hampshire and Maine. Although the view is impressive, it's worth pointing out that in a region so rich in scenery, it arguably doesn't justify the cost.

Running alongside Rte-7A are the tracks of the old **Rutland Railway**, built in the 1850s and setting Vermont on its way toward prominence as a crossroads for north–south New York–Montréal and east–west Boston–Chicago rail traffic. "The Rutland" still traverses Bennington County, but its track bed is in need of such extensive repairs that a 10mph speed limit restricts the line to local freight use. Passenger traffic was mostly phased out by 1950.

Route 7: Manchester and north

With its abundance of designer-clothes outlets, fast-food chains, and gift shops, **MANCHESTER** comes dangerously close to Strip Mall, USA. Fortunately the mountain town does have a few saving graces. It has served as a summer resort hot spot for more than two hundred years, a spirit that lives on in the rambling, colonnaded **Equinox**, Rte-7A (☎802/362-4700; ⑦–⑨), full of restored Victorian-style rooms and luxurious amenities that should satisfy anyone looking for an all-inclusive getaway. Manchester is also well situated for other outdoor pursuits, especially skiing on nearby Stratton and Bromley mountains, and **fly-fishing** in its many trout streams, particularly the Batten Kill River. It's no small coincidence that **Charles Orvis**, founder of fly-rod manufacturer Orvis Company, is a Manchester native.

The Town and around

Route 7A heads right through the town center, known as **Manchester Village**; the first spot of interest here is **Historic Hildene** (mid-May–Oct daily 9.30am–5.30pm; $6; *www.hildene.org*), the 24-room Georgian Revival mansion belonging to longtime Manchester resident Robert Todd Lincoln, son of Abraham Lincoln, but a prominent diplomat and businessman in his own right. It's a magnificent estate, set on more than four hundred acres, and many of the Lincoln family's personal effects – hairbrushes, mirrors and such – are on display inside, along with an antique working pipe organ. More Vermont residents are celebrated at the **Gallery North Star**, Rte-7A (daily 10am–5pm; ☎802/362-4541), which shows paintings, sculptures, and limited-edition prints of local artists, as does the somewhat larger and less Vermont artist-centric **Southern Vermont Art Center**, Rte-7A (Mon–Sat 10am–5pm; ☎802/362-1405).

Further up Rte-7A, you'll arrive at **Manchester Center**, the shopping domain of the city, a fact that should be immediately noticeable. Aside from the main outlets found at the Manchester Commons and Manchester Square factory stores, you might try **Boxology!** at An American Craftsman on Rte-7A, where owner Richard Rothbard manufactures intriguing puzzle boxes, or the **Old Game Store**, on Rte-11/30, worth a look for its clutter of strange games from Penny Hockey to Skittles (not the candy) to Wadjet, a made-in-Vermont item.

On a less commercialized note, the **Vermont Institute of Natural Science**, 109 Union St (☎802/362-4374), offers natural history walks around the region. The **Bushee Battenkill Valley Farm**, 2545 Richville Rd (hours and days vary; ☎802/362-4088), is more entertaining, with its demonstrations of wool processing and milking, and its petting corrals. Throughout July and August, the **Vermont Symphony Orchestra** (☎800/VSO-9293) plays at the amphitheatre in Hunter Park. The tickets are reasonable, ranging from $9 on the lawn, to $29 seats.

Practicalities

You'll find plenty of information at **Manchester and the Mountains Chamber of Commerce**, 5046 Main St, Suite 1, Manchester Center, VT 05255-3451 (☎802/362-2100; *mmchambr@sover.net*). **Accommodation** in town can prove a bit pricey on account of Manchester's resort status; of the higher-priced options, consider the *Reluctant Panther Inn*, West Road (☎802/362-2568; ⑦), splendid rooms with deluxe modern furnishings and optional fireplaces and jacuzzis. Another luxury option is the *1811 House,* right across the street (☎802/362-1811 or 800/432-1811; ⑦–⑨), with fourteen immaculate rooms, each with private bath and shower, plus friendly owners and homebaked cookies. Of course, for the truly discriminating visitor, the only choice is the *Charles Orvis Inn*, next door to the *Equinox* (☎802/362-4700; ⑨). A measly $600+ a night gets you access to a billiards room, a self-serve honor bar (with cigars), free copies of *Millionaire* magazine in your room, and numerous other luxuries, all in the former home of Charles Orvis himself. More moderately priced lodgings can be found along Routes 7, 11 and 30, including the *Four Winds Motel*, Rte-7A (☎802/362-0905; ④), which boasts large rooms and better than expected service. The *Stamford Motel*, Rte-7A, Manchester Center (☎802/362-2342; ③–④), is a tastefully decorated budget motel with surprising amenities, including a heated pool, and great mountain views from most rooms. Another decent choice would be the *Toll Road Motor Inn*, Rte-11/30, Manchester Center (☎802/362-1711; ③–④), a quiet, smoke-free hotel with a huge fireplace in its lobby, which serves as a communal gathering spot.

For **food** and **drink**, the *Panther Bar*, in the *Reluctant Panther Inn*, serves good bar fare along the meat and potatoes line. The longstanding *Quality Restaurant*, 735 Main St (☎802/362-9839), also offers fine American food at fairly reasonable prices.

ROUTE 7: NORTH TO RUTLAND

Shortly after the end of Rte-7A, US-7 opens up into the "Valley of Vermont," between the Green Mountain and Taconic Mountain ranges, making for a lovely drive, though there are few convenient stopping places, and the presence of a four-lane highway doesn't encourage a leisurely pace.

If you're looking to stop longer, **camping** can be done at the **Emerald Lake State Park**, US-7 (late May to late Oct; ☎802/362-1655 summer, ☎802/483-2001 winter), which offers 105 campsites, 36 lean-tos, and easy access to the Long Trail, all on 430 acres that sit alongside Dorset Mountain. Unfortunately, the traffic noise from US-7 penetrates the tranquility. The 84-acre **Lake Shaftsbury State Park**, Rte-7A (☎802/375-9978 summer, ☎802/483-2001 winter), is a little less rough and farther from the highway, and has a developed beach, too.

Rutland

When Vermonters describe **RUTLAND**, halfway between Bennington and Burlington along US-7, as "a little bit of New Hampshire in Vermont," it is not meant as a compliment. Rather, the indictment is of a bland town dominated by a steady, though modest, industrial base and afflicted by a burgeoning strip mall aesthetic. It is, in fact, the state's second largest city after Burlington, with a population of about thirty thousand, most of whom are local laborers. Rutland's history as a marble-manufacturing center is still evident in its extensive use in the construction or embellishment of its downtown buildings. You may very well pass through, as Rutland is a key travel hub, but passing through is about all you'd need – or want – to do here.

Rutland's few attractions lie outside of town, most notably the **Norman Rockwell Museum**, east along US-4 (May–Oct daily 10am–5pm; Nov–April Mon–Fri 10am–4pm, Sat–Sun 10am–5pm; $3; ☎802/773-6095), which displays more than two thousand reproductions of Rockwell paintings, including early material and all of his *Saturday Evening Post* covers. It's a well-contextualized retrospective of his work, which is at times irritatingly wholesome but nevertheless an important contribution to American graphic art. The **Vermont Marble Exhibit**, 62 Main St (June–Oct daily 9am–5.30pm; rest of year Tues–Thurs 9.30am–4pm; $5; ☎802/459-2300), in the town of **PROCTOR**, northeast of Rutland, has two stories of displays on the state's favorite rock. The displays are a treasure trove of kitsch, particularly the "Hall of Presidents," featuring inexpertly carved marble busts of the 41 chief execs; a vast warehouse filled with marble kitchen and bathroom fixtures; and a hilariously self-serious 1950s-documentary-style film on the history of Vermont marble. A short drive southwest from Proctor, the **Wilson Castle** (May–Oct daily 9am–6pm; $7) is an intriguing relic of an aristocrat's past glory. The castle was built in 1867 by Dr. John Johnson, who had married into English nobility and decided to take advantage of his wife's fortune by constructing a castle in a "blend of European styles." He spared no expense, recruiting the best craftsmen and materials from across Europe. The Wilson family owns it today, having added to the already oversized manor complete with Italian woodwork and stained-glass ceilings. One of the strangest rooms that the Wilsons completed is the "art gallery", constructed before they realized that they had no *art*. Now it contains a small collection of works by local artists and designers. Upstairs in the bedrooms, the paint is peeling a bit, adding strangely to the air of faded grandeur.

Practicalities

Most of Rutland's **places to stay** are nondescript, independent motels, but they're generally cheap, clean and located close to major highways. Among the almost indistinguishable accommodation that lines US-7 are the *Cold River Motel* (☎802/ 747-6922; ②); the *Sun-Set Motel* (☎1-800/231-1709 or 802/773-2784; ③); and the *Green-Mont Motel* (☎802/775-2575; ③). *Iröquois Land* (May–mid-Oct; ☎802/ 773-2832), three miles south of Rutland in Clarendon, is an adequate **campground**, though it tends to be dominated by the RV crowd. The Rutland area **visitors center**, intersection of Routes 7 and 4B (☎802/775-0831), is only open from mid-May to mid-October, making the area's **Chamber of Commerce**, 256 N Main St (☎802/ 773-2747; *www.rutlandvermont.com*), open year-round, a better bet for information.

Should you be waiting for a bus or train, there are, surprisingly, a few quite good **places to eat** interspersed among the fast-food joints. *Sweet Tomatoes Trattoria*, 88 Merchant's Row (☎802/747-7747), has light modern Italian dishes in a sleek setting. The selection of vino at *Bistro Cafe's* wine bar, 103 Merchant's Row (☎802/747-7199), is excellent, as is its continental menu, though both are on the expensive side. The *Coffee Exchange*, at the corner of Merchant's Row and Center St (☎802/775-3337), is good for a light snack and a caffeinated beverage. *Pony's*, Center St (☎802/773-6171), is an occasionally raucous bar and dance venue, featuring **live music** for no cover.

Middlebury

In 1800, a small group of local citizens banded together to form a "town's college," primarily to train young men for the ministry. Two centuries later, Middlebury College, in the center of the town of **MIDDLEBURY**, is one of the most endowed (and expensive) colleges in the US, while the eponymous village numbers among the prettiest and most diverse in Vermont. Located at the intersection of Routes 125, 30 and 7, about equidistant from Rutland and Burlington, the town was actually named for its central location between Salisbury and New Haven, two Vermont towns whose prominence has receded substantially in the past two centuries. All roads converge at the **Middlebury Town Green**, an idyllic place with a pretty and ornate **Congregational Church** at its northern end. Middlebury's small downtown has a fairly hip collection of shops, with a few bookstores, a record shop, and the **Vermont Craft Center at Frog Hollow** at 1 Mill St (☎802/388-3177, *www.froghollow.com*), a bright space showcasing high-quality crafts from all over the state. The **Henry Sheldon Museum of Vermont History**, 1 Park St (Mon–Sat 10am–5pm; $3), is an endearingly quirky collection of tools, household objects and "one-of-a-kind oddities," such as the alleged remains of the "Petrified Indian Boy," actually a mid-nineteenth-century hoax bought into by, among others, the collector who established this museum.

Catch Rte-125 west to the **Middlebury College Museum of Art**, off Rte 30 (Tues–Fri 10am–5pm, Sat–Sun noon–5pm; free), for a look at the small permanent collection of nineteenth-century European and American sculpture and modern prints on display; the campus spreads out around it, with no other indivudual compelling sights, though it makes for a nice wander.

Further down Rte-125, turn north on Rte-23 for the **UVM Morgan Horse Farm** (May–Ocober daily 9am–4pm) where you can tour the stables and admire the beautiful world-famous descendants of Justin Morgan's stallion, the first native breed in North America.

Practicalities

There are a few **motels** on Rte-7 South of town; of these, the *Greystone Motel* (☎802/388-4935; [4]) and the *Blue Spruce Motel* (☎802/388-4091 or 1-800/640-7671; [3]–[5]) are recommended as clean and comfortable places to spend the night. The village green boasts two lovely **inns**, the aptly named *Inn on the Green* (☎802/388-7512 or 888/244-7512; [5]–[7]), eleven rooms in a graceful landmark building, with continental breakfast in bed included, and the *Middlebury Inn* (☎800/842-4666, *www.middleburyinn.com;* [7]), running as an inn since 1827, with 75 rooms and an attached restaurant. Television junkies will want to make sure to check out the *Waybury Inn* (☎802/388-4015 or 800/348-1810, *www.wayburyinn.com*; [5]–[7]), whose exterior was used on the TV show *Newhart.* The relationship with the show ends there, but it has fourteen comfortable, well-kept rooms inside.

The **restaurant** scene in Middlebury is pretty good for a town of this size. *Fire and Ice*, Seymour St (☎802/388-7166), is a cavernous steak-and-seafood place, with a massive salad bar. *Woody's Restaurant* (☎802/388-4182), 5 Bakery Lane, is more of a chic urban bistro, with sleek interior and views of Otter Creek. *The Dog Team Tavern*, Dog Team Road, off Rte-7, two miles north of Middlebury, in New Haven(☎802/388-7651), lets you have a proper Vermont feast, with local produce and specialties like maple oatmeal pie. Less expensive are *Rosie's*, Rte-7 South (☎802/388-7052), for hearty diner-style fare;. *Green Peppers* on the Grand Union Plaza (☎802/388-3164), for the best pizza in town; and *Baba's Market and Deli*, 6 College St (☎802/388-6408), with Middle Eastern specialties like felafel.

East on Hwy-125: Robert Frost country

Robert Frost spent 23 summers in Vermont on land that has been overrun by Hwy-125 (also called the Robert Frost Memorial Highway). The small cabin where he stayed, now a National Historic Landmark and owned by Middlebury College, still stands a few miles down a dirt road from the **Robert Frost Wayside**, a small, peaceful picnic area right by the highway (a quiet two lane road). Across the street from the Wayside is the **Robert Frost Interpretative Trail**, a mile-long loop trail punctuated by placards displaying poems and excerpts. Although it may not sound like much, it is actually quite evocative – an affecting environment in which to read his deceptively simple, old-fashioned works.

A few miles east of along 125 is the small campus of **Bread Loaf**, the highly-regarded summer writers' conference initiated at Frost's suggestion while a professor at Middlebury College. Though there's nothing much to see, just a few sturdily constructed beige wooden buildings, budding writers may want to stroll here and commune with the spirits of the notables, such as Frost, Willa Cather and John Gardner, who have taught or studied here.

Rochester

Smack on Rte-100, five miles south of Highway 125, lies pleasant **ROCHESTER**, a good base for exploring the Green Mountains, thanks to its absence of tourist traffice and a few nice places to stay. It's not much more than a town green and some pretty white houses, but it's as close as you get to a city in these parts. It also has three very different **B&Bs** to please any taste, the most central of which is the *Cooper-Webber House* (☎802/767-4742; [4]), right on the green, an eighteenth-century home decorated in high-Yankee style, with white walls, sturdy wooden furniture, and traditional open kitchen. South of town, the unpretentious *New Homestead*

(☎802/767-4751; ②) has a lived-in appearance rare in fancy guesthouses, five comfortable, simply decorated rooms, and good breakfasts. Finally, there's the *Apple Hill Farm* (☎802/767-6088; ④), the most secluded option, on Rte-73 just off Rte-100 about three miles out of town. It is an 1850s farmhouse, with wooded hiking paths, grazing sheep, and a three-story barn in the back.

Killington

The ski resort of **KILLINGTON**, twelve miles east of Rutland off US-4, has grown out of nothing since 1957 to become the most popular ski resort in the state. Its permanent population is still tiny (around fifty), but it's estimated that in season there are enough beds within twenty miles to accommodate some ten thousand people each night. Sometimes called the "Beast of the East," on account of its size – its 212 trails sprawl over seven mountains – and its notoriously rowdy nightlife, Killington sports a freewheeling and wild attitude that can be fun, if a bit dangerous in the early season (call ☎802/422-6200 or 1-800/621-6867 for ski information; lift tickets $49 per day, $349 per season). A less boisterous option is nearby **Pico Mountain**, along US-4 which is officially a part of Killington but in style and scale much tamer and smaller. Its 42 trails are best for skiers of mid-range ability, and there's not as much hotdogging as you'll find on the other peaks (call ☎1-800/621-6867 for ski information; lift tickets $39 per day, Killington lift tickets valid here). **Hiking** is one of the few things that goes on in the area during the summer. The Long and Appalachian trails meet here. Hikers can take the K-1 Gondola ($9 one-way, $13 dollars round-trip) to the summit of Killington and hike down. If you must, there is also an **Alpine slide** ($7) at the base of Pico.

Practicalities

You're spoiled for choice in terms of **accommodation** around these parts, though you may wind up paying a pretty penny, especially during prime skiing season. Wise Vacations (☎1-800/639-4680, *www.wisevacations.com*) rents private homes in and about Killington in every style (including the inevitable Vermont clapboard) and size to those who long for the comforts of someone else's home. Prices vary depending on the home you choose, but they are only a bit higher than the average inn or B&B. The *Cortina Inn*, US-4 (☎802/773-3333 or 1-800/451-6108; ⑤), is an excellent luxury inn, offering reduced summer rates. Closer to the ski areas, the *Inn of the Six Mountains*, on Killington Access Rd (☎802/422-4304 or 1-800/228-4676; ⑥), offers well-appointed quarters and proximity to skiing and Killington village. The popular *Mountain Meadows Lodge*, RR1, Box 4080 (☎802/775-1010, *www.mtmeadowslodge.com*; ⑥), to the side of Killington Rd off US-4, is about five minutes from Killington and offers a relatively unspoiled lakeside farm setting on the Appalachian Trail; it also sports an above-average restaurant. Cheaper options include the quiet *Val Roc Motel* (☎802/422-3881 or 1-800/238-8762; ②–③) and the *Cedarbrook Motor Inn* (☎802/422-9666 or 1-800/446-1088; ③), both of which are out on US-4 just after its junction with Hwy-100.

In winter, the Killington Access Road up from US-4 is jammed with **restaurants**. *Panache* at the *Woods Resort* (☎802/422-8622) does grill fare with a spicy modern twist. Bizarre offerings on the meaty menu include emu, wild boar and yak. *Mother*

VERMONT SKIING

Killington is probably the best known of all Vermont ski resorts, but in a mountainous state that gets plenty of snow, certainly not the only one. Consider other options, like Stowe (see p.365), Haystack Mountain (see p.343), Burke Mountain (see p.382) and Jay Peak (see p.383).

Shapiro's (☎802/422-9933) serves up American comfort food all day long, and is quite popular with locals. *Hemingway*'s, back on US-4 (☎802/422-3886), is one of Vermont's finest restaurants, with a formal waitstaff, impeccable surroundings and presentation, and excellent, vegetarian-friendly (though expensive) *nouvelle cuisine*. There are a ton of **bars** on Killington Road as well. *Moguls Saloon* has cheap draft specials during happy hour, and the *Pickle Barrel* (☎802/422-3035) has a rowdy bar and a dance scene that gets crazy on winter weekends.

Woodstock and around

Since its settlement in the 1760s, **WOODSTOCK**, a few miles west of the Connecticut River on US-4, has considered itself a bit more refined than its rural neighbors, making much, for instance, of its status as the home of a few minor artists, such as sculptor Hiram Powers and novelist Sinclair Lewis. The town has only submitted to the most cultured elements of the tourist industry, hence the distinguished houses that surround its oval green, most of which have been taken over by antiques stores and tearooms, and its tiny downtown area, which is populated by art galleries and upscale eateries. In any case, it should most certainly not be confused with the Woodstock, New York, of festival fame. This Woodstock draws well-heeled WASPs looking for a genteel getaway, and the closest it came to radical action during the Sixties was to build a new covered bridge.

Information and getting around

The **Woodstock Area Chamber of Commerce**, 18 Central St (☎802/457-3555 or 1-888/4WOODSTOCK, *www.woodstockvt.com*), has tons of visitors' information, and also operates an information booth on the oval town green (June–Oct 9am–5pm; ☎802/457-1042); from there you can take walking tours of the village (Mon, Wed & Sat 10.30am).

Accommodation

Places to stay in Woodstock's center are plentiful and luxurious but expensive. Sites farther from town get less expensive; there are relatively cheap motor cookie-cutter lodges along US-4 east of town.

3 Church Street, 3 Church St (☎802/457-1925, *www.scenesofvermont.com/3church*). Rates rise during fall foliage season. Impressive, pet friendly Georgian-mansion with eleven bedrooms, a music room, and a library. Its lawns and gardens adjoin the Ottauquechee river which runs through the heart of Woodstock. Breakfasts are herculean and made to order. There's a clay tennis court and a large swimming pool. ⑤.

1830 Shiretown Inn, 31 South St, Rte-106 (☎802/457-1830, *www.1830shiretowninn.com*). In downtown Woodstock, this tiny (three distinct rooms) restored 1830 farmhouse offers mammoth beds, clawfoot tubs, and good breakfasts, all across the street from Vail Field. [5].

Applebutter Inn, US-4 in Taftsville (☎802/457-4158, *www.bbonline.com/vt/applebutter*). Cozy B&B with comfortable beds, personable proprietors, and breakfasts featuring homemade granola. Four miles east out of town. [3]–[4].

Braeside Motel, US-4 (☎802/457-1366 or 1-800/303-1366 in-state only). Not quite a mile east of the village on US-4, you'll find clean and basic family-owned motel digs with very few extra amenities, save for a swimming pool. [3].

HI-Trojan Horse Hostel, 44 Andover St, Ludlow (☎802/228-5244 or 1-800/547-7475). Though it's some twenty miles south of town, this is prime budget accommodation, with dorm beds for $12 in summer, $17 winter.

Shire Motel, 46 Pleasant St (☎802/457-2211, *www.shiremotel.com*). A little better appointed than your average motel, but only a few steps away from being an overpriced hostel/dorm. [4]–[6].

Village Inn of Woodstock, 41 Pleasant St (☎802/457-1255 or 1-800/722-4571, *www.villageinnofwoodstock.com*). Quaint B&B with an inviting front porch. Dinner served as well, for which you don't have to be a guest. [6].

Woodstock Inn and Resort, 4 The Green (☎802/457-1100 or 1-800/448-7900, *woodstock.resort@connriver.net*). The fanciest – and best – accommodation around, with sumptuous rooms, beautiful grounds, and a gourmet restaurant. [6]–[8].

The Town

Woodstock's center is an oval green at the convergence of Elm, Central and Church streets, which are lined with architecturally diverse houses – New England clapboard is not nearly as prevalent here – that provide a genteel foreground to the landscape of rolling hills. The **Woodstock Historical Society**, 26 Elm St (May–Oct Mon–Sat 10am–4pm, Sun & holidays noon–4pm; $2; ☎802/457-1822), has well-organized multimedia displays include tape recordings of older residents' reminiscences and an admirably complete town archive. It's one of the best museums of its kind, an interesting exercise in social history. Next door to the multimedia center, and included in the admission, is a slightly musty old house with a varied collection of artifacts. Don't miss the assemblage of children's toys and dolls and the elegant drawing room with an antique harpsichord and gilt mirror from the 1790s. Also in this area are the town's many galleries, most notable of which are **Woodstock Folk Art Prints and Antiquities**, 6 Elm St (☎802/457-2012), which displays surprisingly bold, provocative local folk art prints, and **Steven Huneck Gallery**, 49 Central St (☎1-800/449-2580), full of idiosyncratic sculpture and furnishings employing animal forms.

Three of the town's attractions located further afield are devoted to the inimitable pleasure of seeing animals close up. The museum section of **Billings Farm and Museum**, off Rte-12 north of town (May–Oct daily 10am–5pm; Nov weekends 10am–4pm; $8; ☎802/457-2355), puts on not overly exciting demonstrations of antiquated skills, while the grounds are run as a modern dairy farm where you can pet cows and churn a bit of butter if you're so inclined. Across the street from the Billings Farm, the **Marsh-Billings-Rockefeller National Historic Park** (house tours: May–Oct daily 10am–4pm, $6; grounds open year-round 24 hours, free) was originally the home of George Perkins Marsh, whose 1864 book *Man and Nature*, inspired by his distress at the deforestation of his native Vermont, is a seminal work of ecological thought. The house was later purchased in 1869 by

Frederick Billings, who, greatly influenced by Marsh's image of responsible farming and sustainable forestry, decided to put those principles into action on the property. The 553 acres of forest, replanted by Billings in the late nineteenth century, contain a network of **hiking trails**, some leading to splendid vistas with Mount Tom in the distance. The **Vermont Raptor Center**, on Church Hill Road south of town (May–Oct daily 10am–5pm; Nov–April Mon–Sat 10am–4pm; $5; ☎802/457-2779), treats injured birds of prey and offers tours of their grounds, where you can see the process by which rescues are made and view a few recovering falcons in the flesh. Most popular is **Sugarbush Farm**, Hillside Road (Mon–Fri 7am–5pm, Sat–Sun 9am–5pm; ☎802/457-1757), which prides itself, however exaggerated a claim, on producing a more authentic cheddar and maple syrup than other Vermont farms.

Eating and drinking

Woodstock's **restaurants** cater to an upscale crowd, but while they're expensive, they're undeniably good; in any case, it's a good bet to make reservations ahead of time. Restaurants attached to inns and B&Bs tend to be just a bit cheaper.

Bentley's, 3 Elm St (☎802/457-3232). Upmarket versions of traditional bar food (buffalo wings, nachos, turkey burgers, and the like) and a good range of microbrews. Live jazz on weekends.

The Jackson House Inn and Restaurant, US-4, 1.5 miles west of the village green (☎802/457-2065). Very upscale New American cuisine and a good wine list. Try to get a table offering a view of the lovely four-acre garden. Extensive wine list and knowledgeable sommelier on staff.

Lincoln Inn, US-4, three miles west of town (☎802/457-3312). Riverside inn with a very reasonable dining room which serves meat-and-potatoes fare.

Mountain Creamery, 33 Central St (☎802/457-1715). Filling country breakfasts and lunch fare served daily, as well as some fine ice cream.

Pane Salute, 61 Central St (☎802/457-4882). The fresh pastries don't quite match the quality of their cappuccino, Woodstock's best.

The Prince and the Pauper, 24 Elm St (☎802/457-1818). Expensive continental cuisine – braised veal, filet mignon, and the like – in an incongruously casual dining room.

Wild Grass, US-4, a mile east of the village green (☎802/457-1917). *Nouvelle cuisine*, American style, with organic game meats featured regularly, though still fairly vegetarian-friendly. More expensive but worth it.

East of Woodstock: Quechee

Six miles east of Woodstock, **QUECHEE** is a peculiar mixed bag: the **town** proper is a combination of quaint Vermont village and expensive tract housing development, where you'll find several upmarket restaurants and B&Bs; just down US-4 is **Quechee Gorge**, Vermont's greatest natural wonder, and a great place to camp; and adjacent **Quechee Village** is a mire of cheap tourist kitsch, hard not to notice but very easy to skip.

Even if you're just passing through the area, be sure to stop and ogle Quechee Gorge, so-called "Grand Canyon" of Vermont. A delicate bridge spans the 165ft chasm of the Ottauquechee River, and hiking trails lead down through forests to the base of the gorge, where its scale seems even more impressive. If you have more time, hit the town of Quechee, where a waterfall on the river turns the turbines of

Simon Pearce Glass on Main Street (daily 9am–5pm; ☎802/295-2711). Housed in a former wool mill, this is an unusual combination of glass-blowing center and restaurant, where you can watch bowls and pots being made and then eat off them. The hills behind Quechee Town have challenging trails for hiking and cross-country skiing in season. Wilderness Trails, on Dewey's Mills Road (☎802/295-7620), have information about trailheads, and they organize tours and rent equipment.

Practicalities

Most **restaurants** in the area are either painfully chichi affairs or dreary "family" establishments. The most notable exceptions are *Firestone's*, at Waterman Place along US-4 (☎802/295-1600), serving creative pasta dishes and traditional Vermont fare like game and fish and chips that you can enjoy on their pleasant rooftop patio, and *Grondin's on the Green* (☎802/295-2786), which has basic but tasty soups and sandwiches. Also, the restaurant at *Simon Pearce Glass* (☎802/295-1470; see above for more details) serves inventive New American-type entrees starting at around $15.

If you're equipped to **camp**, the best place to stay is in the **Quechee State Park** off US-4 (summer ☎802/295-2990, winter ☎802/886-2434), which has 47 well-maintained sites (no hookups) ensconced in a forest of fir trees, and offers foot trail access to the Gorge. The *Quality Inn*, between the Gorge and the Village (☎802/295-7600 or 1-800/732-4376; ④), offers the least expensive accommodation in the area. But if you're willing to shell out more, the town of Quechee has a few sumptuous B&Bs, including the *Parker House Inn*, located in a beautiful red-brick Victorian building at 16 Main St (☎802/295-6077; ⑤), and the *Quechee Bed & Breakfast* (☎802/295-1776; ④), an eighteenth-century colonial estate at the intersection of US-4 and Waterman Hill Road. The gracious *Quechee Inn at Marshland Farm* is located just outside the village of Quechee, on Quechee Main Street (☎802/295-3133; ⑤–⑥). In addition to its comfy 24 rooms with period furnishings that overlook Dewey's Mills Pond, visitors can take advantage of its association with Wilderness Trails and the Vermont Fly-fishing School (☎802/295-7620). Information is available from the **Quechee Chamber of Commerce**, at 15 Main St in Quechee Town (☎802/295-7900), or the summer-only **information booth** on US-4 across from Quechee Village.

White River Junction and around

Perhaps the most exciting thing ever to happen in **WHITE RIVER JUNCTION** was the first use of nitrous oxide (laughing gas) as an anesthetic, in 1844. Still, it's an important travel hub – as far back as the mid-1860s five different railroads had terminal points in White River, and the community grew steadily until the rail transport industry went bust in the early part of last century. The town hosts an annual downtown street party celebrating its railroading history each September. Weary Amtrak Vermonter trains stop right by North Main Street, and buses come and go from the station right off I-91 exit 11, running east into New Hampshire – **Hanover** (see p.418) is just across the river – and throughout Vermont.

The pride of White River Junction these days is the **Northern Stage,** at Briggs Opera House across from the train station (☎802/296-7000), an ambitious year-round stage company who perform, with the help of some topnotch local and imported talent, a varied program of contemporary and classic pieces, musicals and straight drama. In the past three years, they've even scooped Boston to present the New England premieres of such world-class plays as Martin McDonagh's hit *The Beauty Queen of Lehane* and Margaret Edson's Pulitzer Prize-winning *Wit*.

If you're going to be here **overnight**, the best place to stay is the *Hotel Coolidge*, 17 Main St (☎802/295-3118; ③–④), right in the town center, an old-fashioned railroad hotel with good old-fashioned prices. The HI-affiliated hostel wing has clean dorm beds and kitchen access for $15 per night. The *Super 8 Motel* on the outskirts of town, at I-91 exit 11 (☎802/295-7577 or 1-800/800-8000; ④), has more spacious rooms with far less character, and the most convenient camping option is the Maple Leaf Campground, 406 N Hartland Rd (☎802/295-2817), with twenty sites including plumbing and hookups. In the same building as the *Coolidge*, the *River City Café*, serves light **lunch** fare – mostly cheap soups and sandwiches – with nostalgic Americana on the walls and books to peruse. The *Polka Dot Restaurant*, 1 N Main St (☎802/295-9722), is a shrine to camp, looking as if it were decorated largely by kids, but fixing up good milkshakes and patty melts. Far and away the most interesting culinary option in town is *Karibu Tuk*, Main St (☎802/296-3756), serving African cuisine such as curries and stews.

Fifteen miles north of White River Junction along I-91, in the town of **NOR-WICH**, is the **Montshire Museum of Science**, One Montshire Rd, exit 13 off I-91 (daily 10am–5pm; $5.50, children $3; ☎802/649-2200), intended for kids but well worth the detour even for adults. You'll see several aquaria with peculiar species of fish as well as machines illustrating the weirder side of physics, but most engaging displays are the interactive brain teasing puzzles. Admission includes access to its several easy hiking trails and picnic areas as well.

Windsor

WINDSOR, tucked into a bend in the Connecticut River just this side of the New Hampshire border, about fifteen miles south of White River Junction, is where the original constitution of the Republic of Vermont was drawn up in 1777, an event which led it to be termed the "birthplace of Vermont." Today, the distinction is preserved in one of its two excellent museums, the **Old Constitution House**, Main Street (late May to mid–Oct Wed–Sun 11am–5pm; $2). Housed in the original tavern where the delegates met and constitutional debates took place, it contains a well-preserved re-creation of the tavern's interior plus a fascinating series of history-related displays, featuring rare artifacts like coins and, more interestingly, newspapers from the brief republican period. Further south on Main Street along the banks of a Connecticut River tributary, the **American Precision Museum** (May–Nov Mon–Fri 9am–5pm, Sat–Sun 10am–4pm; $4) is oriented around the idea of mechanization – the construction, function, and historical significance of machinery, with a particular focus on the Industrial Revolution. The small but impressive displays of items (many still in working condition) such as "Mississippi" rifles and sewing machines incorporate original antique machine tools and creative interactivity to illustrate not only the importance of technology, but the peculiar beauty of its precision. Halfway between the two museums, Bridge Street branches off to the east from Main Street; at its terminus, you'll find the **Cornish/Windsor covered bridge**, the longest such bridge in the US, which is open to traffic crossing over to New Hampshire.

For affordable **accommodation**, it's best to backtrack to White River Junction, or farther afield in Woodstock or Quechee (see pp.355 & 357). However, the *Juniper Hill Inn*, off US-5 on Juniper Hill Rd (☎802/674-5273 or 1-800/359-2541; ⑤), has thirty fastidiously kept rooms in a mansion overlooking the town. They also serve excellent, if rather formally presented, continental-style food which is not restricted to inn guests. Up US-5 a few miles in **HARTLAND**, the *Skunk Hollow Tavern*, Hartland Four Corner (☎802/436-2139), has a cozy, convincingly authentic country English atmosphere, with friendly games of darts and hearty pub grub to boot. **Mount Ascutney State Park**, off Rte-44A, nine miles west of Windsor (May–Oct; ☎802/674-2060), maintains several campsites in a secluded setting along with hiking trails and excellent views of the Green Mountains.

Montpelier

With fewer than ten thousand residents, **MONTPELIER** (mont-PEEL-er), situated in a beautiful valley on the Winooski and North Branch rivers, is the smallest state capital in the country. Its residents have cultivated a vital downtown area around the **capitol** building, urban in style but not in scale, lined exclusively with nineteenth-century buildings – some with a slightly Southern antebellum flavor – and boasting a number of fine restaurants, museums, and theaters. Despite its considerable charms, the city still bears a low tourist profile, and it is this lack of commercialism that makes Montpelier a refreshing counterpoint to the cultivated rural quaintness that pervades the rest of the state.

Arrival, information and getting around

Knapp Airport, a postage stamp-sized airport about four miles from I-89 exit 7 serves Montpelier and surrounding communities. Montpelier shares a stop on Amtrak's Vermonter line with its neighbor Barre.

In town, the **Vermont Division of Travel and Tourism**, 134 State St (daily 8am–8pm; ☎802/828-0587), offers plenty of info on local and statewide attractions. The nearby **kiosk**, just down State Street across from the capitol, crams a large assortment of brochures and guides to area attractions into a small but well-kept space. Check out the daily *Times-Argus* for arts and entertainment schedules and listings. Students and locals take advantage of the town's free **shuttle bus**, hopping on at any downtown Montpelier stop.

Accommodation

There's a decent range of **places to stay** in Montpelier, with some of the better options being, unsurprisingly, bed-and-breakfasts. The riverside *Green Valley Campground*, northeast of town at the intersection of Rte-2 and Rte-302, four miles from exit 7 or 8 off I-89 (☎802/223-6217, open May–Oct), offers 35 campsites, swimming, showers, convenience store, and a laundry room.

Betsy's Bed & Breakfast, 74 E State St (☎802/229-0466, *www.central-vt.com/web /betsybb*). Affordable Victorian mansion with enormous and comfy beds, cable TV, and telephone; hearty breakfasts are included in the price. ③–④.

Capitol Plaza Hotel and Conference Center, 100 State St (☎802/274-5252, *www.capitolplaza .com*). Luxurious digs adjacent to the State House and across from the gorgeous Art Deco Capitol Theater. Friendly, exceptionally helpful staff. ⑤–⑦.

Gamble's Bed and Breakfast, 16 Vine St (☎802/229-4810). Three large and colorful rooms with shared baths show a little wear and tear, but you can't beat the price. No in-room phones or TV. ③.

Inn at Montpelier, 147 Main St (☎802/223-2727, *members.aol.com/innvt*). Spacious, well-appointed rooms in a pair of Federal-style buildings. The continental breakfast is a bit skimpy but access to common areas and a pleasant wraparound porch are both welcome. ⑤–⑦.

Montpelier Guest Home, 22 North St (☎802/229-0878, *www.guesthome.com*). Three comfortable rooms with handmade quilts, hand-stenciled walls and shared bath. Pleasant deck and gardens, central location. No smoking, no pets. ②–③.

Vermonter Motel, 509 Barre-Montpelier Rd, on US-302 just off I-89 exit 7 (☎802/476-8541). Generic, very affordable rooms located several miles southeast of town on the Barre-Montpelier Road. ③.

The Town

Diminutive **downtown Montpelier** is home to four college campuses – New England Culinary Institute, Woodbury College, Vermont College of Norwich University, and Community College of Vermont – though it feels nothing like a college town. Its most visible landmark, the gilt-domed **State Capitol** (Mon–Fri 8am–4pm; July–Oct also Sat 11am–3pm; ☎802/828-2228), rises high above the town center on State Street. While most visitors just stroll around the impeccably kept exterior gardens (particularly brilliant during fall) and photograph the statue of **Ethan Allen** guarding the front doors, you should feel free to take a pass through the capitol's recently refurbished vaulted marble hallways to see the vast mural representing the Battle of Cedar Creek, a Civil War skirmish in which Vermonters played a pivotal role, and the permanent exhibit of Vermont artists.

Next door, the **Vermont Historical Society Museum**, 109 State St, first floor of the Pavillion Building (Tues–Fri 9am–4.30pm, Sat 9am–4pm, Sun noon–4pm; $3; ☎802/828-2291, *www.state.vt.us/vhs*), provides an engaging view into the state's past. You'll see some real gems among the usual complement of dusty muskets and period clothes, most notably the Clement Clock, a monolithic 12.5-foot tall oak timepiece bearing elaborately wrought Rococo artwork. There's also one of a very few remaining pieces by nineteenth-century narrative sculptor and Vermonter John Rogers, as well as one of John Adams' early diaries from his time at college and an elegant Persian sword that belonged to Lord Byron.

East of the Capitol district, in College Hall on the campus of Norwich, lies the small but distinguished **T.W. Wood Gallery**, College Street (Tues–Sun noon–4pm; $2; ☎802/828-8743), highlighted by a fascinating array of Vermont painter T.W. Wood's oil paintings of Civil War residents and experimental WPA American folk art and photos.

Montpelier's best spot for outdoor recreation is **Hubbard Park**, north of town on Hubbard Park Drive, 180 acres of grassy space, picnic areas, ponds, and trails. Ascend the fifty-foot stone **observation tower** in the park's center for spectacular views of the Montpelier area. Several hiking and mountain biking trails wind through the hills, and in winter the trails are used for cross-country skiing and the ponds freeze over for ice skating. Onion River Sports, 20 Langdon St (☎802/229-9409), rents athletic equipment, including bikes, hiking gear, and cross-country skis.

Eating, drinking and entertainment

Students from the New England Culinary Institute (NECI) have lent their influence to Montpelier's cuisine, resulting in a number of less expensive, experimental **restaurants**. The area is blissfully resistant to fast-food and chain joints – it's the only US state capital without a *McDonald's*, though a *Dunkin' Donuts* reared its sugared head a few years back. Montpelier's **Farmers Market** (May–Oct Sat 9am–2pm) sells the produce, herbs, flowers, and baked goods of numerous organic gardeners and farmers.

The main drama venue is the **Capital City Theater**, in the City Hall Arts Center on Main Street, where the local Lost Nation Theater Company performs everything from Shakespeare epics to experimental contemporary plays (✆802/229-0492 for current production). Across the street, the **Savoy Theater** (✆802/229-0598) shows first-rate foreign and classic films. During the summer the city band holds well-attended evening concerts on the State House lawn and the Vermont Philharmonic stops by in July.

Coffee Corner, cnr of State and Main sts (✆802/229-9060). A Montpelier standard for over sixty years. Scarf cheap diner food at formica tables or rub elbows with Vermont's political potentates at the lunch counter. Serves breakfast all day.

Fiddleheads, 54 State St (✆802/229-2244). Excellent, inventive American cuisine like marinated salmon patties and pine nut risotto in a spacious restaurant and bar that's casual but classy – despite the faux-wood curtains and Christmas lights.

Horn of the Moon Cafe, 8 Langdon St (✆802/223-2895). Wholesome vegetarian food served by happy hippies whose menu generated a nationally renowned cookbook of the same name. Closed Mondays.

Julio's, 44 Main St (✆802/229-9348). Pretty good Tex-Mex for this area of New England. Cheap, filling taco plates (just upwards of $4) and zippy margaritas. Don't blink or you'll miss the unobtrusive green door entrance.

La Brioche Bakery & Cafe, 89 Main St (✆802/229-0443). Cheerful, pottery-filled, well-designed bakery run by NECI. Good bread, espresso drinks, and the smell of the on-site bakery (but only so-so pastries) lure townies of all stripes.

Main Street Grill and Bar, 118 Main St (✆802/223-3188). Delectable, inventive specialties from NECI alums, sort of pricey but worth it. American grill fare and shellfish are standouts. Also serves breakfast. The next-door *Chef's Table* (✆802/229-9202), run by the same folks, doesn't serve breakfast and is a bit pricier, but also very good.

McGillicuddy's Irish Pub, 14 Langdon St (✆802/223-2721). Standard bar fare, most notable for its really hot hotwings. Wide selection of microbrews, and a ripping Long Island Iced Tea. Draws a lively, younger crowd and gets loud and busy on weekends.

Wayside Restaurant and Bakery, 1873 Barre–Montpelier Rd/Rte-302 (✆802/223-6611). Classic Yankee cooking, with New England standards such as baked haddock and pot roast at moderate prices.

SOUTH OF MONTPELIER: ROUTE 12

If you're in no hurry on your way from Montpelier to points south, a worthwhile alternative to Interstate 89 is little-travelled **Rte-12**, which passes through the towns of Riverton, Northfield, Randolph and Bethel. You won't find a single B&B or country store along this road, just thirty miles of rolling hills, farmland and lakes. This is the real Vermont, and its lush beauty and traditional charm are utterly unposed. Be advised, though, that this is also a road with a fairly high concentration of "Take back Vermont" signs (see p.336).

Barre

BARRE (pronounced "berry") is Vermont's immigrant center, having attracted Scots, Italians, and other ethnic groups almost a hundred years ago to work for the city's booming granite industry. Even today, a visitor to Barre may hear several languages spoken freely on the streets and in the stores – not that people come here to note its diversity. Indeed, the main draw these days is the same thing that lured immigrants a century ago: granite, the rock on which this city was literally built.

Barre's main sight, the **Rock of Ages Quarry**, I-89 exit 6, Graniteville (May–Oct Mon–Sat 8.30am–5pm, Sun noon–5pm; tours Mon–Fri 9.30am–3pm; $4; ☎802/476-3119, *www.rockofages.com*), is actually southeast of town, in the municipality of **Graniteville** on Hwy-63. This is the world's biggest granite quarry, as you'll almost certainly be told by the fleet of helpful guides who will rush to greet you as soon as you enter the visitors center. You can check out one of the smaller but still connected quarries, grab a piece of granite, and watch a campy ("You'll dig the Rock of Ages!") informational film all for free – ask for the map of the self-guided tour. If you've come all this way, though, it's just as well to shell out a few bucks for the narrated shuttlebus tour that takes you to the far more impressive fifty-acre working quarries and through the manufacturing centers where artisans busy themselves making fleets of tombstones.

In Barre proper, the city's turbulent early history – its laborers have long been famed for their militancy – is outlined in the **Barre Museum and Archives**, on the second floor of the Aldrich Public Library, near the intersection of Main and River streets. Newspaper articles, photos, and transcribed oral histories detail various immigrant fracases; even the naming of the town in 1793 spurred a fist-fight (won by Jonathan Sherman of Barre, Massachusetts). This free collection also contains cultural paraphernalia and radical socialist political tracts from the early twentieth century.

Barre's cultural heritage is also painfully evident in a pair of ostentatious granite monuments downtown. The 23-foot-tall **Italian-American Stonecutters' Monument**, at the intersection of North Main and Maple streets, captures a stoneworker in action and pays homage to the town's immigrant past. Similarly, the **Robert Burns Monument**, at Academy and Washington streets, celebrates the great Scottish poet. More interesting than either are the elaborate gravestones of **Hope Cemetery**, just north of town on Hwy-14. While the city's stonecutters lived modestly, they knew how to die in grand style, commemorating themselves and their families with massive, elaborately wrought granite tombstones ranging to ten feet in height, and bearing impressively detailed artwork.

On a more contemporary cultural note, dance and musical performances take place at Main Street's **Barre City Hall and Opera House** (☎802/476-8188), a fanciful building that has seen the likes of John Philip Sousa and Helen Keller on its stage.

Practicalities

Low demand makes for cheap **accommodation** in Barre. The *Hollow Inn and Motel*, 278 Main St (☎802/479-9313 or 1-800/998-9444, *www.central-vt.co/web/hollow*; ④), is on the fancy side, with a fitness center and complimentary continental breakfast. *Reynold's House B&B*, 102 S Main St (☎802/479-9960; ④), offers three well-lit, spacious guest rooms with detailed wood molding, birds-eye maple, and well-chosen antiques. The *Days Inn*, 173–175 S Main St (☎802/476-6678 or 1-800/325-2525; ③), has clean and reasonably priced rooms, along with an indoor pool.

Barre's Italian-American population may be deeply entrenched in the granite industry but it hasn't created the profusion of authentic ethnic **restaurants** you might expect. The exception is *Del's*, 248 N Main St (☎802/476-6685), which serves up cheap, tasty pasta dinners and pizza on classic red-and-white checked tablecloths. For a quick, light lunch, *Simply Delicious*, 160 N Main St (☎802/479-1498), vends a complement of homey soups and sandwiches, which you can enjoy while reading volumes donated by its next-door neighbor, Barre Books, a cozy independent bookstore.

For additional **visitor information**, stop in at the kiosk in the Price Chopper parking lot along Main Street at the intersection with Hwy-14, or contact the Chamber of Commerce, 2 Granger Rd, Berlin (☎802/223-3433); there's also the Central Vermont Chamber of Commerce, PO Box 336, Barre, VT 05641 (☎802/229-4619).

Waterbury

Few people gave much notice to **WATERBURY** before 1978; even then, no one could have expected the opening of a homemade ice-cream stand on the forecourt of a Burlington gas station to excite any interest. But since ageing hippies Ben Cohen and Jerry Greenfield started their mini-empire (and chose Waterbury as its headquarters), **Ben and Jerry's Ice Cream Factory**, one mile north of I-89 in Waterbury Center, on the way up to Stowe, has grown so huge, so fast, that it is now the number-one tourist destination in Vermont. Half-hour tours run by friendly, almost evangelical youths (daily: July–Aug 9am–8pm; Sept–Oct 9am–6pm; Nov–June 10am–5pm; $2; ☎802/224-TOUR; *www.benjerry.com*), feature a short film on the boys' early days, then head into the production factory where machines

---

ICE-CREAM SWIRL

Ben and Jerry's 1960s roots have made for an uneasy combination of hippie culture and multinational corporate conglomerate. Their homespun image and eco-friendly policies won them years of generally congratulatory press, and helped grow the little local company into a household name. Ben and Jerry's later began to come under fire for things like squeezing out the (minimal) competition in their home state (after having won their own battle against Pillsbury-owned Haagen Daz in the distribution wars), and for more complex issues like disagreements with the Food and Water Department over dairy farm water run-off. Still, the company maintained a good PR profile, donating one percent of its profits to peace-related causes, setting limits to its CEO's salary (at one time the company had a highly progressive policy that no one would earn more than ten times as much as the lowest-paid employee), and opposing RBgH, the controversial bovine growth hormone. Then, in April of 2000, shortly after going public, the big blow came: Ben and Jerry's had been bought out for a reputed $326m by the European chemical conglomerate Unilever. Although the conditions of the takeover stipulated maintaining many of the company's progressive stands, Ben Cohen himself summed up the deal bitterly as "Ben and Jerry's sold out."

turn cream, sugar and other natural ingredients into over fifty flavors. Afterwards, you get a free mini-scoop of the stuff that made it all possible – you can buy more at the top-price gift shop and ice-cream stall outside.

There's not really much else to see in Waterbury; even the **culinary outlet shops** clustered together along Hwy-100, each of which offer free samples of their wares in an attempt to seduce travelers into purchasing them, fail to raise much excitement. However, if you're really looking for something to do, stop by the Waterbury Public Library at 28 North Main St and ask the librarians to let you into the **Waterbury Historical Society and Museum** (Mon, Wed 1–8pm, Tues 10am–8pm, Fri 10am–5pm, Sat 9am–2pm; ☎802/244-7036) upstairs, where they'll have to turn on the lights to let you into the small collection of musty Civil War and medical memorabilia. There are plenty of **craft** outlets too on the road, if you're so inclined. Otherwise, you might opt for the surprisingly thrilling goings-on at **Thunder Road**, Thunder Road International Speedway ($6; ☎802/244-6963), which offers weekly stock car racing on a short-track, high-banked, motor speedway. It's loud, cheap, pulsating entertainment.

Practicalities

There are several top-notch **accommodation** options in and around town. The Cape Cod-clapboard *Inn at Blush Hill*, just off Rte-100 (☎1-800/736-7522 or 802/244-7529; [5]), sits atop a hill with fantastic views, and has colonial antiques and canopy beds in each room. The Teutonic-themed *Grunberg Haus* (☎1-800/800-7760 or 802/244-7726; [4]), on Rte-100, is a woodsy A-frame with great breakfasts and reasonable rates. Other quality establishments along Rte-100 near Waterbury Center include the *Black Locust Inn* (☎802/244-7490 or 1-800/366-5592; [4]) and the *Old Stagecoach Inn* (☎1-800/262-2206 or 244-5056; [5]). One of the better **restaurants** around is *Arvad's*, 3 S Main St (☎802/244-8973), which serves up fresh grill fare with tasty pints of ale. For a light lunch, the deli sandwiches and soups at *Park Row Cafe*, Park Row (☎802/244-5111), are cheap and satisfying. *K.C.'s Bagel Cafe*, Stowe St (☎802/244-1740), has fresh bagels and other light breakfast foods baked daily. For more information on accommodation, contact the **Waterbury Tourism Council** (☎802/244-1209) on Rte-100 near its intersection with Stowe Street.

Stowe

Unlike most of Vermont's other ski towns, there is still a beautiful nineteenth-century village at the heart of **STOWE**, with a white-spired meetinghouse and a green to stroll around. Though Stowe was actually a popular summer destination even before the Civil War, what really put the town on the map as a ski resort was the arrival of the **Von Trapp family**, of *The Sound of Music* fame. After fleeing Austria during World War II, they settled here and established a lodge – since burned down – where Maria Von Trapp held her singing camps. A complex composed of a newly rebuilt lodge, restaurant and mini-theme park devoted to the celebration of Alpine culture has taken its place. Interfamily squabbling over the direction the lodge and its offshoots will take in the future doesn't seem to have interfered with its popularity. Regardless, a century's worth of experience catering to increasingly large crowds of skiers has rather swamped the approach road to the main ski area with malls, equipment stores, and sprawling condominium complexes – extremely at odds with the village below. Nonetheless, the setting remains spectacular, at the foot of Vermont's highest mountain, the 4393 foot **Mount Mansfield**.

Arrival and information

Mountain Road (Rte-108) is Stowe's primary thoroughfare, stretching from the main village up through the mountain gap known as "Smugglers' Notch," so named because forbidden trade with Canada passed through here during the War of 1812 at the time of Jefferson's Embargo Act. It has also lived up to its nickname via its popularity with fugitive slaves on their way to Canada and, in the early part of this century, Prohibition-era bootleggers. It's generally closed during winter. The staff at the **visitors' center**, at Main Street and Mountain Road (Mon–Fri 9am–5pm, Sat–Sun 10am–5pm; ☎802/253-7321 or 1-800/24-STOWE, *www.stoweinfo.com*), are very helpful. The closest Amtrak **train** station is over in Waterbury, ten miles to the south.

Accommodation

Multiple **accommodation** options line Mountain Road, and range from luxury resorts to modest B&Bs to hostels. During winter, reserve as far ahead as possible; otherwise, you'll probably be shut out. In summertime, many places close, but those that stay open can usually find a room for you and you might even be able to wrangle a discount if you're bold enough to ask the innkeeper. The closest **campground** is *Gold Brook Campground* (☎802/253-7683), two miles south on Rte-100.

Alpenrose Hotel, 2619 Mountain Rd (☎1-800-962-7002 or 802/253-7277). Affordable, small hotel located halfway between the ski slopes and Stowe Village, just off the Recreation Path. Rooms and efficiencies with private baths, cable TV, and refrigerators. German spoken. ③–④.

Green Mountain Inn, 1 Main St (☎1-800/253-7302 or 802/253-7301, *www.greenmountaininn .com*). Stately hotel built in 1833, centrally located (at a busy intersection) and amply accoutered. Offers not one but two good restaurants, complimentary health club and afternoon tea and cookies. ⑤–⑦.

Inn at Turner Mill, 56 Turner Mill Lane (☎802/253-2062). Quaint streamside quarters in log-cabin buildings. Swimming pool and excellent homemade breakfasts. ④–⑥.

Notch Brook Resort, 1229 Notch Brook Rd (☎1-800/253-4882). A secluded complex of fully equipped studio apartments with fireplaces and patios, good for large groups. Well-behaved pets welcome. ⑤–⑦.

The Pines Motel, 1203 Waterbury Rd (☎802/253-4828) Cheap, fairly clean, basic motel rooms, one step above your average hostel. ②.

Riverside Inn, 1965 Mountain Rd (☎802/253-4217 or 1-800/966-4217). Modest, basic hostelry with all the essentials including bed, bath, and phones, though not much more. ③–⑤.

Stoweflake Inn and Resort, 1746 Mountain Rd (☎1-800/253-7355 or 253-2232, *www .stoweflake.com*). Sumptuous rooms filled with tasteful antiques and homemade quilts, coffee and snacks throughout the day, well-informed and courteous staff, all set on sweeping grounds with pool, sauna, weight room. Definitely the best place to stay if you can afford it. ⑦–⑨.

Trapp Family Lodge, 42 Trapp Hill Rd (☎1-800/826-7000 or 802/253-8511, *info@trappfamily .com*). On the site of the original Trapp family house, also the first cross-country ski center in America. Now a Teutonically themed ski resort with nightly entertainment, as fancy as it is expensive, occasionally graced by some of the original Trapp kids, who are now in their eighties. Concerts in the Trapp Meadow. ⑦–⑨.

Skiing and other outdoor recreation

Alpine experts hotly debate whether Stowe is still the "ski capital of the east," a distinction it clearly held until Killington and other eastern ski centers began to challenge its supremacy a decade or so ago. Regardless, it's an excellent mountain, refurbished to the tune of $20 million a few years back, and its popularity remains intact, as traffic through Stowe Village on winter weekends makes all too painfully clear. There are 46 well-kept trails in all, with excellent options for skiers of every level (lift ticket $56 per day). A less crowded option is **Smugglers' Notch** (☎802/664-8851 or 1-800/451-8752), on the other side of the mountain, a dramatic narrow pass with high cliffs on either side that actually has more trails than Stowe (60), and is cheaper ($48 per day).

Stowe offers almost as much to do in the summer, when the crowds thin out considerably. Ascending to the peak of **Mount Mansfield** is a challenge no matter how you do it, and rewards with spectacular views all the way to Canada and the shores of Lake Champlain. Weather permitting, the easiest approach is the **Toll Road**, a winding ascent that starts seven miles up (late May to mid-Oct daily 10am–5pm; $12 per car), or by **gondola** (mid-June to mid-Oct daily 10am–5pm; $10; ☎802/253-7311), which affords great views and drops off at Cliff House, a brief hike from the summit. If you've got the stamina, the most rewarding approach is to **hike** the full way to the Mansfield summit, a steep, steady, 4.7-mile climb up a section of the Long Trail with a trailhead on Rte-108 halfway through Smugglers' Notch. The notch is laced with miles of **hiking trails**; some of the best start out from Smugglers' Notch State Park, 7248 Mountain Rd (mid-May–Oct; ☎802/253-4014).

Stowe's cross-country ski trails double as **mountain bike routes** during summer. AJ's Mountain Bikes, Mountain Road (☎1-800/226-6257 or 802/253-4593, *ajssports@pwshift.com*), offers rentals and organized tours for which advance reservations are highly recommended (mid-May–Oct; rentals $30–36 per day, tours $25–30). Nearby streams and small rivers offer ample opportunity for **canoeing** and **kayaking**: Umiak Outdoor Outfitters, 849 S Main St (☎802/253-2317), rents full sets of equipment, including watercraft, paddles, and life jackets, for $25–35 per day. There's also an in-line skate park ($10 a day) that offers lessons and rentals, plus an Alpine slide ($7.50 a ride).

People who would rather keep to lower elevations would do well to use the **Stowe Recreation Path**, a 5.5-mile paved trail for bikers, runners, walkers, and in-line skaters that starts in the village behind the Community Church. Despite its heavy usage, it never feels too crowded; better still, it offers scenic views of the West Branch River and Mt Mansfield along the way. Be warned, though – the path does not make a full circuit, so plan ahead if you're going the entire length.

Eating and drinking

There is a big choice of places to **eat** in and around Stowe, ranging from low-budget delis, bakeries and pizza joints to rather pricey restaurants, frequently run by a nearby inn or resort. Its **drinking** and **entertainment** scene draws together lounging apres-skiers, hard-boiled locals, and well-heeled yuppies in its various watering holes.

Asagio Wood Grill & Noodle Bar, 294 Mountain Rd (☎802/253-2125). Wood-fired cuisine featuring handcut pastas, flatbreads, smoky entrees, and vegetarian dishes that draw on Asian and Mediterranean roots. An unexpected find in the mountains.

Austrian Tea Room, 42 Trapp Hill Rd (☎802/253-5705). The high prices are more for the kitschy, Germanic atmosphere than the food, but the cuisine's still authentic enough and the setting fun (in season, try to get seated on the flower-lined balcony).

Blue Moon Cafe, 35 School St (☎802/253-7006). Inventive, surprisingly inexpensive New American fare featuring local game (braised venison and the like) and seafood, prepared by chef Jack Pickett; probably Stowe's best all-round dining choice. Good wine list.

Gracie's, in the Carlson Building, 2 Main St (☎802/253-8741). Good for lunchtime salads and sandwiches, many of them Mexican style; also open well into night for fuller dinners.

Hapelton's, two miles south on Rte-100 (☎802/253-4653). *Hapelton's* has a sunken lounge popular with the mellow apres-ski set, good for a snack and a drink.

McCarthy's, Mountain Rd (☎802/253-8626). Irish-themed joint with great heaping breakfasts.

Mes Amis, Mountain Rd (☎802/253-8669). A local favorite serving affordable French cuisine for dinner. Excellent service.

Miguel's Stowe Away, 3148 Mountain Rd (☎802/253-7574). Spicy, tangy Mexican and Tex-Mex treats, excellent by New England standards. Its lively margarita bar can get rowdy on weekends.

Olive's Bistro, Mountain Rd (☎802/253-2033). Top-notch tapas bar in addition to other French-inspired Mediterranean specialties. Great selection of martinis, single malt scotches, and assorted cocktails.

Pie in the Sky, 492 Mountain Rd (☎802/253-5100). Casual café offering wood-fired specialty pizzas you can design yourself, plus vegetarian entrees.

Shed Restaurant and Brewery Pub, Mountain Rd (☎802/253-4364). Hearty American fare, specializing in the ample "Mighty Shed Burger." The attached bar has great daily specials on pints and bar chow. Open late night.

LAKE CHAMPLAIN

The 150-mile-long **Lake Champlain** forms the boundary between Vermont and New York, and just nudges its way into Canada in the north, never exceeding twelve miles across at its widest point – in all, an area of about 490 square miles, making it the sixth largest body of freshwater in the US. Across the water from the flatlands of the Champlain Valley, the impassive Adirondack Mountains are always visible, looming up in the west. The first non-native to see the lake, French explorer **Samuel de Champlain** in 1609, who named it in his own honor, was also the first to claim that it held a sinuous Loch-Ness-type monster. The people in the region take a bit too much pride in this legend: the Vermont House of Representatives has passed protective legislation for the beast, and "Champ" is now familiar as an informal symbol of Lake Champlain, with his own failed line of snack foods ("Champ's Chips").

Monsters aside, the life and soul of the valley is the French-Canadian-influenced city of **Burlington**, whose longstanding trade connections with Montréal have filled it with elegant nineteenth-century architecture. Within just a few miles of the center, US-2 leads north onto the supremely rural **Champlain Islands**, covered in meadows and farmlands.

Lake Champlain Ferries (☎802/864-9804, *www.ferries.com*) cross the lake from Vermont to New York from **Burlington** (to Port Kent; hourly; $12.75); **Charlotte** (to Essex; hourly; $6.75); and **Grand Isle** (to Plattburgh; every 20min; $6.75). All these rates are one-way for a car and driver; additional charge for passengers, cyclists, and walk-ons ($2–3.25).

Burlington

The closest Vermont gets to a city, with a population of just around forty thousand, lakeside **BURLINGTON** is one of New England's most purely enjoyable destinations, a hip, relaxed fusion of Montréal, eighty miles to the north, and Boston, over two hundred miles southeast. In fact, from its earliest days, Burlington looked as much to Canada as to the south. Shipping connections with the St Lawrence River were far easier than the land routes across the mountains, and the harbor became a major supply center. The city's founders included Ethan Allen and family – far from being some impoverished Robin Hood figure, Ethan was a wealthy landowner, having purchased large tracts of Vermont land from New Hampshire royal governor Benning Wentworth, and his brother Ira set up the University of Vermont.

Burlington today is the definitive youthful university town. From its waterfront walkways to its lively brewpubs, the city is at once cosmopolitan and pleasantly manageable in scale. It's one of the few American cities to offer something approaching a café society, with a downtown – especially around the Church Street Marketplace – you can stroll around on foot, and plenty of open-air terraces. Politically, too, it's unusual: Bernard Sanders, the former "socialist" mayor of Burlington, was in 1990 elected to the House of Representatives from Vermont, the first political independent to go to Congress in forty years.

Arrival, information and getting around

Burlington sits at the confluence of several major highways, US-7, US-2, and I-89. Amtrak Vermonter **trains** haul into the town of Essex Junction an inconvenient five miles northeast of town (connecting buses run every half-hour 6.30am–9.30pm; $1). Vermont Transit **buses**, on the other hand, stop right in downtown Burlington, beside City Hall Park at the corner of St Paul and Main streets. The airport is several miles east of town along US-2.

Practical information is available from the **Lake Champlain Regional Chamber of Commerce**, 60 Main St (July–Sept Mon–Fri 8.30am–5pm, Sat–Sun 11am–3pm; Oct–June Mon–Fri 8.30am–5pm; ☎802/863-3489). Burlington's Web site (*www.burlingtonvt.together.com*) has up-to-the-minute information on area attractions, dining, events and weather.

The local **CCTA** bus company connects points all over the downtown area, and travels to the nearby cities of Winooksi, Essex and Shelburne ($1). Bus stops are plentiful, though, oddly enough, the bus stop signs don't list route numbers. You can get a map downtown at the Merchants Bank on Church Street, or call ☎802/864-CCTA anytime for route, schedule, and service info. CCTA also operates a very convenient – and free – shuttle, which runs along College Street between University of Vermont and the waterfront with stops at the Fleming Museum and the Church Street Marketplace (every 15–30min; Mon–Fri 6.30am–9pm, Sat–Sun 11am–9pm).

Lake Champlain Ferries (see p.368) leave from the jetty at the end of King Street, as do informative sightseeing cruises with Lake Champlain Cruise and Charter (☎802/864-9804; $7). Somewhat more convivial cruises set out from nearby Perkins Pier at the end of Maple Street on the *Spirit of Ethan Allen* (☎802/862-8300; $9). Ski Rack, 85 Main St (☎802/658-3313), and Northstar Cyclery, 100 Main St (☎802/863-3832), rent bikes and in-line skates.

MORE POLITICS, VERMONT-STYLE

In a case of life imitating art, **Fred Tuttle**'s political career began in a movie, *Man With a Plan*, a 1996 mock documentary directed by Fred's neighbor, filmmaker John O'Brien. In the film, a dairy farmer named Fred (played by Fred) needs a job that will help him pay his ailing father(played by Fred's 98-year-old father)'s medical bills. In a moment of inspiration, he discovers "the only job that requires no previous experience or education and pays $129,500 a year" – that of US Senator. He runs under the aegis of the Regressive Party, with the slogan, "Why Not?" The movie was barely a blip on the box office charts, but gained a cult following in Vermont.

So when Massachusetts management consultant Jack McMullen, whose only claim to Vermont was a ski cabin and an apartment in Burlington, turned up as the Republican nominee for Senate in 1998, Tuttle (with O'Brien's encouragement) managed his own campaign. McMullen spent anywhere from a quarter to a half a million dollars; Tuttle spent $261, one for each town in the state. In the debates, Fred challenged McMullen to pronounce town names like "Calais" (locally, "callous"; Ivy Leaguer McMullen gave it the proper – but not in Vermont – French ring "Cah-lay"). McMullen responded with a combination of joking condescension, righteous indignation, and attempts to imitate Fred's folksy style. Yet in the end, Tuttle came out of the Republican Primary with 55 percent of the vote.

Tuttle's reaction to his victory was just as untraditional. Now just a popular vote away from going to DC, a place he once described with the words "I never hated a place so bad in my life," he endorsed Democratic incumbent Patrick Leahy. In November, to no one's surprise, Leahy won, and Tuttle went back to his farm.

Accommodation

The Burlington area has no shortage of moderately priced **accommodation**, though most are removed from the downtown area, along Williston Road (just west along US-2, off I-89 exit 14), and south of town along US-7. For **camping**, the lakeside Northbeach Campsites (☎802/862-0942) is less than two miles north of town on Institute Road, and Lone Pine Campsites, 104 Bay Rd (☎802/878-5447), is equally proximate and offers oodles of facilities.

Hostels

Mrs Farrell's Home Hostel (HI-AYH), 27 Arlington Court (☎802/865-3730). Only a few dorm beds, so reservations are essential, at $15 for HI members, $18 nonmembers. Three miles out from the town center. 10pm curfew. Closed Nov–April.

YWCA, 278 Main St (☎802/862-7520). Strictly women-only budget option very close to downtown. Dorms $11, doubles $24.

Bed and breakfasts

Burlington Redstone B&B, 497 S Willard St (☎802/862-0508, *www.burlingtonredstone.com*). Red-brick home, a little cluttered with antiques and work by local artists, convenient to downtown. Nice lake and mountain views from patios and porches. Singles from $100. Reservations recommended. [4].

Heart of the Village Inn, 2130 Shelburne Rd, Shelburne (☎802/985-2800 or 1-877/808-1834, *www.heartofthevillage.com*). Nine beautifully decorated rooms in a pair of Victorian houses with period antiques and delectable continental breakfast. Cable TV available on request. [5].

Inn at Shelburne Farms, 102 Harbor Rd, Shelburne (☎802/985-8498). Posh digs, perhaps the nicest around, in a mansion on the lovely Shelburne Farms (see p.375). May–Oct. ⑥–⑦.

Lang House on Main Street, 360 Main St (☎1-877/919-9799, *www.langhouse.com*). Handsome Victorian conveniently located between UVM campus and downtown, offers 11 rooms, many with views of Lake Champlain. ⑥.

Hotels and motels

Colonial Motor Inn, 462 Shelburne Rd, Shelburne (☎802/862-5784). The 1960s-era decor lends a campy touch to this meticulously clean motel featuring pool and cable TV. ④.

Comfort Inn, 1285 Williston Rd (☎802/865-3400). Chain motel with clean basic rooms, pool and spa, coffee round the clock, and free continental breakfast. Most rooms are non-smoking. ④.

Ho-Hum Motel, 1660 Williston Rd (☎802/863-4551). This simple and reasonably priced motel, three miles east of downtown, almost lives up to its name. Four adjacent restaurants and a bike path nearby help liven it up. ③.

Radisson, 60 Battery St (☎802/658-6500, *www.Radisson.com/burlingtonvt*). Extravagant – and extravagantly expensive – hotel conveniently located on a hillside right on the Lake Champlain shore. The lounge hosts surprisingly popular comedy nights on weekends. ⑥.

Ramada Inn, 1117 Williston Rd (☎802/658-0250 or 1-800/2RAMADA). Good-quality rooms in this chain hotel, plus outdoor pool in a big courtyard. Popular with business travelers. ④.

The City

Your natural inclination on setting out to explore Burlington might be to head for the **waterfront**. Once surprisingly underdeveloped, it's been undergoing a facelift in the 1990s – though renovations are currently at a standstill, and there's a half-done look to the whole thing. Nevertheless, it has become one of the city's top destinations; indeed, kayaks seem to be strapped to the roof of every third car in Burlington. The aptly named **Waterfront Park** stretches a couple miles along Lake Champlain, with ample green spaces, gorgeous swing benches that people tactfully fight to get to, and a popular dog run. At its northern end, **Battery Park** makes a particularly good place to watch the sun go down over the Adirondacks – especially when there's a band playing, as there usually is on weekends. Winding on and about the shoreline, the 6.5-mile **bike path** follows a scruffy former railroad bed from the south end of the city to the north, a good way to see the waterfront and some of the city beaches if you've got wheels. If you're looking to actually get on the water, rather than just admire it from the path, Winds of Ireland in the Community Boathouse, at the foot of College Street (☎802/863-5090), rents motorboats and jet-skis. Next to the boathouse, the **Lake Champlain Basin Science Center** (daily 11am–5pm; $2) affords the opportunity to handle all sorts of slimy lake-dwelling fauna and has intriguing exhibits on area marine life, though kids will find it more to their liking than adults.

A better target perhaps is the **Church Street Marketplace**, a pedestrian mall, just a few blocks from the waterfront, that holds Burlington's finest old buildings – including an attractive City Hall – and most of its modern cafés and boutiques. Although locals will complain that the Marketplace has become inundated with chainstores in recent years, it still supports a number of unique businesses. Avoid the huge new Border's and head instead to the Crow Bookshop, 14 Church St (☎802/862-0848) or North Country Books, 2 Church St (☎802/862-6413), two of the better **independent bookstores** that pepper downtown. The market's busiest on nights and weekend days, both good people-watching times.

Up College Street from the marketplace is the sleepy campus of the University of Vermont (better known as UVM, for Universitas Viridis Montis, a Latin rendering of the state's alleged, and grammatically dubious, French nomenclature), a comprehensive research university which houses Vermont's largest collection of art and anthropological pieces. The Robert Hull Fleming Museum (May–Aug Tues–Fri noon–4pm, Sat & Sun 1–5pm; Sept–April Tues–Fri 9am–4pm, Sat & Sun 1–5pm; $3) houses some good examples of European Baroque paintings and pre-Columbian artifacts. To catch more art, arrive on the first Friday of each month, when the Burlington City Arts (℅802/865-7166) sponsors a free trolley that traverses downtown's galleries.

North of the city: Winooski

North of Burlington along Rte-127, in the town of **WINOOSKI**, lies the **Ethan Allen Homestead** (mid-May to mid-June daily 1–5pm; mid-June to mid-Oct Mon–Sat 10am–5pm, Sun 1–5pm; rest of year call ☎802/865-4556 for hours; $4), the 1787 farmhouse and 1400-acre farmland on which the Revolutionary War hero spent the last years of his life. The attached museum is housed in a re-created eighteenth-century tavern, where you can quaff an ale while viewing a fairly intriguing video and slide show as you sit on uncomfortable, but true to period, furniture.

ETHAN ALLEN AND HIS GREEN MOUNTAIN BOYS

*"I am as resolutely determined to defend the independence of Vermont
as Congress are that of the United States ..."*

Flamboyant and controversial, folk hero Ethan Allen (1738–1789) represents to many the independent ethos Vermont has long been known for, ironic considering his humble beginnings as a Connecticut farmer. An early convert to the concept of republicanism, Allen would gain renown as a statesman who united Vermonters in their cause for independence and their right to own land. He also helped establish the image of the rugged individualist, contemptuous of federal authority (be it the Crown or Congress) that is carried on by second-amendment fanatics and militia-men to this day.

In the 1760s, Benning Wentworth, the royal governor of New Hampshire, under the assumption that his authority would naturally extend to the unclaimed territory to the north and west, began giving New Hampshire Grants for the area now known as Vermont. After Wentworth had been distributing these grants for more than a decade, the King decided that New York's governor actually wielded the rightful authority over the territory, and the original settlers and their townships were sub-jected to burdensome New York fees or, worse, had their lands confiscated.

The settlers responded by forming a citizens' militia, the **Green Mountain Boys**, to protect their rights, electing Ethan Allen as their colonel. Shortly thereafter, Allen and other family members formed the Onion River Land Company to speculate on the contested Wentworth land grants. This appears to have been a brilliant double strategy: as the Allens sold off the cheap grants to would-be settlers in Massachusetts and Connecticut, they increased the strength of their numbers opposing the Yorkers. And as the numbers increased to back up their claim to the land, the previously worthless grants increased in value accordingly. Eventually, the Allens were selling grants purchased at ten cents an acre for five dollars an acre, a pretty profit indeed. In the meantime, Allen and his fellow settlers were developing the area, building roads and establishing a population center on Burlington Bay.

Allen and (future traitor) Colonel Benedict Arnold were behind the assault on Fort Ticonderoga, the first British property taken by America. Allen eventually became commander of the armed forces of the Commonwealth of Vermont. While defending America's northern border from a renewed British assault from Canada, Allen and other Vermont representatives petitioned Congress to recognize Vermont and to admit her into the American Confederacy. When New York suc-ceeded in blocking Vermont's attempts, the Allens began secret negotiations with the *British* to guarantee their sovereignty. These negotiations became considerably less attractive after the defeat of Cornwallis (1781) and the Treaty of Paris (1783).

With the coming of peace, Ethan Allen had begun to put together an impressive farm on the Winooski (Onion) River at Burlington, now known as the Ethan Allen Homestead (see p.372), where he settled down to become a philosopher and writer. The self-taught Allen wrote Reason, the Only Oracle of Man, a collection of reflections and ideals that drew inspiration from European deism of the period. Allen died in 1789, only six years after peace with England, with Vermont still yet to join the Union.

More raucous fun can be had at the **Magic Hat Brewing Company**, five min-utes south of downtown at 180 Flynn Ave (store open Mon–Thurs & Sat 10am–6pm, Fri 10am–9pm, mid-May to Dec also Sun noon–5pm; tours every half-hour Wed–Fri 3.30–5pm, Sat 1–2.30pm; ☎802/658-BREW), which offers free tours that make the science of beer-making look fun, and free samples that enhance the experience even further.

The Shelburne Museum

It takes a whole day, if not more, to fully appreciate the fabulous fifty-acre collection of unalloyed Americana gathered at the **Shelburne Museum**, three miles south of Burlington on US-7 in Shelburne (late May to late Oct daily 9am–5pm, guided tours at 1pm; select buildings only, open April 1 to late May and mid-October to Dec 31 daily except holidays 1-4pm; $17.50, valid for two successive days). The brainchild of heiress Electra Havemeyer Webb, who aimed to create a distinctly American "collection of collections," the museum centers on her parents' nineteenth-century French Impressionist paintings, housed in a reconstruction of their New York apartment. However, Electra's own interests ran far wider, and she put together what is probably the nation's finest celebration of its own inventive past.

More than thirty buildings, some original and some newly constructed, dot the grounds. Besides seven fully furnished historic houses, moved intact from other locations in the region, there's a blacksmith, a jail, and a general store, all of which aim to re-create aspects of everyday life over the past two centuries. Of the several buildings devoted to American high art, the most notable is the **Webb Gallery**, which focuses on nineteenth-century pieces. Much of this collection consists of naturalist work, such as a fine range of James Audubon's bird prints, and there is also an intriguing portrait of Seneca Indian leader Sagayewatha and one of twentieth-century painter Anna Mary Robertson Moses' (known also as Grandma Moses) few cityscapes, *Cambridge, ca. 1944*. However, the collection is most notable for its assemblage of folk art, including decoys, weather vanes, tools, quilts, carriages, and circus memorabilia. The carnivalesque theme continues over at the **Circus Museum**, a homage to spectacle, American-style, featuring Barnum and Bailey ads with harrowing representations of clowns and wild animals, as well as Roy Arnold's woodcarving, *Circus Parade*, a cortege in miniature. Don't miss, too, the **Stagecoach Inn**, which holds a wonderfully nostalgic assemblage of trade and tavern signs, most notably "cigar store Indians," and the hilariously grotesque burled woodcarvings of Gustav Hertzberg.

The collections go beyond Americana – one of the best buildings is a meticulous reconstruction of Electra Webb's New York apartment, the Greek Revival **Electra Havemeyer Webb Memorial Building**, constructed between 1960 and 1967. Despite the towering Ionic columns that front the place, it's the interior that makes a visit worthwhile: each of the six rooms duplicates the arrangements of furniture and decorative arts – including works by Rembrandt, Manet, and Degas – from Webb's extravagant Manhattan home.

The museum grounds themselves are a joy to browse; a stroll around will bring you past lilac gardens in spring and stunning foliage in fall, over covered bridges, and to a working blacksmith shop. The village includes a **Shaker barn**, a **schoolhouse**, a railroad station, even an enormous, fully reconstructed steam **paddlewheeler**, the *SS Ticonderoga*, with its own rock-surrounded lighthouse.

Shelburne Farms

Next to the Shelburne Museum, **Shelburne Farms**, 102 Harbor Rd (mid-May to mid-Oct 9am–5pm; $9 walking trails plus tour, $5 for just trails; ☎802/985-8686), a working farm reborn as a nonprofit environmental center on Lake Champlain. A guided tour of railroad mogul Dr Seward Webb's estate reveals his descendants' commitment to sustainable farming – though on an incongruously large and impressive scale. The undulating landscape is punctuated by three massive buildings: the main house, which overlooks Lake Champlain and the Adirondacks, a coach barn, and a horseshoe-shaped farm barn. The farm's mansion is the *Inn at Shelburne*, open mid-May to mid-October, with 26 deluxe guest rooms and a dining room which serves breakfast, dinner, and Sunday brunch.

Eating

Burlington's best **restaurants** are located along Main and Church streets and feature a few ethnic eateries as alternatives to the American cuisine which often seems to dominate the town. The presence of ten thousand students insures that there are plenty of inexpensive places to eat, while the academic tone brings a certain sophistication to the café culture. Keep in mind that this is one of the most vehement anti-smoking towns in the state, and smoking is banned in most eateries.

Bourbon Street Grill, 211 College St (☎802/865-2800). Crowded and dimly lit restaurant serving spicy Cajun specials like po' boy sandwiches and fried catfish from $8.

Daily Planet, 15 Center St, behind the Church Street Marketplace (☎802/862-9647). This brightly colored spot offers a creative menu melding Asian and Mediterranean cooking with old-fashioned American comfort food, a la *satay* burgers and *saag paneer* with mashed potatoes. Highly recommended.

Five Spice Cafe, 175 Church St (☎802/864-4045). Excellent Southeast Asian fare, with vegetarian options and dim sum and elaborate, delightfully named dishes like Evil Jungle Prince (chicken and veggies in a sort of coconut milk curry).

Gateway Cafe, 30 Main St (☎802/862-4930). Moderately priced homestyle cooking near the waterfront – grilled *pannini* and rotisserie chicken are served up alongside burgers and milkshakes. Outdoor seating available in season.

Leunig's Bistro, 115 Church St (☎802/863-3759). Sleek, modern bistro serving contemporary continental cuisine at surprisingly reasonable prices. Outdoor dining when weather permits and live jazz on Tues, Wed and Thurs nights.

Pauline's Café and Restaurant, 1834 Shelburne Rd, South Burlington (☎802/862-1081). Inventive American cuisine with a continental flavor, using much local produce. Light meals in a casual setting downstairs, more formality and higher prices upstairs.

Red Onion, 140 Church St (☎802/865-2563). The best sandwiches in town are made to order here in this small shop with a mouth-watering menu, which includes some good vegetarian options. The "red onion" sandwich is a standout, and can easily fill two people for the price of one.

Shanty on the Shore, 181 Battery St (☎802/864-0238). Absolutely fresh seafood in a laid-back setting with views of Lake Champlain. Burlington's best raw bar.

Smoke Jack's, 156 Church St (☎802/658-1119). Innovative American cuisine as well as standard steak and seafood, all smoked over an oak-wood grill.

Sneakers, 36 Main St, Winooski (☎802/655-908). This is the place for breakfast, and you ought to arrive early for it on weekends. Delicious waffles, home made granola, eggs Benedict (try the smoked turkey eggs Benedict) and fresh squeezed juices served in a diner-like decor with Art Deco mirrors lining the walls. Good weekday lunches too.

Sweetwaters, 120 Church St (☎802/864-9800). American grill standards in a converted bank with sidewalk dining, most notable for its excellent salads, a daily stir fry and extensive Sunday brunch.

Trattoria Delia, 152 St Paul St (☎802/864-5253). Modern Italian fare that goes beyond the usual pasta fare – try the polenta pie and marinated shrimp – and a great wine list, at reasonable prices.

Zabby's Stone Soup, 211 College St (☎802/862-7616). Excellent "mostly vegetarian" café, featuring a wide variety of sandwiches, home-made soups, cakes and the like.

Entertainment: bars, coffeehouses and nightlife

The **drinking** scene here is at its most active when school is in session, but Burlington's cafés and bars come to life during the summer as well. Though there are a handful of dance clubs, the **nightlife** in Burlington revolves mostly around live music. Several of its concert venues are big enough to draw indie bands from New York and around New England, but the local band scene is a formidable presence in its own right. Downtown's Art Deco style **Flynn Theater**, 153 Main St, across from City Hall and the Church Street Marketplace (☎802/863-5966), plays host to a wide array of talent, from concerts by local hippie heroes Phish to works by Broadway touring companies. The Comedy Zone, inside the *Radisson Hotel Burlington*, 60 Battery St (☎802/658-6500), hosts nationally acclaimed comics twice a night on Saturdays and Sundays at 8 and 10pm. Beware that because this is a college town, bars and clubs are quite strict with checking IDs. Make sure to have proper proof of age with you when venturing out for the evening or you are guaranteed to be disappointed.

Club Metronome, 188 Main St (☎802/865-4563). This very hip club above *Nectar's* (see below) hosts some live acts, but is mainly a funked-out dance scene with house and techno music being spun. Saturday nights is "Retronome" when Seventies and Eighties music dominates the dance floor. Over 21 only.

Millennium, 165 Church St (☎802/660-2088). The fancy Art Deco interior here (formerly *Club Toast*) serves as the backdrop for dancing, usually to hip-hop and techno, with the occasional theme night thrown in for variety.

Muddy Waters, 184 Main St (☎802/658-0466). Crazy interior lined with used furniture and thrift store rejects, and colorful, crunchy clientele adorn this popular coffeehouse. Extremely potent caffeine beverages.

Nectar's, 188 Main St (☎802/658-4771). Follow the rotating neon sign to this retro lounge lined with vinyl booths and formica tables. Sip a stylish cocktail, smoke a Lucky Strike, and tap your feet to lounge acts. This was the inspiration for Phish's 1995 album title *In the Face of Nectar* as it hosted many of their earliest shows.

Rasputin's, Church St (☎802/864-9324). Popular UVM hangout with a rowdy drinking scene that carries on until late in the evening. Good DJs bring the energy level to eleven on weekends.

Red Square, 136 Church St (☎802/859-8909). For those in the mood for a cosmopolitan experience in the depths of the Green Mountains, *Red Square* is the place to sip cocktails amidst a highbrow clientele. The food menu is also quite inviting and worth investigating further.

Ruben James, 153 Main St (☎802/864-0744). This joint brings in a slightly older crowd for delectable microbrews and loud live bar music.

Three Needs, 207 College St (☎802/658-0889). This bar does a fine job of taking care of its customers' three most important needs: great beer, cheap pool and Sunday night *Simpsons* parties with excellent drink specials.

Vermont Pub and Brewery, 144 College St (☎802/865-0500). Roomy and convivial brew-pub, offering free tastes of its various beers – Dogbite Bitter is the best – plus a good menu with live music on some weekends.

What Ales You, 152 St Paul St (☎802/862-1362). Terrific brewpub with a wide selection of local microbrews.

South of Burlington: underwater preserves

Vermont is one of the few states with designated **Underwater Historic Preserves** (details on ☎802/828-3226), where divers can see wrecks on the lake floor. There are several of the underwater "state parks" close to Burlington, and the best place to find out about them is at the **Lake Champlain Maritime Museum** in Basin Harbor, six miles east of Vergennes (May–Oct daily 10am–5pm; $5; ☎802/475-2022). The museum boasts a life-size replica of the 1776 gunboat *Philadelphia II*, displays on Lake Champlain shipwrecks and the technology used to research them, and details of the horse-powered ferry that plied the lake at the turn of the century. The museum is on the grounds of the Basin Harbor Club, where the *Red Mill Restaurant* serves three meals a day in summer, breakfast only at other times.

Mount Independence

Outside of the town of Orwell, 25 miles south of Vergennes at the very southeastern tip of Lake Champlain, is **Mount Independence**, site of a major American defeat in the Revolutionary War. Mount Independence was built as a fort in 1776, along with the more famous Fort Ticonderoga on the opposite shore, to repel a British attack from Canada. The two forts initially provided such an intimidating sight that British General Guy Carleton aborted his invasion in October 1776. However, the following winter was brutal, and most of the troops deserted, leaving 2500 American soldiers behind to fall ill or freeze to death. Springtime brought reinforcements insufficient to withstand an attack from General Burgoyne, and the fort was abandoned on July 5, 1777. The British occupied the Mount until November of the same year, when they burned the fort in response to General Burgoyne's surrender across the water at Saratoga. Today, the **Mount Independence State Historic Site** (late May to mid-Oct daily 8.30am–5pm) is a pleasingly low-key affair, just a small museum with a few artifacts and some documentation of that dreadful winter, plus four hiking trails around the Mount, with a few spots marking relics of the fort (mostly piles of rocks that had been foundation). It's a relaxing place, with relatively few visitors and nice views of the lake by which to enjoy the solitude.

Champlain Islands

The sparsely populated **Champlain Islands** curl southward into Lake Champlain from Canada, comprising four narrow, oblong land masses – **NORTH HERO**, **GRAND ISLE**, **ALBURG**, and **ISLE LA MOTTE** – that never really caught on development-wise, despite being the site of the first settlement in Vermont, way back in 1666. After the Revolutionary War, Vermonters Ira and Ethan Allen, staked claims to much of the islands' area, modestly naming them North and South Hero (the latter was later changed to Grand Isle). Today, though, the islands' only real industry is farming, evidenced by the silo-dotted hayfields and ubiquitous bovine odor.

French explorer Pierre de St-Paul's short-lived encampment is now occupied by **St Anne's Shrine**, West Shore Road, Isle La Motte, a statue of a prayerful St Anne that during the season is surrounded by visiting groups of devoted Catholics and amateur miracle purveyors; the shrine is right near a popular beach. Also on the island is a massive granite statue of **Samuel de Champlain**, who first landed here in 1609. Grand Isle's claim to historical fame is the **Hyde Log Cabin**, US-2 (July 4–Labor Day Thurs–Mon 10am–4pm; free), built in 1783 and housing a modest museum, notable for its collection of household artifacts like churns, rusty bedpans, and makeshift ovens from Vermont's earliest frontier days.

There is surprisingly little outdoor activity in these parts save for hunting and fishing, though some good opportunities exist for swimming during summertime. The area's best beach is the nearly half-mile strand at **Sand Bar State Park**, actually on the mainland just below the US-2 bridge to Grand Isle. If that one's too crowded (as it often is in summer), head to **Knights' Point State Park**, North Hero (☎802/372-8389), a placid, sandy shoreline enclosed by a bay.

Practicalities

For information on attractions and **accommodation**, contact the Lake Champlain Islands Chamber of Commerce, US-2, North Hero (☎802/372-5683). Should you desire to stay overnight in the islands, the *Thomas Mott Homestead*, along Rte-78, Alburg, is the superior B&B choice, with large rooms, comfortable beds, modern furniture and fantastic cooking (☎802/796-3736 or 1-800/348-0843; ④) in its accompanying restaurants. Less expensive is *Charlie's Northland Lodge*, along US-2 in North Hero, a cozy hostelry with shared baths (☎802/372-8822; ③). The Champlain Islands do offer some of Vermont's best **camping**. Knight's Island State Park is enormously secluded, with a multitude of unspoiled nature trails, though you should reserve early to get one of the ten primitive campsites (☎802/524-6353). Grand Isle State Park, 36 E Shore South, Grand Isle (☎802/372-4300), provides a suitable alternative, with 120 highly developed campsites, replete with restrooms, hot showers, and RVs galore.

The islands offer nothing special in the way of **eating**, though carnivores will enjoy *Sandbar Restaurant*, US-2, Grand Isle (☎802/372-6911), an all-American steakhouse with sweeping lake views. The *Ruthcliffe Lodge and Restaurant*, Old Quarry Rd, Isle La Motte (☎802/928-3200 or 1-800/769-8162), serves decent steak-and-potatoes type fare for daily dinner, though lodgers get breakfast too.

St Albans

Sleepy **ST ALBANS**, about halfway between Burlington and the Canadian border along I-89, is a town only by Vermont's standards, able to be seen by foot in less than an hour. Although there's some ugly mall sprawl to the north, St Albans' center has a large town green, landscaped on the slope of a hill, lined with churches at the top and small, mostly local, shops at the bottom. It's most notable for its curious distinction as the site of the northernmost engagement of the Civil War. The "St Albans Raid" took place on October 22, 1864, when disguised Confederate soldiers entered the town from Canada, robbed its three banks of over $200,000, took some hostages, killed one citizen, and decamped to Quebec, where they were arrested and tried but never extradited back to the US. The town makes much of this event, particularly during the Civil War Days festival in late October, when history buffs descend here to re-create the event. Meanwhile, the **St Albans Historical Museum**, Church and Bishop streets (June–Sept 1–4pm or by appointment; ☎802/527-7933), also has displays on the raid, as well as a range of exhibits that vary greatly in quality. The best of these are the collections of artifacts from the town's earliest days, including military memorabilia, a re-created railroad sta-

THE MYSTERIOUS LEGACY OF CHESTER A. ARTHUR

One of the least celebrated famous figures in Vermont history, President **Chester A. Arthur**, hailed from the small community of Fairfield, about seven miles east of St Albans along Rte-36. Or did he? His rather undistinguished presidency came under fire over a dispute about his upbringing.

Arthur, widely regarded as an ineffectual man with a few powerful connections, ascended from the vice-presidency to the office of president when James Garfield was shot. He was not made more popular by the fact that the assassin's last words were, "I am a Stalwart and Arthur will be President," implying that Garfield was killed not for anything he had done, but to make way for an Arthur presidency. This controversy was followed by the publication of a political tract entitled "How a British Subject Became President of the United States," by feisty journalist A.P. Hinman, who claimed that Arthur had actually been born over the Canadian border, rendering him ineligible for the presidency. No hard evidence was ever produced, just a lot of debate and argument. Regardless, the president failed to win reelection (or even his party's nomination); indeed, he was dogged by kidney disease that would fell him not two years after the end of his term.

Today, you can visit the **Chester A. Arthur Historic Site** (Memorial Day–Columbus Day daily 10am–4pm) in Fairfield, which celebrates his humble origins and otherwise unremarkable presidency while painting a pleasant picture of the murkiness surrounding the actual site of his birth.

tion, and arcane remedies and antique medical devices recovered from local physicians and apothecaries. St Albans is also, as seat of the largest maple-producing county in the US, home to Vermont's Annual Maple Festival, held in April, locally known as the "Sugarin' Off" party.

Accommodation in and around St Albans is reasonable compared to the rest of the state. Least expensive is the *Cadillac Motel*, 213 S Main St (☎802/524-2191; ③), which is low on amenities but very clean. The area's best B&B is the *Old Mill River Place*, Georgia Shore Rd (☎802/524-7211; ④), featuring antique-filled rooms in a restored 1799 farmhouse with views of Lake Champlain. **Eating** options won't dazzle or disappoint. Hearty meat-and-potatoes fare can be had at *Diamond* Jim's Grille, north of town along US-7 (N Main St), in the Highgate Mall Shopping Center (☎802/524-9280). *Simple Pleasures Café*, 84 N Main St (☎802/527-0669), serves tasty light lunches, while the ethnically confused bar-restaurant *McGuel's Irish Burro*, 18 Lake St (☎802/527-1276; closed Sun), has south-of-the-border fare and a dizzying array of beers. There's also *The Brew Lab*, 201 Main St (☎802/524-2772), home of Franklin County Brewery, for quality microbrews.

Around St Albans

The coast of Lake Champlain beckons a mere three miles west of town along Rte-36, where the **Kill Kare State Park** (summer only; ☎802/524-6021) has some decent swimming and boating facilities, though it tends to be crowded. Better to take the $2 ferry to the state park on nearby **Burton Island** (summer only; ☎802/524-6353), much more secluded, with three miles of shoreline, hiking trails, and boat and canoe rentals as well as 43 campsites. North of St Albans along I-89, just below the Canadian border, Rte-78 veers west to the **Missisquoi National Wildlife Refuge** in SWANTON (☎802/868-4781; free), a remote lakeside nature preserve where you can meet Vermont's native beasts face-to-face. The fauna range from the mundane (ducks, deer, and turtles) to the borderline scary (vampire bats). Best to bring along bug repellent, especially during summer.

NORTHEAST KINGDOM

Remote and relentlessly rural, Vermont's **northeast kingdom** takes its name from a remark made by Vermont Senator George Aiken in 1949, referring to the several counties that bulge out eastward to form the state's uppermost corner. The only locales approaching town status are **St Johnsbury** and **Newport**, at the region's southern and northern boundaries, each of which has less than nine thousand inhabitants. I-91 slices through the kingdom, but you can't really appreciate the area's intense quiet and natural beauty without traveling along its innumerable back roads. Here you can drive for hours, passing through vast expanses of green as well as a side of the region that the state tries to downplay – pockets of intense rural poverty. Aside from its idyllic character, the region offers little in the way of formal sights, with a few notable exceptions such as Glover's **Bread and Puppet Museum**, though opportunities for recreation abound; indeed two of the state's least crowded and most challenging ski areas, **Jay Peak** and **Burke Mountain**, are in this region.

St Johnsbury

The hamlet of **ST JOHNSBURY** imagines itself a thriving metropolis in the midst of Vermont's sparsely populated northeast corner; however, its abundance of elaborate architecture, all turrets and marble and stained glass, seem terribly out of proportion to its size. Still, it's the biggest municipality around (the nearest town is Barre, 35 miles away on US-2), and an important travel hub if you happen to be heading this far up.

St J, as it's referred to by locals, grew from a frontier outpost to its current size thanks to the ingenuity of resident **Thaddeus Fairbanks**, the "scale king," who earned his fortune and a minor place in history by inventing the platform scale in the 1830s. Much of his riches were showered on the city in the form of funding for new municipal buildings and elaborate churches. One place that celebrates his legacy, the Romanesque **Fairbanks Museum and Planetarium**, Main and Prospect streets (July–Aug Mon–Sat 10am–6pm, Sun 1–5pm, planetarium shows 11am Mon–Fri, 1.30pm daily; Sept–June Mon–Sat 10am–4pm, Sun 1–5pm, planetarium shows Sat & Sun 1.30pm; museum $5, planetarium $2; ☎802/748-2372, *www.fairbanksmuseum.org*), has the predictable range of platform scales, plus a varied collection of historical and scientific artifacts, from Civil War pieces to Zulu war shields to various Japanese handicrafts, including an excellent collection of tiny *netsuke* figurines. It also serves as an official US weather station, though much of this is out of sight of the viewing public. Just down Main Street, the **St Johnsbury Athanaeum** (Mon & Wed 10.30am–8pm, Tues, Thurs & Fri 10am–5.30pm, Sat 9.30am–4pm, closed Sun; free; ☎802/748-8291) houses a number of excellent paintings from the Hudson River school, including Andrew Bierstadt's gargantuan *Domes of the Yosemite*.

If you're caught in this part of the world with a yearning for something to *do*, you may find your needs fulfilled by the surprisingly eclectic offerings at the **Catamount Arts Center**, 139 East Ave (☎802/748-2600). The small brick building houses a movie theater showing foreign and art films, a concert hall where the offerings focus on jazz, New Age, and world music, a café and an excellent video store, specializing in foreign films.

Practicalities

Accommodation in St J is limited mostly to relatively cheap, independent motels packed with weary travelers taking respite from their sojourns along I-91. One of the more well-accoutered is the *Fairbanks Motor Inn*, 32 Western Ave (☎802/748-5666; ⑤), which has a heated pool, putting green, and cable TV. There's also the *Yankee Traveler Motel*, 65 Portland St (☎802/748-3156; ③–④), a 42-room hotel with a pool, cable TV, and a cheerful staff. Cheaper and closer to St Johnsbury's center, the *Maple Center Motel*, 20 Hastings St (☎802/748-2393; ④), and the *Holiday Motel*, 25 Hastings St (☎802/742-8192; ③), have comfortable rooms with all the basics. But perhaps the best place to stay is the *HI-Sleepers River Home Hostel* (call for reservations and address before 9pm; ☎802/748-1575; closed Dec 20–Jan 2), a snug six-room establishment run by friendly proprietors.

There is not as much choice as far as **eating** goes. Try *Gerardo's*, 43 Eastern Ave (☎802/748-4778; closed Mon), which serves light, inexpensive modern Italian dishes. For a quick pastry or sandwich and some strong coffee, there is the *Northern Lights Book Shop and Cafe*, 79 Railroad St (☎802/748-4463), where you can also browse a quirky collection of books. The Northeast Kingdom **Chamber of Commerce**, at 30 Western Ave (Mon–Sat 10am–5pm; ☎1-800/639-6379), dispenses info and has a **booth** at the intersection of Main and Prospect streets during summer.

West of St Johnsbury

DANVILLE, a nondescript town that lies about ten miles west of St Johnsbury at the intersection of US-2 and Rte-15, stakes its limited claim to notoriety as the headquarters of the American Society of Dowsers, based in **Dowser's Hall**, on Danville Green (☎802/684-3417), where you'll find displays and literature on the practice of intuitively identifying underground water sources using a forked branch or pendulum.

CRAFTSBURY, further north on slow, bumpy Rte-14, is just about in the middle of nowhere – which is exactly its appeal. This is as perfectly lovely a tiny Vermont town as you're likely to see, with a history that stretches back to the mid-eighteenth century and includes one native son who served as Vermont's governor. It has seen virtually no growth in the 200-plus years since its inception; the town center, **Craftsbury Common**, consists of little more than a post office and some lovely inns, best of which are the *Inn on the Common* (☎802/586-9619 or 1-800/521-2233, *www.innonthecommon.com*; ⑨), whose dining room serves excellent traditional American fare, and the homey *Whetstone Brook B&B* (☎802/586-6916; ④). While the main recreation here is getting away from activity, the surrounding hills are crisscrossed with a web of trails popular for mountain biking and skiing. **Craftsbury Outdoor Center** (☎802/729-7751) provides service for all your needs in these activities.

North to Canada

From St Johnsbury, I-91 runs north up to Canada; everything east of the highway is fairly mountainous, and there are a few good diversions not too far off the main road – though if you wander too far off you could easily get lost, as much of the region is undeveloped.

Burke Mountain, Mount Hor and Mount Pisgah

The cream of the United States' crop of young downhill skiers train at **BURKE MOUNTAIN**, Mountain Road, East Burke (☎802/626-3305 or 1-800/541-5480), best approached from I-91 exit 23 onto US-5, then north on Rte-114. Because of the mountain's isolation, Burke's slopes are virtually deserted compared to places like Killington and Stowe, but they're all tough; indeed, intermediate range is as easy as it gets (lift tickets $15 Mon–Fri, $38 Sat–Sun). Venture up US-5 to its intersection with Rte-5A and continue north for several miles to be rewarded with views of spectacular **Lake Willoughby**, which is flanked on either side by **Mounts Hor** and **Pisgah**. The two towering mountains take their remarkably ugly names from biblical accounts of the life of Moses. Recreational opportunities abound, from jet-skiing (rental shacks line the shore) to swimming (there are sand beaches at the lake's north and south ends). Be sure to take note of the **waterfalls** that line the mountainsides along Rte-5A. Few people **stay** in areas this remote, but the *Willough Vale Inn* (☎802/525-4123 or 1-800/594-9102, *www.willoughvale.com*; [5]–[6]) just off Rte-5A offers both rooms and lakefront cottages in a wonderfully secluded setting; there's also a first-rate restaurant.

Glover and Newport

The only reason to hit **GLOVER**, fifteen miles north of St Johnsbury on Rte-122, is to stop by the **Bread and Puppet Museum** (June–Oct daily 10am–5pm; free; ☎802/525-3031), which got its start in the 1960s from a traveling dramatic troupe that performed anti-Vietnam War puppet shows. The remarkably oversized puppets – they can be as big as five feet and require up to four people to operate – can now be viewed in this peaceful barn setting, a far cry from the group's more volatile protest days. There are free performances every Sunday.

The obscurely located **Old Stone House**, about ten miles south of Newport, just off Rte-58 in Brownington (July–Aug daily 10am–5pm; mid-May–June & Sept–mid-Oct Fri–Tues 10am–5pm; $5; ☎802/754-2022), is tricky to find but worth the trouble. Originally a schoolhouse built by the **Reverend Alexander Twilight**, said to be the country's first African-American college graduate and legislator (a point contested by some historians, due to Twilight's mixed-race background), today the building is home to an array of Vermont artifacts, including, most interestingly, schoolroom supplies from the period.

The final stop on I-91 before the Quebec border, unassuming **NEWPORT** seems more French-Canadian than New England in character. Its main draw is **Lake Memphremagog**, which spans the international border and was once a choice resort area surrounded by grand homes. The lake area is no longer quite so upscale, but still popular enough with vacationing Quebecois, who flock here to boat, jet-ski, and swim. The town's drag, Main Street, is lined with quaint brick buildings, many of which are restored relics from the Victorian era and house twee **cafés** with bilingual menus. The best of these are *Miss Newport Diner*, 985 E Main St (☎802/334-7742), a classic American-style diner serving breakfast all day, and *Brown Cow*, 900 E Main St (☎802/334-7887), for fresh salads and excellent soup. Should you need to **stay** in Newport, the *Newport City Motel*, 974 E Main St (☎802/334-6558 or 1-800/338-6558; ③), is a decent, if bland, option.

Jay Peak

The 4000-foot summit of **JAY PEAK**, on Rte-242 (☎802/988-2611 or 1-800/451-4449), looms just south of the Canadian border, about fifteen miles west of I-91. Jay's are some of New England's toughest slopes, and typically only serious skiers venture this far out (unless coming down from Quebec). The most popular accommodation is *Hotel Jay* (☎1-800/451-4449; ④), a snazzy ski lodge at the base of the peak; the hotel has deals on lift tickets, a hot tub, and the *Golden Eagle Lounge*, which hosts the area's best apres-ski scene. The nearby *Jay Village Inn*, Jay Village (☎1-800/227-7452 or 802/988-2643; ④), offers fifteen snug rooms, a busy recreation room, and a quaint French-Canadian restaurant. For a good meal, venture a few miles from Jay, where *The Belfry*, on Rte-242 in Montgomery Center (☎802/326-4400), has a relaxed pub atmosphere and meaty specials.

CHAPTER SEVEN

NEW HAMPSHIRE

S imilar to Rhode Island, **New Hampshire** is a relatively small state (the 44th largest in the United States), with surprisingly diverse terrain. The short coastline is strewn with mellow, sun-drenched beaches and capped by **Portsmouth**, a well-preserved colonial town with a crop of excellent restaurants and stylish inns. Further inland, there are over 1300 lakes to explore, the largest, **Lake Winnipesaukee**, ringed with both developed tourist resorts and quiet villages. To the north, the splendor of the **White Mountains** spreads right across the state, culminating in the highest peak in New England, the formidable **Mount Washington**. Apart from these obvious attractions, quaint and relaxing communities scatter in particular abundance across the southern part of the state, connected by shaded winding country roads and the enduring small-town pride of their residents.

These days most visitors visit New Hampshire for its outdoor activities. In the warm summer months you can kayak, canoe, swim, fish, hike, climb, or bike, while during winter you can cross-country and downhill ski at one of over a dozen ski areas – the **Franconia Notch** area has a high concentration of downhill resorts, while tiny **Jackson** is famous for cross-country skiing. As with much of the rest of New England, fall is a popular time to come, when the trees turn vibrant shades of red, orange, and yellow, and the air temperature drops refreshingly.

All of which makes New Hampshire a busy place, even by New England standards. Much of the state is blanketed with bucolic rural scenery – around **Canterbury Shaker Village** near Concord, for example – but the current tourist authority's motto, "The Road Less Traveled," is not entirely accurate. Some of the major destinations, such as **Weirs Beach**, **North Conway**, and **Hampton Beach**, are extremely well traveled. But if you steer clear of these main draws, the lakes, islands, and snowcapped peaks that define New Hampshire remain both resoundingly spectacular and remote.

Some history

The people of New Hampshire have been an independent and individualistic lot ever since the first settlers of the region survived out of sheer persistence. Though originally explored by Martin Pring in 1603, the first European settlement here did not come until 1623, when the Englishman David Thomson brought a small group to **Odiorne Point**, at the mouth of the Piscataqua River. However, four years later, tired of long winters and failing crops, Thomson abandoned his settlement for Boston.

By then, Sir Ferdinando Gorges and John Mason had received land grants from the recently established Royal Council of New England and founded the Laconia Company with the intention of turning a profit in the fur trade. Without ever having laid eyes on the land, Mason named the region New Hampshire, after his home county in England. Their colony struggled, and after Mason died in 1635, the company was dissolved. A small group of settlers endured at **Strawbery Banke**, now Portsmouth, ignoring land ownership laws and taking large plots for themselves.

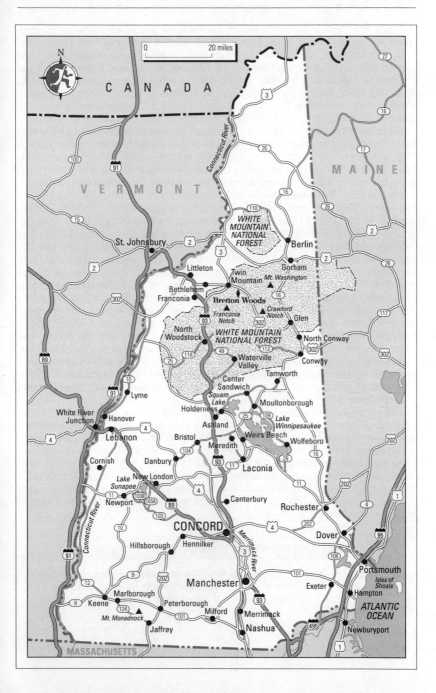

While only the few miles of seashore held sizeable seventeenth-century communities of European settlers, the harsh, glacier-scarred interior of New Hampshire, with its dense forests and forbidding mountains, remained the exclusive preserve of the Abenaki and Pennacook tribes of the **Algonquin Indians**. Relations with the Indians, though initially amiable, turned sour as settlers became more ambitious, damming rivers, logging the forests, introducing livestock, and scaring away game. Fearing they would lose their natural resources to the new settlers forever, the Indians attacked European settlements throughout New Hampshire in 1675. The conflict, known as King Philip's War, continued for several decades, but by the turn of the century the Indian population had been reduced from tens of thousands to less than a thousand. Sadly, after the provincial government offered high bounties for Indian scalps in the early eighteenth century and following the defeat of their French allies in Canada, Native Americans had almost vanished from the state by 1730.

By this time, **Portsmouth** was a thriving port, and the financial backbone of the colony. Timber companies and shipbuilding businesses flourished as loggers pushed further inland from Portsmouth and up the Connecticut River from the south. By the mid-eighteenth century, an extremely profitable mast trade had been established, fueled by the region's dense supply of pine trees and the expansion of England's merchant marine fleet, and a wealthy upper class had developed in the thriving colony. Portsmouth resident Benning Wentworth was appointed the colony's governor in 1741, and under his leadership settlement continued to spread west. Just before the Revolutionary War, upon hearing that the king had issued an edict forbidding shipment of gunpowder to the colonies, some 400 New Hampshire residents invaded **Fort William and Mary**, one of the first overt acts in defiance of England. Without firing a shot, the angry residents procured 100 barrels of gunpowder that were later put to good use in the Battle of Bunker Hill. Though no battles were actually fought in New Hampshire, the state provided valuable resources and manpower in the Revolutionary War. In January 1776, New Hampshire became the first American state to declare its independence.

Life remained a struggle for many of the settlers of New Hampshire's rugged interior. When it became clear that farmers could make little agricultural impact on the rocky terrain of the "granite state," many laborers departed for more fertile lands to the west. With the coming of the Industrial Revolution, however, towns in the Merrimack Valley, such as Nashua, Concord, and Manchester, became major manufacturing centers. Water-powered textile mills were set up along the Merrimack River, and at one point the enormous brick **Amoskeag mills** in Manchester produced more cloth than any other textile facility in the world.

ACCOMMODATION PRICE CODES

All accommodation prices in this book have been coded using the symbols below; prices are for the least expensive **double rooms** in each establishment. For a full explanation see p.28 in Basics. Individual rates rather than price codes are given for **hostels**.

① up to $30	④ $60–80	⑦ $130–175
② $30–45	⑤ $80–100	⑧ $175–250
③ $45–60	⑥ $100–130	⑨ $250+

M. BLEWETT/TRIP

Mystic Seaport, CT

B. TURNER/TRIP

DAVID THOMSEN

Barre rock quarry, VT

Covered bridge, NH

AMANDA HALL/ROBERT HARDING

Stowe, VT

T. MACKIE/TRIP

Lighthouse and coast, Portland, ME

R. WEAVER/GREG EVANS INTL

Mount Washington Cog Railway, NH

White Mountains and Mount Washington, NH

Mount Desert Island, Acadia National Park, ME

Camden Harbor, Camden Hills State Park, ME

Connecticut pumpkins

BRAKE
FOR MOOSE
IT COULD SAVE
YOUR LIFE
HUNDREDS OF COLLISIO

Typical Maine road sign

For a while, the ruthless timber companies looked set to strip all northern New Hampshire bare. Although very few of the trees you see now are original growth, the loggers were brought under control when it became appreciated that the pristine landscape of the White Mountains might turn out to be the state's greatest asset. Indeed, large-scale summer tourism began in the latter half of the nineteenth century, when cityfolk checked into one of several dozen grand resort hotels (the *Mount Washington* in Bretton Woods and the *Balsams* in Dixville Notch are the only two that remain), which stood majestically at the foot of the mountains. The peaks' various passes – here called notches – have long since been penetrated by the convenience of paved roads, but early tourists relied upon the then-burgeoning rail network; at one stage, fifty trains brought travelers to the mountains daily to see such increasingly famous sites as the **Old Man of the Mountain**, now the ubiquitous state symbol. Many also rode the rickety **Cog Railway** (still operational) to the harsh and unpredictable summit of Mount Washington.

Tourism has now surpassed industry as the state's top money earner, but many long-time New Hampshire residents remain suspicious and unaccepting of outsiders. Long known as one of the most conservative states in New England, perhaps even in the nation, many New Hampshire residents retain the stubborn individualism and independent spirit of the original settlers, opting for a less intrusive government with fewer laws and regulations. There is no sales or even personal income tax here – in fulfilment of the state motto, "Live Free or Die." Alternative sources of revenue include meal, hotel, and hefty property taxes, in addition to state-owned liquor stores – set up after prohibition and enthusiastically promoted: they even have them in freeway rest areas.

New Hampshire has also gained inordinate political clout as the venue of the **first primary election of each presidential campaign**, with its villages well used to playing host to would-be presidents on the stump. The New Hampshire presidential primary is viewed by many as a make-or-break event, and since the first one in 1952 the state has picked the candidates eventually nominated by both the Democrats and the Republicans eleven out of thirteen times, although 2000 (in which New Hampshire Republicans picked John McCain by a wide margin over current president George W. Bush) was one of the off years. Though residents are ordinarily rather oblivious to celebrity and public attention, the presidential primary has become the state's quadrennial fifteen minutes of fame. When perpetual rival Vermont suggested that it might have its primary first, New Hampshire quickly passed a law stating that its primaries would be held "on the Tuesday preceding the date on which any other New England state shall hold a similar election."

THE SEACOAST REGION

New Hampshire's **coastline** stretches for just eighteen miles, the shortest of any US state with ocean access. Its sandy length, filling up the area between Hampton Beach on the south end and Portsmouth on the north, is well developed, but it's not difficult to find sparsely populated beaches.

Though separated by such a short distance, the two main coastal towns couldn't be less similar. **Portsmouth**, New Hampshire's resurgent cultural center, is bursting with well-preserved Colonial architecture, gourmet restaurants, and historic attractions; **Hampton Beach** is a sprawling arc of sand packed in summer with giggling teenagers and lined with a corresponding collection of arcades, ice-cream parlors, and waterslides. In between, sleepy towns – small collections of a few elegant white-clapboard buildings and some ill-placed strip malls, really – blend into each other, spilling into laid-back beaches, such as **Jenness State Beach**, **Wallis Sands State Beach**, and **Rye Beach**.

West of busy I-95 – situated three miles inland and the main thoroughfare up from Massachusetts – the density of attractions (and people) drops off sharply. The handsome and historically significant town of **Exeter**, with its shady streets lined with stately mansions, is home to the country's premier college preparatory school, Phillips Exeter Academy; to the north, **Durham** is centered around the University of New Hampshire's flagship campus.

Hampton Beach and around

It's difficult to understand why **HAMPTON BEACH** is so popular. The favorite vacation spot of many thousands of East Coasters, who gorge happily in the town's bad restaurants and pack themselves onto the crowded band of white sandy beach that stretches along the tacky strip, the town's ugly sprawl of cheaply constructed condominiums spreads across the flat, narrow peninsula that juts into the mouth of the Hampton River. It's a decidedly family-friendly resort, with plenty of arcades and waterparks to keep youngsters happy for days, but that aside there aren't many good reasons to stop here, unless you enjoy watching sunburnt vacationers waddle from hot dog stand to ice-cream shop to the beach and back again. One bright spot is the well-known *Hampton Beach Casino Ballroom*, a large performance venue right along the strip at 169 Ocean Blvd (call ☎603/929-4100 for information; tickets $15–30). This is the top choice for touring performers in the state, hosting nationally known rock bands and comedians. If you absolutely must **stay** here, the **Hampton Beach Chamber of Commerce** (☎603/926-8717 or 1-800/438-2826, *www.hamptonbeach.com*) will help with room reservations. If you're **hungry**, you could stop at *Jack's Seafood*, 539 Ocean Blvd (☎603/926-0444), for lobster "in the rough" and other seacoast specialties, but keep your expectations moderate.

The beach is more pleasant a few miles north along Route 1A at **NORTH HAMPTON BEACH**, a more peaceful stretch of sand with abundant metered parking – though it still catches a bit of the slough from Hampton Beach. If you're in the area, you might also stop by the colorful **Fuller Gardens** (mid-May to mid-Oct daily 10am–6pm; $4), at the junction of Route 1A and Route 111. Designed in 1939 for Massachusetts governor Alvin Fuller, the gardens include over 2000 rose bushes and a Japanese section complete with bonsai trees.

Continuing north, Route 1A winds along a picturesque strip of rocky coastline that includes "millionaires' row," where a collection of stately homes greets the ocean from enormous bay windows. There's a paved **walking path** along the water if you decide you'd like to take in the finely restored private oceanfront mansions at a more leisurely pace. In **RYE HARBOR**, at the State Marina, you can go **whale-watching** with New Hampshire Seacoast Cruises (☎603/964-5545 or 1-800/964-5545; $20; call for departure times). Popular with surfers and families alike, **Jenness State Beach**, a little further north along Route 1A, is even more serene, with few buildings and a protected stretch of white sand. Nearby **Wallis Sands State Beach** is also a good bet for swimming and sunning.

North towards Portsmouth

The mouth of the Piscataqua River along Route 1A, **Odiorne Point State Park** (☎603/436-7406; $2.50) marks the site of New Hampshire's first settlement, established in 1623 but vacated shortly after in favor of what is now Portsmouth. The park consists of some 330 acres of protected coastline with a well-maintained network of trails that includes a beautiful seaside bike path and picnic benches (see p.392 for information on bike rental). The park is also home to the **Seacoast Science Center**, 570 Ocean Blvd (daily 10am–5pm; $1), which presents a vaguely diverting array of science and natural history exhibits and has an indoor tide pool touch tank and a small aquarium.

Along the eastern shore on the island of **New Castle**, a wealthy suburb of Portsmouth, there are a couple of historically relevant forts. **Fort Constitution** (formerly Fort William and Mary), along Rte-1B at the mouth of Portsmouth Harbor, was the site of one of the first overt acts of rebellion against the British, when, at the urging of Paul Revere, angry colonists attacked, pilfering gunpowder and cannons from unsuspecting British soldiers. Only the base of the walls remains, however. Just south stands **Fort Stark,** active in every war from the Revolutionary War through World War II. You can make a self-guided tour of the ten-acre site, including parts of the remodeled fort, but the ocean views are more eye-catching.

SEABROOK NUCLEAR POWER STATION

Talk of a New England nuclear power plant began as early as the 1950s, but it wasn't until the energy crisis of the mid-1970s that legislators got serious. Construction of the **Seabrook nuclear power station**, with funding from First National Bank, began in 1976, and vocal **protest** followed soon after. What started as a grassroots campaign, however, exploded into a national debate about the safety and feasibility of nuclear power. The construction spawned an outburst of vocal environmental groups, most notably the so-called **Clamshell Alliance**, which by the early 1980s had thousands of members. New Hampshire residents and politicians – including then-governor John Sununu – generally supported the construction, seeing it as a long-term energy saver, while residents of neighboring Massachusetts and their governor, Michael Dukakis, fearing negative environmental impacts, remained staunchly opposed. Even ice-cream maker **Ben and Jerry's** out in Vermont got involved in the fray, erecting a billboard in Boston that read "Stop Seabrook. Keep our customers alive and licking." Nevertheless, construction continued, and in 1990, after four years of testing and safety inspections, the nuclear plant began producing power. In the process, as expenses ballooned a staggering $4 billion over budget, New Hampshire's largest utility, the Public Service Company of New Hampshire, went bankrupt. The station is now owned jointly by eleven utility companies, providing power for about one million New England homes, and spewing out more than 8 million megawatt hours of electricity per year. New Hampshire residents currently pay the highest electric rates in the country, roughly twice the national average.

One small consolation that accompanied Seabrook's construction was the opening of the **Science and Nature Center at Seabrook Station** (Mon–Fri 10am–4pm; free; ☎603/474-9521) on US-1 in Seabrook, where you can explore various rather bland exhibits about nuclear energy, electricity, and the environment, including displays of flora and fauna that populate the salt marshes nearby.

Portsmouth

Surprisingly attractive **PORTSMOUTH**, off of I-95 at the mouth of the Piscataqua River, blends small town accessibility with the enthusiasm of a rejuvenated city. Having endured the many cycles of prosperity and hardship typical of many New England colonial towns – including, most devastatingly, several major fires and the inevitable loss of its prominence as a port – Portsmouth has found its most recent triumphs in the cultural arena. Artists, musicians, writers, tourists, and, notably, gourmet chefs, attracted by Portsmouth's affordability, authentic colonial flavor, and youthful exuberance, have converged on the quaint seaside town in recent years, paving the way for the yuppies who now populate the town's streets with their BMWs and modern brewpubs.

Optimistic residents will volunteer unprompted that Portsmouth was named one of the top ten places to live in the US by *Money* magazine – and the magazine's claims aren't easily refuted. Though racially monotonous, the town is exceptionally young (the average age is 24); it boasts a good-looking town center, a famous wealth of good restaurants, clean, uncongested streets, an inviting riverside park, and an unusual abundance of well-preserved colonial buildings – not to mention some excellent bed-and-breakfasts.

Some history

Founded in the 1620s by English merchants hoping to turn a quick profit in the fur and fish trade, Portsmouth was, after Jamestown, the second New World commercial settlement of any size. Though initial efforts faltered with the death of leader John Mason in 1635, the immigrants soon established Portsmouth as a premier **seaport**, with thriving **shipbuilding** and commercial **fishing** industries. Demand for manual labor at the busy port was high, and religious dissenters and common criminals from Puritan Massachusetts fled to Portsmouth during its early years, prompting complaints that the settlement attracted, and even welcomed, "desperately wicked" characters. With an abundance of timber in the surrounding regions, which was easily transported along the fast-flowing Piscataqua River, the prosperous shipyards produced enormous masts, entire trading vessels, and warships more cheaply than their British counterparts, and Portsmouth's boats were soon carrying goods – and fighting wars – all over the world.

As industry flourished, so did a well-heeled aristocratic class of merchants and ship captains, who constructed many of the fine eighteenth-century mansions and commercial buildings that remain prominent in the town today. However, the city's golden age peaked in 1800, after which the combination of the 1807 Embargo Act, the War of 1812, and three devastating **fires** plunged the city into decline.

Portsmouth went on to become a major center for **beer and ale** production after the Civil War, when the brick buildings along Market Street all housed breweries – though this industry, too, was to practically disappear half a century later with the onset of Prohibition. By the turn of the twentieth century, the **Portsmouth Naval Shipyard**, founded in 1800 by John Paul Jones as the US government's first shipyard (and still active, just across the Piscataqua River), had become the area's largest employer. As a result, Portsmouth became notorious as a seedy port of call, complete with a busy **red-light district**, a skyrocketing crime rate, and a raucous assortment of grungy taverns.

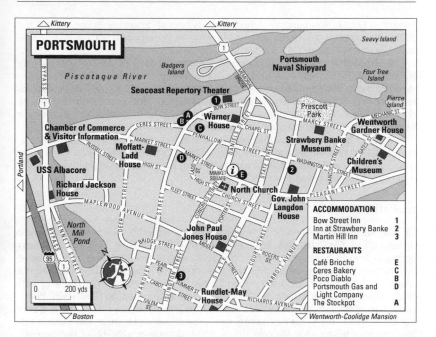

After angry citizens drove the revelers and prostitutes from their city in the early part of this century, Portsmouth settled into a long period of stagnation, still heavily dependent on the government-sponsored shipyard for its well-being. It wasn't until the 1950s that the city began to actively preserve and restore its colorful colonial past, as citizens organized to save the area now known as the "Strawbery Banke Museum" from demolition. Their efforts were largely successful, and today Portsmouth remains one of the best-preserved colonial towns in New England.

Arrival and information

Portsmouth's city center is huddled along the southern bank of the **Piscataqua River**, at the mouth of one of the finest natural harbors on the east coast, just across from Kittery, Maine. Surrounded by water on three sides (South Mill Pond, North Mill Pond, and the Piscataqua), the town is compact and easily manageable on foot. At its heart, **Market Square** is flanked by the towering North Church, an easily located landmark.

Portsmouth is surprisingly accessible via **public transport**, with three companies providing **bus services** to and from the city. C&J Trailways (☎1-800/258-7111) offers frequent daily service from Boston, Newburyport (MA), and Dover (NH) to their stop at the Pease International Tradeport off of Route 16 (you'll have to take a taxi into the city center for roughly $5). Vermont Transit Lines (☎603/436-0163) runs buses five times daily along the coast between Boston and Bar Harbor (ME), stopping in Portsmouth at the Federal Cigar Store, 1 Market

Square. COAST (Cooperative Alliance for Seacoast Transportation; ☎603/862-2328) also stops at the Cigar Store and connects Portsmouth with smaller cities in the Seacoast region.

The **Greater Portsmouth Chamber of Commerce**, 500 Market St (Mon–Fri 8.30am–5pm, plus Sat & Sun 11am–4pm in summer; ☎603/436-3988, *www .portcity.org*), a fifteen-minute walk from Market Square at 500 Market St, houses an enormous collection of brochures and can help you find a room, although your choices will be limited to chamber members. They also operate an information **kiosk** in Market Square during the summer (daily 9am–5pm).

For **travel books, guides, and maps**, you can't do much better than Gulliver's, downstairs at 7 Commercial Alley near Market Square (☎603/431-5556, *www .gulliversbooks.com*), which has an extensive local travel section in addition to titles covering most parts of the world.

Getting around

By **car**, the easiest way to reach downtown Portsmouth is via exit 7 (Market Street) off of **I-95**. **Rte-1A**, which becomes Miller Avenue, and **US-1**, which becomes Middle Street, both pass directly through the city center and continue into Kittery (ME), across the Memorial Bridge. **Parking** near the waterfront is scarce in the summer; there's a public garage at the intersection of Hanover and High streets. You can usually find non-metered parking next to South Mill Pond, along Parrot Avenue, a short walk from Market Square. If you want to **rent a car**, National (☎603/431-4707) has an office on the outskirts of town at 155 Mirona Rd. You can rent **bikes** from Bicycle Bob's, 990 Lafayette St (Rte-1), in Portsmouth (☎603/436-2453) – $25 a day.

The **Coast Trolley** (Mon–Sat 6am–10.30pm; ☎603/427-5091; $1) runs in a small loop around the city, stopping at most attractions to pick up and drop off visitors. It makes for a good way to get an overview of what sites the city has to offer. The **Seacoast Trolley** (☎603/431-6975; $2 all day, $4 for hour-long narrated tours) links historic Portsmouth with several beaches, shopping malls, and local sights, and stops at Market Square hourly.

Several companies run **cruises** of varying lengths in Portsmouth Harbor and beyond. Portsmouth Harbor Cruises, at the Ceres Street Dock (☎603/436-8084 or 1-800/776-0915, *www.portsmouthharbor.com*; harbor cruise $12, 90min; Isles of Shoals $16, 150min; evening cruise $8.50, 60min; call for departure times), features several trips, including hour-long evening and sunset journeys, and has a full bar aboard every boat. The Isles of Shoals Steamship Company, nearby at 315 Market St (☎603/431-5500 or 1-800/441-4620, *www.islesofshoals.com*), offers similar trips, including a $20 journey to the Isles of Shoals, with three hours on Star Island. With both companies, you need to call to make reservations, or to buy your tickets well in advance, to guarantee a spot. If you'd rather see the coastline up close, Atlantic Exposure Kayaking (☎603/772-4433 for information and reservations; $55) runs two three-hour trips daily from Pierce Island near Strawbery Banke.

Accommodation

As might be expected, **accommodation** in and around Portsmouth's historic district can be expensive – in high season on weekends you'll likely pay $100 or more for a good room in a bed-and-breakfast. A collection of slightly cheaper – and less pleasant – **motels** can be found at the traffic circle where I-95, the Route 1 bypass, and Routes 4 and 16 intersect. If you can afford it, staying in a restored old bed-and-breakfast is well worth the extra cash. Call ahead to reserve a room on summer weekends or holidays and be aware that prices can go up by as much as forty percent during high season; midweek accommodations can also be considerably less expensive. **Camping** in the area is limited to crowded RV-type parks, such as the *Shel-Al Camping Area*, US-1, North Hampton (☎603/964-5730; $12), *Tidewater Campground*, US-1, Hampton (☎603/926-5474; $23), and the *Wakeda Campground*, Rte-88, Hampton Falls (☎603/772-5274; $17).

In town

Bow Street Inn, 121 Bow St (☎603/431-7760). Portsmouth's only waterfront inn is centrally located and comfortable. The ten cozy rooms occupy a remodeled brick brewery; two rooms offer full harbor views. Continental breakfast included. ⑥.

Inn at Christian Shore, 335 Maplewood Ave (☎603/431-6770). Early-1800s Federal-style house with six rooms full of tasteful antique furnishings, and big, tasty gourmet breakfasts. ④–⑤.

Inn at Strawbery Banke, 314 Court St (☎1-800/428-3933 or 603/436-7242). The most central of Portsmouth's bed-and-breakfasts, in a sumptuous old colonial home near the waterfront. Reservations strongly recommended. ⑤.

Martin Hill Inn, 404 Islington St (☎603/436-2287, *www.bbhost.com/martinhillinn*). Meticulously furnished nineteenth-century house with seven guest rooms and a shaded garden within walking distance of the city center. Excellent full breakfast and helpful innkeepers. ⑤–⑥.

Oracle House Inn, 38 Marcy St (☎603/433-8827). Painstakingly restored 1702 home located just outside Strawbery Banke with period furniture and views of Prescott Park. Breakfast included. ⑥.

Sise Inn, 40 Court St (☎603/433-1200). One of the larger inns in Portsmouth, with phones and televisions in 34 elegantly appointed luxurious rooms and a Queen Anne-style exterior. The breakfast is a delicious self-serve buffet. ⑤–⑥.

Near the traffic circle

Anchorage Inn, 417 Woodbury Ave (☎603/431-8111 or 1-800/370-8111). A large and comfortable modern hotel with 93 rooms, an indoor pool, sauna, and whirlpool. ④.

Fairfield Inn, 650 Borthwick Ave (☎603/436-6363). Independent hotel that was formerly a Susse Chalet, and still has all you'd expect of a modern hotel – clean, basic rooms with cable TV and phones, and an outdoor pool. Children under 18 stay free with parents. ④.

Port Motor Inn, Route 1 Bypass South (☎603/436-4378 or 1-800/282-PORT). These simple rooms, some with microwaves and refrigerators, are (depending on the season and day) among the cheapest in Portsmouth. ④

The Town

Market Square, where Daniel, Pleasant, Congress, and Market streets converge, has been Portsmouth's commercial center since the mid-1700s. Once a military training site, the brick-dominated square is now surrounded by a bustling assortment of cafés and gift shops. Despite the upscale shopping, the square maintains an unpretentious, lived-in feel – almost everywhere you turn, evidence of the town's history reveals itself in the architecture of old brick buildings like the **Athenaeum**, 9 Market Square (open to the public Thurs 1–4pm; ☎603/431-2538), one of the oldest private libraries in the country. The 1854 **North Church**, also constructed with bricks, flanks the southwest side of the square, and its towering spire makes it the tallest building you'll see in town. It's the best spot to get oriented and begin your wanderings; in fact, this is where you pick up the informative **Portsmouth Harbor Trail** walking-tour guide and map (call ☎603/436-1118 for information; free), a series of three well-detailed walks tracing the city's history that originate in the square.

If you are around on the second Saturday of June, it is pretty tough to miss **Market Square Day** (☎603/431-5388 for information), when the streets are closed to traffic so that craft booths, musical entertainment, good food, and over 30,000 pedestrians can fill them up. For a scaled-down version, check out the **Portsmouth Marketplace** (☎603/431-4333 for information), where artisans sell their works and local restaurants showcase their food every summer weekend in the parking lot adjacent to Eagle Photo.

Market Street

Scanning the chic boutiques and fashionable restaurants that line **Market Street**, it's hard to believe the brick buildings that house them were once occupied by breweries. In the late nineteenth century, when Portsmouth's **beer and ale industry** was booming, Frank Jones, its most famous brewer and founder of the Portsmouth Brewery Company, created and brewed what was once considered to be the best beer in the States here – aptly named "Frank Jones Ale." Jones and his competitors were shut down during Prohibition and never recovered. The company's old brick warehouse, at 125 Bow St, was transformed in 1979 into a theater (see p.399), presenting mostly mainstream plays and musicals. You can learn more about Jones and Portsmouth's brewing history and get drunk on modern microbrews from all over New England during the **Grand Old Portsmouth Brewers Festival**, held the last weekend in September at the Strawbery Banke Museum (see overleaf; admission to the festival is $5).

Of the striking selection of grand old timber mansions in Portsmouth, the **Moffatt-Ladd House**, 154 Market St (mid-June to mid-Oct Mon–Sat 11am–5pm, Sun 1–5pm; $5), is one of the most impressive. Completed in 1763, after no less than 467 days of construction, the house is particularly notable for its Great Hall, which occupies more than a quarter of the first floor. Using inventories left by Captain John Moffatt, who designed the home and later monitored his lucrative shipping business from an office on the second floor, historians have transformed the Yellow Chamber (also on the second floor) into one of the best-documented eighteenth-century American rooms. Portraits of past occupants by artists such as Gilbert Stewart hang throughout the home and include a painting of William Whipple, who signed the Declaration of Independence and lived here in the late eighteenth century. For information on other historic homes that are open to the public, see p.396.

Further up Market Street, next to the salt piles along the river, is the departure point for **harbor cruises** and for boats that take you to the **Isles of Shoals**, a summer meeting place for many well-known writers of the nineteenth century, including Nathaniel Hawthorne and Annie Fields, ten miles off the coast. See p.392 for more details.

Still further along Market Street, at no. 600, you'll find the **USS Albacore Park and Port of Portsmouth Maritime Museum** (May to mid-Oct 9.30am–5.30pm; rest of year 9.30am–4pm; $5), a worthwhile diversion highlighted by the 205-foot, 1200-ton **submarine**. Built in 1952, it was then the fastest electric/diesel submarine in the world. Tours of the underwater vessel offer glimpses of the cockpit, cramped living quarters, and the engine room.

Marcy Street and the Strawbery Banke Museum

At the other end of the historic district, along the river and adjacent to the Strawbery Banke Museum, is beautiful **Prescott Park**, 105 Marcy St (☎603/431-8748 for information), a welcoming expanse of grass and shrubbery that slopes gently toward the water's edge. Featuring free music and entertainment throughout the summer, the park is immaculately maintained – especially the colorful All-American Show Garden – and is a great spot for a picnic or afternoon nap. You could also check out the **Sheafe Warehouse Museum**, which houses a mildly engaging free collection of mostly nautical ephemera. The **Point of Graves cemetery**, a creepy plot of crumbling headstones on the southeast corner of Mechanic Street near the bridge to Pierce Island, is the oldest in the city – the oldest headstone dates from 1682.

Though you'd never suspect it now, **Marcy Street**, which borders the park on its west side, was once home to a strip of notorious brothels, patronized by sailors from across the river. A source of town shame, and with an international reputation, the street's name was changed from Water to Marcy in the early 1900s, after prostitution had subsided. Few reminders of those days are left, but the otherwise undistinguished home of one of Portsmouth's most prominent madames, **Alta Roberts**, who greeted her customers with a mouthful of gold teeth, still stands at 57 Marcy St. Somewhat ironically, the **Children's Museum of Portsmouth**, with hands-on exhibits that investigate a range of diverse topics, such as anatomy, lobstering, sound, and earthquakes, is close by at 280 Marcy St (summer Mon–Sat 10am–5pm, Sun 1–5pm; closed Mon rest of year; $4).

Although historic buildings can be found all over Portsmouth, for a more concentrated look at American architecture over the last three centuries, pay a visit to the **Strawbery Banke Museum** 64 Marcy St (mid-April–Oct daily 10am–5pm; $12 adults, $8 kids under 18; tickets good for two consecutive days; *www.strawberybanke.org*), a fenced-off ten-acre neighborhood that takes in a collection of meticulously restored and maintained old wooden buildings. This area began life as the home of wealthy shipbuilders and was successively the lair of privateers and a red-light district before turning into a respectable – and, in the 1950s, decaying – suburbia. It was decided to re-create its former appearance, mainly by clearing away the newer buildings (only two of the houses on display had to be moved here). A few people still live here, tucked away on the upper floors, but the complex really serves as a living museum that you can explore either on a guided tour or at your own whim; in either case, several of the houses have well-informed attendants.

Each building is shown in its most interesting former incarnation, whether that be 1695 or 1955; in the **Drisco House**, the first you come to, each individual room dates from a different era. The 1766 **Pitt Tavern** holds the most historic significance, having acted as a meeting place during the Revolution for patriots and loyalists (it still functions as a Masonic lodge – one of the four oldest in the US – which explains why you can't go upstairs). Tiny glasses remind you that its clientele drank gin rather than beer. The museum also contains the boyhood home of novelist **Thomas Bailey Aldrich** (1836–1907), which he depicted in his most famous novel, *The Story of a Bad Boy*.

Although you may have to struggle to keep ahead of school groups, Strawbery Banke continues to host serious academic research. Traditional crafts are studied and practiced here; in the **Dinsmore Shop**, an infinitely patient cooper manufactures barrels with the tools and methods of 1800. The **Mils Zoldak pottery shop**,

PORTSMOUTH'S HISTORIC HOMES

Beyond the walls of Strawbery Banke, Portsmouth is home to an uncharacteristi-cally large offering of painstakingly restored **Colonial homes**, which, during the summer, are open to the public. Almost as impressive as the buildings themselves is the unrelenting resolve of the people who devote their lives to the structures' impossibly finicky restoration, with attention given even down to the exact pattern and dye-type used in eighteenth-century wallpapers. The hourly tours, led by schol-ars full of arcane knowledge and stories, can be fascinating, although after one or two, you will have probably had your fill. Most cost $5 and last about an hour. A group called the Historic Associates publishes an informative **free walking-tour guide** to the historic homes, available at the Chamber of Commerce.

Governor John Langdon House, 143 Pleasant St (June to mid-Oct Wed–Sun 11am–5pm; $5; ☎603/436-3205). Three-term governor, New Hampshire Senate president, and delegate to the 1787 Constitutional Convention John Langdon and his wife, Elizabeth, hosted many big-name visitors here, including George Washington. The home, constructed in 1784 with particular attention to interior detailing and woodwork, is in every way a tribute to his afflu-ence and influence.

John Paul Jones House, 43 Middle St (mid-May to mid-Oct Mon–Sat 10am–4pm, Sun noon–4pm; $5; ☎603/436-8420). Home to the Portsmouth Historical Society's museum, this 1761 Georgian structure was where John Paul Jones, the US' first great naval com-mander, stayed while his ships, the *Ranger* and the *America,* were being outfitted in the Langdon shipyards. Inside the boxy yellow structure – featured in Sears paint commercials – you can view some of his naval memorabilia and period-furnished rooms.

Rundlet-May House, 364 Middle St (June–mid-Oct Sat & Sun 11am–5pm; $5; ☎603/433-2494). Wealthy merchant-importer James Rundlet had this symmetrical Neoclassical man-sion built in 1807, when he was 35 years old. The walls are adorned with imported English wallpaper and the rooms filled with a fine collection of Federal period furniture – most built by local craftsmen. Notable features include an indoor well and an early coal-fired heating system.

Warner House, 150 Daniel St (June–Oct Tues–Sat 10am–4pm, Sun 1–4pm; $5; ☎603/436-5909). Built for local merchant and shipowner Captain Archibald MacPhaedris in 1716, the Warner House was one of the first buildings in America to be designated a national historic landmark – and examining its laundry list of other "firsts," it's not hard to see why: it was the first brick house constructed in the state; it contains New Hampshire's oldest murals, painted on the staircase wall; and the murals contain some of the earliest known images of Native Americans. Additionally, Benjamin Franklin is said to have installed the lightning rod on the west wall.

Wentworth-Coolidge Mansion, 375 Little Harbor Rd, off of Rte-1A (May–Oct Tues & Thurs–Sat 10am–3pm, Sun noon–5pm; admission and tour $2.50; ☎603/436-6607). Home to Royal Governor Benning Wentworth, who was in office from 1741 to 1766, this massive 42-room, mustard-yellow mansion hosted the Royal Council meetings of the earliest New Hampshire state government. The rambling mansion, which is beautifully situated on an isolated plot overlooking Little Harbor, now hosts occasional concerts and classes during the summer. It is not furnished, but the wallpaper in several of the rooms is original (though faded), and there are some original Wentworth items on display – among them some fancy imported Chinese porcelain.

Wentworth-Gardner House, 50 Mechanic St (mid-June to mid-Oct Tues–Sun 1–4pm; $5; ☎603/436-4406). Painstakingly restored, and complete with a gray blocked facade, this house is considered one of the finest examples of Georgian architecture in America. The 1760 home was given by Madam Mark Hunking to her son Thomas Wentworth, nephew of Benning. Her other son, John, was the last royal governor of the province of New Hampshire.

open year-round, produces attractive low-priced ceramics. The museum opens its gates after 5pm, and you can wander around for free and observe the building's exteriors in the waning hours of the day (though it's hardly the same experience).

If you've had your fill of historic houses and are looking for something a bit less serious, try vampire hunting with **Ghostly Tours** (June 20–Sept 4 8pm; Sept 5–Oct 31 7pm; ☎603/433-8888, *www.ghostlytours.com*), which offers walking candlelit tours through town, while the guides share various maudlin lore from these parts. One shouldn't take this tour expecting to come across hard historical information, but it can be fun; reservations are recommended.

Eating

Portsmouth likes to bill itself as the "food capital of New England," and while this may be an exaggeration, there are undoubtedly plenty of good spots in town to grab an excellent – even gourmet – meal. Portsmouth's **restaurants** include both expensive high-brow **bistros** and cheap, down-to-earth **cafés**. You can still stretch your culinary dollar quite a long way in this town, although the recent surge in tourism is already effecting menu prices at the most well-known spots. There is a particularly high concentration of places to eat along Ceres Street and Bow Street, and you should treat yourself to at least one waterfront meal at one of the outdoor patios or decks that line the Piscataqua River.

Budget

Annabelle's Natural Ice Cream and Yogurt, 49 Ceres St (☎603/436-3400). Packed on warm summer nights with hungry patrons, and for good reason – this local institution serves up the best (and most creative) ice-cream flavors around. The peanut butter fantasy and the mocha mud pie are both outstanding.

Café Brioche, 14 Market Square (☎603/430-9225). A good selection of pastries, sandwiches, and gourmet coffees, with outdoor seating right in the center of town. Perfect for a relaxing afternoon tea.

Celebrity Sandwich, 171 Islington St (☎603/433-2277). Great, enormous deli sandwiches (all named after celebrities, though only a few, such as the "David Letterman ham sandwich," make much sense) with cheap daily specials and a few tables.

Ceres Bakery, 51 Penhallow St (☎603/436-6518). Excellent fresh breads and an assortment of fine pastries behind a bright blue exterior.

The Friendly Toast, 121 Congress St (☎603/430-2154). Kitschy thrift-store decor with an interesting selection of sandwiches and omelettes, a huge drink menu that includes mixed drinks, shakes, and coffees, and an equally eclectic crowd. The portions are enormous – try Matt's Sandwich, with black beans, avocado, and cheese. Open 24hr on weekends, 7am–midnight during the week.

The Stockpot, 53 Bow St (☎603/431-1851). Reasonably priced hearty American food, including bulging sandwiches, salads, burgers, and lobster, with a superb view of the Piscataqua and a popular outdoor seating area.

Moderate to expensive

Anthony Alberto's, 59 Penhallow St (☎603/436-4000). Excellent, cozy Italian restaurant, frequent recipient of *Yankee Travel* and *Wine Spectator* awards. Try the *fettucine con gamberetti*, or ask for the homemade ravioli of the day.

BG's Boathouse, 191 Wentworth Rd, take Route 1A south to 1B (☎603/431-1074). A basic but good seafood restaurant – featuring lobster, clams, and oysters – that is popular with locals. Along the river, south of the town center.

Blue Mermaid, Hanover and High St (☎603/427-BLUE). Lunch is a bargain at this real wood-burning grill, with a selection of pizzas burgers, and quesadillas, most under $8. For the more pricey dinners (still reasonable at $12–20), there's fresh seafood with your choice of sauce and a mouth-watering array of tapas.

Cafe Mediterraneo, 152 Fleet St (☎603/427-5563). Reasonably priced (entrees are $7–15) authentic, fresh, and delicious southern Italian meals near Market Square.

Dunfey's Aboard the John Wanamaker, 1 Harbor Place Marina, beside Memorial Bridge (☎603/433-3111). American cuisine, but best known for their freshly prepared seafood dishes, such as grilled marinated salmon, served aboard a floating, previously fully operational steam tugboat. Dinner entrees from $18. Closed Sun & Mon during winter.

Karen's Restaurant, 105 Daniel St (☎603/431-1948). A cute and unpretentious tiny restaurant, serving heaping home-cooked portions of creative American *nouvelle cuisine*. Try the warm noodle salad with Thai coconut curry. Breakfast and lunch daily, dinner Thurs–Sat 5.30–9pm.

Lindbergh's Crossing Bistro and Wine Bar, 29 Ceres St (☎603/431-0887). One of Portsmouth's newer eateries is fast becoming one of the most popular. The creative French cuisine is expensive – around $19 per entree – but worth it. The almond-crusted halibut over warm salad niçoise is particularly delicious.

The Oar House, 55 Ceres St (☎603/436-4025). One of Portsmouth's several slightly old-fashioned gourmet standbys, serving standard seafood and grilled meat entrees for around $18. There's a great deck outside.

Portsmouth Gas Light Co, 64 Market St (☎603/430-8582, *www.gaslightco.com*). Portsmouth's favorite pizza joint, with a wide selection of brick-oven pizzas that includes the "Strawbery Banke," a bizarre but tasty combination of tomato, teriyaki chicken, crushed pineapple, sliced almonds, and mozzarella cheese. All-you-can-eat pizza special for $6.50, weekdays 11.30 am–2 pm.

The Rosa Restaurant, 80 State St (☎603/436-9715, *www.therosa.com*). Longstanding straightforward Italian dining in an intimate, friendly setting. Most dishes, including the delicious Chicken Rosa, a lightly breaded chicken breast sautéed in garlic over fresh pasta, go for $8–16.

Sakura, 40 Pleasant St (☎603/431-2721, *www.sakuranh.com*). The best Japanese restaurant in the area, with fresh sushi, sashimi, tempura, and teriyaki. Try the chirashi rice bowl for $16. You can dine at the bar or at a table.

Drinking, entertainment, and nightlife

Despite its size, Portsmouth's **social scene** can be pretty stimulating. Although the place tends to shut down well before midnight, on summer weekends the streets – particularly around **Market Square** and along **Bow Street** and **Ceres Street** – are full of well-dressed couples, noisy high school kids, tattooed slackers, and fun-seeking tourists. The city is home to several vibrant **cafés**, a host of well-attended **bars**, and its several **live music** venues present a diverse range of bands – from punk to folk to jazz. The *Portsmouth Herald*, prints an exhaustive **entertainment** supplement every Thursday, while the town's other newspaper, *Foster's Daily Democrat*, prints entertainment listings more sporadically. The monthly *Portfolio* magazine (*www.seacoastnh.com/arts/portfolio*) focuses exclusively on New Hampshire Seacoast art, theater, music, and literature, and has a lengthy events calendar.

Breaking New Grounds, 16 Market St (☎603/436-9555). This friendly coffee shop is more low-key than its neighbor across the street, *Café Brioche* (see above). Grab an excellent cup of freshly ground coffee and relax with a book or a friend at one of several indoor tables.

The Elvis Room, 142 Congress St (☎603/436-9189, *www.spwa.com/elvisroom*). The outlandish interior at this fun coffee bar-cum-bar is complete with a cheesy oil painting of Mick Jagger. The club presents loud local and nationally touring college/punk rock almost every night for $4–10.

The Music Hall, 28 Chestnut St (☎603/436-2400). Boasting some 900 seats, Portsmouth's largest performance space hosts well-known nationally touring folk, rock, jazz, and blues bands, classical concerts, plus dance, theater, and other performances throughout the year.

Poco Diablo, 37 Bow St (☎603/430-9122). The passable food is typical Mexican fare, but the real reason to come here is for great margaritas (and perhaps a plate of nachos) on the riverfront patio.

Portsmouth Brewery, 56 Market St (☎603/431-1115). A typical microbrew pub, with attractive wood paneling, extensive pizza and burger menu, visible beer tanks, towering ceilings, and a rowdy young crowd. But the beer here is exceptional; don't miss the Old Brown Dog. Open until 1am nightly with occasional live music.

Press Room, 77 Daniel St (☎603/431-5186). Popular for its nightly live jazz, blues, folk, and bluegrass performances, which feature local and national talents. Also serves inexpensive salads, sandwiches, and soups in a casual pub-style setting.

Seacoast Repertory Theatre, 125 Bow St (☎603/433-4472 or 1-800/639-7650). Portsmouth's major performing arts theater, in a converted brewery, presents mainstream professional stage productions, such as *Joseph and the Amazing Technicolor Dreamcoat*, the *Rocky Horror Show*, and *Grease*.

Around Portsmouth

Inland from Portsmouth, the area between I-95 and Rte-125 has a few notable cities, namely **Exeter**, **Durham**, and **Dover**, although aside from Exeter's Colonial charm and historic architecture, there's really not much to see here. With most of the tourists heading the opposite way toward Hampton Beach and Portsmouth, however, the region's small towns and deserted backcountry roads can be refreshing.

Exeter

Situated just eight miles west of the Atlantic down Rte-101 from Portsmouth, along the banks of the Squamscott River, friendly **EXETER** was settled in 1638 by a rebellious Bostonian preacher, the Rev John Wheelwright. With an abundance of timber, Exeter, like other coastal New Hampshire towns, thrived in the eighteenth century, selling masts and lumber to both local and English shipbuilders. It became the state capital in 1775 (the Revolution was fast approaching, and Portsmouth, the previous capital, was too Loyalist), and by early 1776, the provincial congress had signed a state constitution, making New Hampshire the first state to formally declare its independence from England. Its tree-shaded avenues and stately old neighborhood architecture make the charming town worth a stop, if only for a couple of hours. There are a couple of excellent old inns near the town center, making it a good base from which to explore the coast.

The Town

Phillips Exeter Academy, one of the top college preparatory schools in the United States, occupies a large portion of the attractive town center, its heavy-set regal brick buildings sprawling over several acres of well-manicured lawns. Founded in 1781 by Dr John Phillips, the school counts among its long list of prominent alumni the great orator Daniel Webster (see p.428). Along Front Street (Rte-111), near Elm Street south of the center of town, the school's boxy brick **library**, featured in many architecture textbooks, was designed by architect Louis Kahn in 1971. Though the building's exterior is rather plain, inside, the space is both practical and inviting – each symmetrical floor looks out through a huge circular window into a naturally lit central atrium. You can get free **Internet access** here – just ask at the circulation desk. For a self-guided walking tour of the campus, stop by the admissions office (☎603/777-3433) on Front Street across from the Phillips Church.

The well-preserved Art Deco **Ioka Theater**, right in the center of town at 55 Water St, has been in continuous operation since it opened with a screening of *The Birth of a Nation* in 1915. It now shows middle-of-the-road Hollywood blockbusters (call ☎603/772-2222 for listings), though you can usually take a peek inside during off hours. A hundred yards down the street, in the center of the traffic circle, the **Swasey Pavilion**, a prominent circular bandstand, was designed by Henry Bacon, the architect of the Lincoln Memorial. The Exeter Brass Band, founded in 1847, still plays concerts in the bandstand during the summer. Exeter native Daniel Chester French, who sculpted the sternly seated Abe Lincoln inside the Lincoln Memorial, also created **Exeter's WWI Memorial**, in Gale Park on Front Street.

The **American Independence Museum**, in the Ladd-Gilman House at 1 Governors Lane, just north on Water Street (tours hourly, May 1–Oct 31 Wed–Sun noon–5pm; $5), houses an important, if slightly dull, collection of documents and artifacts investigating New Hampshire's role in the American Revolution, including the copy of the Declaration of Independence that was read to the Exeter townspeople by a fiery John Taylor Gilman, only 22 years old at the time. Gilman was a resident of the Ladd-Gilman House and later served fourteen years as governor of the state. The museum also has annotated draft copies of the US Constitution and a few oddities, including a ring containing a piece of George Washington's hair in a tiny glass case. Exeter stages the elaborate **Revolutionary War Festival** (☎603/772-2411 for details) every year during the third weekend in July, when the grounds of the museum are transformed into a militia encampment. During the event, some 10,000 people descend upon the town, many in full colonial militia garb; the vigor with which the battles and costumes are re-created is both frightening and fascinating – if you're in the area, don't miss it.

The **Gilman Garrison House**, at 12 Water St (Jun–mid-Oct Tue, Thur, Sat & Sun noon–5pm; $4), a massive seventeenth-century log cabin (clapboards have covered the logs), offers tours that reflect 300 years of Exeter's history through furniture, decorations, and narrative. The **Moses-Kent House Museum**, 1 Pine St (summer Thurs & Sat 1–4pm; $5; ☎603/772-2044), built in 1868 for Henry Moses, a local wool merchant, and later occupied by George Kent, who owned the Exeter Cotton Mill, retains its original furnishings and is open to the public. Its grounds were laid out by Frederick Law Olmsted, best known for designing New York City's Central Park.

Practicalities

There are several upscale **places to stay** in Exeter's town center, although the affluence of parents visiting their Exeter children keeps the rates relatively expensive. The *Inn by the Bandstand*, at 4 Front St in the center of town (☎603/772-3652 or 1-800/665-9335; [6]), is a lovingly restored Federal-style inn, constructed in 1809; many rooms have brick fireplaces. Down the road, the *Inn of Exeter*, 90 Front St (☎603/772-5901 or 1-800/782-8444, *www.exeterinn.com*; [6]), offers easygoing elegance and superior service in a three-story brick Georgian-style building. There's also a decent gourmet yet casual restaurant here that serves breakfast, lunch, and dinner. The *Governor Jeremiah Smith House Inn*, 41 Front St (☎603/778-7770; [5]), is a friendly bed-and-breakfast across from the Exeter campus with eight antique furnished rooms; a full breakfast is included. You can **camp** at the wooded *Exeter Elms Family Campground*, two miles south on Rte-108, 188 Court St (☎603/778-7631), for $18 per night.

While Exeter does not have any great wealth of good **places to eat**, there are a few affordable options worth noting. The *Green Bean on Water*, 33 Water St (closed Sun; ☎603/778-7585), serves cheap, fresh sandwiches on home-made bread and creatively prepared salads in a casual café with a walk-up counter and outdoor seating. The *Tavern at River's Edge*, 163 Water St (closed Sun; ☎603/772-7393), has a good range of international cuisine in a cozy, more formal Victorian dining room along the river. As its name suggests, *Penang and Tokyo,* 97 Water St (☎603/778-8388), offers well-prepared Malaysian and Japanese cuisine, something of a rarity in these parts. For pastries, fresh breads, light salads, coffee, and espresso, head to the *Baker's Peel*, at 231 Water St (☎603/778-0910). On the outskirts of town, *Fusco's Pizzeria*, 159 Front St (☎603/778-1666), is a family-run bare-bones pizza joint making tasty and quick pizzas. Well worth the ride, *Memories Ice Cream*, Rte-111, four miles outside of town in **Kingston** (☎603/642-3737), has a peaceful farm setting and delicious home-made ice cream.

Durham and Dover

Along US-4 northwest of Portsmouth, the University of New Hampshire's flagship campus dominates **DURHAM**, which was originally settled in 1635, and the university maintains the youthful exuberance of a typical college town during the school year. Between 1675 and the early eighteenth century, the town was the site of some of the worst Indian massacres in America. Commanded by the French, the natives attacked repeatedly and often, destroying homes and killing British settlers; a painting that hung in the Durham Post Office (☎603/868-2151) for many years depicted a Native American poised to set fire to a local garrison. With no other references to this rather bloody past, Durham's **Main Street** is a collection of used bookstores, such as the Durham Book Exchange, 36 Main St (☎603/868-1297), and cafés like the *Licker Store*, 44 Main St (☎603/868-1863), which serves coffee, ice cream, sandwiches, and baked goods. The campus' main **theater**, in the Paul Creative Arts Center (☎603/862-2290 for information), puts on several respectable productions each year.

DOVER, a former mill town just off of the Spaulding Turnpike (Rte-16) near the Maine border, was one of the first four cities to be established in the state. You might stop off for a meal at one of the several affordable **eateries** along its pleasant downtown strip – try *Firehouse One*, at 1 Orchard St (☎603/749-2220), which serves an interesting mix of seafood with an Asian emphasis. Otherwise, there's nothing to see here.

THE MERRIMACK VALLEY

The financial and political heartland of New Hampshire is the **Merrimack Valley**, which – first by water along the Merrimack River and now by road via I-93 – has always been the main thoroughfare north to the lakes, the White Mountains, and Quebec. First settled by the Penacook Indians, early pioneers had established a trading post near Concord by 1660, and by the 1720s large groups of Protestant Anglo-Saxons were calling the area home. In the nineteenth century, the valley was booming with industrialization and Nashua, Manchester, and Concord were all major manufacturing centers. **Concord** became the state's capital in 1784 and it remains the center of New Hampshire's political life – particularly evident during the quadrennial presidential primaries – while **Manchester** is the most populous city in the state, with ample evidence of its gritty industrial past.

Manchester

Although **MANCHESTER** is New Hampshire's largest city (population 102,000) and a major business hub, it does not hold much interest for visitors. Indeed, the Chamber of Commerce's tourist guide lists the city's proximity to everywhere else in the state as its major attraction, and aside from an excellent art museum, there is little to see here. The place is rugged and unmistakably urban, and, although town officials are constantly dreaming up new ways to revitalize the downtown and riverfront areas, most of these efforts reek more of desperation than genuine civic improvement.

Once a prosperous mill-town, Manchester has been in a perpetual state of recovery ever since the **Amoskeag Manufacturing Company** went belly-up here in 1935. From 1838 to 1920, the company was the world's largest textile manufacturer, employing 17,000 people at its peak – many of them women, dubbed "mill girls" – and spewing out over four million yards of cloth per week. The textile company, and the entire town of Manchester, for that matter, was the brainchild of a group of Boston entrepreneurs, who purchased 15,000 acres of land around the Amoskeag Falls, acquired the rights to water power along the entire length of the Merrimack River, built a dam, and constructed the enormous brick Amoskeag Mills in the early 1830s. The mills stretch for over a mile along the east side of the river and are equal in floor space to the entire World Trade Center. Once cutting-edge examples of manufacturing efficiency, they are now run-down and largely deserted – depressing reminders of the prosperity the city once enjoyed.

That isn't to say that the entire grouping of buildings remains dormant; a group of local businessmen bought the crumbling structures for $5 million, and the slow process of converting the mills into apartments, offices, classrooms, and retail space is well underway. Optimistic residents claim Manchester is going through a "renaissance" of sorts, and it's hard not to admire their gumption, but they're still a long way from restoring the booming prosperity of the early part of the century.

The City

It's impossible not to notice all the empty storefronts along Manchester's main commercial drag, **Elm Street**, which runs north–south along the Merrimack River and doubles as US-3. The **Amoskeag Mills** are several blocks west along the banks of the river between Bridge and Granite streets. You can get a good look at the mills, the **Amoskeag Dam**, and the city skyline from the **Amoskeag Falls Scenic Overlook** (mid-April–Oct daily 8am–6.30pm; free), along the river north of Bridge Street. For a more detailed exploration of the mills' history and architecture (as well as other parts of the city), take a **Heritage Walking Tour** (☎603/625-4827; $5), led by enthusiastic local historians.

As New Hampshire's best fine arts museum, the **Currier Gallery of Art**, just north of Bridge Street between Union and Beech streets at 201 Myrtle Way (Mon, Wed, Thur & Sun 11am–5pm, Fri 11am–8pm, Sat 10am–5pm; *www.currier.org*; $5, free Sat 10am–1pm), featuring works by such well-known European and American painters as Monet, O'Keeffe, Hopper, Matisse, and Wyeth, is well worth the stop. Notable paintings include Picasso's colorful *Spanish Woman Seated in a Chair*, from 1941, and Winslow Homer's straightforward watercolor *American in the Woods*. There's also a fair number of local paintings, such as Jasper Francis

Cropsey's glowing *American Indian Summer Morning in the White Mountains,* from 1857. The museum also maintains the **Zimmerman House** close by (Fri–Mon; tours $7; ☎603/626-4158), designed in 1950 by Frank Lloyd Wright. Tours of the house, a one-story wooden structure epitomizing Wright's vision of form in harmony with landscape, depart from the Currier Gallery.

West of the river, **West Manchester** is best known for its ethnic neighborhoods, most notably a large French-Canadian contingent, whose ancestors came in droves to work in the textile mills. Making up nearly forty percent of the population, there are still pockets of French speakers and the Franco American Centre, on the east side of the river at 52 Concord St (Mon–Fri 9am–4.30pm; free), is a leading source of information about French culture, heritage, and history in North America, with a small art gallery. The town also features considerable Greek, Polish, Italian, and Turkish populations.

Practicalities

The **Greater Manchester Chamber of Commerce**, 889 Elm St (☎603/666-666, *www.manchester-chamber.org*), has brochures and the like, though you're unlikely to find any of them much use while in town. The city is one of New Hampshire's few transportation hubs, and **getting around** in the city itself is not particularly difficult. The **Manchester Transit Authority** (☎603/623-8801) runs an extensive network of buses all over town.

From the **Manchester Transportation Center**, 119 Canal St at Granite Street (☎603/668-6133), you can get just about anywhere in the state – and beyond. Peter Pan Trailways (☎413/781-3320 or 1-800/343-9999), Concord Trailways (☎1-800/639-3317), and Vermont Transit Lines (☎1-800/552-8737 or 802/864-6811) all offer frequent bus services to Boston and places further afield. **Manchester Airport** (☎603/624-6556), off of Rte-3A, is served by Air Canada, American Eagle, Delta, Continental, Metro Jet, Northwest, Southwest, United, and US Airways. Many of the major **car rental** companies have offices at the airport.

With little tourism to speak of, the city's few **hotels** count the infrequent presidential primary as their major source of business. You might try the *Rice Hamilton*, 123 Pleasant St (☎603/627-7281; [4]), which has surprisingly well-kept, spacious rooms with kitchens in a run-down brick boarding house, or the *Susse Chalet Inn*, at 860 S Porter St (☎603/625-2020 or 1-800/258-1980; [4]), a fairly standard but quite clean and adequate place for a night's sleep. Most of the politicos stay at the centrally located *Holiday Inn*, 700 Elm St (☎603/625-1000 or 1-800/465-4329; [6]), which becomes a media circus during the primary. The *Derryfield Bed and Breakfast*, 1081 Bridge St (☎603/627-2082; [4]), has three quiet, affordable rooms and great breakfasts. You can **camp** at the family-oriented *Calef Lake Camping*, thirteen minutes outside of town off of Rte-121 in Auburn, 593 Chester Rd (☎603/483-8282; $17).

Manchester does not boast any great wealth of **restaurants** either, although there are a couple of note. Local institution *Red Arrow Lunch*, at 61 Lowell St (☎603/626-1118), is a greasy diner open 24hr and usually filled with talkative patrons, while the newer *Richard's Bistro*, across the street at no. 36 (☎603/644-1180), serves up creative California cuisine in a modern dining room. For good Italian food, head to the elegant *Cafe Pavone*, 75 Arms Park Drive (☎603/622-5488), or the bustling *Fratello's*, 155 Dow St (☎603/624-2022). The *Bean-n-Bagel*, 25 Stark St (☎603/623-2328), is good for gourmet **coffee** and snacks. The city's younger people **drink** beer and listen to live music at *Jillian's*, right along the river at 50 Phillippe Cote (☎603/626-7636).

HORACE GREELEY

Northwest of Nashua, the tiny, unassuming town of **AMHERST** is the birthplace of **Horace Greeley**, prominent entrepreneur, orator, politician, and the most celebrated newspaperman of his time. Born in 1811, Greeley founded the *New York Tribune* in 1841 and turned it into one of the major public opinion vehicles of the mid-nineteenth century. At its height in the late nineteenth century, the *Tribune* counted among its contributors Henry Wadsworth Longfellow, Charles Dickens, Mark Twain, Bret Harte, and Karl Marx. Self-educated, Greeley had no problems matching wits with such intellectual luminaries, impressing them with his astute editing. He was also always amazingly adept at placing himself at the center of attention. He challenged slavery (his political maneuverings helped Abraham Lincoln win the presidency in 1860) as morally wrong, contested exploitive corporations, and opposed capital punishment. But he also opposed women's suffrage and dismissed Native Americans as "slaves of appetite and sloth." Perhaps best known for popularizing the phrase, "Go West, young man, and grow up with the country," Greeley's robust personality was well known throughout the country. A politician at heart, Greeley served for a brief time in Congress, but his New York gubernatorial and senatorial aspirations were repeatedly denied by voters and colleagues, apparently wary of his somewhat unpredictable behavior, which included a strong fondness for the bottle. He even made a bid for the presidency in 1872, which failed miserably, and when he returned to the *New York Tribune* offices expecting to resume his former position, his old associates refused to relinquish control. He died several months later, after suffering a nervous breakdown, at the age of 61, on November 29, 1872. His small one-story **boyhood home**, just off of Route 101 on Horace Greeley Road, is privately owned, but there is a historical marker nearby that is inscribed with a list of his greatest accomplishments.

South of Manchester

South of Manchester along US-3 near the Massachusetts border, **NASHUA**, New Hampshire's second largest city (population 82,000), does not hold much interest for tourists, its suburban sprawl dominated by strip malls and car dealerships. Plenty of its citizens still choose to work in Boston, though Massachusetts no longer allows employees to escape state taxes by living across the border in New Hampshire. The **downtown** area, along Main Street, is pleasant enough, with a short strip of shops and *Michael Timothy's*, which serves creative wood-grilled fare, such as sea bass, duck, and pizza, at 212 Main St (☎603/595-9334); this is one of the state's finer restaurants.

Alongside the Daniel Webster Highway (Rte-3) in **MERRIMACK**, the massive **Anheuser Busch Brewery** (May–Oct daily 9.30am–5pm; Nov–April Thurs–Mon 10am–4pm; ☎603/595-1202, *www.budweisertours.com*), the largest beer brewer in the world, offers free tours of its beer-making facility – one of thirteen it operates nationwide. Afterwards, you're treated to complimentary tastings of several of its well-known (and lesser-known) products. Outside, you can wander over to see the **Clydesdale stables**, where the enormous horses associated with the brewery are groomed, trained, and usually on display.

The **Robert Frost Farm** (June 24 to Labor Day daily 10am-5pm; Memorial Day to June 23 & Labor Day to Columbus Day daily Sat & Sun 10am–5pm; $2.50), just off of Rte-28 (take exit 4 from I-93), north of Salem and south of Derry, is slightly difficult to find, but worth a stop for its small exhibit of Frost's handwritten poems and photos, a short house tour, and an annotated nature trail. Frost lived here between 1900 and 1911, and composed or drew inspiration for many of his most famous poems here, including "Stopping by Woods on a Snowy Evening" and "Mending Wall." He gave such a moving reading of his poem "Tuft of Flowers" to the local Derry Village Men's Club that the teachers in the group convinced him to take up a position teaching English at the nearby Pinkerton Academy, where he worked for two years before deciding to turn to writing full time. Another of the poet's homes can be found in Franconia (see p.443).

Of possible interest is **America's Stonehenge**, off of Rte-111 in North Salem (daily Feb–June 20 & Sept 5–Oct 31 9am–5pm; June 21–Sept 4 9am–7pm, Nov–Jan 9am–4pm; $7; ☎603/893-8300, *www.stonehengeusa.com*). This grouping of stone slabs and tunnels purports to be a site of ancient and mysterious origins – perhaps some sort of sacrificial altar. There is undoubtedly an atmosphere to the place, but note that it has been private property for the last 250 years, and that all the experts featured in the portentous documentary that visitors are shown are employed by the site.

Concord and around

Just twenty minutes north by car from Manchester along I-93, New Hampshire's state capital, **CONCORD** (pronounced "conquered"), like its larger neighbor, does not hold much fascination for travelers. With only 37,000 people, the city is considerably smaller than Manchester, though much of its population lies in the rather spread-out suburbia that surrounds the town.

Arrival and information

The helpful **Greater Concord Chamber of Commerce**, 244 N Main St (Jun–Sept Mon–Fri 8.30am–5pm; ☎603/224-2508), maintains an information kiosk in front of the state house (weekends 9am–5pm) that distributes historical walking-tour brochures. The local newspaper, the *Concord Monitor*, is widely available and offers entertainment listings.

Concord is readily accessible via **public transport** and easily reached by **car** from I-93, which passes through the eastern side of the town. Concord Trailways (☎1-800/639-3317, *www.concordtrailways.com*), Peter Pan Trailways (☎1-800/343-9999, *www.peterpan-bus.com*), and Vermont Transit Lines (☎1-800/552-8737) all stop at the **Concord Trailways Terminal**, 30 Stickney Ave, and provide service to other parts of New Hampshire and New England. Concord Area Transit (CAT) provides a decent local transportation service (☎603/225-1989).

Accommodation

Concord is short on remarkable **accommodation**, although a minimum of basic, cheap lodging is available on the outskirts of town near the Interstate. Smaller towns in the surrounding countryside, such as Henniker (see p.352), feature some first-rate bed-and-breakfasts.

Brick Tower Motor Inn, 414 S Main St (☎603/224-9565). Basic, comfortable rooms, two miles from downtown. ④.

Centennial Inn, 96 Pleasant St (☎603/225-7102, *www.someplacesdifferent.com*). The upper-crust alternative among Concord's lodging options, with spacious rooms, grand Victorian touches, and modern amenities like in-room phones and cable television. ⑦.

Econo Lodge, 3 Gulf St (☎603/224-4011). One of the cheapest lodging options in Concord, with basic rooms near the Interstate. ③.

A Touch of Europe, 85 Centre St (☎603/226-3771). Three guest rooms in a tiny but friendly Victorian-style bed-and-breakfast. ④.

The Town

Government is the main focus in Concord, employing almost a third of the its res-idents, and the town consequently seems to revolve, both physically and spiritual-ly, around the gold-domed **State House**, Main Street (Mon–Fri 8am–4.30pm; call for weekend hours July–Oct; ☎603/271-2154). The building's handsome stone facade was quarried from local granite (once a major local export) using convict labor. Designed by Stuart J. Park, the original structure was completed in 1819, to be expanded and twice remodeled later. The state legislature – the largest in the country, with some 400 members – has met continuously in the same chambers since June 2, 1819, the longest such tenure in the US. Inside, haunting portraits of over 150 legislators hang on all three floors. Both guided and self-guided tours are available from the visitors' center, on the first floor. Outside, bronze statues of New Hampshire political notables, including Daniel Webster and President Franklin Pierce, strike dignified poses.

The small **Museum of New Hampshire History** (Tues, Wed & Sat 9.30am–5pm, Thurs & Fri 9.30am–8.30pm, Sun noon–5pm; July–Oct 15 and December, also open Mon 9:30am–5pm; ☎603/226-3189, *www.newww.com /org/nhhs*) is tucked behind the brick buildings on Main Street across from the State House, in **Eagle Square**, a large open space between buildings back from the road. In the gallery on the first floor, you can browse the well-presented col-lection of paintings, photographs, maps, and artifacts, including a restored Concord coach (see opposite) and a Native American canoe, that chronologically trace the state's history. Upstairs is devoted to rotating exhibits.

At the north end of Main Street, at 14 Penacook St is the **Pierce Manse** (mid-June to Labor Day 11am–3pm; $3), where Franklin Pierce lived with his family between 1842 and 1848. Notable mainly as one of the United States' least success-ful presidents (see box, p.355), Pierce set up a successful private law practice while in residence here. The restored white two-story 1838 home is now a museum filled with the former president's personal effects, such as his top hat and some period furniture, including the family's writing table. It's open for tours during the sum-mer. Pierce is buried in the **Old North Cemetery**, near the intersection of North State Street and Keane Avenue, in the northern end of the downtown area.

Across the river, the **Christa McAuliffe Planetarium**, 3 Institute Drive (Mon–Wed 10am–2pm, Thurs–Sat 10am–5pm, Sun noon–5pm; $7; ☎603/ 271-7827), named for the Concord High School teacher who perished in the Space Shuttle *Challenger* disaster in 1986, stages impressive public astronomy shows in its 92-seat theater and hosts various skywatch events. The planetarium also has interactive exhibits, such as the Pathfinder, where you rescue a team of three astronauts lost in space in the year 2058. McAuliffe was selected from a pool of 11,500 applicants to participate in the tragic space trip that ended her life just 73 seconds after lift-off.

Canterbury Shaker Village

A little way north of Concord, in **Canterbury Center**, Canterbury Shaker Village, exit 18 off I-93, 288 Shaker Rd (May–Oct daily 10am–5pm; Nov, Dec & Apr Sat & Sun 10am–5pm; $10; ☎603/783-9511, *www.shakers.org*), is New England's premier museum of Shaker life (though see also p.242, in Chapter Three, "Central and Western Massachusetts"), and perhaps the most fascinating tourist destination in New Hampshire. The tranquil village, a collection of simple, box-like buildings, is beautifully spread out over a set of rolling hills, overlooking the greenery of the countryside, and the site's quiet isolation is soothing. Founded by Mother Ann Lee in 1774, the Shakers, after breaking off from the Quakers, were one of the religious sects that sought refuge in the New World. In 1792, Canterbury became the sixth of nineteen Shaker communities, and, at its zenith in the mid-1800s, there were some 300 people living on the grounds. Sister Ethel Hudson, the last Shaker living in Canterbury, died in 1992 at age 96; today, only a handful of Shakers remain in the world – all live in New Gloucester, Maine (see p.476).

So named because of their tendency to dance in church (thereby shaking off sins and evil), the Shakers lived apart from the world in communities devoted to efficiency, equality, pacifism, a strong work ethic, co-operative living, and celibacy. Shakers relied upon conversion and adoption to expand their influence; orphans were readily accepted into the community, and at one point the state of New Hampshire opened a foster home in Canterbury Village. However, in the face of industrialization and the opening of the West, the Shakers' decline in the early twentieth century was ultimately exacerbated by their self-imposed sexual chastity.

CONCORD COACHES

Carriage manufacturing became one of Concord's best-known industries in the mid-nineteenth century, when Abbot, Downing & Co became the major supplier for Ben Holladay's Overland Trail Stage Route. Locals Lewis Downing and Stephen Abbot had constructed the first Concord coach in 1827, and their beautifully painted stagecoaches were soon known throughout the developing West as the best mode of transportation available. In addition to durable construction and dependable quality, Concord coaches earned a good reputation for their wheels, which were made with seasoned white oak and fitted with handmade spokes, making them more likely to maintain a round shape. The coaches used three-inch-thick leather bands rather than springs to support the passenger compartment, prompting Mark Twain to describe a Concord coach as a "cradle on wheels" in his novel *Roughing It*. Weighing over a ton and costing roughly $1000 at the time, Concord coaches carried up to twelve passengers, and, with four to six horses out front, could travel fifteen miles an hour. Used by Wells Fargo Bank, they soon became familiar sights in such far-off places as South America and Australia. You can see a real one at the Museum of New Hampshire History (see opposite).

Believing that technology would create more time for worship, the Shakers were creative and industrious inventors. Several of these inventions, such as a seed spreader used in agriculture, as well as some fine examples of Shaker furniture craftsmanship, are presented during three different thirty-minute **tours** of the village. Led by Shaker experts, the engrossing tours also introduce the ideals, day-to-day life, and architecture (there are 25 perfectly restored buildings on the site) of these people as you wander from building to building – including the church, the schoolhouse, and the laundry room. There is also an acclaimed restaurant on the property, the **Creamery**, serving Shaker specialties (see overleaf). On Fridays and Saturdays, the restaurant's four-course meal includes a candlelight tour of the village, storytelling, and light entertainment.

Eating

Concord's **restaurants** can seem uninspired when compared with those of Portsmouth. However, you can find some good-value lunches around the State House; and Loudon Road, east of the Merrimack River is lined with fast-food and national chain restaurants. Other than a couple of basic, typical bars, there is really no **nightlife** to speak of here.

The Creamery, 288 Shaker Rd, Canterbury (☎603/783-9511). Imaginative Shaker-inspired specialties like iced strawberry soup, seared salmon on creamed corn topped with herbal tartar sauce, and chocolate zucchini cake. Lunches served daily, four-course candlelight dinner served Friday and Saturday. Reservations required for dinner, which includes a tour of the Village ($36 per person).

Eagle Square Deli, 5 Eagle Square (☎603/228-4795). Excellent deli sandwiches-to-go across from the History Museum. You can eat outside on the patio. Closed weekends.

Hermanos Cocina Mexicana, 11 Hills Ave (☎603/224-5669). Slightly more expensive than the other Mexican restaurant in town (see below), but the food is more authentic and the scene less noisy. The quesadillas are particularly good. Live jazz Sun–Wed.

Margaritas, 1 Bicentennial Square (☎603/224-2821). Housed in a former police station, this popular place serves some of the biggest Mexican dishes around. You can sit in a former jail cell downstairs while you sip your margarita and carouse with local singles – very atmospheric.

Tea Garden Restaurant, 184 N Main St (☎603/228-4420). Despite its dirty yellow sign and grim-looking exterior, this place serves some of the most authentic Chinese food in the state. Try the sesame sparkling beef or the Mandarin crispy shrimp.

West of Concord: Henniker

The pleasant, relatively untouristed residential town of **HENNIKER** ("The only Henniker in the world!"), west of Concord on Route 114 along the border of the Merrimack Valley, was settled by families from the *Mayflower*, many of whose descendants still live in the area. Residents enjoy the peaceful seclusion so much that they raised $100,000 in a successful campaign to keep retail giant Rite Aid Pharmacy from building a store in the quaint downtown area.

In Henniker's center, along the **Contoocook River** ("Tooky"), **Main Street** is home to an agreeable group of shops, including the nostalgic *Henniker Pharmacy* (☎603/428-3456), where you can order ice cream and sandwiches at an old-fashioned soda counter in back. The Old Number Six Book Depot, 26 Depot Hill Rd (up the hill from Town Hall), with an enormous stock of new and used **books** on all subjects, is worth a browse. Just across the double-arched Edna Dean Proctor Bridge, along Bridge Street, **New England College**, with some 1000 students, lends a youthful feel to the area during the school year. There are also a couple of good **hikes** in the area: try the Mount Liberty Extension trail, which winds up a gentle slope to the top of Mount Liberty, one mile west of the center of town off of Western Avenue at the end of Liberty Hill Road. Baseball great Ted Williams regularly went **fly-fishing** along the Contoocook River between Henniker and Hillsborough (see p.411), and it's still a popular spot between May and October. During the winter, you can **ski** at the family-oriented **Pats Peak Ski Area** (☎603/428-3245), although with only 700 vertical feet of trails the terrain is rather limited.

Practicalities

Henniker has several excellent **accommodation options**, none better than the *Colby Hill Inn*, half a mile from the center of town off of Western Ave (☎603/428-3281 or 1-800/531-0330, *www.colbyhillinn.com*; [6]), a romantic 1795 country farmhouse with friendly owners, an enormous dog named Delilah, delicious breakfasts, and a gourmet restaurant. The *Meeting House Inn*, 35 Flanders Rd (☎603/428-3228; [5]), is a similarly cozy and romantic bed-and-breakfast. Closer to town, the *Henniker House*, 2 Ramsdell Rd (☎603/428-3198; [4]), offers unpretentious lodging along the river in a converted hospital. You can **camp** at the family-oriented *Keyser Pond Campground*, 47 Old Concord Rd (☎603/428-7741), or *Mile-Away Campground*, 41 Old W Hopkinton Rd (☎603/428-7616).

There are also a few good **places to eat** in Henniker. The *Colby Hill Inn* (see above) features expertly prepared upscale food, including sesame-encrusted swordfish and lobster-stuffed chicken breast (entrees are $17–27), in a relaxed but elegant setting overlooking a garden. The *Meeting House Restaurant*, also part of an inn (see above), is another gourmet spot, serving American food in a converted old barn. Along the river, *Daniel's Restaurant and Pub*, on Main St (☎603/428-7621), serves reasonably priced soups and salads, pastas, and meat entrees. The *Coffee Grind*, 9 Bridge St (☎603/428-6397), is a cute little spot with sandwiches, bagels, salads, and good coffee.

THE MONADNOCK REGION

Known as the "quiet corner," the **Monadnock region**, which occupies the southwestern portion of New Hampshire, traverses deserted country roads and typically quaint church spire-filled New England towns that center around the lonely 3165-foot peak of **Mount Monadnock**. Aside from the gentle slopes of the mountain itself, which attracts plenty of outdoor enthusiasts, the region boasts no real stand-out tourist attractions, and, although the slow pace and rolling hills can be infectious, you may very well find yourself restless with the desire to move on after a day or so of exploring.

Although you can get a good feel for small-town New England living at any of the region's many picturesque villages, several are worth highlighting. **Keene**, an amiable place with a provincial disposition and a range of services and stores, is the area's most populous community; **Peterborough**, along US-202, is the region's – perhaps the state's – artistic center. **Hillsborough** was the birthplace of New Hampshire's only US president, Franklin Pierce, and **Jaffrey** rests quietly at the base of Mount Monadnock next to the state park. **Fitzwilliam**, a classic New England community incorporated in 1773, has some nice accommodations, and **Harrisville** recalls its days as an eighteenth-century mill-town.

Information and getting around

Most of the towns in the region have a **chamber of commerce**, good for a few brochures and friendly words of advice. You might try the **Peterborough Chamber of Commerce**, at the junction of Rte-101 and US-202 (☎603/924-7234), or the **Greater Keene Chamber of Commerce**, 48 Central Square (☎603/352-1303), for help with accommodation. The *Monadnock Magazine*, published in Peterborough and distributed throughout the region, has entertainment listings and local-interest stories.

Public transport in the Monadnock region is almost non-existent. There is a Vermont Transit Lines bus terminal in Keene (☎603/352-1331) which has service south to Boston or North to Montréal, stopping in Fitzwilliam. By far the best way to get around here is by **car**, which will allow easy access to the region's many quiet backcountry roads. You can **rent a car** in Keene from National (☎603/357-4045) or Enterprise (☎603/358-3345), or in Peterborough from Enterprise (☎603/924-9058). **Biking** is a good way to explore the pleasant countryside of the Monadnock region, although the terrain can at times be a bit hilly. To **rent bikes**, head to Eclectic Bike, 109 Grove St, Peterborough (☎603/924-9797); they'll also give you plenty of advice on potential routes. Monadnock Bicycle Tours, in Harrisville (☎603/827-3925), organizes on- and off-road biking tours for groups or individuals.

Accommodation

None of the picturesque towns in the Monadnock region offer a large selection of **places to stay**. However, some of the state's finest **bed-and-breakfasts** and **country inns** are scattered about the region, and if "getting away from it all" is your goal, the area's meandering backcountry setting will not disappoint. The region also has several good **campgrounds**; to make a reservation, call the State Parks Reservation Center (☎603/271-3628).

Inns, bed-and-breakfasts, and hotels

Amos Parker House, Rte-119, Fitzwilliam (☎603/585-6540). This small, homely bed-and-breakfast, maintained by a knowledgeable hostess, is surrounded with beautifully manicured gardens. [5].

Apple Gate, 199 Upland Farm Rd, Peterborough, two miles from downtown (☎603/924-6543). Country elegance in an 1832 colonial home. Four rooms, all with private bath. Full breakfasts are included. [4].

Benjamin Prescott Inn, 433 Turnpike Rd off of Rte-124 E, Jaffrey (☎603/532-6637). Friendly, antique-filled upscale bed-and-breakfast with ten quiet rooms just outside of town. [5].

Birchwood Inn, Rte-45, Temple (☎603/878-3285). In a tiny town just east of Peterborough and close to downhill skiing, this cozy, brick bed-and-breakfast once hosted Henry David Thoreau. [4]–[5].

Carriage Barn Bed and Breakfast, 358 Main St, Keene (☎603/357-3812, *www.carriagebarn.com*). Four guest rooms with private bath in a cozy house just a few minutes walk from the shops, restuarants, and entertainment of Keene. [4].

Econo Lodge, Rte-47, Bennington (☎603/588-2777). Affordable basic rooms from the national chain, halfway between Peterborough and Hillsborough. [4].

Fitzwilliam Inn, Rte-119, on the common, Fitzwilliam (☎603/585-9000). This longstanding late eighteenth-century inn is one of the region's better value options, with basic but comfortable rooms. At the center of relaxing Fitzwilliam, the on-site restaurant serves hearty American cooking adjacent to a friendly pub. Some rooms with shared bath. Family-friendly. ④–⑤.

Goose Pond Guest House, E. Surrey Rd, Keene (☎603/352-2828, *goosepond@monnad.net*). Elegant 1790 country home situated among orchards and berry patches just outside the center of town. ④–⑤.

Hancock Inn, 33 Main St (Rte-123), Hancock (☎603/525-3318 or 800/525-1789). One of the oldest continuously operating inns in the country, a beautiful and spacious 1789 tavern in a lovely village where every building is a registered historic landmark. Elegant restaurant in-house. ⑤–⑥.

Hannah Davis House, 106 Rte-119 W, Fitzwilliam (☎603/585-3344). Another fine bed-and-breakfast, this 1820s Federal-style home has been elegantly restored and furnished. ④–⑤.

Jack Daniels Motor Inn, Route 202 N, Peterborough (☎603/924-7548). Comfortable and spacious rooms with modern amenities close to downtown. ⑤.

Peterborough Manor, 50 Summer St, Peterborough (☎603/924-9832, *www. peterboroughmanor.com*). Ten sunny rooms with private bath in an 1890s Victorian mansion. Breakfast is included. ③.

Camping

Emerald Acres Campground, Jaffrey (☎603/532-8838). Fifty-two pleasant sites in a pine forest bordering a small pond. Open May 1–Columbus Day. $15.

Greenfield State Park, Greenfield (☎603/547-3497 or 271-3628 to make reservations). Enormous and popular camping area along Rte-136 north of Peterborough, with 252 tent sites, nature trails, and hot showers. $14.

Monadnock State Park, Jaffrey (☎603/532-8862). Twenty-one scenic tent sites at the base of Mount Monadnock. Open year-round. $12.

Hillsborough

The tiny town of **HILLSBOROUGH** – actually a grouping of four small villages (Hillsborough Bridge Village, Center Village, Lower Village, and Upper Village) – is the birthplace of Franklin Pierce (see box overleaf), fourteenth president of the United States and the only New Hampshire native to have attained the position. You can tour his painstakingly restored boyhood home, the **Franklin Pierce Homestead**, at the intersection of Rte-9 and Rte-31 (July & Aug Mon–Sat 10am–4pm, Sun 1–4pm; June & Sept weekends only; $3), where the docents downplay Pierce's shortcomings – alcoholism, ineffective leadership – to portray him as a misunderstood hero. The building is a fine (if slightly larger) example of the Federal-style homes that were common in the region, and Franklin lived here on and off until he was thirty. The rooms inside are relatively bare, though there are a few nicely painted wallpapers, including one that depicts the harbor at Naples.

The house was built by Franklin's father, **Benjamin Pierce**, who first came to Hillsborough in 1786, after having served as a general in the Revolutionary War under George Washington. He was elected a representative to the legislature for the towns of Hillsborough and Henniker in 1789 and went on to a 57-year career in public office, including two terms as governor of New Hampshire.

The outside of Hillsborough is the site of some stunningly ugly development, courtesy of Rite Aid and McDonald's, but if you follow the roads off Rte-9 to **Hillsboro Center,** ironically not the center of anything anymore, you'll pass through some rolling countryside criss-crossed by stone fences.

One of Hillsborough's four municipalities, **Hillsborough Bridge Village**, at the intersection of Rte-9 and Rte-149, is home to the area's one-street downtown area. You can still see the structural remnants of the nineteenth-century **Contoocook Mills**, abandoned in the early 1900s, along the banks of the river, reminders of the town's once successful textile manufacturing industry. Also worth a quick look, the **Kemps Truck Museum**, along the river on River Street off of Rte-149, is really more like a parking lot full of rusting old trucks, though it supposedly holds the biggest collection of Mack trucks in the world.

Once you've tired of the **antique shops** in the center of town, head for the **Fox State Forest**, a state-maintained nature preserve south of town, which has some good hiking trails. You can get a trail map and advice at the Fox Forest Headquarters (☎603/464-3453), along Center Road south of town.

Less notably, the quiet country roads of Hillsborough span some well-constructed old **stone arch bridges**. Built by skilled Scotch-Irish stonemasons in the mid-1800s, the bridges, some built without mortar, are still in use. The finest bridge can be seen near the Pierce House, at the junction of Rte-9 and US-202, where there is also a small park with picnic benches.

FRANKLIN PIERCE

Not highly rated in history's annals, **Franklin Pierce** was born in Hillsborough, New Hampshire, on November 23, 1804. Though Ralph Waldo Emerson wrote that Pierce was "either the worst, or one of the weakest of all our Presidents," modern New Hampshire residents overlook his shortcomings in the White House and have in fact transformed him into something of a local hero. The biographical brochure published by the New Hampshire Historical Society, for example, dramatically proclaims Pierce's presidency as "one of the great tragedies of our history," although the Friends of Franklin Pierce maintain their mission is to "rescue him from the obscurity he so richly deserves."

Handsome, charming, and amiable in his younger years, Pierce studied law at Bowdoin College in Maine before returning to New Hampshire to win his first election to public office. Only 25 years old at the time, he served in the state legislature under his father, Benjamin, and became speaker of the New Hampshire House at age 28. Pierce served five terms in the House of Representatives before being elected to the United States Senate. But his love of the law ultimately led him to return to Concord, where he set up a successful private law practice. After serving in the Mexican War, he unexpectedly received the nomination for president at the Democratic National Convention in 1852, when his party could not make a decision on any of the other four candidates. Even more surprisingly perhaps, Pierce edged out Whig candidate Whitfield Scott in the general election.

Pierce's presidency began on a particularly black note, when his only remaining son, Bennie, was killed in a train accident just before the inauguration. Pierce's wife, Jane, was rarely seen in public afterwards, and it was said that Pierce himself never recovered. At a time when the nation was severely divided over slavery, Pierce remained staunchly opposed to antislavery legislation, wrongly believing that his status as a Northerner with Southern values would strike an acceptable compromise with the nation. With his signing of the 1854 Kansas-Nebraska Act, which allowed settlers to choose whether to allow slavery, conflict erupted in Kansas, and Pierce effectively lost his authority over the American people. By then he'd become a problem alcoholic, and it is said that Pierce's parting words from the White House were, "Well, I guess there's nothing left to do but go get drunk." To this day, Pierce is the only US president not to be nominated by his party for a second term.

Peterborough

The proud riverfront town of **PETERBOROUGH**, south of Hillsborough along Route 202, has a youthful artistic focus these days. Immortalized by Thornton Wilder in the play *Our Town* and now boldly claiming to be "an entire community devoted to the arts," Peterborough is home to a wide range of cultural activities, but really centers on the **MacDowell Colony**, 100 High St (☎603/924-3886), which hosts over 200 artists – including musicians, painters, filmmakers, and photographers – in its 32 private studios each year. Dedicated to providing an environment free of distraction since its founding in 1907, the privately funded colony has hosted such notables as Alice Walker, Studs Terkel, Milton Avery, Thornton Wilder, Oscar Hijuelos, and Willa Cather. Artists open their studios to the public only once a year, usually in mid-August (☎603/924-3886 for information, *www.macdowellcolony.org*). The main building, **Colony Hall**, is open to visitors most afternoons, but there's nothing particularly of interest inside.

The tiny brick-dominated **downtown**, centered around **Grove Street**, was largely the inspiration of architect Benjamin Russell, who designed the Town House, where the city still holds town meetings, the Historical Society, and the Guernsey Building, an office space just across the street. Inside the **Historical Society** building, 19 Grove St (Mon–Fri 10am–4pm; ☎603/924-3235), a dusty hodgepodge of old artifacts, including photographs and farming tools, describes the "story of a typical New Hampshire town."

Three miles east of Peterborough, along Rte-101, **Miller State Park** (☎603/924-3672; $2.50) has a few excellent hikes. Try the **Wapack Trail**, which takes you to the summit of **Pack Monadnock** (2.8 miles round-trip, 2290 feet), from which you can sometimes see the Boston skyline to the southeast and Mount Washington to the north. The **Summit Loop Trail**, which circumvents the peak (0.4 miles), offers additional scenic vistas.

Practicalities

Of several **places to eat** in Peterborough, *Latacarta at the Boilerhouse*, US-202 south of town in an old mill building (closed Mon; ☎603/924-6878), is the most interesting, serving delicious creative fusion food, such as beef tenderloin with wild mushrooms and roasted poblano peppers stuffed with shrimp and ricotta cheese; they're devoted to fresh ingredients and thoughtful presentation, and there's a four-course dinner special for two that costs $55 – quite a deal. *Donna's Riverside Cafe*, in Depot Square (☎603/924-2002), has good seafood, sandwiches, and salads at reasonable prices overlooking the river. *Harlow's Deli and Café*, 3 School St (☎603/924-6365), serves

---

ARTS IN PETERBOROUGH

Each year in mid-July, Peterborough hosts the **Monadnock Festival for the Arts** (☎603/924-7234 for information), a weekend of dance, art, theater, and music. You can attend performances year-round at a number of local venues. The **Peterborough Players** stages acclaimed traditional and experimental theater performances in a renovated nineteenth-century barn on Hadley Road off of Hancock Middle Road, a few miles outside of town (☎603/924-7585).

up good sandwiches and pizza as well as a healthy dose of town gossip in a friendly, relaxed pub where the bartender knows all the customers by name. For upscale gourmet sandwiches, head to *Twelve Pine*, 11 School St (☎603/924-6140), which also serves espresso and fresh juice and has café seating. One of the finest **bookstores** in the state, the Toadstool Bookshop, 12 Depot Square (☎603/924-3543), has a huge selection of fiction, nonfiction, and travel books.

Jaffrey and the Monadnock State Park

The area commonly referred to as **JAFFREY** actually takes in the towns of Jaffrey and Jaffrey Center. Not much goes on in the former, and you're better off concentrating on picturesque Jaffrey Center, long the domain of novelist Willa Cather, who came to Jaffrey Center every fall during the early twentieth century to work and enjoy the quiet countryside. In a studio in the woods, Cather wrote parts of the novels *My Antonia* (1918) and *One of Ours* (1922). Cather is buried beside her lover, Edith Lewis, in the **Old Town Burial Ground**, along Rte-124 in Jaffrey Center.

Beyond that you really visit Jaffrey for **Mount Monadnock**, reputedly the most climbed mountain in North America and the centerpiece of **MONADNOCK STATE PARK**, just outside town heading west on Rte-124 (☎603/532-8862; $2.50 per day). The park is the most striking natural feature of the Monadnock region, a rolling countryside carpeted with dense stands of birch and pine trees. Although the mountain is only 3165 feet high, its gently sloping peak seems dominant because it is so isolated. The peak was a popular spot with nineteenth-century writers and artists; indeed, by 1900 it was so renowned that *Webster's Dictionary* recognized its name as a noun meaning "a hill or mass of rock rising above a peneplain." Henry David Thoreau hiked and camped around the top of the mountain many times, writing of the experience, "It is a very unique walk . . . it often reminded me of my walks on the beach, and suggested how much both depend for their sublimity on solitude and dreariness. In both cases we feel the presence of some vast, titanic power." You can read more from Thoreau's journals and learn about the history of the park at the visitor center, near the parking lot. They also have information about the park's forty miles of scenic hiking trails; the "White Dot Trail" is the most popular and direct route to the summit, taking about three-and-a-half hours round-trip. The "Spellman Trail" also links the park headquarters to the top, and although it traverses the steepest terrain on the mountain, it features excellent eastern views. Once you've reached the crowded peak, on a clear day, you can see all six New England states. For additional guidance, you can buy the *Monadnock Guide*, a dense look at the geology, wildlife, history, and hiking in the park, for $9 at the park entrance.

Keene

KEENE, with 22,400 residents, is the most populated of the cities in the Monadnock region, though in truth it has little competition, and you would hardly call it cosmopolitan. The architecture here is noticeably more modern, and, although the town manages to maintain a friendly, if somewhat dull charm, there's not much to do other than shop and eat in the downtown area, along the unusually wide **Main Street**, allegedly the "widest Main Street in the U.S.," which culminates in the lovely **Keene Common**. For what it's worth, the town was a well-known crafts center in the early nineteenth century, when **glass** and **pottery** production was at its peak; a marker along Main Street denotes the site of the **Hampshire Pottery Works**, the most successful of the local manufacturers. Still standing at 399 Main St, the **Wyman Tavern** (June–Labor Day Thurs–Sat 11am–4pm; ☎603/352-1895; $2) was built in 1762 by Isaac Wyman, a staunch patriot who later led a group of Minute Men from the tavern south to fight in the Revolutionary War. The tavern was also the sight of the first official meeting of the trustees of Dartmouth College, which was founded in 1769. The restored taproom, living quarters, and ballroom are open to the public. While you're down in that part of town, it's worth stopping in at the **Thorne-Sagendorph Art Gallery** (Sat–Wed 12–4pm, Thurs–Fri 12–7pm; free) on the attractive campus of Keene State College. It's pretty tiny, one room for the permanent collection and one for temporary exhibits, but the eclectic permanent collection ranges from African statues to Robert Mapplethorpe photographs to a Goya print. Take some time to peruse Peter Milton's print, *20ᵗʰ Century Limited*, which depicts the past century's culture as a train wreck, from which only a select few artifacts have been rescued.

Practicalities

If you decide to stop in Keene, there are a couple of **places to eat** worth noting. The popular *176 Main*, 176 Main St (☎603/357-3100), has a huge varied menu of excellent value salads, soups, sandwiches, and main meals, served in a rustic and intimate dining room, as well as sixteen beers on tap. For authentic Italian food in a warm plant-decorated setting, head to *Nicola's Trattoria*, 39 Central Square (☎603/355-5242), which serves traditional pasta and meat entrees for $10–16. *Piazza*, at 149 Main St (☎603/352-5133), offers a mind-boggling array of ice-cream flavors, yogurts, sundaes, and freezes. *Brewbakers*, 97 Main St (☎603/355-4844), is a hip coffee joint with comfy couches that also serves cheap soups, sandwiches, and salads. One of the top spots for **shopping** is the Colony Mill Marketplace, 222 West St, a converted brick woolen mill with an interesting grouping of relatively upscale shops. The Marketplace also houses the best **place to drink** in town, the *Elm City Brewery and Pub* (☎603/355-3335), which serves hearty American meals in addition to its own microbrewed beers.

Lake Sunapee

Although relatively small, **LAKE SUNAPEE** has had a varied history. The lake had been popular as a summer escape since the beginning of the nineteenth century, but with the arrival of train connections to Newbury Harbor at the lake's southern tip, the area exploded with a booming tourist trade. Steamboats full of vacationing Bostonians and New Yorkers plied the waters, while mansions and luxury hotels began appearing on the coast. Among the notables who made their homes here were the Colgates (of Colgate-Palmolive fame) and Secretary of State John Milton Hay, whose mansion **The Fells** still stands. The advent of the automobile effectively ended Sunapee's boom time and saved it from development on the atrocious scale of its huge northern neighbor, Winnipesaukee. Today, the Sunapee region is a very low-key place, although the big resort developer

Okemo's plans for the area, while no doubt providing a new boom, may also sound the death knell for its secluded charm. Enjoy it while it lasts, and know that you're still in rockin' good company – Aerosmith's Steven Tyler has a house on the lake.

The action, such as it is, is all on **Sunapee Harbor**. A far cry from the lake's heyday, the only boats on the clear, clean waters (Sunapee is a spring-fed lake) now are the occasional mail boat and regular **boat tours**. Sunapee Cruises (☎603/763-4030, *www.sunapeecruises.com*) runs two daily, mid-June to Labor Day, 10am and 2:30pm; mid- May to mid-June and Labor Day to mid-Oct, 2.30pm only; $12. The knowledgeable captain will share Sunapee lore and point out the sights, such as the former Colgate estate and the lake's three lighthouses. True boat aficionados won't want to miss the annual **Classic Boat Parade** in August.

On the opposite shore stands the Hay family estate, The Fells, off Rte-103A (grounds open year-round, dawn to dusk; $3; house tours, weekends and holidays, Memorial Day–Columbus Day; $4, including grounds admission). John Milton Hay was an advisor and friend of Abraham Lincoln who, forty years later, became Secretary of State under Teddy Roosevelt. He built his mansion here in the 1870s, and it was passed on to his son, Cecil, who just happened to be a talented landscape artist and designed the grounds of the mansion in a pleasing mix of Asian and European styles. Cecil was also a concerned preservationist, and his distress at the rapid deforestation of the area led him to donate 675 acres of **forest** to the Society for the Protection of New Hampshire Forests. These days, the mansion itself is empty, and the guided tours, while enjoyable, tend to make one feel as if one were being shown the house for prospective purchase. Far more interesting are the **gardens** that surround the house, with the borrowed scenery of the lake and forests adding to their charm. There are also **nature trails** through those 675 acres, a good spot for bird-watching.

Practicalities

If you're looking for **places to stay**, the friendly folks at the Lake Sunapee Business Association (☎1-800/258-3530 or 603/763-2495) will happily help you find accommodation. The biggest town hereabouts, Newport, is nothing like its opulent namesake in Rhode Island, and won't prompt more than a glance, but its Chamber of Commerce (☎603/863-1510, *www.newportnh.org*), in a small booth right on the town green, may also be able to help you out. Up above the lake, with a view as well of nearby Mount Sunapee, the *Inn at Sunapee*, Burkehaven Hill Road (☎603/763-4444 or 1-800/327-2466, *www. innatsunapee.com*; ④–⑤), is a converted 1875 farmhouse with sixteen rooms decorated with a mixture of period items and Asian antiques. There's also an attached restaurant, specializing in creative, fresh American food with an Asian flair.

The Connecticut River Valley

The **Connecticut River** forms the entire western border of New Hampshire, originating in Canada and emptying into the Atlantic after flowing through Massachusetts and Connecticut. Along its banks, a smattering of typically quaint New England villages, connected by empty winding country roads, are spread between serene stretches of misty rolling green farmland. At the region's heart, **Hanover** is New Hampshire's intellectual center, the home of arch-conservative

---

BURDICK CHOCOLATES

Northwest of Keene, off of Rte-12, in the tiny white-clapboard town of **Walpole**, where Louisa May Alcott summered, and where documentary filmmaker Ken Burns currently lives, you can find one of the region's most delectable stores, **Burdick Chocolates** (☎603/756-3701 or 1-800/229-2419, *www.burdickchocolate .com*). Situated in an unassuming storefront along Main Street, the chocolate here has been rated the best in the country by *Consumer Reports* magazine – and deservedly so. Swiss-trained Larry Burdick makes his home-made treats from French Valrhona chocolate before shipping them to the nation's finest restaurants and shops, such as *Bouley* in New York City. If the chocolate isn't enough, you can get coffee and pastries in the adjoining café.

Dartmouth College, which draws some of the country's best students and maintains an active arts scene. Nearby, **West Lebanon** and **Lebanon** are more laidback than Hanover but less interesting, with ample shopping malls in their quiet suburban sprawl. To the south, the tiny village of **Cornish** was once a popular artists' colony, while **Lyme**, north of Hanover, is centered around a particularly attractive town green.

Information and getting around

Good **maps** of the region are available at the **Hanover Chamber of Commerce** (☎603/643-3115, *www.hanoverchamber.org*), which has an office along Main Street and an **information booth** on the Dartmouth Green during the summer. In and around Hanover, Advance Transit (☎802/295-1824, *www.communityinfo.com/rides*; $1.25 one-way) provides a comprehensive **bus** service, stopping in front of the *Hanover Inn* and at the Dartmouth Bookstore and connecting Hanover with Lebanon, West Lebanon, Norwich (VT), Wilder (VT), Hartford Village (VT), and White River Junction (VT). Trips within Hanover or between Hanover and Lebanon are free. You can get a schedule and route map at the Chamber of Commerce. The Dartmouth Mini Coach (☎603/448-2800 or 1-800/637-0123; $35) provides service to and from Boston's Logan Airport five times daily, stopping in New London along the way. Vermont Transit Lines (☎802/864-6811) stops in Hanover at Dartmouth Travel (☎603/643-2121). They have a major terminal across the river in White River Junction (☎802/295-3011), with buses south to Boston, via Manchester (NH), and as far north as Toronto, via Burlington (VT) and Montréal. Other routes head for Springfield (MA), Hartford (CT), and New York City.

Amtrak's *Ethan Allen Express* **train** stops in White River Junction once a day. The southbound train, terminating in Washington, DC, departs at 10.35am daily; the northbound train, heading towards Montréal, leaves at 6.25pm daily.

Like the rest of the state, the upper Connecticut River Valley is most easily accessible by **car**. From the south, **I-91** blasts up the western side of the Connecticut River in Vermont, while **Rte-12A** and **Rte-10**, the slower, more scenic choices, trace the riverbank on the New Hampshire side. From Concord, I-89 passes through Lebanon and West Lebanon before crossing into Vermont; to get to Hanover, take Rte-120 north from Lebanon or Rte-10 north from West Lebanon. A good place to **rent an automobile** is Upper Valley Rent-a-Car, on Rte-120 in Lebanon (☎603/448-3770).

Hanover and around

Almost everyone in **HANOVER** has some connection to **Dartmouth College**. Indeed the city and college are pretty much one and the same thing. Hanover received its official charter in 1761, just eight years before Dartmouth was founded. The college's reputation as one of the more conservative Ivy League schools is not unfounded; in fact, as you walk around, you'll notice that many of the students look strikingly alike: clean-cut preppy-types, most of them white. Stereotypes aside, though, it's an active place, with all the cultural and other benefits you expect from a college town – a good museum; regular performances by international musicians, dancers, and actors; good bookstores; and a scattering of decent places to eat and drink.

Accommodation

Accommodation in Hanover tends to be tidy, expensive, and luxurious – just the sort visiting parents, scholars, and performers appreciate. Things are mellower – though usually just as expensive – in the surrounding countryside. The highbrow *Hanover Inn*, with dozens of spacious, elegantly furnished rooms overlooking Dartmouth Green from the corner of Main and Wheelock streets (☎603/643-4300 or 1-800/443-7024; ⑧), represents the top end of Hanover's accommodation options. For luxury accommodations in a quieter country setting, there's *Trumbull House Bed and Breakfast*, 40 Etna Rd, four miles east of the green (☎603/643-2370 or 1-800/651-5141; ⑦). Just east of Hanover, in **Etna**, the *Moose Mountain Lodge*, nestled in the hills at the end of Moose Mountain Rd (☎603/643-3529; ⑦), is marvelously remote all year, but is best as a base in winter for cross-country skiing. The *Chieftain Motor Inn*, 84 Lyme Rd (☎603/643-2550 or 1-800/845-3557; ④), is the best of the few budget accommodations in the area. If you want to **camp**, head for the *Storrs Pond Recreation Area*, in Hanover on Route 10 off of I-89 (☎603/643-2134 in summer, ☎603/643-2408 in winter; $18).

The Town

Fittingly, the town's focal point remains the grassy **Dartmouth Green**, bounded by Main, Wheelock, Wentworth, and College streets. The Dartmouth-owned **Hood Museum of Art**, on Wheelock Street on the green, is Hanover's main thing to see off the central campus (Tues & Thurs–Sat 10am–5pm, Wed 10am–9pm, Sun noon–5pm; ☎603/646-2808, *www.dartmouth.edu/~hood*; free), with paintings by Picasso and Monet as well as outstanding works by several American artists – Gilbert Stuart, Thomas Eakins, and John Sloan. The standouts include Frederick Remmington's hauntingly realistic painting of three Native Americans and a settler, *Shotgun Hospitality*, a fine collection of portraits, including Joseph Steward's *Portrait of Eleazar Wheelock*, the founder of Dartmouth College, and a selection of detailed etchings by Rembrandt. In addition to a collection of Greek, Assyrian, and African objects, the museum also stages special exhibits of works from around the world. The adjacent cultural complex, the **Hopkins Center for the Creative and Performing Arts** (☎603/646-2422, *www.dartmouth.edu/~hop*), screens international art and classic movies year-round (tickets $6). They also present internationally acclaimed musicians, acting companies, and dance troupes, as well as student performances.

Next door, the venerable **Hanover Inn**, founded by General Ebenezer Brewster in 1780, is a longstanding local landmark, standing five stories high with a classic-looking brick facade. Although devastating fires and extensive renovations have obscured the inn's colonial charm, its lobby is still bustling with visiting parents, scholars, and performers. Recent guests at the inn, owned and operated by the college, include then-President Clinton, dancer Mikhail Baryshnikov, and the rock band Kiss. **South Main Street**, which runs along the west side of the inn, holds most of the town's eateries, bars, and shops, and is pleasant enough to wander around.

Dartmouth College

Majestic **Dartmouth College** (*www.dartmouth.edu*), founded by Rev Eleazar Wheelock in 1769, is the ninth oldest college in the United States. The school was initially an outgrowth of a school for Native Americans that Wheelock had established in Connecticut, but in reality few Native Americans ever studied here. Named for its financial backer, the earl of Dartmouth, the Ivy League institution attracts some of the top students in the world today, with particularly strong programs in medicine, engineering, and business.

The stately 200-acre campus is spread out around **Dartmouth Green**, and this is a good starting point for a look at the grounds. Hanover and Dartmouth jointly maintain an **information booth** on the green during the summer, which is usually attended by enthusiastic alumni eager to spread the word about their old

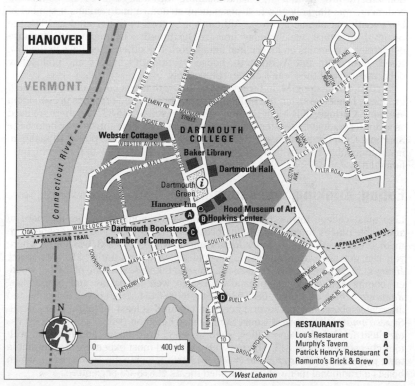

RESTAURANTS	
Lou's Restaurant	B
Murphy's Tavern	A
Patrick Henry's Restaurant	C
Ramunto's Brick & Brew	D

stomping grounds. You can catch a guided (slightly prospective-student-oriented) **tour** of the college here during the summer (call ☎603/646-1110 for times and winter meeting place).

Flanking the north end of the green, along Wentworth Street, the looming **Baker Library**, with its 207-foot bell tower, is an imposing landmark. Inside, it holds the most arresting attraction on the campus, José Clemente Orozco's series of enormous **frescoes**, on the lower level. The Mexican artist painted these politically rousing murals, commissioned by the trustees of the college, between 1932 and 1934, while he was an artist-in-residence and visiting professor at Dartmouth. It's easy to see why conservative college officials and alumni viewed the violent depiction of the artist's stated theme, *An Epic of American Civilization*, as a direct insult. On one of the detailed, realistic panels, for example, a skeleton gives birth while lying upon a bed of dusty books, as a group of arrogant, robed scholars look on. In another panel, a large Jesus-like figure stands angrily next to a felled cross with an axe in his hand. Though college officials initially threatened to paint over the murals, they soon backed down, careful to avoid living up to Orozco's vision. Upstairs on the ground floor, check out the library's map room, which holds 150,000 sheet maps and 7000 atlases.

On the east side of the green stands **Dartmouth Row**, a collection of four impressive old buildings that look out over the grass from a slightly raised position. **Dartmouth Hall**, a large white building with a large "1784" on its hulking pediment, was the college's first permanent structure and remains a symbol of Dartmouth's academic prowess. Although it burned to the ground in 1904, the restored structure, which today houses Dartmouth's language and literature departments, remains on its original foundation. The other three halls in the row, **Reed**, **Thornton**, and **Wentworth**, house Dartmouth's history and philosophy departments, and the Dean's office, respectively.

Further north along Main Street, the memory of the school's most celebrated graduate, Daniel Webster, the brilliant lawyer, senator, and orator, is preserved in **Webster Cottage**, 30B Main St (May–Oct only; ☎603/646-3371), where he lived as an undergraduate. Webster later succeeded in defending the college before the Supreme Court in a landmark case that determined that the power to make an institution public rests with those who control it, rather than with those who have funded it.

Eating, drinking, and shopping

Like most college towns, Hanover and the surrounding area has its share of affordable **places to eat**. For a filling breakfast (the lunches and dinners here are mediocre at best), head to *Lou's Restaurant* on Main St (☎603/643-3321), where you can get tasty hashbrowns, eggs, and sausages for under $10. At *Patrick Henry's*, 39 S Main St (☎603/643-2345), you can take a seat at one of the big wooden booths and enjoy cheap sandwiches, as well as pastas and quesadillas. *Ramunto's Brick and Brew*, 68 S Main St (☎603/643-9500), serves delicious and affordable pizzas and has several beers on tap until at least midnight every night. *Sweet Tomatoes Trattoria*, 1 Court St in nearby Lebanon (☎603/448-1711), serves excellent fresh Italian specialties, such as wood-fired pizzas and tortellini with four cheeses for under $13. The most elegant (and most expensive) restaurant in town is the *Daniel Webster Room* (☎603/643-4300), inside the *Hanover Inn*, which boasts a traditional menu of finely grilled meats at $18–28 per entree.

OUTDOOR ACTIVITIES IN THE CONNECTICUT RIVER VALLEY

Quick to take advantage of their rather isolated location, Dartmouth students and Hanover residents alike take their **outdoor** time seriously. Hiking, biking, rowing, and swimming are all popular during the warmer months, while skiing (both cross-country and downhill) and skating are the activities of choice during the winter. The town's residents include best-selling travel author Bill Bryson, whose most recent book, *A Walk in the Woods*, chronicled his adventures along the 3000-mile Appalachian Trail, which runs right through Hanover along Rte-10A – during the summer, grizzled hikers trudge into town with some regularity. The Dartmouth Outing Club, in Robinson Hall (call ☎603/646-2428 for information), maintains hundreds of additional miles of **hiking trails** in the area and also leads group **bike rides**.

You can **rent bikes** (and snowshoes in the winter) for $25 per day from Omer and Bob's Sportshop, 7 Allen St (☎603/643-3525). **Rowing** on the Connecticut River remains an extremely popular way to take in the scenery while getting some exercise; Dartmouth Recreation Rowing (☎603/646-3434) and the Ledyard Canoe Club (☎603/643-6709) rent **canoes** and **kayaks** and can suggest routes. In the winter, Dartmouth's very own **alpine ski** area, the Dartmouth Skiway, ten miles north in Lyme (☎603/795-2143; $22 weekdays, $31 weekends), rents skis and snowboards. The Silver Fox Ski and Ice Skate Center, in Hanover (☎603/646-2440), maintains 35km of **cross-country skiing** trails and rents skiing and **ice skating** equipment.

If you're in the mood for an Ivy League-flavored **workout**, Dartmouth's enormous athletic facility (☎603/646-2109, *www.Dartmouth.edu/~athfac*), centered around the **Alumni Gymnasium**, along East Wheelock Street, has a modern fitness center, two pools, tennis courts, racquetball and squash courts, and a basketball court. Nonstudents can buy an all-day guest pass for $10.

The place to **drink** in town is *Murphy's*, at 11 S Main St (☎603/643-4075), which also has a popular restaurant serving an eclectic array of healthy American cuisine. For **books**, head to the sprawling Dartmouth Bookstore, 33 S Main St, which has been owned and operated by the same family since 1883. The place is so big it publishes its own four-page map and guide, available at the door. Another place to shop in the area is the **Powerhouse Mall**, on Rte-10 in West Lebanon, where forty specialty stores are housed in an old brick electric powerhouse.

Around Hanover: Lyme and Cornish

Time stands still in tiny **LYME**, only ten miles north of Hanover along Rte-10. The grassy town center is perfect for an evening stroll, which will take you past the attractive 1811 white-clapboard **Lyme Congregational Church**, featuring a bell supposedly cast by Paul Revere. After checking out the church's beautiful interior woodwork, have a look at the creepy old cemetery in back. Of a couple of **places to stay** in Lyme, the *Alden Country Inn*, 1 Market St, off Rte-10, on the common in the center of town (☎603/795-2222 or 1-800/794-2296, *www.aldencountryinn.com*; ⑥), is the best, offering fourteen sizeable upstairs rooms and a full breakfast. On the first floor, the candle-lit *Tavern and Grille* serves hearty portions of New England chow.

Other than a collection of scenic pastures and a few covered bridges, there's not much left in the town of **CORNISH**, south of Hanover along Rte-120, which was a well-known artistic center in the late nineteenth century. The thing to see here is the **Saint-Gaudens National Historic Site**, off Rte-12A (late May to late Oct daily 9am–4.30pm; ☎603/675-2175, *www.nps.gov/saga*; $4), where sculptor Augustus Saint-Gaudens lived and worked between 1885 and 1907, when he died. Saint-Gaudens was best known for his lifelike heroic bronze sculptures, including the Shaw Memorial in Boston and the General William T. Sherman Monument in New York City. Many well-known artists, writers, poets, and musicians, including Maxfield Parrish, Kenyon Cox, and Charles Platt, followed Saint-Gaudens to Cornish, establishing the **Cornish Colony**, an informal and supportive group. Saint-Gaudens' house, his studio, and several galleries displaying his sculptures, are open to the public. Take the time to wander around the beautiful grounds, which feature well-cared-for gardens, two wooded nature trails, and a relaxing expanse of green grass. You can also check out works in progress by the artist-in-residence at the **Ravine Studio**, in the woods along the northern edge of the property. Just north along Rte-12A, works by many of the area's famed artists are on display at the small **Cornish Colony Gallery and Museum** (Memorial Day–Oct 9am–5pm; ☎603/675-6000; $5), whose gardens were designed by Rose Standish Nichols, the first female landscape architect in America.

A few minutes south of town off of Rte-12A, the **Cornish-Windsor covered bridge**, connecting New Hampshire with Vermont, is the longest covered bridge in the United States, though unless you're an enthusiast, it may not be worth seeking out. It was constructed in 1866 and restored in 1989. A little further south, on Springfield Road just off of Rte-11 in **Charleston**, the **Fort at No. 4** (Wed–Mon 10am–4pm; $7) hokily reenacts colonial life in the 1740s and 1750s. Costumed interpreters roam the grounds, acting out the chores and activities of the day in various re-created living quarters and work areas, including old blacksmith and candlemaking shops.

If you're looking for a comfortable **place to stay**, the best around is the luxurious *Chase House Bed and Breakfast*, on Rte-12A (☎603/675-5391 or 1-800/401-9455, *chasehouse1@fcgnetworks; www.chasehouse.com*; ⑥). The well-decorated nineteenth-century mansion is also the birthplace and one-time residence of Salmon Portland Chase, Chief Justice of the US Supreme Court in the 1860s, in whose honor the Chase Manhattan Bank was posthumously named. Today the inn features seven exquisitely furnished rooms and delicious breakfasts (included).

THE LAKES REGION

The vacation-oriented **LAKES REGION**, occupying the state's central corridor, east of I-93, almost doubles its population between May and September, when throngs of visitors crowd the area's restaurants, hotels, lakefront cottages, beaches, and crystal-clear waters. The lakes themselves – **Winnipesaukee**, **Squam**, and **Winnisquam** are the three largest – are the obvious attractions here, and on warm summer weekends they can seem overrun with pleasure craft, all of which are available for rent at the many town marinas. Fishing, swimming, camping, and relaxing on the beach are also popular, and you can enjoy a view of the lakes from afar after hiking to the top of one of several peaks that wrinkle the countryside.

There are literally hundreds of lakes here, created by the snowmelt flowing south from the White Mountains, and the biggest by far is **Lake Winnipesaukee**, which forms the definitive center of the region. Long segments of the enormous lake's shoreline, especially in the east, are carpeted with thick forests that sweep

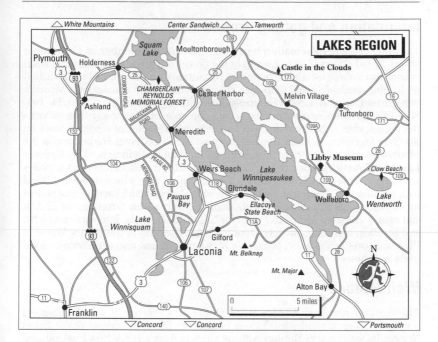

down from surrounding hills to the water's edge. Covering some 72 square miles, the lake is dotted with 274 islands – most of which are privately owned – and its irregular shape, a seemingly endless continuum of inlets and peninsulas, resembles that of a giant paint splatter. The eastern and western shores of Lake Winnipesaukee are quite distinct: sophisticated **Wolfeboro** is the center of the sparsely populated and more upscale region to the east of the lake, while **Weirs Beach** is the most developed stretch of the crowded western shore. Further north, the down-to-earth nineteenth-century towns around beautiful **Squam Lake** are some of the most inviting in the region.

The western Winnipesaukee shore

It's pleasant enough, but the western Winnipesaukee shore is the most visited part of the Lakes Region. Once inhabited by the Abenaki Indians, its position on the major north–south stagecoach route in the early nineteenth century, and, later, the railroad route north to the increasingly popular White Mountains, made it a major stopover. Nowadays, gas stations, cheap hotels, and convenience stores line the major roadways, such as US-3 and Rte-11, although nearly every town in the area boasts sweeping views of some body of water. Downtown **Meredith**, squeezed between Lake Waukewan and Lake Winnipesaukee, is an appealing collection of shops and restaurants, but **Weirs Beach**, south along US-3, is the epitome of summertime overkill, with enough arcades, ice-cream parlors, and roadside fun-parks to keep the kids happy for weeks. Undistinguished **Laconia** is the biggest town in the area, while the resort town of **Gilford** maintains a more relaxed disposition.

Information and getting around

The best source of **information** here is the **Meredith Chamber of Commerce** (☎603/279-6121), on US-3 just south of the downtown area. They distribute loads of brochures about local attractions and restaurants, and can provide information on lodging availability and help with reservations. Public **transport** is virtually non-existent around Lake Winnipesaukee, although Concord Trailways (☎1-800/639-3317, *www.concordtrailways.com*), the sole **bus** company that services the region, calls at 331 S Main St in Laconia, the Wallace Convenience Store on Rte-25 in Meredith, Robbins General Store on Rte-25 in Center Harbor, and at the Moultonborough Emporium along Rte-25 in Moultonborough. The **Greater Laconia Transit Agency** (☎603/528-2496 or 1-800/294-2496) operates a trolley and double-decker bus Memorial Day through Labor Day, which connects Gilford with Laconia, and Tilton and Weirs Beach with Meredith and Laconia, stopping at major restaurants and shopping spots along the way; all-day tickets go for $2. You can **rent a car** from Meredith Ford (☎603/279-4521), at the intersection of US-3 and Rte-25 in Meredith. **Bicycles** rent for $15–24 per day at the Greasy Wheel in Plymouth (☎603/536-3655), 40 S Main St, where you can also get advice on local trails and routes.

Weirs Beach

The short boardwalk at **WEIRS BEACH**, the very essence of seaside tackiness – despite being fifty miles inland – is in summer the social center of the Lakes Region. Its wooden jetty throngs with vacationers from all over New England, and its amusement arcades jingle with cash – there's even a little crescent of sandy beach, suitable for family swimming. The roads are lined with neon signs, mini-golf courses, waterslide playland extravaganzas, and motels clogged with family-filled minivans in summer, when the crowds can be almost overwhelming.

You'd best head elsewhere if you're looking for a relaxing lakeside afternoon. If you're up for a few hours of slippery diversion in the sun, however, you might try the better of the two competing **water parks**, Surf Coaster (summer daily 10am–7pm, sometimes 8pm; $20), which offers dramatic rides and a wave machine on Rte-11B just south of town. Failing that, a great way to take in Winnipesaukee's beautiful expanse of inlets and peninsulas while getting away from the ugliness of Weirs Beach is a cruise aboard the landmark **MS Mount Washington** (mid-May to mid-Oct; ☎603/366-5531 or 1-888/843-6686, *www.msmountwashington.com*; $18, 150min), a 230-foot monster of a boat that departs from the dock in the center of

---

THE NEW HAMPSHIRE INTERNATIONAL SPEEDWAY

Twenty miles south of Laconia in **LOUDON**, the **New Hampshire International Speedway** (☎603/783-4931, *www.nhis.com*) holds weekly NASCAR and motorcycle races from April through October, attracting large crowds of beer-swilling motorsports enthusiasts. The Winston Cup, held in mid-July, is the most popular event here, and during this time many of the hotels and inns in the Lakes Region fill up well in advance. Tickets for the races cost $15–50. If watching fast cars whirl around the track in a deafening frenzy while shielding your eyes from the burning sun is your idea of a good time, this may be just the event for you.

town several times per day to sail to Wolfeboro on the western side of the lake. The ship also sets sail for dinner and dance cruises several times per week (around $30). If you'd rather not listen to the whir of the *Mount Washington*'s engine as you take in the sights, hop aboard the **Queen of Winnipesaukee** (mid-June–Sept; ☎603/366-5005), a 46-foot sailing yacht, which departs for ninety-minute jaunts ($12) daily at 11.15am, 1.15pm, and 3.15pm, and two-hour trips ($16) at 5.15pm (Tues–Sun) and 8pm (Wed & Sat) from the public docks between the beach and the railroad station.

Meredith

MEREDITH, four miles north of Weirs Beach, is more upscale than its neighbor, though still lacking in sophistication. The friendly town center, up the hill behind the massive Mill Falls Shopping Center development, spills into the pleasant **Meredith Marina**, 2 Bayshore Drive (☎603/279-7921), where you can rent a motor boat for a mere $195 per day, $145 per half-day. The **Winnipesaukee Railroad** (☎603/745-2135) operates scenic trips ($8.50 for 1hr, $9.50 for 2hr) along the lakeshore between Meredith and Weirs Beach, on weekends from Memorial Day, and then daily between mid-June and mid-October, including special fall foliage excursions (even a Santa Claus special!). The sandy town **beach**, with mountain views, is located on Waukewan Street along the shores of tiny **Lake Waukewan**. Right outside the center of town, a pretty little **lakeside park** makes for a pleasant stroll; while you're there, you can wonder who decided to mount the anti-aircraft gun from a WWII battle cruiser there on the grass.

Just outside Meredith, off of US-3, the only thing to admire is **Annalee's Doll Museum** (summer daily 9am–5pm; rest of year closes earlier ☎603/279-6542), in reality a hard-sell toy shop, specializing in painted-felt dolls. Those items onto which they've managed to stitch the heads back to front are offered at a 25 percent reduction.

Practicalities

The center of Meredith is compact and walkable, though you'll need a **car** to fully realize what this side of the lake has to offer. During the summer, the intersection of Routes 3 and 25 is one of the busiest in the region. If you need a **place to stay**, the *Inns at Mill Falls* (☎603/279-7006 or 1-800/622-6455, *www.millfalls-baypoint.com*; ⑧) is an exceptionally comfortable – if somewhat expensive – place to rest your head, with clean, modern rooms and attentive service. The *Tuckernuck Inn*, at 25 Red Gate Lane (☎603/279-5521, *www.thetuckernuckinn.com*; ⑤)-is a good-value B&B near the center of town; some rooms have shared bath. Another good bet near the center of town is the *Meredith Inn*, at the corner of Main and Waukewan streets (☎603/279-0000, *www.meredithinn.com*; ⑥). Rooms at the *Olmec Motor Lodge* on Pleasant St (☎603/279-8584; ④) are more basic, although the lakeside setting is nice. The family-oriented *Harbor Hill* **camping** area (mid-May to mid-Oct; ☎603/279-6910; $18), at 189 Rte-25 E, has 33 tent sites, 82 full hookup RV sites, a pool, and a children's playground. *Clearwater Campground*, on Rte-104 (☎603/279-7761), has 150 shaded sites and hot showers.

One of the better places to **eat** in Meredith, just off of the main drag in an old brick building at 8 Plymouth St, is *Mame's* (☎603/279-4631), which does an excellent selection of creative and affordable sandwiches for lunch, and more expensive ($9.95–18.95) seafood, chicken, and steak dinners; there's also a cozy **pub**, which can get crowded on weekend nights. *Phu Jee*, at 55 Main St (☎603/279-1129), offers a dizzying array of authentic Chinese food ($10.95–14.50). The *Boathouse Grill*, 1 Bay Point, at the intersection of Rte-3 and Rte-25 (☎603/279-2253), with a relaxed dining room on the water, is a nice place to eat seafood (entrees are $11–18).

Laconia, Gilford, and Glendale

LACONIA, southwest from Lake Winnipesaukee on the shores of **Winnisquam Lake**, has long been the most populated town in the Lakes Region, established as a trading and manufacturing center after the railroad reached the city in 1848. Some of the factories in use back then – when they produced such things as nails and hosiery – continue as office space. Unfortunately, they do not comprise much of a reason to stop here; Laconia is mostly just convenient as a place to pick up supplies. If you do get past the commercial strip of malls, car dealerships, and fast-food joints to Laconia's downtown, the payoff will be a short and fairly depressed stretch of empty storefronts.

The pleasant twin villages of **GILFORD** and **GLENDALE**, east of Laconia along Rte-11A, are flanked by a huge marina filled with the pleasure craft of wealthy visitors, who frequent the upscale resorts and hotels nestled in the thick greenery along the quiet roads that wind through town. For excellent views of the lake and surrounding region, head for the top of **Mount Belknap**, which at 2384 feet is the highest peak in the Belknap Range, along the west side of the lake, east of Laconia. The easiest and shortest route up the mountain begins along Belknap Mountain Carriage Road; turn off of Rte-11A at the lights in the center of Gilford, drive through the village on Cherry Valley Road and follow the signs for the Fire Tower on Belknap. Along Rte-11 east of Glendale, **Ellacoya State Beach** (May–Oct; ☎603/293-7821) is one of the finer sandy beaches – and the only one that's state maintained – on Lake Winnipesaukee, with 600 feet of sand, and a **campground** that affords some great views of the lake from many of its 38 sites ($30).

Practicalities

If you're planning on **staying**, the *Belknap Point Motel*, at 107 Belknap Point Rd (☎603/293-7511, *www.bpmotel.com*; ⑤–⑥), offers somewhat modern lakeside accommodations in a boxy, white building with a good view of the lake and surrounding mountains. Some rooms have full kitchens and can be rented by the week. Slightly more upscale, *B Mae's Inn & Suites* (☎603/293-7526 or 1-800/458-3877; ⑥), 17 Harris Shore Rd (Rte-11), has two pools, a Jacuzzi, and an exercise room – all within walking distance of the beach. Just past Gilford on Rte-11A, *Gunstock* (☎603/293-4341 or 1-800/486-7862, *www.gunstock.com*) doubles as an alpine ski area during the winter and a recreation area during the summer. Summer activities include mountain-bike riding (you can rent bikes for $30 per day at the camp store), horseback riding ($25 for a one hour trailride), and hiking (visit the store for trail maps and advice). **Campsites** are available for $20 per night, while camping cabins, with electricity and water, can be had for $50 per night or $310 per week.

The Meadowbrook Farm Musical Arts Center in Gilford (☎603/225-1111 or 1-888/563-2369, *www.meadowbrookevents.com*) is the largest **musical venue** in the Lakes Region, presenting such shows as the Indigo Girls and the Dave Matthews Band. For a **drink** or hearty snack in Gilford, try *Patrick's Pub*, at the intersection of Rte-11 and Rte-11B (☎603/293-0841).

The eastern Winnipesaukee shore

The eastern shore of Lake Winnipesaukee is a lot less developed than the western shore, and has a more polished and elegant air about it, although the refined quality of the food, lodging, and atmosphere is reflected in steeper prices. First established as a popular summer destination in the late 1700s by Governor John Wentworth, tourism is still the major industry here, but in a much more relaxed fashion: there are no putt-putt courses and waterslides, and fewer children. Wealthy families vacation year after year at the many stately privately owned homes along Lake Winnipesaukee's shore, and couples flock to the many secluded country B&Bs of the region. This side of the lake is also better for walking and outdoor activities, although most in search of rugged adventure head further north for the popular peaks of the White Mountains. Water-based activities are the rule here, and there are several good public beaches around **Wolfeboro**, the most populated and interesting town in the area. At the northern end of Lake Winnipesaukee, the quiet town of **Moultonborough** has one of the oldest country stores in the country, and at the southern end, **Alton Bay** was once a railroad hub but has settled into a low-key summer resort town. **Melvin Village** and **Tuftonboro** are unobtrusive and sparsely populated, with winding tree-shaded country roads, the occasional antique shop, and some alluring nineteenth-century architecture. North, in the foothills of the White Mountains, the all-season small town of **Tamworth** is home to a fine theater and a few pleasant old inns.

Information and getting around

The best source for information on the eastern shore is the **Wolfeboro Chamber of Commerce**, in the old red railroad building on Railroad Street in the center of town (☎603/569-2200 or 1-800/516-5324, *www.wolfeboro.com*). They stock a dizzying array of brochures and will give the lowdown on local attractions and lodging. **Public transport** is scarce, although the Wolfeboro Trolley Company (☎603/569-5257; $3) operates a short narrated loop around Wolfeboro and tickets are good for an entire day. **Driving** in the area is pleasant. None of the roads along the peaceful and sparsely populated eastern shore are more than two lanes wide, and although traffic is rarely a problem, Rte-28 in and around Wolfeboro can be somewhat congested during the peak of the summer season. To get to the eastern side of the lake from the western side, the drive along Rte-25 and Rte-109 is the easiest and most scenic route; using Rte-11 and Rte-28 through Alton Bay around the south end of the lake is slightly faster. From Boston or Portsmouth, take the Spaulding Turnpike off of I-95, then Rte-11 W, followed by Rte-28 N in Alton. Miller Rent-a-car has an office in Wolfeboro along Rte-28 (☎603/569-1068), where you can **rent a car** for $35 per day or $200 per week.

Accommodation

Cheap **places to stay** on Winnipesaukee's eastern shore are difficult to find, although romantic **inns** and **bed-and-breakfasts** are everywhere. Family-oriented **cottages** are also prevalent, with weekly and monthly rentals available. Many hotels and inns are only available seasonally, so call to be sure, especially in winter months. **Camping** in the quiet birch forests that crowd the lake's shore is also a pleasant summer option, although insect repellent is an absolute must. The only real **budget** options are further east, in **Ossipee**.

Hotels, Inns, and B&Bs

The Lake Motel, 280 S Main St, Wolfeboro (☎603/569-1100, *www.thelakemotel.com*). Modern accommodation, with tennis courts and private sandy beach. Some rooms with kitchen. ⑤.

Lakeview Inn and Motorlodge, 120 N Main St, Wolfeboro (☎603/569-1335). Nicely decorated rooms with modern amenities overlooking Wolfeboro in a restored inn and two-story hotel. ③–⑤.

Old Orchard Inn, Lee Rd, Moultonborough (☎603/476-5004). Relaxing B&B in the middle of an apple orchard. Six rooms are decorated with quilts and antiques. ⑤–⑥.

Pine View Lodge, Rte-109, Melvin Village (☎603/544-3800). The best thing about this basic hotel is the price – it's one of the cheaper places around. ④.

Tamworth Inn, Main St, Tamworth (☎603/323-7721 or 1-800/642-7352, *www.tamworth.com*). Pleasant 1833 inn just across the street from the Barnstormer's Summer Theater (see p.433) in the center of town. Also has elegant dining room serving gourmet home-made American cuisine Tues–Sat. Full breakfast included. ⑥.

Tuc' Me Inn B&B, 118 N Main St (Rte-109 N), Wolfeboro (☎603/569-5702). Homely 1850 Federal/Colonial inn with tastefully furnished rooms and full breakfast close to the lake and town. ⑤.

Wolfeboro Inn, 90 N Main St, Wolfeboro (☎603/569-3016 or 1-800/451-2389, *www .wolfeboroinn.com*). Built in 1812 with 44 well-appointed rooms, this stately inn is situated along the waterfront just a few yards from the town proper. ⑤–⑥.

Camping

Willey Brook Campground, Rte-28 north of Wolfeboro (☎603/569-9493). Tent sites three miles from downtown Wolfeboro and one mile from Wentworth State Beach. $16–25.

Wolfeboro Campground, 61 Haines Hill Rd, Wolfeboro (☎603/569-9881). Fifty wooded family campsites with hot showers and facilities for $18 per night. May 15–Oct 12.

BIRTHPLACE OF DANIEL WEBSTER

New Hampshire's best-known statesman, orator, and public figure, **Daniel Webster**, was born in 1782 in the tiny two-room farmhouse on Flaghold Road off of Rte-127 in **FRANKLIN**. Now known simply as the **Daniel Webster Birthplace** (mid-May to mid-Oct; ☎603/934-5057; $2.50), the restored home contains period furniture, antiques, and some Webster memorabilia, including books he read as a child. Webster attended Phillips Exeter Academy, graduated from Dartmouth College in 1801, and went on to build a successful law practice before serving in Congress from 1813 to 1817 and in the US Senate from 1827 to 1841. He loomed large on the political scene in his day, delivering persuasive speeches on topics as far ranging as states' rights, slavery, the Union, the US–Canadian border, and Dartmouth College. As Secretary of State under presidents William Henry Harrison, Tyler, and Fillmore, Webster remained a staunch defender of the Union. During a particularly heated discussion in 1850, in which Webster debunked the ideal of states' rights, he coined the memorable phrase "Liberty and Union, now and forever, one and inseparable." In perhaps his most famous debate, the Dartmouth College Case of 1817, Webster defended his alma mater before the Supreme Court, which decided that states could not interfere with royal charters.

Wolfeboro

Because Governor John Wentworth built his summer home nearby in 1768, upscale **WOLFEBORO** claims to be "the oldest summer resort in America." Sandwiched between Lakes Winnipesaukee and Wentworth, at the intersection of Rte-109 and Rte-28, it has little to show for that history, but it's a relaxing place to spend a few hours, along the short but bustling Main Street (Rte-109). The governor's 4300-square-foot summer mansion, known as the Wentworth House Plantation, with its own saw mill, orchards, workers' village, and 600-acre deer park, was, at the time, a sort of Hearst Castle of New Hampshire. It burned to the ground in 1820 and was never rebuilt, but the area once occupied by the plantation, on Rte-109 three miles southeast of Rte-28, is now the **Governor John Wentworth State Historic Site** (summer only; free), an undeveloped park and archeological site.

A great way to take in Lake Winnipesaukee's grandeur is aboard the famous **MS Mount Washington** (see p.424), a 230-foot cruiser that departs from the dock in the center of town near *PJ's Dockside* restaurant. The relaxing two-and-a-half-hour **scenic cruises** connect Wolfeboro with Weirs Beach across the lake and are complete with historic narration. You could also hop aboard the smaller *Winnipesaukee Belle* (summer only; ☎603/569-3016; 90min; $10), a 75-passenger excursion boat that departs from the *Wolfeboro Inn* and tours the eastern end of the lake.

One fascinating stop-off, a few miles north of downtown Wolfeboro on Rte-109, is the **Libby Museum** (June 1 to mid-September, Tues–Sat 10am–4pm, Sun noon–4pm; $2), where turn-of-the-century dentist Henry Forset Libby's obsession with evolution is manifested by various ineptly stuffed animals (one can only hope he was a better dentist than taxidermist) and the skeletons of bears, orangutans, and humans. There's also a mastodon's tooth, a "Niddy-Noddy" spinning device, a random collection of fossils and insects, Native American artifacts, and a fingernail supposedly pulled out by its Chinese owner to demonstrate his new-found Christian faith. The setting of the museum, in a 1912 Historic Landmark house with a superb view of the lake from the front steps and a grassy lakefront park, makes the detour even more rewarding.

Moultonborough

Other than some remote B&Bs and quiet country roads, there's not much to the sprawling town of **MOULTONBOROUGH**, north of Lake Winnipesaukee on Rte-25. If you're passing through, however, you might stop off in the **Old Country Store**, at the intersection of Routes 25 and 109. One of the oldest of its kind, it sells everything from homemade dill pickles to penny candy to brass door knockers and carved wooden ducks. The bizarre "museum" upstairs houses a dusty collection of artifacts, including axes, saws, and carved Indian sculptures. If, on the other hand, you'd like to spend some time in the sun, off of Rte-25, near the end of Moultonborough Neck Road on Long Island, the **town beach** is a particularly good spot for picnicking and swimming. There's also a popular **beach** at the intersection of Routes 25 and 25B.

A little way east of town on Rte-171, **Castle in the Clouds** (May 9–Jun 5 weekends only; Jun 6–Labor Day daily 9am–5pm; Labor Day–Oct 18 daily 9am–4pm; $10 for tours or $4 for access to the grounds; ☎1-800/729-2468), the 5200-acre mountain estate of eccentric millionaire Thomas Plant, stops just short of being a complete tourist trap. It's saved by the uniqueness of the house itself, an interesting amalgamation of various architectural styles from around the world, betraying Spanish, Japanese, and Swiss influences. The roof, for example, is covered with red tiles, while the facade recalls a ski chalet. Built in 1913 and designed by Plant, the massive hilltop mansion was somewhat advanced for its time, with a centralized vacuum system, intercom, and a self-cleaning oven. These days, they've also added a brewery (whose Lucknow Beer can be found at local stores) and spring mountain water bottling plant, also included in the tour.

The Loon Preservation Committee maintains the small **Loon Center,** along quiet Lee's Mills Road off of Blake Road (June 1–Columbus Day, 9am–5pm; free; ☎603/476-5666), which houses a collection of exhibits about the endangered and much-loved birds, focusing on environmental awareness and the negative impact of pollution. You can view Lake Winnipesaukee from several vantage points along the **Loon Nest Trail,** which begins at the Loon Center and winds through upland forests and marshes near the lakeshore, and maybe even catch a glimpse (or at least hear the distinguished sounds) of one of the speckled birds.

Eating and drinking

There are plenty of high-class **places to eat** along Lake Winnipesaukee's eastern shore, although you'll pay for it along with all the other tourists. Seafood and panoramic lake views are the norm and reservations are suggested; budget options are limited. Hidden along the area's quiet rambling country roads, there are several out-of-the way eateries that are worth hunting down. The quiet **nightlife** centers around a few low-key local pubs.

The Cider Press, Middleton Rd, South Wolfeboro (☎603/569-2028). Hearty American food – ribs, steak, grilled salmon – in a rustic, candlelit dining room.

East of Suez, Rte-28, just south of Wolfeboro (☎603/569-1648). Huge portions of Asian food, from Thai to Chinese to Korean, authentically prepared and served in a high-ceilinged dining room. The Pad Thai is especially good. Entrees go for $11–15. Summer only.

Lydia's Cafe, Main St, Wolfeboro (☎603/569-3991). Fruit smoothies, espresso drinks, bagels, and excellent sandwiches in a cute little café in the center of town.

The Strawberry Patch, Main St, Wolfeboro (☎603/569-5523). Excellent, freshly prepared breakfasts and lunch in a homely and unpretentious dining room just off Main St. Open daily 7.30am–2pm (until 1pm on Sun).

Wolfeboro House of Pizza, Main St, Wolfeboro (☎603/569-8408). Good Greek-owned place, serving solid pizza and pastas.

The Wolfeboro Inn, 90 N Main St, Wolfeboro (☎603/569-3016). The fancy *1812 Room* serves good expensive New England-style cuisine, but *Wolfe's Tavern*, a dark pub-like eatery with a huge selection of burgers, sandwiches, pasta, soups, and salads, is the better value of the two. The tavern also has 72 beers on tap; if you want to get your own iron mug (check the ceiling for the 1300 or so that have already been claimed) you have to drink one of each type and then kiss the stuffed moosehead (only two beers count per day).

Wolfetrap Grill and Rawbar, 19 Bay St, Wolfeboro (☎603/569-1047, *www.wolfetrap.com*). Unpretentious and basic restaurant just outside of town with a range of seafood plates including lobster, clams, and softshell crab dinners.

The Woodshed, Lee's Mills Road, Moultonborough (☎603/476-2311). Prime rib is the specialty at this old barn-turned-restaurant. Ask for a table in the screened-in patio on warm summer evenings. Dinner only, with moderate prices.

EASTERN SHORE OUTDOOR ACTIVITIES

The eastern shore has enough **outdoor activities** to keep even the most avid enthusiast busy. Hiking, boating, sailing, fishing, swimming, mountain biking, and kayaking are all big in summer, while cross-country skiing and snowmobiling satisfy outdoor urges during the winter.

The best public **beach** for swimming and picnicking in the Wolfeboro area is **Clow Beach** in Wentworth State Park on Lake Wentworth. **Brewster Beach** (summer only; ☎603/569-1532) on Lake Winnipesaukee at the end of Clark Road south of town is also good for sunning and swimming. Once you've done sunning yourself, there are a couple of decent, if gentle, local **hiking routes**. The **Mount Major Trail**, north of Alton on Rte-11, offers excellent lake views and takes about an hour and a half. The scenic trail to the top of **Bald Peak**, at the Moultonborough–Tuftonboro town line on Rte-171, is a mile long. The Mount Flag Trail in Tuftonboro is a strenuous seven-mile loop. For a shorter jaunt (half a mile), with rewarding panoramic views of the lake and surrounding forests, try the **Abenaki Tower Trail**, off of Rte-109 in Tuftonboro across from Wawbeek Road. **Snowmobiles** and **cross-country skiers** fill the trails during winter months. Call the Cross Country Ski Association (☎603/569-3151) or the New Hampshire Snowmobile Club (☎603/271-3254) for information and guidance.

As for **watersports**, Goodhue Hawkins Navy Yard, at 244 Sewall Rd in Wolfeboro (☎603/569-2371), rents several types of **boats,** ranging from $85 to $275 per day. Wet Wolfe Rentals, 19 Bay St, Wolfeboro (☎603/569-1503), rents boats by the hour and gives tours of the lake in its antique wooden boat. You can take an all-inclusive guided **fishing** trip with *Gadabout Golder*, in Wolfeboro (☎603/569-6426), for $100 per person for half a day on the lake. The Winnipesaukee Kayak Company, 17 Bay St in Wolfeboro (☎603/569-9926), rents **kayaks** for $40 per day and canoes for $50 per day and also leads various tours and multi-day excursions. For a truly unique lake experience, try a **seaplane** ride, which departs from Wolfeboro and costs $50 per flight (☎603/569-1310 for information).

Squam Lake

Much smaller than its sprawling neighbor, but still the second largest body of water in the state, beautiful **Squam Lake** can actually hold more appeal than Lake Winnipesaukee. The pace here is slower, the roads less crowded, and, thanks to a conscientious group of old-money landowners, the land has been less developed. In fact, over a century ago, one wealthy man from Boston, whose relatives still own a sizeable portion of the lakefront property, is said to have exclaimed while building his summer home that he wanted to "buy everything I can see, because I don't want anything getting in the way of my view."

Most of the activities here revolve around the **outdoors**; hiking, boating, swimming, or simply relaxing on the beach are all popular during the summer months. It's easy to see why producers chose this lake as the setting for the 1981 film *On Golden Pond*, starring Jane and Henry Fonda – the lake is pristine and glassy and the setting sun brings a quiet calm over the water and surrounding forests. With a population of 1700, **Holderness** is the largest town on the lake, although it's really nothing more than a gas station, a few stately old inns, a couple of restaurants and a dock. **Center Sandwich**, along the north edge of Squam Lake, and **Center Harbor**, squeezed between Lake

Winnipesaukee and Squam Lake, also maintain their nineteenth-century quaintness, while **Ashland**, closer to I-93, near Little Squam Lake, has several good restaurants and a slightly more comospolitan feel.

Holderness

Named for the earl of Holderness, a friend of Governor Wentworth's, **HOLDER-NESS**, at the intersection of US-3 and Rte-113, was granted its original town charter in 1751. The popular statesman, Samuel Livermore, had acquired half of the town's land by the late eighteenth century through grants and purchases, building a church and housing, and although nothing of much historical significance ever happened here, the Holderness School has remained a prestigious college preparatory school since its founding in 1879. The unpretentious village brings together a loosely defined grouping of buildings along the lakeshore next to a well-used public dock. The general store in town is the place to come for supplies and provisions before you head out for a day on the lake.

Squam Lakes Tours (☎603/968-7577; $10) is the best of several companies offering **boat rides** in and out of the picturesque lake's many coves and inlets. Its two-hour jaunts, which depart from the dock a half-mile south of town at 10am, 2pm, and 4pm, include a look at the **Thayer Cottage**, where the bulk of *On Golden Pond* was filmed. If you'd rather steer your own boat, rent a five-person motorboat for $79 per day or a three-person canoe for $49 per day from *Squam Lakeside Farm*, on US-3 (☎603/968-7227). The **Squam Lakes Association** (SLA), through its helpful office on US-3 (☎603/968-7336, *www.squamlakes.org*), remains "dedicated to conserving the natural beauty, peaceful character, and unique resource values of the lakes and surrounding area." They also rent **canoes** ($45/day), **kayaks** ($40/day), and **sailboats** ($50/day) and sell trail guides to the region ($3). They also run half-day kayak tours for $50 and give two-and-a-half-hour kayak lessons for $45.

The best local **beach** is accessible along a short trail through the **Chamberlain-Reynolds Memorial Forest**, off of College Road. To get there from Holderness, follow US-3 south, take a left on Rte-25B, and a left on College Road. The forest is on your right; park in the small lot and follow the Ant Hill Trail for about twenty minutes – be sure to bring some insect repellent. The most popular **hike** in the area begins at the Rattlesnake Trailhead along Rte-113 and follows the **Old Bridle Path** to the top of **Rattlesnake Mountain**, providing spectacular views of Squam Lake and the surrounding hills, with only half an hour of effort. Other trails to the top of Rattlesnake Mountain, such as the **Ramsey Trail**, begin along Pinehurst Road, off of Rte-113. The **Mount Morgan Trail**, which begins at the trailhead along Rte-113, 5.4 miles northeast of US-3, and ascends 1400 feet along a 2.1-mile trail, is also a rewarding hike. Additional hiking suggestions are available at the SLA headquarters (see above).

A delicate glimpse of the area's natural habitat and inhabitants is afforded by the **Science Center of New Hampshire at Squam Lake**, near the intersection of Rte-113 and Rte-25 in the center of town (May–Nov daily 9.30am–4.30pm; $8 July & Aug, $6 rest of year; *www.sciencecentrofnh.org*), which features live animals – including bears, bobcats, owls, and otters – housed in settings that resemble their natural habitats along a quarter-mile nature walk. Compared to a typical zoo, it's refreshingly spacious, though you may find it overrun with large groups of schoolchildren.

Practicalities

By far the ritziest and most expensive **place to stay** is the *Manor on Golden Pond*, on US-3 overlooking the lake (☎603/968-3348 or 1-800/545-2141; ⑧), an elegant mansion complete with crystal chandeliers, sweeping vistas, and roaring stone fireplaces. Their *Wine Spectator* Award-winning dining room offers five-course prix-fixe gourmet meals for $50 ($38 for three courses). Less expensive and more down-to-earth, the welcoming *Inn on Golden Pond*, on US-3 along Little Squam (☎603/968-7269, *www.innongoldenpond.com*; ⑤–⑦); has ten large rooms, friendly hosts, full breakfasts, and table tennis in the game room. Though its rooms are nothing special, the well-situated *White Oak Motel*, at the intersection of Rte-25 and US-3 (☎603/968-3673; ③), is the cheapest place around. They also rent cottages for $250–300 per week. The **SLA** maintains primitive **camping sites** on Moon Island, Bowman Island, and in the Chamberlain Reynolds Forest, costing $36 per site (up to six people) on weekends, $32 per site weekdays, and requiring reservations (call ☎603/968-7336 ext 3).

The only waterfront **restaurant** in town, *Walter's Basin*, on US-3 (☎603/968-4412), serves decent seafood and pasta for $10–15 per entree in a pleasant carpeted dining room. The *Golden Pond Country Store* (daily 6am–10pm; ☎603/968-3434), at the intersection of US-3 and Rte-113, sells pizza, deli sandwiches, fishing supplies, groceries, beer, newspapers, gas, and just about anything else you might need while traveling in the area.

THE BARNSTORMERS

Founded in 1931 by Francis Cleveland (son of 22nd President Grover Cleveland), his wife, Alice, and Edward Goodnow, the **Barnstormers** is the oldest professional summer theater group in the state. It is also one of the few theater companies in the country in which the same actors perform a different play each week, rehearsing the following week's play during the day while acting in the current production at night. Presenting a wide range of productions – from classics like Arthur Miller's *Death of a Salesman* to comedies such as *Lady from Maxim's*, by Georges Feydeau – the theater company plays to consistently large crowds. Housed in a refurbished old store in the center of **Tamworth Village** since 1935, the company typically produces eight plays per summer. Call ☎603/323-8500 for schedule and ticket information.

Center Harbor and Center Sandwich

The relaxing village of **CENTER HARBOR**, nicely situated near Squam's eastern shore, is a good base from which to explore the Lakes Region, especially if you have a car. There isn't much here, but it's close to the larger settlements of Lake Winnipesaukee if you're looking for some action. The *Red Hill Inn*, at the junction of Rte-25B and College Road in Center Harbor (☎603/279-7001 or 1-800/573-3445, *www.redhillinn.com*; ⑥–⑦), is a favorite year-round **place to stay**, with panoramic views of the lakes and mountains and good cross-country skiing in the winter. The *Watch Hill B&B*, on Old Meredith Road (☎603/253-4334; ④), is a nicely appointed four-room inn with great gourmet breakfasts and a screened porch. Larger and more luxurious, with a country club atmosphere, the *Kona Mansion Inn* (☎603/253-4900; 6) has tennis, golf, and swimming in a tranquil lakeside setting. At the south end of town, on the shore of Lake Winnipesaukee, the enormous (151-site) family-oriented *Arcadia Campground* (☎603/253-6759) offers such amenities as a grocery store and video room. Three Legged Tours (☎603/253-7635) offers all-inclusive day-long canoe ($48), walking ($32), and biking ($54) trips around the area.

Nine miles northeast along Rte-113, at the base of the Sandwich Range, **CENTER SANDWICH** groups another string of white-clapboard buildings, including a general store and typically steepled church, in a quaint version of a New England town. Though it's right next to Squam Lake, you'd never know it; the dense forest along the shoreline, which is largely privately owned, obscures the view. The best **place to stay** in town is the *Corner House Inn* (☎603/284-6219; 5), an inviting, informal, and popular bed-and-breakfast that's been around for over 150 years. You could also try the *Overlook Farm B&B*, 14 Mountain Rd (☎603/284-6485, *www.ivacation.com/p6025.htm*; 4–5), with four cozy rooms (some with shared bath) in a quiet setting.

Ashland

Though tiny **ASHLAND** (population 1900) was a thriving manufacturing town in the nineteenth century, producing lumber, wool, gloves, and paper, it's now little more than a sleepy lakeside village. There's not much to stop for, unless you need a quick bite to eat or a place to sleep without straying too far from I-93. If you decide to **stay the night**, the *Glynn House Inn*, 43 Highland St (☎603/968-3775 or 1-800/637-9599, *www.nettx.com/glynnhouse.html*; 5–6), with ornate woodwork and a wraparound porch, is one of the better-looking B&Bs in the state. Slightly cheaper, the well-situated *Black Horse Motor Court*, on US-3 (☎603/968-7116; 3), offers modest rooms and housekeeping cottages that are available nightly or weekly. The *Common Man*, a rustic brick building in the center of town along Main Street (☎603/968-7030), serves great lunches ($5–10) and gourmet dinners ($10–20), specializing in lobster bisque and roast prime rib. For something cheaper and less formal, try the *Ashland House of Pizza*, also on Main Street (☎603/968-3686), which serves good pizzas and sandwiches.

North to the White Mountains

US-3 west from Ashland intersects with I-93, which heads north to Lincoln and North Woodstock in the White Mountains. At the foot of the mountains, in **Plymouth**, you can either continue north along the Interstate or head another five miles west to the **Polar Caves** (mid-May–Oct daily 9am–5pm; $8) – though these are not so much caves as a cascade of clammy granite boulders tumbled against a hillside, between which visitors find pleasure in squeezing themselves – while paying handsomely for the privilege. A large giftshop sells some supremely irrelevant "souvenirs." A good place to get **cheap eats** in Plymouth is *Jigger Johnson's* (☎603/536-4386), where you can gorge on big sandwiches, hamburgers, pizzas, and salads as well as more expensive steak and seafood entrees.

THE WHITE MOUNTAINS

Thanks to their accessibility to both Montréal and Boston, the **WHITE MOUN-TAINS** have become a year-round tourist destination, popular with summer hikers and winter skiers alike, and attracting some six million annual visitors. It's a commercialized region, with quite a lot of tourist development flanking the main highways, but the great granite massifs retain much of their majesty and power. **Mount Washington**, the highest peak not only in the range, but in the entire Northeast, can claim some of the severest weather in the world – conditions harsh enough to produce a timberline at four thousand feet, as compared to around ten thousand feet in the Rockies.

Vacationing in these mountains is not a new thing, and they have long been appreciated for their exquisite beauty. After railroads were built through here during the mid-nineteenth century, lumber companies bought up much of the land and began to log the forest. However, quick to recognize the value of the mountains' beauty, local residents formed influential conservationist groups, such as the **Appalachian Mountain Club**, and eventually ensured the passage of the Weeks Act in 1911, which allowed the federal government to purchase the land to preserve it. The national forest area here now encompasses some 750,000 acres, covering much of the northern part of the state and even spilling over into Maine.

Only a few high passes – here called "notches," discovered by early pioneers through arduous crossings – pierce the range, and the roads through these gaps, such as the **Kancamagus Highway** between Lincoln and Conway, make for predictably scenic routes. However, you won't really have made the most of the White Mountains unless you also set off, on foot, bike, or skis, across the long expanses of thick evergreen forest that separate them, with snow-capped peaks poking out in all directions.

Getting to the White Mountains

The only company that provides regular **bus services** to the White Mountains from the southern part of the state is Concord Trailways (☎1-800/639-3317, *www.concordtrailways.com*). They make stops in Conway, on West Main Street; Franconia, at Kelly's Foodtown, I-93 exit 38; in Glen, at the *Storybook Motor Inn*, Routes 16 and 302; Jackson, at Ellis Grocery Store, Rte-16; Lincoln, at the Lincoln Quik Mart, Main Street; Littleton, at the Irving Service Station, Cottage Street; and at the Pinkham Notch AMC Camp, Rte-16. The bus connects with other major cities in New Hampshire, as well as Boston, from where you can get services to just about anywhere.

WHITE MOUNTAINS PARKING FEE

You will need a **parking pass** for your vehicle when you park and leave it unattended in the White Mountains National Forest, though not if you're just stopping briefly to take pictures or use restrooms, nor if you're staying in a National Forest campground. Passes cost $5 for seven consecutive days, or $20 for an annual pass. You can buy them from many local stores and at all Forest Service offices. If you don't have a pass, you'll most likely get a notice on your windshield instructing you where to send the $5 within fourteen days.

Waterville Valley

East of I-93 along Rte-49, the sparkling "town" of **WATERVILLE VALLEY** was the brainchild of shrewd developer Tom Corcoran, who bought the *Waterville Valley Inn* and its surrounding land in 1965 with the intent of creating a happy family-oriented outdoor center. The many resort-goers enjoying rollerblading, mountain biking, boating, tennis, hiking, and golf during the summer, and skiing, snowmobiling, and ice skating in the winter, are evidence enough that he succeeded – not altogether surprising considering the stunning tree-covered setting.

At the center of the resort is the creatively named **Town Square**, a contrived development of shops and restaurants alongside the smallish **Corcoran's Pond**, where you can lounge on a short strip of sand or rent a kayak ($9/hr), canoe ($11/hr), or paddleboat ($13/hr). Nearby, the Adventure Center (☎603/236-4666) rents **bikes** for $30 per day and sells trail maps for $2.50. You can also rent bikes and ride the lift to the top of the hill at **Snow's Mountain** ($35 per day). In **Campton**, back where Rte-49 first veers off I-93, Ski Fanatics, Rte-49 (☎603/726-4327), rents mountain bikes for $25 per day and has delivery service with advance notice.

Though relatively active in summer, Waterville Valley really comes to life in the winter months, and the intermediate slopes of the **ski** area (☎603/236-8311; lift tickets $37 weekdays, $43 weekends; equipment rental $26), a network of chairlifts covering 2020 vertical feet on Mount Tecumseh and Snow's Mountain, is usually packed. The Nordic Center at Waterville Valley has 105 km of **cross-country trails** (☎603/236-4666; $13 trail fee, $17 equipment rental).

The rugged area surrounding Waterville Valley makes for excellent **hiking** and **camping**. Of several notable hikes that originate along Tripoli Road, a partially unpaved alternate route between I-93 and Waterville Valley, the **Mount Osceola Trail**, originating four miles from town and winding five miles to a ridge at 4300 feet, is the best. If you plan to park your car at the trailhead, or anywhere in the National Forest for that matter, you'll need a **weekly pass** (see box p.435), available locally at the Waterville Valley Recreation Department, Noon Peak Road (☎603/236-4695; $5), and at the Tripoli Road Fee Station, just past the Russell Pond Road.

Practicalities

The **Waterville Valley Region Chamber of Commerce** (daily 9am–5pm; ☎603/726-3804 or 1-800/237-2307, *www.watervillevalleyregion.com*) is your best bet for information on hiking, camping, and lodging in the area; they stock the usual range of brochures and have helpful attendants and good maps. The **Pemigewasset Ranger District** office on Rte-175 in Plymouth (☎603/536-1310) is also a good source of information on hiking and camping in the region. The **Waterville Valley Recreation Department** (☎603/236-4695) sells trail maps, passports to the White Mountains National Forest, and fishing licenses.

Accommodation alternatives in the immediate Waterville Valley area are geared towards families and all-inclusive vacationers, though, in nearby Campton, you'll find a selection of more intimate bed-and-breakfasts and inns. During the summer, prices are surprisingly reasonable, and rates at all nine of the resort's lodges, inns, and condos include use of the athletic club, mountain bike rental, golf, tennis courts, and kayak rental. The *Silver Fox Inn* (☎1-800/468-2553,

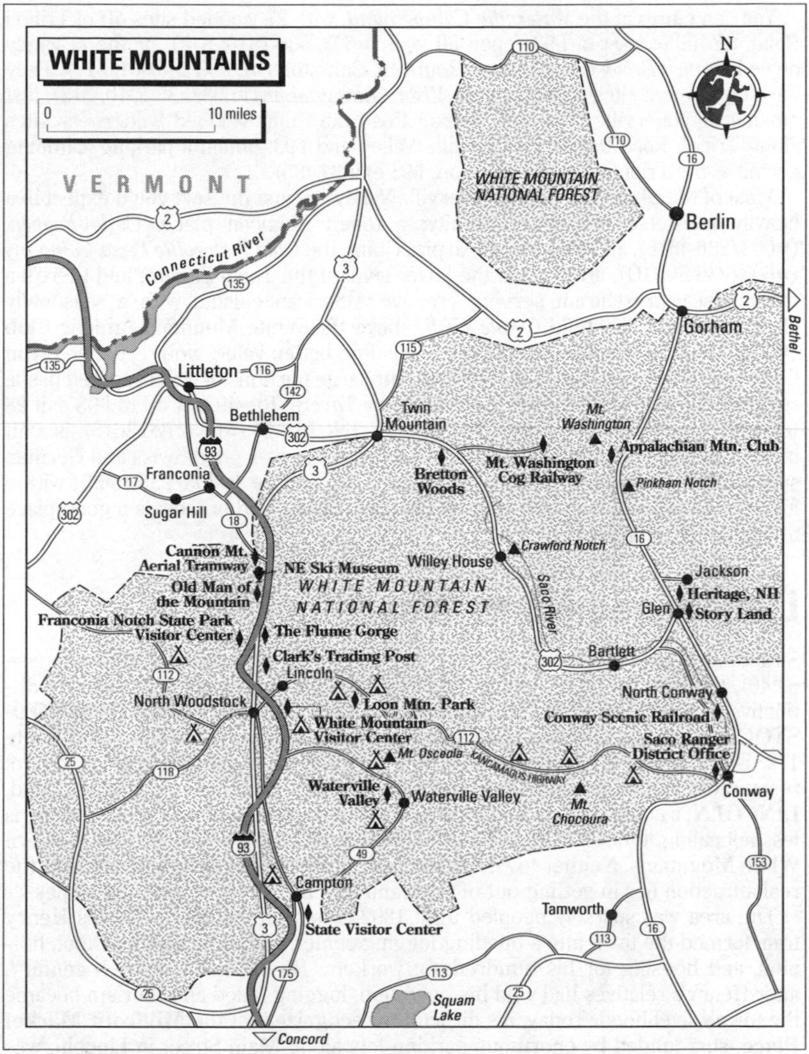

www.waterville.com; [5]) is the cheapest place in the resort, and at the *Black Bear Lodge*, 3 Village Rd (☎1-800/349-2327; [6]), you can get a room that sleeps four for under $100 outside of tourist season. The *Snowy Owl Inn* (☎603/236-4501 or 1-800/766-9969; [5]) has 84 rooms with cozy fireplaces and homely furnishings, and feels least like a huge lodging complex. Be aware, though, that prices go up by as much as fifty percent in winter. In Campton, the *Osgood Inn* (☎603/726-3543; [4]) is one of the better B&Bs, housed in a stately old home; some rooms come with a shared bath.

You can **camp** at the *Waterville Campground*, with 27 wooded sites off of Tripoli Road, ten miles east of I-93 (open all year; ☎603/536-1310; $14), or the privately owned *Branch Brook Campground*, Route 49, Campton (☎603/726-7001; $19). They have eleven tent sites at the *Osceola Vista Campground* (☎603/536-1310; $12), just outside of Waterville Valley on Tripoli Road, and undeveloped wilderness sites along Tripoli Road between Waterville Valley and I-93; obtain a parking/camping permit at the Tripoli Road Fee Station, I-93 exit 31 ($5).

Most of the **places to eat** in Waterville Valley are just the sort you'd expect in a heavily marketed resort community; a token Mexican place, *Chile Peppers* (☎603/236-4646), and a no-nonsense pizza joint, the *Olde Waterville Pizza Company* (☎603/236-FOOD), are both in the lower level of the Town Square, and there's a more upscale restaurant serving creative American cuisine with a seasonally changing menu, the *Wild Coyote Grill*, above the White Mountain Athletic Club (☎603/236-4919, *www.wildcoyotegrill.com*). For better value, you're better off in Campton, where you can stuff your face with large portions of well-prepared pasta, seafood, chicken, and steak at the *Mad River Tavern*, Rte-49 just off of I-93 exit 28 (closed Tues; ☎603/726-4290). The *William Tell*, Rte-49 (☎603/726-3618), is a bit more expensive and less relaxed, but nonetheless serves good Swiss and German specialties. The *Jugtown Country Store*, in Town Square (☎603/236-3669), with a full-service deli and wide selection of cheeses, meats, and breads, is a good place to buy picnic supplies.

Lincoln and North Woodstock

Straddling opposite sides of I-93 at the entrance to the Kancamagus Highway (see p.440), the twin towns of Lincoln and North Woodstock maintain relatively distinctive personalities while catering to both skiers and hikers. **NORTH WOOD-STOCK**, a small-town mountain retreat at the intersection of Route 3 and Route 112, is the nicer and more low-key of the two, with a short, attractive row of restaurants and shops and a couple of good places to stay. On the other hand, **LINCOLN**, a continuous strand of strip malls and condominium-style lodgings, is less appealing, though it makes a good base from which to explore the western White Mountains. Neither town offers much in the way of things to see, and the real attraction lies in getting out of town and into the forest or onto the slopes.

The area was sparsely peopled until 1892, when lumber baron James Henry transformed the town into a bustling logging center, complete with a school, hospital, and housing for his hundreds of workers. By the mid-twentieth century, after Henry's relatives had sold his operation, logging faded and tourism became the town's livelihood. Today, it's difficult to recognize that the **Millfront Market Place**, surrounded by enormous parking lots along Main Street in Lincoln, was once a timber mill, although logging trucks from points further north still occasionally rumble past town along I-93.

Though Lincoln and North Woodstock are relatively busy in summer months, they really come to life in the winter with enthusiastic skiers and snowboarders who hit the slopes at nearby **Loon Mountain** (☎603/745-8111, *www.loonmtn.com*), two miles west of I-93 on the Kancamagus Highway. Lift tickets for adults cost $42 at Loon ($49 on weekends), and equipment rental is available at the base of the mountain for $28. During the summer, Loon offers many of the activities you'd expect from a large full-service mountain resort – swimming, tennis, aerobics, horseback riding, mountain biking, etc – and if you'd like a nice view of the surrounding terrain without going through the trouble of hiking or biking up the mountain, you can ride the **gondola** to the top for $10.00 (☎603/745-6281). You can rent a **mountain bike** for $30 per day at the base of the mountain ($50 with unlimited gondola service; ☎603/745-6281) or rent in-line skates for $8 per hour. There's a stable offering **horseback** trail rides for about $30 per hour. In Lincoln, you can rent bikes at White Mountain Cyclists, Main Street (☎603/745-6466; high-performance bike, $35 per day; basic bike, $20 per day). For **guided alpine adventures** in the surrounding White Mountains, including ice climbing, rock climbing, and wilderness treks, contact Profile Mountaineering (☎603/745-3106, *www.profilemountaineering.com*; $40–200 per person).

A mile north of town along Route 3, local landmark **Clark's Trading Post** (Memorial Day to mid-Oct daily 10am–5pm, closed weekdays June, Sept & Oct; ☎603/745-8913, *www.clarkstradingpost.com*; $7) is a much-touted, family-friendly collection of tourist attractions, including a haunted house, an 1890s fire station, bumper boats, a functional wood-burning steam locomotive, and a thirty-minute black bear show, in which a group of bears do tricks for their longtime trainer – just the ticket if you're in the mood for some hokey tourist fodder, or have kids in tow.

Practicalities

The enormous **White Mountains Visitor Center** in Lincoln near I-93 (daily 9am–5pm; ☎603/745-8720) gives lodging advice and sells maps of the region, including the excellent *Trail Map & Guide to the White Mountain National Forest* ($4.95), which lists 250 trail descriptions and is essential if you plan on embarking on any extended hiking expeditions. The **Lincoln-Woodstock Chamber of Commerce**, in the Depot Mall on the east side of town along Main Street (daily 9am–5pm, winter until 7pm; ☎603/745-6621 or 1-800/227-4191), has more brochures and serves as a room reservation center for the region.

The *Russell Pond Campground*, south of town off of I-93 exit 31 (May to mid-Oct; ☎603/726-7737 or 1-888/CAMPSNH; $16), has 87 well-maintained **camping spots** and coin-operated hot showers in a scenic setting next to the **Russell Pond**, where you can swim and boat. You can also camp nine miles west of town along Route 112 at the *Wildwood Campground* (May 15 to Dec 1; ☎603/726-7737 or 1-888/CAMP-SNH; $14), well maintained by the USDA Forest Service. The *Lost River Valley Campground* (May 15 to Oct 11; ☎603/745-8321; $22–30), just over four miles west of North Woodstock at 951 Lost River Rd (Rte-112), has swimming and a kids' playground near its 125 wooded sites.

North Woodstock has a better selection of **accommodations**, though they also tend to be slightly more expensive. In the center of town, the friendly *Woodstock Inn* (☎603/745-3951 or 1-800/321-3985, *www.woodstockinnnh.com*; ④–⑥) has comfortable carpeted rooms and offers reasonable ski/lodging packages. At the intersection of US-3 and Courtney Street, just south of Rte-112, the *Wilderness Inn* (☎603/745-3890 or 1-800/321-3985, *www.wildernessinn.com*; ④–⑤) has seven antique-furnished guest rooms and sumptuous breakfasts. Cheaper lodging is available along an alarmingly tacky strip of US-3 near exit 33 in Lincoln; you can get a room at the *Franconia Notch Motel*, US-3 (☎603/745-2229 or 1-800/323-7829, *www.franconianotch.com*; ②–③), for under $40 in low season. Down the road, the *Drummer Boy Motor Inn* (☎603/745-3661 or 1-800/762-7275, *www.drummerboy motorinn.com*; ④–⑥) is slightly more luxurious, with a pool, sauna, and Jacuzzi.

The best **place to eat** in Woodstock is the atmospheric and homely *Govoni's* (summer only, 4.30–9pm; ☎603/745-8042), which serves delicious Italian specialties, such as veal parmigiana and baked penne casserole ($10–16 per entree), in an inviting old building perched above the river along Route 112 west of town. *Truant's Tavern*, Main St, North Woodstock (☎603/745-2239), is a cozy, affordable restaurant serving well-cooked standard American grill fare. North Woodstock's most elegant dining experience is at the *Clement Room*, Main St, in the *Woodstock Inn* (☎603/745-3951), where you can feast on duck, veal, seafood, or steak. Down the hall under the same roof, you can get a great range of hearty (and cheaper) food, including pizza, burgers, pasta, steak, seafood, and burritos at the *Woodstock Station*, which also happens to be the place to go in North Woodstock for **drinks**. They have live entertainment nearly every night here, and the beer is brewed on the premises; a crowd of rowdy locals usually sticks around until well past midnight in the *Brewpub* downstairs, where you can also get free **Internet access**.

In Lincoln, the majority of the **places to eat** are of the fast-food or family restaurant variety. *GH Pizza*, on Main St (☎603/745-6885), has the best pizza in town, though not a particularly pleasant dining room. *Chieng Gardens*, also on Main St (☎603/745-8612), has a typically enormous menu of traditional Chinese dishes for $10 or so, including good choices such as lemon chicken and beef with broccoli. Catering to the jovial after-ski crowd, *Gordi's*, on Main St (☎603/745-6635), is a more upscale place specializing in seafood and straightforward meat dishes (entrees $9–$16). For sandwiches and deli salads, head to *Kimber Lee's Deli*, in the Lincoln Depot on the east edge of town (☎603/745-3354). **Entertainment** in Lincoln is in short supply, though the *Papermill Theatre Company*, in the Mill at Loon Mountain on Main St (☎603/745-2141), presents "Broadway blockbusters" and children's plays during the summer. During the ski season, you can listen to bad cover bands at the *Olde Timbermill Restaurant and Pub*, in the Millfront Market Place on Main St (☎603/745-3603), while sipping one of the sixteen beers on tap.

The Kancamagus Highway

Affording plenty of panoramic glimpses of the tree-coated peaks and valleys that fade into a sunny horizon to the south, the **KANCAMAGUS HIGHWAY**, running 34 miles between Lincoln and Conway, lives up to its recent billing as an official "US Forest Service Scenic Byway." You can easily pass a pleasant afternoon driving the length of the road and parking briefly at a couple of the designated lookouts, but you'll gain a better appreciation for the area if you get out of the car and take a hike or have a swim in the Swift River, which runs parallel to the highway for twenty miles. Better still, plan to camp at one of the many well-maintained campgrounds along the road (see below).

The road is named for **Chief Kancamagus** ("Fearless One"), whose grandfather united seventeen Indian tribes into the Panacook Confederacy in 1627. Though Chief Kancamagus struggled to maintain peace between the Indians and pioneering whites, bloodshed eventually forced the tribes to scatter to the north. The region was finally re-settled in the late eighteenth century, though the **Russell Colbath House**, roughly thirteen miles west of Conway – built in 1800 and now a historic site, with a small display of antique furniture and old cooking gear – is the only remaining evidence. There are convenient car pullouts all along the road, and many have picnic tables, though no motorist services are available; don't forget to pick up your supplies and gas in Lincoln or Conway.

Hiking along the Kancamagus

The **Saco Ranger Station**, 33 Kancamagus Highway near Route 16 in Conway (☎603/447-5448), is staffed with friendly rangers who can give advice on hiking and camping along the road. They sell trail maps, which you are well advised to pick up. You can also get information about hiking and camping at the **Pemigewasset Wilderness Center**, just past the *Hancock Campground* on the highway (☎603/536-1310). Among the particularly good **hikes** along the Kancamagus are the **Lincoln Woods Trail**, an easy 2.8-mile walk to the Franconia Falls, five miles east of I-93; the **Greeley Ponds Trail**, a five-mile jaunt to a dark aqua body of water nine miles east of I-93; the **Mount Potash Hike**, a more difficult four-hour round-trip to the summit of Mount Potash thirteen miles west of the Saco Ranger Station; and the **Sabbaday Falls Hike**, a half-mile walk to the waterfalls originating fifteen miles west of the Saco Station.

Camping along the Kancamagus

The **campgrounds** along the well-traveled Kancamagus Highway are usually populated with vacationing families, and most crowded in July and August; for reservations, call ☎1-800/280-2267. *Hancock Campground*, with 56 campsites and a swimming hole (all year; ☎603/536-1310; $12), is the first along the highway, five miles east of Lincoln. Two miles on, *Big Rock* (all year; ☎603/536-1310; $12) has 28 secluded wooded sites. The *Passaconway Campground*, fifteen miles west of Conway (May 13–Oct 24; ☎603/447-5448; $12), is rather primitive, with vault toilets, while the *Jigger Johnson Campground* (May 27–Oct 11; ☎603/447-5448; $14), situated twelve-and-a-half miles west of Conway near the Russell Colbath House, has hot showers and flush toilets. You might also camp at the *Blackberry Crossing Campground* (all year; ☎603/447-5448; $12) or the *Covered Bridge Campground* (May 13–Oct 24; ☎603/447-5448; $12), across the street from one another six miles from Conway.

Franconia and around

North on I-93, past Lincoln and North Conway, the White Mountains continue to rise dramatically above either side of the freeway, boldly announcing their presence with enormous tree-covered peaks. **Franconia Notch State Park** is the highlight of the area, with miles of hiking trails and several natural wonders, including the well-known **Old Man of the Mountain**. Past the White Mountains, along I-93, the landscape flattens into an inviting valley dotted with former resort towns turned quiet mountainside retreats. The pleasant town of **FRANCONIA** began attracting summer vacationers, such as the literary notables Nathaniel Hawthorne and Henry Wadsworth Longfellow, soon after railroad tracks made the town accessible in the mid-nineteenth century; today skiers and leaf-peepers come in droves to check out the area's fall foliage and snow-covered slopes at **Cannon Mountain**. Just west, secluded **Sugar Hill** is scattered with wide open farms and winding country roads. Once a popular escape for Victorian-era socialites, sleepy

Bethlehem still has a sizeable portion of superior lodgings, while counting among its regular summer visitors a large sect of Hasidic Jews. **Littleton**, the largest town in the area, gathers a compact grouping of shops, restaurants, and nineteenth-century brick-dominated architecture in its attractive downtown, though the surrounding land is plagued with ugly strip mall developments.

Information

The **Franconia Notch Chamber of Commerce** has an information office on Rte-116 next to the church (☎603/823-5661 or 1-800/237-9007), while the **Littleton Area Chamber of Commerce** information booth in downtown Littleton across from *Thayer's Inn* (June–Oct; ☎603/444-6561 or 1-888/822-2687 for room reservations) is a good bet for information on lodging and area activities. For advice about the outdoors, head to the **Franconia Notch State Park Visitor Center**, at the *Lafayette Campground* off of I-93 (☎603/271-3628). There's more information at the Flume visitor center (see p.444), while the **Ammonoosuc Ranger Station**, Trudeau Road, Bethlehem (☎603/869-2626), is particularly good with backcountry wilderness help.

Accommodation

Most of the **accommodations** in Franconia and the surrounding area are discerning **B&Bs**. Bethlehem in particular is a haven for B&B hospitality, and you wouldn't have trouble spending over $150 per night on a luxury room, though some of the more low-key spots – especially in spring and early summer – are great value. When checking prices, be sure to inquire about room taxes and surcharges, which can run as much as fifteen percent. Budget lodgings are harder to come by, though the region is particularly well suited for **camping**, at least in the warmer months. *Lafayette Campground*, I-93, Franconia Notch State Park (☎603/823-9513; $14), is a bit close to the Interstate, but if you get a site along the western edge of the grounds, car noise will be minimized. The *Sugarloaf Campground*, Zealand Road, Twin Mountain (May 15–Dec 1; ☎603/869-2626; $12), is maintained by the US Forest Service. You can also camp at the family-oriented *Fransted Campground* in Franconia on Route 18 (May 1–Oct 17; ☎603/823-5675; $20), a developed site with private streamside tent sites.

Adair Country Inn, 80 Guider Lane, Bethlehem (☎603/444-2600 or 1-888/444-2600, *www.adairinn.com*). Deluxe antique furnished rooms, sweeping views of the landscaped grounds, and an impeccable staff make this a first-class inn, reflected in the prices. ⑦–⑧.

Beal House Inn, 2 W Main St, Littleton (☎603/444-2661 or 1-888/616-2325). Charming and friendly inn, housed in an 1833 farmhouse. Some rooms have fireplaces and satellite TV. The adjoining restaurant, the *Flying Moose Café*, is one of the best in the area. ⑤.

Bungay Jar, Easton Valley Rd, Franconia (☎603/823-7775 or 1-800/421-0701, *www .bungayjar.com*). Mountain views from all six rooms in a superb woodland setting. Popular place with skiers in winter. ⑤.

Eastgate Motor Inn, US-302, I-93 exit 41, Littleton (☎603/444-3971, *www .eastgatemotorinn.com*). Nothing fancy, but in the off-season at least (Oct 12–June 25) it's one of the better deals around. Continental breakfast included. ③.

Foxglove Country Inn, Rte-117, Sugar Hill (☎603/823-8840). Secluded and romantic renovated turn-of-the-century inn with private porches. ⑤.

Franconia Inn, Easton Valley Rd/Rte-116, Franconia (☎603/823-5542 or 1-800/473-5299, *www.franconiainn.com*). Thirty-bed inn two miles south of Franconia, with great views, a relaxing porch, and an excellent restaurant (see p.445). A good cross-country ski base. ⑤.

Gale River Motel, 1 Main St, Franconia (☎603/823-5655 or 1-800/255-7989). A sweet little ten-room motel, with three cottages, sleeping four to six people, also available. ④.

Hilltop Inn, Main St (Rte-117), Sugar Hill (☎603/823-5695 or 1-800/770-5695, *www .hilltopinn.com*). 1895 country inn close to skiing and hiking with quilted beds, a quiet atmos-phere, and full breakfasts. For longer stays, there's a two-bedroom cottage out back with kitchen and fireplace. ④.

The Little Guest House, 1167 Prospect St, Bethlehem (☎603/869-5725). Meticulously fur-nished rooms in a peaceful setting. Continental breakfast included; no credit cards. ④.

Lovett's Inn, Rte-18, Franconia (☎603/823-7761 or 1-800/356-3802, *www.lovettsinn.com*). Complete with a swimming pool, a comfortable common area, cozy rooms, an excellent restaurant and charming staff, this 1784 Cape Cod-style home is peacefully set at the foot of Cannon Mountain. Breakfast and four-course dinner are included in the room rate. ⑦.

Mulburn Inn, 2370 Main St, Bethlehem (☎603/869-3389 or 1-800/457-9440). Spacious rooms in a relaxing B&B near the center of Bethlehem. ④.

Thayer's Inn, Main St, Littleton (☎603/444-6469 or 1-800/634-8179, *www.thayersinn.com*). A landmark since it was built in 1843, this creaky but comfortable and classy old inn right in the center of Littleton has hosted such notables as Ulysses S. Grant and Richard Nixon. ③–④.

Wayside Inn, US-302 at Pierce Bridge, Bethlehem (☎603/869-3364 or 1-800/448-9557, *www.thewaysideinn.com*). In addition to the sixteen rooms in the 170-year-old inn, originally a homestead for Franklin Pierce's nephew, there's a twelve-room motel overlooking the Ammonoosuc River. ④.

Franconia

FRANCONIA, a friendly village along I-93 in the rolling grassy hills just north of Franconia Notch State Park and the White Mountains, is best known as the one-time home of poet **Robert Frost**. After owning a small farm in Derry, NH (see p.404) and living for a stint in England, Frost settled here in 1915 at the age of forty. You can visit his old home, now known as the **Frost Place**, Ridge Road off of Bickford Hill Road one mile south on Rte-116 (July–Columbus Day Wed–Mon 1–5pm; June weekends only; $3), where he lived with his wife and children for five years and wrote many of his best-known poems, including "The Road Not Taken." Memorable largely for the inspiring panorama of mountains in its backdrop, the poet's former home is now a Center for Poetry and the Arts, with a poet in resi-dence, readings, workshops, and a small display of Frost memorabilia, such as signed first editions and photographs. There's a short **nature trail** complete with placards displaying Frost's poetry and signs that supposedly mark the exact spot certain poems were composed. A longer and more rewarding hike begins 3.4 miles south of Franconia on Coppermine Road off of Rte-116, following the **Coppermine Trail** to the beautifully cascading **Bridalveil Falls**. The wooden Coppermine Shelter, near the end of the 2.5-mile excursion, is a good spot to camp, although there are no facilities. For advice on **bike routes** in the area and to rent bikes ($19 per day), stop in at the Franconia Sport Shop, Main Street, Franconia (☎603/823-5241).

Northeast of Franconia along US-302, **BETHLEHEM**, an attractive community composed mostly of old resorts, boasts one of the more remarkable sights in the area at the **Crossroads of America**, corner of US-302 and Trudeau Road (June to late Oct Tues–Sun noon–5pm; $3.50), where an obsessively detailed model railroad set – one of the largest in the world – is on display.

To the west, **LITTLETON**, straddling the Ammonoosuc River, has a compact Main Street that's lined with attractive old brick buildings and the largest population in the area at 6000, and though there's really not much to see, it's a good place to find reasonably priced accommodations. Main Street, with a number of good shops, such as the Village Book Store, 81 Main St (☎603/444-5263 or 1-800/640-9673), is good for an hour or so of browsing.

Franconia Notch State Park

I-93, speeding up towards Canada, and the more leisurely US-3 merge briefly about ten miles beyond Lincoln, to pass through **Franconia Notch State Park**. Though it's dwarfed by the surrounding national forest, and split in two by the noisy Interstate, the park, which features excellent hiking and camping, has several sights that are well worth a visit, including the overdone Old Man of the Mountain – for which the area is famous.

From the park **visitor center**, I-93 exit 33 (May–Oct daily 9am–4.30pm; ☎603/745-8391), where they have a helpful information desk, a cafeteria, and a gift shop, you can walk or ride the shuttle bus to the short trail that leads through the **Flume** (entry $7). Formed nearly 200 million years ago, but discovered in 1808 by 93-year-old "Aunt" Jess Guernsey, the 800-foot gorge has been fitted with a wooden walkway that weaves back and forth across cascading falls and between towering sheer granite walls. With the sound of rumbling water echoing through the damp and misty crevice, it's more impressive than you might expect, though during high season the tourist crush can be overwhelming. From the visitor center parking lot, the 1.4-mile **Mount Pemigewasset Trail** leads up a moderate incline to the 2557-foot summit of Mount Pemigewasset, affording views of the Franconia Range.

A mile or so north, you can admire the **Basin**, a curious 25,000-year-old 20-foot-wide granite pothole that catches the surging waters of a cascading waterfall. From the Basin, a marked trail links with the **Cascade Brook Trail**, traversing three miles to **Lonesome Pond**. Back on I-93, follow the signs to a roadside pull-out, from where you can look upwards at the diminutive **Old Man of the Mountain**. This natural rock formation, resembling an old man's profile, will no doubt already be familiar from scores of powerfully magnified photographs – and New Hampshire's license plates. Much less impressive from a thousand feet below, it nevertheless inspired Daniel Webster to pen the following lines:

> *Men hang out their signs indicative of their respective trades.*
> *Shoemakers hang out a gigantic shoe;*
> *Jewelers, a monster watch;*
> *Even the dentist hangs out a gold tooth;*
> *But in the Franconia Mountains, God Almighty has*
> *Hung out a sign to show that in New England He makes men.*

These days, it all has to be held together with wires, and one particular family has the annual responsibility of climbing up to plug the cracks made by the winter's ice.

Three miles or so south of Franconia, state-owned **Cannon Mountain** offers rides to the top of its 4100-foot peak in an aerial tramway (mid-May–June & Sept–mid-Oct 9am–4.30pm; July & Aug 9am–5.30pm; ☎603/823-5241, *www .cannonmt.com*; $9 round-trip, $7 one-way), displaying panoramic views of the surrounding mountains that are especially impressive – and popular – during the early fall foliage season. During the winter, Cannon Mountain (☎603/823-5563; adult full-day lift ticket, $37) offers some of the more challenging **alpine skiing** terrain in the state. You can browse through a collection of old ski equipment and photos or watch a vintage ski flick at the **New England Ski Museum**, next to the tramway (late May to mid-Oct & Dec–March noon–5pm; ☎603/823-7177; free). If you'd rather hike to the top of the mountain, take the slightly difficult **Kinsman Ridge Trail** from the southwest corner of the tramway parking lot. An equally rewarding, but shorter and less strenuous hike leads to **Artists Bluff**; the trail begins in the parking area on the north side of Rte-18, across from the Peabody Base Lodge. At **Echo Lake**, you can swim, rent a canoe ($10 per hr), or just enjoy the short stretch of sand (for a $2.50 entry fee).

Eating and drinking

The Franconia region is not known for fine **dining**, although many of the inns and B&Bs in the area serve excellent (if expensive) food in dining rooms that welcome non-guests. The **nightlife** here is more active in the winter, when young skiers are in abundance. Cheap food can be had in most towns at typically grimy local pizza/burger joints.

Burrito Alley, 89 Main St, Littleton (☎603/444-2200). The burritos are barely mediocre here, but it's still the best (and cheapest) Mexican food for miles.

Flying Moose Cafe, 247 W Main St, Littleton (☎603/444-2661). Intimate bistro serving a mix of classic cuisines with contemporary flair, such as filet mignon with chipotle butter sauce, with a less expensive tavern menu featuring well-prepared steak and seafood dishes.

Franconia Inn, Easton Valley Rd, Franconia (☎603/823-5542). Elegant first-class service in a candlelit dining room, featuring well-prepared steak and seafood dishes.

Grateful Bread, Main St, Franconia (☎603/823-5228). Delicious-smelling bakery selling a dozen types of home-made organic breads, muffins, and croissants.

Littleton Diner, 170 Main St, Littleton (☎603/444-3994). Large greasy portions of typical diner food and extra-thick shakes served up at the counter or in one of seven booths. Daily 6am–9pm.

Lloyd Hills, Main St, Bethlehem (☎603/869-2141). A comfortable and popular spot to munch a sandwich or nurse a beer, with a huge five-page menu that includes burgers, pasta, and steak. Also serves a decent Sunday brunch. Open all year.

Lovett's Inn, Rte-18, Franconia (☎603/823-7761 or 1-800/356-3802). This old inn continues to serve some of the best gourmet food in the area, featuring well-prepared classics like grilled salmon and stuffed chicken breast. Entrees go for $15–20. Reservations required.

Polly's Pancake Parlor, I-93 exit 38, Rte-117, Sugar Hill (daily mid-May to mid-Oct, weekends only April, early May, late Oct and Nov; ☎603/823-5575). Yes, it's in the middle of nowhere, but well worth the schlep if you love pancakes. All-you-can-eat pancakes cost around $10 – the record is apparently 56 in one sitting.

Rosa Flamingo's, Main St (US-302), Bethlehem (☎603/869-3111). They serve a good variety of basic Italian dishes at this informal restaurant which doubles as one of the area's more popular and lively places to drink.

Bretton Woods

The ease with which US-302 now crosses the middle of the mountains belies the effort that went into cutting a road through **Crawford Notch**, a twisty and beautiful pass halfway between Franconia and Conway. Just north, the magnificent **Mount Washington Hotel** (☎603/278-1000 or 1-800/258-0330; [8]) stands in splendid isolation in the wide mountain valley of **BRETTON WOODS**. At the hotel's grand opening in the summer of 1902, developer Joseph Stickney reputedly exclaimed, "Look at me gentlemen . . . for I am the poor fool who built all this!" Its glistening white facade, capped by red cupolas and framed by the western slopes of Mount Washington rising behind it, has barely changed since then. In its heyday, a stream of horse-drawn carriages brought families (and servants) up from the train station, deliberately located at a distance to increase the sense of grandeur. Displays in the lobby commemorate the **Bretton Woods Conference** of 1944, which laid the groundwork for the postwar financial structure of the capitalist world, by setting the gold standard at $35 an ounce (it's now about $260) and creating the International Monetary Fund and the World Bank.

Restoration by a group of investors who purchased the decaying building and surrounding property in 1991 for a mere $3.1 million has insured that the cruise-ship-sized hotel remains marvelously – if somewhat eerily – evocative of past splendor, with its quarter-mile terrace and white wicker furniture. The hotel is not the one featured in the movie *The Shining*, but it's said to have inspired the story and is worth checking out even if you're not staying. None other than Babe Ruth reputedly got sauced in the former speakeasy downstairs – fittingly known as the "Cave" because of its faux-rocky walls – before sauntering to the indoor pool down the hall and taking a fully clothed dip; these days, the bar hosts more mellow live entertainment nightly, though the rock walls are still there. Weekend golfing and tennis packages are available, and in the 1990s the resort opened its doors to the winter ski crowd. On the property, the 34-room *Bretton Arms Country Inn* (☎603/278-1000; [6]) has more affordable rooms, while the *Bretton Woods Motor Inn* (same phone; [4]–[5]), across US-302, has modern rooms even cheaper.

It took a hundred men three years to build the **Mount Washington Cog Railway**, off of Mount Clinton Road at the base of Mount Washington. Completed in 1869, its rickety trains lumber up gradients as steep as 38 percent – the second steepest railway in the world – while consuming a ton of coal and thousand gallons of water and spewing out thick gray clouds of heavy smoke. It's a truly momentous experience, inching up the steep wooden trestles while avoiding descending showers of coal smut – although anyone who's not a bona fide antique train aficionado might find it not really worth the money. The three-hour round-trip costs $44, and trains leave hourly (May–mid-Oct 9am–5pm; 11am–5pm before June 19; ☎603/278-5404 or 1-800/922-8825).

If you'd rather **hike** up Mount Washington, the **Ammonoosuc Ravine Trail** starts in the Cog parking lot, hooking up with the Crawford Path at the AMC's *Lakes of the Clouds* hut (see p.453). If you're in good physical shape (this hike is not for the faint of heart), the four-mile trip takes roughly four and a half hours one-way. Take warm clothing (temperatures above the tree line can be fifty degrees colder than at the base), plenty of water, and food, and do not hesitate to turn back if the weather turns foul; several hikers die of exposure to the harsh weather atop the mountain every year. Another option, the **Jewell Trail**, also originating in the parking lot, zigzags up the north shoulder to the summit in 4.6 miles (roughly 4 hours).

Twin Mountain

Five miles west, **TWIN MOUNTAIN**, a blue-collar town that spreads out around the intersection of US-302 and US-3, is mostly notable for its grouping of cheap, no-frills **motels**. If you're not bothered by run-down surroundings and are cash-conscious, this is a good place from which to explore the area. In late July, the town hosts a **Native American Cultural Weekend** (☎603/869-3326 for schedule), a lively celebration of song and dance. The Abenaki claim they are native to New Hampshire, though they have never been recognized by the state or federal government, which is content to perpetuate the idea that the tribe immigrated from Canada in post-colonial times. The best bets for **places to stay** include the *Four Seasons Motor Inn*, US-3 (☎603/846-5708 or 1-800/228-5708, *www.4seasonsmotorinn .com*; ③), the *Northern Zermatt Inn*, US-3 (☎603/846-5533 or 1-800/535-3214; ③), and *Carlson's Lodge*, US-302 (☎603/846-5501 or 1-800/348-5502; ②–③).

Crawford Notch State Park

Crawford Notch State Park is split in two by US-302, which winds through the dramatic gap formed by the steep slopes of Mount Field to the west and Mount Jackson to the east. Discovered in 1771 by hunter Timothy Nash, who was tracking a moose through the woods, the notch was soon recognized as a viable route through the White Mountains to points further north. A railroad was completed at great expense in 1857, and the old Crawford Depot along US-302 south of Bretton Woods across from tiny Saco Lake is now a helpful **information center** and retail store selling backcountry necessities (May–Oct Mon–Sat 9am–5pm; ☎603/466-2727), maintained by the Appalachian Mountain Club. Recommended **hikes** in the area include the **Mount Willard Trail**, a 1.4-mile (1hr) jaunt up to amazing views of Crawford Notch starting at the Crawford Depot, and the **Zealand Trail**, which begins at the end of Zealand Road and ends, 2.7 miles and ninety minutes later, at the Zealand Pond, Zealand Falls, and the AMC *Zealand Falls* hut (see p.453). In the shadow of Mount Crawford, the **Willey House**, named for a family who lived on the site and died in a terrible landslide in 1826, now serves as the **park headquarters** (☎603/374-2272), selling maps and trail guides and offering advice on camping; they also maintain a small café. Behind the headquarters, the **Ethan Pond Trail** leads to the *Ethan Pond* shelter, a somewhat remote **camping** spot with no facilities. Half a mile south, the **Arethusa Falls Trail** is a short but steep walk to the highest falls in the state. Just across US-302, the *Dry River Campground* (☎603/374-2272; $12) has 31 wooded sites. Another inexpensive place to stay in the area is the AMC's *Crawford Notch Hostel*, US-302 just north of the park (☎603/466-2727; $18), with two heated twelve-bunk cabins, a self-service kitchen, and free showers.

The Mount Washington Valley

There are no clear boundaries to the **Mount Washington Valley**, though it is generally thought to center around the crowded town of **North Conway**, a once-beautiful mountainside hamlet now overwhelmed by outlet malls and other mod-

ern encroachments. In general, the region is more congested than the western
White Mountains, but if you can avoid the crowds that cram their cars onto the
mile-long strip of Rte-16/US-302 south of downtown North Conway, there's plenty to do around here. In the winter, there are numerous trails for **cross-country
skiers**, while in the summer **rock climbers** test their skills on the highly popular **Cathedral Ledge**. North of North Conway, the pace slows and opportunities
for solitary hiking and camping are more accessible. The low-key town of **Glen**
is home to **Storyland**, a children's fantasy park, while peaceful **Jackson** has an
unusual concentration of first-class lodging and eating, presenting a good opportunity to spoil yourself amid the quiet splendor of the greenery.

Information and getting around

The **Mount Washington Valley Chamber of Commerce** in North Conway
(☎603/356-3171 or 1-800/367-3364) has a reservation service and information on
local attractions. The **Conway Village Chamber of Commerce**, south of town
along Rte-16 (☎603/447-2639), will also help with places to stay and has hiking maps.

The AMC runs a **shuttle service** daily from June to October with vans that
make stops at many of the trailheads and AMC lodges throughout the region (call
☎603/466-2727 for information and reservations), including the Crawford Notch
Depot and the Pinkham Notch headquarters. Drivers will stop anywhere along
the route if requested, and the trips cost $8, no matter how long you ride.

Accommodation

The Mount Washington Valley offers good **accommodation** for every budget. In
general, the cheapest (and tackiest) hotels are in Conway and North Conway,
while the more expensive (and elegant) are in Jackson.

Hostels and motels

Albert B Lester Memorial HI/AYH Hostel, 36 Washington St, Conway (☎603/447-1001
or 1-800/886-4284). Particularly clean dorm lodging for $17 per night on the southern edge
of the White Mountains. Private rooms are also available for around $35. Closed for the
month of November. ①.

Covered Bridge Motor Lodge, Rte-16, Jackson (☎603/383-6630 or 1-800/634-2911). A fairly standard roadside hotel with clean rooms, popular with ski families in winter. ④.

School House Motel, Rte-16, North Conway (☎603/356-6829 or 1-800/638-6050). Basic,
clean roadside motel near the outlets. ③.

Swiss Chalets, Rte-16A, Intervale (☎603/356-2232 or 1-800/831-2727, *www.swisschaletsvillage
.com*). One of the nicest motels in the North Conway area, with 42 comfortable, renovated
rooms away from the bustle of the main drag. ④.

Will's Inn, US-302, Glen (☎603/383-6757 or 1-800/233-6780). Family-friendly, cheap, and
adequate accommodations with a heated pool. There's a deluxe two-bedroom cottage that
sleeps up to eight people that goes for $105–165 a night. ③.

B&Bs, hotels, and inns

The **1785 Inn**, Rte-16, North Conway (☎603/356-9025 or 1-800/421-1785, *www
.the1785inn.com*). Though it's right on the busy main road, the spacious rooms, gracious
hosts, delicious food, and mountain view make this a good base from which to explore the
area (or to shop). ⑤.

The Bernerhof Inn, US-302, Glen (☎603/383-9132 or 1-800/548-8007, *www.bernerhofinn.com*). Comfortable, elegant country inn with nine guest rooms and conscientious service. There's a pub and a gourmet restaurant on the first floor. [5].

Christmas Farm Inn, Rte-16B, Jackson (☎603/383-4313 or 1-800/443-5837). All the amenities of a modern hotel, but in a tastefully restored 1778 farmhouse, owned by former US Congressman Bill Zeliff and his family. Outdoor pool, game room, and cozy gourmet candlelit restaurant. Rates include dinner and breakfast. [7].

Covered Bridge House, US-302, Glen (☎603/383-9109 or 1-800/232-9109). Quilted beds, pleasantly decorated rooms, and a homely feel for a reasonable price. [4]–[5].

Darby Field Inn, Bald Hill Rd, Conway (☎603/447-2181 or 1-800/426-4147, *www.darbyfield.com*). Three miles outside of Conway, this converted 1826 farmhouse is nicely secluded, with a view of the White Mountains. [6]–[7].

Inn at Thorn Hill, Thorn Hill Rd, Jackson (☎603/383-4242 or 1-800/289-8990, *www.innatthornhill.com*). First-class luxurious hillside inn designed by renowned architect Stanford White (of McKim, Mead & White), complete with designer furnishings and linens, whirlpool tubs, and private cottages in back. The gourmet restaurant will satisfy the most discerning of palates. Rates include three-course dinner ($30 less without dinner). [8].

Nereledge Inn, River Rd, North Conway (☎603/356-2831, *www.nettx.com/nereledge.html*). Reasonably priced friendly and informal colonial inn near skiing, the Saco River, and rock climbing. Hearty country breakfast included. [4].

Sunny Side Inn, Seavey St, North Conway (☎603/356-6239 or 1-800/600-6239, *www.sunnyside-inn.com*). A friendly, quiet spot, well off the main drag with nine homely rooms. Popular with rock climbers and other outdoors types. Breakfast included. [4]–[5].

Village House, Rte-16A, Jackson (☎603/383-6666 or 1-800/972-8343). A pleasant B&B just beyond the covered bridge, with private baths and a great big porch. [5].

Wildcat Inn & Tavern, Rte-16A, Jackson (☎603/383-4245 or 1-800/228-4245, *www.wildcatinnandtavern.com*). Cozy, unpretentious, and friendly inn right in the center of town with a comfortable ski cabin feel. It's especially popular in the winter (as is the tavern), so call for reservations. Rooms between Oct 26 and Dec 22 are just $79. [6].

Camping

Saco River Camping Area, off of Rte-16, North Conway (☎603/356-3360). Both wooded and open sites, well enough away from the highway nicely located along the Saco River. Open all year, $18–22.

White Ledge Campground, Rte-16 five miles south of Conway, Albany (☎603/447-5448). Twenty-eight campsites maintained by the US Forest Service. $10 per night; open May 13–Oct 24.

North Conway

Whichever way you approach **NORTH CONWAY**, you're in for a depressing time. From the north, the joining of Rte-16 and US-302 eventually becomes a veritable turmoil of shopping malls and theme parks, while from the south, the strip between Conway and North Conway is an orgy of factory outlets, fast-food places, and the over-eager shoppers who have sought them out. Fortunately, there is some relief in the town itself, a touristed village that manages to maintain a hint of rustic backcountry appeal. The centerpiece of downtown is the **North Conway Railroad Station**, a hulking brown and yellow 1874 Victorian structure that you won't miss along Main Street. From here, the **Conway Scenic Railroad** (April to Dec, call for reservations and schedule; ☎603/356-5251 or 1-800/232-5251, *www.conwayscenic.com*) runs antique steam trains to Bartlett ($16.50 round-trip, 2hr); Conway ($9.50 round-trip, 55min); and the Fabyan Station in Bretton Woods

($37 round-trip, 5hr). The trains are especially worth the money in early fall, when the trees are at their brightest – reservations are a must.

West of town along River Road, you can go for a swim at refreshing **Echo Lake** beneath the towering granite face of the White Horse Ledge. Just north off of West Side Road, scores of rock climbers test their skills on the wall of the steep, sheer faces of towering **Cathedral Ledge**, the most popular spot for the sport in the state. Chauvin Guides in North Conway (☎603/356-8919) offers various **guided climbs** and lessons starting at $80. You might also check with Eastern Mountain Sports in North Conway for guidance (☎1-800/310-4504). If you'd rather not spend agonizing hours (and lots of money) tethered to the cliff's sheer face, you can simply drive to the top, where you're presented with views of the entire area. You can also hike to the ledge, along the **Bryce Path**, a steep trail that originates at the base of the auto road and takes about an hour each way. North of the entry to **Cathedral Ledge State Park** on North River Road, you can hike to **Diana's Bath**, an easy half-mile hike to a cool running mountain stream along the Moat Mountain Trail. For a longer hike, head to the top of **Mount Kearsarge** from the north side of Hurricane Mountain Road, one and a half miles west of Rte-16; it's a three-hour jaunt that is rewarded with panoramic views.

Just outside of Conway lies **Mount Chocoura**. Although only 3475 ft, the little curved granite notch on the top, looking like a perched cap, makes it one of the most distinctive mountains visible from this area. It's an easy climb, and it should take about two hours to reach the summit if you're in good shape via the Champney Falls Trail (parking lot ten miles west of Rte-16 on the Kancamagus Highway). The top – that notch you can see – is particularly beautiful, as you emerge from the forest to a stretch of pure rock. The views, including the "Presidential Range," are, of course, stunning.

Jackson and Glen

With a high concentration of first-class lodgings and restaurants, a close-knit local population, and hundreds of miles of trails within easy reach, **JACKSON** is one of the premier **cross-country ski** centers in the country. Indeed, the **Jackson Ski Touring Foundation** (☎603/383-9355; $14 Saturdays and holidays, $12 weekdays; 10–15 years half-price, children under 10 free), with 160km of trails over 60 square miles, was recently rated the number one cross-country ski area in the East by *Ski*, *Skiing*, and *Snow Country* magazines. On hot summer days, a great place to cool off is at **Jackson Falls**, which tumble down a stretch of boulders and rocks in the riverbed along Rte-16B.

If you're traveling with children, don't miss New Hampshire landmark **Story Land**, on Rte-16 in **GLEN** (mid-June to Labor Day, daily 9am–6pm; Labor Day–Columbus Day weekends only 10am–5pm; $18), a colorful children's theme park, akin to a miniature Disneyland, with immaculately maintained grounds, rides like the "Turtle Twirl" and the "Bamboo Chutes," and lots of places for climbing and exploring – including the "Oceans of Fun Sprayground" and "Professor Bigglestep's Loopy Labs." Next door, **Heritage New Hampshire** (mid-May to mid-Oct daily 9am–5pm; ☎603/383-9776; $10) takes a somewhat hokey and outdated Anglocentric look at New Hampshire history through interactive exhibits and badly animated mannequins. You start with a simulated ride aboard a creaky ship bound for the New World and end with a rickety "train ride" through the White Mountains.

The Red Jersey Cyclery on US-302 in Glen (☎603/383-4660) is the place to go for **mountain-bike** trail advice, with a knowledgeable staff and lots of **rental** bikes ($20 per day, $30 with suspension). They lead free **guided group trail rides** every Saturday at 9am during the summer. Next door, Northern Extremes rents bikes, canoes, and kayaks (☎603/383-8117, *www.northernextremes.com*).

Mount Washington Valley eating and drinking

The best **dining** experiences in the Mount Washington Valley can be found in the many inns and B&Bs that populate the outskirts of the region, though these meals are often somewhat formal affairs that are priced accordingly. The few bars here come alive with skiers in the winter; during the summer they are more relaxed, attracting vacationers looking for an after-dinner drink or two.

The 1785 Inn, Rte-16, North Conway (☎603/356-9025 or 1-800/421-1785, *www.the1785inn .com*). Highly praised expensive gourmet food, such as boned rabbit in a cream sherry sauce ($17.85) in a dark, romantic dining room.

As You Like It, Jackson Falls Marketplace, Jackson (☎603/383-6425). Great coffee cake, home-made cookies, pies, brownies, and bread. There's a good deli too.

Bellini's, 33 Seavey St, North Conway (☎603/356-7000, *www.bellinis.com*). The best place around for big portions of freshly prepared Italian dishes like fettuccini chicken pesto ($13) and baked rigatoni ($11), all served in a nicely decorated romantic dining room. Reservations recommended.

Horsefeather's, Main St (Rte-16) at Kearsarge, North Conway (☎603/356-6862, *www .horsefeathers.com*). Friendly service in a somewhat typical informal American bistro/pub setting, serving what many call the best burgers in town in addition to large salads, sandwiches, and steak.

Inn at Thorn Hill, Thorn Hill Rd, Jackson (☎603/383-4242). A romantic spot that's good for special occasions, serving "New England fusion" dishes like Atlantic salmon with a crisp coconut, black pepper, plantain, and basil crust, in a cilantro ginger dressing, using seasonally grown organic produce and featuring an extensive wine list. Reservations recommended.

Margarita Grill, US-302, Glen (☎603/383-6556). The concept is a bit cliched and the Tex-Mex food is slightly overpriced, but nevertheless good – eat in a tastefully decorated Southwestern-style dining room or outside on the shaded patio.

Red Parka Pub, US-302, Glen (☎603/383-4344). Local favorite is especially lively on weekend nights and during the ski season. Lots of large-portion hearty home-cooked steak entrees and buffalo wing-type appetizers. There's live music several nights per week.

Shalimar, 27 Seavey St, North Conway (☎603/356-0123). A huge menu of reasonably priced authentic Indian dishes, with a good selection of vegetarian specialties. The *tandoori reshimi kabob* – tender pieces of marinated chicken over rice – is excellent. Lunch is a bargain.

The Shannon Door, Rte-16, Jackson (☎603/383-4211). Longstanding Irish pub with a suitably dark bar/eating area and lively atmosphere. They serve good cheap pub fare, including shepherd's pie ($7.95), chopped sirloin ($7.95), a selection of appetizers, burgers, pizza, and of course, Guinness. Live entertainment Thurs–Sun.

Thompson House Eatery (T.H.E.), Rte-16 and Rte-16A, Jackson (☎603/383-9341). They serve their own root beer and renowned home-made ice cream. In the dining room, you can get great salads, fresh seafood, steak, and sandwiches. Lunch and dinner seven days a week.

Wildcat Inn and Tavern, Rte-16A, Jackson (☎603/383-4245 or 1-800/228-4245). There's gourmet country cuisine in the dining room, with dishes like roasted loin of lamb ($18.95) and stuffed chicken breast ($15.95), and cheaper sandwiches and appetizers in the less formal tavern. The couch-filled tavern is lively with skiers in from a day on the slopes in winter. They have live music most weekends.

Yesterday's, Rte-16A, Jackson (☎603/383-4457). The place to go for big, cheap American breakfasts. Open daily 6.30am–2pm.

Pinkham Notch and Mount Washington

Roughly ten miles north of Jackson along Rte-16, **PINKHAM NOTCH**, along the eastern base of towering **MOUNT WASHINGTON**, is as beautiful a mountain pass as there is in the National Forest, with a reputation for serious outdoors activity. The Appalachian Trail and a number of other remote wilderness trails converge here, making the Notch overrun with bearded adventurers during the summer. Luckily, the crowds don't detract too much, and they're easy to forget once you've made your way into the forest.

The best place to get information on hiking, camping, and a whole range of other outdoor activities is at the AMC's **Pinkham Notch Visitor Center**, Rte-16 (daily 8am–10pm; ☎603/466-2727), where you can buy the indispensable and exhaustive *AMC White Mountain Guide* ($17), good hiking maps, supplies, and basic camping/mountaineering equipment. The center organizes workshops, guided trips, and programs that cost anywhere from a couple of dollars to a couple hundred dollars. They serve three hearty family-style **meals** per day at long picnic tables in a huge, noisy dining room at the visitor center; the prix-fixe dinner ($14) includes salad, soup, vegetables, home-made breads and dessert, an entree, and plenty of conversation about the day's hike. As if that weren't enough, the club maintains the *Joe Dodge Lodge* (☎603/466-2727), where you can rent a bunk ($30) or a private room ($65 double, $80 quad) and hang out with fellow adventurers. The *Dolly Copp Campground* (☎603/466-2713; $12) has 176 **campsites** and is open from mid-May to mid-Oct.

On the east side of Rte-16 across from the visitor center, local favorite **Wildcat Mountain** (☎603/466-3326 or 1-800/255-6439, *www.skiwildcat.com*) offers some of the best and most challenging **skiing** ($39 mid-week, $46 weekends and holidays) in the state during the winter, as well as **mountain biking** and **tram rides** (mid-June to Oct weekends only; $9).

Mount Washington

The 6288-foot **MOUNT WASHINGTON**, the highest peak in the northeastern US, was named for George Washington before he even became president. Over the years, other mountains in this "Presidential Range" have taken the names of Madison, Jefferson, and even Eisenhower – though it should be noted that Mount Nancy was called that long before the Reagans were in the White House, and Mount Deception just happens to be close by.

On a clear day, you can see all the way to the Atlantic and into Canada from the top of Mount Washington, once called the "second greatest show on earth" by P.T. Barnum, but the real interest in making the ascent lies in the extraordinary severity of the weather up here. The wind exceeds hurricane strength on over a hundred days of the year, and in 1934 it reached the highest speed ever recorded anywhere in the world – 231mph. On the summit, you'll see the remarkable spectacle of buildings actually held down with great chains; many have been blown away over the years, including the old observatory, said to have been the strongest wooden building ever constructed. At the newer (and hopefully stronger) **weather observatory** (☎603/356-8345; *www.mountwashington.org*), scientists research the various effects of wind, ice, and fog; their various findings are displayed at a small museum downstairs (entry $4). You can climb the few

AMC MOUNTAIN HUTS

The Appalachian Mountain Club (AMC) operates eight delightfully remote mountain huts in New Hampshire along a 56-mile stretch of the famed Appalachian Trail. Generally open from June through October, these spots offer full-service lodging in season, and two hot meals per day, for $62 per night, making them a fairly popular choice – reservations are required (☎603/466-2727). At some of the huts, self-service lodging is available (without sheets, heat, or food) for $18. For additional information, contact the Appalachian Mountain Club, 5 Joy St, Boston, MA 02108 (☎617/523-0636, *www.outdoors.org*).

Carter Notch (self-service all year). Accessible via the Nineteen Mile Brook Trail and the Wildcat Ridge Trail, both originating along Rte-16 north of Jackson.

Galehead (full service in season: early June to mid-Oct). On the Garfield Range, this is the most remote hut in the chain. Accessible via the Gale River Trail and the Garfield Ridge Trail, both originating off of US-3 south of Bethlehem.

Greenleaf (full service in season: early June to mid-Oct). Accessible via the Greenleaf Trail and the Old Bridle Path Trail, off of I-93 in Franconia Notch State Park (see p.444).

Lakes of the Clouds (full service in season: early June to mid-Sept). On the southern shoulder of Mount Washington, this is the highest of the huts. Accessible via the Ammonoosuc Ravine Trail and Crawford Path, off of Mount Clinton Road, just south of Bretton Woods.

Lonesome Lake (full service in season: early June to early Sept). Good family destination, with daily hikes and activities. Accessible via the Cascade Brook Trail, Dodge Cutoff Trail, Fishin' Jimmy Trail, Lonesome Lake Trail, and the Whitehouse Trail, west of I-93 in Franconia Notch State Park.

Madison (full service in season: early June to mid-Sept). Great sunsets from a perch above the Madison Gulf. Accessible via the Crawford Path, Gulfside Trail, Westside Trail, and the Valley Way Trail, southwest of Gorham off of US-2.

Mizpah Springs (full service in season: early June to mid-Oct). On Mount Clinton above Crawford Notch. Accessible via the Mount Clinton Trail and the Webster Cliff Trail near Crawford Notch State Park along US-302.

Zealand Falls (full service in season: early June to mid-Oct). Open all year, near waterfalls and good backcountry skiing. Accessible via the Zealand Trail, off of Zealand Road south of Twin Mountain.

remaining feet to the actual summit point, sadly surrounded with cement structures – including a large viewing platform – and smothered by photo-snapping tourists. The **Tip Top House**, once a hotel for wealthy travelers, has been turned into an unremarkable historic museum (entry $2), providing "a link between the mountain's past and present" through antique furniture and a restored interior.

On the way to the top, you pass through four distinct climatic zones, with century-old fir and ash trees so stunted as to be below waist height, before emerging amid Arctic tundra. The drive up the **Mount Washington Auto Road**, ascending eight miles up the east side of the mountain from Rte-16 south of Gorham (mid-May to late Oct only – weather permitting, 7.30am–6pm in peak season, and 7.30am–5.30pm after Labor Day; call ☎603/466-2222 to check weather conditions), is not quite as hair-raising as you may expect, although the hairpin bends

and lack of guard-rails certainly keep you alert. There's a $15 toll for private cars
and driver (plus $6 for each additional adult and $4 for kids). Specially adapted
minibuses, still known as "stages" in honor of the twelve-person horse-drawn carriages that first used the road, give narrated **tours** (daily 8.30am–5pm, 90min
round-trip; ☎603/466-3988, *www.mt-washington.com*; $20) as they carry groups of
tourists up the mountain. Driving takes thirty or forty minutes under normal conditions, though rally drivers have been known to do it in under seven minutes in
the yearly "Climb to the Clouds" auto race, held in late June. The record for the
annual running race up the mountain, also held each June, currently stands at an
incredible 58 minutes 20 seconds.

Some fifteen **hiking trails** – in addition to the Appalachian Trail itself – lead to
the summit of Mount Washington. Unequalled vistas, beautiful flora, and the satisfaction of reaching the top make this hike a particularly thrilling experience.
The most direct route on the eastern side of the mountain is the **Tuckerman
Ravine Trail**, which originates at the AMC Pinkham Notch Visitor Center (see
p.452) and traverses the often snow-filled Tuckerman Ravine, a popular place for
backcountry skiing. If you're in good condition, the 4.1-mile trail can be completed in about four and a half hours, and it is possible to hike up and back in one day,
but don't forget that the weather at the top of the mountain is very unpredictable,
and potentially very dangerous: even when it's seventy degrees and sunny at the
base, the summit, some 4000 feet above, can be below freezing. The weather can
change very quickly, and you should not hesitate to turn back should any signs of
a storm become apparent; indeed, each year the conditions claim several lives –
although the roll-call of the 103 victims to die on the mountain does include the
duo that attempted to slide down on "improvised boards."

For hikes to the summit that originate on the west side of the mountain, see
p.446. You can also ride to the top on the coal-fired steam train of the **Mount
Washington Cog Railway**, originating in Bretton Woods – also detailed on p.446.
Incidentally, unless otherwise posted, you can **camp** anywhere on Mount
Washington below the tree line 200 feet from the trail and water sources, and a
quarter mile from any road or facility.

Gorham and beyond

Spread out along the northern reaches of the White Mountain National Forest,
working-class **GORHAM** can be used as an inexpensive base from which to visit
Mount Washington and other peaks in the "Presidential Range." Basic, affordable
accommodations can be found at the *Hikers Paradise Hostel*, 370 Main St,
Gorham (☎603/466-2732 or 1-800/470-4224; ①), where you can get a bed, sheets,
full kitchen, and full (shared) bath for $12. *Moose Brook State Park*, Jimtown Road,
off Rte-2 in Gorham (mid-May to mid-Oct; ☎603/466-3860), has 56 secluded
campsites. Reasonably priced home-made Italian **food** can be had at *La Bottega
Saladino* on Main Street (☎603/466-2520), while the *Golden Maple*, across the
street at 245 Main St (☎603/466-2766; closed Mon), is good for cheap Cantonese
and Polynesian specialties.

Continuing north along increasingly desolate Rte-16, you'll come across eminently missable **BERLIN**, a crumbling factory town plagued by unemployment,
though the enormous papermill on the east side of town along the shores of the
Androscoggin River still pumps fumes into the sky from its towering smokestacks.

Things get a bit better up in **DIXVILLE NOTCH,** a quiet hideaway centered on the sprawling turn-of-the-century *Balsams Grand Resort Hotel* (Dec 20 to late March and mid-May to mid-Oct; ☎1-800/255-0800 in NH or 1-800/255-0600 outside NH; *www.thebalsams.com*; ⑧), like Bretton Woods another of the last grand White Mountain resort hotels. Built in the 1860s, the enormous red roof-capped palace has 220 guest rooms, its own lake, 15,000 acres of land, a golf course, and a ski area.

Incidentally, if you've ventured this far north, don't miss the chance to **eat** a down-home meal at *Errol Restaurant,* at the intersection of Rte-16 and Rte-26 in **ERROL VILLAGE** (☎603/482-3852), where they serve cheap steaks, eggs, seafood, sandwiches, and "mooseburgers."

CHAPTER EIGHT

MAINE

A s big as the other five New England states combined, **MAINE** has barely the population of Rhode Island. In principle, therefore, there's plenty of room for its massive summer influx of visitors; in practice, the majority of these make for the extravagantly corrugated **coast**. In the shoreline's southern reaches, the beach resort towns of **Ogunquit** and **Old Orchard Beach** quickly lead up to Maine's most cosmopolitan city, **Portland**. The **mid-coast**, between the quiet college town of Brunswick and blue-collar Bucksport, is characterized by a wildly irregular seashore, with plenty of dramatic, windswept peninsulas and sheltered inlets to explore, though in the well-touristed towns of **Boothbay Harbor** and **Camden**, you'll certainly have company on your wanderings. **Down East**, beyond the moneyed Blue Hill Peninsula, **Mount Desert Island** holds Maine's most popular outdoor escape, **Acadia National Park**, in addition to the bustling summer retreat of **Bar Harbor**. Further still up the coastline, you'll find less cooperative weather and increasingly desolate scenery, capped by the candy-striped lighthouse at **Quoddy Head**, the easternmost part of the country.

You only really begin to appreciate the size and space of the state, however, further north or **inland**, where vast tracts of mountainous forest are dotted with lakes and barely pierced by roads – more like the Alaskan interior than the RV-clustered roads of the Vermont and New Hampshire mountains, and ideal territory for hiking and canoeing (and spotting moose), particularly in **Baxter State Park**. In the northwestern part of the state, closer to the New Hampshire border, a cluster of ski resorts lie scattered about the mountains, highlighted by **Sugarloaf USA**, perhaps the finest place to ski in all New England.

Although Maine is in many ways inhospitable – the **Algonquin** called it the "Land of the Frozen Ground" – it has been in contact with Europe ever since the **Vikings** explored it, around 1000 AD. For the navigator Verrazano, in 1524, the "crudity and evil manners" of the Indians made this the "Land of Bad People," but before long European fishermen were setting up camps each summer to dry their catch. Francis Bacon in turn said that the English settlers were "worse than the very Savages, impudently lying with their Women, teaching their men to drink drunke, and . . . to fall together by the eares."

North America's first agricultural **colonies** were in Maine: de Champlain's **French** Protestants near Mount Desert Island in 1604, and an **English** group that survived one winter at the mouth of the Kennebec River three years later. In the face of the unwillingness of subsequent English settlers to let them farm in peace, local Indians formed long-term alliances with the French and, until as late as 1700, regularly drove out streams of impoverished English refugees. By 1764, however, the official census could claim that even Maine's black population was more numerous than its Native Americans.

At first considered part of Massachusetts, Maine became a separate entity only in 1820, when the Missouri Compromise made Maine a free and missouri a slave state. In the nineteenth century, its people had a reputation for conservatism and

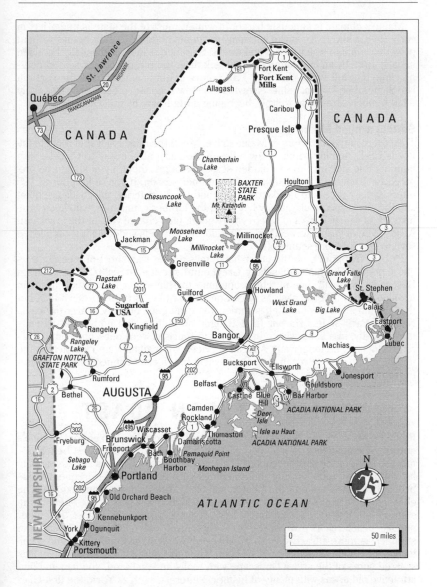

resistance to immigration, manifested in anti-Irish riots. Today, the **economy**
remains heavily based on the sea, although many of those who fish also farm, and
long expeditions are rare. Recently they have been selling their catch direct to
Russian factory ships anchored just offshore. Lobster fishing in particular has
defied gloomy predictions and has boomed again, as evidenced by the many thriving **lobster pounds**.

Maine's climate is famously harsh. In winter, most of the state is under ice; in early 1998, a severe ice storm left many residents huddled in their homes without power or running water for several weeks. Summer is short and usually heralded in early June by an infestation of tiny black flies, though the tourist season doesn't come into full swing until July. **Fall colors** begin to spread from the north in late September – when, unlike elsewhere in New England, off-season prices apply – but temperatures drop sharply, becoming quite frosty by mid-October.

Getting around Maine

The vast majority of visitors to Maine **drive**. Much the most enjoyable route to follow is US-1, running within a few miles of the coast all the way to Canada, with innumerable side turnings to hidden seaside villages, though you should be prepared for backups at the height of the summer season. If you're in a hurry, I-95 offers speedy access to Portland and beyond. In the interior, the roads are quiet and the views spectacular; many belong to the lumber companies, who keep careful track of who you are and where you're going (and charge you for the privilege). At any time of year, bad weather can render these roads suddenly impassable; be sure to check before setting off.

Public transport, on the other hand, falls a long way short of meeting travelers' needs. The nine-times-daily Greyhound service (☎1-800/231-2222) from Boston to Portland, five of which continue to Bangor, at least links the main towns of the southern coast, as does Concord Trailways (☎1-800/639-3317), but that's about all. Except in high summer, you can't get a bus any nearer to Acadia National Park or Bar Harbor than Bangor or Belfast, and nothing at all runs north. Sadly, in a state whose industry and tourism were once built on its railroads, there is no longer any Amtrak service. A Canadian train runs across the middle of the state to reach New Brunswick, but doesn't connect anywhere useful within Maine itself.

THE SOUTHERN COAST

Running between the two shopping hubs of **Kittery** and **Freeport**, Maine's **southern coast** is its most settled part. Blessed with the state's best **beaches** – indeed, most of the state's beaches – the southern coastline was already a popular summer vacation spot by the mid-nineteenth century, when frequent trains brought city-dwellers up from Boston and New York or down from Canada. The eleven-mile strip of sand at **Old Orchard Beach** is still one of the finest in the country, attracting correspondingly huge crowds in July and August. The other popular beach resort town in the area, **Ogunquit**, only slightly less overrun in summer, is more attractive, with a long-established artist community and a collection of excellent restaurants to boot. Though commercial development has scarred some of the area's landscape with malls and fast food, you can still find attractive old towns with plenty of historical interest, such as **York**, the first chartered city in America, and beautiful **Kennebunkport**, best known as the site of ex-president George Bush's summer home. In the northern part of the region, the coastline becomes more varied and prone to peninsulas, harbors, inlets, and islands. At the mouth of the Fore River, Maine's largest city, **Portland**, has experienced a cultural resurgence over the past few years, with a young population, respected art museum, lively music scene, and creative restaurants.

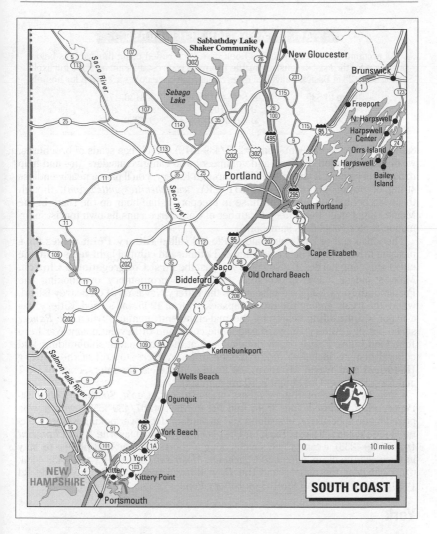

If your aim is to blast north toward lesser populated (and visited), more physically dramatic stretches of the coast, stick to fast-moving **I-95**; otherwise, **US-1** is the major artery, with turnoffs every few miles that lead to the coastal villages.

Kittery and York

KITTERY is only just in Maine, right across the Piscataqua from Portsmouth, NH (see p.390), and it makes for an excellent place to get oriented, namely at its very complete **information center** at the intersection of I-95 and US-1 (daily: summer

---

ACCOMMODATION PRICE CODES

All accommodation prices in this book have been coded using the symbols below; prices are for the least expensive **double rooms** in each establishment. For a full explanation see p.28 in Basics. Individual rates rather than price codes are given for **hostels**.

① up to $30	④ $60–80	⑦ $130–175
② $30–45	⑤ $80–100	⑧ $175–250
③ $45–60	⑥ $100–130	⑨ $250+

8am–6pm; rest of year 9am–5pm; ☎207/439-1319), which has scads of brochures, weather information services, and volunteers who can give insiders' tips and help make reservations. If you follow US-1 through Kittery, you'll pass a nearly endless string of **outlet shops** (☎1-888/KITTERY, *www.thekitteryoutlets.com*), though these lag behind the quality of those in Freeport, a half-hour up the road. In the Maine Outlet mall, the Kittery Chamber of Commerce runs its own tourist information center (weekdays 9am–5pm).

The small spit of land south along Rte-103 called **Kittery Point** makes for a pleasant drive, taking you a few miles and a thousand cultural light-years from the outlet-shopping hordes. It also takes you past the **First Congregational Church**, Maine's oldest house of worship, to a rocky promontory overlooking the Portsmouth Naval Shipyard (also called the Kittery Naval Yard) on Seavey Island, where the treaty ending the Russo-Japanese War of 1905 was signed. Kittery was a major **shipbuilding** center by the mid-eighteenth century, when the *Ranger* sailed out of a Kittery shipyard under the command of Revolutionary War hero John Paul Jones. For an overly detailed look at the city's naval, shipbuilding, and cultural history, including a 12ft model of the *Ranger*, stop off at the **Kittery Historical and Naval Museum**, on Rogers Road near the intersection of US-1 and Rte-236 (June–Oct Mon–Fri 10am–4pm; $3).

Close by is one of Kittery's best places to **eat**, *Cap'n Simeon's Galley*, 90 Pepperrell Rd (closed Tues from mid-Oct to May; ☎207/439-3655), with a well-priced menu specializing in seafood and an outdoor deck overlooking Kittery's picturesque Pepperrell Cove. Back on US-1 is longtime local favorite *Bob's Clam Hut* (☎207/439-4233), a campy fish shack dating to the 1950s. The best **places to stay** in town are the clean, adequate *Coachman Motor Inn*, 380 US-1 (☎207/439-4434; ⑤), right near the outlets, and the *Deep Water Landing B&B*, 92 Whipple Rd (☎207/439-0824; ④), off Rte-103 on Kittery Point.

York

YORK, a few miles north of Kittery off US-1, bears the distinction of being America's first chartered city, incorporated as Georgeana in 1642 – though it was subsequently demoted to the status of "town" in 1670. Its past is very well preserved in the series of seven buildings that comprise Old York. **Jefferd's Tavern**, 5 Lindsay St, offers a starting place for the tour of the old buildings (mid-June to mid-Oct Tues–Sat 10am–5pm, Sun 1–5pm; $2 per building or $6 for all six, free Wed during July & Aug), with a visitor's center where tickets are sold. There are occasional hearth-cooking demonstrations in its working kitchen. Foremost among the structures is the **Old Jail**, 207 York St, the earliest British Colonial public structure still standing on its original site, dating to 1653. It was used as Maine's primary prison until the

SURFING MAINE'S SOUTHERN COAST

A small number of hardy souls brave the cold tumult of the Northern Atlantic to pursue the unlikely pastime of **surfing** off Maine's coast; indeed, it's said that there are only a hundred or so Maine residents who surf regularly year-round (twenty of those in Portland), no matter the weather. While 50°F waters in Northern California are considered cold, the water here in January can dip below 40°F, daunting even with new developments in wet-suit technology. Though wave and tide conditions are usually best in fall and winter, on certain warm summer days, the waves come up and the crowds swell with the tides. The best spots are at **Higgins Beach**, south of Portland in Scarborough, **Fortune Rocks** in Biddeford, **Gooch's Beach** in Kennebunkport, **Old Orchard Beach**, **York Beach**, and **Wells Beach**. For equipment **rentals** and **information** on conditions, contact Bill's Surf and Skate, 61 India St, Portland (☎207/761-0174), or Stickman Surf & Sport, 24 Shore Rd, Ogunquit (☎207/646-0565).

Revolution and continued to confine York County prisoners until the Civil War. Inside, a museum reconstructs the surprisingly plush jailer's quarters, traces York's tumultuous history of threats from Indian raids and pestilence, and has displays on some of the more colorful criminals to do time here. Other highlights in Old York include the **Old Schoolhouse**, which houses exhibits on education in the eighteenth century; the **John Hancock Warehouse and Wharf**, which has displays on early American maritime history and navigation; and the **Old Burying Yard**, where it's rumored that a grave covered with a stone slab was thus protected to prevent its occupant, reputedly a witch, from escaping. In fact, the slab was actually placed there by her husband to prevent cattle from grazing on her grave. As well as its historical attractions, York boasts several fine **beaches**, and invigorating cliff walks. Head beyond Old York, for example, towards **Nubble Light**, at the end of Shore Road, off Rte-103, at York Beach, where you'll find one of Maine's most picturesque lighthouses, situated on an island of its own and observable from a rocky promontory.

Practicalities

York boasts some fine **accommodation**, of which the best is the 40-room *York Harbor Inn*, on Rte-1A in York Harbor (☎207/363-5119 or 1-800/343-3869, *www.yorkharborinn.com*; [7]), a beautifully appointed inn on the shore with several very inviting common areas. It also has a restaurant, which serves inventive takes on seafood, as well as the less expensive *Cellar Pub*, for burger-and-beer cuisine. The *Bell Buoy*, 570 York St (☎207/363-7264; [5]), is one of many B&Bs that crowds the area, a lovely spot that's within walking distance of the shore and with trolley access to historic Old York. A number of cheaper motels and B&Bs can be found along Long Beach Avenue, including *The Willows*, at Number 3 (☎207/363-9900; [4]), a cozy Victorian home.

As for **food**, the *Lobster Barn*, on US-1 in York Village (☎207/363-4721), has a relaxed atmosphere and well-priced lobster dinners that are served outdoors under a tent when weather permits. *Fazio's*, 38 Woodbridge Rd, York Village (☎207/363-7019), has traditional Italian dining at great prices. In York Village's main square, *Village Café*, 226 York St (☎207/363-7171), is good for a light snack or lunch. Out at York Beach, *The Goldenrod*, 2 Railroad Ave (☎207/363-2621), has been churning out saltwater taffy for over a hundred years; they also have an old-fashioned soda fountain. Just north in Cape Neddick, local institution *Flo's*, US-1 across from Mountain Road (closed Wed), cooks up nothing but juicy hotdogs, flavored with a special sauce, in its nondescript roadside shack.

Ogunquit

Approaching the small oceanside town just north of York, it's not difficult to imagine why Maine's Native Americans named the place **OGUNQUIT**, meaning "beautiful place by the sea" in their dialect. Though the place was much more attractive before it was developed into a summertime resort, its most prominent and stunning feature – the beach – still manages to make it a worthwhile spot for a visit. In the nineteenth and twentieth centuries, Ogunquit enjoyed fame as the vacation spot of choice for such rich and famous folks as Bette Davis and Tommy Dorsey, and its beachfront was lined with wooden luxury hotels, most of which are gone today. Also gone is the town's reputation as an artists' colony, though a few galleries remain to illustrate that chapter of its history.

Information and getting around

The **Ogunquit Chamber of Commerce**, just south of Ogunquit Village on US-1 (Mon–Fri 9am–5pm; ☎207/646-2939 or 1-800/639-2442, *www.ogunquit.org*), has brochures year-round and operates as a fully staffed **information center** from May to Oct (Sun–Thurs 9am–5pm, Fri–Sat 9am–8pm; ☎207/646-5533). The town is tiny, but parking can be tricky, so it may be a good idea to use the **trolley** ($1), which connects Perkins Cove, Ogunquit Square, the beach, and the strip of motels along US-1 to the north. Bikes by the Sea, a mile north of Ogunquit Square along US-1 (☎207/646-5898), rents **mountain bikes** and has maps of local cycling trails.

You may well wish to get on the water when you are so near it. A number of **sailing cruises** depart from Perkins Cove: Silverlining runs four cruises daily from May–Oct on its 42-foot sloop (☎207/361-9800) and the *Deborah Ann* charters whale-watching expeditions from mid-June to Aug (☎207/646-2214).

Accommodation

The pier at the beach has some decent **hotels** that tend to be high-priced due to their proximity to the ocean. Shore Road has a number of good-quality **B&Bs** within walking distance of the beach, town square, and Marginal Way. The stretch above Ogunquit Square along US-1 North has cheap **motels**, and once you get to the town of **Moody**, a mile out, prices drop precipitously. The best **camping** in the area is at *Cape Neddick Oceanside Campground*, on Shore Road between York and Ogunquit (☎207/363-4366).

Beachmere Inn, Shore Rd (☎207/646-2021 or 1-800/336-3983, *www.beachmereinn.com*). Beautiful rooms in quirky, turreted old wooden hotel on the shore. The restored inn also operates a more modern motel-style building on the same property as well as three other nearby buildings. ⑦.

Chestnut Tree Inn, 93 Shore Rd (☎207/646-4529 or 1-800/362-0757, *www.chestnuttreeinn.com*). Victorian B&B inn with 22 guest rooms (some with shared bath). ⑤.

Joan's Hideaway, 65 S Main St (☎207/646-3787). Rates start at around $40 at this funky, no-frills guesthouse. May–Oct only. ②.

Juniper Hill Inn, 196 US-1 N (☎207/646-5401 or 1-800/646-4544). Luxury beachside accommodation with pool, weight room, and spacious (somewhat plain) rooms. ⑦.

The Nellie Littlefield House, 9 Shore Rd (☎207/646-1692). Individually designed, well-appointed B&B rooms just outside the square. ④

Pine Hill Inn, 13 Pine Hill Rd (☎207/361-1004). Quiet, secluded B&B in a Victorian cottage off of Shore Rd closer to Perkins Cove. [5].

Seacoast Motel, US-1 N (☎207/646-2187). Cheap, basic, and clean motel north of the square. [4]

Terrace by the Sea, 11 Wharf Lane (☎207/646-3232). Plush motel located on the water's edge with spectacular views from many of its rooms. [5].

Wells-Moody Motel, US-1 N at the corner of Bourne Rd, Moody (☎207/646-5601). Impeccably kept modern motel rooms with cable and refrigerators. April–Oct only. [3].

The Town

Ogunquit Square, along Main Street (US-1), is the center of town, home to most of Ogunquit's best restaurants, coffeehouses, and quirky shops. East of the square, Beach Street leads over the Ogunquit River to the three-mile spit of white sand that is Maine's finest **beach**. The water is always freezing, but the tide is mellow and the sand great for sunbathing. Parking near the pier costs $4, but there's a better way to access the beach: take US-1 north of Ogunquit Square and go left on Ocean Road, which leads to a less populated area of the beach – with free parking.

Perkins Cove, a pleasant knot of restaurants and shops a few miles south of Ogunquit Square, is best reached by walking along **Marginal Way**, a windy path that traces along the shoreline from Ogunquit Beach. The two-mile trail offers unspoiled views of the Atlantic's rocky coast, particularly stunning in fall when the sea contrasts with the changing foliage. The folk art shops and galleries in and around the cove itself warrant maybe an hour's browse, and there are a few places to grab some saltwater taffy for a sweet treat. A half-mile south of Perkins Cove along Shore Road is the **Ogunquit Museum of American Art** (July–Sept Mon–Sat 10.30am–5pm, Sun 2–5pm; $3), which has a decent collection of twentieth-century work, only a fraction of which is on display at any given time. Best are the Marsden Hartleys and the Rockwell Kent seascapes inspired by the surrounding area. The views of the Atlantic from the plate-glass windows provide a stunning complement to the art.

Eating, drinking and entertainment

You'll find the standard profusion of **lobster shacks** and touristy seafood restaurants all over Ogunquit, but the best eateries are in the town square and around Perkins Cove. There are also a couple of decent pubs and **bars** in town, offering occasional live musical acts and friendly piano bar sing-alongs.

For more serious entertainment, the **Ogunquit Playhouse** along US-1 south of town (June 23–Aug 30; ☎207/646-5511) has been called "America's foremost summer theater" and usually attracts a few big-name performers each season.

Arrows Restaurant, Berwick Rd, just outside Ogunquit Square (☎207/646-9898). Excellent, though super-expensive, New American cuisine in a Victorian house surrounded by gardens. Reservations recommended. Weekends only in winter.

Hamilton's, 2 Shore Rd, Ogunquit Square (☎207/646-5262). Basic American comfort food, and a bar that's as lively as the town gets by evening.

Hurricane, Oarweed Lane, Perkins Cove (☎207/646-6348). Great views of the Atlantic from nearly every seat in this simple seaside eatery, where fresh seafood is the specialty. Entrees go for $15–20, but cheaper appetizers such as lobster gazpacho can be a meal in themselves.

Jackie's Too, 59 Perkins Cove (☎207/646-4444). The most popular of the cove area restaurants, with super-fresh seafood and outdoor dining when weather permits.

Jonathan's, 2 Bourne Lane (☎207/646-4777). Live entertainment – musical and otherwise – nightly from April to Oct, with a decent restaurant serving seafood, pasta, and creatively prepared meats. Reservations recommended.

Native Grounds, 139 Main St, Ogunquit Square (☎207/646-0955). Funky joint for light lunch fare. Create-your-own sandwiches and good soups of the day, to be enjoyed in pleasant outdoor yard seating.

The Old Village Inn, 30 Main St (☎207/646-7088). Upmarket seafood with a New American twist. Try the Asian-style crab cakes, lobster *relleno*, or duckling *au poivre*; the lobster bisque, too, is locally famous. There's also a cheaper pub menu if you're strapped for cash.

Poor Richard's Tavern, 2 Pine Hill Rd (☎207/646-4722). Authentic old-time New England pub grub in an old 1780 colonial building that was once a coach stop on the road between Boston and Portland.

North to Portland

The coast meanders on a bit from Ogunquit, with worthwhile stops slightly more spread out than at its most southern reaches. In this thirty or so mile stretch up to Portland, the main points of interest are in **Kennebunkport** and **Old Orchard Beach**.

Kennebunkport

The recent history of **KENNEBUNKPORT** illustrates the truth of Oscar Wilde's famous aphorism, "There is only one thing in the world worse than being talked about, and that is not being talked about." Kennebunkport was perfectly happy as a self-contained and exclusive residential district before its worldwide exposure as the home of **George Bush**'s "summer White House." If anything, locals seemed to feel that George lowered the tone of the place by becoming president. There were complaints at having to bear the extra cost of policing (the far smaller and poorer Plains, Georgia, home of Jimmy Carter, paid up with pride), and talk of a "lower class" of gawking visitor clogging the streets and driving the old money away. However, interest has subsided significantly since Bush lost the presidency to Clinton in 1992, and now it's quite apparent that Kennebunkport isn't that different from anywhere else along the coast – which bothers the locals even more. Bush's son, current President George W. Bush, has not been a regular visitor here.

The only sight worth stopping for in the area is the **Seashore Trolley Museum**, on Log Cabin Road off Rte-9 or US-1 (May–Oct daily 10am–5pm; $7; *www. gwi.net/trolley*), which holds a surprisingly engaging display on the history of the trolley car (of all things) in northern New England. You can take a twenty-minute ride on a vintage trolley car through the Maine woods, along a stretch of track that used to be part of a line that allowed travelers to go from Bangor to Washington, DC, entirely by trolley. Moose have occasionally been spotted along the way. Last, and best, is the collection of old trolleys from around the world, including the original New Orleans trolley that ran along Desire Street, inspiring the Tennessee Williams play *A Streetcar Named Desire*.

While there's really nothing else to see or do here, there are some good **places to eat** if you're passing through. *Alisson's*, 8 Dock Square (☎207/967-4841), is a fun, relaxed place to hang out and chow on seafood. They have a late-night menu, for this area at least (food is served in the pub until 11pm Fri & Sat, until 10pm the rest of the week), as well as a lively bar. In the Lower Village section of town, *Grissini Trattoria and Panificio*, 27 Western Ave (☎207/967-2211), has reasonably priced Italian food that you can eat on an outdoor patio. *Federal Jack's*, off Rte-9, makes great appetizers – try the Goat Island mussels or Maine steamers – and features an on-site **microbrewery** that produces the excellent Shipyard Ale.

Old Orchard Beach

During the late nineteenth and early twentieth centuries, **OLD ORCHARD BEACH** (OOB, in local parlance) stood alongside Ogunquit as a classic New England resort town, drawing upper-crust citizens from all over the eastern seaboard to stay in its massive wooden seafront hotels. After WWII, its popularity and property values declined steadily, and in 1980 the town attempted to rectify the situation by refurbishing its decaying, carnivalesque pier. Almost overnight, OOB regained its status as a major hotspot, though it resembled the spring-break town of Fort Lauderdale more than the posh resort of old. Things have calmed down a bit, even if a slightly corny party atmosphere remains, especially along the waterfront.

The main draw here is the **beach**, a fantastic seven-mile strip of white sand that competes with any in New England. It can get intolerably crowded during summer and holiday weekends, in which case you'd do better to find another stretch of shore. It's free, but **parking** can be pricey; lots that charge $4 per day are reasonable. Just off the beach is the **pier** (☎207/934-2001), with classic amusement-park attractions such as a Ferris wheel, bumper cars, and a vintage carousel dating from 1906. The entirety of **Old Orchard Street** (which leads down to the pier and beach) and **Grand Avenue** (which runs parallel to the ocean), are dotted with carnival attractions, including instant-photo booths, cotton-candy vendors, and stores where you can design your own souvenir T-shirt. It's hopelessly tacky, but at least an alternative to its sedate neighbors.

Practicalities

The **Old Orchard Beach Chamber of Commerce**, on First Street (☎207/934-2500, *www.oldorchardbeachmaine.com*), operates an information center of sporadic availability and can help arrange accommodation. In any case, you shouldn't have a hard time finding a room; the town is packed with **places to stay**. The seafront is dotted with pricey motels, though they sometimes have the advantage of owning a small strip of private beach – an invaluable respite from the maddening crowds. Quality doesn't really vary that much, but two of the nicer establishments are the *Grand Beach Inn*, 198 E Grand Ave (☎207/934-4621 or 1-800/834-9696, *www.oobme.com/grand*; ⑥)), which also has relatively affordable kitchen suites, and the *Edgewater Inn*, 97 W Grand Ave (☎207/934-3731 or 1-800/203-2034, *www.janelle.com*; ⑥)), which also operates the less pricey *White Lamb Cottages*, a series of stand-alone beach cottages done up in 1940s-era style. More downmarket options include the *Friendship Motor Inn*, 167 E Grand Ave (☎207/934-4644 or 1-800/969-7100, *www.friendshipmotorinn.com*; ④)), and the *Skylark Motel*, 8 Brown St (☎207/934-4235; ④)), each of which offer unremarkable motel digs.

Eating in OOB is not such a treat. Many of the restaurants are holdovers from the 1980s commercial boom, and you'll find an overabundance of pizza and burger joints crowding the main thoroughfares. There are a few nearby exceptions, most notably *Joseph's by the Sea*, 55 W Grand Ave (☎207/934-5044), whose deservedly expensive menu includes – but, thankfully, does not focus exclusively on – seafood; the great ocean views are a bonus. *Danton's*, 16 Old Orchard St (☎207/934-7701), makes passable and inexpensive American standards, particularly good if you're in a hurry. For hanging out, there's *The Hobo's Jungle*, 32 E Grand Ave (☎207/943-4266), a hip coffeehouse with faux-jungle environs, a pool table, vintage arcade games, and Internet access.

Portland

The largest city in Maine, with a population hovering around 65,000, **PORTLAND** was founded in 1632 at a superb point on the Casco Bay Peninsula, and quickly prospered, building ships and exporting its great supply of inland pines for use as masts. A long line of wooden **wharves** stretched along the seafront, with the merchants' houses on the hillside above. From the earliest days it was a cosmopolitan city, with a large free black population who traditionally worked as longshoremen; there was great bitterness when Irish immigrants began to muscle in on the scene in the 1830s. When the **railroads** came, the Canada Trunk Line had its terminus right on Portland's quayside, bringing the produce of Canada and the Great Plains one hundred miles closer to Europe than it would have been at any other major US port. Some of the wharves are now taken up by new condo developments, though **Custom House Wharf** remains much as it must have looked when Anthony Trollope passed through in 1861 and said, "I doubt whether I ever saw a town with more evident signs of prosperity." Most of the town he saw, including half the churches, nearly all of the public buildings, and hundreds of houses, was destroyed by an accidental fire in 1866 that was started during a Fourth of July celebration (Indians in 1675, and the British in 1775, had previously burned Portland deliberately).

Grand Trunk Station was torn down in 1966, and downtown Portland appeared to be in terminal decline until a group of committed residents undertook the energetic redevelopment of the area now known as **Old Port Exchange**. In more recent years, downtown Portland, particularly along **Congress Street**, has also undergone a renaissance of sorts, spurred by a high concentration of artists, some wise city planning, and the opening of a new L.L. Bean outlet in the late 1990s. These successes have revitalized the city, keeping it at the heart of Maine life – but you shouldn't expect a hive of energy. Portland is simply a pleasant, sophisticated, and in places very attractive town, not a major urban center.

Arrival, information, and getting around

Both I-95 and US-1 skirt the promontory of Portland, within a very few miles of the city center; **Portland International Jetport** (☎207/774-7301) is next to I-95. Most major carriers serve the airport, as do smaller airlines such as Downeast Express (☎1-800/983-3247), Business Express (☎1-800/345-3400), and Pine State Airlines (☎1-800/353-6334), which provide connections to points throughout the state. The airport is connected with downtown by regular **city buses** (#5; no service Sun; ☎207/774-0351; $1).

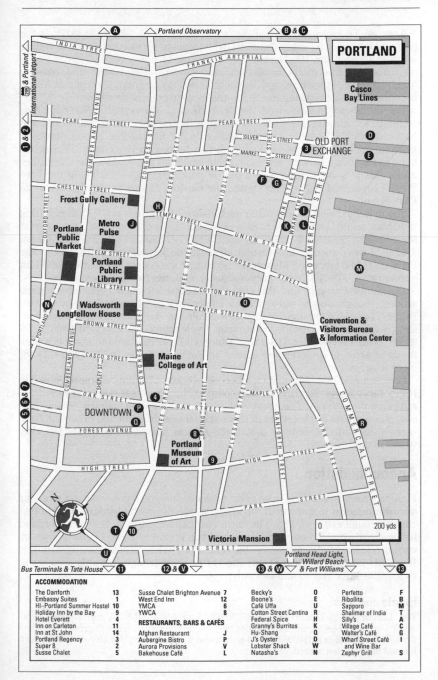

PORTLAND

Casco Bay Lines

Portland Observatory

INDIA STREET

FRANKLIN ARTERIAL

295 & Portland International Jetport

PEARL STREET

PEARL STREET

SILVER STREET

MARKET STREET

OLD PORT EXCHANGE

EXCHANGE STREET

CHESTNUT STREET

Frost Gully Gallery

Metro Pulse

Portland Public Market

Portland Public Library

Wadsworth Longfellow House

BROWN STREET

CASCO STREET

OAK STREET

DOWNTOWN

FOREST AVENUE

HIGH STREET

Maine College of Art

Portland Museum of Art

Victoria Mansion

STATE STREET

Bus Terminals & Tate House

TEMPLE STREET

ELM STREET

PREBLE STREET

CENTER STREET

COTTON STREET

CROSS STREET

UNION STREET

Convention & Visitors Bureau & Information Center

MAPLE STREET

OAK STREET

SPRING STREET

PLEASANT STREET

DANFORTH STREET

HIGH STREET

PARK STREET

COMMERCIAL STREET

FORE STREET

WHARF STREET

MILK STREET

MIDDLE STREET

FEDERAL STREET

CONGRESS STREET

CUMBERLAND AVENUE

OXFORD STREET

PORTLAND ST

PEARL STREET

YORK STREET

Portland Head Light, Willard Beach & Fort Williams

0   200 yds

N

ACCOMMODATION

The Danforth	13	Susse Chalet Brighton Avenue	7	
Embassy Suites	1	West End Inn	12	
HI–Portland Summer Hostel	10	YMCA	6	
Holiday Inn by the Bay	9	YWCA	8	
Hotel Everett	4			
Inn on Carleton	11	**RESTAURANTS, BARS & CAFÉS**		
Inn at St John	14	Afghan Restaurant	J	
Portland Regency	3	Aubergine Bistro	P	
Super 8	2	Aurora Provisions	V	
Susse Chalet	5	Bakehouse Café	L	

Becky's	O	Perfetto	F
Boone's	E	Ribollita	B
Café Uffa	U	Sapporo	M
Cotton Street Cantina	R	Shalimar of India	T
Federal Spice	H	Silly's	A
Granny's Burritos	K	Village Café	C
Hu-Shang	Q	Walter's Café	G
J's Oyster	D	Wharf Street Café	I
Lobster Shack	W	and Wine Bar	
Natasha's	N	Zephyr Grill	S

Concord Trailways, 100 Sewall St (☎207/828-1151 or 1-800/639-3317), is the principal **bus** operator along the coast, with frequent service to Boston, as well as north to Bangor and Bar Harbor. Vermont Transit Lines (☎207/772-6587 or 1-800/552-8737) has direct connection service with Greyhound and runs to Montréal, New Hampshire, and Vermont as well as to points throughout Maine from its station at 950 Congress St, on the eastern edge of downtown.

Car rentals are available from the local offices of Alamo (☎207/775-0855), Avis (☎207/874-7500), Budget (☎207/774-8663), Enterprise (☎207/772-0030), and National (☎207/773-0036); consult Basics (p.21) for toll-free phone numbers. **Parking** can be a real hassle in Portland. The parking meters charge 25¢ per half hour, but finding a parking place can seem well-nigh impossible. The city makes up for this to some degree with a glut of parking garages, including the Fore Street Garage at 439 Fore Street, and the Custom House Square Garage at 25 Pearl Street.

The rather unhelpful **Convention and Visitors Bureau** is at 305 Commercial St (mid-May to mid-Oct Mon–Fri 8am–6pm, Sat & Sun 10am–6pm; rest of year Mon–Fri 8am–5pm, Sat & Sun 10am–3pm; ☎207/772-5800, *www. visitportland.com*). There's a more friendly information office at the Jetport (☎207/775-5809). The Portland Public Library, 5 Monument Square, at the corner of Congress and Elm streets (☎207/871-1700, *www. portlandlibrary.com*), has free **Internet access**.

Downtown Portland and the Old Port are each compact enough to stroll around, though they're served by a comprehensive **bus** and trolley system (☎207/774-0351; $1); stop by the Metro Pulse at the Elm Street Garage near Congress Street for a detailed route map. Cyclemania, 59 Federal St (☎207/774-2933), rents **bicycles** for $15 a day, which you can ride around the city's hundreds of acres of undeveloped land. Call Portland Trails (☎207/775-2411) for more information.

Between mid-May and mid-October, the Prince of Fundy Company's *Scotia Prince* **ferry** leaves Portland for Yarmouth in Nova Scotia at 9pm every evening, returning the next day. The standard high-season fare is $93 per car, $68 per person, plus extra for a cabin, though there are various discount and excursion fares (details on ☎207/775-5616 or 1-800/482-0955 in Maine, ☎1-800/341-7450 elsewhere in the US).

Accommodation

Finding a room in Portland is no great problem, but you'll generally pay more for **accommodation** in town than for space in one of several **budget motels** that cluster around exit 8 off I-95. The extra cost can be worth it, however; Portland has some great old renovated hotels and you'll save in transportation costs by staying closer to downtown or the Old Port. The closest **campground** is *Wassamki Springs*, 56 Saco St, off Rte-114 in Scarborough, towards Westbrook (☎207/839-4276; May to mid-Oct only).

Hotels and inns

The Danforth, 163 Danforth St (☎207/879-8755 or 1-800/991-6557, *www.danforthmaine .com*). Portland's best accommodation has twelve spacious rooms, ten with private baths and working fireplaces, in an 1820s Federal-style home within walking distance of the Old Port. Elegant full breakfast served. ⑥.

Eastland Park Hotel, 157 High St (☎207/775-5411, *www.eastlandparkhotel.com*). Luxury accommodation, centrally located. [6].

Embassy Suites, 1050 Westbrook St (☎207/775-2200 or 1-800/753-8767). Spacious suites for the price of a hotel room, overlooking Portland's tiny Jetport. Rates include full breakfast and afternoon cocktails. [7].

Holiday Inn by the Bay, 88 Spring St (☎207/775-2311 or 1-800/345-5050, *www.innbythebay.com*). Fairly standard link in the *Holiday Inn* chain, with 239 rooms, many of which overlook Casco Bay. [5]–[6].

Hotel Everett, 51A Oak St (☎207/773-7882). Cozy rooms and friendly atmosphere, near the Wadsworth-Longfellow House in the Arts District. [4].

Inn on Carleton, 46 Carleton St (☎207/775-1910 or 1-800/639-1779, *www.innoncarleton.com*). A nicely restored clean Victorian brownstone on a quiet street in Portland's historic district. Breakfast included. [6].

Inn at St John, 939 Congress St (☎207/773-6481 or 1-800/636-9127, *www.innatstjohn.com*). Quaint, comfortable rooms located a short drive from the museums and convenient for public transport to the Old Port. Breakfast included. [3].

Portland Regency Hotel, 20 Milk St (☎207/774-4200 or 1-800/727-3436, *www. theregency.com*). Fancy rooms – some with bay views – in a beautifully renovated brick armory building not far away from the Old Port. [6].

Susse Chalet Inn, 340 Park Ave (☎207/871-0611 or 1-800/5-CHALET, *www.sussechalet.com*). Good value chain offers affordable doubles on the western edge of the peninsula near the Maine Medical Center; there's another *Susse Chalet* at 1200 Brighton Ave (☎207/774-6101; [4]) farther north and slightly less expensive. [5].

West End Inn, 146 Pine St (☎207/772-1377 or 1-800/338-1377). Charming 1871 town house in the historic district. Full breakfast included. [5]–[6].

Hostels and budget accommodation

HI-Portland Summer Hostel, 645 Congress St, in Portland Hall (☎207/874-3281). Open June through late August; office hours 6 to 11am & 5pm to midnight. Members $15, non-members $18.

Super 8, 208 Larrabee Rd (☎207/854-1881 or 1-800/800-8000, *www.super8.com*). Budget suites with kitchenettes and free continental breakfast near I-95. [3]–[4].

YMCA, 70 Forest Ave (☎207/874-1105). Gritty men-only hostel accommodation north of Congress St near Deering Oaks Park. $26.25 per night; often full.

YWCA, 87 Spring St (☎207/874-1130). Very near the Museum of Art, charging $25 single, or $20 per bed in a double room. Women only.

The City

Central Portland consists of two main districts. **Downtown** refers to the city's business district, bisected by Congress Street, where you'll also find several museums, the Civic Center, and a smattering of good restaurants. The **Old Port**, to the southeast, is lively and bustling with shops, bars, and eateries. Commercial Street runs along the water's edge, but Fore Street, just inland, has most of the area's attractions.

Downtown

Portland's best single destination, the **Portland Museum of Art** (PoMA), in the heart of downtown at 7 Congress Square (Tues, Wed & Sat 10am–5pm, Thurs–Fri 10am–9pm, Sun noon–5pm; Memorial Day–Columbus Day Mon 10am–5pm; $6;

☎207/775-6148 or 1-800/639-4067, *www.portlandmuseum.org*), was built in 1988 by the renowned I.M. Pei and Partners. All parts of the museum afford superb views of the bay, including some through porthole windows; indeed, in the museum's first few years, the design tended to overshadow the collection, though the latter has since improved considerably, even if space for extensive displays remains scarce. Ships and images of the sea are prevalent, such as Jamie Wyeth's chromatically layered *Island Friendship* and Winslow Homer's sentimental seascape *Enchanted*, while Maine geography is well depicted by naturalist Frederic Church's romantic *Mount Katahdin from Millinocket Camp* and Edward Hopper's gloomy *Lime Rock Quarry No. 1*. Some of the work by local artists is also striking, like Alan Magee's photorealist *Quartet II* and Joseph Nicoletti's brooding *Night Still Life*. The second floor contains rotating exhibits alongside more seascapes by Winslow Homer, some abstracted nature scenes from Marsden Hartley, and a series of Andrew Wyeths. The top floor houses a little of everything: Impressionist works, a couple of good Henry Moore sculptures, and a Picasso bust from his rose period called *Tête de Fou*. The basement is usually occupied by temporary exhibitions, and there's a lovely garden café as well. Adjoining the main building is the impressive Federal-style **McLellan-Sweat** Mansion, built for a city shipping magnate in 1800.

Among several excellent smaller art galleries in the newly resurgent downtown area, the best is the **Frost Gully Gallery**, 411 Congress St (Mon–Fri noon–6pm; ☎207/773-2555), which usually has a fine display of oil paintings by both local and nationally known artists. Down the street, the **Institute of Contemporary Art at Maine College of Art**, 552 Congress St (Tues–Sun 11am–4pm; ☎207/775-5152), stages interesting modern art exhibits such as "Do It," with do-it-yourself artworks crafted in accordance to the written instructions of several well-known artists from around the world. Nearby, along Cumberland Avenue between Elm and Preble streets, is the **Portland Public Market** (Mon–Sat 9am–7pm, Sun 10am–5pm; ☎207/772-8140, *www.portlandmarket.com*), a sleek 37,000-square-foot indoor food bazaar built in 1998, where you can buy gourmet pasta, fresh breads, organically grown vegetables, specialty cheeses, and a whole host of other yuppyish eats.

Thanks to the various fires, not all that much of old Portland survives, though various grand mansions can be seen along Congress and Danforth streets in the downtown area. A few of the oldest houses are open to the public, most notably the **Wadsworth-Longfellow House** at 485 Congress St (June–Oct Tues–Sun 10am–4pm; Nov–May Wed–Sat noon–4pm; $6), Portland's first brick house, built in 1785 by Revolutionary War hero Peleg Wadsworth, grandfather of poet Henry Wadsworth Longfellow. Longfellow spent his boyhood here and wrote a number of pieces about the local harbor and lighthouses. The house is furnished with the Longfellow family's own housewares. Next door, at 489 Congress St, the **Maine History Gallery** (June–Oct daily 10am–4pm; free with admission to Wadsworth-Longfellow House, otherwise $4; *www.mainehistory.org*) has rotating displays of art and Maine-related historical artifacts, as well as an extensive library. Another building that survived the fires, slightly west of downtown, the period-furnished **Tate House**, 1270 Westbrook St (mid June–Sept Tues–Sat 10am–4pm, Sun 1–4pm; Oct Fri–Sun same times; $5; *www.nentug.org/museums/tatehouse*), was the home of Captain George Tate, mast agent for the British Royal Navy, from 1755 to 1794. The exterior of the building merits attention for its clerestory, an indented wall rising above the gambrel roof on the second story, while the furnishings and decorations inside reflect a style typical of a wealthy eighteenth-century official.

Closer to the Old Port, the **Victoria Mansion**, at 109 Danforth St (May–Oct Tues–Sat 10am–4pm, Sun 1–5pm; $5; *www.portlandarts.com/victoriamansion*), an Italianate brownstone constructed in 1859 for a wealthy hotel magnate, is blessed with an exquisite interior. The walls and ceilings are ornamented with frescoes, and there's a freestanding staircase made of Santo Domingo mahogany. Stained glass and floor-to-ceiling gold-leaf mirrors are also prevalent. Tours of Portland's historic houses and architecture can be arranged through Greater Portland Landmarks, 165 State St (☎207/774-5561; $7 for tours).

Old Port district

For relaxed wandering, the restored **Old Port Exchange** near the quayside, between Exchange and Pearl streets, is quite entertaining, with all sorts of red-brick antiquarian shops, specialist book and music stores (especially on Exchange Street), and other esoterica. Several companies operate **boat trips** from the nearby wharves. The *Palawan*, a vintage 58-foot ocean racer, sails around the harbor and to the Casco Bay islands and lighthouses from DeMillo's Marina off Commercial Street (daily in summer; 2hr trip morning $20, afternoon $35; ☎207/773-2163 or 1-800/284-PAL1), while Bay View Cruises, 184 Commercial St, offers seal-watching excursions all year (May–Oct daily; Nov–April weekends; $8; ☎207/642-3270). Casco Bay Lines runs a twice-daily **mailboat** all year, and additional **cruises** in summer, to six of the seemingly innumerable Calendar Islands in Casco Bay, from its terminal at Commercial and Franklin streets ($8–13.75; ☎207/774-7871, *www.cascobaylines.com*). Long, Peaks, and Cliff islands all have accommodation or camping facilities.

If you follow Portland's waterfront to the end of the peninsula, you'll come to the Eastern Promenade, which became almost exclusively residential after the last fire and is remarkably peaceful for so close to downtown. A big beach lies below the headland, while above, at the top of Munjoy Hill, is the shingled, eight-sided 1807 **Portland Observatory** (June, Sept & Oct Fri–Sun 1–5pm; July to Labor Day Wed–Sun noon–5pm; $3), the oldest remaining operational signal tower on the Atlantic; you can climb its 102 steps for an exhilarating view of the bay and the city.

South Portland

Across the harbor, in South Portland at Fort Williams State Park, lies the **Portland Head Lighthouse** (take Rte-77 south and follow the signs), the oldest in America, commissioned in 1790 by George Washington. Though it is no longer functional, it houses an excellent **museum** on the history of Maine's lighthouses (June–Oct daily 10am–4pm; April–May & Nov–Dec weekends only 10am–4pm; $2). The small but intelligent collection traces lighthouse history back to 300BC when Ptolemy II built a lighthouse on the island of Pharos at Alexandria Harbor. Best are the displays combining lighthouse literature and art, such as Longfellow's paean *The Lighthouse* and Edward Hopper's forlorn watercolors, each of which were inspired by Portland Head. Five miles south of Portland, another lighthouse commissioned by George Washington, the **Cape Elizabeth Lighthouse**, is one of the more recognizable landmarks of the state, captured on countless postcards and posters. Nearby, **Two Lights State Park** has easy shore-side trails and picnic areas (day use fee $1). The lighthouse is still operational, as the occasional and unpredictable ear-splitting blasts from its horn alert anyone in the vicinity.

Eating

Portland's relatively low rents and young, hip population have given rise to a concentration of experimental, though still quite affordable, **restaurants**. Throw a rock in the Old Port district and you'll hit one; also check around the downtown area near the Portland Museum of Art. Be wary of the larger, more touristed restaurants along the waterfront, where the ambiance may be grand, but the food is probably bland. People eat out a lot here, so be sure to call for reservations Thursday through Sunday.

Inexpensive

Afghan Restaurant, 419 Congress St (☎207/773-3431). Cheap, authentic Afghani food with plenty of lamb and veggie options in the heart of downtown.

Aurora Provisions, 64 Pine St (☎207/871-9060). Upscale market/deli with mouth-watering sandwiches, a full selection of coffee, drinks, pastries, salads, desserts, and a small seating area. Closed Sun.

Becky's, 390 Commercial St (☎207/773-7070). The best breakfast spot in Portland, serving hearty American portions, including home-made muffins, from 4am until 9pm. On weekends, the place is open all night.

Cotton Street Cantina, 10 Cotton St (☎207/775-3222). Fancy smoothies with mixtures of papaya, mango, ginger, and cinnamon (the "Reggae Runner") or peanut butter and banana (the "Elvis"). Also Caribbean food like African fire pork stew and "voodoo stuffed" chops.

Federal Spice, 225 Federal St (☎207/774-7777). Eclectic international fare influenced by South American, Southeast Asian, and Caribbean cuisine, all very hot, spicy, and cheap.

Granny's Burritos, 420 Fore St (☎207/761-0751). Super-cheap burritos and quesadillas served on no-frills benches downstairs. There's a new bar area upstairs. Open until midnight on Fri and Sat.

Hu-Shang, 1 Forest Ave (☎207/772-1000). Deservedly popular Chinese restaurant, where a good lunch can easily cost under $10.

Shalimar of India, 675 Congress St (☎207/874-6342). Good tandoori dishes and lunchtime and evening specials. The outdoor deck is the place to sit in summer.

Silly's, 40 Washington St (☎207/772-0360). Burgers, pies, and particularly fine milkshakes in a space adorned with wacky Americana.

Moderate to expensive

Aubergine Bistro, 555 Congress St (☎207/874-0680). Classic French cooking with an American flair in a sophisticated setting. Try the swordfish loin with lemon and ginger or rump steak with red leek bearnaise. Extensive wine bar. Closed Mon; brunch only Sun 11am–2pm.

Bakehouse Café, 205 Commercial St (☎207/773-2217). Relaxing and casual dining with candlelit tables in a small but sleek bakery/restaurant. The wine list isn't too expensive and light pasta entrees cost $8–12.

Boone's, 6 Custom House Wharf (☎207/774-5725). Traditional waterfront restaurant in old wharf buildings, overlooking the fishing docks since 1898. Good lobster and grilled seafood in general.

Café Uffa, 190 State St (☎207/775-3380). Reasonably priced creative fare – the grilled fish is particularly savory – in a funky neighborhood café.

J's Oyster, 5 Portland Pier (☎207/772-4828). Classic old-school raw bar serving oysters and steamers right on the waterfront.

Lobster Shack, five miles south of Portland, just below the Cape Elizabeth Lighthouse (☎207/799-1677). Great for fresh seafood – try the clamburger or lobster stew.

Natasha's, 40 Portland St (☎207/774-4004). New American cuisine, featuring wraps, pasta, salads, paella, ravioli, eggplant casserole, and risotto. Closed Mon.

Perfetto, 28 Exchange St (☎207/828-0001). Modern Italian and New American cuisine in Ikea-dominated environs. Best are the North Beach cioppino, a light seafood stew, and pomegranate chicken.

Ribollita, 41 Middle St (☎207/774-2972). Reasonably priced fresh handmade pasta in a cozy narrow dining room with brick walls.

Sapporo, at Union Wharf, 230 Commercial St (☎207/772-1233). Sushi bar on the water with fresh seafare, teriyaki, tempura, and Japanese beer.

Village Café, 112 Newbury St (☎207/772-5320). No-nonsense, reasonably priced family dining; well-cooked steak and seafood plus a selection of Italian dishes.

Walter's Café, 15 Exchange St (☎207/871-9258). New American cuisine in a hip, high-ceilinged dining room with an open kitchen. Most entrees go for $11–17.

Wharf Street Café and Wine Bar, 38 Wharf St (☎207/773-6667). Really more a restaurant than either a café or wine bar. They do serve good vino by the glass and bottle, and have inventive French/New American fusion fare, such as lobster and brie ravioli and chicken and apple burritos.

Zephyr Grill, 653 Congress St (☎207/828-4033). Zesty country Italian grill fare and artsy interior. Try the pan-seared sea bass fillet with shellfish risotto and roasted vegetables. Wed–Sun only.

PORTLAND'S FESTIVALS

As with many larger New England cities, Portland hosts its share of **festivals** outside of the typical holiday celebrations. Craft booths, plenty of food, and lots of people-watching are standard. In some cases, you should call ahead to double-check dates.

Old Port Festival, first Sun in June. Old Port Exchange. Crafts and food booths, music and other live entertainment (☎207/772-6828).

Greek Heritage Festival, last weekend in June. 133 Pleasant St. Greek food (especially good fresh-baked pastries), traditional music and folk dancing exhibitions (☎207/774-0281).

Portland Symphony Orchestra Independence Pops Concert, Sun of Independence Say Weekend. Free outdoor concert by the PSO followed by fireworks (☎207/773-8191).

OpSail Maine, July 28–31. Tall ships on display, sail parade, ship tours, fireworks.

Italian Street Festival, weekend before Aug 15, Feast of Assumption. Federal Street. Ethnic celebration featuring band music, kids' games, Italian food (☎207/773-0748).

Alive's Sidewalk Art Festival, Sun after Aug 15. Congress Street. Downtown area blocked off for 350 booths featuring work from artists from all over the US and Canada (☎207/828-6666).

Old Port Equinox Art Fair, weekend after Labor Day. Exchange and Fore streets. Over 100 local artists display their work; musical presentations, too (☎207/772-8766).

Victorian Holiday, Nov 29–Dec 31. Downtown and the Old Port feature holiday- and winter-themed events during the month in Old Victorian style.

New Year's Portland, Dec 31. Music, dancing, arts and crafts city-wide. "Family"-oriented events mean no alcohol (☎207/772-9012).

Entertainment and nightlife

The bar-restaurant distinction is blurry in Portland; most watering holes serve food, and many eateries have good selections of microbrews and wine. There are a good many **bars** scattered throughout the Old Port District, of which a number feature live rock music. ID policies are strict and bars aren't allowed to serve after 1am. **Cafés** are becoming increasingly popular with Portland's youthful population and frequently offer Internet access. They're generally as crowded and lively as bars on the weekends. The **club scene** is somewhat tamer, but there are a few intense dance and music venues. One entertainment option that defies category but is very worth a visit is the *Keystone Theatre Café*, 504 Congress St (☎207/772-0606), a sort of bar-theater hybrid where you can watch the latest films while enjoying food and drinks.

There are several options for the **performing arts**, ranging from the tiny and adventurous Mad Horse Theater Company at 955 Forest Ave (☎207/797-3338) up to the large productions at the Portland Performing Arts Center, 25A Forest Ave (☎207/774-0465). Maine Arts, Inc (☎207/772-9102, *www.mainearts.org*) and Portland Parks and Recreation (☎207/874-8793, *www.ci.portland.me.us*) both sponsor free outdoor noontime and evening jazz and blues **concerts** at various locations throughout the city during the summer. The free *Casco Bay Weekly* (*www.cascobayweekly.com*) and *Face Magazine* have **listings** of all local events; Maine's biggest gigs take place each summer at Old Orchard Beach, roughly ten miles south of Portland, but some mid-level shows come to town at the Merrill Auditorium, 20 Myrtle St. Call PorTix (☎207/842-0800) for all area ticketing sales and information.

Sports fans should take a trip to Haddock Field, an intimate baseball stadium on Park Avenue where the minor-league **Portland Sea Dogs** play from May to October. Call ☎207/879-9500 for ticket and schedule information.

Cafés

Arabica Coffee House, 16 Free St (☎207/879-0792). Mellow café with numerous brands of imported java.

Habana Cigar Café, 398 Fore St (☎207/874-4055). Wide selection of stogies and specialty coffees, including banana split latte and almond joy latte.

Java Joe's, 13 Exchange St (☎207/761-JOES). Sleek but warm two-story interior, packed with young hipsters and commonly known as "JJs." Particularly strong caffeine beverages.

JavaNet Café, 37 Exchange St (☎1-800/JAVA-NET). It's part of a burgeoning chain, but the coffee's good, the couches are comfy, and there's Internet access.

Portland Roasting Co, 111 Commercial St (☎207/761-9525). Euro-styled coffeehouse with in-store roasted beans and the standard cappuccinos and lattes.

Bars and microbreweries

Bitter End Microbrewery, 446 Fore St (☎207/874-1933). Slightly more upmarket than the average fratboy bar, with pool, video games, and live bar bands most nights.

Brian Boru Public House, 57 Center St (☎207/780-1506). Traditional Irish pub serving Guinness, with a big, if typical, menu and plenty of benches.

Double Diamond Bar and Grill, 41 Wharf St (☎207/761-0069). Basic American bar with plenty of beer on tap and a sort of Texan-cowboyish atmosphere. Restaurant with outside dining when weather permits. *Penguin's* dance club located upstairs gets raucous on weekends.

Gritty McDuff's, 396 Fore St (☎207/772-2739, *www.grittys.com*). Portland's first brewpub, making Portland Head Pale Ale and Black Fly Stout. Food, folk music, long wooden benches, and a friendly (if a little self-consciously British) atmosphere, which can get rowdy on Saturday nights.

Old Port Tavern, 11 Moulton St (☎207/774-0444). Relaxed downstairs pub in the heart of the Old Port with great burgers and a good selection of brews. Live entertainment some nights.

The Shipyard Brewing Co, 86 Newbury St (☎207/761-0807 or 1-800/BREW-ALE, *www .shipyard.com*). Maker of one of Maine's finest microbrews. Free tours 3–5pm daily.

Stone Coast Brewing Co, 14 York St (☎207/773-BEER). Three-story complex featuring restaurant, cigar lounge, microbrewery, and nightclub with live entertainment.

Three Dollar Dewey's, 230 Commercial St (☎207/772-3310). Raucous beer hall, with a wide selection of micro- and macrobrews. They also have a typical burger menu.

Dance clubs and music venues

Asylum, 121 Center St (☎207/772-8274). Loud, somewhat stylish dance club/bar popular with Portland's twenty-something singles set. DJ and dancing on weekends as well as occasional mid-level bands. Cover $5–12.

The Basement, at the corner of Fore and Exchange streets, below *Punky's Pizza* (☎207/828-1111). Mixed bag of music acts, including progressive rock, punk, funk, and folk. Cheap beer specials from 5 to 7pm weeknights.

Big Easy Blues Club, 55 Market St (☎207/871-8817). Mellow blues joint with local acts, mostly blues with some jazz and rockabilly shows, rather tame on weekdays, more active on weekends.

Geno's, 13 Brown St (☎207/772-7891). Rock venue featuring mostly local indie acts.

Millennium, 35 India St (☎207/773-5700). Alternative, mostly gay dance club with the wildest scene in Portland, probably all of Maine. Call ahead for rapidly changing schedule. Wed is Fetish Night, featuring exotic male dancers. Open until 3am Fri–Sun, closed Mon.

Moon Dance Club, 16 Mussey St, #407, South Portland (☎207/772-1983). Popular top-40 style dance club. Outdoor patio in summer. 21+.

Raoul's Roadside Attraction, 865 Forest Ave (☎207/773-6886). Music venue – R&B, punk, reggae, etc – which is also a restaurant with vegetarian specials, a mile from downtown.

Sisters, 45 Danforth St (☎207/774-1505). Lively lesbian dance club.

Zootz, 31 Forest Ave (☎207/773-8187). "Progressive" dance club hosting world-beat discos and some concerts.

Freeport

Sixteen miles north of Portland along the coast, **FREEPORT** is one long outlet shopping mall, though the town was once one of Maine's primary shipbuilding centers, where huge logs were shipped from the northern pine forests to make masts for schooners; this is still evident in the wide shape of the town square at Main and Bow streets, which was created to give the gigantic logs plenty of room to swing as they were turned on their way to the mast landing. Freeport's prominence was such that it was chosen as the place where the treaty to separate Maine from Massachusetts was signed in 1820, in the **Jameson Tavern**.

The shipping industry fell into disrepair following the Civil War, but Freeport managed a big comeback fifty years later when a fishing-boot maker by the name of **Leon L. Bean** planted the seeds of what was to be an unbelievably successful outdoors wear manufacturer. L.L. Bean's store stood alone along Freeport's Main Street for decades, until the advent of the greed-driven 1980s, when it was joined by countless factory outlets and Freeport developed its current character.

SABBATHDAY LAKE SHAKER COMMUNITY

North of Portland off of Rte-26, at 707 Shaker Rd in **NEW GLOUCESTER**, is the Sabbathday Lake Shaker Community, the last remaining active settlement of its kind. Founded in 1783, the village is made up of seventeen buildings, all constructed in the beautifully functional fashion typical of the Shakers. Though their numbers have dwindled to a mere seven, the remaining Shaker members remain true to their simple, celibate, and religious lives; they welcome visitors to their 10am Sunday worship service. Tours of the grounds ($6 introductory tour, $7.40 extended tour) take in several of the buildings, including the meetinghouse, where the Shaker Museum has many of the religious community's innovative furniture, textile, and farm tool designs on display (Memorial Day–Labor Day Mon–Sat 10am–4.30pm; ☎207/926-4597). It's all well worth the detour, though the Canterbury Shaker Village in New Hampshire (see p.407) is more impressive.

Arrival and information

The best way to get to Freeport is by **car** – there's no public transport, and the closest a bus comes is sixteen miles away in Portland, from where you'll need to take a **taxi** or van the rest of the way. Try Classy Taxi (☎207/865-0663 or 1-800/499-0663) or Freeport Taxi (☎207/865-9494). Mermaid Transportation (☎1-800/696-2463; *www.gomermaid.com*) also offers **van** service to Freeport from Portland for $15 round-trip. Drop by the incredibly complete Freeport Merchants' Association (☎207/865-1212 or 1-800/865-1994) on Mill Street in a restored old tower, for reams of area **information** as well as public restrooms, an ATM, and a staff of senior citizens who will provide far more assistance than you really want.

Accommodation

There's no shortage of quality **B&Bs** in town very proximate to the shopping areas, but if you're low on cash, some cheap motels line US-1 south of Freeport. (Better still, stay in Portland and make a quick trip through Freeport.) The best nearby **camping** is at the oceanside *Recompense Shores*, 8 Burnett Rd (☎207/865-9307), near Casco Bay, which has over one hundred well-kept and spaced sites. You can also camp along the shores of the bay at the *Winslow Park and Campground*, Staples Point Road (☎207/865-4198), which is near nature trails and the town beach.

Brewster House, 180 Main St (☎207/865-4121 or 1-800/865-0822). B&B set in a beautifully restored Queen Anne cottage with antique furnishings. ⑥.

Freeport Inn & Café, 31 US-1 S (☎207/865-3106 or 1-800/99-VALUE). Excellent-value rooms, clean and comfortable, and a café serving hearty breakfasts all day. ⑤.

Harraseeket Inn, 162 Main St (☎207/865-9377 or 1-800/342-6423). Wonderful clapboard B&B inn with some 50 rooms. ⑧.

Maine Idyll Motor Court, 1411 US-1 N (☎207/865-4201). Basic cottage quarters in woodsy area a few miles north of town. ③.

Village Inn, 186 Main St (☎207/865-3236). Motel-style units in the rear building, breakfast in the dining room of the proprietors' home. ⑤.

White Cedar Inn, 178 Main St (☎207/865-9099 or 1-800/853-1269). Seven rooms in a pleasant Victorian home. Breakfast served in bright sunroom. ⑥.

The Town

Freeport owes virtually all of its current prosperity to the invention by Leon Leonwood Bean, in 1912, of a particularly ugly rubber-soled fishing boot. The boot is still available, and **L.L. Bean's** has grown into a multinational clothing conglomerate, housed in an enormous 90,000-square-foot factory outlet building on Main Street (☎1-800/441-5713 or 207/552-6879, *www.llbean.com*) that literally never closes. In theory, this is so pre-dawn hunting expeditions can stock up; all the relevant equipment is available for rent or sale, and the store runs regular workshops to teach backcountry lore. However, with the outdoor look in vogue, L.L. Bean's is now more of a fashion emporium. It's worth a spin just to gawk at the four stories packed with more camping supplies and dense plaid outerwear than the eye can see; there's also a full café, a trout pond with a waterfall, and a self-congratulatory chronicle of the chain's history located just inside the main entrance. There are plenty of other **outlet stores** nearby, classier than most perhaps, with chic fashion stops like Donna Karan, Kenneth Cole, and Calvin Klein, alongside the ones geared toward rugged outdoorsmen (Patagonia, Timberland, and North Face).

Now a lone reference to the city's life before Bean, the **Soldiers and Sailors Monument**, on Bow Street, was dedicated by Civil War General Joshua Chamberlain. The monument's cannons were used at the Battle of Bull Run and on Sherman's march to the sea. To get even further away from the shops, however, head a mile south of Freeport to the sea, where the very green cape visible just across the water is **Wolfe's Neck State Park**. In summer, for just $1, you can follow hiking and nature trails along the unspoiled fringes of the headland. For another – and rather bizarre – change of pace, check out the **Desert of Maine**, on Desert Road off I-95 exit 19 (May–mid-Oct; $7; ☎207/865-6962), a vast expanse of privately owned sand deposited just inland from Freeport by a glacier that slid through eight thousand years ago. The result was a tiny, self-contained desert ecosystem that engulfed the surrounding homes and trees, which you can still see half-buried in sand. There's a kitschy gift shop good for souvenirs, too, and a small museum housed in a 1783 barn.

Eating and drinking

Restaurants in the area cater to the upscale crowd that seeks out the outlets. They're all done up to match the town's strict aesthetic zoning laws; even the *McDonald's* is disguised by a weathered-clapboard motif.

Broad Arrow Tavern, 162 Main St, in the *Harraseeket Inn* (☎207/865-9377). Traditional Maine food prepared over wood-fired oven and grill.

China Rose, 10 School St (☎207/865-6886). Reputed to be some of Maine's best Szechuan and Hunan cuisine. Also has a surprisingly good sushi bar.

Gritty McDuff's Brewpub, 183 US-1 (☎207/865-4321). Standard bar food with a really good selection of local microbrews, including many made on the premises. Seasonal outdoor dining.

Harraseeket Lunch & Lobster Co, off Rte-1, South Freeport (☎207/865-4888). Extending on its wooden jetty into the peaceful bay, this makes a great outdoor lunch spot.

Jameson Tavern, 115 Main St (☎207/865-4196). Excellent traditional American fare in a historical setting – this is where the papers were signed that separated Maine from Massachusetts. Meat-oriented menu highlighted by steak au poivre and pan-blackened haddock. Wash it down with the house brew, Jameson's Black and Tan. The taproom menu offers lighter, less expensive fare.

Lobster Cooker, 39 Main St (☎207/865-4349). A particularly good roadside seafood shack specializing in lobster and crabmeat rolls.

THE MID-COAST

Stretching roughly from the quiet college town of **Brunswick** up to blue-collar **Bucksport**, Maine's central coast is a study in geographic, economic, and cultural contrasts. The shore here is physically different than the southern coast, prone to dangling peninsulas such as the **Harpswells** and **Pemaquid Point** where you can diverge from the well-traveled US-1, which traverses the jagged coastline. Much of this region prospered in the late nineteenth century as a major shipbuilding and trading center, as evidenced by its wealth of attractive old captains' homes; today, only **Bath** remains as a ship manufacturer. Throughout, the focus is still unquestionably the sea, be it for livelihood, nourishment, or entertainment. Consequently, one of the best ways to see the area is by boat; from most coastal towns, you can catch a scenic boat tour. Indeed, purposefully remote **Monhegan Island**, somewhat of an artists' retreat eleven miles off the coast near New Harbor, is only accessible by boat.

Lobsters are a way of life in Maine, and the state's largest producer of the ugly crustaceans is **Rockland**, which is also home to the Farnsworth Museum. Busy **Camden**, just beyond Rockland, is known for its fleet of recreational **windjammers** and as the New England headquarters of MBNA Bank. Picturesque fishing villages such as **Round Pond** and **Tenants Harbor** – tiny windows into the real Maine – can be found throughout, somehow managing to coexist with overrun summer tourist resorts like **Boothbay Harbor**, which is all but deserted in the winter. In the face of dwindling industry, it's hard to say what might happen to these smaller settlements, though sadly many have already reluctantly begun to promote tourism.

Brunswick and the Harpswells

Only a few miles further on from Freeport is **BRUNSWICK**, home since 1794 of the private, well-respected Bowdoin College (*www.bowdoin.edu*). The town is attractive enough, with a concentration of old brick and clapboard homes and buildings, but apart from the small campus itself – at the south end of Maine Street – and a couple of unobtrusive cafés, there's little evidence of student life here.

Information and getting around

The Bath-Brunswick **Chamber of Commerce** at 59 Pleasant St in Brunswick (☎207/725-8797, *www.midcoastmaine.com*) is particularly helpful, with a typical array of brochures and a knowledgeable staff.

Public transport to and from Brunswick is infrequent but nevertheless available. Vermont Transit stops at the depot at 9 Pleasant St (☎207/725-5573), from where you can catch **buses** to most other parts of New England. Concord Trailways stops at 162 Pleasant St before continuing north to Searsport or south to Boston on its coastal route.

Accommodation

There isn't an abundance of **places to stay** in Brunswick, though most of the time you shouldn't have trouble finding a good-value room. The best place to **camp** is at the *Orrs Island Campground*, on the island of the same name in the **Harpswells** along Rte-24 (☎207/833-5595; end May to mid Sept).

Brunswick B&B, 165 Park Row (☎207/729-4919). A gracious old inn decorated with antiques and quilts within easy walking distance of the town center and the college. [5]–[6].

Harriet Beecher Stowe House, 63 Federal St (☎207/729-7869). This rambling old house (see box overleaf) is now a motel – guests stay in modern rooms around the back, but can use the lounge of the original house. [4]–[5].

Hazel-Bea House, south of town along Rte-24 towards Bailey Island (☎207/725-6834). It's a bit out of the way and only open May to Oct, but there are cozy rooms and great breakfasts on the outdoor deck. [4]–[5].

Siesta Motel, 130 Pleasant St (☎207/729-3364 or 1-800/457-3364). The Siesta is a more modest, no-frills hotel a half a mile from the town center. [4].

The Town

Free tours of **Bowdoin College**, which counts among its alumni Henry Wadsworth Longfellow, Nathaniel Hawthorne, and Franklin Pierce (see p.412), begin at the Moulton Union (Mon–Fri at 9am, 11am, 2pm & 4pm; ☎207/725-3000) and take in the intriguing **Peary-MacMillan Arctic Museum** (Tues–Sat 10am–5pm, Sun 2–5pm; ☎207/725-3416; free). After decades of disagreement, experts now generally conclude that former student Admiral Robert Peary was the first man to reach the North Pole in 1909; whatever the truth, his assembled equipment and notebooks hold a powerful fascination.

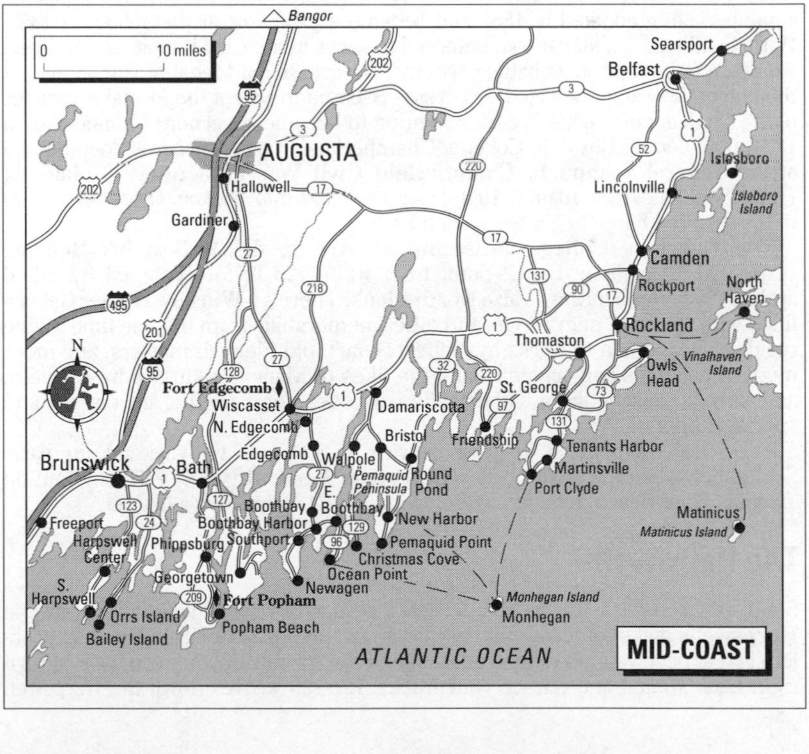

HARRIET BEECHER STOWE

Harriet Beecher Stowe (1811–1896), a native of Litchfield, Connecticut, moved to Brunswick with her family from Ohio in the summer of 1850 when her husband, Calvin, took a position as a professor of religion at Bowdoin College. While her family struggled financially, it was here that Stowe formulated and wrote *Uncle Tom's Cabin*, the emotional anti-slavery novel that would go on to sell millions of copies all over the world. The book is credited with bringing morality and respectability to the abolitionist cause, and when Abraham Lincoln met Stowe several years later he reportedly remarked, "So you're the little lady who wrote the book that started the war."

It is said that Stowe conceived of the death of Uncle Tom while sitting at worship in Brunswick's historic **First Parish Church**, 223 Maine St (☎207/729-7331), and then proceeded to write the entire story in a fiery passion in just a few weeks. The passage of the 1850 Fugitive Slave Act, which stipulated that it was illegal for any citizen to assist an escaped slave and demanded that escaped slaves be apprehended and deported back to the "rightful" owner, further outraged Stowe, who, encouraged by her husband, published her violent story serially in the *National Era*, an abolitionist weekly. The **Harriet Beecher Stowe House**, 63 Federal St (☎207/725-5543), is now a remodeled motel with modern rooms, though guests can still use the intact lounge of the original house.

Another distinguished alum of the college, Civil War hero General Joshua Chamberlain, graduated in 1852 and became a professor at the school in 1855. With no military training, he volunteered to serve in the Civil War at its onset, and would go on to fight in 24 battles, win the Congressional Medal of Honor, and, at the end of the war, be selected by Ulysses S. Grant to accept the formal surrender of the Confederate troops. He later went on to become governor of Maine and, in 1871, president of Bowdoin College. Chamberlain's varied career is documented at the **General Joshua L. Chamberlain Civil War Museum**, 226 Maine St (June–Sept Tues–Sat 10am–3.15pm; $4; *www.curtislibrary.com/pejepscot*). Tours of his restored home begin twice each hour.

The **Bowdoin College Museum of Art**, in the Walker Art Building (Tues–Sat 10am–5pm, Sun 2–5pm; free; ☎207/725-3275), designed by noted architect Charles McKim, is also worth a look. There's a Winslow Homer Gallery filled with etchings, engravings, and other memorabilia from the one-time Maine resident, in addition to works by Gilbert Stuart, old Flemish masters, and more modern paintings and sculptures by the likes of Mary Cassatt, Andrew Wyeth, and Robert Rauschenberg. Other galleries house photography, ancient art, and special exhibits.

The ideal moment to visit Brunswick is Labor Day weekend, in early September, when the town hosts a **Bluegrass Festival** (☎207/725-6009) out on Thomas Point Beach, reached by following Rte-24 from Cook's Corner.

The Harpswells

South of Brunswick the narrow forested peninsulas collectively known as the **Harpswells** make for a welcome escape from the bustle of US-1. The only problem is that once you get to the end of one of the thrusts of land, you have to turn right back around and retrace your tracks. Rte-123 weaves down the Harpswell

Neck past Maine's **oldest meeting house** (1757) in Harpswell Center, and clear down to South Harpswell, where the Basin Cove Falls, created by the tidal flows, are popular with canoeists and kayakers. Rte-24 heads down another long, finger-like strip to **Bailey Island** (one of Casco Bay Cruise Line's stops), first crossing Orrs Island and then the **Cobwork Bridge**, which allows tides to flow right through it. Bailey Island's highlight is the **Giant Staircase**, off of Rte-24 on the eastern shore of the island, a massive waterfront stone stairway that's fun to explore and traverse. On Orrs Island, you can rent **kayaks** from H2Outfitters (☎207/833-5257 or 1-800/649-5257); they also provide instruction and lead day-and multi-day trips.

Eating and drinking

Bohemian Coffee Company, 111 Maine St (☎207/725-9095). Brunswick's hip crowd hangs at this pleasant sidewalk café.

Bombay Mahal, 99 Maine St (☎207/729-5260). Inexpensive Indian specialties, such as a good chicken curry for $7.95.

Cook's Lobster House, Garrison Cove Rd (Rte-24), Bailey Island (☎207/833-2818). They've been dishing out deliciously fresh lobster, shrimp, scallops, and shellfish on their outdoor decks since 1955 – be warned that it can get busy when the Casco Bay Lines cruiser dumps passengers off at the docks in summer.

Dolphin Marine, Basin Point Rd, South Harpswell (☎207/833-6000). A tiny, almost hidden restaurant that serves up reasonably priced and simple yet robust seafood meals overlooking the ocean – don't miss the fish chowder.

Kitchen, 4 Pleasant St (☎207/729-5526). Cheap calzones, sandwiches, soups, and other flavorful dinners in a cafeteria-type dining room.

Richard's, 115 Maine St (☎207/729-9673). Tasty German and American cuisine and fairly good deals for lunch; the bratwurst, goulash, and fish dinner entrees are more expensive ($8–17).

Star Fish Grill, 100 Pleasant St (☎207/725-7828). Relatively new restaurant, and easily Brunswick's best, with a catch of fresh local seafood, fresh produce, and vegetarian dishes and an informal yet sophisticated atmosphere.

Bath

Approaching the small, community-minded town of **BATH** on US-1, it's hard to miss the rather enormous and industrial-looking supply cranes, tools of the massive **Bath Iron Works** shipyard, that hulk rigidly towards the sky along the Kennebeck River. In fact, the town of Bath has an exceptionally long history of **shipbuilding**; the first vessel to be constructed and launched here was the *Virginia* in 1607, by Sir George Popham's short-lived colony, just south of Bath in Phippsburg. Shipbuilding continued to be a major industry in the region throughout the eighteenth century, and between 1800 and 1830, some 288 ships set sail out of Bath's port. Bath Iron Works, founded in 1833, attracted job-seeking Irishmen in such numbers as to provoke a mob of anti-immigrant "Know Nothings" to burn down the local Catholic church in July 1854. Smaller trading vessels gave way to larger ships and in 1841, Clark & Sewall, one of the major builders at the time, launched the *Rappahannock*, then the largest ship in the world at 1133 tons. Despite changes in the shipbuilding market, Bath's military contracts were never in short supply, and during World War II, more destroyers were built here than in all Japan.

Accommodation

Bath is not short on good-value **accommodations**, mostly of the inexpensive bed-and-breakfast variety. There's **camping** south of town along the water in Perry Cove at the Meadowbrook Camping Area, Meadowbrook Road (May–Oct; ☎1-800/370-2267). Two more campgrounds lurk further south along the Phippsburg Peninsula: *Hermit Island* at the end of Rte-216 (late June to mid-Oct; ☎207/443-2101), where you can rent small boats and camp near a white-sand beach, and *Ocean View Park*, near Popham Beach (mid-May–Sept; ☎207/389-2564).

Benjamin F Packard House, 45 Pearl St (☎207/443-6069 or 1-800/516-4578). Their period-furnished rooms are a very good deal; full breakfast is included. ④.

Fairhaven Inn, on North Bath Rd (☎207/433-4391 or 1-888/443-4391). You'll find a bit of a rural flavor here – hiking and cross-country skiing trails are right nearby – plus a fine breakfast. Private or shared bathrooms. ⑤.

Galen C Moses House, 1009 Washington St (☎207/442-8771). A colorful restored mansion whose proprietors are almost as eccentric as the decorations; a delicious gourmet breakfast is included. ④.

Glad II, 60 Pearl St (☎207/443-1191). Small B&B very close to the museum. ④–⑤.

Inn at Bath, 969 Washington St (☎207/443-4294, *www.innatbath.com*). An 1810 Greek Revival house, with friendly service and tastefully decorated rooms. ⑤.

Small Point B&B, 312 Small Point Rd (Rte-216), south of town in Sebasco Estates (☎207/389-1716). Inexpensive bed-and-breakfast, though you'll have to share a bathroom; isolated coastal location. ③–⑤.

The Town

With more than seven thousand employees, **Bath Iron Works**, two miles south of the town center, is the largest private employer in the state – and, thanks to a continuous stream of government contracts, the only shipbuilder remaining in Bath. As the place churns out massive destroyers and cruisers, shift workers keep the factory running around the clock; you should take care to avoid driving anywhere in Bath around 3.30pm, when shifts change and the town's roads come to a halt. The works are only open to visitors for special occasions such as ceremonial launchings – grand affairs that take place twice yearly and feature speeches by senators and the like. However, at the **Maine Maritime Museum**, 243 Washington St, next to the Iron Works (daily 9.30am–5pm; $8.75; ☎207/443-1316, *www .bathmaine.com*), you can tour the old Percy & Small shipyard, check out the mildly intriguing lobstering exhibit, explore several visiting historic vessels, or browse the Maritime History Building, where galleries house an interesting range of ship-related paintings, models, photographs, and artifacts. The museum also runs **boat trips** along the Kennebeck River (for an extra charge; call for schedules). To fully enjoy the museum, take advantage of the detailed one-hour guided **tours** of the shipyard that are offered at 10.30am and noon from mid-April through October.

Walking tours of another sort, led by enthusiastic town historians, begin at the 1847 **Chocolate Church**, 804 Washington St – now an arts center housing a theater and gallery – and lead up and down Bath's streets, highlighting examples of Georgian, Federal, Italianate, and Gothic Revival architecture. If you'd rather not cough up the dough for a live tour guide ($8; ☎207/442-8455), you can pick up one of several exhaustive brochures at the church that annotate various routes.

A pretty fourteen-mile drive south along Rte-209 leads to the inviting crescent-shaped **Popham Beach** ($2; ☎207/389-1335), at the end of the Phippsburg Peninsula, and part of a 529-acre state park. Outside of its scenic sands, there's **Fort Popham**, a nineteenth-century granite fort, with some nicely situated picnic benches that face the ocean and a marker that locates the **Popham Colony** site, where the first attempt at English settlement of the northeast coast was made in 1607. You can catch a **boat ride** at the Sebasco Harbor Resort, at the end of Rte-217 (☎207/389-1161), where the *Ruth* cruises the Casco Bay during the summer ($8).

The **Georgetown Peninsula**, just east from Bath and down Rte-127, contains another superior beach at **Reid State Park** (☎207/371-2303), where the dunes flatten out into 1.5 miles of beautiful sandy seashore.

AMC HUTS ON GEORGETOWN ISLAND

The **Appalachian Mountain Club** (☎617/523-0636, *www.outdoors.org*) maintains a couple of excellent low-budget **accommodations** on Georgetown Island. At the *Knubble Bay Camp*, a friendly riverfront cottage with a nice porch and a kitchen on Georgetown Island (open all year; $60 per 2-day weekend, $90 per 3-day weekend, $25 per weekday; ☎207/465-9732), there's bunk space for twelve as well as tent sites. The site is accessible by car and parking is available ($1 per day). You can also rent canoes for $10 per day and kayaks for $15 per day. A much more primitive option is the secluded wilderness campground at Beal Island (closed in winter; $5 per night; ☎207/465-9732), which is only accessible by canoe or kayak from *Knubble Bay Camp*.

Eating

The majority of Bath's **restaurants** are hearty no-nonsense grub-holes that cater to off-duty BIW employees.

Beale Street Barbeque and Grill, 215 Water St (☎207/442-9514). Slightly more upscale than most in-town restaurants, with hickory-smoked barbecue plates in an airy, modern dining room.

The Cabin, 552 Washington St (☎207/443-6224). Near the museum, the *Cabin* dishes out thick, cheesy pizzas in dark, wooden booths.

Five Islands Lobster Company, Rte-127, on the wharf in Five Islands (☎207/371-2990). A good, casual lobster pound, where you're encouraged to get messy while eating.

Front Street Deli, 128 Front St (☎207/443-9815). Beer on tap and sixteen different varieties of "Destroyers" (sandwiches), each named for a US battleship.

Kennebec Tavern, 119 Commercial St (☎207/442-9636). A huge selection of seafood, at a tavern pretty much right on the water.

Kristina's, 160 Centre St (☎207/442-8577). Inventive American dishes and great home-made breads and desserts.

Robinhood Free Meetinghouse, Robinhood Road, Georgetown, south of Bath along Rte-127 (☎207/371-2188). This is one of Maine's premier restaurants, and well worth the detour. Housed in Georgetown's former town hall, the creative American bistro integrates interesting touches of Cajun, Italian, Szechuan, and German cuisine into its many entrees, all of which cost over $20.

Wiscasset

WISCASSET, ten miles on from Bath, is dominated by the bridge which carries US-1 over the Sheepscot River – and in the summer, the gently arching span is itself dominated by slow-moving automobiles usually headed to or from the coast further north. Tourism, though, is catching on here, perhaps partially on account of Wiscasset's easily accessible town center, right where the bridge meets the river's west bank; in fact, the town lumberyard, grocery, and newsstand have all been replaced by antique shops and art galleries to welcome visitors (changes that have been very unwelcome to locals). Further removal of the town's character occurred in 1997, when two famous **shipwrecks**, the four-masted schooners *Luther Little* and the *Hesper*, which had sat in the shallow waters of its narrow and picturesque bay more than sixty years were carted away – rotted beyond recognition.

The Town

Like many of Maine's coastal towns, Wiscasset prospered in the late eighteenth century as a shipbuilding and lumbering center. The large homes and mansions of wealthy shipping merchants and lumber barons still stand in the town's **historic district**, situated near US-1 and the waterfront, the best example of which is the towering white Federal-style **Nickels-Sortwell House** on US-1 (Main Street) at Federal Street in the center of town (Jun–mid-Oct Wed–Sun 11am–4pm; $4). Commissioned by shipmaster William Nickels in 1807 (he lost his fortune only a few years later due to the devastating effect of the Embargo Act of 1807 and the War of 1812), the house features fine woodwork throughout and a restored garden. Hourly historical tours lead through the period furnished rooms and up the handsomely curved, three-floor stairway.

The **Musical Wonder House**, 18 High St (June–Oct daily 10am–5pm; $1; *www.musicalwonderhouse.com*), is proof that if you amass enough of an obsolete technology, the collection will someday hold a mysterious fascination. This 1852 sea captain's mansion is stuffed with player pianos, phonographs, and antique music boxes, most still in working order, and the eccentric owner of the place takes particular delight in showing off his bizarre treasures. Daily listening tours are separated into two parts following a roughly chronological order ($6.50 for one half or $12 for both); one half is enough.

Along the water, two blocks south of US-1, the **Maine Coast Railroad** (May–Oct; $10 round-trip; ☎207/882-7499 or 1-800/795-5404) offers scenic train rides through the wilderness between Wiscasset, Bath, and Newcastle, ten miles to the east. As restored 1930 railcars wobble down the tracks, passengers are afforded views of Maine's backcountry (though the route is really only about a mile from US-1). The train departs twice daily at 11am and 2pm, traveling to Bath more frequently in summer. The round-trip takes about 1 hour.

A couple of blocks off the main drag, the **Maine Art Gallery**, housed in an old schoolhouse building on Warren Street (mid-May–Sept Tues–Sat 10am–4pm, Sun 1–4pm; rest of year Thurs–Sun 10am–4pm, Sun 1–4pm; free; ☎207/882-7511), exhibits (and sells) the works of up-and-coming Maine artists.

Practicalities

Accommodation possibilities in the area include the comfortable and modern *Wiscasset Motor Lodge* (Apr–Nov only; ☎207/882-7137 or 1-800/732-8168; [3]), around three miles south at 596 Bath Rd (US-1), and the down-to-earth *Edgecomb Inn* (☎207/882-6343; [4]), just across the bridge. The *Cod Cove Inn* on Rte-1 (April–Oct; ☎207/882-9586 or 1-800/882-9586; [5]) is a bit more upmarket, with balconies, views of the sea, cable television, and phones. The good-value *Marston House*, on Main Street (☎207/882-6010 or 1-800/852-4157; [4]), has homely rooms and a tasty light breakfast. The lakeside **campground** *Downeast Family Camping*, at Gardiner Pond, four miles north on Rte-27 (Memorial Day–Columbus Day; ☎207/882-5431), features an impressive cathedral stand of Norway pines.

For **food**, head to *Sarah's Café* on US-1 in the center of town (☎207/882-7504), where you can get pizzas, salads, sandwiches, pasta, and even some Mexican dishes at the right price. Just across the street, *Treats* (☎207/882-6192) has a great selection of gourmet baked and picnic goods, including sandwiches, fresh breads, imported cheeses, pastries, a huge wine selection, and good fresh coffee. For the best view in town, try *Le Garage*, on Water Street (☎207/882-5409), where seafood, steak, and vegetarian entrees ($8–18) are served in the glassed-in porch.

Boothbay Harbor

Due south from Wiscasset on Rte-27, the seaside town of **BOOTHBAY HARBOR** is for no obvious reason one of Maine's most crowded resorts. Much of the town's history as a prosperous fishing and shipbuilding center has been obscured by tourism, which has been an active pursuit here since the late nineteenth century, resulting in a wealth of predictable shops and restaurants. Nevertheless, the village is beautifully situated on a well-protected harbor, and has a lively town center, some good inns, and ample opportunities to explore the sea and surrounding coast. For a more genuine Maine experience, however, you might fare better in the less popular neighboring Pemaquid Peninsula (see p.488) or even the Blue Hill Peninsula (see p.500), closer to Bar Harbor.

Arrival, information, and getting around

Less than fifteen miles south of US-1 along Rte-27, several towns near the end of the Boothbay Peninsula share similar names, the most happening of which, Boothbay Harbor, is crowded into a tiny strip of land on the western edge, along **Commercial Street** and Townsend Avenue. The rest of the settlement spreads out around a tiny cove, thinning into quaint residential neighborhoods southwest on Southport Island and southeast towards Ocean Point. Oak and Commercial streets are one-way headed west, while Townsend is one-way east, heading back to Rte-27.

The town is not easily reached via **public transport**; Concord Trailways stops in Wiscasset twice daily, from where you can catch a taxi; call Boothbay Stage Line at ☎207/633-7380 for information. The *Rocktide Inn* and *Cap'n Fish's* both run **courtesy trolleys** from the Boothbay Harbor Region Chamber of Commerce to various points in the town during summer days until 5pm. The chamber, just north of town on Rte-27 (☎207/633-2353), is a very good source of **information**, with binders on local accommodations and a reservation service. The Boothbay Harbor Memorial Library, 4 Oak St (☎207/633-3112), has free **Internet access**.

Though it's quite likely you'll have arrived by car, Boothbay Harbor is not well designed for auto travel and best explored **on foot**. The town's short, windy, and narrow streets are packed with cars all summer long and **parking** can be a nightmare. It's a good idea to park further out – say along West, Howard, or Sea streets – or take the shuttle into town from the information center on Rte-27.

Accommodation

You can always find some sort of **place to stay** in Boothbay Harbor, but if you want a shorefront room in the summer, plan to call ahead at least a month in advance. In addition to several large undistinguished resort-style motels, complete with all the modern conveniences, there are lots of smaller bed-and-breakfasts in the town center and on the eastern shore of the harbor. Prices drop considerably in the beginning and end of the tourist season – early June and September – and many places close down completely by mid-October.

Anchor Watch B&B, 3 Eames Rd (☎207/633-7565, *www.maineguide.com/boothbay/anchorwatch*). Pamper yourself in this beautiful little B&B on a quiet peninsula just outside of the town center. [5].

Captain Sawyer's Place, 55 Commercial St (☎207/633-2290). The rooms are not huge and the view is partially obscured, but the price is cheaper than most of the other places along Commercial Street. Continental breakfast included. [4].

Jonathan's, 23 Eastern Ave (☎207/633-3588). Three nicely decorated rooms in an old Cape-style house with a deck and fireplace a few minutes walk from the town center. Breakfast included. [5].

Linekin Bay B&B, Ocean Point Rd (Rte-96), East Boothbay (☎207/633-9900). Cozy and romantic 1850s-era home overlooking Linekin Bay, though only two of the rooms have ocean views. Open all year. [5]–[6].

Topside Inn, 60 McKown St (☎207/633-5404). Pleasant rooms in an old sea captain's house on the top of a hill, giving you a great view of the harbor. Open May to Oct 17. [4].

Water's Edge B&B, 8 Eames Rd (☎207/633-4251 or 1-800/791-2026). Upscale, spacious accommodations with the best ocean view in town at the end of a quiet, dead-end street. Enjoy a basic breakfast on the huge porch. [6].

Welch House, 36 McKown St (☎207/633-3431). This gabled white-clapboard house perched on a hill affords excellent views from its rooftop deck. Light and airy guest rooms are tastefully furnished and a buffet breakfast is included. [5]–[6].

The Town and around

Aside from taking a quick stroll around the town's hilly, shop-lined streets, Boothbay Harbor's main attraction lies in the inordinate number of **boat trips** on offer from the harbor behind Commercial Street. Some depart for Monhegan Island (see p.490), while others circle along the rocky coast, taking in the dramatic scenery from the water. Balmy Days Cruises (☎207/633-2284 or 1-800/298-2284) is as good as any of the outfits on the waterfront, with all-day trips to Monhegan Island costing $30 and harbor tours for $9. A cruise aboard the traditional windjammer *Appledore V*, departing from the wharf four times daily (May–Oct; 2hr 30min round-trip; ☎207/633-6598), costs $20. In general, smaller boats depart from Ocean Point; try Captain Roger Marin's 40ft sailboat (☎207/882-1020). If you'd rather explore the coast under your own power, contact the Tidal Transit Company (☎207/633-7140), which offers **kayak** rentals ($12 per hour) and tours ($30) and also rents **bikes** ($20 per day).

On foot, the most immediate view of the harbor is from the 1000-foot-long wooden **footbridge** that connects downtown to the east side of town. If you venture all the way across, head south along Atlantic Avenue to the well-lighted and highly visible **Our Lady Queen of Peace** church, which has a lobster trap next to the altar and some fine architectural details.

Unless you're traveling with small children, skip the rather unimpressive **Marine Resources Aquarium** on McKown Point Road in West Boothbay Harbor (June–Sept daily 10am–5pm; ☎207/633-9542; $3), which houses a touch tank in addition to a small number of other displays.

There's plenty of less-crowded land to explore in the area surrounding the busy town. At the end of the pretty fifteen-minute drive south along Rte-96 to desolate **Ocean Point**, you are rewarded with views of the horizon across the open ocean, interrupted only by Squirrel Island, a sparsely populated fishing village, Fisherman Island to the south, and Ram Island, with its prominent lighthouse. A few miles north on the same peninsula, the **Linekin Preserve** maintains a few miles of **hiking** trails on nearly a hundred acres of wilderness between Rte-96 and the coast.

On relatively deserted **Southport Island**, south on Rte-27, you can drive all the way down to Newagen, affording views of the Cuckolds Lighthouse, a half-mile out to sea. Along the western side of the island, the keepers of **Hendrick's Head Light** (now privately owned and visible only from the water) once adopted the only survivor of a terrible shipwreck – a tiny baby girl that they found floating in the debris, tucked away inside a feather-lined box.

Eating

For all the big tourist money that comes into Boothbay Harbor every summer, the culinary scene is surprisingly drab. While standard gourmet meals are available at several of the smaller inns, prices are often prohibitively high. Your best bet probably is to head to one of a handful of **lobster pounds** on the outskirts of town. Many restaurants close between October and May.

The Black Orchid, 5 By Way (☎207/633-6659). Upscale family-owned bistro serving traditional Italian dishes for $13–25 per entree.

Blue Moon Café, Commercial St (☎207/633-2349). Of the places right on the water, this is probably the least expensive; better still, it serves a variety of delicious hot and cold sandwiches including veggie specials, grilled portobello mushrooms, hummus, smoked salmon, and burgers. There's indoor and outdoor seating.

Ebb Tide, 43 Commercial St (☎207/633-5692). You can get cheap, greasy breakfasts all day at this plain blue-collarish joint right in the center of town. Dinners are also cheap and greasy.

Joey's Breakfast & Lunch, Rte-27 (☎207/653-5090). All that you'd expect in a no-frills diner, including large portions.

King Brud, intersection of McKown and Commercial streets (no phone). As famous as a hot-dog stand can be in these parts, operated by the same man for more than fifty years.

Lobsterman's Co-op, 97 Atlantic Ave (☎207/633-4900). Working lobster pound that dishes up ultra-fresh lobsters at minimal prices, as well as a range of sandwiches.

Robinson's Wharf, Rte-27, Southport Island (☎207/633-3830). Lots of indoor and outdoor seating at this lobster pound, where you can pick out your very own lobster. In addition to fresh seafood, they serve burgers, sandwiches, and all-American desserts.

Spruce Point Inn, Atlantic Ave (☎207/633-4152 or 1-800/553-0289). Boothbay's finest formal dinner spot, with New American fare such as chicken with tropical salsa, shrimp amaretto, and lobster spring rolls. There's a great view of the water, too, but it all comes with a price; entrees go for $15–25. Reservations recommended.

Damariscotta and the Pemaquid Peninsula

The compact town of **DAMARISCOTTA**, just off US-1 across the Damariscotta River from neighboring Newcastle, does not have any sights worth noting, although its Main Street is a good place to stop for lunch or a stroll.

From town, River Road leads south to **Dodge Point**, where you can **hike** along several miles of trails or hang out on the sandy **beach** along the Damariscotta River in summer. It's also a popular spot for **fishing**, where anglers fish for striped bass, bluefish, and mackerel. You can dig for clams in the offshore tidal flats – contact the Newcastle Town Office (☎207/563-3176) for rules and regulations.

Damariscotta is a pleasant place to stay while exploring the rest of the Pemaquid Peninsula; the best **accommodation** can be found at the *Flying Cloud B&B*, on River Road in Newcastle (☎207/563-2484; ④), an immaculately restored 1840s sea captain's home with five guest rooms and an elegant yet homely atmosphere. You might also try the *Brannon-Bunker Inn* on Rte-129 in Walpole (☎207/563-5941 or 1-800/563-9225; ④), where the owner is a bit obsessed with World War I. The *Salt Bay Café*, on Main Street (☎207/563-1666), is a local **restaurant** favorite, with simple but fresh seafood, soups, sandwiches, and steaks. On US-1 east of town in **Waldoboro**, *Moody's Diner* (☎207/832-7785) is a longstanding haunt of police and truckers – open 24hrs and oozing nostalgia – that offers a typical selection of burgers and fries.

The Pemaquid Peninsula

Meaning "long finger" in the native language, the **Pemaquid Peninsula** points some fifteen miles south of US-1 along Routes 129 and 130, culminating in the rocky **Pemaquid Point**. Controversial archeological studies have made as yet unsubstantiated claims that the first European settlers touched down here before they landed at Plymouth. A small state-run museum on the site of the would-be settlement, **Colonial Pemaquid**, just west of New Harbor off of Rte-130 (Memorial Day–Labor Day daily 9.30am–5.30pm; $2), houses ancient pottery, farming tools, and other household items. Over the years, ongoing excavation has also unearthed stone walls and foundations dating back to the seventeenth century. Within the eight-acre historical site stands a replica of **Fort William Henry**, the original built in 1677 by English settlers to ward off pirates, the French, and Indians, who are believed to have inhabited the peninsula as early as two thousand years ago. Though the robust fortress was thought to be rather impenetrable, it was defeated three times in the seventeenth century. There are good **ocean views** from the top of the massive stone citadel.

Nearby, the sands of **Pemaquid Beach**, just off Snowball Hill Road, are some of the most inviting in the state, correspondingly crowded on sunny summer weekends. Nevertheless, it's a great place to catch some rays, and even though the water can be cold, swimming is not impossible (parking $1). There's another smaller **beach** all the way around the bend near the end of Rte-129 on Rutherford Island at **Christmas Cove**, so named by Captain John Smith after the day he discovered it.

Just north of Pemaquid Beach, from Shaw's Fish and Lobster Wharf in quaint **New Harbor**, Hardy Boat Cruises runs daily (9am) **boat trips** out to Monhegan Island for $26 round-trip, in addition to all-day "ocean safaris" ($30), puffin watches ($17), and shorter scenic cruises ($9 and up).

There is probably no better place to observe **lighthouses** than on the Maine coast, where some 61 of the structures direct ships of all sizes through the varied rocky inlets and along the jutting peninsulas from Kittery up to Quoddy Head. For centuries much of Maine's economy has centered on the sea, and the lighthouses here have become symbols of this dependence (not to mention the saving grace of many a passing ship). Consequently a series of museums serves to illustrate their history and importance, none more prominent than the **Shore Village Lighthouse Museum** in Rockland (see p.493). There's even a quarterly publication, *Lighthouse Digest*, devoted to the curious structures. Some of Maine's most dramatic lighthouses include the lonely **West Quoddy Head Light** (p.515), a candy-striped beauty in Lubec, the scenic **Pemaquid Point Light** (see below), south of Damariscotta, and the **Cape Elizabeth Lighthouse** (p.471), near Portland, which was commissioned by none other than George Washington. The *Elms B&B* in Camden runs structured **lighthouse tours** of varying lengths in conjunction with one of the local boats – call ☎207/236-6250 or 1-800/755-3567 for more information.

South along Rte-130, at the tip of Pemaquid Point, the **Pemaquid Point Lighthouse** ($1) sits on a dramatic granite outcrop constantly battered by the violent Atlantic surf. You can wander around the small park for a good view of the salt-stained lighthouse, built in 1827 and still operational, but be careful not to get too close to the waters. The adjoining keeper's quarters have been transformed into the small **Fishermen's Museum** (May–Oct 10am–5pm; donation requested), containing uninspired exhibits related to the local fishing trade and, more interestingly, a map of Maine with a photo and description of each and every one of the state's 61 lighthouses.

Another potential diversion on the Pemaquid Peninsula is the **Thompson Ice House**, Rte-129 north of South Bristol (July & Aug Mon, Wed & Fri 1–4pm). While modern refrigeration has eliminated the ice industry, this ice house was in operation for 150 years, harvesting ice from a nearby pond and shipping it to points as far as South America. Business mostly halted here in 1986, but the building, which sports ten-inch-thick sawdust-insulated walls, has been restored into a museum and working ice-harvesting facility. In the summer, you can check out a display of the tools of the defunct trade and gaze at photos depicting ice harvesters in action. In February, townspeople still gather to collect ice from a local pond using old-fashioned tools before burying the clear blocks in hay until summer, when they are sold to local fishermen.

Practicalities

Just back from the Pemaquid Lighthouse, you can enjoy reasonably priced American **food** with a fine view of the water at the small café that adjoins the Sea Gull Gift Shop (☎207/677-2374). The *Anchor Inn* on Harbor Road in Round Pond (☎207/529-5584) is another good bet, with crab cakes, lobster, pastas, and succulent steaks in a rustic dining room overlooking the harbor. There are also a number of traditional **lobster pounds** on the peninsula in New Harbor and Round Pond, all of which are good.

If you'd like to **stay** close to the lighthouse, the *Hotel Pemaquid*, only 100 yards away at 3098 Bristol Rd, Rte-130 (May–Oct; ☎207/677-2312; ④–⑥), offers Victorian furnishings in casual surroundings – some rooms share baths. Other options on the peninsula include the attractive *Apple Tree B&B* off of Snowball Hill Road in New Harbor (☎207/677-3491; [4]), where you can enjoy delectable breakfasts outside on the patio, and the *Briar Rose B&B*, on Rte-32 in Round Pond (☎207/529-5478; [4]–[5]), with country furnishings and a commanding view of the picturesque town. Basic **campsites** are available up the road near Pemaquid Beach at the *Sherwood Forest Campsite*, on Pemaquid Trail in New Harbor (☎207/677-3642 or 1-800/274-1593; $18), which has its own swimming pool.

Monhegan Island

Deliberately low-tech **MONHEGAN ISLAND**, eleven miles from the mainland, has long attracted a hardy mix of artists and fishermen. It also attracts its fair share of tourists, but for good reason: it's the most worthwhile jaunt away from the mainland along the entirety of the Maine coast. Sailor David Ingram recorded the first description of the place in 1569, calling it "a great island that was backed like a whale." Indeed, not much has changed since artist Robert Henri first came here in the early 1900s looking for tranquility and solitude – there are no banks, credit cards are not readily accepted, very few public phones are available, and there's only one public restroom ($1). Though there were already a few artists residing on the island at the time, Henri introduced the place to his students George Bellows and Rockwell Kent, which solidified the place as a genuine artist colony. Edward Hopper also spent time painting here, and the youngest of the Wyeth family, Jamie, currently calls Monhegan his summertime home.

The small village – occupying only twenty percent of the island – huddles around the tiny harbor, protected by Manana and Smutty Nose islands. Other than a few old hotels and some good restaurants, there's not much here – even automobiles are seldom heard, just as well, because there are some seventeen miles of **hiking trails** that crisscross the eastern half of the island, leading

LOUDS ISLAND

A mile off the coast near Round Pond, **Louds Island** – once known as Muscongus Island – sports a rather odd history. Though the place was inhabited as early as 1650, it was left off the official government maps of the Maine coast. Oblivious, residents voted in nearby Bristol and cooperated with its tax authorities until 1860, when Abraham Lincoln was up for election on the Republican ticket. While the mainlanders voted staunchly Republican, the residents of Louds Island caused the Bristol vote to swing to the Democratic side, sparking a mild uproar among town officials. The Republicans parried by discounting the votes of Louds' residents, citing the official maps.

Outraged, the islanders actually seceded and declared Louds an independent republic. When recruiting officers subsequently came to round up the men who had been drafted into the Civil War, they were met by the entire male population of the island, who announced that they would attack if anyone set foot on the island. Having no quarrel with the United States (only the town of Bristol), the island arranged their own draft and sent additional funding to the government to be used in the war.

Today, the quiet island is accessible only by boat and inhabited by a few families. Nothing will really tempt you over here – there's just a small church, a couple of homes, a store, dirt roads, and a post office – but if it does, be warned that there are no hotels or restaurants.

GETTING TO MONHEGAN ISLAND

To insure a spot with one of the three boats that connect the mainland with Monhegan Island, you should call in advance. The *Laura B* and the faster *Elizabeth Ann* (☎207/372-8848, *www.monheganboat.com*; $14 one-way, $25 round-trip) depart from **Port Clyde** for Monhegan three times daily during the summer and less often during the winter, arriving a little less than or a little more than an hour later, depending on which boat is in service. From **Boothbay Harbor** (see p.486) you can take the *Balmy Days III* (Memorial Day–Columbus Day; ☎207/633-2284 or 1-800/298-2284, *www.anchorwatch.com/balmy*; $28 round-trip), which departs once daily and takes ninety minutes. The *Hardy Boat* takes 70min to get from Shaw's Wharf in **New Harbor** (see p.488) to Monhegan (late May & early Oct departs Wed, Sat & Sun at 9am; June–Sept daily at 9am; ☎207/677-2026 or 1-800/278-3346, *www.hardyboat.com*; $26 round-trip).

through dense stands of fir and spruce to the headlands, 160ft above the island's eastern shore. Monhegan Associates publishes a reliable **trail map**, available at most island stores.

The **Monhegan Island Lighthouse**, on a hill overlooking the village (and a great place to watch the sunset), was erected in 1824 and automated in 1959. You can check out the **Monhegan Historical and Cultural Museum** inside the former keeper's house (July–Sept daily 11.30am–3.30pm; donation), which recently opened a new building to house the work of Monhegan artists, including a few paintings by Rockwell Kent and Jamie Wyeth. Other rooms display artifacts, photographs, and documents relating to the island's history and natural features.

In summer, some of the artists in residence on the island open their **studios** to visitors. For times and locations, check the bulletin boards around town. You can also see works by local artists at one of several **galleries** – the Lupine Gallery (☎207/591-8131) has a consistently good grouping of local works on display.

Practicalities

There's not a great deal of **accommodation** choice on the island, so you should plan on reserving your room well in advance of your visit. The largest place to stay is the *Island Inn* (May–Oct; ☎207/596-0371; ⑥–⑦), a remodeled 1807 structure overlooking the harbor. Many of the rooms at the funky *Trailing Yew* (May–Oct; ☎207/596-0440; ②–③), spread out among several buildings, do not have heat or electricity. The *Shining Sails B&B* (☎207/596-0041, *www.shiningsails .com*; ⑤) does have modern rooms with private baths and lower rates off-season. The *Hitchcock House*, at the top of Horn's Hill (☎207/594-8137; ④), offers efficiencies, a cabin, and several rooms.

The island's several sit-down **restaurants** are all good, hearty, and surprisingly affordable affairs. At the *Trailing Yew* (see above), big family-style seafood dinners cost just $17 per person. The *Monhegan House Café* (☎207/594-7983) is a little more formal, with a menu featuring simple meat, fish, and vegetarian dishes. You can get good pizza and sandwiches at *North End Pizza*, up the hill and to the right from the wharf (☎207/594-5546). For light **snacks and coffee**, head to the *Barnacle* (late May to mid-Oct) overlooking the wharf; it houses the only espresso machine on the island and serves salads, sandwiches, and home-baked goodies. In the heart of the village, the Monhegan Store (☎207/594-4126) sells groceries, alcohol, and sandwiches.

Rockland

Seaside **ROCKLAND** was once a solidly working-class factory town, not only Maine's largest distributor of lobster (which it still is), but home to prosperous sardine canneries. However, the last of these closed down in the late 1990s, and residents have been forced to cultivate tourism to make ends meet. Clearly a city in transition, unpretentious locals have begun to accept their newfound dependence on outsiders – slowly replacing no-nonsense appliance stores with cute little gift shops.

LOBSTER

Though August is Maine's official Lobster Month, **lobsters** are everywhere in the state all year: on corny T-shirts, in countless restaurants, even on the state's license plates. Indeed, lobstering is a way of life around here and many residents in the smaller coastal towns depend on the crustaceans for their well-being. It's hard to believe, considering their status today, but lobsters were once so plentiful that they washed ashore, where they were easily collected – and even fed to servants in the seventeenth and eighteenth centuries.

Though financially and physically difficult, **lobstering** is a profession steeped in tradition and pride. Lobstermen stake their territory over many years, and it can be difficult for rookies to break into the business. Lobsters are caught with basic traps, their ownership denoted by a series of colored bands on a floating marker, which you can see bobbing on the water's surface all up and down the Maine coast. Lobstermen have been known to draw guns when their traps are tampered with, so you'd be well advised to leave them alone.

Though some 45.5 million pounds were caught commercially in 1998, there are strict laws governing the capture of lobsters – the minimum size is 3 and 3/16 inches from the eye to the end of the main body (the carapace) and the maximum length is 5 inches. It takes roughly seven years for a lobster to grow to this size, which usually translates to about 1.5 pounds. The largest lobster ever recorded, measuring 3.5ft and weighing in at an astounding 44 pounds, was caught off the coast of Nova Scotia in 1977.

When being prepared for consumption, lobsters are usually boiled, upon which their color changes from a greenish brown to the familiar bright red that you see gracing so many signs and brochures. Despite the myth, lobsters do not have vocal cords – the "screaming" noise sometimes heard while cooking is air escaping from the lobster's body cavity. Though lobsters have long been believed to contain high levels of cholesterol, the Lobster Promotion Council has been spreading word that newer studies reveal cholesterol levels on par with chicken. Heaps of butter and mayonnaise are in fact the main culprits in a fattening lobster meal.

Unless you're enjoying lobster prepared in a gourmet restaurant, the task of **eating a lobster** is not a clean or easy one. Using your hands, the claws must be pulled off and cracked open, the hard-shelled body and tail snapped apart, and the pale flesh dug out with fingers or forks. It's acceptable – even encouraged – to suck the very last bit of the soft white meat from inside the legs and flippers. If you're having trouble getting to the meat, your waiter – or just about any other local – will be more than happy to assist you.

Lobster festivals are held yearly in several cities along the coast. The largest is the **Rockland Lobster Festival**, when some 50,000 people gather to eat, drink, and listen to music. Call ☎207/596-0376 for more information.

The Town

The town's centerpiece is the outstanding **Farnsworth Museum**, 352 Main St (Memorial Day–Columbus Day daily 9am–5pm; rest of year Tues–Sat 10am–5pm, Sun 1–5pm; $9; ☎207/596-6457), established in 1935 at the bequest of reclusive spinster Lucy Farnsworth, who rather surprised the town when her will left $1.3 million to build a museum in her father's honor. Spreading over several buildings, including the **Wyeth Center**, a beautiful gallery space in a converted old church that holds two floors worth of works by Jamie, Andrew, and N.C. Wyeth, the impressive collection spans two centuries of American art – much of it Maine-related. In fact, the highlight is the permanent "Made in Maine" exhibit, which features landscapes and seascapes by Fitz Hugh Lane, portraits by Frank Benson, familiar watercolors by Winslow Homer, and, of course, more big canvases from the Wyeths. The museum does not own *Christina's World*, Andrew Wyeth's most famous work (it's at the Museum of Modern Art in New York), but you can visit the field and home depicted in the painting at the **Olson House**, Hathorn Point Road, just outside of town in Cushing (Memorial Day–Columbus Day daily 11am–4pm; $3 or free with museum admission). Admission to the museum also gets you into the **Farnsworth Homestead**, tucked between museum buildings on Elm Street (Memorial Day–Columbus Day Mon–Sat 10am–5pm, Sun 1–5pm; Dec Sat & Sun only), a fine example of preserved Victorian opulence.

Another worthwhile museum in town, the **Shore Village Lighthouse Museum**, 104 Limerock St (June–mid-Oct daily 10am–4pm, rest of year by appointment ☎207594-4950; donation), lets you peruse one of the largest collections of lighthouse memorabilia and artifacts in the country. It's fun to press the buttons that trigger various foghorns and bells, but the real attraction is the curator, who probably knows more about lighthouses than anyone in existence. The **Owls Head Transportation Museum**, two miles south of Rockland on Rte-73 at Owls Head (April–Oct daily 10am–5pm; rest of year daily 10am–4pm; *www.ohtm.org*; $6), is a similarly niche-oriented spot, with an interesting (mostly working) collection of cars, motorcycles, trains, and planes from a bygone era, including a full-scale replica of the Wright Brothers' 1903 *Flyer*.

From Rockland's enormous **harbor**, a number of powerboats and **windjammers** compete for your business with offers of everything from leisurely morning breakfast cruises to week-long island-hopping charters. The majority set sail for three to six days at a time, costing a little more than $100 per night, including all meals. If you've got the time and money, do it. You really can't go wrong with any of the options, but a few boats to try include the 68-foot *Stephen Taber* (☎207/236-3520 or 1-800/999-7352), the 92-foot *American Eagle* (☎207/594-8007 or 1-800/648-4544), or the 95-foot *Heritage* (☎1-800/648-4544). If you're having trouble finding what you want, stop by the Chamber of Commerce at Harbor Park, call the Maine Windjammer Association (☎1-800/807-9463), or call the North End Shipyard (☎1-800/648-4544). In late June, the Rockland breakwater serves as the finish line for the **Great Schooner Race**, predecessor to early July's **Schooner Days**, when the harbor fills up with a fleet of the sailing ships and the town occupies itself with live music, crafts, and lots of food.

Down the road at 517A Main St, the **Maine State Ferry Service** (☎207/596-2202 or 1-800/491-4883) runs modern vessels at frequent intervals out to the summer retreats of Vinalhaven (75min; $9) and North Haven (1hr; $9), and less frequently to remote Matinicus Island (call ☎1-800/491-4883 for schedule), all of which make for relaxing day-trips from the mainland. For views of the harbor and the sea beyond without actually boarding a boat, head to the **Rockland Breakwater**, a manmade cement and rock structure jutting not quite a mile into the water and providing additional protection for the harbor. To get there, take Waldo Avenue south from US-1 (just past the Penobscot Bay Medical Center) to Samoset Road. Go right on Samoset and the road will dead-end into Marie Reed Park, at the base of the breakwater.

St George Peninsula

South of Rockland, the pretty **St George Peninsula**, in particular the village of Tenants Harbor, inspired writer Sarah Orne Jewett's classic Maine novel *Country of the Pointed Firs*, which gives descriptions of the landscape so deft that you can still pick out many of the sites depicted in the book. Jewett wrote much of the book in a tiny schoolhouse in Martinsville, though it's since been rebuilt. Boats sail from the hamlet of Port Clyde, at the tip of the peninsula, to **Monhegan Island** (see p.490). You may recognize Port Clyde's picturesque 1857 Marshall Point Lighthouse from the Tom Hanks movie *Forrest Gump*; there's a small historical museum in the old keeper's house.

Thomaston

The attractive little town of **THOMASTON**, straddling US-1 just west of Rockland, has the largest cement manufacturing plant in New England, but it's best known as the home of the **State Prison**, on Main Street. The bleak facility – used for the Tim Robbins film *Shawshank Redemption* – maintains the adjacent store that sells various inmate handicrafts (daily 9am–5pm; ☎207/354-2535). You might also want to check out **Montpelier**, at the junction of Rte-131 and US-1, a faithful 1926 reproduction of a huge white mansion built on the same site in 1794 by Harry Knox, Secretary of War under President George Washington (June–mid-Oct Tues–Sat 10am–4pm, Sun 1–4pm; $5).

Practicalities

Thanks to Colgan Air you can **fly** to Rockland's Knox County Regional Airport direct from Boston for about $150 round-trip. The **bus station** is at the Maine State Ferry building, 517A Main St, just a short walk away from the **Chamber of Commerce**, at the public landing off of South Main Street (summer Mon–Fri 9am–5pm; rest of year 8am–4pm; ☎207/596-0376), which has comprehensive listings and information.

A good **place to stay** in the town center is the *Captain Lindsey House Inn*, 5 Lindsey St just off Main Street (☎207/596-7950 or 1-800/523-2145; ⑥–⑦), snugly decorated with down comforters and puffy pillows, in an updated 1837 house. The *Old Granite Inn*, 546 Main St (☎207/594-9036 or 1-800/386-9036, *www.midcoast .com/~ogi*; ⑤–⑦), has clean, basic rooms right across from the ferry terminal. South of town, along the water in Tenants Harbor, the *East Wind Inn* (☎207/372-6366 or 1-800/241-8439, *www.eastwindinn.com*; ⑤–⑥) is a cozy old building with a huge porch and a formal dining area.

The best **food** in town can be had at funky and perennially crowded *Café Miranda*, tucked away at 15 Oak St just off Main Street (☎207/594-2034); the appetizing array of international entrees ranges from saffron risotto with roasted mussels ($14.50) to Armenian lamb ($14). Situated in a dark, crumbling old shack at the public landing along the waterfront, *Conte's Fish Market and Restaurant* (☎207/596-5579) has an ever-changing menu that centers on hearty portions of seafood. The atmospheric *Waterworks Pub and Restaurant*, 7 Lindsey St just off Main Street (☎207/596-2753), is half sit-down restaurant, half easygoing pub, that is deservedly popular. Another popular spot, the *Brown Bag*, 606 Main St (☎207/596-6372 or 1-800/287-6372), makes scrumptious breakfasts, freshly baked goods, and creative veggie options for lunch. *Second Read*, 328 Main St (☎207/594-4123), is a friendly place to drink **coffee**, with light lunch offerings, pastries, an **Internet connection** ($7 per hour), a broad selection of used books for sale, and occasional live music.

Camden

The adjacent communities of **Rockport** and **CAMDEN** split into two separate towns in 1891 over a dispute as to who should pay for a new bridge over the Goose River between them. Rockport was at that time a major lime producer, manufacturing some two million casks of the stuff in the late nineteenth century, but a fire at the kilns in 1907 not only put an end to that business but also destroyed the icehouses that were the town's other main source of income. Now it's a quiet working port, among the prettiest on the Maine coast, home to numerous lobster boats, pleasure cruisers, and, other than an impressive grouping of rather wealthy-looking homes, little else. Camden, on the other hand, has clearly won the competition for tourists; indeed, it's one of the few towns in Maine that attracts visitors year-round. The place feels a bit more sophisticated than most coastal spots, thanks to the success of MBNA Bank, which set up their New England headquarters here in the late 1980s. The essential stop in town is **Camden Hills State Park**, which affords beautiful coastal views and has good camping. Camden's other highlight is its huge fleet of wind-powered schooners known as **windjammers**, many of which date back to the late nineteenth century, when the town was successful in the now-defunct shipbuilding trade.

Information and arrival

Camden's **information office**, down at the Public Landing (☎207/236-4404), is usually a big help with finding a place to stay; they also stock a typically dizzying array of brochures. You can get free **Internet access** at the brand-new Camden Public Library, located partially underground across from Harbor Park. Published every Thursday and available at many shops, *The Free Press* has comprehensive **listings** of all the goings-on in the area.

Concord Trailways' closest **bus** stop is in Rockport at the Clipper Mart on US-1. The **Camden Shuttle** (Mon–Fri 7.30am–6.30pm, Sat & Sun 9am–6.30pm; ☎207/596-6605) runs up and down US-1 between the *Country Inn* and Camden Hills State Park, stopping at several points along the way, including downtown, which is actually compact enough to be explored **on foot**. If you've got your car, know that **parking** can be a problem, but with patience you can usually find something on Chestnut Street or in the quiet residential areas just outside of town.

Accommodation

While **accommodations** in Camden are plentiful, they are not cheap; it's very difficult to find a room for less than $100. The budget spots congregate along US-1 further north in Lincolnville. There are over a dozen B&Bs in the immediate area, but you'd still be well advised to call in advance if you plan on staying here, especially on summer weekends; Camden Accommodations runs a **reservation service** (☎207/236-6090). Most of the hotels and B&Bs stay open all year here. Camden Hills State Park (see overleaf) is one of the best places to **camp** along the coast (☎207/236-3109), though it's often filled.

The Belmont, 6 Belmont Ave (☎207/236-8053 or 1-800/238-8053, *www.thebelmontinn.com*). Decorated with conservative elegance, this stately inn sits on an unassuming residential street just beyond the commercial district. The dining room is open to the public, serving gourmet meals in a formal atmosphere. ⑥.

Captain Swift Inn, 72 Elm St (☎207/236-8113 or 1-800/251-0865, *www.swiftinn.com*). Four rooms in a restored 1810 house – ask for one in the rear if possible, as the traffic on US-1 (Elm St) can be bothersome. ⑤–⑥.

The Elms B&B, 84 Elm St (☎207/236-6250 or 1-800/755-3567, *www.midcoast.com/~theelms*). A colonial home on the southern end of a long strip of B&Bs along Elm Street. The rooms are cozy, if a bit cramped, and the friendly owners – also lighthouse experts – offer a range of lighthouse tours. ⑤.

Good Guest House, 50 Elm St (☎207/236-2139). There are only two guest rooms in this pleasant home, which happens to be one of the cheapest options in the center of town. ④.

Goodspeed Guest House, 60 Mountain St (☎207/236-8077). Breakfast is included in your stay at this informal hikers' favorite, a short walk from town. Some rooms have shared bath. ④–⑤.

Maine Stay Inn, 22 High St (☎207/236-9636). Three-story white-clapboard 1813 inn, with eight inviting rooms, of which two share a bathroom. ⑦.

Snow Hill Lodge, US-1, Lincolnville (☎207/236-3452 or 1-800/476-4775). Basic, budget option north of town. ④.

Swans House B&B, 49 Mountain St (☎207/236-8275 or 1-800/207-8275). A beautiful little B&B that's nicely situated outside of town near the hiking trail to Mount Battie. ⑤.

The Town

As in Rockland, Camden's specialty is organizing sailing expeditions of up to six days in the large schooners known as **windjammers**. Daysailers, which tour the seas just beyond the harbor for anywhere from two hours to all day, include the *Appledore* (☎207/236-8353), the *Surprise* (☎207/236-4687), and the *Olad* (☎207/236-2323), which cost anywhere from $20 to $80 and can often be booked on the same day – each boat usually has an information table set up along the public landing. Longer **overnight trips** usually cost from $350 to $1000 (including all meals) and should be booked in advance; the boats stop at various points of interest along the coast, such as Castine, Stonington, and Mount Desert Island. Contact the Maine Windjammer Association (☎207/374-2955 or 1-800/807-9463), the Windjammer Wharf (☎1-800/999-7352), or the North End Shipyard (☎207/594-8007 or 1-800/648-4544) for information and schedules.

In the center of town, immaculately maintained **Harbor Park**, right where the whitewater of the Megunticook River spills into the sea, is a good spot to relax or have a picnic after wandering the town's small shopping district, which runs south from Main Street along the water. Further down Bayview Street, which holds many of the shops, tiny **Laite Beach** looks out onto the Penobscot Bay.

EDNA ST VINCENT MILLAY

Edna St Vincent Millay came to Camden with her divorced mother, Cora, and two sisters in 1900, when she was eight years old. Her mother encouraged all the sisters in the arts, and Edna (she insisted on being called "Vincent") excelled in writing. As a young child, she had poems published in *St Nicholas*, a children's magazine, and by the age of twenty, she won international recognition with her poem, *Renascence*, which she first recited aloud at the *Whitehall Inn*, 52 High St (☎207/236-3391 or 1-800/732-8168). Today, the inn maintains a small collection of writings, photos, and scrapbooks that depict her playful childhood in Camden. Millay reputedly lived a rather carefree adulthood as well – an acknowledged bisexual, she had many affairs with women, and when she finally married a man, it was on quite open terms. A lifelong smoker, she died of heart failure in 1950. Her locally famous poem, *Afternoon on a Hill*, supposedly describing her wanderings in the Camden Hills, was published in 1917.

> *I will be the gladdest thing*
> *Under the sun!*
> *I will touch a hundred flowers*
> *And not pick one,*
> *I will look at cliffs and clouds*
> *With quiet eyes,*
> *Watch the wind bow down the grass*
> *And the grass rise,*
> *And when lights begin to show*
> *Up from the town,*
> *I will mark which must be mine*
> *And then start down.*

Just north of town, US-1 leads toward **Camden Hills State Park**, the best spot around for **hiking** and camping. Rather than drive, pick up the **Mount Battie Trail** (45min) that begins at the north end of Megunticook Street, a short walk from the town center. The panoramic views of the harbor and Maine coastline from the top of 790-foot Mount Battie are hard to beat; on the summit, you can climb to the top of the circular World War I memorial for the best vantage point. It was here that poet Edna St Vincent Millay (see box above) penned part of her most recognized poem, *Renascence*, which is commemorated with a small plaque. There's a variety of other trails in the area, including ones that head to the summits of **Ocean Lookout** and **Zeke's Lookout**; you can get a decent free hiking map at the ranger station in the parking lot at the park entrance just off of US-1.

Eating and drinking

Camden has a satisfying array of **eating and drinking** spots – from gourmet restaurants to casual seafood joints to busy bars. One thing is for sure: on summer weekends, they're all going to be packed, so plan on waiting for a table. There's also a somewhat active **nightlife**, for Maine at least.

Camden Bagel Café, 26 Mechanic St (☎207/236-2661). Popular morning spot with tables in a sunny dining area; lots of fresh bagels, coffee, sandwiches, and salads.

Camden Deli, 37 Main St (☎207/236-8343). Great variety of bulging sandwiches and deli salads, right in the center of town overlooking the harbor. They also serve beer and wine.

Cappy's Chowder House, 1 Main St (☎207/236-2254). This cramped, child-friendly bar and restaurant is the place to go in town for a casual drink or meal.

Chez Michel, US-1, Lincolnville Beach (☎207/789-5600). A few miles north of Camden, this unassuming seaside restaurant specializes in fine French cuisine.

Frogwater Café, 31 Elm St (☎207/236-8998). A lively, informal joint with tasty renditions of steak, seafood, pasta, chicken standbys, and plenty of veggie options. Closed on Sundays.

Gilbert's Publick House, Bayview Landing (☎207/236-4320). With lots of beer signs and a big-screen TV, the *Publick House* looks a little like a fraternity basement, but that doesn't stop people from filling up the dance floor to the tune of cheesy Top 40 hits and alternative rock, sometimes live.

Lobster Pound Restaurant, US-1, Lincolnville Beach (☎207/789-5550). Casual and wildly popular restaurant serving heaps of the bright-red crustaceans.

Sea Dog Brewing Co, 43 Mechanic St (☎207/236-6863). The food portions are hearty, but the real treats are the handcrafted beers, brewed on-site. It gets loud on weekend nights.

Waterfront Restaurant, Bay View St (☎207/236-3747). The delicious clam chowder, fisherman's stew, and fresh seafood pastas are a bit expensive ($15–23), but you can't beat the dockside seating.

Zaddik's Pizza, 20 Washington St (☎207/236-6540). Family-friendly joint that serves up the best pizza around, in addition to salads and a small selection of Mexican entrees.

Rockport

Just south of Camden, **ROCKPORT** preserves its past in the remnants of the old **lime kilns** by pleasant Marine Park, next to the harbor, which is also a good place for a picnic. The tiny town center holds a couple of decent galleries, such as the **Maine Coast Artists Gallery**, 162 Russell Ave (☎207/236-2875), where local artists display their works, and the **Maine Photographic Workshops**, nearby at 2 Central St (☎207/236-8581), somewhat well known for its school of photography. Right across the street, the friendly *Corner Shop* (☎207/236-8361) serves up one of the best **breakfasts** in the area, with big and cheap omelettes in a sunny dining room.

Belfast

Homely **BELFAST** feels like the most lived-in and livable of the towns along the Maine coast. Here the shipbuilding boom is long since over (and the chicken-processing plant that regularly turned the bay blood-red has also gone), but the inhabitants have had the waterfront declared a historic district, sparing it from over-commercialization and condo development. As you stroll around, look out for the old-fashioned Western Union office (complete with jukebox) and any number of whitewashed Greek Revival houses, particularly prevalent along the wide avenues in the southern half of town between Church and Congress streets. Belfast was a lively center in the 1960s and its stores, community theater groups, festivals, and the WBYA (101.7 FM) radio station attest to its continued vibrance.

The convivial **information office** (☎207/338-2896), at the foot of Main Street by the bay, is next to the old railroad station, used by the **Belfast and Moosehead Lake Railroad** (☎207/948-5500 or 1-800/392-5500). Ninety-minute excursions ($16) in reconditioned Pullman cars run from here up the lush banks of the Passagassawakeag River, along tracks laid in 1870 to connect logging operations with the sea – though whatever impression you might get from their advertisements, the trains are pulled by diesel, not steam. En route to the villages of Brooks and Burnham Junction, you pass through thick forests, at their most colorful in the fall. The same company offers cruises on an old-style paddleboat in Penobscot Bay ($16); a combination ticket saves $3.

Practicalities

Up from the rail terminal, *90 Main* (☎207/338-1106) is a good bet for **food**, with creative fare such as blueberry chicken with a bagel and cream cheese on the side, a full-service bakery downstairs, and live music on weekends. Across the bay at 4 Mitchell St, *Young's Lobster Pound* (☎207/338-1160) serves up $10 fresh-boiled lobster dinners, among the best in the state, with sunset views. *Darby's*, at 105 High St (☎207/338-2339), is a bit overpriced but nevertheless serves up delicious food such as pecan haddock, pad Thai, and filet mignon; the adjoining **pub** specializes in Scotch whiskeys. *Rollie's Café*, back up the hill at 37 Main St (☎207/338-5217), is a rough-and-ready bar open until 1am every day of the year. The *Gothic*, 4 Main St (☎207/338-9901), is a nice little spot for **coffee**, ice cream, and pastries.

For **accommodation**, try the *Alden House*, 63 Church St (☎207/338-2151, *www.bbonline.com/me/alden*; [4]–[5]), a beautiful 1840 Greek Revival house run as a B&B by two genial hostesses, the comfortable *Thomas Pitcher House*, 19 Franklin St (☎207/338-6454 or 1-888/338-6454; [4]), or the *Jeweled Turret Inn*, 40 Pearl St (☎207/338-2304 or 1-800/696-2304; [5]). Along US-1 across the Passagassawakeag River in East Belfast are several inexpensive motels, including the *Gull* (☎207/338-4030; [4]). East of town, in **Searsport**, there's an *HI-AYH Hostel* at 132 West Main St (closed Nov–April; ☎207/548-2506) with a kitchen, and $15 **dorm beds**; reservations are essential.

Bucksport

Named after founder Colonel Jonathan Buck, who's buried at the Bucksport Cemetery near the Verona Bridge, quiet **BUCKSPORT** was first settled as a trading post in 1762. Today, the Champion International Paper Company's enormous riverside factory dominates the town's skyline and employs a high percentage of its 4900 inhabitants. The town is trying hard to shed its workaday image to attract more visitors, but the problem is, there's not a whole lot to do here. One place worth checking out is **Northeast Historic Film**, in the restored 1916 Alamo Theater building at 379 Main St (☎207/469-0924, *www.acadia.net/oldfilm*), which collects and screens film and video related to the heritage, culture, and history of northern New England. There's a tiny exhibit in the lobby, but the real treat is the chance to watch one of the regularly scheduled matinees.

Even if you hold no particular interest in the military, the hulking **Fort Knox**, just across the Penobscot River from Bucksport (May–Nov daily 9am–sunset; $2; ☎207/469-7719), still merits a wander round its castle-like structure. You can climb up and down circular stairways, stagger through countless tunnels that disappear into total darkness, investigate officers' quarters, and clamber to the top of thick granite walls, from which you can admire Bucksport's factory skyline. With all the cannon mounts – there are over 130 in all – it's hard to believe that this place never saw any action, though it was manned from 1863 to 1866 during the Civil War.

Riverside **camping** is available at the *Flying Dutchman Campground* (☎1-888/541-2267) just off of US-1 on **Verona Island**. Just up the road, past Orland, you can **rent canoes** ($25 half day), paddleboats ($15), and powerboats ($40) from Toddy Boat Rentals (April 15–Oct 12; ☎1-888/537-2822) and explore **Toddy Pond**, which stretches some twelve miles south of US-1.

DOWN EAST

So called because sailors heading east along the coast were also usually heading downwind, **Down East** Maine has engendered plenty of debate over its boundaries – some wishing to draw its western line at Ellsworth, or Belfast, or even include the entire state in their definition. It's all a matter of pride, of course; to be a downeaster means to be tough and fiercely independent – though it would be unfair to say unfriendly. For the purposes of this book at least, we've defined "Down East" as the Maine coast east of Bucksport, including the **Blue Hill Peninsula**, home to several wealthy summer towns, **Mount Desert Island**, the most visited place in the state, and the nearly deserted shoreline that stretches a hundred lonely miles between the strip mall town of Ellsworth and the point furthest east in the United States at **West Quoddy Head**.

As you make your way up the coast – particularly once you pass Mount Desert Island and **Acadia National Park** – the terrain and the population become more rugged and less prone to tourism. The weather here is also less forgiving, and the coast near the Canadian border is normally foggy for half the year.

The Blue Hill Peninsula

It used to be that the **Blue Hill Peninsula**, reaching south from Bucksport, was a sleepy expanse of land, too far off the primary roads to attract much attention. But word is slowly getting out about this beautiful area, blanketed with crimson fields of wild blueberries, and dotted with both dignified old-money towns like **Castine** and **Blue Hill** and hardcore fishing villages like **Stonington** and **Deer Isle**. Even further off the established tourist trail, **Isle au Haut** is a remote outpost accessible only by mail boat. In the smaller towns between, you'll find close-knit communities of people who can trace their ties to the peninsula back for several generations. At once friendly and suspicious, year-round residents are understandably protective of the privacy they have come to cherish. As you might expect, the main draw down here is the quiet tranquility that comes with isolation, and while the area presents ample opportunities for exploration, you might find yourself content with a good book, an afternoon nap, a gourmet meal, and a night in a posh B&B.

COMMUNITY RADIO

In Bucksport and the surrounding area, tune your radio to community-run **WERU**, 89.9 FM, which broadcasts a wide range of lesser-known music, local news, and liberal commentary from its headquarters in East Orland.

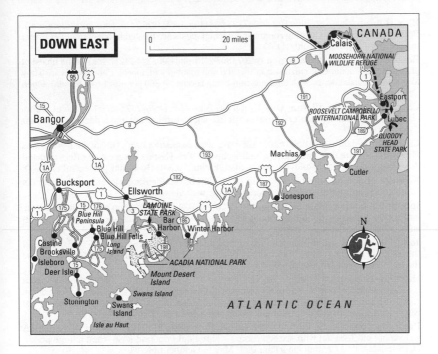

Arrival, information, and getting around

The Blue Hill Peninsula is deceptively large, and, with somewhat indirect roads, it can take well over an hour to reach its southernmost point. It's a good idea to pick up a detailed DeLorme map before you set out to explore the area – even some of the locally produced plans can't seem to keep all the different numbered roads straight. **Cycling** is a good way to get around; your best bet for renting is probably at the Activity Center in Blue Hill on Rte-172 (☎207/374-3600). Public transport is not available, though if you're really in a bind, you can grab a **taxi** by calling Airport & Harbor Taxi (☎207/667-5995) or G&M Taxi (☎207/667-7030).

The only formal **information center** is way down on Little Deer Isle (☎207/348-6124), but most inns and shopkeepers can provide just about all the information you need, including regional maps. The local Chamber of Commerce maintains a useful **Web site** at *www.bluehillme.com*.

Accommodation

Cheap **accommodations** on the Blue Hill Peninsula are non-existent, unless you make it clear down to Stonington. If you're not traveling in the off-season, plan to spend $100 or more per night. There are only two official places to **camp** here, both on Deer Isle. *Sunshine Campground*, near the end of Sunshine Road way out on Sunshine (☎207/348-6681), has 22 sites from Memorial Day through mid-October, while *Greenlaws*, in Stonington (☎207/367-5049) is more RV-oriented.

Blue Hill Inn, Union St, Blue Hill (☎207/374-2844 or 1-800/826-7415, *www.bluehillinn.com*). Romantic 1830 inn with inviting rooms and decor. Guests are treated to outstanding gourmet meals. May to November only. ⑥–⑧.

Boyces Motel, Main St, Stonington (☎207/367-2421 or 1-800/224-2421). It's not the nicest of places, but the somewhat run-down ambiance still manages to appeal. Plus, it's cheap. They also have full apartments, with kitchens and living rooms for $60 per night (off-season). Open all year. ③.

Captain Isaac Merrill Inn, One Union St, Blue Hill (☎207/374-2555). Ancient white-clapboard house in the center of town with fireplaces throughout and a decent restaurant downstairs. ⑥–⑦.

Castine Inn, Main St, Castine (☎207/326-4365, *www.castineinn.com*). One of the few old inns (1898) in the state that was actually built as an inn, this Castine fixture now offers updated amenities and friendly, helpful hosts. See also "Eating," p.504. Open May to December. ⑤–⑥.

Heritage Motor Inn, Rte-172, Blue Hill (☎207/374-5646). Pleasingly located and moderately priced motor inn with good-sized rooms, some with views.④.

Inn on the Harbor, Main St, Stonington (☎207/367-2420). Stonington's fanciest (and priciest) accommodations, though that's not saying a whole lot. It also has the best location, with a fine view of the harbor. Breakfast included. ⑥.

John Peters Inn, half mile north of Blue Hill just off Rte-176 E (☎207/374-2116). Some of the rooms in this impressive brick mansion have private decks and fireplaces. Guests can use the inn's canoe and sailboat. ⑥–⑧.

Oakland House, 435 Herrick Rd, Brooksville (☎207/359-8521 or 1-800/359-7352, *www.acadia.net/oaklandhouse*). Stay in the immaculately refurbished old stone inn or in one of the rustic cabins strewn about the property, situated in an impossibly remote area along the Eggemoggin Reach; you'll need to follow the signs down Rte-15 to get there. ⑦.

Pentagoet Inn, Main St, Castine (☎207/326-8616 or 1-800/845-1701, *www.pentagoet.com*). A welcoming old 1894 inn with sixteen rooms – kitted out in period style – and a huge porch. Occasional mellow evening entertainment. May to October only. ⑥.

Pres du Port B&B, W Main St at Highland Ave, Stonington (☎207/367-5007). This old house, filled with quirky furniture, overlooks the bay; call ahead for reservations. May to October only. ④–⑤.

Blue Hill

Though wealthy **BLUE HILL**, at the intersection of Routes 172, 176, and 15 adjacent the Blue Hill Harbor, makes a fairly good portion of its living from tourism, you'd be hard pressed to find a Maine T-shirt or even a lighthouse figurine around town. It's not that there's much to see here, but plenty come for its quietude nevertheless.

Several well-known writers, among them E.B. White, have made their home in Blue Hill, whose population supports two excellent bookstores. North Light Books, on Main Street (☎207/374-5422), is a great source for **travel books** and maps as well as fiction and specialty titles, while the larger Blue Hill Books, 2 Pleasant St (☎207/374-5632), is a more comprehensive independent bookseller.

It's a relatively short walk (30–45min) up to the top of **Blue Hill Mountain**, from which you can see across the Blue Hill Bay to the dramatic ridges of Mount Desert Island. The trailhead is not difficult to find, halfway down Mountain Road between Rte-15 and Rte-172. South on Rte-175, **Blue Hill Falls** is a good spot to give kayaking a try: the Phoenix Center, along Rte-175 (☎207/374-2113), offers tours and lessons, while at Maine Coast Experience, further south in Brooklin on Reach Road (☎207/359-5057 or 1-888/559-5057), you can rent a kayak ($50 per day) and set your own agenda. They also offer **whale-watching** trips and, for the romantically inclined, sunset cruises.

Castine

CASTINE, nearly surrounded by water on the northern edge of the Penobscot Bay, is one of New England's most majestic towns, with nicely kept streets and gardens, enormous elm trees arching over many of the hilly streets, and a quiet sophistication found in only the wealthiest of communities. Named for Jean Vincent d'Abbadie de St Castin, a Frenchman who was deeded the land in 1667, the historically disputed peninsula has been occupied at various times by the French, British, Dutch, and, obviously, Americans. The British assumed control in 1779 when General Francis McLean stormed ashore with seven hundred men and built **Fort George**, now little more than a few mounds along Wadsworth Cove Road. The Americans responded by sending 32 vessels carrying some 1400 men, and what followed was arguably the worst American naval defeat in history. Unable to agree on a plan of attack on the weaker British forces on land, the Americans sat in the bay until a larger British fleet arrived, forcing them to retreat up the Penobscot, abandon their ships, and walk back to Boston. Among the officers court-martialed upon their return was Paul Revere, whose military career never really recovered. The military battles that occurred here are noted throughout town with various plaques and signs; a brochure and **map** entitled *Welcome to Castine* is available at any local shop for a full listing of all the historic sites.

Castine's small population is a mix of summer residents, a number of well-known poets and writers (Elizabeth Hardwick, founder of *The New York Review of Books* among them) and year-round people, many of whom are employed by the **Maine Maritime Academy**, with buildings both along the water and back on Pleasant Street. It's pretty tough to miss the *State of Maine*, the huge ship that's usually docked at the landing and used to train the academy's students, who give tours in the summer (call ☎207/326-4311 for schedules, or ask around). Take a stroll down **Perkins Street** to check out the string of enormous mansions looking out over the water. Between these ostentatious summer retreats are a number of old historic buildings, such as the 1665 **John Perkins House**, the town's earliest, which is occasionally open to the public. When you tire of wandering around the town, the New England Outdoor Center (☎207/326-9045 or 1-800/766-7238, *www.neoc.com*) runs various **sea kayaking** tours ($40–90, includes equipment and instruction) from Dennett's Wharf next to the public boat landing.

Stonington and Isle au Haut

When you cross over the enormous suspension bridge onto Little Deer Isle and traverse the causeway onto **Deer Isle**, be prepared for a shock. It's said that many locals never even bother to leave the island, and by the time-warped feel of the place, that doesn't seem too far-fetched. Clear down at the end of Rte.15, it doesn't get much more remote than **STONINGTON**, a working-class town whose residents have long had a reputation for superior seamanship; many pirates and smugglers reputedly made port here in the late nineteenth century – no doubt due to its incredible isolation. Over the last hundred years, the place has found hard-earned prosperity in the sardine canning and granite quarrying businesses. The history of the granite quarries is brought to life at the newly opened **Deer Isle Granite Museum**, on Main Street (Memorial Day–Labor Day Mon–Sat 10am–5pm, Sun 1–5pm; donation), which counts as its centerpiece a working model of the quarry as it stood in 1900.

Mailboats headed for **ISLE AU HAUT** ("I'll ah hoe") depart from the Stonington landing several times daily (no service Sunday; ☎207/367-5193; $25 round-trip). On this lonely island, you can explore the less-visited part of **Acadia National Park**, clambering over the rocky shoreline and feeling your way through the cool foggy breeze and dense stands of spruce trees. Alternatively, you can charter your own boat for a reasonable price from Old Quarry Charters, in Stonington (☎207/367-8977), who, in addition to Isle au Haut, will take you anywhere on the Maine coast, 24 hours a day, 365 days a year (so they claim).

Eating

Most of the **eateries** on the peninsula cater to the expensive tastes (and fat wallets) of wealthy summer residents; **Castine** and **Blue Hill** have the best concentration of places, though even on the remote **Deer Isle** there are a couple of prix-fixe gourmet spots.

Castine Inn, Main St, Castine (☎207/326-4365). Bold flavors from dishes such as olive-crusted salmon, grilled foie gras with candied rhubarb, and beef tenderloin with a red wine port sauce. There's also a friendly little pub.

Castine Variety, Main St, Castine (☎207/326-8625). The real draw here is not the food – although you can get a pretty good milkshake – but rather the opportunity to catch up on the town news while sitting at the tiny counter in the back of the store and chatting with the well-connected proprietor.

Dennett's Wharf, 15 Sea St, Castine (☎207/326-9045). Dine on typical seafood fare and then wash it down with one of several Maine microbrews on tap, all while enjoying a fine view of the sea.

Firepond, Main St, Blue Hill (☎207/374-9970). Enjoy a romantic candlelit gourmet feast – for a price – in this intimate dining room near the town center. Entrees such as fresh local sea scallops on a bed of tomato pasta, veal with sundried tomatoes, and vegetarian risotto cost $15–19.

Fisherman's Friend, School St, Stonington (☎207/367-2442). Packed with semi-friendly locals, this no-nonsense eatery serves up just what you'd expect to find in a remote fishing community: fresh, delicious, and sometimes greasy seafood.

Harbor Café, Main St, Stonington (☎207/367-5099). A very casual spot for sandwiches, coffee, and muffins in the center of town.

Jonathan's, Main St, Blue Hill (☎207/374-5226). Imaginatively prepared seafood and eclectic cuisine in a romantic, candlelit dining room. There's an extensive wine list. Entrees $15–20.

Left Bank Bakery and Café, Rte-172, Blue Hill (☎207/374-2201). Fresh-baked goods, delectable salads, and some vegetarian offerings. During the summer, there are frequent musical performances.

Morning Moon Café, Rte-175 and Naskeag Point Rd, Brooklin (☎207/359-2373). Popular gathering spot for breakfast and lunch. Known as simply "The Moon."

The Pantry Restaurant, Water St, Blue Hill (☎207/374-2229). Cute little breakfast and lunch restaurant serving incredibly cheap and simple sandwiches, waffles, eggs, and the like.

East to Mount Desert Island

Aside from a short strip of quaint brick gift shops and a couple of cafés along the old part of Main Street (US-1), most of **ELLSWORTH** has been overdeveloped into a disastrous sprawl of parking lots and chain stores. There's predictably little to see, although on a cloudy day you might check out the **Colonel Black Mansion**, on Rte-172 just south of US-1 (June–Oct Mon–Sat 10am–5pm, last tour

4.30pm; $5), a huge old house that's been restored to its nineteenth-century splendor. Otherwise, stop here only for provisions or a quick bite to eat before heading south to Mount Desert Island. The *Riverside Café*, at 52 Main St (☎207/667-7220), is a friendly local **breakfast and lunch** joint.

If you're arriving in the Acadia region in high season (July and August) and the traffic is unbearable along busy Rte-3, head off down Rte-184 to **Lamoine State Park** ($2), just north of Mount Desert Island along the shores of Frenchman Bay. There are no hiking trails, but there are plenty of beautiful spots to have a picnic or wander the coast. The 61-site **campground** (mid-May to mid-Oct; ☎207/667-4778; $15 per night) here is rarely full – maybe because it offers no hookups or hot showers – and has some well-situated tent sites that offer views of the island. Nearby, Lamoine Beach is the best **swimming** beach in the area. If you'd rather not camp, the *Lamoine House*, on Rte-184 in a farmhouse across from the shore (☎207/667-7711; ②–③), is quite a bargain, at around $40 per room (shared bath), including breakfast.

Mount Desert Island

Considering that five million visitors come to **Mount Desert Island** each year, that it contains most of New England's only national park, and that it boasts not only a genuine fjord but also the highest headland on the entire Atlantic coast north of Rio de Janeiro, it is quite an astonishingly small place, measuring just sixteen by thirteen miles. It is, of course, simply one among innumerable rugged granite islands along the Maine coast; the reason to come here is that it is the most accessible, linked to the mainland by bridge since 1836, and has the best facilities.

The island was named *Monts Deserts* (bare mountains) by Samuel de Champlain in 1604 and fought over by the French and English for the rest of the century. Although all existing settlements date from long after the final defeat of the French, the name remains, still pronounced in French (more like *dessert*, actually). After landscape painters Thomas Cole and Frederic Church depicted the island in mid-nineteenth-century works, word spread about its barren beauty, and by the end of the century, tourism was a fixture here. America's wealthiest families – among them the Rockefellers, Pulitzers, and Fords – erected palatial estates in **Bar Harbor**, and later (under the leadership of Harvard University President Charles Eliot) established the public land trust that would later become Acadia National Park, the first national park donated entirely by private citizens. In 1947, a fire destroyed many of the grand cottages, including Bar Harbor's "Millionaire's Row," putting an end to the island's grand resort era. The fire didn't entirely tarnish the island's luster, however, and the place now attracts vacationing middle-class families and outdoors enthusiasts in addition to the frighteningly rich.

Somes Sound roughly divides the island in half; the east side is more developed and ritzy, holding the island's social center and travel hub Bar Harbor, and **Northeast Harbor**, which provides huge summer homes for many a CEO. The west side, known to some as the "quiet side," is rather sedate, with a few genuine fishing villages and year-round settlements like low-key **Southwest Harbor**, actually fast catching on as a popular destination in its own right. **Acadia National Park**, which covers much of the island, can offer less sedate travelers camping, cycling, canoeing, kayaking, hiking, and bird-watching, though you're hardly ever very far from civilization.

Arrival and information

If you're **driving**, Mount Desert is easy enough to get to, along Rte-3 off US-1, though in high summer roads on the island itself get congested (and the horse-drawn tours don't help). **Public transport**, however is minimal. Vermont Transit Lines (☎207/772-6587) **buses** run to Bar Harbor (stopping at Fox Run Travel, 4 Kennebec St; ☎207/288-3366) from Boston, Bangor, and Portland for a couple of months in summer, starting in mid-June. Concord Trailways (☎207/942-8686) has a line linking Bangor with Ellsworth and Bar Harbor. West Coastal Connections (☎207/546-2823 or 1-800/596-2823) goes as far as Ellsworth and Bar Harbor, as does Downeast Transportation (☎207/667-5796), which also runs buses across the island from Bar Harbor to Southwest Harbor and Northeast Harbor.

Mount Desert is surprisingly accessible via airplane, though **flights** are relatively infrequent and expensive. Bar Harbor/Hancock County Airport on Rte-3 in Trenton (☎207/667-7432) has a limited service run by Colgan Air; Bangor International Airport, 45 miles away, is served by Northwest, Delta, and Continental. The 55mph

"Cat" **ferry** takes two and three quarter hours to link Bar Harbor with Yarmouth, Nova Scotia (June–Aug, cars $55, people $41.50; Sept–Oct, cars $50, people $27.25; ferries leave Bar Harbor daily at 8am, return from Yarmouth at 4.30pm; ☎207/288-3395 or 1-888/249-7245).

Information

The **Acadia Information Center**, on Rte-3 just before you cross the bridge to Mount Desert Island (May–Oct daily 9am–6pm; ☎207/667-8550 or 1-800/248-9250), is an advisable stop for lodging and camping information if you don't already have a reservation, and they have decent free maps of the island. There's also a tourist information office in Bar Harbor at the ferry terminal (☎207/288-5103).

There are three **information** outlets at Acadia during the summer, the best of which is the Hulls Cove Visitor Center, just off of Rte-3 at the entrance to the Park Loop Road (mid-April to Oct daily 8am–4.30pm, until 6pm in July & Aug; ☎207/667-8550 or 1-800/358-8550). Here you can inquire about hiking routes and purchase maps. You can also obtain more information about the park by writing or calling the National Park Service at **Park Headquarters**, PO Box 177, Bar Harbor, ME 04609 (☎207/288-3338, *www.nps.gov/acad*).

Accommodation

Rte-3 into and out of Bar Harbor (which becomes Main Street on the way south) is lined with budget **motels**, which do little to improve the look of the place but satisfy an enormous demand for accommodation. Rates increase drastically in July and August, and anywhere offering sea views will cost a whole lot more. In season, it's difficult to find a room for less than $100 in **Bar Harbor**; elsewhere, prices are a little less exorbitant. Despite the island's 4500 rooms, everywhere tends to be booked up early, so call ahead to check for availability. For help with **reservations**, call or stop in at the Acadia Information Center on Rte-3 just north of the island (☎207/667-8550 or 1-800/248-9250). If you're really pressed for cash, it's cheaper to stay in **Ellsworth** and drive onto the island each day, though the drive to the far south end can be quite time consuming. **Camping** in Acadia National Park is a better (and prettier) budget option but in short supply; here too you will need to call well in advance in July and August, although smaller private campgrounds scattered about the island are usually not full (see box p.508).

Bar Harbor

Acadia Hotel, 20 Mount Desert St (☎207/288-5721 or 1-888/876-2463, *www.acadiahotel .com*). One of the more affordable spots in town, the rooms in this old hotel are newly renovated but a bit overdone. You get a discount if you reserve through the Web site. ④.

Bass Cottage in the Field, 14 In the Field (☎207/288-3705). Authentic Victorian relic from the golden age of Bar Harbor. Some rooms share baths, singles available. ⑤.

Hatfield B&B, 20 Roberts Ave (☎207/288-9655, *www.hatfieldinn.com*). On a quiet side street a short walk from the center of town, this small country-style B&B offers friendly service and a laid-back atmosphere. ⑤.

Johnson Cottage, 108 Cottage St (☎207/288-3743 or 667-5142). Clean and basic guesthouse with shared baths. ③.

Maples Inn, 16 Roberts Ave (☎207/288-3443, *www.acadia.net/maples*). Peaceful little B&B with antique four-poster and canopy beds. Open all year. Prices are thirty percent less in winter. ⑥.

Mount Desert Island HI/AYH Hostel, 27 Kennebec St (☎207/288-5587). Pay just $12 per night for a dorm bed in this basic hostel. Reservations a necessity; credit cards not accepted. Closed Sept to mid-June.

Mount Desert YWCA, 36 Mount Desert St (☎207/288-5008). Centrally located women-only accommodation. Open sporadically – call ahead. Beds in shared rooms start at $25, go up to $50. Beds also available for $85 per week (single) or $140 (double).

The Tides, 119 West St (☎207/288-4968). On a fairly residential street but still within a few minutes of the center of town, this elegant, somewhat formal white mansion affords ocean views from several of its luxurious rooms. ⑦–⑧.

Ullikana B&B, 16 The Field (☎207/288-9552). The place to go in town for a romantic splurge; nicely decorated rooms and unbelievably sumptuous breakfasts. ⑦.

Southwest Harbor and the west side

The Claremont, Claremont Rd, Southwest Harbor (☎207/244-5036 or 1-800/244-5036; *www.acadia.net/claremont*). Classic old-fashioned wooden hotel with tennis and croquet, a few minutes from Acadia National Park on the quieter side of the island. Mid-May to mid-Oct. ⑦.

Emery's Cottages on the Shore, Sand Point Rd (☎207/288-3432 or 1-888/240-3432). Well-equipped individual cottage units in green parkland overlooking Fisherman's Bay. From $320 per week off-season to $480/week peak season.

Inn at Southwest Harbor, Main St, Southwest Harbor (☎207/244-3835, *www.acadia.net /innatsw*). Brilliant old Victorian inn in the center of town with a cozy living room, cheery bedrooms, and an attentive innkeeper. Very inexpensive off-season rates. ⑤.

Jeannie's Place B&B, Swans Island (☎207/526-4116). Three guest rooms share a bath in the only accommodations on Swans Island, a 45-minute ferry ride from Bass Harbor. There's also a housekeeping cottage with a full kitchen for rent. ③–④.

Lindenwood Inn, 118 Clark Point Rd, Southwest Harbor (☎207/244-5335 or 1-800/307-5335). This first-class inn offers tastefully redecorated rooms and African accents in a stylish turn-of-the-century captain's home. Breakfast included. ⑥.

CAMPING ON MOUNT DESERT ISLAND

There are two **public campgrounds** in Acadia National Park. **Blackwoods**, near Seal Harbor (☎207/288-3274), is available all year and reservations are taken from June to September (through Biospherics; ☎1-800/365-2267; $16). At **Seawall**, off Rte-102A near Bass Harbor (☎207/244-3600; $14), campsites are available on a first-come first-served basis (closed Oct–April). The Appalachian Mountain Club maintains the **Echo Lake Camp** (Jun 27–Aug 29; ☎207/244-3747; $377 per week), an extremely popular lakefront camp in Acadia National Park between Somesville and Southwest Harbor, with tent sites, beds, a dining room, kitchens, shared bathhouses with hot showers, canoes, and kayaks; rates here include family-style meals. The following list of privately owned campgrounds on the island is not exhaustive but it should be sufficient; for a more complete guide, contact the information center. Most charge about $25 per night.

Barcadia, Rte-3, Bar Harbor (mid-May to mid-Oct; ☎207/288-3520).

Bass Harbor, Bass Harbor (mid-June to Sept; ☎207/244-5857).

Mount Desert, Bar Harbor Rd (Rte-198), Somesville (mid-May to Sept; ☎207/244-3710).

Mount Desert Narrows, Rte-3, Bar Harbor (May–Oct; ☎207/288-4782).

Quietside, West Tremont (mid-June to mid-Oct; ☎207/244-5992).

Spruce Valley, Rte-102, Bar Harbor (mid-May to Oct; ☎207/288-5139).

White Birches, 195 Seal Cove Rd, Southwest Harbor (mid-May to mid-Oct; ☎207/244-3797).

The Yellow Aster, 53 Clark Point Rd, Southwest Harbor (☎207/244-4422 or 1-800/724-7228, *www.acadia.net/yellowaster*). Spotless and bright with wholesome organic breakfasts and a bit of a new-agey feel. ⑤.

Bar Harbor

The town of **BAR HARBOR** began life as an exclusive resort, summer home to the Vanderbilts and the Astors; the great fire of October 1947 that destroyed their opulent "cottages" ended all that. Many of the old-money families have subsequently rebuilt their summer estates in hyper-rich **Northeast Harbor**, southwest along Rte-3, and Bar Harbor is now firmly geared towards tourists – though it's by no means downmarket. There's not all that much to do in town, even in high summer. However, the ambiance is sufficient for it to take a while to realize that once you've strolled around the village green, and walked along the **Shore Path** past the headland of the *Bar Harbor Inn* and along the coast for views of the ocean and Frenchman Bay, you've seen most of what Bar Harbor has to offer.

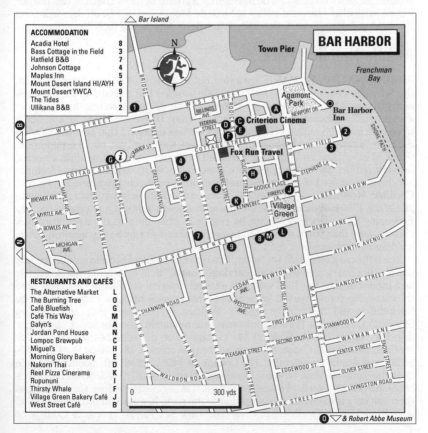

In high season up to 21 different **sea trips** set off each day, for purposes ranging from deep-sea fishing to cocktail cruises. Among the most popular are the
whale-watching trips run by Bar Harbor Whale Watch Company, 1 West St
(☎207/288-2386 or 1-800/WHALES-4). Cruises, which depart adjacent to the
Town Pier, take about two hours and cost around $30. You can also enjoy two-hour
cruises on the impressive **schooners** *Sylvina W Beal* and *Margaret Todd* from the
Bar Harbor Inn (three trips daily June–Oct; ☎207/288-4585; $22–27.50). If you'd
rather steer your own ship, rent a powerboat from Harbor Boat Rentals, at the
town pier (☎207/288-3757; $40 per hour).

One of the town sights in its heyday was the "Indian Village," a summer encampment where Native Americans came to sell pottery, necklaces, and trinkets to
tourists; it was cleared away in the 1930s to make room for a new ballpark. Now
the only signs of the island's first inhabitants are the artifacts at the **Robert Abbe
Museum**, which were found at Fernald Point near Southwest Harbor and attributed to a nomadic people who made birch-bark canoes. What became of them is
encapsulated by a classic understatement on a map contrasting the tribal areas of
1600 with the modern reservations: "The native population did not view territorial
boundaries as we do today." The museum is a couple of miles south of Bar Harbor
– not a particularly pleasant walk – at Sieur de Monts Spring, just off the Park Loop
Road (May & June, Sept & Oct daily 10am–4pm; July & Aug daily 9am–5pm; $2).

Acadia National Park

ACADIA NATIONAL PARK, sprawled out over most of Mount Desert Island,
the Schoodic Peninsula to the east, and little-traveled Isle au Haut, is the most visited place in Maine. It's visually stunning, with dramatic rolling hills carving
smooth rocky silhouettes into the misty horizon. Dense stands of fir and birch
trees hide over 120 miles of **hiking trails** (see box opposite) that pop into view on
the island's several boulder-like summits. In fact, there's all you could want here in
terms of mountains and lakes for secluded rambling, and such **wildlife** as seals,
beavers, puffins, and bald eagles is not scarce. The two main geographical features
are the narrow fjord of **Somes Sound**, which almost splits the island in two, and
Cadillac Mountain, an unbelievable place to watch the sunrise, though the summit of the 1530-foot mound offers tremendous ocean views at any time of the day
(assuming clear weather). It can be reached either by a moderately strenuous
climb – more than you'd want to do before breakfast – or by a very leisurely drive,
winding up a low-gradient road.

Much the most enjoyable way to explore is to ride a rented **bicycle** around the fifty
miles of one-lane gravel-surfaced "**carriage roads**," built by John D. Rockefeller Jr
as a protest against the 1913 vote that allowed "infernal combustion engines" onto
the island. Keep your eye out for several ornate **granite bridges**, commissioned by
Rockefeller and built by architects William Welles Bosworth and Charles
Stonington. Three Bar Harbor companies rent mountain bikes for about $25–30 per
day: Bar Harbor Bicycle Shop, at 141 Cottage St on the edge of town (☎207/288-
3886), Acadia Bike & Canoe, across from the post office at 48 Cottage St (☎207/288-
9605), and Acadia Outfitters, at 106 Cottage St (☎207/288-8118). Southwest Cycle
does the same on Main Street in Southwest Harbor (☎207/244-5856 or 1-800/649-
5856). All provide excellent maps and are good at suggesting routes. Carry water, as
there are very few refreshment stops inside the park. **Kayaks** can be rented ($45 all
day) from May to October from National Park Sea Kayak Tours, 39 Cottage St

HIKING ON MOUNT DESERT ISLAND

It's no secret that Mount Desert Island offers some of the most exhilarating **hiking** in New England – most of its 100 miles of trails are only deserted in the dead of winter. Though by no means exhaustive, the following list highlights some of the best hikes. If you plan on exploring the island's trails extensively, get your hands on a copy of the detailed guidebook, *A Walk in the Park*, published locally ($12) and available at the park visitor center. The Southwest Harbor Chamber of Commerce (☎207/244-9624 or 1-800/423-9264) prints a decent map (free) of the west side of the park, detailing some two dozen hikes.

Acadia Mountain Trail, a few miles south of Somesville, on the east side of Rte-102. A relatively steep ascent to the top of the 700-foot mountain, with fine views of the Somes Sound. 2.5 miles round-trip.

Beehive Trail, just north of the Sand Beach parking area. A short one-mile trip up iron rungs on exposed ledges. There's a swimming pond near the top called the Bowl.

Flying Mountain Trail, five minutes north of Southwest Harbor, just off of Rte-103 on Fernald Point Road. This short hike takes about an hour round-trip, affording beautiful views at the top of 284-foot Flying Mountain.

Great Head Loop, beginning at Sand Beach on the Park Loop Road. Scenic 1.5-mile trail leads along towering cliffs right above the sea.

Jordan Pond Loop Trail, from the Jordan Pond parking area. A 3.3-mile loop that roughly follows the water's edge.

Mansell Mountain, at the south end of Long Pond, near Southwest Harbor. Trees impair the views from the 950-foot summit, but the two-mile hike along the Perpendicular Trail features stairways carved into the rock and unparalleled seclusion.

Penobscot Mountain, departing from near the Jordan Pond House. Panoramic views, second only perhaps to those from Cadillac Mountain, the highest point on the island at 1530ft.

Ship Harbor Nature Trail, at the southern end of the park off of Rte-102A near the Bass Harbor Head Light. An easy 1.3-mile trail that loops out along the coast and back.

South Ridge Trail, departing from Rte-3, near the Blackwoods Campground. This trail is the best way to get to the top of Cadillac Mountain. The 7.4-mile round trip is not particularly strenuous but very rewarding.

(☎207/288-0342 or 1-800/347-0940, *www.acadiakayak.com*), which also leads guided sea kayaking trips and downhill bike rides from the top of Cadillac Mountain. Just up the street at 48 Cottage St, Coastal Kayaking Tours offers similar kayaking trips, including overnight island camping packages (☎207/288-9605 or 1-800/526-8615).

The park is open all year, with a summer-only **visitor center** in Hull's Cove at the entrance to the Loop Road north of Bar Harbor (see "Information," p.507). The entrance fee is $10 per car for a seven-day pass, or $5 if you enter on foot or bike. Many visitors do nothing more than drive the length of the Park Loop Road, which admittedly winds through some of the park's most arresting areas – and you should do this too – but also make the effort to get onto the trails. The only fee collection station is on Park Loop Road near **Sand Beach**, five miles south of Bar Harbor, a gorgeous strand bounded by twin headlands, though the water, sadly, is usually arctic. Because there are so few parking spots near the beautifully sheltered cove, you should either bike over from Bar Harbor or arrive early in the day.

THE SCHOODIC PENINSULA

A small section of Acadia National Park lies isolated at the end of the **Schoodic Peninsula**, some eight miles south of US-1 along Rte-186, where Schoodic Point overlooks a rocky shoreline that spills out into the crashing surf, creating many natural picnic benches. Watch out for the menacing gulls, who easily quell their fear of humans in search of sandwiches to grab.

The Point's the most scenic of stops on the peninsula, though there are plenty of places to pull off Rte-186 and explore a bit of the coast on foot. The pleasant little village of **WINTER HARBOR**, northwest of the park along Rte-186, is a worthwhile stop, if for no other reason than to grab a thick milkshake at local hangout *JM Garrish*, 352 Main St (☎207/963-5575), an old-fashioned soda fountain where you can also munch on huge home-made muffins and cheap sandwiches. If you're in the area, don't miss the yearly **lobster festival** in Winter Harbor, held the second Saturday in August, when lobster lovers converge on the tiny town to down heaps of the tender meat, shop for crafts, listen to live music, and watch a parade.

Southwest Harbor and the west side

The western half of Mount Desert Island was for many years unflatteringly called the "Backside" by well-heeled (and snooty) residents of Bar Harbor. But while its quiet hamlets still maintain a much slower pace than Bar Harbor, the area is not without appeal, especially if you're seeking solace from the crowds.

SOUTHWEST HARBOR, along Rte-102 across from Northeast Harbor, is the center of this side's action, so to speak. The small downtown – if you could call it that – is graced with a couple of top-notch restaurants and the surrounding town has a smattering of cozy, out-of-the-way accommodations. The streets here are quiet at 8pm on Saturday nights in high summer – exactly the appeal, though how long it will hold on to that in the face of increased tourist traffic is up in the air. Regardless, Southwest Harbor makes for a good base from which to explore the western half of Acadia National Park, and, if you plan on visiting the neighboring Swans Island or Long Island, the state ferry is only a couple of miles away in Bass Harbor.

South along Rte-102, **BASS HARBOR** is even further removed, the simple homes that line its streets reflecting the modest middle-class lifestyle of its residents. At the southernmost tip of the island, just off of Rte-102A, you'll find the much-photographed **Bass Harbor Head Light**, perched on the rocks and tucked behind the trees. Though the 1858 structure is not open to visitors, you can walk down a short seaside path for excellent views of the lighthouse and the ocean beyond. If you prefer to explore the water itself, take a three-hour lunch **cruise** from Little Island Marine, at the end of Little Island Way off of Shore Road ($18, lunch not included), to the fishing village of Frenchboro on Long Island, or a two-hour nature cruise aboard the *R.L. Gott* (mid-June to Labor Day; ☎207/244-5785; $14). The Maine State Ferry also runs **boats** between Bass Harbor, Swans Island, and Frenchboro several days per week (☎207/244-3254).

Eating and drinking

Mount Desert's most memorable **eating** experiences are to be found in the many **lobster pounds** all over the island, but for nightlife as such, Bar Harbor is where the people are. Cottage Street is a much more promising area to look for food and evening atmosphere than the surprisingly subdued waterfront. As per usual, **seafood** is everywhere, although, thankfully, there are some more creative options available. The Art Deco Criterion cinema at Cottage Street (☎207/288-3441) puts on 2pm matinees on rainy days and looks exactly as it did when it was built in 1932.

Bar Harbor

The Alternative Market, 16 Mount Desert St (☎207/288-8225). Bag lunches, big sandwiches, soups, smoothies, and fresh squeezed juices.

The Burning Tree, Rte-3, Otter Creek (☎207/288-9331). A few miles south of Bar Harbor, this outwardly unimpressive seafood restaurant spices up its brilliant entrees ($15–20) with tasty Southwestern and Caribbean touches. Reservations a must in July and August. Closed mid-Oct to mid-June.

Café Bluefish, 122 Cottage St (☎207/288-3696). Cute, eclectically decorated little restaurant specializing in basic seafood and poultry dishes with a twist, such as apricot chicken ($14.95) and curry crusted tuna ($17.95).

Café This Way, 14.5 Mount Desert St (☎207/288-4483). Creative light California cuisine, the likes of cashew-crusted chicken over sautéed greens or butternut squash ravioli (entrees $11–15). Breakfast daily, dinner Mon–Sat 6–9pm.

Galyn's, 17 Maine Rd (☎207/288-3070). A good bet for relatively affordable (around $15 per entree) fresh gourmet seafood, with an attractively understated decor and candlelit tables.

Jordan Pond House, Park Loop Rd, Acadia National Park (☎207/276-3316). Worthy concession restaurant in the heart of Acadia National Park between Bar Harbor and Northeast Harbor. Serves light meals, ice cream, and popovers (light, puffy egg muffins, a longtime Acadia tradition). Tea is served in the beautiful lakeside garden 11.30am–6pm.

Lompoc Brewpub & Café, 36 Rodick St (☎207/288-9392). A healthy Middle Eastern and Italian menu for $10–15, with local Bar Harbor Real Ale on draft and live music every night. Open 3pm–midnight.

Miguel's, 51 Rodick St (☎207/288-5117). Hopping Mexican joint with a typically calorie-laden menu and a happy, margarita-swilling crowd.

Morning Glory Bakery, 39 Rodick St (☎207/288-3041). Fresh-baked breads and pastries across from the *Lompoc Brewpub*.

Nakorn Thai, 30 Rodick St (☎207/288-4060). Large selection of authentic Thai food with polite service; most entrees cost under $10.

Reel Pizza Cinerama, 33 Kennebec Place (☎207/288-3828). Eat pizza and watch intelligent films on the big screen. It's a simple concept, but it works. Movie tickets are $4.50.

Rupununi, 119 Main St (☎207/288-2886). Late-night overpriced pub grub – stick to the burgers. The bar stays open until 1am.

Thirsty Whale, 44 Cottage St (☎207/288-9335). As rowdy as Bar Harbor gets. Live music every night of the week in season.

Village Green Bakery Café, 150 Main St (☎207/288-9450). Great pastries, plus a full range of lunches and dinners, including the requisite boiled lobsters. Low prices, good for families.

West Street Café, 195 West St (☎207/288-5242). Family restaurant serving basic seafood at reasonable prices.

Southwest Harbor and the west side

Beal's Lobster Pier, Clark Point Rd, Southwest Harbor (☎207/244-7178). Fresh seafood for under $10, on a rickety wooden pier crammed full of lobsters. Closed Nov–Apr.

Chef Marc & Eat a Pita, 326 Main St, Southwest Harbor (☎207/244-4344). A great casual, cozy, and affordable spot with delicious, healthy gourmet food (pastas, salads, pita sandwiches, seafood), candlelit tables, and friendly service. Lunch and dinner served. Credit cards not accepted.

Preble Grill, 14 Clark Point Rd, Southwest Harbor (☎207/244-9265). Classy and deservedly popular spot with flavorful grilled meats for $15–19 or pastas for about $12.

Restaurant XYZ, Shore Rd, Manset (☎207/244-3508 or 1-800/580-6811). A pleasant surprise amongst the island's typical offering of traditional seafood, this authentic Mexican restaurant offers freshly prepared appetizers such as chilled avocado soup with cilantro ($4.50) and entrees like chile rellenos ($12.50).

Seafood Ketch, Bass Harbor (☎207/244-7463). Great super-fresh seafood overlooking Bass Harbor. Reservations recommended.

Thurston's Lobster Pound, Steamboat Wharf Rd, Bernard (☎207/244-3320 or 1-800/235-3320). Dine on your lobster of choice at the only true lobster pound on the island with a casual cafeteria-style layout overlooking Bass Harbor. Open Memorial Day–Oct.

East to Canada

Looking at a typical map of the United States, you'd never dream that Canada stretches for five hundred miles beyond Maine to the east. In fact, few travelers venture far along the hundred miles of Maine coast beyond Acadia National Park, which is one reason the bulk of Down East Maine remains so little touched by change. Another reason is that this is bleak and windswept country, where high cliffs are battered by harsh seas. In summer, though, the weather is usually no worse than in the rest of Maine, and the coastal drive can be exhilarating. At those points where the road runs next to the sea, you get a real sense of the overwhelming power of the ocean, sweeping in to create the highest tides in the nation. Tourism is not big business in these parts, but each village has one or two B&Bs and low-priced restaurants. Outside of just the rugged scenery, highlights include **West Quoddy Head**, the easternmost point in the United States, and the quiet seaside town of **Eastport.**

Jonesport and Machias

The fishing harbor at **JONESPORT** on Rte-187 holds *Tootsies B&B* (☎207/497-5414; ④). A glorious high-arched iron bridge leads to the nature reserve of Beal's Island. **MACHIAS**, back on US-1, is even more picturesque, with a little waterfall right in the middle, and was the unlikely location of the first naval battle of the Revolutionary War, in 1775, when the townsfolk, brandishing pitchforks, swords, and firearms' commandeered the British schooner *Margaretta* after refusing to provide it with provisions. The attack was planned in the still-standing gambrel-roofed **Burnham Tavern**, Rte-192 just off of US-1 (June–mid-Sept Mon–Fri 9am–5pm; ☎207/255-4432; $2), which is set up as the tavern probably looked two hundred years ago, serving as a small museum to commemorate its place in history.

The best place to **eat** here is the *Artist's Café*, 3 Hill St (☎207/255-8900), with its moderately priced and frequently changing menu; chicken parmesan and lobster linguini are typical offerings. Meals are also good value at *Helen's Restaurant*, 32 Main St (☎207/255-8423), part of the *Machias Motor Inn* (☎207/255-4861; ④–⑤), which has sundecks and superb views. The restored *Riverside Inn and Restaurant*, on US-1 in East Machias (☎207/255-4134; ④–⑤), overlooks the Machias River and has a tasty prix-fixe menu six days a week. Cheaper and less romantic, but still comfortable, is the *Maineland Motel*, a mile east of town on US-1 (☎207/255-3334; ③–④).

East of town, Rte-191 heads along a regal and desolate portion of shoreline known as the **Bold Coast**. From the parking lot along Rte-191, just a little ways

east of **CUTLER**, two **hiking loops** head out to the windswept coast and back.
There's a small beach at Long Point Cove and you can sometimes catch a glimpse
of humpback whales from the cliffs. The Quoddy Regional Land Trust
(☎207/733-5509) has information on the trails and campsites along the way.

West Quoddy Head, Lubec, and Campobello Island

With a distinctive red-and-white striped lighthouse dramatically signaling its end-
point, **WEST QUODDY HEAD** is the easternmost part of the United States, jutting defiantly into the stormy Atlantic. You can see Canada just across the Bay of
Fundy, though for a better view, take the east three-mile trail in **Quoddy Head
State Park** that traces a winding line along precipitous cliffs.

Just beyond the turnoff for Quoddy Head, tiny **LUBEC** was once home to more
than twenty sardine packing plants. The number has dwindled to just one, but the
remnants of **McCurdy's Fish Company**, on Water Street, are enough to evoke
visions (and maybe even smells) of more prosperous times. Of several decent B&Bs
in town, try the *Peacock House*, 27 Summer St (☎207/733-2403; *www.nemaine
.com/peacock_house*; ④), the largest and most elegant, or the *Home Port Inn*, 45 Main
St (mid-June to mid-Oct; ☎207/733-2077 or 1-800/457-2077; ④), an old 1880 house
with seven guest rooms. The *Sunset Point Trailer Park*, on the west end of town, has
several cheap **campsites** overlooking the water (☎207/733-2150).

Campobello Island

Lubec is the gateway to **CAMPOBELLO ISLAND**, in New Brunswick, Canada,
where President Franklin D. Roosevelt summered from 1909 to 1921, before he
became president, and returned to sporadically during his presidency. The barn-
like house is now open to the public, and it's furnished just as the Roosevelts left
it. Perhaps the most interesting room, however, is the photo gallery on the south
end, depicting FDR at various stages in his political career. The rest of **Roosevelt
Campobello International Park** (mid-May to mid-Oct daily 9am–5pm; free;
www.fdr.net), located on Canadian soil but established jointly with the United
States, is good for a couple of hours of wandering. There are several coastal trails
and picnic areas and the drive out to **Liberty Point** is worth the effort.

Eastport

The seaside town of **EASTPORT**, poking into Cobscook Bay at the end of Rte-190,
is attractive and welcoming, though it's quite a ways off the beaten track. Canada
is only several miles away, but the closest border crossing is thirty miles north in
Calais; the bridge to Campobello Island in Lubec is forty miles from here by car –
you have to drive all the way around Cobscook Bay. Despite its remote location,
the town has capitalized on its deepwater commercial port, near the downtown
area. A second shipping pier was recently constructed at Estes Head on the south
edge of town, but it remains to be seen if the expansion will develop into a profitable venture. Cargo ships aside, the quiet town maintains the lonely air of a
remote outpost, with spotty weather, lots of old brick and clapboard buildings, and
hills that slope gently toward a collection of Canadian islands, just across the bay.
A result of the somewhat active local arts community, the **Eastport Gallery**, on
Water Street (☎207/853-4166), is worth a spin, usually housing an interesting collection of works by Maine artists in its two-story exhibit space.

Practicalities

There's not a whole lot to do in Eastport, but there are several decent **restaurants** grouped along Water Street, and some good-value **accommodation** is spread throughout the town's empty streets. *La Sardina Loca* at 28 Water St (☎207/853-2739) serves a host of Mexican entrees for less than $10 in a wonderfully eclectic interior. The *Baywatch Café*, 75 Water St (☎207/853-6030), dishes up cheap steaks, seafood, and sandwiches in a casual setting right next to the bay. Upstairs at 60 Water St, the funky *Blue Moon Coffee House* (☎207/853-2330) is a great place to fill up on caffeine, beer, wine, or light-vegetarian fare; there's also occasional live music. The *Weston House*, a boxy 1810 Federal-style home on 26 Boyton St (☎207/853-2907 or 1-800/853-2907; [4]–[5]), has huge rooms that overlook the water, while the *Kilby House Inn*, 122 Water St (☎207/853-0989 or 1-800/435-4529; [3]–[4]), is a snug old Victorian. Halfway between Eastport and Lubec off of US-1, **Cobscook Bay State Park** has the best **camping** around (mid-May to mid-Oct; ☎207/726-4412), with over a hundred beautifully situated campsites and good facilities.

Calais

The border between the United States and Canada weaves through the center of **Passamaquoddy Bay**; the towns to either side get on so well that they refused to fight in the US–UK War of 1812, and promote themselves jointly to tourists as the **Quoddy Loop** (information on ☎207/454-2597). It's perfectly feasible to take a "two-nation vacation," but each passage through customs and immigration between **CALAIS** (pronounced "callous") in the States and **St Stephen** in Canada does take a little while – and watch out for the confusion stemming from the fact that they're in different time zones. No trace now remains of Samuel de Champlain's 1604 attempt to found a colony on the diminutive St Croix Island, which you can see from an overlook on the main road. In town, the *Wickachee*, on Main Street (☎207/454-3400), serves big plates of seafood and steak. West Coastal Connections (☎207/546-2823 or 1-800/596-2823) runs a once-daily van from Calais to Ellsworth and Bar Harbor. The **visitor center**, 7 Union St (☎207/454-2211), has loads of information on activities and accommodations and a helpful staff.

Nearby, the Baring division of the **Moosehorn National Wildlife Refuge**, between Rte-191 and Charlotte Road (☎207/454-7161), is a good place to catch a glimpse of a bald eagle or woodcock; they maintain some fifty miles of hiking trails – also good for cross-country skiing in winter.

INLAND MAINE

The vast expanses of the **Maine interior**, stretching up into the cold far north, consist mostly of evergreen forests of pine, spruce, and fir, interspersed by the white birches and maples responsible for the spectacular fall colors. Only in the remote north is much of it genuine wilderness, however; elsewhere what you see is more likely to be woodlands cultivated by the timber companies.

Distances are large. Once you get away from the two largest cities nearer the sea – **Augusta**, the capital, and **Bangor** – it's roughly two hundred miles by road to the northern border at **Fort Kent**, while to drive between the two most likely inland bases, **Greenville** and **Rangeley** (where exiled psychologist Wilhelm Reich lived and is buried), takes three hours or more. Driving (there's no public transport) through this mountainous scenery can be a great pleasure, but you do need to know where you're going. There are few places to stay, even fewer gas stations, and beyond Bangor many roads are tolled access routes belonging to the lumber companies: gravel-surfaced, vulnerable to bad weather, and in any case often not heading anywhere in particular.

This landscape has evolved in a very unusual way. Many waterfront communities grew up without roads to serve them, back in the days when the timber harvest was floated downriver to the sea; other more recent settlements have only ever been accessible by seaplane. Now that mighty trucks carry the tree-trunks instead, roads are finally being pushed through, amid complaints that they are ruining the whole feel of the place.

If you have the time, this is great territory in which to **hike** – the **Appalachian Trail** starts its 2000-mile course down to Georgia at the top of Mount Katahdin – or **raft** on the swift **Penobscot** or **Kennebec** rivers. **Skiing** too is a popular activity, particularly at **Sugarloaf** or in the area around **Bethel** near the New Hampshire border, where the White Mountains National Forest extends into Maine.

Especially around the beautiful **Baxter State Park** and enormous **Moosehead Lake**, the forests are home to deer, beaver, a few bears, some recently introduced caribou, and plenty of **moose**. These endearingly gawky creatures (they look like badly drawn horses and are virtually blind) tend to be seen at early morning or dusk; in spring they come to lick the winter's salt off the roads, while in summer you may spot them feeding in shallow water. They do, however, cause major havoc on the roads, particularly at night, and each year significant numbers of drivers are killed in collisions with these hefty creatures.

Augusta and Hallowell

The capital of Maine since 1827, **AUGUSTA**, thirty miles north of Brunswick, is much quieter and less visited now than it was a hundred years ago. The lumber industry here really took off after the technique of making paper from wood was rediscovered in 1844, and Augusta also had a lucrative sideline at the time: each winter hundreds of thousands of tons of **ice**, cut from the Kennebec river, were shipped out as far as the Caribbean, in a trade now all but forgotten by history. There are informative displays on that past in the **Maine State Museum** (Mon–Fri 9am–5pm, Sat 10am–4pm, Sun 1–4pm; free), housed inside the ugly governmental complex that's shared by the Maine State Library and Archives just south of the capitol on State Street. Walking through dimly lit hallways past the well-designed and intriguing (if slightly outdated) "Twelve Thousand Years in Maine" exhibit, you actually get quite a good sense of how the state has developed over the centuries. Also of note is "Made in Maine," centered on a functional three-story water-powered mill and including re-created shops, factories, and homes from the eighteenth and nineteenth centuries.

Next door, the 180-foot dome of the imposing **Maine State House** (Mon–Fri 8.30am–4.30pm), a Charles Bulfinch design, is visible from nearly anywhere in Augusta. The rather impressive granite structure, completed in 1832, has been subject to several renovations that have nearly doubled its size. You can take a self-guided **tour**, though unless you have a particular interest in politics or architecture, this should kill no more than twenty minutes of your time. If you're so inclined, free guided tours can be arranged by calling ☎207/287-1408.

Hallowell

Just two short miles south of Augusta beside the gently sloping banks of the Kennebec River, the quaint haven of **HALLOWELL** is far more pleasant than its governmentally focused neighbor, especially along its main drag, **Water Street**, lined with some excellent **restaurants** and a couple of diverting bookstores and antique shops. Once a major port for lumber and granite, as well as a shipbuilding center, the place boasts a number of stately historic homes left over from those prosperous times, mostly perched in the picturesque hills above town. A small population of artists and craftsmen have arrived in recent years; for **information** on visiting one of the many studios in the area, contact the Kennebec Valley Chamber of Commerce (☎207/623-4559).

Practicalities

If you plan to stay in the Augusta area, the best-value **accommodation** is the *Susse Chalet Motor Lodge* on Whitten Road at the Maine Turnpike's Augusta Winthrop exit (☎207/622-3776; ③–④). The sole **B&B** is over in Hallowell, the *Maple Hill Farm*, set on 62 acres on Outlet Road, off of Shady Lane (☎207/622-2708 or 1-800/622-2708, *www.maplebb.com*; ④–⑤); you can feed the farm animals in the morning before enjoying a delicious breakfast. Decent family **camping** is available in Winthrop at the *Augusta West Lakeside Resort* (May 15–Oct 15; ☎207/377-9993).

For **food**, the lobster rolls at *Burnsie's Homestyle Sandwiches*, on Hitchhorn Street next to the capitol (☎207/622-6425), are favorites with the politicians, while *Curly's*, 750 Main St (☎207/933-2745), does tasty, moderately priced seafood. The *Thai Star*, 611 Civic Center Drive (☎207/621-2808), is another good bet, with an authentic ethnic menu featuring spicy crispy duck, yellow curry, and jasmine rice. Along the short main drag of Hallowell, *Slates*, 167 Water St (Tues–Sat; ☎207/622-9575), is one of the best restaurants in the state, with a friendly atmosphere, fair prices, and original entrees like Indian grilled snapper with apple banana chutney. Nearby, the *River Café*, 119 Water St (☎207/622-2190), gets high marks for its huge portions of Lebanese, Middle Eastern, and occasionally Indian food, while *Michelle's*, 144 Water St (☎207/629-9151), doubles as an art gallery and restaurant, serving both German and French cuisine in an intimate dining room.

Bangor

BANGOR, 120 miles northeast of Portland at the intersection of Rte-1A and I-95, is not a place to spend much time, although its plentiful motels and the big new Bangor Mall on Hogan Road north of town make it a good last stop before the interior. As Maine's third largest city (33,000 people), the place is noticeably more urban and rough around the edges (for Maine, at least) than the state's smaller towns, serving as a major source of goods and services for the stretch of coast twenty miles south. The town is also along the main transportation route between Portland and points further east and north, so if you're using public transport, you may well find yourself here with an hour or two to kill.

A-1 DINER

The state of Maine boasts a decent array of authentic diners; one that tries to combine this authenticity with a modern flair – and succeeds in doing so – is the **A-1 Diner**, 3 Bridge St, in the town of **Gardiner** just south of Hallowell (☎207/582-4804). In addition to your typical burgers, shakes, and fries (all excellent), this 1946 throwback, complete with vinyl booths and a long counter, ventures into the atypical realm of gourmet food and vegetarian specials. Owned by a pair of professionally trained chefs who rather enjoy experimenting behind the guise of a greasy spoon – don't be surprised if you find banana almond French toast, Greek lemon soup, or Cajun meatloaf on the perpetually changing menu.

Arrival, information and accommodation

Many of the major airlines service the newly renovated **Bangor International Airport** (☎207/947-0384) on the western edge of town. Frequent **bus service** is available from Bangor to most other parts of the state. Concord Trailways, which docks at the Transportation Center at 1039 Union St (☎207/945-4000 or 1-800/639-3317), can take you to Bar Harbor, Ellsworth, Portland, Camden, and other smaller coastal cities. The CYR Bus Line (☎1-800/244-2335) heads north from the Trailways Center to Caribou, stopping in several small towns along the way. Vermont Transit Lines has a terminal at 158 Main St (☎207/945-3000 or 1-800/894-3355), from which you can travel to Boston via Portland and Portsmouth or connect with Greyhound routes to other destinations. If you're spending any time at all in Bangor, you will find **The Bus** (☎207/947-0536; 75¢, carnet of five tickets $3), to be a handy means of getting around. Pick up a route map at the Bangor Depot on Main Street.

There's a helpful **information** center at the Bangor Region Chamber of Commerce, 519 Main St (☎207/947-0307, *www.bangorregion.com*), which has the typical collection of brochures and hotel information. Right in the center of town is Bangor's best **place to stay**, the *Phenix Inn*, 20 Broad St (☎207/947-0411; ④–⑤), an old green brick building with 33 comfortably furnished rooms. Cheaper are the *Motel 6*, at 1100 Hammond St (☎207/947-6921 or 1-800/466-8356; ②–③), and the *Main Street Inn*, opposite Paul Bunyan at 480 Main St (☎207/942-5282; ④).

The Town

In its prime, Bangor was the undisputed "Lumber Capital of the World." Every winter its raucous population of "River Tigers" went upstream to brand the felled logs, which they then maneuvered down the swiftly flowing Penobscot River as the thaw came in April, reaching Bangor in time to carouse the summer away in the grog shops of Peppermint Row. Bangor also exported ice to the West Indies – and got rum in return. The forests were thinning and the prosperous days were coming to an end, however, when in October 1882 Oscar Wilde addressed a large crowd at the new Opera House and spoke diplomatically of "such advancement . . . in so small a city." A devastating fire in 1911 leveled much of the city, although a fair amount of the lumber barons' lavish mansions survived. One such mansion, along West Broadway, complete with a spider web-shaped iron gate, is now the suitably Gothic residence of horror author **Stephen King**, a Maine native who relocated here in 1980. You can browse the full collection of King's works, including some limited editions and collectibles, at Bett's Bookstore, 26 Main St (☎207/947-7052).

Bangor's other claim to fame, the 31-foot **Paul Bunyan** statue along Main Street south of downtown, is perhaps the largest such statue in the world – excepting one or two in Minnesota – though it looks more like a brightly painted model airplane kit than a statue. Bunyan was allegedly born here in 1834, though several other prominent logging towns across the US would probably dispute that claim. From mid-May until the end of July there's **harness racing** at Bass Park on Main Street (☎207/947-6744), just behind the statue; admission is $1 but the potential to lose money is unlimited. The same venue hosts the **Bangor State Fair**, in the last week of July and the first in August.

Closer to downtown, a few short blocks off Main Street in a building designed by notable Boston architect Richard Upjohn (who also built the Isaac Farrar Mansion across the street), the **Bangor Historical Society Museum**, 159 Union St (April–Dec Tues–Fri noon–4pm; June–Sept also Sat; noon–4pm ☎207/942-5766; $5), presents some of the state's better historical exhibits in its stately first-floor galleries and more modern upstairs space. The society also conducts special guided "Best of Bangor" bus tours Thursdays and the first Saturday of the month, July through September, departing from the Chamber of Commerce at 10.30am ($5).

If you've got the time, drive up to the **Thomas Hill Standpipe**, off of Union Street on Thomas Hill Road. The massive cylindrical water tank was constructed in 1897 and still provides 1.75 million gallons of water to the residents of Bangor. Though there's really not much to it, the strange shingled structure is set on a hilltop with a partial view of the landscape. Once a year, usually in the first week of October, the standpipe's observatory is opened to the public, providing panoramic views of the surrounding countryside. Call the Chamber of Commerce (☎207/947-0307) for details.

A few miles north of Bangor, the Maine Center for the Arts (☎207/581-1755), at the University of Maine in **Orono**, runs a series of big-name concerts each summer. Orono is named after the eighteenth-century Chief Joseph Orono; a small island nearby is now a rather sad reservation running summer bingo sessions.

Eating and drinking

Bangor does not have any great wealth of good **places to eat**, though there's an incongruous amount of ethnic eats. For fresh, authentic bagels and a huge selection of other kosher foods, you can't beat the *Bagel Shop*, 1 Main St (☎207/947-1654). The *Bahaar Pakistan Restaurant*, 23 Hammond St (☎207/945-5975), does a decent lunch buffet for only $5.95, while the *Siam Garden*, 411 Main St (☎207/947-7911), serves a wide selection of authentic curries and noodles in an unlovely setting.

The place to **drink** in town is the *Sea Dog Brewing Company*, 26 Front St near the marina along the Penobscot (☎207/947-8004 or 1-888/4-SEADOG; *www .seadogbrewing.com*), which has frequent live music and a good selection of hand-crafted brews. The brewery also offers lunch, cocktail, and lobster-bake boat trips of varying lengths on the *River Dog* cruise boat (May–Columbus Day; ☎207/947-7194; $8–15). The *Whig and Courier*, 18 Broad St (☎207/947-4095), is a straightahead pub, with burgers, cheesesteaks, and a wide variety of beers on tap. Across the street, the *New Moon Café*, 21 Main St (☎207/990-2233), is a favorite hangout for Bangor's hip younger set, with snacks, coffee and espresso, and live music.

Bethel and around

The remote, quintessentially New England town of **BETHEL**, nestled in the Maine woods about seventy miles north of Portland, may appear rather sleepy, but it's an excellent year-round base from which to explore the outdoors, most notably in the **White Mountains** and **Grafton Notch State Park**. With a prestigious college preparatory school, the Gould Academy (*www.gouldacademy.org*), and a well-known managerial training center, the NTL Institute (*www.ntl.org*), Bethel has long attracted a rather academic and prosperous population; in fact, the town was once home to famous neurobiologist Dr John Gehring's clinic for people with neurological disorders.

The Town

The **Bethel Common**, at the south end of Main Street along Broad Street, is flanked by a number of stately white-clapboard nineteenth-century homes and dominated by the sprawling **Bethel Inn and Country Club** (see "Practicalities" overleaf), whose yellow Victorian buildings and first-rate golf course spread out over several acres of grassy terrain. The 1813 Federal-style **Dr Moses Mason House**, also on the common (July & Aug Tues–Sun 1–4pm; other months by appointment; $2; ☎207/824-2908), holds an engaging and worthwhile museum that includes murals by painter Rufus Porter, period furnishings, and special exhibits relating to Bethel's history (the building also houses Bethel's active Historical Society). Depending on who's working, you might also get a quick look at the **John Hastings Homestead**, the former home of a founder of the Gould Academy across the street, that was built in 1820 and has been preserved as it stood at the turn of the century. For a more detailed look at the town's architectural highlights, pick up the **walking tour** brochure at the historical society or the Chamber of Commerce.

Just a few miles north of Bethel off of Rte-2 on Sunday River Road, the **Sunday River Ski Resort** ($49 full-day lift ticket; ☎207/824-3000 or 1-800/543-2754, *www .sundayriver.com*), is fast becoming one of the major alpine ski areas in New England. Their snowmaking system guarantees skiing between November and May, with seventeen lifts servicing eight mountain peaks. In summer, Sunday

---

MEAD PAPER COMPANY FOREST AND MILL TOURS

Though it seems a blatant public-relations stunt, the forest and **mill tours** offered by the Mead Paper Company in **RUMFORD**, a few miles east of Bethel along Rte-2 (July–Sept; call ☎207/369-2045 for reservations), are rather interesting and informative. As expected, the guides make everything the company does seem absolutely environmentally sound, so you should listen with a skeptical ear. The first part of the seven-hour tour is devoted to wildlife habitat, harvest technologies, and reforestation, while the second half takes you inside a quarter-mile-long manufacturing facility that produces sixty tons of paper per day. You'll come away having a pretty good concept of the papermaking process in addition to understanding a bit about (one side of) logging politics. Though the tours are prohibitively long, free snacks and lunch are provided. Shorter (2hr) mill-only tours are given Tuesdays and Thursdays at 10am in the administration building at 35 Hartford St in Rumford.

River doubles as a popular **mountain bike** park. The attraction here is the chance to ride the lifts up the hill with your bike so you can speed down at breakneck pace. The White Cap Base Lodge distributes maps, sells lift passes ($8 one-time only, $22 all day), rents bikes, and offers instruction. The logging and farming roads around Bethel offer other good (free) opportunities for mountain biking. Stop by Bethel Outdoor Adventures, 121 Mayville Rd (☎207/824-4224 or 1-800/533-3607), for route advice, maps, and **bike rentals** ($25 per day). They also rent **canoes** and **kayaks** and do guided trips.

Bethel is also known for its **cross-country skiing**, and there are several privately owned resorts in addition to the trails maintained in the White Mountain National Forest and Grafton Notch State Park. Some 25 miles of cross-country ski trails penetrate the wilderness at the beginner-oriented *Sunday River Inn* and Cross Country Ski Center, on Sunday River Road (☎207/824-2410). Don't miss the trail that leads to the 1872 **Artist's Covered Bridge**, off of Sunday River Road, which is a good spot for **swimming** during the summer. You can also cross-country ski at Carter's Cross Country Ski Center, with eighteen miles of trails at its location off of Rte-26 in Oxford, and forty miles of groomed trails in Bethel on Intervale Road (☎207/539-4848).

Practicalities

Bethel is not accessible via public transport. As a last resort, you can catch a ride from Portland on the Bethel Express (☎207/824-4646) or the Airport Car Service (☎1-800/649-5071) for about $90 (it works out considerably less the more passengers there are); call at least 24hrs in advance. A similar service is operated by Airport Limo & Taxi (☎207/893-1962 or 1-800/517-9442). Bethel does, however, have a good concentration of **places to stay** once you do get there. In town, the *Bethel Inn and Country Club*, on the Common (☎207/824-2175 or 1-800/654-0125; ⑦–⑧), is the town's full-service four-star **resort**, with a golf course, tennis courts, a health club, and fine dining. More affordable are the *Briar Lea B&B*, 150 Mayville Rd (☎207/824-4717 or 1-888/479-5735, *www.nettx.com/briarlea*; ④), a renovated 150-year-old Georgian farmhouse, and the *Chapman Inn*, right in the center of town on the common (☎207/824-2657, *www.bethelmaine.com/chapmaninn*; ④–⑤), which also has **dorm beds** for $25, including breakfast. The *Holidae House*, Main Street (☎207/824-3400), is another decent option, with double rooms starting at $45. The local Chamber of Commerce, Cross Street (Mon–Fri 8am–5pm, Sat 10am–6pm, Sun noon–5pm; ☎207/824-2282 or 1-800/442-5826, *www.bethelmaine.com*), can help you out in any case, and is also a good source for maps and brochures.

The quiet *Crocker Pond Campground*, off of Songo Pond Road (Rte-5) just south of town (mid-May to mid-Oct; ☎207/824-2134; $12), has eight secluded and rather primitive **campsites** that are maintained by the US Forest Service, while the more family-oriented *Riverside Campground*, 121 Mayville Rd (☎207/824-4224 or 1-800/553-3607), has both RV and tent sites on the banks of the Androscoggin River.

Bethel's best **restaurant** is *Mother's*, Upper Main Street (☎207/824-2589), where you can dine on concoctions like grilled breast of duck with honey-ginger and soy glaze, and crepes with pecan and sweet potato stuffing in a cozy book-lined dining room (entrees $12–19). Excellent pizza can be had at *Breau's Pizza & Subs*, Rte-2 (☎207/824-3192), which also serves ice cream, clam chowder, lobster rolls, and hearty breakfasts. *Café Di Cocoa,* Lower Main Street (☎207/824-5282), serves bold vegetarian and ethnic specialties, sandwiches, soups, and espresso in a funky dining room (winter breakfast, lunch, and dinner; rest of year no dinner). Surprisingly flavorful Chinese food – including a $5.95 lunch buffet – can be had at the *Sun Garden*, in the Mountain View Mall along Walker's Mill Road (☎207/824-3707). In town, the place to **drink** is the *Suds Pub*, Lower Main Street (☎207/824-6558), with live entertainment five nights per week and a good selection of microbrews until 1am. Tamer is *Java House*, Lower Main St, near the railroad tracks (☎207/824-0562), for coffee and fresh baked goods. North of town along Rte-2 at Sunday River Road, the *Sunday River Brewing Co* (☎207/824-4253) is particularly popular with skiers, serving freshly brewed ales and hearty pub fare, with occasional live music.

Maine's White Mountains

Bethel sits just on the edge of the fifty thousand acres of the **White Mountain National Forest** that fall within Maine's borders, the center of which is **Evans Notch**, just as spectacular as any found in New Hampshire. Stop by their helpful **visitor center**, 18 Mayville Rd, Bethel, ME 04217 (☎207/824-2134), for maps, hiking suggestions, and information on campsite availability. Particularly good **hikes** through stands of birch and pine in the forest include the difficult 9.8-mile (about 7hr) **Baldface Circle Trail**, starting at the trailhead parking area just beyond the AMC's Cold River Camp (☎603/694-3291), and the easier 1.8-mile loop that begins on Rte-113, across the bridge just north of *Hastings Campground* and leads up to the **Roost**, a granite overlook providing views of the Wild River Valley and Evans Notch.

North from Bethel: Grafton Notch State Park

North of Bethel, Rte-26 bisects beautiful **Grafton Notch State Park** (May–Oct; $2; ☎207/287-3821), a patch of rugged mountains, gurgling streams, cascading waterfalls, and bizarre geological formations. Among these, the **Screw Auger Falls**, where the Bear River has carved out a twisting gorge through the solid granite, is good for wading. Just north, easy trails lead to **Moose Cave Gorge** and through the 900-foot-long **Mother Walker Falls Gorge**, which features several natural stone bridges. More difficult trails head up **Old Speck Mountain**, Maine's third highest. Follow the 3.8-mile (one-way) **Old Speck Trail** from the Grafton Notch trailhead parking area up numerous switchbacks and past the Cascade Brook Falls to the Mahoosuc Trail, which affords sweeping views at the summit. A slightly shorter option is the **Table Rock Loop**, a two hour jaunt that

---

BACKCOUNTRY SHELTERS IN MAINE'S WHITE MOUNTAINS

The Evans Notch Ranger District maintains five **backcountry shelters**. Some are nothing more than a sleeping platform with a pit toilet, while others have stoves, insulation, and a small staff. All are accessible only on foot and charge a small fee, depending, of course, on what is offered. For more information on this unique experience contact the **Evans Notch Visitor Center** (see above) or the White Mountain National Forest, Backcountry Facilities, Androscoggin Ranger District, 80 Glen Rd, Gorham, NH 03581 (☎603/466-2713).

also departs from the main trailhead parking area up Baldplate Mountain to Table Rock, where you are treated for your efforts with mountain views. There is no camping in Grafton Notch State Park.

Rangeley

RANGELEY is only just in Maine, a little way east of New Hampshire and even shorter distance from Quebec, at the intersection of routes 4 and 16. Furthermore, as the café-bar *Doc Grant's*, Main Street (☎207/864-3449), makes a great show of telling you, it is equidistant from the North Pole and the equator (3107.5 miles), though that doesn't mean it's on the main road to anywhere. It has always been a resort, served in 1900 by two train lines and several steamships, with the real attraction then being the fishing in the spectacularly named Mooselookmeguntic Lake.

Today there's still one primary, albeit unorthodox, attraction, the remote **Wilhelm Reich Museum**, Dodge Pond Rd, about halfway along the north side of Rangeley Lake, a mile up on a side track off Rte-16 (July & Aug Wed–Sun 1–5pm; Sept Sun 1–5pm; $4; ☎207/864-3443, *www.somtel.com/~wreich*), where Wilhelm Reich eventually made his American home after fleeing Germany in 1933. Although he was an associate of Freud in Vienna and wrote the acclaimed *Mass Psychology of Fascism*, Reich is best remembered for developing the orgone energy accumulator. He claimed it could create rain and dissipate nuclear radiation; skeptical authorities focused on the not very specific way in which it was said to collect and harness human sexual energy. In a tragic end to his career, Reich was imprisoned after a wayward student broke an injunction forbidding the transportation of his accumulators across state lines, and he died in the federal penitentiary in Lewisberg, PA, in November 1957. He is buried here, amid the neat lawns and darting hummingbirds, and his house remains a center for the study of his work.

South of town along Rte-17, it's worth seeking out **Angel Falls**, which, at ninety feet, are the highest in Maine. There's a good **swimming** spot at the base. Getting there is a bit complicated; take Rte-17 eighteen miles south of Oquossoc, go west onto the dirt road and across the bridge at highway mile marker 6102, turn right onto the railroad line, after 3.5 miles, turn left on the gravel road and follow the marked trail. Nearby, in the old mining town of Byron, you can also swim in the crystal clear waters of **Coos Canyon**, just off of Rte-17.

Practicalities

The *Rangeley Inn* on Main Street (☎207/864-3341, *www.rangeleyinn.com*; ⑤–⑥) stands between Rangeley Lake and the smaller bird sanctuary of Haley Pond, so you can stay right in town and have a room that backs onto a scene of utter tranquility; there's also a gorgeous old wooden dining room. *Northwoods B&B* on Main Street (☎207/864-2440; ⑤–⑥) is a good second choice. Otherwise, the Chamber of Commerce (see below) can provide lists of private home/condo rentals and "remote campsites" around the lake – which really are remote, several of them inaccessible by road. The *Red Onion*, 77 Main St (☎207/864-5022), is good for an array of inexpensive **food** including pizza, steak, and pasta; the *People's Choice Café*, also on Main St (☎207/864-5220), is pricier, though the portions are huge and the desserts divine.

Twenty miles north of Rangeley, the peaceful *Grants Camps* beside Kennebago Lake (☎207/864-3608 or 1-800/633-4815) arranges fishing, canoeing, and windsurfing, with accommodation in comfortable cabins overlooking the lake, including all meals, costing around $100 per person per day; there are lower weekly rates. A more accessible **campground** is *Cathedral Pines* (☎207/246-3491), just north of Stratton on Eustis Road. At its entrance stands a memorial to **Benedict Arnold's** expedition to Quebec in 1775, which passed this way, and to Colonel Timothy Bigelow, who climbed the mountain in a "vain endeavor to see the city of Québec."

Rangeley Lakes' **Chamber of Commerce**, down by Lakeside Park (☎207/864-5364 or 1-800/MT-LAKES, *www.rangeley.maine.com*), has details of various activities, including snowmobiling and moose-watching **canoeing** expeditions. One fun thing to do is take a **seaplane** trip with the Mountain Air Service (☎207/864-5307) – a fifteen-minute tour, flying low over vast forests and tiny lakes, costs $25 per person.

Sugarloaf USA and Kingfield

The road east of Rangeley cuts through prime moose-watching territory – in fact, locals call Rte-16 E "Moose Alley." After about fifty miles, in the Carrabassett Valley, looms the huge mountain of **SUGARLOAF USA**, Maine's biggest ski resort (☎207/237-2000 or 1-800/843-5623, *www.sugarloaf.com*). A spectacular place for skiers of all abilities, this condo-studded center would be a more popular destination if it weren't for the fact that the nearest airport is a two-hour drive away in Portland. Summer activities include guided **mountain bike tours** with Bigelow Bikes (☎207/237-6830) and the Sugarloaf Bike Park, which maintains an extensive trail system on the ski mountain and has a full-service bike shop (☎207/237-2000). There's also a **golf** course here, designed by Robert Trent Jones Jr. Near the base of the Sugarloaf access road, just off of Rte-27, the amiable *Sugarloaf Brewing Company* (☎207/237-2211) brews up seven delicious original beers and also has a decent menu of filling pizzas and pub food.

The best base for Sugarloaf is fifteen miles south in the tiny town of **KINGFIELD**. The gorgeous *Inn on Winter Hill*, Winter Hill (☎207/265-5425 or 1-800/233-9687; ⑤), is a lovingly restored Georgian Revival house with big rooms, an outdoor pool, hot tub, tennis court, and the excellent *Julia's* dining room (winter only). Down on the main street, the *Herbert Hotel* (☎207/265-2000; ④) has less attractive but functional rooms and a good restaurant. On Rte-142 in Weld, southwest of Kingfield, the *Lake Webb House* (☎207/585-2479; ③) offers very affordable accommodations in an old farmhouse with a huge porch; breakfast is included. For **food**, *Longfellows Restaurant* on Main Street (☎207/265-4394) serves pastas, sandwiches, and chicken; entrees are two-for-one on Tuesdays, while *The Village Inn Restaurant*, Rte 27, Belgrade Lakes (☎207/495-5553), is *the* place to get award-winning roast duckling.

Kingfield was the birthplace of twins Francis and Freelan Stanley, who invented, among other things, a steam-powered car and the dry-plate photographic process (which they sold to Kodak, amassing a considerable fortune). The **Stanley Museum** on School Street (May–Nov Tues–Sun 1–4pm; Dec–Apr Mon–Fri 9am–5pm; ☎207/265-2729, *www.stanleymuseum.org*; $2) celebrates their story. Part of the main room is given over to their sister Chansonetta, a remarkable photographer whose studies of turn-of-the-century rural and urban workers have been widely published. Other exhibits include working steam cars from the early 1900s – ask nicely and you just may get a ride.

Moosehead Lake and around

Serene waters lap gently at the miles of deserted thickly wooded shores around desolate **Moosehead Lake**, which at 117 square miles is the largest in Maine. As part of Maine's remote interior, the region was once relatively unknown, visited by Maine families, snowmobile fanatics, and serious hunters and fishermen; it's only now that more widespread discovery is taking place. **Greenville** is the sole settlement of any size on the lake, and it makes a good base from which to explore the area, especially if you're after moose sightings or if you intend to go whitewater rafting, though **The Forks**, a sporty settlement along the **Kennebec River** and US-201, has emerged as the center of the industry. West of the lake along Rte-15, gritty **Jackman**, big with the **snowmobile** crowd in winter, is the last stop before the Canadian border on the way to Quebec.

Getting to Moosehead Lake

Moosehead Lake is roughly two and a half hours from Portland by car; the best way is via I-95 as far as Newport to Rte-11, Rte-23, and then Rte-6 N. While the majority of the **roads** in northern Maine are owned and maintained by huge logging and paper conglomerates, the public is often permitted access. On the **Golden Road**, for example, which connects Millinocket with the Quebec border, travelers can pay a $4 fee at one of several gates for the privilege of driving its 96-mile length. Keep in mind, however, that the often unpaved roads are used primarily by logging trucks and that services are few and far between. Use caution and always yield to passing logging trucks. Distances are great and poor road conditions dictate slow travel speeds; be sure you have a good map and plenty of gas before you set out. In the towns especially, pay attention to the posted **speed limits** – local police are not shy about giving tickets if you're going only a few miles per hour too fast. For **information** on road availability and fees, call the Northern Paper Company at ☎207/723-2229.

Greenville

With a population of 1800, the rugged outpost of **GREENVILLE**, at the southern end of Moosehead Lake, is another nineteenth-century lumber town that now makes its living primarily from tourism. People come from all over to see wild **moose**, indigenous to the area, and which the town has been quick to exploit; there is nary a business around here that doesn't somehow incorporate the animal into its name. For several weeks in June, there's even an annual celebration, creatively named **Moosemania** (call ☎207/695-2702 for more information). The Beaver Creek Guide Service (☎207/695-2265 or 695-3091) offers three-hour guided moose-watching tours daily during summer and early fall, while the *Birches Resort* (☎207/534-7305 or 1-800/825-9453) offers, for $25, moose-spotting cruises, where you're also likely to spot eagles, bears, and peregrine falcons.

The town isn't exceptionally pretty and it's certainly not very large, but it is well positioned for explorations throughout the Maine woods. With a bank, grocery store, post office, and a handful of shops and restaurants, it is also the area's commercial center. The main attraction is the restored **steamboat**, *Katahdin*, which tours the lake and serves as the floating (nonprofit) Moosehead Marine Museum (July & Aug cruises at 10am & 12.30pm Tues, Wed, Sat & Sun; Sept weekends only; ☎207/695-2716; 3-hour cruise $18, 8-hour cruise $35). Near the dock, tiny **Thoreau Park** has a couple of picnic tables and a sign commemorating and describing the writer's 1857 visit to Moosehead Lake. Also close by is the **Gallery** (☎207/695-0311), where a chatty husband-and-wife team sells useless junk and paints animal portraits. You'll soon want to get out of town, however, and a good way to explore is on a **mountain bike**; you can rent them ($25 per day), along with canoes, kayaks, and camping equipment at Northwoods Outfitters, on Main Street (☎207/695-3288 or 1-800/530-8859, *www.northwoodsoutfitters.com*).

Practicalities

The **Chamber of Commerce**, just south of town on Rte-6/15 (summer daily 10am–5pm; rest of year Thurs–Tues 10am–4pm; ☎207/695-2702), has lots of information about area activities and accommodations. As an alternative, the **Maine Forest Service** (☎207/695-3721) can provide information on their many free campsites in the area. There's not much in the way of interesting **food** options here; the local favorite is *Flatlander's*, on Main Street (☎207/695-3373), which grills up cheap burgers and hotdogs along with a selection of basic seafood and meat dishes. South of town in quiet Monson, the *Appalachian Station* (☎207/997-3648), on Rte-15, is an especially good place for a hearty down-home breakfast or lunch.

Accommodations are generally upscale wilderness retreats that were built for rugged hunters, though there are exceptions. The *Birches Resort*, north of Greenville near the small village of Rockwood (☎207/534-7305 or 1-800/825-9453, *www.birches.com*; ③–⑦), for example, offers both rustic and first-class

WHITEWATER RAFTING

The **Penobscot** and the **Kennebec** are the two most popular rivers in Maine for the exhilarating sport of **whitewater rafting**, which has caught on in the past decade as a major recreational activity here (and in the rest of the country). **The Forks**, along Hwy-201 between Kingfield and Greenville, is the undisputed rafting center, and the majority of the outfitters are based there, along with the deluxe lodges and camps they've built to house the eager outdoors enthusiasts. Run between mid-May and mid-October, most trips depart in the early morning and return by mid-afternoon. Levels of difficulty vary, but the rafting companies insist that people of all athletic abilities are welcome on most trips, which, as dictated by state law, are all led by certified "Maine guides." Raft Maine (☎1-800/723-8633, *www.raftmaine.com*) is an association comprised of several outfitters that can answer your questions. The following is but a partial list of potential – and reliable – options.

Magic Falls, The Forks (☎207/663-2220 or 1-800/207-7238, *www.magicfalls.com*). One of the smaller, more personal rafting companies. Runs the Kennebec, Penobscot, and Dead rivers. One-day trips cost $65–90. There's a new lodge with a bar and riverside cabins.

Mountain Magic Expeditions, The Forks (☎207/672-3994). This friendly company offers personal service and an unpretentious attitude. They run the Dead and Kennebec rivers and their downscale base camp on Hwy-201 offers camping, a communal lodge, and warm showers. Trips cost $65 weekdays and $75 on weekends.

New England Outdoor Center, Hwy-201, thirteen miles past Bingham in Caratunk (☎207/723-5438 or 1-800/766-7238, *www.neoc.com*). A family-oriented outfit that puts on trips on the Kennebec, Penobscot, and Dead rivers, with campsites, cabin-tents, housekeeping cabins, or B&B accommodations. They operate facilities both in Caratunk, south of The Forks, and at the Rice Farm, near Millinocket. There are also lakeside cabins on Millinocket Lake. Rafting trips cost $79–114 and combination packages are available.

Northern Outdoors, Hwy-201, The Forks (☎207/663-4466 or 1-800/765-7238, *www.northernoutdoors.com*). The oldest and largest of Maine's whitewater outfitters, running both the Kennebec and the Penobscot and offering longer overnight trips. One-day trips cost $79–114, including lunch. Operates relatively upscale facilities at the *Forks Resort Center* and the Penobscot Outdoor Center, near Baxter State Park.

Professional River Runners, Hwy-201, West Forks (☎207/663-2229 or 1-800/325-3911, *www.proriverrunners.com*). Smaller outfit that runs both single-day and overnight trips; their guides are particularly good. No accommodations, but will help with referrals. Full-day trip on the Penobscot and Kennebec costs $69–100.

Wilderness Expeditions, *The Birches Resort*, off of Rte-15, Rockwood (☎1-800/825-9453, *www.birches.com*). Another of the large, full-scale resorts, with a base off of Rte-157 near Baxter State Park, along Hwy-201 just north of The Forks, and on Moosehead Lake near Rockwood. In addition to whitewater rafting, they offer many other activities, including kayaking, moose-cruises, eco-tours, and, in winter, cross-country skiing and snowmobiling. The facilities are top-notch. One-day rafting trips cost between $85 and $1159, depending on the month, day, and river. Half-day trips are also available.

accommodations along with a host of outdoor activities. There's also a rather gourmet dining room overlooking the lake. More traditional choices back in Greenville include the Victorian *Pleasant Street Inn*, on Pleasant Street

(☎207/695-3400; ④–⑤), and the comfortable *Devlin House*, on Lily Bay Road (☎207/695-2229; ⑤), which also has excellent lake views. Also on Lily Bay Road, the *Lodge at Moosehead* (☎207/695-4400; ⑦) is the region's luxury hotel, with a beautiful hillside location.

North of Greenville, the *Kineo House*, an old cottage with six guest rooms (☎207/534-8812; ④), is the only place to stay on **Kineo,** an isolated nature preserve in the middle of the lake; boat shuttle service and breakfast are included. Even if you're not staying there, you can still get a shuttle boat to Kineo in Rockwood (daily 8am–5pm; ☎207/534-8812; $5). Island trails lead to the top of dramatic **Mount Kineo**, whose flint-like cliff face rises some 800ft above the lake's surface.

Other good **hikes** in the area include the trip through the **Gulf Hagas**, a 300-foot gorge fifteen miles east of town off of Greenville Road, the walk to an old B-52 crash site, and difficult climbs to the summits of 3196-foot **Big Squaw Mountain** and 3230-foot **Big Spencer Mountain**. Contact the Chamber of Commerce for more information.

Greenville is also the largest **seaplane** base in New England; contact Currier's Flying Service (☎207/695-2778) or Folsom's (☎207/695-2821) for flight times and prices.

Jackman

Fifty miles west of Greenville, there's not much to **JACKMAN**, another old logging town that's somewhat reluctantly attempting to make the transition into a tourist destination. Situated next to deserted Wood Pond, less than twenty miles from the Canadian border (many of the radio stations here are in French), its main attraction is as a haven for **snowmobiles**, which take over the parking lots and surrounding lumber roads in winter. You can rent one of the noisy craft at the New England Outdoor Center, 240 Katahdin Ave (1-800/766-7238) or the *Sky Lodge* on Hwy-201 (☎207/668-2171), for about $130 per day. **Ice fishing** is also popular in winter and several local businesses sell non-resident licenses, bait, and tackle. In summer, a forty-mile circuit known as the Moose River **Bow Trip** is one of the better flat-water **canoe trips** in the state, with good fishing and several **campsites** scattered along the way. The Jackman Moose River Chamber of Commerce, Main Street (☎207/668-4171), can help you locate a guide, if you so desire. The newly refurbished *Bishops Motel*, right in the center of town at 461 Main St (☎207/668-3231 or 1-888/991-7669, *www.maineguide.com/jackman/bishops*; ④), provides basic, clean **rooms** at reasonable rates. *Sally Mountain Cabins* (☎207/668-5621 or 1-800/644-5621; ②) has rustic cabins along the lake with full kitchens and private baths. The *Moose Point Tavern*, just off Main Street (☎207/668-4012), is the best place to **eat** in town, not just for its views of the lake, but its hearty selection of meat dishes, including venison steak with blackberry sage sauce ($16.95); there's also a pleasant bar on the premises.

Baxter State Park and the far north

Driving through northern Maine can feel as though you're trespassing on the private fiefdoms of the logging companies; only **Baxter State Park** is public land. However, you're pretty much free to hike, camp, and explore anywhere you like, so long as you let people know what you're doing (only a sensible precaution, after all). The scenery is pretty much the same everywhere, although of course to get the best of it – to experience what Thoreau described in *Maine Woods* – you need to leave your car at some point and set off into the backwoods. You can read an excerpt from *Maine Woods* in the Contexts section of the Guide: "New England in Literature," p.549.

Katahdin Iron Works and Millinocket

Five miles north of Brownsville Junction on Rte-11, an inconspicuous left turn leads to the **Katahdin Iron Works** at Silver Lake (summer daily 9am–5pm), built in 1843. It's quite remarkable how little remains of what one hundred years ago was a thriving industrial community: one solitary brick oven and the tower of the blast furnace, stark and forlorn at the end of a few miles of gravel track. In good summer weather, it's possible to continue along the track across the hills to Greenville.

Further north, **Millinocket** is a genuine company town, built on a wilderness site by the Great Northern Paper Company in 1899–1900 as the "magic city of the North." Public curiosity was so great that three hundred people came on a special train from Bangor to see what was happening. In 1990 the company was taken over by multinational Bowater Incorporated, and although the townspeople made a killing from cashing in their stock, their homes were almost unsalable, and their jobs became tentative at best. The hundred-year-old manufacturing facilities still churn out nearly twenty percent of the newsprint produced in the United States. There's nothing to see or do here, but you might consider stopping off to pick up some supplies or grab a hot meal at the *Appalachian Trail Café*, 210 Main St (☎207/723-6720).

It's also not a bad place to **stay** if the weather's bad; try the standard *Pamola Motel*, 973 Central St/Rte-11 (☎207/723-9746; ③), which provides a free continental breakfast. Next to Millinocket Lake, ten miles northwest, several whitewater rafting companies have set up lodgings and **campsites** as bases for their trips down the Penobscot River (see box on p.528 for details). There are dogsled races in February and March.

The park

By now you're approaching the southern end of sprawling and unspoiled **BAXTER STATE PARK** itself, with (on a clear day) the 5268-foot peak of imposing and beautiful **Mount Katahdin** visible from afar. Entrance to the park, collected at the Togue Pond Gate on Park Tote Road, costs $8 per car, and you should plan to arrive early in the day, as only a limited number of visitors are permitted access each day (though this limit rarely comes into effect outside of July and August). The enormous park – covering over 200,000 acres – was the single-handed creation of former Maine Governor Percival P. Baxter, who, having failed to persuade the state to buy the imposing Katahdin and the land around it, bought it himself between the 1930s and 1960s and deeded it bit by bit to the state on condition that it remain "forever wild." A 2600-acre parcel was recently added and, amid some controversy, the State Park Authority refused to prohibit hunting and trapping on the newly acquired land. Nevertheless, the park's majestic green peaks (46 in all) and deserted ponds remain tremendously remote and pristine, and sightings of bears, bald eagles, and (of course) moose are not uncommon.

Hiking is the major pursuit here; indeed, the **Appalachian Trail** originates in the park at the top of Mount Katahdin. Among the park's 175 miles of trails, don't miss **Knife's Edge**, a thrilling walk across a narrow path that connects Katahdin's two peaks. The higher and typically more crowded of these, **Baxter Peak**, can also be reached via the **Hunt Trail**, the Cathedral Trail, and the Saddle Trail. For a less crowded but equally rewarding jaunt, head to the top of Hamlin Peak on the two-mile **Hamlin Ridge Trail**, which originates at Chimney Pond. Wherever you plan to hike, stop beforehand at either the headquarters in Millinocket, 64 Balsam Drive behind *McDonalds* (☎207/723-5140), the visitor center at Togue Pond (at the south entrance to the park – also a good place to **swim**), or at any of the park's campgrounds for a detailed **hiking map**. Water in the park is not treated and you should take care to carry as much as you'll need.

There are ten designated places to **camp** in Baxter, providing an array of options from basic tent sites to cabins equipped with beds, heating stoves, and gas lighting. Prices range from $6 to $17 per person per night and most sites are open from mid-May to mid-October. Reservations are accepted only via regular mail – again, try the Millinocket park headquarters.

North to Canada

The northernmost tip of Maine is taken up by **Aroostook County**, which covers an area larger than several individual states. Although its main activity is the large-scale cultivation of potatoes, it is also the location of the **Allagash Wilderness Waterway**, where several whitewater rafting companies put their boats in (see box, p.528).

Britain and the United States all but went to war over Aroostook in 1839; at **Fort Kent**, the northern terminus of US-1 (which runs all the way from Key West, Florida), the main sight is the solid cedar **Fort Kent Blockhouse**, built to defend American integrity and looking like a throwback to early pioneer days. *Doris' Café* (☎207/834-6262) at Fort Kent Mills on Rte-161, just off Rte-11 towards Eagle Lake, can provide big breakfasts.

PART THREE

THE CONTEXTS

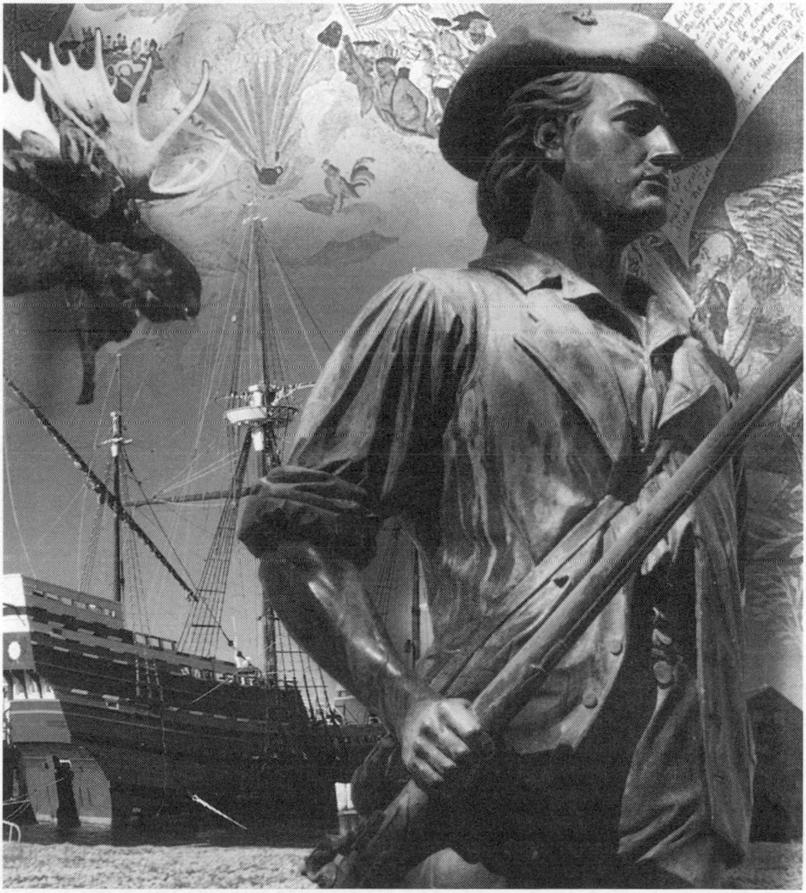

A BRIEF HISTORY OF NEW ENGLAND

NATIVE PEOPLES AND EARLY SETTLERS

It's generally accepted that people of mixed Mongolian descent, from northeast Asia, crossed the frozen Bering Straits and established settlements on the American continent sometime between 12,000 and 25,000 years ago, gradually spreading eastwards over the next several millennia, and arriving in New England between 9000 and 3000 BC. It's unclear whether or not they were the ancestors of the Algonquins, who greeted the Europeans when they arrived in the sixteenth and seventeenth centuries, or whether they became extinct.

The first documented **Europeans** to visit these shores were not English, but Norse. In about 1000AD King Olaf of Norway commissioned Leif Erikson to bring Christianity to a new Viking settlement in Greenland. Like the pilgrims who were to follow six centuries later, Erikson was blown off course, and came ashore somewhere between Newfoundland and Massachusetts. Discovering a new land where wild grapes grew in abundance, he dubbed it Vinland the Good.

Early European settlers applied the name **Algonquin** to the various groups of hunting peoples they encountered on the east coast of North America. Fiercely independent of each other, yet linked by the various dialects of the Algonquin tongue, and by common cultural ties and organizational structures, it's unlikely that they arrived in New England much before the fourteenth or fifteenth centuries – not long before the first European settlers. By 1600, there were only about 25,000 of them, broken into a dozen or so tribal nations, among them the **Narragansetts** of Rhode Island, the **Abnaki** of Maine and smaller groups like the **Niantics** and **Pequot** in Connecticut. They all took great advantage of the land, hunting, fishing, and growing crops such as beans, squash, tobacco and corn.

EUROPEAN EXPLORERS

In the sixteenth century, Spanish conquistadors had focused almost exclusively on the southern regions of what is now North America, leaving the Dutch, English, Portuguese, and French to explore the inhospitable shores of New England – motivated not so much by the spirit of adventure, as by the determination to find an easy passage to the Orient and its treasures. Six years after Columbus's first voyage, in 1492, **John Cabot** nosed by the shores of New England, in search of the elusive Northwest Passage. Cabot, who came ashore somewhere in Labrador, claimed all America east of the Rockies and north of Florida for England and was awarded a generous $30 a year pension by King Henry VII on his return. Meanwhile, **Giovanni de Verazzano**, for Francis I of France, traveled as far north as Rhode Island's Narragansett Bay, though the thought of establishing a settlement scarcely crossed his mind.

In 1583, **Sir Humphrey Gilbert** became the first Englishman to attempt the settlement of North America. Sailing from Plymouth, in the English county of Devon, he aspired to set up a trading post at the mouth of the Penobscot River, but he lost his life in a violent storm on the crossing over. More Englishmen followed him. Between 1602 and 1606, Bartholomew Gosnold, Martin Pring and George Weymouth set out to tap New England's lucrative sassafras bark, used by the Indians to cure many ailments, and regarded in Europe as an effective panacea for all ills. Meanwhile, further north, the French were making inroads: Samuel de Champlain had traversed the lake that today bears his name as early as 1609.

In 1606, King James I granted a charter to the **Virginia company of Plymouth**, with permission to establish a colony between North Carolina and Nova Scotia. In 1607, a hundred adventurous souls led by Pring, Raleigh and Sir Fernando Gorges, set out from Plymouth, their ships laden with trinkets to barter, food and livestock. Arriving on Parker's Island off the coast of Maine, they made a short go of it, but were soon repelled by the hostile winter weather.

Despite their lack of success, they took home with them stories of a land of fast-flowing streams and rivers, of verdant forests and friendly native peoples – so positive a picture, in fact, that the Plymouth Company commissioned distinguished surveyor **John Smith** to research the region's potential for development. Sailing along the Massachusetts coast in 1614, he named the region **"New England."** It was his book, *A Description of New England*, that persuaded the pilgrims to migrate to these shores.

THE PILGRIM FATHERS

By the early 1600s, Europe was in religious turmoil; on mainland Europe, Luther, Calvin, and the other Protestant reformers had started a religious revolution against Roman Catholicism. The new **Church of England** that was created claimed to be both Catholic and reformed in an attempt to appease the varying factions within its ranks. The religious zealots who opposed all aspects of Catholicism, called **Puritans** on account of their apparent purity, enjoyed a degree of respectability during the reign of Elizabeth I, with growing numbers of followers in all walks of life. However, after the accession of the Catholic king, James I, in 1603, the Puritans found themselves increasingly harassed by the authorities.

In 1601, a small group from Lincolnshire decided to emigrate to Leiden, in Holland, but found the loose morals they encountered there not to their taste. Sixty-six of them negotiated a deal with the Plymouth Company to finance a permanent settlement in North America, where they would be free to practice their own religion. Chartered by Separatist leader John Carver, the *Mayflower's* passenger list included the English Separatists, plus hired help, including Myles Standish, professional soldier, and John Alden, a cooper. In all, just over one hundred passengers set sail aboard the *Mayflower* from Southampton, England, on September 16.

After two months at sea, they reached the North American coast at **Provincetown, Cape Cod**, on November 11, 1620. The same day, 41 men signed the so-called **Mayflower Compact**, in which they agreed to establish a "Civic Body Politic" (temporary government) and to be bound by its laws:

IN THE NAME OF God, Amen. We, whose names are underwritten, the loyal subjects of our dread sovereigne Lord, King James, by the grace of God, of Great Britaine, France and Ireland king, defender of the faith etc., having undertaken, for the glory of God, and advancement of the Christian faith, and honour of our king and country, a voyage to plant the first colony in the Northerne parts of Virginia, doe, by these presents, solemnly and mutually in the presence of God, and one of another, covenannt and combine ourselves together into a civill body politick, for our better ordering and preservation and furtherance of the ends aforesaid; and by virtue hereof to enacte, constitute and frame such just and equall laws, ordinances, acts, constitutions and offices, from time to time, as shall be thought most meete and convenient for the generall good of the Colonie unto which we promise all due submission and obedience. In witness whereof we have hereunder subscribed our names at Cape-Codd the 11, of November, in the year of the raigne of our sovereigne lord, King James, of England, France, and Ireland, the eighteenth, and of Scotland the fiftie-fourth. Anno. Dom. 1620.

The Compact became the basis of government in the Plymouth Colony and **John Carver** was elected their first governor. The new arrivals had landed on a virtually barren stretch of the coast, and soon resettled across the bay, arriving at what is now Plymouth on December 26, 1620.

THE EARLY COLONISTS

Only half of the colonists survived the first winter on American soil. Unaccustomed to the extreme cold, and living in shelters built of tree bark, many died from pneumonia, and scurvy and other infections killed many more. It would have been even worse but for **Squanto**, a Native American who had spent time in England. He managed to enlist the support of Massassoit, the local Wampanoag sachem, who signed a Treaty of Friendship, and plied the visitors with food. Exactly a year after their arrival in Plymouth, the surviving Separatists could sit down with the Indians to enjoy a feast of roast game, eel, fruits, vegetables, and cornbread. Weeks later, they were joined by 35 more, laden with provisions, and by 1624 Plymouth had become a thriving village of thirty cottages. News of the community's success reached England, and in 1629 another group, led by London lawyer John Winthrop, obtained a royal charter as the "Company of the Massachusetts Bay in New England." In the summer of 1629, Winthrop and more than 300 settlers arrived at Salem, 1500 more in 1630, a figure that increased to 2000 annually between 1630 and 1635, as persecution of Puritans, led by Charles I's sidekick, Archbishop William Laud, intensified. Dozens of new communities were formed, many, like Dorchester, Ipswich, and Taunton, named after the towns and villages the settlers had left behind in England. By 1640, the **Massachusetts Bay Company** had a population of about 10,000.

As the European population grew, so did the perceived need for clergy, preferably trained in New England. In 1636 **Harvard College** was established for that specific purpose, while a General Court was formed to administer the colony's affairs, including justice.

At this stage, new arrivals in the colonies were not limited to Massachusetts. In **Connecticut**, the Rev. Thomas Hooker established the community that became Hartford, while Theophilus Eaton and John Davenport founded New Haven. But frictions were already developing between the more zealous settlers, rapidly showing themselves to be even less tolerant than their oppressors back in England. The **Rev. Roger Williams**, hounded out of the Massachusetts Bay Colony in 1636 for his liberal views, established a new settlement of twenty families at Providence in 1638, on land made available by two Indian sachems he'd befriended. The new **State of Rhode Island and Providence Plantations**, in its 1663 charter, guaranteed religious freedom for all; Jews, Huguenots, even the despised Quakers. Communities were also established in New Hampshire in 1638, and Maine in 1652.

Meanwhile, zealous Puritans worked at **converting** the Indians to their faith, translating the Bible into Algonquin, and setting up special communities for Christian Indians along the Connecticut River and on Cape Cod, which became known as "praying towns." Several Algonquins were sent to Harvard to train as Christian clergy – although only one completed the training successfully – and by the 1660s, the Christian faith accounted for one-fifth of all Indians. The settlers' arrogant attempt to persuade the Indians to give up their native culture and traditions, and mirror their own culture and beliefs, however, led to profound unhappiness, and eventually bloodshed.

At first, the new settlers and the Native Americans were able to coexist peacefully, though it's likely that **diseases** introduced by the colonists may have been directly responsible for a plague which killed more than a third of all the Algonquins. As the colonists ventured south, they began to meet growing resistance from the Indians, particularly the proud Pequot tribe, with whom war erupted in 1636, at Fort Mystic and Fairfield; many lives were lost on both sides. Then, in 1675, Narragansett leader Metacom, also known as Philip, persuaded feuding groups of Indians, principally the Nipmuck, Narragansetts and Wampanoags, to bury their differences and join in a concerted campaign against the settlers. Known as **King Philip's War**, hostilities culminated in the **Great Swamp Fight** in Kingston, Rhode Island. More than 2000 Indians were slain, including Metacom himself. Even more significantly, it signaled the breaking of the Indian will.

GROWING UNREST

Up until the middle of the seventeenth century, the colonies had largely been left to take care of their own political structures. England, after all, was preoccupied with its own domestic concerns – a bloody civil war, the beheading of Charles I and the establishment of Oliver Cromwell's parliamentary republic – and was scarcely interested in events happening three thousand miles away. The resulting vacuum was a breeding ground for the seeds of separatism, sentiment fueled by speculation that the Crown would soon seek to appoint its own governor to take charge of colonial affairs.

In 1686, King James II revoked the northern colonies' charters and attempted to create a **Dominion of New England** stretching from Maine to New Jersey. Spun as a security measure to protect the English communities from the French and the Indians, it was in reality an attempt to keep tabs on an increasingly defiant and potentially troublesome populace. The king's first gubernatorial appointee, Joseph Dudley, an Anglican, was succeeded by Edmund Andros, who imposed taxes as the disenfranchised populace grew increasingly frustrated.

A new respect between the Crown and colonies was temporarily forged in 1689, when the "Glorious Revolution" brought Protestants William and Mary to the British throne. The despised Andros was removed and put in jail, and the old powers of self-government restored. When King George III came to the throne in1760, he demanded obedience from America and soon demonstrated that he would go to any lengths to get it. In a move designed not so much to raise revenue as to remind the colonists who was boss, he was responsible for the **Revenue Act of 1764**, imposing taxes on sugar, silk, and wine, which resulted in a boycott of British goods and supplies.

The situation deteriorated further in 1765, with London's introduction of the **Stamp Act** and the imposition of taxes on commercial and legal documents, newspapers, even playing cards. Throughout New England, protests erupted. Tax officials were the defendants in mock trials, and their effigies hanged. The bulk of the demonstrations were peaceful, but in Boston, the houses of stampman Andrew Oliver and Governor Thomas Hitchinson were plundered. The British prime minister William Pitt **repealed** the Act in March 1766.

Then, in the summer of 1767, new British prime minister Charles Townshend arrogantly taunted the colonies with his famous remark, "I dare tax America." The subsequent **Townshend Acts**, which introduced harsh levies on imports such as paper, glass, and, most provocatively, tea, prompted the dispatch to Boston of two regiments of Redcoats. On March 5, 1770, a crowd of several hundred Bostonians gathered to ridicule a solitary "lobster-back" standing sentinel outside the customs house. Initially peaceful, the scene turned ugly as stones and rocks were thrown, and seven nervous reinforcements arrived, one firing on the crowd without orders. In the panic, more shots followed. Three colonists were pronounced dead; two were mortally wounded, the first martyrs in an event that was to become known as the **Boston Massacre**.

Things would have deteriorated more rapidly but for the **economic prosperity** that New England, and particularly Boston, was beginning to enjoy. Eventually, the Townshend Acts were repealed, though not the tax on East India tea, which was boycotted by the colonists. Dutch blends were smuggled in, and a special brew called Liberty Tea concocted from sage, currant, or plantain leaves. Britain responded in September 1773 by flooding the market with its own, subsidized blend – half a million pounds of the stuff.

Resistance focused on Boston, where the **Massachusetts Committee of Correspondence**, an unofficial legislature, and the local chapter of the **Sons of Liberty**, a fast-growing pseudo-secret society, organized the barricading of the piers and wharves and demanded Governor Hutchinson send home the tea-filled clipper *Dartmouth*. When he refused, sixty men disguised as Mohawk Indians, Samuel Adams and John Hancock among them, surreptitiously climbed aboard and dumped 350 crates of the tea into Boston Harbor. The date was December 16, 1773, and the event captured the world's imagination as the **Boston Tea Party**.

This blatant act of defiance rattled parliament, which introduced the so-called "**Coercive Acts**": the Boston Port Act sealed off the city with a massive naval blockade. Meanwhile, American patriots from Massachusetts, Rhode Island, and other states gathered in Philadelphia for the **First Continental Congress**, convened on September 5, 1774. Though British garrisons still controlled the major towns, such was the antagonism in rural areas that policing them was becoming virtually impossible for the British. All the while, locals continued to stockpile arms and munitions.

In April 1775, London instructed its Boston commander General Thomas Gage to put down rebellion in rural Massachusetts, where the Provincial congress had assumed de facto political control. On the night of April 18, Gage dispatched 700 soldiers to destroy the arms depot in Concord, while at nearby Lexington seventy colonial soldiers, known as Minute Men, lay in wait, having been pre-warned of the plan by Paul Revere and William Dawes.

On Concord's Town Common, British musket fire resulted in the deaths of eight Americans. The British moved on to Concord, oblivious to the ambush which resulted in the deaths of 273

British soldiers, British retreat, and American jubilation. As news of the victory spread, rumors of plunder and pillage by British troops further fueled American resentment.

A couple of months later, the war intensified with the **Battle of Bunker Hill**, on Boston's Charlestown peninsula, which General Artemus Ward of the Continental Army had ordered to be fortified – though it was actually nearby Breed's Hill where the American forces were stationed. On June 17, the redcoats attacked Breed's Hill twice, but were twice rebuffed. The third attempt succeeded, because the Americans ran out of ammunition. For this reason alone, the much-celebrated order "don't fire until you see the whites of their eyes" was given – some say by Col. William Prescott, others General Isaac Putnam – specifically to save on ammunition. Bunker Hill, with 1000 British casualties, was an **expensive triumph for the Crown**. Worn down by lack of manpower, low morale and growing American resistance, less than a year later, an embattled General Gage ordered a **British withdrawal** to Halifax, Nova Scotia.

The **Declaration of Independence**, with fifty-six signatories, fourteen of whom were from the New England states of **Massachusetts**, **Connecticut**, **New Hampshire**, and **Rhode Island**, was adopted by the Continental Congress on July 4, 1776.

Even after victory, all was not plain sailing. In a move designed to protect the states' newly independent status, the thirteen independent colonies hammered out an integrated union in 1781, though not without the concern that a centralized federal system would be just as bad as British rule. For that reason, heroes Sam Adams and John Hancock gave only grudging support to the Constitution, and Rhode Island consistently voted against it, only ratifying it after the Bill of Rights was added.

With the Declaration of Independence, the families who had settled **Vermont** pondered their future. In a series of conventions the idea of independence was mooted, and at Windsor in July 1777, seventy delegates unanimously adopted a constitution that was almost an exact replica of Pennsylvania's. Vermont was admitted to the Union as the **fourteenth state** on March 4th 1791.

Maine's statehood was not gained until 1820, after the eastern part of the state had been occupied by the British during the War of 1812. According to the Missouri Compromise of 1820, Maine was admitted to the Union as a free (anti-slavery) state, balanced by Missouri, a slave state.

AGRICULTURAL BEGINNINGS AND ECONOMIC TRANSITION

New England had started out as a predominantly **agricultural region**, particularly the areas away from the coast, where maritime trading and commerce was found. Maine and New Hampshire developed important trades in timber, agriculture, and fishing, with some shipbuilding on the coast at Bath, Maine, and Portsmouth, New Hampshire. The opening of the **Champlain Canal**, connecting Lake Champlain to the Hudson River, made it possible for Vermont farmers to ship goods to New York City, stimulating agriculture and wool production, at least until the 1860s when dairy farming began to take hold. But, apart from some lush pockets of Vermont, the soil was generally poor; plowing was difficult, and the long, cold New England winters meant that for a large part of the year the ground was frozen solid. The land lent itself to little more than subsistence farming – small farms, barns, wheat, corn, pigs, cattle – and New England could never compete with the vast wheat- and dairy-producing areas of the growing mid-west.

MARITIME TRADE

New England's true prosperity came first as a result of its **connection with the sea**; fishing, especially for cod, was important, as was the production of whale derivatives, especially oil, used for heating and lighting. More adventurous sea captains, many of them based in Boston or Salem, ventured further afield, and brought back great treasures from India and China including tea, spices, silk, and opium.

Several communities, like Newport, Rhode Island, flourished on the back of the **Triangular trade**; ships unloaded West Indian molasses, reloaded with rum, then sailed to Africa, where the rum was exchanged for slaves, in turn shipped to the West Indies and traded for molasses. **Shipbuilding** industries flourished, particularly in places like Essex, Massachusetts, which earned a reputation for manufacturing swift, easily maneuverable vessels. But the first two decades of the nineteenth century showed how volatile maritime trade was, especially with so many political uncertainties, notably the Napoleonic Wars, Thomas Jefferson's Embargo Acts, prohibiting all exports to Europe and restricting imports from Great Britain – a response to British and French interference with American ships – and the War of 1812. There was a clear need for New England to diversify its economy if its prosperity were to increase.

THE INDUSTRIAL REVOLUTION

In 1789, **Samuel Slater**, a skilled mechanic from England, sailed from his native land to New York disguised as a laborer. The emigration of skilled mechanics was forbidden by the British government, and there were serious penalties for those found smuggling the specifications and drawings for the pioneering industrial machinery that had earned Britain her nickname as the "workshop of the world." Slater, though, had been able to memorize the specifications of his boss Richard Arkwright's factory-sized cotton spinning machine, which was set to revolutionize the highly inefficient existing system of individual looms. Financed by Moses Brown, a Providence Quaker, he set up the nation's first successful **cotton mill** at Pawtucket, Rhode Island. The working conditions here were hellish, and these, together with the poor rates of pay, meant that this was the site of the nation's first industrial strike in 1800.

Another entrepreneur determined to duplicate British weaving feats was Bostonian **Francis Cabot Lowell**, a self-styled "industrial tourist." Determined to duplicate British ingenuity in America, he spent $10,000 of his own money plus $90,000 from his "Boston Associates" to set up a small mill with a power loom and 1700 spindles at Waltham, west of Boston. Lowell's **Merrimack Manufacturing Company** proved extremely profitable, with sales at $3000 in 1815 and reaching $345,000 in 1822. In 1826, having already uprooted to Chelmsford, the business moved again, to a purpose-built community named "Lowell" after its founder. Lowell's enlightened, anthropological approach was continued by his associates after his death: young female workers lived in dorms to protect their honor, received education, and were given sufficient time off to engage in a variety of leisure pursuits.

New England was fast becoming the **industrial center** of the US, home to some two-thirds of the nation's cotton mills, half of which were in Massachusetts. Tiny Rhode Island processed twenty percent of the nation's wool and in Connecticut, **Sam Colt** and **Eli Whitney**, known for his invention of cotton gin, manufactured the first firearms with interchangeable parts. Connecticut also became home to a thriving watch- and clock-making industry. In the fields of paper and shoe manufacture and metalworking New England, and particularly New Hampshire, was unsurpassed.

CULTURE AND EDUCATION

New England, particularly Boston, had always set a strong standard as far as **education** and **literature** were concerned. The nation's first secondary school, Boston Latin, opened in 1635, closely followed by Harvard in 1636. In Connecticut, Yale University was established in 1701, while Rhode Island's Brown University, originally Rhode Island College, came into being in 1764. Further north, New Hampshire's Dartmouth College dates from 1769, and Bowdoin College in Maine from 1769.

In 1639, America's first printing press was set up in Cambridge, where the *Bay Psalm Book*, *New England Primer* and freeman's oath of loyalty to Massachusetts were among the first published works. The colonies' first newspaper, *Publick Occurrences, Both Foreign & Domestick*, came into being in 1690, and was succeeded by the more popular *Boston News-Letter* in 1704. By the 1850s, more than 400 periodicals were in print. Libraries such as Hartford's famous Wadsworth Atheneum and the Providence Atheneum both came into existence in the mid-1800s, while in 1854 the Boston Public Library, with 750,000 volumes, became the world's first free municipal library.

At the same time, the region became home to some of the nation's greatest thinkers, philosophers, essayists, artists, and architects. Among them were Henry David Thoreau, the **transcendentalist** philosopher and essayist; Louisa May Alcott, author of *Little Women*; Winslow Homer, noted for his marine watercolors; Emily Dickinson, poetess; and novelists such as Nathaniel Hawthorne, whose most famous book, *The House of the Seven Gables*, was set in Salem, Massachusetts. In Connecticut, Mark Twain had set up home at Nook Farm, near Hartford, as had Harriet Beecher Stowe – author of *Uncle Tom's Cabin*.

Not coincidentally, a strong cultural identity developed, focusing again on Boston, where the 1871 founding of **the Museum of Fine Arts** was followed a decade later by the Boston Symphony Orchestra and the Boston Pops. New Haven became an important focus for theater in Connecticut, with the establishment of the Long Wharf, Schubert, and Yale Repertory Theaters.

THE CIVIL WAR

The type of **anti-slavery** sentiment Stowe had advocated in *Uncle Tom's Cabin* was echoed by a number of northerners, though in general, when it came to **slavery**, New Englanders held ambivalent views. Laws in all the New England states had **outlawed** the practice. Still, it would prove to be the catalyst for the bloodiest conflict ever seen on American soil, the **Civil War**.

From the moment of its inception, the unity of the nation had been based on shaky foundations. Great care had gone into devising a Constitution that balanced the need for a strong federal government with the aspirations for autonomy of its component states. That was achieved by giving Congress two separated chambers – the House of Representatives, in which the number of representatives from each state depended on its population, and the Senate, where each state elected two members, regardless of size. Thus, although in theory the Constitution remained silent on the issue of slavery, it allayed the fears of the less populated southern states, that the voters of the north might destroy their economy by forcing them to abandon their "peculiar institution." However, it soon became apparent that the system only worked so long as there were roughly equal numbers of "free" and slave-owning states.

At first, it seemed possible that the balance could be maintained – in 1820, under the Missouri Compromise, Missouri was admitted to the Union as a slave-owning state at the same time as Maine was admitted as a "free" one. In 1854, the **Kansas-Nebraska Act** forced the issue to a head, allowing both prospective states self-determination on the issue. John Brown's raid on the Armory at Harpers Ferry, West Virginia, in which he intended to raid arms for a slave rebellion, was quashed, and Brown hanged. The Civil War began. Though **no battles** were fought in New England, the region sent thousands of men to bolster the Union cause, many of whom would

never return. In the end, it was not so much the brilliance of the generals as sheer economic power that won the War for the Union. It was the north, with New England leading the way, that could maintain full trading with the rest of the world while diverting spare resources to the production of munitions.

TIME FOR CHANGE

Civil War, the industrial revolution, a vast intellectual flowering, all these things and more combined to create the vast sea change for New England in the latter half of the nineteenth century. Perhaps most important, the frontiers of the US moved west, and other regions began to play their part in the development of the nation. Despite its **diminishing influence** on the national stage, New England continued the strong tradition of social reform exemplified by William Lloyd Garrison and others long before the Civil War started, paving the way in the field of prison reform, health and mental health provision.

Meantime, the ethnic and religious make-up of New England was changing rapidly. No longer was it the preserve of white Anglo-Saxon Protestants; **Irish immigrants** began pouring over in the 1840s following the potato famine, and soon more than 1000 Irish immigrants a month were arriving in Boston, while Catholics from Italy, French Canada, Portugal, and Eastern Europe accounted for two-thirds of the total population growth during the nineteenth century. Indeed, by 1907, seventy percent of Massachusett's population could claim to be of non-Anglo-Saxon descent. Even in less developed New Hampshire, one out of every five had adopted, not inherited, the US flag.

Such waves of immigration provoked some backlash, with the openly racist **Know-Nothing** party gaining governorships in Massachusetts, Rhode Island, Connecticut, and New Hampshire; membership of the American Protective Association and Immigrant Restriction League increasing dramatically; and signs like "No Irish Need Apply" being easily found on the doorstep of many a business.

Still, immigrants soon found ways of working the political system, especially the Irish, and in 1881 John Breen from Tipperary became the first Irishman to take up an establishment position – as mayor of Lawrence, Massachusetts. This had a profound motivating effect on his fellow countrymen, and three years later, Hugh O'Brien won the Boston mayorship, while Patrick Andrew Collin represented Suffolk County with a congressional seat in the nation's capital. By the turn of the twentieth century, immigrants were represented at all levels of government.

But political scandal and **corruption** were never far away. "Boss" Charlie Brayton and the *Providence Journal* ring bought their way to office in Rhode Island, individual votes costing $2 to $5, and up to $30 in hotly contested elections. Others abused the privileges of the solid ethnic support they enjoyed: **James Michael Curley**, elected Boston mayor four times, and voted governor of Massachusetts 1934–1938, did much to improve the welfare of the poor, but also doled out jobs and money to community leaders who carefully manipulated the electorate and its votes.

With the huge influx of mainly poor immigrants, especially from Catholic countries, a **"New Puritanism"** began to take hold. Encouraged by Catholic leader William Cardinal O'Connell and the closely associated **Watch and Ward Society**, moralists lobbied for the prohibition of, among other things, Hemingway's *The Sun also Rises* and a variety of plays and books.

THE SOUTHERN EXODUS

As time passed, other regions began to challenge New England's claim to be the manufacturing capital of the US. Many companies **moved south**, where costs were much lower, and by 1923 more than half the nation's cotton goods were being woven there. Industrial production in Massachusetts alone fell by more than $1 billion during the 1920s, while unemployment skyrocketed in some towns to 25 percent, and up to 40 percent after the Wall Street crash. The **Great Depression** hit New England particularly hard, and, with few natural resources to draw upon, and the drain of human resources to the south, industry in New England never really recovered. From the boom days of the late nineteenth century, when hundreds of thousands of New Englanders were engaged in textiles, the figure had dropped to fewer than 70,000 by the 1970s. By 1980, the region which had given birth to America's industrial revolution was headquarters to only fourteen of the nation's top five hundred companies.

MODERN TIMES

Political collaboration, instead of confrontation, between New England's "Brahmin" political set, and the second- and- third-generation sons and daughters of immigrants, began to pay off in a common quest to find an answer to New England's economic and social problems, and by the 1980s the region was beginning to experience something of an **industrial resurgence**. New industries, like the production of biomedical machinery, electronics, computer hard- and software, and photographic materials sprang up throughout the region, but especially along Route 128 west of Boston, which has become New England's so-called Silicon Valley. During this period, Boston became the country's mutual fund capital, Hartford's insurance industry continued to flourish, and tourism became the region's second largest source of income. The region became known for its political stability, at the same time as leading the way with anti-pollution laws, consumer rights, handgun controls, and civil rights legislation.

The nationwide economic slump in the late 1980s and early 1990s continued to cause problems in those larger urban centers which had failed to address the social consequences of the demise of traditional manufacturing industries, and a serious **banking crisis** in Rhode Island sent shock waves throughout New England.

The area rebounded again. Increasing, almost unparalleled prosperity accompanied by low unemployment – especially in the latter half of the 1990s – meant that more money was freed up for the benefit of long-neglected areas that needed attention: roads and infrastructure, crime prevention, schools, and social provision, although significant problems remain to be tackled. At the same time **urban regeneration**, sometimes on a spectacular scale (for example in Providence, RI), and the continued development of new, mostly computer-related and service industries, has put the region back on track.

THE PRESENT AND FUTURE

New England continues to grow – not only in population, and prosperity, but also in maturity. Ethnic tensions remain, but are less of a problem than they have ever been. Significant measures to protect the environment have been enacted in several states, and improvement in the frequency and duration of rail services along the northeast corridor –and in commuter services generally – will lead, planners hope, to fewer cars on the road, though the never-ending, multi-million dollar "Big Dig", which will take most of Boston's north–south traffic underground, would appear to contradict that trend.

Politically, liberalism and, to an extent, libertarian values, remain prominent. Vermonter Bernie Sanders has a claim as the lone **socialist/independent** congressman; the storied **Kennedy** family of Massachusetts continues to hold sway in the national consciousness, if less political influence; and both tickets in the 2000 presidential campaign had strong ties to New England. Democratic vice-presidential candidate **Joe Lieberman** comes from New Haven, CT, while the country's new president, **George W. Bush**, matriculated in the same city and has connections with Maine, where his family owns a home at Kennebunkport – though liberalism is certainly something he cannot be faulted for, and he was mostly rejected by New England voters in favor of Al Gore.

NEW ENGLAND ON FILM

As picturesque and as rich in narrative as New England is, the region has always seemed inhospitable to the young turks of Hollywood. For one thing it is as far from Los Angeles, both geographically and psychologically, as you can get in the continental United States; for another, the weather, though undeniably cinematic, is expensively unpredictable.

Nevertheless, there are plenty of films set in New England. They're often films with a particularly local subject matter – academia, witchcraft – or sometimes literary adaptations; indeed Hollywood has gamely hacked away at whole schools of unfilmable New England novels, going after such impossible white whales as *Moby Dick* and *The Scarlet Letter* with vigor, and usually failing more spectacularly with each attempt.

The following films are all set in one or other of New England's six states (though, needless to say, Massachusetts, and especially Boston, predominate). They weren't, however, necessarily filmed in New England: many were shot in California, some in England, and quite a number conveniently across the border in Canada.

The Actress (George Cukor, 1953). A unique portrait of Boston in the early 1910s, *The Actress* is based on a play by Ruth Gordon about her early life in nearby Wollaston. Though the film, which stars Jean Simmons as Gordon and

a deliciously cantankerous Spencer Tracy as her father, is largely studio-bound, it is full of historical tidbits.

Affliction (Paul Schrader, 1998). One of the best New England movies of recent years, though this brooding tale of the violence shattering the placid surface of a snowbound New Hampshire town will hardly do wonders for the tourist trade. Nick Nolte is superb as the divorced small-town cop stumbling through middle age, whose father's legacy of abuse is too heavy a load to bear.

Alice's Restaurant (Arthur Penn, 1969). Built around Arlo Guthrie's hit song of the same name, this quizzical elegy for counterculture brought the hippie nation to the Berkshire town of Stockbridge in western Massachusetts.

All That Heaven Allows (Douglas Sirk, 1955). Sirk's splendid technicolor masterpiece recounts the forbidden romance of a middle-aged widow (Jane Wyman) and her strapping, Thoreau-quoting gardener (Rock Hudson). Sirk's devastating portrait of small minds of the local country club set served to show that the Puritanism of the seventeenth century was alive and well in postwar New England.

Between the Lines (Joan Micklin Silver, 1977). Shot on location, this multi-character comedy-drama documents the dying throes of counterculture in late 1970s Boston by focusing on the ragtag staff of underground newspaper *The Back Bay Mainline* (based on the real-life *Real Paper*).

The Bostonians (James Ivory, 1984). Merchant Ivory's high-minded Henry James adaptation is set in 1875 Boston. New England women's libbers and a Southern male chauvinist battle for the soul of one very pliable young woman in the drawing rooms of Cambridge, on the lawns of Harvard and on the beaches of Martha's Vineyard. Vanessa Redgrave and Christopher Reeve, as the opposing armies, are superb.

The Boston Strangler (Richard Fleischer, 1968). The "usually reserved city of Boston" is set on edge by a series of brutal murders. Shot like a documentary, with a panoply of split-screen effects, this true-life crime story, starring a jittery Tony Curtis as the titular handyman, starts out well but soon gets bogged down in psychobabble.

Christmas in Conneticut (Peter Godfrey, 1945). Barbara Stanwyck plays a Manhattan magazine writer who has faked her way to being the Martha Stewart of her day. When her publisher asks her to invite a war hero to her Connecticut farm for Christmas, Stanwyck has to conjure up the idyllic New England existence she'd only written about. Unfortunately the results are convoluted, and the studio-built Connecticut is – ironically – clearly a fake.

Cider House Rules (Lasse Hallstrom, 1999). Surprisingly well-received adaptation of John Irving's novel (see Books), in which a shifting Maine backdrop sets the stage for a somewhat didactic, if winning, meditation on love, suffering, and the thorny issue of abortion.

A Civil Action (Steve Zaillian, 1998). John Travolta struts his stuff as a cocky ambulance-chasing Boston lawyer who loses everything but regains his soul when he takes up the case of a group of families in nearby Woburn, Massachusetts who believe their children developed leukemia after drinking contaminated local water. A rainy, wintry vision of New England enlivened by Robert Duvall as a devilish old pro who'd rather be at Fenway Park than in court.

The Crucible (Nicholas Hytner, 1996). A riveting adaptation of Arthur Miller's classic allegory of McCarthyism set during the Salem Witch Trials of 1692. Winona Ryder and her friends are spied dancing by firelight, and accused of witchcraft; to save themselves they start naming names. Daniel Day-Lewis is suitably tortured as Ryder's Puritan lover caught between Plymouth Rock and a hard place.

Dead Poets Society (Peter Weir, 1989). This inspirational film, pitting arch-conservative academe versus freethinking progress, seems like the classic New England movie. It was in fact shot in Delaware and the film itself makes no mention of specific locale. However, if any movie deserves mention as an honorary New England movie, this is it.

Dolores Claiborne (Taylor Hackford, 1995). On a dreary island off the coast of Maine, a housekeeper (Kathy Bates) is suspected of murdering her wealthy employer, and even her neurotic journo daughter from New York (Jennifer Jason Leigh) thinks she's guilty. This lovingly crafted Gothic sleeper was adapted from a Stephen King novel, and, although it succeeds admirably in conveying the weather-beaten charms of the Maine coast, it was actually shot in Nova Scotia.

The Europeans (James Ivory, 1979). Shot against the gorgeous fall foliage of New Hampshire and Massachusetts, Merchant Ivory's genial adaptation of Henry James' novella pits New English sobriety ("There must be a thousand ways to be dreary and sometimes I think we make use of them all" pines Lisa Eichhorn) against the dizzy charms of a couple of European visitors to the suburban countryside of nineteenth-century Boston.

Ghost and Mrs. Muir (Joseph Mankiewicz, 1947). Much-beloved film that hasn't aged especially well.

Good Will Hunting (Gus Van Sant, 1997). When money-minded producers suggested shooting their script up in Canada, Beantown buddies Ben Affleck and Matt Damon insisted that the verisimilitude of Boston locations was essential to their script about a South Boston townie tough who is a closet math wizard. They got their way, and the rest is history.

The House of the Seven Gables (Joe May, 1940). Fusty superstition battles liberal enlightenment in eighteenth-century Massachusetts in this histrionic adaptation of Nathaniel Hawthorne's Gothic family saga. George Sanders and Vincent Price play yin-yang siblings fighting for control of their accursed family mansion, against a background of abolitionism and the birth of photography.

The Ice Storm (Ang Lee, 1997). Suburban living in 1970s Connecticut – bell-bottoms, key-parties, etc – is laid bare in all its formica-covered splendor, in this rather dour adaptation of Rick Moody's novel starring Kevin Kline, Sigourney Weaver and Joan Allen. The production design, if nothing else, is priceless, and the titular squall that climaxes the film a magnificent specimen of New England weather.

Jaws (Steven Spielberg, 1975). Spielberg's toothsome blockbuster took the well-worn New England trope of the destructive outsider disrupting the well-ordered life of the community and gave it its ultimate id-like expression in the form of a killer shark who wreaks havoc on the shores of Martha's Vineyard (known here as Amity Island).

The Last Hurrah (John Ford, 1958). The great John Ford was born and raised in Maine, but this is one of his few depictions of the Northeast. Spencer Tracy plays the no-nonsense Irish-American mayor of a New England town (a thinly veiled Boston) whose career is on the wane. It's talky and sentimental, but pulls no punches in its depiction of the snobbery of the local bluebloods towards the Boston Irish.

Leave Her to Heaven (John M. Stahl, 1945). A stunning, too-little-known gem (and, incidentally, the Spanish director Pedro Almodovar's favorite film of all time), in which Gene Tierney plays a woman who loves too much. Half of this gorgeously colorful movie takes place in New Mexico, but the scenes in Maine, most especially a devastating scene involving a rowboat, a lake, and a pair of sunglasses, are indelible.

Little Women (George Cukor, 1933; Gillian Armstrong, 1994). Despite the reams of New England literature massacred by Hollywood, Louisa May Alcott's timeless classic, set in Concord, has fared remarkably well, with not one but two wonderful adaptations. The first, made by George Cukor in 1933, stars a rambunctious Katherine Hepburn as Jo; the second, made some sixty years later by Gillian Armstrong, has Winona Ryder in the lead role and Susan Sarandon as the ever-wise Marmee.

Love Story (Arthur Hiller, 1970). The Harvard preppie (Ryan O'Neal) and the working-class Radcliffe wiseacre (Ali McGraw) fall head over heels against a backdrop of library stacks, falling leaves, tinkling pianos, and low-rent Cambridge digs. The tragedy in this four-hankie blockbuster only kicks in when the lovebirds relocate to New York.

Malice (Harold Becker, 1993). In a small college town in Massachusetts (the film was shot at Smith College in Northampton) the blissful life of newlyweds Bill Pullman and Nicole Kidman is rocked by the arrival of diabolically charismatic Harvard doctor Alec Baldwin – a surgeon with a "God complex." A devilish little thriller.

Me, Myself, and Irene (Farrelly Brothers, 2000). Jim Carrey stars as split personalities in love with the same woman in this slapstick comedy, set in Rhode Island. The directors have done better (see *There's Something about Mary*, below).

Misery (Rob Reiner, 1990). Adaptation of popular Stephen King novel, and certainly one of the more successful screen transformations, with a chilling Kathy Bates as novelist James Caan's biggest fan. With a perfectly dreary and ominous New England backdrop – though most action takes place inside a house.

Moby Dick (Lloyd Bacon, 1930; John Huston, 1956). Melville's great white novel, which begins in New Bedford, Massachusetts, has been given at least two very different treatments by Hollywood. Lloyd Bacon's early version, starring John Barrymore, runs a skimpy 75 minutes and turns Captain Ahab's monomaniacal quest into a love story with a happy ending. John Huston's reverential 1956 version, with Gregory Peck as Ahab, is visually striking, but still unequal to the task.

Mystic Pizza (Donald Petrie, 1988). The film that put both Julia Roberts and Mystic, Connecticut, on the national map. Shot on location in Mystic and nearby Rhode Island, this mildly entertaining tale of the romantic travails of three young waitresses at the local pizza joint is located in the town's Portuguese lobster-fishing community.

Next Stop Wonderland (Brad Anderson, 1998). The twee title of this thinking woman's indie romance actually refers to the greyhound racing stadium at the end of one of Boston's subway lines where luckless nurse Hope Davis finally crosses paths, after many a false start, with the man of her dreams. The Boston aquarium has a major supporting role.

On Golden Pond (Mark Rydell, 1981). The pond of the title is actually Squam Lake in New Hampshire's Lakes Region, where, one schmaltzy summer, a crabby Boston professor (Henry Fonda in his final film) and his wife (Katherine Hepburn) get in touch with their inner grandchild. A breathtakingly picturesque tear-jerker that probably did more for New England tourism than all the other films listed here combined.

One Crazy Summer (Savage Steve Holland, 1986). This unbearably broad teen comedy set on the island of Nantucket stars John Cusack as a lovelorn cartoonist who spends his vacation saving Demi Moore from moustache-twirling condo developers. Shot on location, the film climaxes, none too soon, at the Nantucket regatta.

The Raid (Hugo Fregonese, 1954). A brutal Civil War tale of a band of escaped Confederate prisoners, who, in 1864, infiltrated the picturesque

Vermont town of St Albans intending to raze it to the ground. Based on a true story, this little-known gem stars Van Heflin, Lee Marvin, and Anne Bancroft as the beautiful Yankee widow whose hospitality puts a spanner in the Rebs' plan of action.

Reversal of Fortune (Barbet Schroeder, 1990). Opening with a jaw-dropping aerial sequence of the mansions of Newport strung along the Rhode Island coastline, this devastatingly witty film dramatizes the case of Claus von Bülow, who was convicted of attempting to murder his heiress wife Sunny, and then acquitted in the Rhode Island Supreme Court with the help of Harvard lawyer Alan Dershowitz.

The Russians Are Coming! The Russians Are Coming! (Norman Jewison, 1966). A comic vision of Cold War paranoia in which a Russian submarine runs aground off fictional "Gloucester Island" somewhere on the New England coast, causing panic in this archetypally dozy community. A precursor to *Jaws*, of sorts, but this blockbuster farce was actually shot on the coast of Northern California.

The Scarlet Letter (Victor Seastrom, 1926; Wim Wenders, 1973; Roland Joffe, 1995). Hawthorne's masterpiece has been treated about as woefully by Hollywood as Hester Prynne was treated by the good people of Salem. The first silent adaptation of the book, starring Lillian Gish, is the best, though it reduces Hawthorne's symbol-laden complexities to a tragic pastoral romance. Wim Wenders' 1973 version – filmed in Spain with German actors – is about as much fun as Salem on the Sabbath; while the recent Demi Moore vehicle supplies the story with some racy sex scenes and a new happy ending.

September (Woody Allen, 1987). Woody's dullest film – an attempt to do Chekhov in New England – takes place during one angst-ridden weekend in Vermont. But, due no doubt to Woody's professed dislike for the countryside ("I am at two with nature"), the entire gabfest was shot in a studio in Queens.

Splendor in the Grass (Eli Kazan, 1961). Though its handful of scenes set at Yale University are confined to studio sets, Kazan's Kansas melodrama bears mention for the pivotal role that New Haven's legendary pizza pie plays in the proceedings. To wit, Warren Beatty reneges on his promise to return to high school

sweetheart Nathalie Wood when he is seduced by a New Haven slice and marries the pizza-maker's daughter.

Starting Over (Alan J. Pakula, 1979). Burt Reynolds leaves his unfaithful, song-writing wife in their swanky Manhattan pad and moves to a cold-water Boston flat to start over. A wonderful and little-known comedy romance, co-starring Jill Clayburgh, written by James L. Brooks, and shot by Bergman's cinematographer Sven Nykvist as through Boston were in the midst of a blackout.

State and Main (David Mamet, 2000). A slick Hollywood film crew lands in uptight small-town Vermont after having been run out of New Hampshire for unknown and undoubtedly lurid reasons. Mamet uses all his trademarks to take on sometimes obvious targets, but this screwball comedy, by virtue of its winning performances and often hilarious dialogue, still feels fresh.

The Swimmer (Frank Perry, 1968). A splendid curio adapted from a John Cheever short story, in which upscale rural Connecticut is imagined as a lush Garden of Eden through which broad-chested, swimsuited Burt Lancaster makes his allegorical way home one summer afternoon, going from swimming pool to swimming pool.

There's Something About Mary (Farrelly Brothers, 1998). If Rhode Island is to go down in the annals of cinema history it would have to be as the site of Ben Stiller's notorious pre-prom mishap with a zipper in this gross-out masterpiece. There are some nice views of the Providence waterfront before the film relocates to Miami in pursuit of the eponymous object of desire.

Tough Guys Don't Dance (Norman Mailer, 1987). Set in Provincetown, on the beckoning fingertip of Cape Cod, Mailer's bizarre retelling of his own novel is a purplish affair involving an over-intoxicated writer (Ryan O'Neal), a gay-bashing sheriff, a flamboyant Southern millionaire, a buxom Bible-bashing gold digger, drug-dealing lobster men, and the ghosts of Helltown whores.

The Trouble With Harry (Alfred Hitchcock, 1955). A black comedy painted in the reds and golds of a perfect Vermont fall. The trouble with Harry is that he keeps turning up dead and everybody, including his young wife (Shirley MacLaine in her debut), thinks they may have killed him. The trouble, meanwhile, with perfect Vermont falls is the weather, and, though shooting began on location, Hitchcock's crew eventually had to beat a retreat to Hollywood with truckloads of leaves to finish the film.

The Verdict (Sidney Lumet, 1982). Gripping courtroom thriller, with Paul Newman as an alcoholic has-been lawyer given one last lease on life – trying a medical malpractice suit against a big Massachusetts hospital.

Vermont is for Lovers (John O'Brien, 1993). A charming, semi-documentary, indie comedy about a New York couple who travel to Vermont to get married, come down with a bad case of cold feet, and turn to the locals – all real Vermonters and neighbors of O'Brien – for advice. Scene-stealing septuagenarian sheep farmer Fred Tuttle then had a spin-off in O'Brien's spoof of Vermont politics, *Man with a Plan* (1995).

Walk East on Beacon (Alfred L. Werker, 1952). A very matter-of-fact thriller about FBI agents ferreting out communists in Cold War Boston. Shot documentary-style, the film tempers its pinko-bashing paean to Hoover's boys with the more engaging nuts and bolts of their activities and plenty of vivid location footage.

White Christmas (Michael Curtiz, 1954). Singing and dancing army buddies Bing Crosby and Danny Kaye take a break from hoofing in Manhattan and take the train up to Vermont for a skiing holiday, only to find there hasn't been snow all year. One of the very few musicals to be set in New England, beloved for its Irving Berlin score, and that magical snowy finale.

The Witches of Eastwick (George Miller, 1987). An arch, handsome, but ultimately hollow adaptation of John Updike's novel about three love-starved women who conjure up a rather unwelcome visitor to their sleepy Massachusetts town. The film was shot in Cohasset, just south of Boston – as picture-perfect a New England town as you, or the Warner Brothers production designers, could hope to find.

NEW ENGLAND
IN LITERATURE

New England is as literary a landscape as the United States has to offer; indeed the region's writers perhaps figure more prominently in the American literary canon than those of any other region. There are the early nineteenth-century nature writers, Thoreau and Emerson; the poets, Emily Dickinson, Henry Wadsworth Longfellow, Robert Frost, and Wallace Stevens; nineteenth-century novelists like Nathaniel Hawthorne, Henry James, and Edith Wharton, not to mention more recent authorial heavyweights like John Updike and Richard Ford. And, of course, Boston and Cambridge have long been centers of academic research and writing.

We've selected deliberately wide-ranging pieces of writing below, and printed them chronologically. First there is the opening passage of Thoreau's posthumously published account of trekking through Maine in the mid-nineteenth century; second a flight of fantasy from H.P. Lovecraft, but one very deeply rooted in the landscapes and cultural traditions of New England; and, last, a contemporary piece of reportage about the sea and the fishing industry by adventure writer Sebastian Junger.

THE MAINE WOODS

Henry David Thoreau was born in Concord, Massachusetts, in 1817 and spent all his life in New England before dying of tuberculosis at the age of 45. He was a nature writer above all, but only published two books during his lifetime, A Week on the Concord and Merrimack Rivers, *published in 1849, and* Walden, *a searching and introspective story of the two years he spent living in a home-made hut not far from his home. He was unrecognized as a writer while he was alive, and in fact was regarded as something of an eccentric, both locally and by the literary establishment. "If I seem out of step with the world," he said, "it is because I hear another drummer." The following extract is taken from the opening pages of* The Maine Woods, *a story of several walks undertaken between 1846 and 1857, through what was in those days a relatively wild and*

undiscovered part of the region, still inhabited by native tribes and where the main activity was logging. It was published posthumously, having been edited by his sister Sophie and a friend, Ellery Channing, and is nowadays available as a Penguin paperback.

On the 31st of August, 1846, I left Concord in Massachusetts for Bangor and the backwoods of Maine, by way of the railroad and steamboat, intending to accompany a relative of mine, engaged in the lumber trade in Bangor, as far as a dam on the west branch of the Penobscot, in which property he was interested. From this place, which is about one hundred miles by the river above Bangor, thirty miles from the Houlton military road, and five miles beyond the last log-hut, I proposed to make excursions to Mount Ktaadn, the second highest mountain in New England, about thirty miles distant, and to some of the lakes of the Penobscot, either alone or with such company as I might pick up there. It is unusual to find a camp so far in the woods at that season, when lumbering operations have ceased, and I was glad to avail myself of the circumstance of a gang of men being employed there at that time in repairing the injuries caused by the great freshet in the spring. The mountain may be approached more easily and directly on horseback and on foot from the northeast side, by the Aroostook road, and the Wassataquoik River; but in that case you see much less of the wilderness, none of the glorious river and lake scenery, and have no experience of the batteau and the boatman's life. I was fortunate also in the season of the year, for in the summer myriads of black flies, mosquitoes, and midges, or, as the Indians call them, "no-see-ems," make traveling in the woods almost impossible; but now their reign was nearly over.

Ktaadn, whose name is an Indian word signifying highest land, was first ascended by white men in 1804. It was visited by Professor J. W. Bailey of West Point in 1836; by Dr. Charles T. Jackson, the State Geologist, in 1837; and by two young men from Boston in 1845. All these have given accounts of their expeditions. Since I was there, two or three other parties have made the excursion, and told their stories. Besides these, very few, even among backwoodsmen and hunters, have ever climbed it, and it will be a long time before the tide of fashionable travel sets that way. The mountainous region of the State of Maine stretches from near the White Mountains, northeasterly one hundred and sixty miles, to the head of the Aroostook River, and is about sixty miles wide. The wild or unsettled portion is far more extensive. So that some hours only of travel in this direction will carry the curious to the verge of a primitive forest, more interesting, perhaps, on all accounts, than they would reach by going a thousand miles westward.

The next forenoon, Tuesday, September 1, I started with my companion in a buggy from Bangor for "up river," expecting to be overtaken the next day night at Mattawamkeag Point, some sixty miles off, by two more Bangoreans, who had decided to join us in a trip to the mountain. We had each a knapsack or bag filled with such clothing and articles as were indispensable, and my companion carried his gun.

Within a dozen miles of Bangor we passed through the villages of Stillwater and Oldtown, built at the falls of the Penobscot, which furnish the principal power by which the Maine woods are converted into lumber. The mills are built directly over and across the river. Here is a close jam, a hard rub, at all seasons; and then the once green tree, long since white, I need not say as the driven snow, but as a driven log, becomes lumber merely. Here your inch, your two and your three inch stuff begin to be, and Mr. Sawyer marks off those spaces which decide the destiny of so many prostrate forests. Through this steel riddle, more or less coarse, is the arrowy Maine forest, from Ktaadn and Chesuncook, and the head-waters of the St. John, relentlessly sifted, till it comes out boards, clapboards, laths, and shingles such as the wind can take, still, perchance, to be slit and slit again, till men get a size that will suit. Think how stood the white-pine tree on the shore of Chesuncook, its branches soughing with the four winds, and every individual needle trembling in the sunlight,—think how it stands with it now,— sold, perchance, to the New England FrictionMatch Company! There were in 1837, as I read, two hundred and fifty saw-mills on the Penobscot and its tributaries above Bangor, the greater part of them in this immediate neighborhood, and they sawed two hundred millions of feet of boards annually. To this is to be added the lumber of the Kennebec, Androscoggin, Saco, Passamaquoddy, and other streams. No wonder that we hear so often of vessels which are becalmed off our coast, being surrounded a week at a time by floating lumber from the Maine woods. The mission of men there seems to be, like so many busy demons, to drive the forest all out of the country, from every solitary beaver-swamp and mountain-side, as soon as possible.

At Oldtown, we walked into a batteaumanufactory. The making of batteaux is quite a business here for the supply of the Penobscot River. We examined some on the stocks. They are light and shapely vessels, calculated for rapid and rocky streams, and to be carried over long portages on men's shoulders, from twenty to thirty feet long, and only four or four and a half wide, sharp at both ends like a canoe, though broadest forward on the bottom, and reaching seven or eight feet over the water, in order that they may slip over rocks as gently as possible. They are made very slight, only two boards to a side, commonly secured to a few light maple or other hard-wood knees, but inward are of the clearest and widest white-pine stuff, of which there is a great waste on account of their form, for the bottom is left perfectly flat, not only from side to side, but from end to end. Sometimes they become "hogging" even, after long use, and the boatmen then turn them over and straighten them by a weight at each end. They told us that one wore out in two years, or often in a single trip, on the rocks, and sold for from fourteen to sixteen dollars. There was something refreshing and wildly musical to my ears in the very name of the white man's canoe, reminding me of Charlevoix and Canadian Voyageurs. The batteau is a sort of mongrel between the canoe and the boat, a furtrader's boat.

The ferry here took us past the Indian island. As we left the shore, I observed a short, shabby, washerwoman-looking Indian—they commonly have the woebegone look of the girl that cried for spilt milk,—just from "up river,"—land on the Oldtown side near a grocery, and, drawing up his canoe, take out a bundle of skins in one hand, and an empty keg or half-barrel in the other, and scramble up the bank with them. This picture will do to put before the Indian's history, that is, the history of his extinction. In 1837 there were three hundred and sixty-two souls left of this tribe. The island seemed deserted to-day, yet I observed some new houses among the weather-stained ones, as if the tribe had still a design upon life; but generally they have a very shabby, forlorn, and cheerless look, being all back side and wood-shed, not homesteads, even Indian homesteads, but instead of home or abroad-steads, for their life is domi aut militae, at home or at war, or now rather venatus, that is, a hunting, and most of the latter. The church is the only trim-looking building, but that is not Abenaki, that was Rome's doings. Good Canadian it may be, but it is poor Indian. These were once a powerful tribe. Politics are all the rage with them now. I even thought that a row of wigwams, with a dance of pow-wows, and a prisoner tortured at the stake, would be more respectable than this.

We landed in Milford, and rode along on the east side of the Penobscot, having a more or less constant view of the river, and the Indian islands in it, for they retain all the islands as far up as Nicketow, at the mouth of the East Branch. They are generally well-timbered, and are said to be better soil than the neighboring shores. The river seemed shallow and rocky, and interrupted by rapids, rippling and gleaming in the sun. We paused a moment to see a fish-hawk dive for a fish down straight as an arrow, from a great height, but he missed his prey this time. It was the Houlton road on which we were now traveling, over which some troops were marched once towards Mars' Hill, though not to Mars' field, as it proved. It is the main, almost the only, road in these parts, as straight and well made, and kept in as good repair as almost any you will find anywhere. Everywhere we saw signs of the great freshet, —this house standing awry, and that where it was not founded, but where it was found, at any rate, the next day; and that other with a waterlogged look, as if it were still airing and drying its basement, and logs with everybody's marks upon them, and sometimes the marks of their having served as bridges, strewn along the road. We crossed the Sunkhaze, a summery Indian name, the Olemmon, Passadumkeag, and other streams, which make a greater show on the map than they now did on the road. At Passadumkeag we found anything but what the name implies,— earnest politicians, to wit,— white ones, I mean,—on the alert to know how the election was likely to go; men who talked rapidly, with subdued voice, and a sort of factitious earnestness you could not help believing, hardly waiting for an introduction, one on each side of your buggy, endeavoring to say much in little, for they see you hold the whip impatiently, but

always saying little in much. Caucuses they have had, it seems, and caucuses they are to have again,—victory and defeat. Somebody may be elected, somebody may not. One man, a total stranger, who stood by our carriage in the dusk, actually frightened the horse with his asseverations, growing more solemnly positive as there was less in him to be positive about. So Passadumkeag did not look on the map. At sun-down, leaving the river road awhile for short-ness, we went by way of Enfield, where we stopped for the night. This, like most of the localities bearing names on this road, was a place to name which, in the midst of the unnamed and unincorporated wilderness, was to make a distinction without a difference, it seemed to me. Here, however, I noticed quite an orchard of healthy and well grown apple-trees, in a bearing state, it being the oldest settler's house in this region, but all natural fruit and comparatively worthless for want of a grafter. And so it is generally, lower down the river. It would be a good speculation, as well as a favor conferred on the settlers, for a Massachusetts boy to go down there with a trunk full of choice scions, and his grafting apparatus, in the spring.

THE DUNWICH HORROR

*Much like Thoreau, **Howard Phillips Lovecraft** was a literary outsider. Born in Providence, Rhode Island, in 1890, apart from a brief and unsuccessful marriage (when he lived in New York), he spent all his life in New England until his death in 1937. He was something of a cult author while he was alive, read only by a handful of readers of mystery and fantasy fiction, and he remains relatively unknown to this day. He's perhaps best known for his creation of the so-called **Cthulhu Mythos**, a pantheon of ancient gods that lurk beneath the surface of our everyday lives, influencing terrible events and destined one day to rise again. It's this combination of ancient horrors and every-day occurrences that makes Lovecraft's stories so distinctive – and still so resonant and frightening. They have all the classic motifs of horror fiction, but mix with this a local sensibility and evocations of ancient and sinister New England landscapes. Like many of his tales, the following extract, from the opening of **The Dunwich Horror**, is not describing real locations or events, but it is typical in the authority – and underlying fear – it brings to its subject.*

When a traveller in north central Massachusetts takes the wrong fork at the junction of the Aylesbury pike just beyond Dean's Corners he comes upon a lonely and curious country. The ground gets higher, and the brier-bordered stone walls press closer and closer against the ruts of the dusty, curving road. The trees of the frequent forest belts seem too large, and the wild weeds, brambles, and grasses attain a luxuriance not often found in settled regions. At the same time the planted fields appear singularly few and barren; while the sparsely scattered houses wear a surprisingly uniform aspect of age, squalor, and dilapidation. Without knowing why, one hesitates to ask directions from the gnarled, solitary figures spied now and then on crumbling doorsteps or on the sloping, rock-strewn meadows. Those figures are so silent and furtive that one feels somehow confronted by forbidden things, with which it would be better to have nothing to do. When a rise in the road brings the mountains in view above the deep woods, the feeling of strange uneasiness is increased. The summits are too rounded and symmetrical to give a sense of comfort and naturalness, and sometimes the sky silhouettes with especial clearness the queer circles of tall stone pillars with which most of them are crowned.

Gorges and ravines of problematical depth intersect the way, and the crude wooden bridges always seem of dubious safety. When the road dips again there are stretches of marshland that one instinctively dislikes, and indeed almost fears at evening when unseen whippoorwills chatter and the fireflies come out in abnormal profusion to dance to the raucous, creepily insistent rhythms of stridently piping bull-frogs. The thin, shining line of the Miskatonic's upper reaches has an oddly serpent-like suggestion as it winds close to the feet of the domed hills among which it rises.

As the hills draw nearer, one heeds their wooded sides more than their stone-crowned tops. Those sides loom up so darkly and precipitously that one wishes they would keep their distance, but there is no road by which to escape them. Across a covered bridge one sees a small village huddled between the stream and the vertical slope of Round Mountain, and wonders at the cluster of rotting gambrel roofs bespeaking an earlier architectural period than that of the neighbouring region. It is not reas-

suring to see, on a closer glance, that most of the houses are deserted and falling to ruin, and that the broken-steepled church now harbours the one slovenly mercantile establishment of the hamlet. One dreads to trust the tenebrous tunnel of the bridge, yet there is no way to avoid it. Once across, it is hard to prevent the impression of a faint, malign odour about the village street, as of the massed mould and decay of centuries. It is always a relief to get clear of the place, and to follow the narrow road around the base of the hills and across the level country beyond till it rejoins the Aylesbury pike. Afterward one sometimes learns that one has been through Dunwich.

Outsiders visit Dunwich as seldom as possible, and since a certain season of horror all the signboards pointing toward it have been taken down. The scenery, judged by any ordinary esthetic canon, is more than commonly beautiful; yet there is no influx of artists or summer tourists. Two centuries ago, when talk of witch-blood, Satan-worship, and strange forest presences was not laughed at, it was the custom to give reasons for avoiding the locality. In our sensible age – since the Dunwich horror of 1928 was hushed up by those who had the town's and the world's welfare at heart – people shun it without knowing exactly why. Perhaps one reason – though it cannot apply to uninformed strangers – is that the natives are now repellently decadent, having gone far along that path of retrogression so common in many New-England backwaters. They have come to form a race by themselves, with the well defined mental and physical stigmata of degeneracy and inbreeding. The average of their intelligence is woefully low, whilst their annals reek of overt viciousness and of half-hidden murders, incests, and deeds of almost unnamable violence and perversity. The old gentry, representing the two or three armigerous families which came from Salem in 1692, have kept somewhat above the general level of decay; though many branches are sunk into the sordid populace so deeply that only their names remain as a key to the origin they disgrace. Some of the Whateleys and Bishops still send their eldest sons to Harvard and Miskatonic, though those sons seldom return to the mouldering gambrel roofs under which they and their ancestors were born.

No one, even those who have the facts concerning the recent horror, can say just what is the matter with Dunwich; though old legends speak of unhallowed rites and conclaves of the Indians, amidst which they called forbidden shapes of shadow out of the great rounded hills, and made wild orgiastic prayers that were answered by loud crackings and rumblings from the ground below. In 1747 the Reverend Abijah Hoadley, newly come to the Congregational Church at Dunwich Village, preached a memorable sermon on the close presence of Satan and his imps; in which he said:

> *It must be allow'd, that these Blasphemies of an infernall Train of Daemons are Matters of too common Knowledge to be deny'd; the cursed Voices of Azazel and Buzrael, of Beelzebub and Belial, being heard now from under Ground by above a Score of credible Witnesses now living. I my self did not more than a Fortnight ago catch a very plain Discourse of evill Powers in the Hill behind my House; wherein there were a Rattling and Rolling, Groaning, Screeching, and Hissing, such as no Things of this Earth cou'd raise up, and which must needs have come from those Caves that only black Magick can discover, and only the Divell unlock.*

Mr. Hoadley disappeared soon after delivering this sermon; but the text, printed in Springfield, is still extant. Noises in the hills continued to be reported from year to year, and still form a puzzle to geologists and physiographers.

Other traditions tell of foul odours near the hill-crowning circles of stone pillars, and of rushing airy presences to be heard faintly at certain hours from stated points at the bottom of the great ravines; while still others try to explain the Devil's Hop Yard – a bleak, blasted hillside where no tree, shrub, or grass-blade will grow. Then too, the natives are mortally afraid of the numerous whippoorwills which grow vocal on warm nights. It is vowed that the birds are psychopomps lying in wait for the souls of the dying, and that they time their eery cries in unison with the sufferer's struggling breath. If they can catch the fleeing soul when it leaves the body, they instantly flutter away chittering in daemoniac laughter; but if they fail, they subside gradually into a disappointed silence.

These tales, of course, are obsolete and ridiculous; because they come down from very old times. Dunwich is indeed ridiculously old –

older by far than any of the communities within thirty miles of it. South of the village one may still spy the cellar walls and chimney of the ancient Bishop house, which was built before 1700; whilst the ruins of the mill at the falls, built in 1806, form the most modern piece of architecture to be seen. Industry did not flourish here, and the nineteenth century factory movement proved short-lived. Oldest of all are the great rings of roughhewn stone columns on the hilltops, but these are more generally attributed to the Indians than to the settlers. Deposits of skulls and bones, found within these circles and around the sizeable table-like rock on Sentinel Hill, sustain the popular belief that such spots were once the burial-places of the Pocumtucks; even though many enthnologists, disregarding the absurd improbability of such a theory, persist in believing the remains Caucasian.

THE PERFECT STORM

Sebastian Junger *is a freelance journalist; he contributes to* Outside *magazine, the* New York Times *and* Men's Journal, *among other publications. The extract below is taken from his bestselling book,* **The Perfect Storm**, *which describes the horrendous hurricanes of October, 1991, that took place off the New England and northeast Canada coasts. As well as depicting the frightening conditions experienced by deep-sea fishermen during a storm at sea, the book examines the nature and history of the Massachusetts fishing industry, and reconstructs, from interviews and a great deal of poetic license, the lives of those involved. It's a compelling read, and one which shows another, far grittier side to New England's twee fishing towns and clapboard cottages. The extract below is reprinted by kind permission of W.W. Norton and Fourth Estate.*

Early fishing in Gloucester was the roughest sort of business, and one of the deadliest. As early as the 1650s, three-man crews were venturing up the coast for a week at a time in small open boats that had stones for ballast and unstayed masts. In a big wind the masts sometimes blew down. The men wore canvas hats coated with tar, leather aprons, and cowhide boots known as "redjacks." The eating was spare: for a week-long trip one Gloucester skipper recorded that he shipped four pounds of flour, five pounds of pork fat, seven pounds of sea biscuit, and "a little New England rum." The meals, such as they were, were eaten in the weather because there was no below-deck where the crews could take shelter. They had to take whatever God threw at them.

The first Gloucester fishing vessels worthy of the name were the thirty-foot chebaccos. They boasted two masts stepped well forward, a sharp stern, and cabins fore and aft. The bow rode the seas well, and the high stern kept out a following sea. Into the fo'c'sle were squeezed a couple of bunks and a brick fireplace where they smoked trashfish. That was for the crew to eat while at sea, cod being too valuable to waste on them. Each spring the chebaccos were scraped and caulked and tarred and sent out to the fishing grounds. Once there, the boats were anchored, and the men handlined over the side from the low midship rail. Each man had his spot, called a "berth," which was chosen by lottery and held throughout the trip. They fished two lines at twenty-five to sixty fathoms (150–360 feet) with a ten-pound lead weight, which they hauled up dozens of times a day. The shoulder muscles that resulted from a lifetime of such work made fishermen easily recognizable on the street. They were called "hand-liners" and people got out of their way.

The captain fished his own lines, like everyone else, and pay was reckoned by how much fish each man caught. The tongues were cut out of the fish and kept in separate buckets; at the end of the day the skipper entered the numbers in a log book and dumped the tongues overboard. It took a couple of months for the ships to fill their holds—the fish was either dried or, later, kept on ice—and then they'd head back to port. Some captains, on a run of fish, couldn't help themselves from loading their ship down until her decks were almost underwater. This was called deep-loading, and such a ship was in extreme peril if the weather turned ugly. The trip home took a couple of weeks, and the fish would compress under its own weight and squeeze all the excess fluid out of the flesh. The crew pumped the water over the sides, and deep-loaded Grand Bankers would gradually emerge from the sea as they sailed for port.

By the 1760s Gloucester had seventy-five fishing schooners in the water, about one-sixth of the New England fleet. Cod was so important to the economy that in 1784 a wooden effigy—the "Sacred Cod"—was hung in the Massachusetts

State House by a wealthy statesman named John Rowe. Revenue from the New England codfishery alone was worth over a million dollars a year at the time of the Revolution, and John Adams refused to sign the Treaty of Paris until the British granted American fishing rights to the Grand Banks. The final agreement held that American schooners could fish in Canada's territorial waters unhindered and come ashore on deserted parts of Nova Scotia and Labrador to salt-dry their catch.

Cod was divided into three categories. The best, known as "dun fish," was caught in the spring and shipped to Portugal and Spain, where it fetched the highest prices. (Lisbon restaurants still offer bacalao, dried codfish.) The next grade of fish was sold domestically, and the worst grade "refuse fish"—was used to feed slaves in the West Indian canefields. Gloucester merchants left for the Caribbean with holds full of salt cod and returned with rum, molasses, and cane sugar; when this lucrative trade was impeded by the British during the War of 1812, local captains simply left port on moonless nights and sailed smaller boats. Georges Bank opened up in the 1830s, the first railway spur reached Gloucester in 1848, and the first ice companies were established that same year. By the 1880s—the heyday of the fishing schooner—Gloucester had a fleet of four or five hundred sail in her harbor. It was said you could walk clear across to Rocky Neck without getting your feet wet.

Cod was a blessing but could not, alone, have accounted for such riches. In 1816, a Cape Ann fisherman named Abraham Lurvey invented the mackerel jig by attaching a steel hook to a drop-shaped piece of cast lead. Not only did the lead act as a sinker, but, jiggled up and down, it became irresistible to mackerel. After two centuries of watching these elusive fish swirn past in schools so dense they discolored the sea, New England fishermen suddenly had a way to catch them. Gloucester captains ignored a federal bounty on cod and sailed for Sable Island with men in the crosstrees looking for the telltale darkening of mackerel in the water. "School-O!" they would shout, the ship would come around into the wind, and ground-up baitfish— "chum"—would be thrown out into the water. The riper the chum was, the better it attracted the fish; rotting chum on the breeze meant a mackerel schooner was somewhere upwind.

Jigging for mackerel worked well, but it was inevitable that the Yankee mind would come up with something more efficient. In 1855 the purse seine was invented, a 1,300-foot net of tarred twine with lead weights at the bottom and cork floats at the top. It was stowed in a dory that was towed behind the schooner, and when the fish were sighted, the dory quickly encircled them and cinched the net up tight. It was hauled aboard and the fish were split, gutted, beheaded, and thrown into barrels with salt. Sometimes the school escaped before the net was tightened and the crew drew up what was called a "water haull"; other times the net was so full that they could hardly winch it aboard.

Purse seining passed for a glamorous occupation at the time, and it wasn't long before codfishermen came up with their own version of it. It was called tub trawling and if it was more efficient at killing fish, it was also more efficient at killing men. No longer did groundfishermen work from the relative safety of a schooner, now they were setting out from the mother ship in sixteen-foot wooden dories. Each dory carried half a dozen 300-foot trawl lines that were coiled in tubs and hung with baited hooks. The crews rowed out in the morning, paid out their trawls, and then hauled them back every few hours. There were 1,800 hooks to a dory, ten dories to a schooner, and several hundred ships in the fleet. Groundfish had several million chances a day to die.

Pulling a third of a mile's worth of trawl off the ocean floor was backbreaking work, though, and unspeakably dangerous in bad weather. In November of 1880, two fishermen named Lee and Devine rowed out from the schooner Deep Water in their dory. November was a hell of a time to be on the Grand Banks in any kind of vessel, and in a dory it was sheer insanity. They took a wave broadside while hauling their trawl and both men were thrown into the water. Devine managed to clamber back into the boat, but Lee, weighed down by boots and winter clothing, started to sink. He was several fathoms under when his hand touched the trawl line that led back up to the surface. He started to pull.

Almost immediately his right hand sunk into a hook. He jerked it away, leaving part of his finger on the barbed steel like a piece of herring-bait, and kept pulling upwards towards the light. He finally broke the surface and heaved himself back into the dory. It was almost awash and Devine, who was bailing like mad, could do nothing to help him. Lee passed out from the pain and when he came to, he grabbed a bucket and started bailing as well. They had to empty the boat before they were hit by another freak wave. Twenty minutes later they were out of danger and Devine asked Lee if he needed to go back to the schooner. Lee shook his head and said that they should finish hauling the trawls. For the next hour he pulled gear out of the water with his mangled hand. That was dory fishing in its hayday.

There are worse deaths than the one Lee almost suffered, though. Warm Gulf Stream water meets the Labrador Current over the Grand Banks, and the result is a wall of fog that can sweep in with no warning at all. Dory crews hauling their gear have been caught by the fog and simply never seen again. In 1883, a fisherman named Howard Blackburn—still a hero in town, Gloucester's answer to Paul Bunyan – was separated from his ship and endured three days at sea during a January gale. His dorymate died of exposure, and Blackburn had to freeze his own hands around the oar handles to continue rowing for Newfoundland. In the end he lost all his fingers to frostbite. He made land on a deserted part of the coast and staggered around for several days before finally being rescued.

Every year brought a story of survival nearly as horrific as Blackburn's. A year earlier, two men had been picked up by a South American trader after eight days adrift. They wound up in Pernambuco, Brazil, and it took them two months to get back to Gloucester. From time to time dory crews were even blown across the Atlantic, drifting hopelessly with the trade winds and surviving on raw fish and dew. These men had no way to notify their families when they finally made shore; they simply shipped home and came walking back up Rogers Street several months later like men returning from the dead.

For the families back home, dory fishing gave rise to a new kind of hell. No longer was there just the grief of losing men at sea; now there was the agony of not knowing, as well. Missing dory crews could turn up at any time, and so there was never a point at which the families knew for sure they could grieve and get on with their lives. "We saw a father go morning and evening to the hilltop which overlooked the ocean," recorded the Provincetown Advocate after a terrible gale in 1841. "And there seating himself, would watch for hours, scanning the distant horizon . . . for some speck on which to build a hope."

And they prayed. They walked up Prospect Street to the top of a steep rise called Portagee Hill and stood beneath the twin bell towers of Our Lady of Good Voyage church. The bell towers are one of the highest points in Gloucester and can be seen for miles by incoming ships. Between the towers is a sculpture of the Virgin Mary, who gazes down with love and concern at a bundle in her arms. This is the Virgin who has been charged with the safety of the local fishermen. The bundle in her arms is not the infant Jesus; it's a Gloucester schooner.

BOOKS

Below are some of the best books to use New England as a backdrop for storytelling and otherwise; publishers are listed after the title, US/UK if not published in both territories, and o/p denotes out of print.

James Chenoweth *Oddity Odyssey* (Henry Holt US). Fun little book that tries to point out some of the more intriguing and humorous episodes and myths surrounding the sights and major players in New England's history.

Emily Dickinson *The Complete Poems* (Little, Brown). The ultimate New England poet, who spent all her life in the same town – indeed the same house – and quietly recorded the seasons, local incidents, and her own thoughts on life in a series of insightful poems.

Robert Frost *The Collected Poems* (Henry Holt). Frost's poems skilfully evoke the New England landscape, especially "New Hampshire," and remain classics, despite their sometimes too-familiar feel.

Robert Lowell *Life Studies and For the Union Dead* (Noonday Press). Unbelievably affecting stuff from arguably New England's greatest twentieth-century poet, tackling family and social issues with striking aim.

Henry Wadsworth Longfellow *Poems and Other Writings* (Library of America). Longfellow celebrated both common and heroic New Englanders in his sometimes whimsical verse; perhaps a bit light for some, but very much central to New England society over the mid-nineteenth century.

Henry David Thoreau *Cape Cod; The Maine Woods; Walden* (Penguin US). Walden is basically a transcript of Thoreau's attempt to put his transcendentalist philosophy into practice, by constructing a cabin on the banks of Walden Pond, near Concord, Massachusetts, and living the simplest of lives based on self-reliance, individualism, spiritual enlightenment, and material frugality. Nature also plays a part in *Cape Cod* and *The Maine Woods*, accounts of the writer's walking trips published after his death. An extract from *The Maine Woods* is published on pp.549–551.

William Corbett *Literary New England: a History and Guide* (Faber). A guide to the literary haunts of New England – full of trivia, basically, but entertainingly so.

Malcolm Cowley *New England Writers and Writing* (University Press of New England). A compilation of previously published essays on nineteenth- and twentieth-century New England writers (some of whom Cowley knew personally), and including discussion of the work of Hawthorne, Whitman, and John Cheever, among others. Also included are writings by Cowley himself on aspects of New England life.

Sebastian Junger *The Perfect Storm* (Fourth Estate UK; HarperCollins US). A dramatized account of a storm off the New England coast in 1993, part of which is extracted on pp.553–556.

Mark Kurlansky *Cod* (Penguin). Does a fish merit this much obsessive attention? Only in New England. Kurlansky makes a good case for viewing the cod as one of the more integral parts of the region's fabric.

Nat Philbrick *In the Heart of the Sea: The Tragedy of the Whaleship Essex* (Penguin). Basically the story behind *Moby Dick*, and a true one at that, exploring the Nantucket whaling industry through the *Essex's* saga. Gripping, if a bit too straightforward.

Dan Shaughnessy *The Curse of the Bambino* (Penguin). Shaughnessy, a Boston sportswriter, strikes a chord with every long-suffering Red Sox fan by examining the team's "curse" – no championships since 1918 – that began just after they sold Babe Ruth to the Yankees.

Scott Turow *One L: The Turbulent True Story of a First Year at Law School* (Warner Books). Turow, author of the thriller *Presumed Innocent*, recounts his first year at Harvard Law, and all the trials, tribulations, and tension that it entailed. It's quite a well-written, evocative book, but mainly of interest to law students and lawyers.

Elaine Louie and Solvi dos Santos *Living in New England* (Simon & Schuster). Newish, and well-illustrated coffee-table book about the interiors, rather than architectural styles, of New England homes.

Naomi Miller and Keith Morgan *Boston Architecture 1975–1990* (Prestel). Contextualizes Boston's transformation into a modern city, with emphasis on the building boom of the 1980s, but also detailing the early development and architectural trends of centuries before. Plenty of photographs, too.

Susan and Michael Southworth *AIA Guide to Boston* (Globe Pequot US). The definitive guide to Boston architecture, organized by neighborhood. City landmarks and dozens of notable buildings are given exhaustive but readable coverage.

NATURE AND SPECIFIC GUIDES

Appalachian Mountain Club *Maine Mountain Guide: The Hiking Trails of Maine* (Appalachian Mountain Club). Thorough and meticulous hiking guide, with detailed color maps, that should get you through both the popular and more backwoods sections of the state.

Marilyn Dwelley, Fay Hyland *Trees and Shrubs of New England* (Down East Books). Accessible field guide to outdoor New England, useful if you'll be doing some hiking and camping through various parks and mountains.

Tom Wessels, *Reading the Forested Landscape: Natural History of New England* (Countryman Press). Less an outdoors guide than a deconstruction of why the land and trees are like they are today. Uniquely informative.

FICTION

Louisa May Alcott *Little Women* (Puffin). A semi-autobiographical novel, drawing on her own family experiences, Alcott's novel remains a classic to this day.

Gerry Boyle *Lifeline* (Berkley). Hard-hitting suspense novel about an ex-big city reporter looking for solace in small-town Maine, only to find that crime exists there, too. Others in the series include *Bloodline* and *Deadline*.

James Casey *Spartina* (Vintage). Set in the fishing world of Narragansett Bay, Rhode Island, this memorable, spare work about a man struggling with pretty much every imaginable aspect of his life captured the National Book Award in 1989.

John Cheever *The Wapshot Chronicle* (Vintage). Better known for his short stories, this was Cheever's first novel, and documents the weird doings of the Wapshot family, of St Botolph's, Massachusetts. The sequel, *The Wapshot Scandal*, continues the family saga.

Bret Easton Ellis *The Rules of Attraction* (Picador UK; Vintage US). Another of Ellis' sex-drug- and booze-driven narratives, this time charting the romantic progress of a few students through Vermont's fictional Camden College. Still, strangely compelling.

Mary Eleanor Freeman *A New England Nun and Other Stories* (Penguin Books). Relatively unknown these days, Freeman enjoyed quite a fashion about 100 years ago for her tales of rural New England life. Worth seeking out.

Elizabeth Graver *Unravelling* (Hyperion). In distinct and compelling fashion, Graver charts a young woman's progress on the bleaker edges of New England life: its farms and factory mills.

Nathaniel Hawthorne *The House of the Seven Gables; The Scarlet Letter*. Born in Salem, Massachusetts, in 1804, one of Hawthorne's ancestors was a judge at the famous witch trials, and this (and the curse that ensued) provides the story for *The House of the Seven Gables*. *The Scarlet Letter* is a moral tale of guilt, judgment, and redemption. Both Penguin and Bantam do low-priced paperback editions.

George V. Higgins *Penance for Jerry Higgins* (Abacus UK). Ace crime writer and former district attorney who portrays the seamier side of Boston life in this and most of his other novels.

John Irving *The Cider House Rules* (Black Swan UK; Vintage US). Irving writes huge, sprawling novels set all over New England. This one, suitably Dickensian in scope, is neither his most popular (*The World According to Garp*) or beloved (probably *A Prayer for Owen Meany*). But it is perhaps his best – a fascinating meditation on, of all things, abortion.

Henry James *The Bostonians* (Penguin). James' soporific satire traces the relationship of Olive Chancellor and Verena Tarrant, two fictional feminists, in the 1870s.

Sarah Orne Jewett *A Country Doctor* (Bantam US). One of the lesser-known late-nineteenth-century New England novelists, but one of the most locally evocative. This is a novel about a Maine woman who refuses marriage so she can pursue her ambition to become a doctor. Packed full of period detail, its a marvellous account of life in rural Maine in the last century.

Denis Johnson *The Resuscitation of a Hanged Man* (Penguin). Not Johnson's best work, but still a diverting, suspenseful read, in which a Provincetown disc jockey starts tracking the life of a lesbian with whom he becomes enamored.

Jack Kerouac, *Maggie Cassidy* (Penguin). The proto beatnik grew up in New England; here, he traces the arc of a youthful romance, to fine effect, with an equally fine setting in a small Massachusetts mill town.

Stephen King *Different Seasons; Dolores Claiborne* (Penguin). Born in Maine, King is incredibly prolific, and doesn't always hit the mark; some of his writings do manage, though, quite well to evoke his home state and region; these are two of the better ones.

Wally Lamb *She's Come Undone* (Simon & Schuster). This debut novel is a harrowing and brutal story of a young girl in harsh circumstances, which is lightened by hopeful humor. Its first-person female narrative, despite being written by a man, is credible and moving.

Dennis Lehane *Darkness, Take My Hand* (Avon). Lehane sets his mysteries on the working-class streets of South Boston; they are all excellent and evocative, but this is probably the cream of the crop. His most recent, *Mystic River* (William Morrow), is highly recommended, too.

H.P. Lovecraft *The Best of H.P. Lovecraft: Bloodcurdling Tales of Horror and the Macabre* (Ballantine). The best stories from the author who Stephen King called "the twentieth century's greatest practitioner of the clasic horror tale". An extract from his story, *The Dunwich Horror*, is published on pp.551–553.

Herman Melville *Moby Dick* (Penguin). The incomparable story of a man's obsession with a great white whale. Plenty of descriptive prose on the whaling industry and its effect on places like New Bedford and Nantucket.

Grace Metalious *Peyton Place* (Northeastern University Press US). A saucy and sexy, if not particularly well-written, romp through a small New England town's existence. The book that inspired the TV show and movie of the same name.

John Miler and Tim Smith (eds) *Cape Cod Stories* (Chronicle US). Well-selected stories, essays and excerpts from a mostly predictable crop of writers – Thoreau, Updike, and so on.

Rick Moody *The Ice Storm* (Warner). Two neighboring families from Connecticut whose process of collapse is a tawdry Seventies tale of alcoholic excess, wife-swapping and adultery, and alienation – all brought to a shuddering and tragic climax by the storm of the book's title. Made into a stylish and affecting movie.

E. Annie Proulx *Heartsongs* (Fourth Estate UK; Macmillan US). Gritty stories of life in rural and blue-collar New England – beautifully crafted tales that evoke elemental themes.

George Santayana *The Last Puritan* (MIT Press). The philosopher's brilliant "memoir in the form of a novel," set around Boston, chronicles the short life and education of protagonist Oliver Alden coming to grips with Puritanism.

Wallace Stegner *Crossing to Safety* (Penguin).The saga of two couples who form a lifelong bond, set partly in Vermont. It might seem a bit slow and sentimental at a glance, but Stegner's strong writing should win you over.

John Steinbeck *The Winter of Our Discontent* (Penguin). A late work by Steinbeck, published in 1961, and examining the collapse of an old New England family under pressure from the modern world.

Donna Tartt *The Secret History* (Penguin UK; Ballantine US). An "It" book from the early 1990s, and one that actually resonates, this centers on a small group of students at a fictional Vermont college, modeled after Bennington University, and the murderous turns their elite cadre takes. Short on landscape, but a surprisingly diverting tale.

Edith Wharton *Ethan Frome* (Penguin). A distilled portrait of stark, icy New England that belies the fiery emotions blazing underneath. The title character's perverse, tragic odyssey is riveting; the writing simple and superb, especially evocative of the Massachusetts farmscape in which the story is set.

INDEX

ROUGH GUIDE FAVORITES
College Towns

**ROUGH GUIDE FAVORITES
Scenic Drives**

ROUGH GUIDE FAVORITES
America

N

O

P

ROUGH GUIDE FAVORITES
Coastal Towns

Q

R

S

ROUGH GUIDE FAVORITES
Outdoor Activities

T

ROUGH GUIDE FAVORITES
Literary Landmarks

V

W

Y

stay in touch

roughnews

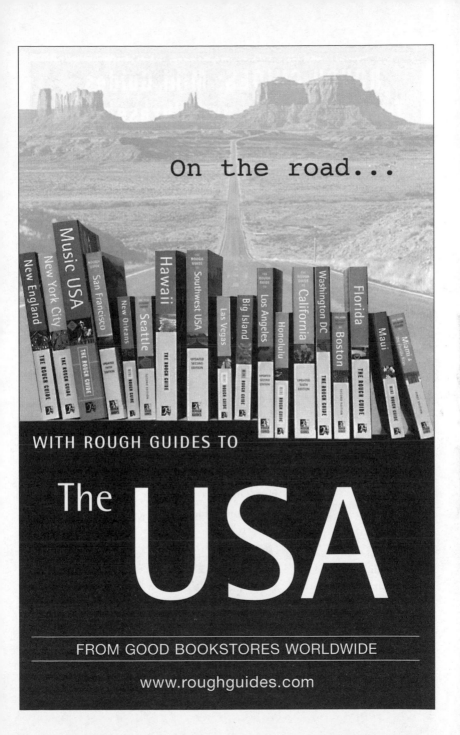

ROUGH GUIDES: Mini Guides, Travel Specials and Phrasebooks

MINI GUIDES

Antigua
Bangkok
Barbados
Beijing
Big Island of Hawaii
Boston
Brussels
Budapest
Cape Town
Copenhagen
Dublin
Edinburgh

Florence
Honolulu
Ibiza & Formentera
Jerusalem
Las Vegas
Lisbon
London Restaurants
Madeira
Madrid
Malta & Gozo
Maui
Melbourne
Menorca

Montreal
New Orleans

Paris
Rome
Seattle
St Lucia
Sydney
Tenerife
Tokyo
Toronto
Vancouver

TRAVEL SPECIALS

First-Time Asia
First-Time Europe
Women Travel

PHRASEBOOKS

Czech
Dutch
Egyptian Arabic
European
French
German
Greek

Hindi & Urdu
Hungarian
Indonesian
Italian
Japanese
Mandarin Chinese
Mexican Spanish
Polish
Portuguese
Russian
Spanish
Swahili
Thai
Turkish
Vietnamese

ROUGH GUIDES:
Reference and Music CDs

REFERENCE

Blues:
  100 Essential CDs
Classical Music
Classical:
  100 Essential CDs
Country Music
Country:
  100 Essential CDs
Drum'n'bass
House Music
Hip Hop
Irish Music
Jazz

Music USA
Opera
Opera:
  100 Essential CDs
Reggae
Reggae:
  100 Essential CDs
Rock
Rock:
  100 Essential CDs

Soul:
  100 Essential CDs
Techno
World Music

World Music:
  100 Essential CDs
English Football
European Football
Internet
Money Online
Shopping Online
Travel Health

ROUGH GUIDE MUSIC CDs

Music of the Andes
Australian Aboriginal
Bluegrass
Brazilian Music
Cajun & Zydeco
Music of Cape Verde
Classic Jazz
Music of
  Colombia
Cuban Music
Eastern Europe

Music of Egypt
English Roots Music
Flamenco
Music of Greece
Hip Hop
India & Pakistan
Irish Music
Music of Jamaica
Music of Japan
Kenya & Tanzania
Marrabenta
  Mozambique
Native American
North African
Music of Portugal
Reggae
Salsa
Samba
Scottish Music
South African Music
Music of Spain
Sufi Music
Tango

Tex-Mex
West African Music
World Music
World Music Vol 2
Music of Zimbabwe

AVAILABLE AT ALL GOOD BOOKSHOPS

Will you have enough stories to tell your grandchildren?

Yahoo! Travel

Do You YAHOO!?

SEP 1 8 2001